中 文 字 譜

Chinese Characters

A Genealogy and Dictionary

Printed in the United States of America.

ISBN: 978-0-966-07500-7

前 言

Alone among modern languages, Chinese integrates both semantic and phonetic components in its characters. *Chinese Characters: A Genealogy and Dictionary* deciphers this rich information to help students understand, appreciate and remember Chinese characters. Following traditional Chinese etymologies, each character is decomposed into smaller composite characters suggesting the character's meaning and/or pronunciation. Successive decomposition traces the over 4000 characters in this dictionary back to less than 200 pictographs and ideographs. This creation of new characters from simpler elements is depicted in a series of genealogical charts (字譜) which form the dictionary's organizing structure. Any character can be found by moving through these unique charts as long as the reader knows any part of the character or knows any character which shares the same part. The 字譜 method generalizes the "radical" (部首) system based loosely on the semantic components of characters, extending it to all components whether semantic or phonetic.

Written for the growing number of English speakers studying Chinese rather than the usual readership of Chinese speakers studying English, this dictionary integrates the study of etymology and vocabulary by including a total of nearly 20,000 words, characters, and phrases. Many early Chinese-English dictionaries were also written explicitly for foreigners, primarily the many missionaries settling in China, and their designs also reflected the particular needs of non-native speakers in learning Chinese characters. While this dictionary's use of diagrams and extensive cross-referencing is unique, several early dictionaries including Soothill's *Chinese Student's Pocket Dictionary* (1899), Wieger's *Chinese Characters* (1915) and Karlgren's *Analytic Dictionary of Chinese and Sino-Japanese* (1923) were similarly structured around character etymology.

As evidenced by the title of this dictionary, it is tempting to use genetic metaphors to explain the connections between Chinese characters. Of course, characters are just symbols that cannot be traced along a true genealogy. To the extent possible, the 字譜 decompose characters according to 許慎's 說文解字 (c.100), one of China's first and still most influential dictionaries. Exceptions arise due to omissions from the 說文, to new characters postdating the 說文, to the remarkably few inconsistencies within that work, and to my own misunderstandings and oversights. Since the 說文 is based on the 小篆 characters of the 秦 dynasty, it does not include information about earlier forms, such as the 甲骨文 characters. While no longer an authoritative source on character origins, the 說文 remains the reference point for all subsequent scholarship and for this reason was chosen as the basis of the 字譜.

After each character's dictionary entry, a brief explanation of the character's "etymology" (字源) follows. Many of these stories are from later commentaries on the 說文 and are more speculative about how the elements combine to suggest a certain idea. In choosing among explanations from different commentaries I relied on what seems plausible, on what can be succinctly presented, and on the judgments of tertiary sources, primarily the extremely helpful 形音義綜合大字典 by 高樹藩. I have resisted the temptation to insert my own stories, though readers should by no means feel similarly

bound. Please keep in mind that this dictionary does not incorporate the large and growing body of research on pre-秦 characters. While these characters are the primary attention of current research, they are of little practical interest to students of modern Chinese. For instance, while it may be true that the character bright 明 once was composed of window 囧 and moon 月 rather than sun 日 and moon 月, this distinction is only of academic interest as the current form has included sun and moon for over two thousand years. The traditional etymologies miss many of these subtleties, but they represent a remarkable amount of insight and information that many linguists are once again beginning to appreciate. With the visual assistance of the 字譜 it is hoped that these etymologies can become an integral part of learning Chinese.

This dictionary began as a distraction from my master's studies in economics at National Taiwan University and continued to serve this purpose during my economics studies at the University of Pittsburgh. I thank 林欣吾, 薛琦, 楊東連, 林宜民, 譚敬南, 羅瑋, 盧珊珊, 于慶, 陳麗眞, 牟嶺 and other friends and teachers for their encouragement of this long digression. For help in correcting many of the numerous errors in this dictionary, I thank 羅瑋, 李兵, 卓意雯, 陸金福, 安琨, 顏菁玉, 吳怡春, 王亞祥, 任彤 and especially 莊斐雯 and 劉康. In compiling this work I consulted a number of printed dictionaries, including 遠東漢英大辭典, 東方國語辭典, 精選英漢漢英詞典, 辭海, 漢英辭典, 牛津高級英英漢雙解辭典, *ABC Chinese-English Dictionary*, and online dictionaries including 國語辭典, the *Unicode Unihan Database*, and the *World Wide Web CJK-English Dictionary Database*. The ability to check word usage and frequency by searching Chinese homepages and discussion boards on the web was also of great help. Readers are invited to visit the website for this dictionary at http://www.zhongwen.com where etymology references for each character and more information on the above resources can be found.

李克
Rick Harbaugh
zhongwen@zhongwen.com

漢 字 的 發 展

According to legend, Chinese characters were invented by the historian 倉頡 under China's founder 黃帝 about 4500 years ago. Archeological research indicates that Chinese characters may have first appeared as early as 7000 years ago and formed a complete system of writing by about 3500 years ago. Approximately 2000 years ago the popularization of the ink brush fundamentally altered the shape of characters, changing them from the rounded "seal characters" (still carved on official seals) to the more angular characters used for most purposes today. Though convenient, the new writing style obscured the original logic of the characters, resulting in miswritings and the creation of illogical new characters. The scholar 許慎 responded with the etymological dictionary 説文解字 based on surviving samples of earlier scripts. By explaining the underlying logic of each character, this work succeeded in stabilizing the writing of characters in forms essentially comparable to, though differently shaped, than the seal characters.

Traditionally, characters are differentiated into six types. The basic units are pictographs (象形) portraying objects, e.g. tree 木, and ideographs (指事) suggesting abstractions, e.g. one 一. These pictographs and ideographs (collectively known as 文) combine to create two additional types of characters, logical aggregates (會意) and phonetic complexes (形聲). Logical aggregates combine the meanings of different characters to create a new meaning, e.g. a person 人 agains a tree 木 means rest 休. Phonetic complexes combine the meaning of one character with the sound of another, e.g. in the character 忠 the meaning of loyal is suggested by heart 心 and the pronunciation is the same as that of 中. The final two types of characters represent transformations in the meanings of these four types. Associative transformations (轉注) extend the meaning of a character to a related concept. Borrowings (假借) give an unrelated meaning to a character, generally that of a spoken word which has the same pronunciation as the borrowed character but lacks its own character.

Chinese Characters: A Genealogy and Dictionary follows the basic etymologies set by 許慎 and elaborated on by Chinese scholars over the centuries. These etymologies are based on the seal characters rather than on earlier forms, such as the characters on early bronzes, which sometimes have different etymologies. Note that the distinction between phonetic complexes and logical aggregates is often blurred by the phonetic component also suggesting a character's meaning. In the above example 中 contributes its meaning of centered to help suggest loyal 忠 ("centered heart"). For almost every phonetic complex some meaning contribution of the phonetic component has been suggested by a noted scholar. The most fanciful have been excluded, although some dubious ones are still included for their mnemonic value and insight into Chinese culture. The reader will note that the phonetic component of some characters is not closely related to the character's modern pronunciation. This problem, along with occasional alteration in the shapes of phonetic and semantic components, reflects the evolution of the written and spoken languages.

查 字 方 法

Each character (字) is listed under one of about two hundred genealogical charts (字譜), each of which starts with a basic pictograph or ideograph (文). In the indexes and cross-referencing, characters are always referenced by two numbers to the right of the character, one above the other. The top number is the 文 number indicating the genealogical chart that the character is listed under, and the bottom number is the 字 number indicating the position of the character in that chart. Using this reference system, you can find characters as follows:

I. If you know the character's pronunciation:

(1) Locate the character in either of the character pronunciation indexes (拼音索引表 or 注音索引表).

(2) Using the 文 reference number at the top and right of the character in the index, go to the appropriate genealogical chart. For instance, if the 文 number is 69 go to the 69th genealogical chart according to the large chart numbers at the top left of each page. Now using the 字 reference number at the bottom and right of the character in the index, you can find the character within this chart. For instance if the 字 number is 25 look down the chart until you find the 25th character. The character's definition, etymology, and derivative words are all shown in the accompanying dictionary text (字典) under the same 文 and 字 reference numbers. Usually this character entry will be on the same page as the character in the chart, though it may be on the previous or next page.

II. If you know the radical (部首):

Look up the 部首 in the radical index (部首索引表) as in a regular dictionary. Follow step (2) above.

III. If you know nothing about the character:

Count the number of strokes and look up the character in the stroke number index (筆劃索引表). Follow step (2) above.

IV. If you know a component character, a character that shares a component part, or a character that is derived from the character:

Find the known character by any of the above methods. After locating the known character in the 字譜, find the desired character in the same chart. If the character is printed in smaller type, then this character is not listed in the dictionary text next to the genealogical chart. Instead, use the accompanying 文 and 字 numbers to find the character according to step (2) above.

字 譜 及 字 典

This section contains the genealogical tables or trees (字譜) and the accompanying dictionary text (字典).

Genealogical Tables:

These 字譜 depict the relations between characters and serve as a means of locating characters. Each of the nearly two hundred tables begins with a simple pictograph or ideograph. Branching off from this character are all characters which derive immediately from it. Note that some of these characters are shown separately in large type and some are grouped together in small type. Large type indicates the primary listing of the character. Small type indicates that the primary listing is in a different table as given by the accompanying reference numbers. For instance, the character 想 (114-24) is found in small type under the character 心 (83-1) in table 83, but in large type under the character 相 (114-20) in table 114. Large type characters are followed by any characters which derive from them, but this chain is broken following small type characters.

Since every character other than the basic pictographs and ideographs is composed of more than one component character, a choice must be made where to put the character's primary listing. While some arbitrariness is unavoidable, the primary listing generally follows the phonetic rather than semantic component when both are present. This complements the emphasis on semantic components found in the 部首 method, and also allows for richer genealogical tables since the phonetic components are more numerous and generally contain more levels of composition.

Character etymology as suggested by character shape sometimes differs from the actual component as identified in the traditional etymology. In such cases the character is listed under all actual and apparent components. In cases where an apparent component is particularly suggestive relative to the actual components, the primary listing is made under that component. In these cases a vertical line segment in the table such as that before 絕 (33-17) signifies deviation from the actual etymology.

Since the tables attempt to show the full sequence of character evolution, some characters are included because they form important etymological links between characters rather than because they are inherently important. A "missing link" problem also arises in which characters identified in ancient writings are no longer used in modern Chinese. These characters have all their definitions labeled as "古".

Dictionary Text:

Characters are listed in the dictionary text near their primary listing in the genealogical tables. Pronunciations of each character are listed on the top line adjacent to the character. In cases where the Mandarin standards used in mainland China and Taiwan diverge, both pronunciations are included and differentiated by usage warnings. (See the following 略語表).

A brief etymology of each character begins on the second line. Almost all of the characters are consistent with the 說文 in that the listed parts are the same. Many of the descriptions are more elaborate as they incorporate later commentaries.

Definitions of the character then follow. Note that some definitions are not common in modern Chinese but are included to help clarify the character's etymology. When such a definition is no longer used it is noted with a "古" usage warning. Different definitions are separated by small boxed characters indicating the parts of speech. After the definitions is a double arrow followed by a referenced list of words which include the character in a non-initial position.

Words that begin with the listed character are shown in alphabetical order by phoneticization. Word pronunciations follow the Mandarin standard used in Taiwan. Word definitions are separated by parts of speech markers in the same manner as character definitions.

In cases where word definitions or usage vary in Taiwan and mainland China, these differences are indicated with usage warnings in the same manner as character pronunciation differences.

略 語 表

文 表

一											
1 一	20 凵	40 尸	61 勹	81 气	102 予	121 禾	142 臣	161 雨	179 鹿		
2 丨	21 厂	41 彳	62 毛	82 火	103 爪	122 庀	143 凶	162 隹	180 魚		
3 丿	22 匚	42 业	63 宀	83 心	爪	123 羊	七	163 易	十三		
4 乀	23 冂	43 夊	64 才	84 牙	五	124 羽	144 函	164 兔	181 鼠		
5 丶	24 宀	44 今	65 弓	85 巴	104 瓜	125 虫	145 匡	165 朋	十四		
6 亅	25 卜	45 丌	66 屮	86 勿	105 矛	126 衣	146 豸	166 亞	182 齊		
7 丿	26 卜	46 丌	67 山	87 斗	106 牛	127 兆	147 身	167 阜			
8 乙	27 卩	47 凡	68 口	88 止	107 玉	128 至	148 盲	九			
9 乙	28 乃	48 阝	69 口	89 手	108 禾	129 舟	149 角	168 韭			
二	29 八	49 彡	70 土	90 毛	109 瓦	130 西	150 貝	169 飛			
10 人	30 九	50 干	71 宀	91 犬	110 出	131 臼	151 呂	170 鹵			
11 儿	31 十	51 工	72 夕	92 牛	111 田	132 肉	152 克	171 爲			
12 匕	32 卜	52 匸	73 午	93 午	112 甲	133 爪	153 糸	172 象			
13 匕	33 卩	53 巾	四	94 方	113 由	134 而	154 雨	173 米			
14 又	34 力	54 女	74 丫	95 毋	114 目	135 曲	155 豖	十			
15 メ	35 刀	55 子	75 丐	96 斤	115 冊	136 単	156 采	174 兩			
16 ㄟ	36 丁	56 也	76 日	97 井	116 皿	137 耳	157 串	175 幕			
17 ㄐ	37 几	57 已	77 木	98 文	117 且	138 米	158 車	176 菐			
18 ㄅ	38 几	58 巳	78 戶	99 天	118 疒	139 自	159 酉	177 馬			
三	59 厶	79 丰	100 氏	120 永	140 由	八	十一				
19 厶	39 大	60 广	80 月	101 氹	六	141 缶	160 來	178 鳥			

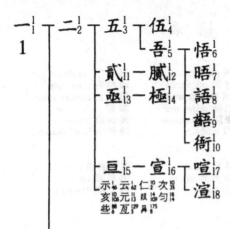

一¹₁ ─┬─ 二¹₂ ─┬─ 五¹₃ ─┬─ 伍¹₄
      │   │   └─ 吾¹₅ ─┬─ 悟¹₆
      │   │   ├─ 晤¹₇
      │   │   ├─ 語¹₈
      │   ├─ 貳¹₁₁ ─ 膩¹₁₂   ├─ 齬¹₉
      │   ├─ 亟¹₁₃ ─ 極¹₁₄   └─ 衙¹₁₀
      │   │
      │   ├─ 亘¹₁₅ ─ 宣¹₁₆ ─┬─ 喧¹₁₇
      │   │   └─ 渲¹₁₈
      │   └─ 示 云 仁 次
      │   亥 元 叚 勾
      │   些 亙 頁 易

一 ¹yī

1 Ideograph representing one. In composition can represent the horizon, a bar or line, or heaven. **yī:** ● one ⇨ 曇花一現, 不一, 同一, 九牛一毛, 打成一片, 統一, 萬一, 獨一無二, 單一, 逐一, 唯一, 惟一

一般 yībān ● generally: 一般來說 generally speaking ● average

一半 yībàn ● half

一輩子 yībèizi ● ● lifetime

一邊 yībiān ● one side ● simultaneously

一併 yībìng ● together, as a group

一旦 yīdàn ● as soon as, once

一道 yīdào ● together

一點 yīdiǎn ● a little, somewhat, a bit

一定 yīdìng ● certainly: 不一定 not necessarily

一度 yīdù ● once

一二 yīèr ● one or two, a little: 略知一二 know just a little

一概 yīgài ● all, totally

一個 yīgè ● a, one

一共 yīgòng ● in total, altogether

一貫 yīguàn ● consistent

一回 yīhuí ● once

一會兒 yīhuǐer ● a moment: 等一會兒 wait a moment

一塊兒 yīkuàier ● together

一流 yīliú ● first-rate

一路 yīlù ● all the way: 一路平安 bon voyage

一律 yīlù ● all

一面 yīmiàn ● one side, one aspect ● simultaneously

一模一樣 yīmóyīyàng ● identical

一齊 yīqí ● simultaneously, together

一起 yīqǐ ● together, altogether

一切 yīqiè ● everything

一群 yīqún ● a group

一生 yīshēng ● lifetime

一時 yīshí ● momentarily, temporarily

一塌糊塗 yītāhútú ● in a great mess

一同 yītóng ● together

一味 yīwèi ● persistently, obsessively

一下 yīxià ● a while: 請等一下. Please wait a moment. ● all at once, all of a sudden

一下子 yīxiàzi ● once ● all at once, all of a sudden

一向 yīxiàng ● all along

一些 yīxiē ● some

一心 yīxīn ● wholeheartedly

一樣 yīyàng ● the same

一一 yīyī ● one by one, individually

一再 yīzài ● again and again, repeatedly

一早 yīzǎo ● early in the morning

一陣子 yīzhènzi ● a while

一直 yīzhí ● always ● straight: 一直走 walk straight ahead

一致 yīzhì ● consistent: 不一致 inconsistent

二 ¹èr

2 One 一 doubled. ● two ⇨ 一二, 獨一無二

二胡 èrhú ● erhu - a two-stringed Chinese musical instrument

二手 èrshǒu ● second hand: 二手貨 second-hand goods

二元化 èryuánhuà ● dichotomous

五 ¹wǔ

3 The two 二 principles yin and yang (⇨ 陰陽) that form the five (an early pictograph showing four sides and the center) elements (⇨ 五行) between heaven and earth. ● five

五彩 wǔcǎi ● multicolored

五花八門 wǔhuābāmén ● rich in variety

五經 wǔjīng ● the Five Classics - 詩經, 書經, 易經, 禮記, 春秋

五行 wǔxíng ● five primary elements - 金, 木, 水, 火, 地

伍 wǔ 4 Five 五 (phonetic) men 人. unit of five soldiers in ancient times, a surname, five (complex form) ⇔ 落伍, 退伍, 隊伍

吾 wú 5 Mouth 口 with five 五 phonetic. I, we ⇔ 維吾爾族

悟 wù 6 Heart 心 with 吾 phonetic. realize, comprehend ⇔ 覺悟, 省悟, 領悟, 醒悟, 禪悟
悟性 wùxìng comprehension

晤 wù 7 Sun 日 with 吾 phonetic. meet ⇔ 會晤
晤面 wùmiàn meet face to face
晤談 wùtán meet and talk

語 yǔ 8 [语] Words 言 from me 吾 (phonetic). talk, words, language ⇔ 標語, 私語, 歇後語, 評語, 漢語, 英語, 成語, 國語, 新語, 母語, 台語, 口語, 言語, 俗語, 外語, 日語, 片語, 滬語, 手語, 論語, 耳語, 謎語, 自言自語, 華語
語錄 yǔlù quotations, sayings: 毛主席語錄 Sayings of Chairman Mao
語氣 yǔqì tone
語文 yǔwén spoken and written language
語系 yǔxì language family
語言 yǔyán language

齬 yǔ 9 [龉] Tooth 齒 with 吾 phonetic. crooked teeth

⇔ 齟齬

衙 yá 10 March 行 with 吾 phonetic. government department
衙門 yámén government office

貳 èr 11 [贰] Originally two 二 (phonetic) halbards 戈, with shell 貝 added later. two (complex form)

膩 nì 12 [腻] Meat 肉 twice 貳. fat, grease, greasy, bored with: 吃膩了 sick of eating something ⇔ 油膩, 細膩

亟 jí 13 Person 人 (in center, altered) struggling with mouth 口 and hands 又 between both 二 heaven and earth. urgently, anxiously
亟待 jídài urgently await
亟欲 jíyù urgently desire to

極 jí 14 [极] Wood 木 in anxious 亟 position. Simplified form uses 及. ridgepole, extreme, extremely: 好極了 excellent ⇔ 北極, 消極, 南極, 太極, 積極
極度 jídù extreme
極端 jíduān extreme, extremist
極力 jílì make every effort
極其 jíqí extremely
極權 jíquán totalitarian rule: 極權主義 totalitarianism
極為 jíwéi extremely
極限 jíxiàn extreme limit

亙 xuān 15 Swirling 回 (altered) between top and bottom 二

宣 xuān 16 Roof 宀 over swirling 亙 expanse. imperial hall, announce, proclaim
宣佈 xuānbù announce, declare
宣布 xuānbù announce, declare
宣稱 xuānchēng assert
宣傳 xuānchuán publicize, propaganda
宣導 xuāndǎo inform and guide
宣告 xuāngào announce, proclaim
宣言 xuānyán declaration, manifesto: 獨立宣言 declaration of independence
宣揚 xuānyáng publicize

喧 xuān 17 Mouth 口 proclaiming 宣 (phonetic). clamor
喧嘩 xuānhuá hubbub, uproar

渲 xuàn 18 Water 水 proclaiming 宣 (phonetic). paint
渲染 xuànrǎn paint, embellish

三 sān 19 Ideograph representing heaven, earth, and humanity. three ⇔ 兩三, 再三
三八 sānbā exaggeratedly feminine
三國 sānguó Three Kingdoms - 魏, 蜀 and 吳 - that coexisted from 222 to 265 A.D.: 三國演義 The Romance of the Three Kingdoms - an historical novel
三合會 sānhéhuì triad
三角 sānjiǎo triangle: 三角洲 delta
三輪車 sānlúnchē tricycle
三民主義 sānmínzhǔyì Three Principles of the People - nationalism 民族, people's rights 民權, and the people's

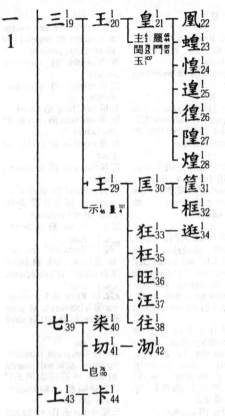

一
1

三₁₉
王₂₀ 皇₂₁ 凰₂₂
王₆ 璽₇₀ 蝗₂₃
閨₇₈ 門₁₀₇ 惶₂₄
玉₁₀₇ 遑₂₅
徨₂₆
隍₂₇
煌₂₈

王₂₉ 匡₃₀ 筐₃₁
框₃₂
狂₃₃ 逛₃₄
枉₃₅
旺₃₆
汪₃₇
七₃₉ 柒₄₀ 往₃₈
切₄₁ 沏₄₂
臯₇₆₁₁₀
上₄₃ 卡₄₄

示₄₆ 壬₄₅

livelihood 民生¹¹⁹ - promoted by Sun Yat-sen
三明治 sānmíngzhì 图 sandwich
三峽 sānxiá 图 Three Gorges - a scenic spot on the Yangtze River
三專 sānzhuān 图 图 technical college

王 1 wáng
20 The one 一 who connects heaven, humanity and earth 三↓ᵤ 图 king 图 a surname ⇔ 大王²ᴾ, 國王⁴⁶,

女王³⁴, 魔王²³, 帝王²³, 霸王¹⁶¹
王八 wángbā 图 tortoise 图 cuckolded husband: 图 王八 蛋 son-of-a-bitch
王妃 wángfēi 图 royal concubine 图 princess (crown prince's wife)
王國 wángguó 图 kingdom
王牌 wángpái 图 trump card
王子 wángzǐ 图 prince

皇 1 huáng
21 Original 自¹³⁹ (alter-

ed to 白²⁶) kings 王↓ₐ. 图 three legendary rulers of ancient China - 伏羲⁶⁴, 神農⁶⁰, and 黃帝²⁵ 图 emperor ⇔ 教皇³⁷, 天皇⁵⁵, 堂皇⁵⁵
皇帝 huángdì 图 emperor
皇宮 huánggōng 图 imperial palace
皇后 huánghòu 图 empress

凰 1 huáng
22 Emperor 皇↓ₐ (phonetic) phoenix 鳳⁴⁷ (abbreviated to 凡¹⁷). 图 phoenix (female) ⇔ 鳳凰⁴⁷

蝗 1 huáng
23 Insect 虫¹²⁵ emperor 皇↓ₐ (phonetic). 图 locust
蝗蟲 huángchóng 图 locust

惶 1 huáng
24 Heart 心⁸³ and emperor 皇↓ₐ (phonetic). 图 anxious, frightened
惶恐 huángkǒng 图 frightened, terrified

遑 1 huáng
25 Movement 辵¹³ with 皇↓ₐ phonetic and suggestive of fear 惶₂₄. 图 hurry
遑論 huánglùn 图 not to mention, much less

徨 1 huáng
26 Step 彳⁴⁴ with 皇↓ₐ phonetic. 图 irresolute ⇔ 彷徨²⁷, 徬徨²⁷

隍 1 huáng
27 Hill 阜¹⁶⁷ and emperor 皇↓ₐ (phonetic). 图 dry moat, ditch ⇔ 城隍²⁹

煌 1 huáng
28 Fire 火⁸² and emperor 皇↓ₐ (phonetic). 图 bright, brilliant ⇔ 敦煌²⁵, 輝煌¹⁷⁵

王 1 huáng
29 Growth 之⁶⁵ (altered) shooting up from the ground 土³⁰. 图 flourish

匡 1 kuāng
30 Container 匸⁵² with

王ᵇ phonetic. ⊕ container ⊞ rectify, correct

匡正 kuāngzhèng ⊞ rectify

筐 31 Bamboo 竹 container 匡ᵇ (phonetic). ⊞ wicker basket ⇔ 籮筐

筐子 kuāngzi ⊞ basket

框 32 Wooden 木 container 匡ᵇ (phonetic). ⊞ frame ⇔ 相框

狂 33 Dog 犬 uncontrolled 王ᵇ (phonetic). ⊕ rabid dog ⊞ crazy ⇔ 瘋狂, 猖狂, 發狂

狂飆 kuángbiāo ⊞ hurricane

狂風 kuángfēng ⊞ strong breeze

狂歡 kuánghuān ⊞ rejoice wildly, revel: 狂歡會 orgy

狂怒 kuángnù ⊞ rage, fury

狂熱 kuángrè ⊞ fanatic zeal, fanaticism

狂人 kuángrén ⊞ lunatic, madman

狂妄 kuángwàng ⊞ crazy, deranged ⊞ deluded.

逛 34 Move 辵 and think crazy 狂ᵇ (phonetic) thoughts. ⊞ stroll ⇔ 閒逛

逛逛 guàngguang ⊞ take a walk, stroll

逛街 guàngjiē ⊞ window shop

枉 35 Tree 木 growing rapidly 王ᵇ (phonetic). ⊞ crooked ⇔ 冤枉

枉費 wǎngfèi ⊞ try in vain

枉然 wǎngrán ⊞ in vain, futilely

旺 36 Sun 日 with 王ᵇ (originally 往ᵇ) phonetic. ⊕ lustrous ⊞ prosperous 興旺

旺季 wàngjì ⊞ busy season

旺盛 wàngshèng ⊞ prosperous

汪 37 Water 水 growing rapidly 王ᵇ (phonetic). ⊞ deep and vast ⊞ a surname

汪洋 wāngyáng ⊞ deep and vast body of water

往 38 Step 彳 and progress 王ᵇ (phonetic, altered to resemble 主). ⊞ depart for, go toward ⊞ to, toward past, previous ⇔ 嚮往, 交往, 以往, 開往, 前往, 來往

往常 wǎngcháng ⊞ in the past

往後 wǎnghòu ⊞ in the future

往來 wǎnglái ⊞ come and go ⊞ contacts, dealings

往日 wǎngrì ⊞ in days past

往事 wǎngshì ⊞ things of the past

往往 wǎngwǎng ⊞ frequently

往昔 wǎngxí ⊞ in former times ⊞ former times

七 39 One 一 crossed by a curved line, suggesting imperfection short of ten 十. ⊞ seven ⇔ 亂七八精

柒 40 Water 水 and wood 木 with 七ᵇ phonetic. ⊕ a tree name ⊞ seven (complex form)

切 41 Knife 刀 with 七ᵇ phonetic. qiē: ⊞ cut, slice qiè: ⊞ correspond to ⇔ 一切, 殷切, 密切, 親切, 關切, 深切, 熱切, 迫切, 確切

切磋 qiēcuō ⊞ learn by exchanging views, compare notes

切斷 qiēduàn ⊞ cut off, nip

沏 42 Water 水 cutting 切ᵇ (phonetic). ⊞ infuse

沏茶 qīchá ⊞ make tea

上 43 Originally a horizontal line 一 topped by a short horizontal line, later by a vertical line, and then finally by both. Original form appears in composition, e.g. 示. ⊞ above, upper ⊞ previous: 上次 last time; ⊞ get on, go up: 上車 get in a car ⇔ 路上, 比不上, 北上, 跟上, 考上, 染上, 加上, 趕上, 樓上, 地上, 以上, 之上, 山上, 街上, 早上, 愛上, 穿上, 爬上, 放上, 晚上, 馬上

上班 shàngbān ⊞ go to work, go to the office: 上班族 office workers

上層 shàngcéng ⊞ upper level

上床 shàngchuáng ⊞ go to bed ⊞ have sex

上次 shàngcì ⊞ last time

上當 shàngdàng ⊞ be cheated, be fooled

上帝 shàngdì ⊞ God

上都 shàngdū ⊞ Xanadu

上風 shàngfēng ⊞ windward advantage: 佔上風 have the advantage

上海 shànghǎi ⊞ Shanghai

上級 shàngjí ⊞ high-grade

上課 shàngkè ⊞ attend class

上口 shàngkǒu ⊞ easily spoken ⊞ euphonious

上來 shànglái ⊞ come up to

上面 shàngmiàn ⊞ ⊞ top, above

上前 shàngqián ⊞ come forward

上去 shàngqù ⊞ go up to

上升 shàngshēng ⊞ ascend

上市 shǎngshì ⊞ go on the market

上述 shàngshù ⊞ above-mentioned

上司 shàngsī ⊞ boss, superior

上訴 shàngsù ⊞ appeal

一
1

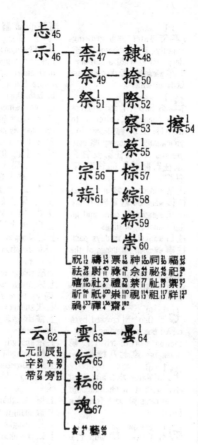

卡車 kǎchē 图 truck
卡片 kǎpiàn 图 card
卡通 kǎtōng 图 cartoon

志 45 tǎn Rising 上 heart 心. 图 timid
志忑 tǎntè 图 apprehensive, disturbed 图 indecisive

示 46 shì The three 三 (written vertically to resemble 小) elements, sun, moon and stars, of heaven above 上 (early form resembling 二) which reveal the truths of gods. 图 teach, show ⇔ 指示, 揭示, 展示, 暗示, 啓示, 提示, 出示, 表示, 顯示
示範 shìfàn 图 demonstrate, show, set an example
示威 shìwēi 图 demonstrate: 示威遊行 demonstration, protest march

奈 47 nài Tree 木 with 示 phonetic. 图 a kind of apple

隸 48 [隶] Seize by the tail 隶 with 奈 phonetic. 图 attached to, belong to 图 be subordinate to 图 servant, slave ⇔ 奴隸
隸書 lìshū 图 clerical script - a calligraphy style
隸屬 lìshǔ 图 belong to, be affiliated

奈 49 nài A miswriting of 柰. 图 what ⇔ 無可奈何, 無奈

捺 50 nà Hand 手 with 奈 phonetic. 图 press with the hand 图 right-falling calligraphy stroke ⇔ 按捺

祭 51 jì Meat 肉 offered with

上台 shàngtái 图 go on stage
上天 shàngtiān 图 heaven
上午 shàngwǔ 图 morning
上下 shàngxià 图 above and below: 上下文 context 图 about
上校 shàngxiào 图 colonel
上學 shàngxué 图 attend school
上旬 shàngxún 图 first ten days of a month
上癮 shàngyǐn 图 become addicted to
上元 shàngyuán 图 Lantern Festival
上漲 shàngzhǎng 图 rise

卡 44 kǎ Controls movement up 上 and down 下 图 checkpoint 图 block, make stuck: 卡住了 stuck 图 card ⇔ 賀卡, 刷卡, 綠卡, 關卡

hand 又 [14] to win revelations 示 ⳑ. 图 sacrifice 图 festival

祭祀 jìsì 图 religious ceremony 回 offer sacrifices: 祭祀祖先 offer sacrifices to ancestors

祭壇 jìtán 图 altar

祭祖 jìzǔ 回 offer sacrifices to ancestors

際 52 [际] Embankment 阜 [67] with 祭 ⳑ phonetic. 回 border, boundary ⇔ 人際 [10], 交際 ⳑ, 國際 ⳑ, 實際 ⳑ, 邊際 [39]

察 53 Hut 宀 [61] with 祭 ⳑ phonetic. 回 investigate, examine ⇔ 檢察官 ⳑ, 考察 ⳑ, 警察 ⳑ, 勘察 ⳑ, 洞察 ⳑ, 偵察 ⳑ, 視察 ⳑ, 監察 ⳑ, 觀察 ⳑ

察覺 chájué 回 perceive

察看 chákàn 回 observe

擦 54 Hand 手 [79] examining 察 ⳑ (phonetic). 回 rub 回 wipe ⇔ 摩擦 ⳑ

擦傷 cāshāng 图 回 scratch

擦拭 cāshì 回 clean

蔡 55 Grass 艸 [57] with 祭 ⳑ phonetic. 图 grass 图 a surname: 蔡倫 Cai Lun - Eastern Han Dynasty inventor of paper

宗 56 Building 宀 [61] of worship 示 ⳑ. 图 ancestors 图 religion ⇔ 教宗 ⳑ, 正宗 ⳑ, 祖宗 ⳑ, 禪宗 ⳑ

宗教 zōngjiào 图 religion: 宗教自由 freedom of religion

宗派 zōngpài 图 sect

宗旨 zōngzhǐ 图 objective, purpose

棕 57 Modern form shows tree 木 [77] with 宗 ⳑ phonetic. 图 palm tree

棕櫚 zōnglú 图 palm tree

棕色 zōngsè 图 brown

綜 58 [综] Threads 糸 [53] with 宗 ⳑ phonetic. 回 weaving tool 回 synthesize ⇔ 錯綜 ⳑ

綜觀 zòngguān 图 overview

綜合 zònghé 回 synthesize: 綜合大學 comprehensive university

綜藝 zòngyì 图 variety show

粽 59 Modern form shows rice 米 [38] with 宗 ⳑ phonetic.

粽子 zòngzi 图 rice dumplings wrapped in leaves

崇 60 Mountain 山 [67] great like ancestors 宗 (phonetic). 图 lofty 回 worship, idolize ⇔ 推崇 ⳑ

崇拜 chóngbài 回 worship, idolize

崇高 chónggāo 图 lofty, high

崇敬 chóngjìng 回 revere, esteem

崇洋 chóngyáng 回 worship foreign things

蒜 61 Plant 艸 [57] and a phonetic element resembling a pair of the character 示 ⳑ. 图 garlic ⇔ 大蒜 ⳑ

云 62 Vapors (resembling ㄙ [79]) rising 上 ⳑ (early form written as 二 ⳑ). 图 clouds (⇔ 雲 ⳑ) 回 say, speak: 人云亦云 parrot others

雲 63 [云 ⳑ] Rising vapors 云 ⳑ (phonetic) that form rain 雨 [61] 图 clouds ⇔ 彩雲 ⳑ

雲彩 yúncǎi 图 clouds

雲海 yúnhǎi 图 sea of clouds

雲南 yúnnán 图 Yunnan Province

雲霧 yúnwù 图 mist

曇 64 [昙] Sun 日 [76] blocked by clouds 雲 ⳑ. 图 cloud cover 曇花一現 tánhuāyīxiàn 回 flash in the pan

紜 65 [纭] Modern form shows thread 糸 [53] jumbled like clouds 云 ⳑ (phonetic). 图 tangled, disorderly ⇔ 紛紜 ⳑ

耘 66 Modern form shows plow 耒 ⳑ with 云 ⳑ phonetic. 回 weed ⇔ 耕耘 ⳑ

魂 67 Vaporous 云 ⳑ (phonetic) spirit 鬼 [40]. 图 soul ⇔ 鬼魂 ⳑ, 靈魂 ⳑ

魂魄 húnpò 图 soul

下 68 Analogous to 上 ⳑ, originally a longer horizontal line 一| above a shorter horizontal line with a vertical line | added later. 回 below, lower 图 next: 下禮拜見. See you next week. 回 go down, get off: 下車 exit a vehicle ⇔ 一下 ⳑ, 一下子 ⳑ, 上下 ⳑ, 閣下 ⳑ, 落下 ⳑ, 鄉下 ⳑ, 陛下 ⳑ, 剩下 ⳑ, 跪下 ⳑ, 四下 ⳑ, 南下 ⳑ, 天下 ⳑ, 吞下 ⳑ, 丟下 ⳑ, 零下 ⳑ, 如下 ⳑ, 每況愈下 ⳑ, 樓下 ⳑ, 地下 ⳑ, 以下 ⳑ, 當下 ⳑ, 之下 ⳑ, 坐下 ⳑ, 掉下 ⳑ, 留下 ⳑ, 爬下 ⳑ, 足下 ⳑ, 手下 ⳑ, 跌下 ⳑ, 放下 ⳑ, 底下 ⳑ, 買下 ⳑ, 蹲下 ⳑ

下巴 xiàbā 图 chin

下班 xiàbān 回 get off work

下邊 xiàbiān 图 图 underneath, below

下次 xiàcì 图 next time another time

下風 xiàfēng 图 图 leeward disadvantage

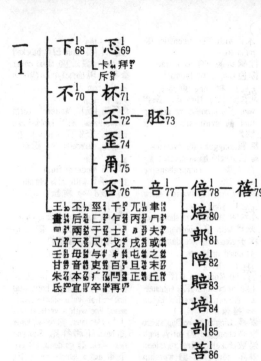

不够, 岂不够, 心不在焉[83]
巴不得[87], 毫不[87], 看不起[88], 想不到[89], 永垂不朽[90], 来不及[90], 免不了[91], 对不起[76]

不安 bùān [形] uneasy
不必 bùbì [副] need not
不便 bùbiàn [形] inconvenient
不測 bùcè [名] contingency
不啻 bùchì [副] tantamount to, equivalent to
不錯 bùcuò [形] not bad, good
不但 bùdàn [副] not only
不當 bùdàng [形] inappropriate
不得 bùdé [副] cannot
不得不 bùdébù [副] cannot help but, must
不得了 bùdéliǎo [形] extremely [副] amazing
不得已 bùdéyǐ [副] cannot help but, must
不斷 bùduàn [副] continuously
不對 bùduì [形] wrong, incorrect
不對勁 bùduìjìn [形] unsatisfactory
不凡 bùfán [形] exceptional, extraordinary
不妨 bùfáng [副] no harm in: 不妨去一下? Why not go for a bit?
不敷 bùfū [形] insufficient, inadequate
不敢 bùgǎn [副] dare not
不顧 bùgù [副] regardless of
不管 bùguǎn [副] regardless of [动] disregard
不過 bùguò [连] however
不合 bùhé [动] not conform to [形] incompatible
不會 bùhuì [副] cannot
不及 bùjí [介] inferior to, inadequate: 來不及 too late
不見 bùjiàn [形] missing, not in sight
不見得 bùjiàndé [副] not necessarily
不禁 bùjīn [副] cannot help but
不僅 bùjǐn [副] not only

下海 xiàhǎi [动] go to sea [动] go commercial
下降 xiàjiàng [动] descend, drop
下課 xiàkè [动] dismiss class
下來 xiàlái [动] come down
下流 xiàliú [形] obscene, dirty
下落 xiàluò [名] whereabouts: 下落不明 whereabouts unknown
下面 xiàmiàn [名] below, underneath
下麵 xiàmiàn [动] make noodles
下棋 xiàqí [动] play chess, play go
下去 xiàqù [动] go down [动] go on, continue: 不能這樣繼續下去。It can't continue to go on like this.
下手 xiàshǒu [动] begin, start
下午 xiàwǔ [名] afternoon
下鄉 xiàxiāng [动] go to the countryside

下旬 xiàxún [名] last ten days of a month
下游 xiàyóu [名] downstream
下雨 xiàyǔ [动] rain: 下大雨 rain heavily

忑 [1] tè [69] Falling 下 heart 心 [形] timid ⟷ 忐忑

不 [1] bù [70] Pictograph of a bird rising to heaven 一乚 [动] soar away [副] no, not ⟷ 說不定, 比不上, 怪不得, 差不多, 供不應求, 要不然, 迥然不同, 喋喋不休, 無不, 捨不得, 好不, 屢見不鮮, 孜孜不倦, 了不起, 莫

不盡 bùjìn endlessly
不久 bùjiǔ not long, soon
不堪 bùkān unbearable, extremely
不可思議 bùkěsīyì unimaginable
不肯 bùkěn unwilling
不快 bùkuài displeased, unhappy
不理 bùlǐ ignore
不利 bùlì disadvantageous
不料 bùliào unexpectedly
不論 bùlùn regardless of
不滿 bùmǎn dissatisfied
不免 bùmiǎn unavoidable, unavoidably
不妙 bùmiào bode ill
不耐煩 bùnàifán impatient
不能 bùnéng cannot
不能不 bùnéngbù cannot help but
不偏不倚 bùpiānbùyǐ unbiased
不然 bùrán otherwise
不忍 bùrěn cannot bear to
不如 bùrú inferior to, incomparable to
不少 bùshǎo not a few, many
不勝 bùshèng extremely
不時 bùshí occasionally
不俗 bùsú uncommon, original
不停 bùtíng nonstop
不通 bùtōng obstructed, impassable: 講不通 unable to communicate
不同 bùtóng different
不肖 bùxiào unworthy, degenerate
不孝 bùxiào unfilial
不行 bùxíng impossible
不幸 bùxìng unfortunately, unfortunate, adversity
不朽 bùxiǔ immortal
不一 bùyī varying
不宜 bùyí inappropriate, inadvisable
不已 bùyǐ endlessly

不用 bùyòng need not
不悅 bùyuè upset, unhappy
不再 bùzài no longer, never again
不在 bùzài absent
不知不覺 bùzhībùjué unconsciously, imperceptibly

杯 bēi 71 Modern form shows wood 木 with 不 phonetic. cup: 世界杯 World Cup ⟺ 茶杯, 乾杯
杯葛 bēigé boycott
杯子 bēizi cup

丕 pī 72 Unique 一 with 不 phonetic. great

胚 pēi 73 Modern form shows flesh 肉 with 丕 phonetic. embryo
胚胎 pēitāi embryo

歪 wāi 74 Not 不 straight 正. crooked, askew
歪曲 wāiqū distort, twist, distorted
歪斜 wāixié crooked, askew

甭 béng 75 Not 不 necessary 用 (together phonetic). do not, unnecessary

否 fǒu 76 No 不 (phonetic) from the mouth 口. no 是否, 能否
否定 fǒudìng negate, deny, negation, denial
否決 fǒujué veto: 否決權 veto power
否認 fǒurèn deny, denial
否則 fǒuzé otherwise

咅 dòu 77 Deny 否 (phonetic, altered) with dot on top. spit in contempt.

倍 bèi 78 Person 人 opposing

咅 (phonetic). rebel, times, multiple ⟺ 加倍
倍數 bèishù multiple

蓓 péi bèi 79 Plant 艸 multiplying 倍 (phonetic). bud
蓓蕾 bèilěi bud

焙 bèi 80 Fire 火 with 咅 phonetic. bake ⟺ 烘焙

部 bù 81 City 邑 with 咅 phonetic. part, section, department, section ⟺ 頸部, 胸部, 北部, 臀部, 腰部, 局部, 腹部, 內部, 南部, 全部, 大部, 大部份, 大部分, 頭部, 幹部, 東部, 西部, 俱樂部
部分 bùfēn part, section
部份 bùfèn part, section
部落 bùluò tribe
部門 bùmén section, division
部首 bùshǒu radical (of a Chinese character)
部署 bùshǔ deploy
部長 bùzhǎng minister, section chief

陪 péi 82 Hill 阜 with 咅 phonetic and suggestive of multiple 倍. pile up (⟹ 培) accompany
陪伴 péibàn accompany, keep company
陪嫁 péijià dowry
陪酒 péijiǔ drink with patron
陪審 péishěn serve jury duty: 陪審團 jury; 陪審員 juror

賠 péi 83 [赔] Money/shells 貝 with 咅 phonetic. compensate, lose (money) ⟺ 索賠
賠償 péicháng compensate: 賠償費 compensation, damages

字譜及字典

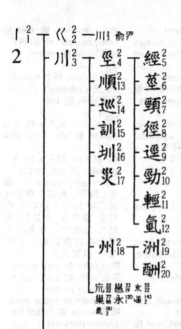

經常 jīngcháng 副 usually, normally

經典 jīngdiǎn 名 classics 形 classical

經度 jīngdù 名 longitude

經費 jīngfèi 名 budget, appropriations

經過 jīngguò 動 pass through

經濟 jīngjì 名 economy: 經濟學 economics; 經濟學家 economist; 經濟特區 special economic zone 形 economical: 經濟艙 economy class

經紀人 jīngjìrén 名 agent, broker

經理 jīnglǐ 動 manage 名 manager: 總經理 general manager

經歷 jīnglì 名 experience

經書 jīngshū 名 classics, scriptures: 佛教經書 Buddhist scriptures

經緯 jīngwěi 名 warp and woof 名 longitude and latitude

經驗 jīngyàn 名 experience: 有經驗 experienced

經營 jīngyíng 動 manage, operate

經由 jīngyóu 介 through, via, by way of

scriptures ⇔ 五經, 書經, 神經, 詩經, 念經, 已經, 財經, 佛經, 聖經, 月經, 正經, 歷經, 曾經, 易經

賠錢 péiqián 動 lose money 名 compensate

培 1 péi 84 Earth 土ㄊ with 咅ㄅ phonetic. 動 pile up 動 cultivate ⇔ 栽培

培養 péiyǎng 動 foster, nurture, train: 培養人材 nurture talent

培育 péiyù 動 cultivate, breed

培植 péizhí 動 cultivate, raise

剖 1 pōu/pōu 85 Conflict 咅ㄅ (phonetic) divided 刀ㄉ. 動 analyze, dissect ⇔ 解剖

剖析 pōuxī 動 analyze, dissect

菩 1 pú 86 Plant 艸 with 咅ㄅ phonetic. 名 sacred Buddhist tree

菩薩 púsà 名 Bodhisattva

丨 2 chuān
1 Pictograph of a small stream of water.

巛 2 kuài
2 Two small streams 丨丨.

川 2 chuān
3 Streams 丨丨 巛 joining. Also used in composition as pictograph of hair. 名 river ⇔ 河川, 四川, 山川

巠 2 jīng
4 River 川 under the surface 一, with 㞢 (altered to resemble 工) phonetic. 名 water course

經 5 [经] Threads 糸 following course 巠 (phonetic). 名 warp (of a fabric) 動 pass through, experience 名

莖 6 [茎] Plant's 艸 internal river 巠 (phonetic). 名 stalk, stem ⇔ 陰莖

頸 7 [颈] Course 巠 (phonetic) to head 頁. 名 neck, throat ⇔ 長頸鹿, 瓶頸

頸部 jǐngbù 名 neck, throat

徑 8 [径] Step 彳 along a course 巠 (phonetic). 名

字譜及字典

path, track 图 way, means 图 diameter ⇔ 路徑, 行徑, 途徑, 口徑, 捷徑, 半徑, 田徑

逕 9 [迳] Variant of 徑 showing movement 辵 along a course 巠 (phonetic). path, track

逕行 jìngxíng proceed without authorization

逕自 jìngzì without authorization

勁 10 [劲] Internal river 巠 (phonetic) of strength 力. jìn: 图 vigor, energy jìng: 圈 strong, powerful ⇔ 不對勁, 後勁, 起勁, 強勁, 使勁, 幹勁, 卯勁

勁敵 jìngdí 图 powerful adversary

輕 11 [轻] Cart 車 moving swiftly on course 巠 (phonetic). 圈 light, easy, simple 圓 slight, belittle ⇔ 年輕, 減輕, 看輕

輕浮 qīngfú frivolous, flighty

輕忽 qīnghū slight, neglect, belittle neglectfully

輕快 qīngkuài brisk, agile, spry light-hearted, lively

輕聲 qīngshēng softly (speak) 图 neutral tone (in Chinese)

輕視 qīngshì look down on, belittle

輕率 qīngshuài neglect rash, indiscreet

輕鬆 qīngsōng relaxed

輕微 qīngwéi slight, minor

輕易 qīngyì easy, simple

輕盈 qīngyíng slim and graceful

氫 12 [氢] Air 气 with 巠 phonetic and suggestive of

light 輕 图 hydrogen

氫彈 qīngdàn 图 hydrogen bomb

順 13 [顺] Head 頁 orderly like stream 川 (phonetic). 圈 arrange 圈 obey, follow 圈 smooth, flowing, hitchless ⇔ 孝順, 溫順, 通順

順便 shùnbiàn 圈 at one's convenience, conveniently: 順便一題 by the way

順從 shùncóng 圈 obey, submit

順口 shùnkǒu 圈 easily spoken 圈 mention in passing

順利 shùnlì 圈 smoothly, without a hitch

順手 shùnshǒu 圈 smoothly

順序 shùnxù 圈 sequence, order

巡 14 xún Travel 辵 down like a river 川 (phonetic). 圈 imperial inspection tour 圈 patrol

巡查 xúnchá 圈 patrol

巡航 xúnháng 图 圈 cruise: 巡航導彈 cruise missile

巡迴 xúnhuí 圈 tour

巡邏 xúnluó 圈 patrol

巡視 xúnshì 圈 make an inspection tour

巡弋 xúnyì 圈 cruise: 巡弋飛彈 cruise missile

訓 15 xùn [训] Words 言 like stream 川 (phonetic). instruct, counsel ⇔ 教訓, 受訓

訓導 xùndǎo 圈 guide, counsel

訓詁 xùngǔ 图 annotations (on ancient texts)

訓誡 xùnjiè 圈 admonish

訓練 xùnliàn 圈 train 图 training, discipline

圳 16 圈 jùn zhèn Dirt 土 river 川 (phonetic). irrigation ditch ⇔ 深圳

災 17 [灾] River 川 and fire 火. Simplified form is an ancient form with roof 宀. 图 disaster ⇔ 旱災, 火災

災害 zāihài 图 disaster

災荒 zāihuāng 图 famine

災禍 zāihùo 图 disaster

災難 zāinàn 图 disaster

州 18 Land, represented by dots, between rivers 川. 图 state, province ⇔ 神州, 廣州, 加州, 杭州, 徐州, 滿州, 貴州, 蘇州

州長 zhōuzhǎng 图 governor

洲 19 Dots of land 州 (phonetic) with water redundant. 图 island in a river continent ⇔ 綠洲, 歐洲, 中美洲, 美洲, 澳洲, 亞洲, 非洲

酬 20 Liquor 酉 with 州 phonetic. 圈 toast 圈 reward ⇔ 報酬, 應酬

酬報 chóubào 图 remuneration

酬金 chóujīn 图 remuneration

酬勞 chóuláo 图 remuneration

酬謝 chóuxiè 圈 offer a gift in appreciation

水 21 shuǐ Pictograph of streams (⇨ 丨 冫) flowing together. 图 water ⇔ 泉水, 飲水, 潛水, 露水, 落水, 汲水, 洪水, 河水, 污水, 冷水, 鼻水, 風水, 膠水, 汗水, 薪水, 海水, 流水, 山水, 潑水, 淚水, 開水, 汽水, 淡水, 溪水, 香水, 自來水, 墨水, 雨水, 排水

水壩 shuǐbà 图 dam

水槽 shuǐcáo 图 sink

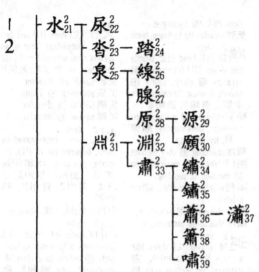

水²₂₁ ┬ 尿²₂₂
      ├ 沓²₂₃ — 踏²₂₄
      ├ 泉²₂₅ ┬ 線²₂₆
      │   ├ 腺²₂₇
      │   ├ 原²₂₈ — 源²₂₉
      └ 臦²₃₁ ┬ 淵²₃₂ — 願²₃₀
              └ 肅²₃₃ ┬ 繡²₃₄
                      ├ 鏽²₃₅
                      ├ 蕭²₃₆ — 瀟²₃₇
                      ├ 簫²₃₈
                      └ 嘯²₃₉

水車 shuǐchē 图 waterwheel: 水車屋 mill
水池 shuǐchí 图 pond
水稻 shuǐdào 图 paddy rice
水滴 shuǐdī 图 drop of water
水痘 shuǐdòu 图 chickenpox
水溝 shuǐgōu 图 gutter, drain
水管 shuǐguǎn 图 water pipe
水果 shuǐguǒ 图 fruit
水壺 shuǐhú 图 kettle
水餃 shuǐjiǎo 图 (steamed) dumpling
水晶 shuǐjīng 图 crystal
水庫 shuǐkù 图 reservoir
水力 shuǐlì 图 water power
水利 shuǐlì 图 water conservancy, irrigation projects
水流 shuǐliú 图 flow, current
水泥 shuǐní 图 cement
水鳥 shuǐniǎo 图 waterfowl
水牛 shuǐniú 图 water buffalo
水平 shuǐpíng 图 图 level, standard
水手 shuǐshǒu 图 sailor, seaman
水塔 shuǐtǎ 图 water tower

水塘 shuǐtáng 图 pool, pond
水土 shuǐtǔ 图 water and soil 图 natural environment: 水土不服 unadjusted to local climate and conditions
水源 shuǐyuán 图 headwaters
水準 shuǐzhǔn 图 level, standard

尿² niào
22 Water 水³₂₁ from the tail 尾⁹₇ (abbreviated to 尸¹⁰). 图 urine 图 urinate ⇔ 糖尿病³₄, 泌尿器⁹₄, 撒尿²₂
尿布 niàobù 图 diaper

沓² tà 图 dá
23 Speech 曰⁴₈ flowing like water 水³₂₁. 图 reiterated, repeated: 人聲雜沓 hubbub 图 pile

踏² tà
24 Foot 足⁹₈ and repeated 沓²₂₃ (phonetic). 图 step on, tread on ⇔ 踐踏⁴₅, 腳踏車⁶⁰
踏實 tàshí 图 practical, realistic

泉² quán
25 Modern form shows white 白²⁶ water 水³₂₁. 图 spring ⇔ 礦泉⁸⁴, 溫泉⁹⁷
泉水 quánshuǐ 图 spring water
泉源 quányuán 图 wellspring, fountainhead

線² xiàn
26 [线] A thread 系¹⁵³ of spring water 泉²₂₅ (phonetic). Simplified form based on alternate form with 戔⁹⁵ thread, string, wire 图 line 路線⁴⁹, 縫線⁴⁸, 光線⁴¹, 有線¹¹⁶, 電線¹³⁹, 佔線²⁶, 界線²⁷, 直線³₃, 無線⁷⁷, 天線⁷⁹, 航線⁵⁹, 地平線⁵⁸, 幹線²⁹, 曲線¹³⁵, 戰線¹³⁶, 陣線⁵⁹
線路 xiànlù 图 line, circuit
線索 xiànsuǒ 图 clue
線條 xiàntiáo 图 line
線性 xiànxìng 图 linear

腺² xiàn
27 Body 肉¹³² and spring 泉²₂₅ (phonetic). 图 gland

原² yuán
28 Spring 泉²₂₅ (altered, phonetic) emanating from a cliff 厂⁷². 图 original, former 图 raw, unprocessed ⇔ 平原²₃, 草原⁹⁶
原本 yuánběn 图 original
原稿 yuángǎo 图 manuscript, original
原告 yuángào 图 plaintiff
原故 yuángù 图 reason
原來 yuánlái 图 original, former: 原來如此! Oh, so that's how it is!
原理 yuánlǐ 图 principle
原諒 yuánliàng 图 forgive
原料 yuánliào 图 raw material
原始 yuánshǐ 图 primitive, aboriginal
原文 yuánwén 图 original text 图 original language
原先 yuánxiān 图 at first, orig-

inally

原因 yuányīn 图 reason

原有 yuányǒu 图 originally possessed

原則 yuánzé 图 principle: 有原則 principled

原住民 yuánzhùmín 图 aborigine

原子 yuánzǐ 图 atom: 原子彈 atomic bomb; 图 原子筆 ballpoint pen

源 29 Water's 水 origin 原 (phonetic). 图 fountain-head 图 source ⇔ 水源, 泉源, 淵源, 資源, 根源, 電源, 溯源, 字源, 起源, 能源, 來源

源流 yuánliú 图 origin and development

源自 yuánzì 图 originate from, come from

願 30 [愿] Source 原 (phonetic) and head 頁. Simplified form uses heart 心. 图 hope, desire 图 be willing, consent to ⇔ 志願, 如願, 甘願, 意願, 情願, 請願, 但願, 心願, 寧願, 自願

願望 yuànwàng 图 hope, aspiration, wish

願意 yuànyì 图 wish, want be willing, consent to

㳇 31 Contained 口 (altered) water 水 (altered) swirling. 图 whirlpool, abyss (⇨ 淵)

淵 32 [渊] Watery 水 abyss 㳇 (phonetic). 图 abyss deep, profound

淵藪 yuānsǒu 图 cesspool of evil

淵源 yuānyuán 图 origin, source

肅 33 [肅] Dexterous actions on the edge of an abyss 㳇. 图 solemn ⇔ 甘肅, 整肅, 嚴肅

肅穆 sùmù 图 solemn and peaceful

肅清 sùqīng 图 eliminate, purge

繡 34 [绣] Work thread 糸 solemnly 肅 (phonetic). Simplified form uses 秀. 图 embroider ⇔ 錦繡

繡花 xiùhuā 图 embroider

鏽 35 [锈] Metal 金 with 肅 phonetic. Simplified form uses 秀. 图 rust: 不鏽鋼 stainless steel ⇔ 生鏽

蕭 36 [萧] Plant 艸 and solemn 肅 (phonetic). 图 a kind of artemisa 图 gloomy a surname

蕭瑟 xiāosè 图 bleak, desolate

蕭條 xiāotiáo 图 depression: 經濟蕭條 economic depression

瀟 37 [潇] Water 水 with 蕭 phonetic. 图 sound of wind and rain

瀟灑 xiāosǎ 图 easy-going

簫 38 [箫] Bamboo 竹 that makes solemn 肅 (phonetic) sounds. 图 a panpipe

嘯 39 [啸] Mouth 口 making solemn 肅 (phonetic) sounds. 图 whistle, howl ⇔ 呼嘯, 海嘯

丿 1 A falling line suggesting motion. Now 撇.

乂 2 Lines 丿 乀 cutting left and right. 图 mow

刈 3 Churning 乂 (phonetic) blades 刀. 图 mow

艾 4 Plant 艸 with 乂 phonetic. 图 moxa

哎 5 Mouth 口 with 艾 phonetic. 图 an interjection expressing regret

哎呀 āiyā 图 an interjection expressing regret or surprise

凶 6 Pictograph of a pit 凵 crossed 乂. 图 unlucky 图 fierce, evil

凶多吉少 xiōngduōjíshǎo 图 bode ill

凶惡 xiōngè brutal, vicious (⇨ 兇惡)

凶猛 xiōngměng 图 ferocious

兇 7 [凶] Person 儿 under evil 凶 (phonetic) influence. 图 cruel, fierce ⇔ 元兇, 行兇, 幫兇

兇惡 xiōngè brutal, vicious (⇨ 凶惡)

兇狠 xiōnghěn 图 fierce, malicious

兇猛 xiōngměng 图 ferocious, violent

兇手 xiōngshǒu 图 murderer

㐰 8 Difficulty walking 夂 with 兇 phonetic. 图 hesitate

傻 9 Person 人 and hesitate 㐰 (altered). 图 stupid

傻瓜 shǎguā 图 fool, idiot

傻笑 shǎxiào 图 silly smile

傻子 shǎzi 图 fool, idiot

匈 10 Wrap 勹 with 凶 phonetic and suggestive of pit 凵. 图 chest, bosom (⇨ 胸)

匈奴 xiōngnú 图 Huns

渲 汪 柴 沏 洲 源 淵 瀟
淘 淯 注 氿 漱 潛 洛 況
洗 混 泥 浪 滄 濤 津 康
凄 浸 汲 波 洪 港 澱 暴
瀑 鹽 漂 淹 淺 泰 涵 涵
氾 泡 潑 潰 范 茫 渴 淘
涼 沈 洞 漫 冰 滌 沾 河
汗 污 沙 渺 消 瀾 沛 渤
染 汁 沽 湖 渡 演 漢 灤
汾 灑 梁 沼 沒 沉 泣 汰
添 決 法 測 衍 象 洽 涂
減 滅 泌 淇 滲 汗 溯
澤 滓 江 渠 深 演 涕 沸
流 潦 治 滋 深 演 涕 沸
漠 沌 泛 澡 活 谷 溶 浴
沿 溫 沖 溝 博 浦 澄 澎
洼 涯 澆 涇 清 汐 液 滿
滿 濱 泊 湯 渣 瀚 潮 潭
沐 淋 泪 潤 溜 淛 潔 漱
漿 灃 淚 潤 溜 淛 汔
淡 澄 瀨 涉 涎 湃 求 浩
滸 激 淅 漸 浙 沃 溪 淨
潰 灑 黍 油 湘 渝 潯 益
溢 沮 渡 沙 泑 泯 永 泳
派 淑 濾 洋 漾 灘 泳
滕 滷 滔 灑 滑 渦 冽 洶
濫 涵 測 汗 混 灕 半
潘 瀋 澳 渾 酒 酋 淮 準

丿 3/1 — 乂 3/2 — 刈 3/3
— 艾 3/4 — 哎 3/5
— 凶 3/6 — 兇 3/7 — 燮 3/8 — 傻 3/9
— 匈 3/10 — 胸 3/11
— 酗 3/13 — 洶 3/12
— 爻 3/14 — 㸚 3/15 — 爽 3/16
— 駁 3/17 — 爾 40
— 肴 3/18 — 淆 3/19

匈牙利 xiōngyálì 國 Hungary

胸 3
11 Chest 匈 (phonetic)

bosom
胸懷 xiōnghuái 國 cherish
胸脯 xiōngpú 國 breast, bosom
胸膛 xiōngtáng 國 chest
胸罩 xiōngzhào 國 bra
胸針 xiōngzhēn 國 brooch

洶 3
12 [洶] Water 水 like a heaving chest 匈 (phonetic). 國 turbulent
洶洶 xiōngxiōng 國 roaring
洶湧 xiōngyǒng 國 dashing

酗 3
13 Alcohol-induced 酉 violence 凶. 國 drunken rage
酗酒 xùjǐu 國 be addicted to alcohol 國 alcoholism

爻 3
14 Interactive 乂 movement. 國 cross, intersect 國 a unit of the Eight Diagrams (⇨ 八卦)

㸚 3
15 Doubly intersect 爻. 國 lattice

爽 3
16 Large 大 with lattices 㸚. 國 clear, open 國 refreshing ⇨ 清爽
爽快 shuǎngkuài 國 refreshed 國 quickly and clearly (decide)

駁 3
17 [駁] Horse 馬 with mixed 爻 colors. 國 variegated 國 refute ⇨ 反駁
駁斥 bóchì 國 refute
駁回 bóhuí 國 reject, refuse

肴 3
18 Mixed 爻 (phonetic) meats 肉. 國 prepared meat dishes ⇨ 菜肴
肴饌 yáozhuàn 國 courses at a banquet

淆 3
19 Water 水 with 肴 phonetic. 國 confused ⇨ 混淆

with flesh 肉 redundant. 國 chest, bosom
胸部 xiōngbù 國 chest, bust,

希 3 xī
20 Specially interwoven 交[3/14] cloth 巾[1/53]. 【形】 rare 【動】 hope
希罕 xīhǎn 【形】 rare, scarce
希臘 xīlà 【地】 Greece
希特勒 xītèlè 【人】 Hitler
希望 xīwàng 【動】【名】 hope

稀 3 xī
21 Grain 禾[1/108] rare 希[3/20] (phonetic). 【形】 sparse, scarce
稀飯 xīfàn 【名】 rice porridge
稀奇 xīqí 【形】 rare, unusual
稀少 xīshǎo 【形】 rare, scarce

网 3 wǎng
22 Covering 冖[1/24] with 乂[3/2] representing interwoven ropes. 【名】 net (⇨ 網[3/24])

罔 3 wǎng
23 Net 网[3/22] to prevent escape 亡[27/13]. 【名】 net (⇨ 網[3/24]) 【副】 not

網 3 wǎng
24 [网[3/22]] Thread 糸[1/53] net 罔[3/23] (phonetic). 【名】 net, web: 互聯網 (網) internet; 萬維網 (網) world wide web ⇔ 蛛網[77/45], 羅網[162/14]
網路 wǎnglù 【名】(網) network: 網際網路 internet
網羅 wǎngluó 【動】 recruit, enlist
網絡 wǎngluò 【名】(網) network
網膜 wǎngmó 【名】 retina
網球 wǎngqiú 【名】 tennis
網站 wǎngzhàn 【名】 website

岡 3 gāng
25 [冈] Mountain 山[1/67] covered in net 网[3/22] (phonetic) of clouds. 【名】 mountain ridge (⇨ 崗[3/29])

剛 3 gāng
26 [刚] Ridge 岡[3/25] (phonetic) of a knife 刀[1/35]. (古) chop 【形】 tough, firm 【副】 just now 【副】 just, exactly
剛纔 gāngcái 【副】 just now
剛才 gāngcái 【副】 just now
剛剛 gānggāng 【副】 just
剛好 gānghǎo 【形】 just right
剛强 gāngqiáng 【形】 indomitable, firm

綱 3 gāng
27 [纲] Thread 糸[1/53] with 岡[3/25] phonetic. 【名】 rope for pulling nets ⇔ 大綱[1/39], 題綱[181/54]
綱領 gānglǐng 【名】 outline, guideline
綱目 gāngmù 【名】 outline
綱要 gāngyào 【名】 outline

鋼 3 gāng
28 [钢] Metal 金[3/44] with 岡[3/25] phonetic and suggestive of firm 剛[3/26]. 【名】 steel ⇔ 煉鋼[82/108]
鋼筆 gāngbǐ 【名】 fountain pen
鋼筋 gāngjīn 【名】 steel reinforcing bar
鋼琴 gāngqín 【名】 piano
鋼絲 gāngsī 【名】 steel wire
鋼鐵 gāngtiě 【名】 steel, iron and steel

崗 3 gǎng
29 [岗] Mountain ridge 岡[3/25] (phonetic) with mountain 山[1/67] redundant. 【名】 mountain ridge 【名】 sentry post
崗哨 gǎngshào 【名】 sentry, lookout
崗位 gǎngwèi 【名】 sentry post

丨 4 gěn
1 Ideograph representing vertical things.

亅 5 juē
1 Pictograph of a hook.

丶 6 zhǔ
1 Pictograph of a flame. (古) flame (⇨ 炷[6/3])

主 6 zhǔ
2 Pictograph of a lamp and flame 丶[6/1]. (古) flame (⇨ 炷[6/3]) 【名】 master 【名】 owner 【形】 primary, main 【動】 advocate ⇔ 三民主義[1/19], 人本主義[1/10], 君主[14/40], 公主[19/2], 沙文主義[29/15], 眞主[31/32], 天主教[39/35], 地主[56/6], 幫主[20/25], 債主[70/69], 雇主[78/5], 民主[1/19], 自主[1/39], 霸主[161/10]
主辦 zhǔbàn 【名】 sponsor
主播 zhǔbō 【名】 news anchor
主持 zhǔchí 【動】 preside over, be in charge of: 主持人 master of ceremonies, host 【動】 uphold
主導 zhǔdǎo 【形】 guiding, dominant
主動 zhǔdòng 【形】 active 【名】 initiative
主婦 zhǔfù 【名】 housewife: 家庭主婦 housewife 【名】 hostess
主觀 zhǔguān 【形】 subjective
主管 zhǔguǎn 【名】 supervisor
主角 zhǔjiǎo 【名】 leading role: 男主角 leading actor; 女主角 leading actress
主教 zhǔjiào 【名】 bishop
主流 zhǔliú 【形】 mainstream: 主流派 mainstream faction; 非主流派 non-mainstream faction
主權 zhǔquán 【名】 sovereignty
主人 zhǔrén 【名】 master 【名】 host
主任 zhǔrèn 【名】 director, chair: 系主任 department chair
主題 zhǔtí 【名】 theme, subject
主席 zhǔxí 【名】 chair: 毛主席 Chairman Mao
主修 zhǔxiū 【動】 major in 【名】(網) major
主演 zhǔyǎn 【動】 star, play leading role: 主演員 leading actor
主要 zhǔyào 【形】 main, principal
主義 zhǔyì 【名】 doctrine, ideology: 社會主義 socialism
主意 zhǔyì 【名】 idea
主因 zhǔyīn 【名】 primary cause
主宰 zhǔzǎi 【動】 dominate, control
主張 zhǔzhāng 【動】 advocate, promote

炷 6 zhù
3 Fire 火[1/82] of lamp 主[6/2] (phonetic). 【名】 wick 【量】 stick (of incense)

住 6 zhù
4 Person 人[1/10] still like a

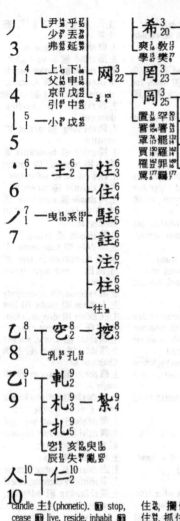

住院 zhùyuàn 動 be hospitalized

住宅 zhùzhái 图 residence: 住宅區 residential area

住址 zhùzhǐ 图 address

駐 6 zhù
5 [驻] Horse 馬 still like a candle 主 (phonetic). 動 halt, stop 图 station

駐防 zhùfáng 動 station defensive troops

駐軍 zhùjūn 動 station troops

駐守 zhùshǒu 動 garrison, defend

駐紮 zhùzhá 動 be stationed at

註 6 zhù
6 [注] Words 言 that enlighten 主 (phonetic). 图 footnote, annotation ⇔ 批註

註冊 zhùcè 動 register

註定 zhùdìng 動 predestined, doomed to ⇨ 注定

註解 zhùjiě 動 annotate 图 annotation

註釋 zhùshì 图 annotation, footnote

注 6 zhù
7 Water 水 with 主 phonetic. 動 pour 動 concentrate 图 stake (gambling) ⇔ 全神貫注, 關注, 轉注, 賭注, 灌注

注定 zhùdìng 動 predestined, doomed to

注目 zhùmù 图 attention

注射 zhùshè 動 inject

注視 zhùshì 動 stare at

注意 zhùyì 動 pay attention, note: 注意力 attention

注音 zhùyīn 動 add phonetic notation for Chinese characters: 注音符號 a system of phonetic symbols for Chinese characters

注重 zhùzhòng 動 emphasize, stress

柱 6 zhù
8 Wood 木 that is

candle 主 (phonetic). 動 stop, cease 動 live, reside, inhabit 動 (verbal complement indicating fixity): 記住 remember ⇔ 原住民, 守住, 塞住, 站住, 居住, 拿住, 按住, 記住, 堵住, 攔住, 壓住, 愣住, 抓住, 招住

住處 zhùchù 图 residence

住家 zhùjiā 图 residence

住口 zhùkǒu 動 Shut up!

住手 zhùshǒu 動 Hands off!

住所 zhùsuǒ 图 residence

primary 主² (phonetic). 图
pillar, column ⇔ 冰柱²

柱石 zhùshí 图 pillar, mainstay

丿 7 yì
1 Ideograph suggesting a dragging motion.

乙 8 yàn
1 Ideograph representing bird's call. 古 swallow

空 8 wā
2 Hole 穴² like burrowed by a swallow 乙² (phonetic). 图 hollow, hole

挖 8 wā
3 Hand 手² making a hole 空² (phonetic). 图 dig, excavate, gouge

挖掘 wājué 图 excavate

乙 9 yǐ
1 Ideograph suggesting effort of sprouting seed. 图 second Heavenly Stem (⇨ 干支²)

軋 9 yà
2 [轧] Cart 車 over sprouting plant 乙² (phonetic). 图 crush

札 9 zhá
3 Wood 木² with 乙² phonetic. 图 ⑦ wooden writing tablet 图 document

札記 zhájì 图 sundry notes

紮 9 图 zhá 图 zā
4 [扎²] Tablets 札² (phonetic) bound with thread 糸¹⁵³. 图 tie, bind ⇔ 駐紮²

紮根 zhágēn 图 take root
紮營 zháyíng 图 encamp

扎 9 zhā 图 zhá
5 Hand 手² pulling up a sprouting 乙² plant. zhá: 图 struggle 图 bind (⇨ 紮²) zhā: 图 prick ⇔ 掙扎²

扎啤 zhāpí 图 draft beer
扎實 zhāshi 图 sturdy, sound

人 10 rén
1 Pictograph of a human. 图 human, person, people ⇔

狂人², 經紀人², 主人², 眾
人², 客人², 鄰人², 老
人², 老人家², 友人², 唐
人街², 婦人², 學人², 神
人², 犯人², 驚人², 私
人², 農人², 盲人², 熟
人², 富人², 病
人², 何人², 小人², 詩
人², 古人², 做人², 個
人², 黃種人², 漢人², 世
人², 候選人², 男人², 別
人², 超人², 大人², 夫
人², 嚇人², 行人², 感
人², 成人², 國人², 凡
人², 親人², 工人², 笨
人², 巨人², 女人², 他
人², 窮人², 仙人², 某
人², 媒人², 逗人², 證
人², 聖人², 情人², 名
人², 外人², 外星人², 白
人², 動人², 本人², 敵
人², 害人², 愛人², 近
人², 哲人², 文人², 殺
人², 野人², 騙人², 洋
人², 美人², 猿人², 黑
人², 懶人², 僧人², 黑
人², 家人², 軍人², 爲
人², 華人², 僕人², 罵
人²

人本主義 rénběnzhǔyì 图 humanism

人才 réncái 图 talented person, human resources

人潮 réncháo 图 human tide

人道 réndào 图 humanity, charity: 人道主義 humanitarianism, humanism; 不人道待遇 inhumane treatment

人犯 rénfàn 图 criminal

人格 réngé 图 personality, character

人工 réngōng 图 artificial: 人工智慧 artificial intelligence

人海 rénhǎi 图 sea of people

人際 rénjì 图 interpersonal: 人際關係 interpersonal relations

人家 rénjiā 图 others 图 house-hold

人間 rénjiān 图 human world

人口 rénkǒu 图 population: 人口調查 census

人類 rénlèi 图 human, humanity, humankind: 人類學 anthropology

人力 rénlì 图 laborpower: 人力車 rickshaw; 人力資源 human resources

人們 rénmen 图 people

人民 rénmín 图 the people: 人民日報 People's Daily; 人民幣 renminbi; 人民公社 people's commune

人情 rénqíng 图 favor 图 sympathy, human feelings: 人情味 human warmth; 他一點人情味都沒有. He is a very cold person.

人權 rénquán 图 human rights: 侵犯人權 violate human rights

人群 rénqún 图 crowd

人人 rénrén 图 everyone

人瑞 rénruì 图 venerable old man

人參 rénshēn 图 ginseng

人身 rénshēn 图 human body

人生 rénshēng 图 human life: 人生觀 philosophy of life

人世 rénshì 图 human life

人士 rénshì 图 important person

人事 rénshì 图 personnel

人手 rénshǒu 图 laborpower

人數 rénshù 图 number of people

人體 réntǐ 图 human body

人頭 réntóu 图 number of people

人為 rénwéi 图 artificial

人文 rénwén 图 culture, humanities

人物 rénwù 图 personage

人心 rénxīn 图 morale 图 will of the people

人性 rénxìng 图 human nature

人行道 rénxíngdào 图 sidewalk

人影 rényǐng 图 human shadow

人員 rényuán 图 personnel

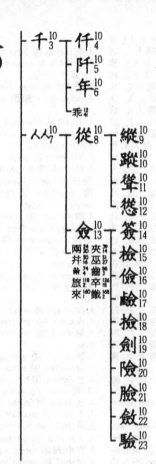

人緣 rényuán 圖 popularity, relations
人造 rénzào 圖 artificial
人質 rénzhì 圖 hostage
人種 rénzhǒng 圖 race

仁 10 rén
2 Feelings between two
二 people 人. 圖 love,
benevolence ⇔ 蝦仁, 同
仁, 杏仁

仁愛 rénài 圖 benevolence,
humanity
仁慈 rénci 圖 kindness, benevolence, charity

千 10 qiān
3 Ten 十 lifespans of
person 人. 圖 thousand ⇔
秋千
千里 qiānlǐ 圖 a long distance:
千里之行, 始於足下. A
journey of a thousand miles
begins with a single step.

千萬 qiānwàn 圖 ten million 圖
must, definitely: 你千萬不
要去. You definitely must not
go.

仟 10 qiān
4 Person 人 leading a
thousand 千 (phonetic). 圖
leader 圖 thousand (complex
form)

阡 10 qiān
5 Mounds 阜 in the
thousands 千 (phonetic).
圖 paths between rice paddies
阡陌 qiānmò 圖 paths between
rice paddies

年 10 nián
6 Thousands 千 (phonetic) of grains 禾 (altered). 圖 圖 year ⇔ 老年,
少年, 去年, 後年, 終
年, 今年, 成年, 新
年, 每年, 幼年, 當
年, 中年, 週年, 青
年, 青少年, 童年, 陳
年, 末年, 壯年, 閏
年, 明年, 拜年, 近
年, 歷年, 翌年, 前
年, 過年, 逐年, 隔
年

年初 niánchū 圖 beginning of
the year
年代 niándài 圖 period, era, age
圖 decade: 九十年代 the
nineties
年底 niándǐ 圖 year-end
年度 niándù 圖 year: 會計年
度 fiscal year
年糕 niángāo 圖 New Year's cake
年級 niánjí 圖 year, grade: 一
年級學生 freshman
年紀 niánjì 圖 age: 年紀大 old
年鑑 niánjiàn 圖 yearbook,
almanac
年齡 niánlíng 圖 age
年年 niánnián 圖 every year
年輕 niánqīng 圖 young: 年輕
人 young people, youth
年青 niánqīng 圖 young, youthful

年少 niánshào 國 young
年歲 niánsuì 國 age
年尾 niánwěi 國 end of the year

人人 10/7 cóng
One person 人[?] behind another. 國 follow, obey (⇒ 從[?])

從 10/8 [从] cóng 國 zòng cōng
Follow 人人[?] step by step 足[?]. cóng: 國 follow, obey 國 from zòng: 國 secondary cōng: 國 lax ⇔ 順從[?], 侍從[?], 服從[?], 屈從[?], 自從[?], 遵從[?]
從此 cóngcǐ 國 from now on
從而 cóngér 國 thereby, thus
從犯 cóngfàn,zòngfàn 國 accomplice
從來 cónglái 國 always, all along: 從來沒有 never; 從來如此. It has always been like this.
從前 cóngqián 國 formerly
從容 cōngróng,cóngróng 國 calmly
從事 cóngshì 國 engage in, undertake
從未 cóngwèi 國 never

縱 10/9 [纵] zòng Threads 糸[?] with 從[?] phonetic. 國 slack zòng: 國 indulge: 縱酒 binge drink 國 although 國 vertical ⇔ 操縱[?], 放縱[?]
縱橫 zònghéng 國 horizontal and vertical
縱火 zònghuǒ 國 commit arson
縱然 zòngrán 國 even if
縱容 zòngróng 國 countenance, condone
縱使 zòngshǐ 國 even if

蹤 10/10 [踪] zōng From the foot 足[?] follows 從[?] (phonetic). Simplified form uses 宗[?]. 國 footprint, trace ⇔ 失蹤[?], 追蹤[?]
蹤跡 zōngjī 國 trace, track

慫 10/11 [怂] sǒng Follow 從[?] (phonetic) and ear 耳[?]. incite, alarm
慫動 sǒngdòng 國 urge, incite

慫 10/12 [怂] sǒng Heart 心[?] following 從[?] (phonetic). incite
慫恿 sǒngyǒng 國 incite, instigate

僉 10/13 [佥] qiān Gathering 亼[?] of talking 吅[?] people 人人[?]. 國 all

簽 10/14 [签] qiān Bamboo 竹[?] with 僉[?] phonetic. 國 signature 國
簽訂 qiāndìng 國 sign, conclude
簽名 qiānmíng 國 sign 國 signature
簽署 qiānshǔ 國 sign
簽證 qiānzhèng 國 visa
簽字 qiānzì 國 sign 國 signature

檢 10/15 [检] jiǎn Wooden 木[?] tablets with 僉[?] phonetic. affix seal to official documents 國 examine ⇔ 體檢[?]
檢查 jiǎnchá 國 check
檢察官 jiǎncháguān 國 prosecutor
檢舉 jiǎnjǔ 國 denounce, inform on
檢視 jiǎnshì 國 examine
檢討 jiǎntǎo 國 self-criticism self-criticize: 你要檢討檢討. You should reflect on your mistakes.
檢驗 jiǎnyàn 國 examine

儉 10/16 [俭] jiǎn Person 人[?] conserving everything 僉[?] (phonetic). thrifty 國 動 儉[?], 節儉[?]
儉樸 jiǎnpú 國 thrifty, simple

鹼 10/17 [硷] jiǎn Salt 鹵[?] with 僉[?] phonetic. Simplified form uses stone 石[?]. 國 lye
鹼性 jiǎnxìng 國 alkaline

撿 10/18 [捡] jiǎn Hand 手[?] with 僉[?] phonetic. 國 gather
撿骨 jiǎngǔ 國 gather bones from grave for placement in ancestral hall

劍 10/19 [剑] jiàn Knife 刀[?] (originally blade 刃[?]) carried by all 僉[?] (phonetic). 國 sword
劍道 jiàndào 國 kendo
劍橋 jiànqiáo 國 Cambridge

險 10/20 [险] xiǎn All 僉[?] (phonetic) hills 阜[?]. 國 obstructed 國 dangerous ⇔ 危險[?], 冒險[?], 陰險[?], 風險[?], 保險[?]
險惡 xiǎnè 國 dangerous, perilous 國 sinister
險些 xiǎnxiē 國 dangerously close to, narrowly

臉 10/21 [脸] liǎn Flesh 肉[?] with 僉[?] phonetic. 國 face 洗臉[?], 丟臉[?], 刮臉[?], 嘴臉[?], 翻臉[?]
臉紅 liǎnhóng 國 blush
臉盆 liǎnpén 國 washbasin
臉皮 liǎnpí 國 face, cheek: 臉皮很厚 thick-skinned, shameless
臉譜 liǎnpǔ 國 Chinese opera facial paintings
臉色 liǎnsè 國 facial expression

斂 10/22 [敛] liǎn Everything 僉[?] (phonetic) arranged 攵[?] (early meaning). 國 collect ⇔ 收斂[?]

驗 10/23 [验] yàn Horse 馬[?] with

人
10

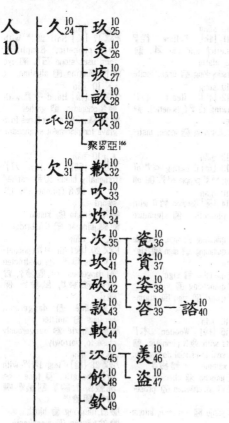

久²⁴₁₀
├ 玖²⁵₁₀
├ 灸²⁶₁₀
├ 疚²⁷₁₀
└ 畝²⁸₁₀

乑²⁹₁₀ ┬ 眾³⁰₁₀
　　　└ 聚¹²⁷ 亞¹⁶⁶

欠³¹₁₀
├ 歉³²₁₀
├ 吹³³₁₀
├ 炊³⁴₁₀
├ 次³⁵₁₀ ┬ 瓷³⁶₁₀
├ 坎⁴¹₁₀ ├ 資³⁷₁₀
├ 砍⁴²₁₀ ├ 姿³⁸₁₀
├ 款⁴³₁₀ └ 咨³⁹₁₀ — 諮⁴⁰₁₀
├ 軟⁴⁴₁₀
├ 沈⁴⁵₁₀ ┬ 羡⁴⁶₁₀
├ 飲⁴⁸₁₀ └ 盜⁴⁷₁₀
└ 欽⁴⁹₁₀

僉¹³ phonetic. 🔲 examine, check ⇔ 經驗¹³, 檢驗¹³, 考驗¹³, 試驗³⁴, 體驗⁵⁴, 實驗²⁵, 抽驗⁴⁷, 測驗⁹⁰
驗屍 yànshī 🔲 autopsy

久²⁴ jiǔ
Person 人¹⁰ whose walk is hindered, as represented by extra mark. 🔲 a long time ⇔ 不久¹⁰, 長久³⁴, 悠久²⁴, 持久³¹, 好久⁵⁴, 多久⁷, 許久⁹⁷, 永久¹²⁰, 恆久¹⁰

久而久之 jiǔérjiǔzhī 🔲 as time passes
久遠 jiǔyuǎn 🔲 ancient, long past

玖²⁵ jiǔ
Jade 玉¹⁰⁷ that lasts 久⁴ (phonetic). 🔲 a black stone 🔲 nine (complex form)

灸²⁶ jiǔ
Fire 火⁸² with 久⁴ phonetic. 🔲 moxibustion ⇔ 針灸⁴⁴

疚²⁷ jiù
Long-lasting 久⁴ (phonetic) sickness 疒¹³⁴. 🔲 lengthy illness 🔲 guilt, remorse ⇔ 內疚⁴²

畝²⁸ mǔ
Unchanging 久⁴ measurement of field 田¹¹¹ by ten 十³ (altered) steps. 🔲 mu - 1/15th of a hectare

乑²⁹ zhòng
Three people 人¹⁰ gathering together. 🅐 crowd (⇨ 眾)

眾³⁰ zhòng
[众] Eye 目¹¹⁴ seeing many people 乑¹⁰ (phonetic). 🔲 crowd ⇔ 群眾⁴⁴, 公眾⁴, 聽眾³⁴, 大眾⁴, 當眾⁴⁴, 民眾¹⁷, 觀眾⁴⁴, 嘩眾取寵¹⁷
眾多 zhòngduō 🔲 numerous (people)
眾怒 zhòngnù 🔲 public anger
眾人 zhòngrén 🔲 the masses, the public
眾所周知 zhòngsuǒzhōuzhī 🔲 as everyone well knows
眾議 zhòngyì 🔲 majority opinion: 眾議院 lower house, House of Commons, House of Representatives

欠³¹ qiàn
Person 人¹⁰ (originally 儿¹) with strokes above indicating breath. 🔲 yawn 🔲 lack 🔲 owe: 我欠你五塊. I owe you five dollars. ⇔ 哈欠⁴⁷, 賒欠⁵⁴
欠缺 qiànquē 🔲 lack

歉³² qiàn
Doubly 兼⁹⁴ lacking 欠⁴³ (phonetic). 🔲 poor harvest 🔲 regret ⇔ 抱歉¹⁹, 道歉¹⁴⁸
歉收 qiànshōu 🔲 poor harvest
歉意 qiànyì 🔲 apology: 表示歉意 offer apologies, express regrets

吹 10 chūi
33 Mouth 口 exhaling 欠. blow boast, brag play (a wind instrument) ⇔ 鼓吹

吹風 chūifēng blow-dry: 吹風機 blow-dryer
吹牛 chūiníu brag, boast, bullshit

炊 10 chūi
34 Fire 火 blown on 吹 (phonetic, abbreviated to 欠). cook
炊具 chūijù cooking utensils

次 10 cì
35 Second 二 (often altered to resemble 冫) and lacking 欠. second-rate, inferior next, second order, sequence times: 三次 three times ⇔ 上次, 下次, 其次, 每次, 屢次, 逐次, 歷次, 倫次, 依次, 層次, 首次, 再次
次日 cìrì next day
次數 cìshù number of times
次序 cìxù sequence, order
次於 cìyú second to, inferior to
次元 cìyuán dimension

瓷 10 cí
36 Pottery 瓦 fired second 次 (phonetic) time with glaze. ceramics ⇔ 陶瓷
瓷器 cíqì porcelain, china

資 10 zī
37 [资] Well-ordered 次 (phonetic) money/shells 貝. capital, funds ⇔ 投資, 合資, 薪資, 工資, 外資, 物資
資本 zīběn capital: 資本家 capitalist; 資本主義 capitalism
資產 zīchǎn property, assets: 資產階級 bourgeoisie

資格 zīgé qualifications: 沒有資格 unqualified
資金 zījīn funds
資歷 zīlì qualifications, experience: 資歷很深 well-experienced
資料 zīliào data, information: 收集資料 gather data; 資料庫 database
資深 zīshēn senior, experienced
資訊 zīxùn information
資源 zīyuán resources: 自然資源 natural resources

姿 10 zī
38 Woman 女 with 次 phonetic. manner
姿勢 zīshì posture, pose
姿態 zītài deportment, bearing pose

咨 10 zī
39 Ask a second 次 (phonetic) mouth 口. inquire

諮 10 zī
40 [谘] Words 言 of inquiry 咨 (phonetic). inquire
諮詢 zīxún consult, inquire, seek advice: 諮詢台 information desk

坎 10 kǎn
41 Ground 土 inducing exhalation 欠 (phonetic). dip
坎坷 kǎnkě bumpy

砍 10 kǎn
42 Stone 石 with 欠 phonetic. chop
砍掉 kǎndiào cut down, chop off
砍伐 kǎnfá chop down

款 10 kuǎn
43 Evil spirit 祟 (altered) and exhale 欠. sincere funds section (of a document) ⇔ 貨款, 付款, 公款, 條款, 貸款, 墊款, 存款, 罰款, 借款, 撥款, 提款, 放款, 現款, 捐款, 匯款
款待 kuǎndài entertain cordially: 款待客人 entertain guests hospitality
款式 kuǎnshì style
款項 kuǎnxiàng amount of money

軟 10 ruǎn
44 [软] Cart 車 and lack 欠 (phonetic). weak soft gentle ⇔ 疲軟, 鬆軟, 柔軟
軟件 ruǎnjiàn software
軟禁 ruǎnjìn put under house arrest
軟體 ruǎntǐ software

次 10 xián
45 Water 水 exhaled 欠 (phonetic). salivate (⇨ 涎)

羨 10 xiàn
46 Mutton 羊 inducing salivation 次 (phonetic). envy, covet
羨慕 xiànmù envy

盜 10 dào
47 [盗] Salivate 次 over vases 皿. Simplified form uses 次. steal, rob ⇔ 海盜, 強盜, 竊盜
盜匪 dàofěi bandit
盜賣 dàomài steal and resell
盜墓 dàomù grave rob
盜印 dàoyìn copy illegally, pirate: 盜印本 pirated book
盜賊 dàozéi robber

飲 10 yǐn
48 [饮] Modern form shows food 食 with 欠 phonetic. drink
飲茶 yǐnchá drink tea dim sum
飲料 yǐnliào beverage
飲食 yǐnshí food and beverages: 飲食文化 culinary

字譜及字典

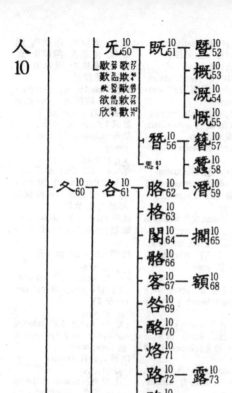

culture
飲水 yǐnshuǐ 🔲 drink water 圖 drinking water: 飲水機 drinking fountain

欽 10 qīn [钦] Metal 金 suggesting heavy, and inadequate 欠 (phonetic), suggesting politeness. 🔲 respect
欽佩 qīnpèi 🔲 admire

旡 10 jì 50 Breath 欠 reversed or stopped as swallow. 🔲

swallow

既 51 jì Meal 皀 swallowed 旡 (phonetic). 🔲 already 🔲 since, now that 🔲 both: 既好吃，又便宜 both tasty and cheap
既得 jìdé 🔲 vested: 既得利益 vested interest, special interest
既定 jìdìng 🔲 decided
既然 jìrán 🔲 since, because
既是 jìshì 🔲 since, in that case

暨 10 jì 52 Dawn 旦 with 既 phonetic. 🔲 and

概 10 gài 53 Wood 木 instrument for measuring when already 既 (phonetic) full. 🔲 striker 🔲 estimate, measure roughly, overall ⇔ 一概, 梗概, 大概, 氣概
概括 gàikuò 🔲 summarize
概念 gàiniàn 🔲 concept, idea

溉 10 gài 54 Water 水 with 既 phonetic. 🔲 irrigate ⇔ 灌溉

慨 10 kǎi 55 Heart 心 with 既 phonetic. 🔲 indignant 🔲 sigh 🔲 generous ⇔ 慷慨, 感慨, 憤慨
慨然 kǎirán 🔲 generous

朁 10 zǎn 56 Speak 曰 with an ancient character resembling two 旡 phonetic. 🔲 murmur

簪 10 zān 57 [簮] Bamboo 竹 with 朁 phonetic. 🔲 hairpin

蠶 10 cán 58 [蚕] Insect 虫 with 朁 phonetic. Simplified form uses 天. 🔲 silkworm ⇔ 桑蠶
蠶豆 cándòu 🔲 broad bean
蠶繭 cánjiǎn 🔲 silkworm cocoon
蠶絲 cánsī 🔲 silk

潛 10 qián 59 [潜] Water 水 with 朁 phonetic. Simplified form uses 替. 🔲 dive 🔲 latent
潛伏 qiánfú 🔲 latent, hidden: 潛伏期 incubation period
潛力 qiánlì 🔲 potential, latent ability
潛能 qiánnéng 🔲 latent ability

潛入 qiánrù 動 sneak in
潛水 qiánshuǐ 動 dive, snorkel
潛逃 qiántáo 動 abscond
潛艇 qiántǐng 名 submarine
潛心 qiánxīn 動 concentrate
潛在 qiánzài 形 latent, hidden

10 zhǐ
夂 60 A person 人 with extra mark suggesting pursuit. 意 catch up

10 gè
各 61 Pursue 夂 but speak 口 at odds. 形 separate 意 each, every

各地 gèdì 名 each place
各個 gège 形 each 副 one by one
各式各樣 gèshìgèyàng 形 every kind of
各位 gèwèi 名 everyone
各種 gèzhǒng 形 every kind of
各自 gèzì 形 each, respective 副 individually

10 gē
胳 62 Flesh 肉 with 各 phonetic. 名 arm
胳臂 gēbei 名 arm
胳膊 gēbo 名 arm

10 gé
格 63 Wood 木 with 各 phonetic. 名 pattern, standard 名 line 名 shelf ⇔ 人格, 資格, 及格, 價格, 規格, 合格, 風格, 品格, 性格, 表格, 嚴格, 蘇格蘭
格局 géjú 名 structure, form
格式 géshì 名 pattern, form
格外 géwài 形 exceptional, unusual
格言 géyán 名 proverb

10 gé
閣 64 [阁] Doors 門 separated 各 (phonetic). 意 doorstop 名 room, chamber 名 pavilion 名 government cabinet ⇔ 內閣, 亭閣
閣樓 gélóu 名 attic, loft
閣下 géxià 敬 Your Excellency

閣員 géyuán 名 cabinet member

10 gē
擱 65 [搁] Hand 手 and doorstop 閣 (phonetic). 動 stop, delay 動 put, leave
擱置 gēzhì 動 put off, table

10 gé
骼 66 [骼] Bones 骨 with 各 phonetic. 名 animal bones 名 bone, skeleton ⇔ 骨骼

10 kè
客 67 House 宀 with 各 (phonetic). 名 guest 名 customer ⇔ 說客, 乘客, 嫖客, 作客, 載客, 好客, 常客, 請客, 刺客, 顧客, 掮客, 政客, 旅客, 遊客
客艙 kècāng 名 passenger cabin
客車 kèchē 名 bus
客店 kèdiàn 名 hotel
客觀 kèguān 形 objective, impartial
客戶 kèhù 名 customer
客家 kèjiā 名 Hakka
客滿 kèmǎn 形 full, sold out
客氣 kèqì 形 polite: 不客氣 don't be so polite, don't mention it
客人 kèrén 名 guest, visitor
客套 kètào 名 civilities: 客套話 polite words
客廳 kètīng 名 living room

10 é
額 68 [额] Head 頁 with 客 phonetic. 名 forehead 名 quota ⇔ 限額, 差額, 份額, 超額, 金額, 餘額, 互額, 鉅額, 數額, 配額, 名額, 匾額, 總額
額定 édìng 形 specified (amount), fixed (amount)
額頭 étóu 名 forehead
額外 éwài 形 additional, extra

10 jiù
咎 69 People 人 pursuing separate 各 interests. 動 blame ⇔ 歸咎

10 lào luò
酪 70 Alcohol 酉, suggesting fermentation, with 各 phonetic. 名 cheese ⇔ 奶酪, 乳酪, 乾酪

10 lào
烙 71 Fire 火 with 各 phonetic. 動 burn 動 bake in a pan
烙餅 làobǐng 名 pancake
烙印 làoyìn 動 名 brand

10 lù
路 72 Feet 足 going separate 各 ways. 名 path, road 名 a surname ⇔ 一路, 線路, 網路, 公路, 銷路, 岔路, 大路, 斜路, 築路, 讓路, 鋪路, 繞路, 鐵路, 問路, 走路, 出路, 死路, 迷路, 道路, 馬路
路邊 lùbiān 名 roadside
路標 lùbiāo 名 road sign
路程 lùchéng 名 journey, traveling distance
路徑 lùjìng 名 path
路上 lùshàng 名 on the road 副 en route
路途 lùtú 名 road, journey: 路途遙遠 long way
路線 lùxiàn 名 route

10 lù lòu
露 73 Rain 雨 with 路 phonetic. lù: 名 dew 動 reveal lòu: 動 reveal ⇔ 披露, 暴露, 淺露, 揭露, 透露, 流露, 裸露, 表露, 顯露
露出 lòuchū 動 reveal
露面 lòumiàn 動 appear in public
露骨 lùgǔ 形 undisguised
露水 lùshuǐ 名 dew
露營 lùyíng 動 camp out

字譜及字典

洛 10 77 — 落 10 78
絡 10 79
駱 10 80
夅 10 81 — 夆 10 82 — 降 10 83 — 隆 10 84 — 窿 10 85
夅 10 82
外 10 86 — 桀 10 87 — 傑 10 88
乘 12 42
舛 10 89 — 燐 10 90
磷 10 91
鄰 10 92
遴 10 93
憐 10 94
舜 10 95 — 瞬 10 96
韋 10 97 — 達 10 98
舞 31 119
圍 10 99
偉 10 100
葦 10 101
緯 10 102
衛 10 103
諱 10 104
韌 韓 76

略 (phonetic). 🔲 leave behind
撂開 liàokāi 🔲 put aside

洛 10 77 lùo
Water 水 with 各 phonetic. 🔲 name of a river ⇔ 日洛 76
洛杉磯 lùoshānjī 🔲 Los Angeles

落 10 78 lùo là
Plant 艸 with 洛 phonetic. lùo: 🔲 fall 🔲 decline 🔲 fallen là: 🔲 leave out, omit ⇔ 下落, 部落, 降落, 村落, 墮落, 段落, 沒落, 失落, 低落, 奚落, 衰落, 角落, 墜落
落後 lùohòu 🔲 fall behind 🔲 outdated
落空 lùokōng 🔲 fall through, come to nothing
落寞 lùomò 🔲 lose popularity 🔲 lonely
落入 lùorù 🔲 fall into
落水 lùoshuǐ 🔲 fall into water, fall overboard
落伍 lùowǔ 🔲 become outdated
落下 lùoxià 🔲 drop
落葉 lùoyè 🔲 shed leaves

絡 10 79 [络] Thread 糸 joining separate 各 (phonetic) objects. 🔲 net, web ⇔ 網絡, 聯絡, 脈絡, 籠絡

駱 10 80 lùo Horse 馬 with 各 phonetic. 🔲 a white horse with black mane 🔲 a surname
駱駝 lùotúo 🔲 camel

夅 10 81 kuà Inversion of 夂 surpass

夆 10 82 jiàng xiáng One person 夂 above another ㄓ, implying higher and lower rank. 🔲 obey

賂 10 74 lù [赂] Shell/money 貝 with 各 phonetic. 🔲 bribe ⇔ 賄賂

略 10 75 lùe Each 各 (phonetic) field 田. 🔲 survey fields 🔲 strategy 🔲 approximate, rough 🔲 omit 🔲 invade ⇔ 侵略, 省略, 大略, 謀略, 策略, 簡略, 忽略, 粗略, 戰略

撂 10 76 liào Hand 手 and omit

降 10 jiàng xiáng
83 Hill 阜⁶⁷ with 夅 phonetic and suggestive of rank. jiàng: 🀄 decline xiáng: 🀄 surrender ⇔ 下降, 投降

降低 jiàngdī 🀄 lower, reduce, decrease
降臨 jiànglín 🀄 arrive
降落 jiàngluò 🀄 land, touch down

隆 10 lóng
84 Germinate 生 with 降 (abbreviated) phonetic. 🀄 flourishing 🀄 grand, glorious ⇔ 興隆, 基隆
隆冬 lóngdōng 🀄 depth of winter
隆重 lóngzhòng 🀄 solemn and impressive, grand

窿 10 lóng
85 Hole 穴 with 隆 phonetic. 🀄 cavity ⇔ 窟窿

舛 10 chuǎn
86 Persons 夂 中 back to back. 🀄 oppose 🀄 error
舛誤 chuǎnwù 🀄 mistake, error

桀 10 jié
87 Persons hung back to back 舛 on a tree 木. 🀄 gallows 🀄 cruel 🀄 perch

傑 88 [杰] Person 人 perched 桀 (phonetic) above others. Simplified form is related character using fire 火. 🀄 outstanding
傑出 jiéchū 🀄 outstanding
傑作 jiézuò 🀄 masterpiece

舜 10 lín
89 Flames 炎 (altered to resemble 米) dancing 舛 over old battlefields. 🀄 ghostly light (⇨ 燐)

燐 10 lín
90 [磷] Fire 火 flickering 舛 (phonetic). 🀄 ghostly light 🀄 phosphorus
燐光 línguāng 🀄 phosphorescence

燐火 línhuǒ 🀄 phosphorescence

磷 10 lín
91 Stone 石 and flicker 舛 (phonetic). 🀄 phosphorus (⇨ 燐)

鄰 10 lín
92 [邻] Village 邑 with 舛 phonetic. Simplified form uses 令. 🀄 group of five homes neighbor ⇔ 毗鄰, 睦鄰
鄰國 línguó 🀄 neighboring country
鄰接 línjiē 🀄 adjoin
鄰近 línjìn 🀄 nearby, in the vicinity
鄰居 línjū 🀄 neighbor
鄰人 línrén 🀄 neighbor
鄰舍 línshè 🀄 next door

遴 10 lín
93 Movement 辵 with 舛 phonetic. 🀄 difficult walking 🀄 select, choose
遴選 línxuǎn 🀄 select, choose

憐 10 lián
94 [怜] Heart 心 upon seeing ghostly light of dead 舛 (phonetic). Simplified form uses 令. 🀄 pity, sympathize with ⇔ 可憐, 哀憐
憐憫 liánmǐn 🀄 pity
憐惜 liánxī 🀄 pity

舜 10 shùn
95 Pictograph of growing plants with 舛 phonetic. 🀄 a creeping plant 🀄 Shun - legendary king of China c. 2200 B.C. ⇔ 堯舜

瞬 10 shùn
96 Eye 目 with 舜 phonetic. 🀄 blink
瞬間 shùnjiān 🀄 in a flash, in a blink of an eye
瞬時 shùnshí 🀄 instantaneously

韋 10 wéi
97 [韦] Oppose 舛 (rearranged) with 口 phonetic. 🀄 oppose 🀄 leather 🀄 a surname

違 10 wéi
98 [违] Move 辵 in opposition 韋 (phonetic). 🀄 defy, disregard ⇔ 暌違
違背 wéibèi 🀄 disobey, violate
違法 wéifǎ 🀄 break the law
違反 wéifǎn 🀄 violate
違犯 wéifàn 🀄 break, violate
違規 wéiguī 🀄 violate the rules
違建 wéijiàn 🀄 illegal buildings
違禁 wéijìn 🀄 violate a prohibition: 違禁品 contraband
違抗 wéikàng 🀄 defy, disobey

圍 10 wéi
99 [围] Surround 口 with 韋 phonetic. 🀄 encircle, surround ⇔ 範圍, 包圍, 周圍
圍城 wéichéng 🀄 lay siege
圍攻 wéigōng 🀄 besiege
圍巾 wéijīn 🀄 scarf
圍棋 wéiqí 🀄 go - a board game
圍牆 wéiqiáng 🀄 fence
圍裙 wéiqún 🀄 apron
圍繞 wéirào 🀄 revolve around

偉 10 wěi
100 [伟] Person 人 standing in contrast 韋 (phonetic). 🀄 outstanding, great ⇔ 宏偉, 雄偉
偉大 wěidà 🀄 great

葦 10 wěi
101 [苇] Plant 艸 with 韋 phonetic. 🀄 reed ⇔ 蘆葦

緯 10 wěi
102 [纬] Thread 糸 opposing 韋 (phonetic). 🀄 woof ⇔ 經緯
緯度 wěidù 🀄 latitude
緯線 wěixiàn 🀄 latitude line

衛 10 wèi
103 [卫] Modern form

字譜及字典

人
10

夂 10 105 ── 夏 舛 退 复 後 贛 夌 愛 致 憂 夏 麥 慶

亥 10 106 ┬ 孩 10 107
         ├ 骸 10 108
         ├ 駭 10 109
         ├ 該 10 110
         ├ 核 10 111
         ├ 閡 10 112
         ├ 劾 10 113
         ├ 咳 10 114
         └ 刻 10 115

諱 104 [讳] Words 言 that oppose 韋 (phonetic). 围 taboo, proscription ⇔ 忌諱, 隱諱
諱言 huìyán 囫 conceal, avoid telling

夂 105 sūi Person 人 with mark suggesting shackles. 围 walk with difficulty

亥 106 hài Two persons 人, above 上 (early form) and sprouting seed 乙. 圄 twelfth Earthly Branch (⇨ 干支) ⇔ 辛亥

孩 107 hái Child 子 making sound like 亥. 围 laugh 圄 child ⇔ 小孩, 小孩兒, 小孩子, 男孩, 男孩子, 女孩, 女孩兒, 女孩子
孩子 háizi 圄 child: 孩子氣 childlike

骸 108 [骸] Bone 骨 with 亥 phonetic. 圄 shinbone 圄 skeleton ⇔ 殘骸

駭 109 [骇] Horse 馬 with 亥 phonetic. 围 startle, frighten ⇔ 驚駭
駭異 hàiyì 圈 shocked, astonished

該 110 [该] Words 言 with 亥 phonetic. 围 military obligation 圖 should: 我該不該去? Should I or shouldn't I go? 围 be one's turn: 該你 your turn 围 that ⇔ 活該, 應該
該死 gāisǐ 圄 damn: 該死的 damned

核 111 hé Wood 木 with

伍 倍 傻 住 仟 儉 咎 傑 偉 俊
傾 仏 化 老 佬 儘 健 伊 侵 付
俯 及 假 佐 右 俾 供 伸 俺 便
倦 广 仄 佝 信 乍 作 尤 倆 價 攸
佔 偵 何 倚 介 俏 你 仇 仕
侍 值 什 仗 做 個 僅 侯 侯
候 仰 色 倒 份 停 佇 夾 俠 位
优 伶 伐 戍 儀 仔 佟 他 似
倖 僻 任 巫 佈 毎 佟 似
傳 夐 償 倘 寅 弔 佛 仙 倡 信
億 俗 囚 仲 使 佣 俑 傭 備 傅
佳 僥 坐 捧 伎 多 偶 佰 伯
儲 但 傷 借 倏 体 債 異 休 僱
們 閃 伙 僚 企 促 伏 件 件 仿
傲 傍 伕 佩 佃 佃 倜 俚
偏 倫 佯 依 偷 倪 例 攸 儆
傀 臥 僧 僵 側 負 俱 侶 係 偶
傢 儒 催 雁 隺 偽 像 僕

shows walk 行 and opposition 韋 (phonetic). 围 guard ⇔ 守衛, 警衛, 侍衛, 捍衛, 保衛, 門衛, 防衛, 自衛
衛兵 wèibīng 圄 guard: 紅衛兵 red guard

衛道 wèidào 圄 defend traditional values
衛生 wèishēng 圄 hygiene: 衛生紙 toilet paper
衛星 wèixīng 圄 satellite: 衛星天線 satellite dish

亥ㄏㄞˋ phonetic. 图 pit, kernel, core 图 check, verify ⇔ 稽 核ㄏㄜˊ, 考核ㄎㄠˇ, 陰核ㄧㄣ, 審 核ㄕㄣˇ

核電 hédiàn 图 nuclear power
核定 hédìng 图 assess and decide
核對 hédùi 图 verify
核能 hénéng 图 nuclear energy
核桃 hétáo 图 walnut
核武 héwǔ 图 nuclear weapons
核心 héxīn 图 core, nucleus: 核心家庭 nuclear family
核准 hézhǔn 图 approve
核子 hézǐ 图 nucleus: 核子彈 nuclear bomb

閡 10 hé
112 [阂] Door 門ㄇㄣˊ with 亥ㄏㄞˋ phonetic. 图 obstruct ⇔ 隔閡ㄍㄜˊ

劾 10 hé
113 [劾] Strength 力ㄌㄧˋ with 亥ㄏㄞˋ phonetic. 图 accuse ⇔ 彈劾ㄊㄢˊ

咳 10 ké
114 Mouth 口ㄎㄡˇ with 亥ㄏㄞˋ phonetic. 图 laugh cough
咳嗽 késòu 图 cough

刻 10 kè
115 Knife 刀ㄉㄠ with 亥ㄏㄞˋ phonetic. kè: 图 carve, engrave 图 quarter (of an hour) 图 moment 图 cruel 图 kē: 图 carve, engrave ⇔ 頃刻ㄑㄧㄥˇ, 苛刻ㄎㄜ, 時刻ㄕˊ, 即刻ㄐㄧˊ, 立刻ㄌㄧˋ, 篆刻ㄓㄨㄢˋ, 深刻ㄕㄣ, 鐫刻ㄐㄩㄢ, 雕刻ㄉㄧㄠ, 銘刻ㄇㄧㄥˊ, 片刻ㄆㄧㄢˋ
刻版 kèbǎn 图 engrave 图 inflexible, stereotyped: 刻版印象 stereotype
刻薄 kèbó 图 caustic, mean
刻骨 kègǔ 图 deeply engrained: 刻骨銘心 engraved in one's mind
刻畫 kèhuà 图 depict
刻苦 kèkǔ 图 assiduous 图

simple and frugal
刻意 kèyì 图 deliberately
刻印 kěyìn 图 engrave a chop

儿 11 rén
1 Pictograph of human legs. 图 human, person

兄 11 xiong
2 Person 儿ㄦˊ whose mouth 口ㄎㄡˇ does the talking. 图 brother (elder) ⇔ 弟兄ㄉㄧˋ, 師兄ㄕ
兄弟 xiōngdì 图 brother: 兄弟姊妹 siblings; 兄弟會 fraternity
兄長 xiōngzhǎng 图 brother (elder)

兌 11 dùi
3 Person 儿ㄦˊ with mouth 口ㄎㄡˇ split 八ㄅㄚ. 图 rejoice (⇨ 悦ㄩㄝˋ) 图 exchange, trade
兌換 dùihuàn 图 exchange

銳 11 rùi
4 [锐] Metal 金ㄐㄧㄣ with 兌ㄩˋ phonetic. 图 sharp, acute ⇔ 尖銳ㄐㄧㄢ, 敏銳ㄇㄧㄣˇ
銳利 rùilì 图 sharp

閱 11 yuè
5 [阅] Door 門ㄇㄣˊ with 兌ㄩˋ phonetic. 图 examine, inspect 图 read 图 experience
閱兵 yuèbīng 图 review troops
閱讀 yuèdú 图 read
閱覽 yuèlǎn 图 read: 閱覽室 reading room
閱歷 yuèlì 图 图 experience

悦 11 yuè
6 Heart 心ㄒㄧㄣ rejoicing 兌ㄩˋ (phonetic). 图 joy ⇔ 不悦ㄅㄨˋ, 喜悦ㄒㄧˇ, 愉悦ㄩˊ, 取悦ㄑㄩˇ
悦目 yuèmù 图 pleasant, visually appealing

稅 11 shùi
7 Grain 禾ㄏㄜˊ with 兌ㄩˋ phonetic. 图 tax ⇔ 納稅ㄋㄚˋ, 關稅ㄍㄨㄢ, 賦稅ㄈㄨˋ, 租稅ㄗㄨ, 逃稅ㄊㄠˊ, 徵稅ㄓㄥ, 免稅ㄇㄧㄢˇ
稅捐 shùijuān 图 taxes

稅率 shùilǜ 图 tax rate
稅收 shùishōu 图 tax revenue
稅制 shùizhì 图 tax system

說 11 shūo shùi yuè
8 [说] Words 言ㄧㄢˊ of rejoicing 兌ㄩˋ (phonetic). shūo: 图 explain 图 speak, say 图 theory shùi: 图 persuade, urge yuè: 图 rejoice (⇨ 悦ㄩㄝˋ) ⇔ 假說ㄐㄧㄚˇ, 小說ㄒㄧㄠˇ, 聽說ㄊㄧㄥ, 胡說ㄏㄨˊ, 雖說ㄙㄨㄟ, 關說ㄍㄨㄢ, 傳說ㄔㄨㄢˊ, 換句話說ㄏㄨㄢˋ, 演說ㄧㄢˇ, 邪說ㄒㄧㄝˊ, 訴說ㄙㄨˋ, 述說ㄕㄨˋ, 遊說ㄧㄡˊ, 據說ㄐㄩˋ
說服 shūifú, shūofú 图 persuade, lobby
說客 shùikè 图 lobbyist
說不定 shūobùdìng 图 perhaps, maybe
說道 shūodào 图 say
說到 shūodào 图 refer to, touch on
說法 shūofǎ 图 way of speaking
說話 shūohuà 图 speak: 無話可說 speechless
說謊 shūohuǎng 图 lie: 說謊者 liar
說明 shūomíng 图 explain 图 explanation

蛻 11 tùi
9 Insect 虫ㄔㄨˊ trading 兌ㄩˋ (phonetic) skin. 图 molted skin or shell 图 molt, slough
蛻變 tùibiàn 图 metamorphose 图 decay
蛻化 tùihuà 图 degenerate (⇨ 退化)

脫 11 tūo
10 Flesh 肉ㄖㄡˋ splitting 兌ㄩˋ (phonetic). 图 flay 图 take off, strip: 脫衣服 take off one's clothes ⇔ 超脫ㄔㄠ, 掙脫ㄓㄥ, 擺脫ㄅㄞˇ, 解脫ㄐㄧㄝˇ, 灑脫ㄙㄚˇ
脫光 tūoguāng 图 strip bare: 脫光光 naked
脫節 tūojié 图 separate, disjoint
脫臼 tūojìu 图 dislocate

字譜及字典

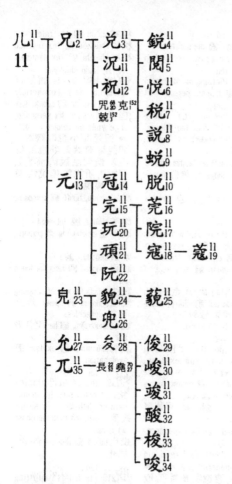

脱口而出 tuōkǒuérchū 🔲 blurt out

脱離 tuōlí 🔲 separate from, diverge from: 脱離實際 divorced from reality

脱身 tuōshēn 🔲 get away

脱下 tuōxià 🔲 take off

況¹¹ kuàng
11 [况] Water 水½ with 兄¹⁷ phonetic. Simplified form uses ice 冫ᵖ. 🔲 cold water 🔲 situation ⇔ 何況½, 盛況½, 每況愈下½, 情況½, 狀況½

況且 kuàngqiě 🔲 moreover

祝¹¹ zhù
12 [祝] Omens 示½ from person's 儿¹ mouth 口ᵖ. wish well, pray for: 祝你成功! I wish you success! 🔲 a surname ⇔ 慶祝½

祝福 zhùfú 🔲 bless

祝賀 zhùhè 🔲 congratulate

元¹¹ yuán
13 Top 上⅜ (early form resembling 二⅓) of a person 儿¹ (phonetic). 🔲 head 🔲 primary, original 🔲 yuan, dollar ⇔ 二元化½, 上元½, 次元⅜, 公元½, 紀元½, 多元化½, 美元½, 西元¹⁰

元旦 yuándàn 🔲 New Year's Day

元件 yuánjiàn 🔲 element, part

元老 yuánlǎo 🔲 elder statesman

元氣 yuánqì 🔲 vitality, vigor

元帥 yuánshuài 🔲 marshal

元素 yuánsù 🔲 (chemical) element

元宵 yuánxiāo 🔲 15th night of the first month of the lunar calendar 🔲 Lantern Festival 🔲 dumplings eaten on the Lantern Festival

元兇 yuánxiōng 🔲 chief culprit, ring-leader

元月 yuányuè 🔲 January

冠¹¹ guān guàn
14 Covering 冖 ⁱᵛ hand 寸⅜ places on the head 元⅓ (phonetic). guān: 🔲 hat (traditional) guàn: 🔲 wear a heat ⇔ 桂冠½

冠詞 guàncí 🔲 article (grammar): 定冠詞 definite article; 不定冠詞 indefinite article

冠軍 guànjūn 🔲 champion

完¹¹ wán
15 Roof 宀ᵖ with 元⅓ phonetic. 🔲 finish, complete ⇔ 做完½

完畢 wánbì 🔲 finish, complete

完成 wánchéng 🔲 complete

完蛋 wándàn 🔲 doomed, ruined: 我完蛋了. I'm done for.

完美 wánměi 彫 perfect: 完美主義者 perfectionist
完全 wánquán 彫 complete
完善 wánshàn 彫 perfect
完整 wánzhěng 彫 complete, intact

莞 11 guān wǎn 16 Plant 艸 with 完 phonetic. guān: 图 an aquatic grass wǎn: 图 smiling
莞爾 wǎněr 图 smiling

院 11 yuàn 17 Walls/hills 阜 surrounding completely 完 (phonetic). 图 courtyard 图 government office 图 public place ⇔ 住院, 學院, 醫院, 四合院, 寺院, 法院, 議院, 戲院, 庭院, 劇院
院士 yuànshì 图 academician, fellow
院長 yuànzhǎng 图 director of an institute, dean
院子 yuànzi 图 yard, courtyard

寇 11 kòu 18 Strike 攵 what is complete 完 图 rob, pillage 图 robber 图 a surname

蔲 11 kòu 19 Plant 艸 with 寇 phonetic. 图 nutmeg ⇔ 荳蔲

玩 11 wán wàn 20 Jade 玉 with 元 phonetic. wán: 图 play wàn: ⇔ 電玩, 古玩, 好玩
玩具 wánjù 图 toy
玩命 wánmìng 图 reckless
玩弄 wánnòng 图 play with, toy with (somebody)
玩偶 wánǒu 图 doll
玩耍 wánshuǎ 图 play
玩物 wánwù 图 plaything
玩笑 wánxiào 图 joke: 開玩笑: joke, tease

頑 11 wán 21 [顽] Head 頁 with 元 phonetic. 图 stupid 图 obstinate ⇔ 冥頑
頑固 wángù 图 obstinate, stubborn
頑皮 wánpí 图 naughty, mischievous
頑強 wánqiáng 图 stubborn

阮 11 ruǎn 22 Hill 阜 with 元 phonetic. 图 a surname

皃 11 mào 23 Person 儿 with head written as 白. 图 countenance

貌 11 mào 24 Countenance 皃 with 豹 (contracted to 豸) phonetic. 图 countenance ⇔ 容貌, 禮貌, 外貌, 相貌, 美貌, 面貌
貌似 màosì 图 look like, appear to be

藐 11 miǎo 25 Plant 艸 and appearance 貌 (phonetic). 图 a plant used for dyeing 图 belittle
藐視 miǎoshì 图 despise, belittle

兜 11 dōu 26 Countenance 皃 with an ancient character for encase. 图 helmet 图 peddle
兜風 dōufēng 图 joyride, cruise
兜售 dōushòu 图 peddle, hawk

允 11 yǔn 27 Exhaling 㠯 (altered to resemble 厶) person 儿 (phonetic). 图 consent, approve ⇔ 應允
允諾 yǔnnuò 图 promise, consent
允許 yǔnxǔ 图 allow, permit

夋 11 qūn 28 Difficulty walking 夊 with 允 phonetic. 图 hesitate

俊 11 jùn 29 Person 人 with 夋 phonetic. 图 talented 图 handsome ⇔ 英俊

峻 11 jùn 30 Mountain 山 with 夋 phonetic. 图 lofty 图 severe ⇔ 嚴峻
峻嶺 jùnlǐng 图 lofty mountains

竣 11 jùn 31 Stand 立 with 夋 phonetic. 图 complete
竣工 jùngōng 图 complete (a construction project)

酸 11 suān 32 Liquor 酉 with 夋 phonetic. 图 sour 图 acidic ⇔ 硫酸, 甜酸
酸菜 suāncài 图 pickled cabbage
酸辣湯 suānlàtāng 图 hot and sour soup
酸奶 suānnǎi 图 yogurt
酸痛 suāntòng 图 ache
酸雨 suānyǔ 图 acid rain

梭 11 suō 33 Wood 木 that moves back and forth 夋 (phonetic). 图 shuttle ⇔ 穿梭

唆 11 suō 34 Mouth 口 moving back and forth 夋. 图 incite ⇔ 教唆
唆使 suōshǐ 图 incite, instigate

兀 11 wù 35 Flat surface 一 supported by legs 儿. 图 high and level 图 stool ⇔ 突兀
兀鷹 wùyīng 图 vulture

先 11 xiān 36 Progress 之 (altered) with one's feet 儿. 图 first 图 before ⇔ 原先, 領先, 事先, 預先, 祖先, 首先, 優先
先鋒 xiānfēng 图 vanguard: 少年先鋒隊 Young Pioneers
先後 xiānhòu 图 successively
先進 xiānjìn 彫 advanced: 先進

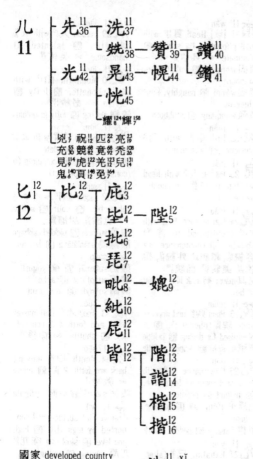

洗刷 xǐshuā 🔲 scrub
洗衣 xǐyī 🔲 do laundry: 洗衣機 washing machine
洗澡 xǐzǎo 🔲 shower, bathe: 洗個澡 take a shower

兟 11 xiǎn
38 Advance 先½ repeatedly. (古) call on, visit

贊 11 zàn
39 [赞] Call on 兟½ (phonetic) bearing shells/money 貝⁵⁰. 🔲 assist, aid
贊成 zànchéng 🔲 approve of, agree with
贊同 zàntóng 🔲 endorse, approve of
贊助 zànzhù 🔲 support, assistance

讚 11 zàn
40 [赞½] Words 言 aiding 贊½ (phonetic). 🔲 praise ⇔ 稱讚¹⁷⁵
讚美 zànměi 🔲 praise, compliment
讚賞 zànshǎng 🔲 appreciate, admire
讚歎 zàntàn 🔲 gasp in admiration, praise highly
讚揚 zànyáng 🔲 glorify, exalt

鑽 11 zuān zuàn
41 [钻] Metal 金 with 贊½ phonetic. Simplified form uses 占 zuān: 🔲 drill, bore zuàn: 🔲 drill 🔲 diamond ⇔ 刁鑽
鑽石 zuànshí 🔲 diamond
鑽研 zuānyán 🔲 study thoroughly
鑽營 zuānyíng 🔲 take advantage of loopholes

光 11 guāng
42 Person 儿 carrying fire 火⁸². 🔲 light 🔲 smooth, glossy 🔲 merely, purely 🔲 completely: 望光 completely forget; 吃光 eat up ⇔ 燐光, 脫光, 眼光, 霞光, 曝光, 沾光, 時

國家 developed country
先烈 xiānliè 🔲 martyr
先民 xiānmín 🔲 ancients
先前 xiānqián 🔲 before, previously
先驅 xiānqū 🔲 pioneer
先生 xiānshēng 🔲 Mr., sir: 王先生 Mr. Wang 🔲 gentleman, man 🔲 husband
先行 xiānxíng 🔲 go first

洗 11 xǐ
37 Water 水 with 先½ phonetic. 🔲 wash ⇔ 盥洗, 刷洗, 沖洗, 清洗, 乾洗
洗滌 xǐdí 🔲 wash, rinse
洗臉 xǐliǎn 🔲 wash one's face 🔲 wash up
洗手 xǐshǒu 🔲 wash one's hands: 洗手間 washroom, bathroom

光孔, 燈光㵾, 精光㶳, 日
光⁷⁶, 曙光㶇, 陽光㶝, 散
光㶷, 閃光㶮, 月光ᴵᴾ, 火
光ᴵᴾ, 螢光㶯, 發光㶭, 激
光㶲, 爭光㶹, 目光ᴵᴵ⁴, 燭
光㶶, 觀光㶺

光標 guāngbiāo 图 ⑦ cursor
光彩 guāngcǎi 图 brilliance
光碟 guāngdié 图 CD ROM
光復 guāngfù ⑪ recover, recapture
光顧 guānggù ⑪ patronize
光滑 guānghuá 㑇 smooth
光輝 guānghuī 㑇 radiant
光景 guāngjǐng 图 scene 图 about, around
光亮 guāngliàng 㑇 shiny, bright
光臨 guānglín 图 presence, attendance: 歡迎光臨! Welcome!
光芒 guāngmáng 图 radiance, rays of light
光明 guāngmíng 图 brilliance 㑇 open: 光明磊落 open and honest
光榮 guāngróng 图 honor
光纖 guāngxiān 图 optical fiber
光線 guāngxiàn 图 light, light ray
光耀 guāngyào 图 magnificent
光陰 guāngyīn 图 time
光澤 guāngzé 图 luster, sheen

晃⁴³ huǎng huàng Sun's 日⁷⁶ light 光㎏ (phonetic). huǎng: 㑇 dazzling ⑪ flash by huàng: ⑪ sway ⇔ 搖晃㵷
晃蕩 huàngdàng ⑪ sway, rock
晃動 huàngdòng ⑪ sway, rock

幌⁴⁴ huǎng Cloth 巾ᴵ³ that stops sunlight 晃㎏ (phonetic). 图 curtain
幌子 huǎngzi 图 ⑦ store banner 图 facade

恍⁴⁵ huǎng Heart/mind 心ᴵ³ seeing the light 光㎏ (phonetic). 图 sudden insight
恍惚 huǎnghū 㑇 absent-minded
恍然 huǎngrán 㑇 suddenly: 恍然大悟 suddenly understand

七¹² bǐ 1 Person 人ᴵ⁰ turned around. Early form of compare 比ᴵ². Also used to represent a spoon or other object.
七首 bǐshǒu 图 dagger

比¹² bǐ 2 Two persons 七ᴵ² next to each other. ⑪ compare: 不能比 incomparable 㞢 compared to ⇔ 無比㎏, 好比㑇, 利比亞ᴵᴾ, 相比㎏, 盧比ᴵᴾ, 對比ᴵ⁶
比不上 bǐbùshàng ⑪ incomparable to
比方 bǐfāng 图 for instance
比較 bǐjiào ⑪ compare 图 comparison 㘘 relatively, comparatively
比例 bǐlì 图 proportion
比利時 bǐlìshí 图 Belgium
比率 bǐlǜ 图 ratio
比擬 bǐnǐ ⑪ compare 图 analogy, metaphor
比起 bǐqǐ ⑪ compare
比如 bǐrú 图 for example
比薩 bǐsà 图 Pisa 图 pizza
比賽 bǐsài ⑪ compete 图 competition, match, game, race
比喻 bǐyù 图 analogy, metaphor

庇¹² bì 3 Together 比ᴵ² (phonetic) under shelter 广⁴⁰. 图 harbor, shield ⇔ 包庇ᴵ⁸
庇護 bìhù ⑪ shelter, shield: 政治庇護 political asylum

坒¹² bì 4 Together 比ᴵ² (phonetic) sitting on the earth 土⁷⁰. 图 connected

陛¹² bì 5 Hill 阜ᴵ⁶⁷ connected 坒ᴵ² (phonetic). 图 steps to the throne

陛下 bìxià ⑦ Your Majesty

批¹² pī 6 Modern form shows hand 手⁹⁰ with 比ᴵ² phonetic. ⑪ slap ⇔ critique, criticize 图 batch ⇔ 分批ᴵ³, 大批ᴵ³
批發 pīfā ⑪ sell wholesale
批改 pīgǎi ⑪ correct
批判 pīpàn ⑪ judge, criticize
批評 pīpíng ⑪ criticize: 批評家 critic
批註 pīzhù ⑪ critique and annotate 图 commentary, annotation
批准 pīzhǔn ⑪ grant, approve

琵⁷ pí 7 Jade pieces 玨⁹⁷ with 比ᴵ² phonetic. 图 lute
琵琶 pípá 图 pipa, lute

毗⁸ pí 8 Head 囟ᴵ⁴³ (altered to resemble 田ᴵᴵ) with 比ᴵ² phonetic. 图 navel ⑪ adjoin
毗鄰 pílín 图 adjacent (⇔ 比鄰ᴵ²)

媲⁹ pì 9 Woman 女ᴵ⁴ and adjoin 毗ᴵ² (phonetic). ⑪ match, be compatible 图 comparable
媲美 pìměi ⑪ rival, compare well with

紕¹⁰ pī [纰] Thread 糸ᴵ⁵³ connected 比ᴵ². 图 fringe, hem 图 mistake
紕漏 pīlòu 图 error, mistake

屁¹¹ pì 11 Lower body 尸ᴵ⁰ with 比ᴵ² phonetic. 图 fart 图 ass, buttocks ⇔ 狗屁㎏, 放屁㎏
屁股 pìgǔ 图 ass, buttocks: 打屁股 spank

皆¹² jiē 12 Each person 自ᴵ³⁹ (abbreviated form resembling 白⁷⁶) together 比ᴵ². 图 all, every ⇔ 啼笑皆非㎏

30   字譜及字典

比
12

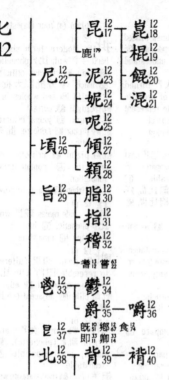

昆 12/17
　鹿 1/79
尼 12/22 ─ 泥 12/23
　　　妮 12/24
　　　呢 12/25
頃 12/26 ─ 傾 12/27
　　　穎 12/28
旨 12/29 ─ 脂 12/30
　　　指 12/31
　　　稽 12/32
　　　耆 1/2 嘗 2/2
卽 12/33 ─ 鬱 12/34
　　　爵 12/35 ─ 嚼 12/36
旣 12/37 ─ 旣 1/17 鄉 1/5 食 1/4
　　　　即 1/7 卿 1/4
北 12/38 ─ 背 12/39 ─ 揹 12/40

崑 12/18
棍 12/19
餛 12/20
混 12/21

階 12/13 jiē
[阶] Hill 阜 1/67 with
皆 1/2 phonetic. Simplified
form uses 介 1/8. 图 steps ⇔
臺階 1/28
階層 jiēcéng 图 stratum
階段 jiēduàn 图 phase, stage
階級 jiējí 图 rank, class: 階級
鬥爭 class struggle; 無產階
級 proletariat
階梯 jiētī 图 stairs

諧 12/14 xié
[谐] Words 言 1/6 for
all 皆 1/2 (phonetic). 图
harmonious ⇔ 詼諧 1/2, 和
諧 1/2

楷 12/15 kǎi
Wood 木 1/7 and all 皆 1/2
(phonetic). 图 standard, model
楷模 kǎimó 图 model, pattern
楷書 kǎishū 图 standard
calligraphy style

揩 12/16 kāi
Hand 手 1/9 and all 皆 1/2
(phonetic). 图 wipe

昆 12/17 kūn
Together 比 1/2 under
the sun 日 1/6. 图 multitudes
descendants
昆蟲 kūnchóng 图 insects
昆明 kūnmíng 图 Kunming
昆仲 kūnzhòng 图 brothers

崑 12/18 kūn
[昆] Multitude 昆 1/9
(phonetic) of mountains 山 1/67.
崑崙 kūnlún 图 Kunlun Moun-
tains - mountain range
between Tibet and Xinjiang

棍 12/19 gùn
Wood 木 1/7 with 昆 1/9
phonetic. 图 stick, club ⇔
冰棍 1/2, 曲棍球 1/35
棍子 gùnzi 图 stick, club

餛 12/20 hún
[馄] Food 食 1/9 with
昆 1/9 phonetic. 图 wonton
餛飩 húntun 图 wonton

混 12/21 hùn 图 hǔn hún
Multitude 昆 1/9 (pho-
netic) of rushing water 水 1/9.
hùn: 图 confuse, mix hǔn:
图 confused, indistinguishable
hún: 图 turbid, murky ⇔ 鬼
混 1/40, 蒙混 1/95
混蛋 húndàn,hùndàn 图 (⼑) damn
fool
混沌 hùndùn 图 primordial chaos
混合 hùnhé,hǔnhé 图 mix, blend
混亂 hǔnluàn,hùnluàn 图 confusion
混血 hùnxiě,hùnxuè 图 mixed
race
混淆 hǔnyáo 图 confuse
混雜 hùnzá,hǔnzá 图 mix, mingle
混濁 húnzhúo 图 turbid, murky

尼 12/22 ní
Body 尸 1/40 and turned-
around person 匕 1/2. (⼑)
approach from behind 图 nun
⇔ 印尼 1/8
尼泊爾 níbóěr 图 Nepal
尼姑 nígū 图 nun
尼克森 níkèsēn (⼏) Nixon

泥 12/23 ní nì
Water 水 1/9 with 尼 1/22
phonetic. nì: 图 mud nì:
图 mired in old ways, conservative ⇔ 水泥 1/9, 拘泥 1/9, 污
泥 1/9, 印泥 1/8, 淤泥 1/111
泥濘 nínìng 图 mud, mire

泥土 nítǔ 📖 mud

妮 ní
[12] / 24 Woman 女[54] who is close 尼[45] (phonetic). 📖 maid

呢 ní ne
[12] / 25 Mouth 口[68] with 尼[45] phonetic. ní: 🔲 murmur woolen ne: 📖 a particle indicating a question or emphasis: 你呢? And you?

呢喃 nínán 🔲 murmur

頃 qǐng
[12] / 26 [顷] Turned-around 匕[12] head 頁[98]. 🔲 lean, incline 📖 hectare ⇔ 公頃[92]

頃刻 qǐngkè 📖 instantly

傾 qīng
[12] / 27 [倾] Person 人[10] leaning 頃[45] (phonetic). 🔲 lean, bend ⇔ 左傾[12], 右傾[12]

傾倒 qīngdǎo 🔲 topple, fall for, be infatuated with
傾倒 qīngdào 🔲 empty, dump: 傾倒垃圾 empty the trash
傾訴 qīngsù 🔲 pour out one's heart
傾聽 qīngtīng 🔲 listen carefully
傾向 qīngxiàng 🔲 incline toward, lean toward
傾銷 qīngxiāo 🔲 dump, sell below cost
傾斜 qīngxié 🔲 tilt, slant

穎 yǐng
[12] / 28 [颖] Grain 禾[08] leaning 頃[45] (phonetic) under own weight. 📖 ear of grain 🔲 outstanding, talented ⇔ 新穎[92], 聰穎[144]

穎慧 yǐnghuì 📖 clever, bright

旨 zhǐ
[12] / 29 Spoonful 匕[12] (phonetic) of sweetness 甘[49] (altered to resemble 日[76]). 📖 tasty 📖 purpose ⇔ 宗旨[45]

脂 zhī
[12] / 30 Meat 肉[132] that is tasty 旨[45] (phonetic). 📖 fat ⇔ 油脂[113]

脂肪 zhīfáng 📖 fat
脂粉 zhīfěn 📖 cosmetics

指 zhǐ
[12] / 31 Part of hand 手[97] used for tasting 旨[45] (phonetic). 🔲 finger to point ⇔ 戒指[92], 拇指[12], 手指[97]

指標 zhǐbiāo 📖 target, quota
指出 zhǐchū 🔲 point out
指導 zhǐdǎo 🔲 guide: 指導教授 academic advisor
指點 zhǐdiǎn 🔲 instruct
指定 zhǐdìng 🔲 appoint, assign, specify
指揮 zhǐhuī 🔲 direct, command
指甲 zhǐjiǎ 📖 fingernail
指教 zhǐjiào 🔲 advise
指控 zhǐkòng 🔲 accuse
指令 zhǐlìng 🔲 command, order
指明 zhǐmíng 🔲 point out
指南 zhǐnán 📖 guidebook, guide: 指南針 compass
指示 zhǐshì 🔲 indicate, instruct
指事 zhǐshì 📖 type of Chinese character representing an abstraction (⇒ 六書[89])
指數 zhǐshù 📖 index number 📖 exponent
指望 zhǐwàng 🔲 hope, expect
指紋 zhǐwén 📖 fingerprint
指責 zhǐzé 🔲 blame
指針 zhǐzhēn 📖 indicator, pointer

稽 jī
[12] / 32 Stunted tree (ancient character resembling 禾[08]) and especially 尤[54] with 旨[45] phonetic. 🔲 delay 🔲 inspect ⇔ 滑稽[137]

稽核 jīhé 🔲 audit

鬯 chàng
[12] / 33 Ladle 匕[12] and bowl-shaped 凵[70] vessel holding rice 米[138] wine. 📖 sacrificial wine

鬱 yù
[12] / 34 [郁] Forest 林[70] and an ancient character showing the offering of a vessel 缶[141] of wine 鬯[45] with decorative markings 彡[17]. 📖 lush ⇔ 蔓鬱[19]

鬱悶 yùmèn 🔲 depressed

爵 jué
[12] / 35 Hand 寸[43] holding sacrificial wine 鬯[45] with lid on top (altered to resemble 爪[103] and 目[94]). 📖 an ancient wine pitcher 📖 feudal title ⇔ 侯爵[23], 伯爵[74]

爵士 juéshì 📖 jazz
爵位 juéwèi 📖 feudal title

嚼 jiáo jué
[12] / 36 Mouth 口[68] used as vessel 爵[45] (phonetic). 🔲 chew: 味如嚼蠟 bland, tasteless ⇔ 咀嚼[117]

嚼食 juéshí 🔲 chew

匕 xiāng bǐ
[12] / 37 Spoon 匕[12] and a pictograph of a rice pot.

北 běi
[12] / 38 Two persons turned 匕[12] back to back. 📖 disagree 🔲 flee 📖 north ⇔ 河北[82], 湖北[82], 台北[58], 東北[78], 敗北[150]

北部 běibù 📖 northern part
北方 běifāng 📖 north 📖 the North
北海道 běihǎidào 🌐 Hokkaido
北極 běijí 📖 Arctic: 北極點 North Pole
北京 běijīng 🌐 Beijing, Peking: 北京烤鴨 Peking duck; 北京大學 Peking University
北平 běipíng 🌐 📖 Beiping, Peking
北上 běishàng 🔲 go up north

背 bèi bēi
[12] / 39 Back to back 北[45] (phonetic) and body 肉[132]. bèi: 🔲 back 🔲 memorize 🔲 violate bēi: 🔲 carry on the back, shoulder ⇔ 違背[92], 駝背[15]

背包 bèibāo 📖 backpack, knapsack

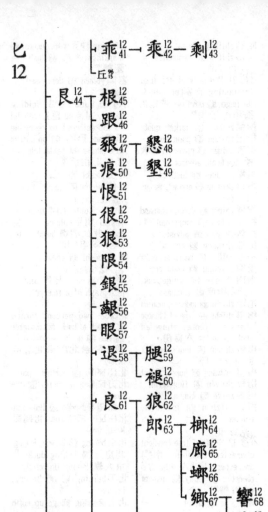

memory

背痛 bèitòng 图 backache

褙 12 bèi
40 Cloth 衣¹²⁶ backing 背² (phonetic). 動 mount (paintings or calligraphy) ⇔ 裱褙¹²

乖 12 guāi
41 Horns ㅜ ⁷⁴ cracked 兆¹²⁷ (altered to resemble 北²). 動 contradict, oppose 图 obedient, well-behaved
乖乖 guāiguāi 图 obedient, well-behaved
乖巧 guāiqiǎo 图 clever, ingenious

乘 12 chéng
42 Person 大 ⁷ (or enter 入 ⁷) on a perch 桀²² (together altered to resemble 乖⁴¹). 由 cover 動 ride 動 multiply by ⇔ 搭乘²²
乘法 chéngfǎ 图 multiplication
乘機 chéngjī 動 seize the opportunity
乘客 chéngkè 图 passenger
乘涼 chéngliáng 動 enjoy the cool

剩 12 shèng
43 Multiply 乘⁴² (phonetic) and knife 刀 ⁷. 動 be left over, remain: 還剩多少? How much is left? ⇔ 過剩¹³³
剩下 shèngxià 動 be left over, remain: 剩下的 remainder
剩餘 shèngyú 图 surplus

艮 12 gěn gèn
44 Turn around 匕¹² and look in the eye 目¹⁴ (abbreviated). gěn: 图 rude gèn: 图 one of the Eight Diagrams (⇒ 八卦 ⁷)

根 12 gēn
45 Tree 木 ⁷ with 艮⁴⁴ phonetic. 图 root 動 measure-word for long and thin objects ⇔ 紮根⁴⁴, 阿根廷²², 生根⁴⁴, 草根⁵⁶, 雷根¹¹, 里根¹¹

背負 bēifù 動 carry on the back, shoulder
背後 bèihòu 图 back
背脊 bèijǐ 图 spine
背景 bèijǐng 图 background

背離 bèilí 動 deviate from
背面 bèimiàn 图 reverse side
背叛 bèipàn 動 betray, forsake
背棄 bèiqì 動 abandon
背誦 bèisòng 動 recite from

根本 gēnběn [名] roots, essence [副] completely: 根本不行 utterly impossible
根除 gēnchú [動] exterminate, eradicate
根基 gēnjī [名] foundation
根據 gēnjù [動] according to
根深蒂固 gēnshēndìgù [成] deep-rooted
根源 gēnyuán [名] source
根子 gēnzi [名] root

跟 12 gēn
46 Foot 足[88/80] with 艮[12/44] phonetic. [名] heel [動] follow [介] with ⇔ 腳跟[48/117]
跟前 gēnqián [副] in front of
跟上 gēnshàng [動] catch up with: 跟不上 fall behind
跟隨 gēnsúi [動] follow behind

豤 12 kěn
47 Boar 豕[155/1] with 艮[12/44] phonetic. [動] gnaw

懇 12 kěn
48 [恳] Heart 心[83/1] intent like gnawing boar 豤[12/47] (phonetic, altered). [副] earnestly ⇔ 誠懇[45/38]
懇求 kěnqíu [動] beseech

墾 12 kěn
49 [垦] Gnaw 豤[12/47] (phonetic, altered) at the ground 土[70/1]. [動] cultivate
墾荒 kěnhuāng [動] settle new land

痕 12 hén
50 Sickness 疒[73/136] with 艮[12/44] phonetic. [名] scar, mark ⇔ 創痕[12/83], 傷痕[76/63], 疤痕[85/3]
痕跡 hénjī [名] trace, mark

恨 12 hèn
51 Heart 心[83/1] that is rude 艮[12/44] (phonetic). [動] hate ⇔ 仇恨[30/4], 悔恨[53/25], 痛恨[48/45], 怨恨[73/9], 憎恨[144/10]

很 12 hěn
52 Step 彳[41/1] rudely 艮[12/44] (phonetic). [古] disobey [副] very

狠 12 hěn
53 Dog 犬[91/1] with 艮[12/44] phonetic. [形] vicious ⇔ 兇狠[3/7], 心狠手辣[83/1]

限 12 xiàn
54 Hill 阜[167/1] rudely 艮[12/44] (phonetic) blocking travel. [動] restrict, limit [名] limit ⇔ 極限[1/4], 有限[15/118], 無限[71/117], 期限[96/3]
限度 xiàndù [名] limit
限額 xiàné [名] quota
限期 xiànqí [名] deadline
限於 xiànyú [動] restricted to
限制 xiànzhì [動] limit, restrict

銀 12 yín
55 [银] Metal 金[44/3] with 艮[12/44] phonetic. [名] silver
銀行 yínháng [名] bank
銀河 yínhé [地] Milky Way [名] galaxy
銀色 yínsè [名] silver (color)
銀子 yínzi [名] silver

齦 12 yín
56 [龈] Teeth 齒[98/3] with 艮[12/44] phonetic. [名] gums ⇔ 牙齦[84/1]

眼 12 yǎn
57 Eye 目[114/1] with 艮[12/44] phonetic. [名] eye ⇔ 親眼[90/75], 字眼[55/2], 眨眼[66/61], 媚眼[114/19], 耀眼[124/8], 肉眼[132/1]
眼光 yǎnguāng [名] sense of quality, taste: 他很有眼光. He has good taste.
眼紅 yǎnhóng [形] envious [名] envy
眼睛 yǎnjīng [名] eyes
眼鏡 yǎnjìng [名] eyeglasses
眼看 yǎnkàn [動] see
眼淚 yǎnlèi [名] tears
眼皮 yǎnpí [名] eyelid: 雙眼皮 folded eyelids
眼前 yǎnqián [副] before one's eyes [副] presently
眼神 yǎnshén [名] gleam in one's eyes

退 12 tùi
58 Walk 辵[41/3] trudgingly 夊[10/105] like sun 日[76/1] (together resembling 艮[12/44]). [動] retreat, withdraw [動] recede ⇔ 撤退[55/19], 衰退[126/5]
退步 tùibù [動] regress, step back
退房 tùifáng [動] check out (of a hotel)
退化 tùihuà [動] deteriorate
退換 tùihuàn [動] exchange, return
退票 tùipiào [動] return a ticket
退讓 tùiràng [動] yield
退伍 tùiwǔ [動] be discharged, be decommissioned
退休 tùixīu [動] retire

腿 12 tǔi
59 Flesh 肉[132/1] and retreat 退[12/58] (phonetic). [名] leg, thigh ⇔ 大腿[79/1], 火腿[82/1]

褪 12 tùi [又] tùn
60 Clothing 衣[126/1] and retreat 退[12/58] (phonetic). [動] strip [動] fade
褪色 tùnsè,tùisè [動] fade

良 12 liáng
61 Abundant 畐[23/54] with 亡[29/13] phonetic (together altered to resemble 艮[12/44]). [形] good ⇔ 改良[57/6], 善良[123/17]
良好 liánghǎo [形] good
良心 liángxīn [名] conscience
良友 liángyǒu [名] good friend

狼 12 láng
62 Dog 犬[91/1] with 良[12/61] phonetic. [名] wolf ⇔ 色狼[33/16]

郎 12 láng
63 City 邑[33/18] with 良[12/61] phonetic. [名] an ancient city [名] an ancient title ⇔ 法郎[39/69], 新郎[90/77], 女郎[54/1], 牛郎[92/1]

榔 12 láng
64 Tree 木[77/1] product offered to honored 郎[12/63] (phonetic) guest. [名] betel nut ⇔ 檳榔[75/4]

廊 12 láng
65 Open roof 广[60/1] with 郎[12/63] phonetic. [名] corridor, veranda ⇔ 走廊[88/58], 髮廊[91/15]

螂 12 láng
66 Insect 虫[125/1] with 郎[12/63]

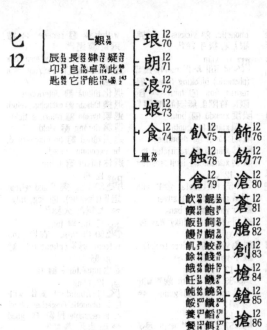

look forward to

琅 12 láng
70 Jade 玉[107] that is good
良 (phonetic). 圖 a jade-
like stone ⇔ 琳琅[7]

朗 12 lǎng
71 Good 良 (phonetic)
moon 月[9]. 圈 bright, clear
⇔ 伊朗[49], 開朗[79], 明朗[9]
朗讀 lǎngdú 勔 recite
朗誦 lǎngsòng 勔 recite

浪 12 làng
72 Water 水 with 良
phonetic. 圖 wave 圈 disso-
lute ⇔ 波浪[106], 流浪[89], 放
浪[17], 孟浪[16]
浪潮 làngcháo 圖 tide, wave
浪費 làngfèi 勔 waste
浪漫 làngmàn 圈 romantic
浪子 làngzǐ 圖 prodigal son

娘 12 niáng
73 Woman 女[14] who is
good 良 (phonetic). 圖 girl,
woman 圈 wife 圖 mother ⇔
姑娘[8], 新娘[9], 師娘[12]

食 12 shí
74 Collected ∠[14] rice
皀[9]. 圖 food ⇔ 飲食[9],
嚼食[9], 吸食[9], 絕食[7], 零
食[7], 糧食[6], 速食[7], 覓
食[7], 膳食[12], 美食[9], 素
食[153]
食量 shíliàng 圖 appetite
食品 shípǐn 圖 foods
食譜 shípǔ 圖 recipe
食堂 shítáng 圖 dining hall
食物 shíwù 圖 food
食用 shíyòng 勔 edible
食慾 shíyù 圖 appetite

飲 12 shí
75 Give food 食 (pho-
netic) to a person 人[10]. 匎 feed

飾 12 shì
76 [饰] Towel 巾[31] with
𠂤 phonetic. 勔 polish 勔
adorn, decorate ⇔ 掩飾[9],
修飾[9], 服飾[9], 裝飾[9]
飾物 shìwù 圖 decorations,

phonetic. 圖 cockroach ⇔
蟑螂[9]

鄉 12 xiāng
67 [乡] Region between
cities 邑[72] that produces grain
皀[9]. Simplified form is
abbreviation of 邑[9]. 圖
countryside 圖 hometown 圖
village 圖 township ⇔ 下
鄉[1], 老鄉[4], 返鄉[9], 同
鄉[9], 故鄉[9], 家鄉[155]
鄉村 xiāngcūn 圖 countryside
鄉間 xiāngjiān 圖 countryside
鄉土 xiāngtǔ 圖 hometown
鄉下 xiāngxià 圖 countryside:
鄉下人 country people,
villagers
鄉長 xiāngzhǎng 圖 village elder
圖 township leader
鄉鎮 xiāngzhèn 圖 village: 鄉
鎮企業 township enterprise

響 12 xiǎng
68 [响] Homeward 鄉
(phonetic) returning sound
音[49]. Simplified form uses
口[14] and 向[9]. 圖 echo 圖 勔
sound 勔 noisy, loud ⇔ 影
響[9], 聲響[9], 音響[9], 回
響[9], 迴響[9]
響亮 xiǎngliàng 圈 loud and clear
響應 xiǎngyìng 勔 respond
favorably

嚮 12 xiàng
69 [向] Toward 向
home 鄉 (phonetic). 囵
towards
嚮導 xiàngdǎo 圖 guide
嚮往 xiàngwǎng 勔 aspire to,

ornaments

飭 12 chì 77 [饬] Strength 力[74/1] with 飤[12/75] phonetic. 【動】 order ⇔ 整飭[88/43]

飭令 chìlìng 【動】 【書】 edict

蝕 12 shí 78 [蚀] Modern form shows food 食[12/74] (phonetic) and insect 虫[125/1]. 【動】 eat away at 【名】 eclipse ⇔ 腐蝕[14/72], 日蝕[76/1], 月蝕[80/1]

蝕本 shíběn 【動】 lose money

倉 12 cāng 79 [仓] Food 食[12/74] (abbreviated) contained 口[69/1]. 【名】 granary, storehouse ⇔ 穀倉[37/11], 義倉[45/51], 糧倉[76/100]

倉促 cāngcù 【副】 hurriedly

倉頡 cāngjié 【人】 Cang Jie - legendary inventor of Chinese characters

倉庫 cāngkù 【名】 warehouse, storehouse

滄 12 cāng 80 [沧] Water 水[2/21] with 倉[12/79] phonetic. 【形】 blue

滄海 cānghǎi 【名】 blue sea

蒼 12 cāng 81 [苍] Plant 艸[66/2] with 倉[12/79] phonetic. 【形】 green ⇔ 穹蒼[65/4]

蒼白 cāngbái 【形】 pale

蒼翠 cāngcùi 【形】 emerald

蒼老 cānglǎo 【形】 old

蒼茫 cāngmáng 【形】 vast

蒼蠅 cāngyíng 【名】 fly

艙 12 cāng 82 [舱] Ship's 舟[129/1] storehouse 倉[12/79] (phonetic). 【名】 cabin, hold ⇔ 客艙[10/67], 船艙[68/121]

創 12 chuāng chuàng 83 [创] Knife 刀[35/1] with 倉[12/79] phonetic. chuāng: 【名】 wound chuàng: 【動】 create, found ⇔ 開創[78/29], 手創[89/1], 獨創[125/12]

創辦 chuàngbàn 【動】 found

創痕 chuānghén 【名】 scar

創見 chuàngjiàn 【形】 original idea

創立 chuànglì 【動】 found, establish

創傷 chuāngshāng 【名】 wound

創始 chuàngshǐ 【動】 found: 創始者 founder

創新 chuàngxīn 【動】 create

創業 chuàngyè 【動】 start a business

創造 chuàngzào 【動】 create: 創造力 creativity

創作 chuàngzùo 【動】 create 【名】 creation

槍 12 qiāng 84 [枪] Wood 木[77/1] with 倉[12/79] phonetic and suggestive of wound 創[12/83]. 【名】 lance 【名】 gun ⇔ 標槍[15/91], 機槍[59/5], 手槍[89/1]

槍斃 qiāngbì 【動】 execute by firing squad

槍殺 qiāngshā 【動】 shoot dead

槍枝 qiāngzhī 【名】 guns

鎗 12 qiāng 85 [枪[12/84]] Metal 金[44/3] with 倉[12/79] phonetic. 【名】 gun (⇨ 槍[12/84])

搶 12 qiǎng 86 [抢] Hand 手[89/1] with 倉[12/79] phonetic. 【動】 rob 【動】 rush

搶案 qiǎngàn 【名】 robbery case

搶奪 qiǎngdúo 【動】 loot, plunder

搶購 qiǎnggòu 【動】 rush to buy

搶劫 qiǎngjié 【動】 rob, hold up

搶救 qiǎngjìu 【動】 rescue

嗆 12 qiàng 87 [呛] Mouth 口[68/1] with 倉[12/79] phonetic. 【動】 cough, choke ⇔ 夠嗆[18/34]

匕 13 huà 1 Pictograph of a person upside down. 【古】 transform

化 13 huà 2 Person 人[10/1] transformed 匕[13/1]. 【動】 transform, change ⇔ 二元化[1/2], 蛻化[11/9], 退化[12/58], 腐化[14/72], 同化[24/3], 消化[29/26], 漢化[31/97], 分化[35/4], 綠化[42/12], 孵化[55/6], 深化[63/4], 演化[63/40], 溶化[68/108], 熔化[68/109], 多元化[72/4], 焚化[77/10], 簡化[78/24], 淡化[82/12], 造化[92/20], 文化[98/1], 僵化[111/7], 洋化[123/2], 變化[153/5], 惡化[166/3], 融化[174/3]

化肥 huàféi 【名】 chemical fertilizer

化合物 huàhéwù 【名】 chemical compound

化名 huàmíng 【名】 alias

化石 huàshí 【名】 fossil: 恐龍化石 dinosaur fossil

化學 huàxué 【名】 chemistry: 化學療法 chemotherapy

化妝 huàzhuāng 【動】 apply makeup 【名】 makeup: 化妝品 makeup, cosmetics

花 13 huā 3 Modern form shows plant 艸[66/2] and change 化[13/2] (phonetic). 【名】 flower 【動】 spend: 很花時間 time-consuming 【形】 flowery, florid ⇔ 五花八門[1/3], 曇花一現[1/64], 繡花[2/34], 爆米花[15/55], 菊花[18/23], 荷花[27/20], 黃花[31/82], 天花板[37/35], 梅花[54/20], 澆花[70/31], 雪花[70/83], 百花齊放[76/3], 棉花[76/11], 蘭花[70/105], 開花[78/29], 葵花[88/23], 桃花[127/3], 插花[131/23], 櫻花[150/4], 蓮花[158/12]

花瓣 huābàn 【名】 petal

花茶 huāchá 【名】 herbal tea

花店 huādiàn 【名】 flower store

花朵 huādǔo 【名】 flower

花費 huāfèi 【名】 cost

花粉 huāfěn 【名】 pollen: 花粉熱 hayfever

花花公子 huāhuāgōngzǐ 【名】 playboy

花卉 huāhùi 【名】 flowering plants

花籃 huālán 【名】 flower basket

花蓮 huālián 【地】 Hualian - a city in Taiwan

花瓶 huāpíng 【名】 flower vase

花錢 huāqián 【動】 spend money

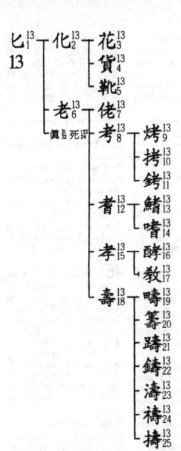

靴₅ xuē
Leather 革? changed
化? (phonetic) into. 图 boots
靴子 xuēzi 图 boots

老₆ lǎo
Person 人? (altered)
whose hair 毛? (altered)
changes 匕?. 图 old ⇔ 元
老?, 蒼老?, 耆老?, 父老?,
長老?, 古老?, 養老?, 衰老?

老闆 lǎobǎn 图 owner, boss
老板 lǎobǎn 图 owner, boss: 老板娘 proprietress, proprietor's wife
老兵 lǎobīng 图 veteran
老大 lǎodà 图 eldest sibling 图 gang leader
老爹 lǎodiē 图 father
老公 lǎogōng 图 husband
老虎 lǎohǔ 图 tiger: 紙老虎 paper tiger
老繭 lǎojiǎn 图 callus
老君 lǎojūn 囚 Lao-tse ⇨ 子?
老年 lǎonián 图 old age: 老年人 the elderly; 老年癡呆 senility
老婆 lǎopó 图 wife: 小老婆 mistress, second wife
老人 lǎorén 图 old man 图 the elderly
老人家 lǎorénjiā 图 图 old person
老師 lǎoshī 图 teacher
老實 lǎoshí 图 honest
老是 lǎoshì 图 always
老鼠 lǎoshǔ 图 rat, mouse: 米老鼠 Mickey Mouse
老太太 lǎotàitài 图 old woman
老天 lǎotiān 图 My God!
老頭 lǎotóu 图 old man
老外 lǎowài 图 图 foreigner
老鄉 lǎoxiāng 图 fellow villager
老爺 lǎoyé 图 master
老鷹 lǎoyīng 图 eagle
老友 lǎoyǒu 图 old friend
老遠 lǎoyuǎn 图 afar, distant

花圈 huāquān 图 wreath
花生 huāshēng 图 peanut
花壇 huātán 图 flower terrace
花園 huāyuán 图 garden

貨₄ huò [货] Money 貝? and change 化? (phonetic). commodity money ⇔ 賤
貨?, 期貨?, 存貨?, 通貨?, 百貨?, 卸貨?, 雜貨?, 售貨?

貨幣 huòbì 图 currency
貨車 huòchē 图 truck
貨船 huòchuán 图 cargo vessel
貨櫃 huòguì 图 shipping container
貨款 huòkuǎn 图 payment
貨品 huòpǐn 图 goods, commodities
貨物 huòwù 图 product, merchandise
貨運 huòyùn 图 freight

老者 lǎozhě 图 the elderly
老子 lǎozǐ 囚 Lao-tse - founder of Taoism

佬 13 lǎo
7 Person 人¹⁰ and old/familiar 老¹³ (phonetic). 图 fellow ⇔ 閩佬² , 鬼佬⁴⁰

考 13 kǎo
8 Old 老¹³ (phonetic, abbreviated) and obstructed breath 丂 ⁷⁷. 图 deceased father 冊 test ⇔ 高考³⁷ , 參考⁷ , 聯考⁸⁸ , 補考⁸⁸ , 思考¹⁴³
考察 kǎochá 冊 examine, observe
考古學 kǎogǔxué 图 archeology
考過 kǎoguò 冊 pass a test
考核 kǎohé 冊 check, evaluate
考卷 kǎojuàn 图 test paper
考慮 kǎolǜ 冊 consider
考上 kǎoshàng 冊 pass a test
考生 kǎoshēng 图 examinee
考試 kǎoshì 图 test, exam
考題 kǎotí 图 test question
考驗 kǎoyàn 图 test, trial

烤 13 kǎo
9 Fire 火⁸² that withers 考¹³ (phonetic). 冊 roast, toast
烤肉 kǎoròu 图 冊 barbecue
烤鴨 kǎoyā 图 roast duck: 北京烤鴨 Peking duck

拷 13 kǎo
10 Hand 手⁷⁹ with 考¹³ phonetic. 冊 beat 冊 torture
拷貝 kǎobèi 冊 图 copy
拷打 kǎodǎ 冊 beat up
拷問 kǎowèn 冊 torture to extract a confession

銬 13 kào
11 [铐] Metal 金³¹ with 考¹³ phonetic. 图 shackles ⇔ 手銬⁷⁹

耆 13 qí
12 Old 老¹³ with 旨⁸ (merged) phonetic. 圈 old
耆老 qílǎo 图 the elderly

鰭 13 qí
13 [鳍] Fish 魚¹⁸⁰ with

耆¹³ phonetic. 图 fin

嗜 13 shì
14 Mouth 口⁶⁸ used to old 耆¹³ (phonetic) tastes. 图 habit 冊 become addicted to
嗜好 shìhào 图 habit
嗜酒 shìjiǔ 冊 addicted to alcohol

孝 13 xiào
15 Child 子¹⁵ supporting aged 老¹³ (abbreviated) parent. 图 filial piety 圈 pious ⇔ 不孝¹⁰ , 忠孝¹³⁷
孝道 xiàodào 图 filial piety
孝順 xiàoshùn 冊 be filial
孝子 xiàozǐ 图 filial son

酵 13 xiào
16 Alcohol 酉¹⁵⁹ and care for 孝¹³ (phonetic). 冊 ferment, leaven ⇔ 發酵⁷⁰
酵母 xiàomǔ 图 yeast
酵素 xiàosù 图 enzyme

教 13 jiāo jiào
17 Strikes 攵³⁸ to make learn (ancient character resembling 孝¹³ from child 子¹⁵ under influence 爻¹⁰). jiāo: 冊 teach jiào: 冊 advise, instruct 图 a religion ⇔ 宗教⁵⁶ , 主教⁵ , 指教⁸¹ , 天主教⁸⁹ , 領教⁸⁸ , 新教⁹⁹ , 傳教⁸⁵ , 佛教⁸⁹ , 回教⁹⁷ , 諸教⁴⁷ , 東正教⁹⁷ , 助教¹¹⁷ , 道教¹⁴⁰ , 家教¹⁵⁵ , 管教¹⁶⁷
教材 jiàocái 图 teaching material
教導 jiàodǎo 冊 instruct, guide
教官 jiàoguān 图 military instructor
教皇 jiàohuáng 图 pope
教誨 jiàohuǐ 冊 teach
教會 jiàohuì 图 church: 教會學校 missionary school
教科書 jiàokēshū 图 textbook
教練 jiàoliàn 图 冊 coach
教師 jiàoshī 图 teacher
教室 jiàoshì 图 classroom
教授 jiàoshòu 图 professor
教書 jiāoshū 冊 teach
教唆 jiàosuō 冊 instigate, abet

教堂 jiàotáng 图 church: 大教堂 cathedral
教條 jiàotiáo 图 dogma 圈 dogmatic
教徒 jiàotú 图 follower of a religion, believer
教學 jiàoxué 图 teaching
教訓 jiàoxùn 图 lesson, moral
教養 jiàoyǎng 冊 raise, bring up: 沒有教養 uncultured, unmannered
教義 jiàoyì 图 doctrine
教育 jiàoyù 冊 educate 图 education: 再教育 reeducation
教員 jiàoyuán 图 teachers, faculty
教職員 jiàozhíyuán 图 faculty and staff
教宗 jiàozōng 图 pope

壽 13 shòu
18 [寿] Old 老¹³ (at top, abbreviated) with an ancient character for fields (now 疇¹³) phonetic. 图 longevity 图 age ⇔ 長壽⁸⁸
壽命 shòumìng 图 life span
壽司 shòusī 图 sushi
壽星 shòuxīng 图 birthday person

疇 13 chóu
19 [畴] Field 田¹¹¹ with 壽¹³ (originally a pictograph of furrows) phonetic. 图 field ⇔ 範疇¹⁶

籌 13 chóu
20 [筹] Bamboo 竹⁷¹ with 壽¹³ phonetic. 图 chip 冊 plan
籌備 chóubèi 冊 prepare, plan
籌劃 chóuhuà 冊 plan
籌集 chóují 冊 raise (funds)
籌碼 chóumǎ 图 bargaining chip
籌募 chóumù 冊 raise (funds)

躊 13 chóu
21 [踌] Feet 足⁸⁵ and age 壽¹³ (phonetic). 圈 hesitant
躊躇 chóuchú 冊 vacillate,

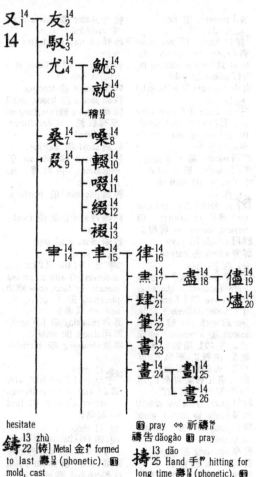

It's not that simple. 圖 also

友 14 2 yǒu
Two right hands 又¹⁴ (one now written to resemble left hand ㇓ ¹³) working in concert. 图 friend 圖 friendly ⇔ 良友, 老友, 男友, 校友, 密友, 摯友, 親友, 工友, 女友, 好友, 室友, 朋友

友好 yǒuhǎo 圖 friendly
友情 yǒuqíng 图 friendship
友人 yǒurén 图 friend
友善 yǒushàn 图 friendly, nice
友誼 yǒuyí 图 friendship

馭 14 3 yù [驭] Horse 馬 handled 又¹⁴ (phonetic). 圖 drive ⇔ 駕馭

尤 14 4 yóu Right hand 又¹⁴ (phonetic, altered) and sprout 乙?. 圖 especially 图 a surname
尤其 yóuqí 圖 especially

魷 14 5 yóu [鱿] Fish 魚¹⁸⁰ that is special 尤¹⁴ (phonetic). 图 squid
魷魚 yóuyú 图 squid

就 14 6 jiù Hill 京²⁷ that is special 尤¹⁴. 图 tall hill 圖 become, assume 圖 undertake 圖 immediately 图 regarding 圖 exactly, namely: 就是她. It's her. 圖 only, merely 圖 even if 圖 already: 我昨天就說了. I already said so yesterday. 圖 (indicating indifference) 丟了就丟了. What's lost is lost. 圖 (indicating a sufficient condition) 他去我就不去. If he goes I won't. 遷就, 成就, 將就
就此 jiùcǐ 圖 now, at this point
就讀 jiùdú 圖 read
就範 jiùfàn 圖 yield, be subdued
就任 jiùrèn 圖 take office

hesitate

鑄 13 22 zhù [铸] Metal 金³¹ formed to last 壽¹³ (phonetic). 圖 mold, cast
鑄造 zhùzào 图 mold, cast

濤 13 23 tāo [涛] Water 水³¹ with 壽¹³ phonetic. 图 large wave ⇔ 波濤

禱 13 24 dǎo [祷] Seek omen 示³⁶ of long life 壽¹³ (phonetic).

圖 pray ⇔ 祈禱
禱告 dǎogào 圖 pray

擣 13 25 dǎo Hand 手¹⁹ hitting for long time 壽¹³ (phonetic). 圖 pound (⇔ 搗)

又 14 1 yòu Pictograph of the right hand. 圖 again 图 both...and: 又高又快 both tall and fast 圖 (used in negative statements or rhetorical questions for emphasis) 又沒那麼簡單.

就是 jiùshì 🔲 exactly, precisely
就算 jiùsuàn 🔲 even if, granted that
就緒 jiùxù 🔲 completed (preparations)
就學 jiùxué 🔲 study, be a student
就要 jiùyào 🔲 about to
就業 jiùyè 🔲 employment
就職 jiùzhí 🔲 assume office

桑 7 sāng Tree 木 picked by many hands 又. 🔲 mulberry tree
桑蠶 sāngcán 🔲 silkworm

嗓 8 sǎng Mouth 口 with 桑 phonetic. 🔲 throat
嗓音 sǎngyīn 🔲 voice
嗓子 sǎngzi throat: 嗓子痛 🔲 sore throat

叕 9 chuò Pictograph of stitches, now written as hands 又. 🔲 connect

輟 10 [辍] chuò Cart 車 with 叕 phonetic. 🔲 stop, cease
輟學 chuòxué 🔲 drop out of school

啜 11 chuò Mouth 口 with 叕 phonetic. 🔲 sip 🔲 sob
啜泣 chuòqì 🔲 sob

綴 12 [缀] zhuì Threads 糸 united 叕, stitch together, combine ⇔ 點綴

裰 13 dúo Cloth 衣 united 叕 (phonetic). 🔲 mend, patch

聿 14 niè Hand 又 wielding a towel 巾 or other object. Early form shows hand with pen. 🔲 dexterity

聿 15 yù Write 聿 a line 一 (phonetic). 🔲 pen

律 16 lǜ Step 彳 according to what is written 聿 (phonetic). 🔲 tuning instrument 🔲 law, rule ⇔ 一律, 規律, 法律, 紀律, 旋律, 韻律, 菲律賓
律師 lǜshī 🔲 lawyer

肃 17 jìn Hand holding a pen/stick 聿 over a fire 火. ashes (⇨ 燼)

盡 18 [尽] jìn Only ashes 肃 (phonetic) in a plate 皿. Simplified form uses 尺. exhaust 🔲 utmost 🔲 entirely ⇔ 不盡, 無窮無盡, 罄盡, 殆盡, 詳盡
盡力 jìnlì 🔲 do one's best
盡量 jìnliàng 🔲 as hard as one can (⇨ 儘量)

儘 19 [尽] jǐn Person 人 trying the utmost 盡 (phonetic). 🔲 to the utmost 🔲 utmost
儘管 jǐnguǎn 🔲 despite, though
儘快 jǐnkuài 🔲 as soon as possible
儘量 jǐnliàng 🔲 as hard as one can (⇨ 盡量)

燼 20 [烬] jìn Fire 火 leaving nothing 盡 (phonetic). 🔲 ashes ⇔ 餘燼, 灰燼

肆 21 sì Lengthy 長 and grab 隶 (changed to write 聿). 🔲 indiscreet, unrestrained 🔲 four (complex form) ⇔ 大肆, 酒肆
肆虐 sìnüè 🔲 devastate, ravage
肆意 sìyì 🔲 wantonly, without restraint

筆 22 [笔] bǐ Bamboo 竹 pen 聿. Simplified form uses hair 毛. 🔲 pen, pencil, writing brush 🔲 writing style 🔲 brush stroke 🔲 a measure-word for money: 一大筆錢 a large sum of money ⇔ 鋼筆, 隨筆, 粉筆, 鉛筆, 毛筆, 伏筆, 圓珠筆, 蠟筆
筆畫 bǐhuà 🔲 brush stroke
筆記 bǐjì 🔲 notes
筆錄 bǐlù 🔲 take notes
筆名 bǐmíng 🔲 pen name
筆墨 bǐmò brush and ink 🔲 words, writing: 難以用筆墨來形容 hard to describe in words
筆試 bǐshì 🔲 written test
筆者 bǐzhě 🔲 writer

書 23 [书] shū Pen 聿 with 者 (abbreviated) phonetic. 🔲 write 🔲 book 🔲 letter 🔲 document ⇔ 隸書, 經書, 楷書, 教科書, 教書, 聘書, 四書, 六書, 釘書, 篆書, 念書, 唸書, 秘書, 梵書, 書館, 百科全書, 草書, 焚書坑儒, 藏書, 文書, 曆書, 叢書, 讀書, 家書
書包 shūbāo 🔲 bookbag
書本 shūběn 🔲 book: 書本知識 book knowledge
書店 shūdiàn 🔲 bookstore
書法 shūfǎ 🔲 calligraphy
書房 shūfáng 🔲 den, study
書籍 shūjí 🔲 books, works, literature
書架 shūjià 🔲 bookcase
書經 shūjīng 🔲 Book of History (⇨ 五經)
書面 shūmiàn 🔲 written
書名 shūmíng 🔲 title (of a book)
書寫 shūxiě 🔲 write

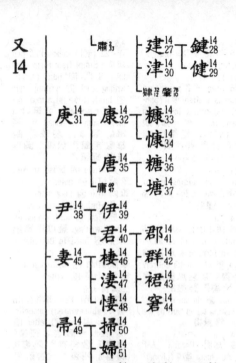

又
14

庸

建 14/27 ── 鍵 14/28
津 14/30 ── 健 14/29
肄　肇

庚 14/31 ┬ 康 14/32 ┬ 糠 14/33
　　　　　　　　└ 慷 14/34
　　　　├ 唐 14/35 ┬ 糖 14/36
　　　　│　　　　　└ 塘 14/37
　　　　庸

尹 14/38 ┬ 伊 14/39
　　　　　└ 君 14/40 ── 郡 14/41
妻 14/45 ┬ 樓 14/46 ── 群 14/42
　　　　　├ 淒 14/47 ── 裙 14/43
　　　　　└ 悽 14/48 ── 窘 14/44
帚 14/49 ┬ 掃 14/50
　　　　　├ 婦 14/51
　　　　　└ 侵 14/52 ── 寢 14/53 ── 浸 14/54
歸

書信 shūxìn letter, correspondence
書齋 shūzhāi study, den
書桌 shūzhuō desk

畫 14/24 [画] huà Write 聿 boundary lines 一 around a field 田. delineate, delimit draw, paint drawing, painting ⇔ 刻畫, 筆畫, 漫畫, 計畫, 國畫, 壁畫, 圖畫, 動畫, 油畫, 絹畫, 繪畫
畫報 huàbào picture magazine
畫地自封 huàdìzìfēng limit oneself
畫畫 huàhuā paint, draw
畫家 huàjiā painter
畫蛇添足 huàshétiānzú add feet to drawing of a snake - make superfluous additions
畫圖 huàtú draw, paint drawing, painting
畫展 huàzhǎn art exhibition

劃 14/25 [划] huà Delineate 畫 (phonetic) with a knife 刀. divide delimit plan ⇔ 籌劃, 計劃, 規劃, 策劃

劃分 huàfēn divide

晝 14/26 [昼] zhòu Delineated 畫 (abbreviated) by sun 日. Simplified form uses measure 尺 and sunrise 旦. daytime ⇔ 白晝
晝夜 zhòuyè day and night

建 14/27 jiàn Write 聿 rules governing behavior/steps 廴. establish, found build, erect, construct ⇔ 違建, 興建, 福建, 封建, 營建
建國 jiànguó found a nation
建交 jiànjiāo establish diplomatic relations
建立 jiànlì establish, found
建設 jiànshè construct, build: 基礎建設 infrastructure
建議 jiànyì suggest: 提出建議 suggest, make suggestions
建造 jiànzào construct
建築 jiànzhú building, structure construct: 建築師 architect; 建築物 building

鍵 14/28 [键] jiàn Metal 金 with 建 phonetic. key (on a keyboard) ⇔ 關鍵
鍵盤 jiànpán keyboard

健 14/29 jiàn Person 人 erect 建 (phonetic). healthy strengthen ⇔ 保健, 穩健
健康 jiànkāng health: 健康保險 health insurance healthy
健全 jiànquán sound, perfect
健壯 jiànzhuàng robust, vigorous

津 14/30 jīn Modern form shows water 水 and pen 聿. ferry ⇔ 天津
津貼 jīntiē subsidy, fringe

benefit

庚[14] gēng
[31] Hands 廾[55] (altered) holding a shield 干[70] (altered). 图 seventh Heavenly Stem (⇨ 干支[70])
庚子之役 gēngzǐzhīyì 图 Boxer Rebellion

康[14] kāng
[32] Rice 米[138] (resembling 水[41]) with 庚[51] phonetic. 图 rice husks (⇨ 糠[53]). 图 healthy 图 a surname ⇔ 健康[53], 小康[3]
康復 kāngfù 动 recover from illness
康熙 kāngxī 名 Kang-Hsi - a Qing Dynasty emperor: 康熙字典 a dictionary compiled during Kang Hsi's reign

糠[14] kāng
[33] Rice husks 康[51] (phonetic) with rice 米[138] redundant. 图 rice husks, rice chaff

慷[14] kāng
[34] Heart 心[83] and healthy 康[51] (phonetic). 形 fervent
慷慨 kāngkǎi 形 generous, fervent

唐[14] táng
[35] Mouth 口[66] with 庚[51] phonetic. 形 bold, rude 图 a surname ⇔ 荒唐[2]
唐朝 tángcháo 名 Tang Dynasty
唐代 tángdài 名 Tang Dynasty
唐人街 tángrénjiē 名 Chinatown
唐山 tángshān 名 Tangshan - a city in Hebei Province
唐詩 tángshī 名 Tang poetry
唐突 tángtú 形 rude, offensive, blunt

糖[14] táng
[36] Rice 米[138] with 唐[51] phonetic. 图 candy 图 sugar ⇔ 砂糖[87], 蔗糖[34], 楓糖[7], 口香糖[66]
糖醋 tángcù 形 sweet and sour: 糖醋魚 sweet and sour fish

糖果 tángguǒ 图 candy
糖尿病 tángniàobìng 图 diabetes

塘[14] táng
[37] Earth 土[70] with 唐[51] phonetic. 图 dike 图 pool ⇔ 水塘[41], 池塘[41]

尹[14] yǐn
[38] Hand 又[14] controlling as symbolized by 丿[7]. 图 rule 图 a surname

伊[14] yī
[39] Person 人[10] with 尹[51] phonetic. 图 he, she 图 a surname
伊拉克 yīlākè 图 Iraq
伊朗 yīlǎng 图 Iran
伊斯蘭 yīsīlán 图 Islam

君[14] jūn
[40] Rule 尹[51] by spoken 口[66] orders. 图 lord, monarch 图 gentleman ⇔ 老君[13], 暴君[51], 國君[51]
君權 jūnquán 图 monarchy
君主 jūnzhǔ 图 monarch
君子 jūnzǐ 图 gentleman: 偽君子 hypocrite

郡[14] jùn
[41] Lord's 君[51] (phonetic) villages 邑[77]. 图 prefecture, county

群[14] qún
[42] Sheep 羊[123] with 君[51] phonetic. 图 group, herd, swarm, flock ⇔ 一群[1], 人群[10]
群島 qúndǎo 图 archipelago
群集 qúnjí 动 swarm
群體 qúntǐ 图 colony, community, group: 群體利益 group interest
群眾 qúnzhòng 图 crowd 图 the masses: 群眾運動 mass movement

裙[14] qún
[43] Clothing 衣[126] with 君[51] phonetic. 图 skirt ⇔ 圍裙[39]

裙子 qúnzi 图 skirt

窘[14] jiǒng
[44] Lord 君[51] (phonetic) in a hole 穴[41]. 形 distressed, impoverished
窘境 jiǒngjìng 图 poverty
窘迫 jiǒngpò 形 distressed, hard-pressed

妻[14] qī
[45] Woman 女[4] holding 又[14] a broom-like object 屮[45]. 图 wife ⇔ 夫妻[37]
妻子 qīzi 图 wife

棲[14] qī
[46] [栖] Tree 木[7] with wife 妻[51] phonetic and suggestive of settling down. 动 perch
棲身 qīshēn 动 reside temporarily
棲息 qīxí 动 rest, perch

淒[14] qī
[47] [凄] Water 水[41] with 妻[51] phonetic. Simplified form uses ice 冫[75]. 形 rainy and cloudy
淒涼 qīliáng 形 dreary, bleak

悽[14] qī
[48] [凄] Heart 心[83] with 妻[51] phonetic and suggestive of dreary 淒[51]. 形 sad
悽慘 qīcǎn 形 miserable, tragic

帚[14] zhǒu
[49] Hand 又[14] sweeping area 冂[77] with broom of rags 巾[53]. 图 broom ⇔ 掃帚[51]

掃[14] sǎo sào
[50] [扫] Hand 手[90] holding a broom 帚[51]. sǎo: 动 sweep. sào: 图 broom ⇔ 打掃[3]
掃除 sǎochú 动 sweep away, eliminate
掃蕩 sǎodàng 动 mop up
掃地 sǎodì 动 sweep the floor
掃瞄 sǎomiáo 动 scan (with the eyes)
掃描 sǎomiáo 动 scan (electronically): 掃描器 scanner

字譜及字典

又 14

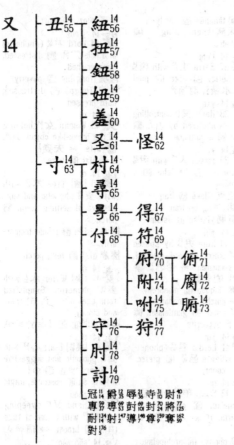

丑 14 55 ─┬ 紐 14 56
        ├ 扭 14 57
        ├ 鈕 14 58
        └ 妞 14 59

羞 14 60
圣 14 61 ─ 怪 14 62
寸 14 63 ─┬ 村 14 64
          ├ 尋 14 65
          ├ 尋 14 66 ─ 得 14 67
          ├ 付 14 68 ─┬ 符 14 69
          │   ├ 府 14 70 ─ 俯 14 71
          │   ├ 附 14 74 ─ 腐 14 72
          │   └ 咐 14 75 ─ 腑 14 73
          ├ 守 14 76 ─ 狩 14 77
          ├ 肘 14 78
          └ 討 14 79

冠 14 爵 76 辱 9 寺 40 尉 40
專 82 傳 83 封 10 封 124 將 77
耐 134 射 147 導 9 尊 159 尊 162
對 5   176

掃墓 sǎomù 🔲 sweep ancestors' graves
掃興 sǎoxìng 🔲 disappointed
掃帚 sàozhǒu 🔲 broom

婦 14 51 [妇] Woman 女 54 holding a broom 帚 (abbreviated) in hand 又. 🔲 wife ⇔ 主婦 孕婦 少婦 寡婦 夫婦 悄婦 潑婦 媳婦
婦女 fùnǚ 🔲 women

婦人 fùrén 🔲 woman 🔲 married woman
婦孺 fùrú 🔲 women and children

侵 14 52 Person 人 sweeping forward with broom 帚 (abbreviated) in hand 又. 🔲 encroach 🔲 invade ⇔ 入侵
侵犯 qīnfàn 🔲 infringe upon, violate
侵略 qīnlüè 🔲 invade

侵入 qīnrù 🔲 invade
侵襲 qīnxí 🔲 encroach 🔲 make a sneak attack

寢 14 53 [寝] Modern form shows bed/plank 爿 under a roof 宀 with 侵 (abbreviated) phonetic. 🔲 bedroom
寢室 qǐnshì 🔲 bedroom, dorm room

浸 14 54 Water 水 with 寢 (early form) phonetic and suggestive of encroach 侵. 🔲 permeate ⇔ 沈浸
浸入 jìnrù 🔲 permeate
浸透 jìntòu 🔲 soak through, saturate
浸淫 jìnyín 🔲 absorb into

丑 14 55 Hand 又 bound as suggested by extra vertical line. 🔿 bind (⇨ 紐) 🔲 second Earthly Branch (⇨ 干支) 🔲 clown ⇔ 小丑

紐 14 56 [纽] Thread 糸 binding 丑 (phonetic). 🔲 knot 🔲 bind ⇔ 樞紐
紐西蘭 nǐuxīlán 🔲 🔲 New Zealand
紐約 nǐuyuē 🔲 New York

扭 14 57 Hand 手 binding 丑 (phonetic). 🔲 twist, wrench
扭曲 nǐuqū 🔲 distort
扭轉 nǐuzhuǎn 🔲 turn around

鈕 14 58 [钮] To metal 金 bound 丑 (phonetic). 🔲 knob 🔲 button ⇔ 按鈕
鈕釦 nǐukòu 🔲 button

妞 14 59 Woman 女 with 丑 phonetic. 🔲 🔲 girl

羞 14 60 Goat 羊 bound 丑

(phonetic). 🈯 offer 🈯 ashamed ⇔ 遮羞弘, 害羞?, 蒙羞以

羞慚 xiūcán 🈯 ashamed
羞恥 xiūchǐ 🈯 shame: 不知羞恥 shameless
羞愧 xiūkuì 🈯 ashamed
羞辱 xiūrù 🈯 disgrace, humiliation 🈯 disgrace, humiliate
羞澀 xiūsè 🈯 embarrassed, ashamed

圣 14 kū
61 Hand 又 working the land 土. Also used as simplified form of sage 聖.

怪 14 guài
62 Heart 心 with 圣 phonetic. 🈯 strange, weird ⇔ 作怪弘, 奇怪弘, 古怪弘, 難怪弘, 責怪弘, 妖怪?, 鬼怪

怪不得 guàibùdé 🈯 no wonder
怪僻 guàipì 🈯 eccentric
怪物 guàiwù 🈯 monster

寸 14 cùn
63 Hand 又 with the dot representing point one inch from wrist where pulse is felt. In composition can represent hand or law. 🈯 inch ⇔ 尺寸

村 14 cūn
64 Modern form shows tree 木 with 寸 phonetic. 🈯 village ⇔ 鄉村, 農村
村落 cūnluò 🈯 village, hamlet
村民 cūnmín 🈯 villagers
村莊 cūnzhuāng 🈯 village, hamlet
村子 cūnzi 🈯 village

尋 14 xún
65 [寻] Hand 又 and mouth 口 working 工 with 寸 phonetic. 🈯 seek, search for ⇔ 找尋, 追尋
尋常 xúncháng 🈯 usually
尋覓 xúnmì 🈯 seek, search for
尋求 xúnqiú 🈯 seek, search for

尋找 xúnzhǎo 🈯 seek, search for

尋 14 dé
66 Hand 寸 on shells 貝 (now written as 旦). 🈯 get, obtain (⇨ 得)

得 14 dé de děi
67 Go 彳 obtain 尋 (phonetic). dé: 🈯 get, obtain, gain děi: 🈯 need, must ⇔ 不得, 不得不, 不得了, 不得已, 不見得, 既得, 怪不得, 學得, 覺得, 贏得, 長得, 值得, 難得, 認得, 捨不得, 捨得, 了得, 記得, 只得, 使得, 曉得, 懂得, 懶得, 所得, 巴不得, 取得, 變得, 顯得, 獲得, 免得

得病 débìng 🈯 fall sick
得逞 déchěng 🈯 prevail
得到 dédào 🈯 achieve, get
得分 défēn 🈯 score points
得獎 déjiǎng 🈯 win an award
得勢 déshì 🈯 gain power, have the advantage
得以 déyǐ 🈯 able to
得意 déyì 🈯 self-satisfied, complacent
得知 dézhī 🈯 know, learn: 你如何得知這個消息？ How did you find out this news?
得罪 dézuì 🈯 offend

付 14 fù
68 Hand 寸 offering something to a person 人. 🈯 hand over, consign 🈯 pay 🈯 a surname ⇔ 交付, 託付, 償付, 支付, 應付, 對付
付出 fùchū 🈯 pay
付款 fùkuǎn 🈯 make payments
付錢 fùqián 🈯 pay
付帳 fùzhàng 🈯 pay a bill

符 14 fú
69 Bamboo 竹 seal offered 付 (phonetic) for comparison. 🈯 match, accord 🈯 symbol, sign 🈯 charm, talisman ⇔ 相符
符號 fúhào 🈯 sign, notation, mark, symbol
符合 fúhé 🈯 match, conform to

府 14 fǔ
70 Building 广 where official documents are consigned 付. 🈯 archives 🈯 government office 🈯 official residence: 總統府 presidential palace 🈯 prefecture ⇔ 省府, 政府, 華府

俯 14 fǔ
71 Person 人 before government 府 (phonetic) official. 🈯 bow
俯瞰 fǔkàn 🈯 look down over
俯首 fǔshǒu 🈯 bow (in submission)

腐 14 fǔ
72 Meat 肉 with archives 府 phonetic and suggestive of old. 🈯 rotten, spoiled ⇔ 迂腐, 豆腐, 陳腐
腐敗 fǔbài 🈯 corrupt
腐化 fǔhuà 🈯 corruption
腐爛 fǔlàn 🈯 rotten, spoiled
腐蝕 fǔshí 🈯 corrode, corrupt: 腐蝕思想 to corrupt morals
腐朽 fǔxiǔ 🈯 rotten, decayed

腑 14 fǔ
73 Body 肉 archives 府 (phonetic). 🈯 bowels, entrails ⇔ 肺腑

附 14 fù
74 Hill 阜 with 付 phonetic. 🈯 add to 🈯 attach 🈯 depend on ⇔ 依附
附帶 fùdài 🈯 append, attach
附加 fùjiā 🈯 attach, append
附近 fùjìn 🈯 nearby, close
附錄 fùlù 🈯 appendix
附屬 fùshǔ 🈯 be affiliated
附庸 fùyōng 🈯 vassal state

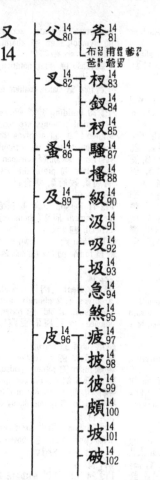

咐 14 fù
75 Mouth 口⁶⁶ giving 付 (phonetic). instruct ⇔ 吩咐, 嘱咐

守 14 shǒu
76 House 宀⁶³ of laws 寸. abide by guard, defend ⇔ 駐守, 成守, 操守, 保守, 把守, 防守, 看守, 堅守, 遵守
守法 shǒufǎ obey the law, law-abiding
守候 shǒuhòu wait, bide time
守護 shǒuhù guard, protect
守時 shǒushí punctual
守歲 shǒusuì stay up on New Year's Eve

守衛 shǒuwèi guard, defend
守信 shǒuxìn trustworthy
守住 shǒuzhù guard

狩 14 shòu
77 Dog 犬 on guard. 守 (phonetic). hunt
狩獵 shòuliè hunt

肘 14 zhǒu
78 Flesh 肉¹² above the wrist 寸. elbow ⇔ 掣肘

討 14 tǎo
79 [讨] Speak 言 about laws 寸. govern discuss ⇔ 檢討, 商討, 研討, 探討, 乞討
討價 tǎojià haggle, bargain
討論 tǎolùn discuss
討厭 tǎoyàn disgusting, disgusted by, loathe

父 14 fù
80 Hand 又 enforcing rules with stick. father ⇔ 神父, 國父, 義父, 繼父, 伯父, 岳父, 祖父, 叔父, 師父
父老 fùlǎo elders
父母 fùmǔ parents
父母親 fùmǔqīn parents
父親 fùqīn father
父權 fùquán patriarchal: 父權制 patriarchy
父系 fùxì patrilineal: 父系社會 patrilineal society

斧 14 fǔ
81 Axe 斤 with 父 phonetic. axe
斧頭 fǔtóu axe, hatchet
斧子 fǔzi axe, hatchet

叉 14 chā
82 Hand 又 with crossed finger. cross, interlace fork ⇔ 刀叉, 交叉, 魚叉

杈 14 chā
83 Tree 木 fork 叉 (phonetic). branch pitchfork

釵 14 chāi
84 [钗] Metal 金³⁴ fork-like 叉⁵⁹ (phonetic) object. 名 hairpin

衩 14 chà
85 Fork 叉⁵⁹ (phonetic) in clothing 衣¹²⁶. 名 vent on the side of a gown ⇔ 開衩²⁸⁶

蚤 14 zǎo
86 [蚤] Insect 虫¹²⁵ and a form of claw 爪¹⁰³ based on hand 又¹⁴ with dots representing claws. 名 flea ⇔ 跳蚤²⁷

騷 14 sāo
87 [骚] Horse 馬¹⁷⁷ and flea 蚤⁸⁵ (phonetic). 動 agitate ⇔ 牟騷⁷⁸
騷動 sāodòng 名 disturbance
騷擾 sāorǎo 動 harass: 性騷擾 sexual harassment

搔 14 sāo
88 [搔] Hand 手⁸⁹ and flea 蚤⁸⁵ (phonetic). 動 scratch
搔癢 sāoyǎng 動 scratch an itch

及 14 jí
89 Hand 又¹⁴ grabbing a person 人¹⁰. 動 reach, attain 動 and ⇔ 不及⁴⁰, 波及¹⁵³, 埃及³, 普及²⁷, 顧及⁷, 涉及²⁰⁸, 來不及²¹⁰
及格 jígé 動 pass, qualify
及時 jíshí 副 on time, promptly
及早 jízǎo 副 as soon as possible

級 14 jí
90 [级] Thread 糸⁵³ attaining 及⁸⁹ (phonetic) quality. 名 rank, level 量 grade, year: 三年級學生 third-year student, junior ⇔ 上級⁴³, 年級¹⁰, 階級⁴⁸, 高級²⁷, 等級³¹, 超級⁸⁸, 初級⁴⁵, 升級⁸⁷, 低級⁷⁷, 班級¹⁰⁷

汲 14 jí
91 Water 水⁵¹ attained 及⁸⁹ (phonetic). 動 draw
汲取 jíqǔ 動 draw, derive
汲水 jíshuǐ 動 draw water

吸 14 xī
92 Mouth 口⁶⁸ attaining (phonetic) 及⁸⁹. 動 inhale suck 動 absorb 動 attract ⇔ 呼吸²⁷
吸塵器 xīchénqì 名 vacuum cleaner
吸毒 xīdú 動 take drugs
吸管 xīguǎn 名 straw (for drinking)
吸取 xīqǔ 動 absorb, assimilate
吸食 xīshí 動 take (drugs)
吸收 xīshōu 動 absorb 動 enlist, enroll
吸鐵石 xītiěshí 名 (物) magnet
吸煙 xīyān 動 smoke cigarettes
吸引 xīyǐn 動 attract: 吸引力 attraction, attractiveness

圾 14 sè 动 jī
93 Dirt 土⁷⁰ added 及⁸⁹ (phonetic). 名 garbage ⇔ 垃圾²³

急 14 jí
94 Heart 心⁸³ and attain 及⁸⁹ (early form, phonetic). 形 anxious 形 urgent 副 quickly ⇔ 著急²⁴, 緊急²⁷, 焦急¹⁶²
急救 jíjiù 名 first aid, emergency treatment
急劇 jíjù 副 sudden, abrupt
急遽 jíjù 副 sudden, rapidly
急忙 jímáng 副 urgently
急迫 jípò 形 urgent
急需 jíxū 動 need urgently
急於 jíyú 動 anxious to
急躁 jízào 形 rash, impetuous
急診 jízhěn 名 emergency care

煞 14 shā shà
95 Reach 及⁸⁹ (early form), strike 攵⁹⁶ and fire 火⁸². shā: 動 stop, halt shà: 名 evil spirit
煞車 shāchē 動 brake

皮 14 pí
96 Hand 又¹⁴ and markings representing an animal's hide. 動 flay 名 skin: 皮很厚 thick-skinned 形 naughty ⇔ 臉皮⁸², 頑皮⁸², 眼皮⁴³, 俏皮⁸², 頭皮⁸², 樹皮⁸², 嬉皮⁸², 橡皮⁷²
皮包 píbāo 名 wallet
皮帶 pídài 名 belt
皮蛋 pídàn 名 thousand-year-old egg
皮膚 pífū 名 skin
皮革 pígé 名 leather
皮毛 pímáo 名 fur
皮箱 píxiāng 名 suitcase

疲 14 pí
97 Sickness 广⁷⁴ with 皮⁹⁶ phonetic. 形 weary
疲憊 píbèi 形 weary, fatigued
疲乏 pífá 形 tired, exhausted
疲倦 píjuàn 形 weary, fatigued
疲勞 píláo 形 tired, exhausted
疲累 pílèi 形 tired, weary
疲軟 píruǎn 形 tired, fatigued

披 14 pī
98 Hand 手⁸⁹ removing skin/cover 皮⁹⁶ (phonetic). 動 open, unroll 動 drape 所向披靡
披風 pīfēng 名 cloak
披肩 pījiān 名 shawl
披露 pīlù 動 reveal, disclose

彼 14 bǐ
99 Move 彳⁴⁴ with 皮⁹⁶ phonetic. 代 that
彼此 bǐcǐ 代 each other, mutually: 彼此誤會 mutual understanding
彼時 bǐshí 代 at that time

頗 14 pō 动 pǒ
100 [颇] Head 頁¹⁹⁰ with 皮⁹⁶ phonetic. pō: 形 tilted pǒ: 副 quite, rather ⇔ 偏頗¹¹⁵
頗為 pǒwéi 副 quite

坡 14 pō
101 Earth 土⁷⁰ with 皮⁹⁶ phonetic. 名 slope 形 斜 坡度⁹⁰, 新加坡⁸⁹, 山坡⁶⁷
坡度 pōdù 名 slope, gradient

破 14 pò
102 Stones 石⁸⁹ with 皮⁹⁶ phonetic. 動 break: 破舊立

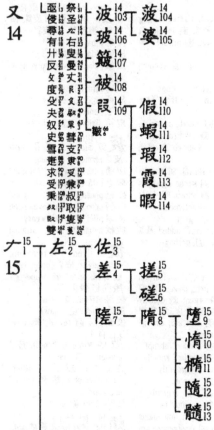

acter when its pronunciation differs from its most common form

破綻 pòzhàn [图] flaw, weak point

波 103 Water 水 with 皮 phonetic. ⇔ 風波, 軒然大波, 奔波, 短波, 微波

波動 bōdòng [图] fluctuate, vary [图] variance

波及 bōjí [图] spread

波蘭 bōlán [图] Poland

波浪 bōlàng [图] waves

波士頓 bōshìdùn [图] Boston

波濤 bōtāo [图] large waves

波折 bōzhé [图] twists and turns, obstacle

菠 104 Plant 艸 with wavy 波 (phonetic) leaves. [图] spinach

菠菜 bōcài [图] spinach

菠蘿 bōluó [图] pineapple

婆 105 Modern character from woman 女 with 波 phonetic. [图] old woman [图] mother-in-law (husband's mother) ⇔ 老婆, 巫婆, 外婆

婆婆 pópo [图] mother-in-law (husband's mother): 婆婆媽媽 like an old lady

婆娑 pósuō [图] sway

玻 106 Jade 玉 with 皮 phonetic. [图] glass

玻璃 bōlí [图] glass: 玻璃窗 glass window

簸 107 Winnowing basket 箕 with 皮 phonetic. bǒ: [图] winnow bò: [图] winnowing basket ⇔ 顛簸

簸箕 bòji [图] dustpan

被 108 Clothing 衣 with

新 destroy the old and build the new - a revolutionary slogan [图] broken, worn-out ⇔ 打破, 突破, 砸破

破案 pòàn [图] solve a case

破產 pòchǎn [图] go bankrupt [图] broke

破除 pòchú [图] eliminate, root out: 破除迷信 root out superstition

破壞 pòhuài [图] break, destroy, ruin

破舊 pòjiù [图] broken down, worn-out

破爛 pòlàn [图] tattered, worn-out

破裂 pòliè [图] rupture, break off: 談判破裂了 negotiations collapsed

破滅 pòmiè [图] evaporate, fall through, shatter (hopes)

破碎 pòsuì [图] broken, shattered

破音字 pòyīnzì [图] [图] a char-

皮⁵⁵ phonetic. 图 quilt 图 by
⇨ 棉被⁷⁹

被逼 bèibī 動 compelled,
forced: 我是被逼去的. I
was forced to go.
被单 bèidān 图 sheet
被动 bèidòng 图 passive: 被动
態 passive tense
被告 bèigào 图 defendant
被害 bèihài 動 be hurt: 被害人
victim; 被害者 victim
被迫 bèipò 動 compelled, forced
被子 bèizi 图 quilt, blanket

叚 14 jiǎ
109 Second 二⁵ skin 皮⁵⁵
(altered). 意 borrow (⇨ 假¹¹⁰)

假 14 jià jiǎ
110 Person 人¹⁰ with
borrowed skin 叚⁵. jiǎ: 形
fake, bogus, pseudo- 連 if
borrow jià: 图 holiday ⇨ 寒
假¹², 度假³⁹, 请假²⁷, 暑
假⁹⁴, 休假⁷⁵, 放假⁶²
假定 jiǎdìng 動 suppose, assume
假借 jiǎjiè 名 borrow: 假借名
义 under false pretenses 图
type of Chinese character
incorporating meaning of an
unrelated spoken word (⇨ 六
书⁶)
假日 jiàrì 图 holiday
假如 jiǎrú 連 if, supposing
假若 jiǎrùo 連 if, supposing
假设 jiǎshè 動 assume 图
assumption
假使 jiǎshǐ 連 if, supposing
假释 jiǎshì 名 parole
假说 jiǎshuō 图 hypothesis
假象 jiǎxiàng 图 semblance
假装 jiǎzhuāng 動 pretend

蝦 14 xiā
111 [虾] Insect 虫¹²⁵
with 叚⁵₀ phonetic. 图 shrimp
⇨ 龍蝦¹²
蝦仁 xiārén 图 shelled shrimp

瑕 14 xiá
112 Jade 玉¹⁰⁷ with
叚⁵₀ phonetic. 图 defect in

jade
瑕疵 xiácī 图 flaw, blemish

霞 14 xiá
113 Clouds/rain 雨¹⁶¹
with 叚⁵₀ phonetic. 图 clouds
of sunset or sunrise ⇨ 晚
霞¹⁰⁸
霞光 xiáguāng 图 light of sunset
or sunrise

暇 14 xiá
114 Sun 日⁷⁶ with 叚⁵₀
phonetic. 图 leisure, free time
⇨ 閒暇⁶⁶

ナ 15 zuǒ
1 Pictograph of the left
hand. 意 left hand

左 15 zuǒ
2 Left hand ナ⁵ (pho-
netic) helping with the work
工⁵. 图 left
左边 zuǒbiān 图 left side
左派 zuǒpài 图 left wing
左倾 zuǒqīng 形 leftist
左手 zuǒshǒu 图 left hand
左翼 zuǒyì 图 left wing
左右 zuǒyòu 副 or so, about
influence, control

佐 15 zuǒ
3 Person 人¹⁰ helping
左⁵ (phonetic). 動 assist
⇨ 辅佐⁸⁵
佐料 zuǒliào 图 condiment
佐证 zuǒzhèng 图 corroboration

差 15 chā chà chāi cī
4 Left 左⁵ and falling
leaves 来¹⁷³ (altered). chā:
動 discrepancy 图 error chà:
動 differ, fall short chāi: 動
dispatch cī: 形 uneven ⇨ 時
差¹¹, 误差²⁷, 参差²⁷, 逆
差²⁷, 兼差¹⁰⁰, 出差¹⁰, 郵
差⁷³
差别 chābié 图 difference,
disparity
差不多 chābùduō 副 more or
less, about
差额 chāé 图 difference
(amount)

差距 chājù 图 disparity, gap
差异 chāyì 图 difference, distinction, divergence
差遣 chāiqiǎn 動 dispatch
差役 chāiyì 图 messenger

搓 15 cūo
5 Hand 手⁷⁹ with 差⁵
phonetic. 動 rub ⇨ 揉搓⁸⁵

磋 15 cūo
6 Stone 石³⁴ with 差⁵
phonetic and suggestive of
rub 搓⁵. 動 polish ⇨ 切磋⁸⁵
磋商 cūoshāng 動 negotiate

陰 15 duò
7 Ramparts 阜¹⁶⁷ with
左⁵ phonetic and suggesting
opposing action. 意 besiege,
destroy (⇨ 堕⁹)

隋 15 duò suí
8 Meat 肉¹³² destroyed
陰⁵ (phonetic, abbreviated).
duò: 图 meat scraps suí: 图
Sui Dynasty
隋朝 suícháo 图 Sui Dynasty

堕 15 duò
9 [堕] Earthen 土⁴⁰
ramparts in pieces 隋⁵ (phonetic). Simplified form uses
有⁵⁵. 動 fall, sink
堕落 dùolùo 動 degenerate
堕胎 dùotāi 動 abort 图 abortion

惰 15 duò
10 Heart 心⁸³ with 隋⁵
(abbreviated) phonetic and
suggestive of sink 堕⁵. 形
lazy, indolent ⇨ 怠惰²⁷, 懒
惰⁷³
惰性 dùoxìng 图 inertia

椭 15 tǔo
11 Wood 木⁷ with 隋⁵
phonetic. 形 oval
椭圆 tǔoyuán 图 形 oval

隨 15 suí
12 [随] Move 辵⁹ with
隋⁵ phonetic. Simplified
form uses 有⁵₅. 動 follow 動
accompany 動 comply with
⇨ 跟随²⁷, 尾随²⁷, 伴随²⁷,

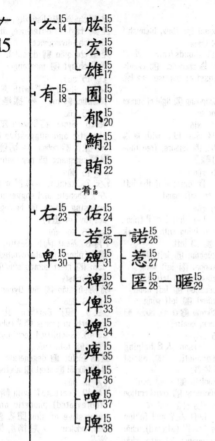

netic). 圖 marrow ⇔ 骨髓²³³

左 15 gōng
14 Right hand 又|⁴ (written like left hand 厂|⁵) and a pictograph of an elbow. 古 forearm (⇒ 肱¹⁵)

肱 15 gōng
15 Forearm 左 (phonetic) with flesh 肉¹³² redundant. 圖 forearm

宏 15 hóng
16 House 宀⁶³ with forearm 左 phonetic and suggesting extend. 圖 vast, grand
宏大 hóngdà 圖 grand, immense
宏觀 hóngguān 圖 macroscopic: 宏觀經濟 macroeconomics
宏偉 hóngwěi 圖 grand, magnificent

雄 15 xióng
17 Bird 隹¹⁶² with forearm 左 (phonetic) suggesting strength. 圖 male (bird or other animal) 圖 brave, heroic
高雄, 英雄, 雌雄, 梟雄
雄厚 xiónghòu 圖 plentiful, considerable: 資產雄厚 abundant assets
雄赳赳 xióngjiūjiū 圖 valiant, gallant
雄偉 xióngwěi 圖 imposing, magnificent
雄性 xióngxìng 圖 male

有 15 yǒu
18 Right hand 又|⁴ (phonetic, altered to left hand 厂|⁵) grasping the abundance of the moon 月⁹⁰ (or, alternatively, meat 肉¹³²). 圖 have, possess 圖 exist, be present 圖 (indicating comparison) as: 你有他高嗎? Are you as tall as he? ⇔ 原有, 共有, 公有, 私有, 享有, 富有, 佔有, 持有, 擁

追隨¹⁶⁷
隨筆 súibǐ 圖 casual notes, jottings
隨便 súibiàn 圖 casual 圖 casually 圖 act as one pleases: 隨便你. Do whatever you want.
隨和 súihé 圖 friendly, amiable, obliging
隨後 súihòu 圖 soon afterwards
隨機 súijī 圖 random: 隨機因

素 random factors
隨即 súijí 圖 immediately
隨身 súishēn 圖 portable: 隨身聽 walkman
隨時 súishí 圖 anytime
隨意 súiyì 圖 as you please
隨著 súizhe 圖 accordingly, along with

髓 15 suǐ
13 [髓] Bone 骨¹³³ destroyed 陸 (altered, pho-

有[?], 沒有[?], 含有[?], 國有[?], 存有[?], 只有[?], 保有[?], 所有[?], 祇有[?], 現有[?], 還有[?], 具有[?], 患有[?], 唯有[?], 烏有[?]

有的 yǒude 囲 some
有點 yǒudiǎn 囲 a little
有關 yǒuguān 囲 relevant, related
有力 yǒulì 囲 powerful
有利 yǒulì 囲 advantageous
有名 yǒumíng 囲 famous, well-known
有錢 yǒuqián 囲 rich
有趣 yǒuqù 囲 interesting
有如 yǒurú 囲 like, as if
有時 yǒushí 囲 sometimes
有限 yǒuxiàn 囲 limited
有線 yǒuxiàn 囲 wired: 有線電視 cable television
有效 yǒuxiào 囲 effective
有些 yǒuxiē 囲 some
有心 yǒuxīn 囲 intentionally, on purpose
有意 yǒuyì 囲 intend: 有意的 intentional
有用 yǒuyòng 囲 useful
有助於 yǒuzhùyú 囲 beneficial to

圃 19 yòu Have 有[?] (phonetic) in an enclosure 口[?]. 囲 confine: 囿於成見 closed-minded

郁 20 yù City 邑[?] with 有[?] phonetic. 囲 a surname
郁郁 yùyù 囲 lush, luxuriant

鮪 [鲔] 21 wěi Fish 魚[?] with 有[?] phonetic. 囲 tuna
鮪魚 wěiyú 囲 tuna

賄 [贿] 22 huì Money/shells 貝[?] owned 有[?] (phonetic). 囲 wealth 囲 bribe ⇔ 行賄[?]
賄賂 huìlù 囲 bribe
賄選 huìxuǎn 囲 buy votes

右 23 yòu Right hand 又[?] (phonetic, now written as left hand ナ[?]) working with mouth 口[?]. 囲 assist 囲 囲 right ⇔ 左右[?], 反右[?], 座右銘[?]
右邊 yòubiān 囲 right side
右派 yòupài 囲 right wing
右傾 yòuqīng 囲 rightist
右手 yòushǒu 囲 right hand
右翼 yòuyì 囲 right wing

佑 24 yòu Person 人[?] helping 右[?] (phonetic). 囲 protect, bless ⇔ 保佑[?]

若 25 ruò Plants 艸[?] picked by right hand 右[?]. 囲 pick vegetables 囲 if 囲 seem, like ⇔ 假若[?], 倘若[?]
若干 ruògān 囲 some, several
若是 ruòshì 囲 if

諾 [诺] 26 nuò Words 言[?] that seem 若[?] (phonetic) true. 囲 promise ⇔ 允諾[?], 承諾[?]
諾言 nuòyán 囲 promise

惹 27 rě Heart 心[?] with 若[?] phonetic. 囲 provoke
惹禍 rěhuò 囲 court disaster

匿 28 nì Box 匚[?] with 若[?] phonetic. 囲 conceal ⇔ 藏匿[?]
匿藏 nìcáng 囲 conceal
匿名 nìmíng 囲 anonymous: 匿名信 anonymous letter; 匿名投票 secret vote

暱 [昵] 29 nì Sun 日[?] with 匿[?] phonetic. Simplified form uses 尼[?]. 囲 intimate ⇔ 親暱[?]
暱稱 nìchēng 囲 pet name

卑 30 bēi Left hand ナ[?] holding a common mug (written as

甲[?]). 囲 vulgar, inferior ⇔ 謙卑[?], 自卑[?]
卑鄙 bēibǐ 囲 depraved, base, amoral

碑 31 bēi Stone 石[?] with 卑[?] phonetic. 囲 stone tablet ⇔ 石碑[?], 墓碑[?]
碑記 bēijì 囲 inscription on a stone tablet
碑文 bēiwén 囲 inscription on a stone tablet

裨 32 bì Clothing 衣[?] with 卑[?] phonetic. 囲 supplement
裨益 bìyì 囲 benefit

俾 33 bì / bǐ Person 人[?] with 卑[?] phonetic. 囲 enable 囲 in order to

婢 34 bì Girl 女[?] who is low 卑[?] (phonetic). 囲 maidservant
婢女 bìnǚ 囲 maidservant

痹 35 bì Sickness 疒[?] with 卑[?] phonetic. 囲 paralysis ⇔ 麻痹[?]

牌 36 pái Plank 片[?] with 卑[?] phonetic and suggestive of tablet 碑[?]. 囲 signboard 囲 brand 囲 cards 囲 dominoes 囲 medal: 金牌 gold medal ⇔ 王牌[?], 盾牌[?], 攤牌[?], 招牌[?], 打牌[?], 擋箭牌[?], 名牌[?], 獎牌[?], 橋牌[?], 骨牌[?]
牌坊 páifāng 囲 commemorative gate
牌價 páijià 囲 list price
牌樓 páilóu 囲 commemorative building
牌位 páiwèi 囲 memorial tablet
牌照 páizhào 囲 license, license plate
牌子 páizi 囲 brand

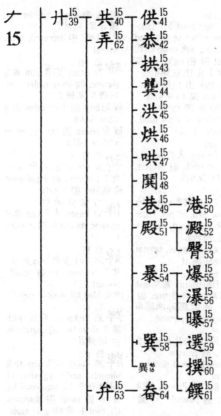

產主義 communism
共處 gòngchǔ 🔲 coexist
共存 gòngcún 🔲 coexist
共匪 gòngfěi 🔲 🔲 "communist bandit"
共和 gònghé 🔲 republican: 共和黨 Republican Party; 共和國 republic
共鳴 gòngmíng 🔲 resonance
共識 gòngshì 🔲 shared values
共通 gòngtōng 🔲 universally applicable
共同 gòngtóng 🔲 common, shared: 共同點 commonality
共享 gòngxiǎng 🔲 enjoy together, share
共有 gòngyǒu 🔲 jointly owned, common

供 15 gōng gòng
41 For all 共⅕ (phonetic) people 人⅕. gōng: 🔲 supply, provide gòng: 🔲 confess ⇔ 口供, 提供
供不應求 gōngbùyìngqiú 🔲 shortage
供詞 gòngcí 🔲 confession
供奉 gòngfèng 🔲 religious sacrifice
供給 gōngjǐ 🔲 supply
供認 gòngrèn 🔲 confess
供需 gōngxū 🔲 supply and demand
供養 gōngyǎng 🔲 provide for, support
供應 gōngyìng 🔲 supply

恭 15 gōng
42 Hearts 心⅓ together 共⅕ (phonetic). 🔲 respectful
恭賀 gōnghè 🔲 congratulate: 恭賀新禧! Happy New Year!
恭敬 gōngjìng 🔲 polite
恭維 gōngwéi 🔲 flatter, praise
恭喜 gōngxǐ 🔲 congratulate 🔲 Congratulations!: 恭喜發財! Have a happy and prosperous year!

啤 15 pí
37 Mouth 口 with 卑⅕ phonetic. 🔲 beer ⇔ 扎啤⅕
啤酒 píjiǔ 🔲 beer: 啤酒屋 beer hall

脾 15 pí
38 Flesh 肉¹² in the lower 卑⅕ (phonetic) body. 🔲 spleen
脾氣 píqì 🔲 temper, temperament: 發脾氣 lose one's temper; 脾氣不好 temperamental

廾 15 gǒng
39 Left ナ¹⁵ and right 又¹⁴ hands joined in gesture of respect.

共 15 gòng
40 Twenty 廿⅕ pairs of hands 廾⅕. 🔲 together, collectively 🔲 altogether 🔲 common, general 🔲 share ⇔ 一共, 公共, 反共, 同舟共濟, 中共, 總共
共產 gòngchǎn 🔲 communist: 共產黨 Communist Party; 共

拱 15 gǒng
43 Hands 手$^{89}_{1}$ together 共$^{15}_{40}$ (phonetic). 動 cup hands and bow 名 arch

拱門 gǒngmén 名 arch, archway

拱橋 gǒngqiáo 名 arched bridge

拱手 gǒngshǒu 動 cup hands and bow

龔 15 gōng
44 [龚] Offer 共$^{15}_{40}$ with 龍 phonetic. 古 give 姓 a surname

洪 15 hóng
45 Water 水$^{2}_{21}$ together 共$^{15}_{40}$ (phonetic). 名 floods 形 vast 姓 a surname

洪水 hóngshuǐ 名 flood

烘 15 hōng
46 With fire 火$^{82}_{1}$ together 共$^{15}_{40}$ (phonetic). 動 dry by fire

烘焙 hōngbèi 動 cure (tea or tobacco leaves)

烘乾 hōnggān 動 dry by fire: 烘乾機 dryer

哄 15 hōng hǒng
47 Voices 口$^{68}_{1}$ together 共$^{15}_{40}$ (phonetic). hōng: 名 roar (of the crowd) hǒng: 動 fool, defraud

哄騙 hǒngpiàn 動 cheat, defraud

哄抬 hōngtái 動 drive up (prices)

鬨 15 hòng
48 [哄$^{15}_{47}$] Struggle 鬥$^{89}_{10}$ together 共$^{15}_{40}$ (phonetic). 動 quarrel ⇔ 起鬨$^{57}_{5}$

巷 15 xiàng
49 City 邑$^{33}_{18}$ (abbreviated) area open to all 共$^{15}_{40}$ (phonetic). 名 lane, alley

巷子 xiàngzi 名 lane, alley

港 15 gǎng
50 Water 水$^{2}_{21}$ lane 巷$^{15}_{49}$ (phonetic). 名 harbor, port ⇔ 香港$^{108}_{25}$, 漁港$^{180}_{2}$

港澳 gǎngào 地 Hong Kong and Macau

港幣 gǎngbì 名 Hong Kong dollar

港口 gǎngkǒu 名 port, harbor

殿 15 diàn
51 Strike 殳$^{37}_{2}$ with an early form of buttocks 臀$^{15}_{53}$ (resembling 尸$^{40}_{1}$ and 共$^{15}_{40}$) phonetic. 名 rear 名 palace ⇔ 宮殿$^{151}_{6}$

殿軍 diànjūn 名 fourth place

殿堂 diàntáng 名 palace hall, temple

澱 15 diàn
52 [淀] At water's 水$^{2}_{21}$ bottom/rear 殿$^{15}_{51}$ (phonetic). Simplified form uses 定$^{88}_{49}$. 名 sediment ⇔ 沈澱$^{23}_{57}$

澱粉 diànfěn 名 starch

臀 15 tún
53 Rear 殿$^{15}_{51}$ (phonetic) flesh 肉$^{132}_{1}$. 名 buttocks

臀部 túnbù 名 buttocks, ass 名 hips

暴 15 bào 又 pù
54 Modern form shows sun 日$^{76}_{1}$ together 共$^{15}_{40}$ with water 水$^{2}_{21}$. 形 violent 形 suddenly ⇔ 鎮暴$^{31}_{33}$, 風暴$^{47}_{4}$, 强暴$^{65}_{6}$, 粗暴$^{117}_{3}$

暴動 bàodòng 名 rebellion

暴發 bàofā 動 break out 動 get rich suddenly: 暴發戶 nouveau riche (⇨ 爆發$^{15}_{55}$)

暴風 bàofēng 名 storm, windstorm: 暴風雨 rainstorm, tempest

暴君 bàojūn 名 tyrant, despot

暴力 bàolì 名 violence 形 violent

暴利 bàolì 名 exorbitant profits

暴戾 bàolì 形 tyrannical

暴烈 bàoliè 形 violent, fierce

暴亂 bàoluàn 名 rebellion

暴虐 bàonüè 形 tyrannical, despotic

暴行 bàoxíng 名 atrocity

暴雨 bàoyǔ 名 rainstorm

暴政 bàozhèng 名 tyranny

暴露 pùlù 動 expose, reveal

爆 15 bào
55 Fire 火$^{82}_{1}$ and sudden 暴$^{15}_{54}$ (phonetic). 動 explode

爆發 bàofā 動 erupt, explode ⇨ 暴發$^{15}_{54}$

爆米花 bàomǐhuā 名 popcorn

爆炸 bàozhà 動 explode

爆竹 bàozhú 名 firecracker

瀑 15 pù
56 Water 水$^{2}_{21}$ moving suddenly 暴$^{15}_{54}$ (phonetic). 名 waterfall

瀑布 pùbù 名 waterfall

曝 15 pù
57 Sunlight 日$^{76}_{1}$ suddenly 暴$^{15}_{54}$ (phonetic). 動 expose to sunlight

曝光 pùguāng 名 exposure (photography)

巽 15 xùn
58 Official seals 卩$^{33}_{1}$ placed by hands 廾$^{15}_{39}$ on a table 丌$^{46}_{1}$ (together resembling 共$^{15}_{40}$). 姓 a surname 名 fifth of the Eight Diagrams (⇨ 八卦$^{29}_{1}$)

選 15 xuǎn
59 [选] Movement 辵$^{41}_{3}$ with 巽$^{15}_{58}$ phonetic. Simplified form uses 先$^{11}_{36}$. 動 choose, select 動 elect 名 selection, anthology ⇔ 遴選$^{10}_{93}$, 賄選$^{15}_{22}$, 候選人$^{32}_{26}$, 當選$^{63}_{28}$, 競選$^{68}_{82}$, 精選$^{70}_{72}$, 揀選$^{77}_{100}$, 文選$^{98}_{1}$, 民選$^{119}_{1}$, 挑選$^{127}_{4}$, 甄選$^{130}_{4}$, 推選$^{162}_{12}$, 膺選$^{162}_{54}$, 篩選$^{167}_{14}$

選拔 xuǎnbá 動 select, choose

選集 xuǎnjí 名 selection, anthology

選舉 xuǎnjǔ 動 elect 名 election

選民 xuǎnmín 名 voters, electorate

選手 xuǎnshǒu 名 contestant

選擇 xuǎnzé 動 choose 名 choice

撰 15 zhuàn
60 Hand 手$^{89}_{1}$ with 巽$^{15}_{58}$ phonetic. 動 author, compose ⇔ 杜撰$^{70}_{5}$, 編撰$^{115}_{7}$

撰述 zhuànshù 動 narrate

撰寫 zhuànxiě 動 compose, write

白 65 (15) ── 盥 66 (15)

學 67 (15) ── 覺 68 (15) ── 攪 69 (15)

舁 70 (15) ── 與 71 (15) ── 舋 72 (15)

與 73 (15) ── 嶼 74 (15)

與 77 (15) ── 譽 75 (15)

叟 78 (15) ── 搜 79 (15) ── 舉 76 (15)

瘦 80 (15)

艘 81 (15)

嫂 82 (15)

絽 83 (15) ── 要 84 (15) ── 腰 85 (15)

饌 61 [饌] Food 食 with 巽 phonetic. 動 eat and drink ⇔ 肴饌.

弄 62 Hands 廾 holding jade 玉. nòng: 動 play with 動 make, do lòng: 图 lane, alley ⇔ 玩弄, 逗弄, 愚弄, 嘲弄
弄錯 nòngcuò 動 err, mistake
弄好 nònghǎo 動 complete

弁 63 Hands 廾 putting on a hat (resembling ㄙ). 图 ⊛ hat
弁言 biànyán 图 preface

畚 64 Vessel (ancient character altered to 田) with hat 弁 phonetic and also suggestive of container. 图 basket
畚箕 běnjī 图 dustpan

白 65 Two hands lowered, inversion of 廾.

盥 66 Water 水 pouring over lowered hands 白 into a basin 皿. 動 wash
盥洗 guànxǐ 動 wash: 盥洗室 washroom

學 67 [学] Hands 白 (phonetic) reaching down through covered 冖 mind to teach 教 (abbreviated). 動 learn study ⇔ 上學, 化學, 考古學, 教學, 就學, 輟學, 醫學, 同學, 小學, 漢學, 力學, 初學, 大學, 法學, 數學, 佛學, 中學, 休學, 獎學金, 開學, 留學, 科學, 升學, 求學, 哲學, 文學, 理學, 助學金, 遊學, 美學, 易學

學報 xuébào 图 academic journal
學到 xuédào 動 learn
學得 xuédé 動 learn
學弟 xuédì 图 schoolmate (younger male)

學費 xuéfèi 图 tuition
學好 xuéhǎo 動 learn
學會 xuéhùi 图 academic association
學姐 xuéjiě 图 schoolmate (elder female)
學歷 xuélì 图 educational background
學妹 xuémèi 图 schoolmate (younger female)
學派 xuépài 图 school of thought
學期 xuéqī 图 semester
學人 xuérén 图 scholar
學生 xuéshēng 图 student
學識 xuéshì 图 learning, knowledge
學士 xuéshì 图 bachelor's degree
學術 xuéshù 图 academics: 學術界 academia; 學術自由 academic freedom
學堂 xuétáng 图 school
學童 xuétóng 图 school children
學徒 xuétú 图 apprentice
學位 xuéwèi 图 academic degree
學問 xuéwèn 图 knowledge
學習 xuéxí 图 study
學校 xuéxiào 图 school
學業 xuéyè 图 education, studies
學院 xuéyuàn 图 college, institute
學運 xuéyùn 图 student movement (學生運動)
學長 xuézhǎng 图 schoolmate (elder male)
學者 xuézhě 图 scholar

覺 68 [觉] See 見 and learn 學 (phonetic, abbreviated). jué: 動 perceive 動 feel 图 sense jiào: 動 sleep ⇔ 察覺, 不知不覺, 警覺, 直覺, 知覺, 感覺, 幻覺, 錯覺, 發覺, 嗅覺, 午覺, 視覺, 自覺, 睡覺
覺得 juédé 動 feel
覺悟 juéwù 图 consciousness

覺醒 juéxǐng 動 awaken, become aware

攪 69 [搅] Hand 手⁹⁷ and percieve 覺⁵⁵ (phonetic). 動 annoy 動 mix, stir ⇔ 招攪⁵⁵, 打攪⁵⁵
攪拌 jiǎobàn 動 mix, stir
攪動 jiǎodòng 動 mix, stir
攪局 jiǎojú 動 spoil (a party)
攪擾 jiǎorǎo 動 agitate, disturb

舁 70 Hands reaching down 白⁵⁵ and hands pushing up 廾⁵⁵. 動 lift

與 71 [兴] Lift 舁⁷⁰ together 同³⁴. xīng: 動 prosper, flourish 動 undertake xìng: 名 enthusiasm ⇔ 掃興⁵⁵, 振興⁵⁵, 高興⁵⁵, 復興⁵⁵, 紹興⁵⁵, 新興⁵⁵
興奮 xīngfèn 形 excited: 興奮劑 stimulant
興建 xīngjiàn 動 build
興隆 xīnglóng 形 flourishing
興起 xīngqǐ 動 rise up
興趣 xìngqù 名 interest: 有沒有興趣? Are you interested? 感興趣 be interested
興衰 xīngshuāi 名 rise and fall
興旺 xīngwàng 形 prosperous
興致 xìngzhì 名 interest, enthusiasm: 興致勃勃 very enthusiastic

釁 72 [衅] Jar 酉⁵⁹ and separate 分³⁵ with an ancient character related to 與⁷¹ phonetic. 動 anoint ceremonially with blood ⇔ 挑釁¹²⁷
釁隙 xìnxì 名 rift, enmity

與 73 [与] Hands 舁⁷⁰ giving 与⁶¹. yǔ: 動 give 連 介 with yù: 動 participate ⇔ 參與⁷, 賦與⁷

嶼 74 [屿] Mountain 山⁴⁷ with 與⁷³ phonetic. 名 island ⇔ 蘭嶼⁷⁸, 島嶼¹⁷⁸

譽 75 [誉] Words 言⁵⁶ given 與⁷³ (phonetic). Simplified form uses 與⁷³ simplification. 名 honor, reputation ⇔ 聲譽²⁷, 信譽⁵⁹, 名譽²⁷, 榮譽⁹²

舉 76 [举] Hand 手⁹⁷ with 與⁷³ phonetic. Simplified form uses 與⁷³ simplification. 動 lift, raise 形 whole, entire ⇔ 檢舉⁷⁵, 選舉⁷³, 壯舉⁷⁶, 科舉⁸⁷, 列舉¹²³
舉辦 jǔbàn 動 hold, run
舉動 jǔdòng 名 action, deed 名 conduct, behavior
舉例 jǔlì 動 give examples
舉起 jǔqǐ 動 raise
舉世 jǔshì 副 worldwide, universally
舉行 jǔxíng 動 hold, conduct
舉止 jǔzhǐ 名 bearing, manner

輿 77 [舆] Cart 車¹⁵⁸ lifted by many hands 舁⁷⁰ (phonetic). 名 sedan chair
輿論 yúlùn 名 public opinion
輿情 yúqíng 名 public sentiment

叟 78 Ancient form shows hand 又⁴ and a flame 火⁹² in a house 宀⁶³. 名 search (⇒ 搜⁷⁹) 名 venerable old man ⇔ 智叟³²

搜 79 Hand 手⁹⁷ searching 叟⁷⁸ (phonetic). 動 search
搜查 sōuchá 動 search (a person or house): 搜查證 search warrant
搜集 sōují 動 collect ⇒ 蒐集¹²⁵
搜索 sōusuǒ 動 search for

瘦 80 Sickness 疒⁷⁶ of the eldery 叟⁷⁸ (phonetic). 形 thin, skinny ⇔ 消瘦⁸⁹
瘦弱 shòuruò 形 thin and weak, frail

艘 81 Boat 舟¹⁷⁹ with 叟⁷⁸ phonetic. 名 a measureword for boats

嫂 82 Woman 女⁵⁴ with 叟⁷⁸ phonetic. 名 sister-in-law (elder brother's wife) ⇔ 大嫂⁷⁹
嫂嫂 sǎosao 名 sister-in-law (elder brother's wife)

舀 83 Hands 白⁵⁵ and head 凶¹⁴³. 形 high

要 84 Earliest form shows hands girding a waist and meant waist (now 腰⁵⁵). Later forms modified to include hands and head 西¹³⁰) (altered to resemble 西¹³⁰) and woman 女⁵⁴. yào: 動 want, need 動 must, should 動 have to 動 will, going to 連 if 形 important yāo: 動 ask for, demand ⇔ 綱要⁵⁷, 主要⁵⁵, 就要⁵⁵, 扼要⁵⁵, 必要⁵⁵, 須要⁵⁵, 只要⁵⁵, 重要⁵⁷, 摘要⁵⁷, 將要⁵⁵, 正要⁵⁵, 提要⁵⁵, 祇要⁵⁷, 想要¹¹⁴, 緊要⁵²; 首要¹⁴⁶, 需要⁶¹
要不 yàobù 連 otherwise
要不然 yàobùrán 連 otherwise, lest
要點 yàodiǎn 名 important point
要緊 yàojǐn 形 critical, urgent
要命 yàomìng 副 desperately, extremely
要求 yāoqiú 動 request
要塞 yàosài 名 fortress
要是 yàoshì 連 if
要素 yàosù 名 main factor

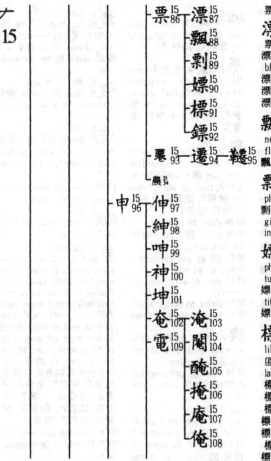

票 ⁱ⁵⁄₄₂, 郵票 ⁱ⁷³

漂 87 Water 水 ⅜ and rise 票 ⅜ (phonetic). piāo: 動 float
漂白 piǎobái 動 bleach: 漂白劑 bleach
漂浮 piāofú 動 float, drift
漂亮 piàoliàng 形 beautiful
漂流 piāolíu 動 drift

飄 88 [飘] Rising 票 ⅜ (phonetic) wind 風 ⁷. 動 float, flutter
飄逸 piāoyì 形 elegant, graceful

剽 89 Knife 刀 ³⁵ with 票 ⅜ phonetic. 動 plunder
剽竊 piàoqiè 動 steal 動 plagiarize: 剽竊專利權 infringe on a patent

嫖 90 Woman 女 ⁵⁴ with 票 ⅜ phonetic. 動 patronize prostitutes
嫖妓 piáojì 動 patronize prostitutes
嫖客 piáokè 名 john

標 91 [标] Wood 木 ⁷ pointed like flames 票 ⅜ (phonetic). 名 javelin point 名 動 mark, label ⟷ 路標 ⁹⁄₅₉, 光標 ⁴⁄₄₂, 指標 ⅜, 商標 ⁸⁄₅₁, 招標 ³⁄₉₂, 座標 ⁵⁷⁄₂₇, 錦標 ⁷⁶⁄₇₅, 目標 ¹⁄₁₄, 游標 ⁹⁄₉
標榜 biāobǎng 動 boast of
標點 biāodiǎn 動 punctuate: 標點符號 punctuation
標會 biāohùi 名 private loan association
標明 biāomíng 動 indicate, label, mark clearly
標籤 biāoqiān 名 label, tag
標槍 biāoqiāng 名 javelin
標題 biāotí 名 headline, title
標語 biāoyǔ 名 slogan
標誌 biāozhì 名 sign, symbol 動 symbolize

腰 85 yāo Waist 要 ⅜ (phonetic) with flesh 肉 ¹³² redundant. 名 waist ⟷ 撐腰 ⁴⁄₃₉
腰部 yāobù 名 waist
腰帶 yāodài 名 belt
腰果 yāoguǒ 名 cashew

票 86 Fire 火 ¹² (altered to resemble 示 ⁴⁶) and upper body 垔 ⅜ (phonetic, altered to resemble 西 ¹³⁰). 名 rising flames 名 ticket 名 bill ⟷ 退票 ⁵⁄₄₂, 鈔票 ⁹⁄₇₇, 訂票 ⁸⁄₄, 股票 ⅜, 投票 ⁵⁄₄₂, 拉票 ⁵⁄₃₄, 機票 ⁷⁄₈, 綁票 ⁴⁄₄₅, 支票 ⁷⁄₁, 糧票 ⁷⁶⁄₅₀, 門票 ⁴⁄₆₅, 彩票 ⁵⁄₆₃, 跳票 ⁵⁄₅₉, 車票 ¹⁹⁄₄₄, 售票 ⁴⁶⁄₄₂, 匯

標準 biāozhǔn 图 standard, criterion 图 standard: 你的發音很標準. Your pronunciation is very standard.

鏢 15 biāo [镖] Metal 金 pointed like flames 票 (phonetic). 图 spear point 图 escort, guard ⇔ 保鏢

襄 15 xiān 93 Hands 廾 (altered to resemble 大) raising (altered to resemble 西) with scepter suggesting promotion. 图 rise

遷 15 qiān 94 [迁] Rise 襄 (phonetic) and move 辵. Simplified form uses 千. 图 move, migrate ⇔ 升遷, 喬遷, 變遷
遷就 qiānjiù 图 accommodate, compromise
遷居 qiānjū 图 move, migrate
遷徙 qiānxǐ 图 move out
遷移 qiānyí 图 move, migrate

韆 15 qiān 95 [千] Leather 革 moving 遷 (phonetic). 图 swing ⇔ 鞦韆

申 15 shēn 96 Hands 臼 girding pole-like 丨 body. 图 extend 图 state 图 ninth Earthly Branch (⇨ 干支) ⇔ 重申
申斥 shēnchì 图 rebuke, reprimand
申請 shēnqǐng 图 apply; request: 申請表 application form
申訴 shēnsù 图 appeal

伸 15 shēn 97 Person 人 extending 申 (phonetic). 图 stretch ⇔ 延伸
伸出 shēnchū 图 stretch out
伸手 shēnshǒu 图 reach for, ask for help
伸展 shēnzhǎn 图 stretch, extend

紳 15 shēn 98 [绅] Silk 糸 extended 申 (phonetic) across the body. 图 sash 图 gentry
紳士 shēnshì 图 gentleman

呻 15 shēn 99 Mouth 口 extended 申 (phonetic). 图 groan
呻吟 shēnyín 图 groan, moan

神 15 shén 100 Omen 示 with 申 phonetic and suggestive of lightning 電. 图 soul, spirit ⇔ 眼神, 無神論, 全神貫注, 凝神, 女神, 傳神, 灶神, 精神, 門神
神風隊 shénfēngduì 图 kamikaze
神父 shénfù 图 priest
神話 shénhuà 图 myth
神經 shénjīng 图 nerve: 神經病 ⓖ mental illness: 你有神經病! You are crazy!
神秘 shénmì 图 mysterious
神農 shénnóng 囚 Shen Nong - legendary inventor of agriculture and herbal medicine
神奇 shénqí 图 miraculous, mystical
神氣 shénqì 图 appearance, expression 图 proud, dignified 图 put on airs
神情 shénqíng 图 facial expression, appearance
神人 shénrén 图 holy man
神色 shénsè 图 look, expression
神聖 shénshèng 图 sacred, holy
神態 shéntài 图 look, expression
神童 shéntóng 图 child prodigy
神仙 shénxiān 图 supernatural being, immortal
神州 shénzhōu 图 China

坤 15 kūn 101 Soil 土 from which all things extend 申. 图 earth 图 female 图 one of the Eight Diagrams (⇨ 八卦) ⇔ 乾坤

奄 15 yān 102 Person 大 stretching 申 (phonetic). 图 cover

淹 15 yān 103 Water 水 and covering 奄 (phonetic). 图 a river name 图 inundate
淹沒 yānmò 图 submerge, inundate
淹死 yānsǐ 图 drown

閹 15 yān 104 [阉] Gate 門 with 奄 phonetic. 图 eunuch
閹割 yāngē 图 castrate

醃 15 yān 105 [腌] Cover 奄 (phonetic) in a jar 酉. Simplified form is a variant based on meat 肉. 图 pickle, salt

掩 15 yǎn 106 Hand 手 covering 奄 (phonetic). 图 cover up, conceal 图 shut, close ⇔ 遮掩
掩蔽 yǎnbì 图 cover up, conceal
掩蓋 yǎngài 图 cover up, conceal
掩護 yǎnhù 图 cover, shield, screen
掩埋 yǎnmái 图 bury
掩飾 yǎnshì 图 cover up

庵 15 ān 107 Covered 奄 (phonetic) shelter 广. 图 hut, cottage 图 nunnery
庵堂 āntáng 图 nunnery

俺 15 ǎn 108 Person 人 with 奄 phonetic. 图 I, we

電 15 diàn 109 [电] Extends 申 (phonetic) down from rain-cloud 雨. 图 lightning 图 electricity ⇔ 核電, 充電, 閃電, 發電, 手電筒, 雷電, 觸電, 家

泰 15/123 — 寅 69 — 革 74/2
奏 15/124 — 揍 15/125
湊 15/126

曳 15/110 — 洩 15/111
            拽 15/112
更 15/113 — 梗 15/114
            埂 15/115
            便 15/116 — 鞭 15/117
            硬 15/118
            甦 15/119
叓 15/120 — 腴 15/121
            諛 15/122

春 15/127 — 椿 15/128 — 暢 76/62   陳
秦 15/129 — 臻 15/130
舂 15/131 — 蠢 15/132
夬 15/133 — 卷 15/134 — 倦 15/135
                        捲 15/136
                        圈 15/137

電 155
電報 diànbào 名 telegram
電池 diànchí 名 battery
電燈 diàndēng 名 electric light
電動 diàndòng 形 electric powered: 名 電動玩具 video games
電鍋 diànguō 名 hotpot
電話 diànhuà 名 telephone: 電話簿 telephone book; 行動電話 cell phone; 電話卡 phone card 名 phone call: 打電話給他 call him; 國際電話 international phone call
電匯 diànhuì 名 telegraphic transfer, money order
電晶體 diànjīngtǐ 名 transistor
電纜 diànlǎn 名 electric cable

電力 diànlì 名 electric power
電腦 diànnǎo 名 computer
電器 diànqì 名 electric appliances
電扇 diànshàn 名 electric fan
電視 diànshì 名 television: 電視機 television set; 電視台 television station
電台 diàntái 名 radio station
電玩 diànwán 名動 video games (電動玩具)
電線 diànxiàn 名 electric wire
電信 diànxìn 名 telecommunications
電訊 diànxùn 名 telecommunications
電壓 diànyā 名 voltage
電影 diànyǐng 名 movie: 電影院 cinema

電源 diànyuán 名 power supply
電子 diànzǐ 名 electron 形 electronic: 電子品 electronics; 電子琴 electronic organ; 電子字典 electronic dictionary; 電子遊戲 video games; 電子郵件 e-mail

曳 15/110 yì yè Stretch 申 and drag ノ (phonetic). 動 haul, drag ⇔ 搖曳[4]

洩 15/111 xiè [泄] Water 水 and drag 曳 (phonetic). Simplified form is variant character with 世 phonetic. 動 drain, vent, leak ⇔ 外洩, 發洩
洩漏 xièlòu 動 leak, disclose
洩露 xièlù 動 reveal, disclose
洩氣 xièqì 動 lose heart

拽 15/112 zhuāi Modern form shows hand 手 and drag 曳. 動 drag

更 15/113 gèng gēng Strike 攴 (altered) with 丙 (altered) phonetic. gēng 動 transform, alter 副 alternate gèng: 副 further, more ⇔ 自力更生, 變更[5]
更迭 gēngdié 動 alternate
更動 gēngdòng 動 change, shift
更多 gèngduō 副 more
更改 gēnggǎi 動 change, alter
更換 gēnghuàn 動 replace, switch
更加 gèngjiā 副 still more, even more
更為 gèngwéi 副 more so
更新 gēngxīn 動 renew
更正 gēngzhèng 動 correct

梗 15/114 gěng Tree 木 with 更 (phonetic). 古 a tree name 名 stalk, stem
梗概 gěnggài 名 gist, synopsis
梗阻 gěngzǔ 動 block, obstruct

埂 15/115 gěng Earth 土² with 更 phonetic. ⇔ embankment between fields ⇔ 田埂¹¹¹

便 15/116 biàn pián Person 人¹⁰ who improves 更 biàn: 圏 advantageous, convenient 圏 casual, informal then pián: 圏 inexpensive ⇔ 不便⁶, 順便⁶, 隨便⁶, 小便⁶, 即便⁶, 大便⁷, 搭便車⁹⁵, 糞便⁹⁵, 以便⁹⁵, 方便⁹¹
便當 biàndāng 图 lunch box
便服 biànfú 图 casual clothes
便利 biànlì 圏 convenient: 便利商店 convenience store
便衣 biànyī 图 civilian clothes: 便衣警察 plainclothes policeman
便於 biànyú 圏 convenient for
便宜 piányí 圏 inexpensive, cheap

鞭 15/117 biān Leather 革² with 便 phonetic. 圖 whip, spur 图 whip
鞭炮 biānpào 图 firecracker
鞭撻 biāntà 圖 whip, lash
鞭子 biānzi 图 whip

硬 15/118 yìng Stone 石⁸ with 更 phonetic. 圏 hard, stiff inflexible, obstinate ⇔ 強硬⁸⁵, 僵硬³¹, 堅硬⁶²
硬碟 yìngdié 图 hard-drive
硬件 yìngjiàn 图 图 hardware
硬體 yìngtǐ 图 图 hardware

甦 15/119 sū [蘇¹⁰⁰] Again 更 alive 生⁸. 圖 revive, resurrect ⇔ 復甦⁸
甦醒 sūxǐng 圖 revive, come to

臾 15/120 yú Stretch 申 and effort 乙. 圖 pull 图 moment, instant ⇔ 須臾⁶

腴 15/121 yú Flesh 肉¹³² needing support 臾 (phonetic). 图 belly ⇔ 豐腴⁹

諛 15/122 [谀] Words 言 with 臾 phonetic and suggestive of fat 腴. 圖 flatter ⇔ 阿諛⁴³

泰 15/123 tài Water 水 slipping through a person's 大⁷ (phonetic) hands 廾 (altered). 图 slippery 圏 peaceful
泰國 tàiguó 图 Thailand
泰然 tàirán 圏 calm, composed
泰山 tàishān 图 Taishan - a sacred mountain in Shandong Province

奏 15/124 zòu Enter (ancient character resembling 天) and offer 廾 an object 屮 (altered). 圖 report to the emperor 圖 play (an instrument) ⇔ 節奏⁸⁵, 演奏⁸⁵
奏捷 zòujié 圖 report victory
奏效 zòuxiào 圖 be effective, perform
奏樂 zòuyuè 圖 play music

揍 15/125 zòu Hand 手⁷ with 奏 phonetic. 圖 beat, hit ⇔ 挨揍⁴³

湊 15/126 còu Water 水 with 奏 phonetic. 圖 pool, put together 图 by chance
湊巧 còuqiǎo 图 fortuitously 图 fortuitous

舂 15/127 chōng Hands 廾 holding pestle 午¹³ (altered) over mortar 臼¹³¹. 圖 mill or pound rice
舂米 chōngmǐ 圖 pound rice

椿 15/128 zhuāng [桩] Wood 木⁷ pounded 舂 (phonetic). Simplified form uses simplification of 莊⁸⁵. 图 stake, post ⇔ 木椿⁷⁷

秦 15/129 qín Rice 禾¹⁰⁸ ready to be milled 舂²⁷ (abbreviated). 图 a variety of rice 图 an ancient kingdom in China Qin Dynasty: 秦始皇 founder of the Qin Dynasty - China's first emperor 图 a surname
秦朝 qíncháo 图 Qin Dynasty

臻 15/130 zhēn Reach 至¹²⁰ with 秦 phonetic. 圖 reach, attain 圏 utmost

春 15/131 chūn Plants 艸⁹⁶ (altered) growing 屯⁹⁸ (altered) in the sun 日⁷⁶. 图 change seasons 图 spring ⇔ 長春⁸², 長春藤⁸², 青春⁸², 賣春¹⁰
春分 chūnfēn 图 spring equinox
春節 chūnjié 图 New Year (Chinese), Spring Festival
春捲 chūnjuǎn 图 spring roll
春聯 chūnlián 图 New Year's couplet
春秋 chūnqiū 图 year 图 spring and autumn: 春秋時代 Spring and Autumn Period (770-476 B.C.) 图 The Spring and Autumn Annals (⇨ 五經⁸)
春天 chūntiān 图 spring
春意 chūnyì 图 thoughts of spring, thoughts of love

蠢 15/132 chǔn Insects 虫¹²⁵ in the spring 春 (phonetic). 圏 wriggle ⇔ 愚蠢²⁷
蠢動 chǔndòng 圖 wriggle, writhe

奍 15/133 juàn Hands 廾 with 釆¹⁵⁶ (altered) phonetic. 图 roll rice into balls

卷 15/134 juàn Roll 奍 (phonetic)

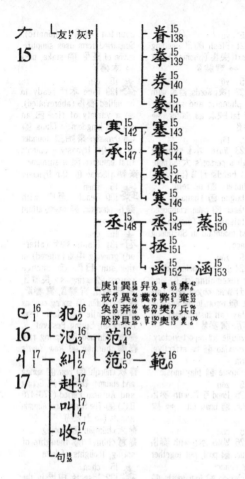

大
└友 ¹⁴ 灰 ²⁷
15

├ 眷 15
│ 138
├ 拳 15
│ 139
├ 券 15
│ 140
└ 豢 15
    141

寒 15   塞 15
  142   143
├承 15   賽 15
│ 147   144
│   寨 15
│   145
│   寒 15
│   146
└丞 15   烝 15 ── 蒸 15
    148   149   150
         ├ 拯 15
         │   151
         └ 函 15 ── 涵 15
             152   153

庚 ¹⁴ 異 ¹⁵ 异 ¹⁵ 畢 ¹⁵ 彝 ⁴²
戒 ¹⁷ 異 ¹⁵ 糞 ⁴⁶ 弊 ⁵² 棄 ⁵²
奐 ¹² 莽 ⁴⁵ 樊 ²⁷ 兵 ⁹⁶
胅 ¹²⁷ 具 ¹⁵⁰ 與 ¹⁴⁹ 奥 ¹³¹ 舁 ¹⁷⁶

巳 16   犯 16
  1   2
16   └ 氾 16 ── 范 16
            3   4
            └ 范 16 ── 範 16
                5   6
丩 17   糾 17
  1   2
17   ├ 赳 17
         │   3
         ├ 叫 17
         │   4
         ├ 收 17
         │   5
         └ 句 18
              26

and kneeling person 卩 ¹³. 囲
knee 囮 roll 囮 volume ⇔ 考
卷 ⁵⁷, 問卷 ⁵⁷

倦 15 juàn
   135 Person 人 ¹⁰ rolled up
卷 ¹⁵₅ (phonetic). 囮 weary
⇔ 疲倦 ⁵⁷, 孜孜不倦 ³⁷, 困
倦 ¹⁷, 厭倦 ⁹⁷

捲 15 juǎn
   136 [卷 ¹⁵₄] Hand 手 ⁹⁹
and roll 卷 ¹⁵₄ (phonetic). 囮
roll, curl ⇔ 春捲 ¹⁵₅, 席捲 ¹⁵,
膠捲 ¹⁵₄, 龍捲風 ¹³²
捲入 juǎnrù 囮 draw in, embroil

圈 15 juàn juān quān
   137 Rolled up 卷 ¹⁵₄ (phonetic) in confines 囗 ⁶⁹. juàn:

圈 pen, sty: 豬圈 pig sty juān:
囮 pen in, confine quān: 囹
circle, ring ⇔ 花圈 ²⁷, 項
圈 ³¹, 圓圈 ¹⁵⁰
圈套 quāntào 囮 trap, trick
圈子 quānzi 囮 circle, ring

眷 15 juàn
   138 Eyes 目 ¹⁴ with 类 ¹⁵₅
phonetic. 囮 care for ⇔ 家
眷 ²₅
眷顧 juàngù 囮 care for
眷戀 juànliàn 囮 feel attached
to, feel sentimental about
眷念 juànniàn 囮 feel nostalgic
about
眷屬 juànshǔ 囹 dependents

拳 15 quán
   139 Hand 手 ⁹⁹ and roll
类 ¹⁵₅ (phonetic). 囹 fist
拳頭 quántóu 囹 fist

券 15 quàn
   140 Knife 刀 ²⁵ with 类 ¹⁵₅
phonetic. 囹 ticket, coupon
⇔ 證券 ⁹², 債券 ²⁷, 獎券 ²⁷,
彩券 ¹⁰³

豢 15 huàn
   141 Boar 豕 ¹⁵₅ with
类 ¹⁵₅ phonetic and suggestive of sty 圈 ¹⁵₇. 囮 raise with
grainfeed
豢養 huànyǎng 囮 raise, rear

寒 15 sāi
   142 Hands 廾 ¹⁵ filling a
room 宀 ⁶³ with objects
(originally written as 工 ⁵¹, now
altered). 囲 wall in, block (⇔
塞 ¹⁵₃)

塞 15 sāi sè sài
   143 Block 寒 ¹⁵₂ (phonetic) with earth 土 ⁷⁰. sāi,sè: 囮
block, clog sài: 囹 stronghold
⇔ 要塞 ⁴⁵, 填塞 ²¹, 壅塞 ²⁷,
鼻塞 ¹⁴, 閉塞 ⁴⁷, 堵塞 ²⁶, 阻
塞 ¹⁷
塞車 sāichē 囹 ⓖ traffic jam
塞外 sàiwài 囹 beyond the Great
Wall (to north and west)
塞住 sāizhù 囮 plug, stop up

賽 15 sài
144 [賽] Shell 貝¹⁵⁰ with 塞¹⁴⁶ phonetic. 🈔 match, contest 🈔 race, contest 🈔 a surname: 賽珍珠 Pearl Buck ⇔ 比賽¹², 競賽¹², 球賽⁸² 賽跑 sàipǎo 🈔 race (on foot)

寨 15 zhài
145 Modern form shows block 塞¹⁴⁶ (phonetic) with wood 木⁷⁷. 🈔 stockade 🈔 stronghold ⇔ 山寨⁷⁷, 柬埔寨⁷⁷

寒 15 hán
146 Person 人¹⁰ (altered) stuffing straw 艸⁵⁹ into shelter 宀⁶³ (together resembling 塞¹⁴²) to ward off the cold 冫⁷⁵. ⇔ 禦寒⁹⁷
寒帶 hándài 🈔 frigid zone
寒假 hánjià 🈔 winter vacation
寒冷 hánlěng 🈔 cold, frigid
寒舍 hánshè 🈔 ⑩my home: 光臨寒舍. Welcome to my humble home.

承 15 chéng
147 Respectfully 廾¹⁵ (altered) hand 手⁹⁹ over a seal 卩³³ (altered). 🈔 receive, accept 🈔 undertake ⇔ 繼承, 奉承⁹², 秉承¹³
承包 chéngbāo 🈔 contract for
承擔 chéngdān 🈔 undertake
承諾 chéngnuò 🈔 promise
承認 chéngrèn 🈔 acknowledge, admit
承受 chéngshòu 🈔 bear, stand
承襲 chéngxí 🈔 follow (a tradition)

丞 15 chéng
148 Hands 廾¹⁵ (altered) holding a seal 卩³³ (altered) before heights 山⁶⁷ (altered). 🈔 assist 🈔 deputy official
丞相 chéngxiàng 🈔 ⑩ prime minister

烝 15 zhēng
149 Fire 火⁸² with 丞¹⁵ᵇ phonetic. 🈔 rise (as steam)

蒸 15 zhēng
150 Plants 艸⁵⁹ burned for steam 烝¹⁴⁹ (phonetic). 🈔 kindling 🈔 🈔 steam
蒸發 zhēngfā 🈔 evaporate
蒸汽 zhēngqì 🈔 steam

拯 15 zhěng
151 Hand 手⁹⁹ assisting 丞¹⁵ᵇ (phonetic). 🈔 raise
拯救 zhěngjiù 🈔 rescue

函 15 hán
152 Unrelated to 丞¹⁵ or 凵⁷⁰. Early form shows tongue 舌⁵⁸ withdrawn into the mouth 口⁶⁸ with 弖¹⁶ phonetic. 🈔 contain 🈔 letter, correspondence
函數 hánshù 🈔 function, correspondence (mathematics)

涵 15 hán
153 Contain 函¹⁵² (phonetic) water 水³⁶. 🈔 damp 🈔 contain (⇨ 含⁴⁸) ⇔ 蘊涵⁵⁹
涵蓋 hángài 🈔 include
涵養 hányǎng 🈔 self-restraint: 有涵養 restrained

弖 16 hǎn
1 Pictograph of a budding flower. 🈔 spring up

犯 16 fàn
2 Dog 犬⁹¹ springing 弖¹⁶ (phonetic). 🈔 attack 🈔 commit (error or crime) 🈔 criminal ⇔ 人犯¹⁰, 從犯¹³, 違犯¹⁴, 侵犯¹², 囚犯⁷⁰, 竊犯²⁴, 嫌犯¹⁴, 觸犯¹³, 逃犯²⁷, 戰犯¹³, 罪犯¹⁵⁶
犯錯 fàncuò 🈔 make a mistake, err
犯法 fànfǎ 🈔 break the law
犯規 fànguī 🈔 break the rules
犯人 fànrén 🈔 convict 🈔 criminal
犯罪 fànzuì 🈔 commit a crime, break the law: 犯罪率 crime rate

氾 16 fàn
[泛弖] Water 水³⁶ springing 弖¹⁶ forward. 🈔 flood
氾濫 fànlàn 🈔 flood, overflow

范 16 fàn
4 Plant 艸⁵⁹ with 氾¹⁶ phonetic. 🈔 an ancient plant 🈔 a surname

笵 16 fàn
5 Bamboo 竹⁷¹ with 氾¹⁶ phonetic. 🈔 bamboo form 🈔 law, principle

範 16 fàn
6 [范弖] Cart 車⁵⁸ following law 笵¹⁶ (phonetic, abbreviated). 🈔 sacrifice to road gods 🈔 model, example ⇔ 示範⁴⁶, 就範⁸⁵, 規範²⁷, 模範⁸⁹, 防範⁹¹, 典範¹⁹, 師範⁹²
範疇 fànchóu 🈔 category
範例 fànlì 🈔 example, model
範圍 fànwéi 🈔 scope

丩 17 jiū
1 Pictograph of intertwined vines. 🈔 curved, entangled

糾 17 jiū
2 [纠] Thread 糸⁵³ intertwined 丩¹⁷ (phonetic). 🈔 braid
糾纏 jiūchán 🈔 entwine, entangle
糾紛 jiūfēn 🈔 dispute
糾葛 jiūgé 🈔 dispute, entanglement
糾正 jiūzhèng 🈔 correct, rectify, redress

赳 17 jiū
3 Walk 走⁹⁵ with 丩¹⁷ phonetic. 🈔 gallant ⇔ 雄赳赳¹³

叫 17 jiào
4 Mouth 口⁶⁸ with 丩¹⁷ phonetic. 🈔 call, summon: 她在叫你 she's calling for you 🈔 shout 🈔 call, name: 這叫

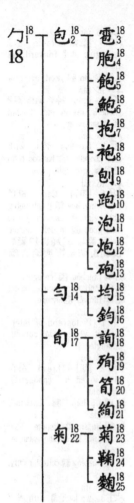

勹 18/1
18

包 18/2

電 18/3
胞 18/4
飽 18/5
鮑 18/6
抱 18/7
袍 18/8
刨 18/9
跑 18/10
泡 18/11
炮 18/12
砲 18/13

匀 18/14
均 18/15
鈞 18/16

旬 18/17
詢 18/18
殉 18/19
筍 18/20
絢 18/21

芻 18/22
菊 18/23
鞠 18/24
麴 18/25

什麼? What's this called? tell: 叫他過來 tell him to come over ⇔ 呼叫, 尖叫, 喊叫, 名叫
叫囂 jiàoxiāo clamor
叫醒 jiàoxǐng awaken (sb.)
叫做 jiàozuò be called

叫作 jiàozuò be called

收 17/5 shōu
Entangle 丩 and hit 攵. catch, trap, collect, gather, accept, receive ⇔ 歉收, 稅收, 吸收, 沒收, 接收, 回收, 豐

收藏 shōucáng collect, store
收成 shōuchéng harvest
收到 shōudào receive
收費 shōufèi charge, collect fees
收購 shōugòu purchase, buy
收回 shōuhuí take back, recall
收穫 shōuhuò results, gains
收集 shōují collect
收據 shōujù receipt
收斂 shōuliàn restrain oneself
收買 shōumǎi buy, purchase
收起 shōuqǐ stop, desist, lay off
收訖 shōuqì paid
收取 shōuqǔ collect, gather
收入 shōurù earnings, gain
收拾 shōushí tidy up, put in order
收縮 shōusuō contract, shrink
收養 shōuyǎng adopt
收益 shōuyì income, revenue
收支 shōuzhī revenue and expenditure

勹 18/1 bāo
Pictograph of person bent over something. envelop

包 18/2 bāo
Embryo 巳 enveloped 勹 (phonetic). pregnant wrap: 把它包起來 wrap it up, include, contain, surround, bundle, package, packet ⇔ 背包, 書包, 皮包, 承包, 紅包, 蛋包, 麵包
包辦 bāobàn take responsibility for: 包辦婚姻 arranged marriage
包庇 bāobì shelter
包袱 bāofu burden, bundle wrapped in cloth
包括 bāoguā include: 包括我在內 including me
包裹 bāoguǒ package
包含 bāohán include

包容 bāoróng 🉑 forgive, tolerate 🉑 contain, hold

包商 bāoshāng 🉑 contractor

包圍 bāowéi 🉑 surround, encircle

包裝 bāozhuāng 🉑 package 🉑 pack

包子 bāozi 🉑 steamed bun (stuffed)

雹 3 báo Rain 雨¹⁶¹ packet 包²ᵇ (phonetic). 🉑 hail ⇔ 冰雹²⁵

胞 4 bāo Flesh 肉¹³² wrapped 包²ᵇ (phonetic). 🉑 afterbirth ⇔ 同胞³⁴, 細胞¹⁴³, 雙胞胎¹⁶²

飽 5 [饱] bǎo Pregnant 包²ᵇ (phonetic) with food 食⁴⁵, full, satisfied ⇔ 溫飽²⁷, 吃飽⁹ᵇ

飽和 bǎohé 🉑 saturation 🉑 saturated

飽滿 bǎomǎn 🉑 full, plump

鮑 6 [鲍] bào Fish 魚¹⁸⁰ with 包²ᵇ phonetic. 🉑 a surname

鮑魚 bàoyú 🉑 abalone

抱 7 bào Hands 手⁷⁹ enwrapping 包²ᵇ (phonetic). 🉑 hug, embrace 🉑 harbor, cherish 擁抱²⁷, 摟抱²⁷

抱負 bàofù 🉑 ambition, aspiration

抱歉 bàoqiàn 🉑🈂 "excuse me"

抱怨 bàoyuàn 🉑 complain

抱著 bào zhe 🉑 embrace

袍 8 páo Clothing 衣²⁶ that wraps 包²ᵇ (phonetic) around. 🉑 gown, robe ⇔ 旗袍²⁶

刨 9 páo Knife 刀¹⁵ digging out what is wrapped 包²ᵇ (phonetic). 🉑 excavate

跑 10 pǎo Feet 足²⁰⁶ with 包²ᵇ phonetic. 🉑 run 🉑 flee ⇔ 賽跑¹⁵⁴, 慢跑⁷ᵇ, 奔跑⁶⁰, 逃跑¹⁷⁷

跑步 pǎobù 🉑 run

跑道 pǎodào 🉑 track, running path

跑堂 pǎotáng 🉑 waiter

跑走 pǎozǒu 🉑 run off, flee

泡 11 pào Watery 水²₂ packets 包²ᵇ (phonetic). 🉑 bubble 🉑 soak 🉑 氣泡³⁹

泡菜 pàocài 🉑 pickled vegetables, kimchee

泡茶 pàochá 🉑 make tea, steep tea

泡麵 pàomiàn 🉑🍜 make instant noodles 🉑 instant noodles

泡沫 pàomò 🉑 foam, froth

泡湯 pàotāng 🉑 make soup

炮 12 páo pào bāo Fire 火⁸² with 包²ᵇ phonetic. páo: 🉑 decoct pào: 🉑 cannon (⇔ 砲¹³) bāo: 🉑 saute ⇔ 鞭炮¹³⁵

砲 13 [炮¹²] pào Stone 石⁸⁹ with 包²ᵇ phonetic. 🉑 catapult 🉑 cannon ⇔ 大砲²⁹

砲兵 pàobīng 🉑 artillery

砲彈 pàodàn 🉑 shell

勻 14 yún Bundle 勹¹⁸ divided in two 二²₂ (often written as 冫 ³ᵇ). 🈂 small, few 🈺 even ⇔ 均勻¹⁵

勻稱 yúnchèn 🈺 balanced, symmetric

均 15 jūn Earth 土⁷ᵇ even 勻¹⁸ (phonetic). 🈺 fair, equal: 不均 unfair 🈺 even, level 🈺 all ⇔ 平均²⁸

均等 jūnděng 🈺 fair, impartial

均衡 jūnhéng 🈺 equilibrium, balance

均勻 jūnyún 🈺 even, balanced

鈞 16 [钧] jūn Metal 金²⁷ measured evenly 勻¹⁸ (phonetic). 🉑 thirty pounds 🈺 🈂 you

鈞鑒 jūnjiàn 🈂 a respectful salutation used in letters

鈞啓 jūnqǐ 🈂 a respectful phrase used on envelopes

旬 17 xún Days 日⁷⁶ wrapped 勹¹⁸. 🉑 ten days 🈺 decade ⇔ 上旬⁴₁, 下旬⁵₂, 中旬⁵⁸

詢 18 [询] xún Words 言⁹⁸ evenly measured 旬¹⁹ (phonetic). 🉑 inquire ⇔ 諮詢⁹³, 查詢⁵⁶, 質詢⁹⁸, 徵詢¹³⁴

詢問 xúnwèn 🉑 inquire

殉 19 xùn Death 歹¹²⁷ with 旬¹⁹ phonetic. 🈂 bury living persons to accompany the dead 🉑 die for a cause

殉道 xùndào 🉑 die a martyr's death: 殉道者 martyr

筍 20 [笋] sǔn Bamboo 竹⁷₁ growing in ten days 旬¹⁹ (phonetic). Simplified form uses 尹⁸₁. 🉑 bamboo shoot ⇔ 竹筍⁷₁

絢 21 [绚] xuàn Silk 糸¹⁵³ with 旬¹⁹ phonetic. 🈺 gorgeous

絢爛 xuànlàn 🈺 glittering, bright

絢麗 xuànlì 🈺 gorgeous, magnificent

菊 22 jú Bundle 勹¹⁸ of grain 米¹³ᵇ. 🈂 offer handful of grain

菊 23 jú Modern form shows plant 艸²⁷ with 匊²² phonetic. 🉑 chrysanthemum

菊花 júhuā 🉑 chrysanthemum

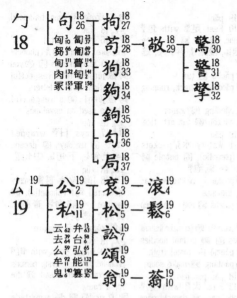

敬您一杯酒. Drink a toast to you.

敬佩 jìngpèi 🔟 respect and admire

敬畏 jìngwèi 🔟 hold in awe

驚 18 jīng
馬 30 [惊] Horse 馬 [17] with 敬 [29] phonetic. Simplified form uses 心 [13] and 京 [21]. 🔟 startle, alarm ⇔ 震驚 [?], 吃驚 [?]

驚動 jīngdòng 🔟 disturb, alarm

驚愕 jīngè 🔟 stunned, terror stricken

驚駭 jīnghài 🔟 terrified

驚恐 jīngkǒng 🔟 frightened, terrified

驚奇 jīngqí 🔟 amaze, surprise

驚人 jīngrén 🔟 astonishing, startling

驚歎 jīngtàn 🔟 marvel, exclaim: 驚歎號 exclamation point

驚喜 jīngxǐ 🔟 pleasantly surprised

驚嚇 jīngxià 🔟 frighten

驚訝 jīngyà 🔟 surprised, astonished

驚異 jīngyì 🔟 surprised, astonished

警 18 jǐng
言 31 Words 言 [?] with 敬 [?] phonetic. 🔟 warn ⇔ 火警 [82]

警報 jǐngbào 🔟 alarm, warning

警察 jǐngchá 🔟 police: 警察員 police officer; 警察局 police station

警方 jǐngfāng 🔟 police

警告 jǐnggào 🔟 warn

警戒 jǐngjiè 🔟 warn, admonish

警覺 jǐngjué 🔟 alertness

警惕 jǐngtì 🔟 be vigilant, be alert

警衛 jǐngwèi 🔟 guard, sentry

警員 jǐngyuán 🔟 police officer

擎 18 qíng
手 32 Hand 手 [99] with 敬 [?] phonetic. 🔟 lift ⇔ 引擎 [65]

勹 18 — 句 18/26 — 拘 18/27
匈 [10] 匐 [?]
勼 [?] 匍 [?] 苟 18/28 — 敬 18/29 — 驚 18/30
匋 [11] 曆 [14] 狗 18/33 警 18/31
肉 [13] 匎 [14] 夠 18/34 擎 18/32
冢 [14] 軍 [158] 鈎 18/35
勾 18/36
局 18/37

厶 19/1 — 公 19/2 — 袞 19/3 — 滾 19/4
19 私 19/11 松 19/5 — 鬆 19/6
云 [?] 弁 [?] 訟 19/7
去 [?] 台 [?] 頌 19/8
厷 [?] 弘 [65]
牟 [?] 能 [132] 翁 19/9 — 蓊 19/10
鬼 [140] 篹 [150]

鞠 18 🔟 jú 🔟 jū
革 24 Leather 革 [?] bundle 匊 [?] (phonetic). 🔟 leather ball 🔟 bow

鞠躬 júgōng 🔟 bow

麴 18 🔟 qú 🔟 qū
麥 25 [麹] Wheat 麥 with 匊 [?] phonetic. Simplified form is variant form using 曲 [135]. 🔟 brewer's yeast

句 18 jù gōu
口 26 Mouth 口 [60] stopped/entangled 丩 [?] (phonetic, written to resemble 勹 [?]). jù: 🔟 🔟 sentence: 說幾句話 say a few words gōu: 🔟 a surname ⇔ 換句話說 [61], 造句 [?]

句號 jùhào 🔟 period

句子 jùzi 🔟 sentence

拘 18 jū
手 27 Hand 手 [99] stopping 句 [?] (phonetic). 🔟 arrest

拘捕 jūbǔ 🔟 arrest

拘謹 jūjǐn 🔟 reserved

拘禁 jūjìn 🔟 detain, imprison

拘留 jūliú 🔟 detain, imprison

拘泥 jūnì 🔟 inflexible, rigid by the book

拘束 jūshù 🔟 restrain

苟 18 gǒu
艸 28 Plant 艸 with 句 [?] phonetic. 🔟 careless

苟安 gǒuān 🔟 appease

苟且 gǒuqiě 🔟 unprincipled 🔟 perfunctorily, carelessly

敬 18 jìng
攵 29 Strike 攵 [?] and self-restraint (an ancient character resembling 苟 [?]). 🔟 respect 🔟 respectfully: 敬請 respectfully request ⇔ 崇敬 [?], 恭敬 [?], 致敬 [28], 尊敬 [159]

敬愛 jìngài 🔟 love and respect

敬酒 jìngjiǔ 🔟 propose a toast:

字譜及字典

狗 18 gǒu
33 Dog 犬 with 句 phonetic. 图 dog ⇔ 哈巴狗, 走狗
狗屁 gǒupì 图 ㊀ nonsense, bullshit

够 18 gòu
34 [够] Much 多 until stop 句 (phonetic). 形 enough, sufficient 副 quite ⇔ 足够, 能够
够多 gòuduō 形 enough, sufficient
够嗆 gòuqiàng 形 ㊀ hard to swallow, unbearable

鉤 18 gōu
35 [钩] Metal 金 with 句 phonetic and suggestive of hook 勾. 图 hook ⇔ 掛鉤, 魚鉤

勾 18 gōu
36 A variant of 句. 图 hook 图 check, mark
勾結 gōujié 動 collaborate
勾引 gōuyǐn 動 tempt, entice

局 18 jú
37 Measure 尺 and speak/mouth 口. 動 compel 图 situation 图 game 图 office, bureau ⇔ 格局, 攪局, 結局, 分局, 佈局, 當局, 支局, 政局, 定局, 僵局, 郵局
局部 júbù 图 part 形 partial
局面 júmiàn 图 situation, aspect
局勢 júshì 图 circumstances
局長 júzhǎng 图 bureau chief

厶 19 sī
1 Curved line suggesting lack of straightforwardness. 形 selfish (⇒ 私)

公 19 gōng
2 Divide 八 what was private 厶. 形 fair, just public 图 metric male (animal) 图 father-in-law (husband's father) 图 grandfather ⇔ 花花公子, 老公, 辦公室, 充公, 蒲公英
公安 gōngān 图 動 public security, police
公報 gōngbào 图 bulletin, communique
公佈 gōngbù 動 announce, make public
公布 gōngbù 動 announce, make public
公車 gōngchē 图 图 public bus (公共汽車)
公尺 gōngchǐ 图 图 meter
公費 gōngfèi 图 public expense
公分 gōngfēn 图 centimeter
公告 gōnggào 動 announce, make public
公公 gōnggōng 图 grandfather 图 father-in-law
公共 gōnggòng 形 public: 公共汽車 public bus; 公共關係 public relations
公關 gōngguān 图 public relations (公共關係)
公害 gōnghài 图 environmental damage
公會 gōnghuì 图 association
公雞 gōngjī 图 rooster
公斤 gōngjīn 图 kilogram
公開 gōngkāi 形 public, open publicly, openly: 公開討論 discuss openly
公克 gōngkè 图 gram
公款 gōngkuǎn 图 public funds
公釐 gōnglí 图 millimeter
公理 gōnglǐ 图 axiom
公里 gōnglǐ 图 kilometer
公立 gōnglì 形 publicly established: 公立學校 public school, state school
公路 gōnglù 图 highway
公論 gōnglùn 图 public opinion
公民 gōngmín 图 citizen
公牛 gōngniú 图 bull
公平 gōngpíng 形 fair
公僕 gōngpú 图 civil servant
公頃 gōngqǐng 图 hectare

公然 gōngrán 副 openly
公認 gōngrèn 動 generally acknowledged
公社 gōngshè 图 commune
公升 gōngshēng 图 liter
公事 gōngshì 图 public affairs
公式 gōngshì 图 formula
公司 gōngsī 图 corporation, company
公孫 gōngsūn 图 a surname
公務 gōngwù 图 official business: 公務員 public official; 公務人員 public official
公益 gōngyì 图 public good
公營 gōngyíng 形 government-operated
公用 gōngyòng 形 public use: 公用電話 public phone
公有 gōngyǒu 形 publicly owned
公寓 gōngyù 图 apartment
公元 gōngyuán 图 A.D.: 公元前 B.C.
公園 gōngyuán 图 park
公約 gōngyuē 图 convention, treaty
公債 gōngzhài 图 government bonds
公正 gōngzhèng 形 fair
公制 gōngzhì 图 metric system
公眾 gōngzhòng 图 the public
公主 gōngzhǔ 图 princess

衮 19 gǔn
3 [袞] Official 公 (in center, with bottom altered to 口) clothes 衣. 图 imperial robes

滾 19 gǔn
4 [滚] Water 水 flowing like robes 衮 (phonetic) 動 bubble, billow 動 boil ⇔ 搖滾
滾滾 gǔngǔn 動 roll, billow, surge
滾燙 gǔntàng 形 boiling hot, scalding

松 19 sōng
5 Tree 木 straight and unchanging like justice 公

字譜及字典

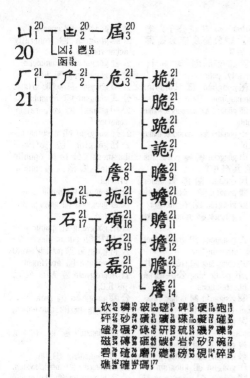

(phonetic). 图 pine
松鼠 sōngshǔ 图 squirrel
松樹 sōngshù 图 pine tree

鬆 19 sōng
6 [松髟] Modern form shows long hair 髟髟 with 松髟 phonetic. 图 loose 图 relax:
鬆口氣 sigh in relief ⇔ 輕鬆髟, 放鬆髟
鬆綁 sōngbǎng 图 untie, free
鬆弛 sōngchí 图 limp, flabby 图 lax
鬆動 sōngdòng 图 become uncrowded 图 loosen
鬆軟 sōngruǎn 图 soft
鬆散 sōngsǎn 图 loose 图 inattentive

鬆懈 sōngxiè 图 inattentive, lackadaisical

訟 19 sòng
7 [讼] Words 言言 for the public 公公 (phonetic). 图 argue 图 lawsuit ⇔ 訴訟髟
訟案 sòngàn 图 law case

頌 19 sòng
8 [颂] Public 公公 (phonetic) forehead 頁頁. 图 appearance, looks 图 praise 图 ode, eulogy
頌揚 sòngyáng 图 praise, laud, extol

翁 19 wēng
9 Feathers 羽羽 with 公公 phonetic. 图 neck feathers

图 father 图 old man 图 a surname ⇔ 富翁髟

蓊 19 wěng
10 Plant 艸艸 and neck feathers 翁髟 (phonetic). 图 lush

私 19 sī
11 Grain 禾禾 held for self 厶厶. 图 selfish: 無私 selfless 图 personal, private 图 secret 图 illicit ⇔ 走私髟, 隱私髟, 緝私髟, 自私髟
私產 sīchǎn 图 private property
私酒 sījiǔ 图 bootleg liquor
私立 sīlì 图 private: 私立大學 private university
私利 sīlì 图 private interest
私人 sīrén 图 private
私事 sīshì 图 private matters
私塾 sīshú 图 private school
私下 sīxià 图 privately
私心 sīxīn 图 selfish
私營 sīyíng 图 privately operated: 私營公司 private company; 私營化 privatization
私有 sīyǒu 图 privately owned
私語 sīyǔ 图 whisper

凵 20 kǎn
1 Pictograph of an open mouth or a pit.

坴 20 kuài
2 Clump of earth 土土 from a pit 凵凵. 图 piece (⇔ 塊髟)

屆 20 jiè
3 [届] Person 尸尸 with 坴髟 phonetic. 图 session
屆滿 jièmǎn 图 expire (term of office)
屆時 jièshí 图 when the time comes, at the appointed time

厂 21 hǎn
1 Pictograph of a cliff. 图 cliff dwelling

厃 21 wéi
2 Person 人人 atop a cliff 厂厂. 图 danger

危 21 Ⓔ wéi Ⓔ wēi
3 Danger 厂 ⁷⁵ (phonetic) with a crouching figure 厂 ⁷³ below. Ⓝ danger
危害 wéihài Ⓥ endanger
危機 wéijī Ⓝ crisis
危險 wéixiǎn Ⓐ dangerous

桅 21 wéi
4 Wooden 木 ⁷⁷ pole in dangerous 危 ³ (phonetic) position. Ⓝ mast
桅杆 wéigān Ⓝ mast

脆 21 cùi
5 Modern form shows flesh 肉 ¹³² in danger 危 ³ (phonetic). Ⓐ fragile, brittle Ⓐ crisp (voice) ⇔ 乾脆
脆弱 cùiruò Ⓐ weak

跪 21 gùi
6 Feet 足 ⁸⁶ and dangerous 危 ³ (phonetic). Ⓥ kneel
跪拜 gùibài Ⓥ kowtow
跪下 gùixià Ⓥ kneel

詭 21 [诡] Words 言 ⁹⁰ gǔi
7 endangering 危 ³ (phonetic): accuse. Ⓥ deceive
詭辯 gǔibiàn Ⓝ sophistry
詭計 gǔijì Ⓝ trick
詭譎 gǔijué Ⓐ treacherous, unpredictable
詭祕 gǔimì Ⓐ secretive, mysterious
詭異 gǔiyì Ⓐ odd, weird
詭詐 gǔizhà Ⓐ cunning

詹 21 zhān
8 Danger 厂 ?, separate 八 ⁷, and words 言 ⁹⁰. Ⓐ verbose Ⓝ a surname

瞻 21 zhān
9 Eye 目 ¹¹⁴ with 詹 ⁸ phonetic. Ⓥ look into the distance
瞻望 zhānwàng Ⓥ look into the distance
瞻仰 zhānyǎng Ⓥ look up to, show respect to

蟾 21 chán
10 Insect-like 虫 ¹²⁵ animal with 詹 ⁸ phonetic. Ⓝ toad Ⓝ the moon

贍 21 shàn
11 [赡] Money/shells 貝 ¹⁵⁰ and verbose 詹 ⁸ (phonetic). Ⓥ support financially
贍養 shànyǎng Ⓥ support financially: 贍養費 alimony, child support

擔 21 dān dàn
12 [担] Hand 手 ⁹⁹ with 詹 ⁸ phonetic. Simplified form uses 且 ⁴⁰ dān: Ⓥ carry, shoulder Ⓥ assume, bear dàn: Ⓝ burden ⇔ 承擔 ²⁵, 分擔 ²⁵, 扁擔 ¹⁵, 負擔 ¹⁹
擔當 dāndāng Ⓥ assume, undertake
擔負 dānfù Ⓥ burden Ⓥ bear, undertake
擔任 dānrèn Ⓥ serve as
擔心 dānxīn Ⓥ worry
擔憂 dānyōu Ⓥ worry
擔子 dànzi Ⓝ burden

膽 21 dǎn
13 [胆] Flesh 肉 ¹³² with 詹 ⁸ phonetic. Simplified form uses 且 ⁴⁰. Ⓝ gall bladder Ⓝ courage ⇔ 大膽 ⁷
膽敢 dǎngǎn Ⓥ dare
膽固醇 dǎngùchún Ⓝ cholesterol
膽量 dǎnliàng Ⓝ courage
膽怯 dǎnquè Ⓐ timid
膽子 dǎnzi Ⓝ courage: 膽子大 courageous; 膽子小 cowardly

簷 21 yán
14 [檐] Bamboo 竹 ⁷¹ used verbosely 詹 ⁸ (phonetic). Simplified form is variant form based on wood 木 ⁷⁷. Ⓝ eaves ⇔ 屋簷 ¹²⁸

厄 21 è
15 Crouched figure 厂 ⁷³ under an overhang 厂 ?. Ⓐ cramped, tight Ⓝ hardship

厄運 èyùn Ⓝ bad luck

扼 21 è
16 Modern form shows hand 手 ⁹⁹ holding tight 厄 ¹⁵ (phonetic). Ⓥ grip
扼殺 èshā Ⓥ strangle
扼腕 èwàn Ⓝ regret, disappointment
扼要 èyào Ⓐ concise

石 21 shí dàn
17 Cliff 厂 ⁷³ piece (written as 口 ⁶⁸). shí: Ⓝ stone, rock dàn: Ⓝ picul ⇔ 柱石 ⁴, 鑽石 ¹¹, 化石 ¹³, 吸鐵石 ²³, 砂石 ²⁷, 岩石 ⁶⁷, 絆腳石 ⁷², 寶石 ¹⁴¹, 隕石 ¹⁵⁰, 礁石 ¹⁶²
石碑 shíbēi Ⓝ stone tablet
石壁 shíbì Ⓝ stone wall
石灰 shíhuī Ⓝ lime
石窟 shíkū Ⓝ grotto: 雲岡石窟 Yungang grottoes - famous grotto site in Shanxi Province
石塊 shíkuài Ⓝ rock, stone
石器 shíqì Ⓝ stone tools: 石器時代 stone age
石頭 shítou Ⓝ rock, stone
石英 shíyīng Ⓝ quartz
石油 shíyóu Ⓝ petroleum

碩 21 shuò
18 [硕] Head 頁 ¹⁴⁹ big like a stone 石 ¹⁷ (phonetic). Ⓐ large
碩大 shuòdà Ⓐ large, huge
碩士 shuòshì Ⓝ master's degree: 碩士班學生 master's student

拓 21 tuò tà
19 Hand 手 ⁹⁹ pushing stone 石 ¹⁷. tuò: Ⓥ push Ⓥ develop (new lands) Ⓥ tà: Ⓥ make stone rubbings ⇔ 開拓 ²⁹
拓荒 tuòhuāng Ⓥ develop new lands
拓展 tuòzhǎn Ⓥ expand and develop

磊 21 lěi
20 Stones 石 ¹⁷ together.

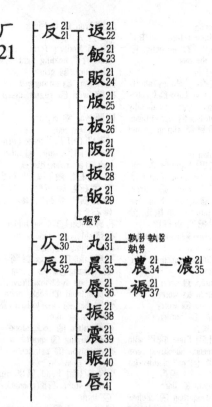

反²¹₂₁

返²¹₂₂
飯²¹₂₃
販²¹₂₄
版²¹₂₅
板²¹₂₆
阪²¹₂₇
扳²¹₂₈
飯²¹₂₉
叛⁹ᵖ

仄²¹₃₀ — 丸²¹₃₁ — 執⁹ᵖ 執⁹²
執⁹ᵖ

辰²¹₃₂

晨²¹₃₃ — 農²¹₃₄ — 濃²¹₃₅
辱²¹₃₆ — 褥²¹₃₇
振²¹₃₈
震²¹₃₉
賑²¹₄₀
唇²¹₄₁

囲 pile of stones

反 21 fǎn
反 21 Hand 又⁴ turned cliff-like 厂 ⁷ᵗ. 囲 turn over, flip, reverse 囲 oppose ⇔ 違反⁹², 平反⁹², 相反⁵², 易如反掌¹⁶³

反駁 fǎnbó 囲 refute, rebut
反常 fǎncháng 囲 abnormal
反芻 fǎnchú 囲 ruminate
反動 fǎndòng 囲 reactionary: 反動份子 reactionary elements; 反動派 reactionary faction, reactionaries
反對 fǎnduì 囲 oppose, counter

反而 fǎnér 囲 on the contrary
反覆 fǎnfù 囲 repeatedly
反感 fǎngǎn 囲 disgust, antipathy 囲 disgusted
反攻 fǎngōng 囲 囲 counterattack
反共 fǎngòng 囲 囲 anti-communist
反過來 fǎnguòlái 囲 turn over 囲 on the other hand
反華 fǎnhuá 囲 anti-Chinese
反擊 fǎnjí 囲 囲 counterattack
反抗 fǎnkàng 囲 resist: 反抗軍 resistance army
反饋 fǎnkuì 囲 囲 feedback

反美 fǎnměi 囲 anti-American
反面 fǎnmiàn 囲 reverse side
反撲 fǎnpū 囲 counterattack
反射 fǎnshè 囲 reflect 囲 reflection
反彈 fǎntán 囲 rebound, bounce back
反向 fǎnxiàng 囲 opposite direction
反省 fǎnxǐng 囲 introspection, reflection
反應 fǎnyìng 囲 react, respond 囲 reaction, response
反映 fǎnyìng 囲 reflect
反右 fǎnyòu 囲 囲 anti-rightist: 反右運動 anti-rightist campaign
反正 fǎnzhèng 囲 anyway, anyhow
反證 fǎnzhèng 囲 counterproof, counterexample
反之 fǎnzhī 囲 conversely: 反之而言 on the other hand

返 21 fǎn 22 Movement 辵⁷ in reverse 反⁹ (phonetic). 囲 return ⇔ 流連忘返⁹², 重返⁹²

返回 fǎnhuí 囲 return
返鄉 fǎnxiāng 囲 return home

飯 21 fàn 23 [饭] Food 食⁹² with 反⁹ phonetic. 囲 cooked rice 囲 meal ⇔ 稀飯²¹, 炒飯⁹², 白飯⁷², 煮飯⁹², 早飯⁹², 吃飯⁹², 午飯¹⁷, 米飯¹⁷³, 晚飯¹⁶⁴, 齋飯¹⁸²

飯店 fàndiàn 囲 restaurant 囲 hotel
飯鍋 fànguā 囲 rice pot: 電飯鍋 rice cooker
飯館 fànguǎn 囲 restaurant
飯碗 fànwǎn 囲 rice bowl: 鐵飯碗 iron rice bowl – permanent job

販 21 fàn 24 [贩] Money/shells 貝¹⁵⁰ in reverse 反⁹ (pho-

netic). 图 speculator, merchant 团 buy and sell, deal ⇔ 小販, 攤販, 毒販

販毒 fàndú 团 sell drugs

販賣 fànmài 团 sell

販子 fànzi 图 peddler

版 25 bǎn Wooden piece 片 with 反 phonetic. 图 board, plank 图 printing plate 图 edition: 中文版 Chinese edition 图 newspaper page ⇔ 刻版, 頭版, 出版, 西雙版納

版本 bǎnběn 图 edition

版權 bǎnquán 图 copyright

板 26 bǎn Tree 木 cut into opposing 反 (phonetic) pieces. 图 board, plank ⇔ 老板, 天花板, 地板, 舢板, 木板, 呆板, 紙板, 看板, 樓板, 滑板, 死板, 黑板

板凳 bǎndèng 图 bench

阪 27 bǎn Hill 阜 with 反 phonetic. 图 hillside ⇔ 大阪

扳 28 bān Hand 手 and reverse 反 (phonetic). 团 pull

扳機 bānjī 图 trigger

扳手 bānshǒu 图 wrench

皈 29 guī Bright 白 and return 反. Variant of 歸.

皈依 guīyī 团 convert (to Buddhism)

仄 30 zé Person 人 leaning as climbs hillside 厂. 图 oblique

丸 31 wán Oblique 仄 reversed, representing curves on all sides. 图 ball 图 pill ⇔ 睪丸, 藥丸

辰 32 chén Sprouting 乙 (altered) plants like daggers 七 following stars above 上, with 厂 phonetic. (altered) a constellation appearing in spring 图 celestial bodies 图 time, period 图 fifth Earthly Branch (⇨ 干支) ⇔ 時辰, 星辰, 誕辰

晨 33 chén Starry 日 (originally 晶) early morning constellation 辰 (phonetic). 图 daybreak, dawn ⇔ 凌晨, 清晨, 早晨

農 34 [农] nóng Daybreak 晨 (variant form) with head 囟 (altered) phonetic. 图 farming 图 farmer ⇔ 神農, 佃農

農場 nóngchǎng 图 farm

農村 nóngcūn 图 village countryside

農地 nóngdì 图 farmland

農夫 nóngfū 图 farmer

農戶 nónghù 图 farmer household

農曆 nónglì 图 Chinese calendar, lunar calendar

農民 nóngmín 图 peasant

農人 nóngrén 图 farmer

農田 nóngtián 图 farmland

農藥 nóngyào 图 pesticide, insecticide

農業 nóngyè 图 agriculture

濃 35 [浓] nóng Water 水 with 農 phonetic. 嘢 dense, concentrated

濃厚 nónghòu 嘢 dense, thick

濃縮 nóngsuō 团 condense, concentrate

辱 36 rù / rǔ Hand 寸 mistaken under the stars 辰. 图 disgrace ⇔ 羞辱, 污辱, 侮辱, 凌辱, 榮辱, 屈辱, 恥辱

辱罵 rùmà 团 insult, vilify

辱沒 rùmò 团 disgrace, dishonor

褥 37 rù Cloth 衣 with 辱 phonetic. 图 cushion

振 38 zhèn Hand 手 just in time 辰 (phonetic). 团 rescue 团 flap, shake 团 invigorate

振動 zhèndòng 团 vibrate, shake 图 shock

振奮 zhènfèn 团 inspire, stimulate

振興 zhènxīng 团 promote, develop

振作 zhènzuò 团 bestir

震 39 zhèn Rain 雨 with 辰 phonetic. 图 lightning bolt 团 shake, tremble ⇔ 地震

震盪 zhèndàng 团 vibrate, oscillate

震驚 zhènjīng 团 shock, astonish

賑 40 [赈] zhèn Money/shell 貝 with 辰 phonetic. 团 relieve, aid

賑濟 zhènjì 团 relieve, aid

唇 41 chún Mouth 口 shaking 辰 (phonetic). (altered) startled 图 lip ⇔ 嘴唇

后 42 hòu Person leaning forward (written as 厂 and 一) to mouth 口 orders. (altered) prince 图 empress 图 behind (⇨ 後) ⇔ 皇后, 太后

詬 43 [诟] gòu Words 言 with 后 phonetic. 团 insult

詬病 gòubìng 团 find fault with, criticize

詬罵 gòumà 团 berate

垢 44 gòu Dirt 土 left behind

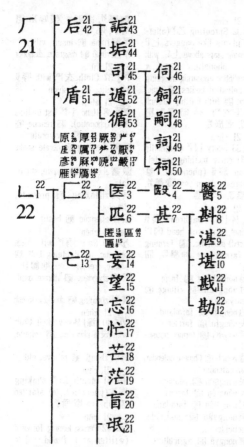

伺機 sìjī 围 await an opportunity

飼
21 sì
47 [伺] Food 食⁶⁵ with
司⁴⁵ phonetic. 围 raise
(animals)
飼料 sìliào 围 feed, fodder
飼養 sìyǎng 围 raise, breed

嗣
21 sì
48 Mouth 口⁶⁸ documents
冊¹¹⁵ proclaiming rule 司⁴⁵
(phonetic). 围 succeed to the
throne 围 inherit
嗣後 sìhòu 围 thereafter, from
then on

詞
21 cí
49 [词] Words 言⁹⁵
managing 司⁴⁵ (phonetic).
围 speech, statement ⇔ 冠詞¹¹⁴, 供詞⁹⁶,
副詞⁶⁷, 介詞⁹⁷, 嘆詞¹⁰⁴, 名
詞⁹⁷, 致詞¹²⁸, 單詞¹³⁰, 連
詞¹¹⁸
詞典 cídiǎn 围 围 dictionary ⇔
辭典⁹⁷
詞彙 cíhuì 围 vocabulary
詞類 cílèi 围 part of speech

祠
21 cí
50 Offering 示⁴⁶ with
司⁴⁵ phonetic. 围 temple
祠堂 cítáng 围 ancestral hall

盾
21 dùn
51 Eye 目¹¹⁴ behind cliff-
like 厂²¹ shield with cross-like
十³¹ handle. 围 shield ⇔ 後
盾²¹, 矛盾¹⁰⁵
盾牌 dùnpái 围 shield

遁
21 dùn
52 Movement 辵³¹ with
shield 盾⁵¹ (phonetic). 围 flee
遁形 dùnxíng 围 vanish

循
21 xún
53 Step 彳⁴¹ with shield
盾⁵¹ (phonetic). 围 proceed
smoothly 围 comply with, abide
by ⇔ 遵循¹²⁰
循環 xúnhuán 围 circulate, cycle
围 circulation, cycle: 惡性循

后⁴² (phonetic). 围 dirt, filth
围 disgrace ⇔ 污垢⁴³, 油
垢²¹¹³

司
21 sì
45 Prince 后⁴² reversed.
围 manage 围 government
office ⇔ 上司⁴³, 壽司⁷⁹,
公司⁷², 官司¹⁶⁷
司法 sìfǎ 围 judiciary
司機 sìjī 围 driver, chauffeur
司令 sìlìng 围 commander

司馬 sìmǎ 围 minister of war 围
a surname: 司馬光 Sima
Guang - a Song Dynasty statesman and author; 司馬遷 Sima
Qian - a Han Dynasty historian

伺
21 sì cì
46 Person 人¹⁰ and
manage 司⁴⁵ (phonetic). sì:
围 watch for, await cì: 围 wait
on ⇔ 窺伺⁷⁹
伺候 cìhòu wait upon, serve

環 vicious cycle

22 yǐn
└ 1 Pictograph suggesting a curve or corner. (古) conceal, cover

22 xǐ
2 Conceal └ 22 with a cover 一└. (古) box, chest

22 yì
医 3 Arrows 矢 22 in a container 匚 22. (古) quiver

22 yī
殹 4 Arrows from quiver 医 22 (phonetic) shot 殳 22. (古) sound of striking arrow

22 yī
醫 5 [医] Ill sounds 殹 22 (phonetic) cured with alcohol 酉 19. (動) treat, cure (名) medical science, medicine (名) doctor
牙醫, 獸醫, 西醫
醫療 yīliáo (名) medical treatment
醫生 yīshēng (名) doctor
醫師 yīshī (名) doctor
醫學 yīxué (名) medicine, medical science; 醫學院 medical school
醫藥 yīyào (名) medicine
醫院 yīyuàn (名) hospital
醫治 yīzhì (動) cure, heal, treat

22 pǐ pī
匹 6 Separate 八 22 and roll up in chest 匚 22. pǐ: bolt (of cloth) (動) equal, match (動) measureword for horses ⇔ 馬匹
匹敵 pǐdí (動) be competitive with, be equal of

22 shèn shé
甚 7 Sweetness 甘 22 of marriage match 匹 22. happiness shèn: (形) very ⇔ 爲甚麼
甚麼 shéme what ⇨ 什麼
甚爲 shènwéi (動) very
甚至 shènzhì even to the point that

22 zhēn
斟 8 Wine jug 斗 22 with 甚 22 phonetic. (動) fill (動) consider
斟酌 zhēnzhuó (動) consider, deliberate

22 zhàn
湛 9 Water 水 22 excessive 甚 22 (phonetic). (動) immerse, sink (形) deep, profound ⇔ 精湛

22 kān
堪 10 Ground 土 22 excessive 甚 22 (phonetic). (動) mound (動) bear, endure (動) able ⇔ 不堪, 難堪

22 kān
戡 11 Exceeding 甚 22 (phonetic) lance 戈 22. (古) pierce (動) suppress
戡亂 kānluàn (動) suppress a rebellion

22 kān
勘 12 Exceeding 甚 22 (phonetic) strength 力 22. (動) investigate
勘察 kānchá (動) reconnaissance
勘探 kāntàn (動) explore

22 wáng
亡 13 Enter 入 22 concealed └ 22 place. (動) flee (動) die
滅亡, 流亡, 存亡, 傷亡, 逃亡, 死亡
亡故 wánggù (形) dead
亡國 wángguó (動) conquered nation (名) national ruin

22 wàng
妄 14 Flee 亡 22 (phonetic) and woman 女 22. (形) rash absurd ⇔ 狂妄
妄動 wàngdòng (動) rash, impetuous
妄想 wàngxiǎng (動) delude oneself (名) delusion

22 wàng
望 15 [望] Moon 月 22 and stand 壬 22 with 亡 22 (phonetic) suggestive of wane. Simplified form uses 王 22. (名) full moon (動) watch, gaze at (動) hope, expect ⇔ 願望, 希望, 指望, 瞻望, 渴望, 張望, 寄望, 仰望, 絕望, 盼望, 聲望, 展望, 期望, 探望, 欲望, 慾望, 奢望, 瞭望, 企望, 失望, 眺望, 觀望
望見 wàngjiàn (動) see from afar
望遠鏡 wàngyuǎnjìng (名) telescope

22 wàng
忘 16 Escape 亡 22 (phonetic) the mind/heart 心 22. (動) forget: 忘不了 unforgettable ⇔ 流連忘返, 備忘錄, 遺忘
忘本 wàngběn (形) ungrateful
忘掉 wàngdiào (動) forget
忘懷 wànghuái (動) forget
忘記 wàngjì (動) forget

22 máng
忙 17 Mind/heart 心 22 lost 亡 22 (phonetic). (動) busy busily (動) hurry ⇔ 急忙, 慌忙, 趕忙, 繁忙, 幫忙, 匆忙, 連忙
忙碌 mánglù (形) busy

22 máng
芒 18 Grass 艸 22 with 亡 22 phonetic. (形) sharp ⇔ 光芒
芒果 mángguǒ (名) mango

22 máng
茫 19 Grass 艸 22 sea (ancient character from water 水 22 with 亡 22 phonetic). (形) boundless (形) vague ⇔ 蒼茫, 渺茫
茫茫 mángmáng (形) boundless, vast
茫然 mángrán (形) ignorant, uncertain

22 máng
盲 20 Lost 亡 22 (phonetic) eyes 目 22. (形) blind ⇔ 文

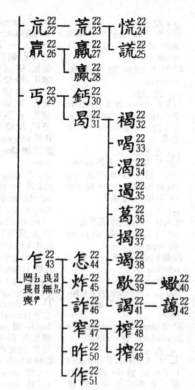

22

亡22/22 — 荒22/23 ┬ 慌22/24
贏22/26 ── 贏22/27 ┬ 謊22/25
                  └ 贏22/28
└ 丐22/29 ── 鈣22/30
└ 曷22/31 ┬ 褐22/32
         ├ 喝22/33
         ├ 渴22/34
         ├ 遏22/35
         ├ 蔼22/36
         ├ 揭22/37
乍22/43 ┬ 怎22/44 ├ 竭22/38
罔23/良12 ├ 炸22/45 ├ 歇22/39 — 蠍22/40
長22/無31/117 ├ 詐22/46 ├ 謁22/41 — 藹22/42
喪68 ├ 窄22/47 ┬ 榨22/48
   ├ 昨22/50 └ 搾22/49
   └ 作22/51

---

remote

荒唐 huāngtáng 形 preposter-
ous

荒野 huāngyě 名 wilderness

荒淫 huāngyín 形 debauched,
dissolute

荒塚 huāngzhǒng 名 abandoned
grave

慌22/24 huāng
Heart 心心 run wild
荒荒 (phonetic). 形 scared:
不要慌. Don't panic. ⇔ 恐
慌5/, 發慌5/

慌忙 huāngmáng 副 hurriedly

謊22/25 [谎] huǎng
Words 言 that
are wild 荒荒 (phonetic). 名
lie ⇔ 說謊1/, 撒謊

謊話 huǎnghuà 名 lie

贏22/26 lúo
Enclose 亡户 captured
羊8/ (altered to 凡1?) animal
in a pen 口68 and fatten up its
meat 肉132. 古 an animal name

贏22/27 léi
Lamb 羊123 requiring
fattening 贏荒 (phonetic).
形 frail

贏弱 léiruò 形 frail

贏22/28 [赢] yíng
Fatten 贏荒 with
money/shells 貝150. 動 gain,
profit 動 win, beat

贏得 yíngdé 動 win, gain

丐22/29 gài
Person 人10 (altered)
seeking refuge 亡户 (altered).
動 beg ⇔ 乞丐9/

鈣22/30 [钙] gài
Metal 金44 with
丐荒 phonetic. 名 calcium

曷22/31 hé
Speak 曰 with 丐荒
(early form) phonetic. 疑 who,
what

褐22/32 hé 颰 hè
Clothing 衣126 with
曷荒 phonetic. 名 coarse cloth

盲98
盲腸 mángcháng 名 appendix:
盲腸炎 appendicitis
盲目 mángmù 形 blind 副 blindly
盲人 mángrén 名 blind person

氓22/21 máng méng
Lost 亡户 (phonetic)
people 民119. máng:
immigrant, vagrant, vagabond
méng: 名 common people ⇔
流氓

亡22/22 huāng
Death 亡户 (phonetic)
from rivers 川15. 古 flood

荒22/23 huāng
Plant 艸94 flood 亡荒
(phonetic). 形 wild, uncultivated 形 desolate, barren 名
famine ⇔ 災荒5/, 墾荒12/,
拓荒5/, 飢荒5/

荒草 huāngcǎo 名 weeds
荒島 huāngdǎo 名 desert island
荒地 huāngdì 名 wasteland
荒廢 huāngfèi 動 lie waste 動
waste 動 neglect
荒涼 huāngliáng 形 desolate,
barren
荒謬 huāngmiù 形 absurd
荒僻 huāngpì 形 desolate and

圈 brown
褐色 hésè 圈 brown

喝 22 hē hè
33 Mouth 口⁶⁸ with 曷⁹⁷
phonetic. hē: 圈 drink hè: 圈
shout
喝采 hēcǎi 圈 applaud, acclaim
喝酒 hējiǔ 圈 drink alcohol
喝令 hèlìng 圈 shout a command
喝醉 hēzuì 圈 become drunk: 你
喝醉了。You're drunk.

渴 22 kě
34 Water 水⁶₃ with 曷⁹⁷
phonetic. 圈 thirst 圈 thirsty
渴望 kěwàng 圈 thirst for, yearn
for

遏 22 è
35 Movement 辵⁹¹ with
曷⁹⁷ phonetic. 圈 restrain
遏止 èzhǐ 圈 stop, hold back
遏制 èzhì 圈 suppress, restrain,
curb
遏阻 èzǔ 圈 stop, curb

葛 22 gé gě
36 Plant 艸⁵₆ with 曷⁹⁷
phonetic. gé: 圈 a plant used
to make cloth gě: 圈 a surname
⇔ 杯葛ₐ, 糾葛⁹₇, 瓜葛¹⁰⁴

揭 22 jiē
37 Hand 手⁹⁹ with 曷⁹⁷
phonetic. 圈 expose, uncover
揭穿 jiēchuān 圈 expose, unveil
揭發 jiēfā 圈 expose (a plot)
揭開 jiēkāi 圈 uncover
揭露 jiēlù 圈 expose, uncover
揭示 jiēshì 圈 reveal 圈
announce, make public

竭 22 jié
38 Stand 立⁹⁷ with 曷⁹⁷
phonetic. 圈 endeavor 圈
exhaust ⇔ 枯竭₃₅, 耗竭⁹⁰
竭力 jiélì 圈 to the best of one's
ability

歇 22 xiē
39 Exhale 欠⁵⁹ with 曷⁹⁷
phonetic. 圈 rest ⇔ 間歇₆₃
歇後語 xiēhòuyǔ 圈 proverb
歇宿 xiēsù 圈 stop for the night

歇息 xiēxí 圈 rest

蠍 22 xiē
40 [蝎] Insect 虫¹²⁵ with
歇 phonetic. Simplified form
is a variant form. 圈 scorpion
蠍子 xiēzi 圈 scorpion

謁 22 yè
41 [谒] Words 言⁷₆ with
曷⁹⁷ phonetic. 圈 meet with a
superior

藹 22 ǎi
42 [蔼] Plant 艸⁵₆ with
謁⁹⁷ phonetic. 圈 lush 圈
amiable ⇔ 和藹₁⁰⁸

乍 22 zhà
43 Try to hide 亡₁₀ (al-
tered) but meet obstacle 一ₗ.
圈 suddenly
乍見 zhàjiàn 圈 glimpse

怎 22 zěn
44 Mind/heart 心⁸₃
suddenly 乍⁹⁷ (phonetic)
uncertain. 圈 why, how, what
怎麼 zěnme 圈 what: 怎麼辦?
What should be done? 圈 why:
你怎麼不去呢? Why aren't
you going? 圈 how: 怎麼樣?
How is it? How about it? 圈
(indicating inadequacy) 不
怎麼好 not very good
怎樣 zěnyàng 圈 how: 最近怎
樣? How have you been
recently?

炸 22 zhá zhà
45 Fire 火⁸² working
quickly 乍⁹⁷ (phonetic). zhá:
圈 fry zhà: 圈 explode ⇔ 爆
炸₁₂₅, 轟炸₁⁵⁸
炸彈 zhàdàn 圈 bomb
炸毀 zhàhuǐ 圈 blow up
炸醬麵 zhàjiàngmiàn 圈 noodles
with fried bean and meat sauce
炸藥 zhàyào 圈 explosive

詐 22 zhà
46 [诈] Words 言⁷₆ that
work briefly 乍⁹⁷ (phonetic).
圈 deceive, cheat ⇔ 詭詐⁹⁷,
敲詐⁹⁷, 欺詐⁹⁴, 奸詐⁹⁷

詐騙 zhàpiàn 圈 deceive, cheat
詐欺 zhàqī 圈 fraud
詐取 zhàqǔ 圈 extort

窄 22 zhǎi
47 Hole 穴⁹⁷ with 乍⁹⁷
phonetic. 圈 narrow ⇔ 狹
窄⁹⁷

榨 22 zhà
48 Wood 木⁷₇ squeezing
窄⁹⁷ (phonetic). 圈 juice
extractor 圈 press, extract ⇔
壓榨⁹⁰

搾 22 zhà
49 [榨] Hand 手⁹⁹ and
narrow 窄⁹⁷ (phonetic). 圈
press, extract (⇔ 榨⁹⁷)
搾取 zhàqǔ 圈 extract

昨 22 zuó
50 Day 日⁷₆ suddenly
乍⁹⁷ (phonetic). past. 圈
yesterday
昨日 zuórì 圈 yesterday
昨天 zuótiān 圈 yesterday
昨晚 zuówǎn 圈 last night,
yesterday evening
昨夜 zuóyè 圈 last night

作 22 zuò
51 Person 人¹⁰ suddenly
乍⁹⁷ (phonetic) active. 圈 do,
make 圈 act as 圈 regard as
圈 work, product ⇔ 傑作⁹₅,
創作₁₂₅, 叫作⁹₇, 振作⁹₉, 做
作⁹₃, 大作⁹⁷, 合作⁹₃, 工
作⁵¹, 當作⁹₈, 操作⁹₉, 著
作⁹₃, 動作⁹₇, 製作⁹₇, 裝
作⁹₆, 發作⁹₈, 耕作⁹⁷, 拙
作₁⁰, 寫作₁₅₄, 運作⁴⁵⁸
作弊 zuòbì 圈 cheat
作成 zuòchéng 圈 make into
作對 zuòduì 圈 oppose, antagonize
作法 zuòfǎ 圈 method
作風 zuòfēng 圈 style: 生活作
風 lifestyle
作怪 zuòguài 圈 make trouble
圈 mischievous
作家 zuòjiā 圈 author
作客 zuòkè 圈 be a guest

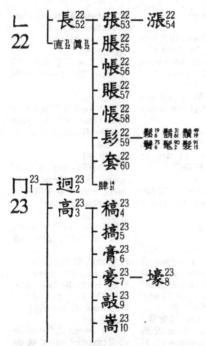

作夢 zuòmèng 動 dream
作孽 zuòniè 動 do evil, harm
作品 zuòpǐn 名 creative works
作曲 zuòqǔ 動 compose (music): 作曲家 composer
作勢 zuòshì 動 pretend
作祟 zuòsuì 動 make mischief
作為 zuòwéi 名 conduct, behavior 動 serve as 動 regard as
作物 zuòwù 名 crop
作秀 zuòxiù 動 show off, grandstand
作業 zuòyè 名 homework 名 operation, task
作用 zuòyòng 名 function, effect: 副作用 side-effect
作戰 zuòzhàn 動 make war
作者 zuòzhě 名 writer, author
作證 zuòzhèng 動 testify

長 22 cháng zhǎng
52 [长] Early form shows high table 兀, changed person 七, and death 亡 (phonetic). cháng: 名 duration, length 形 long 名 strength, forte zhǎng: 動 grow 形 senior 名 a surname ⇔ 部長, 州長, 兄長, 院長, 鄉長, 學長, 局長, 漫長, 省長, 消長, 處長, 冗長, 拉長, 校長, 成長, 滋長, 專長, 廠長, 市長, 船長, 生長, 擅長, 延長, 班長, 里長, 助長, 組長, 增長, 首長, 家長, 隊長, 酋長, 師長...

張 22 zhāng
53 [张] Bow 弓 that grows 長 (phonetic). 動 stretch, spread 量 measureword for flat objects, sheet 名 a surname ⇔ 主張, 誇張, 擴張, 囂張, 緊張
張開 zhāngkāi 動 stretch open, open

長安 chángān 地 Changan - ancient name of 西安 [30]
長白山 chángbáishān 地 Changbaishan - a mountain range in Northeast China
長程 chángchéng 形 long-distance
長城 chángchéng 地 Great Wall
長處 chángchù 名 strength, advantage
長春 chángchūn 地 Changchun - capital of Jilin Province
長春藤 chángchūnténg 名 ivy: 長春藤大學 Ivy League
長度 chángdù 名 length
長短 chángduǎn 名 length
長江 chángjiāng 地 Yang-tze River ⇨ 楊子江 [?]
長頸鹿 chángjǐnglù 名 giraffe
長久 chángjiǔ 形 a long time
長期 chángqí 形 long-term
長沙 chángshā 地 Changsha - capital of Hunan Province
長壽 chángshòu 形 longevity
長途 chángtú 形 long distance: 長途電話 long-distance call
長征 chángzhēng 名 the Long March
長輩 zhǎngbèi 名 elders
長成 zhǎngchéng 動 grow up, grow into
長大 zhǎngdà 動 grow up, mature: 在美國長大 grow up in America
長得 zhǎngde 動 grow up: 她長得很漂亮. She is very pretty.
長老 zhǎnglǎo 名 elders
長相 zhǎngxiàng 名 appearance
長子 zhǎngzǐ 名 son (eldest)

張望 zhāngwàng look around
張揚 zhāngyáng publicize (confidential matters)

漲 22 zhǎng zhàng 54 [涨] Water 水 spreading 張 (phonetic). zhǎng: rise zhàng: swell ⇔ 上漲, 高漲
漲價 zhǎngjià raise prices

脹 22 zhàng 55 [胀] Flesh 肉 growing 長 (phonetic). bloat, expand ⇔ 膨脹

帳 22 zhàng 56 [帐] Cloth 巾 extended 長 (phonetic). spread out tent account ⇔ 付帳, 認帳, 呆帳, 賴帳, 蚊帳, 算帳
帳單 zhàngdān bill, check
帳戶 zhànghù bank account
帳目 zhàngmù account
帳篷 zhàngpéng tent
帳棚 zhàngpéng tent

賬 22 zhàng 57 [账] Money/shells 貝 growing 長 (phonetic). Variant of 帳.

悵 22 chàng 58 [怅] Heart 心 and long 長 (phonetic). disappointed, frustrated ⇔ 惆悵

髟 22 biāo 59 Long 長 hair 彡. long hair

套 22 tào 60 Of right size 大 and length 長. cover, case set ⇔ 客套, 圈套, 枕套, 外套, 手套
套房 tàofáng suite, apartment
套牢 tàoláo lock up, trap: 被錢套牢 trapped by money
套用 tàoyòng apply mechanically

冂 23 jiōng 1 Ideograph representing outer limits. countryside, wilds

迥 23 jiōng 2 Walk 辵 and a variant of distant 冂 (phonetic). distant
迥然不同 jiōngránbùtóng completely different, worlds apart
迥異 jiōngyì very different

高 23 gāo 3 A room 口 on the bottom, topped by 冂 and a pictograph of a pavilion. high, tall high level a surname ⇔ 崇高, 提高, 最高
高矮 gāoǎi height
高昂 gāoáng high: 價格高昂 expensive; 士氣高昂 jubilant, spirited
高傲 gāoào arrogant
高潮 gāocháo high tide climax: 性高潮 orgasm
高等 gāoděng high level
高低 gāodī height
高調 gāodiào high-pitched
高度 gāodù high degree
高峰 gāofēng peak, summit: 交通高峰時間 rush hour; 高峰會 summit meeting
高幹 gāogàn high-level cadre (高級幹部)
高估 gāogū overestimate
高貴 gāoguì noble elegant, classy
高級 gāojí high-class
高架橋 gāojiàqiáo overpass, expressway
高亢 gāokàng resounding
高考 gāokǎo university entrance exam
高空 gāokōng high altitude
高粱 gāoliáng sorghum: 高粱酒 sorghum wine
高棉 gāomián Cambodia

高明 gāomíng wise, brilliant
高蹺 gāoqiāo stilts
高球 gāoqiú golf
高尚 gāoshàng classic, noble, lofty
高聲 gāoshēng loudly
高手 gāoshǒu expert
高速 gāosù high-speed: 高速公路 highway
高興 gāoxìng happy
高雄 gāoxióng Kaohsiung - a city in Taiwan
高於 gāoyú higher than, above
高漲 gāozhǎng surge upwards
高中 gāozhōng senior high school

稿 23 gǎo 4 Grain 禾 with 高 phonetic. straw manuscript, draft ⇔ 原稿, 初稿, 投稿, 校稿, 底稿
稿費 gǎofèi payment for a written work
稿子 gǎozi manuscript, draft

搞 23 gǎo 5 Hand 手 with 高 phonetic. do: 搞清楚 clarify; 搞不懂 don't understand organize obtain
搞錯 gǎocuò misunderstand
搞鬼 gǎoguǐ make trouble: 你在搞什麼鬼? What trouble are you up to?
搞砸 gǎozá bungle

膏 23 gāo 6 Thick/high 高 (phonetic) flesh 肉. grease, fat ointment ⇔ 牙膏
膏藥 gāoyào medicinal plaster

豪 23 háo 7 Boar 豕 with high 高 (phonetic, abbreviated) bristles. porcupine person of outstanding talent ⇔ 富豪, 自豪
豪富 háofù the rich and

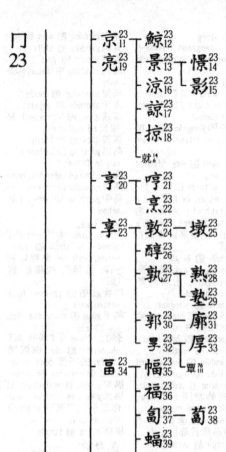

京 23/11 jīng — Tall 高邛 (abbreviated) and vertical 丨. capital city great ⟺ 北京, 南京, 東京
京都 jīngdū Kyoto
京劇 jīngjù Peking opera

鯨 23/12 [鲸] Fish 魚 which is great 京邛 (phonetic). whale
鯨吞 jīngtūn annex, swallow up
鯨魚 jīngyú whale

景 23/13 jǐng — Sun 日 above hill 京邛 (phonetic). bright view, scene, scenery ⟺ 光景, 背景, 盆景, 風景, 情景
景觀 jǐngguān view, vista
景氣 jǐngqì economic prosperity: 經濟不景氣 recession
景色 jǐngsè landscape, scenery
景象 jǐngxiàng prospects
景致 jǐngzhì scenery, view

憬 23/14 jǐng — Heart 心 aware of scene 景邛 (phonetic). realize ⟺ 憧憬

影 23/15 yǐng — Scene 景邛 (phonetic) with 彡 suggestive of shape 形. shadow ⟺ 人影, 電影, 投影, 錄影, 陰影, 攝影
影片 yǐngpiàn film, movie
影響 yǐngxiǎng affect, influence: 影響力 power, influence; 有影響力 influential
影像 yǐngxiàng image
影星 yǐngxīng movie star
影印 yǐngyìn photocopy: 影印機 photocopier
影展 yǐngzhǎn film festival

powerful (⟹ 富豪)
豪華 háohuá luxurious
豪雨 háoyǔ pouring rain
壕 23/8 háo — Earth 土 with 豪 phonetic. moat, trench
壕溝 háogōu moat, trench
敲 23/9 qiāo — Strike 攵 high 高邛 (phonetic). rap, knock: 敲門 knock on the door ⟺ 推

敲
敲打 qiāodǎ knock, rap
敲擊 qiāojí knock, beat
敲詐 qiāozhà extort
嵩 23/10 sōng — Tall 高邛 mountain 山. Song Mountain - a sacred mountain in Henan Province
嵩山 sōngshān Song Mountain

影子 yǐngzi 图 shadow

涼 23 liáng liàng
涼 16 [凉] Like water 水幺
and high hills 京阝 (phonetic).
Simplified form uses ice 冫冫.
liáng: cool liàng: 助 cool off
⇔ 乘涼幺, 凄涼幺, 荒涼幺,
清涼幺, 著涼幺
涼菜 liángcài 图 salad (Chinese
style), cold dish
涼快 liángkuài 图 cool, refreshing
涼蓆 liángxí 图 sleeping mat
(for the summer)
涼鞋 liángxié 图 sandals

諒 23 liàng
諒 17 [谅] Words 言幺 that
are grand 京阝 (phonetic). 助
trust 助 forgive ⇔ 原諒幺,
見諒幺

掠 23 lüè
掠 18 Hand 手阝 building hill
京阝 (phonetic). 助 plunder
助 brush past ⇔ 劫掠幺, 搶
掠幺
掠奪 lüèduó 助 loot, plunder,
pillage
掠過 lüèguò 助 brush past

亮 23 liàng
亮 19 [亮] Tall 高阝 (abbre-
viated) person 儿阝. Simplified
form uses 几阝. 图 clear 助
bright 助 light up ⇔ 光亮幺,
響亮幺, 漂亮幺, 照亮幺, 閃
亮幺, 月亮阝, 明亮阝, 發
亮幺

亨 23 hēng
亨 20 Variant of 享幺 with
tall 高阝 (abbreviated) on top
and form now written to
resemble 了幺 on bottom. 图
gift to a superior 助 proceed
smoothly
亨通 hēngtōng 助 proceed
smoothly

哼 23 hēng
哼 21 Mouth 口阝 making
亨幺 sound. 助 hum 助 grunt

烹 23 pēng
烹 22 Fire 火阝 offering
亨幺 (phonetic). 助 cook
烹飪 pēngrèn 图 cooking
烹調 pēngtiáo 助 cook

享 23 xiǎng
享 23 Tall 高阝 (abbre-
viated) on top and an object
(now written to resemble 子阝)
on bottom. 助 gift to a superior
助 enjoy ⇔ 共享幺, 分享幺
享受 xiǎngshòu 助 enjoy
享用 xiǎngyòng 助 enjoy use of
享有 xiǎngyǒu 助 enjoy (rights
or privileges)

敦 23 dūn dùi
敦 24 Strike 攵阝 with an
ancient character for lamb
(now written as 享幺) pho-
netic. dùi: 图 an ancient bronze
container dūn: 助 urge ⇔ 倫
敦幺
敦促 dūncù 助 urge sincerely
敦厚 dūnhòu 图 honest, sincere
敦煌 dūnhuáng 图 Dunhuang —
a town in Gansu Province: 敦
煌石窟 Dunhuang grottoes

墩 23 dūn
墩 25 Dirt 土阝 with 敦幺
phonetic. 图 block ⇔ 橋
墩幺

醇 23 chún
醇 26 Alcohol 酉阝 with an
ancient character for lamb
(now written as 享幺) pho-
netic. 图 rich wine ⇔ 膽固
醇幺
醇厚 chúnhòu 图 mellow, rich

孰 23 shú
孰 27 Lamb (ancient character written as 享幺) taken
丮阝 (written as 丸幺). 助
cooked 图 ripe 图 which, who

熟 23 shóu 助 shú
熟 28 Cooked 孰幺 (phonet-
ic) on fire 火阝. 图 cooked 图
ripe 图 well-versed, familiar
with, experienced ⇔ 成熟幺,

純熟幺, 嫻熟幺
熟練 shóuliàn 图 well-trained,
skilled
熟人 shóurén 图 acquaintance,
friend
熟睡 shóushùi 助 sleep soundly
熟悉 shóuxī 图 familiar with

塾 23 shú
塾 29 Earth 土阝 with 孰幺
phonetic. 图 home school ⇔
私塾阝

郭 23 guō
郭 30 City 邑阝 with 享幺
phonetic. 图 city wall 图 a
surname

廓 23 kuò
廓 31 Shed 广阝 and city wall
郭幺 (phonetic). 图 boundless
⇔ 輪廓幺
廓清 kuòqīng 助 clear away

亯 32 Inverse of 享幺, indi-
cating gift from superior to
inferior. 图 generosity

厚 23 hòu
厚 33 Cliff-sized 厂阝 generosity 亯幺. 图 generous,
considerate 图 thick ⇔ 雄
厚幺, 濃厚幺, 敦厚幺, 醇
厚幺, 深厚阝, 忠厚幺, 豐
厚幺, 優厚阝
厚薄 hòubó 图 thickness
厚度 hòudù 图 thickness

富 23 fú
富 34 Fields 田阝 piled high
高阝 (abbreviated). 图 abun-
dance

幅 23 fú
幅 35 Cloth 巾阝 abundant
富幺 (phonetic). 图 width 助
measureword for paintings and
scrolls ⇔ 篇幅阝
幅度 fúdù 图 range
幅員 fúyuán 图 extent of a
country: 幅員遼闊的國家
a vast country

福 23 fú
福 36 Omen 示幺 and abun-

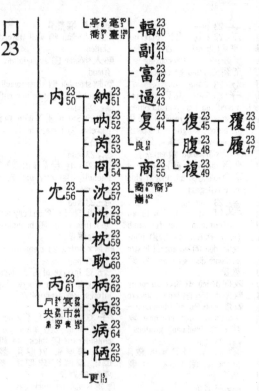

冂 23

亭 毫 喬 臺
輻 40 / 副 41 / 富 42 / 逼 43 / 复 44 — 復 45 — 覆 46 / 履 47 / 腹 48 / 褚 49
商 55（啇 啻 嫡）

内 50 → 納 51 / 呐 52 / 芮 53（良）/ 冏 54
尢 56 → 沈 57 / 忱 58 / 枕 59 / 耽 60
丙 61 → 柄 62 / 炳 63 / 病 64 / 陋 65
冏 央 市 … 更

---

dance 富彐 (phonetic). 图 fortune, happiness ⇔ 祝福12, 幸福彖, 口福彷, 祈福竹, 羅斯福142

福建 fújiàn 图 Fujian Province: 福建話 Fukienese

福利 fúlì 图 welfare

福祉 fúzhǐ 图 welfare

匐 23 fú
37 Bundle 勹彐 with 富彐 phonetic. 图 crawl ⇔ 匍匐彷

葡 23 bó
38 [卜艹] Plants 艸彐 that crawl 匐彐 (phonetic) under-ground. 图 plants with edible roots ⇔ 蘿蔔162

蝠 23 fú
39 Insect 虫125 with 富彐 phonetic. 图 bat ⇔ 蝙蝠115

輻 23 fú
40 [辐] Cart 車158 and abundant 富彐 (phonetic). 图 spoke

輻射 fúshè 图 radiate 图 radiation

副 23 fù
41 Knife 刀彐 with 富彐 phonetic. 图 vice-, assistant: 副總統 vice-president

副詞 fùcí 图 adverb

富 23 fù
42 Roof 宀彷 covering abundant 富彐 (phonetic) reserves. 图 wealthy ⇔ 豪富尸, 阿富汗彸, 財富尤, 豐富尨, 致富128

富貴 fùguì 图 wealth and status

富豪 fùháo 图 the rich and powerful

富強 fùqiáng 圈 rich and strong

富人 fùrén 图 rich person

富翁 fùwēng 图 rich man: 百萬富翁 millionaire; 億萬富翁 billionaire

富有 fùyǒu 圈 rich, abundant 圈 full of

富裕 fùyù 圈 wealthy

逼 23 bī
43 Movement 辵彷 with 富彐 phonetic. 图 close in 图 force, compel ⇔ 被逼尨

逼近 bījìn 图 press in, close in

逼迫 bīpò 图 force, compel

逼真 bīzhēn 圈 lifelike, realistic

复 23 fù
44 Go 夂彸 with 富彐 (altered) phonetic. 动 return (⇨ 復彷)

復 23 fù
45 [复] Step 彳彷 and repeat 复彐 (phonetic). 图 return 图 recover ⇔ 光復42, 康復彸, 報復彸, 恢復82

復辟 fùbì 图 restore a monarchy

復仇 fùchóu 图 avenge 图 vengeance

復甦 fùsū 图 revive, recover 图 recovery: 經濟復甦 economic recovery

復習 fùxí 图 review

復興 fùxīng 图 revive 图 renaissance

覆 23 fù
46 Cover 襾彐 with repeat 復彐 (phonetic) suggesting reversal. 图 overturn 图 cover 图 reply ⇔ 反覆尨, 顛覆尨,

答覆^指, 回覆^罗, 重蹈覆轍⁷⁶
覆蓋 fùgài 🔟 cover

履 23 lǚ
47 Modern form shows body 尸⁴⁰ and return 復^罗. 🔟 shoes 🔟 walk ⇔ 步履^器
履歷 lǚlì 🔟 resume, vita
履行 lǚxíng 🔟 implement

腹 23 fù
48 Flesh 肉³² with 复^罗 phonetic. 🔟 abdomen ⇔ 心腹⁸³
腹部 fùbù 🔟 abdomen
腹地 fùdì 🔟 heartland

複 23 fù
49 [复^罗] Cloth 衣¹²⁶ returning 复^罗 (phonetic). 🔟 innerlined garment 🔟 complex ⇔ 重複⁷⁶
複數 fùshù 🔟 plural (grammar)
複印 fùyìn 🔟 🔟 photocopy: 複印機 photocopier
複雜 fùzá 🔟 complicated, complex
複製 fùzhì 🔟 duplicate: 複製品 replica, reproduction

內 23 nèi
50 Enter 入¹² from outside 口尸. 🔟 inside 🔟 internal ⇔ 河內^罗, 國內^器, 室內¹²⁸
內部 nèibù 🔟 interior 🔟 internal 🔟 🔟 restricted, classified
內地 nèidì 🔟 hinterland
內閣 nèigé 🔟 cabinet (government)
內行 nèiháng 🔟 expert
內疚 nèijiù 🔟 regret, guilty conscience
內陸 nèilù 🔟 inland
內容 nèiróng 🔟 contents
內外 nèiwài 🔟 inside and outside
內向 nèixiàng 🔟 introverted
內心 nèixīn 🔟 heart
內衣 nèiyī 🔟 underwear, underclothes
內在 nèizài 🔟 inherent, internal
內臟 nèizàng 🔟 internal organs

內戰 nèizhàn 🔟 civil war

納 23 nà
51 [纳] Threads 糸⁵³ entering 內^罗 (phonetic) water. 🔟 wet silk 🔟 receive, accept 🔟 offer, pay ⇔ 接納^罗, 容納^器, 繳納^罗, 採納¹⁰³, 出納¹⁰, 西雙版納¹³⁰, 歸納¹⁶⁷
納粹 nàcuì 🔟 Nazi
納罕 nàhǎn 🔟 marvel, wonder
納悶 nàmèn 🔟 depressed
納入 nàrù 🔟 bring into
納稅 nàshuì 🔟 pay taxes
納西族 nàxīzú 🔟 Naxi - a people in Yunnan

吶 23 nà
52 Mouth 口⁶⁸ and inside 內^罗 (phonetic). 🔟 stammer 🔟 shout
吶喊 nàhǎn 🔟 cheer, whoop

芮 23 ruì
53 Grass 艸^罗 with 內^罗 phonetic. 🔟 fine grass 🔟 tiny

冏 23 nà jiǒng
54 Speak in 內^罗 one's mouth 口⁶⁸. Modern form also represents an ancient pictograph of a window. nà: 🔟 stammer jiǒng: 🔟 window

商 23 shāng
55 Stammer 冏^罗 with 章^罗 (abbreviated) phonetic. 🔟 discuss 🔟 trade 🔟 business, commerce 🔟 merchant ⇔ 磋商^器, 包商^罗, 協商^罗, 殷商^罗, 洽商^罗, 研商^罗, 廠商^器, 外商^罗, 會商^器, 官商^罗
商標 shāngbiāo 🔟 trademark: 註冊商標 registered trademark
商場 shāngchǎng 🔟 market place
商朝 shāngcháo 🔟 Shang Dynasty
商店 shāngdiàn 🔟 store, shop
商量 shāngliáng 🔟 discuss

商品 shāngpǐn 🔟 good, commodity
商榷 shāngquè 🔟 discuss
商人 shāngrén 🔟 businessperson, merchant
商討 shāngtǎo 🔟 discuss
商務 shāngwù 🔟 commercial affairs
商業 shāngyè 🔟 business, commerce
商議 shāngyì 🔟 negotiate, discuss
商酌 shāngzhuó 🔟 discuss and think over

尢 23 yín
56 Person 人¹⁰ going outside 囗尸. 🔟 leave

沈 23 chén shěn
57 Water 水^罗 with 尢^罗 phonetic. chén: 🔟 sink, submerge shěn: 🔟 a surname ⇔ 消沈^罗, 深沈^罗, 低沈^罗
沈澱 chéndiàn 🔟 settle, precipitate 🔟 sediment, precipitate
沈寂 chénjí 🔟 silent, still
沈浸 chénjìn 🔟 immerse
沈靜 chénjìng 🔟 placid, calm
沈淪 chénlún 🔟 drown (in vice): 沈淪於電玩中 addicted to video games
沈悶 chénmèn 🔟 depressed 🔟 oppressive (heat and humidity)
沈湎 chénmiǎn 🔟 wallow in
沈默 chénmò 🔟 silence: 沈默寡言 reticent, taciturn
沈睡 chénshuì 🔟 fast asleep
沈思 chénsī 🔟 contemplate, ponder
沈吟 chényín 🔟 ponder aloud
沈重 chénzhòng 🔟 heavy 🔟 serious, formal
沈醉 chénzuì 🔟 addicted to

忱 23 chén
58 Heart 心⁸³ with 尢^罗 phonetic. 🔟 sincere ⇔ 熱忱^罗

枕 23 zhěn
59 Wood 木¹⁷ with 尢^罗

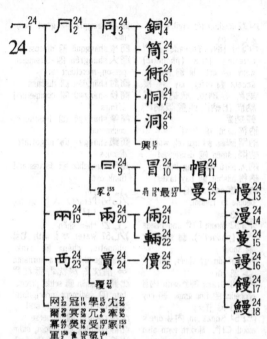

病人 bìngrén 图 patient
病逝 bìngshì 圃 die of illness
病症 bìngzhèng 图 disease 图 symptom

陌 23 lòu
65 Hills 阜 [67] with an ancient character based on 丙 [23] and 匚 [52] phonetic. 图 narrow 图 ugly 图 crude, inferior ⇔ 鄙陋 [67], 簡陋 [24], 醜陋 [159]
陋規 lòuguī 图 bad practices
陋習 lòuxí 图 corrupt customs

冖 24 mì
1 Pictograph of an edged cover. 图 cover (⇒ 幂 [49])

冃 24 mào
2 Cover 冖 [24] an object 一凵 图 cover

同 24 tóng
3 Objects (written as 口 [4]) under the same cover 冃 [24]. 图 same, similar 圖 similarly 圆 together ⇔ 一同 [1], 不同 [16], 贊同 [16], 共同 [16], 迥然不同 [16], 志同道合 [16], 認同 [16], 大同 [16], 合同 [16], 如同 [16], 雷同 [16], 相同 [16]
同班 tóngbān 图 in the same class: 同班同學 classmate
同伴 tóngbàn 图 companion
同胞 tóngbāo 图 compatriot
同行 tóngháng 图 same profession
同化 tónghuà 圃 assimilate
同居 tóngjū 圃 live together, cohabitate
同類 tónglèi 图 of the same kind
同僚 tóngliáo 图 colleague
同盟 tóngméng 图 ally, alliance
同謀 tóngmóu 圃 conspire 图 accomplice
同情 tóngqíng 圃 sympathize, empathize 图 sympathy, empathy
同仁 tóngrén 图 colleague
同時 tóngshí 圆 at the same time
同事 tóngshì 图 colleague

phonetic. 图 pillow
枕套 zhěntào 图 pillowcase
枕頭 zhěntou 图 pillow

耽 23 dān
60 Ear 耳 [17] with 尢 [23] phonetic. 图 large and drooping (ears) 圃 addicted to
耽擱 dāngē 圃 delay 圃 stop over
耽誤 dānwù 圃 hold up: 耽誤你的時間 take up your time

丙 23 bǐng
61 One 一 [1], representing yang, entering 入 [12] a space 冂 [23]. 图 bright 图 fire 图 third Heavenly Stem (⇒ 干支 [9])

柄 23 bǐng
62 Wood 木 [7] with 丙 [23] phonetic. 图 handle ⇔ 把柄 [32], 笑柄 [77]

炳 23 bǐng
63 Fire 火 [82] bright 丙 [23] (phonetic). 图 bright ⇔ 彪炳 [122]

病 23 bìng
64 Illness 疒 [24] spreading like fire 丙 [23] (phonetic). 图 disease, illness 圃 fall sick: 病了 ill, sick ⇔ 糖尿病 [55], 得病 [33], 詬病 [92], 肺病 [82], 疾病 [83], 弊病 [91], 生病 [22], 性病 [57], 愛滋病 [83], 毛病 [9], 養病 [122], 患病 [57]
病毒 bìngdú 图 virus: 電腦病毒 computer virus
病房 bìngfáng 图 sickroom
病患 bìnghuàn 图 sickness
病情 bìngqíng 图 patient's condition

同鄉 tóngxiāng 图 person from the same hometown

同性 tóngxìng 圈 same sex: 同性戀 homosexuality; 同性戀者 homosexual

同學 tóngxué 图 schoolmate

同樣 tóngyàng 圈 alike, similar, same

同業 tóngyè 圈 of the same profession

同一 tóngyī 圈 same

同意 tóngyì 图 agree, accept

同志 tóngzhì 图 comrade 图 國 @ homosexual

同舟共濟 tóngzhōugòngjì 图 pull together in a crisis

銅 24 tóng
4 [铜] Metal 金字 that mixes with others together 同字 (phonetic). 图 copper ⇔ 黃銅字, 青銅字

銅鏡 tóngjìng 图 bronze mirror

銅鑼 tónglúo 图 gong

銅器 tóngqì 图 bronzeware, copperware, brassware

銅錢 tóngqián 图 copper money

筒 24 tǒng
5 Bamboo 竹字 with 同字 phonetic and suggestive of hole 洞字. 图 cylinder ⇔ 甜筒字, 手電筒字, 郵筒字

衕 24 tòng
6 Go 行字 with 同字 phonetic. 图 lane, alley ⇔ 衚衕字

恫 24 dòng
7 Heart 心字 with 同字 phonetic. 图 threaten

恫嚇 dònghè 图 threaten

洞 24 dòng
8 Formed by water 水字 rushing together 同字 (phonetic). 图 hole, cavity ⇔ 空洞字, 山洞字, 窯洞字, 漏洞字

洞察 dòngchá 图 have insight into: 洞察力 insight

洞房 dòngfáng 图 nuptial chamber: 鬧洞房 tease newly-weds on wedding night

洞窟 dòngkū 图 cave, cavern

洞悉 dòngxī 图 understand thoroughly

冃 24 mào
9 Cover 冂字 with 一 representing head. 侚 hat (⇔ 帽字)

冒 24 mào
10 With eyes 目字 covered 冃字 (phonetic). 图 rashly, imprudently 图 emit, billow 图 risk, brave: 冒風險 take risks ⇔ 感冒字, 甘冒字, 仿冒字

冒充 màochōng 图 pose as, pass off as: 冒充内行 pose as an expert

冒號 màohào 图 colon

冒進 màojìn 图 proceed rashly

冒昧 màomèi 图 venture to, presume to 图 presumptuous

冒失 màoshī 圈 rash, reckless, imprudent

冒險 màoxiǎn 图 risk danger 图 adventure

帽 24 mào
11 Cloth 巾字 that covers eyes 冒字 (phonetic). 图 hat

帽子 màozi 图 hat

曼 24 màn
12 Hand 又字 with 冒字 phonetic. 图 stretch, lengthen

曼谷 màngǔ 图 Bangkok

慢 24 màn
13 Heart 心字 and lengthen 曼字 (phonetic). 图 slow: 慢走! Take care! ⇔ 怠慢字, 傲慢字, 緩慢字

慢跑 mànpǎo 图 jog

漫 24 màn
14 Water 水字 and lengthen 曼字 (phonetic). 图 overflow 图 uncontrolled ⇔ 浪漫字, 彌漫字, 瀰漫字, 爛漫字

漫步 mànbù 图 stroll

漫長 màncháng 圈 endless

漫畫 mànhuà 图 comics, manga

漫談 màntán 图 discuss informally

蔓 24 màn
15 Plant 艸字 that extends 曼字 (phonetic). 图 vine

蔓延 mànyán 图 spread, extend

謾 24 màn
16 [谩] Words 言字 extending 曼字 (phonetic). 图 malign

謾罵 mànmà 图 malign, vilify

饅 24 mán
17 [馒] Food 食字 with 曼字 phonetic.

饅頭 mántou 图 mantou, steamed bun

鰻 24 mán
18 [鳗] Extended 曼字 (phonetic) fish 魚字. 图 eel

鰻魚 mányú 图 eel

网 24 liǎng
19 Covering 冂字 with objects hanging on either side. 侚 scale

兩 24 liǎng
20 [两] Scale 网字 with a redundant bar 一. 图 tael 图 two ⇔ 半斤八兩字

兩邊 liǎngbiān 图 both sides

兩三 liǎngsān 图 a couple, a few

兩樣 liǎngyàng 圈 different: 沒有兩樣 the same

倆 24 liǎ liǎng
21 [俩] Person 人字 balancing 兩字 (phonetic). liǎng: 图 ability liǎ: 图 two (people) ⇔ 他倆字, 伎倆字

輛 24 liàng
22 [辆] Cart 車字 with 兩字 phonetic. 图 a measure-word for vehicles ⇔ 車輛字

亞 24 yà
23 Cover 冂字 from top and bottom. 侚 cover

賈 24 gǔ jiǎ
24 [贾] Cover 西字 (phonetic) cost with shells/money 貝字. gǔ: 图 trade jiǎ: 图 a

字譜及字典

冫 25/1
冰 25/2
馮 25/3 — 憑 25/4

寒 凝 冬 冷 冶 凌 漢 凋 凍 列 准

卜 26/1
攵 26/2 — 攸 26/3 — 悠 26/4
扑 26/11 — 枚 26/9 — 修 26/5
朴 26/12 — 玫 26/10 — 倏 26/6
赴 26/13 — 條 26/7 — 滌 26/8
計 26/14

敏 寇 教 煞 更 收 敬 敝 救 故 赦 效 敘 攻 敵 敏 數 孜 改 敻 敞 敕 林 敲 救 肇 敢 政 救 牧 放 務 啓 敢 敗 變

占 26/15
佔 26/16
站 26/17
沾 26/18
點 26/19
店 26/20 — 惦 26/21
坫 26/22
黏 26/23
貼 26/24
帖 26/25
貞 26/26 — 偵 26/27
卦 外

surname
價 24/25 【价】 Person 人 and

trade 賈 (phonetic). Simplified form uses 介. 图 price 图 value ⇔ 討價, 牌價,

---

漲價, 評價, 削價, 估價, 減價, 代價, 市價, 物價, 定價, 殺價, 廉價, 售價, 講價

價格 jiàgé 图 price
價錢 jiàqián 图 price, cost
價值 jiàzhí 图 value: 價值觀 values, morals

冫 25/1 bīng
Pictograph of ice crystals. freeze

冰 25/2 bīng
Frozen 冫 (phonetic) water 水. 图 ice ⇔ 溜冰, 滑冰

冰棒 bīngbàng 图 popsicle
冰雹 bīngbáo 图 hail
冰茶 bīngchá 图 iced tea
冰島 bīngdǎo 图 Iceland
冰凍 bīngdòng 图 freeze
冰棍 bīnggùn 图 popsicle
冰河 bīnghé 图 glacier
冰塊 bīngkuài 图 ice cube
冰淇淋 bīngqílín 图 ice cream
冰山 bīngshān 图 iceberg
冰箱 bīngxiāng 图 refrigerator, freezer
冰鞋 bīngxié 图 ice skates
冰柱 bīngzhù 图 icicle

馮 25/3 【冯】 píng féng
Horse 馬 with 冫 phonetic and suggesting galloping sound. píng: gallop féng: a surname

憑 25/4 【凭】 píng
Heart 心 with 馮 phonetic. Simplified character is an ancient form from table 几 and assume responsibility 任. rely on, be based on lean on evidence no matter, regardless of ⇔ 任憑, 文憑
憑弔 píngdiào pay homage (to the deceased)
憑藉 píngjiè rely on: 憑藉自己的努力 rely on one's

own efforts
憑據 píngjù 图 proof, basis
憑空 píngkōng 图 without basis

卜 26 bǔ
1 Pictograph of cracks in tortoise shells. In composition can represent a stick. 图 foretell, divine ⇔ 占卜
卜辭 bǔcí 图 oracle bone inscriptions
卜卦 bǔguà 图 divine, foretell
卜筮 bǔshì 图 divination

攵 26 pū
2 Hand 又 holding a stick 卜 (phonetic). 图 strike (⇒ 扑)

攸 26 yōu
3 Person 人 holding a stick 攵 and crossing a stream 水 (abbreviated to 丨). 图 destination
攸關 yōuguān 图 concerning, relating to

悠 26 yōu
4 Heart 心 and destination 攸 (phonetic). 图 pensive, distant
悠久 yōujiǔ a long time
悠閑 yōuxián 图 leisurely, unhurried
悠揚 yōuyáng 图 melodious: 悠揚旋律 pleasant melody

修 26 xiū
5 Hair 彡 with 攸 phonetic. 图 adorn, decorate 图 fix, repair 图 study ⇔ 主修, 裝修, 維修
修補 xiūbǔ 图 repair, mend
修訂 xiūdìng 图 revise
修改 xiūgǎi 图 revise
修課 xiūkè 图 take a class
修理 xiūlǐ 图 repair
修女 xiūnǚ 图 nun
修繕 xiūshàn 图 repair
修飾 xiūshì 图 decorate, adorn
修行 xiūxíng 图 practice moral or religious teachings
修養 xiūyǎng 图 recuperate

修正 xiūzhèng 图 revise, amend: 修正主義 revisionism; 修正液 white-out fluid

倏 26 shù
6 Dog 犬 with 攸 phonetic. 图 suddenly
倏忽 shùhū 图 suddenly

條 26 tiáo
7 [条] Wood 木 with 攸 phonetic. 图 twig 图 article, item 图 line, strip 图 a measureword for fish ⇔ 線
條件 tiáojiàn 图 condition, term 图 qualification, requirement
條款 tiáokuǎn 图 clause, article
條理 tiáolǐ 图 order, arrangement: 有條理 organized, methodical; 沒條理 incoherent, disorganized
條例 tiáolì 图 regulations, rules
條文 tiáowén 图 text
條紋 tiáowén 图 stripe, streak
條約 tiáoyuē 图 treaty: 不平等條約 unequal treaties

滌 26 dí
8 [涤] Water 水 and twigs 攸. 图 wash away ⇔ 洗滌
滌除 díchú 图 wash away

枚 26 méi
9 Wood 木 for striking 攵. 图 measureword for small objects

玫 26 méi
10 Modern form shows jade 玉 and strike 攵. 图 black mica
玫瑰 méiguī 图 rose

扑 26 pū
11 Hand 手 holding a stick 卜. 图 strike, beat

朴 26 pú
12 Wood 木 with 卜 phonetic. 图 bark 图 a type of oak tree 图 simple (⇒ 模)

赴 26 fù
13 Go 走 with 卜 phonetic. 图 attend, go to

訃 26 fù
14 [讣] Words 言 and foretold 卜 (phonetic). 图 obituary
訃告 fùgào 图 obituary

占 26 zhān
15 Ask/mouth 口 tortoise shell cracks 卜. 图 divine
占卜 zhānbǔ 图 divine

佔 26 zhàn
16 [占] Person 人 with 占 phonetic. 图 occupy, seize: 佔便宜 take advantage of 图 constitute, account for ⇔ 獨佔, 霸佔
佔據 zhànjù 图 occupy
佔領 zhànlǐng 图 seize, occupy
佔線 zhànxiàn 图 busy (phone line)
佔用 zhànyòng 图 appropriate
佔有 zhànyǒu 图 occupy, hold

站 26 zhàn
17 Stand 立 with 占 phonetic. 图 stand: 站起來 stand up 图 station, stop: 火車站 train station ⇔ 網站, 驛站, 車站
站立 zhànlì 图 stand
站住 zhànzhù 图 Halt!

沾 26 zhān
18 Water 水 with 占 phonetic. 图 moisten
沾光 zhānguāng 图 benefit from reflected glory
沾染 zhānrǎn 图 be corrupted by: 我沾染了你的惡習. I've been corrupted by your bad habits.

點 26 diǎn
19 [点] Black 黑 with 占 phonetic. 图 spot, dot 图 drop, a bit: 一點點 just a little

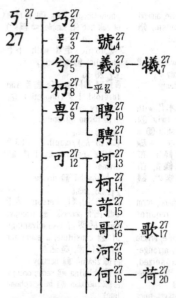

图 point: 零點三 zero point three 圖 dot 圖 select: 點菜 order dishes 圖 light, ignite o'clock: 三點半 three-thirty ⇔ 一點, 指點兒, 有點兒, 要點兒, 標點兒, 污點兒, 特點兒, 缺點兒, 終點兒, 地點兒, 沸點兒, 重點兒, 鐘點兒, 早點兒, 半點兒, 斑點兒, 論點兒, 弱點兒, 優點兒, 據點兒, 焦點兒, 觀點兒
點滴 diǎndī 圖 drop
點名 diǎnmíng 圖 call the roll
點燃 diǎnrán 圖 light, ignite, kindle
點頭 diǎntóu 圖 nod
點香 diǎnxiāng 圖 burn incense
點心 diǎnxīn 圖 dessert 圖 dim sum
點鐘 diǎnzhōng 圖 hour, o'clock: 三點鐘 three o'clock
點綴 diǎnzhuì 圖 embellish, adorn

點子 diǎnzi 圖 speck 圖 idea

店 26 diàn
20 Shed 广⁶⁰ with 占兒 phonetic: storehouse. 圖 shop, store ⇔ 客店兒, 花店兒, 書店兒, 飯店兒, 商店兒, 藥店兒, 旅店¹¹⁸, 酒店¹⁵⁹
店鋪 diànpù 圖 shop, store
店員 diànyuán 圖 salesclerk

惦 26 diàn
21 Heart 心⁸³ and storehouse 店兒 (phonetic). 圖 think of
惦記 diànjì 圖 remember, think of
惦念 diànniàn 圖 worry about 圖 miss

玷 26 diàn
22 Jade 玉¹⁰⁷ with 占兒 phonetic and suggestive of cracks 卜²⁶. 圖 defect in jade
玷污 diànwū 圖 stain, smear (reputation)

黏 26 nián
23 Glutinous millet 黍兒 with 占兒 phonetic. 圖 sticky 圖 stick
黏貼 niántiē 圖 stick, glue, paste
黏土 niántǔ 圖 clay
黏性 niánxìng 圖 stickiness, adhesiveness

貼 26 tiē
24 [贴] Shell/money 貝¹⁵⁰ with 占兒 phonetic. 圖 stick, glue 圖 allowance, subsidy ⇔ 津貼兒, 黏貼兒, 補貼兒, 體貼兒, 鍋貼¹⁷³
貼補 tiēbǔ 圖 subsidize 圖 supplement
貼心 tiēxīn 圖 intimate
貼紙 tiēzhǐ 圖 sticker

帖 26 tiē tiě
25 Cloth 巾⁵³ with 占兒 phonetic. tiē: 圖 write on silk tiě: 圖 note, card ⇔ 字帖兒, 請帖兒

貞 26 zhēn
26 [贞] Money 貝¹⁵⁰ given to obtain fortune 卜²⁶. 圖 divine 圖 chaste, virtuous
貞操 zhēncāo 圖 chastity
貞節 zhēnjié 圖 chastity

偵 26 zhēn
27 [侦] Person 人¹⁰ divining 貞兒 (phonetic). 圖 investigate
偵查 zhēnchá 圖 investigate
偵察 zhēnchá 圖 reconnoiter, scout
偵探 zhēntàn 圖 detective: 偵探小說 detective story
偵訊 zhēnxùn 圖 investigate

5 27 kǎo
1 Pictograph of breath against an obstacle.

巧 27 qiǎo
2 Work 工⁵¹ to overcome an obstacle 5²⁷ (phonetic). 圖 skillful 圖 coincidental: 真巧! What a coincidence! ⇔ 乖巧兒, 湊巧兒, 恰巧兒, 精

巧另, 技巧另
巧合 qiǎohé 图 coincidental, serendipitous
巧克力 qiǎokèlì 图 chocolate
巧妙 qiǎomiào 图 skillful, ingenious, clever

丂 27 háo hào
3 Mouth 口⁶⁸ and difficulty in breathing 丂⁷. 㒰 howl (⇨ 號²⁷)

號 27 háo hào
4 [号] Tiger's 虎¹²² howl 丂 (phonetic). háo: 图 howl hào: 图 number: 幾號? Which number? 图 mark, sign 图 title, name ⇔ 符號..., 句號..., 冒號..., 等號..., 分號..., 國號..., 訊號..., 引號..., 頓號..., 口號..., 括號..., 信號..., 暗號..., 逗號..., 掛號..., 外號..., 綽號..., 問號...
號稱 hàochēng 圖 known as, called
號碼 hàomǎ 图 number
號召 hàozhào 圖 call for appeal, call

兮 27 xī
5 Separated 八⁷ breath 丂⁷. 圙 ⊗ a particle indicating a pause

義 27 xī
6 Pause 兮⁷ with 義 phonetic. 㒰 exhale ⇔ 伏義...

犧 27 xī
7 [牺] Ox 牛⁷ with 義⁷ phonetic. Simplified form uses 西¹³⁰. 圙 sacrifice
犧牲 xīshēng 圙 sacrifice

朽 27 xiǔ
8 Wood 木⁷ with 丂⁷ phonetic. 图 rotten ⇔ 不朽..., 腐朽..., 永垂不朽...

粤 27 píng
9 Through 由¹¹³ cries 丂⁷. 㒰 assist

聘 27 pìn
10 Listen 耳¹⁷ and assist 粤⁷ (phonetic). 圙 visit, call on 圙 employ
聘禮 pìnlǐ 图 betrothal gifts (from groom's family), bride-price
聘請 pìnqǐng 圙 appoint, hire
聘任 pìnrèn 圙 employ
聘書 pìnshū 图 appointment letter, employment contract
聘用 pìnyòng 圙 employ

騁 27 chěng
11 [骋] Horse 馬¹⁷ with 粤⁷ phonetic. 圙 gallop
馳騁...

可 27 kě
12 Mouth 口⁶⁸ consenting (obstructed breath 丂⁷ reversed). 圙 approve 圙 may 圙 but ⇔ 不可思議..., 無可奈何..., 認可..., 許可..., 寧可..., 炙手可熱...
可愛 kěài 图 cute, adorable
可觀 kěguān 图 sizable, appreciable
可貴 kěguì 图 valuable
可見 kějiàn 圙 as can be seen
可靠 kěkào 图 dependable, reliable: 不可靠 unreliable
可口 kěkǒu 图 tasty
可樂 kělè 图 cola: 可口可樂 Coca-Cola
可憐 kělián 图 pitiful 圙 pity, show mercy
可能 kěnéng 圙 perhaps, maybe: 可能性 possibility, probability; 不可能 impossible
可怕 kěpà 图 fearful, terrifying
可取 kěqǔ 图 desirable
可是 kěshì 圙 but, however
可惡 kěwù 图 abominable
可惜 kěxí 图 unfortunate, pitiful 圙 unfortunately
可笑 kěxiào 图 ridiculous, laughable
可行 kěxíng 图 feasible: 可行性 feasibility
可疑 kěyí 图 dubious
可以 kěyǐ 圙 can, may 图 good, acceptable, o.k.: 還可以 all right, o.k.

坷 27 kě
13 Ground 土⁷ inducing exhalation 可⁷ (phonetic). 图 bumpy ⇔ 坎坷...

柯 27 kē
14 Wood 木⁷ with 可⁷ phonetic. 图 axe handle 㒰 a surname

苛 27 kē
15 Plant 艸⁶⁶ with 可⁷ phonetic. 㒰 small grass 图 harsh
苛刻 kēkè 图 merciless, harsh
苛求 kēqiú 图 exacting, demanding

哥 27 gē
16 Repeated exhales 可⁷ (phonetic). 㒰 song (⇨ 歌⁷) 图 brother (elder) ⇔ 阿兵哥..., 大哥..., 大哥大..., 堂哥..., 芝加哥..., 表哥..., 墨西哥..., 帥哥...
哥哥 gēge 图 brother (elder)

歌 27 gē
17 Song 哥⁷ (phonetic) exhaled 欠⁸⁶. 圙 chant, sing 图 song ⇔ 詩歌..., 秧歌..., 國歌..., 唱歌..., 民歌...
歌唱 gēchàng 圙 sing
歌詞 gēcí 图 lyrics
歌劇 gējù 图 opera
歌曲 gēqǔ 图 song
歌手 gēshǒu 图 singer
歌廳 gētīng 图 song hall
歌星 gēxīng 图 singing star
歌謠 gēyáo 图 folksong

河 27 hé
18 Water 水⁴⁰ with 可⁷ phonetic. 图 river ⇔ 銀河系..., 冰河..., 黃河..., 恆河..., 運河..., 淮河...
河岸 héàn 图 river bank
河北 héběi 圙 Hebei Province
河邊 hébiān 图 river bank

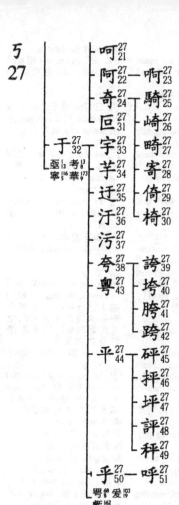

何嘗 hécháng 〔〕 how can it be
何處 héchù 〔〕 where
何等 héděng 〔〕 what kind 〔〕 how, such (exclamatory)
何妨 héfáng 〔〕 why not, what's the harm
何故 hégù 〔〕 why, for what reason
何況 hékuàng 〔〕 much less, let alone, not to mention
何人 hérén 〔〕 who
何時 héshí 〔〕 when, what time
何以 héyǐ 〔〕 why

荷 27 20 Plant 艸 with 何 phonetic. hé: 〔〕 lotus hè: 〔〕 burden ⇨ 負荷
荷爾蒙 héěrméng 〔〕 hormone
荷花 héhuā 〔〕 lotus flower
荷蘭 hélán 〔〕 Holland

呵 27 21 Mouth 口 exhaling 可 (phonetic). 〔〕 laugh exhale
呵呵 hēhē 〔〕 laugh: 呵呵大笑 roar with laughter

阿 27 22 Hill 阜 with 可 phonetic. ā: 〔〕 a prefix used before names ē: 〔〕 flatter
阿兵哥 ābīnggē 〔〕 〔〕 〔〕 soldier
阿富汗 āfùhàn 〔〕 Afghanistan
阿根廷 āgēntíng 〔〕 Argentina
阿拉伯 ālābó 〔〕 Arab
阿里山 ālǐshān 〔〕 Alishan - a mountain in Taiwan
阿姨 āyí 〔〕 aunt (maternal)
阿彌陀佛 ēmítuófó 〔〕 Amitabha - a Buddhist figure
阿諛 ēyú 〔〕 flatter

啊 27 23 Mouth 口 with 阿 phonetic. 〔〕 ah

奇 27 24 Person 大 exhaling 可 in wonder. qí: 〔〕 strange, unusual jī: 〔〕 odd (number)

河川 héchuān 〔〕 rivers
河道 hédào 〔〕 river channel
河南 hénán 〔〕 Henan Province
河內 hénèi 〔〕 Hanoi
河水 héshuǐ 〔〕 river water
何 27 19 Person 人 exhaling

可召. 〔〕 load, burden (⇨ 荷召) 〔〕 what, which 〔〕 a surname ⇨ 無可奈何, 任何, 如何, 幾何, 為何
何必 hébì 〔〕 why is it necessary (rhetorical): 我們何必去呢? Why must we go?

稀奇 xīqí, 神奇 shénqí, 驚奇 jīngqí, 新奇 xīnqí, 好奇 hàoqí, 傳奇 chuánqí, 離奇 líqí

奇數 jīshù 名 odd number
奇怪 qíguài 形 strange, weird
奇蹟 qíjī 名 miracle
奇妙 qímiào 形 intriguing, marvelous
奇特 qítè 形 unusual, peculiar
奇異 qíyì 形 bizarre, unusual: 奇異果 kiwi

騎 25 [骑] qí Horse 馬 with 奇 phonetic and suggestive of lean on 倚. 動 ride
騎車 qíchē 動 ride a bicycle or motorcycle
騎馬 qímǎ 動 ride a horse
騎士 qíshì 名 knight

崎 26 qí Mountain 山 inducing wonder 奇 (phonetic). 形 rugged
崎嶇 qíqū 形 rugged, bumpy

畸 27 jī Fields 田 oddly-shaped 奇 (phonetic). 形 irregular fields
畸戀 jīliàn 名 incestuous relationship
畸形 jīxíng 形 abnormal, unbalanced: 畸形發展 abnormal development

寄 28 jì Roof 宀 with 奇 phonetic. 動 consign 動 mail, send ⇨ 郵寄 yóujì
寄給 jìgěi 動 mail to
寄生 jìshēng 動 be parasitic: 寄生蟲 parasite
寄宿 jìsù 動 board, lodge
寄託 jìtuō 動 consign
寄望 jìwàng 動 place hope in
寄信 jìxìn 動 mail a letter

倚 29 yǐ Person 人 with 奇 phonetic. 動 lean on ⇨ 不偏不倚 bùpiānbùyǐ

倚賴 yǐlài 動 depend on, rely on
倚重 yǐzhòng 動 entrust

椅 30 yǐ Tree 木 that is strange 奇 (phonetic). 名 idesia 名 chair
椅子 yǐzi 名 chair

叵 31 pǒ Can 可 reversed. 形 unable
叵測 pǒcè 形 unpredictable

于 32 yú Breath 𠂉 (altered, though original form reappears in some derivatives) spreading 一. 動 exhale 介 at, to 名 a surname

宇 33 yǔ Roof 宀 spreading 于 (phonetic). 名 eaves 名 roof ⇨ 廟宇 miàoyǔ
宇宙 yǔzhòu 名 universe

芋 34 yù Plant 艸 with 于 phonetic. 名 taro ⇨ 洋芋片
芋頭 yùtou 名 taro

迂 35 yū Movement 辵 with 于 phonetic. 動 close in 動 detour
迂腐 yūfǔ 形 trite
迂迴 yūhúi 形 circuitous

汙 36 [污汙] wū Water 水 with 于 phonetic. Variant of 污.

污 37 wū Water 水 with 于 phonetic. 名 filth ⇨ 玷污 diànwū, 貪污 tānwū
污點 wūdiǎn 名 stain, spot
污垢 wūgòu 名 dirt, filth
污衊 wūmiè 動 slander
污泥 wūní 名 mud
污染 wūrǎn 名 pollution 動 pollute
污辱 wūrù 動 insult, humiliate, dishonor

污水 wūshuǐ 名 sewage
污濁 wūzhuó 形 muddy, dirty

夸 38 kuā Large 大 and exhale 于. 動 boast (⇨ 誇)

誇 39 [夸] kuā Speak 言 boastfully 夸 (phonetic). 動 boast, brag ⇨ 自誇 zìkuā
誇大 kuādà 動 exaggerate
誇獎 kuājiǎng 動 praise
誇耀 kuāyào 動 flaunt, show off
誇張 kuāzhāng 動 exaggerate: 你太誇張了! Stop exaggerating!

垮 40 kuā Boasts 夸 (phonetic) come down to earth 土. 動 collapse
垮台 kuǎtái 動 collapse

胯 41 kuà Flesh 肉 with 夸 phonetic. 名 hip
胯骨 kuàgǔ 名 hipbone

跨 42 kuà Feet 足 and boast 夸 (phonetic). 動 stride
跨越 kuàyuè 動 leap over, stride across

粤 43 yuè [粵] Exhale 于 and examine 釆 (ancient variant). 形 cautious 助 a particle 名 Guangdong Province

平 44 píng Exhalation 于 separating 八. 形 even, level, flat 形 peaceful 動 pacify ⇨ 水平 shuǐpíng, 北平 Běipíng, 公平 gōngpíng, 太平 tàipíng, 地平線 dìpíngxiàn, 生平 shēngpíng, 和平 hépíng
平安 píngān 形 peaceful, safe
平常 píngcháng 形 common
平等 píngděng 形 equal
平定 píngdìng 動 stabilize
平凡 píngfán 形 ordinary
平反 píngfǎn 動 reverse a sentence, rehabilitate, redress

字譜及字典

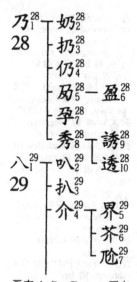

乃²⁸₁
28
奶²⁸₂
扔²⁸₃
仍²⁸₄
及²⁸₅ — 盈²⁸₆
孕²⁸₇
秀²⁸₈ — 誘²⁸₉
— 透²⁸₁₀
八²⁹₁ — 叭²⁹₂
29
扒²⁹₃
介²⁹₄ — 界²⁹₅
— 芥²⁹₆
— 尬²⁹₇

平方 píngfāng 🔲 square: 平方公尺 🔲 square meter; 平方米 🔲 square meter
平衡 pínghéng 🔲 equilibrium, balance
平静 píngjìng 🔲 tranquil
平劇 píngjù 🔲 🔲 Peking opera
平均 píngjūn 🔲 average, mean: 平均收入 average income
平民 píngmín 🔲 common people, civilians
平平 píngpíng 🔲 so-so, mediocre
平壤 píngrǎng 🔲 Pyongyang - capital of North Korea
平日 píngrì 🔲 usually
平時 píngshí 🔲 usually
平坦 píngtǎn 🔲 flat, level, smooth
平穩 píngwěn 🔲 steady, stable, smooth
平息 píngxī 🔲 calm down, subside 🔲 quell, suppress
平原 píngyuán 🔲 plain: 華北平原 North China plain

砰²⁷ pēng
45 Stone 石⁹ with 平⁵⁸ phonetic. 🔲 bang

抨²⁷ pēng
46 Hand 手⁹ with 平⁵⁸ phonetic. 🔲 criticize
抨擊 pēngjī 🔲 attack, criticize

坪²⁷ píng
47 Ground 土⁹ even 平⁵⁸ (phonetic). 🔲 flat ground 🔲 🔲 six feet square ⇔ 草坪⁷⁸

評²⁷ píng
48 [评] Words 言⁸⁸ that are fair and even 平⁵⁸ (phonetic). 🔲 critique, judge ⇔ 批評⁴², 議評⁸³
評分 píngfēn 🔲 judge, mark
評估 pínggū 🔲 assess, judge
評價 píngjià 🔲 evaluate, appraise 🔲 appraisal
評論 pínglùn 🔲 comment, review 🔲 commentary
評判 píngpàn 🔲 judge (a contest), critique

評審 píngshěn 🔲 judge, evaluate
評議 píngyì 🔲 arbitrate
評語 píngyǔ 🔲 comment, remark

秤²⁷ chèng
49 Grain 禾⁰⁸ measured evenly 平⁵⁸ (phonetic). 🔲 scale, balance

乎²⁷ hū
50 Pause 兮³⁷ (altered) with top mark suggesting rising. exhale. Now 呼⁵¹ exclamatory particle ⇔ 合乎⁵⁸, 似乎⁸⁷, 幾乎⁷⁷, 在乎⁵⁴

呼²⁷ hū
51 Mouth 口⁰⁹ exhaling 乎⁵⁰ (phonetic). 🔲 exhale 🔲 call, shout ⇔ 招呼⁴³, 傳呼²⁰, 歡呼¹⁰², 稱呼⁷⁵
呼喚 hūhuàn 🔲 call, shout to
呼叫 hūjiào 🔲 call, shout to: 呼叫器 beeper, pager
呼聲 hūshēng 🔲 shouts, cries
呼吸 hūxī 🔲 breathe
呼嘯 hūxiào 🔲 roar, scream
呼應 hūyìng 🔲 work in concert
呼籲 hūyù 🔲 appeal for, call for

乃²⁸ nǎi
1 Pictograph of air exhaled in a sigh. 🔲 difficulty 🔲 is 🔲 hence, therefore, consequently
乃是 nǎishì 🔲 but 🔲 is
乃至 nǎizhì 🔲 and even, even to the point that

奶²⁸ nǎi
2 Women 女⁹⁴ with 乃²⁸ phonetic. 🔲 breasts ⇔ 酸奶⁵⁵, 牛奶⁹⁷, 餵奶¹⁴⁰
奶茶 nǎichá 🔲 milk tea
奶房 nǎifáng 🔲 breasts
奶粉 nǎifěn 🔲 powdered milk
奶酪 nǎilào 🔲 cheese
奶媽 nǎimā 🔲 nursemaid
奶奶 nǎinai 🔲 grandma
奶頭 nǎitou 🔲 nipple
奶油 nǎiyóu 🔲 butter

奶子 nǎizi 图 圈 breasts

扔 3 rēng [28]
Hand 手 and difficulty 乃 (phonetic). 图 throw 图 discard ⇔ 亂扔罗
扔掉 rēngdiào 图 throw away, discard

仍 4 réng [28]
Person 人 persevering through difficulty 乃 (phonetic). 图 in accord with 图 still
仍舊 réngjiù 图 as usual, still
仍然 réngrán 图 still
仍是 réngshì 图 still is

及 5 gǔ [28]
Overcome 人 difficulty 乃. 图 augment

盈 6 yíng [28]
Add to 及 vessel 皿. 图 become full ⇔ 輕盈
盈虧 yíngkuī 图 profit and loss
盈利 yínglì 图 earnings, profit
盈餘 yíngyú 图 surplus

孕 7 yùn [28]
Child 子 consequently 乃. 图 pregnant 避孕, 懷孕
孕婦 yùnfù 图 pregnant woman
孕育 yùnyù 图 nurture, breed

秀 8 xiù [28]
Stalk 禾 struggling 乃 from weight of abundant grain. 图 form ears of grain 图 outstanding, excellent 图 elegant, graceful 图 show, show off ⇔ 作秀, 娟秀, 優秀
秀麗 xiùlì 图 elegant, graceful
秀美 xiùměi 图 elegant, graceful

誘 9 [诱] yòu [28]
[诱] Excellent 秀 (phonetic) words 言. 图 guide, teach 图 entice, lure 引誘
誘導 yòudǎo 图 induce, guide
誘惑 yòuhuò 图 tempt, lure

誘因 yòuyīn 图 圈 incentive, inducement

透 10 tòu [28]
Movement 辶 with 秀 phonetic. 图 penetrate 图 thoroughly, quite ⇔ 浸透, 滲透, 穿透, 看透
透徹 tòuchè 图 penetrating, in-depth 图 clear, lucid
透過 tòuguò 图 by way of, via
透露 tòulù 图 reveal, divulge
透明 tòumíng 图 transparent: 透明度 transparency
透視 tòushì 图 see through

八 1 bā [29]
Ideograph representing division. 图 separate ⇔ eight ⇔ 五花八門, 三八, 王八, 半斤八兩, 亂七八糟
八股 bāgǔ 图 hackneyed, formulaic (writing)
八卦 bāguà 图 the Eight Diagrams - an ancient divination system
八戒 bājiè 图 eight prohibitions in Buddhism

叭 2 bā [29]
Mouth 口 with 八 phonetic. 图 trumpet ⇔ 喇叭

扒 3 pá bā [29]
Hand 手 acting to separate 八 (phonetic). pá: 图 gather bā: 图 strip
扒竊 páqiè 图 pickpocket
扒手 páshǒu 图 pickpocket

介 4 jiè [29]
Divisions 八 between people 人. 图 between ⇔ 媒介, 仲介, 簡介
介詞 jiècí 图 preposition
介入 jièrù 图 get involved
介紹 jièshào 图 introduce 图 introduction: 介紹信 letter of introduction 图 explain, brief 图 recommend

介意 jièyì 图 mind, heed: 不介意 don't mind

界 5 jiè [29]
Fields 田 divided 介 (phonetic). 图 boundary 图 world, realm ⇔ 世界, 境界, 外界, 政界, 疆界, 租界, 邊界
界線 jièxiàn 图 boundary, borderline

芥 6 jiè [29]
Plant 艸 with 介 phonetic. 图 mustard plant
芥菜 jiècài 图 mustard plant
芥蒂 jièdì 图 grudge
芥末 jièmò 图 mustard

尬 7 gà [29]
[尬] Walk unevenly 尢 with 介 phonetic. ⇔ 尷尬

小 8 xiǎo [29]
Line 丨 dividing 八. 图 small ⇔ 渺小, 大小, 國小, 縮小, 頭小利, 微小, 細小
小便 xiǎobiàn 图 urine 图 urinate
小吃 xiǎochī 图 snack
小蟲 xiǎochóng 图 bug
小丑 xiǎochǒu 图 clown
小弟 xiǎodì 图 brother (younger)
小販 xiǎofàn 图 peddler
小費 xiǎofèi 图 tip, gratuity
小孩 xiǎohái 图 child
小孩兒 xiǎoháier 图 child
小孩子 xiǎoháizi 图 child
小伙子 xiǎohuǒzi 图 lad
小雞 xiǎojī 图 chick
小腳 xiǎojiǎo 图 bound feet: 綁小腳 bind feet
小姐 xiǎojiě 图 图 Miss, Ms. 图 young woman
小看 xiǎokàn 图 belittle
小康 xiǎokāng 图 middle-class
小麥 xiǎomài 图 wheat
小米 xiǎomǐ 图 millet
小氣 xiǎoqì 图 stingy
小覷 xiǎoqù 图 ignore
小人 xiǎorén 图 low-class person

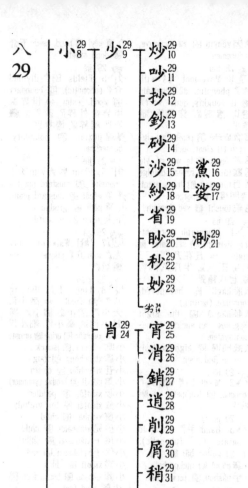

少 29 shǎo shào
9 Take away ノ亅 from what is already small 小²⁹ (phonetic). shǎo: 形 few, little 動 missing, short shào: 形 young ⇔ 不少²⁹, 凶多吉少²⁹, 稀少²⁹, 年少²⁹, 缺少²⁹, 減少²⁹, 青少年²⁹, 多少²⁷, 鮮少¹²⁷, 至少¹²⁸

少婦 shàofù 图 young wife
少見 shǎojiàn 形 rare
少來 shǎolái 成 ⊟ "Cut it out!", "Give me a break!"
少林寺 shàolínsì 圐 Shaolin temple - a Buddhist temple in Henan Province
少年 shàonián 图 youth, juvenile: 少年犯罪 juvenile delinquency
少女 shàonǚ 图 young girl
少數 shǎoshù 图 minority: 少數民族 minority peoples
少校 shàoxiào 图 major

炒 29 chǎo
10 Modern form shows fire 火⁸² with 少²⁹ phonetic. 動 stir-fry, fry, saute
炒蛋 chǎodàn 图 scrambled egg
炒飯 chǎofàn 图 fried rice
炒賣 chǎomài 動 buy and sell, speculate
炒麵 chǎomiàn 图 chow mein, fried noodles

吵 29 chǎo
11 Mouth 口¹⁶ with 少²⁹ phonetic. 動 quarrel 形 noisy ⇔ 爭吵³⁷
吵架 chǎojià 動 quarrel, brawl
吵鬧 chǎonào 動 quarrel loudly, brawl
吵嚷 chǎorǎng 動 quarrel

抄 29 chǎo
12 Hand 手⁷ and a few 少²⁹ (phonetic). 動 seize 動 plagiarize, transcribe
抄襲 chāoxí 動 plagiarize
抄寫 chāoxiě 動 transcribe

形 mean person
小時 xiǎoshí 图 hour
小事 xiǎoshì 图 trivial matter
小時候 xiǎoshíhòu 图 childhood
小說 xiǎoshūo 图 novel: 小說家 novelist
小廝 xiǎosī 图 ⑪ servant, underling
小偷 xiǎotōu 图 petty thief

小心 xiǎoxīn 動 be careful
小型 xiǎoxíng 形 small-scale
小學 xiǎoxué 图 elementary school
小篆 xiǎozhuàn 图 an ancient calligraphy style
小子 xiǎozi 图 ⑪ boy
小組 xiǎozǔ 图 group

字譜及字典

鈔 29 chāo
[钞] Gold 金 with 少 phonetic. banknote ⇔ 現鈔, 偽鈔
鈔票 chāopiào banknote

砂 29 shā
Stones 石 with 少 phonetic. sand
砂石 shāshí gravel
砂糖 shātáng granular sugar

沙 29 shā
Visible when little 少 (phonetic) water 水. sand ⇔ 長沙
沙發 shāfā sofa
沙拉 shālā salad
沙龍 shālóng salon
沙漠 shāmò desert: 戈壁沙漠 Gobi Desert
沙鷗 shāōu sea gull
沙丘 shāqiū sand dune
沙灘 shātān beach
沙文 shāwén chauvinist
沙文主義 shāwénzhǔyì chauvinism
沙啞 shāyǎ hoarse
沙豬 shāzhū chauvinist pig
沙子 shāzi sand

鯊 29 shā
[鲨] Fish 魚 and sand 沙 (phonetic). shark
鯊魚 shāyú shark

娑 29 suō
Woman 女 shifting like sand 沙 (phonetic). dance ⇔ 婆娑

紗 29 shā
[纱] Few 少 (phonetic) threads 糸. gauze ⇔ 紡紗, 面紗
紗窗 shāchuāng screen window

省 29 shěng xǐng
Contract 少 eye 目 to see closely. shěng: examine, reflect on economize, save: 省時間 save time

omit, abridge province
xǐng: be conscious ⇔ 反省, 節省, 本省, 自省

省府 shěngfǔ provincial government
省會 shěnghuì provincial capital
省籍 shěngjí provincial citizenship
省略 shěnglüè abridge, omit
省錢 shěngqián save money economical
省事 shěngshì simplify matters, save trouble
省長 shěngzhǎng governor
省親 xǐngqīn visit parents
省悟 xǐngwù realize realization, awakening

眇 20 miǎo
Eye 目 made small 少 (phonetic). tiny, fine.

渺 29 miǎo
Water 水 with 眇 phonetic. infinitesimal vast, unbounded
渺茫 miǎománg dim: 前途渺茫 have a dim future
渺小 miǎoxiǎo negligible, paltry

秒 29 miǎo
Grain stalk's 禾 little 少 (phonetic) end. grain spike second
秒鐘 miǎozhōng second

妙 29 miào
Young 少 (phonetic) woman 女. wonderful subtle ⇔ 不妙, 巧妙, 奇妙, 玄妙, 莫名其妙, 美妙, 微妙, 奧妙

肖 29 xiào
Smaller 小 (phonetic) embodiment 肉. resemble (parents) ⇔ 不肖, 生肖
肖像 xiàoxiàng portrait

宵 25 Same 肖 (phonetic) darkness indoors 宀 and outdoors. evening ⇔ 元宵, 通宵
宵禁 xiāojìn curfew
宵夜 xiāoyè late-night snack

消 29 xiāo
Like 肖 (phonetic) water 水. vanish, disappear ⇔ 打消, 取消
消沈 xiāochén depressed, dispirited
消除 xiāochú eliminate
消毒 xiāodú disinfect
消防 xiāofáng fire fighting: 消防隊 fire department
消費 xiāofèi consume: 消費者 consumer consumption, expenditure: 高消費 expensive
消耗 xiāohào consume consumption
消化 xiāohuà digest
消極 xiāojí negative, passive
消弭 xiāomǐ stop, terminate
消滅 xiāomiè exterminate
消磨 xiāomó while away: 消磨時間 kill time
消遣 xiāoqiǎn diversion, pastime
消失 xiāoshī disappear
消逝 xiāoshì die away, fade away
消瘦 xiāoshòu become thin, waste away
消息 xiāoxí news, information: 消息封鎖 information blockade; 有沒有他的消息? Do you have any news of him?
消長 xiāozhǎng ups and downs, vicissitudes

銷 27 [销] Metal 金 with 肖 phonetic. melt sell, market ⇔ 傾銷, 直銷, 行銷, 滯銷, 撤銷, 吊

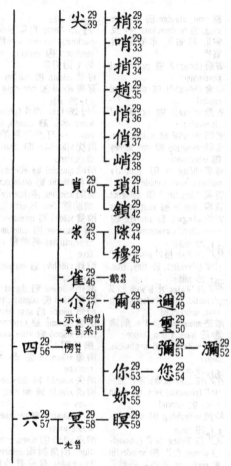

body 尸 with 肖 phonetic.
圖 crumb, flake ⇔ 瑣屑

稍 29 shāo
31 Grain stalk's 禾 smaller embodiment 肖 (phonetic). 古 stalk tip 圖 little, slight
稍候 shāohòu wait a moment: 請稍後 please wait a moment
稍微 shāowéi 圖 slightly: 稍微多一點 a little bit more

梢 29 shāo
32 Tree's 木 smaller embodiment 肖 (phonetic). 圖 tip of a branch, tip ⇔ 盯 椿梢, 樹梢

哨 29 shāo
33 Mouth 口 with 肖 phonetic. 圖 whistle ⇔ 崗 哨, 口哨

捎 29 shāo
34 Hand 手 with 肖 phonetic. 圖 take, carry

趙 29 zhào
35 [趙] Walk 走 with 肖 phonetic. 圖 a surname: 趙紫陽 Zhao Ziyang – a former premier of China

悄 29 qiāo 或 qiǎo
36 Heart 心 with 肖 phonetic. 圖 quiet
悄悄 qiāoqiāo 圖 silently, secretly
悄然 qiǎorán 圖 quietly

俏 29 qiào
37 Person 人 embodying 肖 (phonetic) ideal. 圖 pretty
俏麗 qiàolì 圖 pretty, attractive
俏皮 qiàopí 圖 sarcastic, witty: 俏皮話 witticism

峭 29 qiào
38 Mountain 山 with 肖 phonetic and suggestive of cutting 削. 圖 steep ⇔ 陡峭
峭壁 qiàobì 圖 cliffside

尖 29 jiān
39 From small 小 to big

銷路 xiāolù 圖 market demand 圖 marketing channels
銷售 xiāoshòu 圖 sell, market

逍 29 xiāo
28 Walk 辵 with 肖 phonetic. 圖 saunter
逍遙 xiāoyáo 圖 carefree

saunter

削 29 xiāo 或 xuè 亦 xuē
29 Knife 刀 with 肖 phonetic. 圖 pare, cut ⇔ 剝削
削價 xiāojià 圖 cut prices
削減 xiāojiǎn 圖 cut down, reduce

屑 29 xiè
30 Modern form shows

大尸. 𡕒 sharp, pointed
尖端 jiānduān 图 point
尖叫 jiānjiào 动 shriek
尖銳 jiānruì 图 sharp

貨 29 suǒ 40 Small 小尸 shells 貝[90]. 古 tinkle of shells

瑣 29 suǒ 41 [琐] Jade 玉[10] and small shells 貨 (phonetic). 古 tinkle of jade and shells 图 trifles
瑣事 suǒshì 图 trivial matters
瑣碎 suǒsuì 图 fragmentary
瑣屑 suǒxiè 图 trivial

鎖 29 suǒ 42 [锁] Metal 金 small object 貨 (phonetic). 图 动 lock ⇔ 枷鎖, 封鎖, 連鎖

㿱 29 xì 43 Small, small 小尸 ray of light 白. 古 crevice, crack (⇒ 隙)

隙 29 xì 44 Wall/hill 阜[167] crevice 㿱 (phonetic). 图 crevice, fissure 图 leisure ⇔ 縫隙, 空隙, 嫌隙
隙地 xìdì 图 vacant land

穆 29 mù 45 Grain 禾[10] and fine lines (variant of 㿱 with lines 彡 added in place of small 小). 图 rice paddy 图 peaceful ⇔ 肅穆
穆斯林 mùsīlín 图 Muslim

雀 29 què 46 Small 小尸 bird 隹[162]. 图 sparrow ⇔ 孔雀, 麻雀
雀斑 quèbān 图 freckles
雀躍 quèyuè 动 jump for joy

尒 29 ěr 47 Breath, represented by 丨, drawn in 入 and separated 八尸. 古 word 图 you (⇒ 爾).

爾 29 ěr 48 [尔] Lattice and cover 冖 with 尒 phonetic. 古 intricate lattice 图 you ⇔ 莞爾, 尼泊爾, 荷爾蒙, 達爾文, 哈爾濱, 威爾斯, 偶爾, 愛爾蘭, 維吾爾族
爾後 ěrhòu 图 thereafter, henceforth

邇 29 ěr 49 [迩] Walk 辵 with 爾 phonetic. 图 near 副 recently
邇來 ěrlái ⊗ recently

璽 29 xǐ 50 [玺] Jade 玉[10] with 爾 phonetic. 图 imperial seal ⇔ 國璽

彌 29 mí 51 [弥] Bow 弓[65] with 璽, abbreviated to 爾 phonetic. 动 fill, complete ⇔ 阿彌陀佛
彌補 míbǔ 动 make up, supplement
彌漫 mímàn 动 permeate

瀰 29 mí 52 [弥] Water 水 filling 彌 (phonetic). 动 overflowing
瀰漫 mímàn 动 brimming, overflowing 动 permeate

你 29 nǐ 53 Person 人[9] and you 尒. 图 you ⇔ 迷你
你好 nǐhǎo 嘆 hello
你們 nǐmen 图 you all

您 29 nín 54 You 你 (phonetic) from the heart 心[61]. 图 嘆 you

妳 29 nǐ 55 [你] Female 女[38] you 尒. 图 you (feminine form)
妳們 nǐmén 图 you all (feminine form)

四 29 sì 56 Pictograph of a square 口 divided 八尸 in parts. 图 four
四處 sìchù 副 everywhere
四川 sìchuān 图 Sichuan Province
四海 sìhǎi 图 the whole world
四合院 sìhéyuàn 图 quadrangle, courtyard (a style of residence in Northern China)
四季 sìjì 图 four seasons, all year
四面 sìmiàn 图 on all sides: 四面八方 all directions
四聲 sìshēng 图 the four tones of Mandarin
四書 sìshū 图 the Four Books - 大學, 中庸, 論語, 孟子 - classics of Confucianism
四下 sìxià 副 everywhere
四肢 sìzhī 图 arms and legs, limbs
四周 sìzhōu 图 on all sides, all around

六 29 liù 57 Even number entering 入 (altered) eight 八尸. 图 six
六書 liùshū 图 six forms of Chinese characters (⇒ 象形[172], 指事, 會議, 形聲, 轉注, 假借)

冥 29 míng 58 Moon waning in sixth 六 sun 日[76] of middle third of month, with 冂尸 phonetic. 图 dark, obscure 图 deep, profound
冥誕 míngdàn 图 birthday (of a deceased person)
冥頑 míngwán 图 obstinate
冥想 míngxiǎng 图 meditation
冥紙 míngzhǐ 图 paper money burnt as an offering to the dead

暝 29 míng 59 Eyes 目[14] dark 冥

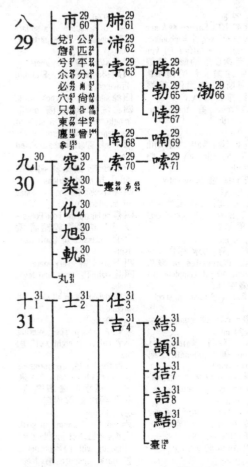

沛 29 pèi
62 Water 水29 and multiply
市 (phonetic). abundant
⇔ 充沛

孛 29 bèi
63 Multiplicity 市 (phonetic, abbreviated) of offspring
子. lush growth comet

脖 29 bó
64 Flesh 肉 with 孛
phonetic. neck
脖子 bózi neck

勃 29 bó
65 Strength 力 multiplying 孛 (phonetic). push
open suddenly ⇔ 蓬勃
勃勃 bóbó vigorous, flourishing
勃發 bófā begin suddenly
勃起 bóqǐ become erect
erection
勃然 bórán agitatedly

渤 29 bó
66 Water 水 with 勃
phonetic.
渤海 bóhǎi Bohai Sea

悖 29 bèi
67 Heart 心 multiplying 孛 (phonetic).
counter
悖理 bèilǐ irrational
悖謬 bèimìu absurd
悖逆 bèinì revolt, rebel

南 29 nán
68 Multiply 市 with
⼲ phonetic. south
雲南, 指南, 河南, 湖南, 越南, 江南, 台南, 東南, 閩南, 華南, 濟南
南部 nánbù southern part
南方 nánfāng south the South
南非 nánfēi South Africa
南極 nánjí South Pole: 南極洲 Antarctica
南京 nánjīng Nanking - former capital of Republic of

(phonetic). close the eyes
瞑目 míngmù die at peace

市 29 bèi
60 Pictograph of a plant sprouting and dividing 八 (phonetic). multiply (⇔ 市)

肺 29 fèi
61 Flesh 肉 that bifur-
cates 市 (phonetic). lung
肺病 fèibìng tuberculosis, consumption
肺腑 fèifǔ bottom of one's heart: 肺腑之言 words from the bottom of one's heart
肺癌 fèiyán,fèiái lung cancer
肺炎 fèiyán pneumonia
肺臟 fèizàng lung

China

南美 nánměi 🔲 South America: 南美洲 South American continent

南下 nánxià 🔲 go down south

喃 69 nán Mouth 口⁶⁹ with 南 phonetic. 🔲 mumble ⇔ 呢喃

喃喃 nánnán 🔲 mumble, mutter: 喃喃自語 mumble to oneself

索 70 suǒ Multiplicity 市 of threads 糸⁵³. 🔲 rope 🔲 demand, exact ⇔ 線索, 搜索, 勒索, 探索, 摸索, 繩索, 思索

索賠 suǒpéi 🔲 demand compensation

索取 suǒqǔ 🔲 extort, demand 🔲 extract

索性 suǒxìng 🔲 might as well

索引 suǒyǐn 🔲 index

嗦 71 suō Mouth 口⁶⁹ with 索 phonetic. 🔲 shiver ⇔ 哆嗦, 囉嗦

九 1 jiǔ Pictograph of a bent object, suggesting limit as approach ten 十. 🔲 nine 🔲 a large amount ⇔ 重九

九牛一毛 jiǔniúyìmáo 🔲 a drop in the ocean

究 2 jiù 🔲 🔲 jiū In a hole 穴⁶² to the limit 九 (phonetic). 🔲 limit, extreme 🔲 investigate thoroughly ⇔ 終究, 研究, 深究, 探究, 追究, 講究

究竟 jiùjìng 🔲 actually 🔲 after all, in the end: 究竟怎麼樣? So what finally happened?

染 3 rǎn Nine 九 dips into liquid 水 from a tree 木. 🔲 dye 🔲 contaminate ⇔ 渲染, 沾染, 污染, 感染, 傳染, 蠟染

染上 rǎnshàng 🔲 contract a disease 🔲 acquire a habit

仇 4 chóu Person 人¹⁰ with 九 phonetic. 🔲 hatred ⇔ 復仇, 報仇

仇敵 chóudí 🔲 enemy

仇恨 chóuhèn 🔲 hatred, enmity 🔲 hate

仇視 chóushì 🔲 view hostilely

旭 5 xù Sun 日⁷⁶ with 九 phonetic.

旭日 xùrì 🔲 morning sun: 旭日東昇 the sun rises in the East

軌 6 guǐ [軌] Cart 車⁵⁸ with 九 phonetic. 🔲 rail, track ⇔ 雙軌

軌道 guǐdào 🔲 orbit

軌跡 guǐjì 🔲 orbit

十 1 shí Ideograph indicating the four directions and the center. 🔲 complete 🔲 ten

十分 shífēn 🔲 very, completely

十全十美 shíquánshíměi 🔲 perfect in every way

十字 shízì 🔲 cross: 十字路口 crossroads, intersection

十足 shízú 🔲 completely

士 2 shì Person who knows all from one 一 to ten 十 (phonetic). 🔲 scholar, gentleman 🔲 noncommissioned officer 🔲 person ⇔ 人士, 院士, 爵士, 波士頓, 學士, 紳士, 碩士, 騎士, 義士, 女士, 博士, 壯士, 武士, 鬥士, 術士, 隱士, 烈士, 瑞士, 道士, 護士

士兵 shìbīng 🔲 soldiers

士大夫 shìdàifū 🔲 🔲 scholar-official

士林 shìlín 🔲 🔲 intelligentsia, literati

士氣 shìqì 🔲 morale: 鼓舞士氣 boost morale

仕 3 shì Person 人¹⁰ and scholar 士 (phonetic). 🔲 study 🔲 enter government service 🔲 official

仕宦 shìhuàn 🔲 enter government service

仕途 shìtú 🔲 official career, political career

吉 4 jí Words from scholar's 士 mouth 口⁶⁹. 🔲 good, auspicious, lucky ⇔ 凶多吉少

吉利 jílì 🔲 lucky, auspicious

吉林 jílín 🔲 Jilin Province

吉普 jípǔ 🔲 jeep

吉他 jítā 🔲 guitar

吉祥 jíxiáng 🔲 auspicious

吉兆 jízhào 🔲 auspicious sign, good omen

結 5 jié jiē [結] Thread 糸⁵³ with 吉 phonetic. jié: 🔲 tie 🔲 knot: 中國結 Chinese macrame 🔲 unite 🔲 congeal 🔲 settle 🔲 bear fruit jiē: 🔲 tough ⇔ 勾結, 凝結, 終結, 了結, 團結, 凍結, 締結, 巴結, 癥結, 總結, 連結

結構 jiégòu 🔲 structure

結果 jiéguǒ 🔲 result, fruits, outcome

結合 jiéhé 🔲 join, integrate

結婚 jiéhūn 🔲 get married

結交 jiéjiāo 🔲 befriend

結晶 jiéjīng 🔲 crystallize

結局 jiéjú 🔲 outcome, ending

結論 jiélùn 🔲 conclusion

結實 jiēshí 🔲 sturdy, durable

結實 jiēshí 🔲 bear fruit

結識 jiéshì 🔲 get to know
結束 jiéshù 🔲 end, conclude

頡6 jié [颉] Head 頁 with 吉 phonetic. 🔲 straight neck ⇔ 倉頡

拮7 jié Hand 手 with 吉 phonetic. 🔲 work hard
拮据 jiéjū, jiéjù 🔲 hard up, short of money

詰8 jié [诘] Speak 言 with 吉 phonetic. 🔲 interrogate
詰問 jiéwèn 🔲 interrogate

黠9 xiá 🔲 xié Black 黑 with 吉 phonetic. 🔲 shrewd ⇔ 狡黠

寺10 sì Develops 之 (phonetic, now written variously as 士 or 土) laws 寸. 🔲 court 🔲 temple ⇔ 少林寺, 佛寺, 禪寺
寺廟 sìmiào 🔲 temple
寺院 sìyuàn 🔲 monastery

詩11 shī [诗] Words 言 with 寺 phonetic. 🔲 aspire 🔲

poetry, poem ⇔ 唐詩
詩歌 shīgē 🔲 verse, poetry
詩集 shījí 🔲 poetry anthology
詩經 shījīng 🔲 Book of Poetry - a Confucian classic
詩人 shīrén 🔲 poet
詩文 shīwén 🔲 literary works

時12 shí [时] Sun 日 with 寺 phonetic. 🔲 season 🔲 time 🔲 hour 🔲 o'clock 🔲 current ⇔ 一時, 不時, 瞬時, 比利時, 守時, 及時, 彼時, 隨時, 有時, 屆時, 同時, 何時, 平時, 小時, 小時候, 古時, 零時, 按時, 幾時, 當時, 頓時, 臨時, 定時, 暫時, 歷時, 過時, 準時
時差 shíchā 🔲 time difference, time lag
時常 shícháng 🔲 often, frequently
時辰 shíchén 🔲 traditional Chinese hour equaling two modern "small" hours (小時)
時代 shídài 🔲 time, era, period: 中古時代 Middle Ages; 日據時代 Japanese Occupation Period
時光 shíguāng 🔲 time
時候 shíhòu 🔲 time: 到時候 when the time comes, at that time; 有時候 sometimes
時機 shíjī 🔲 opportune moment
時間 shíjiān 🔲 time: 沒有時間 have no time; 趕時間 in a hurry
時刻 shíkè 🔲 time, moment: 時刻表 timetable, schedule
時髦 shímáo 🔲 fashionable
時期 shíqī 🔲 time, period
時時 shíshí 🔲 frequently, continually
時事 shíshì 🔲 current affairs
時勢 shíshì 🔲 contemporary

trends
時速 shísù 图 speed per hour
時鐘 shízhōng 图 clock
時裝 shízhuāng 图 fashionable clothing: 時裝展覽 fashion show

侍 31 shì
13 Person 人 at court 寺 (phonetic). 图 attendant 图 serve ⇔ 服侍
侍從 shìcóng 图 attendants
侍候 shìhòu 图 wait upon
侍女 shìnǚ 图 maid
侍衛 shìwèi 图 bodyguard
侍者 shìzhě 图 waiter

恃 31 shì
14 Heart 心 with court 寺 phonetic. 图 rely on, depend on

峙 31 zhì
15 Mountain 山 and temple 寺 (phonetic). 图 stand tall ⇔ 對峙

持 31 chí
16 Hand 手 with 寺 phonetic. 图 hold, grasp 图 support 图 manage ⇔ 主持, 挾持, 劫持, 支持, 保持, 僵持, 堅持, 維持
持家 chíjiā 图 manage the household
持久 chíjiǔ 图 lasting
持續 chíxù 图 sustain, continue
持有 chíyǒu 图 possess, hold

待 31 dài dāi
17 Small step 彳 and court 寺 dài. 图 wait, await 图 treat dāi: 图 stay: 待了一個禮拜 stayed a week ⇔ 亟待, 款待, 等待, 招待, 拭目以待, 期待, 接待, 虐待, 善待, 優待, 對待
待業 dàiyè 图 awaiting work, unemployed
待遇 dàiyù 图 treatment 图 salary and benefits

等 31 děng
18 Bamboo 竹 tablets arranged at court 寺 图 rank, class 图 equal, same 图 wait, await 图 etc. ⇔ 均等, 高等, 何等, 平等, 劣等, 職等, 頭等, 相等, 對等
等待 děngdài 图 wait for
等到 děngdào 图 wait until
等等 děngděng 图 wait 图 etc., and so on
等號 děnghào 图 equality sign
等候 děnghòu 图 wait for
等級 děngjí 图 grade
等式 děngshì 图 equation
等於 děngyú 图 equals
等著 děngzhe 图 wait for, await

特 31 tè
19 Ox 牛 sacrificed at temple 寺. 图 bull 图 special 图 specially: 特好 excellent ⇔ 希特勒, 奇特, 模特兒, 伏特, 瓦特, 獨特
特別 tèbié 图 special 图 specially
特產 tèchǎn 图 local specialty
特地 tèdì 图 specially
特點 tèdiǎn 图 characteristic, feature
特定 tèdìng 图 particular, specific
特區 tèqū 图 special district
特權 tèquán 图 privilege
特色 tèsè 图 special feature
特赦 tèshè 图 pardon, amnesty: 國際特赦組織 Amnesty International
特使 tèshǐ 图 special envoy
特殊 tèshū 图 special, exceptional
特務 tèwù 图 special service 图 secret agent: 特務活動 espionage
特性 tèxìng 图 special characteristic, peculiarity
特意 tèyì 图 especially, intentionally
特異 tèyì 图 exceptional, distinctive
特徵 tèzhēng 图 characteristic, special feature, trait
特質 tèzhí 图 characteristic

志 31 zhì
20 Develops 之 (phonetic, now written as 士) in the heart 心. 图 will 图 aspiration, ambition ⇔ 同志, 職志, 意志
志同道合 zhìtóngdàohé 图 of one mind
志向 zhìxiàng 图 ambition, aspiration
志願 zhìyuàn 图 ideal 图 volunteer: 志願者 a volunteer

誌 31 zhì
21 [志] Words 言 recording aspirations 志 (phonetic). 图 record ⇔ 標誌, 雜誌

直 31 zhí
22 [直] Ten 十 (phonetic) eyes 目 saw no concealment ∟. 图 straight, direct 图 vertical: 直著寫 write vertically ⇔ 一直, 挺直, 簡直, 正直, 耿直, 垂直
直到 zhídào 图 until, up to
直角 zhíjiǎo 图 right angle
直接 zhíjiē 图 direct 图 directly
直覺 zhíjué 图 intuition
直昇機 zhíshēngjī 图 helicopter
直轄 zhíxiá 图 under direct jurisdiction (of central government)
直線 zhíxiàn 图 straight line, direct line
直銷 zhíxiāo 图 market directly

值 31 zhí
23 [值] Person 人 and direct 直 (phonetic). 图 value 图 be worth: 不值 not worthwhile ⇔ 價值, 貶值, 升值, 產值, 淨

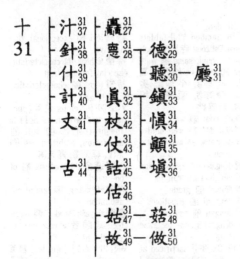

十
31

汁 31/37
針 31/38
什 31/39
計 31/40
丈 31/41
古 31/44

真 31/27
惪 31/28
真 31/32
杖 31/42
仗 31/43
話 31/45
估 31/46
姑 31/47 — 菇 31/48
故 31/49 — 做 31/50

德 31/29
聽 31/30 — 廳 31/31
鎮 31/33
慎 31/34
顛 31/35
填 31/36

値
値得 zhíde worthwhile, worthy: 值得嘉獎 worthy of commendation

殖 31/24 [殖] Bury/death 歹 with 直 phonetic. plant reproduce, propagate ⇔ 繁殖, 生殖, 養殖
殖民 zhímín colonize: 殖民地 colony; 殖民主義 colonialism

植 31/25 [植] Tree 木 with 直 phonetic. plant plants, vegetation ⇔ 培植, 扶植, 移植, 種植
植物 zhíwù plant, flora: 植物學 botany

置 31/26 [置] Net 网 (altered) with 直 phonetic. put place, 擱置, 設置, 處置, 位置, 佈置, 安置, 棄置, 裝置, 閒置, 放置, 購置
置疑 zhìyí doubt

真 27 [真] Straight 直 repeated. upright
真立 chùlì tower

惪 28 Straight 直 heart 心. moral

德 29 Moral 惪 (phonetic) steps 彳. virtue, righteousness ⇔ 功德, 品德, 賢德, 道德
德國 déguó Germany
德育 déyù moral education

聽 30 [听] Ear 耳 learning virtue 惪 with 壬 phonetic. tīng listen heed ⇔ 傾聽, 打聽, 聆聽, 探聽, 竊聽, 重聽, 旁聽, 視聽, 偏聽偏信, 偷聽
聽到 tīngdào hear
聽話 tīnghuà obey obedient
聽見 tīngjiàn hear
聽課 tīngkè audit a class attend a class

聽命 tīngmìng obey orders
聽說 tīngshuō hear reportedly: 聽說他生病了. It is said he is sick.
聽眾 tīngzhòng audience

廳 31 [厅] Shelter 广 for listening 聽 (phonetic). Simplified form uses 厂 and 丁. hall ⇔ 客廳, 歌廳, 大廳, 餐廳

真 32 [真] Transform 匕, eyes 目, hidden ∟ (together often written as 直), and pedestal 丌. spiritual conversion true truly, really ⇔ 逼真, 認真, 天真, 傳真, 當真, 純真, 清真, 果真, 寫真
真誠 zhēnchéng sincere
真空 zhēnkōng vacuum: 權力真空 power vacuum
真理 zhēnlǐ truth
真實 zhēnshí actual, real: 真實狀況 real situation
真是 zhēnshì (口) truly
真絲 zhēnsī silk
真相 zhēnxiàng true situation
真心 zhēnxīn sincere sincerely
真正 zhēnzhèng real, true
真摯 zhēnzhì sincere
真主 zhēnzhǔ Allah

鎮 33 [镇] Metal 金 with 真 phonetic. subdue, suppress township ⇔ 鄉鎮, 城鎮
鎮暴 zhènbào suppress riot control
鎮定 zhèndìng composed, calm
鎮靜 zhènjìng composed, calm
鎮壓 zhènyā suppress, repress

慎 31 shèn
34 [慎] Heart 心 true 眞 (phonetic). 形 scrupulous, cautious ⇔ 謹慎, 審慎
慎重 shènzhòng 形 cautious, prudent

顚 31 diān
35 [顛] Head 頁 with 眞 phonetic. 名 top 動 bump
顚簸 diānbǒ 動 bump, jolt
顚倒 diāndǎo 動 invert: 顚倒是非 confuse right and wrong; 顚三倒四 disorganized, incoherent
顚峰 diānfēng 名 summit, peak
顚覆 diānfù 動 overthrow, subvert: 顚覆活動 subversive activities

填 31 tián
36 [填] Make earth 土 true 眞 (phonetic). 動 fill
填補 tiánbǔ 動 fill up
填塞 tiánsài 動 fill up, clog
填寫 tiánxiě 動 fill out (a form)
填鴨 tiányā 動 force-feed ducks: 填鴨式的教育 force-feed students with knowledge for exams

汁 31 zhī
37 Water 水 with 十 phonetic. 名 juice ⇔ 果汁

針 31 zhēn
38 [针] Metal 金 with 十 suggestive of shape. 名 needle ⇔ 胸針, 指針, 打針, 方針
針對 zhēnduì 動 aimed at 因 regarding
針灸 zhēnjiǔ 名 acupuncture

什 31 shí 蛇 shé 什 shén
39 Men 人 in group of ten 十 (phonetic). shí: 名 squad 形 sundry shé: 代 what ⇔ 爲什麼
什麼 shéme 代 what: 什麼樣的 what kind of
什錦 shíjǐn 形 assorted, mixed (ingredients in a dish)

計 31 jì
40 [计] Say 言 numbers to ten 十. 動 count, calculate 名 plan, scheme ⇔ 詭計, 估計, 設計, 狡計, 統計, 生計, 預計, 會計, 算計, 家計
計程車 jìchéngchē 名 taxi
計畫 jìhuà 名 動 plan
計劃 jìhuà 名 動 plan: 計劃經濟 planned economy
計較 jìjiào 動 haggle, dispute mind, care
計量 jìliàng 動 measure, calculate
計算 jìsuàn 動 calculate: 計算機 名 calculator 俗 computer; 計算器 名 calculator

丈 31 zhàng
41 Ten 十 held up by hand 又 (altered). 名 ten feet 名 elder ⇔ 師丈
丈夫 zhàngfū 名 husband

杖 31 zhàng
42 Wood 木 ten-feet 丈 (phonetic) long. 名 staff, cane ⇔ 拐杖

仗 31 zhàng
43 Person 人 with 丈 phonetic and suggesting cane 杖. 名 weaponry 名 battle, war ⇔ 仰仗, 打仗

古 31 gǔ
44 Retold through ten 十 mouths 口. 形 ancient 因 a surname ⇔ 考古學, 盤古, 蒙古
古巴 gǔbā 名 Cuba
古代 gǔdài 名 ancient times
古典 gǔdiǎn 形 classical: 古典音樂 classical music; 古典文學 classical literature
古董 gǔdǒng 名 antique
古怪 gǔguài 形 peculiar, eccentric
古跡 gǔjī 名 relics
古蹟 gǔjī 名 relics

古籍 gǔjí 名 ancient books
古老 gǔlǎo 形 ancient
古人 gǔrén 名 ancients
古時 gǔshí 名 ancient times
古玩 gǔwàn 名 curio, antique
古雅 gǔyǎ 形 quaint

詁 31 gǔ
45 [诂] Words 言 explaining the ancient 古 (phonetic) classics. 名 annotation ⇔ 訓詁

估 31 gū
46 Person 人 with 古 phonetic. 動 estimate, appraise ⇔ 高估, 評估, 低估, 預估
估計 gūjì 動 estimate
估價 gūjià 動 appraise 名 price estimate
估量 gūliàng 動 estimate
估算 gūsuàn 動 estimate 名 estimation

姑 31 gū
47 Woman 女 and ancient 古 (phonetic). 名 mother-in-law (husband's mother) 名 aunt (father's sister) 名 sister-in-law (husband's sister) 名 nun ⇔ 尼姑
姑姑 gūgu 名 aunt (father's sister)
姑媽 gūmā 名 aunt (father's sister)
姑娘 gūniáng 名 girl 俗 Miss
姑息 gūxí 動 indulge, appease

菇 31 gū
48 Plant 艸 with 姑 phonetic. 名 mushroom 蘑菇, 香菇

故 31 gù
49 Past 古 (phonetic) strike 攵. 名 cause, reason 因 former, previous ⇔ 原故, 亡故, 何故, 緣故, 事故
故此 gùcǐ 連 therefore, for this reason
故宮 gùgōng 名 former palace:

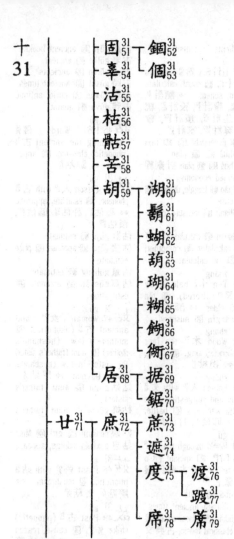

十
31

固 31/51 ─ 鋼 31/52
辜 31/54 ─ 個 31/53
沽 31/55
枯 31/56
骷 31/57
苦 31/58
胡 31/59 ┬ 湖 31/60
　　　　├ 鬍 31/61
　　　　├ 蝴 31/62
　　　　├ 葫 31/63
　　　　├ 瑚 31/64
　　　　├ 糊 31/65
　　　　├ 餬 31/66
　　　　└ 衚 31/67
居 31/68 ┬ 据 31/69
　　　　 └ 鋸 31/70
廿 31/71 ┬ 庶 31/72 ┬ 蔗 31/73
　　　　　　　　　　├ 遮 31/74
　　　　　　　　　　├ 度 31/75 ┬ 渡 31/76
　　　　　　　　　　│　　　　　 └ 踱 31/77
　　　　　　　　　　└ 席 31/78 ─ 蓆 31/79

當做⁵⁰

做愛 zuòài 🈲 make love

做成 zuòchéng 🈲 complete, accomplish

做錯 zuòcuò 🈲 err

做法 zuòfǎ 🈲 way, method

做工 zuògōng 🈲 do manual work

做官 zuòguān 🈲 serve as a public official

做好 zuòhǎo 🈲 finish, complete

做夢 zuòmèng 🈲 dream

做人 zuòrén 🈲 behave, conduct oneself: 他做人很好. He conducts himself well.

做事 zuòshì 🈲 work

做完 zuòwán 🈲 finish, complete

做作 zuòzuò 🈲 affected, pretentious

固 31/51 gù Ancient 古古 (phonetic) enclosure 口口. 🈲 walls, ramparts 🈲 sturdy, solid ⇔ 頑固, 根深蒂固, 膽固醇, 鞏固, 牢固, 穩固, 堅固

固定 gùdìng 🈲 fixed, regular 🈲 fix, set

固然 gùrán 🈲 assuredly, no doubt

固執 gùzhí 🈲 stubborn

鋼 31/52 gù [钢] Metal 金 and sturdy 固 (phonetic). 🈲 imprison ⇔ 禁錮

個 31/53 gè [个] Person 人 with 固 phonetic. Simplified form is ancient form 个. 🈲 a, one ⇔ 一個, 各個, 這個, 整個, 那個, 哪個

個別 gèbié 🈲 individual

個個 gègè 🈲 each, all

個人 gèrén 🈲 individual, personal: 個人電腦 personal computer; 個人主義 individualism

個體 gètǐ 🈲 individual: 🈲 個

故宮博物館 National Palace Museum

故事 gùshì 🈲 story

故鄉 gùxiāng 🈲 hometown

故意 gùyì 🈲 intentionally

故障 gùzhàng 🈲 breakdown, failure

做 31/50 zuò Person 人 and cause 故. 🈲 do, make ⇔ 叫做,

體戶 household operating a private business

個性 gèxìng 图 character, personality

個子 gèzi 图 stature, height: 他的個子很高. He is tall.

辜 31 gū
54 Suffer 辛^罪 under past 古^古 (phonetic). 图 sin 图 a surname ⇔ 無辜^冤

辜負 gūfù 图 be unworthy, disappoint

沽 31 gū
55 Water 水^水 with 古^古 phonetic. 動 buy

沽售 gūshòu 動 buy and sell

枯 31 kū
56 Tree 木^木 that is ancient 古^古 (phonetic). 形 withered ⇔ 乾枯^乾

枯竭 kūjié 形 withered, dried up

枯萎 kūwěi 動 wither away

枯燥 kūzào 形 dry 形 boring, dull

骷 31 kū
57 [骷] Bones 骨¹³³ and old 古^古 (phonetic). 图 skeletal remains

骷髏 kūlóu 图 skeleton: 骷髏頭 skull

苦 31 kǔ
58 Plant 艸^艸 with 古^古 phonetic. 形 bitter 图 pain, suffering 副 painstakingly ⇔ 刻苦^刻, 艱苦^艱, 貧苦^貧, 辛苦^辛, 痛苦^痛, 吃苦^吃, 受苦^受

苦力 kǔlì 图 hard work

苦悶 kǔmèn 形 depressed

苦難 kǔnàn 图 suffering, hardship

苦惱 kǔnǎo 形 vexed, distressed

苦澀 kǔsè 形 bitter, anguished

苦痛 kǔtòng 图 pain, suffering

胡 31 hú
59 Meat 肉¹³² with 古^古 phonetic. 名 ox jowl 图 barbarians to the north and west

in ancient times 图 a surname: 胡耀邦 Hu Yaobang – a former premier of China ⇔ 二胡^二

胡椒 hújiāo 图 black pepper

胡來 húlái 動 bungle

胡亂 húluàn 形 confused

胡說 húshuō 動 talk nonsense: 胡說八道 nonsensical 图 nonsense, drivel

湖 31 hú
60 Water 水^水 with 胡^胡 phonetic. ⇔ 太湖^太, 江湖^江, 澎湖^澎

湖北 húběi 图 Hubei Province

湖泊 húbó 图 lakes

湖南 húnán 图 Hunan Province

鬍 31 hú
61 [胡] Long hair 髟^髟 on jowl 胡^胡 (phonetic). 图 beard ⇔ 刮鬍子^刮

鬍子 húzi 图 beard

蝴 31 hú
62 Insect 虫¹²⁵ with 胡^胡 phonetic. 图 butterfly

蝴蝶 húdié 图 butterfly

葫 31 hú
63 Plant 艸^艸 from barbarian 胡^胡 (phonetic) lands. 图 gourd

葫蘆 húlú 图 gourd

瑚 31 hú
64 Jade 玉¹⁰⁷ with 胡^胡 phonetic. 图 coral ⇔ 珊瑚¹⁵

糊 31 hú
65 Modern form shows rice 米¹³⁸ with 胡^胡 phonetic. 動 paste 形 blurred ⇔ 一塌糊塗^一, 含糊^含, 糨糊^糨, 模糊^模, 迷糊¹³⁸

糊塗 hútú 形 careless, confused

餬 31 hú
66 [糊] Food 食^食 with 胡^胡 phonetic. 图 porridge, gruel

餬口 húkǒu 動 eke out a living

衚 31 hú
67 Go 行^行 with 胡^胡

phonetic. 图 lane, alley

衚衕 hútòng 图 lane, alley

居 31 jū
68 Lower body 尸^尸 with 古^古 phonetic. 動 live, reside ⇔ 鄰居^鄰, 遷居^遷, 同居^同, 移居^移

居留 jūliú 動 reside: 居留證 residence permit

居民 jūmín 图 resident

居然 jūrán 副 unexpectedly

居住 jūzhù 動 live

据 31 jū
69 Hand 手^手 with 居^居 phonetic. 图 sore joints in the hand ⇔ 拮据^拮

鋸 31 jù
70 [锯] Metal 金^金 with 居^居 phonetic. 動 图 saw

廿 31 niàn
71 Ten 十^十 doubled. 数 twenty

庶 31 shù
72 Bright fire (ancient character from twenty 廿^廿 and fire 火⁸²) under shelter 广⁶⁰. 图 commoners

庶民 shùmín 图 commoners

蔗 31 zhè
73 Common 庶^庶 (phonetic) plant 艸^艸. 图 sugarcane ⇔ 甘蔗^甘

蔗糖 zhètáng 图 cane sugar

遮 31 zhē
74 Move 辵^辵 among the dense crowd 庶^庶. 動 block 動 hide, conceal

遮蔽 zhēbì 動 screen, shield, hide

遮蓋 zhēgài 動 cover up

遮羞 zhēxiū 動 hide embarrassment, hush up scandal: 遮羞費 hush money

遮掩 zhēyǎn 動 cover up

度 31 dù
75 Right hand 又^又 and commoners 庶^庶 (abbreviated). 名 legal system 動 measure 图 degree 图 times

字譜及字典

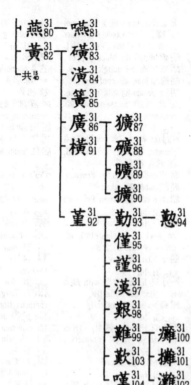

席 31 xí
79 [席蓆] Grass 艸 mat 席 (phonetic). 图 straw mat ⇔ 涼蓆, 竹蓆
席子 xízi 图 straw mat

燕 31 yàn yān
80 Pictograph of a swallow. yàn: 图 swallow yān: 图 an ancient kingdom in China
燕窩 yànwō 图 swallow's nest - a Chinese delicacy
燕子 yànzi 图 swallow

嚥 31 yàn
81 [咽] Use mouth 口 like a swallow 燕 (phonetic). 图 swallow

黃 31 huáng
82 [黄] Bright 光 (ancient form from twenty 廿 fires 火) color of fields 田. 图 yellow, yellow-brown 图 a surname
黃帝 huángdì 囚 Yellow Emperor - legendary founder of China
黃豆 huángdòu 图 soybean
黃瓜 huángguā 图 cucumber
黃河 huánghé 图 Yellow River
黃花 huánghuā 图 chrysanthemum
黃昏 huánghūn 图 dusk
黃金 huángjīn 图 gold
黃牛 huángniú 图 ox 图 ticket scalper: 黃牛票 scalped tickets 图 break a promise
黃色 huángsè 图 yellow 图 obscene, pornographic
黃銅 huángtóng 图 brass
黃油 huángyóu 图 butter
黃魚 huángyú 图 yellow croaker
黃種人 huángzhǒngrén 图 East Asian

磺 31 huáng
83 [磺] Stone 石 and yellow 黃 (phonetic). 图 sulfur ⇔ 硫磺

潢 31 huáng
84 [潢] Water 水 with 黃 phonetic. 图 reservoir

图 pass, spend ⇔ 一度, 極度, 經度, 年度, 緯度, 限度, 坡度, 長度, 高度, 厚度, 幅度, 印度, 尺度, 斜度, 密度, 季度, 深度, 強度, 溫度, 調度, 程度, 制度, 適度, 速度, 寬度, 態度, 過度, 首度, 角度, 濕度, 再度
度假 dùjià 图 holiday

渡 31 dù
76 Water 水 and measure 度 (phonetic). 图 ford, cross ⇔ 引渡, 偷渡, 過渡

踱 31 duò duó
77 Foot 足 and pass 度 (phonetic) 图 stroll, pace

席 31 xí
78 Cloth 巾 that crowd 庶 (abbreviated) sits on. 图 mat 图 seat ⇔ 主席, 缺席, 草席, 筵席, 出席, 酒席
席捲 xíjuǎn 图 roll across, engulf
席位 xíwèi 图 seats (in an elected assembly)

⇔ 裝潢⁵¹

簧 85 [簧] huáng Bamboo 竹⁷¹ with 黃⁸⁵ phonetic. 图 reed (of a musical instrument) ⇔ 彈簧¹³⁶

廣 86 [广] guǎng Open-sided room 广⁶⁰ with 黃⁸⁵ phonetic. (古) large room 图 wide, broad, extensive 动 broaden ⇔ 寬廣¹¹², 推廣⁸²
廣播 guǎngbō 图 broadcast
廣場 guǎngchǎng 图 public square
廣大 guǎngdà 形 vast
廣島 guǎngdǎo 图 Hiroshima
廣東 guǎngdōng 图 Guangdong Province: 廣東話 Cantonese
廣泛 guǎngfàn 形 extensive: 興趣廣泛 wide-ranging interests
廣告 guǎnggào 图 advertisement: 登廣告 advertise
廣闊 guǎngkuò 形 vast
廣西 guǎngxī 图 Guangxi Province
廣義 guǎngyì 图 broad sense
廣州 guǎngzhōu 图 Canton

獷 87 [犷] guǎng Dog 犬⁹¹ with 廣⁸⁶ phonetic. 形 fierce, uncivilized ⇔ 粗獷⁹⁷

礦 88 [矿] kuàng Stone 石⁵⁹ with 廣⁸⁶ phonetic. 图 ore ⇔ 煤礦⁸⁵, 採礦¹⁰²
礦藏 kuàngcáng 图 mineral resources
礦場 kuàngchǎng 图 mine
礦工 kuànggōng 图 miner
礦坑 kuàngkēng 图 mining pit
礦泉 kuàngquán 图 mineral springs: 礦泉水 mineral water

曠 89 [旷] kuàng Open 廣⁸⁶ (phonetic) under the sun 日⁷⁶. (古) bright 形 spacious, unoccupied

⇔ 空曠⁸⁹
曠野 kuàngyě 图 wilderness

擴 90 [扩] kuò Hand 手⁹⁷ broadening 廣⁸⁶. 动 enlarge, expand
擴充 kuòchōng 动 expand, enlarge
擴大 kuòdà 动 extend
擴散 kuòsàn 动 spread, diffuse
擴音 kuòyīn 动 amplify (sound): 擴音器 megaphone
擴展 kuòzhǎn 动 expand, extend
擴張 kuòzhāng 动 expand, spread

橫 91 [横] héng hèng Tree 木⁷⁷ in the yellow 黃⁸⁵ (phonetic) dirt. héng: 形 horizontal: 橫著寫 write horizontally 形 horizontal calligraphy stroke 副 boldly hèng: 形 unexpected 形 unreasonable ⇔ 縱橫⁹⁵, 蠻橫¹⁵³
橫濱 héngbīn 图 Yokohama
橫貫 héngguàn 动 traverse
橫豎 héngshù 副 regardless, anyway
橫軸 héngzhóu 图 horizontal axis

菫 92 [堇] qín Yellow 黃⁸⁵ (abbreviated) earth 土⁸⁰. 图 clay

勤 93 [勤] qín Clay 菫⁹² (phonetic) worked with strength 力⁴. 形 diligent 副 regularly ⇔ 殷勤⁴⁵, 通勤⁸²
勤奮 qínfèn 形 diligent, industrious
勤儉 qínjiǎn 形 diligent and thrifty
勤快 qínkuài 形 diligent, industrious
勤勞 qínláo 形 diligent, industrious
勤勉 qínmiǎn 形 diligent, industrious
勤務 qínwù 图 duty, service

懃 94 [勤] qín Diligent 勤⁹³ (phonetic) heart 心⁴³. 形 cordial ⇔ 慇懃⁴⁵

僅 95 [仅] jǐn Person 人¹⁰ with 菫⁹² phonetic. Simplified form uses 又¹⁴. 副 only ⇔ 不僅¹⁰
僅僅 jǐnjǐn 副 only

謹 96 [谨] jǐn Words 言⁹⁶ like fine clay 菫⁹² (phonetic). 形 cautious ⇔ 拘謹⁴⁵, 嚴謹¹³⁷
謹慎 jǐnshèn 形 cautious, prudent

漢 97 [汉] hàn Water 水³¹ with clay 菫⁹² (phonetic, altered). Simplified form uses 又¹⁴. Han River 图 Han Dynasty 图 the Han people 图 man, fellow ⇔ 大漢³⁷, 好漢⁹⁴, 醉漢⁹⁵
漢城 hànchéng 图 Seoul
漢化 hànhuà 动 sinicize
漢奸 hànjiān 图 traitor to China
漢人 hànrén 图 a Han person
漢學 hànxué 图 sinology: 漢學家 sinologist
漢英 hànyīng 形 Chinese-to-English: 漢英字典 Chinese-English dictionary
漢語 hànyǔ 图 (動) Chinese, Mandarin
漢字 hànzì 图 Chinese characters, kanji
漢族 hànzú 图 the Han people (⇔ 漢人⁹⁷)

艱 98 [艰] jiān Clay 菫⁹² (altered) unfriendly 艮⁴⁸ (phonetic) to cultivation. Simplified form uses 又¹⁴. 形 hard, difficult
艱鉅 jiānjù 形 arduous
艱苦 jiānkǔ 形 arduous
艱難 jiānnán 形 difficult
艱辛 jiānxīn 形 hardship

31

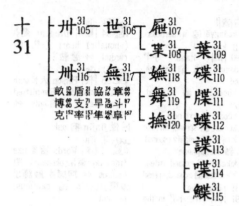

卅³¹₁₀₅ — 世³¹₁₀₆ — 屉³¹₁₀₇
　　　　　└ 枼³¹₁₀₈ — 葉³¹₁₀₉
└ 州³¹₁₁₆ — 無³¹₁₁₇ — 嫵³¹₁₁₈ — 碟³¹₁₁₀
　　　　　　　　　　舞³¹₁₁₉ — 牒³¹₁₁₁
　　　　　　　　　　撫³¹₁₂₀ — 蝶³¹₁₁₂
　　　　　　　　　　　　　　　謀³¹₁₁₃
　　　　　　　　　　　　　　　喋³¹₁₁₄
　　　　　　　　　　　　　　　鰈³¹₁₁₅

畝⁹⁹ 盾¹⁶ 協³⁴ 章⁶⁸
博⁸² 支⁴⁵ 早⁷⁶ 斗⁸⁷
克¹⁵² 率¹⁵³ 隼¹⁶² 阜¹⁶⁷

難³¹₉₉ nán nàn [难] Bird 隹¹⁶² like yellow clay 堇¹⁶² (phonetic, altered). Simplified form uses 又¹⁴. nán: 圈 a bird with golden wings 圈 difficult nàn: 圈 disaster ⇔ 災難, 苦難, 艱難, 刁難, 避難, 困難, 遇難, 受難, 患難¹⁵⁷, 罹難, 非難

難纏 nánchán 圈 hard to deal with

難道 nándào 圈 could it be (for rhetorical questions)

難得 nándé 圈 rare, difficult to come by

難怪 nánguài 圈 no wonder

難過 nánguò 圈 sad

難堪 nánkān 圈 embarrassed 圈 unbearable, intolerable

難看 nánkàn 圈 ugly

難免 nánmiǎn 圈 unavoidable

難民 nànmín 圈 refugee

難受 nánshòu 圈 feel bad, feel sorry 圈 feel sick

難說 nánshuō 圈 hard to say

難題 nántí 圈 dilemma

難以 nányǐ 圈 difficult to: 難以想像 difficult to imagine

癱³¹₁₀₀ tān [瘫] Sickness 疒

making movement difficult 難 (phonetic). 圈 paralysis

癱瘓 tānhuàn 圈 paralysis

攤³¹₁₀₁ tān [摊] Hand 手 with 難 phonetic. 圈 spread out, unfold 圈 share (a burden) 圈 booth, stand ⇔ 分攤

攤販 tānfàn 圈 peddler, vender

攤牌 tānpái 圈 show cards, have a showdown

攤派 tānpài 圈 apportion (costs)

灘³¹₁₀₂ tān [滩] Water 水 with 難 phonetic. 圈 beach ⇔ 沙灘, 海灘

歎³¹₁₀₃ tàn [叹] Exhale 欠 with 堇 (altered) phonetic. Simplified form merged with 嘆. 圈 sigh 圈 exclaim ⇔ 讚歎, 驚歎

嘆³¹₁₀₄ tàn [叹] Mouth 口 with 堇 (altered) phonetic. Simplified form uses 又. 圈 sigh (⇒ 歎) 圈 感嘆, 詠嘆

嘆詞 tàncí 圈 exclamation, interjection

嘆服 tànfú 圈 admire

嘆賞 tànshǎng 圈 admire

嘆息 tànxí 圈 圈 sigh

卅³¹₁₀₅ sà Three times ten 十. 圈 thirty

世³¹₁₀₆ shì Thirty 卅 (altered) years. 圈 generation, lifetime 圈 age, era 圈 world ⇔ 人世, 舉世, 去世, 後世, 厭世, 逝世, 出世, 前世, 過世, 身世

世代 shìdài 圈 generation

世紀 shìjì 圈 century

世家 shìjiā 圈 aristocratic family

世間 shìjiān 圈 world

世界 shìjiè 圈 world: 世界大戰 world war; 世界觀 world view

世人 shìrén 圈 mortals

世事 shìshì 圈 human affairs: 世事多變化 things change

屉³¹₁₀₇ tì Step 彳 and saddlecloth (an earlier form of 屜 from 世 and 尸): insole. 圈 drawer ⇔ 抽屜

枼³¹₁₀₈ yè Generation 世 of a tree 木. 圈 leaf (⇒ 葉)

葉³¹₁₀₉ yè [叶] Leaf 枼 (phonetic) with plant 艸 redundant. Simplified form uses 口 and 十. 圈 leaf 圈 a surname ⇔ 落葉, 茶葉

葉子 yèzi 圈 leaf

碟³¹₁₁₀ dié Leaf-like 枼 (phonetic) stone 石. 圈 dish, plate ⇔ 光碟, 硬碟, 磁碟

碟子 diézi 圈 small plate

牒³¹₁₁₁ dié Leaf-like 枼 (phonetic) piece 片. 圈 official document ⇔ 通牒

蝶 31 dié
112 Leaf-like 枼 (phonetic) insect 虫. 图 butterfly ⇔ 蝴蝶

謀 31 dié
113 [谋] Report 言 from drifting among the enemy leaf-like 枼 (phonetic). 图 espionage ⇔ 間諜

喋 31 dié
114 Speak 口 like rustling leaves 枼 (phonetic). 图 babble, chatter 喋喋不休 diédiébùxiū 图 talk incessantly

鰈 31 dié
115 [鰈] Leaf-like 枼 (phonetic) fish 魚. 图 flounder

卅 31 xì
116 Four times ten 十. 图 forty

無 31 wú
117 [无] Early forms showed a person dancing, now 舞. A later form, much altered, shows forest 林, destroy 亡, multitude 卅 and person 大. Simplified form is ancient variant form. 图 without 图 ⇔ 束手無策, 毫無, 獨一無二 无 比 wúbǐ 图 matchless, incomparable
無邊 wúbiān 图 limitless, infinite
無不 wúbù 图 without exception, invariably
無產 wúchǎn 图 capital: 無產階級 proletariat
無償 wúcháng 图 free of charge
無常 wúcháng 图 impermanent, variable
無恥 wúchǐ 图 shameless
無法 wúfǎ 图 impossible
無妨 wúfáng 图 no harm in, might as well
無非 wúfēi 图 nothing but, only
無辜 wúgū 图 innocent

無關 wúguān 图 irrelevant, unrelated
無可奈何 wúkěnàihé 图 unavoidable, having no alternative
無禮 wúlǐ 图 rude, impolite
無聊 wúliáo 图 boring, annoying: 他很無聊. He is very annoying. 图 bored: 我最近很無聊. I've been very bored recently.
無論 wúlùn 图 regardless: 無論如何 no matter what happens, anyway
無名 wúmíng 图 nameless 图 anonymous
無名氏 wúmíngshì 图 图 anonymous
無奈 wúnài 图 have no choice
無能 wúnéng 图 incompetent
無情 wúqíng 图 heartless
無窮 wúqióng 图 endless, infinite
無窮無盡 wúqióngwújìn 图 endless, infinite
無神論 wúshénlùn 图 atheism
無數 wúshù 图 innumerable
無所謂 wúsuǒwèi 图 inconsequential 图 don't care
無謂 wúwèi 图 pointless, senseless
無限 wúxiàn 图 infinite, limitless
無線 wúxiàn 图 wireless: 無線電 two-way radio
無效 wúxiào 图 invalid, ineffective
無形 wúxíng 图 invisible
無需 wúxū 图 need not
無涯 wúyá 图 limitless
無恙 wúyàng 图 healthy: 別來無恙? Have you been well recently?
無疑 wúyí 图 doubtless, certainly
無意 wúyì 图 unintentionally, inadvertently
無知 wúzhī 图 ignorant
無罪 wúzuì 图 innocent: 被判無罪 found innocent

嫵 31 wǔ
118 [妩] Woman 女 dancing 無 (phonetic). 图 lovely
嫵媚 wǔmèi 图 lovely, charming

舞 31 wǔ
119 Dance 無 (phonetic, abbreviated) back to back 舛. 图 dance ⇔ 鼓舞, 跳舞
舞弊 wǔbì 图 embezzlement, malfeasance
舞蹈 wǔdǎo 图 dance
舞會 wǔhuì 图 dancing party
舞龍舞獅 wǔlóngwǔshī 图 dragon and lion celebration dance
舞台 wǔtái 图 stage

撫 31 fǔ
120 [抚] Hand 手 dancing 無 (phonetic). 图 calm, stroke ⇔ 愛撫
撫摸 fǔmō 图 stroke, caress
撫恤 fǔxù 图 compensate: 撫恤金 compensation, bereavement money
撫養 fǔyǎng 图 bring up, rear
撫育 fǔyù 图 bring up, rear

入 32 rù
1 Pictograph of roots descending into the earth. 图 enter ⇔ 潛入, 落入, 侵入, 浸入, 捲入, 收入, 納入, 介入, 加入, 投入, 滲入, 併入, 深入, 出入, 輸入, 陷入, 插入, 列入, 進入, 匯入
入夥 rùhuǒ 图 join a partnership
入籍 rùjí 图 be naturalized
入境 rùjìng 图 enter a country
入口 rùkǒu 图 entrance
入睡 rùshuì 图 fall asleep

全 32 quán
2 Jade 玉 put 入 away for safe-keeping. 图

字譜及字典

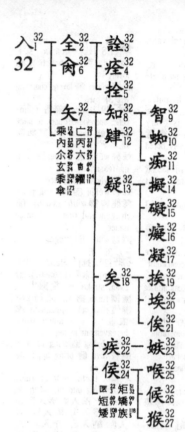

全心投入 put all one's heart in it

詮[32] quán
3 [诠] Words 言[8] to complete 全[32] (phonetic) understanding. 🔟 explain
詮釋 quánshì 🔟 annotation, explanatory note, footnote

痊[32] quán
4 From sickness 疒[8] to complete 全[32] (phonetic) health. 🔟 be healed
痊癒 quányù 🔟 be healed, be cured

拴[32] shuān
5 Hand 手[8] with 全[32] phonetic. 🔟 fasten, tie

肏[32] cào
6 Enter 入[8] flesh 肉[32]. 🔟 fuck

矢[32] shǐ
7 Enter 入[8] with marks for arrowhead and flights. 🔟 arrow

知[32] zhī
8 Arrow-like 矢[8] mouth 口[8]. 🔟 know 🔟 knowledge ⇔ 不知不覺[6], 衆所周知[8], 得知[8], 無知[8], 認知[8], 稔知[8], 須知[8], 已知[8], 通知[8], 明知[8], 告知[8], 預知[8], 諭知[8], 自知[8]
知恥 zhīchǐ 🔟 have a sense of shame
知道 zhīdào 🔟 know
知己 zhījǐ 🔟 close friend
知覺 zhījué 🔟 consciousness 🔟 perception
知名 zhīmíng 🔟 famous
知青 zhīqīng 🔟 students sent to the countryside during the Cultural Revolution (知識青年)
知情 zhīqíng 🔟 informed, aware
知識 zhīshì 🔟 knowledge: 知識份子 an intellectual; 知識介 intelligentsia; 知識

perfect, intact 🔟 complete 🔟 all, whole, entire 🔟 completely, entirely ⇔ 完全[6], 健全[32], 十全十美[8], 安全[8], 周全[8], 百科全書[8]
全部 quánbù 🔟 all
全國 quánguó 🔟 national
全家 quánjiā 🔟 entire family
全壘打 quánlěidǎ 🔟 home run
全力 quánlì 🔟 all one's strength: 全力以赴 overcome with all one's strength
全面 quánmiàn 🔟 completely

全民 quánmín 🔟 national: 全民所有制 state ownership; 全民健保 national health insurance
全能 quánnéng 🔟 omnipotent
全盤 quánpán 🔟 complete, comprehensive
全球 quánqiú 🔟 whole world
全身 quánshēn 🔟 whole body
全神貫注 quánshénguànzhù concentrate completely
全體 quántǐ 🔟 all, entire
全心 quánxīn 🔟 wholeheartedly:

產權 ⑭ intellectual property rights

知曉 zhīxiǎo ⓥ know, learn of

智 32 zhì
9 Modern form shows knowledge 知⁹² (phonetic) and speak 曰⁹⁶. ⑧ wisdom, intelligence ⇔ 機智⁹², 才智⁹⁵, 心智⁹³

智慧 zhìhuì ⑧ intelligence: 智慧財產權 ⑭ intellectual property rights

智力 zhìlì ⑧ intelligence

智謀 zhìmóu ⑧ resourcefulness

智叟 zhìsǒu ⑧ ⑦ sage

智障 zhìzhàng ⑧ mental handicap

蜘 32 zhī
10 Modern form shows insect 虫¹²⁵ and clever 知⁹² (phonetic). ⑧ spider

蜘蛛 zhīzhū ⑧ spider: 蜘蛛網 spider web

痴 32 chī
11 Variant of 癡³² showing sickness 疒⁷⁶ affecting intelligence 知⁹² (phonetic). ⇔ 白痴⁷⁶

肄 32 yì
12 Modern form shows archery 矢⁹⁷, person 七¹² and writing 聿¹⁵ (originally 中¹⁴). ⓥ practice, study

肄業 yìyè ⓥ study at a school

疑 32 yí
13 Person 七¹² and arrow 矢⁹⁷ (phonetic) on left, and child 子⁵⁵ and stop 止⁶⁸ (merged) on right. ⑧ ⓥ doubt ⇔ 可疑⁷², 置疑³³, 無疑³⁵, 猜疑⁹², 遲疑⁹⁷, 懷疑⁴², 質疑⁹³, 嫌疑¹⁰², 懸疑¹⁴⁰

疑案 yí'àn ⑧ mystery case

疑竇 yídòu ⑧ suspicion, doubt: 啓人疑竇 arouse suspicion

疑惑 yíhuò ⑱ uncertain, unconvinced

疑慮 yílù ⑧ misgivings, anxiety

疑問 yíwèn ⑧ questions, doubt, uncertainty

疑心 yíxīn ⑧ suspicion, doubt

擬 32 nǐ
14 [擬] Hand 手⁸⁹ and doubt 疑³² (phonetic). Simplified form uses 以⁹². ⓥ intend, plan ⇔ 比擬⁸³, 模擬⁸⁹

擬定 nǐdìng ⓥ draft, draw up

擬訂 nǐdìng ⓥ draft, draw up

礙 32 ài
15 [碍] Stone 石⁶⁹ with 疑³² phonetic. Simplified form uses 㝵⁵⁵. ⓥ hinder ⇔ 障礙⁶⁶, 妨礙⁹⁴, 阻礙¹¹⁷, 窒礙¹²⁸

癡 32 chī
16 [痴] Sickness 疒⁷⁶ characterized by doubt 疑³² (phonetic). ⑱ idiotic ⇔ 白癡⁷⁶

癡呆 chīdāi ⑱ stupid

凝 32 níng
17 Ice 冫⁷⁹ with 疑³² phonetic. ⓥ freeze, congeal

凝結 níngjié ⓥ condense, congeal

凝聚 níngjù ⓥ condense, congeal

凝神 níngshén ⓥ concentrate, be attentive

凝視 níngshì ⓥ stare at

凝重 níngzhòng ⑱ solemn

矣 32 yǐ
18 Arrow 矢⁹⁷ that has finished 已⁵⁹ (phonetic, written as 厶¹⁹) its journey. ⑩ ⊗ an indicator of the perfect tense

挨 32 āi ⑯ ái
19 Hand 手⁸⁹ with 矣³² phonetic. ⓥ suffer, endure ⓥ delay: 挨時間 play for time ⑱ close to ⓥ in order

挨打 āidǎ ⓥ be beaten up

挨近 āijìn ⓥ close to, near to

挨罵 āimà ⓥ be scolded

挨揍 āizòu ⓥ be beaten up

埃 32 āi
20 Dirt 土⁷⁵ with 矣³² phonetic. ⑧ fine dust ⇔ 塵埃¹⁷⁰

埃及 āijí ⑦ Egypt

俟 32 sì
21 Person 人¹⁰ with 矣³² phonetic. ⓥ wait

俟候 sìhòu ⓥ wait

疾 32 jí
22 Sickness 疒⁷⁶ striking like an arrow 矢⁹⁷ (phonetic). ⑧ disease ⑱ swift, rapid ⇔ 殘疾⁸⁷, 痢疾⁹², 瘧疾⁹⁷

疾病 jíbìng ⑧ disease

嫉 32 jí
23 Woman's 女⁹³ (formerly person's 人¹⁰) disease 疾³² (phonetic). ⓥ envy

嫉妒 jídù ⓥ envy ⑧ envy, jealousy

侯 32 hóu
24 Person 人¹⁰ shooting arrow 矢⁹⁷ at target (once written as 厂²¹, now obscured). ⑧ nobleman ⑭ a surname

侯爵 hóujué ⑧ marquis

喉 32 hóu
25 Mouth's 口⁶⁸ target 侯³² (phonetic). ⑧ throat ⇔ 咽喉²³

喉嚨 hóulóng ⑧ throat: 喉嚨痛 ⑭ sore throat

喉舌 hóushé ⑧ mouthpiece

候 32 hòu
26 Person 人¹⁰ (redundant) shooting an arrow 侯³² (phonetic, altered). ⓥ hope, expect ⓥ wait: 請稍候. Please wait a moment. ⇔ 守候⁴², 伺候⁹², 小時候⁷², 稍候⁹², 時候³³, 侍候⁹², 等候²⁰, 侯候³², 問候³³, 氣候⁹¹, 症候⁹²

候補 hòubǔ ⓥ await a vacancy ⑧ alternate member

106

字譜及字典

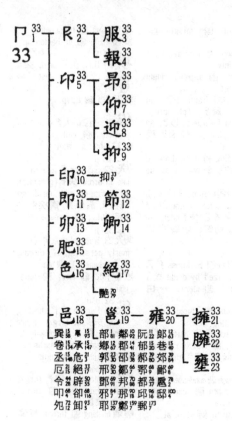

服[卩]33, 和服[卩]33, 屈服[卩]33, 衣
服[卩]33, 克服[卩]52
服從 fúcóng 動 obey: 服從權
威 obey authority
服氣 fúqì 動 concede, be con-
vinced
服飾 fúshì 名 clothing apparel:
服飾店 dress store
服侍 fúshì 動 serve, attend to
服務 fúwù 名 service: 服務員
attendant, servant
服役 fúyì 名 military service
服用 fúyòng 動 take (medicine)
服裝 fúzhuāng 名 clothing: 服
裝店 clothing store; 服裝表
演 fashion show

報[报] bào
報4 [报] Criminals 辛[卩]
subjected to rule 卩[卩]. Simplified form uses hand 扌[卩]. 動
report 動 respond 名 news-
paper: 晚報 evening paper ⇔
酬報[卩], 畫報[卩], 學報[卩], 電
報[卩], 警報[卩], 公報[卩], 快
報[卩], 海報[卩], 回報[卩], 稟
報[卩], 呈報[卩], 情報[卩], 日
報[卩], 預報[卩], 簡報[卩]
報案 bào'àn 動 report a crime
報仇 bàochóu 動 avenge, revenge
報酬 bàochóu 名 remuneration
報答 bàodá 動 repay (kindness)
報導 bàodǎo 動 動 report
article, story
報道 bàodào 動 動 report 名
article, story
報到 bàodào 動 check in, register
報復 bàofù 名 revenge
報告 bàogào 名 report, article 動
report
報捷 bàojié 動 report victory
報名 bàomíng 動 register
報社 bàoshè 名 newspaper
company
報應 bàoyìng 名 karma
報章 bàozhāng 名 newspapers
報紙 bàozhǐ 名 newspaper

印 áng
印5 Turned around person

候選人 hòuxuǎnrén 名 candi-
date
猴 hóu
猴27 Beast 犬[卩] with 侯[卩]
phonetic. 名 monkey ⇔ 猿
猴[卩]
猴子 hóuzi 名 monkey
卩 jié
卩1 Pictograph of an
official seal. Early form shows
pictograph of a kneeling person.
名 seal 名 kneeling person 名
section (⇔ 節[卩])

卩 fú
卩2 Hand 又[卩] holding an
official seal 卩[卩]. 動 rule

服 fú
服3 Boat 舟[卩] (resemb-
ling abbreviated form of 肉[卩])
ruled 卩[卩] (phonetic). 動 steer
動 obey 動 serve: 服兵役 do
military service 動 take
(medicine) 名 clothing ⇔ 說
服[卩], 便服[卩], 嘆服[卩], 佩
服[卩], 信服[卩], 禮服[卩], 制
服[卩], 心服[卩], 征服[卩], 舒

七 |² and kneeling person 卩 卩. 㐁 aspire

昂 33 áng
6 Aspire 印卩 (phonetic) to the sun 日卩. rise, ascend high, lofty expensive ⇔ 高昂卩, 激昂卩
昂貴 ánggùi expensive
昂然 ángrán proudly and boldly

仰 33 yǎng
7 Person 人卩 aspiring 印卩 (phonetic). lift admire, revere ⇔ 瞻仰卩, 信仰卩
仰賴 yǎnglài rely on, look to for help
仰慕 yǎngmù admire
仰韶 yǎngsháo Yangshao - a village in Hunan: 仰韶文化 Yangshao culture - neolithic culture unearthed in Yangshao
仰望 yǎngwàng admire
仰仗 yǎngzhàng rely on, look to for help

迎 33 yíng
8 Move 足卩 forward and look up 印卩 (phonetic). greet, welcome ⇔ 歡迎卩
迎接 yíngjiē greet
迎面 yíngmiàn head-on
迎娶 yíngqǔ escort bride to one's home from her home
迎刃而解 yíngrènérjiě readily solved

抑 33 yì
9 Hand 手卩 stamping 印卩 (altered to 印卩). press restrain ⇔ 壓抑卩
抑或 yìhùo or
抑制 yìzhì repress, control: 抑制力 self-restraint inhibition

印 33 yìn
10 Hand 爪卩 holding a seal 卩 卩. stamp, print, engrave seal, stamp ⇔ 盜印卩, 烙印卩, 刻印卩, 影印卩, 複印卩, 打印機卩, 腳印卩, 手印卩
印表機 yìnbiǎojī printer
印第安 yìndìān Indian, Native American
印度 yìndù India: 印度教 Hinduism; 印度洋 Indian Ocean
印尼 yìnní Indonesia
印泥 yìnní red ink paste for seals
印刷 yìnshuā print
印象 yìnxiàng impression: 印象很深 deep impression; 印象派 impressionism
印章 yìnzhāng seal, chop
印證 yìnzhèng verify, corroborate

即 33 jí
11 Part 卩 卩 of a meal 皀 卩. 㐁 eat moderately immediately even if then ⇔ 隨即卩, 立即卩, 亦即卩, 當即卩
即便 jíbiàn even if, even though
即將 jíjiāng soon, imminently
即刻 jíkè immediately
即使 jíshǐ even though, although

節 33 jié
12 [节] Part 即卩 of bamboo 竹卩. Simplified form uses grass 艸卩 and section 卩 卩. joint section holiday, festival season restrain, control ⇔ 脫節卩, 春節卩, 貞節卩, 季節卩, 關節卩, 音節卩, 中秋節卩, 使節卩, 調節卩, 情節卩, 禮節卩, 枝節卩, 環節卩, 過節卩, 端午節卩, 細節卩, 變節卩, 撐節卩
節儉 jiéjiǎn thrifty
節目 jiémù program, show: 電視節目 television show
節日 jiérì festival, holiday
節省 jiéshěng save, economize
節育 jiéyù birth control, family planning
節約 jiéyuē economize, conserve
節制 jiézhì refrain from, abstain from temperance, abstinence
節奏 jiézòu rhythm, pace

卯 33 qīng
13 Two halves of a seal 卩 卩 (resembling 卯卩). 㐁 authority

卿 33 qīng
14 Official 卯卩 with 皀卩 phonetic. minister: 國務卿 Secretary of State

肥 33 féi
15 Flesh 肉卩 with 卩 卩 (resembling 巴卩) phonetic. fat, plump fat fertile (soil) ⇔ 化肥卩, 減肥卩
肥料 féiliào fertilizer
肥胖 féipàng fat
肥肉 féiròu fatty meat
肥沃 féiwò rich, fertile
肥皂 féizào soap

色 33 sè
16 Person's 人卩 seal 卩 卩 (resembling 巴卩). facial expression color lust salacious, risque ⇔ 棕色卩, 臉色卩, 銀色卩, 褪色卩, 神色卩, 褐色卩, 景色卩, 特色卩, 黃色卩, 天色卩, 綠色卩, 金色卩, 紅色卩, 遜色卩, 起色卩, 以色列卩, 暮色卩, 青色卩, 白色卩, 灰色卩, 秋色卩, 物色卩, 紫色卩, 失色卩, 顏色卩, 彩色卩, 菜色卩, 出色卩, 愧色卩, 藍色卩, 黑色卩, 角色卩, 酒色財氣卩
色彩 sècǎi color
色鬼 sèguǐ sex maniac, pervert
色狼 sèláng sex maniac, pervert

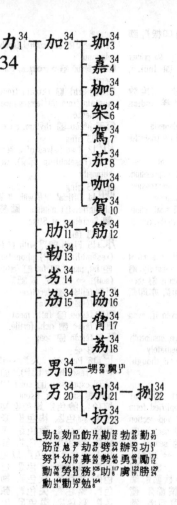

absolutely

絕跡 juéjī 動 disappear, vanish, become extinct

絕食 juéshí 動 图 fast, hunger strike

絕望 juéwàng 動 despair, lose hope

絕種 juézhǒng 图 extinct 图 extinction: 瀕臨絕種 on the verge of extinction

邑 33 yì
18 Surrounding walls 囗[69] and official seal 卩[3] (resembling 巴[85]). 图 citystate

邕 33 yōng
19 River 川[3] surrounding a city 邑[18]. 图 moat

雍 33 yōng
20 Bird 隹[162] that likes moats 邕[57] (altered). 图 wagtail 图 harmonious, peaceful

雍容 yōngróng 图 graceful

擁 33 图 yǒng 图 yōng
21 [拥] Hands 手[97] harmoniously 雍[57] (phonetic) engaged. Simplified form uses 用[57]. 動 embrace 图 crowd, swarm ⇔ 蜂擁[57]

擁抱 yōngbào 動 图 embrace, hug

擁戴 yōngdài 動 support (a leader)

擁護 yōnghù 動 support

擁擠 yōngjǐ 動 crowd, squeeze 图 crowded, packed

擁有 yōngyǒu 動 possess

臃 33 yōng
22 Modern form shows flesh 肉[132] with 雍[57] phonetic. 图 obese

臃腫 yōngzhǒng 图 obese

壅 33 yōng
23 Dirt 土[9] with 雍[57] phonetic. 動 clog

壅塞 yōngsè 图 clogged, congested

色情 sèqíng 图 sexual passion, lust 图 pornographic

絕 33 jué
17 [绝] Knife 刀[35] cutting thread 糸[153] into sections 卩[3] (resembling 巴[85]). 動 sever, break off 图 matchless,

unparalleled 图 used up, exhausted 图 extremely, absolutely ⇔ 戒絕[57], 滅絕[58], 拒絕[58], 斷絕[58], 回絕[57], 杜絕[70], 謝絕[147], 隔絕[14]

絕對 juéduì 图 absolute 图

力 34 lì
1 Pictograph of a tendon. 图 strength 图 power, force ⇔ 極力, 水力, 人力, 潛力, 盡力, 有力, 暴力, 電力, 竭力, 巧克力, 苦力, 全力, 智力, 毅力, 效力, 威力, 戮力, 努力, 引力, 勢力, 活力, 用力, 精力, 體力, 魄力, 重力, 動力, 魅力, 氣力, 努力, 武力, 壓力, 實力, 兵力, 視力, 助力, 阻力, 致力, 能力, 耐力, 自力更生, 角力, 奮力, 權力

力量 lìliàng 图 power, strength
力氣 lìqì 图 physical strength
力求 lìqiú 動 strive for
力圖 lìtú 動 strive to
力學 lìxué 图 mechanics
力爭 lìzhēng 動 struggle for

加 34 jiā
2 Strengthen 力 speech 口. 動 increase add, plus: 一加一等於二 one plus one equals two 動 append ⇔ 附加, 更加, 添加, 參加, 新加坡, 施加, 芝加哥, 增加
加班 jiābān 動 work overtime
加倍 jiābèi 動 double
加法 jiāfǎ 图 addition
加工 jiāgōng 動 process
加緊 jiājǐn 動 intensify
加劇 jiājù 動 exacerbate, aggravate
加快 jiākuài 動 accelerate
加侖 jiālún 图 gallon
加強 jiāqiáng 動 strengthen
加權 jiāquán 動 weighted: 加權指數 weighted index
加入 jiārù 動 participate
加上 jiāshàng 動 add on, attach
加深 jiāshēn 動 deepen
加速 jiāsù 動 accelerate

加以 jiāyǐ 動 take into account: 加以考慮 take into consideration 動 moreover
加油 jiāyóu 動 refuel 動 work harder
加重 jiāzhòng 動 weight aggravate
加州 jiāzhōu 圈 California

珈 34 jiā
3 Jade 玉 with 加 phonetic. 图 an ancient kind of jewelry ⇔ 瑜珈

嘉 34 jiā
4 Drums 壴 added 加 (phonetic). 動 commend 圈 fine, excellent
嘉賓 jiābīn 图 honored guest
嘉獎 jiājiǎng 動 honor, reward
嘉義 jiāyì 圈 Jiayi - a city in Taiwan

枷 34 jiā
5 Wood 木 added 加 (phonetic). 图 thresher pillory
枷鎖 jiāsuǒ 图 shackles, yoke: 擺脫枷鎖 throw off one's shackles

架 34 jià
6 Wood 木 that is added 加 (phonetic) to. 图 frame, rack 動 erect, set up ⇔ 書架, 高架橋, 吵架, 打架, 綁架, 擺架子, 鷹架, 棚架
架構 jiàgòu 图 structure
架式 jiàshì 图 pose, stance
架子 jiàzi 图 frame, rack: 衣架子 clothes hanger 動 outline, framework 動 manner: 架子大 overbearing

駕 34 jià
7 [驾] Add 加 (phonetic) yoke to a horse 馬. 動 drive, pilot ⇔ 凌駕, 勞駕
駕駛 jiàshǐ 動 drive, pilot: 駕駛員 pilot; 駕駛執照 driver's license

駕馭 jiàyù 動 drive, maneuver, direct
駕照 jiàzhào 图 driver's license (駕駛執照)

茄 34 jiā qié
8 Plant 艸 with 加 phonetic. jiā: 图 lotus stem qié: 图 eggplant ⇔ 雪茄, 番茄
茄子 qiézi 图 eggplant

咖 34 kā gā
9 Add 加 (phonetic) to the mouth 口. Used in transliterations of foreign words.
咖哩 gālī 图 curry
咖啡 kāfēi 图 coffee: 咖啡廳 cafe, coffee house; 咖啡因 caffeine; 咖啡色 coffee-colored, brown

賀 34 hè
10 [贺] Add 加 (phonetic) shells/money 貝. 動 congratulate 圈 a surname ⇔ 祝賀, 恭賀, 慶賀
賀卡 hèkǎ 图 congratulatory card

肋 34 lè lèi
11 Strong 力 (phonetic) flesh 肉. 图 rib
肋骨 lègǔ 图 rib

筋 34 jīn
12 Bamboo 竹, flesh 肉 and strength 力. 图 tendon ⇔ 鋼筋, 抽筋, 腦筋
筋骨 jīngǔ 图 physique

勒 34 lè lēi
13 Leather 革 that works like a tendon 力 (phonetic). lè: 图 bridle 動 force lēi: 動 tighten ⇔ 希特勒, 巴勒斯坦, 馬勒
勒索 lèsuǒ 動 extort

劣 34 liè
14 Few 少 strengths 力. 圈 inferior, low quality ⇔ 低劣, 拙劣, 惡劣

$刀^{35}_1$ — $到^{35}_2$ — $倒^{35}_3$

35 — $分^{35}_4$ — $份^{35}_5$

— $紛^{35}_6$

— $氛^{35}_7$

— $吩^{35}_8$

— $芬^{35}_9$

— $忿^{35}_{10}$

— $汾^{35}_{11}$

— $粉^{35}_{12}$

— $扮^{35}_{13}$

劣等 lièděng 圐 inferior

劦 34 xié
15 Join strength 力³⁴.

劦 34 xié
16 [协] Ten 十³⁴ people joining strength 劦³⁴ (phonetic). Simplified form uses 辨劦 simplification. 圐 assist ⇔ 安協¹⁰³

協定 xiédìng 圐 agreement, accord

協會 xiéhuì 圐 association

協商 xiéshāng 圐 negotiate, consult

協調 xiétiáo 圐 coordinate, harmonize 圐 coordination

協議 xiéyì 圐 negotiate

協助 xiézhù 圐 assist, aid

脅 34 xié
17 [胁] Body's 肉¹¹² strength 劦³⁴ (phonetic). Simplified form uses 辨劦. 圐 flank 圐 threaten ⇔ 威脅³⁴

脅迫 xiépò 圐 coerce, force

荔 34 lì
18 Strong 劦³⁴ plant 艸⁶ with pronunciation atavistically from 力³⁴.

荔枝 lìzhī 圐 litchi

男 34 nán
19 Field 田¹¹¹ strength 力³⁴. 圐 male, man 圐 male ⇔ 處男³⁴

男孩 nánhái 圐 boy 圐 son

男孩子 nánháizǐ 圐 boy 圐 son

男女 nánnǚ 圐 men and women: 男女平等 gender equity

男人 nánrén 圐 man

男生 nánshēng 圐 schoolboy 圐 boy

男性 nánxìng 圐 male

男友 nányǒu 圐 boyfriend

男子 nánzǐ 圐 man, male: 男子隊 men's team

另 34 lìng
20 Feed mouth 口¹⁴⁶ with own strength 力³⁴. 圐 separate 圐 separately

另外 lìngwài 圐 separate, another 圐 separately

別 34 bié
21 [别] Knife 刀³⁵ scraping flesh from bone 冎¹³³ (altered). Simplified form uses 另³⁴. 圐 other 圐 difference 圐 differentiate 圐 do not: 別走 don't go ⇔ 差別³⁴ 特別³⁴, 個別³⁴, 分別³⁴, 辨別³⁴, 區別³⁴, 闊別³⁴, 識別³⁴, 性別³⁴, 離別³⁴, 惜別³⁴, 告別³⁴, 辭別³⁴, 甄別¹³⁰, 鑑別¹⁴², 道別⁴⁶, 類別³⁴

別處 biéchù 圐 elsewhere

別的 biéde 圐 other

別名 biémíng 圐 alias, second name

別人 biérén 圐 others

別墅 biéshù 圐 villa, house

別外 biéwài 圐 especially

別緻 biézhì 圐 novel

捌 34 bā
22 [捌] Hand 手⁴ separating 別³⁴ (phonetic). 圐 pull apart (⇨ 扒³⁷) 圐 eight (complex form)

拐 34 guǎi
23 [拐] Hand 手⁴ with 咼¹³³ (altered) phonetic. Simplified form uses 另³⁴. 圐 turn 圐 kidnap

拐騙 guǎipiàn 圐 swindle

拐彎 guǎiwān 圐 turn

拐杖 guǎizhàng 圐 walking stick, cane

刀 35 dāo
1 Pictograph of a knife. 圐 knife, sword ⇔ 剃刀³⁵ 開刀³⁵, 捉刀³⁵, 菜刀¹⁰², 鐮刀¹⁷², 剪刀³⁵

刀叉 dāochā 圐 knife and fork

刀口 dāokǒu 圐 blade

刀刃 dāorèn 圐 blade

刀子 dāozi 圐 knife

到 35 dào
2 Arrive 至¹⁴⁸ with 刀³⁵ phonetic. 圐 arrive 圐 until: 等到明天 wait until tomorrow 圐 go to, leave for: 你到哪裡去? Where are you going? 圐 (indicating completion of an action): 買到 bought; 辨得到

can be done ⇔ 說到做, 得
到, 學到, 收到, 等
到, 直到, 聽到, 報
到, 達到, 碰到, 送
到, 拿到, 找到, 感
到, 趕到, 接到, 遭
到, 回到, 周到, 遇
到, 談到, 提到, 遲
到, 抓到, 受到, 見
到, 看到, 想不到, 想
到, 獨到, 搬到, 來
到

到處 dàochù everywhere
到達 dàodá arrive
到底 dàodǐ after all, in the end
到來 dàolái come
到期 dàoqī expire, come due

倒 35 dǎo dào
3 Person 人 with 到
phonetic. dǎo: fall down
dào: invert, reverse pour
out, empty ⇔ 傾倒, 顛
倒, 打倒, 跌倒, 壓
倒, 絆倒, 昏倒, 摔
倒, 暈倒, 官倒
倒閉 dàobì go bankrupt
倒彩 dàocǎi boos, catcalls:
喝倒彩 boo
倒茶 dàochá pour tea
倒楣 dǎoméi unlucky
倒霉 dǎoméi unlucky
倒數 dàoshǔ count back-
wards: 倒數第三 third from
the bottom
倒塌 dǎotā collapse

分 35 fēn fèn
4 Divide 八 with a
knife 刀 separate
distribute distinguish: 分
清楚 distinguish clearly
point cent minute
fraction: 三分之一 one-third
tenth branch, extension:
分公司 branch office ⇔ 部
分, 劃分, 得分, 春
分, 公分, 評分, 十
分, 處分, 大部分, 天
分, 緣分, 成分, 充

分別, 區分, 萬分, 滿
分, 百分, 秋分, 瓜
分, 養分, 過分
分辨 fēnbiàn distinguish,
differentiate
分別 fēnbié part, separate
distinguish, differentiate:
分別不出來 indistinguish-
able differently, separately
分布 fēnbù distribute
分成 fēnchéng divide into
分擔 fēndān share (a burden)
分割 fēngē partition
分隔 fēngé divide, separate
分工 fēngōng division of labor
分行 fēnháng branch (of a
bank or organization)
分號 fēnhào semicolon
分化 fēnhuà divide
分家 fēnjiā establish separate
households
分解 fēnjiě dissolve
analyze
分局 fēnjú branch office
分開 fēnkāi separate
分類 fēnlèi categorize
category
分離 fēnlí separate
分裂 fēnliè split apart
divided
分泌 fēnmì secrete
分娩 fēnmiǎn childbirth
分明 fēnmíng clear, distinct
分母 fēnmǔ denominator
分配 fēnpèi assign, distribute
分批 fēnpī in groups, in
batches
分歧 fēnqí disagree
分散 fēnsàn disperse, scatter
diffuse, decentralized,
scattered
分社 fēnshè branch office
分手 fēnshǒu separate, break
up (a relationship)
分數 fēnshù fraction point
分攤 fēntān apportion
分析 fēnxī analyze
analysis

分享 fēnxiǎng share (benefits)
分曉 fēnxiǎo solution, outcome
分野 fēnyě boundary
分贓 fēnzāng divide spoils
分支 fēnzhī branch (of an
organization)
分鐘 fēnzhōng minute
分子 fēnzǐ numerator
molecule

份 35 fèn
5 Person's 人 share
分 (phonetic). role
part, portion ⇔ 部份, 股
份, 大部份, 充份, 月
份, 身份
份額 fèné share, portion
份量 fènliàng amount
weight, impact (of a statement)
份子 fènzǐ member

紛 36 [纷] Separate 分
(phonetic) threads 糸.
numerous, varied confused,
disorderly ⇔ 糾紛
紛紛 fēnfēn in droves, in
succession
紛擾 fēnrǎo disturb
紛紜 fēnyún diverse and
contradictory (opinions): 衆多
紛紜 numerous and diverse
紛爭 fēnzhēng dispute

氛 35 fēn
7 Air 气 with 分
phonetic. atmosphere, mood
⇔ 氣氛

吩 35 fēn
8 Mouth 口 with 分
phonetic. instruct, direct
吩咐 fēnfu instruct, direct

芬 35 fēn
9 Plant 艸 with 分
phonetic. fragrance
芬芳 fēnfāng fragrant
芬蘭 fēnlán Finland

忿 35 fèn
10 Divided 分 (phonet-
ic) heart 心. anger

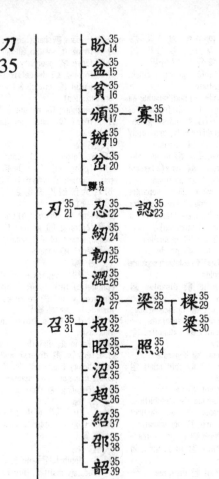

刀 35

汾 35/11 fén — Water 水 that separates 分 (phonetic). name of a tributary to the Yellow River

汾酒 fénjiǔ — a liquor made in Shanxi Province

粉 35/12 fěn — Rice 米 ground to pieces 分 (phonetic). powder, flour ⇔ 脂粉, 花粉, 澱粉, 奶粉, 米粉, 麵粉

粉筆 fěnbǐ — chalk

粉紅 fěnhóng — pink: 粉紅色 pink

粉刷 fěnshuā — whitewash

粉碎 fěnsuì — smash to pieces, crush, shatter

扮 35/13 bàn — Hands 手 and separate 分 (phonetic). dress up as, disguise as ⇔ 打扮, 裝扮

扮演 bànyǎn — act, play the part

盼 35/14 pàn — Eye 目 with 分 phonetic. look hope for ⇔ 期盼, 企盼

盼望 pànwàng — hope for, look forward to

盆 35/15 pén — Dish 皿 with open/separate 分 (phonetic) edges. basin ⇔ 臉盆

盆地 péndì — basin, depression

盆景 pénjǐng — potted landscape, bonsai

盆子 pénzi — washbasin

貧 35/16 pín — [貧] Divided 分 (phonetic) money/shell 貝. poor: 貧富不均 unequal income distribution

貧乏 pínfá — lacking, poor

貧苦 pínkǔ — destitute

貧困 pínkùn — poor, impoverished

貧民 pínmín — the poor

貧窮 pínqióng — poor, impoverished poverty

頒 35/17 bān — [頒] Head 頁 with 分 phonetic. big head bestow, confer distribute

頒佈 bānbù — promulgate, issue

頒發 bānfā — award, issue

寡 35/18 guǎ — Distribute 頒 contents of house 宀. few, scarce widowed ⇔ 多寡

寡婦 guǎfù — widow

掰 35/19 bāi — Separate 分 with the hands 手. pull apart

岔 35 chà
20 Split 分[35] in a mountain 山[67] path. 图 形 fork, branch ⇔ 打岔[35]
岔路 chàlù 图 branch path
岔子 chàzi 图 accident, problem

刃 35 rèn
21 Knife 刀[35] with point indicating blade. 图 blade, edge ⇔ 迎刃而解[35], 刀刃[35], 兵刃[35]

忍 35 rěn
22 [忍] Blade 刃[35] (phonetic) in the heart 心[9]. 動 endure: 忍不住 cannot help but ⇔ 不忍[35], 残忍[35], 容忍[35]
忍耐 rěnnài 動 endure, restrain oneself
忍受 rěnshòu 動 suffer, tolerate, endure
忍者 rěnzhě 图 ninja

認 35 rèn
23 [认] Modern form shows words 言[35] and endure 忍[35] (phonetic). Simplified form uses 人[9]. 動 admit, acknowledge 動 recognize, identify ⇔ 否認[35], 供認[35], 承認[35], 公認[35], 辨認[35], 體認[35], 默認[35], 確認[35]
認出 rènchū 動 recognize, identify
認錯 rèncuò 動 admit an error
認得 rènde 動 recognize, know: 你認得他嗎? Do you know him?
認定 rèndìng 動 decide, conclude
認可 rènkě 動 approve, sanction
認命 rènmìng 動 resigned to fate
認清 rènqīng 動 understand clearly
認識 rènshì 動 know, recognize
認同 rèntóng 動 identify
認為 rènwéi 動 believe, think
認帳 rènzhàng 動 acknowledge a debt or mistake
認真 rènzhēn 動 earnest, serious

認知 rènzhī 動 cognition
認罪 rènzuì 動 confess

紉 35 rèn
24 [纫] Thread 糸[53] and blade 刃[35] (phonetic). 動 sew ⇔ 縫紉[35]

韌 35 rèn
25 [韧] Struggle 韋[35] and blade 刃[35] (phonetic). 形 tenacious
韌帶 rèndài 图 ligament
韌性 rènxìng 图 tenacity, toughness

澀 35 sè
26 [涩] Water 水[35] and stop repeatedly (an ancient character showing stop 止[35] four times, the upper two written upside down and now appearing as 刃[35]). 形 rough, not fluid 形 astringent, puckery ⇔ 羞澀[35], 苦澀[35], 生澀[35]

刅 35 chuāng
27 Blade 刃[35] making mark—丨. 會 cut

梁 35 liáng
28 Cut 刅 (phonetic) trees 木[35] over water 水[35]. bridge 图 beam 图 a surname ⇔ 橋梁[35]

樑 35 liáng
29 [梁樑] Bridge 梁[35] (phonetic) with wood 木[35] redundant. 图 bridge ⇔ 棟樑[35], 橋樑[35]

粱 35 liáng
30 Rice 米[35] stalks leaning over like a bridge 梁[35] (phonetic, abbreviated). 图 sorghum ⇔ 高粱[35]

召 35 zhào
31 Mouth 口[35] with 刀[35] phonetic. 動 summon, convene ⇔ 號召[35]
召喚 zhàohuàn 動 call, beckon
召回 zhàohuí 動 recall: 召回大使 recall ambassador
召集 zhàojí 動 assemble

召開 zhàokāi 動 convene

招 35 zhāo
32 Hand 手[35] calling 召[35] (phonetic). 動 beckon 動 recruit 動 incur
招標 zhāobiāo 動 invite bids
招車 zhāochē 動 hail a cab
招待 zhāodài 動 entertain, host: 招待客人 entertain guests; 招待所 guesthouse, hostel
招呼 zhāohū 動 beckon, call: 打招呼 greet; 跟他打招呼 greet him
招攬 zhāojiǎo 動 solicit
招徠 zhāolái 動 solicit: 招徠顧客 solicit customers
招牌 zhāopái 图 placard, sign: 招牌菜 house specialty
招致 zhāozhì 動 incur

昭 35 zhāo
33 Sun 日[76] convened 召[35] (phonetic). 形 evident, apparent
昭彰 zhāozhāng 形 clear, evident

照 35 zhào
34 Apparent 昭[35] (phonetic) by light of fire 火[35]. 動 illuminate 動 take (a picture) 動 look after 介 according to ⇔ 牌照[35], 駕照[35], 合照[35], 執照[35], 按照[35], 日照[76], 拍照[35], 依照[35], 寫照[35], 護照[35], 觀照[35], 對照[76]
照常 zhàocháng 動 as usual
照顧 zhàogù 動 consider 動 look after, care for
照舊 zhàojiù 動 as before, as usual
照例 zhàolì 動 as a rule
照亮 zhàoliàng 動 illuminate
照料 zhàoliào 動 take care of, look after
照片 zhàopiàn 图 photograph, picture
照相 zhàoxiàng 動 photograph: 我們照個相. Let's take a picture. 照相機 camera

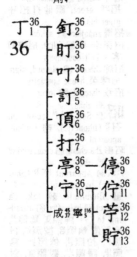

刀 35

┬ 初 35/40

├ 刁 35/41 ─ 叼 35/42

└ 切⁴³ 剖⁴⁴ 刈⁴⁵ 剛⁴⁶ 劍⁴⁷ 刻¹⁰⁵ 剩¹¹⁶ 創¹²⁵
劃¹³⁸ 剷¹⁴³ 券¹⁵⁰ 刨¹⁵¹ 副¹⁵⁶ 削¹⁶¹ 絕¹⁶⁹ 別³⁴
剎⁴⁷ 刷⁴⁸ 剝⁴⁹ 划⁵¹ 刺⁵³ 剌⁵⁴ 班⁵⁷ 利⁶³ 刪⁶⁴ 俞⁷⁸
刮⁷⁹ 割⁸⁰ 判⁸³ 劇⁸⁷ 制⁸⁹ 刺⁹² 剡⁹⁶ 則⁹⁷ 利⁹⁸
前¹⁰⁶ 剪¹¹² 列¹³³ 解¹⁴⁷ 剋¹⁵⁰,¹⁵² 劇¹⁵⁷ 剔¹⁶³
劑¹⁸²

丁 36/1

┬ 釘 36/2

├ 盯 36/3

├ 叮 36/4

├ 訂 36/6

├ 頂 36/6

├ 打 36/7

├ 亭 36/8 ─ 停 36/9

├ 宁 36/10 ─ 佇 36/11

├ 成⁹⁵ 率¹¹⁶ ─ 苧 36/12

└ 貯 36/13

照樣 zhàoyàng 圈 as usual

沼 35 zhǎo
35 Water 水³⁸ with 召³⁹
phonetic. 图 pond
沼澤 zhǎozé 图 marsh, swamp

超 35 chāo
35 Walk 走²⁹ with 召³⁹
phonetic. 图 surpass, exceed
超出 chāochū 图 exceed, overstep
超額 chāoé 图 exceed a quota
超過 chāoguò 图 exceed, surpass
超級 chāojí 图 super: 超級市
場 supermarket
超強 chāoqiáng 图 superpower
超人 chāorén 图 superman

超脫 chāotuō 图 transcendental
图 transcend
超越 chāoyuè 图 surpass, transcend
超重 chāozhòng 图 overweight

紹 35 shào
37 [绍] Thread 糸¹⁵³ and
convene 召³⁹ (phonetic).
connect ⇔ 介紹²⁹
紹興 shàoxīng 图 Shaoxing - a
city in Zhejiang Province: 紹興
酒 a famous wine

邵 35 shào
38 City 邑³⁹ with 召³⁹
phonetic. 图 a surname

韶 35 sháo
39 Music 音 with 召³⁹
phonetic. 图 ancient musical
style ⇔ 仰韶²⁹

初 35 chū
40 Cut/knife 刀³⁵ cloth to
begin making clothing 衣¹²⁶.
图 first, original, initial
early 图 beginning ⇔ 年
初¹⁰, 起初²⁶, 當初²⁹, 月
初²⁹, 最初²⁷
初步 chūbù 图 first step
初稿 chūgǎo 图 rough draft
初級 chūjí 图 basic, elementary
初戀 chūliàn 图 first love
初期 chūqī 图 early times
初學 chūxué 图 begin to study:
初學者 beginner
初中 chūzhōng 图 junior high
school

刁 35 diāo
41 A modern variant of
knife 刀³⁵ (phonetic). 图
wicked
刁蠻 diāomán 图 wilful, obstinate
刁難 diāonán 图 make difficulties for
刁鑽 diāozuān 图 cunning

叼 35 diāo
42 Mouth 口⁶⁸ with 刁³⁵
phonetic. 图 hold in mouth

丁 36 dīng
1 Pictograph of a nail.
图 nail (⇨ 釘³⁶) 图 fourth
Heavenly Stem (⇨ 干支²⁹) 图
man 图 cube, chunk: 雞丁
diced chicken 图 a surname
⇔ 拉丁²⁴

釘 36 dīng
2 [钉] Metal 金³⁹ nail
丁³⁶ (phonetic). dīng: 图 nail
dìng: 图 nail
釘書 dìngshū 图 staple: 釘書
機 stapler
釘子 dīngzi 图 nail

盯 36 dīng
3 Eyes 目¹¹⁴ nailing

丁 ³⁶ (phonetic). 🔲 stare at
盯梢 dīngshāo 🔲 tail (somebody), shadow (somebody)
盯著 dīngzhe 🔲 stare at

叮 ³⁶ dīng
4 Mouth 口⁶⁸ nailing 丁 ³⁶ (phonetic). 🔲 exhort sting, bite
叮噹 dīngdāng 🔲 ding-dong
叮囑 dīngzhǔ 🔲 exhort

訂 ³⁶ dìng
5 [订] Words 言⁹⁶ nailing 丁 ³⁶ (phonetic) down. 🔲 arrange, settle 🔲 subscribe, book: 訂報紙 subscribe to a newspaper; 訂房間 reserve a hotel room ⇔ 簽訂⁹⁵, 修訂⁹⁷, 擬訂⁹⁷, 裝訂⁹⁶, 預訂¹⁰²
訂定 dìngdìng 🔲 set, fix, define
訂購 dìnggòu 🔲 place an order
訂婚 dìnghūn 🔲 become engaged
訂票 dìngpiào 🔲 book tickets

頂 ³⁶ dǐng
6 [顶] Nail's 丁 ³⁶ (phonetic) head 頁¹⁵⁰. 🔲 peak, top 🔲 extremely 🔲 a measureword for hats ⇔ 山頂⁶⁷, 房頂⁹⁷, 屋頂¹²⁸
頂峰 dǐngfēng 🔲 peak
頂樓 dǐnglóu 🔲 loft 🔲 roof

打 ³⁶ dǎ dá
7 Hand 手⁸⁹ nailing 丁 ³⁶. dǎ: 🔲 hit, punch, beat 🔲 fight 🔲 make, do: 打電話 call, make a phonecall; 打電腦 work on the computer 🔲 play: 打球 play ball dá: 🔲 dozen ⇔ 拷打¹²⁵, 敲打²⁷, 全壘打²⁷, 挨打²⁷, 毆打⁹⁵, 武打⁹²
打靶 dǎbǎ 🔲 practice shooting
打敗 dǎbài 🔲 defeat: 被打敗 be defeated
打扮 dǎbàn 🔲 apply makeup 🔲 dress up
打岔 dǎchà 🔲 interrupt

打成一片 dǎchéngyīpiàn 🔲 become one with, unite into a single entity
打倒 dǎdǎo 🔲 overthrow, down with 🔲 knock down
打賭 dǎdǔ 🔲 bet, gamble
打斷 dǎduàn 🔲 interrupt
打發 dǎfā 🔲 dismiss, send away 🔲 easy to please
打工 dǎgōng 🔲🔲 🔲 work part-time 🔲 🔲 work
打鼾 dǎhān 🔲 snore
打火機 dǎhuǒjī 🔲 lighter
打擊 dǎjī 🔲 attack, strike: 打擊樂器 percussion instruments
打架 dǎjià 🔲 fight
打攪 dǎjiǎo 🔲 disturb, bother
打開 dǎkāi 🔲 open
打獵 dǎliè 🔲 hunt
打牌 dǎpái 🔲 play cards
打破 dǎpò 🔲 break
打球 dǎqiú 🔲 play (ball sports)
打擾 dǎrǎo 🔲 disturb, bother
打掃 dǎsǎo 🔲 sweep
打死 dǎsǐ 🔲 beat to death
打算 dǎsuàn 🔲 intend, plan 🔲 intention, plan
打聽 dǎtīng 🔲 ask, inquire
打消 dǎxiāo 🔲 disperse
打印機 dǎyìnjī 🔲 🔲 printer
打仗 dǎzhàng 🔲 fight, go to war
打針 dǎzhēn 🔲 inject
打字 dǎzì 🔲 type: 打字機 typewriter

亭 ³⁶ tíng
8 High 高²⁷ (abbreviated) nail-like 丁 ³⁶ (phonetic) building. 🔲 pavilion
亭閣 tínggé 🔲 pavilion
亭子 tíngzi 🔲 pavilion

停 ³⁶ tíng
9 Person 人¹⁰ resting at a pavilion 亭 ³⁶ (phonetic). 🔲 stop 🔲 park ⇔ 不停⁵, 調停⁵⁵, 暫停²⁷
停車 tíngchē 🔲 park: 停車場 parking lot

停頓 tíngdùn 🔲 stop, pause
停工 tínggōng 🔲 work stoppage
停火 tínghuǒ 🔲 cease fire 🔲 ceasefire
停留 tíngliú 🔲 stop over: 在北京停留三天 stop over three days in Beijing
停止 tíngzhǐ 🔲 stop, cease, suspend
停滯 tíngzhì 🔲 stagnate, come to a standstill

宁 ³⁶ zhù
10 Originally a pictograph of a storehouse, modern form suggests nails 丁 ³⁶ under a roof 宀⁶⁷. Simplified forms of derivatives use 一↓. 🔲 store

伫 ³⁶ zhù
11 [伫] Person 人¹⁰ and store 宁 ³⁶ (phonetic). 🔲 stand still
伫立 zhùlì 🔲 stand still

苎 ³⁶ zhù
12 [苎] Plant 艸²⁶ with 宁 ³⁶ phonetic. 🔲 ramie
苎麻 zhùmá 🔲 ramie

贮 ³⁶ zhù
13 [贮] Shells 貝¹⁵⁰ stored 宁 ³⁶ (phonetic). 🔲 store
贮藏 zhùcáng 🔲 store up, stockpile
贮存 zhùcún 🔲 store up, stockpile

几 ³⁷ shú
1 Pictograph of a short wing. ⓐ flap

殳 ³⁷ shū
2 Hand 又¹⁴ flapping 几 ³⁷ (phonetic). ⓐ strike with stick ⓐ halberd

設 ³⁷ shè
3 [设] Words 言⁹⁶ and strikes 殳 ³⁷ motivating. 🔲 establish, set up 🔲 if ⇔ 建設⁵⁵, 假設⁹⁶, 常設⁹⁸, 陳設⁹⁶, 裝設⁹⁶, 攤設⁹⁷
設備 shèbèi 🔲 equipment

殼 37 qìng
5 Strike 殳📑 stones hanging from a frame (pictograph on left). 🈁 instrument made from hollowed stones (⇨ 磬)

磬 37 qìng
6 Pottery 缶[41] empty like hollowed stones 殼📑 (phonetic). 📖 exhaust
磬盡 qìngjìn 📖 ⊗ use up, exhaust

馨 37 xīn
7 Fragrance 香📑 that resonates like hollowed stones 殼📑 (phonetic). 📖 fragrance ⇔ 溫馨
馨香 xīnxiāng 📖 fragrance, aroma 📖 fragrant

聲 37 shēng
8 [青] Instrument 殼📑 (phonetic) next to ear 耳[37]. 📖 sound tone 📖 fame ⇔ 輕聲, 高聲, 呼聲, 四聲, 大聲, 鈴聲, 風聲, 舒聲, 形聲, 哭聲, 名聲, 屬聲, 心聲, 失聲, 尾聲, 低聲, 雷聲, 相聲, 鑼聲

聲稱 shēngchēng 📖 declare
聲調 shēngdiào 📖 tone
聲名 shēngmíng 📖 fame, reputation
聲明 shēngmíng 📖 declare 📖 declaration, statement
聲勢 shēngshì 📖 threatening force
聲望 shēngwàng 📖 popularity, prestige
聲響 shēngxiǎng 📖 sound 📖 reputation
聲音 shēngyīn 📖 sound, voice
聲譽 shēngyù 📖 reputation
聲援 shēngyuán 📖 express support for

設法 shèfǎ 📖 try, think of a way
設計 shèjì 📖 📖 design
設立 shèlì 📖 erect, found
設施 shèshī 📖 facilities
設想 shèxiǎng 📖 imagine, conceive, envision
設置 shèzhì 📖 set up

股 37 gǔ
4 Flesh 肉[32] long like halberd 殳📑 (phonetic). 📖 thigh 📖 puff, whiff 📖 share, stock ⇔ 屁股, 八股
股東 gǔdōng 📖 shareholder
股份 gǔfèn 📖 share, stock
股金 gǔjīn 📖 capitalization
股票 gǔpiào 📖 stock: 股票市場 stock market
股權 gǔquán 📖 stock equity

毅 37 yì
9 Strike 殳[97] and early form of 毅 showing bristles 辛[8] (abbreviated) of an angry boar 豙[55]. resolute
毅力 yìlì perseverance, willpower
毅然 yìrán firmly, courageously

殼 37 ké qiào
10 [壳] Strike 殳[97] and an ancient character for a covering. shell ⇔ 蚌殼, 貝殼[50]

穀 37 gǔ
11 [谷] Grain 禾[108] and shell 殼[10] (abbreviated). grains
穀倉 gǔcāng granary, barn
穀物 gǔwù grains

殷 37 yīn
12 Halberd 殳[97] and an ancient character for reversed body 身[47]. ceremonial dance ardent, eager Shang Dynasty (latter half) a surname
殷切 yīnqiè ardent, eager
殷勤 yīnqín attentive, warm (⇒ 慇懃[13])
殷商 yīnshāng Shang Dynasty
殷墟 yīnxū Shang Dynasty ruins in Henan

慇 37 yīn
13 [殷] Ardent 殷[12] (phonetic) heart 心[17]. pained
慇懃 yīnqín attentive, warm (⇒ 殷勤[12])

轂 37 jī
14 Strike 殳[97] another cart with tip of axle (ancient character based on cart 車[58]).

擊 37 jí jī
15 [击] Bump 毄[14] (phonetic) with the hand 手[99]. strike, bump, hit ⇔ 反擊[27], 敲擊[27], 抨擊[22], 打擊[?], 攻

擊[?], 突擊[67], 衝擊[?], 撞擊[?], 伏擊[?], 目擊[114], 狙擊[117], 游擊[118], 襲擊[132]
擊敗 jíbài defeat, conquer
擊毀 jíhuǐ smash, wreck
擊中 jízhòng hit the target

繫 37 jì xì
16 [系] Bump 毄[14] (phonetic) and thread 糸[53]. jì: tie: 繫鞋帶 tie shoelaces xì: join, connect ⇔ 聯繫[?], 連繫[?], 維繫[?]

投 37 tóu
17 Hand 手[99] and halberd 殳[97]. throw, toss, cast
投奔 tóubèn flee: 投奔自由 flee to freedom
投誠 tóuchéng surrender, defect
投稿 tóugǎo submit for publication
投機 tóujī speculate, be opportunistic: 投機分子 opportunist
投靠 tóukào rely on, seek patronage of
投票 tóupiào vote
投入 tóurù throw into
投射 tóushè project
投手 tóushǒu pitcher (in baseball)
投訴 tóusù file a complaint
投降 tóuxiáng surrender
投影 tóuyǐng project: 投影機 projector, overhead
投擲 tóuzhí throw
投資 tóuzī invest, investment

役 37 yì
18 March 彳[?] with halberds 殳[97]. defend border military service service battle ⇔ 庚子之役[?], 差役[?], 服役[?], 兵役[?], 戰役[?]

疫 37 yì
19 Warring 役[?] (phonetic, abbreviated to 殳[97])

disease 广[?]. plague, epidemic 鼠疫[81]
疫苗 yìmiáo vaccine

段 37 duàn
20 Growing plant 耑[34] (phonetic, altered) struck 殳[97]. strike, break section, part a surname 階段[?], 片段[?], 手段[99]
段落 duànluò paragraph

鍛 37 duàn
21 [锻] Metal 金[19] with 段[20] phonetic. forge
鍛鍊 duànliàn temper, exercise

緞 37 duàn
22 [缎] Thread 糸[53] with 段[20] phonetic. satin ⇔ 綢緞[?]
緞子 duànzi satin

夋 37 mù
23 Hand 又[14] reaching into swirling 回[?] (altered) waters. immerse (⇒ 沒[24])

沒 37 méi mò
24 [没] Immerse 夋[23] (phonetic) into water 水[31]. Simplified form uses 殳[97]. mò: immerse méi: have not without ⇔ 淹沒[105], 辱沒[?], 埋沒[?], 還沒[?]
沒錯 méicuò correct
沒事 méishì no problem
沒用 méiyòng useless
沒有 méiyǒu have not
沒落 mòluò sink, decline
沒收 mòshōu confiscate, expropriate

殁 37 mò
25 [殁] Death 歹[12] with immerse 夋[23] phonetic and suggesting burial. Simplified form uses 殳[97]. die

朵 37 duǒ
26 Tree 木[7] and a pictograph of a flower (written to resemble 几[?]). a measureword for flowers ⇔

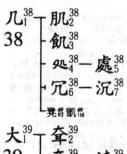

花朵⁹, 耳朵[157]

躲[27] [37] dǔo Body 身[157] with 朵[27] (original form) phonetic. 🈺 hide
躲避 dǔobì 🈺 avoid
躲藏 dǔocáng 🈺 hide
躲開 dǔokāi 🈺 dodge, shirk

剁[28] [37] dǔo Knife 刀[29] cutting flowers 朵[27] (phonetic). 🈺 chop, cut

几₁ [38] jī Pictograph of a small table or stool. Also used as simplified form of 幾[29]. 🈺 small table ⇔ 茶几[12]

肌₂ [38] jī Flesh 肉[132] with 几[38] phonetic. 🈺 muscle
肌膚 jīfū 🈺 skin: 肌膚之親 intimate relations
肌肉 jīròu 🈺 muscle

飢₃ [38] jī [饥] Food 食[95] with 几[38] phonetic. 🈺 hungry, starving 🈺 famine
飢餓 jiè 🈺 hungry, famished 🈺 hunger, starvation
飢荒 jīhuāng 🈺 famine

处₄ [38] chù Find/pursue 夂[50] a stool 几[38] to rest on. 🈺 place

處₅ [38] chù chǔ [处] Later variant of 处[50] with 虍[122] added. Simplified form uses 卜[7]. chù: 🈺 place 🈺 office, department point, feature chǔ: 🈺 manage, handle 🈺 get along with dwell ⇔ 住處⁴, 共處⁵, 長處[58], 何處[66], 四處[62], 別處[59], 去處[52], 好處[59], 深處[72], 短處[61], 害處⁷, 壞處[63], 判處[80], 相處[133], 益處[116], 遠處[126]

處處 chùchù 🈺 everywhere
處罰 chǔfá 🈺 punish
處方 chǔfāng 🈺 prescription
處分 chǔfèn 🈺 punish, discipline
處境 chǔjìng 🈺 circumstances
處理 chǔlǐ 🈺 handle, process
處男 chǔnán 🈺 virgin (male)
處女 chǔnǔ 🈺 virgin (female): 處女地 virgin land; 處女膜 hymen
處事 chǔshì 🈺 handle matters
處於 chǔyú 🈺 located at
處長 chùzhǎng 🈺 department chief
處置 chǔzhì 🈺 handle, dispose of

冗₆ [38] rǒng Person 儿[11] (altered to 几[38]) relaxing in a shed 冖[63] (altered to 冖[38]). 🈺 superfluous
冗長 rǒngcháng 🈺 lengthy, verbose
冗員 rǒngyuán 🈺 redundant workers
冗雜 rǒngzá 🈺 complicated, disorderly

沉₇ [38] chén A variation of 沈[95].

大₁ [39] dà dài Pictograph of a standing person. dà: 🈺 big, large 🈺 great, grand 🈺 greatly ⇔ 偉大[96], 老大[13], 宏大[15], 碩大[74], 長大[58], 誇大[89], 士大夫[87], 廣大[63], 擴大[56], 義大利[95], 軒然大波[95], 巨大[31], 台大[20], 胎笑大方[132], 強大[59], 莫大[95], 意大利[95], 多大⁷, 重大[92], 壯大[73], 浩大[12], 放大[12], 寬大[115], 滔天大罪[131], 龐大[82], 最大[27], 自大[177], 澳大利亞[96]

大阪 dàbǎn 🈺 Osaka
大半 dàbàn 🈺 most 🈺 mostly
大便 dàbiàn 🈺 shit
大部 dàbù 🈺 greater part
大部份 dàbùfèn 🈺 most

大部分 dàbùfèn 图 most
大臣 dàchén 图 minister
大蔥 dàcōng 图 chives
大膽 dàdǎn 围 brave, bold
大道 dàdào 图 avenue 图 virtuous path
大抵 dàdǐ 圖 generally
大地 dàdì 图 the earth
大豆 dàdòu 图 soybean
大都 dàdū 圖 mostly
大隊 dàduì 图 brigade
大多 dàduō 圖 mostly
大多數 dàduōshù 图 majority
大方 dàfāng 围 generous 围 poised 圍 elegant
大概 dàgài 圖 probably 围 approximate
大綱 dàgāng 图 outline
大哥 dàgē 图 brother (eldest) 图 gang leader
大哥大 dàgēdà 图 godfather (of a gang) 图 (t) cell phone
大海 dàhǎi 图 ocean
大漢 dàhàn 图 big fellow
大會 dàhuì 图 conference, congress: 全國人民代表大會 图 National People's Congress
大家 dàjiā 图 everybody
大街 dàjiē 图 avenue
大姐 dàjiě 图 sister (eldest)
大理 dàlǐ 图 Dali - a town in Yunnan Province: 大理石 marble
大量 dàliàng 图 large quantity
大樓 dàlóu 图 large building: 摩天大樓 skyscraper
大陸 dàlù 图 mainland, continent: 中國大陸 mainland China; 歐洲大陸 continental Europe
大路 dàlù 图 boulevard
大略 dàlüè 圖 briefly, roughly
大麻 dàmá 图 marijuana
大門 dàmén 图 front door, main entrance
大米 dàmǐ 图 rice
大名 dàmíng 图 name

大砲 dàpào 图 cannon 图 braggart
大批 dàpī 图 large quantity
大人 dàrén 图 adult
大嫂 dàsǎo 图 sister-in-law (elder brother's wife)
大聲 dàshēng 围 loud
大師 dàshī 图 great master
大使 dàshǐ 图 ambassador: 大使館 embassy
大勢 dàshì 图 general situation
大事 dàshì 图 important event
大肆 dàsì 围 wantonly
大蒜 dàsuàn 图 garlic
大體 dàtǐ 圖 generally, roughly: 大體說來 generally speaking
大廳 dàtīng 图 hall
大同 dàtóng 图 Great Harmony - Confucian utopia
大腿 dàtuǐ 图 thigh
大王 dàwáng 图 king, magnate
大西洋 dàxīyáng 图 Atlantic Ocean
大廈 dàxià 图 large building 图 mansion
大象 dàxiàng 图 elephant
大小 dàxiǎo 图 size
大笑 dàxiào 围 laugh heartily
大寫 dàxiě 围 capitalize
大型 dàxíng 围 large-scale
大學 dàxué 图 university: 大學生 college student 图 The Great Learning (⇨ 四書图)
大衣 dàyī 图 coat, overcoat
大意 dàyì 图 general idea, outline
大約 dàyuē 圖 about, approximately
大躍進 dàyuèjìn 图 Great Leap Forward
大戰 dàzhàn 图 war: 第二次世界大戰 World War II
大致 dàzhì 圖 mostly
大衆 dàzhòng 图 masses: 大衆文化 popular culture
大字 dàzì 图 big character: 大字報 big-character poster
大作 dàzuò 图 围 your work

大夫 dàifū 图 doctor 图 (t) high official

奓 39 dā
2 Big 大 (phonetic) ears 耳. 围 big-eared
奓拉 dālā 围 droop

羍 39 tā
3 Sheep 羊 with 大 phonetic. 图 lamb

達 39 dá
4 [达] Moving 足 sheep 羍 (phonetic). 围 reach, attain 围 convey, express ⇔ 到達, 轉達, 傳達, 練達, 豁達, 發達, 抵達, 雷達, 表達
達成 dáchéng 围 reach, achieve: 達成協議 reach agreement
達到 dádào 围 attain, reach, accomplish
達爾文 dáěrwén 图 Darwin
達摩 dámó 图 Bodhidharma - introduced Zen to China

撻 39 tà
5 [挞] Hand 手 conveying 達 (phonetic). 围 whip ⇔ 鞭撻

尢 39 wāng
6 Person 大 with bent right leg.

尬 7 Leg bent 尢 as exert strength 力 (phonetic).

抛 39 pāo
8 [抛] Hand 手 and coiled leg 尬. 围 throw, toss 围 discard
抛開 pāokāi 围 throw away, dump
抛錨 pāomáo 围 drop anchor 围 break down (vehicular)
抛棄 pāoqì 围 abandon, discard, dump: 抛棄式 disposable
抛售 pāoshòu 围 dump, sell below cost

夫 39 fū
9 Man 大 with a hairpin (represented by 一)

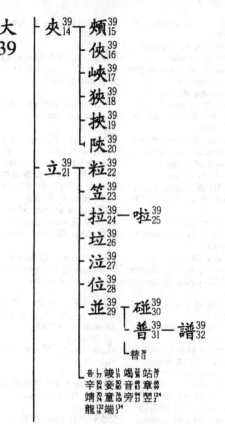

symbolizing adulthood.
man 图 husband ⇔ 農夫扎
士大夫扎, 丈夫扎, 大夫扎,
工夫扎, 功夫扎, 漁夫扎
夫婦 fūfù 图 husband and wife
夫妻 fūqī 图 husband and wife
夫人 fūrén 囶 Mrs. 图 wife
夫子 fūzǐ 囶 囵 Confucian
teacher: 孔夫子 Confucius

扶 39 fú
10 Hand 手扎 of a man
夫扎 (phonetic). 囸 support
with hand 囵 aid, help ⇔ 攙

扶养

扶養 fúyǎng 囸 bring up, raise
扶植 fúzhí 囸 prop up

規 39 guī
11 [规] As husband 夫扎
sees 見扎. 图 rules, regula-
tions ⇔ 違規扎, 犯規扎, 陋
規扎, 法規扎
規程 guīchéng 图 rules, regulations
規定 guīdìng 囸 stipulate 图
rule
規範 guīfàn 图 norm, standard

囵 regulate, standardize
規格 guīgé 图 specification
規劃 guīhuà 图 layout
規矩 guījǔ 图 rules: 規規矩矩
well-behaved; 守規矩 behave
oneself
規律 guīlù 图 regulations
規模 guīmó 图 scale, scope
規勸 guīquàn 囸 admonish
規則 guīzé 图 rule

窺 39 kuī
12 Hole 穴扎 with 規扎
phonetic. 囸 spy on
窺視 kuīshì 囸 spy on
窺伺 kuīsì 囸 watch and wait
窺探 kuītàn 囸 spy on, pry into

替 39 tì
13 Succession 並扎 (al-
tered to resemble two 夫扎)
from 自扎 (altered to 日扎).
囸 replace, substitute for ⇔
代替扎
替代 tìdài 囸 replace, substitute
for

夾 39 囵 jiá 囵 jiā
14 [夹] Person 大扎
holding two people 人扎. 囸
squeeze 囸 place between 图
clip
夾克 jiákè 图 jacket
夾雜 jiázá 囸 mix up
夾子 jiázi 图 clip

頰 39 jiá
15 [颊] Squeezes 夾扎
(phonetic) head 頁扎. 图 jaw
图 cheeks ⇔ 面頰扎

俠 39 xiá
16 [侠] Person 人扎 with
夾扎 phonetic and suggestive
of rescue. 图 knight-errant 图
chivalry ⇔ 武俠扎

峽 39 xiá
17 [峡] Mountains 山扎
squeezed 夾扎 (phonetic). 图
gorge 图 三峽扎, 海峽扎
峽谷 xiágǔ 图 canyon: 大峽谷
Grand Canyon

狭 39 xiá
[狹] Hills 阜¹⁶⁷ (mis-written as dog 犬²⁷¹) squeezed 夹²⁷ (phonetic). 㽞 narrow
狭義 xiáyì 㽞 narrow definition
狭窄 xiázhǎi 㽞 narrow

挟 39 xié xiá
[挾] Hand 手⁹⁰ and squeeze 夹²⁷ (phonetic). ㊀ carry under the arm
挟持 xiáchí ㊀ hold, detain
挟帶 xiádài,xiédài ㊀ carry along ㊁ portable (⇨ 攜帶¹⁶²)

陝 39 shǎn
[陝] Mountains 阜¹⁶⁷ hiding thieves (an ancient character resembling 夹²⁷ showing a person 大⁷⁹ carrying loot under his arms). ㊀ a region in ancient China ㊁ Shaanxi Province
陝西 shǎnxī 㽞 Shaanxi Province

立 39 lì
21 Person 大⁷⁹ (altered) standing on a surface 一. ㊀ stand ㊁ erect ㊂ found, establish ⇔ 創立³⁵, 建立⁵³, 公立⁷⁷, 私立⁷⁷, 站立⁹⁵, 矗立, 佇立³⁵, 設立⁵⁷, 成立⁵⁵, 國立⁵⁵, 市立⁵⁵, 豎立⁵⁵, 屹立⁵⁵, 孤立⁵⁷, 獨立⁵⁷, 對立⁷⁶
立場 lìchǎng 㽞 standpoint
立法 lìfǎ ㊀ legislate: 立法院 ㊁ Legislative Yuan; 立法員 legislator
立即 lìjí ㊌ immediately
立刻 lìkè ㊌ immediately
立體 lìtǐ 㽞 three-dimensional
立意 lìyì 㽞 conception, approach

粒 39 lì
22 Rice 米¹³⁸ standing 立²⁷ (phonetic) apart. ㊀ grain, pellet ⇔ 顆粒²⁴
粒子 lìzi ㊁ particle

笠 39 lì
23 Bamboo 竹⁷¹ standing 立²⁷ (phonetic) on a person. 㽞 bamboo hat ⇔ 斗笠⁸⁷

拉 39 lā
24 Hand 手⁹⁰ and standing person 立²⁷ (phonetic). ㊀ pull, drag ㊁ drag in, involve ㊂ excrete ㊃ play: 拉小提琴 play the violin ⇔ 伊拉克⁵⁵, 阿拉伯⁴⁵, 沙拉⁵⁷, 耷拉⁷⁹, 拖拉機⁵⁵
拉長 lācháng ㊀ prolong, draw out
拉扯 lāchě ㊀ pull and drag ㊁ implicate, drag in
拉出 lāchū ㊀ pull up
拉丁 lādīng 㽞 Latin: 拉丁文 Latin language; 拉丁美洲 Latin America
拉肚子 lādùzi ㊀ have diarrhea
拉開 lākāi ㊀ pull open
拉鍊 lāliàn 㽞 zipper
拉攏 lālǒng ㊀ win over (sb.)
拉票 lāpiào ㊀ canvass votes
拉薩 lāsà 㽞 Lhasa
拉屎 lāshǐ ㊀ shit
拉雜 lāzá 㽞 rambling, incoherent

啦 39 lā la
25 Mouth 口⁶⁸ with 拉²⁷ phonetic. la: ㊀ exclamatory particle ⇔ 嘩啦¹⁷³
啦啦隊 lālāduì 㽞 cheerleading squad

垃 39 ㊀ lè ㊁ lā
26 Dirt 土⁷⁰ standing 立²⁷ (phonetic) in pile.
垃圾 lèsè 㽞 garbage, trash: 垃圾桶 trash can

泣 39 qì
27 Water 水⁵² with 立²⁷ phonetic. ㊀ weep ⇔ 啜泣³⁵, 哭泣⁹⁸

位 39 wèi
28 Person 人¹⁰ standing 立²⁷ in assigned position. 㽞 position, rank 㽞 location, place ㊀ a measureword for people: 幾位? How many people? 㽞 digit, figure: 六位數字 six-digit figure ⇔ 崗位³⁵, 各位³⁷, 爵位⁴⁸, 牌位⁵², 學位⁵⁵, 席位⁵⁵, 祿位⁵⁷, 空位⁵⁷, 數位⁵⁷, 地位⁵⁸, 職位⁵⁷, 舖位⁹⁵, 坐位⁹⁸, 座位⁹⁸, 諸位⁵⁷, 定位⁵⁹, 單位¹⁴⁶, 首位¹⁴⁸, 篡位⁵⁷
位於 wèiyú ㊀ situated at
位置 wèizhì 㽞 position
位子 wèizi 㽞 seat

並 39 bìng
29 [并] Stand 立²⁷ side by side. ㊀ unite, merge ㊁ simultaneously ㊂ and ㊃ (used for emphasis in negative statements): 我並不是傻瓜. I'm not an idiot.
並非 bìngfēi ㊌ and not, by no means
並列 bìngliè ㊀ stand side by side, stand in a row
並且 bìngqiě ㊌ moreover
並重 bìngzhòng ㊀ emphasize equally

碰 39 pèng
30 Stones 石⁸⁹ uniting 並²⁷ (phonetic). ㊀ bump, hit ㊁ bang
碰到 pèngdào ㊀ bump into, meet
碰見 pèngjiàn ㊀ bump into, meet
碰頭 pèngtóu ㊀ bump into, meet
碰撞 pèngzhuàng ㊀ hit, bump into, run into

普 39 pǔ
31 Blurred together 並²⁷ in the weak sun 日⁷⁶. ㊀ overcast ㊁ universal, general ⇔ 吉普²⁷
普遍 pǔbiàn 㽞 widespread, general
普及 pǔjí ㊀ popularize, spread
普通 pǔtōng 㽞 common, ordinary: 普通話 ㊁ Mandarin, Chinese ㊂ all right, average
普陀山 pǔtuóshān 㽞 Mount Puto - a sacred mountain in Zhejiang Province

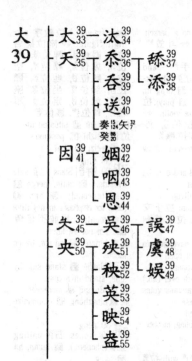

大
39

太 39/33 — 汰 39/34
天 39/35 ┬ 忝 39/36 ┬ 舔 39/37
              │   └ 添 39/38
              ├ 吞 39/39
              ├ 送 39/40
              ├ 奏 124 矢 32
              └ 癸 88
因 39/41 ┬ 姻 39/42
              ├ 咽 39/43
              └ 恩 39/44
矢 39/45 — 吳 39/46 ┬ 誤 39/47
                              └ 虞 39/48
央 39/50 ┬ 殃 39/51 ┬ 娛 39/49
              ├ 秧 39/52
              ├ 英 39/53
              ├ 映 39/54
              └ 盎 39/55

譜 39/32 [谱] pǔ Words 言98 containing all 普37 (phonetic). 图 manual 图 chart, table 动 compose 图 idea, plan ⇔ 臉譜19, 食譜14, 樂譜50, 離譜78, 族譜9, 家譜155
譜曲 pǔqǔ 动 compose, set to music

太 39/33 tài Big 大79 with the dot, once written as two 二1, for emphasis. 形 very big 副 too, excessively 副 too, extremely ⇔ 老太太90, 姨太太88, 猶太9, 亞太166
太后 tàihòu 图 queen mother, empress dowager
太湖 tàihú 地 Taihu lake - a large lake in Jiangsu and Zhejiang Provinces
太極 tàijí 图 Daoist theory of the world: 太極圖 circular symbol of yin and yang; 太極拳 taichi - shadow boxing
太監 tàijiàn 图 eunuch
太空 tàikōng 图 space: 外太空 outer space; 太空人 astronaut; 太空梭 space shuttle
太平 tàipíng 图 peace: 太平洋 Pacific Ocean; 太平洋戰爭 Pacific War; 太平門 emergency exit; 太平天國起義 Taiping Rebellion
太太 tàitai 图 Mrs.: 王太太 Mrs. Wang 图 wife
太陽 tàiyáng 图 sun: 太陽系 solar system; 太陽傘 parasol

太子 tàizǐ 图 prince

汰 39/34 tài Water 水36 with 太29 phonetic. 动 rinse rice ⇔ 淘汰14'

天 39/35 tiān The expanse 一1 above humans 大79. Early pictograph shows a person with enlarged head. 图 heaven 又 God 量 day ⇔ 上天4, 老天12, 春天154, 昨天86, 航天82, 後天47, 冬天43, 今天41, 陰天26, 每天55, 當天59, 青天22, 晴天28, 白天76, 聊天43, 明天27, 秋天17, 整天88, 半天97, 前天157, 西天12, 滔天大罪13, 藍天162, 夏天14, 隔天17
天安門 tiānānmén 地 Gate of Heavenly Peace: 天安門廣場 Tiananmen Square
天才 tiāncái 图 genius
天地 tiāndì 图 universe, world
天鵝 tiāné 图 swan
天分 tiānfèn 图 talent, natural endowment: 沒有語言天分 don't have a talent for languages; 有天分的 talented
天干 tiāngān 图 Heavenly Stems - 甲12, 乙1, 丙40, 丁20, 戊88, 己57, 庚88, 辛88, 壬88, 癸88
天花板 tiānhuābǎn 图 ceiling
天皇 tiānhuáng 图 emperor of Japan
天津 tiānjīn 地 Tianjin - a city near Beijing
天空 tiānkōng 图 sky
天命 tiānmìng 图 mandate of heaven
天氣 tiānqì 图 weather
天橋 tiānqiáo 图 overpass
天然 tiānrán 图 natural: (動) 天然氣 natural gas; 動 天然瓦斯 natural gas
天色 tiānsè 图 color of the sky 图 weather
天生 tiānshēng 形 natural, innate

天使 tiānshǐ 图 angel

天壇 tiāntán Temple of Heaven - temple in Beijing where emperors worshipped

天堂 tiāntáng 图 heaven, paradise

天體 tiāntǐ 图 celestial body 图 nude body

天天 tiāntiān 圆 every day

天文 tiānwén 图 astronomy: 天文學 astronomy; 天文台 observatory

天下 tiānxià 图 under heaven, world

天線 tiānxiàn 图 antenna

天性 tiānxìng 图 disposition, nature

天眞 tiānzhēn 圈 naive, innocent

天主教 tiānzhǔjiào Catholicism: 天主教徒 Catholic

天子 tiānzǐ 图 Son of Heaven - emperor of China

忝 39 tiǎn
36 Heart 心 with 天 phonetic. 圃 disgrace

舔 39 tiǎn
37 Tongue 舌 with 忝 phonetic. 圃 lick

添 39 tiān
38 Water 水 with 忝 phonetic. 圃 add, increase ⇔ 畫蛇添足, 增添

添購 tiāngòu 圃 buy more, make additional purchases

添加 tiānjiā 圃 increase, add

吞 39 tūn
39 Mouth 口 with 天 phonetic. 圃 swallow, gulp ⇔ 鯨吞, 併吞

吞併 tūnbìng 圃 annex, swallow up

吞噬 tūnshì 圃 devour

吞下 tūnxià 圃 swallow

送 39 sòng
40 Movement 辵 and an ancient character for dowry slaves resembling 天. 圃

give 圃 deliver 圃 escort out, see off ⇔ 葬送, 遣送, 遞送, 贈送, 播送, 護送

送出 sòngchū 圃 send out

送到 sòngdào 圃 send to

送給 sònggěi 圃 give

送回 sònghuí 圃 send back

送交 sòngjiāo 圃 deliver

送命 sòngmìng 圃 go to one's doom

因 39 yīn
41 Person 大 and surroundings 口. 图 reason, cause 介 because 介 according to, on the basis of ⇔ 原因, 主因, 誘因, 基因, 起因

因此 yīncǐ 圃 therefore

因而 yīnér 圃 therefore

因果 yīnguǒ 图 cause and effect 图 karma

因素 yīnsù 图 factor

因爲 yīnwèi 圃 because

因應 yīnyìng 圃 react according to circumstances

姻 39 yīn
42 Woman 女 with 因 phonetic. 图 marriage ⇔ 婚姻

姻親 yīnqīn 图 relatives by marriage

咽 39 yān yàn
43 Mouth's 口 source/ cause 因 (phonetic). yān: 图 larynx yàn: 圃 swallow (⇨ 嚥)

咽喉 yānhóu 图 throat

恩 39 ēn
44 Heart's 心 reason 因 (phonetic). 图 kindness, benevolence ⇔ 感恩

恩愛 ēnài 图 marital love

恩惠 ēnhùi 图 favor, grace

恩情 ēnqíng 图 kindness

恩師 ēnshī 图 mentor

恩賜 ēnsì,ēncì 图 charity

恩怨 ēnyuàn 图 gratitude or

resentment: 不計較個人恩怨 unswayed by personal feelings

夨 39 cè
45 Person 大 with head tilted to the side.

吳 39 wú
46 [吴] Talk/mouth 口 with tilted head 夨. 㥀 shout, boast 圃 an ancient kingdom in China 图 a surname

誤 39 wù
47 [误] Words 言 in boast 吳 (phonetic). 图 mistake, error 圃 mistakenly, incorrectly ⇔ 舛誤, 耽誤, 謬誤, 錯誤, 失誤

誤差 wùchā 图 error (statistics)

誤會 wùhuì 圃 misunderstand 图 misunderstanding

誤解 wùjiě 圃 misunderstand, misinterpret 图 misunderstanding

虞 48 yú
48 [虞] Tiger 虍 and shout 吳 (phonetic). 图 anxiety, worry

娛 39 yú
49 [娱] Woman 女 shouting 吳 (phonetic). 图 pleasure, amusement ⇔ 自娛

娛樂 yúlè 图 amusement, entertainment

央 39 yāng
50 Person 大 in the center of a space 冂. 图 middle, center 圃 entreat ⇔ 中央

央行 yāngháng 圃 central bank (中央銀行)

央求 yāngqiú 圃 entreat

殃 39 yāng
51 Death's 歹 midst 央 (phonetic). 图 calamity 圃 bring disaster on ⇔ 遭殃

字譜及字典

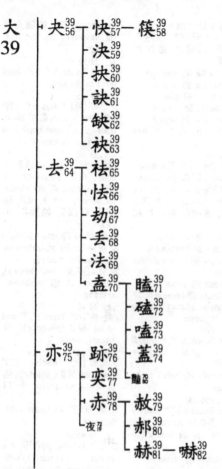

大
39

夬 39/56
去 39/64
亦 39/75

快 39/57 — 筷 39/58
決 39/59
抉 39/60
訣 39/61
缺 39/62
袂 39/63

祛 39/65
怯 39/66
劫 39/67
丟 39/68
法 39/69
盍 39/70

跡 39/76 — 瞌 39/71
磕 39/72
嗑 39/73
蓋 39/74
奕 39/77 — 瞌 39
赤 39/78 — 赦 39/79
郝 39/80
赫 39/81 — 嚇 39/82
夜 39

秧 39/52 yāng Grain 禾 with 央 phonetic. 圖 seedling ⇔ 插秧
秧歌 yānggē 圖 a folk dance (in Northern China)
秧苗 yāngmiáo 圖 rice seedlings

英 39/53 yīng Plant 艸 with 央 phonetic. 圖 flower, petal 圖 hero 圖 English ⇔ 石英, 漢英, 蒲公英
英國 yīngguó 圖 England
英俊 yīngjùn 圖 handsome
英里 yīnglǐ 圖 mile
英文 yīngwén 圖 English (written)
英雄 yīngxióng 圖 hero

英語 yīngyǔ 圖 English (spoken)
英制 yīngzhì 圖 British measurement system

映 39/54 yìng Sun 日 striking center 央 (phonetic). 圖 shine 圖 reflect ⇔ 反映, 放映, 輝映

盎 39/55 àng Well-centered 央 (phonetic) vessel. 圖 an ancient vessel with a large base
盎然 àngrán 圖 abundant, overflowing: 生氣盎然 overflowing with anger

夬 39/56 guài Hand 又 holding half of an object resembling 中. 圄 divide, separate. 圄 one of the Eight Diagrams (⇔ 八卦)

快 39/57 kuài Heart 心 with 夬 phonetic. 圖 happy 圖 fast, quick 圖 soon, shortly ⇔ 不快, 輕快, 爽快, 儘快, 涼快, 勤快, 加快, 趕快, 痛快, 外快, 暢快, 愉快
快報 kuàibào 圖 preliminary report
快餐 kuàicān 圖 fast food: 快餐廳 fast-food restaurant; 快餐麵 instant noodles
快感 kuàigǎn 圖 excitement, high
快活 kuàihúo 圖 cheerful
快樂 kuàilè 圖 happy
快速 kuàisù 圖 fast

筷 39/58 kuài Bamboo 竹 for eating rapidly 快 (phonetic). 圖 chopsticks
筷子 kuàizi 圖 chopsticks

決 39/59 jué [决] Water 水 separating 夬 (phonetic). Simplified form uses ice 冫. 圖 clear a channel 圖 decide

⇔ 否決[16], 判決[82], 堅決[162], 解決[197]
決策 juécè 图 decision
決定 juédìng 动 decide 图 decision
決裂 juéliè 动 rupture
決心 juéxīn 动 determine, resolve 图 determination
決議 juéyì 图 resolution

抉 39 jué
60 Hand 手[9p] separating 夬[59] (phonetic). 动 choose
抉擇 juézé 动 choose 图 choice

訣 39 jué
61 [诀] Words 言[59] of separation 夬[59] (phonetic). 动 bid farewell 图 trick of the trade ⇔ 秘訣[59]
訣竅 juéqiào 图 trick of the trade

缺 39 quē
62 Pottery 缶[141] divided 夬[59] (phonetic). 形 lack: 缺錢 short of money ⇔ 欠缺[92], 空缺[48], 短缺[49]
缺點 quēdiǎn 图 weakness, fault
缺乏 quēfá 动 lack
缺少 quēshǎo 动 lack
缺失 quēshī 动 missing, lacking
缺席 quēxí 动 be absent
缺陷 quēxiàn 图 defect, drawback

袂 39 mèi
63 Clothing 衣[126] that diverges 夬[59] (phonetic). 图 sleeve ⇔ 聯袂[79]

去 39 qù
64 Person 大[9p] (altered to resemble 土[9p]) with an ancient character resembling 厶[19] phonetic. 动 go 动 remove ⇔ 上去[47], 下去[48], 除去[59], 回去[17], 失去[87], 辭去[177], 出去[110], 過去[135], 進去[162]
去除 qùchú 动 eliminate, remove
去處 qùchù 图 place
去過 qùguò 动 been to
去年 qùnián 图 last year

去世 qùshì 动 pass away, die

祛 39 qū
65 Pray 示[46] to remove 去[64] (phonetic) evil spirits. 动 dispel, ward off
祛邪 qūxié 动 ward off evil

怯 39 què 粤 qiè
66 Heart 心[91] anxious to flee 去[64] (phonetic). cowardly ⇔ 膽怯[49]
怯懦 quènuò 图 cowardice
怯弱 quèruò 形 timid, cowardly

劫 39 jié
67 Keep from leaving 去[64] (phonetic) by force 力[24]. 动 coerce, compel 动 rob, plunder ⇔ 搶劫[23], 浩劫[92]
劫持 jiéchí 动 kidnap
劫機 jiéjī 动 hijack
劫掠 jiélüè 动 plunder

丢 39 diū
68 Drop 丿 and go 去. 动 lose, misplace 动 drop 亂丢[92]
丢掉 diūdiào 动 lose, misplace 动 throw away
丢臉 diūliǎn 动 lose face 形 embarrassing
丢下 diūxià 动 throw down

法 39 fǎ
69 As water 水[21] goes 去. 图 law 图 method ⇔ 違法[45], 說法[45], 乘法[45], 書法[46], 守法[46], 犯法[46], 司法[46], 作法[47], 做法[46], 無法[46], 加法[47], 設法[47], 立法[46], 效法[47], 合法[46], 除法[46], 減法[47], 拼法[47], 刑法[46], 辦法[46], 用法[46], 憲法[46], 療法[46], 手法[89], 方法[46], 法[94], 看法[115], 想法[115], 依法[126], 算法[150], 變法[153], 非法[169]
法案 fǎàn 图 bill
法寶 fǎbǎo 图 magic weapon
法官 fǎguān 图 judge
法規 fǎguī 图 laws
法國 fǎguó 图 France

法家 fǎjiā 图 Legalism – a school of thought in ancient China
法郎 fǎláng 图 franc
法令 fǎlìng 图 ordinance, decree
法律 fǎlǜ 图 law
法庭 fǎtíng 图 court
法學 fǎxué 图 legal studies
法院 fǎyuàn 图 law court
法則 fǎzé 图 rule, law
法制 fǎzhì 图 legal system
法子 fǎzi,fází 图 way, method

盍 39 hé
70 Cover (a pictograph resembling 去[64]) on a dish 皿[116] (or 血[16]). 动 cover, shut. 副 why not

瞌 39 kē
71 Eyes 目[114] shut 盍[70] (phonetic). 动 doze off
瞌睡 kēshuì 图 nap: 打瞌睡 take a nap

磕 39 kē
72 Stones 石[59] connecting 盍[70] (phonetic). 图 knocking sound 动 knock, bump
磕頭 kētóu 动 kowtow

嗑 39 kè
73 Mouth 口[68] with 盍[70] (phonetic). 动 speak excessively 动 crack (with the teeth): 嗑瓜子 crack dried melon seeds

蓋 39 gài
74 [盖] Grass 艸[59] roof/cover 盍[70] (phonetic). Simplified form uses 羊[123]. 动 图 cover 动 build, construct 动 imprint ⇔ 掩蓋[48], 涵蓋[46], 覆蓋[22], 遮蓋[34], 瓶蓋[49], 膝蓋[49]
蓋章 gàizhāng 动 stamp, imprint: 蓋個章 imprint a seal
蓋子 gàizi 图 cover, lid

亦 39 yì
75 Person 大[9p] with dots representing sides. 动 armpits (⇒ 腋[49]) 副 also
亦即 yìjí 动 that is, namely

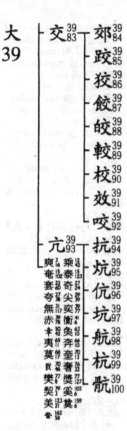

亦然 yìrán likewise, similarly:
反之亦然 vice-versa

跡 39 76 [跡] Feet 足 with
亦 phonetic. track, trace
⇔ 蹤跡, 痕跡, 軌跡,
古跡, 絕跡, 遺跡
跡象 jīxiàng sign, mark,
indication

奕 39 77 yì Big 大 with 亦
phonetic. grand

赤 39 78 chì Large 大 fire 火
(together altered to resemble
亦). red bare
赤膊 chìbó naked to the waist
赤道 chìdào equator
赤腳 chìjiǎo barefoot
赤裸 chìluǒ naked, bare
赤字 chìzì deficit, red ink:
預算赤字 budget deficit

赦 39 79 shè Strike 攵 with 赤
phonetic. pardon ⇔

特赦

赦免 shèmiǎn pardon, absolve
pardon, amnesty

郝 39 80 hǎo City 邑 with 赤
phonetic. a surname

赫 39 81 hè Two fires 赤.
brilliant a surname hertz
⇔ 顯赫

赫然 hèrán terribly (angry)

嚇 39 82 hè xià [吓] Mouth 口 like
two fires 赫 (phonetic).
Simplified form uses 下 hè:
threaten, intimidate xià:
frighten: 嚇我一跳 startled
me ⇔ 驚嚇, 恫嚇, 恐
嚇

嚇唬 xiàhu scare, frighten
嚇人 xiàrén startling

交 39 83 jiāo Pictograph of a person
大 with crossed legs.
cross, intersect hand in,
submit meet: 交朋友 make
friends ⇔ 建交, 結交,
送交, 口交, 性交, 邦
交, 外交, 締交

交班 jiāobān change shifts
交叉 jiāochā cross, intersect
交代 jiāodài hand over
交道 jiāodào social intercourse: 打交道 deal with
交付 jiāofù consign
交給 jiāogěi hand over
交媾 jiāogòu sexual intercourse
交合 jiāohé have sex
交互 jiāohù alternately mutual: 交互作用 synergy
交還 jiāohuán return (something)
交換 jiāohuàn exchange: 語言交換 language exchange
交際 jiāojì socializing: 交際費 entertainment expenses
交流 jiāoliú exchange, inter-

flow: 文化交流 cultural exchange

交配 jiāopéi 動 mate

交情 jiāoqíng 图 friendship

交涉 jiāoshè 動 negotiate

交談 jiāotán 動 converse, chat

交通 jiāotōng 图 transportation, traffic

交往 jiāowǎng 图 social intercourse

交誼 jiāoyí 图 friendship

交易 jiāoyì 图 trade, transaction

郊 39 jiāo
84 Interacts 交 (phonetic) with the city 邑. 图 suburbs ⇔ 市郊

郊區 jiāoqū 图 suburbs

郊遊 jiāoyóu 動 outing, excursion

跤 39 jiāo
85 Feet 足 intertwined 交 (phonetic). 動 trip ⇔ 摔跤

狡 39 jiāo
86 Dog 犬 with 交 phonetic. 彫 cunning

狡猾 jiāohuá 彫 cunning

狡計 jiāojì 图 subterfuge, trick

狡黠 jiāoxiá 彫 crafty, cunning

餃 39 jiāo
87 [饺] Food 食 with 交 phonetic. 图 dumpling ⇔ 水餃

餃子 jiǎozi 图 dumpling

皎 39 jiāo
88 White 白 with 交 phonetic. 彫 bright

皎潔 jiǎojié 彫 shining clean

較 39 jiào
89 [较] Carriage 車 and connect 交 (phonetic). 图 crossbar supporting a carriage seat 動 comparatively, relatively ⇔ 比較, 計較

較爲 jiàowéi 副 comparatively

校 39 xiào jiào
90 Wood 木 with 交 phonetic. xiào: 图 school jiào:

校 compare 動 proofread ⇔ 上校, 學校, 少校, 母校, 夜校

校對 jiàoduì 動 proofread

校稿 jiàogǎo 動 proofread

校正 jiàozhèng 動 correct, proofread

校友 xiàoyǒu 图 alum

校園 xiàoyuán 图 campus

校長 xiàozhǎng 图 school president, principal

效 39 xiào
91 Intersect 交 (phonetic) and strike 攵. 動 mimic, copy 图 effect, efficacy ⇔ 有效, 奏效, 無效, 成效, 功效, 生效, 績效, 仿效

效法 xiàofǎ 動 follow example of

效果 xiàoguǒ 图 result, effect: 反效果 reverse effect

效力 xiàolì 图 effect, efficacy

效率 xiàolù 图 efficiency

效能 xiàonéng 图 efficacy

效益 xiàoyì 图 performance, efficiency

效用 xiàoyòng 图 usefulness, utility

咬 39 yǎo
92 Modern form shows mouth 口 connecting 交 (phonetic). 動 bite

亢 39 kàng
93 Pictograph showing person's 大 head and neck. 图 neck 彫 proud, haughty 副 excessive, extreme ⇔ 高亢

亢奮 kàngfèn 彫 stimulated, excited

抗 39 kàng
94 Hand 手 with 亢 phonetic. 動 resist, combat ⇔ 違抗, 反抗, 抵抗, 對抗

抗衡 kànghéng 動 contend, compete

抗拒 kàngjù 動 resist

抗議 kàngyì 動 protest

抗戰 kàngzhàn 图 resistance war: 抗日戰爭 War of Resistance Against Japan (1937-45)

炕 39 kàng
95 Fire 火 with 亢 phonetic. 图 kang - a brick bed warmable by fire

伉 39 kàng
96 Person 人 with 亢 phonetic. 图 spouse

伉儷 kànglì 图 married couple

坑 39 kēng
97 Earth 土 with 亢 phonetic. 图 pit, hole ⇔ 礦坑, 糞坑, 焚書坑儒, 火坑

航 39 háng
98 Modern form shows boat 舟 with 亢 phonetic. 图 boat, ship 動 navigate, sail ⇔ 巡航

航程 hángchéng 图 voyage: 三天的航程 three days' voyage

航道 hángdào 图 channel, waterway

航空 hángkōng 图 aviation: 航空公司 airline; 航空信 airmail; 航空母艦 aircraft carrier

航天 hángtiān 图 space flight

航線 hángxiàn 图 air route, shipping route

航行 hángxíng 動 navigate

航運 hángyùn 图 shipping

杭 39 háng
99 Wood 木 with 亢 phonetic. 動 Hangzhou

杭州 hángzhōu 動 Hangzhou - capital of Zhejiang Province

骯 39 āng
100 [肮] Bones 骨 with 亢 phonetic. 彫 corpulent

骯髒 āngzāng 彫 dirty

尸 40 shī
1 Pictograph of a person sitting or lying down. 图 corpse (⇔ 屍)

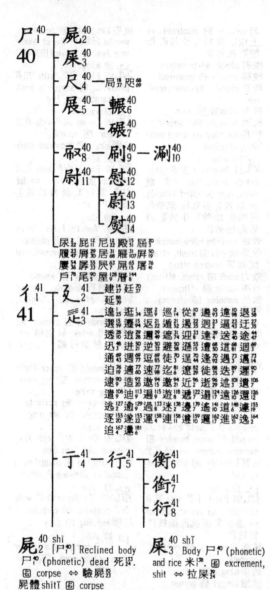

尸 40 [1]
40

屍 40 [2]

屎 40 [3]

尺 40 [4] — 局 15 咫 66

展 40 [5] — 輾 40 [6]
            — 碾 40 [7]

帬 40 [8] — 刷 40 [9] — 涮 40 [10]

尉 40 [11] — 慰 40 [12]
             蔚 40 [13]
             熨 40 [14]

尿 32 屁 17 尼 52 殿 23 屆 9
履 3 屑 33 居 41 屜 23 屏 9
屢 43 屠 75 屍 15 屑 18 屠 76
尸 67 尾 20 屋 128 層 144

彳 41 [1] — 爻 41 [2] — 建 39 廷 29
41   延 28

         辵 41 [3] 遶 25 逛 14 運 21 巡 8 從 97 遯 10 達 11 退 13
                    選 25 邋 13 返 21 遁 16 過 5 迥 13 逼 4 迂 11
                    透 26 逍 27 邇 19 遮 74 迎 3 還 2 送 97 途 11
                    迅 89 進 77 逆 89 避 85 遜 89 遭 77 逅 11 迴 14
                    通 30 週 89 逗 24 徒 45 逞 29 逢 89 遇 90 邁 14
                    迫 91 適 77 速 89 迄 25 遼 89 徙 77 迭 97 遷 9
                    逮 47 造 92 近 99 逝 99 迎 99 逃 9 遺 99 遺 126
                    遣 127 迪 113 遍 99 遊 118 邊 99 遙 10 道 140 遡 99
                    逃 127 逾 179 過 99 迷 18 邊 99 遙 10 道 140 遡 99
                    逐 99 邃 155 運 99 連 158 遣 10 邇 17 進 162 逸 164
                    迫 167 邊 181

         丁 41 [4] — 行 41 [5] — 衡 41 [6]
                                  衛 41 [7]
                                  衍 41 [8]

屍 40 shī
[尸[1]] Reclined body
尸[1] (phonetic) dead 死[17].
📖 corpse ⇔ 驗屍[92]
屍體 shītǐ 📖 corpse

屎 40 shǐ
3 Body 尸[1] (phonetic)
and rice 米[138]. 📖 excrement,
shit ⇔ 拉屎[32]

尺 40 chǐ
4 Body 尸[1] with line
乙[1] suggesting measure-
ment. 📖 foot ⇔ 公尺[1], 咫
尺[66]
尺寸 chǐcùn 📖 measurements,
dimensions, size
尺度 chǐdù 📖 scale, measure

展 40 zhǎn
5 Body 尸[1] and gown
(ancient character based on
clothing 衣[126]). 📖 unroll, unfold
⇔ 畫展[5], 伸展[89], 拓展[26],
影展[57], 擴展[80], 參展[97], 施
展[89], 開展[89], 發展[92], 進
展[162]
展開 zhǎnkāi 📖 launch, unfold
展覽 zhǎnlǎn 📖 exhibition
展示 zhǎnshì 📖 display
展望 zhǎnwàng 📖 forecast,
prospects

輾 40 zhǎn
6 [辗] Cart 車[158] rolling
展[5] (phonetic). 📖 roll over
輾轉 zhǎnzhuǎn 📖 be tossed
about 📖 be passed along

碾 40 niǎn
7 Stone 石[89] rolling
展[5] (phonetic). 📖 mill, grind:
碾米 mill rice

帬 40 shuā
8 Body 尸[1], rag 巾[37]
and hand 又[1]. 古 wipe

刷 40 shuā
9 Wipe 帬[8] (phonetic,
abbreviated) with a knife 刀[5].
📖 scrub, brush ⇔ 洗刷[31],
印刷[25], 粉刷[89], 牙刷[94]
刷卡 shuākǎ 📖 use a credit card
刷洗 shuāxǐ 📖 scrub
刷牙 shuāyá 📖 brush teeth
刷子 shuāzi 📖 brush

涮 40 shuàn
10 Brush 刷[9] (phonetic)
with water 水[34]. 📖 rinse 📖
boil thin slices of meat: 涮羊
肉 dip-boiled mutton slices

尉 40 wèi

11 Fire 火[42] (altered to 小[8]?) and hand 寸[24] with an ancient character from 尸[10] and 二[2] phonetic. ❀ iron, press (⇨ 慰[40]) 图 officer ⇔ 中尉[9]

慰 40 wèi

12 Iron 尉[40] (phonetic) the heart 心[93]. 动 console, comfort ⇔ 安慰[40], 欣慰[40]

慰藉 wèijiè 动 console, comfort

蔚 40 wèi

13 Plant 艸[46] with 尉[40] phonetic. 形 lush

蔚藍 wèilán 形 azure, sky-blue

熨 40 yùn

14 Modern form shows iron 尉[40] (phonetic) with fire 火[42] redundant. 动 iron, press: 熨衣服 iron clothes

熨斗 yùndǒu 图 iron

彳 41 chì

1 Pictograph showing a person taking a small step. 图 step 图 left step

亍 41 yǐn

2 Step 彳[41] extended. ❀ stride

辵 41 chuò

3 Step 彳[41] and stop 止[78] (merged except in derivatives such as 徒[41] and 從[41].) ❀ halting movement

亍 41 chù

4 Reverse of step 彳[41]. 图 stop 图 right step

行 41 xíng háng

5 Step 彳[41] and stop 亍[41]. Also explained as left step and right step. xíng: 动 walk 动 do 形 all right, o.k. 形 capable háng: 图 line, row company, firm 图 line of business, profession: 改行 change careers ⇔ 五行[15], 不行[40], 逐行[3], 人行道[13], 先行[15], 銀行[25], 暴行[15], 舉

行[15], 腹行[47], 內行[41], 同
行[34], 修行[47], 可行[27], 分
行[15], 央行[80], 航行[40], 錢
行[15], 盛行[45], 執行[80], 流
行[33], 施行[47], 言行[94], 通
行[92], 繞行[47], 爬行[80], 發
行[10], 步行[14], 獸行[30], 實
行[14], 暫行[27], 採行[100], 辭
行[93], 雷厲風行[50], 旅行[218], 遊行[118], 自行[139], 推行[142], 進
行[142], 飛行[49]

行家 hángjiā 图 expert

行列 hángliè 图 row or column 图 ranks: 進入先進國家的行列 enter the ranks of developed countries

行情 hángqíng 图 market price

行業 hángyè 图 profession

行動 xíngdòng 动 take action 动 action 动 move about: 行動電話 cell phone

行賄 xínghuì 动 bribe

行徑 xíngjìng 图 conduct, action

行李 xínglǐ 图 baggage

行禮 xínglǐ 动 salute

行囊 xíngnáng 图 luggage and traveling money

行人 xíngrén 图 pedestrian

行駛 xíngshǐ 动 drive, ride

行使 xíngshǐ 动 exercise (power or rights)

行爲 xíngwéi 图 behavior

行銷 xíngxiāo 动 sell, market: 行銷策略 marketing strategy

行星 xíngxīng 图 planet: 小行星 asteroid

行兇 xíngxiōng 动 commit murder

行者 xíngzhě 图 Buddhist monk

行政 xíngzhèng 图 administration: 行政大樓 administrative building; ❀ 行政院 Executive Yuan

行走 xíngzǒu 动 walk

衡 41 héng

6 Large 大[7] piece of wood placed on bull's horns

角[100] with 行[41] phonetic. 图 beam 动 weigh ⇔ 均衡[45], 平衡[45], 抗衡[80], 制衡[80], 失衡[45]

衡量 héngliáng 动 measure, weigh

衡山 héngshān 图 Mount Heng - a sacred mountain in Hunan Province

衡 41 xián

7 Metal 金[91] and go 行[41]. 图 bit (to control a horse) 动 hold in mouth ⇨ 頭衡[41]

衡接 xiánjiē 动 join, connect

衍 41 yǎn

8 Water 水[56] moving 行[41] towards the sea. 动 flow ⇔ 敷衍[41]

衍變 yǎnbiàn 动 evolve 图 evolution (⇨ 演變[40])

衍生 yǎnshēng 动 evolve, derive

後 41 hòu

9 [后[41]] Small 么[76] steps 彳[41] and walk with difficulty 夊[15]. 图 fall behind 图 back, behind 图 afterwards ⇔ 往後[41], 落後[45], 先後[45], 背後[47], 隨後[18], 嗣後[41], 歇後語[47], 爾後[27], 今後[27], 以後[47], 向後[47], 之後[45], 事後[47], 此後[47], 延後[80], 然後[27], 午後[47], 前後[47], 而後[14], 最後[15]

後輩 hòubèi 图 future generations

後邊 hòubiān 图 back, behind

後代 hòudài 图 future generations, posterity

後盾 hòudùn 图 backing, support

後方 hòufāng 图 rear

後果 hòuguǒ 图 result, repercussion

後悔 hòuhuǐ 动 regret

後勁 hòujìn 图 after-effect 图 stamina

後來 hòulái 动 afterwards

後門 hòumén 图 back door: 走後門 use "back door" connec-

彳
41

後 41/9

衝 10, 衛 品, 衛 24
衛 妒, 街 妒, 衝 76/2
術 01/2

徨 ?, 往 ?, 徑 ?, 很 ?, 律 ?, 得 ?
彼 ?, 循 ?, 復 ?, 待 ?, 德 ?, 雁 107
役 ?, 行 41, 徐 ?, 徹 ?, 彿 ?, 徊 ?
征 ?, 御 ?, 彷 ?, 徬 ?, 微 134, 徠 160
徘 159

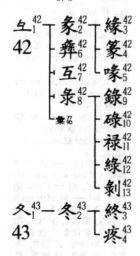

彑 42/1 ── 象 42/2 ── 緣 42/3
          彝 42/6 ── 篆 42/4
          互 42/7 ── 彙 42/5
          彔 42/8 ── 錄 42/9
          彚 ?   碌 42/10
                    祿 42/11
                    綠 42/12
                    剝 42/13

夂 43/1 ── 冬 43/2 ┬ 終 43/3
                   └ 疼 43/4

tions
後面 hòumiàn ⬚ back, behind
後年 hòunián ⬚ year after next
後世 hòushì ⬚ future gener-
ations
後台 hòutái ⬚ backstage
後天 hòutiān ⬚ day after
tomorrow: 大後天 three days
from now
後裔 hòuyì ⬚ descendants
後遺症 hòuyízhèng ⬚ after-
effect, repercussion
後者 hòuzhě ⬚ the latter

彑 42/1
1 Pictograph of a boar's
snout.

彖 42/2 tuàn
2 Boar 豕 155 following
its snout 彑 42.

緣 42/3 yuán
3 [缘] Threads 糸 153
and follow 彖 42 (phonetic).
⬚ hem ⬚ cause, reason ⇔
人緣 ?, 邊緣 ?
緣分 yuánfèn ⬚ destiny, fate:
有緣分的 destined
緣故 yuángù ⬚ cause
緣起 yuánqǐ ⬚ origin
緣由 yuányóu ⬚ reason ⇨ 原
由 ?

篆 42/4 zhuàn
4 Trace/follow 彖 42
(phonetic) on bamboo 竹 ?

tablet. ⬚ transcribe ⇔ 小
篆 ?
篆刻 zhuànkè ⬚ seal carving
篆書 zhuànshū ⬚ seal characters - an ancient calligraphy
style still used on seals

彙 42/5 huì
5 Mouth 口 ? and boar
with snout 彑 42. ⬚ beak, bill

彝 42/6 yí
6 Boar's head 彑 42, rice
米 138, and silk 糸 153 offered
廾 ? to ancestors. ⬚ a sacrificial vessel ⬚ a surname
彝族 yízú ⬚ Yi people

互 42/7 hù
7 Pictograph of a device
for twisting ropes. ⬚ mutual
⇔ 交互 ?, 相互 ?
互惠 hùhuì ⬚ reciprocal ⬚
reciprocate
互利 hùlì ⬚ mutually beneficial
互相 hùxiāng ⬚ mutual: 互相
學習 study from each other
互助 hùzhù ⬚ mutual aid

彔 42/8 lù
8 Pictograph showing
an axe (altered to resemble
彑 42) stripping an overturned
tree (altered to resemble 水 ?).
⬚ carve

錄 42/9 lù
9 [录] Metal 金 ? with
彔 42 phonetic. ⬚ record ⬚
register, record ⇔ 語錄 ?, 筆
錄 ?, 附錄 ?, 紀錄 ?, 記
錄 ?, 備忘錄 ?, 目錄 114, 輯
錄像 lùxiàng ⬚ ⬚ video: 錄像
機 VCR; 錄像帶 videotape
錄音 lùyīn ⬚ record: 錄音機
tape recorder; 錄音帶 recording tape, cassette tape
錄影 lùyǐng ⬚ ⬚ video: 錄影
機 VCR; 錄影帶 videotape

碌 42/10 lù
10 [碌] Stone 石 ? with
彔 42 phonetic. ⬚ stone roller

禍 mediocre ⇔ 忙碌⁷⁹, 庸碌⁹⁷

禄 42 lù
11 [祿] Omen 示₄₆ with 彔⁴² phonetic. 图 luck 图 official salary
祿位 lùwèi 图 salary and rank

綠 42 lù
12 [綠] Silk 糸⁵³ with 彔⁴² phonetic. 形 green ⇔ 碧綠⁷⁶, 翠綠¹²⁶
綠茶 lùchá 图 green tea
綠地 lùdì 图 green space
綠豆 lùdòu 图 pea
綠化 lùhuà 动 greenify, afforest
綠卡 lùkǎ 图 green card
綠色 lùsè 图 green
綠洲 lùzhōu 图 oasis

剝 13 bō bāo
[剝] Strip tree 彔₈ (phonetic) with knife 刀⁵. 动 peel, strip, shell
剝奪 bōdúo 动 deprive, strip
剝削 bōxuē 动 exploit 图 exploitation

夂 43 zhōng
1 Pictograph of a thread skein tied at one end.

冬 43 dōng
2 Cold 冫²⁵ (phonetic) end 夂⁴³ of the year. 图 winter ⇔ 隆冬⁸⁸
冬季 dōngjì 图 winter
冬眠 dōngmián 图 hibernation
冬天 dōngtiān 图 winter
冬至 dōngzhì 图 winter solstice

終 43 zhōng
3 [終] Thread 糸⁵³ with 夂⁴³ phonetic. 图 end, finish 副 finally ⇔ 始終⁶, 最終⁹⁷
終點 zhōngdiǎn 图 terminal point: 終點站 terminal station, last stop
終結 zhōngjié 图 end, conclusion
終究 zhōngjiù 副 finally
終年 zhōngnián 副 all year
終日 zhōngrì 副 all day

終身 zhōngshēn 图 lifelong: 終身職 lifetime employment, tenure
終生 zhōngshēng 形 lifelong
終於 zhōngyú 副 finally
終止 zhōngzhǐ 动 terminate

疼 43 téng
4 Sickness 疒⁷³ with 冬⁴³ phonetic. 动 ache, hurt 形 painful ⇔ 心疼¹³
疼痛 téngtòng 动 图 ache

亼 44 jí
1 Three lines. 形 many, gather (⇨ 集¹²⁴)

今 44 jīn
2 Union 亼⁴⁴ with additional stroke suggesting contact. 形 now, currently 图 this, current 图 recent ⇔ 如今¹⁴, 當今⁸⁹, 迄今⁹¹, 今後¹¹⁶, 至今¹²⁸, 而今¹³⁴
今後 jīnhòu 副 from now on
今年 jīnnián 图 this year
今日 jīnrì 图 today
今天 jīntiān 图 today
今晚 jīnwǎn 图 tonight, this evening

金 44 jīn
3 Nuggets (dots on bottom) in the earth 土⁷ with 今⁴⁴ (altered) phonetic. 图 gold 图 metals 图 money 图 a surname ⇔ 酬金⁶⁶, 資金⁸⁷, 黃金⁹³, 股金⁹⁷, 合金⁹⁸, 基金⁹⁸, 冶金⁹⁹, 佣金⁹⁹, 萬金油¹⁰⁵, 本金¹⁰⁵, 獎金¹¹⁰, 獎學金¹¹⁷, 押金¹¹⁷, 現金¹¹⁵, 助學金¹¹⁷, 租金¹³¹, 淘金¹⁴¹, 贖金¹⁵⁹, 獻金¹⁷⁴
金額 jīné 图 amount of money
金髮 jīnfà 图 blond hair
金瓶梅 jīnpíngméi 图 The Golden Lotus - a Ming Dynasty erotic novel
金錢 jīnqián 图 money: 金錢政治 money politics
金融 jīnróng 图 finance

金色 jīnsè 图 gold color
金屬 jīnshǔ 图 metals
金文 jīnwén 图 characters inscribed on ancient bronzes
金魚 jīnyú 图 goldfish
金字塔 jīnzìtǎ 图 pyramid

鑫 44 xīn
4 Much gold 金⁴⁴. 图 prosperity, profit

侌 44 yīn
5 Clouds 云₄₂ with 今⁴⁴ phonetic. 形 cloudy (⇨ 陰⁴⁴)

陰 44 yīn
6 [阴] Hill's 阜¹⁶⁷ shady 侌⁴⁴ (phonetic) side. 图 north side of a hill 图 yin - feminine or negative principle in Daoist philosophy 图 shade 形 cloudy, overcast 图 genitals 图 hidden, secret ⇔ 光陰⁴²
陰道 yīndào 图 vagina
陰核 yīnhé 图 clitoris
陰莖 yīnjīng 图 penis
陰曆 yīnlì 图 lunar calendar
陰霾 yīnmái 图 haze
陰毛 yīnmáo 图 pubic hair
陰謀 yīnmóu 图 scheme
陰森 yīnsēn 形 gloomy
陰天 yīntiān 图 cloudy day
陰險 yīnxiǎn 形 cunning, treacherous
陰性 yīnxìng 形 negative 图 female
陰陽 yīnyáng 图 yin and yang
陰影 yīnyǐng 图 shadow

吟 44 yín
7 Mouth 口⁶⁶ with 今⁴⁴ phonetic. 动 moan 动 recite, chant ⇔ 呻吟⁹³, 沈吟⁸⁹
吟誦 yínsòng 动 chant, recite

含 44 hán
8 Mouth 口⁶⁶ with 今⁴⁴ phonetic. 动 hold in mouth 动 contain, hold ⇔ 包含¹⁸
含糊 hánhú 图 unclear
含量 hánliàng 图 contents
含蓄 hánxù 形 implicit 形 reserved

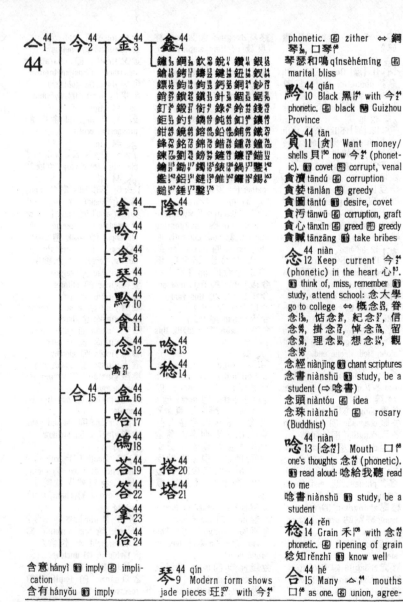

亼 44/1 — 今 44/2 — 金 44/3 — 鑫 44/4

鏞 2/35 鋼 3/28 欽 10/49 鋭 11/4 鑽 11/41 銀 12/53
鎗 12/85 銬 13/11 鑄 13/22 鍵 14/28 鈕 14/58 釵 14/84
鏢 15/92 鈎 18/16 鉤 18/35 鍔 22/30 銅 24/4 鈔 29/13
銷 29/27 鎖 29/42 鎮 31/33 針 31/38 錮 31/52 鋸 31/70
釘 36/2 鍛 37/21 銜 41/7 錄 42/9 鈐 44/32 錢 45/12
鉅 51/33 釣 61/5 鏰 65/17 鈍 66/53 釦 68/3 鑲 68/13
鉗 68/67 鐃 68/93 鎔 68/110 鉛 68/120 鋪 69/73 鐵 70/47
鋒 70/96 銘 72/10 錦 76/10 錯 76/85 鍾 76/93 鐘 76/103
鍊 77/109 劉 78/42 鎊 94/29 鐽 98/13 鐮 108/12 錨 111/32
鑰 115/21 鋤 117/9 鐲 125/10 錶 126/16 鍋 133/7 鑿 142/4
鑑 142/5 鋁 151/3 鏈 158/13 錐 162/3 鑼 162/15 錫 163/6
鎚 167/5 錘 173/3 鑿 176/3

侌 44/5 — 陰 44/6

吟 44/7

含 44/8

琴 44/9

黔 44/10

貪 44/11

念 44/12 — 唸 44/13, 稔 44/14

禽 73/21

合 44/15 — 盒 44/16

哈 44/17

鴿 44/18

荅 44/19 — 搭 44/20, 塔 44/21

答 44/22

拿 44/23

恰 44/24

含意 hányì [動] imply [名] implication
含有 hányǒu [動] imply

琴 44 qín
9 Modern form shows jade pieces 玨 107/2 with 今 44/2 phonetic. [名] zither ⇔ 鋼琴 3/28, 口琴 68/1
琴瑟和鳴 qínsèhémíng [名] marital bliss

黔 44 qián
10 Black 黑 144/17 with 今 44/2 phonetic. [名] black [地] Guizhou Province

貪 44 tān
11 [贪] Want money/shells 貝 150/1 now 今 44/2 (phonetic). [動] covet [形] corrupt, venal
貪瀆 tāndú [名] corruption
貪婪 tānlán [形] greedy
貪圖 tāntú [動] desire, covet
貪污 tānwū [名] corruption, graft
貪心 tānxīn [名] greed [形] greedy
貪贓 tānzāng [動] take bribes

念 44 niàn
12 Keep current 今 44/2 (phonetic) in the heart 心 83/1. [動] think of, miss, remember [動] study, attend school: 念大學 go to college ⇔ 概念 10/53, 眷念 15/138, 惦念 26/21, 紀念 57/2, 信念 69/79, 掛念 70/12, 悼念 76/118, 留念 78/98, 理念 111/20, 想念 114/24, 觀念 162/70
念經 niànjīng [動] chant scriptures
念書 niànshū [動] study, be a student (⇨ 唸書)
念頭 niàntóu [名] idea
念珠 niànzhū [名] rosary (Buddhist)

唸 44 niàn
13 [念 44/12] Mouth 口 68/1 one's thoughts 念 44/12 (phonetic). [動] read aloud: 唸給我聽 read to me
唸書 niànshū [動] study, be a student

稔 44 rěn
14 Grain 禾 108/1 with 念 44/12 phonetic. [名] ripening of grain
稔知 rěnzhī [動] know well

合 44 hé
15 Many 亼 44/1 mouths 口 68/1 as one. [名] union, agree-

ment 📖 join, combine 📖 suit, be appropriate ⇔ 三合會📖, 綜合🖊, 不合🖊, 混合🖊, 化合物🖊, 符合🖊, 巧合🖊, 四合院🖊, 結合🖊, 志同道合🖊, 交合🖊, 配合🖊, 聯合🖊, 回合🖊, 百合🖊, 場合🖊, 適合🖊, 契合🖊, 吻合🖊, 整合🖊, 組合🖊, 撮合🖊, 會合🖊, 集合🖊, 融合🖊

合併 hébìng 📖 merge
合唱 héchàng 📖 sing in chorus: 合唱團 chorus
合成 héchéng 📖 synthesize
合法 héfǎ 📖 legal
合格 hégé 📖 qualified: 不合格 unqualified
合乎 héhū 📖 conform to
合夥 héhǔo 📖 partnership
合金 héjīn 📖 alloy
合理 hélǐ 📖 reasonable
合氣道 héqìdào 📖 aikido
合適 héshì 📖 fitting, suitable, appropriate
合算 hésuàn 📖 worthwhile, profitable
合同 hétóng 📖 contract
合約 héyuē 📖 contract
合照 hézhào 📖 group picture
合資 hézī 📖 joint venture
合作 hézùo 📖 cooperate, collaborate: 合作社 cooperative

盒 44 hé
16 Vessel Ⅲ📖 that can be joined/covered 合📖 (phonetic). 📖 box
盒子 hézi 📖 box

哈 44 hā hǎ
17 Mouth 口📖 together 合📖 (phonetic). hā: 📖 sound of laughter
哈巴狗 hābāgǒu 📖 Pekingese dog 📖 sycophant/ Peke?
哈爾濱 hāěrbīn 📖 Harbin - capital of Heilongjiang Province
哈哈 hāhā 📖 📖 laugh: 哈

哈大笑 laugh heartily
哈密瓜 hāmìguā 📖 Hami melon
哈欠 hāqiàn 📖 📖 yawn

鴿 44 gē
18 [鸽] Bird 鳥📖 with 合📖 phonetic. 📖 pigeon
鴿子 gēzi pigeon: 被她放鴿子 📖 stood up by her

荅 44 dá
19 Plant 艸📖 joined 合📖. 📖 a bean plant

搭 44 dā
20 Hand 手📖 with 荅📖 phonetic. 📖 hang on, attach 📖 ride, travel by
搭便車 dābiànchē 📖 hitchhike
搭乘 dāchéng 📖 travel by
搭配 dāpèi 📖 match
搭腔 dāqiāng 📖 answer, respond
搭訕 dāshàn 📖 strike up a conversation

塔 44 tǎ
21 Earth 土📖 with 荅📖 phonetic. 📖 pagoda, tower, stupa ⇔ 水塔🖊, 金字塔🖊, 佛塔🖊, 燈塔🖊

答 44 dá dā
22 Bamboo 竹📖 joined 合📖. 📖 mend a fence dá: 📖 reply: 答對了! Correct! ⇔ 報答🖊, 回答🖊, 問答🖊, 解答🖊
答案 dáàn 📖 answer
答覆 dáfù 📖 reply
答謝 dáxiè 📖 express appreciation
答應 dāyìng 📖 agree to, promise 📖 respond, reply

拿 44 ná
23 Modern form shows together 合📖 and hand 手📖. 📖 take, get 📖 hold, carry ⇔ 擒拿🖊, 巴拿馬🖊, 捉拿🖊, 緝拿🖊, 推拿🖊
拿出 náchū 📖 take out
拿到 nádào 📖 get hold of
拿回 náhúi 📖 recover, retrieve
拿來 nálái 📖 fetch, retrieve,

bring
拿起 náqǐ 📖 pick up
拿手 náshǒu 📖 specialty 📖 adept
拿著 názhe 📖 holding
拿住 názhù 📖 take hold of
拿走 názǒu 📖 take, walk off with

恰 44 qià
24 Heart 心📖 united 合📖. 📖 fitting, suitable
恰當 qiàdāng 📖 appropriate, fitting
恰好 qiàhǎo 📖 just right, fortunately
恰巧 qiàqiǎo 📖 coincidentally, fortunately

洽 44 qià
25 Water 水📖 and join 合📖. 📖 lubricate 📖 negotiate, consult ⇔ 接洽🖊, 融洽🖊
洽商 qiàshāng 📖 discuss business
洽談 qiàtán 📖 discuss, consult

給 44 gěi jǐ
26 [给] Threads 糸📖 joined 合📖. 📖 give, supply 📖 let, allow: 給我看! Let me see! 📖 for, to: 把這送給她. Give this to her. 📖 by 📖 (indicating emphasis) 把這件事給忘了. Forget this matter. ⇔ 供給🖊, 寄給🖊, 送給🖊, 交給🖊, 帶給🖊, 配給🖊, 借給🖊, 遞給🖊, 捐給🖊, 自給自足🖊, 賣給🖊, 嫁給🖊, 獻給🖊
給予 gěiyǔ 📖 give, grant

拾 44 shí
27 Hand 手📖 joining 合📖. 📖 pick up, collect ten (complex form) ⇔ 收拾🖊

令 44 lìng
28 Join 人📖 a seal 卩📖 to a document. 📖 decree, order 📖 make, cause 📖 good, pleasant ⇔ 指令🖊, 飭令🖊, 司令🖊, 喝令🖊, 法令🖊, 命

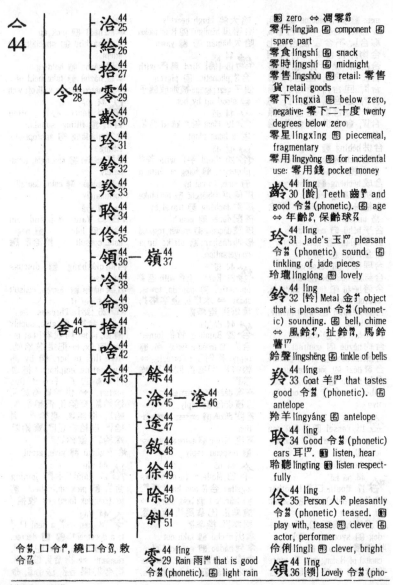

⌒
44

Tree diagram (left side):

- 洽 44/25
- 給 44/26
- 拾 44/27
- 令 44/28
  - 零 44/29
  - 齡 44/30
  - 玲 44/31
  - 鈴 44/32
  - 羚 44/33
  - 聆 44/34
  - 伶 44/35
  - 領 44/36 — 嶺 44/37
  - 冷 44/38
  - 命 44/39
- 舍 44/40 — 捨 44/41
  - 啥 44/42
  - 余 44/43 ┬ 餘 44/44
    - 涂 44/45 — 塗 44/46
    - 途 44/47
    - 敘 44/48
    - 徐 44/49
    - 除 44/50
    - 斜 44/51

令 ⁴⁴/₂₈, 口令 ⁴⁴, 繞口令 ᵈᵉ, 敕令 ⁷⁵

零 29 44 líng
Rain 雨 ¹⁶⁴ that is good 令 ⁴⁴/₂₈ (phonetic). 图 light rain

图 zero ⇔ 凋零 ⁴⁴⁷

零件 língjiàn 图 component 图 spare part

零食 língshí 图 snack

零時 língshí 图 midnight

零售 língshòu 图 retail: 零售貨 retail goods

零下 língxià 图 below zero, negative: 零下二十度 twenty degrees below zero

零星 língxīng 图 piecemeal, fragmentary

零用 língyòng 图 for incidental use: 零用錢 pocket money

齡 30 44 líng
[齡] Teeth 齒 ²¹¹ and good 令 ⁴⁴/₂₈ (phonetic). 图 age ⇔ 年齡 ¹⁰, 保齡球 ⁴⁴

玲 31 44 líng
Jade's 玉 ¹⁰⁷ pleasant 令 ⁴⁴/₂₈ (phonetic) sound. 图 tinkling of jade pieces

玲瓏 línglóng 图 lovely

鈴 32 44 líng
[铃] Metal 金 ¹⁶⁷ object that is pleasant 令 ⁴⁴/₂₈ (phonetic) sounding. 图 bell, chime ⇔ 風鈴 ⁴⁷, 扯鈴 ᵇⁱⁿᵈ, 馬鈴薯 ¹⁷⁷

鈴聲 língshēng 图 tinkle of bells

羚 33 44 líng
Goat 羊 ¹²³ that tastes good 令 ⁴⁴/₂₈ (phonetic). 图 antelope

羚羊 língyáng 图 antelope

聆 34 44 líng
Good 令 ⁴⁴/₂₈ (phonetic) ears 耳 ¹²⁸. 🔲 listen, hear

聆聽 língtīng 🔲 listen respectfully

伶 35 44 líng
Person 人 ¹⁰ pleasantly 令 ⁴⁴/₂₈ (phonetic) teased. 🔲 play with, tease 图 clever 图 actor, performer

伶俐 línglì 图 clever, bright

領 36 44 lǐng
[领] Lovely 令 ⁴⁴/₂₈ (pho-

字譜及字典

135

netic) part of the head 頁. 图 neck 图 collar 图 lead 图 receive, get ⇔ 綱領, 佔領, 帶領, 頭領, 本領, 將領, 首領, 率領

領導 lǐngdǎo 图 lead: 領導人 leader; 最高領導人 supreme leader

領巾 lǐngjīn 图 scarf

領情 lǐngqíng 图 grateful

領事 lǐngshì 图 consul: 領事館 consulate

領土 lǐngtǔ 图 territory

領悟 lǐngwù 图 comprehend

領先 lǐngxiān 图 lead

領袖 lǐngxiù 图 leader

領養 lǐngyǎng 图 adopt

領域 lǐngyù 图 territory, domain, realm

嶺 37 lǐng [岭] Mountain's 山 collar 領 (phonetic). 图 mountain ridge 图 mountain range ⇔ 峻嶺, 山嶺

冷 44 lěng 38 Cold 冫 with 令 phonetic. 图 cold ⇔ 寒冷

冷藏 lěngcáng 图 refrigerate

冷淡 lěngdàn 图 cool, indifferent: 反應冷淡 cool reaction

冷凍 lěngdòng 图 freeze: 冷凍庫 freezer

冷靜 lěngjìng 图 dispassionate, calm, cool

冷酷 lěngkù 图 cold, unfeeling

冷漠 lěngmò 图 aloof, indifferent

冷氣 lěngqì 图 air-conditioning: 冷氣機 air-conditioner

冷卻 lěngquè 图 cool off

冷水 lěngshuǐ 图 cold water

冷戰 lěngzhàn 图 cold war

命 44 mìng 39 Verbal 口 decree 令 (phonetic). 图 order, command 图 life 图 fate, destiny ⇔ 玩命, 壽命, 要命, 送命, 聽命, 認命, 天命, 拼命, 任命, 安非他命, 喪命, 使命, 生命, 性命, 革命, 救命, 致命, 算命, 維他命

命案 mìng'àn 图 murder case

命令 mìnglìng 图 order, command

命題 mìngtí 图 proposition (logic) 图 set exam questions

命運 mìngyùn 图 destiny, fate

舍 44 shè 40 Joining ᐱ of thatch 屮 and walls 口 (together resembling 舌). 图 shed, hut ⇔ 鄰舍, 寒舍, 敝舍, 宿舍, 廬舍

捨 44 shě 41 [舍] Hand 手 with 舍 phonetic. 图 abandon ⇔ 取捨

捨不得 shěbùdé 图 unwilling to give up

捨得 shědé 图 willing to give up

捨棄 shěqì 图 abandon

啥 42 shá / shà From 口 mouth/speak 口 with 舍 phonetic. 图 what

余 44 yú 43 Separate 八 with 舍 (abbreviated) phonetic. 图 exhale I 图 a surname

餘 44 yú [余] Food 食 and exhale 余 (phonetic). 图 surplus, excess 图 more than, over ⇔ 剩餘, 盈餘, 殘餘, 其餘, 多餘, 業餘

餘地 yúdì 图 leeway, latitude

餘額 yúé 图 surplus amount

餘燼 yújìn 图 embers, ashes

涂 45 tú Water 水 with 余 phonetic. 图 name of a river 图 a surname

塗 44 tú 46 [涂] River 涂 (phonetic) of earth 土. 图 mud 图 smear 图 erase ⇔ 一塌糊塗, 糊塗

塗抹 túmǒ 图 smear over, obliterate 图 scribble, doodle

塗鴉 túyā 图 scribbles, graffiti

途 44 tú 47 Movement 足 with 余 phonetic and suggestive of mud 塗. 图 road, way ⇔ 路途, 長途, 仕途, 沿途, 中途, 用途, 半途而廢, 旅途, 前途

途徑 tújìng 图 way, channel

途中 túzhōng 图 en route

敘 44 xù 48 Strike 攵 with 余 phonetic. 图 arrange in order 图 describe, recount

敘述 xùshù 图 describe, recount

徐 44 xú 49 Walk/step 彳 with 余 phonetic. 图 slow, unhurried 图 a surname

徐徐 xúxú 图 steady, slow

徐州 xúzhōu 图 Xuzhou - a city in Jiangsu Province

除 44 chú 50 Hills 阜 with 余 phonetic. 图 remove 图 divide 图 except, besides 图 unless ⇔ 根除, 掃除, 破除, 濰除, 消除, 去除, 戒除, 摒除, 扣除, 清除, 革除, 開除, 割除, 廢除, 拆除, 剷除, 刪除, 解除, 剔除, 免除, 排除

除掉 chúdiào 图 remove, eliminate

除法 chúfǎ 图 division

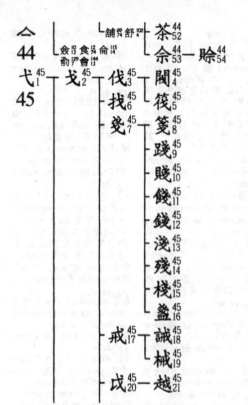

茶園 cháyuán 🔲 tea farm

佘 44 53 shé A variant of 余. 🔲 a surname

赊 54 shē My 佘 (phonetic) shells/money 貝. 🔲 buy on credit

赊購 shēgòu 🔲 buy on credit
赊欠 shēqiàn 🔲 buy on credit

弋 45 1 yì Pictograph of a stake. 🔲 stake, arrow 🔲 shoot ⇔ 巡弋

弋獵 yìliè 🔲 hunt

戈 45 2 gē Stake 弋 with a horizontal 一 blade. 🔲 halberd, lance ⇔ 干戈

伐 45 3 fá Person 人 with a lance 戈. 🔲 cut down, fell 🔲 attack ⇔ 砍伐, 步伐
伐木 fámù 🔲 fell trees

閥 45 4 fá [阀] Gate 門 and attack 伐 (phonetic). 🔲 powerful bloc ⇔ 財閥, 軍閥

筏 45 5 fá Bamboo 竹 with 伐 phonetic. 🔲 raft

找 45 6 zhǎo Hand 手 on lance-like 戈 pole (phonetic). 🔲 punt (a boat) 🔲 seek, look for: 有人找你 someone was looking for you ⇔ 尋找
找出 zhǎochū 🔲 find out
找到 zhǎodào 🔲 find
找錢 zhǎoqián 🔲 return change: 找你三塊錢 return you three dollars' change
找尋 zhǎoxún 🔲 search

戔 45 7 jiān [戋] Lances 戈 destroying. 🔲 small, tiny

除非 chúfēi 🔲 unless
除了 chúle 🔲 except: 除了這個以外 except for this
除去 chúqù 🔲 remove
除外 chúwài 🔲 besides, aside from, excepted
除夕 chúxì 🔲 New Year's Eve

斜 44 51 xié Measure 斗 with 余 phonetic. 🔲 slanting, tilted ⇔ 歪斜, 傾斜
斜度 xiédù 🔲 gradient, slope
斜路 xiélù 🔲 wrong path: 走上斜路 go astray
斜坡 xiépō 🔲 slope

茶 44 52 chá Plant 艸 with 余 (altered) phonetic. 🔲 tea ⇔ 沏茶, 飲茶, 花茶, 泡茶, 冰茶, 奶茶, 倒茶, 綠茶, 紅茶, 烏龍茶
茶杯 chábēi 🔲 teacup
茶房 cháfáng 🔲 teahouse
茶館 cháguǎn 🔲 teahouse
茶壺 cháhú 🔲 teapot
茶几 chájī 🔲 tea table
茶具 chájù 🔲 tea set
茶葉 cháyè 🔲 tea leaf
茶藝館 cháyìguǎn 🔲 teahouse

笸 45 jiān
8 [笺] Bamboo 竹 strips with 戋 phonetic. stationery ⇔ 信箋

踐 45 jiàn
9 [践] Feet 足 destroying 戋 (phonetic). trample ⇔ 實踐
踐踏 jiàntà trample

賤 45 jiàn
10 [贱] Shells/money 貝 tiny 戋 (phonetic). cheap
賤貨 jiànhuò tramp, slut
賤民 jiànmín untouchables

餞 45 jiàn
11 [饯] Food 食 with 戋 phonetic. give farewell dinner
餞行 jiànxíng farewell dinner

錢 45 qián
12 [钱] Metal 金 for breaking to pieces 戋 (phonetic). hoe money a surname ⇔ 賠錢, 花錢, 付錢, 有錢, 銅錢, 價錢, 省錢, 金錢, 找錢, 換錢, 罰錢, 賭錢, 愛錢, 紙錢, 掙錢, 賺錢, 掏錢
錢幣 qiánbì coin
錢財 qiáncái wealth, money, riches
錢莊 qiánzhuāng traditional bank

淺 45 qiǎn
13 [浅] Water 水 small 戋 (phonetic). shallow ⇔ 粗淺, 膚淺

殘 45 cán
14 [残] Death 歹 and destroy 戋 (phonetic). deficient ⇔ 摧殘
殘廢 cánfèi disabled, maimed
殘骸 cánhái wreckage
殘疾 cánjí handicap: 殘疾人 handicapped person
殘酷 cánkù ruthless, cruel

殘忍 cánrěn cruel, brutal
殘殺 cánshā massacre, slaughter
殘餘 cányú remnants
殘渣 cánzhā residue
殘障 cánzhàng handicap: 殘障者 handicapped person

棧 45 zhàn
15 [栈] Wood 木 with 戋 phonetic. shed, storehouse ⇔ 戀棧

盞 45 zhǎn
16 [盏] Tiny 戋 (phonetic) container 皿. small cup a measureword for lamps

戒 45 jiè
17 Hands 廾 holding a lance 戈. guard against, abstain from, quit ⇔ 警戒, 八戒
戒備 jièbèi be on guard, take precautions
戒除 jièchú abstain from, give up
戒酒 jièjiǔ quit drinking
戒絕 jièjué quit a habit: 戒絕菸酒 quit smoking and drinking
戒心 jièxīn vigilance
戒煙 jièyān quit smoking
戒嚴 jièyán martial law: 戒嚴時期 martial law period
戒指 jièzhǐ ring

誡 45 jiè
18 [诫] Words 言 that guard 戒 (phonetic). warn ⇔ 訓誡, 告誡

械 45 xiè
19 Wood 木 that protects 戒 (phonetic) the public. shackles machinery 機械, 器械

戉 45 yuè
20 Lance 戈 and reversed hook ㇄ (phonetic). battle axe

越 45 yuè
21 Walk 走 with 戉 phonetic. traverse exceed the more ... the more 跨越, 超越, 卓越, 穿越, 逾越, 優越
越發 yuèfā more and more
越過 yuèguò cross, exceed
越來越 yuèláiyuè more and more, increasingly
越南 yuènán Vietnam
越野 yuèyě cross-country: 越野車 mountain bike

戊 45 wù
22 Lance 戈 with 丿 indicating large blade. lance fifth Heavenly Stem (⇨ 干支)

戌 45 xū
23 Lance 戊 leaving slash mark 一. wound, kill eleventh Earthly Branch (⇨ 干支)

咸 45 xián
24 Wound 戌 with the mouth 口. bite all
咸信 xiánxìn generally believed

鹹 45 xián
25 [咸] Salt 鹵 with 咸 phonetic. salty
鹹菜 xiáncài pickled vegetables
鹹魚 xiányú salted fish

減 45 jiǎn
26 Water 水 and bite 咸 (phonetic). reduce, decrease subtract ⇔ 削減, 裁減, 縮減, 遞減
減低 jiǎndī reduce, lower
減法 jiǎnfǎ subtraction
減肥 jiǎnféi lose weight
減價 jiǎnjià reduce prices
減輕 jiǎnqīng alleviate
減弱 jiǎnruò weaken, subside
減少 jiǎnshǎo reduce, decrease

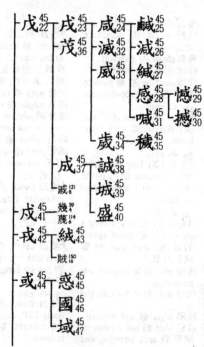

thankful: 非常感謝 extremely thankful

憾 45 hàn
29 Feeling 感紹 (phonetic) with heart 心83 added for emphasis. 動 regret, resent ⇔ 遺憾105

撼 45 hàn
30 Modern form shows hand 手97 and feeling 感紹 (phonetic). 動 shake

喊 45 hǎn
31 Use mouth 口68 with all 咸紹 (phonetic) one's might. 動 shout ⇔ 吶喊紹 喊叫 hǎnjiào 動 shout

滅 45 miè
32 [灭] Kill 戌紹 fire 火82, with water 水31 added later. 動 extinguish 動 exterminate ⇔ 破滅紹, 消滅紹, 泯滅119, 毀滅紹, 熄滅176, 殲滅46, 撲滅176
滅火 mièhuǒ 動 put out a fire: 滅火器 fire extinguisher
滅絕 mièjué 動 become extinct
滅亡 mièwáng 動 perish

威 45 wēi
33 Woman 女34 and kill 戌紹. 图 fear, awe 图 authority, might ⇔ 示威紹, 挪威紹, 夏威夷155, 權威紹
威爾斯 wēiěrsī 图 Wales
威風 wēifēng 图 power and prestige 形 imposing
威力 wēilì 图 force, might
威權 wēiquán 四 authority
威武 wēiwǔ 图 force, might 形 forceful, mighty
威脅 wēixié 動 threaten
威信 wēixìn 图 prestige, credibility
威嚴 wēiyán 图 dignity, majesty 形 majestic, awe-inspiring

歲 45 suì
34 [岁] Step 步紹 with 戌紹 phonetic. Simplified form uses 山67 and 夕7. 图

緘 45 jiān
27 [缄] Threads 糸53 and bite 咸紹 (phonetic). 動 seal
緘口 jiānkǒu 動 keep silent
緘默 jiānmò 動 keep silent

感 45 gǎn
28 Bite 咸紹 (phonetic) the heart 心83. 動 feel, sense 图 feeling, sense ⇔ 反感紹, 快感紹, 好感紹, 敏感紹, 深感紹, 性感紹, 情感紹, 預感102, 美感紹, 靈感164, 觀感162
感觸 gǎnchù 图 emotions and thoughts
感到 gǎndào 動 feel
感動 gǎndòng 動 move, touch 形 moving, touching
感恩 gǎnēn 形 grateful, thankful:

感恩節 Thanksgiving
感官 gǎnguān 图 senses
感激 gǎnjī 形 grateful
感覺 gǎnjué 图 feel 图 feeling
感慨 gǎnkǎi 動 sigh 形 wistful, nostalgic 图 regrets, recollections
感冒 gǎnmào 動 catch cold 图 cold
感情 gǎnqíng 图 affection
感染 gǎnrǎn 動 infect, contaminate 動 influence
感人 gǎnrén 形 moving, touching
感受 gǎnshòu 動 feel
感嘆 gǎntàn 動 exclaim: 感嘆號 exclamation point
感想 gǎnxiǎng 图 reaction, impressions, thoughts
感謝 gǎnxiè 動 thank

years old: 你幾歲? How old are you? ⇔ 年歲, 守歲, 萬歲

歲月 suìyuè years

穢 45 huì 35 [秽] Modern form shows grain 禾 with 歲 phonetic. weeds vile ⇔ 淫穢

茂 45 mào 36 Plants 艸 with 戊 phonetic. luxuriant, flourishing

茂盛 màoshèng luxuriant, flourishing

成 45 chéng 37 Lance 戊 with 丁 phonetic. become complete, accomplish tenth ⇔ 完成, 贊成, 收成, 作成, 長成, 做成, 分成, 打成一片, 達成, 合成, 形成, 換成, 釀成, 製成, 促成, 造成, 現成, 看成, 相成, 相成, 組成, 養成, 變成, 構成

成敗 chéngbài success or failure

成本 chéngběn cost

成分 chéngfèn component, ingredient composition

成功 chénggōng success, achievement

成果 chéngguǒ accomplishment, fruition

成績 chéngjī grade, record: 成績單 report card success

成家 chéngjiā settle down, start a family

成見 chéngjiàn prejudice

成就 chéngjiù achieve achievement

成立 chénglì found, establish

成名 chéngmíng become famous

成年 chéngnián grow up adult

成人 chéngrén adult

成熟 chéngshóu mature, ripen mature, ripe: 不成熟 immature

成為 chéngwéi become

成效 chéngxiào result, effect

成衣 chéngyī tailoring clothing, apparel

成語 chéngyǔ saying, proverb, idiom

成員 chéngyuán member

成長 chéngzhǎng grow growth: 經濟成長率 economic growth rate

誠 45 chéng 38 [诚] Words 言 that become 成 (phonetic) reality. sincere ⇔ 真誠, 投誠, 熟誠, 忠誠, 坦誠, 虔誠

誠懇 chéngkěn sincere, earnest

誠然 chéngrán indeed, certainly

誠實 chéngshí honest

誠意 chéngyì sincerity

誠摯 chéngzhì sincere

城 45 chéng 39 From earth 土 made 成 (phonetic). city, town: 城中心 city center city wall ⇔ 圍城, 長城, 漢城, 都城, 紫禁城

城堡 chéngbǎo castle

城隍 chénghuáng city god: 城隍廟 temple of a city god

城門 chéngmén city gate

城牆 chéngqiáng city wall

城市 chéngshì city

城鎮 chéngzhèn town

盛 45 chéng shèng 40 Vessel 皿 with 成 phonetic. chéng: contain shèng: flourishing, abundant grand a surname ⇔ 旺盛, 茂盛, 強盛, 昌盛, 熾盛, 豐盛, 華盛頓

盛傳 shèngchuán widely rumored

盛況 shèngkuàng grand occasion

盛行 shèngxíng fashionable

戍 45 shù 41 Person 人 with a lance 戈. guard

戍守 shùshǒu guard: 戍守邊疆 guard the frontier

戎 45 róng 42 Lance 戈 and armor 甲 (abbreviated). military barbarians to the west ⇔ 兵戎

戎裝 róngzhuāng military dress

絨 45 róng 43 [绒] Silk 糸 with 戎 phonetic. down ⇔ 鴨絨, 絲絨

絨毛 róngmáo down

或 45 huò 44 Lance 戈, encompass 口, and land represented by 一. region (⇔ 域) or perhaps ⇔ 抑或

或是 huòshì or

或許 huòxǔ perhaps, maybe

或者 huòzhě or perhaps

惑 45 huò 45 Perhaps 或 (phonetic) and heart 心. confused delude ⇔ 誘惑, 疑惑, 困惑, 蠱惑, 迷惑

國 45 gúo 46 [国] Region 或 (phonetic) encompassed 口. Simplified form uses jade 玉. country, nation ⇔ 三國, 王國, 鄰國, 建國, 泰國, 亡國, 德國, 全國, 英國, 法國, 我國, 俄國, 母國, 回國, 中國, 外國, 韓國, 帝國, 敵

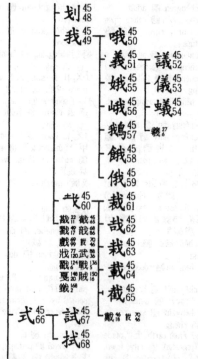

國旗 gúoqí 图 national flag
國慶 gúoqìng 图 National Day
國人 gúorén 图 countrymen
國事 gúoshì 图 national affairs
國手 gúoshǒu 图 national representative: 國手隊 national team
國土 gúotǔ 图 national territory
國外 gúowài 图 abroad
國王 gúowáng 图 king
國文 gúowén 图 图 Chinese (written)
國務 gúowù 图 national affairs: 國務卿 Secretary of State; 國務院 State Department 图 State Council
國璽 gúoxǐ 图 imperial seal, government seal
國小 gúoxiǎo 图 图 elementary school (國民小學)
國營 gúoyíng 图 图 state-operated: 國營企業 state enterprises
國有 gúoyǒu 图 图 state-owned: 國有企業 state enterprises
國語 gúoyǔ 图 图 national language 图 图 Chinese, Mandarin
國宅 gúozhái 图 public housing
國債 gúozhài 图 national debt
國中 gúozhōng 图 图 middle school, junior high school (國民中學)

域 45 yù
47 Region 或 (phonetic) with earth 土 redundant. 图 region ⇔ 領域, 海域, 流域, 地域, 區域, 疆域

划 45 huá
48 Attack 伐 (phonetic, abbreviated to 戈) water as with knife 刀. 图 row, paddle 划船 huáchuán 图 row, paddle 划算 huásuàn 图 worthwhile, profitable

我 45 wǒ
49 Hand 手 holding a halberd 戈. 四1 ⇔ 自我

國弓, 盟國, 寮國, 愛國, 楚國, 叛國, 出國, 祖國, 民國, 美國, 列國, 戰國
國寶 gúobǎo 图 national treasure
國產 gúochǎn 图 domestic goods
國粹 gúocùi 图 essence of China
國都 gúodū 图 capital city
國防 gúofáng 图 national defense
國父 gúofù 图 father of the nation
國歌 gúogē 图 national anthem
國號 gúohào 图 nation's official name
國畫 gúohuà 图 traditional Chinese painting

國會 gúohùi 图 national legislature, congress
國籍 gúojí 图 nationality
國際 gúojì 图 international: 國際化 internationalization
國家 gúojiā 图 nation
國劇 gúojù 图 图 Peking opera
國君 gúojūn 图 king, monarch
國庫 gúokù 图 national treasury: 國庫券 treasury bill
國立 gúolì 图 founded by national government: 國立台灣大學 National Taiwan University
國民 gúomín 图 citizen, national: 國民黨 Kuomintang, Nationalist Party
國內 gúonèi 图 domestic

我國 wǒgúo 图 our country
我家 wǒjiā 图 my home, my family
我們 wǒmen 图 we

哦 45 é ó
50 [哦] Mouth 口⁶⁸ and self 我⁴⁵. é: recite ó: 图 Oh!

義 45 yí
51 [义] Sheep 羊¹²³ with 我⁴⁵ phonetic. 图 dignified, proper 图 justice 图 meaning ⇔ 三民主義¹, 主義², 人本主義³, 敦義⁴, 沙文主義⁵, 廣義⁶, 嘉義⁷, 狹義⁸, 起義⁹, 演義¹⁰, 貶義¹¹, 意義¹², 名義¹³, 正義¹⁴, 定義¹⁵
義倉 yìcāng 图 ⑨ public granary
義大利 yìdàlì ⑩ 图 Italy: 義大利麵 spaghetti (⇨ 意大利⁷)
義父 yìfù 图 foster father
義和團 yìhétuán 图 the Boxers: 義和團運動 Boxer Rebellion
義母 yìmǔ 图 foster mother
義氣 yìqì 图 code of honor personal loyalty: 講義氣 loyal
義士 yìshì 图 righteous person
義務 yìwù 图 duty, obligation
義塚 yìzhǒng 图 ⑨ public cemetery

議 45 yì
52 [议] Words 言⁴⁵ that are proper 義⁵¹ (phonetic). ⑪ discuss 图 opinion ⇔ 不可思議¹⁶, 衆議¹⁷, 建議¹⁸, 商議¹⁹, 評議²⁰, 協議²¹, 決議²², 抗議²³, 異議²⁴, 參議²⁵, 芻議²⁶, 提議²⁷, 爭議²⁸, 會議²⁹, 審議³⁰
議程 yìchéng 图 agenda
議會 yìhùi 图 parliament, council: 市議會 city council; 省議會 provincial legislature
議論 yìlùn ⑪ discuss, argue
議題 yìtí 图 discussion topic

議員 yìyuán 图 legislator, councilor
議院 yìyuàn 图 parliament, council: 參議院 Senate; 衆議院 House of Representatives

儀 45 yí
53 [仪] Propriety 義⁵¹ (phonetic) between people 人⁹. 图 bearing, manner 图 ceremony, rite ⇔ 溥儀³¹, 禮儀³², 獎儀³³
儀器 yíqì 图 instrument, apparatus
儀式 yíshì 图 ceremony, rite

蟻 45 yǐ
54 [蚁] Insect 虫¹²⁵ which behaves properly 義⁵¹ (phonetic). 图 ant ⇔ 螞蟻³⁴

娥 45 é
55 Woman 女¹⁴ with 我⁴⁵ phonetic. 图 beautiful young woman ⇔ 嫦娥³⁵

峨 45 é
56 Mountain 山⁶⁷ with 我⁴⁵ phonetic. 图 high
峨嵋山 éméishān 图 Emei Mountain - a sacred Buddhist mountain in Sichuan Province

鵝 45 é
57 [鹅] Self-important 我⁴⁵ (phonetic) bird 鳥¹⁷⁶. 图 goose ⇔ 天鵝³⁶
鵝毛 émáo 图 goose feather

餓 45 è
58 [饿] Food 食⁴⁵ and self 我⁴⁵ (phonetic). 图 hungry ⇔ 飢餓³⁷
餓死 èsǐ ⑪ starve to death

俄 45 è
59 Person 人⁹ with 我⁴⁵ phonetic. 图 Russia ⇔ 蘇俄³⁸
俄國 èguó 图 Russia
俄羅斯 èlúosī ⑩ Russia

戈 45 cái
60 Lance 戈⁴⁵ with 才⁶⁴ (altered) phonetic. ⑨ wound

裁 45 cái
61 Cut 戈⁴⁵ (phonetic) clothing 衣¹²⁶. ⑪ cut ⇔ 仲裁³⁹, 制裁⁴⁰, 獨裁⁴¹, 總裁⁴²
裁縫 cáiféng 图 图 tailor
裁減 cáijiǎn ⑪ cut, reduce
裁判 cáipàn 图 referee, judge

哉 45 zāi
62 Mouth 口⁶⁸ with 戈⁴⁵ phonetic. ⑪ Alas!

栽 45 zāi
63 Tree 木⁷⁷ with 戈⁴⁵ phonetic. ⑪ plant
栽培 zāipéi ⑪ cultivate ⑪ train, educate
栽種 zāizhòng ⑪ plant, grow

載 45 zài zǎi
64 [载] Cart 車⁵⁸ with 戈⁴⁵ phonetic. zài: ⑪ carry ⑪ record, register zǎi: 图 year ⇔ 記載³⁷
載客 zàikè ⑪ carry passengers
載明 zàimíng ⑪ record clearly

截 45 jié
65 Lance 戈⁴⁵ hitting sparrow 雀⁴⁵ (phonetic, altered). ⑪ cut, sever ⑪ stop, block ⇔ 攔截⁴³
截斷 jiéduàn ⑪ cut off, block
截然 jiérán ⑪ clearly ⑪ completely: 截然不同 completely different
截止 jiézhǐ ⑪ close, end

式 45 shì
66 Work 工⁵¹ and stake 弋⁴⁵ (phonetic). 图 pattern, model ⑪ type, style ⇔ 款式⁴⁴, 各式各樣⁴⁵, 格式⁴⁶, 公式⁴⁷, 等式⁴⁸, 架式⁴⁹, 儀式⁵⁰, 形式⁵¹, 型式⁵², 模式⁵³, 程式⁵⁴, 正式⁵⁵, 方程式⁵⁶, 方式⁵⁷, 和式⁵⁸
式微 shìwéi ⑪ decline
式樣 shìyàng 图 style

試 45 shì
67 [试] Words 言⁴⁵ and pattern 式⁴⁵ (phonetic). ⑪

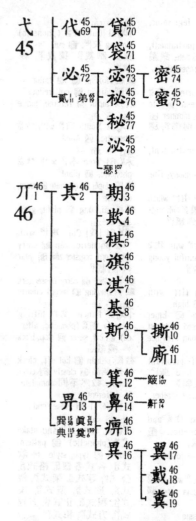

imagine how bad it would be

試驗 shìyàn 图 experiment, test

試用 shìyòng 动 try out, test

拭 45 shì
68 Hand 手 ^{97} with 式 $^{23}_{45}$ phonetic. 动 wipe ⇔ 擦拭 $^{134}_{77}$

拭目以待 shìmùyǐdài 动 wait and see

代 45 dài
69 Person 人 ^{19} with 弋 $^{45}_{1}$ phonetic. 图 generation 图 era, period, dynasty 动 substitute for 图 a surname ⇔ 年代 $^{68}_{75}$, 唐代 $^{16}_{74}$, 時代 $^{76}_{76}$, 古代 $^{24}_{9}$, 世代 $^{80}_{75}$, 替代 $^{80}_{77}$, 交代 $^{76}_{77}$, 後代 $^{42}_{87}$, 當代 $^{50}_{89}$, 周代 $^{80}_{9}$, 朝代 $^{79}_{75}$, 末代 $^{7}_{7}$, 近代 $^{84}_{7}$, 班代 $^{96}_{77}$, 歷代 $^{96}_{77}$, 現代 $^{62}_{75}$, 取代 $^{9}_{77}$

代表 dàibiǎo 动 represent: 代表性 representative, typical 图 representative, envoy: 代表團 delegation

代溝 dàigōu 图 generation gap

代價 dàijià 图 price, cost

代理 dàilǐ 图 agent

代替 dàitì 动 substitute for

貸 45 dài
70 [贷] Substitute 代 $^{45}_{69}$ (phonetic) and money 貝 ^{150}. 动 loan

貸款 dàikuǎn 动 lend 图 loan

袋 45 dài
71 Clothing 衣 ^{126} with 代 $^{45}_{69}$ phonetic. 图 bag, sack: 塑膠袋 图 plastic bag ⇔ 布袋 $^{52}_{77}$, 口袋 ^{68}, 衣袋 ^{126}, 腦袋 ^{143}

袋鼠 dàishǔ 图 kangaroo

袋子 dàizi 图 bag

必 45 bì
72 Stake 弋 ^{45} splitting 八 ^{29}. 动 must, necessarily ⇔ 不必 $^{3}_{72}$, 何必 ^{43}, 勢必 $^{48}_{72}$, 未必 $^{7}_{72}$, 想必 $^{94}_{72}$

必定 bìdìng 助 necessarily

必然 bìrán 助 inevitably

必須 bìxū 助 must

try, test ⇔ 考試 ^{62}, 筆試 ^{152}, 嘗試 ^{52}, 口試 ^{68}, 躍躍欲試 ^{124}, 測試 ^{150}

試辦 shìbàn 动 implement on a trial basis

試試 shìshì 动 try: 試試看 try and see

試圖 shìtú 动 attempt, try

試想 shìxiǎng 动 imagine, consider: 試想會多精

必需 bìxū necessary: 必需品 necessity

必要 bìyào need: 必要性 necessity 必要 necessary

宓 [45] mì [73] Roof 宀[63] with 必[5] phonetic. silent, quiet

密 [45] mì [74] Silent 宓[5] (phonetic) encircling mountains 山[67]. intimate secret dense ⇔ 哈密瓜[5], 祕密[5], 秘密[5], 親密[5], 機密[5], 周密[5], 稠密[5], 精密[5], 保密[5], 告密[5], 嚴密[17], 緊密[12]

密度 mìdù density
密封 mìfēng seal, close off
密集 mìjí dense, concentrated
密碼 mìmǎ secret number, PIN
密切 mìqiè intimate, close
密友 mìyǒu close friend

蜜 [45] mì [75] Insect 虫[125] with 必[5] phonetic. honey ⇔ 甜蜜[5], 蜂蜜[5]
蜜蜂 mìfēng honeybee, bee
蜜月 mìyuè honeymoon: 蜜月旅行 honeymoon trip

祕 [45] mì [76] [秘[5]] Revelation 示[5] with 必[5] phonetic. mysterious, secret ⇔ 詭祕[5], 奧祕[15]
祕密 mìmì secret

秘 [45] mì [77] A miswriting of 祕[5] using 禾[108]. ⇔ 神秘[56]
秘方 mìfāng secret recipe
秘訣 mìjué secret trick
秘魯 mìlǔ Peru
秘密 mìmì secret, confidential
秘書 mìshū secretary

泌 [45] mì [78] Water 水[5] with 必[5] phonetic. seep, secrete

⇔ 分泌[35]
泌尿 mìniào pee, urinate

丌 [46] jī [1] Pictograph of a stool or workbench.

其 [46] qí [2] Stool 丌[46] with a pictograph of a basket on top. 箅 winnowing basket (⇨ 箕[5]) 他 he, she, it 此 this, that ⇔ 極其[5], 尤其[5], 莫名其妙[5], 土耳其[70]
其次 qícì next, secondly
其實 qíshí in fact, actually
其他 qítā other
其它 qítā other
其餘 qíyú remainder
其中 qízhōng among which, of which

期 [46] qī qí [3] Month 月[70] with 其[5] phonetic. period, phase expect ⇔ 限期[5], 學期[5], 長期[5], 時期[5], 到期[5], 初期[5], 任期[5], 如期[5], 短期[5], 星期[5], 日期[5], 早期[5], 末期[5], 延期[5], 定期[5], 預期[102]
期待 qídài expect
期貨 qíhuò futures: 期貨市場 futures market
期間 qíjiān time, period
期刊 qíkān periodical
期末 qímò end of the term: 期末考 final exam
期盼 qípàn anticipate
期望 qíwàng hope, expect hope, expectation
期限 qíxiàn deadline
期許 qíxǔ expectation

欺 [46] qī [4] Owe 欠[5] with 其[5] phonetic. cheat, swindle bully ⇔ 詐欺[5]
欺負 qīfù bully, humiliate, oppress
欺瞞 qīmán deceive, cheat
欺騙 qīpiàn deceive, cheat deception

欺侮 qīwǔ humiliate
欺壓 qīyā oppress
欺詐 qīzhà cheat, swindle

棋 [46] qí [5] Wood 木[77] with 其[5] phonetic. chess piece chess: 西洋棋 chess (Western) ⇔ 下棋[5], 圍棋[5], 跳棋[127], 象棋[172]
棋盤 qípán chessboard
棋子 qízi chess piece

旗 [46] qí [6] Waving 方[118] with 其[5] phonetic. flag, banner ⇔ 國旗[45]
旗杆 qígān flagpole
旗袍 qípáo Chinese gown, cheongsam
旗幟 qízhì flag, banner
旗子 qízi flag, banner

淇 [46] qí [7] Water 水[5] with 其[5] phonetic. a river in Henan Province ⇔ 冰淇淋[25]

基 [46] jī [8] Earth 土[70] with 其[5] phonetic. basis, foundation ⇔ 根基[5], 巴基斯坦[85]
基本 jīběn basic, fundamental
基層 jīcéng grassroots, primary level
基礎 jīchǔ foundation
基地 jīdì base
基督 jīdū Christ: 基督教 Christianity, Protestantism; 基督徒 Christian, Protestant
基金 jījīn funds: 基金會 fund, foundation
基隆 jīlóng Keelung - a city in Taiwan
基因 jīyīn gene
基於 jīyú according to, on the basis of

斯 [46] sī [9] Axe 斤[70] with 其[5]

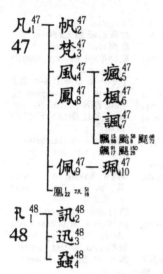

凡⁴⁷₁
47
— 帆⁴⁷₂
— 梵⁴⁷₃
— 風⁴⁷₅ ┬ 瘋⁴⁷₅
— 鳳⁴⁷₈ ┼ 楓⁴⁷₆
┼ 諷⁴⁷₇
飄¹⁵₁₅ 颱⁵⁸₅₈ 颳⁷²₇₂ 飆⁹¹₁₇ 飈¹⁵⁰₂₈
— 佩⁴⁷₉ — 珮⁴⁷₁₀
— 凰¹₂₂ 凧⁵¹₁₆

凡⁴⁸₁
48
— 訊⁴⁸₂
— 迅⁴⁸₃
— 蝨⁴⁸₄

phonetic. 圐 rip, cut 圐 this, here 圐 thus 圐 refined ⇔ 伊斯蘭教, 穆斯林名, 威爾遜斯名, 俄羅斯名, 莫斯科名, 巴基斯坦名, 巴勒斯坦名, 瓦斯名, 羅斯福名 斯文 sīwén 圐 cultured, refined

撕 ⁴⁶ sī
10 Hand 手⁸⁹ ripping 斯名 (phonetic). 圐 rip, tear
撕毀 sīhuǐ 圐 tear, rip
撕開 sīkāi 圐 tear open

廝 ⁴⁶ sī
11 [廝] Shed 广⁶⁰ (or cliff 厂²¹ in early form and simplified form) with 斯名 phonetic. 圐 together ⇔ 小廝
廝殺 sīshā 圐 engage in hand-to-hand combat

箕 ⁴⁶ jī
12 Bamboo 竹名 basket 其名 (phonetic). 圐 winnowing basket 圐 dustpan ⇔ 簸箕名, 畚箕名

昇 ⁴⁶ bì
13 An object (resembling 田名) offered on a table 丌名. 圐 bestow

鼻 ⁴⁶ bí
14 Nose 自³⁹ with 畀名 phonetic. 圐 nose
鼻孔 bíkǒng 圐 nostril
鼻塞 bísè 圐 nasal congestion, stuffy nose
鼻水 bíshuǐ 圐 snivel: 流鼻水 have a runny nose
鼻涕 bítì 圐 snivel
鼻息 bíxí 圐 breath
鼻子 bízi 圐 nose
鼻祖 bízǔ 圐 founder

痺 ⁴⁶ bì
15 Sickness 疒名 with 畀名 phonetic. 圐 paralysis ⇔ 麻痺名

異 ⁴⁶ yì
16 [异] Hands 廾名 making offering 畀名. Simplified form, based on an ancient form, uses 已名 and 廾名. 圐

differing, opposing ⇔ 駭異名, 差異名, 驚異名, 詭異名, 迥異名, 奇異名, 特異名, 詫異名, 歧異名, 優異名
異常 yìcháng 圐 abnormal 圐 abnormality
異性 yìxìng 圐 opposite sex, heterosexual: 異性戀 heterosexuality
異議 yìyì 圐 objection: 異議分子 圐 dissident

翼 ⁴⁶ yì
17 Feathers 羽名 on opposite 異名 (phonetic) sides. 圐 wing ⇔ 左翼名, 右翼名

戴 ⁴⁶ dài
18 Cut 戈名 (phonetic) and different 異名. 圐 separately increase 圐 wear: 戴眼鏡 wear glasses 圐 a surname ⇔ 擁戴名, 穿戴名

糞 ⁴⁶ fèn
19 [粪] Hands 廾名 shoveling 釆名 (together resembling 異名) excrement

night soil
糞便 fènbiàn 圐 night soil, excrement
糞坑 fènkēng 圐 cesspool
糞土 fèntǔ 圐 dirt, muck

凡 ⁴⁷ fán
1 Early form is pictograph of an encompassing square. 圐 all ⇔ 不凡名, 平凡名
凡人 fánrén 圐 common person
凡事 fánshì 圐 all things
凡是 fánshì 圐 every

帆 ⁴⁷ fán
2 Cloth 巾名 with 凡⁴⁷ phonetic. 圐 sail
帆布 fánbù 圐 canvas
帆船 fánchuán 圐 sailboat

梵 ⁴⁷ fàn
3 Forest 林名 with 凡⁴⁷ phonetic. 圐 Bhuddist

字譜及字典   145

梵書 fànshū 图 Buddhist scriptures

梵文 fànwén 图 Sanskrit

風 47 fēng
4 [风] Insects 虫 [125], which are borne by the wind, with 凡 [47] phonetic. 图 wind 图 custom, practice, fashion 图 manner, style ⇔ 狂風 [61], 上風 [43], 下風 [66], 吹風 [92], 兜風 [52], 披風 [52], 暴風 [153], 神風隊 [156], 作風 [92], 威風 [181], 屏風 [59], 朔風 [92], 颱風 [81], 山風 [92], 颶風 [92], 中風 [92], 通風 [92], 傷風 [92], 把風 [95], 雷屬風行 [111], 旋風 [218], 龍捲風 [127], 颶風 [150]

風暴 fēngbào 图 tempest, storm

風波 fēngbō 图 disturbance

風采 fēngcǎi 图 attractive, dashing

風潮 fēngcháo 图 unrest, agitation

風格 fēnggé 图 style, manner

風景 fēngjǐng 图 scenery: 風景區 scenic area

風鈴 fēnglíng 图 chime

風靡 fēngmí 图 become fashionable: 風靡一時 briefly fashionable

風氣 fēngqì 图 custom

風趣 fēngqù 图 humor, wit

風聲 fēngshēng 图 rumor of, wind of

風水 fēngshuǐ 图 fengshui, geomancy: 風水先生 geomancer

風俗 fēngsú 图 customs, traditions

風頭 fēngtou 图 circumstances 图 prominence: 出風頭 be in the limelight, show off

風味 fēngwèi 图 distinctive flavor or style

風險 fēngxiǎn 图 risk, danger

風雨 fēngyǔ 图 trials and tribulations

風韻 fēngyùn 图 charm, grace

風箏 fēngzhēng 图 kite: 放風箏 fly a kite

瘋 47 fēng
5 [疯] Sickness 扩 [76] like a wind 風 [47] (phonetic) swirling in the mind. 图 crazy, insane: 你瘋了。You're crazy. ⇔ 麻瘋 [92], 發瘋 [92]

瘋狂 fēngkuáng 图 insane, crazy

瘋子 fēngzi 图 lunatic, madman

楓 47 fēng
6 [枫] Tree 木 [77] that blows in the wind 風 [47] (phonetic). 图 maple

楓樹 fēngshù 图 maple tree

楓糖 fēngtáng 图 maple syrup

諷 47 fèng 图 fěng
7 [讽] Words 言 [96] flowing like the wind 風 [47] (phonetic). 图 chant 图 satirize ⇔ 譏諷 [92], 嘲諷 [92]

諷刺 fèngcì 图 satirize 图 satirical, sarcastic

鳳 47 fèng
8 [凤] Bird 鳥 [178] with 凡 [47] phonetic. 图 phoenix (male)

鳳凰 fènghuáng 图 phoenix

鳳梨 fènglí 图 图 pineapple

佩 47 pèi
9 Cloth 巾 [53] ornaments worn by all 凡 [47] men 人 [10] in ancient times. 图 wear pendant ⇔ 欽佩 [92], 敬佩 [92]

佩帶 pèidài 图 wear

佩服 pèifu 图 admire

珮 47 pèi
10 [佩 [47]] Jade 玉 [107] pendant 佩 [47] (phonetic, abbreviated). 图 jade pendant

凡 48 xìn
1 Pictograph of a bird flying rapidly, feathers tight together unlike in 飛 [169].

訊 48 xùn
2 [讯] Words 言 [96] flying rapidly 凡 [48] (phonetic). 图 ask, inquire 图 news, information ⇔ 資訊 [92], 電訊 [92], 偵訊 [92], 通訊 [92], 審訊 [156]

訊號 xùnhào 图 signal

訊問 xùnwèn 图 interrogate

訊息 xùnxí 图 message

迅 48 xùn
3 Movement 辵 [91] like rapid flight 凡 [48] (phonetic). 图 fast, speed

迅速 xùnsù 图 quick, rapid

蝨 48 shī
4 [虱] Rapidly 凡 [48] (phonetic) multiplying insect 虫 [125]. 图 louse, lice

蝨子 shīzi 图 louse, lice

彡 49 shān
1 Pictograph of hairs or fine feathers. Also used to indicate markings.

衫 49 shān
2 Clothing 衣 [126] with 彡 [49] phonetic. 图 shirt

襯衫 [92]

杉 49 shān
3 Tree 木 [77] with hair 彡 [49] (phonetic). 图 fir tree

⇔ 洛杉磯 [92]

鬢 49 zhěn
4 Person's 人 [10] hair 彡 [49] (phonetic). 图 fine, dense hair

診 49 zhěn
5 [诊] Words 言 [96] with 㐱 [49] phonetic. 图 examine, diagnose ⇔ 急診 [92], 門診 [92]

診斷 zhěnduàn 图 diagnose 图 diagnosis

診療 zhěnliáo 图 diagnosis and treatment

診所 zhěnsuǒ 图 clinic

診治 zhěnzhì 图 diagnose and treat

疹 49 zhěn
6 Sickness 扩 [76] with 㐱 [49] phonetic. 图 rash

麻疹 [92]

疹子 zhěnzi 图 measles

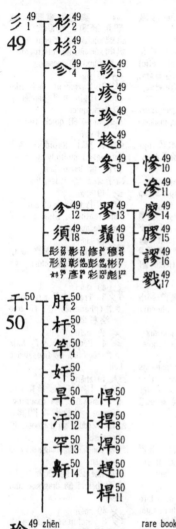

趁[49] chèn
8 Go 走 with ☆ phonetic. catch up, take advantage of (a situation): 趁熱吃. Eat it while it's hot.
趁機 chènjī seize the opportunity
趁早 chènzǎo while it's not too late
趁著 chènzhe take advantage of (a situation)

參[49] cān cēn sān shēn
9 [叅] Three suns 晶 (altered) with ☆ phonetic. shēn: Orion's Belt cān: participate, join consult, refer to sān: three (complex form) cēn: uneven ⟺ 人參, 海參
參觀 cānguān visit
參加 cānjiā participate, join
參見 cānjiàn refer to: 參見第六章 see chapter six
參考 cānkǎo consult, refer to: 參考書 reference book; 參考文獻 bibliography
參謀 cānmóu adviser, counsel
參數 cānshù parameter
參議 cānyì counsel: 參議員 Senator
參與 cānyù participate, join
參展 cānzhǎn tour
參酌 cānzhuó consult and consider
參差 cēncī uneven, irregular: 參差不齊 uneven

慘[49] cǎn
10 [惨] Heart 心 with 參 phonetic. merciless, brutal, tragic, disastrous ⟺ 悽慘, 悲慘
慘敗 cǎnbài crushing defeat
慘淡 cǎndàn gloomy, bleak
慘劇 cǎnjù tragedy
慘痛 cǎntòng bitter, painful
慘重 cǎnzhòng disastrous
慘狀 cǎnzhuàng miserable situation

珍[49] zhēn
7 Jade 玉[107] with ☆ phonetic. precious ⟺ 袖珍
珍藏 zhēncáng collect (art or rare books)
珍貴 zhēnguì precious
珍惜 zhēnxī cherish
珍珠 zhēnzhū pearl: 珍珠港 Pearl Harbor

滲 49 shèn [渗] Water 水 joining 參 (phonetic). seep in

滲入 shènrù permeate, pervade

滲透 shèntòu seep in, permeate, infiltrate

羨 49 shān 12 Short wing 几 with feathers 彡. take flight

翏 49 liáo 13 Wings 羽 flying. soar

廖 49 liào 14 Shelter 广 with 翏 phonetic. a surname

膠 49 jiāo [胶] Flesh 肉 with 翏 phonetic. Simplified form uses 交. glue, rubber ⇔ 塑膠, 橡膠

膠帶 jiāodài tape (adhesive)

膠捲 jiāojuǎn film roll

膠水 jiāoshuǐ glue

膠著 jiāozhuó deadlocked

謬 49 miù [谬] Words 言 flying high 翏 (phonetic). erroneous ⇔ 荒謬, 悖謬

謬誤 miùwù mistake, falsehood

戮 49 lù 17 Fly high 翏 (phonetic) and lance 戈. join forces slaughter ⇔ 殺戮

戮力 lùlì join forces

須 49 xū 18 Hair 彡 on head 頁. beard (⇒ 鬚) must, need to ⇔ 必須

須要 xūyào must, need to

須臾 xūyú moment, instant

須知 xūzhī required knowledge

鬚 49 xū 19 [须] Beard 須 (phonetic) with long hair 髟 redundant. beard, mustache

干 50 gān 1 Pictograph of a shield. Alternatively, pictograph of a pestle. shield offend, attack stem concern 若干, 天干, 相干

干戈 gāngē armaments warfare

干擾 gānrǎo interfere, disturb

干涉 gānshè interfere, meddle: 干涉內政 interfere with internal affairs

干預 gānyù interfere

干支 gānzhī Heavenly Stems and Earthly Branches - basis of the traditional 60-year calendar (⇒ 天干, 地支)

肝 50 gān 2 Flesh 肉 with 干 phonetic. liver 心肝

肝炎 gānyán hepatitis

肝臟 gānzàng liver

杆 50 gān 3 Wooden 木 stem 干 (phonetic). pole, post ⇔ 槍杆, 旗杆, 欄杆

竿 50 gān 4 Bamboo 竹 stem 干 (phonetic). pole, rod ⇔ 竹竿

奸 50 jiān 5 Woman 女 and offend 干 (phonetic). adultery (⇒ 姦) 漢奸

奸詐 jiānzhà crafty, cunning

旱 50 hàn 6 Sun 日 offending 干 (phonetic). drought 乾旱

旱災 hànzāi drought

悍 50 hàn 7 Heart 心 like blazing sun 旱 (phonetic). bold, intrepid

悍然 hànrán brazenly, flagrantly

捍 50 hàn 8 [扞] Hand 手 with 旱 phonetic and suggestive of brave 悍. defend

捍衛 hànwèi defend

焊 50 hàn 9 Fire 火 with 旱 phonetic. weld, solder

焊接 hànjiē weld

趕 50 gǎn 10 [赶] Walk 走 with 旱 phonetic. hurry, hurry after pursue drive, expel ⇔ 驅趕, 追趕

趕到 gǎndào arrive

趕緊 gǎnjǐn hurriedly

趕快 gǎnkuài at once, quickly

趕來 gǎnlái hurry

趕忙 gǎnmáng quickly

趕上 gǎnshàng catch up with

趕走 gǎnzǒu drive out, expel

桿 50 gǎn 11 [杆] Wood 木 with 旱 phonetic. pole, post ⇔ 橫桿

汗 50 hàn 12 Water 水 that offends 干 (phonetic). sweat khan: 成吉思汗 Ghengis Khan ⇔ 阿富汗, 流汗, 出汗

汗水 hànshuǐ sweat

汗顏 hànyán ashamed

罕 50 hǎn 13 Net 网 (altered) on a pole/stem 干 (phonetic). rare, scarce ⇔ 希罕, 納罕

罕見 hǎnjiàn rare, scarce

鼾 50 hān 14 Nose 鼻 offending 干 (phonetic). snore ⇔ 打鼾

鼾聲 hānshēng snores

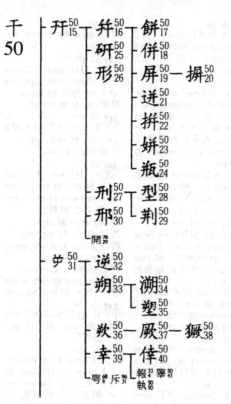

屏幕 píngmù 图 screen
屏障 píngzhàng 图 barrier

摒 50 @ bìng @ bǐng
20 Hand 手⁷ discarding
屏⁷⁹ (phonetic). 🔲 remove
摒除 bìngchú 🔲 remove, eliminate
摒棄 bìngqì 🔲 discard, abandon

迸 50 bèng
21 Movement 辵⁷ of what
was together 并⁷⁹ (phonetic).
🔲 scatter 🔲 burst
迸裂 bèngliè 🔲 crack, split open

拼 50 pīn
22 Hand 手⁷ and together
并⁷⁹ (phonetic). 🔲 put
together 🔲 spell: 怎麼拼?
How is it spelled? 🔲 risk one's
life
拼法 pīnfǎ 图 spelling
拼命 pīnmìng 🔲 risk one's life
🔲 with all one's might
拼死 pīnsǐ 🔲 risk one's life
拼圖 pīntú 图 jigsaw puzzle
拼音 pīnyīn 🔲 phoneticize,
spell: 漢語拼音 the transliteration system used in mainland China

姘 50 pīn
23 With woman 女⁷
together 并⁷⁹ (phonetic). 图
adultery
姘頭 pīntóu 图 (粵) lover (male)

瓶 50 píng
24 Pottery 瓦⁷⁰ that
keeps water together 并⁷⁹
(phonetic). 图 🔲 bottle ⇔
花瓶⁷⁹, 金瓶梅⁷⁷
瓶蓋 pínggài 图 bottle cap
瓶頸 píngjǐng 图 bottleneck
瓶子 píngzi 图 bottle

研 50 yán
25 [研] Stone 石⁷⁹ rubbed
even 开⁷⁷ (phonetic). 🔲 grind
🔲 research ⇔ 鑽研⁴⁴
研究 yánjiū 🔲 图 research: 研
究生 graduate student; 研究
所 graduate school; 研究院

开 50 jiān
15 Two stems 干⁷⁰ of
equal height. 图 level, even

幵 50 bìng
16 [并] Two people 人人⁷⁰
(abbreviated to two dots)
marching side-by-side 开⁷⁹.
and, also (⇨ 並⁷⁹)

餅 50 bǐng
17 [饼] Food 食⁷⁹ with
并⁷⁹ phonetic. 图 biscuit ⇔
烙餅⁷⁹, 燒餅⁷⁹, 月餅⁷⁹, 酥
餅⁷⁹
餅乾 bǐnggān 图 biscuit

併 50 bìng
18 [并⁷⁹] People 人⁷⁰
standing together 并⁷⁹ (phonetic). 🔲 side by side ⇔ 一併⁷,
吞併⁷⁹, 合併⁷⁹, 兼併⁷⁹
併入 bìngrù 🔲 merge
併吞 bìngtūn 🔲 annex, swallow
up
🔲 discard

屏 50 bǐng píng
19 Body 尸⁷⁰ with 并⁷⁹
phonetic. píng: 图 shield bǐng:
🔲 hold one's breath
屏息 bǐngxí 🔲 hold one's breath
屏風 píngfēng 图 screen, partition

---

research institute; 研究員 researcher

研商 yánshāng 🉐 discuss

研討 yántǎo 🉐 study and discuss: 研討會 seminar, symposium

研習 yánxí 🉐 research and study

研製 yánzhì 🉐 develop for manufacture

形 50 xíng
26 Lines 彡 ⁱ⁷ equalling 幵 ⁷⁶ (phonetic) reality. 🈷 pictograph 🈁 shape, form ⇔ 遁形⁸⁵, 畸形⁴⁹, 無形¹¹⁶, 字形⁶⁵, 地形⁵⁴, 弓形¹⁵, 雛形⁴⁶, 形⁴⁶, 圓形⁸⁵, 情形⁸⁶, 球形⁹⁷, 方形⁶⁷, 隱形⁵³, 弧形¹⁰⁴, 身形¹⁴⁷, 圓形¹²⁰, 象形¹⁷²

形成 xíngchéng 🉐 become

形容 xíngróng 🉐 describe: 形容詞 adjective

形聲 xíngshēng 🈁 type of Chinese character in which one part suggests the meaning and the other part the sound (⇒ 六書)

形式 xíngshì 🈁 form 🈁 formality: 流於形式 be reduced to a mere formality

形勢 xíngshì 🈁 situation

形態 xíngtài 🈁 appearance, form, type

形象 xíngxiàng 🈁 image, form

形狀 xíngzhuàng 🈁 form

刑 50 xíng
27 Evened 幵 ⁷⁶ (phonetic) with knife 刀 ¹⁵. 🈷 decapitate 🈁 punishment ⇔ 徒刑⁷, 判刑⁹², 酷刑⁷⁶, 死刑²⁷, 嚴刑⁹³

刑罰 xíngfá 🈁 punishment

刑法 xíngfǎ 🈁 penal code

刑求 xíngqiú 🉐 extract a confession through torture

刑事 xíngshì 🉐 criminal, penal

型 50 xíng
28 Earthen 土 ⁷⁰ mold with

刑 ²⁷ phonetic. 🈁 model, type ⇔ 小型⁵⁴, 大型⁷³, 模型⁸⁸, 體型⁵⁷, 髮型⁷⁶, 造型⁸⁵, 典型¹⁷, 類型¹⁴⁸

型式 xíngshì 🈁 pattern

型態 xíngtài 🈁 type

荆 50 jīng
29 Plant 艸 ²⁶ that punishes 刑 ²⁷ (phonetic). 🈁 thorn

荆棘 jīngjí 🈁 thorns 🈁 thorny

邢 50 xíng
30 City 邑 with 幵 phonetic. 🈁 an ancient kingdom 🈁 a surname

苄 50 nì
31 Attack 干 ⁷⁵ repeated. 🈷 obstructed

逆 50 nì
32 Movement 辵 ⁹⁴ against obstacle 屰 ³¹ (phonetic). 🉐 oppose, counter 🈁 inverse, converse ⇔ 悖逆⁸⁷, 叛逆⁹²

逆差 nìchā 🈁 deficit

逆境 nìjìng 🈁 adversity

逆轉 nìzhuǎn 🉐 deteriorate, turn for the worse

朔 50 shuò
33 Moon 月 ⁸ and obstruct 屰 ³¹. 🈁 new moon 🈁 north ⇔ 陽朔⁴⁸

朔風 shuòfēng 🈁 north wind

溯 50 sù
34 Water 水 ¹ reversing direction 朔 ³³ (phonetic). 🉐 go against the stream 🉐 trace back, recall ⇔ 回溯⁹⁹, 追溯¹⁶⁷

溯源 sùyuán 🉐 trace to the source

塑 50 sù
35 Clay 土 ⁷⁰ with 朔 ³³ phonetic. 🉐 mold ⇔ 雕塑⁸⁹

塑膠 sùjiāo 🈁 plastic

塑料 sùliào 🈁 plastic

塑造 sùzào 🉐 mold

欮 50 quē
36 Obstructed 屰 ³¹ breath

欠 ⁹⁵.

厥 50 jué
37 Cliff 厂 ⁷¹, suggesting stones, and difficulty breathing 欮 ³⁶ (phonetic), suggesting effort. 🉐 dig 🉐 faint ⇔ 昏厥¹⁰⁵

撅 50 jué
38 Beast/dog 犬 ⁷¹ digging 厥 ³⁷ (phonetic). 🈁 wild ⇔ 猖獗⁸⁹

幸 50 xìng
39 Early death 夭 ⁷⁰ (altered to resemble 土 ⁷⁰) reversed 屰 ³¹. 🈁 lucky 🉐 fortunately, luckily ⇔ 不幸⁵⁰, 榮幸⁸⁹, 慶幸¹⁷

幸而 xìngér 🉐 fortunately, luckily

幸福 xìngfú 🈁 happiness

幸好 xìnghǎo 🉐 fortunately, luckily

幸會 xìnghuì 🉐 fortuitous meeting: 幸會,幸會! Glad to meet you!

幸虧 xìngkuī 🉐 fortunately, luckily

幸運 xìngyùn 🈁 lucky, fortunate: 幸運鐵餅 fortune cookie

倖 50 xìng
40 [幸 ³⁹] Person 人 ¹⁰ lucky 幸 ³⁹ (phonetic). 🈁 lucky ⇔ 僥倖⁸⁸

倖存 xìngcún 🉐 survive through luck

羍 50 rěn
41 Offense 干 ⁷⁵ with extra marks indicating severity.

羍 50 niè
42 Person 大 ⁷⁰ (resembling 土 ⁷⁰) and crime 羍 ⁴¹. Note similarity to 幸 ³⁹. 🈷 criminal

睪 50 yì gāo
43 [睾] Keep an eye 目 ¹¹⁴ on criminals 羍 ⁴². yì: 🉐 watch gāo: 🈁 testicles

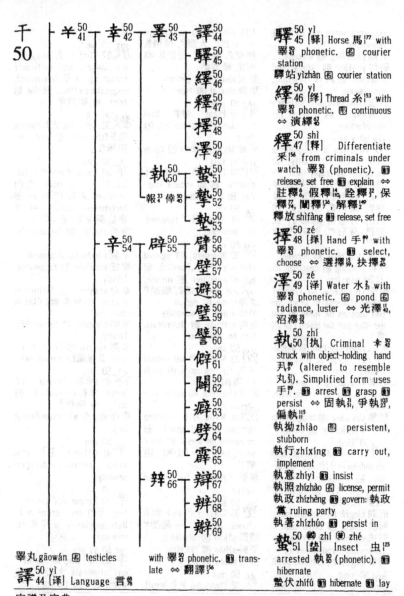

千 50
50

羊 50/41 ── 辛 50/42 ── 睪 50/43 ── 譯 50/44
　　　　　　　　　　　　　 驛 50/45
　　　　　　　　　　　　　 繹 50/46
　　　　　　　　　　　　　 釋 50/47
　　　　　　　　　　　　　 擇 50/48
　　　　　　　　　　　　　 澤 50/49

　　　　　　　　 執 50/50 ── 蟄 50/51
　　　　　　　│　　　　　　　 摯 50/52
　　　　 報 執 倖 執　　　　　 墊 50/53

　　　　　 辛 50/54 ── 辟 50/55 ── 臂 50/56
　　　　　　　　　　　　　 壁 50/57
　　　　　　　　　　　　　 避 50/58
　　　　　　　　　　　　　 璧 50/59
　　　　　　　　　　　　　 譬 50/60
　　　　　　　　　　　　　 僻 50/61
　　　　　　　　　　　　　 闢 50/62
　　　　　　　　　　　　　 癖 50/63
　　　　　　　　　　　　　 劈 50/64
　　　　　　　　　　　　　 霹 50/65

　　　　　　　　 辡 50/66 ── 辯 50/67
　　　　　　　　　　　　　 辨 50/68
　　　　　　　　　　　　　 辮 50/69

驛 50/45 yì [驿] Horse 馬[77] with 睪 phonetic. 🔲 courier station
驛站 yìzhàn 🔲 courier station

繹 50/46 yì [绎] Thread 糸[53] with 睪 phonetic. 🔲 continuous ⇔ 演繹

釋 50/47 shì [释] Differentiate 釆[56] from criminals under watch 睪 (phonetic). 🔲 release, set free 🔲 explain ⇔ 註釋, 假釋, 詮釋, 保釋, 闡釋, 解釋 🔲
釋放 shìfàng 🔲 release, set free

擇 50/48 zé [择] Hand 手[17] with 睪 phonetic. 🔲 select, choose ⇔ 選擇, 抉擇

澤 50/49 zé [泽] Water 水 with 睪 phonetic. 🔲 pond 🔲 radiance, luster ⇔ 光澤, 沼澤

執 50/50 zhí [执] Criminal 辛 struck with object-holding hand 丮 (altered to resemble 丸). Simplified form uses 手[17]. 🔲 arrest 🔲 grasp 🔲 persist ⇔ 固執, 爭執, 偏執
執拗 zhíào 🔲 persistent, stubborn
執行 zhíxíng 🔲 carry out, implement
執意 zhíyì 🔲 insist
執照 zhízhào 🔲 license, permit
執政 zhízhèng 🔲 govern: 執政黨 ruling party
執著 zhízhuó 🔲 persist in

蟄 50/51 zhí 🔲 zhé [蛰] Insect 虫[125] arrested 執 (phonetic). 🔲 hibernate
蟄伏 zhífú 🔲 hibernate 🔲 lay

睪丸 gāowán 🔲 testicles

譯 50/44 yì [译] Language 言 with 睪 phonetic. 🔲 translate ⇔ 翻譯

摯 50 zhì 52 [挚] Hand 手 grasping 執 (phonetic). seize, hold sincere ⇔ 眞
摯友 zhìyǒu close friend

墊 50 diàn 53 [垫] Captured criminal 執 on the earth 土. sink advance (funds) cushion ⇔ 床墊
墊款 diànkuǎn loan, advance money
墊子 diànzi cushion

辛 50 xīn 54 Seriously offend superiors 上 (early form). crime difficult, laborious hardship, suffering eighth Heavenly Stem (⇔ 干支) ⇔ 艱辛
辛亥 xīnhài the 48th year of the traditional 60-year Chinese calendar: 辛亥革命 Revolution of 1911
辛苦 xīnkǔ toilsome, laborious

辟 50 bì 55 Rules 尸 (resembling 尸) to criminals 辛. law ⇔ 復辟

臂 50 bì bèi 56 Flesh 肉 that governs 辟 (phonetic). bì: arm ⇔ 胳臂, 手臂
臂膀 bìbǎng arm and shoulder

壁 50 bì 57 Clay 土 with 辟 phonetic. wall ⇔ 石壁, 峭壁, 牆壁, 隔壁
壁櫥 bìchú closet
壁虎 bìhǔ gecko
壁畫 bìhuà fresco
壁壘 bìlěi barrier, rampart: 貿易壁壘 trade barrier

避 50 bì 58 Move from the law 辟 (phonetic). avoid, evade ⇔ 躲避, 迴避, 逃避
避開 bìkāi dodge, avoid
避免 bìmiǎn avoid
避難 bìnàn seek refuge
避邪 bìxié ward off evil
避孕 bìyùn contraception, birth control: 避孕藥 birth control pills; 避孕套 condom

璧 50 bì 59 Jade 玉 symbol of authority 辟 (phonetic). jade ring

譬 50 pì 60 Words 言 with 辟 phonetic. simile compare
譬如 pìrú for instance

僻 50 pì 61 Person 人 avoiding the law 辟 (phonetic). evade, hide remote ⇔ 怪僻, 荒僻, 偏僻

闢 50 pì 62 [辟] Door 門 with 辟 phonetic. open up refute ⇔ 精闢, 開闢
闢謠 pìyáo refute rumors

癖 50 pǐ 63 Sickness 疒 with 辟 phonetic. addiction
癖好 pǐhào habit, addiction inclination

劈 50 pī pǐ 64 Knife 刀 applying the law 辟 (phonetic). pī: cleave, split pǐ: divide, split
劈開 pīkāi split open
劈頭 pītóu head-on from the very start, immediately

霹 50 pī 65 Rain 雨 with 辟 phonetic. thunder
霹靂 pīlì thunderbolt

辡 50 biàn 66 Criminals 辛 accusing each other.

辯 50 biàn 67 [辩] Words 言 of mutual incrimination 辡 (phonetic). debate, argue ⇔ 詭辯, 爭辯
辯護 biànhù speak in defense of
辯解 biànjiě make excuses, rationalize
辯論 biànlùn debate
辯證 biànzhèng dialectical: 辯證唯物論 dialectical materialism

辨 50 biàn 68 Knife 刀 and mutual incrimination 辡 (phonetic). judge, decide ⇔ 分辨
辨別 biànbié distinguish, differentiate
辨認 biànrèn recognize, identify: 語音辨認 voice recognition
辨識 biànshì recognize, identify

辮 50 biàn 69 [辫] Threads 糸 and mutual incrimination 辡 (phonetic). braid
辮子 biànzi braid, queue

辦 50 bàn 70 [办] Strength 力 with 辡 phonetic. manage, run, host ⇔ 主辦, 創辦, 舉辦, 包辦, 試辦, 外辦, 買辦
辦案 bànàn handle a case
辦法 bànfǎ method
辦公室 bàngōngshì office
辦理 bànlǐ handle, take care of, manage
辦事 bànshì work, handle matters

辮 50 bàn 71 Melon 瓜 with 辡

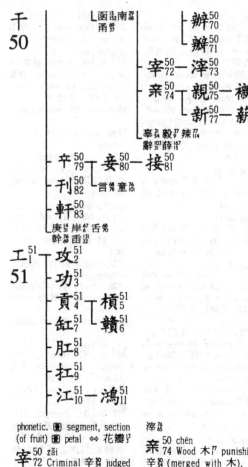

姻親, 母親, 探親, 近親, 相親

親愛的 qīnàide dear, beloved: 親愛的媽媽 Dear Mom
親近 qīnjìn befriend
親密 qīnmì intimate: 親密感 intimacy
親暱 qīnnì affectionate, intimate
親戚 qīnqī relatives
親切 qīnqiè warm, friendly
親熱 qīnrè warm, affectionate
親人 qīnrén close relatives
親身 qīnshēn personal
親手 qīnshǒu with own hands, personally
親屬 qīnshǔ relatives
親吻 qīnwěn kiss
親眼 qīnyǎn with own eyes
親友 qīnyǒu friends and relatives
親自 qīnzì personally, in person
親家 qīngjiā relatives by marriage

襯 76 chèn
[衬] Clothing 衣 and intimate 親 (phonetic). Simplified form uses inch 寸. underwear
襯衫 chènshān shirt
襯托 chèntuō contrast, set off
襯衣 chènyī undershirt

新 77 xīn
Axe 斤 with 親 phonetic. cut firewood (⇒ 薪) new, fresh ⇔ 創新, 更新, 清新, 革新, 重新, 嶄新, 維新

新加坡 xīnjiāpō Singapore
新疆 xīnjiāng Xinjiang Province
新教 xīnjiào Protestantism: 新教徒 Protestant
新郎 xīnláng groom
新年 xīnnián New Year: 新

phonetic. segment, section (of fruit) petal ⇔ 花瓣

宰 72 zǎi
Criminal 辛 judged under court roof 宀. govern slaughter ⇔ 主宰, 屠宰
宰殺 zǎishā slaughter
宰相 zǎixiàng prime minister

滓 73 zǐ
Water 水 with 宰 phonetic. dregs ⇔ 渣

滓

亲 74 chēn
Wood 木 punishing 辛 (merged with 木). thornbush

親 75 [亲] See 見 with 亲 phonetic and suggestive of intertwined. Simplified form uses 亲. qīn: intimate related kiss lightly qìng: relatives by marriage ⇔ 父母親, 父親, 省親,

年卡 New Year's card; 新年快樂! Happy New Year!
新娘 xīnniáng 图 bride
新奇 xīnqí 圀 unusual
新生 xīnshēng 图 new student 圀 newborn 图
新手 xīnshǒu 图 novice
新聞 xīnwén 图 news: 新聞自由 freedom of the press
新西蘭 xīnxīlán 圀 邎 New Zealand
新鮮 xīnxiān 图 fresh
新興 xīnxīng 圀 emerging, burgeoning
新穎 xīnyǐng 图 novel, original
新語 xīnyǔ 图 neologism

薪 50 xīn
78 Grass 艸 and firewood 新界 (phonetic). 图 firewood, fuel 图 salary: 月薪 monthly salary
薪俸 xīnfèng 图 salary
薪水 xīnshuǐ 图 salary
薪資 xīnzī 图 salary

辛 50 qiān
79 Offend 干 the law above 上 (early form). 圇 crime

妾 50 qiè
80 Sentence for crime 辛 by woman 女. 图 maidservant 图 concubine

接 50 jiē
81 Hand 手 and concubine 妾 (phonetic). 圙 receive, accept 圙 welcome, meet 圙 connect, join ⇔ 鄰接, 直接, 迎接, 衝接, 焊接, 間接, 連接
接觸 jiēchù 圙 touch
接待 jiēdài 圙 receive, host
接到 jiēdào 圙 receive
接濟 jiējì 圙 assist (materially)
接近 jiējìn 圙 near, close 圙 approach
接連 jiēlián 圙 continuously, in succession

接納 jiēnà 圙 accept
接洽 jiēqià 圙 deal with, arrange with
接壤 jiērǎng 圙 border on, be contiguous with
接收 jiēshōu 圙 receive, take over
接受 jiēshòu 圙 accept, receive 圙 tolerate: 可以接受的 tolerable
接通 jiētōng 圙 put through
接頭 jiētóu 圙 contact, meet
接吻 jiēwěn 圙 kiss
接著 jiēzhe 圙 immediately following 圙 catch

刊 50 kān
82 Knife 刀 with 干 phonetic. 圙 cut, engrave 图 publication ⇔ 期刊, 週刊
刊出 kānchū 圙 publish
刊登 kāndēng 圙 publish
刊物 kānwù 图 publication

軒 50 xuān
83 [轩] Cart 車 with 干 phonetic. 图 carriage 圀 high
軒然大波 xuānrándàbō 圙 big stir, strong reaction

工 51 gōng
1 Pictograph of a carpenter's square. 图 work 图 worker ⇔ 人工, 竣工, 做工, 礦工, 加工, 分工, 打工, 停工, 施工, 怠工, 職工, 技工, 勞工, 理工, 罷工, 員工
工廠 gōngchǎng 图 factory
工程 gōngchéng 图 engineering: 工程師 engineer
工地 gōngdì 图 building site
工讀 gōngdú 图 work-study
工夫 gōngfū 图 time 图 work, effort 图 skill, technique 图 kung-fu (⇨ 功夫)
工會 gōnghuì 图 labor union
工匠 gōngjiàng 图 craftsman

工具 gōngjù 图 tool
工人 gōngrén 图 worker: 工人階級 working class
工業 gōngyè 图 industry: 工業化 industrialization
工友 gōngyǒu 图 manual worker
工資 gōngzī 图 wages
工作 gōngzuò 图 work, job: 工作站 work station

攻 51 gōng
2 Work 工 (phonetic) and strike 攵. 圙 attack ⇔ 圍攻, 反攻, 專攻
攻擊 gōngjí 圙 attack
攻勢 gōngshì 图 offensive

功 51 gōng
3 Work 工 (phonetic) and strength 力. 图 contribution, achievement ⇔ 成功, 用功, 氣功, 武功
功德 gōngdé 图 meritorious deeds
功夫 gōngfū 图 time 图 work: 下功夫 work hard (⇨ 工夫) kung-fu
功績 gōngjī 图 merits
功課 gōngkè 图 homework
功勞 gōngláo 图 achievement
功利 gōnglì 图 utility
功能 gōngnéng 图 function
功效 gōngxiào 图 effect, efficacy
功勳 gōngxūn 图 eminent contribution
功用 gōngyòng 图 use, effect, function

貢 51 gòng
4 [贡] Work's 工 (phonetic) reward of shells/money 貝. 图 tribute ⇔ 朝貢, 西貢
貢獻 gòngxiàn 圙 contribute, offer 图 contribution

槓 51 gàng
5 [杠] Wood 木 with 貢 phonetic. 图 lever
槓桿 gànggǎn 图 lever

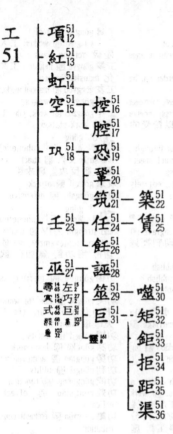

工
51

項 51 12

紅 51 13

虹 51 14

空 51 15 ── 控 51 16
           └ 腔 51 17

巩 51 18 ── 恐 51 19
           ── 鞏 51 20
           ── 筑 51 21 ── 築 51 22

壬 51 23 ── 任 51 24 ── 賃 51 25
           └ 飪 51 26

巫 51 27 ── 誣 51 28

尋 43 45 左 51 巧 37 27
實 68 80 51 筮 51 29 ── 噬 51 30
式 46 66 巨 51
蠱 103 32 巨 51 31 ── 矩 51 32
           鹽 161 8 鉅 51 33
           ── 拒 51 34
           ── 距 51 35
           ── 渠 51 36

贛 51 6 gàn
Modern form shows badge 章 69, walk ㄆ 66 and tribute 貢 24. 图 Jiangxi Province

缸 51 7 gāng
Ceramic 缶 141 with 工 9 phonetic. 图 jar ⇔ 浴缸 68

肛 51 8 gāng
Flesh 肉 132 with 工 9 phonetic. 图 anus
肛門 gāngmén 图 anus

扛 51 9 káng
Hand 手 97 and work 工 9 (phonetic). 图 lift, shoulder

江 51 10 jiāng
Water 水 85 with 工 9 phonetic. 图 river 图 a surname: 江青 Jiang Qing - a wife of Mao Zedong ⇔ 長江 23, 珠江 44, 浙江 59, 黑龍江 19
江湖 jiānghú 图 rivers and lakes 图 itinerant, vagabond

江南 jiāngnán 图 area south of and near the Yangtze River
江蘇 jiāngsū 图 Jiangsu Province
江西 jiāngxī 图 Jiangxi Province

鴻 51 11 [鸿] hóng
River 江 50 (phonetic) bird 鳥 178. 图 wild swan
鴻溝 hónggōu 图 wide gap, chasm

項 51 12 [项] xiàng
Head 頁 12 with 工 9 phonetic. 图 nape 图 item ⇔ 款項 55, 事項 95
項鍊 xiàngliàn 图 necklace
項目 xiàngmù 图 item
項圈 xiàngquān 图 necklace

紅 51 13 [红] hóng
Silk 糸 153 with 工 9 phonetic. 图 图 red 图 popular, fashionable 图 图 revolutionary ⇔ 臉紅 62, 眼紅 39, 粉紅 27, 口紅 64, 通紅 53, 朱紅 21
紅包 hóngbāo 图 red envelope containing money: 送紅包 give a monetary gift
紅茶 hóngchá 图 black tea
紅軍 hóngjūn 图 Red Army
紅利 hónglì 图 bonus, profit share
紅樓 hónglóu 图 boudoir: 紅樓夢 Dream of Red Mansions - a Qing Dynasty novel
紅色 hóngsè 图 red
紅燒 hóngshāo 图 stew, braise

虹 51 14 hóng
Insect/reptile 虫 125, suggesting snake-like, with 工 9 phonetic. 图 rainbow ⇔ 彩虹 105, 霓虹 143

空 51 15 kōng kòng
Hole 穴 91 with 工 9 phonetic. kōng: 图 empty 图 sky 图 in vain 图 merely kòng: 图 free time: 有空請來 come when you have the time 图 vacant, unoccupied 图 leave blank ⇔ 落空 89, 高空 27,

憑空²⁷, 真空³⁵, 太空³⁵, 天空³⁵, 航空³⁵

空白 kòngbái 圈 blank

空地 kòngdì 圈 vacant land

空洞 kōngdòng 圈 empty, hollow

空話 kōnghuà 圈 empty talk, idle talk

空間 kōngjiān 圈 space 圈 leeway

空軍 kōngjūn 圈 air force

空曠 kōngkuàng 圈 spacious

空論 kōnglùn 圈 empty talk

空氣 kōngqì 圈 air

空前 kōngqián 圈 unprecedented

空缺 kòngquē 圈 scarcity

空手道 kōngshǒudào 圈 karate

空調 kōngtiáo 圈 air-conditioning 圈 air-conditioner

空位 kòngwèi 圈 unoccupied seat

空襲 kōngxí 圈 air raid

空隙 kòngxì 圈 crevice

空閒 kòngxián 圈 leisure, free time

空想 kōngxiǎng 圈 fantasize 圈 fantasy, daydream

空虛 kōngxū 圈 hollow, meaningless

空中 kōngzhōng 圈 mid-air: 空中小姐 stewardess

控 51 kòng
16 Hand 手²⁷ moving through space 空³⁵ (phonetic). 圈 pull, draw ⇔ 指控³⁷, 遙控¹⁴¹

控告 kònggào 圈 accuse 圈 accusation

控訴 kòngsù 圈 sue

控制 kòngzhì 圈 圈 control

腔 51 qiāng
17 Flesh 肉¹³² cavity 空³⁵ (phonetic). 圈 chest cavity 圈 accent ⇔ 搭腔³⁵, 陳腔濫調⁴⁹

腔調 qiāngdiào 圈 accent, intonation

鞏 51 gǒng zhù
18 Work 工⁵¹ (phonetic) with object-holding hand 丮⁸² (altered to resemble 凡¹⁷). 圄 hold

恐 51 kǒng
19 Hold 丮 ⁵¹₁₈ (phonetic) heart 心¹³. 圈 fear, dread 圈 terrify ⇔ 惶恐²⁴, 驚恐⁹³, 惟恐¹⁶²

恐怖 kǒngbù 圈 terrifying 圈 terror: 恐怖份子 terrorist

恐嚇 kǒnghè 圈 threaten, intimidate

恐慌 kǒnghuāng 圈 panic 圈 panicky

恐懼 kǒngjù 圈 fear, dread: 恐懼症 phobia

恐龍 kǒnglóng 圈 dinosaur

恐怕 kǒngpà 圈 fear: 我恐怕不行。 I'm afraid it's impossible.

鞏 51 gǒng
20 [巩] Hold 丮 ⁵¹₁₈ (phonetic) with leather 革²⁴. 圈 bind with leather

鞏固 gǒnggù 圈 strengthen, solidify, consolidate

筑 51 zhú
21 Bamboo 竹⁷¹ (phonetic) instrument that is held 丮 ⁵¹₁₈ zhu - an ancient string instrument

築 51 圈 zhú 圈 zhù
22 [筑] Wield wood 木⁷¹ as instrument 筑³⁵ (phonetic). 圈 pack, ram 圈 build, construct ⇔ 建築³⁵

築路 zhúlù 圈 build roads

壬 51 rén
23 Pole 一¹ for carrying work 工⁵¹. 圈 burden (⇨ 任³⁴) 圈 ninth Heavenly Stem (⇨ 干支³⁷)

任 51 rén
24 Person 人¹⁰ assuming a burden 壬³⁵ (phonetic). 圈 assume a post 圈 appoint 圈

allow, let 圈 measureword for official assignments 圈 a surname ⇔ 主任⁸, 就任¹⁴, 擔任²⁹, 聘任²⁹, 繼任³⁸, 專任²⁹, 常任⁴⁵, 信任⁸⁵, 責任⁵⁷, 現任¹⁶³, 前任¹⁹, 勝任¹²⁴, 連任¹³⁵, 膺任⁸⁵

任何 rènhé 圈 any, whichever: 任何人 anyone

任命 rènmìng 圈 appoint

任憑 rènpíng 圈 no matter what

任期 rènqí 圈 term of office, tenure

任務 rènwù 圈 mission

任性 rènxìng 圈 wilful, uninhibited

任意 rènyì 圈 arbitrarily, uninhibitedly

任用 rènyòng 圈 employ

任職 rènzhí 圈 hold office

賃 51 lìn
25 [赁] Assume 任³⁴ (phonetic) for shells/money 貝¹⁵⁰. 圈 rent ⇔ 租賃¹⁶⁷

飪 51 rèn
26 [饪] Food 食³⁵ with 壬³⁵ phonetic. 圈 cook ⇔ 烹飪⁴³

巫 51 wū
27 Work 工⁵¹ of two people 人¹⁰. 圈 sorcery 圈 shaman, sorcerer 圈 a surname

巫婆 wūpó 圈 witch, sorceress

巫術 wūshù 圈 sorcery: 巫術師 sorcerer

誣 51 wū
28 [诬] Words 言⁹⁸ of sorcerers 巫³⁵ (phonetic). 圈 slander

誣害 wūhài 圈 malign

誣賴 wūlài 圈 accuse falsely, slander

誣陷 wūxiàn 圈 frame (someone)

筮 51 shì
29 Bamboo 竹⁷¹ and sorcery 巫³⁵. 圈 divine 卜筮²⁶

筮人 shìrén 圈 fortune teller

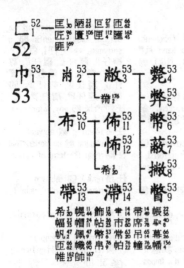

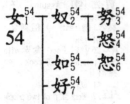

噬 51 shì 30 Mouth 口 with 筮 phonetic. 圗 bite ⇔ 吞噬

巨 51 jù 31 Carpenter's square 工 with marks showing handle. ⑨ carpenter's square (⇒ 矩) 圗 huge

巨大 jùdà 圗 huge, enormous

巨額 jùé 圗 large sum ⇒ 鉅額

巨人 jùrén 圗 giant

矩 51 jǔ 32 Carpenter's square 巨 (phonetic) with arrow 矢 emphasizing straightness. 圗 carpenter's square ⇔ 規矩

矩陣 jǔzhèn 圗 matrix

鉅 51 jù 33 [钜] Metal 金 and big 巨 (phonetic). 圗 strong, stiff 圗 great, large ⇔ 艱鉅

鉅額 jùé 圗 large sum ⇒ 巨額

拒 51 jù 34 Modern form shows hand 手 with 巨 phonetic. 圗 refuse ⇔ 抗拒, 婉拒

拒絕 jùjué 圗 refuse

距 51 jù 35 Foot 足 with 巨 phonetic. 圗 bird's spur 圗 distance ⇔ 差距, 焦距

距離 jùlí 圗 distance

渠 36 qú Water 水 and carpenter's square (phonetic, ancient form including 巨 and wood 木). 圗 channel, ditch ⇔ 溝渠

渠道 qúdào 圗 channel, ditch

匚 52 fāng 1 Pictograph of a hollowed out piece of wood.

巾 53 jīn 1 Pictograph of a hanging handkerchief. 圗 towel, cloth 圍巾, 領巾, 毛巾, 餐巾

㡀 53 bì 2 Cloth 巾 in tatters. 圗 rags

敝 53 bì 3 Beat 攴 to shreds 㡀 (phonetic). 圗 broken, tattered 圗 圗 my, our ⇔ 凋敝

敝舍 bìshè 圗 圗 my home

斃 53 bì 4 [毙] Worn 敝 (phonetic) to death 死. Simplified form uses 比. 圗 collapse, die ⇔ 槍斃

弊 53 bì 5 Modern form shows tattered 敝 (phonetic) and joined hands 廾. 圗 collapse (⇒ 斃) 圗 corruption, fraud ⇔ 作弊, 舞弊, 利弊

弊病 bìbìng 圗 drawback

弊端 bìduān 圗 corruption

幣 53 bì 6 [币] Cloth 巾 with 敝 phonetic. 圗 silk cloth 圗 currency ⇔ 貨幣, 港幣, 錢幣, 台幣, 外幣, 日幣

蔽 53 bì 7 Plant 艸 with 敝 phonetic. 圗 cover, conceal ⇔ 掩蔽, 遮蔽, 隱蔽

撇8 53 piē piě
Hand 手⼿ discarding what is broken 敝⼫ (phonetic). piē: 動 abandon piě: 名 a calligraphy stroke
撇開 piēkāi 動 cast aside
撇清 piēqīng 動 feign innocence

瞥9 53 piē
Eye 目⼨ with 敝⼫ phonetic. 動 glance at
瞥見 piējiàn 動 catch a glimpse of

布10 53 bù
Cloth 巾⼸ with 父 (abbreviated) phonetic. 名 cloth 動 announce 動 deploy ⇔ 宣布, 尿布, 瀑布, 公布, 分布, 帆布, 抹布, 發布, 盧布
布袋 bùdài 名 cloth sack: 布袋戲 puppet show
布施 bùshī 動 donate
布條 bùtiáo 名 strip of cloth

佈11 53 bù
[布] Person 人⼈ with 布 phonetic and suggesting to spread out. 動 announce ⇔ 宣佈, 公佈, 頒佈, 發佈, 攞佈
佈告 bùgào 動 notice, announcement: 佈告欄 bulletin board
佈局 bùjú 名 layout, composition
佈置 bùzhì 動 arrange, decorate

怖12 53 bù
Heart 心⼼ with 布 phonetic. 動 frighten ⇔ 恐怖

帶13 53 dài
[带] Cloth 巾⼸ repeated on the bottom and a pictograph of a belt with pendants on top. 名 belt, sash band 動 carry, take, bring 名 zone, region ⇔ 附帶, 皮帶, 腰帶, 寒帶, 靭帶, 挾帶, 佩帶, 膠帶, 海帶, 磁帶, 熱帶, 溫帶, 鞋帶, 連帶, 攜帶, 繃帶
帶動 dàidòng 動 pull along, spur on, drive
帶給 dàigěi 動 bring to, take to
帶回 dàihuí 動 bring back
帶來 dàilái 動 bring
帶領 dàilǐng 動 lead, guide
帶著 dàizhe 動 carry along
帶走 dàizǒu 動 take, take out, walk off with

滯14 53 zhì
[滞] Water 水⽔ with belt 帶 suggesting restraint. 形 stagnant ⇔ 停滯, 遲滯, 阻滯
滯留 zhìliú 動 be detained, be held up 動 overstay
滯銷 zhìxiāo 形 stagnant sales

女1 54 nǚ
Pictograph of a kneeling woman. 名 woman 形 female ⇔ 婦女, 婢女, 修女, 少女, 侍女, 男女, 處女, 子女, 孫女, 仙女, 甥女, 妓女, 吧女, 淑女, 養女, 美女, 姪女, 兒女
女兒 nǚ'ér 名 daughter
女孩 nǚhái 名 girl
女孩兒 nǚháir 名 girl
女孩子 nǚháizi 名 girl
女郎 nǚláng 名 girl, young woman
女權 nǚquán 名 women's rights: 女權主義 feminism; 女權主義者 feminist
女人 nǚrén 名 woman
女神 nǚshén 名 goddess
女生 nǚshēng 名 schoolgirl, girl, young woman
女士 nǚshì 名 lady
女王 nǚwáng 名 queen
女性 nǚxìng 名 形 female
女婿 nǚxù 名 son-in-law

女友 nǚyǒu 名 girlfriend
女子 nǚzǐ 名 woman, female: 女子隊 women's team

奴2 54 nú
Woman 女⼥ (phonetic) under master's hand 又⼜. 名 slave, servant ⇔ 匈奴
奴隸 núlì 名 slave
奴僕 núpú 名 servant

努3 54 nǔ
Slave's 奴 (phonetic) strength 力⼒. 動 work hard
努力 nǔlì 動 work hard 形 diligent

怒4 54 nù
Slave's 奴 (phonetic) heart 心⼼. 名 rage, fury ⇔ 狂怒, 衆怒, 憤怒, 喜怒哀樂, 激怒, 觸怒, 惱怒
怒氣 nùqì 名 rage, fury

如5 54 rú
Woman 女⼥ following mouthed 口⼝ instructions. 動 listen, heed 動 like, as if 形 comparable to: 不如上次 not as good as last time according to 動 if ⇔ 不如, 比如, 假如, 有如, 譬如, 宛如, 諸如, 例如, 猶如, 易如反掌
如此 rúcǐ 形 like this, such: 希望如此 wish it were so, hope it is so
如果 rúguǒ 連 if, suppose
如何 rúhé 代 how
如今 rújīn 名 nowadays
如期 rúqí 動 as scheduled
如同 rútóng 介 as if, like
如昔 rúxí 動 as of old
如下 rúxià 動 as follows
如意 rúyì 動 as wished: 祝您萬事如意. May everything turn out as you wish.
如願 rúyuàn 動 as wished

恕6 54 shù
As 如 (phonetic) the heart 心⼼ does. 動 forgive

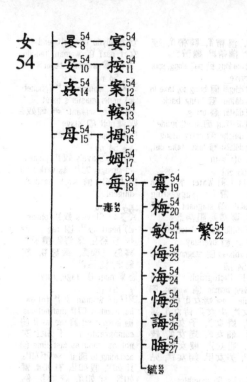

女
54

⇦ 饒恕⁴⁹, 寬恕¹¹⁴

恕罪 shùzuì 🔟 forgive, pardon

好7 Female 女🔟 child
子⁵⁵. hǎo: 🔟 good 🔟 all right
🔟 (indicating completion):
做好了 Finished. 🔟 very, how:
好奇怪 how strange 🔟 easily:
不好發音 difficult to pro-
nounce hào: 🔟 like, love ⇦
剛好³⁶, 良好⁵⁷, 嗜好¹³⁴, 友
好¹², 弄好⁴⁵, 學好⁸⁹, 你
好⁴⁸, 做好²⁴, 恰好³⁴, 幸
好⁴⁵, 癖好²⁸, 約好⁶¹, 只
好⁶⁶, 喜好⁵⁸, 挺好⁴⁷, 問
好⁴⁹, 愛好⁹, 正好⁴⁷, 看
好¹⁴, 偏好¹¹³, 美好¹²⁷, 還

好¹²⁸, 最好¹²⁷

好棒 hǎobàng 🔟 (口) 🔟 excel-
lent

好比 hǎobǐ 🔟 comparable to,
like

好不 hǎobù 🔟 not at all 🔟 very,
how

好吃 hǎochī 🔟 tasty, delicious

好處 hǎochù 🔟 good point,
advantage

好歹 hǎodǎi 🔟 good and bad
anyhow, in any case 🔟 misfortune, accident

好感 hǎogǎn 🔟 good will,
favorable impression

好漢 hǎohàn 🔟 hero

好好 hǎohǎo 🔟 thoroughly,
properly

好話 hǎohuà 🔟 praise: 說你的
好話 say good things about you

好壞 hǎohuài 🔟 good and bad
🔟 quality

好久 hǎojiǔ 🔟 a long time: 好
久不見. Long time no see.

好看 hǎokàn 🔟 good-looking,
attractive, pretty

好客 hàokè 🔟 hospitable

好奇 hàoqí 🔟 curious

好生 hǎoshēng 🔟 good life

好手 hǎoshǒu 🔟 expert

好玩 hǎowán 🔟 fun, enter-
taining

好像 hǎoxiàng 🔟 resemble 🔟
apparently, seemingly

好笑 hǎoxiào 🔟 funny, amusing
🔟 laughable

好些 hǎoxiē 🔟 a little better

好意 hǎoyì 🔟 good intentions

好意思 hǎoyìsī 🔟 have the
nerve to: 不好意思 embar-
rassed

好友 hǎoyǒu 🔟 good friend

好運 hǎoyùn 🔟 good luck: 祝
你好運! Good luck!

好在 hǎozài 🔟 fortunately

好轉 hǎozhuǎn 🔟 turn for the
better, improve 🔟 improvement

晏8 yàn Sunlight
日⁷⁶,
representing man, over woman
女⁵⁴. 🔟 peace

宴9 yàn Tranquility 晏⁵⁴ (phonetic) under a roof 宀⁶¹. 🔟
rest, quiet 🔟 banquet

宴會 yànhuì 🔟 banquet, feast

安10 ān Woman 女⁵⁴ under a
roof 宀⁶¹. 🔟 peaceful, tranquil
🔟 pacify, console 🔟 place,
arrange 🔟 a surname ⇦ 不
安⁵³, 苟安⁴³, 公安¹², 長
安⁴³, 平安³³, 印第安⁵³, 天
安門⁴⁹, 治安⁹, 請安³⁶, 保
安⁵³, 西安¹³, 晚安¹⁰⁰

安定 āndìng 🔳 stabilize
安非他命 ānfēitāmìng 🔳 amphetamine
安徽 ānhuī 🔳 Anhui Province
安靜 ānjìng 🔳 peaceful, quiet
安眠 ānmián 🔳 sleep peacefully: 安眠藥 sleeping pill
安寧 ānníng 🔳 quiet and peaceful
安排 ānpái 🔳 arrange 🔳 arrangement
安全 ānquán 🔳 safe, secure 🔳 safety, security: 安全帶 safety belt, seatbelt; 安全感 sense of security; 安全島 traffic island; 安全理事會 Security Council
安慰 ānwèi 🔳 comfort, console 🔳 consolation: 安慰獎 consolation prize
安穩 ānwěn 🔳 safe and stable
安心 ānxīn 🔳 have peace of mind
安置 ānzhì 🔳 settle 🔳 arrange for
安裝 ānzhuāng 🔳 install

按 54 àn
11 Hand 手 and pacify 安 (phonetic). 🔳 press, push 🔳 restrain 🔳 according to
按理 ànlǐ 🔳 according to reason
按摩 ànmó 🔳 🔳 massage
按捺 ànnà 🔳 repress, contain: 按捺不住 cannot hold back
按鈕 ànnǐu 🔳 button 🔳 push a button
按時 ànshí 🔳 on time, as scheduled
按照 ànzhào 🔳 according to, on the basis of
按著 ànzhe 🔳 according to
按住 ànzhù 🔳 press down 🔳 restrain

案 54 àn
12 Stable/tranquil 安 (phonetic) wood 木. 🔳 display table 🔳 legal case 🔳

record, file 🔳 proposal, plan ⇔ 搶案, 破案, 訟案, 疑案, 報案, 法案, 答案, 命案, 辦案, 專案, 檔案, 圖案, 草案, 提案, 方案, 翻案
案件 ànjiàn 🔳 law case
案子 ànzi 🔳 case, law case

鞍 54 ān
13 Leather 革 ensuring safety 安 (phonetic). 🔳 saddle ⇔ 馬鞍

姦 54 jiān
14 [奸] Many woman 女. 🔳 adultery (⇨ 奸) ⇔ 強姦, 通姦
姦淫 jiānyín adultery 🔳 rape, seduce

母 54 mǔ
15 Woman 女 with dots indicating breasts. 🔳 mother ⇔ 酵母, 父母, 父母親, 分母, 義母, 字母, 繼母, 伯母, 岳母, 祖母, 師母
母國 mǔguó 🔳 motherland
母雞 mǔjī 🔳 hen
母親 mǔqīn 🔳 mother: 母親節 Mother's Day
母系 mǔxì 🔳 matrilineal: 母系社會 matrilineal society
母校 mǔxiào 🔳 alma mater
母語 mǔyǔ 🔳 mother tongue

拇 54 mǔ
16 Hand's 手 mother 每 (phonetic). 🔳 thumb
拇指 mǔzhǐ 🔳 thumb
拇趾 mǔzhǐ 🔳 big toe

姆 54 mǔ
17 Modern form shows woman 女 and mother 母 (phonetic). 🔳 nanny ⇔ 保姆

每 54 měi
18 Blade of grass 屮 with 母 phonetic: flourish. 🔳 each, every

每次 měicì 🔳 every time, whenever
每況愈下 měikuàngyùxià 🔳 getting worse and worse
每年 měinián 🔳 every year
每日 měirì 🔳 everyday
每天 měitiān 🔳 everyday

霉 54 méi
19 Rain 雨 with 每 phonetic. 🔳 mildew ⇔ 倒霉, 發霉

梅 54 méi
20 Wood 木 with 每 phonetic. 🔳 plum ⇔ 金瓶梅
梅花 méihuā 🔳 plum flower
梅雨 méiyǔ 🔳 plum rains – the rainy season in early summer

敏 54 mǐn
21 Strike 攵 with 每 phonetic. 🔳 quick ⇔ 機敏, 過敏, 靈敏
敏感 mǐngǎn 🔳 allergy 🔳 sensitive, touchy: 這個問題很敏感. This is a very sensitive issue.
敏捷 mǐnjié 🔳 agile, nimble
敏銳 mǐnruì 🔳 sharp, keen

繁 54 fán
22 Modern form shows quick 敏 and thread 糸. 🔳 manifold, intricate ⇔ 頻繁
繁華 fánhuá 🔳 flourishing, bustling
繁忙 fánmáng 🔳 hectic
繁榮 fánróng 🔳 prosperous
繁體字 fántǐzì 🔳 traditional Chinese characters
繁雜 fánzá 🔳 numerous and complex
繁殖 fánzhí 🔳 breed, reproduce

侮 54 wǔ
23 Person 人 with 每 phonetic. 🔳 humiliate ⇔ 欺侮, 外侮
侮辱 wǔrù 🔳 humiliate, affront

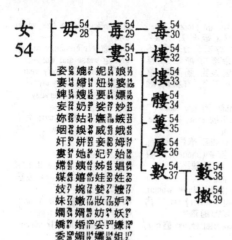

女
54

海嘯 hǎixiào 图 tidal wave, tsunami

海洋 hǎiyáng 图 ocean

海域 hǎiyù 图 sea area

海員 hǎiyuán 图 seaman, sailor

海蜇 hǎizhé 图 jellyfish

悔
25 Heart 心 with 每 phonetic. 图 regret ⇔ 後悔, 懺悔

悔改 huǐgǎi 图 repent and reform

悔過 huǐguò 图 repent

悔恨 huǐhèn 图 regret, feel remorse

誨 54 (動) huì 動 huǐ
26 [诲] Words 言 with 每 phonetic. 图 teach ⇔ 教誨

晦 54 huì
27 Sun 日 with 每 phonetic. 图 dark

晦氣 huìqì 图 unlucky

毋 54 wú
28 Adulterous woman 女 behind barred 一 door. 图 do not

毐 54 ǎi
29 Scholar 士 doing what he should not 毋. 图 immoral

毒 54 dú
30 Plant 屮 that is ruinous 毒 (bottom usually written as 母). 图 poison 图 poisonous 图 malicious 图 drug ⇔ 吸毒, 販毒, 病毒, 消毒, 中毒, 惡毒

毒販 dúfàn 图 drug pusher

毒辣 dúlà 图 cruel, vicious, malicious

毒瘤 dúliú 图 cancerous growth, malignant tumor

毒品 dúpǐn 图 drug

毒梟 dúxiāo 图 druglord

毒藥 dúyào 图 poison

婁 54 lóu
31 [娄] Woman 女 in

海 54 hǎi
24 Where all 每 water 水 goes. 图 sea, ocean 图 a surname ⇔ 上海, 雲海, 下海, 人海, 北海道, 滄海, 四海, 渤海, 大海, 地中海, 沿海, 青海, 碧海, 珠海, 腦海

海岸 hǎiàn 图 coast, shore

海拔 hǎibá 图 elevation, altitude

海豹 hǎibào 图 seal

海報 hǎibào 图 poster

海邊 hǎibiān 图 seaside

海濱 hǎibīn 图 beach

海帶 hǎidài 图 kelp

海盜 hǎidào 图 pirate

海關 hǎiguān 图 customs, customs house

海龜 hǎiguī 图 sea turtle

海軍 hǎijūn 图 navy

海口 hǎikǒu 图 port

海面 hǎimiàn 图 ocean surface

海鷗 hǎiōu 图 sea gull

海權 hǎiquán 图 naval power

海參 hǎishēn 图 sea cucumber

海水 hǎishuǐ 图 seawater

海苔 hǎitái 图 seaweed

海灘 hǎitān 图 beach

海豚 hǎitún 图 dolphin

海外 hǎiwài 图 overseas

海灣 hǎiwān 图 gulf

海峽 hǎixiá 图 straits

海鮮 hǎixiān 图 seafood

the middle 中繇 of doing nothing 毋繇. Simplified form uses 米繇. 團 leisure 圖 a constellation

樓 54 lóu
32 [楼] Wood 木繇 with 婁繇 phonetic. 圖 tower 圖 multi-story building 圖 story, floor: 二樓 second floor ⇔ 閣樓繇, 牌樓繇, 頂樓繇, 大樓繇, 紅樓繇

樓上 lóushàng 圖 upstairs

樓梯 lóutī 圖 stairs

樓下 lóuxià 圖 downstairs

摟 54 lóu lōu lǒu
33 [搂] Hand 手繇 with 婁繇 phonetic. lóu: 圖 drag, pull lōu: 圖 gather 圖 extort: 摟錢 extort money lǒu: 圖 embrace

摟抱 lǒubào 圖 embrace, hug

髏 54 lóu
34 [髅] Bone 骨繇 with 婁繇 phonnetic. 圖 skull 骷髏繇

簍 54 lǒu
35 [篓] Bamboo 竹繇 with 婁繇 phonetic. 圖 basket

簍子 lǒuzi 圖 basket

屢 54 lǚ
36 [屡] Body 尸繇 with 婁繇 phonetic. 圖 repeatedly

屢次 lǚcì 圖 repeatedly, frequently

屢見不鮮 lǚjiànbùxiān 圖 nothing new

數 54 shǔ shù
37 [数] Strike 攵繇 with 婁繇 phonetic. shǔ: 圖 count shù: 圖 number 圖 several ⇔ 倍數繇, 人數繇, 次數繇, 指數繇, 函數繇, 複數繇, 奇數繇, 少數繇, 無數繇, 倒數繇, 分數繇, 大多數繇, 參數繇, 常數繇, 多數繇, 偶數繇, 半數繇, 單數繇, 總數繇, 負數繇, 算數繇, 變數繇, 係數繇, 雙數繇, 對數繇

數額 shùé 圖 quantity

數據 shùjù 圖 data: 數據庫 database; 數據機 modem

數量 shùliàng 圖 quantity

數目 shùmù 圖 number, amount

數位 shùwèi 圖 digit: 數位化 digital

數學 shùxué 圖 mathematics

數字 shùzì 圖 numeral, figure: 六位數字 six-digit figure

藪 54 sǒu
38 [薮] Where grass 艸繇 is numerous 數繇 (phonetic). 圖 marsh ⇔ 淵藪繇

擻 54 sǒu
39 [擞] Hand 手繇 making numerous 數繇 (phonetic) movements. 圖 shake, tremble ⇔ 抖擻繇

子 55 zǐ zi
1 Pictograph of an infant, legs bundled together. 圖 child 圖 son 圖 egg, seed 圖 first Earthly Branch (⇒ 干支繇) ⇔ 一輩子繇, 一下子繇, 一陣子繇, 王子繇, 筷子繇, 粽子繇, 杯子繇, 原子繇, 儍子繇, 孩子繇, 核子繇, 院子繇, 幌子繇, 棍子繇, 根子繇, 銀子繇, 浪子繇, 花花公子繇, 靴子繇, 老子繇, 孝子繇, 嗓子繇, 庚子之役繇, 君子繇, 裙子繇, 妻子繇, 村子繇, 斧子繇, 被子繇, 牌子繇, 巷子繇, 電子繇, 鞭子繇, 圈子繇, 包子繇, 句子繇, 擔子繇, 膽子繇, 販子繇, 蠍子繇, 長子繇, 稿子繇, 影子繇, 帽子繇, 點子繇, 椅子繇, 奶子繇, 小孩子繇, 小伙子繇, 小子繇, 沙子繇, 脖子繇, 個子繇, 鬍子繇, 蓆子繇, 燕子繇, 架子繇, 碟子繇, 猴子繇, 架子繇, 茄子繇, 男孩子繇, 男子繇, 刀子繇, 分子繇, 份子繇, 盆子繇, 岔子繇, 釘子繇, 亭子繇, 緞子繇, 夫子繇, 夾子繇, 粒子繇, 拉肚子繇, 位子繇, 太子繇, 天子繇, 筷子繇, 法子繇, 蓋子繇, 餃子繇, 刷子繇, 盒子繇, 鴿子繇, 袋子繇, 棋子繇, 旗子繇, 鼻子繇, 瘋子繇, 盅子繇, 疹子繇, 瓶子繇, 墊子繇, 辮子繇, 女孩子繇, 女子繇, 案子繇, 簍子繇, 孔子繇, 李子繇, 孫子繇, 梳子繇, 起子繇, 仙子繇, 杓子繇, 弟子繇, 仙子繇, 扣子繇, 鉗子繇, 刮鬍子繇, 鏡子繇, 簿子繇, 凳子繇, 獸子繇, 肚子繇, 鞋子繇, 精子繇, 棒子繇, 竹子繇, 腕子繇, 日子繇, 拍子繇, 渣子繇, 種子繇, 果子繇, 本子繇, 呆子繇, 瞎子繇, 片子繇, 莊子繇, 睏子繇, 毯子繇, 葵瓜子繇, 耗子繇, 胖子繇, 胖子繇, 房子繇, 蚊子繇, 鑷子繇, 橘子繇, 底子繇, 爪子繇, 驢子繇, 櫃子繇, 梨子繇, 騾子繇, 鴨子繇, 匣子繇, 笛子繇, 襪子繇, 箱子繇, 冊子繇, 輪子繇, 孟子繇, 爐子繇, 養子繇, 樣子繇, 扇子繇, 蟲子繇, 繩子繇, 圈子繇, 嫂子繇, 桃子繇, 娃子繇, 屋子繇, 盤子繇, 兒子繇, 絹子繇, 擺架子繇, 轎子繇, 骨子繇, 例子繇, 曲子繇, 彈子繇, 椰子繇, 鬼子繇, 籃子繇, 腦子繇, 窗子繇, 墨子繇, 身子繇, 面子繇, 車子繇, 鏈子繇, 褲子繇, 兔子繇, 館子繇, 獅子繇, 輩子繇, 栗子繇

子彈 zǐdàn 圖 bullet

子宮 zǐgōng 圖 womb, uterus

子女 zǐnǚ 圖 sons and daughters, children

子孫 zǐsūn 圖 descendants

字 55 zì
2 Children 子繇 (pho-

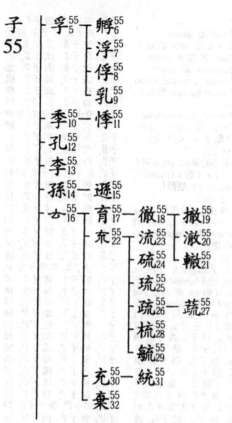

子
55

孚 55/5 ── 孵 55/6
│   浮 55/7
│   俘 55/8
│   乳 55/9
├─ 季 55/10 ── 悸 55/11
├─ 孔 55/12
├─ 李 55/13
├─ 孫 55/14 ── 遜 55/15
└─ 㐬 55/16 ── 育 55/17 ── 徹 55/18 ── 撤 55/19
              充 55/22 ── 流 55/23 ── 澈 55/20
              │   硫 55/24 ── 轍 55/21
              │   琉 55/25
              │   疏 55/26 ── 蔬 55/27
              │   梳 55/28
              │   毓 55/29
              └─ 充 55/30 ── 統 55/31
                 棄 55/32

netic) under a roof 宀⁶³. ㊈
love, care for 圖 character,
logograph, letter 圖 a name
given to a young man upon
coming of age ⇔ 簽字¹⁴², 破
音字¹⁴⁶, 十字²⁷, 漢字³⁹, 打
字³⁷, 大字⁷, 赤字⁹⁹, 金字
塔¹⁷, 繁體字⁸⁶, 數字³⁹, 識
字⁷⁴, 名字⁷, 白字²⁷, 簡體
字⁸⁶, 文字⁷, 寫字¹⁴², 單
字¹³⁰, 測字¹⁹, 逐字¹⁵⁵
字典 zìdiǎn 圖 dictionary (of
Chinese characters)

字母 zìmǔ 圖 letter, alphabet
字幕 zìmù 圖 subtitle
字體 zìtǐ 圖 font, typestyle
字條 zìtiáo 圖 slip of paper 圖
note
字帖 zìtiè 圖 calligraphy copy
book
字形 zìxíng 圖 font, typestyle
字眼 zìyǎn 圖 wording, diction
字源 zìyuán 圖 etymology of a
character

仔 55/3 zǐ zǎi
Person 人¹⁰ and child

子⁵⁵ (phonetic). zǐ: ㊈
assume, take on 圖 careful zǎi:
圖 young animal ⇔ 牛仔⁹²
仔細 zǐxì 圖 careful, detailed

孜 55/4 zī
Strike 攵⁶² with 子⁵⁵
phonetic. 圖 diligent
孜孜不倦 zīzībùjuàn 圖 dili-
gently, untiringly

孚 55/5 fú
Claws 爪¹⁰³ over off-
spring 子⁵⁵. ㊈ hatch (⇔ 孵⁵⁵)
圖 confidence, trust

孵 55/6 fū
Hatch 孚⁵⁵ (phonet-
ic) eggs 卵⁵⁷. 圖 incubate,
hatch
孵化 fūhuà 圖 hatch, spawn

浮 55/7 fú
Water 水⁶¹ with 孚⁵⁵
phonetic. 圖 float 圖 exceed
⇔ 輕浮⁷, 漂浮⁵⁹
浮動 fúdòng 圖 float
浮華 fúhuá 圖 showy, ostentatious

俘 55/8 fú
Person 人¹⁰ held under
claws 孚⁵⁵ (phonetic). 圖
capture 圖 captive ⇔ 戰俘⁵⁵
俘虜 fúlǔ 圖 capture 圖 captive,
prisoner of war

乳 55/9 rǔ
A swallow 乚¹
hatching 孚⁵⁵ (phonetic) its
young. 圖 give birth 圖 breasts
圖 milk ⇔ 哺乳⁶⁰
乳房 rǔfáng 圖 breasts
乳酪 rǔlào 圖 cheese
乳臭未乾 rǔxiùwèigān 圖
young and inexperienced

季 55/10 jì
Immature 稚⁶⁹ (pho-
netic, abbreviated to 禾¹⁰⁸)
child 子⁵⁵ (phonetic). 圖
youngest brother 圖 season 圖
a surname ⇔ 旺季¹⁶, 四
季⁷, 冬季⁶⁷, 淡季⁶³, 夏
季¹⁰⁸, 雨季¹⁶¹

季度 jìdù 图 quarter (of a year)
季節 jìjié 图 season

悸 55 jì
11 Heart 心[fp] of youngest brother 季[phonetic] (phonetic). 图 fear
悸動 jìdòng 圆 palpitate with fear

孔 55 kǒng
12 Where offspring 子[fp] of swallow 乙[fp] raised. 图 hole, opening 囲 a surname ⇔ 鼻孔[fp], 瞳孔[fp], 面孔[fp]
孔廟 kǒngmiào 图 Confucian temple
孔雀 kǒngquè 图 peacock
孔子 kǒngzǐ 囚 Confucius

李 55 lǐ
13 Tree 木[fp] offspring 子[fp]. 图 plum 图 plum tree 囲 a surname: 李白 Li Po - a Tang Dynasty poet ⇔ 行李[fp]
李子 lǐzi 图 plum

孫 55 sūn
14 [孙] Child 子[fp] in the family line 系[fp]. Simplified form uses 小[fp]. 图 grandchild 囲 a surname: 孫中山 Sun Yat-sen; 孫悟空 Monkey King ⇔ 公孫[fp], 子孫[fp], 外孫[fp], 曾孫[fp]
孫女 sūnnǚ 图 granddaughter
孫子 sūnzi 图 grandson (son's son)
孫子 sūnzǐ 囚 Sun Tzu - an ancient military strategist: 孫子兵法 Sun Tzu's Art of War

遜 55 xùn
15 [逊] Movement 辵[fp] like grandchild 孫[fp] (phonetic). 国 retreat 圈 humble inferior ⇔ 謙遜[fp]
遜色 xùnsè 圈 inferior
遜於 xùnyú 圈 inferior to

㐬 55 tú
16 Child 子[fp] inverted, representing the head first position of birth.

育 55 yù
17 Flesh 肉[fp] born [fp]. 国 raise, nurture 圆 breed, reproduce 圆 raise, cultivate ⇔ 培育[fp], 教育[fp], 孕育[fp], 德育[fp], 撫育[fp], 節育[fp], 生育[fp], 體育[fp], 保育[fp], 發育[fp], 養育[fp]

徹 55 chè
18 [彻] Step 彳[fp], cultivate 育[fp], and strike 攴[fp] (phonetic). Simplified form uses 切[fp]. 圈 unobstructed ⇔ 透徹[fp]
徹底 chèdǐ 圈 thoroughly

撤 55 chè
19 Modern form shows hand 手[fp] clearing 徹[fp] (phonetic, abbreviated). 圆 remove, withdraw
撤兵 chèbīng 圆 withdraw troops
撤出 chèchū 圆 withdraw
撤退 chètuì 圆 retreat
撤銷 chèxiāo 圆 revoke, abolish

澈 55 chè
20 Water 水[fp] unobstructed 徹[fp] (phonetic, abbreviated). 圈 clear ⇔ 清澈[fp]

轍 55 chè 粵 zhé
21 [辙] Cart 車[fp] clearing 徹[fp] (phonetic, abbreviated). 图 cart tracks ⇔ 重蹈覆轍[fp]

㐬 55 tú
22 Birth [fp] (phonetic) with river 川[fp] suggesting amniotic fluid. 图 birth

流 55 liú
23 Water 水[fp] flowing 㐬[fp]. 圆 图 flow 图 class, rate ⇔ 一流[fp], 下流[fp], 水流[fp], 源流[fp], 主流[fp], 漂流[fp], 交流[fp], 支流[fp], 外流[fp], 潮流[fp], 氣流[fp], 溪流[fp], 輪流[fp]
流產 liúchǎn 图 圆 miscarriage
流暢 liúchàng 圈 圆 facile and smooth
流出 liúchū 圆 flow out 图 outflow
流傳 liúchuán 圆 pass on, hand down
流動 liúdòng 圆 flow
流汗 liúhàn 圆 sweat, perspire
流覽 liúlǎn 圆 skim, scan, browse (⇨ 瀏覽)
流浪 liúlàng 圆 wander, drift: 流浪漢 drifter, vagrant
流淚 liúlèi 圆 shed tears
流利 liúlì 圈 fluent: 講一口流利的中文 speak fluent Chinese
流連忘返 liúliánwàngfǎn 圖 become enchanted by a place and forget to return home
流露 liúlù 圆 let slip, reveal
流氓 liúmáng 图 hoodlum, delinquent
流失 liúshī 圆 run off
流水 liúshuǐ 图 flowing water
流通 liútōng 圆 circulate
流亡 liúwáng 圆 go into exile: 流亡政府 government in exile
流星 liúxīng 图 meteor
流行 liúxíng 圆 spread: 流行性感冒 influenza; 流行病 epidemic 圈 popular, fashionable
流血 liúxuè 圆 bleed
流鶯 liúyīng 图 streetwalker
流於 liúyú 圆 degenerate into
流域 liúyù 图 river basin: 長江流域 Yang-tze River basin

硫 55 liú
24 Stone 石[fp] that flows 㐬[fp] (phonetic). 图 sulfur
硫磺 liúhuáng 图 sulfur
硫酸 liúsuān 图 sulfuric acid

琉 55 liú
25 Jade-like 玉[fp] and flow 㐬[fp] (phonetic). 图 glaze
琉璃 liúlí 图 glaze: 琉璃瓦 glazed tiles
琉球 liúqiú 图 Ryukyu - islands

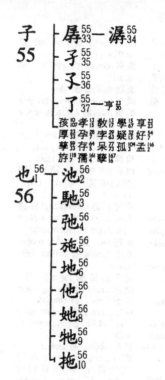

子
55

屏 55/33 — 潺 55/34
子 55/35
孑 55/36
了 55/37 — 亨 38

孩 09 孝 19 教 19 學 20 享 23
厚 24 孕 25 孛 26 疑 27 好 28
孳 29 存 30 呆 31 孤 161 孟 116
斿 117 孺 161 孿 167

也 56/1 — 池 56/2
56
馳 56/3
弛 56/4
施 56/5
地 56/6
他 56/7
她 56/8
牠 56/9
拖 56/10

between Taiwan and Japan

疏 55 shū
26 Moving foot 疋 29 and
flow 束 25 (phonetic). 🄳
clear, remove obstructions 🄳
unfamiliar 🄳 neglect 🄳
sparse, thin ⇔ 生疏 20
疏導 shūdǎo 🄳 dredge
疏忽 shūhū 🄳 neglect
疏失 shūshī 🄳 negligent,
remiss
疏通 shūtōng 🄳 dredge 🄳
mediate, reconcile
疏遠 shūyuǎn 🄳 estranged,
alienated
蔬 55 shū
27 Plant 艸 25 with 疏 22

phonetic. 🄳 vegetable
蔬菜 shūcài 🄳 vegetable
蔬果 shūguǒ 🄳 fruits and vege-
tables

梳 55 shū
28 Wood 木 17 that makes
hair flow 束 25 (phonetic). 🄳
comb 🄳 comb
梳妝 shūzhuāng 🄳 dress and
put on make-up
梳子 shūzi 🄳 comb

毓 55 yù
29 Mother 母 28 (changed
to 每 28) giving birth 束 25.
nurture

充 55 chōng
30 Raise 育 37 (abbre-

viated to 云 38) til standing 儿 6.
🄰 grow, raise 🄳 sufficient
🄳 fill 🄳 fake, pretend ⇔ 冒
充 32, 擴充 33, 補充 37
充斥 chōngchì 🄳 flood, inundate
充當 chōngdāng 🄳 serve as
充電 chōngdiàn 🄳 recharge
充分 chōngfèn 🄳 full, ample:
不充分 inadequate, insuf-
ficient
充份 chōngfèn 🄳 full
充公 chōnggōng 🄳 confiscate,
expropriate
充滿 chōngmǎn 🄳 full of, abound
in
充沛 chōngpèi 🄳 abundant,
plentiful
充實 chōngshí 🄳 substantial,
rich
充裕 chōngyù 🄳 abundant
充足 chōngzú 🄳 ample, suffi-
cient

統 55 tǒng
31 [统] Threads 糸 53
arranged sufficiently 充 26
(phonetic). 🄳 unite 🄳 all
⇔ 傳統 26, 正統 116, 血統 114,
籠統 127, 總統 144, 系統 153
統稱 tǒngchēng 🄳 collectively
known as 🄳 general term
統計 tǒngjì 🄳 statistic
統一 tǒngyī 🄳 unify, unite 🄳
unification, unity
統治 tǒngzhì 🄳 rule: 統治階
級 ruling class

棄 55 qì
32 [弃] Child 云 38 cast
off with hands 廾 39 (altered)
and winnowing shovel 華 136.
🄳 abandon ⇔ 背棄 45, 拋
棄 27, 捨棄 47, 拼棄 28, 揚
棄 24, 廢棄 55, 放棄 65, 遺
棄 25, 嫌棄 55, 唾棄 17
棄權 qìquán 🄳 waive a right,
abdicate
棄置 qìzhì 🄳 abandoned,
vacant

屏[55] chán
33 Body/person 尸[40] with three children 子[55]. 圈 weak, frail
屏弱 chánruò 圈 frail

潺[55] chán
34 Water 水[3] with 屏 phonetic. 圈 murmur (of flowing water)
潺潺 chánchán 圈 murmur (of flowing water)

孑[55] jié
35 Child 子[55] missing right arm. 圈 solitary 圈 mosquito larvae
孑孓 jiéjué 圈 mosquito larvae
孑然 jiérán 圈 solitary, alone: 孑然一身 alone in the world

孓[55] jué
36 Child 子[55] missing left arm. ⇔ 孑孓

了[55] le liǎo
37 Child 子[55] without arms. liǎo: 圈 finish, complete 圈 remarkable 圈 (indicating capability) 受不了 unbearable le: 圈 (indicating change or completion) 做好了沒？ Have you finished? 圈 (indicating a past event) 他已經說了. He already said so. 圈 (indicating imperative) 別說了! Don't say! ⇔ 不得了[5], 除了[35], 罷了[12], 算了[159], 免不了[5], 爲了[171]
了不起 liǎobùqǐ 圈 terrific, incredible
了得 liǎodé 圈 excellent
了結 liǎojié 圈 conclude
了解 liǎojiě 圈 understand (⇒ 瞭解[25])

也[56] yě
1 Pictograph of an ancient funnel or wash basin. Now 匜. 圈 also, too
也許 yěxǔ 圈 perhaps

池[56] chí
2 Modern form shows water 水[3] and wash basin 也[56] (phonetic). 圈 pool, pond: 魚池 fish pond ⇔ 水池[3], 電池[3], 魚池[180]
池塘 chítáng 圈 garden pond

馳[56] chí
3 [馳] Horse 馬[177] with 也[56] phonetic. 圈 speed 圈 propogate ⇔ 奔馳[66]
馳騁 chíchěng 圈 gallop about
馳名 chímíng 圈 famous

弛[56] chí
4 Bow 弓[65] with 也[56] phonetic. 圈 relax ⇔ 鬆弛[19]

施[56] shī
5 Waving motion 方[118] with 也[56] phonetic. 圇 wave, flutter 圈 grant, bestow make, do 圈 a surname ⇔ 設施[37], 布施[38], 措施[24], 實施[56]
施工 shīgōng 圈 construct, build: 施工中 under construction
施加 shījiā 圈 exert, bring to bear: 施加壓力 put pressure on
施行 shīxíng 圈 implement
施展 shīzhǎn 圈 display
施政 shīzhèng 圈 administration

地[56] dì de
6 Soil 土[7] with 也[56] phonetic. dì: 圈 the earth land, soil 圈 ground, floor place 圈 situation, condition de: 圈 particle used to form an adverbial phrase ⇔ 各地[42], 畫地自封[88], 掃地[959], 農地[21], 荒地[88], 腹地[24], 內地[43], 陸地[44], 特地[45], 盆地[47], 大地[7], 天地[84], 綠地[48], 餘地[94], 基地[96], 工地[97], 空地[98], 當地[99], 墳地, 墓地[, 境地[, 陸地[, 土地[, 甘地[, 窪地[, 場地[, 草地[, 本地[, 營地[, 房地
產地[97], 實地[97], 耕地[97], 田地[111], 見地[114], 園地[126], 勝地[127], 道地[148], 奧地利[139]
地板 dìbǎn 圈 floor
地步 dìbù 圈 plight, situation 圈 extent: 已經到了不能回去的地步. It's already gotten to the point of no return.
地點 dìdiǎn 圈 site, place
地方 dìfāng 圈 place, region 圈 local: 地方政府 local government; 地方話 local dialect
地理 dìlǐ 圈 geography
地面 dìmiàn 圈 ground surface
地名 dìmíng 圈 place name
地盤 dìpán 圈 territory, turf
地平線 dìpíngxiàn 圈 horizon
地球 dìqiú 圈 the earth
地區 dìqū 圈 region
地上 dìshàng 圈 on the ground 圈 above ground
地勢 dìshì 圈 topography
地毯 dìtǎn 圈 carpet
地鐵 dìtiě 圈 subway
地圖 dìtú 圈 map
地位 dìwèi 圈 status
地下 dìxià 圈 underground: 地下鐵 subway; 地下室 basement; 地下道 underground walkway
地形 dìxíng 圈 topography
地獄 dìyù 圈 hell, purgatory
地域 dìyù 圈 region
地震 dìzhèn 圈 earthquake
地支 dìzhī 圈 Earthly Branches - 子[55], 丑[45], 寅[55], 卯[55], 辰[45], 巳[56], 午[47], 未[47], 申[45], 酉[159], 戌[45], 亥[45]
地質 dìzhì 圈 geology: 地質學 geology
地址 dìzhǐ 圈 address
地中海 dìzhōnghǎi 圈 Mediterranean Sea
地主 dìzhǔ 圈 landlord

他[56] tā
7 Modern form shows person 人[9] with 也[56] (originally 它[137]) phonetic. 圈

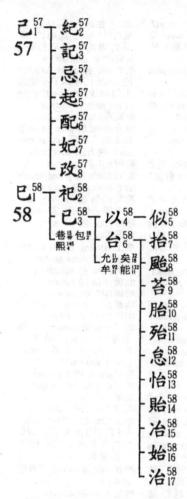

牠 56 tā
9 [它牜] Ox 牛牜 with
也牜 phonetic. 牠 it
牠們 tāmen 牠 they (referring
to animals)

拖 56 tūo
10 Hand 手扌 with 它牜
(now written to resemble 也牜)
phonetic. 拖 pull, drag 拖
delay: 已經拖得太久了 it's
been delayed for too long already
拖把 tūoba 拖 mop
拖車 tūochē 拖 trailer
拖拉機 tūolājī 拖 tractor
拖鞋 tūoxié 拖 slippers, flip-flops
拖延 tūoyán 拖 procrastinate

己 57 jǐ
1 Pictograph of threads
in a loom. 己 sort threads (⇨
紀) 己 self 己 personal 己
sixth Heavenly Stem (⇨干
支牜) ⇔ 知己牜, 自己牜

紀 57 jì
2 [纪] Sort threads 己牜
(phonetic) with thread 糸牜
redundant. 紀 sort threads 紀
arrange 紀 annals 紀 a surname
⇔ 經紀人牜, 年紀牜, 世
紀牜
紀錄 jìlù 紀 紀 record, take notes
紀 minutes, records: 紀錄片
documentary ⇨ 記錄牜
紀律 jìlǜ 紀 discipline
紀念 jìniàn 紀 celebrate, com-
memorate: 紀念日 anniver-
sary; 紀念品 memento, mem-
orabilia; 紀念堂 memorial
hall
紀元 jìyuán 紀 A.D.: 紀元前
B.C.

記 57 jì
3 [记] Words 言牜
arranged 己牜 (phonetic). 記
register, record 記 remember,
keep in mind ⇔ 札記牜, 筆
記牜, 碑記牜, 忘記牜, 帖
記牜, 傳記牜, 史記牜, 登
記牜, 禮記牜, 日記牜, 遊

he 他 other, another ⇔ 吉
他牜, 其他牜, 安非他命牜,
維他命牜, 排他牜
他倆 tāliǎ 他 the two of them
他媽的 tāmāde 他 damn
他們 tāmen 他 they (referring
to men or to men and women)

他人 tārén 他 others

她 56 tā
8 Woman 女牜 with
也牜 phonetic. 她 she
她們 tāmen 她 they (referring
to women)

記[18], 戳記[124]
記得 jìde ▢ remember
記錄 jìlù ▢ record, take notes ▢ record, records: 破記錄 break the record ⇨ 紀錄[97]
記憶 jìyì ▢ memory
記載 jìzài ▢ record
記者 jìzhě ▢ reporter
記住 jìzhù ▢ remember, keep in mind

忌 57 jì
4 Selfish 己[97] (phonetic) heart 心[67]. ▢ envy abstain from ⇔ 猜忌[95], 禁忌[77], 妒忌[95], 顧忌[97]
忌妒 jìdù ▢ envy, be jealous of ⇨ 嫉妒[95]
忌諱 jìhuì ▢ taboo ⇔ avoid as taboo

起 57 qǐ
5 Walk 走[99] with 己[97] phonetic. ▢ rise, get up start, begin ▢ appear, happen ⇔ 一起[95], 興起[95], 舉起[95], 收起[95], 勃起[95], 緣起[97], 拿起[97], 了不起[95], 抬起[97], 引起[97], 鼓起[95], 揚起[95], 爬起來[95], 發起[95], 激起[95], 掀起[97], 呵起[97], 看不起[97], 看起來[95], 想起來[95], 對不起[96]
起初 qǐchū ▢ at first
起床 qǐchuáng ▢ get up, rise
起飛 qǐfēi ▢ take off, lift off
起伏 qǐfú ▢ rise and fall
起鬨 qǐhòng ▢ boo, jeer
起火 qǐhuǒ ▢ catch fire
起勁 qǐjìn ▢ vigorous, energetic
起來 qǐlái ▢ get up, arise
起碼 qǐmǎ ▢ minimum, elementary ▢ at least, minimally
起色 qǐsè ▢ signs of improvement
起身 qǐshēn ▢ get up, rise
起義 qǐyì ▢ revolt
起因 qǐyīn ▢ origin, cause
起源 qǐyuán ▢ origin

起子 qǐzi ▢ bottle opener ▢ screwdriver

配 57 pèi
6 Liquor 酉[159] arranged 己[97] by type. ▢ match, suit ▢ mate ▢ distribute, dispense ⇔ 分配[97], 交配[95], 搭配[95], 調配[95], 支配[97], 裝配[95]
配備 pèibèi ▢ provide, equip
配對 pèiduì ▢ match, pair
配額 pèié ▢ quota
配合 pèihé ▢ coordinate
配給 pèijǐ ▢ ration
配偶 pèiǒu ▢ spouse, mate

妃 57 fēi
7 Woman 女[44] of mine 己[97]. ▢ spouse ▢ royal concubine ▢ princess (crown prince's wife) ⇔ 王妃[95]

改 57 gǎi
8 Self 己[97] struck 攵[56]. ▢ correct ▢ change, transform ⇔ 批改[95], 更改[95], 修改[95], 悔改[95], 勞改[95], 竄改[97]
改編 gǎibiān ▢ reorganize, restructure
改變 gǎibiàn ▢ change: 稍微改變 change slightly
改革 gǎigé ▢ reform: 經濟改革 economic reform
改進 gǎijìn ▢ improve
改良 gǎiliáng ▢ improve
改善 gǎishàn ▢ improve, ameliorate
改爲 gǎiwéi ▢ change to
改寫 gǎixiě ▢ rewrite, paraphrase
改造 gǎizào ▢ reform, transform, restructure
改正 gǎizhèng ▢ correct, rectify
改錐 gǎizhuī ▢ screwdriver

巳 58 sì
1 Pictograph of a snake or possibly fetus. ▢ sixth Earthly Branch (⇨ 干支[95])

祀 58 sì
2 Omen 示[56] with 巳[98] phonetic. ▢ worship ⇔ 祭祀[95]

已 58 yǐ
3 Variant of 巳[98]. ▢ finish, stop ▢ already ⇔ 不得已[95], 不已[95], 早已[95], 而已[134]
已經 yǐjīng ▢ already
已然 yǐrán ▢ already so
已知 yǐzhī ▢ already known

以 58 yǐ
4 Stop 巳[97] inverted (and altered in modern writing). ▢ continue ▢ use ▢ by means of ▢ according to ⇔ 得以[95], 可以[95], 何以[97], 難以[95], 加以[97], 拭目以待[95], 藉以[97], 所以[95], 是以[97], 足以[95], 予以[102]
以便 yǐbiàn ▢ in order to, so that
以後 yǐhòu ▢ afterwards
以及 yǐjí ▢ and, as well as
以來 yǐlái ▢ since
以免 yǐmiǎn ▢ in order to prevent
以前 yǐqián ▢ before, previously
以色列 yǐsèliè ▢ Israel
以上 yǐshàng ▢ above
以外 yǐwài ▢ excluding, besides
以往 yǐwǎng ▢ formerly
以爲 yǐwéi ▢ think, believe
以下 yǐxià ▢ below
以致 yǐzhì ▢ consequently

似 58 sì
5 Person 人[9] and according to 以[97]. ▢ appear, seem ⇔ 貌似[95], 近似[95], 相似[95], 類似[98]
似的 sìde ▢ it seems
似乎 sìhū ▢ apparently, it seems, as if

台 58 yí tái
6 Mouth 口[68] exhaling 巳[97] (altered to resemble 厶[77]) in joy. yí: ▢ happy (⇨ 怡[95]) tái: (simplification of

59

么₁⁵⁹ — 幺₂⁵⁹ — 幽₃⁵⁹
幾₄⁵⁹ — 機₅⁵⁹
饑₆⁵⁹
磯₇⁵⁹
譏₈⁵⁹
邇₉⁵⁹ — 斷₁₀⁵⁹
繼₁₁⁵⁹
玆₁₂⁵⁹ — 關₁₃⁵⁹
茲₁₅⁵⁹ — 聯₁₄⁵⁹

臺⁽¹²⁾ 图 platform, stage 图 table 图 measureword for equipment 图 station, channel: 轉台 change channels ⇔ 上台₄₃, 電台₇₂, 垮台₂₆, 舞台₃₁₆, 後台₉₄, 陽台₂, 妝台₇₅, 茅台酒₁₀⁵, 櫃台₄, 講台₁⁷⁵

台北 táiběi 图 Taipei
台幣 táibì 图 Taiwan dollar
台大 táidà 图 National Taiwan University (國立台灣大學)
台南 táinán 图 Tainan - a city in Taiwan
台球 táiqiú 图 图 pool, billiards
台灣 táiwān 图 图 Taiwan: 台灣海峽 Taiwan Straits
台語 táiyǔ 图 图 Taiwanese, Fukienese

抬₇ ⁵⁸ tái Hand 手⁹⁰ and platform 台₈⁵⁸ (phonetic). 图 lift, raise 图 carry ⇔ 哄抬₄₃
抬起 táiqǐ 图 raise, lift up
抬頭 táitóu 图 raise its head 图 title

颱₈ ⁵⁸ tái [台⁵⁸] Wind 風⁴⁷ with 台₈⁵⁸ phonetic. 图 typhoon

颱風 táifēng 图 typhoon

苔₉ ⁵⁸ tái [苔] Modern form shows plant 艸⁹² with 台₈⁵⁸ phonetic. 图 moss ⇔ 海苔₄₃

胎₁₀ ⁵⁸ tāi Flesh 肉¹³² arising from joy 台₈⁵⁸ (phonetic). 图 fetus, embryo: 一胎化政策 one-child policy ⇔ 胚胎₅₃, 輪胎₁₅, 雙胞胎¹⁶²
胎兒 tāiér 图 embryo, fetus

殆₁₁ ⁵⁸ dài Death 歹¹²² with 台₈⁵⁸ phonetic. 图 dangerous nearly, almost
殆盡 dàijìn 图 nearly exhausted

怠₁₂ ⁵⁸ dài Happy 台₈⁵⁸ (phonetic) heart 心⁸³. 图 idle ⇔ 懈怠₁⁹
怠惰 dàiduò 图 lazy, indolent
怠工 dàigōng 图 slowdown, go-slow strike
怠慢 dàimàn 图 be inhospitable, neglect a guest

怡₁₃ ⁵⁸ yí Heart 心⁸³ joyous 台₈⁵⁸ (phonetic). 图 happy

貽₁₄ ⁵⁸ yí [贻] Money/shells 貝¹⁹⁰ bringing joy 台₈⁵⁸ (phonetic). 图 bequeath, present
貽笑大方 yíxiàodàfāng 图 become a laughingstock

冶₁₅ ⁵⁸ yě Ice 冫¹⁵, suggestive of melting, with 台₈⁵⁸ phonetic. 图 smelt ⇔ 陶冶¹⁵¹
冶金 yějīn 图 metallurgy
冶煉 yěliàn 图 smelt

始₁₆ ⁵⁸ shǐ Woman 女⁵⁴ and joy 台₈⁵⁸. 图 begin, start 图 beginning, start ⇔ 原始₅₆, 創始₄₃, 開始₂₃
始終 shǐzhōng 图 always

治₁₇ ⁵⁸ zhì Water 水₂⁶¹ arranged to bring joy 台₈⁵⁸. 图 a river name 图 harness a river 图 govern, rule 图 treat, cure ⇔ 三明治₁₆, 醫治₂₇, 診治⁹⁹, 統治₄₆, 政治¹⁰², 防治⁹⁷, 自治¹⁹
治安 zhìān 图 public order
治理 zhìlǐ 图 manage, administer
治療 zhìliáo 图 图 cure

么₁ ⁵⁹ yāo Pictograph of a fetus or newborn child. 图 tiny 图 youngest child 图 one

幺₂ ⁵⁹ yōu Doubly small 么¹⁹.

幽₃ ⁵⁹ yōu Small 幺⁹² (phonetic) mountain 山⁶⁷ recesses. 图 secluded
幽會 yōuhuì 图 secret rendezvous, tryst
幽靜 yōujìng 图 secluded
幽靈 yōulíng 图 spirit, phantom
幽默 yōumò 图 humor 图 humorous

幾₄ ⁵⁹ jī jǐ [几³⁸] On guard 戌⁴³

for small 幺幺乡 dangers. jī: 幾
subtle 幽 nearly, almost jǐ: 幾
several, a few 幾 how many
幾何 jǐhé 幾 geometry: 幾何學
geometry
幾乎 jīhū 幽 nearly, almost
幾時 jīshí 幽 when, what time
幾許 jǐxǔ 幽 ⊗ how much, how
many

機5 [机] Wood 木³ for
subtle 幾³ (phonetic) work.
㊑ loom 幽 machine 幽 oppor-
tunity, chance ⇔ 乘機幽,
隨機幽, 危機幽, 扳機幽, 司
機幽, 伺機幽, 時機幽, 直昇
機幽, 印表機幽, 打火機幽,
打印機幽, 投機幽, 劫機幽,
趁機幽, 拖拉機幽, 轉機幽,
當機幽, 班機幽, 動機幽, 契
機幽, 班機幽, 相機幽, 戰
機¹³⁶, 耳機¹³⁷, 飛機¹⁶⁹
機場 jīchǎng 幽 airport
機車 jīchē 幽 motorcycle
機動 jīdòng 幽 mobile, flexible
幽 motorized
機構 jīgòu 幽 organization
機關 jīguān 幽 organization
機會 jīhuì 幽 opportunity,
chance: 機會主義 opportun-
ism; 機會主義者 opportun-
ist
機率 jīlù 幽 probability
機密 jīmì 幽 secret
機敏 jīmǐn 幽 witty
機能 jīnéng 幽 function
機票 jīpiào 幽 plane ticket
機器 jīqì 幽 machine: 機器人
robot
機槍 jīqiāng 幽 machine gun
機械 jīxiè 幽 machine mech-
anical, inflexible
機遇 jīyù 幽 opportunity
機制 jīzhì 幽 system: 市場
機制 market system
機智 jīzhì 幽 witty

饑6 [饥³] Food 食³ with

幾³ phonetic. 幽 famine (⇨
飢³)

磯7 [机] Stone 石³ with
幾³ phonetic. 幽 boulders
obstructing a river ⇨ 洛杉
磯ⁿ

譏8 [讥] Words 言³ with
幾³ phonetic. 幽 satirize
譏諷 jīfěng 幽 satirize, ridicule
譏評 jīpíng 幽 deride
譏笑 jīxiào 幽 ridicule

継9 jué
9 Threads 幺幺 cut into
sections. Simplified forms of
derivatives use 米¹³⁸. ㊑ cut
(⇨ 絕³) 喇

斷10 [断] Cut 㡭³ (reversed
in modern form) with an axe
斤ⁿ⁶. 幽 sever, break 幽 decide,
judge ⇔ 切斷幽, 不斷幽, 打
斷幽, 截斷幽, 診斷幽, 中
斷幽, 果斷幽, 間斷幽, 割
斷幽, 武斷幽, 判斷幽, 折
斷幽, 壟斷幽, 推斷¹⁶², 繼
斷¹⁶⁵, 隔斷¹⁷⁴
斷定 duàndìng 幽 conclude
斷絕 duànjué 幽 sever, cut off
(relations)
斷然 duànrán 幽 resolute, drastic
斷續 duànxù 幽 intermittent:
斷斷續續地學了四年.
Studied on and off for four
years.
斷言 duànyán 幽 assert

繼11 [继] Thread 糸⁵³
reconnected (inverse of cut
㡭³). 幽 continue, follow ⇔
相繼³
繼承 jìchéng 幽 inherit
繼父 jìfù 幽 step-father
繼母 jìmǔ 幽 step-mother
繼任 jìrèn 幽 take over
somebody's position
繼續 jìxù 幽 continue

絲12 Threads 絲 (abbre-
viated to 幺幺³) on a loom
(structure represented by 卝).

關13 [关] Door 門³ with
卝 phonetic. 幽 close, shut
幽 turn off: 關燈 turn off the
lights 幽 relate to, concern 幽
checkpoint, pass: 山海關
Shanhai Guan - eastern termi-
nus of the Great Wall 幽 a
surname ⇔ 有關幽, 公關幽,
攻關幽, 無關幽, 海關幽, 機
關幽, 休戚相關幽, 開關幽,
相關幽, 過關¹³³, 息息相
關¹³⁷, 雙關¹⁶²
關閉 guānbì 幽 close down
關島 guāndǎo 幽 Guam
關掉 guāndiào 幽 shut off, turn
off
關懷 guānhuái 幽 concerned
about
關鍵 guānjiàn 幽 crux, key
關節 guānjié 幽 joint
關卡 guānkǎ 幽 checkpoint
關聯 guānlián 幽 related, connected
關門 guānmén 幽 shut the door
幽 close shop
關切 guānqiè 幽 concerned
about
關稅 guānshuì 幽 tariff
關說 guānshuō 幽 lobby illegally, buy influence
關頭 guāntóu 幽 juncture,
moment
關外 guānwài 幽 beyond the
Great Wall (to the northeast)
關係 guānxì 幽 relations,
connections: 沒關係 it doesn't
matter; 拉關係 use connec-
tions
關心 guānxīn 幽 concerned
about
關於 guānyú 幽 about, regarding, concerning
關注 guānzhù 幽 pay attention

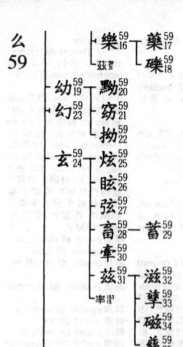

么
59

├─ 樂 59/16 ─ 藥 59/17
│   └ 礫 59/18
│   └ 兹 59/?
│
├─ 幼 59/19 ─ 黝 59/20
├─ 幻 59/23 ─ 窈 59/21
│   └ 拗 59/22
│
├─ 玄 59/24 ─ 炫 59/25
│   ├ 眩 59/26
│   ├ 弦 59/27
│   ├ 畜 59/28 ─ 蓄 59/29
│   ├ 牽 59/30
│   └ 兹 59/31 ─ 滋 59/32
│   ├ 孳 59/33
│   ├ 磁 59/34
│   └ 慈 59/35
└─ 率 153/15

聯 59/14 lián
[联] As ears 耳 17 and threads 絲 153 (now written as 艹 ??). Simplified form uses simplification of 關 ??. 圖 connect, join, ally ⇔ 春聯 15, 關聯 ??, 蟬聯 156, 對聯 176, 蘇聯 ??
聯邦 liánbāng 圖 federal: 聯邦政府 federal government
聯合 liánhé 圖 unite: 聯合國 United Nations
聯歡 liánhuān 圖 have a party: 聯歡會 party
聯軍 liánjūn 圖 allied armies: 八國聯軍 allied Western armies that occupied Beijing after the Boxer Rebellion (⇔ 義和團 ??)

聯考 liánkǎo 圖 圖 joint examination: 大學聯考 joint college entrance examination
聯絡 liánluò 圖 contact, get in touch with
聯袂 liánmèi 圖 ⊗ together
聯盟 liánméng 圖 圖 alliance, coalition: 歐洲聯盟 European Union
聯手 liánshǒu 圖 ally, gang up
聯繫 liánxì 圖 contact 圖 contact, connection: 保持聯繫 keep in touch
聯誼 liányí 圖 promote friendship: 聯誼會 friendship society

兹 59/15 zī
[兹 ??] Grasses 艹 66 like silk 絲 153 (abbreviated to 丝 ??). 圖 lush 圖 this 圖 now

(⇨ 兹)

樂 59/16 yuè lè
[乐] Drums (resembling 白 76 and 丝 ??) on a wooden 木 17 stand. yuè: 圖 music lè: 圖 happy, joyful ⇔ 奏樂 154, 可樂 ??, 娛樂 ??, 快樂 ??, 弦樂 ??, 音樂 ??, 喜怒哀樂 ??, 芭樂 45, 俱樂部 ??, 歡樂 162
樂觀 lèguān 圖 optimistic
樂趣 lèqù 圖 delight, pleasure
樂事 lèshì 圖 joyous matter
樂意 lèyì 圖 happily, willingly 圖 pleased
樂於 lèyú 圖 happy to
樂園 lèyuán 圖 paradise
樂隊 yuèduì 圖 band, orchestra
樂譜 yuèpǔ 圖 musical score
樂器 yuèqì 圖 musical instrument
樂團 yuètuán 圖 band

藥 59/17 yào
[药] Plants 艹 66 that bring happiness 樂 ?? (phonetic). Simplified form uses 約 ??. 圖 medicine ⇔ 農藥 ??, 醫藥 ??, 炸藥 ??, 膏藥 ??, 毒藥 ??, 補藥 ??, 吃藥 ??, 火藥 17, 彈藥 136, 迷幻藥 ??
藥店 yàodiàn 圖 drugstore, pharmacy
藥方 yàofāng 圖 prescription
藥房 yàofáng 圖 drugstore, pharmacy
藥品 yàopǐn 圖 drug, medicine
藥丸 yàowán 圖 pill
藥物 yàowù 圖 drug, medicine

礫 59/18 lì
[砾] Stone 石 ?? with 樂 ?? phonetic. 圖 pebble 圖 shingle ⇔ 瓦礫 ??

幼 59/19 yòu
Small 么 ?? (phonetic) tendon 力 ?. 圖 tender, immature
幼兒 yòuér 圖 infant
幼年 yòunián 圖 childhood

幼稚 yòuzhì immature, childish: 幼稚園 kindergarten

黝 59 yǒu
20 Weak 幼 (phonetic) black 黑. bluish black 黝黑 yǒuhēi dark, swarthy: 黝黑皮膚 dark complexion

窈 59 yǎo
21 Hole 穴 with 幼 phonetic. deep 窈窕 yǎotiǎo charming and attractive deep, profound

拗 59 ǎo ào niù
22 Hand 手 and tender 幼 (phonetic). snap ⇔ 執拗

幻 59 huàn
23 Give 予 (altered) inverted. deceive illusory ⇔ 迷幻藥, 變幻
幻燈 huàndēng slide show: 幻燈片 slide; 幻燈機 slide projector
幻覺 huànjué illusion, hallucination
幻想 huànxiǎng illusion, delusion
幻象 huànxiàng mirage, illusion

玄 59 xuán
24 Cover (written as 入) what is already obscure/tiny 么. obscure, distant dark abstruse
玄妙 xuánmiào abstruse, profound

炫 59 xuàn
25 Fire 火 with 玄 phonetic. dazzling
炫耀 xuànyào show off, flaunt

眩 59 xuàn
26 Eyes 目 and abstruse 玄 (phonetic). dizzy, unfocused ⇔ 暈眩

弦 59 xián
27 Modern form shows bow 弓 with 玄 phonetic. bowstring, string

弦樂 xiányuè string music: 弦樂器 stringed instrument

畜 59 chù xù
28 Dark 玄 fields 田. chù: cattle xù: raise animals ⇔ 牲畜, 家畜
畜生 chùshēng domestic animal beast
畜牧 xùmù animal husbandry

蓄 59 xù
29 Grass 艸 and cattle 畜 (phonetic). save, accumulate ⇔ 含蓄, 儲蓄, 積蓄
蓄意 xùyì deliberate, premeditated

牽 59 qiān
30 [牵] Rope, suggested by 玄 (phonetic), pulling an ox 牛, with resistance represented by marks resembling 冖. Simplified form uses 大. pull, drag
牽扯 qiānchě involve, drag in
牽連 qiānlián involve, implicate
牽涉 qiānshè involve, embroil
牽引 qiānyǐn draw, pull: 牽引機 tractor
牽制 qiānzhì constrain, check

茲 59 zī
31 Doubly dark 玄. Often interchanged with lush 茲. black this now

滋 59 zī
32 Water 水 lush 茲 (phonetic). nourish 愛滋病
滋補 zībǔ nourish, nutrify
滋生 zīshēng reproduce, multiply
滋味 zīwèi taste, flavor
滋養 zīyǎng nourish
滋長 zīzhǎng grow, develop

孳 59 zī
33 Children 子 lush 茲 (phonetic). reproduce prolifically

孳生 zīshēng reproduce, multiply (⇨ 滋生)
孳息 zīxí grow interest (on funds)

磁 59 cí
34 Stone 石 with 茲 phonetic. magneticism
磁帶 cídài tape (magnetic)
磁碟 cídié magnetic disk
磁盤 cípán diskette
磁片 cípiàn diskette
磁鐵 cítiě magnet
磁磚 cízhuān ceramic tiles

慈 59 cí
35 Heart 心 lush 茲 (phonetic). loving ⇔ 仁慈
慈愛 cíài affection, kindness
慈悲 cíbēi mercy
慈善 císhàn charitable, philanthropic: 慈善機構 charity
慈祥 cíxiáng kind (old person)

叀 59 zhuān
36 Small 么 (altered) item 屮. Alternatively, pictograph of a shuttle. concentrate on

專 59 zhuān
37 [专] Hand 寸 concentrating 叀 (phonetic). shuttle concentrate on specialize ⇔ 三專
專案 zhuānàn special case
專長 zhuāncháng specialty, special skill
專攻 zhuāngōng specialize
專家 zhuānjiā expert: 外國專家 foreign expert
專科 zhuānkē special course of study: 專科學校 technical school
專欄 zhuānlán newspaper column
專利 zhuānlì patent exclusive right
專門 zhuānmén specially
專任 zhuānrèn full-time
專心 zhuānxīn single-

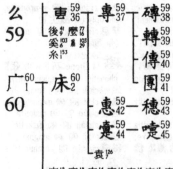

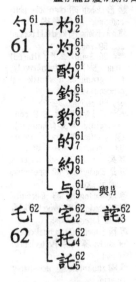

磚 59 zhuān
38 [砖] Stone 石丹 with 專罗 phonetic. 圐 brick ⇔ 磁磚罗

磚頭 zhuāntóu 圐 brick

轉 59 zhuǎn zhuàn
39 [转] Cart 車罗 with 專罗 phonetic. zhuǎn: 圐 convey, transfer 圐 turn: 右轉 turn right zhuàn: 圐 rotate 圐 rotation, revolution ⇔ 扭轉罗, 輾轉罗, 逆轉罗, 好轉罗, 迴轉罗, 週轉罗, 婉轉罗, 旋轉罗

轉變 zhuǎnbiàn 圐 transform, change

轉播 zhuǎnbō 圐 relay (a broadcast)

轉達 zhuǎndá 圐 pass on, convey

轉告 zhuǎngào 圐 relay, pass on

轉換 zhuǎnhuàn 圐 change, transform

轉機 zhuǎnjī 圐 turn for the better

轉捩 zhuǎnliè 圐 turning point

轉盤 zhuǎnpán 圐 lazy Susan

轉身 zhuǎnshēn 圐 turn around

轉彎 zhuǎnwān 圐 turn

轉移 zhuǎnyí 圐 transfer, shift

轉注 zhuǎnzhù 圐 Chinese character in which the meaning has been extended to related meanings (⇨ 六書罗)

傳 59 chuán zhuàn
40 [传] Person 人丹 with 專罗 phonetic. chuán: 圐 pass, transmit zhuàn: 圐 biography, chronicle: 水滸傳 The Water Margin Chronicles ⇔ 宣傳罗, 盛傳罗, 流傳罗, 失傳罗, 遺傳罗, 相傳罗, 自傳罗, 謠傳罗

傳播 chuánbō 圐 spread, disseminate

傳出 chuánchū 圐 pass on

傳達 chuándá 圐 communicate

傳遞 chuándì 圐 deliver

傳呼 chuánhū 圐 page: 傳呼機

mindedly, wholeheartedly

專業 zhuānyè 圐 profession 圐 (圐) major (in college)

專政 zhuānzhèng 圐 autocracy, dictatorship: 無產階級專政 dictatorship of the proletariat

專制 zhuānzhì 圐 autocracy, dictatorship

pager

傳教 chuánjiào 動 proselytize: 傳教士 missionary
傳媒 chuánméi 名 media
傳奇 chuánqí 名 legend
傳染 chuánrǎn 動 infect: 傳染病 infectious disease
傳神 chuánshén 名 vivid portrayal
傳授 chuánshòu 動 teach
傳說 chuánshuō 名 legend
傳統 chuántǒng 名 tradition
傳聞 chuánwén 名 rumor
傳言 chuányán 名 rumor
傳真 chuánzhēn 名 動 fax
傳記 zhuànjì 名 biography

團 59 tuán 41 [团] Surround 囗 with 專 phonetic. 形 circular, spherical 動 unite 名 group, organization: 旅行團 tour group 名 lump ⇔ 義和團, 樂團, 社團, 集團
團結 tuánjié 動 solidify, unite
團聚 tuánjù 動 gather, reunite: 全家團聚 family reunion
團體 tuántǐ 名 group: 團體旅行 group tour; 團體感 group feeling, esprit de corps
團員 tuányuán 名 group member

惠 59 huì 42 Concentrate 車 on the heart 心. 形 benevolent ⇔ 恩惠, 互惠, 受惠, 賢惠

穗 59 suì 43 Grain 禾 benevolently 惠 (phonetic) bestowed by heaven. 名 ear of grain 名 Canton ⇔ 稻穗

疐 59 zhì 44 Concentrate 車 and stop 止, together altered to resemble 市, 田 and 疋. 動 hindered, stumble

嚏 59 tì 45 Mouth 口 with 疐 phonetic. 名 sneeze 名 噴嚏

广 60 yǎn 1 Pictograph showing half of a large room. Also explained as a room formed from the side of a cliff 厂. 名 shelter

床 60 chuáng 2 Modern form shows wood 木 under a shed 广. 名 bed: 雙人床 double bed ⇔ 上床, 起床, 吊床, 臨床
床單 chuángdān 名 sheet
床墊 chuángdiàn 名 mattress
床舖 chuángpù 名 bed, berth

勺 61 sháo 1 Pictograph of a spoon with dot representing its contents. 名 spoon
勺子 sháozi 名 spoon, ladle

杓 61 sháo 2 Wood 木 end of spoon 勺 (phonetic). 名 spoon handle 名 spoon, ladle
杓子 sháozi 名 spoon, ladle

灼 61 zhuó 3 Fire 火 with 勺 phonetic. 動 burn
灼見 zhuójiàn 名 insight
灼傷 zhuóshāng 名 burn

酌 61 zhuó 4 Ladle 勺 (phonetic) from a vessel 酉. 動 pour ⇔ 斟酌, 商酌, 參酌

釣 61 diào 5 [钓] Metal 金 with ladle 勺 phonetic and suggestive of hook. Simplified form uses hook 勾. 動 fish
釣魚 diàoyú 動 fish

豹 61 bào 6 Clawed beast 豸 with 勺 phonetic. 名 leopard ⇔ 海豹

的 61 de dí dì 7 Ladle 勺 out into the sunlight 日 (altered to

白). dì: 形 clear dí: 形 accurate de: 助 of ⇔ 有的, 別的, 親愛的, 他媽的, 似的, 是的, 目的
的確 díquè 副 truly

約 61 yuē 8 [约] Silk 糸 with 勺 phonetic. 動 bind 動 make an appointment: 約她去吃飯 arrange to eat with her 名 treaty 副 about, approximately ⇔ 紐約, 公約, 條約, 節約, 大約, 合約, 綽約, 契約, 盟約, 隱約
約定 yuēdìng 動 agree to, arrange to
約好 yuēhǎo 動 agree to, arrange to
約會 yuēhuì 名 appointment, date 動 make an appointment
約束 yuēshù 動 restrain, bind

与 61 yǔ 9 Ladle 勺 with 一 representing contents. 古 give (⇔ 與)

乇 62 dié 1 Pictograph of a small plant taking root.

宅 62 zhái 2 Building 宀 where one takes root 乇 (phonetic). 名 house ⇔ 住宅, 國宅

詫 62 chà 3 [诧] Words 言 with 宅 phonetic. 動 surprise
詫異 chàyì 動 astonished

托 62 tuō 4 Hand 手 with 乇 phonetic. 動 lift or support with the palm 動 entrust, consign ⇔ 襯托, 摩托, 烏托邦
托兒所 tuōérsuǒ 名 nursery

託 62 tuō 5 [托] Words 言 with 乇 phonetic. Simplified

字譜及字典

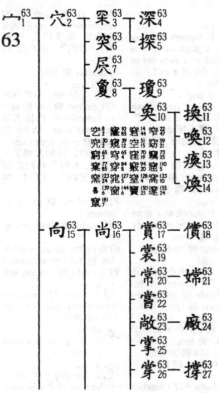

63

深厚 shēnhòu deep, profound
深化 shēnhuà deepen
深究 shēnjiù investigate thoroughly
深圳 shēnjùn Shenzhen
深刻 shēnkè deep: 留下深刻的印象 leave a deep impression
深切 shēnqiè heartfelt
深入 shēnrù thorough
深深 shēnshēn profoundly
深邃 shēnsuì deep, profound, abstruse
深夜 shēnyè deep of night
深造 shēnzào pursue advanced study

探 63 tàn
5 Hand 手 with 罙 phonetic and suggestive of deep 深. explore, search, pay a visit to ⇔ 勘探, 偵探, 窺探, 刺探
探究 tànjiū investigate, inquire into
探親 tànqīn visit relatives
探求 tànqíu seek, search for
探索 tànsuǒ investigate, explore
探討 tàntǎo investigate, inquire into
探聽 tàntīng inquire about
探望 tànwàng visit, call on

突 63 tú tū
6 Dog 犬 rushing from its den 穴. dash, charge, suddenly ⇔ 唐突, 衝突
突出 túchū outstanding, prominent
突擊 tújí assault, raid
突破 tūpò break through, breakthrough
突然 túrán suddenly
突兀 túwù suddenly

屄 63 bī
7 Hole 穴 and reclined body 尸. vagina

form is conflated with 托. entrust, consign use as an excuse ⇔ 寄託, 信託, 拜託, 委託
託辭 tuōcí make excuses, excuse, pretext
託付 tuōfù entrust, consign

宀 63 mián
1 Pictograph of a hut or roof.

穴 63 xuè xué
2 Enclosure 宀 made by removing 八 dirt. cave, hole
穴道 xuèdào acupuncture points

罙 63 shēn
3 Hole 穴 (altered) taking 求 fire 火 (together altered to resemble 木). hearth

深 63 shēn
4 Water 水 with 罙 phonetic. deep, very, deeply ⇔ 資深, 根深蒂固, 加深
深沉 shēnchén deep
深處 shēnchù depths
深度 shēndù depth
深感 shēngǎn feel deeply

夐 63 xiòng
8 Person 人[10] over hole 穴[53] looking (ancient character from see 目[14] and hand with stick 攴[24]). 動 seek

瓊 63 qióng
9 [琼] Jade 玉[07] sought after 夐[63] (phonetic). Simplified form uses 京[37]. 形 fine jade 圈 fine, excellent ⇔ 道瓊[148]
瓊瑤 qióngyáo 名 fine jade

奐 63 huàn
10 [奂] Seek 夐[63] (phonetic, abbreviated) and hands 廾[39] (altered to resemble 大[37]). 動 exchange 圈 splendid, brilliant

換 63 huàn
11 [换] Hand 手[19] with 奐[63] phonetic. 動 exchange, trade 圈 change: 換衣服 change clothes ⇔ 兌換[1], 退換[3], 更換[5], 交換[3], 轉換[2], 變換[153]
換成 huànchéng 動 transform into
換句話說 huànjùhuàshuō 動 in other words
換錢 huànqián 動 change money, convert currencies

喚 63 huàn
12 [唤] Mouth 口[06] with 奐[63] phonetic. 動 summon, call ⇔ 呼喚[2], 召喚[3]
喚醒 huànxǐng 動 awaken (sb.)

瘓 63 huàn
13 [痪] Sickness 疒[36] with 奐[63] phonetic. 名 paralysis ⇔ 癱瘓[30]

煥 63 huàn
14 [焕] Firey 火[82] and brilliant 奐[63] (phonetic). 形 lustrous
煥發 huànfā 動 glow, shine

向 63 xiàng
15 Roof 宀[79] with a ventilation hole 口[06] in the northern wall. 名 direction 動 face 介 towards 圈 a surname ⇔ 一向[1], 傾向[3], 反向[3], 內向[3], 志向[3], 趨向[6], 外向[7], 邁向[8], 所向披靡[3], 方向[14], 欣欣向榮[26], 偏向[15], 取向[37], 導向[48]
向後 xiànghòu 動 backward
向來 xiànglái 動 have always been, all along
向前 xiàngqián 動 forward
向日葵 xiàngrìkúi 名 sunflower
向著 xiàngzhe 動 facing

尚 63 shàng
16 Divide 八[7] in one direction 向[63] (phonetic). 動 esteem, uphold 動 yet, still ⇔ 高尚[3], 俗尚[6], 和尚[08]
尚且 shàngqiě 動 even
尚未 shàngwèi 動 not yet

賞 63 shǎng
17 [赏] Appreciate 尚[63] (phonetic) with money/shells 貝[50]. 動 reward 動 appreciate ⇔ 讚賞[4], 嘆賞[3], 欣賞[26], 鑑賞[42], 觀賞[62]
賞識 shǎngshì 動 appreciate, value
賞賜 shǎngsì,shǎngcì 動 bestow, grant, award

償 63 cháng
18 [偿] Person 人[10] rewarded 賞[63] (phonetic). Simplified form uses 賞 simplification. 動 repay 賠償[43], 無償[37], 補償[3], 清償[3], 抵償[00]
償付 chángfù 動 repay
償還 chánghuán 動 repay, compensate
償債 chángzhài 動 repay debt

裳 63 cháng shāng
19 Valued 尚[63] (phonetic) clothing 衣[126]. cháng: 名 ancient skirt shang: 名 clothing 衣裳[126]

常 63 cháng
20 Cloth 巾[53] upheld 尚[63] (phonetic). 分 lord's banner 名 rule, principle 形 permanent 動 often 形 ordinary, common 圈 a surname ⇔ 往常[3], 經常[3], 尋常[3], 反常[3], 平常[3], 時常[3], 無常[3], 照常[3], 異常[96], 通常[9], 日常[76], 正常[38], 失常[9], 倫常[15], 家常[55], 非常[3]
常常 chángcháng 動 always, frequently
常客 chángkè 名 regular customer
常任 chángrèn 形 permanent, standing (committee)
常設 chángshè 形 permanent, standing (committee)
常識 chángshì 名 common sense
常數 chángshù 名 constant (mathematics)

嫦 63 cháng
21 Woman 女[19] with 常[63] phonetic. 名 moon goddess
嫦娥 cháng'é 名 moon goddess

嘗 63 cháng
22 [尝] Tasty 旨[33] with 尚[63] phonetic. 動 taste 動 try ⇔ 何嘗[23], 品嘗[37]
嘗試 chángshì 動 try

敞 63 chǎng
23 Strike 攴[24] at high 尚[63] land. 動 level off, clear 形 spacious, open ⇔ 寬敞[114]
敞開 chǎngkāi 動 open wide

廠 63 chǎng
24 [厂] Spacious 敞[63] (phonetic) shed 广[90]. 名 workshop, factory ⇔ 工廠[37]
廠房 chǎngfáng 名 factory premises
廠商 chǎngshāng 名 firm, company
廠長 chǎngzhǎng 名 factory director

掌 63 zhǎng
25 Hand 手[19] with 尚[63] phonetic. 名 palm, sole 名 paw

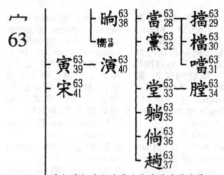

宣¹⁵³ 察³³ 宗⁴⁹ 客⁴⁶ 完⁵⁰ 寝⁵⁷ 守⁵⁶ 宏¹⁵⁸
叟¹⁶⁰ 寞⁴⁴ 寒⁴⁵ 富⁴⁷ 奇⁴⁸ 宇⁵¹ 育⁵² 寡⁵⁴
宁⁵⁵ 冗⁶² 必⁵³ 宰⁵⁹ 寅⁶⁰ 安⁶¹ 字⁵⁵ 宅⁶³
寨⁶⁴ 容⁶⁵ 宛⁶⁶ 寓⁶⁷ 宿⁷⁰ 宿⁷¹ 寐⁷⁴ 害⁷⁵
寮¹⁰³ 定⁷⁹ 牢⁸⁰ 室⁸⁵ 寫¹²⁸ 宙⁹⁰ 寬¹¹⁶ 宜⁷⁸
寂¹²⁸ 它¹⁵⁴ 它¹⁵⁵ 室¹¹¹ 寫¹²⁸ 寵¹⁴⁹ 寶¹⁵⁰ 宦¹⁵¹
家¹⁵² 審¹⁵⁷ 奥¹⁶⁷ 官¹⁶⁷

left column (bottom)

🀄 slap 🀄 control ⇔ 鼓掌⁸⁶, 巴掌⁸⁵, 手掌⁸⁷, 熊掌¹²⁷, 易如反掌¹⁶³

掌舵 zhǎngduò 🀄 steer

掌握 zhǎngwò 🀄 control 🀄 master

掌 63 chēng
26 Tooth 牙¹⁴ with 尚⁴⁸ phonetic. 🀄 prop up

撐 63 chēng
27 [撑] Modern form shows hand 手¹⁷ and prop up 掌² (phonetic). Simplified

middle column (bottom)

form is variant form using 掌².
🀄 prop up, support ⇔ 支撐²⁷
撐腰 chēngyāo 🀄 support, back

當 63 dāng dàng
28 [当] Field 田¹¹ with 尚⁴⁸ phonetic. dàng: equal 🀄 pawn 🀄 take for, regard as 🀄 appropriate, right 🀄 flunk
dāng: 🀄 work as: 當老師 work as a teacher 🀄 when: 當你想要的時候 when you want to 🀄 face ⇔ 上當⁴³, 不當⁹⁰, 便當¹¹⁶, 擔當⁵⁹, 恰

right column

當²⁴, 充當⁸³, 適當⁸⁵, 正當⁹⁷, 妥當⁸⁷, 理當¹²³, 相當¹²⁷, 敢當¹³⁷, 麥當勞⁹⁶⁰, 應當⁹²

當兵 dāngbīng 🀄 do military service

當場 dāngchǎng 🀄 then and there

當初 dāngchū 🀄 originally

當代 dāngdài 🀄 contemporary

當地 dāngdì 🀄 local

當掉 dàngdiào 🀄 (c) flunk

當官 dāngguān 🀄 serve as a public official

當即 dāngjí 🀄 at once, immediately

當機 dàngjī 🀄 crash (computer)

當今 dāngjīn 🀄 currently, nowadays

當局 dāngjú 🀄 authorities

當面 dāngmiàn 🀄 in one's presence, face-to-face

當年 dāngnián 🀄 in those years

當鋪 dàngpù 🀄 pawn shop

當前 dāngqián 🀄 presently

當然 dāngrán 🀄 of course

當日 dāngrì 🀄 that same day

當時 dāngshí 🀄 at that time, then 🀄 concurrent, contemporary

當天 dāngtiān 🀄 that same day

當晚 dāngwǎn 🀄 that same evening

當下 dāngxià 🀄 at that moment

當心 dāngxīn 🀄 look out, be careful, beware

當選 dāngxuǎn 🀄 be elected

當真 dàngzhēn 🀄 really

當中 dāngzhōng 🀄 in the middle of

當衆 dāngzhòng 🀄 publicly

當作 dāngzuò 🀄 regard as, consider as

當做 dāngzuò 🀄 regard as, consider as

擋 63 dǎng
29 [挡] Hand 手¹⁷ with 當²⁸ phonetic. 🀄 block, shield

⇔ 抵擋[90], 阻擋[17]
擋箭牌 dǎngjiànpái 图 shield 图 pretext, excuse

檔 63 [档] dǎng [简] dàng
30 [档] Wood 木[7] with 當[?] phonetic. 图 crosspiece 图 file, record
檔案 dǎng'àn 图 file, record
檔名 dǎngmíng 图 filename

噹 63 dāng
31 [当?] Mouth 口[66] with 當[?] phonetic. 图 dong, bell sound ⇔ 叮噹[36]

黨 63 dǎng
32 [党] Dark 黑[?] with 尚[?] phonetic. Simplified form uses 儿[?]. 图 faction, gang 图 political party ⇔ 政黨[?], 民進黨[?], 黑手黨[?]
黨魁 dǎngkuí 图 party leader
黨外 dǎngwài 图 non-party
黨員 dǎngyuán 图 party member

堂 63 táng
33 Roof held high 尚[?] (phonetic) above ground 土[?]. 图 hall ⇔ 食堂[?], 教堂[?], 殿堂[?], 學堂[?], 庵堂[?], 跑堂[?], 祠堂[?], 天堂[?], 課堂[?]
堂弟 tángdì 图 cousin (younger male on paternal side)
堂哥 tánggē 图 cousin (older male on paternal side)
堂皇 tánghuáng 图 stately, grand
堂姐 tángjiě 图 cousin (older female on paternal side)
堂妹 tángmèi 图 cousin (younger female on paternal side)

膛 63 táng
34 Body's 肉[32] hall 堂[?] (phonetic). 图 chest ⇔ 胸膛[?]

躺 63 tǎng
35 Body 身[47] with 尚[?] phonetic. 图 lie, recline

倘 63 tǎng
36 Person 人[10] with 尚[?] phonetic. 图 if, supposing

倘若 tǎngruò 图 if, supposing
倘使 tǎngshǐ 图 if, supposing

趟 63 tàng
37 Walk 走[?] with 尚[?] phonetic. 图 trip: 白跑一趟 make a wasted trip

晌 63 shǎng
38 Sun 日[76] and direction 向[?] (phonetic). 图 noon 图 brief period of time ⇔ 半晌[?]

寅 63 yín
39 Roof 宀[63] covering a person 人[10] with lowered hands 白[?]. 图 polite 图 third Earthly Branch (⇨ 干支[?])
寅月 yínyuè 图 first month of lunar calendar

演 63 yǎn
40 Water 水[?] with 寅[?] phonetic. 图 evolve 图 practice 图 act, perform ⇔ 主演[?], 扮演[?], 開演[?], 預演[?], 表演[?], 導演[?]
演變 yǎnbiàn 图 evolve 图 evolution: 和平演變 peaceful evolution
演出 yǎnchū 图 perform
演化 yǎnhuà 图 evolve 图 evolution
演技 yǎnjì 图 acting
演講 yǎnjiǎng 图 图 lecture
演說 yǎnshuō 图 speech
演習 yǎnxí 图 rehearse, practice
演繹 yǎnyì 图 deduce: 演繹法 deduction
演義 yǎnyì 图 historical novel: 三國演義 Romance of the Three Kingdoms - a Han Dynasty novel
演員 yǎnyuán 图 actor, actress
演奏 yǎnzòu 图 give a musical performance

宋 63 sòng
41 Wooden 木[7] hut 宀[63]. 图 reside 图 Song Dynasty a surname: 宋美齡 Madame Chiang Kai-Shek
宋朝 sòngcháo 图 Song Dynasty

才 64 cái
1 Pictograph of a sprouting plant. 图 natural talent, gift 图 just 图 only: 才五歲 only five years old 图 (indicating a necessary condition) 有錢才能去。You can only go if you have money. ⇔ 剛才[?], 人才[?], 天才[?], 口才[?], 方才[?], 賢才[?]
才幹 cáigàn 图 ability
才華 cáihuá 图 talent, gift
才能 cáinéng 图 talent, aptitude
才智 cáizhì 图 ability and wisdom

財 64 cái
2 [财] Monetary/shell 貝[90] endowment 才[?] (phonetic). 图 wealth ⇔ 錢財[?], 發財[?], 理財[?], 酒色財氣[?]
財寶 cáibǎo 图 valuables
財產 cáichǎn 图 property, assets
財閥 cáifá 图 magnate, tycoon
財富 cáifù 图 wealth, fortune
財經 cáijīng 图 finance and economics
財務 cáiwù 图 finance
財政 cáizhèng 图 public finance

材 64 cái
3 Wood 木[7] endowment 才[?] (phonetic). 图 timber 图 material ⇔ 教材[?], 木材[?], 題材[?], 身材[?], 素材[?], 棺材[?]
材料 cáiliào 图 material

在 64 zài
4 Endowment 才[?] (phonetic) of earth 土[?]. 图 at, on 图 exist: 還在 still there 图 in the process of: 你在做什麼? What are you doing? ⇔ 不在[?], 潛在[?], 內在[?], 好在[?], 存在[?], 外在[?], 所在[?], 心不在焉[?], 正在[?], 實在[?], 現在[?], 自在[?]
在場 zàichǎng 图 be present, be on the scene

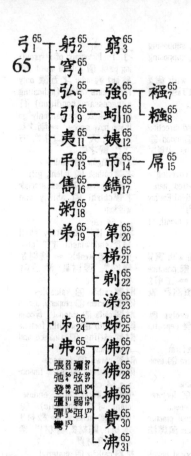

在乎 zàihū 🔟 care

在野 zàiyě 🔟 be out of power, be in opposition: 在野黨 opposition party

在意 zàiyì 🔟 care

在於 zàiyú 🔟 lies in, rests in: 問題在於 the problem is

存 [64] cún 5 Sprouting 才 [64] child 子 [15]. 🔟 exist, live 🔟 deposit, store ⇔ 共存, 貯存, 倖

存, 生存, 儲存, 保存, 庫存

存底 cúndǐ 🔟 reserves: 外匯存底 foreign exchange reserves

存貨 cúnhuò 🔟 stock, inventory

存款 cúnkuǎn 🔟 savings

存量 cúnliàng 🔟 savings

存亡 cúnwáng 🔟 life or death

存心 cúnxīn 🔟 intentionally

存有 cúnyǒu 🔟 existence

存在 cúnzài 🔟 exist: 存在主義 existentialism

荐 [64] jiàn 6 Grass 艸 with 存 phonetic. 🔟 straw mattress 🔟 recommend (⇨ 薦)

閉 [64] bì 7 [闭] Door 門 locked by bars resembling 才. 🔟 close, shut ⇔ 倒閉, 關閉, 封閉

閉門 bìmén 🔟 shut the door

閉塞 bìsè 🔟 stop up, block

閉嘴 bìzuǐ 🔟 🔟 Shut up!

弓 [65] gōng 1 Pictograph of a bow. 🔟 bow 🔟 five feet 🔟 arch

弓箭 gōngjiàn 🔟 bow and arrow

弓形 gōngxíng 🔟 arc

躬 [65] gōng 2 Body 身 [47] bent bow-like 弓 [65] (phonetic). 🔟 bow ⇔ 鞠躬

窮 [65] qióng 3 [穷] Bent over 躬 [65] (phonetic) in a hole 穴 [67]. Simplified form uses 力 [5]. 🔟 poor 🔟 limit ⇔ 無窮, 無窮無盡, 貧窮

窮人 qióngrén 🔟 the poor

穹 [65] qióng 4 Bow-like 弓 [65] (phonetic) cavern/hole 穴 [67]. 🔟 vaulted

穹蒼 qióngcāng 🔟 heaven

弘 [65] hóng 5 Bow 弓 [65] after released by forearm (ancient form of 肱). 🔟 twang 🔟 enlarge ⇔ 恢弘

弘揚 hóngyáng 🔟 expand

強 [65] qiáng qiǎng jiàng 6 Insect 虫 [125] with 弘 [65] phonetic. 🔟 worm qiáng: strong, powerful qiǎng: 🔟 force jiàng: 🔟 stubborn ⇔ 剛強, 頑強, 富強, 加強, 超強, 逞強, 倔強, 列

强[133/18], 堅强[142/18], 增强[144/9], 勉强[164/8]
强暴 qiángbào [形] violent, fierce [動] rape
强大 qiángdà [形] powerful
强盜 qiángdào [動] rob [名] robber
强調 qiángdiào [動] emphasize
强度 qiángdù [名] intensity
强姦 qiángjiān [動] rape
强勁 qiángjìng [形] sturdy, powerful
强烈 qiángliè [形] intense, violent
强迫 qiángpò, qiǎngpò [動] force
强求 qiángqíu, qiǎngqíu [動] forcibly demand
强權 qiángquán [名] power, might
强盛 qiángshèng [形] rich and powerful
强硬 qiángyìng [形] tough
强制 qiángzhì [形] mandatory, forced
强壯 qiángzhuàng [形] strong, vigorous, robust

襁 65 qiǎng
7 Clothing 衣[126/1] that restrains/forces 强[65/6] (phonetic). [名] swaddling clothes

襁褓 qiǎngbǎo [名] swaddling clothes [名] infancy

糨 65 jiàng
8 Rice 米[138/1] that is strong 强[65/6] (phonetic). [名] paste

糨糊 jiànghú [名] paste, glue

引 65 yǐn
9 Draw bow 弓[65/1] string 丨[4/1]. [動] pull [動] attract [動] lead, guide [動] quote, cite [動] cause ⇔ 吸引[14/92], 勾引[18/36], 索引[29/70], 牽引[59/30], 援引[103/20]

引導 yǐndǎo [動] lead, guide
引渡 yǐndù [動] extradite
引發 yǐnfā [動] induce
引號 yǐnhào [名] quotation marks
引進 yǐnjìn [動] bring in, introduce
引力 yǐnlì [名] gravity
引起 yǐnqǐ [動] lead to, induce, cause
引擎 yǐnqíng [名] engine
引述 yǐnshù [動] quote, cite
引用 yǐnyòng [動] quote, cite
引誘 yǐnyòu [動] entice, seduce
引致 yǐnzhì [動] cause

蚓 65 yǐn
10 Insect 虫[125/1] that extends 引[65/9] (phonetic). [名] earthworm ⇔ 蚯蚓[96/17]

夷 65 yí
11 Person 大[39/1] with bow 弓[65/1]. [名] barbarians to the east in ancient times [名] (晋) foreigners ⇔ 鄙夷[69/8], 夏威夷[148/18], 匪夷所思[169/7]

姨 65 yí
12 Woman 女[54/1] on family's foreign 夷[65/11] (phonetic) side. [名] sister-in-law (wife's sister) [名] aunt (maternal) ⇔ 阿姨[37/22]

姨媽 yímā [名] aunt (maternal)
姨太太 yítàitài [名] mistress, concubine

弔 65 diào
13 [吊[65/14]] Person 人[10/1] (altered) holding a bow 弓[65/1], guarding a body from scavengers. Simplified form is variant form 吊[65/14]. [動] mourn, condole [動] hang, suspend (⇨ 吊[65/14]) ⇔ 憑弔[25/4]

弔唁 diàoyàn [動] condole

吊 65 diào
14 A variation of 弔[65/13]. [動] hang, suspend

吊車 diàochē [名] crane
吊床 diàochuáng [名] hammock
吊橋 diàoqiáo [名] suspension bridge
吊死 diàosǐ [動] hang to death
吊銷 diàoxiāo [動] cancel

屌 65 diǎo
15 Hangs 吊[65/14] (phonetic) from body 尸[40/1]. [名] penis

雋 65 juàn
16 [隽] Bird 隹[162/1] shot with bow 弓[65/1]. Simplified form uses 乃[28/1]. [名] fatty meat

雋永 juànyǒng [形] interesting, intriguing

鐫 65 juān
17 [镌] Metal 金[44/3] with 雋[65/16] phonetic. [動] engrave

鐫刻 juānkè [動] engrave

粥 65 zhōu
18 Modern form shows rice 米[138/1] steaming (represented by waving lines written as 弓[65/1]). [名] rice gruel, porridge ⇔ 米粥[138/1]

弟 65 dì
19 Ancient form suggests arrow/stake 弋[45/1] bound with string (resembling 弓[65/1]). (古) sequence of action (⇨ 第[65/20]) [名] brother (younger) ⇔ 兄弟[11/2], 學弟[15/67], 小弟[29/8], 堂弟[63/33], 徒弟[70/3], 表弟[126/14], 師弟[167/12]

弟弟 dìdì [名] brother (younger)
弟兄 dìxīong [名] brothers
弟子 dìzǐ [名] pupil

第 65 dì
20 Bamboo 竹[71/11] strips arranged in sequence 弟[65/19] (phonetic). [名] a prefix for ordinal numbers: 第一 first, number one ⇔ 印第安[38/10], 門第[79/17]

梯 65 tī
21 Wood 木[77/1] in sequence 弟[65/19] (phonetic). [名] ladder, staircase ⇔ 階梯[12/13], 樓梯[53/32]

梯田 tītián [名] terraced field

剃 65 tì
22 Knife 刀[35/1] applied in sequence 弟[65/19] (phonetic). [動] shave

剃刀 tìdāo [名] razor

涕 65 tì
23 Water 水[3/21] in sequence 弟[65/19] (phonetic). [名] tears, snivel ⇔ 鼻涕[96/14]

66

山 66/1 — 艸 66/2 —

蔡 蒜 蓓 菩 莖 蕭 艾 落
蘿 莞 蔻 藐 蒼 花 菠 若
春 蒸 范 菊 筍 蕎 芒 茫
荒 萬 藕 葡 芮 蔓 苛 荷
芋 芥 菇 苦 葫 蔗 蘼 葉
茄 荔 芬 芋 英 蓋 蔚 苔
茶 茂 荊 薪 蔽 芳 苔 苔
茲 藥 蕾 茲 荐 芥 莫 葬
藝 菱 芝 菌 穗 艽 薄 葡
蒲 荳 蓬 藕 萬 蒨 著 薯
蕩 藉 董 草 藷 茉 蒂 蘭
藏 蔣 莊 萌 芯 蕊 芽 芭
葵 蘋 芝 芹 — 荣 芽 芦
莉 萎 苞 薑 蕾 苗 芦 蓂
荶 菽 蘆 蓑 莩 藤 薇 茸
蒐 葡 藍 惠 蓄 薦 蒙 藩
蓮 萊 薔 蘿 蕉 蘭 薛 菲
華 蔦 蘇

芻 66/3 — 雛 66/4
趨 66/5
皺 66/6
鄒 66/7

艸 66/8 — 卉 66/9 — 奔 66/10
芔 66/15 — 莽 66/16 — 賁 66/11 — 憤 66/12
莫 66/17 — 寞 66/18 — 墳 66/13
漠 66/19 — 噴 66/14
蟇 66/20
摸 66/21
膜 66/22
模 66/23
摹 66/24

弔 65 jiě
24 Growth 市 (altered) blocked 一し

姊 65 jiě zǐ
25 Woman 女 with 弔 phonetic. 图 sister (elder) (⇨

姐) ⇔ 師姊

姊姊 jiějie 图 sister (elder) (⇨ 姐姐)

姊妹 jiěmèi 图 sister, sisters (⇨ 姐妹)

弗 65 fú
26 Rods (represented by lines ㇒ ㇀) bound together (written as 弓). 甸 not

佛 65 fó
27 Person 人 with 弗 phonetic. 图 Buddha ⇔ 阿彌陀佛

佛教 fójiào 图 Buddhism

佛經 fójīng 图 Buddhist scriptures, sutras

佛寺 fósì 图 Buddhist temple

佛塔 fótǎ 图 stupa

佛陀 fótúo 图 Buddha

佛像 fóxiàng 图 statue of Buddha

佛學 fóxué 图 Buddhism

彿 65 fú
28 [彷彿] Step 彳 with 弗 phonetic. 图 similar to ⇔ 彷彿

拂 65 fú
29 Hand 手 with 弗 phonetic. 甸 brush, whisk

費 65 fèi
30 [費] No 弗 (phonetic) money/shells 貝 left. 甸 waste: 費時間 waste time 甸 consume 甸 fee, charge: 電費 electric bill ⇔ 枉費 , 經費 , 浪費 , 花費 , 學費 , 收費 , 公費 , 稿費 , 小費 , 消費 , 白費 , 耗費 , 自費 , 車費 , 軍費 , 免費

費解 fèijiě 图 difficult to understand

費心 fèixīn 甸 take the trouble

費用 fèiyòng 图 expenses

沸 65 fèi
31 Water 水 not 弗 (phonetic) in order. 图 bubbling, boiling

字譜及字典

沸點 fèidiǎn ▣ boiling point
沸騰 fèiténg ▣ boiling ▣ seething

屮 66 chè
1 Pictograph of a sprouting plant.

艸 66 cǎo
2 Multiple sprouts 屮⁶⁶. Derivatives relate to plants. ▣ grass

芻 66 chú
3 [刍] Bundles 勹⁸ of grass 屮⁶⁶. ▣ hay, fodder ⇔ 反芻³¹
芻議 chúyì ▣ rough proposal

雛 66 chú
4 [雏] Bird 隹⁶² with 芻⁶⁶ phonetic. ▣ chick ▣ young
雛形 chúxíng ▣ embryonic

趨 66 qū
5 [趋] Walk 走⁸⁸ with 芻⁶⁶ phonetic. ▣ hurry ▣ tend towards
趨緩 qūhuǎn ▣ decelerate
趨勢 qūshì ▣ trend, tendency
趨向 qūxiàng ▣ trend, tendency ▣ incline toward, lean toward

皺 66 zhòu
6 [皱] Skin 皮⁵⁵ like bundled grass 芻⁶⁶ (phonetic). ▣ wrinkle, crease
皺眉 zhòuméi ▣ frown, wrinkle one's brow
皺紋 zhòuwén ▣ wrinkle, crease

鄒 66 zōu
7 [邹] City 邑⁷⁷ with 芻⁶⁶ phonetic. ▣ a surname

芔 66 huì
8 Many sprouts 屮⁶⁶. ▣ grasses

卉 66 huì
9 A variant of 芔⁶⁶. ▣ grasses ⇔ 花卉⁸¹

奔 66 bēn bèn
10 Person 大⁷ʳ (originally bent forward 夭⁷ʳ) in a field of grass 卉⁶⁶. bēn: ▣ run

⇔ 投奔⁴⁷, 飛奔¹⁶⁹
奔波 bēnbō ▣ rush about
奔馳 bēnchí ▣ speed
奔跑 bēnpǎo ▣ run
奔騰 bēnténg ▣ gallop ▣ surge forward

賁 66 bì bēn
11 [贲] Plants 卉⁶⁶ and shells 貝⁵⁰. bì: ▣ ornamental bēn: ▣ forge ahead (⇔ 奔⁶⁶)

憤 66 fèn
12 [愤] Heart 心⁸³ with 賁⁶⁶ phonetic. ▣ anger, resentment ⇔ 氣憤⁹¹
憤慨 fènkǎi ▣ indignation
憤懣 fènmèn ▣ resentful
憤怒 fènnù ▣ anger, wrath

墳 66 fén
13 [坟] Earth 土⁷ʳ with ornaments 賁⁶⁶ (phonetic). Simplified form uses 文⁰⁰. ▣ grave ⇔ 祖墳⁸⁷
墳地 féndì ▣ graveyard, cemetery
墳墓 fénmù ▣ grave

噴 66 pēn
14 [喷] Mouth 口⁶⁸ with 賁⁶⁶ phonetic. ▣ spurt, spray, gush
噴出 pēnchū ▣ jet forth, gush out
噴漆 pēnqī ▣ ▣ spray paint
噴射 pēnshè ▣ spurt, jet
噴嚏 pēntì ▣ sneeze: 打噴嚏 to sneeze

茻 66 mǎng
15 Plants 屮⁶⁶ all around.

莽 66 mǎng
16 Dog 犬⁷ʳ (often written as 大⁷ʳ) chasing prey into bushes 茻⁶⁶ (phonetic, altered). ▣ reckless ⇔ 魯莽¹⁹
莽撞 mǎngzhuàng ▣ rude, reckless

莫 66 mò
17 Sun 日⁷⁶ disappearing behind bushes 茻⁶⁶ (altered). ▣ not ▣ a surname

莫不 mòbù ▣ no one
莫大 mòdà ▣ greatest
莫非 mòfēi ▣ could it be
莫名 mòmíng ▣ difficult to express
莫名其妙 mòmíngqímiào ▣ puzzling, enigmatic
莫斯科 mòsīkē ▣ Moscow

寞 66 mò
18 Modern character shows not 莫⁶⁶ (phonetic) and home 宀⁶³. ▣ lonely ⇔ 落寞⁵⁹, 寂寞¹²¹

漠 66 mò
19 Without 莫⁶⁶ (phonetic) water 水⁴₁. ▣ desert ⇔ 沙漠⁵⁹, 冷漠⁸⁵, 淡漠¹²
漠視 mòshì ▣ ignore

驀 66 mò
20 [蓦] Horse 馬⁷⁷ with 莫⁶⁶ phonetic. ▣ suddenly
驀地 mòdì ▣ suddenly
驀然 mòrán ▣ suddenly

摸 66 mō
21 Hand 手⁹⁷ with 莫⁶⁶ phonetic. ▣ touch, stroke ▣ seek ⇔ 撫摸³⁰, 觸摸¹⁵
摸索 mōsuǒ ▣ grope, fumble ▣ learn by trial and error

膜 66 mó
22 Flesh 肉¹³² with 莫⁶⁶ phonetic and suggestive of curtain 幕⁶⁶. mó,mò: ▣ membrane mó: ▣ kneel and worship ⇔ 網膜²⁴
膜拜 móbài ▣ worship

模 66 mó mú
23 Wood 木⁷ʳ with 莫⁶⁶ phonetic. mó: ▣ model, pattern mú: ▣ mold, form ⇔ 一模一樣¹, 楷模¹⁴₅, 規模⁷⁷
模範 mófàn ▣ model, paragon 勞動模範 model worker ▣ exemplary
模仿 mófǎng ▣ copy, imitate
模糊 móhú ▣ vague, blurred, unclear
模擬 mónǐ ▣ mimic, simulate

字譜及字典

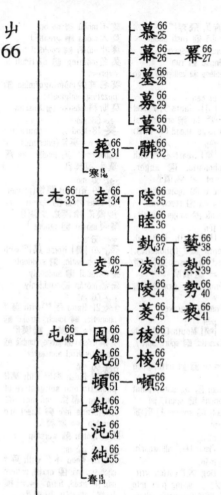

慕 66 mù
25 Heart 心 unclear 莫 (phonetic). yearn for ⇔ 羨慕, 仰慕, 愛慕

幕 66 mù
26 Cloth 巾 that hides 莫 (phonetic). curtain ⇔ 屏幕, 字幕, 鐵幕, 開幕, 螢幕, 序幕, 帷幕

冪 66 mì
27 [冪] Cover 冖 with a curtain 幕 (phonetic). cloth cover exponent (math)

墓 66 mù
28 Earth 土 with 莫 phonetic. grave ⇔ 盜墓, 掃墓, 墳墓, 陵墓
墓碑 mùbēi tombstone, gravestone
墓地 mùdì graveyard, cemetery

募 66 mù
29 Strength 力 with 莫 phonetic. enlist, recruit ⇔ 籌募
募集 mùjí raise (funds)

暮 66 mù
30 Disappearing sun 莫 (phonetic) with sun 日 redundant. dusk
暮色 mùsè dusk, twilight

葬 66 zàng
31 Corpse 死 in a bundle of grass 茻 (altered). bury ⇔ 火葬, 埋葬
葬禮 zànglǐ funeral
葬送 zàngsòng ruin

髒 66 zāng
32 [髒] Bones 骨 buried 葬 (phonetic). dirty ⇔ 骯髒

卉 66 lù
33 Plant 屮 with 六 phonetic. mushroom

坴 66 liù
34 Mushroom-shaped 卉

simulation
模式 móshì model, pattern, formula
模特兒 mótèr fashion model mannequin
模型 móxíng miniature, model paradigm, model

模樣 múyàng appearance about

摹 66 mó
24 Hand 手 with 莫 phonetic. trace, copy ⇔ 臨摹

(phonetic) earth 土. mound

陸 66 lù liù
35 [陆] Hill 阜 and mound 坴 (phonetic). Simplified form uses 擊 simplification. lù: plateau land, shore, a surname liù: six (complex form) ⇔ 内陸, 大陸, 登陸
陸地 lùdì land (in contrast to sea or air)
陸軍 lùjūn army
陸續 lùxù continuously

睦 66 mù
36 Eyes 目 with 坴 phonetic. friendly ⇔ 和睦
睦鄰 mùlín be good neighbors

埶 66 yì
37 Mound 坴 being worked 丮. plant, cultivate

藝 66 yì
38 [艺] Cultivate 埶 (phonetic) with plant 艸 and mist 云 added for elaboration. Simplified form uses 乙. cultivate art, talent ⇔ 綜藝, 茶藝館, 技藝, 武藝, 文藝
藝妓 yìjì geisha
藝術 yìshù art: 藝術家 artist; 藝術品 artwork; 藝術館 art museum

熱 66 rè
39 [热] Needed for cultivation 埶 (phonetic) and fire 火. hot fever: 登革熱 dengue fever ⇔ 狂熱, 親熱, 熾熱, 悶熱, 炎熱, 酷熱, 炙手可熱, 過熱, 酒酣耳熱
熱愛 rèài love passionately passionate love
熱忱 rèchén enthusiasm, zeal earnest

熱誠 rèchéng hospitable
熱帶 rèdài tropics: 亞熱帶 subtropics
熱烈 rèliè enthusiastic, passionate
熱門 rèmén fashion, craze popular, topical
熱鬧 rènào lively, bustling
熱切 rèqiè fervent
熱情 rèqíng enthusiasm, warmth enthusiastic
熱身 rèshēn warm up: 熱身運動 warm-up exercises
熱心 rèxīn ardent, enthusiastic
熱中 rèzhōng crave, fond of

勢 66 shì
40 [势] Cultivate 埶 strength 力. force, influence situation ⇔ 姿勢
得勢, 局勢, 作勢, 時勢, 聲勢, 大勢, 形勢, 攻勢, 地勢, 趨勢, 情勢, 氣勢, 手勢, 預勢, 優勢, 權勢
勢必 shìbì certainly, bound to
勢力 shìlì power, strength, influence

褻 66 xiè
41 [亵] Clothes 衣 with 埶 phonetic. underclothes ⇔ 猥褻
褻瀆 xièdú besmirch, blasphemy

夌 66 líng
42 Walk 夂 over a protruding 坴 mound. traverse

凌 66 líng
43 Ice 冫 and traverse 夌 (phonetic). accumulated ice high traverse insult a surname
凌晨 língchén early morning, pre-dawn hours
凌駕 língjià override
凌厲 línglì swift and powerful

凌亂 língluàn untidy, disarrayed
凌辱 língrù insult, humiliate

陵 66 líng
44 Hill 阜 to be traversed 夌 (phonetic). high mound tomb, mausoleum: 明朝十三陵 the Ming Tombs in Beijing ⇔ 丘陵
陵墓 língmù tomb, mausoleum

菱 66 líng
45 Plant 艸 that traverses 夌 (phonetic) water. water chestnut
菱角 língjiǎo water chestnut

稜 66 léng
46 [棱] Grain 禾 with 夌 phonetic. a type of rice angle, corner (⇔ 棱)
稜角 léngjiǎo angle, corner

棱 66 léng
47 Wood 禾 with 夌 phonetic. angle, corner

屯 66 tún
48 Plant 屮 rising through the surface 一. sprout stockpile 草屯? FEx 屯田 túntián use militia labor to farm

囤 66 tún
49 Stockpile 屯 (phonetic) and enclosure 囗. hoard
囤積 túnjī hoard: 囤積居奇 corner the market

飩 66 tún
50 [饨] Food 食 with 屯 phonetic. dumpling ⇔ 餛飩

頓 66 dùn
51 [顿] Head 頁 with 屯 phonetic. bow pause meal ⇔ 波士頓, 停頓, 困頓, 整頓, 華盛頓
頓號 dùnhào comma (for lists)
頓時 dùnshí suddenly

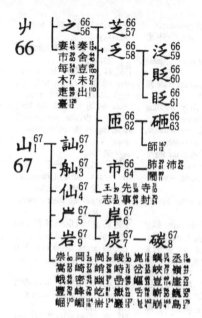

噸 66 52 [吨] dùn / dūn Mouth 口 with 頓 phonetic. ton

鈍 66 53 [钝] dùn Metal 金 cutting with difficulty 屯 (phonetic). blunt ⇔ 遲鈍

沌 66 54 dùn Water 水 with 屯 phonetic. turbid ⇔ 混沌, 渾沌

純 66 55 [纯] chún Silk 糸 with 屯 phonetic. pure ⇔ 單純

純粹 chúncuì pure, unadulterated purely, simply
純潔 chúnjié pure and honest
純淨 chúnjìng pure and clean
純利 chúnlì net profit
純樸 chúnpú honest and simple
純熟 chúnshú proficient, skilled
純眞 chúnzhēn pure, sincere, naive

之 66 56 zhī Plant 屮 (altered) rising from the ground 一. go of it (used only as an object): 總而言之 in summary of what was said ⇔ 久而久之, 庚子之役, 反之, 總而言之, 總之

之後 zhīhòu after, behind
之間 zhījiān between
之前 zhīqián before, in front of
之上 zhīshàng above
之下 zhīxià below, beneath
之中 zhīzhōng among

芝 66 57 zhī Plant 艸 with 之 phonetic. a fungus
芝加哥 zhījiāgē Chicago
芝麻 zhīmá sesame

乏 66 58 fá Reverse of 正. lack exhausted ⇔ 疲乏, 貧乏, 缺乏, 匱乏
乏味 fáwèi bland, dull

泛 66 59 fàn Water 水 with 乏 phonetic. float ⇔ 廣泛

貶 66 60 [贬] biǎn Money/shells 貝 lacking 乏 (phonetic). devalue ⇔ 褒貶
貶義 biǎnyì derogatory
貶值 biǎnzhí devalue, depreciate

眨 66 61 zhǎ Eye 目 lacking 乏 stability. blink
眨眼 zhǎyǎn wink, blink

匝 66 62 zā Ancient form shows grow 之 inverted. circle, encompass

砸 66 63 zá Stones 石 surrounding 匝 (phonetic). pound, mash break: 砸飯碗 lose one's job fail, bungle ⇔ 搞砸
砸破 zápò break, smash

市 66 shì
64 Distant lands 冂 and an early form of accumulate 及 with 之 (altered) phonetic. market, city ⇔ 上市, 股市, 城市, 夜市, 都市, 灰市, 黑市

市場 shìchǎng market: 市場經濟 market economy; 自由市場 free market; 黑市場 black market
市價 shìjià market price
市郊 shìjiāo suburbs
市立 shìlì city-founded
市民 shìmín citizen, citizenry
市區 shìqū urban district
市長 shìzhǎng mayor

山 67 shān
1 Pictograph of mountain peaks. mountain ⇔ 唐山, 泰山, 長白山, 嵩山, 冰山, 阿里山, 普陀山, 衡山, 峨嵋山, 中山, 登山, 爬山, 玉山, 廬山, 恆山, 舊金山, 華山
山崩 shānbēng landslide
山川 shānchuān mountains and streams
山頂 shāndǐng summit
山東 shāndōng Shandong Province
山洞 shāndòng cave
山風 shānfēng mountain breeze
山峰 shānfēng mountain peak
山谷 shāngǔ valley
山嶺 shānlǐng mountain range
山麓 shānlù foothill
山脈 shānmài mountain range
山門 shānmén monastery gate
山坡 shānpō mountain slope
山區 shānqū mountain area
山上 shānshàng mountain-top

山水 shānshuǐ natural scenery, landscape: 山水畫 landscape painting
山頭 shāntóu mountaintop
山西 shānxī Shanxi Province
山崖 shānyái cliff
山羊 shānyáng goat: 山羊鬚 goatee
山岳 shānyuè high mountains
山寨 shānzhài mountain fortress
山莊 shānzhuāng villa

訕 67 shàn
2 [讪] Words 言 with 山 phonetic. ridicule, mock ⇔ 搭訕
訕笑 shànxiào ridicule, mock

舢 67 shān
3 Boat 舟 and mountain 山 (phonetic). sampan
舢板 shānbǎn sampan

仙 67 xiān
4 Person 人 in mountains 山 (phonetic). fairy, god divine ⇔ 神仙
仙丹 xiāndān elixir
仙女 xiānnǚ fairy beautiful woman
仙人 xiānrén immortal
仙子 xiānzǐ immortal, fairy beautiful woman

屵 67 nàn
5 Mountain 山 cliff 厂 (phonetic). high cliff

岸 67 àn
6 High cliff 屵 opposing 干 (phonetic). shore, coast, bank ⇔ 河岸, 海岸, 沿岸, 東岸, 西岸

炭 67 tàn
7 Fire 火 with 屵 phonetic. Often written as mountain 山 and ashes 灰. charcoal ⇔ 煤炭

碳 67 tàn
8 Stone 石 charcoal 炭 (phonetic). carbon: 二氧化碳 carbon dioxide

岩 67 yán
9 Mountain 山 rock 石. cliff ⇔ 熔岩
岩層 yáncéng rock strata
岩石 yánshí rock

口 68 kǒu
1 Pictograph of a mouth. mouth, entrance, opening mouthful ⇔ 上口, 住口, 人口, 脫口而出, 港口, 可口, 餬口, 入口, 刀口, 緘口, 海口, 繞口令, 傷口, 藉口, 漱口, 戶口, 門口, 開口, 出口, 袖口, 目瞪口呆, 胃口, 窗口, 進出口, 進口

口才 kǒucái eloquence
口齒 kǒuchǐ enunciation: 口齒清楚 clear enunciation
口袋 kǒudài pocket
口福 kǒufú lucky attainment of good food
口供 kǒugòng confession
口號 kǒuhào slogan
口紅 kǒuhóng lipstick
口吃 kǒují stammer, stutter
口交 kǒujiāo oral sex
口角 kǒujiǎo quarrel
口徑 kǒujìng caliber
口令 kǒulìng password
口氣 kǒuqì tone
口琴 kǒuqín harmonica
口哨 kǒushào whistle: 吹口哨 to whistle
口試 kǒushì interview, oral examination
口頭 kǒutóu orally: 口頭報告 oral report
口味 kǒuwèi flavor, taste
口香糖 kǒuxiāngtáng gum
口信 kǒuxìn verbal message
口音 kǒuyīn accent

口
68

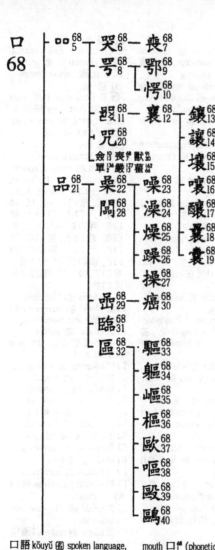

扣留 kòuliú 🈺 confiscate
扣押 kòuyā 🈺 detain, arrest
扣子 kòuzi 🈺 knot, button

鈕 68 kòu
3 [扣第] Metal 金籍 opening 口⁶⁸ (phonetic). 🈺 button ⇔ 鈕釦笳

叩 68 kòu
4 Kneel 卩⁷⁰ with 口⁶⁸ phonetic. 🈺 kowtow 🈺 knock
叩頭 kòutóu 🈺 kowtow

㗊 68 xuān
5 Two mouths 口⁶⁸. 🈺 cry out

哭 68 kū
6 Wailing 㗊⁶⁸ dog 犬?. 🈺 cry, weep ⇔ 啼哭ⁿ
哭泣 kūqì 🈺 weep
哭聲 kūshēng 🈺 sobs, cries

喪 68 sāng sàng
7 [丧] Cry 哭⁶⁸ (altered) over the dead 亡⁵⁷ (altered, phonetic). sāng: 🈺 mourn 🈺 funeral sàng: 🈺 lose ⇔ 沮喪ˡ⁷
喪禮 sānglǐ 🈺 funeral
喪命 sàngmìng 🈺 meet violent or accidental death
喪氣 sàngqì 🈺 despair, lose heart
喪失 sàngshī 🈺 lose

咢 68 è
8 Clamor 㗊⁶⁸ and attack 屰界 (phonetic, altered to resemble early form of 于?). 🈺 startled

鄂 68 è
9 City 邑? with 咢⁶⁸ phonetic. 🈺 an ancient kingdom 🈺 Hubei Province

愕 68 è
10 Heart 心ⁱ? startled 咢⁶⁸ (phonetic). 🈺 startled ⇔ 驚愕ⁱˢ
愕然 èrán 🈺 startled, stunned
愕視 èshì 🈺 stare in amazement

毆 68 nēng
11 Cries 㗊⁶⁸ and

口語 kǒuyǔ 🈺 spoken language, vernacular
口罩 kǒuzhào 🈺 facemask

扣 68 kòu
2 Hand 手? restraining
mouth 口⁶⁸ (phonetic). 🈺 rein in, rope 🈺 detain, arrest 🈺 deduct 🈺 button 🈺 discount ⇔ 回扣ˢ, 查扣笳, 折扣笳
扣除 kòuchú 🈺 deduct

movement 交 [ ] accompanying work 工 [ ].

襄 68 xiāng
12 Shed clothes 衣 [ ] to work 攴 [ ] (phonetic, abbreviated). 會 work, cooperate 會 manager
襄理 xiānglǐ 會 assistant manager

鑲 68 xiāng
13 [镶] Metal 金 [ ] with 襄 [ ] phonetic. 會 inlay, set

讓 68 ràng
14 [让] Words 言 [ ] with 襄 [ ] phonetic. Simplified form uses 上 [ ]. 會 let, allow 會 yield 會 offer: 讓座 offer one's seat 會 退讓 [ ], 謙讓 [ ], 禮讓 [ ]
讓步 ràngbù 會 concede 會 concession
讓路 rànglù 會 give way

壤 68 rǎng
15 Earth 土 [ ] that can be worked 襄 [ ] (phonetic). 會 soil 會 平壤 [ ], 接壤 [ ], 土壤 [ ]

嚷 68 rāng rǎng
16 Mouth 口 [ ] with 襄 [ ] phonetic. 會 shout, yell 會 吵嚷 [ ]
嚷嚷 rāngrang 會 shout, yell: 別嚷嚷了! Stop yelling!

釀 68 niàng
17 [酿] Alcohol 酉 [ ] with 襄 [ ] phonetic. Simplified form uses 良 [ ]. 會 brew, ferment 會 醞釀 [ ]
釀成 niàngchéng 會 bring about, form gradually
釀造 niàngzào 會 brew

曩 68 nǎng
18 Days 日 [ ] already shed 襄 [ ] (phonetic). 會 past formerly
曩昔 nǎngxī 會 formerly, historically

囊 68 náng
19 Ancient character showing bound 束 [ ] enclosure 口 [ ] with 襄 [ ] (abbreviated) phonetic. 會 sack 會 行囊 [ ], 窩囊 [ ]
囊括 nángguā 會 include

咒 68 zhòu
20 From mouth 口 [ ] of big brother 兄 [ ] (altered). 會 curse, scold 會 詛咒 [ ]
咒罵 zhòumà 會 curse, scold

品 68 pǐn
21 Group of people, represented by mouths 口 [ ]. Also explained as a collection of small objects (written as 口 [ ]). 會 commodity, product 會 rank, grade 會 character, personality 會 appraise: 品茶 sample tea 會 食品 [ ], 貨品 [ ], 作品 [ ], 商品 [ ], 毒品 [ ], 藥品 [ ], 補品 [ ], 舶來品 [ ], 產品 [ ], 出品 [ ], 贈品 [ ], 廢品 [ ]
品嘗 pǐncháng 會 taste
品德 pǐndé 會 moral character
品格 pǐngé 會 moral character
品質 pǐnzhí 會 quality
品種 pǐnzhǒng 會 variety, types, assortment

喿 68 zào
22 Mouths 品 [ ] of songbirds on a tree 木 [ ]. 會 chirping of birds (⇨ 噪 [ ])

噪 68 zào
23 Singing birds 喿 [ ] (phonetic) with mouth 口 [ ] redundant. 會 loud chirping 會 clamor
噪音 zàoyīn 會 noise, racket: 噪音污染 noise pollution

澡 68 zào
24 Water 水 [ ] with 喿 [ ] phonetic. 會 bathe 會 bath: 洗個澡 bathe 會 洗澡 [ ]

燥 68 zào
25 Fire 火 [ ] with 喿 [ ] phonetic. 會 arid 會 枯燥 [ ], 乾燥 [ ]

躁 68 zào
26 Foot 足 [ ] with 喿 [ ] phonetic. 會 impetuous 會 急躁 [ ], 煩躁 [ ], 焦躁 [ ]

操 68 cāo
27 Hand 手 [ ] with 喿 [ ] phonetic. 會 hold, handle 會 manage, operate 會 exercise, drill 會 貞操 [ ], 情操 [ ], 體操 [ ], 早操 [ ]
操場 cāochǎng 會 drill ground, playground, sports ground
操守 cāoshǒu 會 integrity, moral strength
操心 cāoxīn 會 worry
操縱 cāozòng 會 manipulate 會 operate
操作 cāozuò 會 operate

闆 68 bǎn
28 [板] Objects 品 [ ] behind a door 門 [ ]. 會 owner, boss 會 老闆 [ ]

嵒 68 yán
29 Mountains 山 [ ] huddled together 品 [ ]. 會 cliffs

癌 68 ái yán
30 Sickness 疒 [ ] with 嵒 [ ] phonetic. 會 cancer: 致癌物 carcinogen 會 肺癌 [ ]
癌症 áizhèng 會 cancer

臨 68 lín
31 [临] Recline 臥 [ ] with 品 [ ] phonetic. 會 face 會 just before 會 降臨 [ ], 光臨 [ ], 瀕臨 [ ], 面臨 [ ], 來臨 [ ]
臨床 línchuáng 會 clinical
臨摹 línmó 會 practice by copying (painting or calligraphy)
臨時 línshí 會 temporary, provisional

區 68 qū
32 [区] Objects 品 [ ] placed in a box 匚 [ ]. 會 differentiate 會 region, area 會 特區 [ ], 郊區 [ ], 地區 [ ], 市區 [ ], 山區 [ ], 社區 [ ], 禁

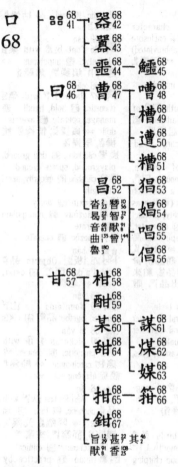

68

口
68

逐出境 deport

軀 68 qū
34 [躯] Body 身147 with
區貿 phonetic. 名 body ⇔
身軀147
軀體 qūtǐ 名 body

崛 68 qū
35 [岖] Modern form
shows mountain 山67 and region
區貿 (phonetic). 形 rugged
⇔ 崎嶇

樞 68 shū
36 [枢] Wood 木77 with
區貿 phonetic. 名 pivot, hub
⇔ 中樞

樞紐 shūniǔ 名 pivot, hub, axis

歐 68 ōu
37 [欧] Stored good 區貿
(phonetic) exhaled 欠界. 動
vomit (嘔貿) 名 a surname
專 Europe ⇔ 東歐, 西歐

歐美 ōuměi 專 Europe and
America: 歐美人 Westerner
歐陽 ōuyáng 專 a surname
歐洲 ōuzhōu 專 Europe: 歐洲
大陸 continental Europe; 歐
洲人 European

嘔 68 ǒu
38 [呕] Mouth 口68 and
store 區貿 (phonetic). 動
vomit
嘔吐 ǒutù 動 vomit

毆 68 ōu
39 [殴] Strike 殳 with
區貿 phonetic. 動 beat up
毆打 ōudǎ 動 beat up

鷗 68 ōu
40 [鸥] Bird 鳥178 with
區貿 phonetic. 名 gull ⇔
沙鷗, 海鷗

品 68 jí
41 Clamor of many mouths
口68.

器 68 qì
42 Collection of cooking
vessels (resembling 品)
guarded by a dog 犬91. 名

區77, 轄區77
區別 qūbié 動 differentiate,
distinguish 名 difference
區分 qūfēn 動 differentiate,
distinguish
區間 qūjiān 名 zone
區區 qūqū 形 trivial
區域 qūyù 名 district, region

驅 68 qū
33 [驱] Horse 馬187 with
區貿 phonetic. 動 drive a
carriage 動 expel ⇔ 先驅, 前驅
驅趕 qūgǎn 動 expel, drive out
驅散 qūsàn 動 disperse, scatter
驅使 qūshǐ 動 order, dictate
驅逐 qūzhú 動 banish, expel: 驅逐

utensil, equipment ⇔ 瓷器, 吸塵器, 電器, 石器, 銅器, 儀器, 機器, 樂器, 容器, 漆器, 武器, 玉器, 藤器, 陶器, 變壓器

器官 qìguān organ
器皿 qìmǐn food container
器械 qìxiè machine, apparatus, instrument

囂 68 xiāo
43 [嚚] Head 頁 surrounded by clamoring mouths 口口. clamor 叫囂
囂張 xiāozhāng arrogant and aggressive

噩 68 è
44 King 王 and clamor 口口. startling
噩夢 èmèng nightmare ⇨ 惡夢

鱷 68 è
45 [鰐] Startling 噩 (phonetic) fish-like 魚 animal. Simplified form uses 咢. crocodile
鱷魚 èyú crocodile

曰 68 yuē
46 Mouth 口 exhaling (indicated by line). say: 子曰 Confucius says

曹 68 cáo
47 Speak 曰曰 to judge in position at court's east 東 (altered). plaintiff and defendant. a surname: 曹雪芹 Cao Xueqin - author of Dream of Red Mansions

嘈 68 cáo
48 Mouths 口 of plaintiff and defendant 曹 (phonetic). noisy
嘈雜 cáozá noisy

槽 68 cáo
49 Wood 木 with 曹 phonetic. trough, groove, slot ⇔ 水槽, 跳槽

遭 68 zāo
50 Movement 辵 of plaintiff and defendant 曹 (phonetic). meet with, incur, suffer
遭到 zāodào encounter
遭逢 zāoféng encounter
遭受 zāoshòu suffer from, be subject to
遭殃 zāoyāng meet with calamity
遭遇 zāoyù encounter vicissitudes

糟 68 zāo
51 Rice 米 with 曹 phonetic. wine sediment in a mess ⇔ 亂七八糟
糟糕 zāogāo messed up, disastrous Damn!
糟蹋 zāotà waste, spoil

昌 68 chāng
52 Sunny 日 speech 曰. flatter flourishing
昌明 chāngmíng flourishing, glorious
昌盛 chāngshèng prosperous

猖 68 chāng
53 Dog/beast 犬 flourishing 昌 (phonetic). reckless
猖獗 chāngjué rampant, unbridled
猖狂 chāngkuáng wild, furious

娼 68 chāng
54 Modern form shows woman 女 and flatter 昌 (phonetic). prostitute
娼妓 chāngjì prostitute

唱 68 chàng
55 Mouth 口 flattering 昌 (phonetic). lead (⇨ 倡) sing ⇔ 歌唱, 合唱
唱歌 chànggē sing
唱片 chàngpiàn record, phonograph

倡 68 chàng
56 Person 人 flattering 昌 (phonetic). sing (⇨ 唱) lead, advocate ⇔ 提倡

甘 68 gān
57 Something 一 in the mouth 口. sweet willingly
甘地 gāndì Gandhi
甘冒 gānmào risk, brave
甘薯 gānshǔ sweet potato
甘肅 gānsù Gansu Province
甘心 gānxīn readily willingly
甘願 gānyuàn willingly
甘蔗 gānzhè sugarcane

柑 68 gān
58 Tree 木 with sweet 甘 (phonetic) fruit. mandarin orange
柑橘 gānjú mandarin orange, tangerine

酣 68 hān
59 Alcohol 酉 enjoyed sweetly 甘 (phonetic). joy ⇨ 酒酣耳熱
酣睡 hānshuì sleep soundly

某 68 mǒu
60 Sweet 甘 tree 木. plum tree (⇨ 梅) some (person or thing)
某某 mǒumǒu so-and-so
某人 mǒurén someone
某些 mǒuxiē some

謀 68 móu
61 [谋] Words 言 with 某 phonetic. scheme, strategize seek, try for ⇔ 同謀, 智謀, 陰謀, 參謀
謀略 móulüè strategize
謀求 móuqiú seek
謀殺 móushā murder
謀生 móushēng make a living
謀職 móuzhí search for a job

煤 68 méi
62 Fire 火 with 某

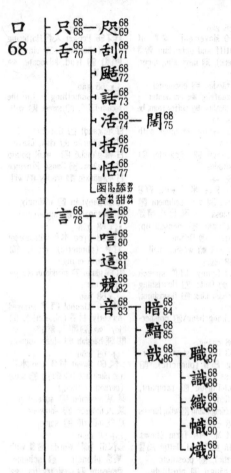

甜蜜 tiánmì 🔲 sweet, happy

甜酸 tiánsuān 🔲 sweet and sour

甜筒 tiántǒng 🔲 ice-cream cone

拑 68 qián
65 [钳势] Hand 手🔲 like mouth on object 甘势 (phonetic). 🔲 grasp

箝 68 qián
66 Bamboo 竹🔲 grasping 拑势 (phonetic). 🔲 pincers
箝制 qiánzhì 🔲 suppress, restrain

鉗 68 qián
67 [钳] Metal 金🔲 clasping as mouth on object 甘势. 🔲 pincers
鉗子 qiánzi 🔲 pincers, tweezers

只 68 zhǐ
68 Mouth 口🔲 exhaling (lines resembling 八🔲). 🔲 but, yet 🔲 only, merely
只得 zhǐdé 🔲 have to, obliged to
只好 zhǐhǎo 🔲 have to, must
只是 zhǐshì 🔲 only, merely
只要 zhǐyào 🔲 provided that, so long as
只有 zhǐyǒu 🔲 only if

咫 68 zhǐ
69 Foot 尺🔲 with 只势 phonetic. 🔲 near
咫尺 zhǐchǐ 🔲 very close

舌 68 shé
70 Mouth 口🔲 with object (resembling 干🔲) emerging. 🔲 tongue ⇔ 喉舌🔲
舌頭 shétou 🔲 tongue

刮 68 guā
71 Knife 刀🔲 with an ancient character resembling 舌势 phonetic. 🔲 scrape, shave
刮鬍子 guāhúzi 🔲 🔲 shave (the face): 刮鬍刀 razor
刮臉 guāliǎn 🔲 🔲 shave (the face): 刮臉刀 razor
刮目相看 guāmùxiāngkàn 🔲 see in a different light, view with new respect

phonetic. 🔲 coal
煤礦 méikuàng 🔲 coal mine
煤氣 méiqì 🔲 gas
煤炭 méitàn 🔲 coal

媒 68 méi
63 Woman 女🔲 with 某势 phonetic. 🔲 matchmaker ⇔ 傳媒🔲
媒介 méijiè 🔲 medium, go-between

media: 多媒體 multimedia between
媒人 méirén 🔲 matchmaker
媒體 méitǐ 🔲 🔲 media: 多媒體 multimedia

甜 68 tián
64 Sweet 甘势 to the tongue 舌势. 🔲 sweet
甜美 tiánměi 🔲 sweet 🔲 pleasant

颳 68 guā
72 [刮] Wind 風 with an ancient character resembling 舌 phonetic. 动 blow
颳風 guāfēng 动 blowing wind

話 68 huà
73 [话] Words 言 with an ancient character resembling 舌 phonetic. 动 words, speech 动 discuss ⇔ 說話, 神話, 電話, 謊話, 聽話, 空話, 好話, 換句話說, 俗話, 回話, 土話, 白話, 閒話, 留話, 談話, 廢話, 壞話, 笑話, 會話, 官話, 講話, 對話
話題 huàtí 动 conversation topic

活 68 huó
74 Water 水 with an ancient character resembling 舌 phonetic. 形 sound of rushing water 动 live 形 lively ⇔ 快活, 生活, 救活, 死活, 靈活
活動 huódòng 动 activity
活該 huógāi 动 "serves you right"
活力 huólì 动 vitality
活潑 huópō 形 vivacious, lively, dynamic
活躍 huóyuè 形 brisk, active
活著 huózhe 动 living, alive

闊 68 kuò
75 [阔] Door 門 with 活 phonetic. 形 wide ⇔ 廣闊, 遼闊, 寬闊
闊別 kuòbié 形 long-separated
闊綽 kuòchuò 形 extravagant, lavish
闊佬 kuòlǎo 动 rich man

括 68 guā kuò
76 Hand 手 with an ancient character resembling 舌 phonetic. 动 embrace, include ⇔ 概括, 包括, 囊括
括號 guāhào 动 parentheses

恬 68 tián
77 Heart 心 and sweet 甜 (phonetic, abbreviated to 舌). 形 tranquil
恬靜 tiánjìng 形 quiet, reserved

言 68 yán
78 Crime 辛 (phonetic, altered) of the mouth 口. 动 word 动 speak ⇔ 語言, 宜言, 格言, 諱言, 諾言, 弁言, 斷言, 傳言, 婉言, 寓言, 緒言, 揚言, 留言, 發言, 方言, 誓言, 文言, 預言, 序言, 前言, 自言自語, 謠言, 總而言之
言論 yánlùn 动 discussion, speech: 言論自由 freedom of speech
言行 yánxíng 动 words and actions
言語 yányǔ 动 spoken language

信 68 xìn
79 Person's 人 word 言. 动 动 trust 动 letter ⇔ 書信, 守信, 電信, 寄信, 咸信, 威信, 口信, 回信, 通信, 篤信, 寫信, 徵信社, 迷信, 自信, 來信
信封 xìnfēng 动 envelope
信奉 xìnfèng 动 believe in
信服 xìnfú 动 believe in
信號 xìnhào 动 signal
信箋 xìnjiān 动 stationery
信件 xìnjiàn 动 mail, letter
信賴 xìnlài 动 动 trust
信念 xìnniàn 动 conviction, belief
信任 xìnrèn 动 动 trust
信徒 xìntú 动 disciple, believer
信託 xìntuō 动 trust, entrust
信息 xìnxí 动 information
信心 xìnxīn 动 confidence: 沒有信心 lack confidence
信仰 xìnyǎng 动 believe in 动

belief, faith, conviction: 政治信仰 political beliefs; 宗教信仰 religious beliefs
信用 xìnyòng 动 trustworthiness: 信用卡 credit card; 信用貸款 loan
信譽 xìnyù 动 reputation, prestige
信紙 xìnzhǐ 动 stationery

唁 68 yàn
80 Mouth 口 words 言 (phonetic). 动 console ⇔ 弔唁

這 68 zhè zhèi
81 [这] Move 辵 and speak 言. Simplified form uses 文. 动 welcome 代 this
這般 zhèbān 代 like this
這邊 zhèbiān 代 here
這次 zhècì 代 this time
這個 zhège, zhèige 代 this
這裡 zhèlǐ 代 here
這麼 zhème 代 so, like this
這兒 zhèr 代 here
這些 zhèxiē 代 these
這樣 zhèyàng, zhèiyàng 动 like this
這種 zhèzhǒng 代 this kind

競 68 jìng
82 [竞] Two people 儿 talking 言 (altered). 动 argue 动 compete
競賽 jìngsài 动 competition
競選 jìngxuǎn 动 run for office
競爭 jìngzhēng 动 动 competition: 競爭力 competitiveness; 競爭者 competitor

音 68 yīn
83 Speak 言 (altered) with 一 representing sound. 动 sound ⇔ 注音, 噪音, 破音字, 擴音, 聲音, 錄音, 拼音, 口音, 噪音, 回音, 重音, 發音, 播音, 雜音, 觀音, 隔音
音節 yīnjié 动 syllable
音響 yīnxiǎng 动 stereo system

口
68

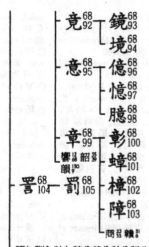

竟 68/92 ── 鏡 68/93
　　　　└─ 境 68/94
意 68/95 ── 億 68/96
　　　　├─ 憶 68/97
　　　　└─ 臆 68/98
章 68/99 ── 彰 68/100
　　　　　　 蟫 68/101
響 韶 韻
罾 68/104 ── 罰 68/105 ── 樟 68/102
　　　　　　　　　　　　└─ 障 68/103

谷 68/106 ── 容 68/107 ── 溶 68/108
　　　　　　　　　　　　├─ 熔 68/109
　　　　　　　　　　　　└─ 鎔 68/110

黯然 ànrán [img] gloomy

戠 68 zhí
86 Lance 戈 and sound 音. watch tower

職 68 zhí
87 [职] Ear 耳 and watch tower 戠 (phonetic). Simplified form uses 只. [img] duty [img] post, position ⇔ 教職員, 就職, 任職, 謀職, 辭職, 兼職, 瀆職, 稱職

職稱 zhíchēng [img] professional title
職等 zhíděng [img] official rank
職工 zhígōng [img] [img] workers and staff
職權 zhíquán [img] authority of office
職位 zhíwèi [img] position, post
職務 zhíwù [img] post, duty
職業 zhíyè [img] occupation, career
職員 zhíyuán [img] staff member
職責 zhízé [img] duty, responsibility
職志 zhízhì [img] aspiration, mission

識 68 [img] shì [img] shí
88 [识] Words 言 with 戠 phonetic. Simplified form uses 只. [img] know [img] knowledge ⇔ 共識, 學識, 結識, 知識, 認識, 辨識, 賞識, 常識, 意識, 見識, 相識

識別 shìbié [img] distinguish, discern, identify
識相 shìxiàng [img] tactful: 不識相 tactless
識字 shìzì [img] learn to read literate: 識字率 literacy rate

織 68 zhī
89 [织] Threads 糸 with 戠 phonetic. Simplified form uses 只. [img] weave, knit ⇔ 紡織, 編織, 組織

音樂 yīnyuè [img] music: 音樂電視 MTV; 音樂團體 band

暗 68 àn
84 Sun 日 with 音 phonetic. [img] dim ⇔ 黑暗
暗號 ànhào [img] password, codeword

暗殺 ànshā [img] assassinate
暗示 ànshì [img] hint, suggest [img] hint
暗中 ànzhōng [img] secretly

黯 68 àn
85 Dark 黑 with 音 phonetic. [img] gloomy

織 90 [帜] Cloth 巾[3] with 戠 phonetic. Simplified form uses 只. 图 banner ⇔ 旗幟

熾 91 [炽] Fire 火[2] with 戠 phonetic. Simplified form uses 只. 图 blazing
熾烈 chìliè 图 blazing
熾熱 chìrè 图 blazing, red-hot
熾盛 chìshèng 图 thriving

竟 92 Person 儿[1] concluding a musical 音 performance. 图 finish, conclude 图 unexpectedly ⇔ 究竟, 畢竟
竟然 jìngrán 图 unexpectedly

鏡 93 [镜] Metal 金 with 竟 phonetic. 图 mirror ⇔ 眼鏡, 望遠鏡, 銅鏡, 借鏡, 顯微鏡
鏡頭 jìngtóu 图 camera lens 图 scene (in a movie)
鏡子 jìngzi 图 mirror

境 94 Ground 土[3] that concludes 竟 (phonetic). 图 border, boundary 图 situation, condition ⇔ 窘境, 入境, 處境, 逆境, 困境, 離境, 心境, 止境, 出境, 環境, 過境, 家境
境地 jìngdì 图 circumstances
境界 jìngjiè 图 border, boundary

意 95 Sound 音 from the heart 心[3]. 图 meaning, idea 图 intention ⇔ 願意, 主意, 注意, 歉意, 刻意, 肆意, 得意, 隨意, 有意, 春意, 同意, 介意, 特意, 故意, 無意, 大意, 立意, 含意, 誠意, 執意, 任意, 如意, 好意思, 樂意, 蓄意, 在意, 生意, 情意, 寓意, 滿意, 酷意, 本意, 留意, 心意, 授意, 民意, 善意, 醉意, 會意, 惡意
意大利 yìdàlì 图 Italy: 意大利麵條 spaghetti
意見 yìjiàn 图 view, suggestion 图 objection: 如果你沒有意見 if you have no objection
意料 yìliào 图 expect, anticipate: 出乎意料 exceed expectations
意氣 yìqì 图 spirit: 意氣風發 high-spirited and energetic
意識 yìshì 图 consciousness: 意識型態 ideology; 潛意識 subconscious; 下意識 subconscious
意思 yìsi 图 meaning 图 interest: 沒意思 uninteresting 图 intention 图 token of appreciation
意圖 yìtú 图 intention, plan
意外 yìwài 图 accident 图 unexpected
意味 yìwèi 图 meaning, implication
意義 yìyì 图 meaning: 沒有意義 meaningless
意願 yìyuàn 图 will, aspiration
意志 yìzhì 图 will, determination: 戰鬥意志 will to fight

億 96 [亿] Modern form shows person 人[1] with 意 phonetic. Simplified form uses 乙. 图 hundred million: 十億 billion
億萬 yìwàn 图 millions and millions

憶 97 [忆] Heart's 心[3] intention 意 (phonetic). Simplified form uses 乙. 图 remember ⇔ 記憶, 回憶

臆 98 Flesh 肉[2] revealing aspiration 意 (phonetic). 图 breast
臆測 yìcè 图 conjecture

章 99 Music/sound 音 completed 十[1]. 图 section, chapter 图 seal, stamp 图 a surname ⇔ 報章, 印章, 蓋章, 圖章, 文章, 徽章, 像章
彰 100 Decorate 彡[1] with 章 phonetic. 图 evident ⇔ 昭彰, 表彰
彰顯 zhāngxiǎn 图 manifest, demonstrate

蟑 101 Insect 虫[2] with 章 phonetic. 图 cockroach
蟑螂 zhāngláng 图 cockroach

樟 102 Tree 木[1] with 章 phonetic. 图 camphor
樟木 zhāngmù 图 camphorwood
樟木箱 camphorwood chest

障 103 Hill 阜[2] separating into sections 章 (phonetic). 图 obstruct ⇔ 故障, 智障, 殘障, 屏障, 保障
障礙 zhàngài 图 obstacle

詈 104 Words 言 against person caught in web 网[2] (altered) of misdeeds. 图 scold

罰 105 [罚] Punish for insults 詈 and threats with knife 刀[1]. 图 penalize, fine ⇔ 處罰, 刑罰, 受罰, 懲罰
罰款 fákuǎn 图 fine
罰錢 fáqián 图 fine
罰球 fáqiú 图 penalty shot, free throw

俗 68 111
欲 68 112 — 慾 68 113
裕 68 114
浴 68 115
卻 68 116 — 腳 68 117
豁 79
凸 68 118 — 沿 68 119
鉛 68 120
船 68 121

吾 兄 唐 叫 閊 哨 邑 吳 命 台 噪 吐 杏 吻 呱 嘯 囉

亟 祝 君 句 同 嘀 加 嗌 啥 噎 嘔 呈 束 嘴 和 咼 唯

喧 唆 尋 局 占 喋 嗦 嚇 咸 喚 哆 名 噹 哨 哩 售

否 呢 吶 附 石 矛 吉 咬 喊 向 唱 名 問 足 龠 嚚

嘛 嗰 吸 可 昏 古 吩 或 哦 噡 吊 嘲 哪 咀 畀

哎 倉 右 呵 瞧 哈 哈 哦 哉 噴 嘛 味 吠 嘹 咱

吹 嗆 啤 啊 嘆 吟 含 哉 喵 嘖 呇 問 嘆 哀 喂

容 嘻 哄 呼 喋 吃 唸 辟 噴 喜 啼 害 告 喩 員

各 嚎 呻 叭 知 喉 食 喻 嚀 嚙 喵 害 哲 呂 呂

咳 嗾 函 吵 喉 咽 哈 如 咒 嘻 呆 吧 者 啄 嗒

吧 串 囉 鳴

谷 68 106 gǔ yù
Water 水 (abbreviated) through ravine's mouth 口. gǔ: valley, gorge yù: a surname ⇔ 曼谷, 峽谷, 山谷, 溪谷

容 68 107 róng
Cover 宀 a valley 谷. contain counenance ⇔ 從容, 縱容, 包容, 內容, 雍容, 形容, 笑容, 寬容, 美容, 面容, 陣容
容量 róngliàng capacity
容貌 róngmào countenance, features
容納 róngnà fit, hold tolerate, accept
容器 róngqì container
容忍 róngrěn tolerate
容許 róngxǔ allow, permit
容顏 róngyán countenance, features
容易 róngyì easy, simple: 好容易 with difficulty (from 好不容易)

溶 68 108 Full 容 (phonetic) of water 水. dissolve, melt
溶化 rónghuà dissolve, melt

熔 68 109 róng
Fire 火 with 容 phonetic. smelt, fuse
熔化 rónghuà smelt, fuse
熔爐 rónglú melting pot: 美國是個大熔爐. America is a great melting pot.
熔岩 róngyán lava

鎔 68 110 róng
[熔] Metal 金 with 容 phonetic. smelt, fuse (⇨ 熔)

俗 68 111 sú
Practices of valley 谷 (phonetic) people 人. custom common, vulgar ⇔ 不俗, 風俗, 通俗, 庸俗, 俚俗, 粗俗, 民俗, 習俗
俗話 súhuà common saying
俗氣 súqì vulgar
俗尚 súshàng customs, conventions
俗語 súyǔ popular saying

欲 68 112 yù
Gaping 谷 (phonetic) needs 欠. desire want ⇔ 亟欲, 躍躍欲試
欲望 yùwàng desire, longing

慾 68 113 yù
[欲] Desire 欲 (phonetic) of the heart 心. passion, lust ⇔ 食慾, 性慾, 獸慾
慾望 yùwàng desire, longing

裕 68 114 Clothing 衣 and other goods flowing like water

through a ravine 谷 (phonetic). 图 abundance ⇔ 富裕, 充裕, 寬裕

浴 68 yù
115 Water 水 in a valley 谷 (phonetic). 图 bath 图 bathe ⇔ 沐浴, 淋浴
浴缸 yùgāng 图 bathtub
浴室 yùshì 图 bathroom, shower room

卻 68 què
116 [却] Restrain 卩 and an ancient character resembling 谷 showing lip above the mouth. Simplified form uses 去. 图 resist desire 图 withdraw, retreat 图 but, yet, however ⇔ 冷卻
卻步 quèbù 图 step back
卻是 quèshì 图 nevertheless

腳 68 jiǎo
117 [脚] Flesh 肉 withdrawn 卻 behind self when sitting ancient style. 图 lower leg foot ⇔ 小腳, 赤腳, 裹腳, 手腳, 絆腳石, 陣腳
腳步 jiǎobù 图 footstep
腳跟 jiǎogēn 图 heel
腳踝 jiǎohuái 图 ankle
腳踏車 jiǎotàchē 图 bicycle
腳印 jiǎoyìn 图 footprint

㕣 68 yǎn
118 Separate 八 (or instead an abbreviation of water 水) drainage outlets 口. 图 ravine

沿 68 yán
119 Water 水 flowing in a ravine 㕣 (phonetic). 图 edge 图 along
沿岸 yánàn 图 coastal
沿海 yánhǎi 图 coastal
沿途 yántú 图 throughout a journey
沿襲 yánxí 图 follow

鉛 68 qiān
120 [铅] Metal 金 that flows in a mold/ravine 㕣 (phonetic). 图 lead
鉛筆 qiānbǐ 图 pencil

船 68 chuán
121 Boat 舟 with 㕣 phonetic. 图 ship, boat 图 货船, 划船, 帆船, 輪船, 翻船, 漁船
船舶 chuánbó 图 ships
船艙 chuáncāng 图 berth
船尾 chuánwěi 图 stern
船長 chuánzhǎng 图 captain

囗 69 wéi
1 Ideograph representing an enclosure. Now 圍.

回 69 huí
2 Pictograph of swirling within an enclosure 口. Also represents double enclosure 口. 图 return 图 times Muslim ⇔ 一回, 駁回, 收回, 返回, 召回, 送回, 拿回, 帶回, 縮回, 來回, 挽回
回報 huíbào 图 repay 图 return (on an investment) 图 report back
回稟 huíbǐng 图 report back
回答 huídá 图 answer
回到 huídào 图 return to
回覆 huífù 图 reply
回顧 huígù 图 look back 图 retrospective
回歸 huíguī 图 regression regress: 北回歸線 Tropic of Cancer; 南回歸線 Tropic of Capricorn 图 retrocession: 香港回歸 Hong Kong retrocession
回國 huíguó 图 return to one's native country
回合 huíhé 图 bout, round
回話 huíhuà 图 reply
回家 huíjiā 图 return home
回教 huíjiào 图 Islam
回絕 huíjué 图 decline, refuse
回扣 huíkòu 图 commission 图 kickback
回饋 huíkuì 图 图 feedback 图 repay a favor
回來 huílai 图 come back
回去 huíqù 图 return
回事 huíshì 图 result: 怎麼回事? What's going on?
回收 huíshōu 图 recycle
回溯 huísù 图 recall, look back on
回頭 huítóu 图 turn around: 不能走回頭路 can't go back to the old ways; 图 later: 回頭見 See you later!
回味 huíwèi 图 aftertaste 图 enjoy in retrospect
回響 huíxiǎng 图 图 echo (⇔ 迴響)
回想 huíxiǎng 图 remember, recall, reflect back on
回信 huíxìn 图 letter of reply
回憶 huíyì 图 recollect recollection, memory: 回憶錄 memoir
回音 huíyīn 图 echo
回族 huízú 图 Hui people - Chinese Moslems

迴 69 huí
3 [回] Return 回 (phonetic) movement 辵. 图 revolve ⇔ 巡迴, 迂迴, 輪迴
迴避 huíbì 图 avoid, evade, withdraw
迴響 huíxiǎng 图 echo, resound (⇔ 回響)
迴轉 huízhuǎn 图 revolve

蛔 69 huí
4 Modern form shows insect 虫 that returns 回 (phonetic). 图 roundworm
蛔蟲 huíchóng 图 roundworm

徊 69 huái
5 Steps 彳 revolving 回 (phonetic). 图 walk back and forth ⇔ 徘徊

囷 69 lǐn
6 Put in 入 storehouse 回. 图 granary (⇔ 廩)

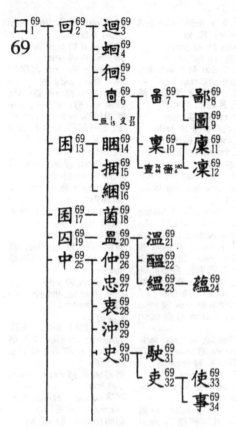

圖章 túzhāng 图 seal, chop

稟 10 [禀] Grain 禾 given to granary 回. Simplified form uses 示. receive report ⇔ 回稟
稟報 bǐngbào report (to one's superior)
稟賦 bǐngfù natural talent
稟告 bǐnggào report (to one's superior)

廩 11 [廪] Shed 广 where grain is recieved 稟 (phonetic). granary stockpile

凜 12 [凛] Ice 冫 with 稟 phonetic. cold
凜冽 lǐnliè biting cold
凜然 lǐnrán stern

困 13 Tree 木 growing in ruined enclosure 囗. poor weary, fatigued difficult ⇔ 貧困, 紓困
困頓 kùndùn exhausted
困惑 kùnhuò perplexed, baffled
困境 kùnjìng predicament
困倦 kùnjuàn fatigued, tired
困難 kùnnán difficulty
困擾 kùnrǎo perplex puzzle

睏 14 [困] Eyes 目 tired 困 (phonetic). sleepy

捆 15 Modern form shows hand 手 and difficult 困 (phonetic). tie, bind

綑 16 [捆] Thread 糸 with 困 phonetic. bundle weave

囷 17 Grain 禾 enclosed 囗. granary

㐭 7 bǐ Enclosed 囗 granary 回.

鄙 8 bǐ Town 邑 with enclosed granary 㐭. garrison town vulgar, base disdain ⇔ 卑鄙
鄙陋 bǐlòu superficial: 鄙陋無知 shallow and ignorant
鄙視 bǐshì despise, disdain
鄙夷 bǐyí scorn, despise

圖 9 tú [图] Encompass 囗 and granary 㐭. Simplified form uses 多. scheme, plan picture, drawing, graph ⇔ 畫圖, 力圖, 貪圖, 試圖, 拼圖, 地圖, 意圖, 企圖, 插圖, 藍圖
圖案 tú'àn pattern
圖畫 túhuà drawing, picture
圖書館 túshūguǎn library
圖形 túxíng sketch, graph

菌 69 jùn / jūn
18 Plant 艸 with 囷 phonetic. mushroom, fungus; bacteria ⇔ 細菌

囚 69 qiú
19 Person 人 confined 囗. imprison; prisoner
囚犯 qiúfàn prisoner
囚禁 qiújìn imprison
囚室 qiúshì prison cell

盟 69 wēn
20 Prisoner 囚 offered plate 皿. Simplified forms of derivatives use sun 日. benevolence

溫 69 wēn
21 [温] Water 水 and warm feeling 盟 (phonetic). a river name; warm; a surname ⇔ 體溫, 保溫, 氣溫
溫飽 wēnbǎo warm and fed
溫帶 wēndài temperate zone
溫度 wēndù temperature: 溫度計 thermometer
溫和 wēnhé gentle
溫暖 wēnnuǎn warm
溫泉 wēnquán hot springs
溫柔 wēnróu gentle, tender
溫順 wēnshùn docile
溫馨 wēnxīn comfortable, intimate

醞 69 yùn
22 [醞] Alcohol 酉 and warm feeling 盟 (phonetic). Simplified form uses 云. ferment
醞釀 yùnniàng ferment, brew

緼 69 yùn
23 [缊] Threads 糸 that give warm feeling 盟 (phonetic). coarse hemp cloth

蘊 69 yùn
24 [蕴] Plants 艸 with 緼 phonetic. accumulate, store
蘊藏 yùncáng contain, store
蘊涵 yùnhán contain

中 69 zhōng zhòng
25 Line 丨 bisecting an enclosure 囗. zhōng: center, middle; among; medium; China zhòng: strike, hit (a target); be struck ⇔ 高中, 初中, 擊中, 途中, 國中, 其中, 空中, 地中海, 當中, 熱中, 之中, 暗中, 心中, 手中, 集中
中彩 zhòngcǎi win a lottery prize
中餐 zhōngcān Chinese food; lunch
中東 zhōngdōng Middle East
中毒 zhòngdú be poisoned
中斷 zhōngduàn break off
中風 zhòngfēng stroke; suffer a stroke
中共 zhōnggòng Communist China
中國 zhōngguó China: 中國大陸 mainland China; 中國人 Chinese person
中華 zhōnghuá China: 中華民國 Republic of China; 中華人民共和國 People's Republic of China
中間 zhōngjiān between, in the center
中獎 zhòngjiǎng win a lottery prize
中美 zhōngměi Sino-American: 中美關係 Sino-American relations
中美洲 zhōngměizhōu Central America
中年 zhōngnián middle age: 中年人 middle-aged person
中秋節 zhōngqiūjié Mid-Autumn Festival, Moon Festival
中山 zhōngshān Sun Yat-sen (孫逸仙): 中山裝 Mao suit
中傷 zhòngshāng malign, vilify
中樞 zhōngshū hub, center
中途 zhōngtú halfway, midway
中尉 zhōngwèi lieutenant
中文 zhōngwén Chinese (written): 中文字 Chinese characters
中午 zhōngwǔ noon
中心 zhōngxīn center
中學 zhōngxué middle school
中旬 zhōngxún middle ten days of a month
中央 zhōngyāng central: 中央銀行 central bank
中庸 zhōngyōng moderation: 中庸之道 golden mean; mediocre; Doctrine of the Mean (⇔ 四書)
中止 zhōngzhǐ stop halfway

仲 69 zhòng
26 Person 人 in the middle 中 (phonetic). between ⇔ 昆仲
仲裁 zhòngcái arbitrate
仲介 zhòngjiè mediate: 仲介人 middleman

忠 69 zhōng
27 Centered 中 (phonetic) heart 心. loyal, faithful, devoted
忠誠 zhōngchéng faithful, loyal
忠告 zhōnggào exhortation
忠厚 zhōnghòu honest and kind
忠實 zhōngshí faithful
忠孝 zhōngxiào loyalty and filial piety
忠心 zhōngxīn loyalty, faithfulness, devotion

衷 69 zhōng
28 Inner 中 (phonetic) clothes 衣. underwear; inner feelings; sincere, virtuous, proper
衷心 zhōngxīn wholehearted, heartfelt

沖 69 chōng
29 [冲] Water 水 with 中 phonetic. Simplified

口
69

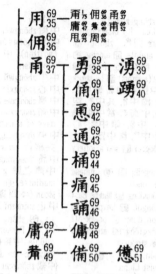

往事^{Ih}, 人事^{IO}, 從事^{I6}, 指
事^I, 公事^I, 私事^{II}, 同事^{Iq},
小事^{Ih}, 省事^{Iq}, 瑣事^{Iq}, 時
事^{Iq}, 故事^{Ih}, 做事^{Ih}, 世
事^{Iq}, 沒事^{Iq}, 處事^{Ih}, 大
事^{Iq}, 領事^{Iq}, 國事^{Iq}, 凡
事^{Iq}, 刑事^{Iq}, 辦事^{Iq}, 樂
事^{Iq}, 回事^{Iq}, 喜事^{Iq}, 幹
事^{Iq}, 董事^{Iq}, 肇事^{Iq}, 心
事^{Iq}, 軼事^{Iq}, 鬧事^{Iq}, 壞
事^{Iq}, 實事求是^{Iq}, 婚事^{Iq},
出事^{IIO}, 理事^{Iq}, 戰事^{I36}, 家
事^{I55}, 軍事^{Iq}, 雜事^{Iq}

事變 shìbiàn 图 incident

事端 shìduān 图 incident,
disturbance

事故 shìgù 图 accident

事後 shìhòu 图 afterwards, ex
post

事件 shìjiàn 图 event, incident

事前 shìqián 图 beforehand, ex
ante

事情 shìqíng 图 matter, affair,
business

事實 shìshí 图 fact: 事實上 in
fact, actually

事事 shìshì 图 everything

事物 shìwù 图 thing

事務 shìwù 图 business, affairs

事先 shìxiān 图 beforehand, ex
ante

事項 shìxiàng 图 item

事業 shìyè 图 business

---

form uses ice 冫⁷⁵. 图 rinse,
flush 图 infuse: 沖茶 make tea
沖淡 chōngdàn 图 dilute
沖洗 chōngxǐ 图 develop
(pictures)

史 69 shǐ
30 Hand 又¹⁴ (altered)
holding a fountain pen resembling 中⁷². 图 scribe 图 history
图 a surname ⇔ 歷史¹⁰⁸
史記 shǐjì 图 Historical Records
- a history written in the
Western Han Dynasty
史料 shǐliào 图 historical ma-
terials

駛 69 shǐ
31 [驶] Modern charac-
ter shows horse 馬¹⁷⁷ with 史⁶⁹
phonetic. 图 fast 图 operate
(a vehicle) ⇔ 駕駛³⁴, 行駛³⁴

吏 69 lì
32 Primary — 丨 scribe
史⁶⁹. 图 official ⇔ 酷吏⁶⁹,
官吏⁶⁷

使 69 shǐ
33 Person 人¹⁰ acting as
official 吏⁶⁹ (pronunciation
atavistically from 史⁶⁹). 图
envoy 图 use 图 cause, make
⇔ 縱使⁶⁹, 唆使⁶⁹, 假使⁶⁹,
特使⁶⁹, 即使⁶⁹, 大使⁶⁹, 天
使⁶⁹, 行使⁶⁹, 倘使⁶⁹, 驅
使⁶⁹, 迫使⁶⁹, 促使⁶⁹
使出 shǐchū 图 exert
使得 shǐdé 图 make, render
使館 shǐguǎn 图 legation
使節 shǐjié 图 envoy
使勁 shǐjìn 图 exert all one's
strength
使命 shǐmìng 图 mission: 使命
感 sense of mission
使用 shǐyòng 图 use, utilize: 使
用者 user

事 69 shì
34 Scribe 史⁶⁹ with 之⁶⁹
(abbreviated) phonetic. 图
job, occupation 图 affair,
matter, business: 不關你的
事 none of your business ⇔

用 69 yòng
35 Divine 卜²⁶ (altered)
and center 中⁶⁹ (altered). 图
use 图 usefulness: 這個有
什麼用? Of what use is this?
⇔ 不用^{Io}, 食用^{Iq}, 有用^{Iq},
公用^{Iq}, 作用^{Iq}, 套用^{Iq}, 享
用^{Iq}, 佔用^{Iq}, 聘用^{Iq}, 服
用^{Iq}, 沒用^{Iq}, 效用^{Iq}, 零
用^{Iq}, 試用^{Iq}, 功用^{Iq}, 任
用^{Iq}, 引用^{Iq}, 費用^{Iq}, 信
用^{Iq}, 使用⁶⁹, 備用^{Iq}, 日
用⁷⁶, 適用^{Iq}, 雇用^{Iq}, 僱
用^{Iq}, 挪用^{Iq}, 御用^{Iq}, 實
用^{Iq}, 採用^{IO3}, 利用^{Iq}, 租

用[1/2], 耐用[1/4], 濫用[1/2], 運用[1/5], 應用[1/2]

用法 yòngfǎ 图 usage
用功 yònggōng 圈 diligent
用戶 yònghù 图 customer
用具 yòngjù 图 utensil, appliance
用來 yònglái 图 used for
用力 yònglì 圈 exert self
用途 yòngtú 图 use
用心 yòngxīn 圈 diligent 圈 diligently

佣 69 yòng
36 For person's 人[p] use 用[务] (phonetic). 图 commission

佣金 yòngjīn 图 commission 图 kickback: 收取佣金 take kickbacks

甬 69 yǒng
37 Bud ㄥ[6] with 用[务] phonetic. 图 bud, burst forth.

勇 69 yǒng
38 Burst forth 甬[务] (phonetic) with strength 力[f]. 圈 brave

勇敢 yǒnggǎn 圈 brave, bold
勇氣 yǒngqì 图 courage

湧 69 yǒng
39 [涌] Water 水[念] rushing forward 勇[务] (phonetic). 圈 gush, surge ⇔ 洶湧[念]

湧現 yǒngxiàn 圈 emerge en masse

踊 69 yǒng
40 [踴] Feet 足[务] rushing forward 勇[务] (phonetic). 圈 leap

踊躍 yǒngyuè 圈 leap 圈 enthusiastically

俑 69 yǒng
41 Person 人[p] with 甬[务] phonetic. 图 tomb figure: 兵馬俑 terra-cotta warriors

慂 69 yǒng
42 Heart 心[83] and bud 甬[务] (phonetic). 图 urge ⇔ 慫慂[2]

通 69 tōng
43 Move 辵[务] forth 甬[务] (phonetic). 圈 passable, open 圈 move unobstructed 圈 all 圈 coherent 图 expert: 中國通 sinologist ⇔ 卡通[务], 不通[么], 共通[务], 亨通[么], 普通[务], 交通[务], 接通[务], 流通[务], 疏通[务], 暢通[么], 開通[务], 貫通[务], 變通[153], 串通[157], 靈通[61], 溝通[75]

通常 tōngcháng 圈 usually, normally
通道 tōngdào 图 passageway, thoroughfare
通牒 tōngdié 图 diplomatic note: 最後通牒 ultimatum
通風 tōngfēng 图 ventilation, circulation 图 leak (information)
通告 tōnggào 圈 announce, notify publicly 图 public notice, announcement
通過 tōngguò 圈 pass through 圈 be approved
通紅 tōnghóng 圈 bright red
通貨 tōnghuò 图 currency: 通貨膨脹 inflation
通姦 tōngjiān 圈 commit adultery 图 adultery
通靈 tōnglíng 圈 mediate with spirits
通勤 tōngqín 圈 commute
通順 tōngshùn 圈 fluid (writing)
通俗 tōngsú 圈 popular, common
通通 tōngtōng 圈 all, without exception
通宵 tōngxiāo 圈 all night
通信 tōngxìn 圈 correspond
通行 tōngxíng 圈 pass through 圈 passable, open to traffic
通訊 tōngxùn 图 communication: 通訊錄 address book
通則 tōngzé 图 general rule
通知 tōngzhī 圈 notify, inform

桶 69 tǒng
44 Wood 木[f] with 甬[务] phonetic. 图 圈 bucket, barrel ⇔ 馬桶[77]

痛 69 tòng
45 Sickness 疒[7/6] with 甬[务] phonetic. 圈 hurt, ache 图 ache, pain ⇔ 酸痛[务], 背痛[务], 苦痛[务], 疼痛[务], 慘痛[务], 頭痛[务], 牙痛[务], 悲痛[务]

痛楚 tòngchǔ 图 agony
痛恨 tònghèn 圈 hate bitterly
痛苦 tòngkǔ 图 suffering, pain
痛快 tòngkuài 圈 delighted, happy, joyful
痛心 tòngxīn 圈 pained, grieved

誦 69 sòng
46 [诵] Words 言[务] budding 甬[务] (phonetic). 圈 chant ⇔ 背誦[务], 朗誦[务], 吟誦[务]

庸 69 yōng
47 Pound 庚[务] and use 用[务] (phonetic). 圈 use 圈 mediocre ⇔ 附庸[务], 中庸[务], 昏庸[务]

庸碌 yōnglù 圈 common, mediocre
庸俗 yōngsú 圈 vulgar, uncultured

傭 69 yōng
48 [佣务] Use 庸[务] (phonetic) a person 人[p]. 圈 employ, hire 图 servant ⇔ 雇傭[务]

傭兵 yōngbīng 图 mercenary

葡 69 bèi
49 Self restraint (abbreviated from an ancient character resembling 苟[务]) in use 用[务]. 图 prepare (⇨ 備[务])

備 69 bèi
50 [备] Person 人[p] prepared 葡[务] (phonetic). Simplified form uses 夂[务] and 田[11]. 圈 prepare 圈 be equipped with 图 equipment ⇔ 籌備[务], 設備[务], 戒備[务], 配備[务], 儲備[务], 責備[务], 裝

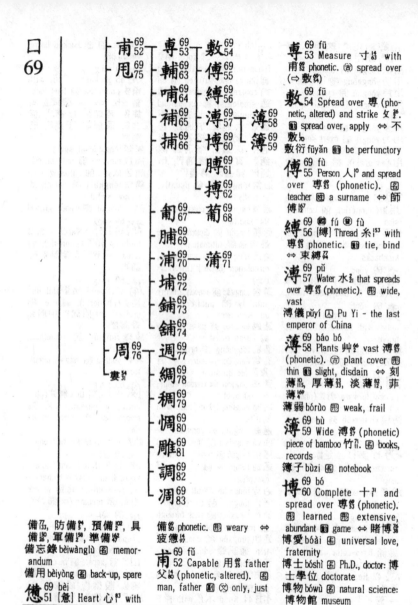

専 69 fū
53 Measure 寸 with 甫 phonetic. spread over (⇨ 敷)

敷 69 fū
54 Spread over 専 (phonetic, altered) and strike 攵. spread over, apply ⇔ 不敷
敷衍 fūyǎn be perfunctory

傅 69 fù
55 Person 人 and spread over 専 (phonetic). teacher a surname ⇔ 師傅

縛 69 fú fù
56 [缚] Thread 糸 with 専 phonetic. tie, bind ⇔ 束縛

溥 69 pǔ
57 Water 水 that spreads over 専 (phonetic). wide, vast
溥儀 pǔyí Pu Yi - the last emperor of China

薄 69 báo bó
58 Plants 艸 vast 溥 (phonetic). plant cover thin slight, disdain ⇔ 刻薄, 厚薄, 淡薄, 菲薄
薄弱 bórùo weak, frail

簿 69 bù
59 Wide 溥 (phonetic) piece of bamboo 竹. books, records
簿子 bùzi notebook

博 69 bó
60 Complete 十 and spread over 専 (phonetic). learned extensive, abundant game ⇔ 賭博
博愛 bóài universal love, fraternity
博士 bóshì Ph.D., doctor: 博士學位 doctorate
博物 bówù natural science: 博物館 museum

備, 防備, 預備, 具備, 軍備, 準備
備忘錄 bèiwànglù memorandum
備用 bèiyòng back-up, spare

憊 69 bèi
51 [惫] Heart 心 with

備 phonetic. weary ⇔ 疲憊

甫 69 fū
52 Capable 用 father 父 (phonetic, altered). man, father only, just

膊 69 bó
61 Flesh 肉[12] with 尃[62] phonetic. 图 upper arms, shoulders ⇔ 胳膊[63], 赤膊[63]

搏 69 bó
62 Hands 手[19] spread out 尃 (phonetic). 励 struggle, wrestle ⇔ 脈搏[120]
搏鬥 bódòu 励 battle, wrestle, fight

輔 69 fǔ
63 [辅] Cart 車[150] with 甫[62] phonetic and suggestive of strength. 图 sidebars on a cart 励 assist ⇔ 相輔相成[152]
輔導 fǔdǎo 励 guide 图 guidance
輔助 fǔzhù 励 support, assist
輔佐 fǔzuǒ 励 assist

哺 69 bǔ
64 Mouth 口[68] with 甫[62] phonetic. 励 nurse
哺乳 bǔrǔ 励 nurse, breast-feed: 哺乳動物 mammal

補 69 bǔ
65 [补] Cloth 衣[26] with 甫[62] phonetic. Simplified form uses 卜[78]. 励 mend, repair, patch 图 supplement ⇔ 修補[29], 貼補[63], 彌補[63], 填補[53], 候補[33], 滋補[33], 遞補[72], 增補[44]
補償 bǔcháng 励 compensate
補充 bǔchōng 励 supplement
補救 bǔjiù 励 rectify, remedy
補考 bǔkǎo 励 retake an exam
補品 bǔpǐn 图 tonic
補貼 bǔtiē 图 subsidy
補習 bǔxí 励 take supplementary classes: 補習班 cram school
補藥 bǔyào 图 tonic
補助 bǔzhù 图 subsidize: 補助金 subsidy, allowance

捕 69 bǔ
66 Hand 手[19] with 甫[62] phonetic. 励 catch, seize ⇔

拘捕[83], 逮捕[87]
捕捉 bǔzhuō 励 catch, capture

匍 69 pú
67 Body doubled over 勹[18] with 甫[62] phonetic. 励 crawl
匍匐 púfú 励 crawl

葡 69 pú
68 Crawling 匍[67] (phonetic) plant 艸[97]. 图 grape-vine
葡萄 pútáo 图 grape: 葡萄酒 wine; 葡萄柚 grapefruit; 葡萄乾 raisin
葡萄牙 pútáoyá 图 Portugal

脯 69 pú
69 Flesh 肉[12] with 甫[62] phonetic. 图 dried meat, dried fruit 图 chest ⇔ 胸脯[4]

浦 69 pú
70 Water 水[3] with 甫[62] phonetic. 图 shore, bank
浦東 pǔdōng 图 Pudong – a region of Shanghai

蒲 69 pú
71 Plant 艸[97] that grows by the riverside 浦[70] (phonetic). 图 rush
蒲公英 púgōngyīng 图 dandelion

埔 69 pǔ
72 Earth 土[7] with 甫[62] phonetic. 图 plain ⇔ 柬埔寨[72]

鋪 69 pū pù
73 [铺] Metal 金[1] with 甫[62] phonetic. pū: 励 lay, spread out pù: 图 store, shop ⇔ 店鋪[63], 當鋪[63]
鋪路 pūlù 励 pave the way

舖 69 pù
74 [铺房] Shed 舍[38] with 甫[62] phonetic. 图 berth, bunk ⇔ 床鋪[63], 臥鋪[42]
舖位 pùwèi 图 bunk, berth

甩 69 shuǎi
75 A modern character from useful 用[62] with elongated stroke suggesting

disposal. 励 throw off, leave behind: 把他甩了 dump him 励 swing

周 69 zhōu
76 How should use 用[62] mouth 口[68]. 图 cautious 图 circuit 围 all around 励 help, assist 图 a surname: 周恩來 Zhou Enlai ⇔ 衆所周知[82], 四周[82], 圓周[50]
周代 zhōudài 图 Zhou Dynasty
周到 zhōudào 围 thoughtful, considerate
周密 zhōumì 围 careful and attentive
周全 zhōuquán 围 thoughtful
周圍 zhōuwéi 图 circumference 图 surroundings
周詳 zhōuxiáng 围 detailed and complete
周旋 zhōuxuán 励 deal with (people)
周易 zhōuyì 图 I-Qing, Book of Changes (⇒ 易經[63])

週 69 zhōu
77 [周期] Modern form shows movement 辵[1] around 周[76] (phonetic). 图 cycle 图 week
週刊 zhōukān 图 weekly magazine
週末 zhōumò 图 weekend
週年 zhōunián 图 anniversary
週轉 zhōuzhuǎn 图 turnover: 週轉不靈 illiquid

綢 69 zhōu
78 [绸] Silk thread 糸[153] with 周[76] phonetic. 图 silk ⇔ 絲綢[153]
綢緞 chóuduàn 图 silk and satin

稠 69 chóu
79 Rice 禾[108] all around 周[76] (phonetic). 围 thick, dense
稠密 chóumì 围 dense

惆 69 chóu
80 Heart 心[83] with 周[76] phonetic. 围 melancholy

字譜及字典

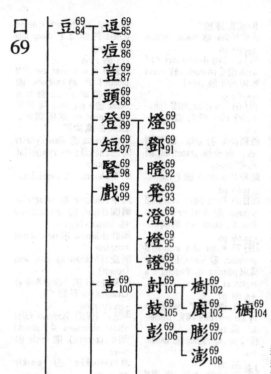

豆 69/84 — 逗 69/85
痘 69/86
荳 69/87
頭 69/88
登 69/89 — 燈 69/90
短 69/97 — 鄧 69/91
豎 69/98 — 瞪 69/92
戲 69/99 — 凳 69/93
澄 69/94
橙 69/95
證 69/96
壹 69/100 — 封 69/101 — 樹 69/102
鼓 69/105 — 廚 69/103 — 櫥 69/104
彭 69/106 — 膨 69/107
澎 69/108

惆悵 chóuchàng ▢ rueful

雕 69/81 diāo Bird 隹162 with 周% phonetic. ▢ hawk ▢ engrave

雕刻 diāokè ▢ carve, engrave ▢ carving, sculpture

雕塑 diāosù ▢ carve, sculpt ▢ sculpture

雕像 diāoxiàng ▢ statue

調 69/82 [调] tiáo diào Words 言% all around 周% (phonetic). tiáo: ▢ mediate, reconcile ▢ adjust diào: ▢ allocate, transfer ▢ tone, tune ⇔ 高調%, 烹調%, 協調%, 聲調%, 空調%, 腔調%, 強調%, 陳腔濫調%,

步調%, 失調%, 論調%, 單調%, 濫調%

調撥 diàobō ▢ allocate (funds)

調查 diàochá ▢ investigate: 調查表 questionnaire

調動 diàodòng ▢ mobilize ▢ transfer, shift

調度 diàodù ▢ dispatch, deploy

調配 diàopèi ▢ allocate, distribute, deploy

調和 tiáohé ▢ mediate, reconcile ▢ compromise

調劑 tiáojì ▢ adjust

調節 tiáojié ▢ adjust, regulate

調解 tiáojiě ▢ mediate, reconcile

調配 tiáopèi ▢ blend, mix

調情 tiáoqíng ▢ flirt

調停 tiáotíng ▢ mediate, intervene

調味 tiáowèi ▢ flavor, season

調整 tiáozhěng ▢ adjust

凋 69/83 diāo Ice 冫25 all around 周% (phonetic). ▢ wither

凋敝 diāobì ▢ exhausted, emaciated

凋零 diāolíng ▢ wither ▢ pass away

凋謝 diāoxiè ▢ pass away

豆 69/84 Pictograph of a serving container 口%. ▢ ceremonial serving dish ▢ bean ⇔ 蠶豆%, 黃豆%, 大豆%, 綠豆%, 土豆%

豆腐 dòufǔ ▢ tofu: 豆腐乾 dried tofu

豆漿 dòujiāng ▢ soy milk

豆芽 dòuyá ▢ bean sprout

逗 69/85 dòu Movement 辶% with 豆% phonetic. ▢ pause ▢ tease, play with: 逗孩子 play with children ▢ funny ⇔ 挑逗%

逗號 dòuhào ▢ comma

逗留 dòuliú ▢ stop over, linger

逗弄 dòunòng ▢ tease

逗趣 dòuqù ▢ amuse

逗人 dòurén ▢ amuse ▢ amusing

逗笑 dòuxiào ▢ amuse

痘 69/86 dòu Sickness 疒% that produces bean-like 豆% (phonetic) bumps. ▢ smallpox ⇔ 水痘%

荳 69/87 dòu [豆%] Bean 豆% (phonetic) plants 艸%. ▢ legumes

荳蔻 dòukòu ▢ nutmeg maiden: 荳蔻年華 teenage years (of girls)

頭 69 tóu tou

88 [头] Head 頁 with 豆 phonetic. Simplified form uses 大. head top beginning: 從頭到尾 from start to finish ⇔ 人頭, 額頭, 老頭, 斧頭, 拳頭, 石頭, 枕頭, 饅頭, 點頭, 芋頭, 奶頭, 碰頭, 磕頭, 念頭, 風頭, 妍頭, 劈頭, 接頭, 抬頭, 磚頭, 山頭, 口頭, 叩頭, 舌頭, 鏡頭, 回頭, 街頭, 外頭, 鐘頭, 木頭, 肩頭, 心頭, 禿頭, 裡頭, 苗頭, 鋤頭, 虎頭蛇尾, 蠅頭小利, 兆頭, 前頭, 箭頭, 插頭, 龍頭, 骨頭, 彈頭, 搖頭, 罐頭, 碼頭

頭版 tóubǎn front page
頭部 tóubù head
頭等 tóuděng first-class
頭髮 tóufǎ hair
頭盔 tóukuī helmet
頭領 tóulǐng chief, leader
頭目 tóumù chief, leader
頭腦 tóunǎo brains
頭皮 tóupí scalp: 頭皮屑 dandruff
頭痛 tóutòng have a headache headache
頭銜 tóuxián title
頭緒 tóuxù lead, clue
頭暈 tóuyūn dizzy

登 69 dēng

89 Feet on vase-like 豆 carriage. mount, step on climb record, register ⇔ 刊登, 攀登

登機 dēngjī board a plane, embark: 登機證 boarding pass
登記 dēngjì register
登陸 dēnglù go ashore
登山 dēngshān mountain climb

燈 69 dēng

90 [灯] Modern form shows fire 火 rising 登 (phonetic). Simplified form uses 丁. lamp, light: 開燈 turn on the light ⇔ 電燈, 幻燈, 檯燈

燈光 dēngguāng lamplight
燈火 dēnghuǒ lights
燈籠 dēnglóng lantern
燈塔 dēngtǎ lighthouse

鄧 69 dèng

91 [邓] City 邑 with 登 phonetic. Simplified form uses 又. an ancient kingdom a surname: 鄧小平 Deng Xiaoping

瞪 92 dèng

Eyes 目 raised 登 (phonetic). stare: 你幹嗎瞪著我? Why are you staring at me? ⇔ 目瞪口呆

瞪著 dèngzhe stare at

凳 69 dèng

93 Small table 几 with 登 phonetic. stool, bench ⇔ 板凳

凳子 dèngzi stool, bench

澄 94 chéng

Water 水 with 登 phonetic. clear

澄清 chéngqīng clarify clear

橙 69 chéng

95 Tree 木 with 登 phonetic. orange ⇔ 柳橙

證 69 zhèng

96 [证] Words 言 with 登 phonetic. testify, prove proof, evidence certificate: 學生證 student I.D. 簽證, 佐證, 反證, 作證, 印證, 辯證, 保證, 實證, 見證, 例證, 罪證

證據 zhèngjù evidence
證明 zhèngmíng proof prove
證券 zhèngquàn, zhèngjuàn security: 證券市場 securities markets
證人 zhèngrén witness
證實 zhèngshí confirm, corroborate

短 69 duǎn

97 Dart/arrow 矢 with 豆 phonetic. short, brief ⇔ 長短, 縮短, 簡短

短波 duǎnbō short wave
短程 duǎnchéng short distance
短處 duǎnchù shortcoming
短絀 duǎnchù shortcoming
短褲 duǎnkù shorts
短篇 duǎnpiān short article: 短篇小說 short story
短期 duǎnqī short-term
短缺 duǎnquē deficient, insufficient
短暫 duǎnzhàn brief

豎 69 shù

98 [竖] Sturdy 取 with 豆 phonnetic. vertical: 豎著寫 write vertically vertical calligraphy stroke ⇔ 橫豎

豎立 shùlì stand erect

戲 69 xì

99 [戏] Lance 戈 with an ancient character from tiger 虍 and dish 豆 phonetic. Simplified form uses 又. play, drama game play 嬉戲, 把戲, 遊戲, 兒戲, 馬戲

戲劇 xìjù drama, play
戲曲 xìqǔ traditional opera
戲院 xìyuàn theater

壴 69 zhù

100 Celebratory dishes 豆 and a stick 屮. drum (⇨ 鼓)

尌 69 shū

101 Drum 壴 held by hand 寸. vertical, standing

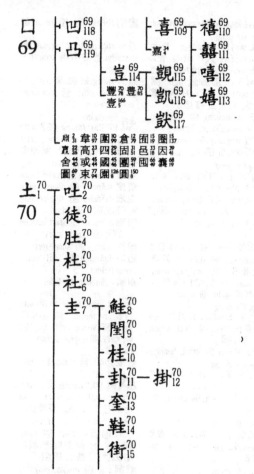

樹 69 shù
102 [树] Wood 木 vertical 尌 (phonetic). Simplified form uses 對's simplification. 🔲 tree ⇔ 松樹, 楓樹, 柏樹, 棗樹, 爬樹, 栗樹.
樹幹 shùgàn 🔲 tree trunk
樹林 shùlín 🔲 forest

樹木 shùmù 🔲 tree
樹皮 shùpí 🔲 bark
樹梢 shùshāo 🔲 twig
樹枝 shùzhī 🔲 tree branch

廚 69 chú
103 [厨] Open-sided roof 厂 with 尌 phonetic. Simplified form uses 厂, 豆 and 寸. 🔲 kitchen

廚房 chúfáng 🔲 kitchen
廚師 chúshī 🔲 cook: 大廚師 chef

櫥 69 chú
104 [橱] Wood 木 in the kitchen 廚 (phonetic). 🔲 cabinet, cupboard ⇔ 壁櫥
櫥窗 chúchuāng 🔲 display window
櫥櫃 chúguì 🔲 cabinet, cupboard

鼓 69 gǔ
105 Drum 壴 struck by stick-holding hand 支. 🔲 drum 🔲 rouse ⇔ 鳴鼓
鼓吹 gǔchūi 🔲 advocate
鼓勵 gǔlì 🔲 encourage
鼓起 gǔqǐ 🔲 rouse: 鼓起勇氣 get up the courage
鼓舞 gǔwǔ 🔲 encourage, inspire
鼓掌 gǔzhǎng 🔲 applaud, clap

彭 69 péng
106 Drum 壴 with 彡 representing beats. 🔲 big 🔲 a surname

膨 69 péng
107 Flesh 肉 big 彭 (phonetic). 🔲 swell
膨脹 péngzhàng 🔲 inflate, swell

澎 69 pēng péng
108 Water 水 beating 彭 (phonetic). pēng: 🔲 roar of waves
澎湖 pénghú 🔲 Pescadores Islands
澎湃 pēngpài 🔲 surge

喜 69 xǐ
109 Mouth 口 and drum 壴. 🔲 happy 🔲 like happiness ⇔ 恭喜, 驚喜, 欣喜, 歡喜
喜愛 xǐ'ài 🔲 like, enjoy
喜好 xǐhào 🔲 like, enjoy
喜歡 xǐhuān 🔲 like, enjoy
喜酒 xǐjǐu 🔲 wedding banquet
喜劇 xǐjù 🔲 comedy
喜怒哀樂 xǐnùāilè 🔲 primary emotions - joy, anger, sorrow and delight

喜鵲 xǐquè 图 magpie
喜事 xǐshì 图 joyous occasion (especially a wedding)
喜筵 xǐyán 图 wedding banquet
喜悦 xǐyuè 图 joy

禧 69 xǐ
110 Omen 示丝 of happiness 喜兹 (phonetic). 图 blessings: 恭賀新禧! Happy New Year!

囍 69 xǐ
111 Double happiness 喜兹. 图 marital bliss

嘻 69 xī
112 Mouth 口⁶⁹ revealing happiness 喜兹 (phonetic). 图 laugh, giggle
嘻笑 xīxiào 图 giggle

嬉 69 xī
113 Woman 女⁴ and happiness 喜兹 (phonetic). 图 play
嬉皮 xīpí 图 hippie
嬉戲 xīxì 图 play about

豈 69 qǐ
114 [岂] Celebratory dish 豆兹 with 微⁴ (abbreviated to 山¹⁷) phonetic. Simplified form uses 己¹⁷. 图 celebrate 豈 is it (rhetorical) 豈不 qǐbù 图 would it not be (rhetorical)

覬 69 jì
115 [觊] See 見¹⁴ with 豈兹 phonetic. 图 covet
覬覦 jìyú 图 covet, desire

凱 69 kǎi
116 [凯] Celebrate 豈 with 几³ phonetic. 图 victory
凱旋 kǎixuán 图 return triumphant

獃 69 dāi
117 [呆另] Dog 犬¹ with 豈兹 phonetic. 图 stupid
獃子 dāizi 图 idiot

凹 69 āo
118 Square (resembling 口⁶⁹) with indented section. 图 indented, concave
凹進 āojìn 图 indented, concave

凸 69 tū 图 tú
119 Square (resembling 口⁶⁹) with protruding section. 图 protrude 图 convex
凸出 túchū 图 convex
凸顯 túxiǎn 图 highlight, accentuate

土 70 tǔ
1 Pictograph of object rising through the earth. 图 soil, earth, dirt 图 land, ground 图 uncultured ⇔ 水土⅔, 泥土⅖, 鄉土⅖, 黏土⅖, 領土⅙, 國土⅖, 糞土⅖, 本土⅗, 塵土¹²
土地 tǔdì 图 land: 土地改革 land reform
土豆 tǔdòu 图 potato
土耳其 tǔěrqí 图 Turkey
土匪 tǔfěi 图 bandit
土話 tǔhuà 图 dialect 图 local expression
土壤 tǔrǎng 图 soil

吐 70 tǔ tù
2 From mouth 口⁶⁹ to ground 土⁷ (phonetic). tǔ: 图 spit tù: 图 vomit, throw up ⇔ 嘔吐⅖, 談吐⅖
吐痰 tǔtán 图 spit: 請勿吐痰. Please do not spit.

徒 70 tú
3 Motion 辵⁹ along the ground 土⁷ (phonetic). 图 go on foot 图 disciple ⇔ 教徒⅖, 學徒⅖, 信徒⅖, 叛徒⅖, 歹徒¹², 師徒⅖, 匪徒⅕
徒步 túbù 图 go on foot
徒弟 túdì 图 disciple
徒然 túrán 图 in vain
徒刑 túxíng 图 prison sentence: 二十年徒刑 20-year sentence

肚 70 dù dǔ
4 Flesh 肉¹² protrud-
ing 土⁷ (phonetic). dù: 图 belly dǔ: 图 stomach ⇔ 拉肚子兹
肚臍 dùjí 图 navel
肚子 dǔzi 图 tripe
肚子 dùzi 图 belly, abdomen: 肚子痛 stomach ache

杜 70 dù
5 Tree 木⁷ with 土⁷ phonetic. 图 sweet pear tree 图 block 图 a surname: 杜甫 Du Fu - a Tang Dynasty poet
杜鵑 dùjuān 图 cuckoo: 杜鵑花 azalea
杜絕 dùjué 图 eradicate
杜撰 dùzhuàn 图 fabricate

社 70 shè
6 Omen 示丝 and earth 土⁷. 图 god of land 图 association, organization, society ⇔ 公社¹⁷, 報社¹⁷, 分社⅖, 旅社⅖, 徵信社¹⁸, 會社¹⁸
社會 shèhuì 图 society: 黑社會 secret societies, triads, underworld; 社會科學 social science; 社會學 sociology; 社會主義 socialism; 社會黨 Socialist Party
社論 shèlùn 图 editorial
社區 shèqū 图 community
社團 shètuán 图 association, club

圭 70 guī
7 Land 土⁷ doubled. 图 feudal lands 图 jade tablet symbolizing feudal authority

鮭 70 guī
8 [鲑] Fish 魚¹⁸⁰ with 圭⁷ phonetic. 图 salmon
鮭魚 guīyú 图 salmon

閨 70 guī
9 [闺] Door 門⁷⁹ with 圭⁷ phonetic. 图 small door
閨房 guīfáng 图 boudoir

桂 70 guì
10 Wood 木⁷ with 圭⁷ phonetic. 图 cinnamon 图 Guangxi Province ⇔ 肉桂¹²

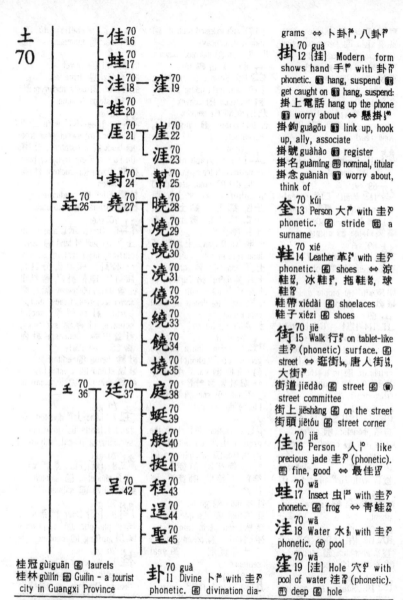

土 70

佳 70 16
蛙 70 17
洼 70 18 — 窪 70 19
娃 70 20
厓 70 21 ┬ 崖 70 22
　　　　 └ 涯 70 23
封 70 24 — 幫 70 25
垚 70 26 — 堯 70 27 ┬ 曉 70 28
　　　　　　　　　 ├ 燒 70 29
　　　　　　　　　 ├ 蹺 70 30
　　　　　　　　　 ├ 澆 70 31
　　　　　　　　　 ├ 僥 70 32
　　　　　　　　　 ├ 繞 70 33
　　　　　　　　　 ├ 饒 70 34
　　　　　　　　　 └ 撓 70 35
壬 70 36 ┬ 廷 70 37 ┬ 庭 70 38
　　　　　　　　　 ├ 蜓 70 39
　　　　　　　　　 ├ 艇 70 40
　　　　　　　　　 └ 挺 70 41
　　　　　 └ 呈 70 42 ┬ 程 70 43
　　　　　　　　　　 ├ 逞 70 44
　　　　　　　　　　 └ 聖 70 45

桂冠 gùiguān laurels
桂林 gùilín Guilin – a tourist city in Guangxi Province

卦 70 11 guà Divine 卜 with 圭 phonetic. divination dia-

掛 70 12 [挂] guà Modern form shows hand 手 with 卦 phonetic. hang, suspend get caught on hang, suspend: 掛上電話 hang up the phone worry about ⇔ 懸掛
掛鉤 guàgōu link up, hook up, ally, associate
掛號 guàhào register
掛名 guàmíng nominal, titular
掛念 guàniàn worry about, think of

奎 70 13 kúi Person 大 with 圭 phonetic. stride a surname

鞋 70 14 xié Leather 革 with 圭 phonetic. shoes ⇔ 涼鞋, 冰鞋, 拖鞋, 球鞋
鞋帶 xiédài shoelaces
鞋子 xiézi shoes

街 70 15 jiē Walk 行 on tablet-like 圭 (phonetic) surface. street ⇔ 逛街, 唐人街, 大街
街道 jiēdào street street committee
街上 jiēshàng on the street
街頭 jiētóu street corner

佳 70 16 jiā Person 人 like precious jade 圭 (phonetic). fine, good ⇔ 最佳

蛙 70 17 wā Insect 虫 with 圭 phonetic. frog ⇔ 青蛙

洼 70 18 wā Water 水 with 圭 phonetic. pool

窪 70 19 [洼] wā Hole 穴 with pool of water 洼 (phonetic). deep hole

窪地 wādì 图 marshland

娃 20 wá Woman 女r with 圭r phonetic. 图 baby
娃娃 wáwa 图 baby: 洋娃娃 doll

厓 21 yái Cliff 厂r with 圭r phonetic. 图 cliff

崖 22 yái yá Mountain 山r cliff 厓r (phonetic). 图 cliff, precipice ⇔ 山崖r, 懸崖r

涯 23 yá Water 水r against a cliff 厓r (phonetic). 图 limit ⇔ 無涯r, 生涯r

封 24 fēng Land 土r and grow 之r (together resembling 圭r) with hand 寸r representing authority. 图 feudal domain 图 seal, block 图 measureword for correspondence ⇔ 畫地自封r, 密封r, 信封r
封閉 fēngbì 图 close, seal
封建 fēngjiàn 图 feudal: 封建主義 feudalism
封面 fēngmiàn 图 cover (of a book or magazine)
封鎖 fēngsuǒ 图 blockade

幫 25 bāng [帮] Sealed 封r (phonetic) by silk 帛r. Simplified form uses 邦r. 图 sides of a shoe 图 help: 請幫我一下。 Please give me a hand. 图 gang: 四人幫 Gang of Four
幫會 bānghuì 图 gang, triad
幫忙 bāngmáng 图 help: 幫不上忙 unable to help; 幫你的忙 help you
幫派 bāngpài 图 gang: 幫派分子 gangster
幫手 bāngshǒu 图 assistant
幫兇 bāngxiōng 图 accomplice

幫主 bāngzhǔ 图 gang leader
幫助 bāngzhù 图 help

垚 26 yáo Earth 土r piled up.

堯 27 [尧] Earth piled up 垚r on a base 兀r. 图 high 囚 Yao - legendary king of ancient China and inventor of calendar 图 a surname
堯舜 yáoshùn 囚 Yao and Shun - legendary kings of ancient China

曉 28 xiǎo [晓] Sun 日r rising high 堯r (phonetic). 图 dawn 图 know ⇔ 知曉r, 分曉r
曉得 xiǎode 图 know: 我不曉得。 I don't know.

燒 29 shāo [烧] Fire 火r burning high 堯r (phonetic). 图 burn 图 bake, roast ⇔ 紅燒r, 焚燒r, 發燒r, 燃燒r
燒餅 shāobǐng 图 baked wheat cake
燒燬 shāohuǐ 图 burn down
燒賣 shāomài 图 steamed dumpling
燒香 shāoxiāng 图 burn incense: 燒香拜佛 burn incense for Buddha

蹺 30 qiāo qiào [跷] Feet 足r up high 堯r (phonetic). 图 raise one's feet ⇔ 高蹺r
蹺課 qiàokè 图 skip class

澆 31 jiāo [浇] Water 水r raised high 堯r (phonetic). 图 sprinkle 图 irrigate, water
澆灌 jiāoguàn 图 irrigate
澆花 jiāohuā 图 water flowers
澆水 jiāoshuǐ 图 water plants

僥 32 jiǎo [侥] Person 人r with 堯r phonetic. 图 lucky
僥倖 jiǎoxìng 图 luckily, fortu-

nately 图 lucky

繞 33 rào [绕] Thread 糸r with 堯r phonetic. 图 go around, circle ⇔ 圍繞r, 縈繞r, 纏繞r, 環繞r
繞口令 ràokǒulìng 图 tongue twister
繞路 ràolù 图 detour, go around
繞行 ràoxíng 图 orbit
繞嘴 ràozuǐ 图 difficult to pronounce

饒 34 ráo [饶] Food 食r piled high 堯r (phonetic). 图 abundant 图 forgive
饒恕 ráoshù 图 forgive, pardon 图 forgiveness

撓 35 náo [挠] Hand 手r piling up 堯r (phonetic) objects. 图 obstruct ⇔ 阻撓r

壬 36 chěng Person 人r like scholar 士r. Alternatively, person on ground 土r. 图 good 图 stand

廷 37 tíng Go 廴r and stand 壬r (phonetic). 图 imperial court ⇔ 阿根廷r, 朝廷r

庭 38 tíng Roofed 广r courtyard 廷r (phonetic). 图 hall 图 court ⇔ 法庭r, 出庭r, 家庭r
庭園 tíngyuán 图 garden
庭院 tíngyuàn 图 courtyard

蜓 39 tíng Insect 虫r with 廷r phonetic. 图 dragonfly ⇔ 蜻蜓r

艇 40 tǐng Boat 舟r with 廷r phonetic. 图 small boat 潛艇r, 艦艇r

挺 41 tǐng Hand 手r with 廷r phonetic. 图 pull up 图

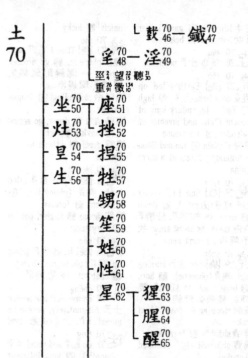

土
70

戴⁷⁰₄₆—鐵⁷⁰₄₇

望⁷⁰₄₈—淫⁷⁰₄₉

坐⁷⁰₅₀┬座⁷⁰₅₁
灶⁷⁰₅₃└挫⁷⁰₅₂

旦⁷⁰₅₄—捏⁷⁰₅₅

生⁷⁰₅₆┬牲⁷⁰₅₇
├甥⁷⁰₅₈
├笙⁷⁰₅₉
├姓⁷⁰₆₀
├性⁷⁰₆₁
└星⁷⁰₆₂┬猩⁷⁰₆₃
├腥⁷⁰₆₄
└醒⁷⁰₆₅

---

straighten 圖 straight, erect
圖 (國) very
挺拔 tǐngbá 圖 tall and straight
挺好 tǐnghǎo (口) (國) excellent
挺直 tǐngzhí 圖 stand upright

呈⁷⁰₄₂ chéng [呈] Make good 土 ❀
with mouth 口 of container.
Simplified form uses 王. (古)
even 圖 report 圖 is 圖 appear,
show ⇔ 辭呈

呈報 chéngbào 圖 report
呈現 chéngxiàn 圖 present,
appear

程⁷⁰₄₃ chéng [程] Grain 禾
measured evenly 呈 (phonetic). 圖 measure 圖 order, procedure 圖 journey 圖 a

---

surname ⇔ 路程, 長程,
計程車, 規程, 航程,
議程, 工程, 短程, 日
程, 課程, 啓程, 方程
式, 歷程, 旅程, 過
程, 進程

程度 chéngdù 圖 degree, extent
程式 chéngshì 圖 computer program
程序 chéngxù 圖 procedure, process

逞⁷⁰₄₄ chéng [逞] Movement 辵
with 呈 phonetic. 圖 fast.
圖 show off: 逞英雄 play the
hero 圖 indulge ⇔ 得逞
逞強 chěngqiáng 圖 show off
one's superiority

聖⁷⁰₄₅ shèng [圣] Hears 耳
reports 呈 (phonetic). 圖
sage 圖 sacred ⇔ 神聖

聖誕 shèngdàn 圖 Christmas: 聖
誕節 Christmas holiday; 聖誕
老人 Santa Claus
聖經 shèngjīng 圖 Bible 圖 holy
book
聖人 shèngrén 圖 sage

戴⁷⁰₄₆ tiě 46 Person 大 (altered)
with an ancient character from
戈 and 呈 phonetic. (古)
large, abundant

鐵⁷⁰₄₇ tiě [铁] Metal 金 that is
abundant 戴 (phonetic).
Simplified form uses 失. 圖
iron ⇔ 鋼鐵, 吸鐵石,
地鐵, 磁鐵
鐵棒 tiěbàng 圖 iron staff
鐵鎚 tiěchuí 圖 hammer
鐵道 tiědào 圖 railroad
鐵路 tiělù 圖 railroad
鐵幕 tiěmù 圖 Iron Curtain
鐵青 tiěqīng 圖 livid, ashen
鐵絲 tiěsī 圖 wire: 鐵絲網 wire
fence

望⁷⁰₄₈ yín 48 Grab 爪 person
王. (古) encroach

淫⁷⁰₄₉ yín 49 Like water 水
encroach 望 (phonetic). 圖
seduce ⇔ 浸淫, 荒淫,
姦淫, 手淫, 賣淫
淫蕩 yíndàng 圖 lewd, licentious
淫穢 yínhuì 圖 obscene, salacious
淫亂 yínluàn 圖 promiscuous

坐⁷⁰₅₀ zuò 50 Two people 人 on the
ground 土. 圖 sit 圖 ride
⇔ 靜坐
坐牢 zuòláo 圖 do time in prison
坐位 zuòwèi 圖 seat
坐下 zuòxià 圖 sit down

座 70 zuò
51 Where sit 坐器 (phonetic) in a room 广只. 图 seat ⇔ 星座器, 插座器

座標 zuòbiāo 图 coordinates

座談 zuòtán 图 group discussion: 座談會 symposium, conference

座位 zuòwèi 图 seat

座右銘 zuòyòumíng 图 motto, maxim

挫 70 cuò
52 Hand 手只 and sit 坐器 (phonetic). 图 defeat ⇔ 受挫器

挫折 cuòzhé 图 frustrate: 挫折感 frustration 图 setback

灶 70 zào
53 Modern form shows fire 火器 in clay 土只. 图 stove 图 kitchen ⇔ 爐灶器

灶神 zàoshén 图 kitchen god

垩 70 niè
54 Clay 土只 hardened in the sun 日只.

捏 70 niè
55 Shaped by the hands 手只 before hardening 垩只. 图 mold, shape 图 pinch

捏造 niēzào 图 fabricate

生 70 shēng
56 Pictograph of a plant rising from ground 土只. 图 grow 图 give birth to, bear, produce: 生孩子 have a child 图 fresh, unripe, raw: 生魚片 sashimi; 图 draft beer ⇔ 一生器, 人生器, 衛生器, 先生器, 花生器, 考生器, 學生器, 醫生器, 寄生器, 男生器, 天生器, 衍生器, 終生器, 新生器, 女生器, 好生器, 畜生器, 滋生器, 孳生器, 謀生器, 陌生器, 刺生器, 門生器, 發生器, 誕生器, 產生器, 僑生器, 野生器, 出生器, 民生器, 前生器, 畢生器, 自力更生器,

優生器, 再生器

生病 shēngbìng 图 get sick, fall ill

生產 shēngchǎn 图 produce 图 production

生存 shēngcún 图 exist, survive

生動 shēngdòng 图 lively, vivid

生根 shēnggēn 图 take root

生活 shēnghuó 图 life 图 live

生計 shēngjì 图 livelihood

生理 shēnglǐ 图 physiology

生命 shēngmìng 图 life: 生命力 vitality

生怕 shēngpà 图 fear

生平 shēngpíng 图 life story

生氣 shēngqì 图 angry: 生他的氣 anger him

生前 shēngqián 图 during lifetime (of deceased person)

生日 shēngrì 图 birthday

生澀 shēngsè 图 confusing, clumsily written

生手 shēngshǒu 图 novice

生疏 shēngshū 图 unfamiliar 图 rusty, out of practice

生死 shēngsǐ 图 life or death

生態 shēngtài 图 ecosystem: 生態學 ecology

生物 shēngwù 图 living creature: 生物學 biology; 生物化學 biochemistry

生肖 shēngxiào 图 (Chinese) zodiac

生效 shēngxiào 图 take effect

生鏽 shēngxiù 图 rust

生涯 shēngyá 图 career, livelihood

生意 shēngyì 图 business: 做生意 do business, be a businessperson

生育 shēngyù 图 bear, give birth: 計劃生育 family planning; 生兒育女 have children

生長 shēngzhǎng 图 grow

生殖 shēngzhí 图 reproduction: 生殖器 genitals

牲 70 shēng
57 Ox 牛只 growing 生器

(phonetic) to maturity. 图 livestock ⇔ 犧牲器

牲畜 shēngchù 图 livestock

甥 70 shēng
58 Birth 生器 (phonetic) and male 男只. 图 nephew (sister's son) ⇔ 外甥器

甥女 shēngnǚ 图 niece (sister's daughter)

笙 70 shēng
59 Bamboo 竹只 that produces 生器 (phonetic) sound. 图 panpipe

姓 70 xìng
60 From a woman 女只 born 生器 (phonetic). 图 surname, family name ⇔ 百姓器

姓名 xìngmíng 图 full name, family and given name

姓氏 xìngshì 图 surname, family name

性 70 xìng
61 One's heart 心只 from birth 生器 (phonetic). 图 nature, disposition 图 sex: 性關係 sexual relations 图 gender ⇔ 悟性器, 線性器, 人性器, 鹼性器, 惰性器, 雄性器, 同性器, 黏性器, 索性器, 特性器, 個性器, 男性器, 韌性器, 天性器, 陰性器, 異性器, 任性器, 女性器, 陽性器, 本性器, 雌性器, 定性器, 理性器, 耐性器, 彈性器, 惡性器

性別 xìngbié 图 sex, gender

性病 xìngbìng 图 venereal disease

性感 xìnggǎn 图 sexy

性格 xìnggé 图 personality

性交 xìngjiāo 图 have sex 图 sexual intercourse

性命 xìngmìng 图 life

性能 xìngnéng 图 function

性情 xìngqíng 图 temperament

性慾 xìngyù 图 sexual desire, libido

土
70

青 66 ┬ 清 70/67
隆 甦 甦 │ 晴 70/68
毒 責 責 │ 蜻 70/69
產 │ 情 70/70
│ 請 70/71
│ 精 70/72
│ 晴 70/73
│ 靖 70/74
│ 猜 70/75
└ 靜 [97]

性質 xìngzhí 图 nature, quality

星 70 xīng
62 Modern character shows sun 日 [76] with 生 phonetic. 图 star ⇔ 衛星, 壽星, 影星, 歌星, 行星, 零星, 流星, 彗星, 外星人, 明星, 剋星

星辰 xīngchén 图 stars
星期 xīngqí 图 week: 星期一 Monday; 星期二 Tuesday; 星期三 Wednesday; 星期四 Thursday; 星期五 Friday; 星期六 Saturday; 星期日 Sunday; 星期天 Sunday
星球 xīngqiú 图 star
星系 xīngxì 图 galaxy
星象 xīngxiàng 图 astrology: 星象學 astrology; 星象家 astrologist
星宿 xīngxiù,xīngsù 图 constellation
星座 xīngzuò 图 constellation, zodiac sign

猩 70 xīng
63 Dog/beast 犬 [9] with 星 phonetic. 图 orangutan
猩猩 xīngxīng 图 orangutan: 黑猩猩 chimpanzee; 大猩猩 gorilla

腥 70 xīng
64 Flesh 肉 [32] with 星 phonetic. 图 smell of carnage ⇔ 血腥

醒 70 xīng
65 Liquor 酉 [159] with 星 phonetic. 動 wake up, come to ⇔ 覺醒, 甦醒, 叫醒, 喚醒, 清醒, 提醒, 睡醒, 蘇醒
醒來 xīnglái 動 wake up
醒悟 xīngwù 動 come to realize

青 70 qīng
66 Color of lush growth 生 that burns red 丹 [7] (often written as 月 [7]). 图 green, blue 图 young ⇔ 年青, 知青, 鐵青, 刺青, 垂青 [173]
青菜 qīngcài 图 green vegetables
青春 qīngchūn 图 youth: 青春痘 acne
青蔥 qīngcōng 图 green onion
青島 qīngdǎo 图 Qingdao – a port city in Shandong Province
青海 qīnghǎi 图 Qinghai Province
青椒 qīngjiāo 图 green pepper
青睞 qīnglài 图 動 favor
青年 qīngnián 图 youth
青色 qīngsè 图 green, blue
青少年 qīngshàonián 图 teenager
青天 qīngtiān 图 blue sky
青銅 qīngtóng 图 bronze: 青銅器 bronzeware; 青銅時代 bronze age
青蛙 qīngwā 图 frog

清 70 qīng
67 Water 水 green/blue 青 (phonetic). 图 clear, pure ⇔ 撇清, 廓清, 認清, 撇清, 澄清, 滿清, 釐清, 濾清
清白 qīngbái 图 innocent, pure, clean
清償 qīngcháng 動 pay off debts
清朝 qīngcháo 图 Qing Dynasty
清澈 qīngchè 图 pure, clear
清晨 qīngchén 图 dawn, early morning
清除 qīngchú 動 purge, liquidate, eliminate
清楚 qīngchǔ 图 clear: 弄清楚 clarify
清單 qīngdān 图 list, inventory
清淡 qīngdàn 图 light (food) 图 calm (life) 图 slack (sales)
清官 qīngguān 图 honest and upright official
清潔 qīngjié 图 clean, sanitary: 清潔劑 detergent
清理 qīnglǐ 動 tidy up 動 settle accounts
清廉 qīnglián 图 honest, incorruptible
清涼 qīngliáng 图 fresh and cool
清明 qīngmíng 图 pure and clear: 清明節 Tomb-Sweeping Day
清爽 qīngshuǎng 图 cool and refreshing 图 relaxed

清算 qīngsuàn [verb] settle accounts

清晰 qīngxī [verb] clear: 清晰度 clarity; 發音清晰 clear pronunciation

清洗 qīngxǐ [verb] wash, cleanse [verb] purge

清新 qīngxīn [adj] refreshing (style)

清醒 qīngxǐng [adj] sober, clear-headed [verb] regain consciousness

清真 qīngzhēn [noun] Islamic: 清真寺 Mosque

晴 70 qíng 68 Modern character shows sun 日76 and blue 青 (phonetic). [adj] clear, sunny

晴天 qíngtiān [noun] clear sky, sunny day

蜻 70 qíng 69 Insect 虫125 with 青 phonetic. [noun] dragonfly

蜻蜓 qīngtíng [noun] dragonfly

情 70 qíng 70 Heart 心61 with 青 phonetic. [noun] feelings [noun] love, passion [noun] situation, condition ⇔ 人情, 友情, 輿情, 神情, 病情, 同情, 無情, 知情, 色情, 恩情, 交情, 行情, 領情, 感情, 熱情, 事情, 調情, 性情, 鍾情, 陳情, 心情, 愛情, 政情, 抒情, 隱情, 煽情, 表情, 濫情

情愛 qíngài [noun] love

情報 qíngbào [noun] intelligence report, information: 中央情報局 C.I.A.

情操 qíngcāo [noun] noble sentiments, integrity

情婦 qíngfù [noun] mistress

情感 qínggǎn [noun] emotion

情節 qíngjié [noun] details [noun] plot (of a movie or play)

情景 qíngjǐng [noun] scene

情況 qíngkuàng [noun] circumstances, situation

情理 qínglǐ [noun] reason, common sense

情侶 qínglǚ [noun] lovers

情趣 qíngqù [noun] appeal

情人 qíngrén [noun] lover: 情人節 Valentine's Day

情勢 qíngshì [noun] situation

情形 qíngxíng [noun] situation

情緒 qíngxù [noun] feeling, emotion: 情緒化 emotional

情誼 qíngyì [noun] friendship

情意 qíngyì [noun] affection, love

情願 qíngyuàn [verb] willing, agree [verb] would rather, prefer to

請 70 qǐng 71 [请] Words 言 with 青 phonetic and suggestive of feelings 情. [verb] request, ask [verb] please: 請坐 please sit down [verb] treat: 我請你. It's on me. [verb] hire, employ ⇔ 申請, 聘請, 邀請, 籲請

請安 qǐngān [verb] pay respects

請假 qǐngjià [verb] ask off, take leave

請柬 qǐngjiǎn [noun] written invitation

請教 qǐngjiào [verb] ask for advice

請客 qǐngkè [verb] host, treat: 我請客. It's on me.

請求 qǐngqiú [verb] request

請帖 qǐngtiě [noun] invitation

請問 qǐngwèn [verb] May I ask...?

請願 qǐngyuàn [verb] petition: 請願書 a petition

精 70 jīng 72 Rice 米73 with 青 phonetic. [adj] select, choice [noun] essence [adj] exquisite, fine ⇔ 味精, 妖精, 酒精

精采 jīngcǎi [adj] brilliant, splendid

精彩 jīngcǎi [adj] brilliant, splendid

精光 jīngguāng [adj] exhausted, completely gone

精華 jīnghuá [noun] essence

精力 jīnglì [noun] stamina, vitality

精煉 jīngliàn [verb] refine, purify

精美 jīngměi [adj] elegant

精密 jīngmì [adj] precise, accurate

精闢 jīngpì [adj] incisive, penetrating

精巧 jīngqiǎo [adj] exquisite, finely crafted

精確 jīngquè [adj] exact, precise

精神 jīngshén [noun] spirit: 精神病 mental illness; 精神污染 spiritual pollution

精細 jīngxì [adj] fine, meticulous

精心 jīngxīn [adv] meticulously

精選 jīngxuǎn [adj] selected, choice

精湛 jīngzhàn [adj] consummate, exquisite

精緻 jīngzhì [adj] exquisite, delicate, fine

精裝 jīngzhuāng [adj] hardbound

精子 jīngzǐ [noun] sperm

睛 70 jīng 73 Eye 目114 with 青 phonetic. [noun] eyeball ⇔ 眼睛

靖 70 jìng 74 Stand 立72 with 青 phonetic. [adj] tranquil [verb] pacify ⇔ 綏靖

猜 70 cāi 75 Dog/beast 犬94 with 青 phonetic. [adj] suspicious [verb] guess: 你猜吧! Guess!

猜測 cāicè [noun] guess

猜忌 cāijì [verb] jealously suspect

猜想 cāixiǎng [verb] guess, suppose

猜疑 cāiyí [verb] suspect

丰 70 fēng 76 Plant growing 生 and taking root. [adj] lush, abundant (⇒ 豐)

丰采 fēngcǎi [adj] attractive, dashing

丰 70 fēng 77 Abundance of plants 丰.

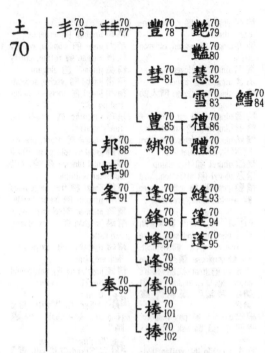

土
70

豐 78 fēng [丰㐱] Container 豆㐱 filled with mountainous 山⁶⁷ abundance 丰㐱 (phonetic). 🔲 abundant, plentiful

豐富 fēngfù 🔲 abundant, plentiful

豐厚 fēnghòu 🔲 plentiful, generous

豐滿 fēngmǎn 🔲 plentiful 🔲 buxom: 身材豐滿 full-figured

豐盛 fēngshèng 🔲 lush 🔲 sumptuous

豐收 fēngshōu 🔲 bumper harvest

豐腴 fēngyú 🔲 plump 🔲 fertile

艶 79 [艳] Prosperous 豐㐱 color 色㐱. 🔲 gorgeous (⇨

豔㐱)

豔 80 [艳㐱] Prosperous 豐㐱 cover 盍㐱. 🔲 gorgeous ⇨ 嬌豔㐱

豔麗 yànlì 🔲 gorgeous

彗 81 Hand 又¹⁴ holding bundle of plants 丰㐱. 🔲 broom

彗星 huìxīng 🔲 comet

慧 82 Well-kept 彗 (phonetic) heart/mind 心¹⁴. 🔲 intelligent ⇨ 穎慧㐱, 智慧㐱, 聰慧㐱⁴⁴

雪 83 Rain 雨¹⁶¹ that requires sweeping 彗㐱 (phonetic, abbreviated). 🔲 snow ⇨ 滑

雪¹⁷³

雪白 xuěbái 🔲 snow-white

雪崩 xuěbēng 🔲 avalanche, snowslide

雪花 xuěhuā 🔲 snowflake

雪茄 xuějiā 🔲 cigar

雪球 xuěqiú 🔲 snowball

鱈 84 xuě [鳕] Fish 魚¹⁹⁰ with flesh white as snow 雪㐱 (phonetic). 🔲 cod

鱈魚 xuěyú 🔲 cod

豊 85 lǐ Vessel 豆㐱 (phonetic) with contents resembling 曲¹³⁵. 🔲 sacrificial vessel

禮 86 lǐ [礼] Obtain revelations 示²₄ with sacrificial vessel 豊㐱. Simplified form uses 乙¹. 🔲 rite, ceremony 🔲 decorum, propriety 🔲 gift ⇨ 聘禮㐱, 無禮㐱, 行禮㐱, 葬禮㐱, 喪禮㐱, 婚禮¹⁰, 典禮¹⁵

禮拜 lǐbài 🔲 week: 禮拜一 Monday; 禮拜二 Tuesday; 禮拜三 Wednesday; 禮拜四 Thursday; 禮拜五 Friday; 禮拜六 Saturday; 禮拜天 Sunday; 禮拜日 Sunday 🔲 religious service: 做禮拜 attend religious services

禮服 lǐfú 🔲 ceremonial dress, formal dress

禮記 lǐjì 🔲 Book of Rites

禮節 lǐjié 🔲 etiquette

禮貌 lǐmào 🔲 polite

禮物 lǐwù 🔲 gift

禮儀 lǐyí 🔲 propriety

體 87 tǐ [体㐱] Bones 骨¹⁷³ and sacrificial vessel 豊㐱 (phonetic). 🔲 body ⇨ 人體¹⁰, 軟體㐱, 群體㐱, 電晶體¹⁵, 硬體¹⁵, 個體㐱, 全體²⁷, 大體²⁷, 立體㐱, 天體㐱, 屍體²⁷, 繁體字㐱, 字體㐱, 團

體²⁷,

字譜及字典 213

體操, 軀體, 媒體, 肢
體, 液體, 晶體, 裸
體, 簡體字, 氣體, 物
體, 整體, 肉體, 身
體, 導體, 具體, 集
體

體操 tǐcāo 图 gymnastics
體會 tǐhuì 動 realize through experience
體檢 tǐjiǎn 图 physical exam
體力 tǐlì 图 physical strength
體面 tǐmiàn 图 dignity, face 形 dignified
體能 tǐnéng 图 physical ability
體認 tǐrèn 動 realize through experience
體貼 tǐtiē 形 considerate, affectionate
體溫 tǐwēn 图 body temperature
體系 tǐxì 图 system
體現 tǐxiàn 動 embody, reflect
體型 tǐxíng 图 body shape
體驗 tǐyàn 動 experience personally, learn through practice
體育 tǐyù 图 athletics: 體育館 gymnasium
體制 tǐzhì 图 system
體重 tǐzhòng 图 body weight

邦 70 bāng
88 City 邑 with 丰 phonetic. 图 country, nation ⇔ 聯邦, 烏托邦
邦交 bāngjiāo 图 diplomatic relations

綁 70 bǎng
89 [绑] Thread 糸 with 邦 phonetic. 動 tie up, bind ⇔ 鬆綁
綁架 bǎngjià 動 kidnap, abduct
綁票 bǎngpiào 動 kidnap and hold for ransom

蚌 70 bàng
90 Insect-like 虫 with 丰 phonetic. 图 clam
蚌殼 bàngké 图 clam shell

夆 70 féng
91 Approach 夂 dense

foliage 丰 (phonetic). 画 meet resistance

逢 70 féng
92 Move 辵 and meet 夆 (phonetic). 動 meet, run into ⇔ 遭逢

縫 70 féng fèng
93 [缝] Thread 糸 meeting 逢 (phonetic). féng: 動 sew fèng: 图 seam ⇔ 裁縫
縫紉 féngrèn 图 sewing: 縫紉機 sewing machine

篷 70 péng
94 Bamboo 竹 with 逢 phonetic. 图 awning ⇔ 帳篷, 斗篷

蓬 70 péng
95 Plant 艸 with 逢 phonetic. 图 an artemisia plant 形 tangled, dishevelled
蓬勃 péngbó 形 vital, vigorous, flourishing

鋒 70 fēng
96 [锋] Modern form shows metal 金 that meets 夆 (phonetic). 图 swordpoint ⇔ 先鋒
鋒利 fēnglì 形 sharp 形 keen, incisive

蜂 70 fēng
97 Insect 虫 that meets 夆 (phonetic) in groups. 图 bee ⇔ 蜜蜂
蜂蜜 fēngmì 图 honey
蜂擁 fēngyǒng 動 swarm

峰 70 fēng
98 Where mountain 山 meets 夆 (phonetic) sky. 图 summit, peak ⇔ 高峰, 顛峰, 頂峰, 山峰

奉 70 fèng
99 Respectfully 廾 hand 手 over an object 丰 (phonetic). 動 offer respectfully 動 receive respectfully 動 admire ⇔ 供奉, 信奉
奉承 fèngchéng 動 flatter

奉告 fènggào 動 inform: 無可奉告 no comment
奉獻 fèngxiàn 動 offer in tribute
奉養 fèngyǎng 動 look after

俸 70 fèng
100 Person 人 and receive respectfully 奉 (phonetic). 图 salary ⇔ 薪俸

棒 70 bàng
101 Wood 木 with 奉 phonetic. 图 stick ⇔ 冰棒, 好棒, 鐵棒
棒球 bàngqiú 图 baseball
棒子 bàngzi 图 stick, club, bat

捧 70 pěng
102 Receive respectfully 奉 (phonetic) with hand 手 redundant. 動 hold in both hands

个 71 gè
1 Pictograph of a bamboo shoot. 图 a, one (⇒ 個)

支 71 zhī
2 Hand 又 stripping a branch 个 (resembling 十). 图 branch, offshoot 動 support, prop up 動 pay, disburse 图 measureword for stick-like objects 動 收支, 分支, 干支, 地支, 開支
支撐 zhīchēng 動 prop up, bolster
支持 zhīchí 動 support 图 support, backing
支出 zhīchū 图 expenditure
支付 zhīfù 動 pay out, disperse
支局 zhījú 图 branch office
支流 zhīliú 图 tributary
支配 zhīpèi 動 allocate, arrange
支票 zhīpiào 图 check: 開支票 write a check
支援 zhīyuán 動 support

枝 71 zhī
3 Tree 木 offshoot 支 (phonetic). 图 branch, twig ⇔ 槍枝, 荔枝, 樹

字譜及字典

土
70

王 培 圳 坎 坒 墾 塘 圣 圾 坡
墮 坤 埂 塞 均 垢 塔 壕 墩
塾 坷 埼 坏 寺 填 董 埃 塞 垃
去 坑 金 塔 塗 城 域 基 型 塑
幸 塾 壁 地 堂 在 墳 墓 坴 壞
境 埔 封 牡 坊 坍 墅 疆 壘 堤
壞 壓 牡 坊 坍 墅 疆 壘 里 埋
塵 墟 塌 至 堊 毀 墁 塊 堅 增
墨 塚 墜 壇 堆 埠 垂 塵

↑
71
1

支 2 ── 枝 71 3
         肢 71 4
         翅 71 5
         技 71 6
         妓 71 7
         伎 71 8
         屐 71 9
         歧 71 10
       ── 鼓 (cross ref)
竹 71 11 ── 篤 71 12

篦 簟 簽 管 簿 筆 符 范
筍 簹 筒 等 簧 節 筋 笠
筷 篆 答 筏 箋 箕 竿 築
笙 簍 第 箱 簿 笙 蓬 籬
籍 笨 策 簡 笆 筵 笑 箏
簾 笛 箱 篇 簫 簇 箭 籠
籃 算 籮 管 節 箭 籤

枝節 zhījié 图 complication 图 secondary, minor: 枝節問題 minor complication

肢 71 zhī 4 Body 肉 offshoot 支 (phonetic). 图 limb ⇔ 四肢
肢體 zhītǐ 图 limbs

翅 71 chì 5 Supporting 支 (phonetic) feathers 羽. 图 wing ⇔ 魚翅
翅膀 chìbǎng 图 wing

技 71 jì 6 Hand 手 with 支 phonetic. 图 skill, technique ⇔ 演技, 科技, 雜技

技工 jìgōng 图 skilled worker
技能 jìnéng 图 technique, mastery
技巧 jìqiǎo 图 technique
技術 jìshù 图 technique 图 technology: 技術性 technical
技藝 jìyì 图 technique

妓 71 jì 7 Woman 女 with 支 phonetic. 图 geisha ⇔ 嫖妓, 藝妓, 娼妓
妓女 jìnǚ 图 prostitute

伎 71 jì 8 Person 人 with 支 phonetic. 图 skill, talent
伎倆 jìliǎng 图 skill, dexterity

屐 71 jī 9 Shoe 履 (abbreviated) with 支 phonetic. 图 clogs ⇔ 木屐

歧 71 qí 10 Stop 止 with 支 phonetic. 图 forked road ⇔ 分歧
歧見 qíjiàn 图 conflicting opinions
歧視 qíshì 图 discriminate against 图 discrimination
歧異 qíyì 图 discrepancy

竹 71 zhú 11 Bamboo shoots ↑. 图 bamboo ⇔ 爆竹
竹編 zhúbiān 图 bamboo weaving
竹竿 zhúgān 图 bamboo pole
竹籃 zhúlán 图 bamboo basket
竹林 zhúlín 图 bamboo grove
竹筍 zhúsǔn 图 bamboo shoot
竹蓆 zhúxí 图 bamboo mat
竹子 zhúzi 图 bamboo

篤 71 dǔ 12 [笃] Horse 馬 with 竹 phonetic. 图 sincere
篤定 dǔdìng 图 confident, assured
篤信 dǔxìn 图 sincerely believe

夕 72 图 xì 图 xī 1 Pictograph of a

crescent moon. 图 evening, dusk ⇔ 除夕 xíxī, 朝夕 zhāoxī, 前夕 qiánxī

夕陽 xìyáng 图 setting sun

汐 72 粵 xì 普 xī
2 Water 水氵 at night 夕 (phonetic). 图 evening tide ⇔ 潮汐 cháoxī

矽 72 xì
3 Stone 石 with 夕 phonetic. 图 silicon: 矽谷 Silicon Valley

多 72 duō
4 Many moons 夕夕. 图 many, much: 太多 too many; 好多了 much better 图 more than: 三十多 more than thirty 图 excessive, extra: 多一個 one extra 圆 how: 多大? How big? 凶多吉少, 衆多, 差不多, 大多, 大多數, 諸多, 許多, 最多

多半 duōbàn 图 most
多大 duōdà 圆 how big 圆 how old
多寡 duōguǎ 图 amount
多久 duōjiǔ 图 how long
多麼 duōme 圆 how, so: 多麼好 excellent
多少 duōshǎo 圆 how many, how much: 多少錢? How much does it cost? 图 more or less, somewhat
多數 duōshù 图 most, majority
多謝 duōxiè 圆 many thanks
多餘 duōyú 图 surplus, leftover, extra
多元化 duōyuánhuà 图 multipolar
多種 duōzhǒng 图 variety

哆 72 duō
5 Mouth 口 with 多 phonetic. 圆 shiver, tremble
哆嗦 duōsuō 圆 shiver, tremble

爹 72 diē
6 Father 父 with 多 phonetic. 图 dad ⇔ 老爹 lǎodiē
爹爹 diēdie 图 daddy

移 72 yí
7 Rice plant 禾 with 多 phonetic. 图 transplant 圆 move, shift 圆 change, alter ⇔ 遷移, 轉移, 挪移
移動 yídòng 圆 shift, move
移居 yíjū 圆 migrate: 移居到美國 emigrate to America
移民 yímín 圆 immigrate, emigrate 图 immigrant, emigrant: 非法移民 illegal immigrant
移植 yízhí 圆 transplant

侈 72 chǐ
8 Person 人 and many 多. 圆 wasteful ⇔ 奢侈
侈談 chǐtán 圆 talk glibly

名 72 míng
9 Mouthed 口 in the dark of evening 夕 to identify. 图 name 图 fame 圆 famous, well-known 圆 a measureword for people: 第一名 first place ⇔ 簽名, 化名, 筆名, 書名, 有名, 匿名, 點名, 無名, 無名氏, 知名, 署名, 別名, 聲名, 大名, 成名, 馳名, 地名, 檔名, 莫名, 莫名其妙, 掛名, 姓名, 著名, 署名, 聞名, 提名, 出名, 排名, 罪名
名產 míngchǎn 图 famous product
名稱 míngchēng 图 name
名詞 míngcí 图 noun: 代名詞 pronoun; 可數名詞 countable noun 图 term
名單 míngdān 图 name list: 黑名單 blacklist
名額 míngé 图 quota
名叫 míngjiào 圆 named, called
名利 mínglì 图 fame and wealth
名目 míngmù 图 term, title 圆 nominal
名牌 míngpái 图 name brand
名片 míngpiàn 图 name card, business card

名氣 míngqì 图 reputation
名人 míngrén 图 celebrity
名聲 míngshēng 图 reputation
名義 míngyì 图 name 图 nominal
名譽 míngyù 图 reputation
名著 míngzhù 图 famous work, masterpiece
名字 míngzì 图 name 图 given name

銘 72 míng
10 [铭] Name 名 (phonetic) in metal 金. 图 inscription ⇔ 座右銘
銘刻 míngkē 圆 inscribe
銘文 míngwén 图 inscription, engraving
銘心 míngxīn 圆 engraved in one's heart

外 72 wài
11 Divine 卜 in the evening 夕, beyond the day's events. 圆 图 outside 圆 foreign ⇔ 格外, 額外, 老外, 賽外, 內外, 另外, 別外, 除外, 國外, 海外, 以外, 關外, 黨外, 意外, 課外, 戶外, 此外, 野外, 媚外, 例外, 排外
外辦 wàibàn 图 粵 foreign affairs office
外幣 wàibì 图 foreign currency
外邊 wàibiān 图 outside
外表 wàibiǎo 图 outward appearance
外賓 wàibīn 图 foreign guest
外國 wàiguó 图 foreign country: 外國人 foreigner
外號 wàihào 图 nickname
外匯 wàihuì 图 foreign exchange
外籍 wàijí 图 foreign nationality
外交 wàijiāo 图 diplomacy
外界 wàijiè 图 outsiders
外科 wàikē 图 surgery: 外科醫生 surgeon
外快 wàikuài 图 supplemental income

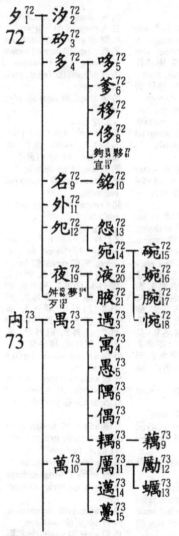

外婆 wàipó 图 grandmother (maternal)
外僑 wàiqiáo 图 foreigner, alien (in China)
外人 wàirén 图 outsider
外商 wàishāng 图 foreign firm
外甥 wàishēng 图 nephew (sister's son): 外甥女 niece (sister's daughter)
外孫 wàisūn 图 grandson (daughter's son): 外孫女 granddaughter (daughter's daughter)
外套 wàitào 图 coat
外頭 wàitou 图 outside
外侮 wàiwǔ 图 foreign aggression
外向 wàixiàng 围 extroverted
外銷 wàixiāo 动 export
外洩 wàixiè 动 leak (information)
外星人 wàixīngrén 图 alien
外溢 wàiyì 图 spillover
外語 wàiyǔ 图 foreign language
外遇 wàiyù 图 lover
外援 wàiyuán 图 foreign aid
外在 wàizài 围 outside
外債 wàizhài 图 foreign debt
外資 wàizī 图 foreign capital

夗 72 yuàn
12 Evening 夕 72 and slumped person 卩 卩. 古 turn in one's sleep

怨 72 yuàn
13 Heart 心 73 and turn in one's sleep 夗 72 (phonetic). 图 resentment, hatred 动 complain, blame ⇔ 抱怨, 恩怨, 埋怨
怨恨 yuànhèn 动 hate, resent 图 resentment
怨氣 yuànqì 图 hatred

宛 72 wǎn
14 Turn 夗 72 under roof 宀 72. 围 bent
宛如 wǎnrú 围 as if

碗 72 wǎn
15 Stone 石 87 with 夗 72

外來 wàilái 围 foreign 外貌 wàimào 图 appearance, looks
外流 wàiliú 图 outflow 外面 wàimiàn 图 outside
外貿 wàimào 图 foreign trade

phonetic. 图 图 bowl ⇔ 飯碗弘

碗盤 wǎnpán 图 dishware

婉 72 wǎn
16 Woman 女阝 with 宛阝 phonetic. 图 gentle 圈 lovely

婉拒 wǎnjù 圈 politely refuse
婉言 wǎnyán 图 tactful words
婉轉 wǎnzhuǎn 圈 tactfully

腕 72 wàn
17 Flesh 肉阝² that bends 宛阝 (phonetic). 图 wrist ⇔ 扼腕弘, 手腕阝

腕子 wànzi 图 wrist

惋 72 wàn = wǎn
18 Heart 心阝³ bent 宛阝 (phonetic). 圈 sigh

惋惜 wànxí 圈 regret

夜 72 yè
19 Sleep on one's side 亦阝 (phonetic, altered) under moon 夕阝. 图 night ⇔ 晝夜弘, 昨夜弘, 宵夜弘, 深夜弘, 日夜阝⁶, 半夜阝, 午夜阝, 熬夜弘, 過夜阝³

夜間 yèjiān 图 nighttime
夜市 yèshì 图 night market
夜晚 yèwǎn 图 night
夜校 yèxiào 图 night school

液 72 yì = yè
20 Water 水弘 condensing at night 夜阝 (phonetic). 图 liquid, fluid ⇔ 血液阝⁶

液體 yètǐ, yìtǐ 图 liquid

腋 72 yè
21 Body 肉阝² part that is dark like night 夜阝 (phonetic). 图 armpit

禸 73 róu
1 Pictograph of an animal's hind legs and tail. track left by an animal (⇨ 蹂阝⁰⁵) 图 rump

禺 73 yù
2 Ghost-like head 由阝⁴⁰ and rump 禸阝. 图 monkey

遇 73 yù
3 Walk 足阝 with 禺阝

phonetic and suggesting coincidental 偶阝. 图 meet, run into ⇔ 待遇阝, 機遇阝, 遭遇弘, 外遇阝

遇到 yùdào 圈 meet, run into
遇見 yùjiàn 圈 meet, run into
遇難 yùnàn 圈 die in an accident

寓 73 yù
4 House 宀阝³ of a monkey 禺阝 (phonetic). 图 sojourn ⇔ 公寓阝

寓所 yùsuǒ 图 accommodation
寓言 yùyán 图 fable
寓意 yùyì 图 moral

愚 73 yú
5 Monkey's 禺阝 (phonetic) mind/heart 心阝³. 圈 foolish

愚笨 yúbèn 圈 stupid, foolish
愚蠢 yúchǔn 圈 stupid, foolish
愚昧 yúmèi 图 ignorance 圈 ignorant
愚弄 yúnòng 圈 dupe, make a fool of

嵎 73 yú
6 Hill 阜阝⁶⁷ with 禺阝 phonetic. 图 corner, nook

偶 73 ǒu
7 Human 人阝⁰ and monkey 禺阝 (phonetic). 图 idol, image 圈 coincidentally ⇔ 玩偶弘, 配偶阝, 木偶阝

偶而 ǒuér 圈 occasionally
偶爾 ǒuěr 圈 occasionally
偶然 ǒurán 圈 by chance, accidentally
偶數 ǒushù 图 even number
偶像 ǒuxiàng 图 idol

耦 73 ǒu
8 Plow 耒弘 with 禺阝 phonetic. 圈 plow side by side

藕 73 ǒu
9 Modern forms shows plant 艸阝⁶ and plow 耦阝 (phonetic). 图 lotus root

萬 73 wàn
10 [万] Rump 禸阝 and an image of a head (like 由 阝⁴⁰)

with claws above (altered to resemble 艸阝). Simplified form follows an ancient simplification. 图 scorpion (⇨ 蠆)
图 ten thousand myriad 图 a surname ⇔ 千萬阝, 億萬弘, 百萬阝

萬分 wànfēn 圈 extremely
萬金油 wànjīnyóu 图 balm
萬歲 wànsuì 图 ten thousand years: 毛主席萬歲! Long live Chairman Mao!
萬一 wànyī 圈 if by any chance

厲 73 lì
11 [厉] Ledge/stone 厂阝 with scorpion 萬阝 suggesting sharp. 图 whetstone 圈 stern, harsh ⇔ 凌厲弘, 雷厲風行阝, 嚴厲阝

厲害 lìhài 圈 fierce 圈 terrific, impressive
厲聲 lìshēng 图 stern voice

勵 73 lì
12 [励] Whetstone 厲阝 and effort 力阝. 圈 exert encourage, rouse ⇔ 鼓勵弘, 獎勵阝, 激勵弘, 勉勵阝⁴

蠣 73 lì
13 [蛎] Insect-like 虫阝² animal with stone-like 厲阝 (phonetic) shell. 图 oyster ⇔ 牡蠣阝

邁 73 mài
14 [迈] Movement 足阝 and ten thousand 萬阝. 圈 stride

邁步 màibù 圈 step
邁進 màijìn 圈 stride forward, advance rapidly
邁向 màixiàng 圈 march toward

躉 73 dǔn
15 [趸] Ten thousand 萬阝 complete 足弘. 图 complete batch

躉售 dǔnshòu 圈 wholesale

离 73 lí
16 Rump 禸阝 and an image of a head with horns on top. 图 yak

字譜及字典

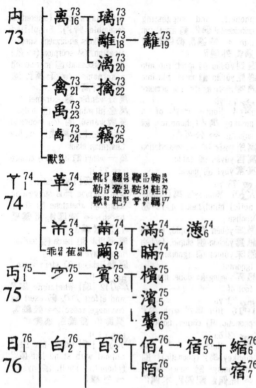

phonetic. 图 drenched ⇔ 淋漓⁷

禽 73 qín
21 Claws/tail 内⁷³ and head ⊞¹⁴⁰ with 今²¹ phonetic. 图 bird
禽獸 qínshòu 团 animals, beasts

擒 73 qín
22 Modern form shows hand 手¹⁹ and bird 禽²¹ (phonetic). 团 catch, capture
擒拿 qínná 团 catch, capture

禹 73 yǔ
23 Legs/tail 内⁷³ and an image of a head. 图 an insect 固 a surname

禼 73 xiè
24 Legs/tail 内⁷³ and an image of a head. 固 an insect

竊 73 qiè
25 [窃] Modern form shows insects 卌²⁴ stealing rice 米¹³⁸ (written to resemble 釆¹⁵⁶) from storage hole 穴⁹⁷. Simplified form uses 切¹⁴. 团 steal ⇔ 剽竊竊⁴, 扒竊⁷, 失竊⁷, 偷竊¹²⁸
竊盜 qièdào 图 thief
竊犯 qièfàn 图 thief, burglar
竊取 qièqǔ 团 steal, usurp
竊聽 qiètīng 团 eavesdrop, bug:
竊聽器 a bug
竊賊 qièzéi 图 thief, burglar

丫 74 guǎi
1 Pictograph of ram horns.

革 74 gé
2 Horned 丫¹⁴ animal flayed by hands 白³⁸ (altered). 图 leather 团 transform ⇔ 皮革⁴⁵, 改革⁷, 文革¹⁹, 變革¹⁵³
革除 géchú 团 eliminate, expel
革命 gémìng 图 revolution: 反革命 counterrevolutionary; 反革命分子 counterrevolutionary element; 革命家 revolutionary

璃 73 lí
17 Jade 玉¹⁰⁷ with 离⁷⁶ phonetic. 图 glass ⇔ 玻璃¹⁵, 琉璃⁹⁸

離 73 lí
18 [离] Bird 佳¹⁶² with 离⁷⁶ phonetic. 图 oriole 团 leave, depart ⇔ 脱離¹⁵, 背離³, 分離²⁵, 距離³¹, 偏離¹¹⁵, 隔離¹⁷⁴
離別 líbié 团 part, leave, bid farewell
離婚 líhūn 团 divorce
離間 líjiàn 团 set one side against another, sow discord

離境 líjìng 团 exit a country
離開 líkāi 团 leave, depart
離譜 lípǔ 图 ridiculous, outrageous: 你這樣講太離譜了. What you're saying is ridiculous.
離奇 líqí 图 odd, strange
離題 lítí 团 digress

籬 73 lí
19 [篱] Bamboo 竹⁷¹ that separates 離¹⁸ (phonetic). 图 hedge, fence ⇔ 藩籬¹⁵⁶
籬笆 líbā 图 bamboo fence

漓 73 lí
20 Water 水³¹ with 离⁷⁶

革新 géxīn [verb] reform [noun] innovation

羋 74 mián
3 Ram horns ⺍ and lines on either side. [phonetic] even

羋 74 mán
4 Even 羋 (phonetic) with weights on either side, suggesting scale. [phonetic] even

滿 74 mǎn
5 [满] Water 水 level 羋 (phonetic) with rim. [adj] full [verb] satisfied [adj] complete, fulfill ⇔ 不滿, 客滿, 飽滿, 屆滿, 充滿, 豐滿, 自滿, 圓滿
滿分 mǎnfēn [noun] perfect score
滿清 mǎnqīng [noun] Qing Dynasty
滿意 mǎnyì [adj] satisfied
滿洲 mǎnzhōu [noun] Manchuria: 滿州國 Manchukuo
滿族 mǎnzú [noun] Manchu people
滿足 mǎnzú [verb] satisfy [verb] be satisfied

懣 74 mèn
6 [懑] Full 滿 (phonetic) heart 心. [adj] resentful, sullen ⇔ 憤懣

瞞 74 mán
7 [瞒] Eyelids level 羋 (phonetic) with the eyes 目. [verb] dim vision [verb] deceive, fool ⇔ 欺瞞, 隱瞞
瞞騙 mánpiàn [verb] deceive

繭 74 jiǎn
8 [茧] Insect's 虫 thread 糸 with 羋 phonetic. [noun] silk cocoon [noun] callus ⇔ 蠶繭, 老繭

丏 75 miǎn
1 Pictograph of a person behind an object. [adj] hidden

宀 75 mín
2 Hidden 丏 (altered) under a roof 宀. [phonetic] home

賓 75 bīn
3 [宾] Brings presents/shells 貝 to the home 宀 (phonetic). Simplified form uses 兵. [noun] guest, visitor ⇔ 嘉賓, 外賓, 貴賓, 來賓, 菲律賓
賓館 bīnguǎn [noun] guesthouse, hotel

檳 75 bīn
4 [槟] Tree 木 product offered to guests 賓 (phonetic). [noun] betel nut ⇔ 香檳酒
檳榔 bīnláng [noun] betel nut

濱 75 bīn
5 [滨] Water 水 with 賓 phonetic. [noun] shore, bank ⇔ 橫濱, 哈爾濱, 海濱

鬢 75 bìn
6 [鬓] Hair 髟 with 賓 phonetic. [noun] hair on temples
鬢髮 bìnfà [noun] hair on temples
鬢毛 bìnmáo [noun] hair on temples

日 76 rì
1 Pictograph of the sun. [noun] sun [noun] day ⇔ 往日, 次日, 假日, 昨日, 平日, 旭日, 節日, 終日, 今日, 每日, 向日葵, 當日, 生日, 昔日, 早日, 明日, 近日, 翌日, 舊日
日報 rìbào [noun] daily newspaper
日本 rìběn [noun] Japan
日幣 rìbì [noun] yen
日常 rìcháng [adj] everyday: 日常生活 everyday life [adv] normally, usually
日程 rìchéng [noun] schedule, itinerary
日出 rìchū [noun] sunrise
日光 rìguāng [noun] sunlight, daylight: 日光燈 fluorescent light
日記 rìjì [noun] diary
日漸 rìjiàn [adv] gradually
日曆 rìlì [noun] solar calendar
日洛 rìluò [noun] sunset
日期 rìqí [noun] date
日前 rìqián [adv] recently, a few days ago
日蝕 rìshí [noun] solar eclipse
日文 rìwén [noun] Japanese written language
日夜 rìyè [noun] day and night
日益 rìyì [adv] increasingly
日用 rìyòng [adj] everyday use: 日用品 daily necessities
日語 rìyǔ [noun] (spoken) Japanese
日圓 rìyuán [noun] yen
日照 rìzhào [noun] sunlight
日子 rìzi [noun] days: 選日子 choose auspicious day

白 76 bái bó
2 Sun 日 with mark indicating it is just rising. bái: [adj] white [adj] pale [adj] clear, pure [adj] blank [adv] in vain [adv] free of charge [noun] a surname ⇔ 蒼白, 漂白, 長白山, 空白, 清白, 雪白, 坦白, 漂白, 明白, 蛋白, 斑白, 表白
白菜 báicài [noun] cabbage
白痴 báichī [noun] idiot
白癡 báichī [noun] idiot
白飯 báifàn [noun] white rice, rice
白費 báifèi [verb] waste
白宮 báigōng [noun] White House
白話 báihuà [noun] vernacular: 白話文 vernacular writing
白酒 báijiǔ [noun] a liquor made from sorghum or maize [noun] white wine
白人 báirén [noun] white person, Caucasian
白色 báisè [noun] white
白天 báitiān [noun] daytime
白晝 báizhòu [noun] daytime, daylight
白字 báizì [noun] incorrect character
白族 báizú [noun] Bai people

百 76 bǎi
3 Clear 白 (phonetic) unit 一. Alternatively, origin

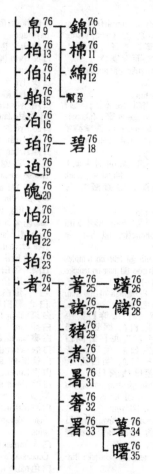

百萬 bǎiwàn million
百香果 bǎixiānggǔo passion fruit
百姓 bǎixìng common people: 老百姓 common people

佰 76 bǎi
4 One hundred 百 (phonetic) people 人. hundred (complex form)

宿 76 sù xiù xǐu
5 Roof 宀 over an ancient character for night (from person 人 and a variant of meat 肉, now written to resemble 佰). sù: spend the night long-standing xiù: constellation xǐu: night: 住一宿 stay one night ⇔ 歇宿, 寄宿, 星宿, 膳宿
宿敵 sùdí archenemy
宿舍 sùshè dormitory
宿醉 sùzùi hangover

縮 76 sūo
6 [缩] Silk 糸 with 宿 phonetic. shrink, contract ⇔ 收縮, 濃縮, 壓縮, 萎縮, 緊縮
縮短 sūoduǎn shorten
縮回 sūohúi retract, recoil
縮減 sūojiǎn cut, reduce
縮小 sūoxiǎo contract, reduce
縮寫 sūoxiě abbreviate abbreviation

蓿 76 sù
7 Grass 艸 with 宿 phonetic. clover ⇔ 苜蓿

陌 76 mò
8 Mounds 阜 in the hundreds 百. paths, roads ⇔ 阡陌
陌生 mòshēng unfamiliar, strange: 陌生人 stranger

帛 76 bó
9 White 白 (phonetic) cloth 巾. silk ⇔ 絹帛

自 (abbreviated form resembling 白) unit 一. hundred
百分 bǎifēn hundred points: 百分比 percentage; 百分之百 one hundred percent, absolutely
百合 bǎihé lily
百花齊放 bǎihuāqífàng Let a hundred flowers bloom.

百貨 bǎihùo general merchandise: 百貨公司 department store; 百貨商店 department store
百家爭鳴 bǎijiāzhēngmíng Let a hundred schools of thought contend.
百科全書 bǎikēquánshū encyclopedia

錦 [76] jǐn
10 [锦] Silk 帛 [76] as valuable as gold 金 (phonetic). brocade / beautiful / glorious ⇔ 什錦
錦標 jǐnbiāo trophy
錦繡 jǐnxìu splendid: 錦繡前途 bright future

棉 [76] mián
11 Bush/tree 木 that produces silk-like 帛 [76] fiber. cotton ⇔ 高棉
棉襖 mián'ǎo cotton coat
棉被 miánbèi cotton quilt
棉花 miánhuā cotton

綿 [76] mián
12 [绵] Threads 糸 like silk 帛 [76]. cotton / soft / continuous ⇔ 連綿
綿亙 miángèn mountain chain
綿延 miányán continuous, unbroken / continue
綿羊 miányáng sheep

柏 [76] bó
13 Tree 木 with 白 [76] phonetic. cypress
柏林 bólín Berlin
柏樹 bóshù cypress
柏油 bóyóu asphalt

伯 [76] bó
14 Person 人 with 白 [76] phonetic. uncle (father's elder brother) ⇔ 阿拉伯, 西伯利亞
伯伯 bóbo uncle(father's elder brother)
伯父 bófù uncle(father's elder brother)
伯爵 bójué count
伯母 bómǔ aunt (wife of father's elder brother)

舶 [76] bó
15 Boat 舟 with 白 [76] phonetic. ship ⇔ 船舶
舶來品 bóláipǐn imported goods

泊 [76] bó
16 Water 水 with 白 [76] phonetic. anchor, moor / lake ⇔ 尼泊爾, 湖泊, 淡泊

珀 [76] pò
17 Jade 玉 with 白 [76] phonetic. amber ⇔ 琥珀

碧 [76] bì
18 Stone 石 with 珀 phonetic. jasper
碧海 bìhǎi blue sea
碧綠 bìlù verdant
碧玉 bìyù jasper

迫 [76] pò
19 Movement 辵 with 白 [76] phonetic. approach force, compel / urgent ⇔ 窘迫, 急迫, 被迫, 逼迫, 脅迫, 強迫, 壓迫, 緊迫
迫害 pòhài persecute
迫切 pòqiè urgent, pressing
迫使 pòshǐ force, compel

魄 [76] pò
20 Ghost 鬼 with 白 [76] phonetic. soul, spirit 魂魄, 氣魄
魄力 pòlì guts, courage

怕 [76] pà
21 Heart 心 with 白 [76] phonetic. fear ⇔ 可怕, 恐怕, 生怕, 害怕, 懼怕

帕 [76] pà
22 Cloth 巾 that is white 白 [76] (phonetic). handkerchief ⇔ 手帕

拍 [76] pāi
23 Hand 手 with 白 [76] phonetic. clap, pat: 拍馬屁 flatter / film, shoot: 拍電影 film a movie
拍賣 pāimài auction
拍攝 pāishè film, shoot
拍手 pāishǒu clap, applaud
拍照 pāizhào photograph
拍子 pāizi racquet

者 [76] zhě
24 Clear/white 白 [76] (dot often dropped to resemble 日 [76]) with an ancient pictograph of grain or sugarcane stalks phonetic. person, thing 老者, 筆者, 學者, 作者, 侍者, 忍者, 行者, 後者, 或者, 記者, 癮者, 前者, 死者, 讀者, 患者, 再者

著 [76] zhù zhúo zháo zhāo zhe
25 [着] Plant 艸 with 者 phonetic. zhù: apparent / write zhúo: wear / apply, attach zháo: touch zhāo: move, trick / catch (a sickness) zhe: (indicating continuation of an action) 看著電視 watching television (used after a verb to form a preposition) 沿著 along; 爲著 for 隨著, 抱著, 等著, 盯著, 拿著, 趁著, 膠著, 執著, 接著, 帶著, 按著, 向著, 活著, 瞪著, 名著, 朝著, 藉著, 穿著, 衣著, 握著, 顯著, 睡著, 對著
著火 zháohǔo catch fire
著急 zhāojí worried: 別著急 don't worry
著涼 zhāoliáng catch cold
著迷 zháomí fascinated, enraptured
著名 zhùmíng well-known
著作 zhùzùo works, writings: 著作權 copyright
著手 zhúoshǒu begin, get started
著重 zhúozhòng emphasize

躇 [76] chú
26 Foot 足 touching 著 (phonetic). hesitate ⇔ 躊躇

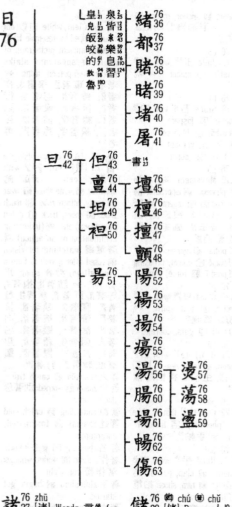

日
76

儲量 chúliàng 图 deposits
儲蓄 chúxù 图 save 图 savings

豬 76 zhū
29 [猪] Boar 豕155 with 者24 phonetic. 图 pig ⇔ 沙豬57, 野豬102
豬肉 zhūròu 图 pork

煮 76 zhǔ
30 Fire 火82 with 者24 phonetic. 🔟 boil 🔟 cook
煮菜 zhǔcài 🔟 cook vegetables 🔟 cook
煮飯 zhǔfàn 🔟 cook rice 🔟 cook

暑 76 shǔ
31 Sun 日76 with 者24 phonetic. 图 hot weather
暑假 shǔjià 图 summer vacation

奢 76 shē
32 Big 大3 with 者24 phonetic. 图 extravagant
奢侈 shēchǐ 图 extravagant, luxurious: 奢侈品 luxury goods
奢望 shēwàng 🔟 entertain wild hopes

署 76 shǔ 图 shù
33 Net 网22 (altered) with 者24 phonetic. shù: 🔟 arrange 🔟 sign shǔ: 图 government office ⇔ 部署41, 簽署19, 官署167
署名 shùmíng 🔟 sign 图 signature

薯 76 shǔ
34 Plant 艸66 with 署33 phonetic. 图 potato, yam ⇔ 甘薯59, 番薯256, 馬鈴薯177
薯條 shǔtiáo 图 french fries

曙 76 shù 图 shǔ
35 Sun 日76 with 署33 phonetic. 图 dawn
曙光 shùguāng 图 dawn, dawn's light

緒 76 xù
36 [绪] Thread 糸153 with 者24 phonetic. 图 end of a thread 图 task ⇔ 就緒14, 頭緒81, 情緒98

諸 76 zhū
27 [诸] Words 言98 for things 者24 (phonetic). 图 various, all
諸多 zhūduō 图 many
諸如 zhūrú 图 such as
諸位 zhūwèi 图 everybody

儲 76 图 chú 图 chǔ
28 [储] Person 人10 collecting everything 諸27 (phonetic). 🔟 store, save
儲備 chúbèi 🔟 reserve, stockpile 图 reserves, savings
儲存 chúcún 🔟 store, stockpile

緒言 xùyán 图 introduction

都 76 dōu dū
37 City 邑 with 者 phonetic. dū: 图 big city dōu: 图图 all ⇔ 上都, 京都, 大都, 國都, 首都
都城 dūchéng 图 capital city
都市 dūshì 图 city

賭 76 dǔ
38 [赌] Money/shell 貝 with 者 phonetic. 图 gamble ⇔ 打賭
賭博 dǔbó 图 gamble
賭場 dǔchǎng 图 casino
賭錢 dǔqián 图 gamble
賭注 dǔzhù 图 stake (gambling): 提高賭注 raise the stakes

睹 76 dǔ
39 Eye 目 with 者 phonetic. 图 see ⇔ 目睹

堵 76 dǔ
40 Dirt 土 with 者 phonetic. 图 stop up
堵車 dǔchē 图 traffic jam
堵塞 dǔsè 图 stop up, block up
堵住 dǔzhù 图 block up

屠 76 tú
41 Prone body 尸 with 者 phonetic. 图 slaughter 图 a surname
屠殺 túshā 图 图 slaughter, massacre: 南京大屠殺 Nanking Massacre
屠宰 túzǎi 图 butcher, slaughter

旦 76 dàn
42 Sun 日 rising above the horizon 一 图 dawn ⇔ 一旦, 元旦

但 76 dàn
43 Person 人 with 旦 phonetic. 图 but ⇔ 不但, 非但
但是 dànshì 图 but
但願 dànyuàn 图 wish but that, if only

亶 76 dǎn
44 Granary 回 like rising sun 旦 (phonetic). 古

overflowing

壇 76 tán
45 [坛] Earth 土 with 亶 phonetic. Simplified form uses 云. 图 platform, altar ⇔ 祭壇, 花壇, 天壇, 政壇, 文壇, 論壇

檀 76 tán
46 Tree 木 with overflowing 亶 (phonetic) scent. 图 sandalwood
檀香 tánxiāng 图 sandalwood
檀香扇 sandalwood fan

擅 76 shàn
47 Hand 手 overflowing 亶 (phonetic). 图 excel at 图 unilaterally
擅長 shàncháng 图 excel at: 擅長於圍棋 excel at go
擅自 shànzì 图 without authorization

顫 76 chàn
48 [颤] Overflowing 亶 (phonetic) head 頁. 图 tremble
顫動 chàndòng 图 vibrate
顫抖 chàndǒu 图 shiver

坦 76 tǎn
49 Earth 土 with 旦 phonetic. 图 level 图 straightforward ⇔ 平坦, 巴基斯坦, 巴勒斯坦, 舒坦
坦白 tǎnbái 图 frank, straightforward
坦誠 tǎnchéng 图 frank and sincere
坦克 tǎnkè 图 tank (military vehicle)
坦然 tǎnrán 图 composed, at ease
坦率 tǎnshuài 图 candid, frank

袒 76 tǎn
50 Clothes 衣 disrobed like sun at dawn 旦 (phonetic). 图 strip, bare ⇔ 偏袒
袒護 tǎnhù 图 shield, make excuses for

易 76 yáng
51 Sun appearing 旦, rays piercing clouds like pennants 勿. 图 bright

陽 76 yáng
52 [阳] Hill's 阜 bright 易 (phonetic) side. Simplified form uses sun 日. 图 south side of a hill 图 sun 图 yang - masculine or positive principle in Daoist philosophy ⇔ 太陽, 陰陽, 歐陽, 夕陽, 朝陽, 瀋陽
陽光 yángguāng 图 sunlight
陽曆 yánglì 图 solar calendar
陽傘 yángsǎn 图 parasol
陽朔 yángshuò 图 Yangshuo - a scenic town near Guilin
陽台 yángtái 图 sundeck, veranda, balcony
陽性 yángxìng 图 positive 图 male

楊 76 yáng
53 [杨] Tree 木 with 易 phonetic. 图 poplar a surname
楊柳 yángliǔ 图 willow
楊桃 yángtáo 图 star fruit

揚 76 yáng
54 [扬] Hold 手 up in the light 易 (phonetic). 图 raise 图 acclaim 图 propagate, spread ⇔ 宣揚, 讚揚, 頌揚, 張揚, 悠揚, 弘揚, 褒揚, 發揚, 表揚
揚起 yángqǐ 图 raise
揚棄 yángqì 图 renounce
揚言 yángyán 图 threaten

瘍 76 yáng
55 [疡] Sickness 疒 with 易 phonetic. 图 sore ⇔ 潰瘍

湯 76 tāng
56 [汤] Water 水 heated by solar rays 易 (phonetic). 图 hot water 图 soup 图 a

日
76

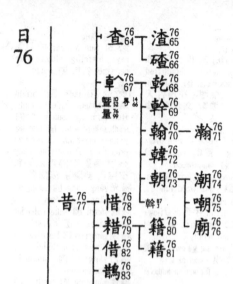

昔⁷⁶₇₇ — 惜⁷⁶₇₈
耤⁷⁶₇₉ — 籍⁷⁶₈₀ — 廟⁷⁶₇₆
借⁷⁶₈₂ — 藉⁷⁶₈₁
鵲⁷⁶₈₃
措⁷⁶₈₄
錯⁷⁶₈₅
醋⁷⁶₈₆

查⁷⁶₆₄ — 渣⁷⁶₆₅
碴⁷⁶₆₆
車⁷⁶₆₇ — 乾⁷⁶₆₈
幹⁷⁶₆₉
翰⁷⁶₇₀ — 瀚⁷⁶₇₁
韓⁷⁶₇₂
朝⁷⁶₇₃ — 潮⁷⁶₇₄
嘲⁷⁶₇₅

surname ⇔ 酸辣湯⁵⁷, 泡湯⁵⁷
湯匙 tāngchí 图 soup spoon
湯圓 tāngyuán 图 glutinous rice ball (eaten on winter solstice)

燙⁷⁶₅₇ [烫] Hot water 湯⁷⁶ (phonetic) further heated by fire 火⁷². 图 hot, scalding, scald ⇔ 滚燙⁵⁷

蕩⁷⁶₅₈ [荡] Modern form shows plant 艸²⁶ and soup 湯⁷⁶ (phonetic). 图 a river name 图 marsh 图 vagrant 图 licentious 图 sway ⇔ 晃蕩⁵⁸, 掃蕩⁵⁸, 淫蕩⁵⁸, 動蕩⁵⁸, 放蕩⁵⁸, 遊蕩⁵⁸, 闖蕩⁷⁷
蕩漾 dàngyàng 图 ripple

盪⁷⁶₅₉ [荡] Saucer 皿¹¹⁶ with soup 湯⁷⁶ phonetic and suggestive of sway 蕩⁵⁸. 图 slosh, sway ⇔ 震盪⁵⁹

腸⁷⁶₆₀ [肠] Flesh 肉¹³² with 易⁵⁷ phonetic. 图 intestine ⇔ 盲腸⁸⁵, 香腸⁵⁷, 臘腸⁸¹

場⁷⁶₆₁ [场] Ground 土⁷⁰ open to the sun 易⁵⁷ (phonetic). 图 open space 图 site, place 图 farm 图 stage 图 scene, act 图 a measureword for recreational events ⇔ 農場⁵⁴, 商場⁸², 廣場⁸³, 礦場⁸², 立場⁵⁴, 機場⁸³, 當場⁶¹, 在場⁵⁴, 市場⁸², 操

場⁵⁹, 賭場⁷⁶, 牧場⁷², 出場¹¹⁰, 現場¹⁵⁴, 戰場¹³, 劇場¹⁹⁵, 官場¹⁶⁷, 排場¹⁶⁹
場地 chǎngdì 图 site
場合 chǎnghé 图 situation, occasion
場面 chǎngmiàn 图 scene
場所 chǎngsuǒ 图 place, site

暢⁷⁶₆₂ [畅] Extend 申⁵⁸ like solar rays 易⁵⁷ (phonetic). 图 smoothly, fluently 图 uninhibitedly ⇔ 流暢⁵⁸
暢快 chàngkuài 图 thrilling
暢通 chàngtōng 图 unimpeded
暢銷 chàngxiāo 图 hot-selling: 暢銷書 bestseller

傷⁷⁶₆₃ [伤] Person 人⁹ with a variant of solar rays 易⁵⁷ phonetic. Simplified form uses strength 力²⁴. 图 harm, injure ⇔ 擦傷⁶⁴, 創傷⁸³, 灼傷⁹¹, 中傷⁸², 重傷⁹⁸, 受傷¹⁰⁷, 死傷²², 憂傷¹⁶⁹, 悲傷¹⁰⁵
傷風 shāngfēng 图 catch cold
傷害 shānghài 图 hurt, injure
傷痕 shānghén 图 scar
傷口 shāngkǒu 图 wound, cut
傷亡 shāngwáng 图 casualties
傷心 shāngxin 图 sad, grieved

查⁷⁶₆₄ Wood 木⁷¹ with 且¹¹⁷ (altered to resemble 且⁸⁸) phonetic. 图 check, examine 图 search: 查辭典 look up in a dictionary ⇔ 巡查⁷⁶, 檢查⁹², 搜查¹⁵, 偵查⁹⁵, 調查⁶⁷, 盤查¹²⁹, 審查⁷⁵, 追查¹⁶⁷
查出 cháchū 图 find out, search out
查對 cháduì 图 verify, check
查獲 cháhùo 图 track down
查看 chákàn 图 look into
查扣 chákòu 图 confiscate
查詢 cháxún 图 inquire about

渣 76 zhā
65 Water 水氵 with 查 phonetic. 图 sediment ⇔ 殘渣
渣滓 zhāzǐ 图 dregs, residue
渣子 zhāzi 图 dregs, residue

碴 76 chá
66 Stone 石 with 查 phonetic. 图 fragment 动 cut
碴兒 chár 图 fragment 图 quarrel: 打碴兒 pick a fight

乾 76 gàn
67 Rising sun's 旦 waves (altered). 形 early light

乾 76 gān qián
68 [干] Plants sprouting 乙 towards early light. qián: 图 heaven 图 first of the Eight Diagrams (八卦). gān: 形 dry ⇔ 烘乾, 餅乾, 乳臭未乾, 曬乾
乾杯 gānbēi 动 drink a toast "Bottoms up!", "Cheers!"
乾脆 gāncuì 形 simply
乾旱 gānhàn 形 arid
乾淨 gānjìng 形 clean
乾枯 gānkū 动 dry up, wither
乾酪 gānlào 图 cheese
乾洗 gānxǐ 动 dry-clean
乾燥 gānzào 形 dry
乾坤 qiánkūn 图 heaven and earth

幹 76 gàn
69 [干] Rising stem 干 (phonetic). 图 trunk 动 do: 你在幹嘛? What are you doing? 动 fuck ⇔ 高幹, 才幹, 樹幹, 能幹, 骨幹
幹部 gànbù 图 cadre, official
幹勁 gànjìn gusto, vigor, enthusiasm
幹事 gànshì 图 clerk 图 executive: 總幹事 general manager
幹線 gànxiàn 图 trunk line

翰 76 hàn
70 Feather 羽 like sun rays (phonetic). 图 long feather
翰墨 hànmò 图 brush and ink

瀚 76 hàn
71 Extending like long feathers 翰 (phonetic) in water-like 水氵 appearance. 地 Gobi Desert 形 vast ⇔ 浩瀚

韓 76 hán
72 [韩] Raise (phonetic, abbreviated) and pull 韋 动 water-raising well mechanism 地 Korea: 南韓 South Korea; 北韓 North Korea 图 a surname
韓國 hánguó 地 Korea, South Korea

朝 76 cháo zhāo
73 Modern form shows sun rising (abbreviated) and 月 moon. cháo: 图 imperial court 图 dynasty 动 face zhāo: 图 morning ⇔ 唐朝, 隋朝, 秦朝, 宋朝, 清朝, 晉朝
朝代 cháodài 图 dynasty
朝貢 cháogòng 动 pay imperial tribute
朝廷 cháotíng 图 imperial court, royal court
朝鮮 cháoxiān 地 Korea: 南朝鮮 South Korea; 北朝鮮 North Korea
朝野 cháoyě 图 government and public 图 government and opposition
朝著 cháozhe 动 facing
朝氣 zhāoqì 图 vitality, vigor
朝夕 zhāoxì 动 day and night, always
朝陽 zhāoyáng 图 morning sun

潮 76 cháo
74 Modern form shows water 水氵 with 朝 phonetic. 图 tide ⇔ 人潮, 浪潮, 高潮, 風潮, 低潮, 思

潮
潮流 cháoliú 图 tidal current 图 trend
潮濕 cháoshī 形 damp, humid
潮汐 cháoxì 图 tide

嘲 76 cháo
75 Mouth 口 facing 朝 (phonetic) target. 动 mock
嘲諷 cháofèng 动 taunt
嘲弄 cháonòng 动 mock, tease
嘲笑 cháoxiào 动 laugh at, ridicule

廟 76 miào
76 [庙] Shelter 广 and court 朝 (phonetic). Simplified form uses 由. 图 temple ⇔ 寺廟, 孔廟
廟宇 miàoyǔ 图 temple

昔 76 xī
77 Pictograph of pieces of meat in the sun 日. 名 dried meat 形 ancient, bygone ⇔ 往昔, 如昔, 曩昔
昔日 xīrì 图 former days

惜 78
78 Heart 心忄 and things past 昔 (phonetic). 动 regret 动 be fond of 动 pity ⇔ 憐惜, 可惜, 珍惜, 惋惜, 愛惜
惜別 xībié 动 say good-bye, part reluctantly

耤 76 jí
79 Plow handle 耒 with 昔 phonetic. 动 lands cultivated for the emperor

籍 76 jí
80 Bamboo 竹 with 耤 phonetic. 图 record, register 图 books 图 nationality: 美籍 American ⇔ 書籍, 省籍, 古籍, 入籍, 國籍, 外籍
籍貫 jíguàn 图 place of origin

藉 76 jiè
81 [借] Grass 艸 with 耤 phonetic. 图 ceremonial

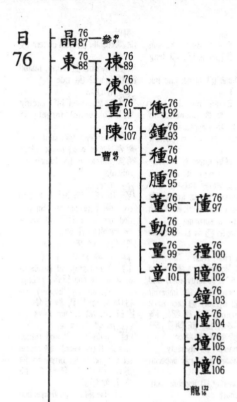

日 76

晶 76 87 — 參 %

東 76 88 — 棟 76 89
　　　　 凍 76 90
　　　　 重 76 91 — 衝 76 92
　　　　 陳 76 107 — 鍾 76 93
　　　　 曹 %8 47 — 種 76 94
　　　　　　　 腫 76 95
　　　　　　　 董 76 96 — 懂 76 97
　　　　　　　 動 76 98
　　　　　　　 量 76 99 — 糧 76 100
　　　　　　　 童 76 101 — 瞳 76 102
　　　　　　　　　　 鐘 76 103
　　　　　　　　　　 憧 76 104
　　　　　　　　　　 撞 76 105
　　　　　　　　　　 幢 76 106
　　　　　　　　　　 龍 132 16

---

mat 🈂 rely on, by means of ⇔ 憑藉 ²⁷, 慰藉 ¹²

藉口 jièkǒu 🈂 excuse

藉以 jièyǐ 🈂 in order to

藉由 jièyóu 🈂 through, by means of

藉著 jièzhe 🈂 through, by means of

借 76 82 jiè Person 人 ¹⁹ lending meat 昔 ⁷⁹ (phonetic). 🈂 lend 🈂 borrow ⇔ 假借 ¹⁶

借給 jiègěi 🈂 lend

借鏡 jièjìng 🈂 learn from other's experience

借款 jièkuǎn 🈂 borrow money 🈂 loan

鵲 76 83 [鹊] Bird 鳥 ¹⁷⁸ with 昔 ⁷⁹ phonetic. 🈂 magpie ⇔ 喜鵲 %6

措 76 84 cuò Hand 手 ⁷⁹ setting in order of old 昔 ⁷⁹ (phonetic). 🈂 place, arrange

措辭 cuòcí 🈂 choose words 🈂 wording, diction

措施 cuòshī 🈂 measure, action

錯 76 85 [错] Metal 金 ³⁴ with 昔 ⁷⁹ phonetic. 🈂 gilt 🈂 mistaken, wrong 🈂 mistake, error ⇔ 不錯 ²⁶, 弄錯 ¹³⁸, 犯錯 ¹⁷, 搞錯 ²⁷, 做錯 ¹⁸, 認錯 ²⁵, 沒錯 ²⁴, 挑錯 ¹²⁷, 算錯 ¹⁵⁰

錯過 cuòguò 🈂 miss, pass by: 錯過好機會 miss a good opportunity

錯覺 cuòjué 🈂 illusion, misconception

錯失 cuòshī 🈂 miss, lose: 錯失良機 miss a good opportunity

錯誤 cuòwù 🈂 mistake, error

錯雜 cuòzá 🈂 jumbled, mixed up

錯綜 cuòzōng 🈂 intricate: 錯綜複雜 complex, intricate

醋 76 86 Wine 酉 ¹⁹⁷ with 昔 ⁷⁹ phonetic. 🈂 vinegar ⇔ 糖醋 ²⁵, 吃醋 ⁹¹

醋意 cùyì 🈂 jealousy

晶 76 87 jīng Suns 日 ⁷⁶. 🈂 radiant, glittering ⇔ 水晶 ²⁵, 電晶體 ¹⁵⁶, 結晶 ³¹

晶片 jīngpiàn 🈂 computer chip

晶體 jīngtǐ 🈂 crystal

晶瑩 jīngyíng 🈂 sparkling

東 76 88 [东] Sun 日 ⁷⁶ rising behind a tree 木 ⁷⁷. 🈂 east 🈂 host, owner ⇔ 廣東 ²⁴, 股東 ²⁷, 山東 ¹⁷, 中東 ⁸², 浦東 %6, 房東 ⁷⁷, 遠東 ¹²⁸

東岸 dōngàn 🈂 East Coast

東北 dōngběi 🈂 northeast

東部 dōngbù 🈂 eastern region

東方 dōngfāng 🈂 the Orient

東京 dōngjīng 🈂 Tokyo

東南 dōngnán 🈂 southeast: 東南亞 Southeast Asia

東歐 dōngōu 🈂 Eastern Europe

東西 dōngxi 🈂 thing

東亞 dōngyà 🈂 East Asia

東正教 dōngzhèngjiào 🈂 Eastern Orthodox Church

棟 76 dòng
89 [栋] Wood 木[7] with 東[88] phonetic. 图 main beam 图 measureword for buildings
棟樑 dòngliáng 图 ridgepole and beam

凍 76 dòng
90 [冻] Ice 冫[7] with 東[88] phonetic. 图 freeze ⇔ 冰凍[87], 冷凍[88]
凍結 dòngjié 图 freeze

重 76 zhòng chóng
91 Standing person 土[92] with 東[88] (altered) phonetic. zhòng: 图 heavy 图 serious 图 emphasize, value: 重男輕女 value males and undervalue females chóng: 图 repeat 图 layer ⇔ 注重[87], 隆重[88], 沈重[89], 倚重[88], 慎重[89], 凝重[88], 加重[88], 超重[88], 並重[88], 慘重[88], 體重[88], 著重[88], 笨重[87], 貴重[88], 看重[88], 偏重[88], 過重[88], 嚴重[88], 自重[88], 鄭重[88], 尊重[88], 雙重[88]
重重 chóngchóng 图 layer upon layer, one after another
重蹈覆轍 chóngdàofùchè 图 follow the track of an overturned cart - repeat the mistakes of others
重疊 chóngdié 图 overlap, superimpose
重返 chóngfǎn 图 return
重複 chóngfù 图 repeat, duplicate
重婚 chónghūn 图 polygamy
重九 chóngjiǔ 图 Double Nine Festival
重慶 chóngqìng 图 Chongqing, Chungking - a city in Sichuan Province
重申 chóngshēn 图 reiterate
重新 chóngxīn 图 anew, afresh
重大 zhòngdà 图 important
重點 zhòngdiǎn 图 key point: 重點在於 the key point is

重力 zhònglì 图 gravity
重量 zhòngliàng 图 weight
重傷 zhòngshāng 图 serious injury 图 seriously injure
重視 zhòngshì 图 emphasize, value
重聽 zhòngtīng 图 hard of hearing
重要 zhòngyào 图 important: 重要性 importance
重音 zhòngyīn 图 stress, accent

衝 76 chōng chòng
92 [冲] Move 行[8] with 重[88] (originally 童[88]) phonetic. 图 open road chōng: 图 charge, rush chòng: 图 toward
衝動 chōngdòng 图 be impetuous 图 impulse, urge
衝擊 chōngjī 图 shock, impact
衝突 chōngtú 图 conflict, clash

鍾 76 zhōng
93 [钟] Heavy 重[88] (phonetic) metal 金[8]. 图 a ceremonial wine vessel 图 concentrate 图 a surname
鍾愛 zhōngài 图 dote on, cherish
鍾情 zhōngqíng 图 fall in love

種 76 zhòng zhǒng
94 [种] Grain 禾[8] repeating 重[88] (phonetic) itself. Simplified form uses 中[88]. zhòng: 图 plant, cultivate zhǒng: 图 seed 图 type, kind ⇔ 人種[88], 各種[88], 黃種人[88], 絕種[88], 栽種[88], 品種[88], 這種[88], 多種[88], 撒種[88], 火種[88], 播種[88]
種類 zhǒnglèi 图 kind, type, category
種植 zhòngzhí 图 plant, cultivate
種種 zhǒngzhǒng 图 various
種子 zhǒngzǐ 图 seed
種族 zhǒngzú 图 race, ethnic group: 種族歧視 ethnic or racial prejudice

腫 76 zhǒng
95 [肿] Flesh 肉[32]

repeated 重[88] (phonetic). Simplified form uses 中[88]. 图 swell ⇔ 臃腫[88]
腫瘤 zhǒngliú 图 tumor

董 76 dǒng
96 Plant 艸[88] with 重[88] phonetic. 图 a type of grass 图 supervise 图 a surname ⇔ 古董[88]
董事 dǒngshì 图 director, trustee: 董事會 board of directors; 董事長 chairman of the board

懂 76 dǒng
97 Heart 心[8] and supervise 董[88] (phonetic) 图 understand: 我不懂. I don't understand. ⇔ 懵懵[88], 看懂[88], 易懂[88]
懂得 dǒngdé 图 come to understand

動 76 dòng
98 [动] Heavy 重[88] (phonetic) strength 力[8]. Simplified form uses 云[8]. 图 act, do 图 move ⇔ 主動[88], 攣動[88], 晃動[88], 騷動[88], 波動[88], 被動[88], 暴動[88], 攪動[88], 舉動[88], 電動[88], 更動[88], 震動[88], 驚動[88], 鬆動[88], 反動[88], 振動[88], 妄動[88], 浮動[88], 感動[88], 帶動[88], 浮動[88], 悸動[88], 流動[88], 機動[88], 活動[88], 調動[88], 生動[88], 移動[88], 顫動[88], 衝動[88], 策動[88], 啟動[88], 勞動[88], 抖動[88], 發動[88], 走動[88], 挪動[88], 激動[88], 出動[10], 煽動[14], 挑動[17], 擺動[17], 自動[19], 搖動[14], 變動[53], 運動[58], 揮動[58], 轟動[58], 推動[62]
動蕩 dòngdàng 图 unrest
動畫 dònghuà 图 animation, anime, cartoon
動機 dòngjī 图 motive
動靜 dòngjìng 图 activity, movement
動力 dònglì 图 power, motiv-

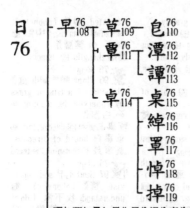

日 76

早 76/108 草 76/109 皂 76/110
覃 76/111 潭 76/112
譚 76/113
卓 76/114 桌 76/115
綽 76/116
罩 76/117
悼 76/118
掉 76/119

晤 旺 疊 晃 昆 退 春 晝 暇
暄 暴 曝 申 春 旬 晨 昨 景
冥 旭 時 曠 昂 昭 替 普 暫
旱 昊 晦 晌 莫 曩 曇 晉 暗
曉 昃 星 晴 暈 暑 曙 昧 間
明 暖 昇 曉 是 昕 暫 昏 暖
曆 曜 旮 晒 灑 晃 曨 曛 暉
易 晚

ation, impetus
動亂 dòngluàn turmoil
動脈 dòngmài artery
動人 dòngrén moving, touching
動手 dòngshǒu begin, get started
動態 dòngtài tendency, trend, dynamic
動彈 dòngtán move, stir
動武 dòngwǔ resort to violence
動物 dòngwù animal, fauna: 動物園 zoo
動搖 dòngyáo falter, waver
動員 dòngyuán mobilize
動輒 dòngzhé at every turn, frequently
動作 dòngzuò action: 動作片 action movie

量 76 liáng liàng 99 Weight 重 (abbreviated) with 良 (abbreviated) phonetic. liáng: measure liàng: quantity, amount ⇔ 食量, 盡量, 儘量, 膽量, 商量, 計量, 估量, 力量, 份量, 大量, 衡量, 含量, 數量, 存量, 容量, 儲量, 重量, 定量, 質量, 產量, 能量, 過量, 測量, 酒量, 劑量

糧 76 100 [粮] liáng Rice 米 measured 量 (phonetic). Simplified form uses 良. provisions, grain
糧倉 liángcāng granary
糧票 liángpiào grain coupon
糧食 liángshí food

童 76 101 tóng Serious 重 (abbreviated) crime 辛 (abbreviated) requiring celibate servitude. unmarried, virgin child a surname ⇔ 學童, 神童, 兒童
童年 tóngnián childhood

瞳 76 102 tóng Eye 目 with 童 phonetic. pupil (of the eye)
瞳孔 tóngkǒng pupil (of the eye)

鐘 76 103 [钟] zhōng Metal 金 struck like servant 童 (phonetic). Simplified form uses 中. bell clock o'clock: 三點鐘 three o'clock ⇔ 點鐘, 秒鐘, 時鐘, 分鐘, 鬧鐘
鐘擺 zhōngbǎi pendulum
鐘錶 zhōngbiǎo clock
鐘點 zhōngdiǎn hour
鐘頭 zhōngtóu hour

憧 76 104 chōng Heart 心 with 童 phonetic. irresolute
憧憬 chōngjǐng long for, longing

撞 76 105 zhuàng Hand 手 with 童 phonetic. collide, bump ⇔ 碰撞, 莽撞
撞車 zhuàngchē crash cars
撞擊 zhuàngjí collide, ram
撞球 zhuàngqiú billiards, pool

幢 76 106 chuáng zhuàng Cloth 巾 long like a child's 童 (phonetic) hair. banner measureword for buildings
幢幢 chuángchuáng flickering, wavering

陳 76 107 [陈] chén City 阜 and wood 木 with 申 phonetic (together written as 東). name of an ancient capital old, stale display a surname
陳腐 chénfǔ stale, trite

陳舊 chénjiù obsolete
陳列 chénliè display, exhibit
陳年 chénnián vintage, aged
陳腔濫調 chénqiānglàndiào cliche
陳情 chénqíng explain one's situation
陳設 chénshè decorate / decorations
陳述 chénshù state, narrate

早 76 zǎo
108 Modern form shows sun 日 rising above all directions 十. morning / early / Good morning! ⇔ 一早, 及早, 趁早, 提早, 遲早, 最早
早餐 zǎocān breakfast
早操 zǎocāo morning exercises
早晨 zǎochén early morning
早點 zǎodiǎn breakfast
早飯 zǎofàn breakfast
早期 zǎoqī earlier times
早日 zǎorì soon
早上 zǎoshàng morning
早晚 zǎowǎn sooner or later, eventually
早已 zǎoyǐ already

草 76 cǎo
109 Grass 艸 with 早 phonetic. grass / coarse / draft, draw up ⇔ 荒草, 割草, 茅草, 香草, 煙草, 雜草
草案 cǎoàn draft plan
草地 cǎodì lawn / grassland
草根 cǎogēn grassroots
草坪 cǎopíng lawn
草書 cǎoshū a cursive calligraphy style
草率 cǎoshuài careless, sloppy
草屋 cǎowū cottage
草席 cǎoxí mat: 日式草席 tatami
草原 cǎoyuán prairie, grasslands, steppe

皂 76 zào
110 A variant of 草 with bottom written as 七 or 七 and top abbreviated to 白. black / soap ⇔ 肥皂, 香皂

覃 76 qín tán
111 Abundance 早 (altered to resemble 早) and salt 鹵 (altered to resemble 西). deep and vast

潭 76 tán
112 Water 水 deep and vast 覃 (phonetic). lake

譚 76 tán
113 [谭] Words 言 deep and vast 覃 (phonetic). talk / a surname

卓 76 zhúo
114 Compare 七 to the rising sun 早. high / a surname
卓越 zhúoyuè brilliant, outstanding

桌 76 zhūo
115 Tall 卓 (phonetic, abbreviated) wood 木. table, desk ⇔ 書桌
桌球 zhūoqiú table tennis, ping-pong
桌子 zhūozi table, desk

綽 76 chùo
116 [绰] Silk 糸 wide and tall 卓 (phonetic). spacious / ample ⇔ 闊綽
綽號 chùohào nickname
綽約 chùoyuē delicate and attractive

罩 76 zhào
117 Net 网 (altered) with 卓 phonetic. cover ⇔ 胸罩, 口罩, 籠罩

悼 76 dào
118 Heart 心 sympathizing highly 卓 (phonetic). grieve ⇔ 哀悼

追悼
悼念 dàoniàn grieve, mourn

掉 76 diào
119 Hand 手 with 卓 phonetic. drop, fall / lose ⇔ 砍掉, 忘掉, 扔掉, 丟掉, 除掉, 關掉, 當掉, 吃掉, 失掉, 拆掉
掉下 diàoxià drop, fall off

木 77 mù
1 Pictograph of a tree. tree / wood ⇔ 伐木, 樟木, 樹木, 麻木, 柚木, 啄木鳥, 灌木, 烏魯木齊
木板 mùbǎn board
木材 mùcái timber
木耳 mùěr edible tree mushroom
木工 mùgōng carpentry
木瓜 mùguā papaya
木屐 mùjī clogs
木匠 mùjiàng carpenter
木蘭 mùlán magnolia / Mulan - an ancient warrior-heroine (also known as 花木蘭)
木偶 mùǒu puppet
木排 mùpái raft
木頭 mùtóu wood
木屋 mùwū cabin
木樁 mùzhuāng stake

沐 77 mù
2 Water 水 with 木 phonetic. shampoo
沐浴 mùyù bathe

林 77 lín
3 Several trees 木. forest / a surname ⇔ 少林寺, 穆斯林, 士林, 吉林, 樹林, 桂林, 竹林, 柏林, 森林, 叢林, 雨林
林業 línyè forestry

琳 77 lín
4 Jade 玉 with 林 phonetic. fine jade

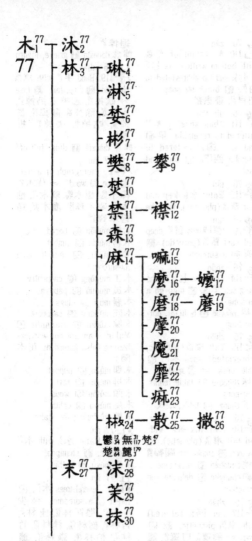

⇨ 貪婪⁴¹

彬 77 bīn
7 Forest 林⁷ (phonetic) of writings/marks 彡². 圖 intelligent and elegant
彬彬 bīnbīn 圖 refined: 文質彬彬 accomplished and refined; 彬彬有禮 polite

樊 77 fán
8 From an old form of hedge showing interwoven 交 trees 林⁷ and from the inverse of 廾 (appearing as 大) representing hands pushing apart. 画 caught in a hedge 圖 a surname

攀 77 pān
9 Hand 手 extracting one from difficulty 樊 (phonetic). 動 climb, clamber
攀登 pāndēng 動 climb
攀爬 pānpá 動 clamber
攀升 pānshēng 動 rise
攀談 pāntán 動 strike up a conversation
攀巖 pānyán 動 rock climb

焚 77 fén
10 Forest 林⁷ on fire 火. 動 burn ⇨ 自焚¹⁹
焚化 fénhuà 動 cremate incinerate: 焚化爐 incinerator
焚燬 fénhuǐ 動 incinerate, burn down
焚燒 fénshāo 動 burn
焚書坑儒 fénshūkēngrú 圖 burn books and bury scholars alive
焚香 fénxiāng 動 burn incense

禁 77 jìn jīn
11 Omen 示 with 林⁷ phonetic. jìn: 動 forbid, prohibit jīn: 動 restrain oneself ⇨ 不禁, 軟禁, 違禁, 拘禁, 宵禁, 囚禁, 紫禁城
禁錮 jìngù 動 imprison, confine
禁忌 jìnjì 圖 taboo
禁區 jìnqū 圖 restricted area

琳琅 línláng 圖 resplendent

淋 5 Streams of water 水 like a forest 林⁷ (phonetic). 動 drench ⇨ 冰淇淋²
淋漓 línlí 圖 dripping wet
淋浴 línyù 圖 shower

婪 77 lán
6 Woman 女 with 林⁷ phonetic. 圖 covetous

禁止 jìnzhǐ 動 forbid, prohibit

襟 77/12 jīn [衤] Clothing 衣 with 禁 phonetic. 名 lapel
襟懷 jīnhuái 名 aspirations, feelings

森 77/13 sēn [木] Trees 木 rising above the forest 林. 名 luxuriant growth 形 gloomy 形 majestic ⇔ 尼克森, 陰森
森林 sēnlín 名 forest
森嚴 sēnyán 形 stern, forbidding

麻 77/14 [麻] Hemp fibers (ancient character resembling 林) drying under a shed 广. 名 hemp, flax ⇔ 苧麻, 大麻, 芝麻
麻痺 mábì 形 numb 名 paralysis, numbness: 小兒麻痺症 polio
麻痺 mábì 形 numb 名 paralysis, numbness
麻煩 máfán 動名 bother, trouble, inconvenience 形 bothersome, inconvenient
麻將 májiàng 名 mahjong
麻辣 málà 形 spicy: 麻辣豆腐 spicy tofu
麻木 mámù 形 numb
麻雀 máquè 名 sparrow 名 mahjong (⇨ 麻將)
麻醉 mázùi 動 anesthetize

嘛 77/15 [嘛] Mouth 口 with 麻 phonetic. 助 a particle indicating obviousness of statement: 對嘛? Right? ⇔ 喇嘛

麼 77/16 [幺] Small 么 with 麻 phonetic. mé: 形 tiny ma: 助 an interrogative particle ⇔ 甚麼? 怎麼? 什麼? 這麼? 多麼? 那麼? 為

什麼, 為甚麼

嬤 77 mā [嬤] Woman 女 with 麼 phonetic. Variant of 媽.

磨 77/18 [磨] Stone 石 with 麻 phonetic. mò: 名 millstone mó: 動 whet, rub ⇔ 消磨, 折磨, 琢磨
磨練 móliàn 動 temper oneself

蘑 77/19 [蘑] Plant 艸 with millstone-shaped 磨 (phonetic) top. 名 mushroom
蘑菇 mógu 名 mushroom

摩 77/20 [摩] Hand 手 with 麻 phonetic. 動 rub ⇔ 達摩, 按摩, 揣摩
摩擦 mócā 動 rub 名 friction: 貿易摩擦 trade friction
摩托 mótuō 名 動 motor: 摩托車 motorcycle

魔 77/21 [魔] Ghost 鬼 with 麻 phonetic. 名 demon ⇔ 惡魔
魔鬼 móguǐ 名 demon, monster
魔術 móshù 名 magic
魔王 mówáng 名 devil

靡 77/22 [靡] Fibers 麻 (phonetic) not 非 in order. mǐ: 動 disperse mí: 動 waste: 靡之音 decadent music ⇔ 風靡, 所向披靡

痲 77 má [痲] Sickness 疒 that leaves skin looking like hemp fibers 麻 (abbreviated). 名 leprosy
痲瘋 máfēng 名 leprosy
痲疹 mázhěn 名 measles

㪔 77/23/24 sàn [㪔] Strike 攵 hemp fibers (ancient character resembling 林). 古 separate

散 77/25 sàn sǎn [散] Separate 㪔 (phonetic, altered) meat 肉. sàn: 動 disperse, scatter 動 distribute, disseminate sǎn: 形 loose 動 diffuse, scattered ⇔ 鬆散, 擴散, 分散, 驅散, 懶散, 拆散, 解散
散播 sànbō 動 disseminate, spread
散步 sànbù 名 動 walk, stroll
散發 sànfā 動 emit 動 distribute
散光 sǎnguāng 名 astigmatism
散會 sànhuì 動 adjourn a meeting
散開 sànkāi 動 disperse, scatter
散文 sǎnwén 名 prose, essay

撒 77/26 sǎ sā [撒] Hand 手 scattering 散 (phonetic). sǎ: 動 spread, sprinkle sā: 動 relax, unleash
撒謊 sāhuǎng 動 spread lies
撒尿 sǎniào 動 pee
撒種 sǎzhǒng 動 sow seeds

末 77/27 mò [末] The top 一 of a tree 木. 名 tip, end ⇔ 芥末, 期末, 週末
末代 mòdài 名 last period of a dynasty
末年 mònián 名 last years of a period
末期 mòqí 名 end of a period, final stage

沫 77/28 mò [沫] Water 水 with 末 phonetic. 名 suds, froth ⇔ 泡沫, 唾沫

茉 77/29 mò [茉] Plant 艸 with 末 phonetic. 名 jasmine
茉莉 mòlì 名 jasmine: 茉莉花茶 jasmine tea

抹 77/30 mǒ mò [抹] Hand 手 with 末 phonetic. mǒ: 動 wipe mò: 動 plaster ⇔ 塗抹
抹布 mǒbù 名 rag, dish cloth

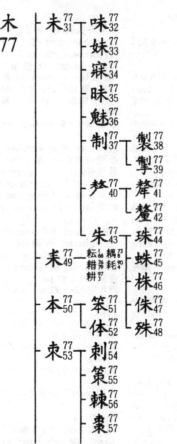

phonetic. flavor smell ⇔ 一味¹, 風味⁷, 滋味⁸², 乏味⁸⁸, 口味⁴⁹, 意味⁴⁸, 回味⁷, 調味⁸², 開味⁵, 香味⁷², 美味⁷², 趣味⁷

味道 wèidào taste, flavor

味精 wèijīng monosodium glutamate, MSG

妹 77 mèi
33 Woman 女 not yet 未 (phonetic) adult. sister (younger) ⇔ 學妹, 堂妹, 姊妹, 姐妹, 表妹, 師妹

妹妹 mèimei sister (younger)

寐 77 mèi
34 Bed 爿 under a roof 宀 with 未 phonetic. sleep ⇔ 夢寐

昧 77 mèi
35 Sun 日 not yet 未 (phonetic) out. dark conceal ⇔ 冒昧, 愚昧, 曖昧

魅 77 mèi
36 Ghost 鬼 with 未 phonetic. demon, elf

魅力 mèilì charisma, glamour

制 77 zhì
37 Chop a large tree 未 (altered) with an axe/knife 刀. chop, cot overpower, control system ⇔ 稅制, 限制, 公制, 遏制, 抑制, 節制, 英制, 法制, 控制, 機制, 牽制, 專制, 強制, 箝制, 體制, 壓制, 抵制, 編制, 克制, 管制

制裁 zhìcái sanctions: 經濟制裁 economic sanctions

制度 zhìdù system

制伏 zhìfú subdue, overpower

制服 zhìfú uniform

制衡 zhìhéng balance

制止 zhìzhǐ check, curb

抹殺 mǒshā wipe out: 抹殺歷史 deny history

未 77 wèi
31 Tree 木 with extra branches 屮. Modern meaning unrelated. not yet, have not eighth Earthly Branch (⇒ 干支) ⇔ 從未, 乳臭未乾, 尚未

未必 wèibì not necessarily

未曾 wèicéng never

未定 wèidìng undecided, indeterminate

未婚 wèihūn unmarried: 未婚妻 fiancee; 未婚夫 fiance

未來 wèilái future

未免 wèimiǎn rather, really

未能 wèinéng could not

未遂 wèisùi abortive, attempted

味 77 wèi
32 Mouth 口 with 未

製 77 zhì
38 [制𢦏] Cut 制𢦏 (phonetic) and make clothing 衣¹²⁶. ⑩ make, produce, manufacture ⇔ 複製𢦏, 研製𢦏, 仿製𢦏, 編製¹⁷⁵
製成 zhìchéng ⑩ make into
製造 zhìzào ⑩ manufacture: 製造業 manufacturing industry
製作 zhìzuò ⑩ manufacture

掣 77 chè
39 Force 制𢦏 (phonetic) with the hand 手⁹⁷. ⑩ pull, tug
掣肘 chèzhǒu ⑩ elbow

敕 77 lì
40 Strike 攵²⁴ a large tree 未𢦏 so it falls (suggested by cliff 厂⁷).

犛 77 lí
41 Ox 牛⁹² with 犛 phonetic. ⑧ yak
犛牛 líníu ⑧ yak

釐 77 lí
42 [厘] Village 里¹⁴⁸ with 犛 phonetic. ⑩ manage ⑧ thousandth of a foot ⑧ tenth of one percent, mill ⇔ 公釐¹⁹
釐定 lídìng ⑩ formulate
釐米 límǐ ⑧ centimeter
釐清 líqīng ⑩ clarify

朱 77 zhū
43 Tree 木⁷ (altered to resemble 未𢦏) with cut mark 一| indicating reddish core. ⑧ a tree name ⑯ red, vermilion ⑧ cinnabar ⑧ a surname: 朱熹 Zhu Xi - Song Dynasty Neoconfucianist
朱紅 zhūhóng ⑯ scarlet

珠 77 zhū
44 Jade 玉¹⁰⁷ from clam's core 朱𢦏 (phonetic). ⑧ pearl ⑧ bead ⇔ 念珠⁶², 珍珠⁹⁷, 淚珠⁸⁸, 圓珠筆¹⁴
珠寶 zhūbǎo ⑧ jewelry
珠海 zhūhǎi ⑧ Zhuhai - a special economic zone near Macau

珠江 zhūjiāng ⑧ Pearl River: 珠江三角洲 Pearl River Delta

蛛 77 zhū
45 Insect 虫¹²⁵ with 朱𢦏 phonetic. ⑧ spider ⇔ 蜘蛛𢦏
蛛網 zhūwǎng ⑧ spider web

株 77 zhū
46 Tree 木⁷ with 朱𢦏 phonetic. ⑧ base of tree ⑩ a measureword for trees
株連 zhūlián ⑩ involve, implicate

侏 77 zhū
47 Person 人¹⁰ with 朱𢦏 phonetic. ⑧ dwarf
侏儒 zhūrú ⑧ dwarf

殊 77 shū
48 Crushed bones 歹¹⁸ bloody 朱𢦏 (phonetic). ⑱ die ⑩ extremely ⑯ special ⇔ 特殊²⁹, 懸殊¹⁴⁸

耒 77 lěi
49 Wood 木⁷ through vegetation 丰⁷. Also interpreted as knotched 丰⁷ wood 木⁷. ⑧ plow ⑧ plow handle

本 77 běn
50 Tree 木⁷ with line 一| emphasizing base. ⑧ stem ⑧ root ⑧ basis, origin ⑧ principal, capital ⑧ book ⑧ edition ⑯ original ⑯ personal, own ⑯ this ⑩ a measureword for books ⇔ 原本⁸, 人本主義¹⁰, 資本⁸⁹, 根本⁸, 蝕本⁸, 書本¹⁵⁵, 版本⁸, 忘本⁸, 成本⁸⁷, 基本⁸⁴, 日本⁷, 課本⁸⁴, 樣本¹²⁷, 還本¹⁵, 謄本¹⁵⁵, 劇本¹⁹⁵, 虧本⁸
本地 běndì ⑧ this locality: 本地人 local person, native
本金 běnjīn ⑧ principal (of a loan)
本科 běnkē ⑯ ⑩ undergraduate: 本科生 undergraduate student

本來 běnlái ⑯ originally: 我本來是想去但是... Originally I intended to go but...
本領 běnlǐng ⑧ ability, talent
本能 běnnéng ⑧ instinct
本人 běnrén ⑧ I, myself
本身 běnshēn ⑧ one's self
本省 běnshěng ⑯ this province: 本省人 provincial native
本土 běntǔ ⑧ local: 本土化 localization
本文 běnwén ⑯ this article
本性 běnxìng ⑧ inherent nature
本意 běnyì ⑧ original intention
本質 běnzhí ⑧ essence
本子 běnzi ⑧ notebook

笨 77 bèn
51 Bamboo 竹⁷¹ with 本𢦏 phonetic. ⑧ bamboo core ⑯ stupid ⑯ clumsy ⇔ 愚笨𢦏
笨蛋 bèndàn ⑧ imbecile, idiot
笨重 bènzhòng ⑯ cumbersome, unwieldy
笨拙 bènzhúo ⑯ clumsy

体 77 tǐ
52 Person 人¹⁰ and trunk 本𢦏. Variant of 體⁸⁷.

朿 77 cì
53 Pictograph of a tree's 木⁷ needles or thorns. ⑧ tree or grass needles

刺 77 cì
54 Use knife 刀¹⁵ like thorn 束𢦏 (phonetic). ⑩ prick, jab ⑩ spur ⑧ thorn ⇔ 諷刺⁸⁶, 魚刺¹⁰⁰
刺耳 cìěr ⑯ grating, piercing
刺激 cìjī ⑩ spur, motivate ⑧ incentive ⑧ shock
刺客 cìkè ⑧ assassin
刺青 cìqīng ⑧ tattoo
刺殺 cìshā ⑩ assassinate
刺生 cìshēng ⑧ ⑩ sashimi (Japanese)
刺探 cìtàn ⑩ pry into

策 77 cè
55 Bamboo 竹⁷¹ whip to spur 束𢦏 (phonetic) horse.

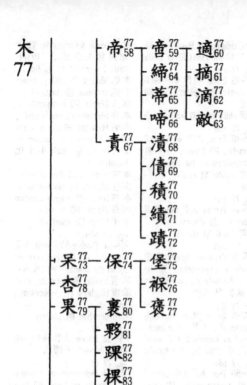

phonetic. tì: 📖 but chì: 📖 only, merely ⇔ 不啻ₙ

適₆₀ shì [适] Movement 辵 with 啻 phonetic. Simplified form uses 舌. 📖 follow 📖 suitable, appropriate ⇔ 合適, 舒適

適當 shìdàng,shìdāng 📖 appropriate, fitting, proper

適度 shìdù 📖 moderate, appropriate

適合 shìhé 📖 suit, fit, be appropriate

適宜 shìyí 📖 suitable

適應 shìyìng 📖 adapt, acclimate: 適應環境 adapt to surroundings

適用 shìyòng 📖 apply, use

適於 shìyú 📖 appropriate for

摘₆₁ zhāi Hand 手 with 啻 phonetic. 📖 pick, pluck, select

摘要 zhāiyào 📖 summary, abstract

滴₆₂ dī Water 水 with 啻 phonetic. 📖 drip 📖 drop ⇔ 水滴, 點滴

敵₆₃ dí [敌] Strike 攵 with 啻 phonetic. Simplified form uses 舌. 📖 enemy 勁敵, 匹敵, 仇敵, 宿敵

敵國 díguó 📖 enemy nation

敵人 dírén 📖 enemy

敵視 díshì 📖 view hostilely

敵手 díshǒu 📖 enemy

締₆₄ [缔] Thread 糸 with 帝 phonetic. 📖 join ⇔ 取締

締交 dìjiāo 📖 establish diplomatic relations

締結 dìjié 📖 conclude, establish

締造 dìzào 📖 found

📖 spur, urge 📖 strategy ⇔ 決策, 束手無策, 政策, 對策

策動 cèdòng 📖 motivate, instigate

策劃 cèhuà 📖 plan, plot

策略 cèluè 📖 strategy

棘₅₆ jí Many thorns 朿. 📖 thorn bush ⇔ 荊棘

棘手 jíshǒu 📖 thorny, difficult

棗₅₇ zǎo [枣] Many thorns 朿. Simplified form uses 二 to indicate plurality. 📖 jujube, Chinese date

棗樹 zǎoshù 📖 jujube tree, Chinese date tree

帝₅₈ dì Above 上 (ancient form) with 朿 (altered) phonetic. 📖 emperor ⇔ 皇帝, 上帝, 黃帝

帝國 dìguó 📖 empire: 帝國主義 imperialism: 打倒美帝國主義! Down with American imperialism!

帝王 dìwáng 📖 monarch

啻₅₉ chì Mouth 口 with 帝

蒂 77 dì
65 Modern form shows plant 艸⁹⁶ with 帝⁵ phonetic. 图 base of a fruit ⇔ 根深蒂固⁶³, 芥蒂⁷, 煙蒂¹³°

啼 77 tí
66 Modern forms shows mouth 口⁶⁸ with 帝⁵ phonetic. 町 cry
啼哭tíkū 町 cry
啼笑皆非tíxiàojiēfēi 圀 not know whether to laugh or cry

責 77 zé
67 [责] Spur 束⁶⁹ (phonetic, altered) to repay shells 貝¹⁵⁰. 町 demand 圀 blame 图 responsibility ⇔ 指責⁹⁷, 職責⁶⁸, 斥責⁹⁷, 譴責¹²⁵, 負責¹⁹⁰
責備zébèi 町 rebuke, blame
責怪zéguài 町 blame
責罵zémà 町 scold
責任zérèn 图 duty, responsibility: 不負責任 irresponsible; 責任感 sense of responsibility

漬 77 zì
68 [渍] Water 水²⁴ with 責⁵ phonetic. 图 stain

債 77 zhài
69 [债] Person's 人¹⁰ responsibility 責⁵ (phonetic). 图 debt ⇔ 公債¹², 國債⁴⁶, 償債⁶², 外債²⁷, 負債¹⁹⁰
債權zhàiquán 图 creditor's rights: 債權人 creditor
債券zhàiquàn 图 bond
債務zhàiwù 图 debt, liability
債主zhàizhǔ 图 creditor

積 77 jī
70 [积] Grain 禾¹⁰⁸ demanded 責⁵ (phonetic). Simplified form uses 只⁹⁶. 町 accumulate, save ⇔ 囤積¹⁴⁶, 淤積¹¹⁸, 面積¹⁴⁰, 堆積¹⁶²
積極jījí 圀 positive, active

積累jīlěi 町 accumulate
積蓄jīxù 图 savings 町 save

績 77 jī
71 [绩] Thread 糸⁵³ with 責⁵ phonetic. 町 spin, weave 图 achievement ⇔ 成績⁸⁷, 功績³ⁱ
績效jīxiào 图 performance

蹟 77 jī
72 [迹⁸³] Foot 足⁶⁸ with 責⁵ phonetic. 图 trace ⇔ 奇蹟⁸³, 古蹟³⁴

呆 77 dāi
73 Baby 子⁵⁵ (early form with head resembling 口⁶⁸) wrapped in a blanket (together resembling 木⁷). 圀 protect (⇨ 保⁷⁴) 圀 stupid (⇨ 獃⁸⁹) ⇔ 癡呆⁸⁸, 發呆⁸⁸, 目瞪口呆¹¹⁴
呆板dāibǎn 圀 boring, dull, rigid
呆呆dāidāi 圀 stupid
呆帳dāizhàng 图 delinquent debt
呆子dāizi 图 idiot: 書呆子 nerd, bookworm

保 77 bǎo
74 Person 人¹⁰ with blanketed child 呆⁵ (phonetic). 町 protect, preserve, guarantee ⇔ 環保¹²⁹, 酒保¹⁵⁹, 確保⁹⁷
保安bǎoān 图 public security
保鏢bǎobiāo 图 bodyguard
保持bǎochí 町 keep, maintain
保存bǎocún 町 keep, preserve
保護bǎohù 町 protect: 保護區 protected area, reservation
保甲bǎojiǎ 图 ⑰ village collective security system
保健bǎojiàn 图 health care
保齡球bǎolíngqiú 图 bowling
保留bǎoliú 町 reserve, retain
保密bǎomì 町 keep a secret
保姆bǎomǔ 图 nanny
保暖bǎonuǎn 町 keep warm: 保暖瓶 thermos
保釋bǎoshì 町 bail out
保守bǎoshǒu 町 preserve, guard

圀 conservative
保衛bǎowèi 町 safeguard, defend
保溫bǎowēn 町 keep warm: 保溫杯 图 thermos
保險bǎoxiǎn 图 insurance 圀 safe: 保險套 condom
保養bǎoyǎng 町 maintain
保有bǎoyǒu 图 possession
保佑bǎoyòu 町 protect, bless 图 blessing
保育bǎoyù 町 wildlife protection
保障bǎozhàng 町 guarantee, ensure, safeguard
保證bǎozhèng 町 guarantee, assure

堡 77 bǎo
75 Protective 保⁷⁴ (phonetic) earth 土⁷. 图 fort ⇔ 城堡⁸⁹
堡壘bǎolěi 图 fort

褓 77 bǎo
76 Clothing 衣¹²⁶ for protected 保⁷⁴ (phonetic) child. 图 swaddling clothes ⇔ 襁褓⁹⁷

褒 77 bāo
77 Modern form shows clothing 衣¹²⁶ with 保⁷⁴ phonetic. 町 commend
褒貶bāobiǎn 町 critique, evaluate 图 criticize
褒揚bāoyáng 町 praise, commend 图 commendation

杏 77 xìng
78 Tree 木⁷ with mouth 口⁶⁸ below. 图 apricot
杏仁xìngrén 图 almond

果 77 guǒ
79 Fruit (resembling 田¹¹) on top of tree 木⁷. 图 fruit, nut ⇔ 水果²⁴, 糖果¹⁴, 腰果⁴⁹, 芒果⁷², 結果³ⁱ, 因果²⁷, 效果²⁷, 後果⁵¹, 成果⁸⁷, 如果⁵⁵, 蔬果⁹⁷, 百香果²⁶, 蘋果¹²⁹
果斷guǒduàn 圀 resolute,

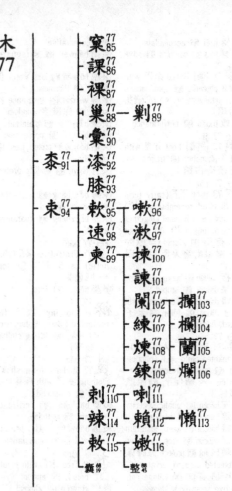

裹¹²

裹腳 guǒjiǎo 🔲 bind feet 🔲 foot-binding

夥 77 huǒ
81 Fruitful 果乃 (phonetic) adundance 多乃². 🔲 numerous 🔲 partner ⇔ 入夥¹², 合夥¹⁵

夥伴 huǒbàn 🔲 partner, companion

踝 77 huái
82 Foot's 足器 fruit-shaped 果乃 (phonetic) part. 🔲 ankle ⇔ 腳踝器, 足踝器

棵 77 kē
83 Tree 木ㄣ with 果乃 phonetic. 🔲 a measureword for trees

顆 77 kē
84 [颗] Head 頁¹² like fruit 果乃 (phonetic). 🔲 measureword for small objects

顆粒 kēlì 🔲 pellet, bead, grain

窠 77 kē
85 Hole 穴⁹ with 果乃 phonetic. 🔲 burrow, nest

窠臼 kējiù 🔲 cliche

課 77 kè
86 [课] Words 言器 producing fruit 果乃 (phonetic). 🔲 test 🔲 class, lesson 🔲 course ⇔ 上課⁴³, 下課⁴⁴, 修課⁹, 聽課³³, 功課³¹, 曉課⁸², 授課¹⁸³, 罷課¹²⁴, 排課¹⁴⁹

課本 kèběn 🔲 textbook
課程 kèchéng 🔲 course 🔲 academic program, curriculum
課堂 kètáng 🔲 classroom
課題 kètí 🔲 exercise, problem
課外 kèwài 🔲 extracurricular

裸 77 luǒ
87 Clothing 衣¹²⁶ with 果乃 phonetic. 🔲 naked ⇔ 赤裸裸

裸露 luǒlù 🔲 exposed, naked
裸體 luǒtǐ 🔲 naked, nude

decisive 🔲 resolutely, decisively

果敢 guǒgǎn 🔲 resolute and courageous
果醬 guǒjiàng 🔲 jam
果然 guǒrán 🔲 as expected
果實 guǒshí 🔲 fruit 🔲 fruits, gains
果蠅 guǒyíng 🔲 fruitfly

果園 guǒyuán 🔲 orchard
果眞 guǒzhēn 🔲 really, as expected
果汁 guǒzhī 🔲 fruit juice
果子 guǒzi 🔲 fruit

裹 77 guǒ
80 Wrap in clothing 衣¹²⁶ like fruit 果乃 (phonetic) around seed. 🔲 bind ⇔ 包

巢 77 cháo
88 Pictograph of a nest upon a tree 木⁷ (together resembling 果⁴⁹) with 川³ suggesting bird feathers. 圖 nest ⇔ 卵巢⁵², 鳥巢¹⁷⁶

剿 77 jiǎo
89 Modern form shows attack nest 巢⁸⁸ and knife 刀³⁵. 圖 exterminate
剿匪 jiǎofěi 圖 suppress bandits

彙 77 huì
90 [汇⁹⁷] Boar's snout ⇌⁴² with stomach and legs now written to resemble 果⁴⁹. 圖 hedgehog 圖 collect, categorize ⇔ 詞彙²⁴

桼 77 qī
91 Tree 木⁷ with drops (merging with trunk to resemble 水³¹) emanating. 圍 sap, lacquer

漆 77 qī
92 Water 水³¹ and lacquer 桼⁹¹ (phonetic). 圖 a river name 圖 lacquer tree 圖 lacquer ⇔ 噴漆¹⁶⁹, 油漆¹¹³
漆黑 qīhēi 圖 pitch-black
漆器 qīqì 圖 lacquerware

膝 77 xī
93 Modern form shows flesh 肉¹² with 桼⁹¹ phonetic. 圖 knee
膝蓋 xīgài 圖 kneecap

束 77 shù
94 Enclose 口⁶⁰ a tree 木⁷. 圖 bind, tie 圖 bundle: 一束花 bouquet ⇔ 拘束³⁹, 結束⁶⁸, 約束⁶⁴
束縛 shùfú 圖 restrain, bind 圖 restraint
束手無策 shùshǒuwúcè 圖 feel helpless

欶 77 shuò
95 Tighten 束⁹⁴ (phonetic) and breath 欠⁸⁵. 圍 suck

嗽 77 sòu
96 Cough 欶⁹⁵ (phonetic) with mouth 口⁶⁰ for emphasis. 圖 cough ⇔ 咳嗽¹⁰⁴

漱 77 shù
97 Such 欶⁹⁵ (phonetic) water 水³¹. 圖 gargle
漱口 shùkǒu 圖 gargle

速 77 sù
98 Movement 辵³¹ with 束⁹⁴ phonetic. 圖 fast, rapid 圖 speed ⇔ 高速⁹⁷, 時速²⁰, 加速²¹, 快速³⁹, 迅速²⁹, 火速⁸²
速度 sùdù 圖 speed
速食 sùshí 圖 fast food: 速食麵 instant noodles

柬 77 jiǎn
99 Separate 八⁷⁸ into bundles 束⁹⁴. Simplified form, used in some derivatives, is based on cursive script. 圖 select ⇔ 請柬²⁹
柬埔寨 jiǎnpǔzhài 圖 Cambodia

揀 77 jiǎn
100 [拣] Hand 手¹⁰⁰ selecting 柬⁹⁹ (phonetic). 圖 select
揀選 jiǎnxuǎn 圖 select

諫 77 jiàn
101 [谏] Words 言⁷⁸ selecting 柬⁹⁹. 圖 admonish

闌 77 lán
102 [阑] Gate 門⁷⁸ selecting 柬⁹⁹ (phonetic). 圖 block
闌尾 lánwěi 圖 appendix: 闌尾炎 appendicitis

攔 77 lán
103 [拦] Hand 手¹⁰⁰ blocking 闌¹⁰² (phonetic). Simplified form uses 蘭¹⁰⁵ simplification. 圖 block ⇔ 阻攔²¹
攔截 lánjié 圖 intercept
攔住 lánzhù 圖 obstruct, block
攔阻 lánzǔ 圖 impede, obstruct

欄 77 lán
104 [栏] Wood 木⁷ blocking 闌¹⁰² (phonetic). Simplified form uses 蘭¹⁰⁵ simplification. 圖 fence, railing ⇔ 專欄⁴⁹, 柵欄¹¹⁵
欄杆 lángān 圖 railing, banister

蘭 77 lán
105 [兰] Plant 艸⁴⁹ with 闌¹⁰² phonetic. Simplified form uses 三⁵. 圖 orchid 圖 a surname ⇔ 伊斯蘭⁸¹, 紐西蘭¹⁸, 波蘭³⁶, 荷蘭²⁵, 芬蘭²⁹, 新西蘭⁸², 木蘭⁷, 愛爾蘭⁹³, 烏克蘭¹⁷, 蘇格蘭¹⁸⁰
蘭花 lánhuā 圖 orchid
蘭嶼 lányǔ 圖 Orchid Island - an island off Taiwan

爛 77 làn
106 [烂] Modern form shows fire 火⁸² with 闌¹⁰² phonetic. Simplified form uses 蘭¹⁰⁵ simplification. 圖 overcooked 圖 fester 圖 poor, bad: 我的中文很爛. My Chinese is horrible. ⇔ 腐爛³⁹, 破爛¹¹⁵, 絢爛³⁹, 燦爛¹⁷
爛漫 lànmàn 圖 bright-colored

練 77 liàn
107 [练] Silk 糸¹⁵³ with 柬⁹⁹ phonetic. 圖 boil raw silk 圖 practice, train ⇔ 訓練²⁹, 教練¹⁹, 熟練⁹⁸, 磨練⁷²
練達 liàndá 圖 experienced, proficient
練習 liànxí 圖 practice, train: 練習簿 exercise book

煉 77 liàn
108 [炼] Fire 火⁸² selecting 柬⁹⁹ (phonetic). 圖 smelt, refine ⇔ 冶煉⁸⁹, 精煉²⁹
煉鋼 liàngāng 圖 make steel
煉油 liànyóu 圖 refine oil

鍊 77 liàn
109 [链¹⁵⁰] Metal 金³⁴

木 77

休 77/117
片 77/118 — 牌 版 牒 牖
爿 77/119 — 戕 77/120 — 臧 77/121 — 贓 77/122
將 77/125 — 漿 77/126 — 藏 77/123 — 臟 77/124
獎 77/127
蔣 77/128
槳 77/129
醬 77/130
壯 77/131 — 莊 77/132
狀 77/134 — 裝 77/133
妝 77/135
疒 77/136 — 疢 痕 疲 痹 瘦 病 癰 痤 痴 癡 疾 疫 疼 痹 瘋 癬 瘓 癌 痛 痘 瘍 痲 瘤 痰 瘓 瘁 疤 疵 症 癒 痢 癮 癢 癒 癥 癀
鼎 77/137

極 框 杠 柴 柰 奈 棕 杯 柱 札
檢 概 格 桀 柯 械 棍 根 柳
槍 桑 棲 村 權 欄 標 梗 椿 寨
松 柢 板 樺 枕 柄 條 枚 朴 朽
柯 椅 梢 染 植 枝 枯 横 東 枷
架 梁 樑 朵 校 杭 棧 械 栽 棋
楓 杉 杆 桿 斉 檳 築 渠 案 梅
樓 李 梳 機 樂 床 杓 宋 檔 梅
材 梯 模 棱 柩 槽 某 樟
困 桶 橙 樹 櫥 杜 桂 棒 枝 横
棉 柏 檀 楊 查 東 棟 陳 桌 森
朱 株 棵 欄 樂 閑 榴 柳 榮 柴
梧 杵 榜 析 橋 采 柔 橘 櫃 梨
柚 楣 相 栅 檬 椒 樣 桃 桎 檔
橄 椰 檻 橙 櫻 櫻 樣 集 椎 權
棚 棺 栗 橡 構 業 樸 梟

selected 柬 (phonetic). 囲 temper, forge ⇔ 鍛鍊, 拉
鍊, 項鍊, 錘鍊

剌 77 lá lǎ 110 Bind 束 and knife
刀. lá: 囲 slash, slit, cut là:

囲 disagreeable

喇 77 lǎ 111 Mouth 口 making
violent 剌 (phonetic)
sounds. 囲 trumpet, horn
喇叭 lǎbā 囲 trumpet, horn 囲
speaker
喇嘛 lǎma 囲 lama: 達賴喇嘛
Dalai Lama; 喇嘛教 Lamaism

賴 77 lài 112 [赖] Money/shell
貝 with 剌 (knife 刀
element above 貝) phonetic.
囲 earn 囲 rely on, depend on
囲 blame 囲 a surname ⇔
倚賴, 仰賴, 誣賴, 信
賴, 依賴
賴帳 làizhàng 囲 repudiate a
debt, break a promise

懶 77 lǎn 113 [懒] Modern form
shows heart 心 and depend-
ence 賴. 囲 lazy ⇔ 偷
懶
懶得 lǎnde 囲 disinclined to,
don't feel like: 我懶得去. I
don't feel like going.
懶惰 lǎnduò 囲 lazy 囲 laziness
懶散 lǎnsàn 囲 listless, lazy

辣 77 là 114 Bitter 辛 with
剌 abbreviated to 束,
phonetic. 囲 hot, spicy ⇔ 酸
辣湯, 毒辣, 麻辣, 心
狠手辣, 潑辣
辣椒 làjiāo 囲 hot pepper: 辣椒
醬 hot sauce

敕 77 chì 115 Bind 束 (phonetic) and strike 攵. 囲 admonish
敕令 chìlìng 囲 imperial decree

嫩 77 nèn 116 Modern form shows
woman 女 and admonish
敕. 囲 delicate, tender ⇔
嬌嫩, 稚嫩

休 77 xiū 117 Person 人 against

a tree 木. 働 rest 働 stop, cease ⇔ 退休, 喋喋不休

休會 xiūhuì 働 adjourn

休假 xiūjià 图 働 holiday

休克 xiūkè 图 shock

休戚相關 xiūqīxiāngguān 图 share good and bad luck

休息 xiūxí 働 rest

休閒 xiūxián 图 leisure

休想 xiūxiǎng 働 dream of, delude oneself

休學 xiūxué 働 take a leave of absence from school

休止 xiūzhǐ 働 stop, cease

片 118 piàn Tree 木 split in half. 働 piece, chip ⇔ 卡片, 影片, 照片, 打成一片, 磁片, 唱片, 名片, 晶片, 鴉片, 底片, 瓦片, 相片, 洋片, 洋芋片, 麥片

片段 piànduàn 图 passage, section, episode

片刻 piànkè 图 moment, instant

片面 piànmiàn 働 unilateral 働 one-sided

片語 piànyǔ 图 phrase

片子 piànzi 图 film, movie

爿 119 bàn qiáng Tree 木 split in half. qiáng: 图 plank bàn: 働 measureword for stores

戕 120 qiáng Split 爿 (phonetic) with a lance 戈. 働 attack

戕害 qiánghài 働 slay, kill

臧 121 zāng Attack 戕 (phonetic) and subjugate 臣. 图 stolen goods 图 a surname

贓 122 [赃] zāng Money/shells 貝 stolen goods 臧 (phonetic). Simplified form uses 莊 simplification. 图 stolen goods ⇔ 分贓, 貪贓

臟物 zāngwù 图 booty, spoils

藏 77 cáng zàng 123 Grass 艸 covering spoils 臧 (phonetic). Simplified form uses 莊 simplification. cáng: 働 conceal 働 save, hoard zàng: 图 storehouse 働 Tibet ⇔ 匿藏, 收藏, 礦藏, 貯藏, 躲藏, 冷藏, 珍藏, 蘊藏, 隱藏, 埋藏, 西藏

藏匿 cángnì 働 conceal

藏書 cángshū 图 book collection

藏族 zàngzú 图 Tibetan people

臟 124 [脏] zàng Flesh 肉 concealed 藏 (phonetic). 图 internal organs ⇔ 內臟, 肺臟, 肝臟, 心臟, 腎臟

將 125 [将] jiàng jiāng Law 寸 with an early form of 醬 phonetic. Also explained as hand 寸 placing flesh 肉 on plank 爿 (phonetic). jiàng: general jiāng: 働 will, going to 働 (indicating inversion of verb and object) 將門關上 close the door ⇔ 即將, 麻將

將近 jiāngjìn 働 nearly, almost

將就 jiāngjiù 働 compromise, make the best of, make do with

將軍 jiāngjūn 图 general

將來 jiānglái 働 in the future

將領 jiànglǐng 图 general

將要 jiāngyào 働 will, going to

漿 126 [浆] jiāng Water 水 with 將 phonetic. 图 paste ⇔ 豆漿

獎 127 [奖] jiǎng Dog 犬 (often written as big 大) following leader's 將 (phonetic) orders. 働 encourage, reward 图 prize, award: 諾貝獎 Nobel Prize ⇔ 得獎, 誇獎, 嘉獎, 中獎, 過獎

獎金 jiǎngjīn 图 award, bonus

獎勵 jiǎnglì 働 reward, encourage materially 働 reward

獎牌 jiǎngpái 图 medal

獎券 jiǎngquàn 图 lottery ticket

獎學金 jiǎngxuéjīn 图 scholarship, fellowship

蔣 128 [蒋] jiǎng Grass 艸 with 將 phonetic. 图 a plant 图 a surname: 蔣介石 Chiang Kai-Shek

槳 129 [桨] jiǎng Commanding 將 (phonetic) wood 木. 图 oar

醬 130 [酱] jiàng Modern form shows vase 酉 with 將 phonetic. 图 jam, paste 图 soy ⇔ 炸醬麵, 果醬

醬油 jiàngyóu 图 soy sauce

壯 131 [壮] zhuàng Scholar/warrior 士 with 爿 phonetic. 働 big, great 图 strong, sturdy 働 strengthen: 壯膽子 get courage up ⇔ 健壯, 強壯, 茁壯

壯大 zhuàngdà 働 strong, robust 働 strengthen, expand

壯舉 zhuàngjǔ 图 heroic act

壯麗 zhuànglì 働 magnificent

壯年 zhuàngnián 图 prime of life

壯士 zhuàngshì 图 hero, warrior

壯族 zhuàngzú 图 the Zhuang people

莊 132 [庄] zhuāng Plants 艸 growing strong 壯 phonetic. Simplified form uses 广 and 土. 图 flourish 图 village 图 solemn 图 a surname ⇔ 村莊, 錢莊, 山莊

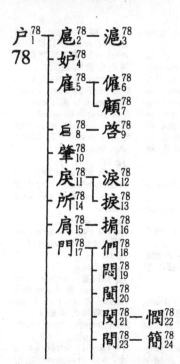

户 78 1	扈 78 2 — 滬 78 3	
78	妒 78 4	
	雇 78 5 — 催 78 6	
		顧 78 7
	启 78 8 — 啓 78 9	
	肇 78 10	
	戾 78 11 — 淚 78 12	
	所 78 14 — 捩 78 13	
	肩 78 15 — 掮 78 16	
	門 78 17 — 們 78 18	
		悶 78 19
		閏 78 20
		閔 78 21 — 憫 78 22
		間 78 23 — 簡 78 24

莊稼 zhuāngjià 图 farm goods

莊嚴 zhuāngyán 图 solemn, dignified

莊子 zhuāngzǐ 囚 Zhuang-zi - a Daoist philosopher

裝 77 zhuāng 133 [裝] Clothing 衣[26] with 壯[56] phonetic. 图 clothing 图 pretend, feign 图 install 假裝[156], 包裝[3], 時裝[5], 服裝[1], 戎裝[62], 安裝[60], 精裝[9], 武裝[8], 喬裝[9], 泳裝[120], 佯裝[15], 西裝[130], 軍裝[158], 晚裝[16], 偽裝[17]

裝扮 zhuāngbàn 图 adorn 图 masquerade, disguise

裝備 zhuāngbèi 图 equip, furnish 图 equipment

裝裱 zhuāngbiǎo 图 mount (paintings or calligraphy)

裝訂 zhuāngdìng 图 bind (books)

裝潢 zhuānghuáng 图 decorate (a room): 室內裝潢 interior decoration

裝配 zhuāngpèi 图 assemble: 裝配工 assembly work

裝設 zhuāngshè 图 install, equip

裝飾 zhuāngshì 图 decorate, adorn 图 decorations

裝修 zhuāngxiū 图 decorate: 室內裝修 interior decoration

裝置 zhuāngzhì 图 equip, install

裝作 zhuāngzuò 图 feign, pretend

狀 77 zhuàng 134 [狀] Dog 犬[91] with 爿[76] phonetic. 图 appearance 图 state, condition 图 describe ⇔ 慘狀[78], 形狀[82], 症狀[88],

現狀[119]

狀況 zhuàngkuàng 图 condition, situation

狀態 zhuàngtài 图 appearance, condition

妝 77 zhuāng 135 [妝] Woman 女[54] with 爿[76] phonetic. 图 put on make up ⇔ 化妝[47], 梳妝[98], 嫁妝[155]

妝台 zhuāngtái 图 dressing table

爿 77 chuáng 136 Lie flat 一| on a plank 爿[76] bed. 图 lie down

鼎 77 dǐng 137 Pictograph of a sacrificial vessel with body resembling 目[14] and handles and legs resembling 爿[76] and 片[76]. 图 ancient bronze tripod

户 78 hù 1 Pictograph of a door leaf. 图 door 图 household ⇔ 客戶[32], 農戶[131], 帳戶[33], 用戶[92], 門戶[76], 佃戶[91], 窗戶[144]

戶口 hùkǒu 图 population: 戶口制 population registration system

戶外 hùwài 图 outdoor

扈 78 hù 2 City 邑[42] with 戶[78] phonetic. 图 an ancient kingdom 图 insolent

滬 78 hù 3 [沪] Water 水[25] with 扈[2] phonetic. 图 local name of a river near Shanghai 图 Shanghai

滬語 hùyǔ 图 Shanghaiese

妒 78 dù 4 Woman 女[54] with 戶[78] phonetic. 图 envy ⇔ 嫉妒[82], 忌妒[87]

妒忌 dùjì 图 envy, be jealous of

雇 78 gù 5 Bird 隹[62] with 戶[78] phonetic. 图 a bird name 图

employ, hire
雇傭 gùyōng 動 employ, hire
雇用 gùyòng 動 employ, hire
雇主 gùzhǔ 名 employer

僱 6 [僱] Employ 雇 (phonetic) a person 人. 動 employ
僱用 gùyòng 動 employ, hire

顧 7 [顾] Head 頁 with 雇 phonetic. 動 turn head and look 動 attend to, look after 圈 a surname ⇔ 不顧, 光顧, 眷顧, 照顧, 回顧, 兼顧
顧及 gùjí 動 consider, take into account
顧忌 gùjì 圈 misgivings, scruples
顧客 gùkè 名 customer
顧慮 gùlǜ 名 concern, apprehension
顧問 gùwèn 名 adviser, consultant

启 8 Door 戶 mouth 口. 圖 open

啓 9 [启] Open 启 (phonetic) student's minds with strikes 攵. 動 explain, enlighten 動 start ⇔ 鈎啓, 開啓
啓程 qǐchéng 動 start on a journey, set out
啓動 qǐdòng 動 start (a machine)
啓發 qǐfā 動 inspire, arouse
啓蒙 qǐméng 動 enlighten
啓示 qǐshì 動 enlighten 名 inspiration, insight

肇 10 Strike 攵 with an ancient character from door 戶 and pen 聿 phonetic. 動 initiate
肇禍 zhàohuò 動 cause trouble
肇事 zhàoshì 動 cause trouble

戾 11 Dog 犬 in a doorway 戶. 動 crouch 圈 rebellious, violent ⇔ 暴戾, 罪戾

淚 12 [泪] Water 水 with 戾 phonetic. Simplified form uses 目. 名 tears ⇔ 眼淚, 流淚
淚水 lèishuǐ 名 tears
淚珠 lèizhū 名 teardrop

捩 13 Hand 手 with 戾 phonetic. 動 twist ⇔ 轉捩

所 14 Axe 斤 swinging like a door 戶 (phonetic). 圈 chopping sound 名 place (enumerating places) 兩所醫院 two hospitals 圈 which: 你所提到的問題 the problems which you mentioned 圈 (indicating passive construction) ⇔ 住所, 眾所周知, 無所謂, 診所, 托兒所, 寓所, 場所, 派出所, 廁所, 匪夷所思
被人所笑 be laughed at
所得 suǒdé 名 income: 所得稅 income tax; 所得分配 income distribution
所謂 suǒwèi 圈 so-called
所向披靡 suǒxiàngpīmǐ 圈 invincible
所以 suǒyǐ 圈 therefore
所有 suǒyǒu 動 own, possess: 所有權 property rights 圈 all
所在 suǒzài 名 place, location

肩 15 Flesh 肉 and door leaf 戶 (in early form suggests shape of shoulder). 名 shoulder ⇔ 披肩
肩膀 jiānbǎng 名 shoulder
肩負 jiānfù 動 shoulder, bear
肩頭 jiāntóu 名 shoulders

搯 16 With hand 手 and shoulder 肩 (phonetic). 動 shoulder
搯客 qiánkè 名 broker

門 17 [门] Double-leafed door 戶. 名 door, gate 名 school of thought 名 class, course: 你在修幾門課? How many classes are you taking? ⇔ 五花八門, 衙門, 部門, 拱門, 大門, 天安門, 後門, 城門, 肛門, 關門, 專門, 閉門, 熱門, 山門, 房門, 竅門, 出門, 柵門, 射門, 廈門, 澳門
門第 méndì 名 family status
門戶 ménhù 名 gate
門檻 ménkǎn 名 threshold
門口 ménkǒu 名 doorway, gateway, entrance
門票 ménpiào 名 admission ticket, cover charge
門神 ménshén 名 door-god
門生 ménshēng 名 pupil
門閂 ménshuān 名 bolt
門衛 ménwèi 名 door guard
門診 ménzhěn 名 out-patient service

們 18 [们] Person 人 with 門 phonetic. 圈 (indicating plurality of persons) 老師們 teachers ⇔ 人們, 你們, 妳們, 我們, 他們, 她們, 牠們, 它們, 咱們

悶 19 [闷] Heart 心 behind a door 門 (phonetic). mèn: 圈 depressed mēn: 圈 stuffy ⇔ 鬱悶, 納悶, 沈悶, 苦悶
悶氣 mēnqì 名 stuffy air 圈 bored
悶熱 mēnrè 圈 sweltering

閩 20 [闽] Snake 虫 with

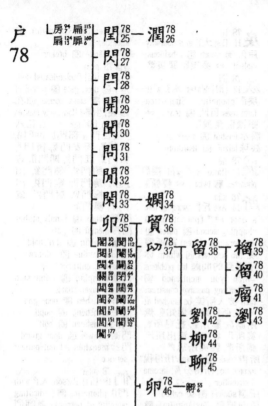

户 78

L房[94]扁[115] 扇[133]扉[169]

閏 78.25 — 潤 78.26
閃 78.27
閂 78.28
開 78.29
聞 78.30
問 78.31
閉 78.32
閑 78.33 — 嫻 78.34
卯 78.35 — 貿 78.36

閆[10].5 閩[10].112
閈[11].5 閬[10].104
閌[45] 闊[30].62
闃[59].17 閉[4].93
閣[68] 閥[76].75
閏[24] 閡[77].102
閘[131].62 閫[102]
閏[151] 闐[162].7
闔[9].177

卯 78.37 — 留 78.38 — 榴 78.39
           — 溜 78.40
           — 瘤 78.41
   劉 78.42 — 瀏 78.43
   柳 78.44
   聊 78.45

卯 78.46 — 孵 55.6

卯[39]

門[79] phonetic. 图 an ancient people in southeastern China 図 Fujian Province

閩南 mǐnnán 図 southern Fujian Province: 閩南話 Fukienese, Taiwanese

閔 78
21 [闵] Cultured 文[96] (phonetic) persons calling at door 門[79]. 動 mourn 图 a surname

憫 78
22 [悯] Heart 心[83] mourning 閔[21] (phonetic). 動 commiserate, sympathize ⇔ 憐憫[69]

間 78
23 [间] jiàn jiān Modern form shows sunlight 日[76] through a door 門[79]. jiàn: 图 space in between 動 divide jiān: 介 between, among 图 specific space or time 图 room 图 a measureword for rooms ⇔ 人間[10], 瞬間[85], 鄉間[48], 時間[37], 世間[100], 期間[56], 空

間[66], 之間[86], 區間[66], 中間[66], 夜間[77], 離間[47], 坊間[67], 房間[94], 民間[119], 車間[98]
間諜 jiàndié 图 spy
間斷 jiànduàn 動 interrupted, disconnected
間隔 jiàngé 图 partition
間接 jiànjiē 照 indirect
間歇 jiànxiē 照 intermittent

簡 78
24 [简] jiǎn Bamboo 竹[71] with 間[23] phonetic. 图 bamboo slips for writing on in ancient times 照 brief, simple
簡稱 jiǎnchēng 图 abbreviation 動 be abbreviated as
簡單 jiǎndān 照 simple
簡短 jiǎnduǎn 照 brief
簡化 jiǎnhuà 動 simplify
簡潔 jiǎnjié 照 succinct, concise
簡介 jiǎnjiè 图 synopsis
簡陋 jiǎnlòu 照 simple and crude
簡略 jiǎnlüè 照 brief, sketchy: 簡略語 abbreviation
簡體字 jiǎntǐzì 图 simplified Chinese characters
簡易 jiǎnyì 照 simple and easy
簡直 jiǎnzhí 動 simply

閏 78
25 [闰] rùn King 王[10] sitting at the door 門[79], as was customary during extra month added to lunar calendar. 图 intercalary month
閏年 rùnnián 图 leap year
閏月 rùnyuè 图 intercalary month

潤 78
26 [润] rùn Water 水[31] added 閏[25] (phonetic). 動 moisten 照 moist ⇔ 利潤[199], 濕潤[153]
潤滑 rùnhuá 動 lubricate

閃 78
27 [闪] shǎn Person 人[10] in a door 門[79]. 图 glimpse 動 flash 動 dodge, duck
閃電 shǎndiàn 图 lightning

閃光 shǎnguāng 🔟 flash, gleam, glitter

閃亮 shǎnliàng 🔡 flash of light

閃閃 shǎnshǎn 🔟 flash, sparkle

閂 78 shuān
28 [闩] A door 門㣎 with bar 一 across. 🔡 bolt, latch ⇔ 門閂閂㣎

開 78 kāi
29 [开] Door leaves 門㣎 spread evenly 幵㣎. 🔟 open 🔟 operate (a machine), drive (a vehicle) 🔟 begin 🔟 turn on 🔟 set out 🔟 hold (an event) 🔟 boil 🔟 (verbal complement indicating separation) 推開 push open ⇔ 撥開㣎, 公開㣎, 揭開㣎, 張開㣎, 分開㣎, 召開㣎, 打開㣎, 躲開㣎, 抛開㣎, 拉開㣎, 展開㣎, 撕開㣎, 避開㣎, 勞開㣎, 撤開㣎, 敞開㣎, 離開㣎, 散開㣎, 走開㣎, 放開㣎, 掀開㣎, 拆開㣎, 睜開㣎, 解開㣎, 推開㣎, 鑿開㣎

開衩 kāichà 🔡 slit, vent (on the side of a gown)

開車 kāichē 🔟 drive a car

開除 kāichú 🔟 dismiss, fire, expel

開創 kāichuàng 🔟 found, initiate

開刀 kāidāo 🔟 operate (on somebody)

開端 kāiduān 🔡 starting point

開發 kāifā 🔟 develop, open up

開放 kāifàng 🔟 bloom 🔟 open: 開放政策 open door policy

開關 kāiguān 🔡 switch

開花 kāihuā 🔟 bloom

開會 kāihuì 🔟 hold a meeting

開口 kāikǒu 🔟 open one's mouth, speak

開朗 kāilǎng 🔢 bright, clear

開鑼 kāiluó 🔟 begin (a performance of Chinese opera)

開明 kāimíng 🔢 enlightened, open-minded

開幕 kāimù 🔟 open, begin

開闢 kāipì 🔟 open up, start

開啓 kāiqǐ 🔟 open

開始 kāishǐ 🔟 start, begin 🔡 start, beginning

開水 kāishuǐ 🔡 boiled water

開通 kāitōng 🔢 enlightened, open-minded 🔟 clear

開拓 kāituò 🔟 open up: 開拓新市場 open up new markets

開往 kāiwǎng 🔟 leave for, be bound for

開味 kāiwèi 🔟 whet the appetite: 開味菜 appetizer

開心 kāixīn 🔢 happy, joyful

開學 kāixué 🔟 begin classes, begin school

開演 kāiyǎn 🔟 begin (a movie or performance)

開業 kāiyè 🔟 start a business

開展 kāizhǎn 🔟 develop

開支 kāizhī 🔡 expenditure, spending

聞 78 wén
30 [闻] Ear 耳㣎 and door 門㣎 (phonetic). 🔟 hear 🔟 smell ⇔ 新聞㣎, 傳聞㣎, 軼聞㣎, 醜聞㣎, 緋聞㣎

聞名 wénmíng 🔡 publicity

問 78 wèn
31 [问] Mouth 口㣎 and door 門㣎 (phonetic). 🔟 ask ⇔ 拷問㣎, 學問㣎, 詢問㣎, 詰問㣎, 疑問㣎, 訊問㣎, 請問㣎, 顧問㣎, 發問㣎, 訪問㣎, 質問㣎, 盤問㣎, 追問㣎

問答 wèndá 🔟 question and answer

問好 wènhǎo 🔟 send one's regards to: 請替我問他好 please send my regards

問號 wènhào 🔡 question mark

問候 wènhòu 🔟 send one's regards to: 請問候他 please wish him well

問卷 wènjuàn 🔡 questionnaire

問路 wènlù 🔟 ask the way

問題 wèntí 🔡 question 🔡 problem

閒 78 xián
32 [闲] Moonlight 月㣎 through a door 門㣎. 🔡 crack 🔢 tranquil 🔡 leisure time 🔡 idle: 我最近很閒. I've been very lazy recently. ⇔ 悠閒㣎, 空閒㣎, 休閒㣎

閒逛 xiánguàng 🔟 stroll

閒話 xiánhuà 🔡 gossip

閒談 xiántán 🔟 chat

閒暇 xiánxiá 🔡 leisure time

閒置 xiánzhì 🔢 idle

閑 78 xián
33 [闲] Door 門㣎 blocked by wood 木㣎. 🔡 barrier 🔢 idle (⇨ 閒㣎)

嫻 78 xián
34 [娴] Modern form shows woman 女㣎 with 閑㣎 phonetic. 🔢 refined

嫻熟 xiánshóu 🔢 adept, skilled

卯 78 mǎo
35 Door 門㣎 opened to spring. 🔢 lush 🔡 fourth Earthly Branch (⇨ 干支㣎)

卯勁 mǎojìn 🔟 make an all-out effort

貿 78 mào
36 [贸] Money/shells 貝㣎 with 卯㣎 phonetic. 🔡 trade ⇔ 外貿㣎

貿然 màorán 🔟 hastily

貿易 màoyì 🔡 trade: 貿易順差 trade surplus; 貿易逆差 trade deficit; 貿易戰 trade war

卬 78 yǒu
37 Open door 卯㣎 barred 一| (missing in modern form). 🔢 stop

留 78 liú
38 Stop 卬㣎 (phonetic) in a field 田㣎. 🔟 remain, stay 🔟 leave, leave behind 🔟 detain, delay ⇔ 拘留㣎, 居留㣎, 停留㣎, 滯留㣎, 扣留㣎, 逗留㣎, 保留㣎, 遺留㣎, 挽留㣎

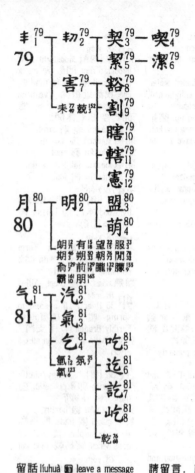

留話 líuhuà 🔊 leave a message
留戀 líuliàn 🔊 have sentimental attachment to
留念 líuniàn 🔊 keep as a memento
留下 líuxià 🔊 leave behind 🔊 remain, stay
留心 líuxīn 🔊 be attentive
留學 líuxué 🔊 study abroad: 留學生 student studying abroad
留言 líuyán 🔊 leave a message:

諸留言. Please leave a message.
留意 líuyì 🔊 keep in mind

榴 78 líu
39 Tree 木 with 留 phonetic. 🔊 pomegranate 🔊 a surname
榴彈 líudàn 🔊 grenade

溜 78 líu
40 Water 水 with 留 phonetic. líu: 🔊 slide 🔊 slip away ⇔ 滑溜
溜冰 líubīng 🔊 ice-skate
溜走 líuzǒu 🔊 slip away, skip out

瘤 78 líu
41 Sickness 疒 that stays 留 (phonetic). 🔊 tumor 🔊 毒瘤, 腫瘤, 腦瘤

劉 78 líu
42 [刘] Metal 金 knife 刀 with 卯 phonetic. Simplified form uses 文. 🔊 slay 🔊 a surname

瀏 78 líu
43 [浏] Water 水 with 劉 phonetic. 🔊 clear (water) 🔊 windy
瀏覽 líulǎn 🔊 skim, scan, browse: 瀏覽器 browser

柳 78 lǐu
44 Wood 木 with 卯 phonetic. 🔊 willow 🔊 a surname ⇔ 楊柳
柳橙 lǐuchéng 🔊 orange: 柳橙汁 orange juice

聊 78 liáo
45 Chat 耳 with 卯 phonetic. 🔊 chat, talk: 明天再聊. Talk to you again tomorrow. ⇔ 無聊
聊天 liáotiān 🔊 talk, chat

卵 78 luǎn
46 Pictograph of fish eggs resembling 卯 but unrelated. 🔊 ova, eggs ⇔ 魚卵
卵巢 luǎncháo 🔊 ovary

丰 79 jiè
1 Pictograph of a flourishing plant. Same character also represents notches cut in bamboo as a primitive record.

韧 79 qì
2 Notches 丰 cut with knife 刀. 🔊 record

契 79 qì
3 Record 韧 (phonet-

ic) of importance 大[罗]. 图 contract ⇔ 默契[罗]

契合 qìhé 图 agree, be consistent

契機 qìjī 图 opportunity

契約 qìyuē 图 contract

喫 79 chī 4 [吃罗] Mouth 口[68] with 契罗 phonetic. Variant of eat 吃罗.

絜 79 xié 5 Thread 糸[53] and notch 㓞罗 (phonetic). 图 bind

潔 79 jié 6 [洁] Water 水[2] with 絜罗 phonetic. Simplified form uses 吉罗. 图 clean ⇔ 皎潔[罗], 純潔[罗], 清潔[罗], 簡潔[罗], 整潔[罗]

潔白 jiébái 图 spotless

潔淨 jiéjìng 图 clean, untainted

害 79 hài 7 Mouth 口[68] speaking at home 宀[63] with 丰罗 phonetic. 图 harm 图 harm, misfortune ⇔ 災害[罗], 被害[罗], 公害[罗], 危害[罗], 誣害[罗], 厲害[罗], 迫害[罗], 傷害[罗], 戕害[罗], 妨害[罗], 殺害[罗], 受害[罗], 利害[罗], 陷害[罗], 禍害[罗], 損害[罗]

害處 hàichù 图 disadvantage

害怕 hàipà 图 图 fear

害人 hàirén 图 harm others

害死 hàisǐ 图 图 trouble

害羞 hàixiū 图 shy 图 shyness

豁 79 huō huò 8 Valley 谷[58] with 害罗 phonetic. huō: 图 图 crack 图 sacrifice huò: 图 generous, liberal

豁達 huòdá 图 open-minded

豁免 huòmiǎn 图 exempt from

豁然 huòrán 图 open and clear

割 79 gē 9 Harm 害罗 with knife 刀[罗]. 图 cut ⇔ 閹割[罗], 分割[罗]

割草 gēcǎo 图 mow grass

割除 gēchú 图 cut out

割斷 gēduàn 图 cut off

瞎 79 xiā 10 Eyes 目[14] harmed 害罗 (phonetic). 图 blind

瞎子 xiāzi 图 blind person

轄 79 xiá 11 [辖] Cart 車[58] and pierce/harm 害罗 (phonetic). 图 sound of cart 图 linchpin 图 govern, administer ⇔ 直轄[罗], 管轄[67]

轄區 xiáqū 图 administrative region

憲 79 xiàn 12 [宪] Eyes 目[14], mind/heart 心[83] and pierce/harm 害罗 (abbreviated). Simplified form uses 先[罗]. 图 intelligent 图 constitution

憲兵 xiànbīng 图 military police

憲法 xiànfǎ 图 constitution

月 80 yuè 1 Pictograph of a crescent moon. 图 图 moon month: 一月 January; 二月 February; 三月 March; 四月 April; 五月 May; 六月 June; 七月 July; 八月 August; 九月 September; 十月 October; 十一月 November; 十二月 December ⇔ 元月[罗], 歲月[罗], 蜜月[罗], 寅月[罗], 閏月[罗], 鬼月[罗]

月餅 yuèbǐng 图 moon cake

月初 yuèchū 图 beginning of the month

月底 yuèdǐ 图 end of the month

月份 yuèfèn 图 month

月光 yuèguāng 图 moonlight

月經 yuèjīng 图 menses, period

月曆 yuèlì 图 lunar calendar

月亮 yuèliàng 图 moon

月球 yuèqiú 图 moon

月蝕 yuèshí 图 lunar eclipse

明 80 míng 2 Sun 日[76] and moon 月[80]. Early form shows window 囧 and moon 月[80]. 图 bright, light 图 clear, evident 图 understand, know ⇔ 三明治[罗], 說明[罗], 光明[罗], 昆明[罗], 指明[罗], 標明[罗], 高明[罗], 明明[罗], 分明[罗], 聲明[罗], 載明[罗], 昌明[罗], 證明[罗], 清明[罗], 開明[罗], 發明[罗], 失明[罗], 文明[罗], 黎明[罗], 鮮明[罗], 表明[罗], 闡明[罗], 賢明[罗], 聰明[罗], 顯明[罗]

明白 míngbái 图 understand, realize: 明白了！I see!

明朗 mínglǎng 图 bright

明亮 míngliàng 图 bright

明瞭 míngliǎo 图 understand clearly 图 clear, simple

明明 míngmíng 图 clearly, definitely

明年 míngnián 图 next year

明確 míngquè 图 unequivocal, clear

明日 míngrì 图 tomorrow

明天 míngtiān 图 tomorrow

明文 míngwén 图 clear statement

明晰 míngxī 图 clear, distinct

明顯 míngxiǎn 图 obvious, apparent

明星 míngxīng 图 star, celebrity

明知 míngzhī 图 know full well

盟 80 méng 3 Clarify 明[80] relationship before gods with sacrificial blood 血[16] (abbreviated to 皿[16]). 图 alliance ⇔ 同盟[罗], 聯盟[罗]

盟國 méngguó 图 ally

盟約 méngyuē 图 alliance treaty

萌 80 méng 4 Plant 艸[罗] appearing 明[80] (phonetic). 图 sprout

萌芽 méngyá 图 sprout 蒙

气 81 qì 1 Pictograph of curling clouds. 图 air (⇔ 氣罗)

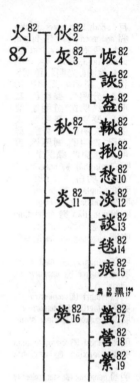

火⁸²₁ ┬ 伙⁸²₂
82   └ 灰⁸²₃ ┬ 恢⁸²₄
              ├ 詼⁸²₅
              └ 盉⁸²₆
         ├ 秋⁸²₇ ┬ 鞦⁸²₈
                 ├ 揪⁸²₉
                 └ 愁⁸²₁₀
         ├ 炎⁸²₁₁ ┬ 淡⁸²₁₂
                   ├ 談⁸²₁₃
                   ├ 毯⁸²₁₄
                   └ 痰⁸²₁₅
                       典 19 黑 144
         └ 熒⁸²₁₆ ┬ 螢⁸²₁₇
                   ├ 營⁸²₁₈
                   └ 縈⁸²₁₉

汽⁸¹₂ qì Watery 水₃ air 气⁸¹ (phonetic). 图 steam ⇔ 蒸汽₁₈

汽車 qìchē 图 car
汽水 qìshuǐ 图 soda
汽油 qìyóu 图 gasoline: 汽油站 gas station

氣⁸¹₃ qì [气⁸¹] Rice 米¹³⁸ dispursed like air 气⁸¹ (phonetic). 图 rice for guests 图 air 图 gas 图 manner, airs 图 spirit, morale 图 anger 图 語氣₄, 客氣₆, 元氣₁₅, 脾氣₅₈, 神氣₂₇, 淺氣₃₄, 景氣₅₀, 小氣₂₇, 士氣₂₁, 服氣₂₇, 力

氣₃⁷⁴, 天氣₇₈, 合氣道₁₃₂, 冷氣₅₈, 義氣₉₇, 風氣₁⁷, 空氣₆₈, 怒氣₉⁴, 晦氣₃₀, 意氣₅₉, 喪氣₉₉, 煤氣₁₈₂, 生氣₃₂, 俗氣₆₆, 勇氣₆₂, 名氣₅₉, 怨氣₆₇, 朝氣₃₉, 悶氣₃₉, 火氣⁸², 廢氣₁₇, 暖氣₃₆, 霧氣₉₅, 和氣₁₂₃, 香氣⁴⁶, 出氣¹⁰, 氧氣₁₄⁴, 骨氣₁₃₃, 喘氣₁³⁴, 淘氣₁₄⁴, 運氣₁₅⁸, 酒色財氣₁⁹, 稚氣⁴⁷

氣喘 qìchuǎn 图 gasp, pant: 氣喘病 asthma
氣氛 qìfēn 图 mood, atmosphere
氣憤 qìfèn 图 angry, furious, enraged

氣概 qìgài 图 spirit: 有男子氣概 macho
氣功 qìgōng 图 qigong
氣候 qìhòu 图 climate, weather
氣力 qìlì 图 physical strength
氣流 qìliú 图 air current
氣餒 qìněi 图 dispirited, discouraged
氣派 qìpài 图 manner: 學者氣派 scholarly manner
氣泡 qìpào 图 bubble
氣魄 qìpò 图 spirit, moral strength
氣球 qìqiú 图 balloon
氣勢 qìshì 图 vehemence, fervor
氣死 qìsǐ 图 anger, infuriate: 氣死人 infuriating 图 angered, infuriated
氣體 qìtǐ 图 gas
氣溫 qìwēn 图 air temperature
氣息 qìxí 图 breath
氣象 qìxiàng 图 weather: 氣象報告 weather report
氣質 qìzhí 图 disposition, temperament

乞⁸¹₄ qǐ Variation of air 气⁸¹. 图 beg
乞丐 qǐgài 图 beggar
乞求 qǐqiú 图 beg, request humbly
乞討 qǐtǎo 图 beg

吃⁸¹₅ chī Mouth 口⁶⁸ swirling like air 乞⁸¹ (phonetic). jí: 图 stammer chī: 图 eat 图 suffer, endure ⇔ 小吃₇, 好吃₃₄, 口吃⁶⁸
吃飽 chībǎo 图 eat until full: 你吃飽了嗎? Are you full?
吃醋 chīcù 图 jealous
吃掉 chīdiào 图 eat up
吃飯 chīfàn 图 eat
吃緊 chījǐn 图 tense, critical
吃驚 chījīng 图 frightened
吃苦 chīkǔ 图 suffer: 吃了很多苦 suffered greatly
吃虧 chīkuī 图 lose money

吃素 chīsù 🔲 be vegetarian
吃藥 chīyào 🔲 take medicine
吃齋 chīzhāi 🔲 be vegetarian (for religious reasons)

迄 81 qì
6 Motion 辵[il] with 乞[il] phonetic. 🔲 up to
迄今 qìjīn 🔲 up to now, so far

訖 81 qì
7 [讫] Words 言[il] with 乞[il] phonetic. 🔲 complete ⇔ 收訖[il]

屹 81 yì
8 Mountain 山[il] high in the air 乞[il] (phonetic). 🔲 rise majestically
屹立 yìlì 🔲 tower, rise majestically

火 82 huǒ
1 Pictograph of rising flames. 🔲 fire, flame 🔲 a surname ⇔ 縱火[il], 燐火[il], 打火機[il], 停火[il], 滅火[il], 起火[il], 燈火[il], 螢火蟲[il], 營火[il], 洋火[il], 煙火[il], 軍火[il]
火把 huǒbǎ 🔲 torch
火柴 huǒchái 🔲 match
火車 huǒchē 🔲 train: 火車站 train station
火光 huǒguāng 🔲 firelight
火鍋 huǒguō 🔲 hot pot
火箭 huǒjiàn 🔲 rocket
火警 huǒjǐng 🔲 fire alarm
火坑 huǒkēng 🔲 fire pit 🔲 hellish situation
火爐 huǒlú 🔲 stove
火氣 huǒqì 🔲 temper
火山 huǒshān 🔲 volcano
火速 huǒsù 🔲 at top speed
火腿 huǒtuǐ 🔲 ham
火焰 huǒyàn 🔲 flame
火藥 huǒyào 🔲 gunpowder
火災 huǒzāi 🔲 fire, conflagration
火葬 huǒzàng 🔲 cremation
火種 huǒzhǒng 🔲 kindling

伙 82 huǒ
2 Person 人[il] at the same fire 火[il] (phonetic). 🔲 partner ⇔ 小伙子[il], 傢伙[il]
伙伴 huǒbàn 🔲 partner

灰 82 huī
3 Fire 火[il] that can be handled (originally right hand 又[il], now written as left hand 𠂇[il]). 🔲 gray ⇔ 石灰[il], 煙灰[il]
灰塵 huīchén 🔲 dust
灰燼 huījìn 🔲 ashes
灰色 huīsè 🔲 gray
灰市 huīshì 🔲 gray market
灰心 huīxīn 🔲 disheartened

恢 82 huī
4 Heart 心[il] with 灰[il] phonetic. 🔲 vast
恢復 huīfù 🔲 recover
恢弘 huīhóng 🔲 extensive

詼 82 huī
5 [诙] Words 言[il] neither black nor white 灰[il] (phonetic). 🔲 funny
詼諧 huīxié 🔲 humorous, funny

盔 82 kuī
6 Gray 灰[il] (phonetic) platter 皿[il] on the head. 🔲 helmet ⇔ 頭盔[il]
盔甲 kuījiǎ 🔲 armor

秋 82 qiū
7 Grain 禾[il] with 火[il] phonetic. 🔲 autumn, fall 🔲 year ⇔ 春秋[il], 中秋節[il]
秋分 qiūfēn 🔲 fall equinox
秋千 qiūqiān 🔲 swing (⇔ 鞦韆)
秋色 qiūsè 🔲 autumn colors
秋天 qiūtiān 🔲 autumn, fall

鞦 82 qiū
8 [秋] Leather 革[il] with 秋[il] phonetic. 🔲 swing
鞦韆 qiūqiān 🔲 swing

揪 82 jiū
9 Hand 手[il] with 秋[il] phonetic. 🔲 grab, clutch
揪出 jiūchū 🔲 ferret out

愁 82 chóu
10 Autumnal 秋[il] (phonetic) heart 心[il]. 🔲 worry ⇔ 憂愁[il]

炎 82 yán
11 Fire 火[il] doubled. 🔲 blaze 🔲 inflammation, infection ⇔ 肺炎[il], 肝炎[il], 發炎[il]
炎熱 yánrè 🔲 blazing hot

淡 82 dàn
12 Water 水[il] with 炎[il] phonetic. 🔲 flavorless 🔲 weak (tea) 🔲 light (color or food) ⇔ 冷淡[il], 慘淡[il], 沖淡[il], 清淡[il]
淡泊 dànbó 🔲 live free of worldly desires
淡薄 dànbó 🔲 weak, faint
淡淡 dàndàn 🔲 light, weak
淡化 dànhuà 🔲 desalinate 🔲 dilute
淡季 dànjì 🔲 off season
淡漠 dànmò 🔲 indifferent, aloof, apathetic
淡水 dànshuǐ 🔲 fresh water

談 82 tán
13 [谈] Words 言[il] with 炎[il] phonetic. 🔲 discuss, chat: 談得來 have a good rapport 🔲 a surname ⇔ 晤談[il], 漫談[il], 交談[il], 洽談[il], 座談[il], 侈談[il], 攀談[il], 閒談[il], 和談[il], 會談[il], 面談[il]
談到 tándào 🔲 speak of
談話 tánhuà 🔲 🔲 talk, chat
談論 tánlùn 🔲 discuss 🔲 discussion
談判 tánpàn 🔲 negotiate, bargain 🔲 negotiations
談談 tántán 🔲 discuss
談吐 tántǔ 🔲 style of speech: 談吐風趣 interesting way of speaking

火
82

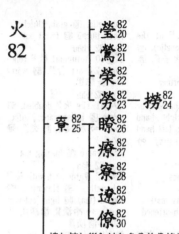

瑩 82 20
鶯 82 21
榮 82 22
勞 82 23 — 撈 82 24
寮 82 25 ┬ 瞭 82 26
療 82 27
寮 82 28
遼 82 29
僚 82 30

煌17 焙18 灾19 炷19 灸19 炊19 烙21 燐21 光42 烤19
熹17 爐19 煞19 烘19 爆19 叟19 票19 烝21 炮22 炸19
烹20 熟21 丙21 炳21 炒22 庶24 燕24 黃21 照21 赤25
炕22 熨23 滅23 焊25 炫26 灼26 杲27 煥29 熱29 炭29
燥24 煤24 爍30 熔30 燈31 燒32 灶32 煮35 燙40 焚42
爛24 煉34 然33 燃37 狄44 熬47 爐44 羔49 煽123 燭125
煎42 朕42 煙47 焰47 鐙48 炙49 熊49 爍49 烈49 耿127
熄49 燴144 照145 煩16 焦26

心 83
1
┬ 芯 83 2
蕊 83 3
惢 83 4 — 愛 83 5 — 曖 83 6

毯 82 14 tǎn
Wool 毛90 with 炎97
phonetic. 图 blanket, rug ⇔
地毯26, 毛毯90
毯子 tǎnzi 图 blanket

痰 82 15 tán
Sickness 疒76
erupting like flames 炎97 (phonetic). 图 spit, phlegm ⇔
吐痰97

炎 82 16 [焱] Lamp fires 火82
in a room 宀24. 图 shining,
glowing
熒熒 yíngyíng 围 luminous 围
luxuriant

螢 82 17 [萤] Glowing 熒82
(phonetic, abbreviated) insect
虫125. 图 lightning bug,
glowworm
螢光 yíngguāng 围 fluores-
cence: 螢光幕 (computer)
screen; 围 螢光屏 (computer)
screen
螢火蟲 yínghuǒchóng 图 firefly
螢幕 yíngmù 图 围 (computer)
screen

營 82 18 [营] Housed legion 官
(abbreviated) with glowing
fires 熒82 (phonetic, abbreviated). 图 encampment 围 围
battalion 围 a surname ⇔
經營3, 紫營3, 露營3, 鑽
營41, 公營12, 私營12, 國營12,
野營12, 民營19, 陣營15
營地 yíngdì 图 campground
營火 yínghuǒ 图 campfire
營建 yíngjiàn 围 construct
營利 yínglì 图 operating profit
围 profit: 非營利 non-profit
營養 yíngyǎng 图 nourishment,
nutrition
營業 yíngyè 围 do business: 營
業時間 business hours
營運 yíngyùn 围 operations
營造 yíngzào 围 construct: 營
造企業 construction company

縈 82 19 [萦] Thread 糸153 with
熒82 (abbreviated) phonetic.
围 entwine
縈繞 yíngrào 围 swirl around

瑩 82 20 [莹] Glow 熒82 (phonetic, abbreviated) of jade
玉97. 图 jade-like stone 围
shining ⇔ 晶瑩20

鶯 82 21 [莺] Bird 鳥178 with
熒82 (or 榮82) phonetic and
suggestive of bright or lush.
图 greenfinch ⇔ 流鶯23

榮 82 22 [荣] Bright 熒82 (phonetic, abbreviated) trees 木77.
围 firmiana tree 围 lush, leafy
glory, honor ⇔ 光榮42,
繁榮32, 欣欣向榮9, 虛
榮27
榮民 róngmín 图 围 veteran
榮辱 róngrù 图 honor or dishonor
榮幸 róngxìng 图 honor
榮耀 róngyào 图 honor, glory
榮譽 róngyù 图 honor, glory

勞 82 láo
23 [劳] Burning 熒營 (abbreviated) strength 力. labor, exert deed, service ⇔ 酬勞, 疲勞, 勤勞, 功勞, 麥當勞

勞動 láodòng labor
勞煩 láofán trouble somebody for a favor
勞改 láogǎi reform through forced labor: 勞改營 reeducation camp, gulag
勞工 láogōng labor
勞駕 láojià May I trouble you...?
勞力 láolì physical labor, manual labor
勞務 láowù service

撈 82 lāo
24 [捞] Hand 手 laboring 勞 (phonetic). dredge for
撈麵 lāomiàn lo mein

寮 82 liáo
25 Fire 火 (altered) and an ancient character for careful. sacrificical fire

瞭 82 liǎo liào
26 [了] Eyes 目 and sacrificial fire 寮 (phonetic). liǎo: bright understand liào: watch from a high place ⇔ 明瞭
瞭解 liǎojiě understand
瞭望 liàowàng watch from a distance

療 82 liáo
27 [疗] Sacrifices 寮 (phonetic) to cure illness 疒. Simplified form uses 了. treat, cure ⇔ 醫療, 診療, 治療
療法 liáofǎ therapy

寮 82 liáo
28 Roof 宀 over a fire 寮 (phonetic). hut
寮國 liáoguó Laos

遼 82 liáo
29 [辽] Movement 辵 with 寮 phonetic. Simplified form uses 了. distant
遼闊 liáokùo vast, boundless
遼寧 liáoníng Liaoning Province

僚 82 liáo
30 Person 人 bright like fire 寮 (phonetic). official colleague ⇔ 同僚, 官僚

心 83 xīn
1 Pictograph of a heart. heart mind feelings center, middle ⇔ 一心, 人心, 潛心, 核心, 良心, 有心, 私心, 擔心, 內心, 點心, 貼心, 小心, 真心, 疑心, 決心, 貪心, 戒心, 安心, 關心, 專心, 當心, 存心, 費心, 熱心, 操心, 甘心, 信心, 中心, 忠心, 衷心, 用心, 痛心, 精心, 銘心, 傷心, 開心, 留心, 灰心, 愛心, 芳心, 放心, 匠心, 野心, 軸心, 偏心, 粗心, 民心, 醉心, 恆心, 死心, 耐心, 細心, 身心, 唯心論, 惡心

心不在焉 xīnbùzàiyān absent-minded
心服 xīnfú admire sincerely
心腹 xīnfù confidential
心肝 xīngān darling, sweetheart
心狠手辣 xīnhěnshǒulà merciless and vicious
心懷 xīnhuái harbor, cherish
心焦 xīnjiāo anxious
心境 xīnjìng mood
心理 xīnlǐ mental state, mentality: 心理學 psychology; 心理學家 psychologist;

心理戰 psychological warfare
心裡 xīnlǐ in one's heart mentally: 心裡不平衡 mentally unstable
心靈 xīnlíng clever soul, spirit
心目 xīnmù heart, mind
心情 xīnqíng mood, mental state: 心情不穩定 emotionally unstable
心聲 xīnshēng intention, thinking
心事 xīnshì private worries
心思 xīnsī thoughts, thinking
心碎 xīnsuì heart-broken
心態 xīntài mentality
心疼 xīnténg love dearly
心跳 xīntiào heartbeat, palpitations
心頭 xīntóu heart, mind
心想 xīnxiǎng wish
心意 xīnyì intention affection
心願 xīnyuàn wish
心臟 xīnzàng heart: 心臟病 heart disease
心智 xīnzhì intelligence, mental power
心中 xīnzhōng in one's heart

芯 83 xīn
2 Plant's 艸 heart 心 (phonetic). xīn: pith xìn: center

蕊 83 ruǐ
3 Plant's 艸 hearts 心. flower bud stamen, pistil

恶 83 ài
4 Heart 心 with an ancient character resembling 无 phonetic. love (⇒ 愛)

愛 83 ài
5 [爱] Love 恶 (altered) and walk 夊. Simplified form uses friend 友. gait love ⇔ 仁愛, 敬

心
83

牙 84₁
├ 芽 84₂
├ 呀 84₃
├ 鴉 84₄
├ 雅 84₅
├ 訝 84₆
├ 邪 84₇
├ 穿 84₈
└ 掌⁶³

巴 85₁
├ 吧 85₂
├ 疤 85₃
├ 芭 85₄
├ 笆 85₅
├ 把 85₆
├ 範 85₇
└ 爸 85₈

愛¹⁹⁸, 可愛²⁷, 做愛¹⁴, 恩愛⁷², 親愛的⁸⁷, 慈愛⁶³, 熱愛⁵⁹, 博愛⁸⁰, 喜愛⁶⁶, 情愛²⁰, 鍾愛²⁹⁸, 酷愛⁹⁷, 相愛¹¹⁴, 偏愛¹¹⁵, 溺愛²⁶, 籠愛¹³², 戀愛¹⁵³

愛爾蘭 àiěrlán 🔲 Ireland
愛撫 àifǔ 🔲 caress
愛國 àigúo 🔲 be patriotic
愛好 àihào 🔲 hobby: 愛好者 fan, lover
愛護 àihù 🔲 cherish, protect
愛慕 àimù 🔲 adore
愛錢 àiqián 🔲 greedy
愛情 àiqíng 🔲 love
愛人 àirén 🔲 🔲 lover 🔲 🔲 spouse
愛上 àishàng 🔲 fall in love with
愛惜 àixí 🔲 cherish
愛心 àixīn 🔲 compassion
愛滋病 àizībìng 🔲 AIDS

暖 83 ài
6 [暖] Sun 日⁷⁶ clouded like judgment is by love 愛³⁷ (phonetic). 🔲 dim
暖昧 àimèi 🔲 ambiguous 🔲 dubious

牙 84 yá
1 Pictograph of a canine tooth. 🔲 tooth ⇔ 匈牙利³, 刷牙⁴, 葡萄牙²⁸, 尾牙³, 西班牙¹⁰, 象牙⁷²
牙齒 yáchǐ 🔲 tooth
牙膏 yágāo 🔲 toothpaste
牙科 yákē 🔲 dentistry
牙籤 yáqiān 🔲 toothpick
牙刷 yáshuā 🔲 toothbrush
牙痛 yátòng 🔲 toothache
牙醫 yáyī 🔲 dentist
牙齦 yáyín 🔲 gums

芽 84 yá
2 Plant 艸⁶ sprouting like canines 牙¹ (phonetic). 🔲 sprout, bud ⇔ 豆芽⁸⁴, 萌芽³⁷, 發芽⁹⁸

呀 84 yā
3 Mouth 口⁶⁶ gaping to reveal teeth 牙¹⁴ (phonetic). 🔲 a particle indicating surprise or emphasis 🔲 creak ⇔ 哎呀³

鴉 84 yā
4 [鸦] Modern form shows bird 鳥¹⁷⁶ with 牙¹⁴

phonetic. 图 raven ⇔ 烏鴉[170]

鴉片 yāpiàn,yǎpiàn 图 opium: 鴉片戰爭 Opium War

雅 84 yǎ
5 Bird 佳[162] with 牙[84] phonetic. 图 raven (⇒ 鴉[170]) 图 refined, elegant ⇔ 古雅[24], 文雅[28], 典雅[119]
雅緻 yǎzhì 图 refined, elegant 图 elegance

訝 84 yà
6 [讶] Words 言[49] with 牙[84] phonetic. 图 meet surprised ⇔ 驚訝[185]

邪 84 xié
7 City 邑[74] with 牙[84] phonetic. 图 a county name 图 evil ⇔ 祛邪[28], 避邪[42], 妖邪[27]
邪惡 xié'è 图 evil
邪路 xiélù 图 evil ways
邪說 xiéshuō 图 heresy

穿 84 chuān
8 Bore a hole 穴[51] with the teeth 牙[84]. 图 cut through 图 wear, put on ⇔ 揭穿[42], 貫穿[77], 看穿[115], 戳穿[124]
穿插 chuānchā 图 weave in
穿戴 chuāndài 图 wear
穿過 chuānguò 图 cut through
穿上 chuānshàng 图 put on, wear
穿梭 chuānsuō 图 shuttle back and forth
穿透 chuāntòu 图 penetrate, pierce
穿越 chuānyuè 图 cross, pass through
穿著 chuānzhuó 图 dress, clothing

巴 85 bā
1 Pictograph of a snake raised on its tail. 图 python 图 await 图 a surname ⇔ 下巴[66], 古巴[24], 哈巴狗[45], 嘴巴[97], 尾巴[89], 啞巴[166]
巴不得 bābude 图 wish anxiously 图 cannot wait to

巴基斯坦 bājīsītǎn 图 Pakistan
巴結 bājié 图 curry favor
巴勒斯坦 bālèsītǎn 图 Palestine
巴黎 bālí 图 Paris
巴拿馬 bānámǎ 图 Panama
巴西 bāxī 图 Brazil
巴掌 bāzhǎng 图 palm: 打巴掌 slap

吧 85 bā ba
2 Mouth 口[48] big like a snake 巴[85] (phonetic). ba: 图 (indicating imperative tense) 走吧! Let's go! 图 (indicating agreement) 好吧 o.k. 图 (indicating uncertainty) 他不來吧? He isn't coming? bā: 图 bar ⇔ 酒吧[159]
吧女 bānǚ 图 bar girl

疤 85 bā
3 Sickness 疒[76] with 巴[85] phonetic. 图 scar
疤痕 bāhén 图 scar

芭 85 bā
4 Plant 艸[65] with 巴[85] phonetic. 图 plantain
芭蕉 bājiāo 图 plantain
芭樂 bālè 图 guava
芭蕾 bālěi 图 ballet

笆 85 bā
5 Bamboo 竹[71] with 巴[85] phonetic. 图 bamboo fence ⇔ 籬笆[79]

把 85 bǎ bà
6 Hand 手[59] gripping python 巴[85] (phonetic). bǎ: 图 hold, grasp 图 measureword for objects with handles (indicating inversion of verb and object): 把筆給我 give the pen to me bà: 图 handle ⇔ 拖把[68], 火把[92], 車把[198]
把柄 bǎbǐng 图 hold 图 handle
把風 bǎfēng 图 stand guard 图 lookout
把守 bǎshǒu 图 guard
把手 bǎshǒu 图 handle
把握 bǎwò 图 grab, grasp

confident, sure
把戲 bǎxì 图 juggling

靶 85 bǎ
7 Leather 革[24] with 巴[85] phonetic. 图 bridle 图 target ⇔ 打靶[36]

爸 85 bà
8 Father 父[53] with 巴[85] phonetic. 图 father, pa
爸爸 bàba 图 father, papa: 爸爸媽媽 mom and dad, parents

爬 85 pá
9 Claw 爪[103] with 巴[85] phonetic. 图 climb, clamber 图 crawl 图 lie prone ⇔ 攀爬[28]
爬起來 páqǐlái 图 get up
爬山 páshān 图 mountain climb
爬上 páshàng 图 climb on
爬樹 páshù 图 climb a tree
爬下 páxià 图 climb off
爬行 páxíng 图 crawl, creep: 爬行動物 reptile

琶 85 pá
10 Jade 玉[97] with 巴[85] phonetic. ⇔ 琵琶[7]

勿 86 wù
1 Pictograph of banners on a pole used to direct troops. 图 do not: 請勿吸煙. No smoking.

忽 86 hū
2 Heart 心[83] with 勿[86] phonetic. 图 neglect 图 suddenly ⇔ 輕忽[26], 倏忽[26], 疏忽[22]
忽見 hūjiàn 图 see suddenly
忽略 hūlüè 图 neglect
忽然 hūrán 图 suddenly
忽視 hūshì 图 neglect, ignore, overlook

惚 86 hū
3 Mind/heart 心[83] neglecting 忽[86] (phonetic). 图 absent-minded ⇔ 恍惚[45]

吻 86 wěn
4 Mouth's 口[48] pennant-like 勿[86] part. 图 lips 图 kiss ⇔ 親吻[27], 接吻[89]

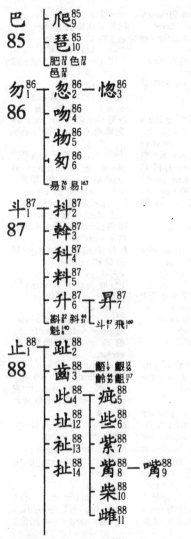

物箔, 作物栽, 植物黏, 穀
物黏, 刊物蕊, 藥物髓, 事
物黏, 博物號, 生物籠, 禮
物黏, 動物籠, 贓物匜, 廢
物階, 文物階, 寵物雞, 唯物
論盜, 購物盜

物價 wùjià 图 commodity prices, prices

物理 wùlī 图 physics: 物理學 physics

物色 wùsè 图 scout for (talent)

物體 wùtī 图 object

物質 wùzhí 图 material: 物質主義 materialism

物資 wùzī 图 supplies, resources

匆 86 cōng
6 Modern form of alarmed 悤 resembling 勿. 图 hurriedly

匆匆 cōngcōng 图 hurriedly

匆促 cōngcù 图 hurriedly: 匆促時間 pressed for time

匆忙 cōngmáng 图 hurriedly

斗 87 dǒu
1 Pictograph of a container. 图 ten liters 图 wine barrel: 北斗七星 Big Dipper ⇔ 熨斗, 煙斗

斗笠 dǒulì conical bamboo hat

斗篷 dǒupéng 图 cape

抖 87 dǒu
2 Hand 手 with 斗 phonetic. 图 shake 图 shiver ⇔ 顫抖, 發抖

抖動 dǒudòng 图 shiver, shake

抖擻 dǒusǒu 图 rouse

斡 87 wò
3 Ten liters 斗 with 倝 phonetic. 图 ladle handle 图 revolve

斡旋 wòxuán 图 mediate

科 87 kē
4 Grain 禾 measured 斗 and sorted. 图 section, division 图 department, branch of study ⇔ 教科書, 專科, 莫斯科, 外科, 百

吻合 wěnhé 图 tally, coincide

物 86 wù
5 Ox 牛 with 勿 phonetic. 图 thing, object ⇔ 人物, 玩物, 食物, 飾物, 化合物, 貨物, 怪

科全書[29], 本科[22], 牙科[14], 前科[19]

科技 kējì [動] technology: 高科技 high-technology

科舉 kējǔ [名] civil service exam
科目 kēmù [名] field of study, subject

科學 kēxué [名] science: 科學家 scientist

料 [87] liào

5 Rice 米[38] measured 斗[17]. [動] calculate [動] predict, expect [名] material ⇔ 不料[40], 原料[24], 資料[95], 飲料[45], 佐料[74], 飼料[42], 肥料[75], 照料[93], 塑料[92], 材料[94], 意料[82], 史料[92], 燃料[97], 預料[102]

料理 liàolǐ [動] arrange, manage [名] cuisine: 日本料理 Japanese food

料想 liàoxiǎng [動] expect, imagine

升 [87] shēng

6 Pictograph based on container 斗[17] (altered). [量] liter [動] rise ⇔ 上升[43], 公升[26], 攀升[87], 提升[35], 擢升[74], 晉升[128]

升級 shēngjí [動] advance to a higher level

升遷 shēngqiān [動] be promoted
升學 shēngxué [動] enter a higher level school

升值 shēngzhí [動] revalue, appreciate

昇 [87] shēng

7 [升[87]] Rise 升[87] (phonetic) sunward 日[76]. [動] ascend ⇔ 直昇機[55], 提昇[35]

昇華 shēnghuá [名] sublimation, distillation

止 [88] zhǐ

1 Pictograph of a foot with protruding toes. [省] toes (⇒趾[88]) [動] stop [動] arrive limit: 不止 not limited to ⇔ 舉止[93], 遏止[128], 停止[26], 終止[97], 截止[128], 中止[28], 禁

止[77], 制止[43], 休止[77], 廢止[97], 防止[97], 靜止[82], 阻止[117], 為止[11]

止步 zhǐbù [動] halt

止境 zhǐjìng [名] limit: 無止境 limitless

趾 [88] zhǐ

2 Toes 止[88] (phonetic) with foot 足[86] redundant. [名] toes ⇔ 拇趾[58]

齒 [88] chǐ

3 [齿] Pictograph of teeth with 止[88] phonetic. [名] tooth ⇔ 口齒[68], 牙齒[14], 犬齒[71], 臼齒[31]

齒輪 chǐlún [名] gear

此 [88] cǐ

4 Stop 止[88] (phonetic) and turn around 匕[17]. [代] this ⇔ 從此[61], 就此[43], 彼此[58], 故此[43], 因此[47], 如此[20], 由此[113], 自此[79], 為此[71]

此後 cǐhòu [副] henceforth, thereafter

此外 cǐwài [連] besides

疵 [88] cī

5 Sickness 疒[26] here 此[88] (phonetic). [名] blemish, flaw ⇔ 瑕疵[112]

些 [88] xiē

6 A couple 二[2] of these 此[88] (phonetic). [量] some, a few ⇔ 一些[1], 險些[72], 有些[52], 好些[57], 某些[60], 這些[97], 那些[97], 哪些[97]

紫 [88] zǐ

7 Silk thread 糸[53] with 此[88] phonetic. [形] purple

紫禁城 zǐjìnchéng [名] Forbidden City

紫色 zǐsè [名] purple

觜 [88] zuǐ

8 Horn-like 角[69] with 此[88] phonetic. [名] owl horns

嘴 [88] zuǐ

9 Horn-like 觜[88] (phonetic) mouth 口[68]. [名] beak,

snout, mouth ⇔ 閉嘴[91], 繞嘴[51], 插嘴[38]

嘴巴 zuǐbā [名] mouth

嘴唇 zuǐchún [名] lip

嘴臉 zuǐliǎn [名] [貶] face, features

柴 [88] chái

10 Wood 木[7] with 此[88] phonetic. [名] firewood [姓] a surname ⇔ 火柴[62]

柴油 cháiyóu [名] diesel fuel

雌 [88] cí

11 Bird 隹[62] with 此[88] phonetic. [形] female (bird or other animal)

雌性 cíxìng [形] female

雌雄 cíxióng [名] female and male

址 [88] zhǐ

12 Soil 土[7] under foot 止[88] (phonetic). [名] foundation site, location ⇔ 住址[5], 地址[93], 遺址[105]

祉 [88] zhǐ

13 Omen 示[10] with 止[88] phonetic. [名] blessings ⇔ 福祉[10]

扯 [88] chě

14 Modern form shows hand 手[28] and foot 止[88]. [動] pull [動] tear, rip ⇔ 拉扯[27], 牽扯[77]

扯鈴 chělíng [名] yo-yo

癶 [88] bò

15 Feet 止[88] (abbreviated) in opposite directions.

發 [88] fā

16 [发] Bow 弓[65] opening path (phonetic, ancient character showing stamp 殳[27] with the feet 癶[88]). [動] shoot, launch [動] issue, distribute [動] become, occur [動] express, utter ⇔ 批發[52], 暴發[65], 爆發[65], 蒸發[116], 揭發[59], 沙發[85], 勃發[60], 頒發[126], 打發[37], 越發[74], 煥發[65], 引發[67], 散發[30], 啟發[68], 開發[79], 告發[25], 激發[55], 出發[110], 觸發[69], 奮發[85], 奮發[85]

發抖 fādǒu 🔲 shiver

發瘋 fāfēng 🔲 go crazy: 你發瘋了。You're crazy.

發光 fāguāng 🔲 shine

發慌 fāhuāng 🔲 become flustered

發揮 fāhuī 🔲 give full play to

發昏 fāhūn 🔲 feel faint 🔲 be in a daze

發覺 fājué 🔲 discover, realize

發掘 fājué 🔲 excavate, unearth

發狂 fākuáng 🔲 go crazy

發愣 fālèng 🔲 be astonished

發亮 fāliàng 🔲 glow

發霉 fāméi 🔲 become mildewed

發明 fāmíng 🔲 invent 🔲 invention

發起 fāqǐ 🔲 initiate: 發起人 initiator, sponsor

發燒 fāshāo 🔲 develop a fever

發射 fāshè 🔲 shoot, launch

發生 fāshēng 🔲 take place, happen

發誓 fāshì 🔲 swear, pledge, vow

發售 fāshòu 🔲 sell, put on the market

發問 fāwèn 🔲 ask a question

發現 fāxiàn 🔲 discover, realize

發酵 fāxiào 🔲 ferment

發洩 fāxiè 🔲 let out, vent

發行 fāxíng 🔲 publish, distribute

發芽 fāyá 🔲 sprout, bud

發言 fāyán 🔲 speak, give a speech: 發言人 spokesperson

發炎 fāyán 🔲 become infected, become inflamed

發揚 fāyáng 🔲 foster, carry on (a tradition)

發音 fāyīn 🔲 pronounce 🔲 pronunciation

發育 fāyù 🔲 grow, develop 🔲 growth, development

發展 fāzhǎn 🔲 develop: 發展中國家 developing country 🔲 development: 經濟發展 economic development

發作 fāzuò 🔲 go into action

發表 fābiǎo 🔲 issue, publish 🔲 state, present: 發表意見 state one's views; 發表文章 present a paper

發布 fābù 🔲 announce

發佈 fābù 🔲 announce

發財 fācái 🔲 get rich

發出 fāchū 🔲 send out

發達 fādá 🔲 developed: 發達國家 developed country

發呆 fādāi 🔲 stupefied

發電 fādiàn 🔲 generate electricity

發動 fādòng 🔲 launch, mobilize

廢 88 fèi
17 [廢] Shelter 广 with 發 phonetic. useless abandon ⇔ 荒廢, 残廢, 半途而廢, 頹廢, 偏廢
廢除 fèichú abrogate, abolish
廢話 fèihuà Nonsense!
廢棄 fèiqì abandon
廢氣 fèiqì exhaust
廢物 fèiwù waste material
廢墟 fèixū ruins
廢止 fèizhǐ abolish
廢紙 fèizhǐ scrap paper

撥 88 bō
18 [拨] Hand 手 issuing 發 (phonetic). allocate stir batch, group ⇔ 調撥, 挑撥
撥款 bōkuǎn issue funds

潑 88 pō
19 [泼] Water 水 issuing 發 (phonetic). sprinkle 潑冷水 throw cold water on, dampen enthusiasm for ⇔ 活潑
潑婦 pōfù shrew
潑辣 pōlà vicious, spiteful

癸 88 guǐ
20 Modern form shows feet and sky. tenth Heavenly Stem (⇒干支)

揆 88 kuí
21 Hand 手 with 癸 phonetic. survey prime minister
揆測 kuícè calculate, guess

暌 88 kuí
22 Sun 日 with 癸 phonetic. separate
暌違 kuíwéi separated (friends)

葵 88 kuí
23 Plant 艸 with 癸 phonetic. sunflower 向日葵
葵瓜子 kuíguāzi sunflower seeds

葵花 kuíhuā sunflower

步 88 bù
24 One foot 止 then the other (reversed, resembling 少). step: 第一步 first step condition, situation ⇔ 退步, 跑步, 漫步, 初步, 地步, 讓步, 卻步, 腳步, 徒步, 邁步, 散步, 止步, 逐步, 進步
步道 bùdào sidewalk, footpath
步調 bùdiào pace, step
步伐 bùfá pace
步履 bùlǚ walk, travel by foot
步行 bùxíng walk
步驟 bùzòu step, measure

頻 88 pín
25 [频] Modern form shows step 步 and head 頁. frequently
頻道 píndào channel, frequency
頻繁 pínfán frequently, often
頻率 pínlǜ frequency
頻頻 pínpín again and again

蘋 88 píng
26 [苹] Plant 艸 with 頻 phonetic. Simplified form uses 平. apple
蘋果 píngguǒ apple

瀕 88 bīn
27 [濒] Water 水 with 頻 phonetic. border on
瀕臨 bīnlín verging on

涉 88 shè
28 Watery 水 steps 步. wade, ford entangle, implicate ⇔ 交涉, 干涉, 牽涉, 跋涉
涉及 shèjí involve, relate to
涉嫌 shèxián be suspected of

走 88 jié
29 Hand 又 and feet 止 struggling to attain object 屮 (phonetic). quick (⇒捷)

捷 88 jié
30 Hand 手 moving quickly 走 (phonetic). triumph quick ⇔ 奏捷, 報捷, 敏捷
捷徑 jiéjìng shortcut
捷克 jiékè Czech Republic
捷運 jiéyùn rapid transit

睫 88 jié
31 Eye 目 and quick 走 (phonetic). eyelashes
睫毛 jiémáo eyelashes

肯 88 kěn
32 Modern form shows stop 止 and flesh 肉. agree, consent ⇔ 不肯, 首肯
肯定 kěndìng affirm

啃 88 kěn
33 Mouth 口 with 肯 phonetic. nibble, gnaw

企 88 qì 88 qǐ
34 Person 人 on toes 止. stand on tiptoes hope
企盼 qìpàn hope, anticipate
企圖 qìtú attempt, try, plot
企望 qìwàng hope, anticipate
企業 qìyè enterprise, business: 企業家 entrepreneur; 中小企業 small business

徙 88 xǐ
35 Move 足 feet 止. migrate ⇔ 遷徙

武 88 wǔ
36 Stop 止 invaders' lances 戈 (altered). military a surname: 武則天 Wu Zetian - a Tang dynasty empress valiant ⇔ 核武, 威武, 動武, 黷武
武打 wǔdǎ martial arts: 武打片 martial arts movie
武斷 wǔduàn arbitrary
武功 wǔgōng martial arts skill
武力 wǔlì military force

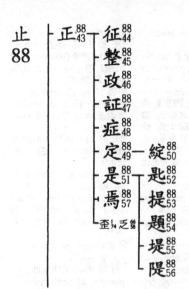

止
88

正 88/43
　征 88/44
　整 88/45
　政 88/46
　証 88/47
　症 88/48
　定 88/49 ─ 綻 88/50
　是 88/51 ┬ 匙 88/52
　　　　　├ 提 88/53
　焉 88/57 ├ 題 88/54
　　　　　├ 堤 88/55
　歪 ¼ 乏 88/58 └ 隄 88/56

武器 wǔqì 圖 weapons, armaments

武士 wǔshì 圖 warrior, knight, samurai

武術 wǔshù 圖 martial arts

武俠 wǔxiá 圖 chivalry: 武俠小說 martial arts novel

武藝 wǔyì 圖 martial arts skill

武裝 wǔzhuāng 圖 arm 圖 weapons, armaments

賦 88/37 fù [賦] Money/shells 貝¹⁵⁰ for the military 武 (phonetic). 圖 tax 圖 fu-type of prose poem ⇔ 稟賦 /⁶⁵

賦稅 fùshuì 圖 taxes

賦予 fùyǔ 圖 bestow, endow

賦與 fùyǔ 圖 bestow, endow

鵡 88/38 wǔ [鵡] Bird 鳥¹⁷⁸ with 武 phonetic. 圖 parrot ⇔ 鸚鵡 /⁵⁰

延 88/39 yán Drag ノ丨 and an ancient character showing stride 辵 ²/ and foot 止/⁷. 圖 prolong, extend 圖 postpone, delay ⇔ 蔓延 /⁷⁸, 拖延 ⁶⁶/⁵, 綿延 /⁷⁸

延長 yáncháng 圖 prolong, extend: 延長線 extension cord

延遲 yánchí 圖 delay

延後 yánhòu 圖 postpone

延攬 yánlǎn 圖 search(for talent)

延期 yánqī 圖 postpone

延伸 yánshēn 圖 extend 圖 extension

延續 yánxù 圖 continue

筵 88/40 yán Bamboo 竹 ⁷/ that is spread out 延 (phonetic). 圖 bamboo mat ⇔ 喜筵 /⁴⁶

筵席 yánxí 圖 banquet

涎 88/41 xián Water 水 ³/ that extends 延 (phonetic). 圖 saliva ⇔ 垂涎 /¹⁷³

誕 88/42 [誕] Words 言 ⁹/ extended 延 (phonetic). 圖

---

preposterous 圖 birth ⇔ 冥誕 /⁵⁷, 聖誕 ²/, 耶誕 /⁷

誕辰 dànchén 圖 birthday (of a famous person)

誕生 dànshēng 圖 be born (said of a famous person)

正 88/43 zhèng zhēng Stop 止/⁷ at the line 一⌐. zhèng: 圖 proper, right 圖 straight 圖 just, fair 圖 positive: 正數 positive number 圖 rectify, correct 圖 main, primary: 正門 main entrance 圖 just, exactly zhēng: 圖 first: 正月 first month of the lunar calendar ⇔ 匡正 ⁴, 更正 ⁴⁶, 糾正 ⁹, 公正 ⁷, 反正 ⁵, 修正 ⁹, 真正 ⁹, 校正 ⁹, 改正 ³, 東正教 ⁵⁵, 矯正 ³, 端正 /³⁴, 嚴正 /³⁷

正常 zhèngcháng 圖 normal

正當 zhèngdāng 圖 just when

正當 zhèngdàng 圖 proper, appropriate

正好 zhènghǎo 圖 just right

正經 zhèngjīng 圖 proper

正面 zhèngmiàn 圖 front side, obverse

正派 zhèngpài 圖 honest, upright

正確 zhèngquè 圖 right, accurate: 正確性 accuracy

正式 zhèngshì 圖 formal

正統 zhèngtǒng 圖 orthodox: 不正統 unorthodox, deviant

正要 zhèngyào 圖 just going to

正義 zhèngyì 圖 justice, right-eousness 圖 just, righteous

正在 zhèngzài 圖 in the process of

正直 zhèngzhí 圖 fair, upright

正宗 zhèngzōng 圖 orthodox

征 88/44 zhēng March 彳/ straight 正 (phonetic) ahead. 圖 journey 圖 conquer 圖 levy (⇨ 徵 /²⁴) ⇔ 長征 ⁴⁶

征服 zhēngfú 圖 conquer

整 88 zhěng
45 Admonish 敕 to make correct 正 (phonetic). ⓥ rectify ⓥ entire, whole ⓥ neat, orderly ⇔ 完整, 調整

整飭 zhěngchì ⓥ put in order
整頓 zhěngdùn ⓥ reorganize, rectify
整個 zhěnggè ⓥ whole, entire
整合 zhěnghé ⓥ integrate
整潔 zhěngjié ⓥ neat and clean
整理 zhěnglǐ ⓥ straighten up, put in order
整齊 zhěngqí ⓥ orderly, neat
整肅 zhěngsù ⓥ strict, rigid ⓥ purge, rectify
整體 zhěngtǐ ⓥ whole, entirety
整天 zhěngtiān ⓥ all day

政 88 zhèng
46 Correct 正 (phonetic) by striking 攵. ⓥ correct, right ⓥ government, administration ⓥ politics ⇔ 暴政, 行政, 執政, 施政, 專政, 財政, 郵政

政變 zhèngbiàn ⓥ coup d'etat
政策 zhèngcè ⓥ policy
政黨 zhèngdǎng ⓥ political party
政府 zhèngfǔ ⓥ government: 無政府狀態 anarchy
政見 zhèngjiàn ⓥ political views
政界 zhèngjiè ⓥ officialdom
政局 zhèngjú ⓥ political situation
政客 zhèngkè ⓥ ⓥ politician
政情 zhèngqíng ⓥ political situation
政權 zhèngquán ⓥ political power: 槍桿子裡面出政權 power comes from the barrel of a gun
政壇 zhèngtán ⓥ political circles
政治 zhèngzhì ⓥ politics: 政治

學 political science; 政治家 politician; 政治犯 political prisoner; 政治改革 political reform

証 88 zhèng
47 [证] Words 言 that show what is right 正 (phonetic). Variant of 證.

症 88 zhèng
48 Reveals the correct 正 (phonetic) disease 疒. ⓥ symptom ⓥ disease ⇔ 病症, 後遺症, 癌症
症候 zhènghòu ⓥ symptom
症狀 zhèngzhuàng ⓥ symptom

定 88 dìng
49 Roof 宀 straight 正. ⓥ stable ⓥ certainly ⓥ decide, determine: 定個時間 set a time ⇔ 一定, 否定, 註定, 注定, 既定, 額定, 核定, 說不定, 指定, 假定, 平定, 特定, 鎮定, 固定, 擬定, 協定, 認定, 訂定, 規定, 決定, 必定, 安定, 斷定, 約定, 篤定, 未定, 驚定, 肯定, 預定, 穩定, 鑑定, 堅定, 測定, 奠定, 確定
定價 dìngjià ⓥ set a price ⓥ list price
定見 dìngjiàn ⓥ fixed opinion
定局 dìngjú ⓥ predetermined situation
定理 dìnglǐ ⓥ theorem
定量 dìngliàng ⓥ fixed quantity ⓥ quantitative
定論 dìnglùn ⓥ final conclusion
定期 dìngqí ⓥ fixed term, fixed period: 不定期 occasional, intermittent
定時 dìngshí ⓥ regularly
定為 dìngwéi ⓥ set at
定位 dìngwèi ⓥ reserve, make reservations

定性 dìngxìng ⓥ qualitative: 定性分析 qualitative analysis
定義 dìngyì ⓥ definition
定則 dìngzé ⓥ rule, law (science)

綻 88 zhàn
50 [绽] Thread 糸 with 定 phonetic. ⓥ ripped seam ⓥ split, burst ⇔ 破綻

是 88 shì
51 Right 正 under the light of day 日. ⓥ correct, right ⓥ yes to be ⓥ (indicating concession) 好是好,但是 alright, but ⓥ (indicating emphasis) 是誰告訴你的? Who told you? ⇔ 既是, 老是, 就是, 若是, 要是, 真是, 或是, 凡是, 只是, 卻是, 但是, 實事求是, 於是, 還是, 而是, 總是, 像是
是的 shìde ⓥ yes, right
是非 shìfēi ⓥ right and wrong ⓥ dispute
是否 shìfǒu ⓥ whether or not
是以 shìyǐ ⓥ therefore, hence

匙 88 chí shi
52 Spoon-like object 匕 with 是 phonetic. chí: ⓥ spoon ⇔ 湯匙, 鑰匙

提 88 tí
53 Hand 手 with 是 phonetic. ⓥ lift, raise ⓥ carry ⓥ propose, mention: 提意見 make a suggestion; 提個小問題 raise a small problem ⇔ 手提
提案 tí'àn ⓥ propose ⓥ proposal
提拔 tíbá ⓥ mentor
提倡 tíchàng ⓥ advocate, encourage
提出 tíchū ⓥ bring up, put forward, propose
提到 tídào ⓥ mention, bring up

字譜及字典

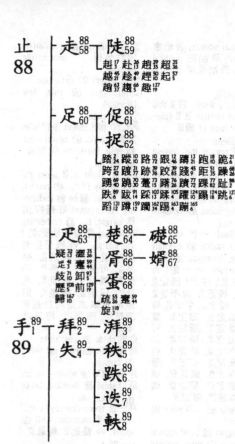

止
88

走 88 / 58
陡 88 / 59
赳 趴 趙 超 越 趁 趕 起 趨 趣 趣

足 88 / 60
促 88 / 61
捉 88 / 62
踏 蹤 路 跟 蹼 跑 跪 跨 蹙 跡 跤 踐 踴 踢 蹺 壹 踏 蹟 踝 趾 跌 跋 踩 踭 蹕 蹋 跳 蹈 蹭 蹣 踢 蹦

疋 88 / 63
楚 88 / 64 — 礎 88 / 65
疑 澀 胥 66 — 婿 88 / 67
正 蹇 蛋 88 / 68
歧 卸 前
歷 歸 疏 蹇 旋

手 89 / 1 — 拜 89 / 2 — 湃 89 / 3
失 89 / 4 — 秩 89 / 5
跌 89 / 6
迭 89 / 7
軼 89 / 8

是 phonetic. forehead topic, subject inscribe ⇔ 主題, 考題, 標題, 難題, 命題, 議題, 話題, 離題, 課題, 問題

題材 tícái theme
題綱 tígāng outline
題目 tímù topic, issue question

堤 88 tí dī
55 Dirt 土 with 是 phonetic. dike
堤防 tífáng dike guard against (⇒ 提防)

隄 88 tí dī
56 [堤] Hill 阜 with 是 phonetic. dike
隄防 tífáng dike guard against (⇒ 提防)

焉 88 yān
57 Pictograph of a bird 鳥 with top resembling 正. here how (rhetorical) ⇔ 心不在焉

走 88 zǒu
58 Person leaning forward 夭 (altered) and foot 止. walk move leave, depart ⇔ 跑走, 行走, 拿走, 趕走, 帶走, 溜走, 逃走

走動 zǒudòng take a stroll
走狗 zǒugǒu running dog, lackey: 帝國主義的走狗 imperialist running dog
走近 zǒujìn approach
走開 zǒukāi Get lost!
走廊 zǒuláng hallway, corridor
走路 zǒulù walk
走私 zǒusī smuggle
走走 zǒuzou take a walk

陡 88 dǒu
59 Hill 阜 and move 走 (phonetic). steep
陡峭 dǒuqiào precipitous

提防 tífáng guard against guard, defense
提高 tígāo heighten, raise
提供 tígōng supply, provide
提款 tíkuǎn withdraw funds: 提款機 ATM; 提款卡 ATM card
提名 tímíng nominate
提前 tíqián in advance, ahead of schedule
提昇 tíshēng promote, advance
提升 tíshēng promote, advance

提示 tíshì point out, prompt, hint hint
提攜 tíxī support, guide support, guidance
提醒 tíxǐng remind
提要 tíyào synopsis, summary
提議 tíyì suggest, propose proposal
提早 tízǎo in advance, ahead of schedule

題 88 tí
54 [题] Head 頁 with

陡然 dǒurán 副 suddenly, abruptly

足 88 zú
60 Foot 止 and lower leg (written as 口). 图 foot, leg 形 sufficient ⇔ 畫蛇添足, 十足, 充足, 滿足, 手足, 失足, 纏足, 自給自足
足夠 zúgòu 形 sufficient, enough
足踝 zúhuái 图 ankle
足球 zúqiú 图 soccer, football: 美式足球 American football
足下 zúxià 代 (term of respect in letters) you
足以 zúyǐ 副 sufficient to

促 88 cù
61 Person 人 on one's heels/feet 足 (phonetic). 形 urgent 動 urge ⇔ 倉促, 敦促, 匆促, 催促
促成 cùchéng 動 facilitate
促進 cùjìn 動 promote
促使 cùshǐ 動 impel, spur

捉 88 zhuō
62 Hands 手 and feet 足 (phonetic). 動 catch, seize, grasp ⇔ 捕捉
捉刀 zhuōdāo 動 ghostwrite
捉拿 zhuōná 動 arrest

疋 88 sū pǐ
63 Foot 止 and lower leg (represented by line at top). sū: 图 lower leg pǐ: 图 bolt (of cloth)

楚 88 chǔ
64 Knee-high 足 (phonetic) forest 林. 图 thornbush 图 suffering 形 clear, neat 姓 a surname ⇔ 痛楚, 清楚
楚國 chǔguó 專 an ancient kingdom in China

礎 88 chǔ
65 [础] Stone 石 with 楚 phonetic. Simplified form uses 出. 图 base,

foundation ⇔ 基礎

胥 88 xū
66 Flesh 肉 with 疋 phonetic. 古 a meat sauce 動 assist

婿 88 xù
67 Woman 女 with 胥 (phonetic). 图 son-in-law ⇔ 女婿

蛋 88 dàn
68 Insect 虫 with 疋, abbreviated from 延, phonetic. 图 egg ⇔ 完蛋, 混蛋, 皮蛋, 炒蛋, 笨蛋, 雞蛋, 渾蛋, 搗蛋
蛋白 dànbái 图 egg white: 蛋白質 protein
蛋包 dànbāo 图 omelet
蛋糕 dàngāo 图 cake

手 89 shǒu
1 Pictograph of a hand. 图 hand ⇔ 二手, 下手, 順手, 水手, 兇手, 住手, 人手, 洗手, 左手, 右手, 拱手, 選手, 伸手, 扳手, 高手, 歌手, 扒手, 分手, 投手, 拿手, 國手, 親手, 新手, 空手道, 好手, 聯手, 幫手, 生手, 拍手, 著手, 動手, 棘手, 敵手, 束手無策, 心狠手辣, 把手, 失手, 放手, 出手, 助手, 舵手, 握手, 插手, 炙手可熱, 能手, 黑手黨, 揮手, 攜手, 對手
手臂 shǒubì 图 arm
手錶 shǒubiǎo 图 wristwatch
手冊 shǒucè 图 manual, handbook
手創 shǒuchuàng 動 originate, pioneer
手電筒 shǒudiàntǒng 图 flashlight
手段 shǒuduàn 图 means, method

手法 shǒufǎ 图 skill
手腳 shǒujiǎo 图 hands and feet
手銬 shǒukào 图 handcuffs
手帕 shǒupà 图 handkerchief
手槍 shǒuqiāng 图 pistol
手勢 shǒushì 图 sign, gesture: 勝利手勢 victory sign
手術 shǒushù 图 surgery
手套 shǒutào 图 gloves
手提 shǒutí 形 portable
手腕 shǒuwàn 图 wrist
手下 shǒuxià 動 under charge of 图 on hand
手續 shǒuxù 图 procedures, formalities
手淫 shǒuyín 图 masturbation
手印 shǒuyìn 图 fingerprint
手語 shǒuyǔ 图 sign language
手掌 shǒuzhǎng 图 palm
手指 shǒuzhǐ 图 finger
手中 shǒuzhōng 图 on hand
手鐲 shǒuzhuó 图 bracelet
手足 shǒuzú 图 brothers

拜 89 bài
2 Hands 手 held down 下 (shown under the right hand) in bow. 動 pay respects: 拜祖先 worship ancestors 動 call on, pay a visit 副 respectfully ⇔ 崇拜, 跪拜, 膜拜, 禮拜
拜拜 bàibài 動 圄 bow with hands together
拜訪 bàifǎng 動 call on, pay a visit
拜年 bàinián 動 make ceremonial visit at New Year's
拜託 bàituō 動 敬request 感 Please! 圄 感 口 Give me a break!

湃 89 pài
3 Water 水 bowing 拜 phonetic. 形 turbulent ⇔ 澎湃

失 89 shī
4 Sprout 乙 (altered) from the hand 手 (altered). 動 lose ⇔ 冒失, 消失,

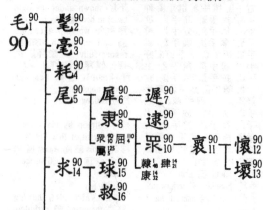

失掉 shīdiào 🈳 lose (faith or contact) 🈳 miss: 失掉機會 miss an opportunity

失衡 shīhéng 🈳 disequilibrium

失靈 shīlíng 🈳 malfunction 🈳 broken, out of order

失落 shīluò 🈳 lose

失眠 shīmián 🈳 lose sleep: 失眠病 insomnia

失明 shīmíng 🈳 become blind

失竊 shīqiè 🈳 stolen

失去 shīqù 🈳 lose

失色 shīsè 🈳 fade 🈳 turn pale

失聲 shīshēng 🈳 lose one's voice

失手 shīshǒu 🈳 slip

失調 shītiáo 🈳 imbalance 🈳 out of tune

失望 shīwàng 🈳 lose hope 🈳 disappointment

失誤 shīwù 🈳 error

失業 shīyè 🈳 become unemployed 🈳 unemployment: 失業率 unemployment rate

失蹤 shīzōng 🈳 disappear

失足 shīzú 🈳 misstep, slip

秩5 89 zhì Grain 禾¹⁰⁷ with 失⁹⁷ phonetic. 🈳 order

秩序 zhìxù 🈳 order, sequence

跌6 89 🈳 dié 🈳 diē Footing 足⁸⁸ lost 失⁹⁷ (phonetic). 🈳 fall

跌倒 diédǎo 🈳 fall down, tumble

跌下 diéxià 🈳 fall

迭7 89 dié Movement 辵¹⁶² when lost 失⁹⁷ (phonetic). 🈳 repeatedly 🈳 alternately ⇔ 更迭¹⁵

軼8 89 yì [轶] Chariot 車¹⁵⁸ losing 失⁹⁷ another. 🈳 pass, surpass 🈳 scattered

軼事 yìshì 🈳 anecdote

軼聞 yìwén 🈳 anecdote

刋9 89 jǐ Hand 手⁹⁷ holding an

缺失, 流失, 疏失, 喪失⁹⁷, 錯失, 遺失¹⁹⁷, 過失¹³⁷, 迷失¹⁹⁸, 損失¹⁸¹

失敗 shībài 🈳 fail, lose 🈳 failure, loss 🈳 downfall, undoing

失常 shīcháng 🈳 abnormal 🈳 abnormality

失傳 shīchuán 🈳 lose (across generations): 失傳的技術

object. 㑷 hold, do

鬥 89 dòu
10 [斗⁸⁷] Warriors raising weapon-holding hands 孔𦥑. 㑷 struggle ⇔ 搏鬥𤴡, 戰鬥𦥑³⁶, 奮鬥𤴡⁷⁸
鬥士 dòushì 㑷 fighter
鬥爭 dòuzhēng 㑷 struggle: 文革時他被鬥爭了三次. He was struggled against three times during the Cultural Revolution.

鬧 89 nào
11 [闹] Wrangling 鬥𦥑⁹ at the market 市𦥑. Simplified form uses gate 門⁷⁹ simplification. 㑷 noisy, clamorous 㑷 disturb, agitate 㑷 suffer from ⇔ 吵鬧𤴡⁷, 熱鬧𤴡⁵⁹
鬧事 nàoshì 㑷 make trouble
鬧鐘 nàozhōng 㑷 alarm clock

毛 90 máo
1 Pictograph of fur. 㑷 fur 㑷 hair 㑷 unrefined, gross 㑷 tenth of a yuan 㑷 a surname: 毛澤東 Mao Zedong ⇔ 皮毛𤴡⁸, 九牛一毛𤴡⁷, 陰毛𤴡¹, 絨毛𤴡⁵, 鵝毛𤴡⁹, 鬢毛𤴡⁵, 睫毛𤴡¹⁴, 眉毛𤴡¹⁴, 羽毛𤴡²⁴
毛筆 máobǐ 㑷 writing brush
毛病 máobìng 㑷 problem, defect
毛蟲 máochóng 㑷 caterpillar
毛巾 máojīn 㑷 towel
毛利 máolì 㑷 gross profit
毛毯 máotǎn 㑷 wool blanket
毛衣 máoyī 㑷 sweater

髦 90 máo
2 Long hair 髟𣬉 with hair 毛⁹⁰ phonetic. 㑷 hair-style with long bangs ⇔ 時髦𤴡¹²

毫 90 háo
3 Tall 高⁹¹ (phonetic, abbreviated) hair 毛⁹⁰. 㑷 fine long hair 㑷 thousandth: 毫米 millimeter ⇔ 絲毫𤴡⁵³
毫不 háobù 㑷 not at all

毫無 háowú 㑷 without the least: 毫無關係 completely unrelated

耗 90 hào
4 Plow 耒𣬉 with 毛⁹⁰ phonetic. 㑷 waste ⇔ 消耗𤴡²
耗費 hàofèi 㑷 waste
耗竭 hàojié 㑷 exhaust
耗子 hàozi 㑷 rat

尾 90 wěi
5 Fur 毛⁹⁰ of the lower body 尸⁴⁰. 㑷 tail ⇔ 年尾𤴡⁹, 船尾𤴡⁹, 闌尾𤴡⁵⁶, 雞尾酒𤴡¹⁰³, 虎頭蛇尾𤴡²²
尾巴 wěibā 㑷 tail
尾聲 wěishēng 㑷 epilogue 㑷 end
尾隨 wěisuí 㑷 follow, shadow, trail
尾牙 wěiyá 㑷 㑷 year-end employee dinner

犀 90 xī
6 Ox 牛⁹² with 尾⁹⁰ phonetic. 㑷 rhinoceros
犀利 xīlì 㑷 sharp 㑷 trenchant
犀牛 xīniú 㑷 rhinocerous

遲 90 chí
7 [迟] Move 辵𦥑¹ with 犀⁹⁰ phonetic. Simplified form uses foot 尺⁴⁰. 㑷 slow 㑷 late, tardy ⇔ 延遲𤴡⁵⁰
遲遲 chíchí 㑷 slowly
遲到 chídào 㑷 arrive late
遲鈍 chídùn 㑷 slow, stupid
遲疑 chíyí 㑷 hesitate 㑷 hesitation
遲早 chízǎo 㑷 sooner or later
遲滯 chízhì 㑷 slow, sluggish

隸 90 dài
8 Hand 又¹⁴ holding a tail 尾⁹⁰ (abbreviated). 㑷 grab, catch Used as simplified form of 隸.

逮 90 dǎi dài
9 Move 辵𦥑¹ to grab 隸⁹⁰ (phonetic). dǎi: 㑷 catch dài: 㑷 reach

逮捕 dàibǔ 㑷 arrest

睬 90 dài
10 Catch 隸⁹⁰ (abbreviated) with the eyes 目¹⁴. 㑷 wink

褱 90 huái
11 Clothes 衣¹²⁶ with 睬⁹⁰ phonetic. 㑷 hide in one's clothes

懷 90 huái
12 [怀] Keep hidden 褱⁹⁰ in one's heart 心⁹³. Simplified form uses 不𣬉. 㑷 cherish 㑷 bosom 㑷 conceive (a child) ⇔ 胸懷𤴡⁷, 忘懷𤴡⁹, 關懷𤴡⁶, 襟懷𤴡⁷, 心懷𤴡³, 耿耿於懷𤴡⁷, 緬懷𤴡⁸
懷疑 huáiyí 㑷 doubt: 值得懷疑 worth questioning 㑷 suspect: 我懷疑是她. I suspect it was her.
懷孕 huáiyùn 㑷 conceive, be pregnant

壞 90 huài
13 [坏] Soiled 土⁴⁰ or stolen 褱⁹⁰ (phonetic). Simplified form uses 不𣬉. 㑷 ruined, useless 㑷 ruin 㑷 bad, poor 㑷 evil, mean ⇔ 破壞𤴡⁶, 好壞𤴡⁷, 寵壞𤴡³², 敗壞𤴡⁵⁰, 損壞𤴡⁰, 變壞𤴡⁵³
壞處 huàichù 㑷 disadvantage
壞話 huàihuà 㑷 malicious talk
壞事 huàishì 㑷 evil deed

求 90 qiú
14 Hand 又¹⁴ grasping fur 毛⁹⁰ (abbreviated) of a coat. 㑷 request, solicit 㑷 seek, strive for ⇔ 懇求𤴡², 尋求𤴡⁵, 供不應求𤴡⁵, 要求𤴡⁷, 苛求𤴡⁷, 力求𤴡⁴, 央求𤴡³, 刑求𤴡⁹, 探求𤴡⁹, 強求𤴡⁵, 謀求𤴡⁵, 請求𤴡⁷, 乞求𤴡⁷, 實事求是𤴡⁹, 祈求𤴡⁷, 予取予求𤴡⁰², 哀求𤴡⁹, 徵求𤴡⁸, 需求𤴡⁷, 追求𤴡⁶⁷, 講求𤴡⁷⁵
求婚 qiúhūn 㑷 propose marriage
求救 qiújiù 㑷 cry for help

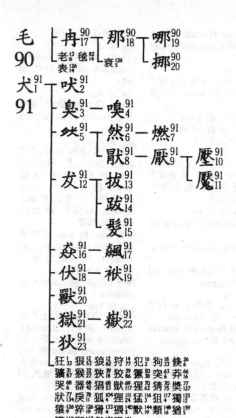

救活 jiùhuó **vb** save a life
救濟 jiùjì **vb** relieve, aid
救命 jiùmìng **vb** Help!
救助 jiùzhù **vb** help, relieve

冉 rǎn
90 17 Pictograph of fur 毛⁹⁰ (altered) doubled. **adv** gradually
冉冉 rǎnrǎn **adv** gradually

那 nà nǎ nèi núo
90 18 City 邑 where furs 冉 (altered, phonetic) were worn. **pn** an ancient barbarian kingdom in Sichuan nà: **pn** that **cj** then, in that case nǎ: **pn** which, what ⇔ 刹那
那邊 nàbiān,nèibiān **pn** there
那個 nǎge **pn** **qw** which
那個 nàge,nèige **pn** that
那裡 nǎlǐ **pn** **qw** where:那裡,那裡 (a modest response to praise)
那裡 nàlǐ **pn** there
那麼 nàme **cj** then, in that case **pn** like that: 沒那麼好 not that great
那兒 nàr **pn** there
那些 nàxiē,nèixiē **pn** those
那樣 nàyàng,nèiyàng **pn** that kind

哪 nǎ
90 19 Mouth 口 asking what 那 (phonetic). **pn** which, what
哪個 nǎge **pn** which
哪裡 nǎlǐ **pn** where
哪兒 nǎr **pn** **qw** where: 哪兒的話 (a modest response to praise)
哪些 nǎxiē **pn** which

挪 núo
90 20 Hand 手 with 那 phonetic. **vb** move, transfer
挪動 núodòng **vb** move, shift
挪威 núowēi **pn** Norway
挪移 núoyí **vb** shift
挪用 núoyòng **vb** divert (funds)

犬 quǎn
91 1 Pictograph of a dog. **n** dog
犬齒 quǎnchǐ **n** fang

求學 qiúxué **vb** study, pursue studies

球 qiú
90 15 Jade 玉 with 求 phonetic. **n** ball, sphere, globe ⇔ 網球, 高球, 全球, 打球, 琉球, 地球, 台球, 罰球, 星球, 雪球, 棒球, 撞球, 桌球, 保齡球, 月球, 氣球, 足球, 壘球, 血球, 曲棍球, 籃球, 排球

求迷 qiúmí **n** sports fan
球賽 qiúsài **n** ballgame, match
球鞋 qiúxié **n** tennis shoes
球形 qiúxíng **adj** spherical
球員 qiúyuán **n** ballplayer, player

救 jiù
90 16 Strike 攴 with 求 phonetic. **vb** rescue ⇔ 搶救, 急救, 拯救, 補救, 求救, 挽救
救護 jiùhù **vb** rescue: 救護車 ambulance

吠 91 fèi
2 From mouth 口[68/1] of dog 犬[91/1]. 【動】 bark

臭 91 chòu
3 Dog 犬[91/1] following its nose 自[139/1]. 【形】 smelly ⇔ 乳臭未乾[55/9]

嗅 91 xiù
4 Mouth 口[68/1] (originally nose 鼻[46/14]) and smell 臭[91/3]. 【動】 sniff, smell

嗅覺 xìujué 【名】 sense of smell

肰 91 rán
5 Dog 犬[91/1] meat 肉[132/1]. 【古】 dog meat

然 91 rán
6 Dog meat 肰[91/5] (phonetic) on fire 火[82/1]. 【古】 roast, burn (⇨燃[91/7]) 【副】 however 【代】 like that, so: 不以爲然 disagree ⇔ 枉然[35], 不然[70], 縱然[10/9], 既然[10/51], 慨然[10/55], 恍然[11/45], 要不然[15/84], 泰然[15/23], 公然[19/2], 茫然[22/19], 迥然不同[23/2], 仍然[28/4], 悄然[29/38], 勃然[29/63], 固然[31/51], 居然[31/68], 昂然[33/6], 毅然[37/9], 天然[38/35], 盎然[38/55], 亦然[39/75], 赫然[39/81], 誠然[41/38], 截然[45/63], 必然[45/72], 悍然[50], 軒然大波[53], 孑然[55/35], 已然[58/3], 斷然[59/10], 突然[63/6], 當然[63/28], 驀然[66], 愕然[68/10], 黯然[68/85], 竟然[69/92], 凜然[69/12], 徒然[70], 偶然[73/7], 坦然[76/49], 果然[77], 貿然[78/36], 豁然[79/8], 忽然[86/2], 陡然[88/99], 欣然[96/4], 井然[97], 猛然[116/3], 依然[126/2], 猝然[126/19], 儼然[137/14], 驟然[137/21], 自然[139/1], 默然[144/19], 戛然[148/20], 顯然[153/10], 遽然[155/19], 幡然[156/4], 雖然[162/57], 譁然[173/10]

然而 ránér 【副】 however, to the contrary

然後 ránhòu 【副】 afterwards, and then

燃 91 rán
7 Roast 然[91/6] (phonetic) with fire 火[82/1] redundant. 【動】 burn ⇔ 點燃[26/19]

燃料 ránliào 【名】 fuel

燃燒 ránshāo 【動】 burn

猒 91 yān
8 Full of sweet 甘[69/57] (altered to resemble 曰[69/46]) dog meat 肰[91/5]. 【古】 satiated

厭 91 yàn
9 [厌] Pile on stones/cliff 厂[71/1] until full 猒[91/8] (phonetic). 【古】 crush (⇨壓[91/10]) 【動】 be disgusted by 【動】 bored with ⇔ 討厭[14/79]

厭惡 yànè 【動】 loathe, detest, be disgusted by

厭煩 yànfán 【動】 annoyed by, bored with

厭倦 yànjuàn 【動】 tired of, weary of

厭世 yànshì 【動】 hate life

壓 91 yā
10 [压] Crush 厭[91/9] (phonetic) dirt 土[70/1]. 【動】 press down, crush 【動】 oppress 【動】 quell ⇔ 電壓[15/109], 鎮壓[31/33], 欺壓[46/4], 血壓[11/116], 變壓器[153/5]

壓倒 yādǎo 【動】 crush, overwhelm: 壓倒性的勝利 overwhelming victory

壓低 yādī 【動】 force down

壓力 yālì 【名】 pressure

壓迫 yāpò 【動】 oppress, force

壓縮 yāsūo 【動】 compress

壓抑 yāyì 【動】 suppress, repress

壓榨 yāzhà 【動】 oppress, extort

壓制 yāzhì 【動】 inhibit, restrain, suppress 【名】 inhibition

壓住 yāzhù 【動】 suppress

魘 91 yǎn
11 [魇] Ghost 鬼[140/6] with 厭[91/9] phonetic. 【名】 nightmare ⇔ 夢魘[114/5]

犮 91 bá
12 Dog 犬[91/1] with leg restrained 丿[7/1] by leash.

拔 91 bá
13 [拔] Hand 手[89/1] holding leashed dog 犮[91/12] (phonetic). 【動】 pull out ⇔ 選拔[15/99], 海拔[54/24], 挺拔[70/41], 提拔[89/53]

跋 91 bá
14 [跋] Foot 足[88/80] with 犮[91/12] phonetic. 【動】 trek

跋涉 báshè 【動】 trek, hike

髮 91 【簡】 fǎ 【繁】 fà
15 [发[88/18]] Long hair 髟[22/59] with 犮[91/12] phonetic. 【名】 hair ⇔ 金髮[44/1], 頭髮[69/88], 鬢髮[75/6], 理髮[11/20]

髮廊 fǎláng 【名】 hair salon

髮型 fǎxíng 【名】 hairstyle

猋 91 biāo
16 Dogs 犬[91/1]. 【古】 pack of dogs

飆 91 biāo
17 [飙] Wind 風[47/4] blowing like a pack of dogs 猋[91/16] (phonetic). 【名】 whirlwind ⇔ 狂飆[1/33]

飆車 biāochē 【動】 joy ride

伏 91 fú
18 Person 人[10/1] crouched like a dog 犬[91/1]. 【動】 prostrate 【動】 hide ⇔ 潛伏[10/99], 蟄伏[50/51], 起伏[57/5], 制伏[23], 埋伏[11/27]

伏筆 fúbǐ 【名】 foreshadowing

伏擊 fújí 【動】 ambush

伏特 fútè 【名】 volt

伏羲 fúxī 【人】 Fu Xi – legendary emperor who invented farming

袱 91 fú
19 Cloth 衣[126/1] hiding 伏[91/18] (phonetic). 【名】 bundle ⇔ 包袱[18/2]

獸 91 shòu
20 [兽] Dog 犬[91/1] and a pictograph showing an animal's ears (resembling 吅[68/5]), head 由[140/1], and paws/tail 内[73/1] (altered). 【名】 beast, animal ⇔ 禽獸[73/21], 野獸[102/8]

獸行 shòuxíng 【名】 bestial behavior, brutality

獸醫 shòuyī 【名】 veterinarian

獸慾 shòuyù 【名】 bestial desire

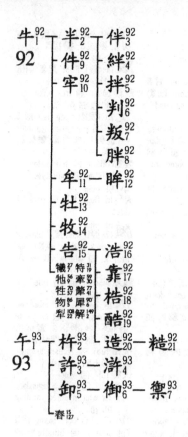

92
牛₁⁹² 半₂⁹² 伴₃⁹²
件₉⁹² 絆₄⁹²
牢₁₀⁹² 拌₅⁹²
判₆⁹²
叛₇⁹²
胖₈⁹²
牟₁₁⁹² 眸₁₂⁹²
牡₁₃⁹²
牧₁₄⁹²
告₁₅⁹² 浩₁₆⁹²
犧 特 靠₁₇⁹²
牲 犛 梏₁₈⁹²
物 犀 酷₁₉⁹²
犁 解

93
午₁⁹³ 杵₂⁹³ 造₂₀⁹² 糙₂₁⁹²
許₃⁹³ 滸₄⁹³
卸₅⁹³ 御₆⁹³ 禦₇⁹³
舂

獄 91 yù
21 Words 言 between fighting dogs (ancient character showing two dogs 犬). lawsuit jail ⇔ 地獄, 監獄, 冤獄

獄 91 yuè
22 [岳階] Mountain 山 tall like jail 獄 (phonetic). high mountain: 五嶽 five sacred mountains in China

狄 91 dí
23 Dog 犬 with red (赤 abbreviated to 火) fur. a type of dog a people to the north of ancient China a surname

牛 92 níu
1 Pictograph of an ox. ox, cattle a surname ⇔ 水牛, 吹牛, 公牛, 九牛一毛, 黃牛, 犛牛, 犀牛, 蝸牛
牛車 níuchē cart, oxcart
牛耳 níuěr ox ears: 執牛耳 be in a dominant position

牛郎 níuláng cowboy gigolo
牛奶 níunǎi milk
牛排 níupái steak
牛肉 níuròu beef
牛仔 níuzǎi cowboy: 牛仔褲 jeans

半 92 bàn
2 Divide 八 an ox 牛. half half, semi- ⇔ 一半, 大半, 多半
半島 bàndǎo peninsula
半點 bàndiǎn the least bit
半斤八兩 bànjīnbāliǎng six of one and a half-dozen of the other, the same
半徑 bànjìng radius
半晌 bànshǎng a long time
半數 bànshù half
半天 bàntiān a long while: 我等了半天. I waited half the day.
半途而廢 bàntúérfèi give up halfway
半夜 bànyè midnight

伴 92 bàn
3 Person's 人 other half 半 (phonetic). companion, partner ⇔ 陪伴, 同伴, 夥伴, 伙伴
伴侶 bànlǚ companion
伴隨 bànsúi accompany

絆 92 bàn
4 [絆] String 糸 with 半 phonetic. fetters trip, stumble ⇔ 羈絆
絆倒 bàndǎo trip, trip over
絆腳石 bànjiǎoshí stumbling block, obstacle

拌 92 bàn
5 Hand 手 with 半 phonetic. mix ⇔ 攪拌

判 92 pàn
6 Cut 刀 in half 半 (phonetic). separate judge ⇔ 批判, 評判, 裁判, 談判, 審判

判處 pànchǔ 🔲 sentence, condemn

判斷 pànduàn 🔲 judge, determine

判決 pànjué 🔲 verdict, judgment

判刑 pànxíng 🔲 sentence

叛 7 Turn against 反⁶ with 半⁷ᵇ phonetic. 🔲 betray ⇔ 背叛⁴⁰ pàn

叛變 pànbiàn 🔲 commit treason

叛國 pànguó 🔲 commit treason, commit sedition

叛亂 pànluàn 🔲 revolt, rebellion, insurrection

叛賣 pànmài 🔲 betray

叛逆 pànnì 🔲 rebel 🔲 rebel

叛逃 pàntáo 🔲 defect

叛徒 pàntú 🔲 traitor

胖 8 Flesh 肉¹² of split bull 半⁷ᵇ (phonetic). 🄐 side of beef 🔲 fat 🔲 gain weight: 你胖了. You've gained weight. ⇔ 肥胖⁸ pàng

胖子 pàngzi 🔲 🄐 fat person

件 9 Person 人¹⁰ dividing an ox 牛⁷ᵇ. 🔲 piece ⇔ 軟件⁸⁵, 元件¹¹, 硬件¹²⁶, 條件⁸⁴, 零件⁹⁶, 案件²⁷, 信件⁶⁹, 事件⁹³, 文件¹⁰, 郵件¹⁷³ jiàn

牢 10 Modern form shows an ox 牛⁷ᵇ under a roof 宀⁶³. 🔲 pen 🔲 prison, jail 🔲 durable, sturdy ⇔ 套牢⁵², 坐牢⁵⁶, 監牢¹⁴² láo

牢固 láogù 🔲 sturdy, firm

牢靠 láokào 🔲 firm, stable, reliable

牢籠 láolóng 🔲 cage, trap

牢騷 láosāo 🔲 discontent, grumbling: 發牢騷 complain, grumble

牟 11 Ox 牛⁷ᵇ exhaling 己⁵⁹ móu

(written as 厶¹⁹). 🔲 moo 🔲 seek

牟利 móulì 🔲 seek profits: 非牟利 non-profit

牟取 móuqǔ 🔲 seek ⇒ 謀取²⁸

眸 12 Eye 目 with 牟⁷ phonetic. 🔲 pupil (of the eye) móu

眸子 móuzi 🔲 pupil (of the eye) 🔲 eye

牡 13 Ox 牛⁷ᵇ with 土⁷⁶ phonetic. 🔲 male mǔ

牡丹 mǔdān 🔲 peony: 牡丹亭 The Peony Pavilion - a Ming Dynasty opera

牡蠣 mǔlì 🔲 oyster

牧 14 Strike 攵²⁶ cattle 牛⁷ᵇ. 🔲 shepherd ⇔ 畜牧³⁸ mù

牧場 mùchǎng 🔲 pasture

牧師 mùshī 🔲 pastor, priest, minister

牧羊 mùyáng 🔲 shepherd: 牧羊者 a shepherd

告 15 Ox 牛⁷ᵇ and mouth 口⁶⁸. 🔲 report, tell 🔲 accuse 🔲 sue ⇔ 宣告⁴², 原告³⁴, 被告¹²⁶, 警告⁹⁷, 公告¹⁴, 計告⁶⁷, 廣告⁸⁵, 報告²⁸, 控告⁸⁵, 佈告⁸⁷, 轉告⁸⁴, 稟告⁶⁸, 忠告³³, 通告⁸⁵, 奉告⁵⁶, 預告¹⁰², 勸告¹⁹ gào

告別 gàobié 🔲 say good-bye, leave

告辭 gàocí 🔲 say good-bye, leave

告發 gàofā 🔲 inform on, accuse

告誡 gàojiè 🔲 warn

告密 gàomì 🔲 inform on, tip off

告訴 gàosù 🔲 tell

告知 gàozhī 🔲 tell, inform, notify

浩 16 Water 水⁴¹ with 告⁷ phonetic. 🔲 vast hào

浩大 hàodà 🔲 vast

浩瀚 hàohàn 🔲 extensive

浩劫 hàojié 🔲 disaster, catastrophe

靠 17 Accuse 告⁷ (phonetic) of wrongs 非¹⁵⁹. 🄐 oppose 🔲 lean on 🔲 rely on 🄐 near, by ⇔ 可靠⁷, 投靠⁵², 牢靠⁹, 依靠¹²⁶ kào

靠近 kàojìn 🔲 near, close to 🔲 approach, draw near

靠攏 kàolǒng 🔲 draw close, narrow

梏 18 Wood 木⁷ for the accused 告⁷ (phonetic). 🔲 manacles ⇔ 桎梏¹²⁸ gù

酷 19 Alcohol 酉¹⁵⁹ with 告⁷ phonetic. 🔲 strong (alcohol) 🔲 cruel 🔲 extremely 🔲 🄐 cool ⇔ 冷酷⁸⁴, 殘酷¹⁴ kù

酷愛 kùài 🔲 painful love

酷吏 kùlì 🔲 cruel official

酷熱 kùrè 🔲 extremely hot

酷刑 kùxíng 🔲 torture, severe punishment

造 20 Movement 辵³ worthy of reporting 告 (phonetic). 🔲 make, create, build, produce ⇔ 人造¹⁰, 創造³⁵, 鑄造¹³⁵, 建造⁴⁵, 塑造⁵³, 改造⁵⁷, 深造⁴⁵, 釀造⁶⁹, 捏造⁸⁵, 製造⁷⁵, 締造⁸⁴, 營造¹⁶², 仿造⁵⁵, 偽造¹²⁸, 構造¹⁷⁵ zào

造成 zàochéng 🔲 compose, form 🔲 cause, result in

造訪 zàofǎng 🔲 visit, call on

造化 zàohuà 🔲 fate

造句 zàojù 🔲 construct sentences

造型 zàoxíng 🔲 model, mold

糙 21 Rice 米¹³⁸ with 造⁹² phonetic. 🔲 coarse ⇔ 粗糙¹⁷ cāo

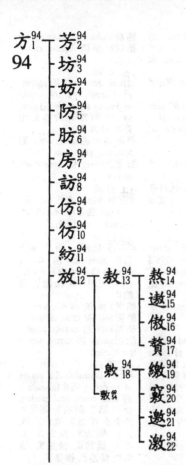

方₁⁹⁴ 94
├ 芳₂⁹⁴
├ 坊₃⁹⁴
├ 妨₄⁹⁴
├ 防₅⁹⁴
├ 肪₆⁹⁴
├ 房₇⁹⁴
├ 訪₈⁹⁴
├ 仿₉⁹⁴
├ 彷₁₀⁹⁴
├ 紡₁₁⁹⁴
└ 放₁₂⁹⁴ ─┬ 敖₁₃⁹⁴ ─┬ 熬₁₄⁹⁴
          │   ├ 遨₁₅⁹⁴
          │   ├ 傲₁₆⁹⁴
          │   └ 贅₁₇⁹⁴
          └ 敫₁₈⁹⁴ ─┬ 繳₁₉⁹⁴
                      ├ 竅₂₀⁹⁴
                      ├ 邀₂₁⁹⁴
                      └ 激₂₂⁹⁴
            └ 敷

午 93 wǔ
1 Pictograph of a pestle. (盦) pestle (⇒ 杵⁹³) seventh Earthly Branch (⇒ 干支⁹³) noon ⇔ 上午, 下午, 中午, 端午節

午餐 wǔcān lunch
午飯 wǔfàn lunch
午後 wǔhòu afternoon
午覺 wǔjiào noon nap, siesta
睡午覺 take a noon nap

午睡 wǔshùi noon nap, siesta
午夜 wǔyè midnight

杵 93 chǔ
2 Wooden 木 pestle 午 (phonetic). pestle

許 93 xǔ
3 [许] Words 言 with 午 phonetic. permit perhaps a surname: 許慎 Xu Shen - Han Dynasty lexicographer ⇔ 允許, 或許,

期許, 也許, 幾許, 容許, 准許
許多 xǔduō many
許久 xǔjiǔ a long time
許可 xǔkě permit, allow

滸 93 hǔ
4 [浒] Modern form shows water 水 with 許 phonetic. water's edge

卸 93 xiè
5 From pestle 午 stop 止 and kneeling person 卩. unload ⇔ 推卸
卸貨 xièhùo unload goods

御 93 yù
6 March 彳 and unload 卸. drive imperial
御用 yùyòng for imperial use

禦 93 yù
7 [御] Omen 示 with 御 phonetic. worship defend, protect ⇔ 防禦, 抵禦
禦寒 yùhán ward off the cold

方 94 fāng
1 Pictograph of two ships tied together. Alternatively, a pictograph of a plow. direction side place, region square prescription, method a surname ⇔ 比方, 北方, 警方, 平方, 南方, 處方, 大方, 後方, 秘方, 地方, 貽笑大方, 藥方, 東方, 坍方, 貴方, 西方, 單方, 雙方, 官方, 對方

方案 fāngàn project, plan
方便 fāngbiàn convenient: 不方便 inconvenient
方才 fāngcái just now
方纔 fāngcái just now
方程式 fāngchéngshì equation
方法 fāngfǎ method: 方法論 methodology
方塊 fāngkuài square: 方塊

字 Chinese characters

方面 fāngmiàn 图 side, aspect: 一方面 on the one hand, in one respect

方式 fāngshì 图 way, style, pattern

方向 fāngxiàng 图 direction

方形 fāngxíng 圐 square

方言 fāngyán 图 dialect

方針 fāngzhēn 图 guiding principle

芳 94 fāng
2 Plant 艸 with 方 phonetic. 圐 fragrant ⇔ 芬芳

芳香 fāngxiāng 图 fragrance

芳心 fāngxīn 图 young woman's heart: 挑動她的芳心 stir her heart

坊 94 囷 fāng 囷 fáng
3 Ground 土 and place 方 (phonetic). 图 neighborhood 图 workshop ⇔ 牌坊

坊間 fāngjiān 圐 on the market

妨 94 fáng
4 Woman 女 with 方 phonetic. 囷 hinder ⇔ 不妨, 何妨, 無妨

妨礙 fángài 囷 hinder

妨害 fánghài 囷 harm

防 94 fáng
5 Hill 阜 with 方 phonetic. 囷 prevent, defend ⇔ 駐防, 消防, 國防, 提防, 堤防, 隄防, 預防

防備 fángbèi 囷 prepare against

防範 fángfàn 囷 guard against

防守 fángshǒu 囷 defend

防衛 fángwèi 囷 defend

防禦 fángyù 囷 defend

防止 fángzhǐ 囷 prevent

防治 fángzhì 图 prevention and cure

肪 94 fáng
6 Flesh 肉 with 方 phonetic. 图 fat ⇔ 脂肪

房 94 fáng
7 Household 戶 place 方 (phonetic). 图 house 图 room 囷 a surname ⇔ 退房, 書房, 套房, 病房, 洞房, 奶房, 茶房, 乳房, 藥房, 廠房, 廚房, 閨房, 茅房, 廂房, 臥房

房地產 fángdìchǎn 图 real estate

房頂 fángdǐng 图 roof

房東 fángdōng 图 landlord

房間 fángjiān 图 room

房門 fángmén 图 door

房屋 fángwū 图 house

房子 fángzi 图 house

房租 fángzū 图 rent

訪 94 fǎng
8 [访] Words 言 with 方 phonetic. 囷 inquire 囷 visit ⇔ 拜訪, 造訪, 採訪, 來訪

訪問 fǎngwèn 囷 call on, interview

仿 94 fǎng
9 Person 人 with 方 phonetic. 囷 imitate ⇔ 模仿

仿冒 fǎngmào 囷 counterfeit: 仿冒品 counterfeit good

仿絲 fǎngsī 图 imitation silk

仿效 fǎngxiào 囷 imitate

仿造 fǎngzào 囷 counterfeit

仿製 fǎngzhì 囷 counterfeit

彷 94 páng fǎng
10 Step 彳 with 方 phonetic. páng: 囷 hesitate fǎng: 囷 resemble

彷彿 fǎngfú 囷 resemble, seem to

彷徨 pánghuáng 囷 pace back and forth 囷 hesitate (⇨ 徬徨)

紡 94 fǎng
11 [纺] Thread 糸 with 方 phonetic. 囷 spin into yarn

紡紗 fǎngshā 图 spin into yarn

紡織 fǎngzhī 图 textiles: 紡織機 loom; 紡織業 textile industry

放 94 fàng
12 Send to place 方 (phonetic) with strikes 攴. 囷 exile 囷 release, let go 囷 act without restraint 囷 put, place, lay ⇔ 釋放, 百花齊放, 開放, 解放, 播放

放出 fàngchū 囷 let out

放大 fàngdà 囷 enlarge

放蕩 fàngdàng 圐 dissolute

放假 fàngjià 囷 take vacation, go on holiday

放開 fàngkāi 囷 release, set free, let go

放寬 fàngkuān 囷 loosen

放款 fàngkuǎn 囷 loan

放浪 fànglàng 圐 debauched

放屁 fàngpì 囷 fart

放棄 fàngqì 囷 abandon, give up

放上 fàngshàng 囷 put on

放射 fàngshè 囷 radiate

放手 fàngshǒu 囷 let go, unhand

放鬆 fàngsōng 囷 relax

放下 fàngxià 囷 let go, lay down

放心 fàngxīn 囷 rest assured

放映 fàngyìng 囷 project: 放映機 projector

放置 fàngzhì 囷 put, place

放逐 fàngzhú 囷 exile, banish

放縱 fàngzòng 囷 indulge

敖 94 áo
13 [敖] Go out 出 (written as 土) and indulge 放. 囷 ramble (⇨ 遨) 囷 leisurely 圐 a surname

熬 94 áo
14 [熬] Leisurely 敖 (phonetic) upon a fire 火. 囷 stew 囷 endure ⇔ 煎熬

熬夜 áoyè 囷 stay up late

遨 94 áo
15 [遨] Walk 辵 leisurely 敖 (phonetic). 囷 ramble, roam

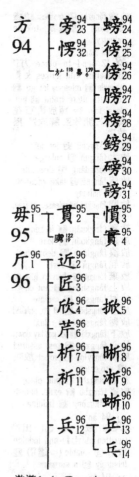

方 94
旁 94/23 ── 螃 94/24
愕 94/32 ── 徬 94/25
── 傍 94/26
── 膀 94/27
── 榜 94/28
── 鎊 94/29
── 磅 94/30
── 謗 94/31

方 118 鼻 139

毋 95/1 ── 貫 95/2 ── 慣 95/3
腐 122 ── 實 95/4

斤 96/1 ── 近 96/2
── 匠 96/3
── 欣 96/4 ── 掀 96/5
── 芹 96/6
── 析 96/7 ── 晰 96/8
── 祈 96/11 ── 淅 96/9
── 蜥 96/10
── 兵 96/12 ── 乒 96/13
── 乓 96/14

邀遊 áoyóu 動 wander, roam

傲 94 ào
16 [傲] Person 人 who treats propriety leisurely 敖 (phonetic). 形 arrogant ⇔ 高傲, 驕傲
傲慢 àomàn 形 arrogant
傲視 àoshì 動 disdain

贅 94 zhuì
17 [贅] Traveling 敖 shells/money 貝. 形 collateral 形 superfluous ⇔ 累贅
贅述 zhùìshù 動 elaborate unnecessarily

敫 94 jiǎo
18 Sunlight 白 emitting

放 敫. 形 shine

繳 94 zhuó jiǎo
19 [繳] Thread 糸 that shoots 敫 (phonetic). zhuó: 图 string attached to an arrow jiǎo: 動 hand in, turn in
繳納 jiǎonà 動 pay (taxes or tuition)

竅 94 qiào
20 [竅] Hole 穴 shined through 敫 (phonetic). Simplified form uses 巧. 图 aperture ⇔ 訣竅
竅門 qiàomén 图 key (to a problem)

邀 94 yāo
21 Movement 辶 with 敫 phonetic. 動 invite
邀集 yāojí 動 invite to a gathering
邀請 yāoqǐng 動 invite

激 94 jī
22 Water 水 shooting out 敫 (phonetic). 動 surge 動 arouse, stir up 形 fierce, heated ⇔ 感激, 刺激
激昂 jīáng 形 spirited
激動 jīdòng 形 excited, stirred up, agitated
激發 jīfā 動 arouse, spur to action
激光 jīguāng 图 形 laser: 激光打印機 laser printer
激進 jījìn 形 radical
激勵 jīlì 動 encourage
激烈 jīliè 形 intense, fierce
激怒 jīnù 動 infuriate, enrage
激起 jīqǐ 動 arouse, stir up
激素 jīsù 图 hormone

旁 94 páng
23 Above 上 (ancient form) and sides (extra marks) with 方 phonetic. 图 side ⇔ 偏旁, 身旁
旁邊 pángbiān 图 side, flank
旁觀 pángguān 動 watch from the sidelines: 旁觀者 onlookers, spectators

旁聽 pángtīng 動 audit, sit in on

螃 94 páng
24 Insect-like 虫[125] with 旁[94] phonetic. 名 crab
螃蟹 pángxiè 名 crab

徬 94 páng
25 [旁] Stepping 彳[41] from side to side 旁[94] (phonetic). 動 pace
徬徨 pánghuáng 動 pace back and forth 動 hesitate

傍 94 bàng
26 Person 人[10] at one's side 旁[94] (phonetic). 動 draw near
傍晚 bàngwǎn 名 evening, dusk

膀 94 bǎng
27 Flesh 肉[132] on the side 旁[94] (phonetic). 名 upper arm, shoulder ⇔ 臂膀[35], 翅膀[7], 肩膀[39]

榜 94 bǎng
28 Wood 木[77] with 旁[94] phonetic. 名 posted list of names ⇔ 標榜[34]
榜首 bǎngshǒu 名 number one on a list
榜樣 bǎngyàng 名 model

鎊 94 bàng
29 [镑] Metal 金[94] with 旁[94] phonetic. 名 pound sterling

磅 94 bàng
30 Stone 石[69] with 旁[94] phonetic. 名 pound

謗 94 bàng
31 [谤] Words 言[98] on all sides 旁[94] (phonetic). 動 slander ⇔ 毀謗[30]

愣 94 lèng
32 Heart 心[83] on all four 四[8] sides 方[94]. 形 stupefied ⇔ 發愣[93]
愣住 lèngzhù 動 stupefied, struck dumb

毋 95 guàn
1 Pictograph of a pierced object.

貫 95 guàn
2 [贯] Pierced 毋[95] (phonetic) money/shells 貝[50]. 名 string of copper coins 動 pierce, pass through 動 follow in a line ⇔ 一貫[1], 橫貫[31], 全神貫注[72], 籍貫[56], 連貫[58]
貫穿 guànchuān 動 pass through
貫通 guàntōng 動 understand thoroughly

慣 95 guàn
3 [惯] Heart 心[83] following in a sequence 貫[95] (phonetic). 動 be used to ⇔ 習慣[84]
慣例 guànlì 名 precedent, convention

實 95 shí
4 [实] Strings of money 貫[95] under a roof 宀[93]. Simplified form uses 頭[43] simplification. 形 wealthy 形 substantial, solid 形 true, actual 名 reality, fact 名 fruit, seed ⇔ 踏實[83], 扎實[17], 老實[12], 結實[29], 真實[34], 誠實[93], 其實[8], 充實[63], 忠實[87], 事實[62], 證實[52], 果實[77], 現實[105], 堅實[62], 確實[30]
實地 shídì 副 on-the-spot: 實地調查 on-the-spot investigation
實際 shíjì 形 real: 實際狀況 true situation 名 reality: 實際上 in reality, actually
實踐 shíjiàn 動 put into practice
實例 shílì 名 instance, example
實力 shílì 名 strength
實施 shíshī 動 put into practice
實事求是 shíshìqiúshì 動 seek truth from facts
實習 shíxí 動 practice, intern: 實習生 trainee
實現 shíxiàn 動 realize, achieve
實行 shíxíng 動 implement, put into practice

實驗 shíyàn 名 experiment: 實驗室 laboratory
實用 shíyòng 形 practical: 實用價值 practical value
實在 shízài 形 true, real 副 really, indeed
實證 shízhèng 名 empirical evidence
實質 shízhí 名 essence

斤 96 jīn
1 Pictograph of an axe. 名 axe 量 pound, catty ⇔ 公斤[77], 半斤八兩[32]

近 96 jìn
2 Movement 辵[41] with 斤[96] phonetic. 形 near, close ⇔ 鄰近[92], 附近[54], 逼近[22], 挨近[29], 親近[85], 接近[27], 將近[76], 走近[89], 靠近[17], 相近[105], 遠近[105], 最近[79]
近代 jìndài 名 modern era: 近代史 modern history
近來 jìnlái 副 recently
近年 jìnnián 名 recent years
近親 jìnqīn 名 close relatives
近人 jìnrén 名 modern people
近日 jìnrì 副 recently
近似 jìnsì 形 approximate: 近似值 approximate value
近於 jìnyú 動 close to, near to

匠 96 jiàng
3 Use an axe 斤[96] to hollow out 匚[92]: carpentry. 名 craftsman, artisan ⇔ 工匠[3], 木匠[77]
匠心 jiàngxīn 名 craftsmanship

欣 96 xīn
4 Exhale 欠[97] with 斤[96] phonetic. 名 joy ⇔ 歡欣[102]
欣然 xīnrán 副 gladly, with pleasure
欣賞 xīnshǎng 動 appreciate, admire
欣慰 xīnwèi 形 delighted, gratified
欣喜 xīnxǐ 形 happy, joyful
欣欣向榮 xīnxīnxiàngróng 形 prosperous, flourishing

斤 96

丘 96/15 — 邱 96/16
        — 蚯 96/17
        — 岳 96/18
        — 虛 122

斬 96/19 — 蘄 96/20
        — 暫 96/21
        — 慚 96/22
        — 漸 96/23

折 96/24 — 哲 96/25
        — 蜇 96/26
        — 淅 96/27
        — 誓 96/28
        — 逝 96/29
質 96/30

斥 96/31 — 拆 96/32
        — 訴 96/33

斧 61 斯 96 新 97
斷 83 所 74

井 97/1 — 阱 97/2
97
       — 耕 97/3
       — 丹 97/4 — 坍 97/5
                 — 青 95

掀 96/5 xiān Hand 手 97 with 欣 96 phonetic. 🈁 lift
掀開 xiānkāi 🈁 lift open
掀起 xiānqǐ 🈁 bring about, set off

芹 96/6 qín Grass 艸 95 with 斤 96 phonetic. 🈁 celery
芹菜 qíncài 🈁 celery

析 96/7 xī Wood 木 77 split with an axe 斤 96. 🈁 divide 🈁 analyze ⇔ 剖析 65, 分析 97, 解析 140

晰 96/8 xī Separable 析 96 (phonetic) in the light of day 日 76. 🈁 clear, distinct ⇔ 清晰 85, 明晰 97

淅 96/9 xī Water 水 85 separating 析 96 (phonetic). 🈁 wash rice
淅瀝 xīlì 🈁 patter of raindrops

蜥 96/10 Insect-like 虫 125 with 析 96 phonetic. 🈁 lizard
蜥蜴 xīyì 🈁 lizard

祈 96/11 qí Omen 示 146 with 斤 96 phonetic. 🈁 pray
祈禱 qídǎo 🈁 pray
祈福 qífú 🈁 pray for luck
祈求 qíqiú 🈁 pray for

兵 96/12 bīng Hands 廾 35 wielding an axe 斤 96. 🈁 armaments, weapons 🈁 soldiers, army ⇔ 衛兵 83, 閱兵 117, 老兵 67, 砲兵 81, 阿兵哥 117, 士兵 31, 撤兵 62, 當兵 80, 傭兵 56, 憲兵 72, 徵兵 63

兵力 bīnglì 🈁 military strength
兵馬 bīngmǎ 🈁 military forces: 兵馬俑 terra-cotta warriors
兵刃 bīngrèn 🈁 weapons
兵戎 bīngróng 🈁 weapons
兵役 bīngyì 🈁 military service

乒 96/13 pīng Weapon 兵 96 phonetic and suggestive of sound of weapons clashing. 🈁 ping
乒乓 pīngpāng 🈁 ping-pong: 乒乓球 ping-pong, ping-pong ball

乓 96/14 pāng Weapon 兵 96 phonetic and suggestive of sound of weapons clashing. 🈁 pong ⇔ 乒乓 96

丘 96 qiū
15 Persons back-to-back
北 (altered to resemble
斤) on a surface 一L 图
mound, small hill 图 a surname
⇔ 沙丘
丘陵 qiūlíng 图 hills

邱 96 qiū
16 Town 邑 with 丘
(phonetic). 图 a place name
图 a surname

蚯 96 qiū
17 Insect 虫 and hill
丘 (phonetic). 图 earth-
worm
蚯蚓 qiūyǐn 图 earthworm

岳 96 yuè
18 Modern form shows hill
丘 and mountain 山. 图
high mountain 图 in-laws
(wife's parents) 图 a surname
⇔ 山岳
岳父 yuèfù 图 father-in-law
(wife's father)
岳母 yuèmǔ 图 mother-in-law
(wife's mother)

斬 96 zhǎn
19 [斩] Cart 車
attacked with axe 斤. 图 chop
图 behead
斬首 zhǎnshǒu 图 behead

嶄 96 zhǎn
20 [崭] Mountain 山
cutting 斬 (phonetic)
through the clouds. 图 towering
嶄新 zhǎnxīn 图 brand-new

暫 96 zhàn 图 zàn
21 [暂] Day 日 cutting
斬 (phonetic) past. 图
briefly, temporarily ⇔ 短
暫
暫緩 zhànhuǎn 图 postpone,
defer
暫且 zhànqiě 图 temporarily,
for the moment
暫時 zhànshí 图 temporary 图
temporarily
暫停 zhàntíng 图 suspend

暫行 zhànxíng 图 provisional

慚 96 cán
22 [惭] Heart 心 cut
斬 (phonetic). 图 ashamed
⇔ 羞慚
慚愧 cánkuì 图 ashamed

漸 96 jiàn
23 [渐] Water 水 and
cutting 斬 (phonetic). 图 a
river name 图 gradually ⇔
日漸, 逐漸
漸漸 jiànjiàn 图 gradually

折 96 zhé
24 Hand 手 using an
axe 斤. 图 break 图 fold (⇔
摺) 图 suffer loss of 图
discount: 打七折 discounted
30% ⇔ 波折, 挫折, 夭
折, 曲折
折斷 zhéduàn 图 break off
折舊 zhéjiù 图 depreciate
折扣 zhékòu 图 discount: 打折
扣 to discount
折磨 zhémó 图 torment
折損 zhésǔn 图 damage

哲 96 zhé
25 Mouth 口 that breaks
折 (phonetic) fallacies.
图 wise
哲人 zhérén 图 sage
哲學 zhéxué 图 philosophy: 哲
學家 philosopher

蜇 96 zhé
26 Insect-like 虫
animal that damages 折
(phonetic). 图 jellyfish ⇔
海蜇

浙 96 zhè
27 Water 水 with 折
phonetic. 图 Zhejiang Province
浙江 zhèjiāng 图 Zhejiang
Province

誓 96 shì
28 Words 言 with 折
phonetic. 图 vow, pledge ⇔
發誓
誓言 shìyán 图 pledge, oath

逝 96 shì
29 Walk 足 with 折
phonetic. 图 depart ⇔ 病
逝, 消逝
逝世 shìshì 图 pass away, die

質 96 zhì 图 zhí
30 [质] Money/shell 貝
with double axe 斤 suggesting mutual nature of exchange.
zhì: 图 pawn zhí: 图 nature,
character 图 quality 图
question ⇔ 人質, 特質,
地質, 品質, 性質, 本
質, 氣質, 物質, 實
質, 素質
質量 zhíliàng 图 quality
質問 zhíwèn 图 question
質詢 zhíxún 图 query
質疑 zhíyí 图 question, doubt

斥 96 shì
31 Early form shows
shelter 广 attacked 屰
(phonetic). 图 expand, enlarge
图 denounce ⇔ 駁斥, 申
斥, 充斥, 排斥
斥責 chìzé 图 rebuke, denounce

拆 96 chāi
32 Hand 手 denouncing
斥 (phonetic). 图 rip open
图 tear down, demolish
拆除 chāichú 图 demolish,
remove
拆掉 chāidiào 图 tear down,
demolish
拆開 chāikāi 图 rip open
拆散 chāisàn 图 dismantle,
break up

訴 96 sù
33 [诉] Words 言
denouncing 斥 (phonetic).
图 accuse 图 tell ⇔ 上訴,
傾訴, 申訴, 投訴, 控
訴, 告訴
訴說 sùshūo 图 tell, relate
訴訟 sùsòng 图 litigation,
lawsuit

井 97 jǐng
1 Pictograph of a field

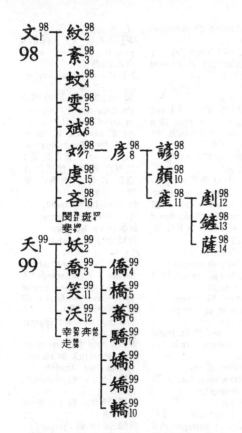

phonetic and suggestive of mine. [img] collapse

坍方 tānfāng [img] cave in [img] landslide

坍塌 tāntā [img] collapse, cave in

文 98₁ wén Pictograph of interlocking lines. [img] script, writing [img] language: 法文 French [img] culture [img] cultured, refined [img] a surname ⇔ 語文₁, 原文₂, 人文₁₃, 碑文₂₇, 條文₂₇, 沙文₂₇, 沙文主義₂₇, 詩文₁₃, 達爾文₂₇, 天文₂₇, 英文₂₇, 金文₂₇, 國文₂₇, 斯文₄₆, 梵文₃₇, 中文₈₃, 銘文₂₇, 日文₁₆, 散文₂₇, 本文₆₃, 明文₉₇, 甲骨文₁₁₂, 論文₁₈

文革 wéngé [img] Cultural Revolution (文化大革命)

文官 wénguān [img] civil servant

文化 wénhuà [img] culture: 文化大革命 Cultural Revolution

文件 wénjiàn [img] document

文具 wénjù [img] stationery

文盲 wénmáng [img] illiteracy illiterate person

文明 wénmíng [img] civilization [img] civilized: 非文明 uncivilized

文憑 wénpíng [img] diploma

文人 wénrén [img] scholar, literati

文書 wénshū [img] official document: [img] 文書處理 word processing

文壇 wéntán [img] literary circles

文物 wénwù [img] cultural objects: [img] 文物展示 cultural exhibition

文獻 wénxiàn [img] literature documents: [img] 文獻片 documentary

文選 wénxuǎn [img] selected writings

文學 wénxué [img] literature

文雅 wényǎ [img] refined, cultured

文言 wényán [img] classical Chinese: 文言文 classical Chinese

divided into lots with well at center. [img] well [img] a surname

井然 jǐngrán [img] orderly

阱 97₂ jǐng Hill 阜 with well 井 (phonetic). [img] pit, trap ⇔ 陷阱₅₇

耕 97₃ gēng Plow 耒 along field lines 井 (phonetic). [img] plow, till

耕地 gēngdì [img] farmland

耕田 gēngtián [img] plow, till

耕耘 gēngyún [img] plow and weed, cultivate

耕作 gēngzuò [img] cultivation, farming

丹 97₄ dān A red mineral, represented by the dot, found in a mine/well 井 (altered). [img] red ⇔ 仙丹₄₇, 牡丹₆₃, 靈丹₆₁, 蘇丹₉₀

丹麥 dānmài [img] Denmark

坍 97₅ tān Earth 土 with 丹

文藝 wényì 图 arts and literature

文章 wénzhāng 图 article, paper

文字 wénzì 图 writing, script: 文字改革 writing reform; 文字處理 word processing

紋 2 [纹] Threads 糸|53 and lines 文|ᵖ (phonetic). 图 stripes, lines ⇔ 指紋ᵖ, 條紋ᵖ, 皺紋ᵖ, 斑紋|ᵖ

紋身 wénshēn 图 tattoo

紊 3 Intersecting 文|ᵖ (phonetic) threads 糸|53. 围 chaotic

紊亂 wènluàn 围 disorderly, chaotic

蚊 4 Insect 虫|25 with 文|ᵖ phonetic. 图 mosquito

蚊帳 wénzhàng 图 mosquito net
蚊子 wénzi 图 mosquito

雯 5 Cloud 雲｜(abbreviated to 雨|ᵖ) writing 文|ᵖ (phonetic). 图 coloring of clouds

斌 6 bīn Culture 文|ᵖ (phonetic) and military 武|. 围 cultured and accomplished

彣 7 wén Culture 文|ᵖ (phonetic) and fine hair 彡|ᵖ. 围 refined

彥 8 yàn [彦] Refined 彣|ᵖ with 厂|ᵖ phonetic. 图 venerable scholar

諺 9 yàn [谚] Words 言|ᵖ with 彥|ᵖ phonetic. 图 proverb

諺語 yànyǔ 图 proverb, saying

顏 10 yán [颜] Head 頁|ᵖ with 彥|ᵖ phonetic. 图 face, countenance 围 a surname ⇔

汗顏ᵖ, 容顏ᵖ
顏面 yánmiàn 图 face
顏色 yánsè 图 color

產 11 chǎn [产] Birth 生ᵖ with 彥|ᵖ (abbreviated) phonetic. 围 give birth to 图 produce 图 product assets ⇔ 資產ᵖ, 破產ᵖ, 共產ᵖ, 私產ᵖ, 特產ᵖ, 無產ᵖ, 國產ᵖ, 流產ᵖ, 財產ᵖ, 生產ᵖ, 名產ᵖ, 房地產ᵖ, 遺產|ᵖ

產出 chǎnchū 围 output, production
產量 chǎnliàng 图 yield, output
產能 chǎnnéng 图 production capacity
產品 chǎnpǐn 图 product, good
產權 chǎnquán 图 围 property rights
產生 chǎnshēng 围 produce
產業 chǎnyè 图 industry 图 property, estate
產值 chǎnzhí 图 production value

剷 12 chǎn [铲铲] Knife 刀|ᵖ with 產|ᵖ phonetic. 围 raze, level

剷除 chǎnchú 围 root out, eradicate

鏟 13 chǎn [铲] Metal 金|ᵖ with 產|ᵖ phonetic. 图 shovel

鏟子 chǎnzi 图 shovel

薩 14 sà [萨] Modern form shows grass 艸|ᵖ, hill 阜|67 and produce 產|ᵖ. 图 Buddha ⇔ 菩薩ᵖ, 比薩ᵖ, 拉薩ᵖ

虔 15 qián Tiger 虍|22 with 文|ᵖ phonetic. 围 sincere

虔誠 qiánchéng 围 pious, devout

吝 16 lìn Mouth 口|ᵖ with 文|ᵖ phonetic. 围 stingy

吝嗇 lìnsè 围 cheap, stingy

夭 1 yǎo 围 yāo Pictograph of a person with head leaning forward. 图 bent over 图 die young

夭折 yǎozhé 围 die young, end prematurely

妖 2 yāo Modern form shows woman 女|ᵖ with 夭|ᵖ phonetic. 围 bewitching 图 demon

妖怪 yāoguài 图 monster, demon
妖精 yāojīng 图 demon, spirit
妖邪 yāoxié 围 wicked, monstrous

喬 3 qiáo [乔] Tall 高|ᵖ (abbreviated) and bent forward 夭|ᵖ. 围 tall 围 disguise 围 a surname

喬遷 qiáoqiān 围 move house
喬裝 qiáozhuāng 围 disguise oneself

僑 4 qiáo [侨] Person 人|ᵖ tall 喬|ᵖ (phonetic). 围 tall 围 travel 围 sojourn overseas ⇔ 外僑ᵖ, 華僑|ᵖ

僑生 qiáoshēng 图 foreign student (in China)

橋 5 qiáo [桥] Tall 喬|ᵖ (phonetic) wood 木|ᵖ. 图 bridge ⇔ 劍橋ᵖ, 拱橋ᵖ, 高架橋ᵖ, 天橋ᵖ, 吊橋ᵖ, 蘆溝橋|ᵖ

橋墩 qiáodūn 图 pier, buttress
橋樑 qiáoliáng 图 bridge
橋梁 qiáoliáng 图 bridge
橋牌 qiáopái 图 bridge (the card game)

蕎 6 qiáo [荞] Plant 艸|ᵖ that is tall and bent 喬|ᵖ (phonetic). 图 buckwheat

驕 7 jiāo [骄] Tall 喬|ᵖ (phonetic) horse 馬|ᵖ. 围 proud, arrogant

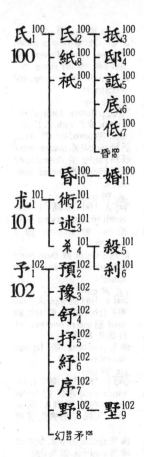

轎車 jiàochē 图 car, sedan
轎子 jiàozi 图 sedan-chair, palanquin

笑 99 xiào
11 Bamboo 竹, suggesting a flute, with 夭 phonetic. 图 smile 图 laugh 图 laugh at, mock ⇔ 傻笑, 玩笑, 可笑, 大笑, 好笑, 貽笑大方, 譏笑, 訕笑, 逗笑, 嘻笑, 嘲笑, 啼笑皆非, 微笑, 恥笑, 歡笑

笑柄 xiàobǐng 图 laughing-stock
笑話 xiàohuà 图 joke
笑容 xiàoróng 图 smiling face: 滿面笑容 full of smiles

沃 99 wò
12 Water 水 with 夭 phonetic. 图 irrigate ⇔ 肥沃

氏 100 shì
1 Pictograph of a plant's roots. 图 surname ⇔ 無名氏, 姓氏, 攝氏, 華氏

氏族 shìzú 图 clan: 氏族制度 clan system

氐 100 dǐ
2 [氐] Roots 氏 into the ground 一. 图 roots, foundation

抵 100 dǐ
3 [抵] Hand 手 on roots 氐 (phonetic). 图 resist 图 prop up ⇔ 大抵
抵償 dǐcháng 图 compensate
抵觸 dǐchù 图 contradict, conflict with
抵達 dǐdá 图 arrive
抵擋 dǐdǎng 图 resist
抵抗 dǐkàng 图 resist
抵銷 dǐxiāo 图 cancel out, offset, neutralize
抵押 dǐyā 图 mortgage, pawn: 抵押品 collateral
抵禦 dǐyù 图 withstand, resist

驕傲 jiāoào 图 proud, arrogant 图 pride: 中國的驕傲 the pride of China

嬌 99 jiāo
8 [娇] Woman 女 with 喬 phonetic. 图 charming 图 pamper, spoil
嬌媚 jiāomèi 图 charming coquettish
嬌嫩 jiāonèn 图 tender, delicate, fragile

嬌豔 jiāoyàn 图 beautiful and charming

矯 99 jiǎo
9 [矫] Straighten a long, bent 喬 (phonetic) arrow 矢. 图 correct, rectify
矯正 jiǎozhèng 图 correct, rectify

轎 99 jiào
10 [轿] Cart 車 held high 喬 (phonetic). 图 sedan-chair

抵制 dǐzhì 🔲 resist ⇔ boycott

邸 100 dǐ
4 [邸] City 邑 with 氏 phonetic. 图 official residence ⇔ 官邸

詆 100 dǐ
5 [诋] Words 言 attacking roots 氏 (phonetic). 🔲 defame
詆毀 dǐhuǐ 🔲 defame, slander

底 100 dǐ
6 [底] Shelter 广 taking root 氐 (phonetic). 图 settle 图 foundation, base, bottom 图 end ⇔ 年底, 到底, 徹底, 存底, 月底, 班底
底稿 dǐgǎo 图 manuscript
底片 dǐpiàn 图 film 图 negative
底細 dǐxì 图 full details
底下 dǐxià 图 underneath
底子 dǐzi 图 foundation, base

低 100 dī
7 [低] Person 人 bowing to the ground 氐 (phonetic). 图 low 图 lower ⇔ 降低, 高低, 減低, 壓低, 最低
低潮 dīcháo 图 low tide
低沈 dīchén 🔲 overcast 图 depressed 图 baritone
低估 dīgū 🔲 underestimate
低級 dījí 图 low class
低廉 dīlián 图 cheap
低劣 dīliè 图 inferior, low quality
低落 dīluò 图 low, downcast
低迷 dīmí 图 turbid
低聲 dīshēng 🔲 in a low voice: 低聲下氣 sheepish
低於 dīyú 🔲 lower than, below

紙 100 zhǐ
8 [纸] Silk 糸 with 氏 phonetic. 图 paper ⇔ 貼紙, 冥紙, 報紙, 信紙, 廢紙, 摺紙, 剪紙
紙板 zhǐbǎn 图 cardboard
紙錢 zhǐqián 图 fake money burnt as an offering to the dead
紙傘 zhǐsǎn 图 paper umbrella, parasol

祇 100 qí zhǐ
9 [只] Omen 示 and roots 氏 (phonetic). 图 qí: god of earth zhǐ: 🔲 only (⇨只)
祇要 zhǐyào 🔲 only
祇有 zhǐyǒu 🔲 only

昏 100 hūn
10 Sun 日 sinking in ground 氐 (written as 氏). 图 dusk ⇔ 黃昏, 發昏
昏倒 hūndǎo 🔲 faint
昏厥 hūnjué 🔲 faint
昏迷 hūnmí 🔲 fall into a coma 图 coma
昏庸 hūnyōng 图 fatuous

婚 100 hūn
11 Woman 女 off into the sunset 昏 (phonetic). 🔲 marry 图 marriage: 婚外情 affair ⇔ 結婚, 訂婚, 離婚, 重婚, 未婚, 求婚
婚禮 hūnlǐ 图 wedding ceremony
婚事 hūnshì 图 marriage
婚姻 hūnyīn 图 marriage

秫 101 shù
1 [术] Pictograph of a top-heavy grain plant. 图 sorghum, millet

術 101 shù
2 [术] Proceed 行 with 秫 phonetic. 图 road 图 method, technique ⇔ 學術, 巫術, 藝術, 技術, 魔術, 武術, 手術, 美術, 算術
術士 shùshì 图 witchdoctor
術語 shùyǔ 图 jargon, terminology

述 101 shù
3 [述] Movement 辵 with 秫 phonetic. 🔲 follow 🔲 state, explain ⇔ 上述, 撰述, 敘述, 引述, 陳述, 贊述, 描述, 闡述
述說 shùshuō 🔲 narrate, recount

秎 101 shā
4 Cut off 乂 ears of grain from sorghum 秫 (phonetic). 图 decapitate.

殺 101 shā
5 [杀] Decapitate 秎 (phonetic) with a halberd 殳. 🔲 kill ⇔ 槍殺, 扼殺, 殘殺, 斯殺, 宰殺, 謀殺, 暗殺, 屠殺, 抹殺, 刺殺, 自殺
殺害 shāhài 🔲 kill, murder
殺價 shājià 🔲 bargain, haggle
殺戮 shālù 🔲 massacre, slaughter
殺人 shārén 🔲 kill, murder
殺死 shāsǐ 🔲 kill, murder
殺嬰 shāyīng 图 infanticide: 殺女嬰 female infanticide

刹 chà
6 [刹] Pagoda rising knife-like 刀 with 杀 phonetic. 图 Buddhist temple
刹那 chànà, chànuó 🔲 instantly, in a flash

予 102 yú
1 Pictograph suggesting exchange of an object. 🔲 give ⇔ 給予, 賦予, 授予, 准予, 賜予
予取予求 yǔqǔyǔqiú 🔲 take at will
予以 yǔyǐ 🔲 give, grant

預 102 yù
2 [预] Head 頁 with 予 phonetic. 🔲 prepare 图 in advance ⇔ 干預
預報 yùbào 图 forecast: 天氣預報 weather forecast
預備 yùbèi 图 prepare
預測 yùcè 🔲 forecast, predict
預訂 yùdìng 🔲 subscribe, place an order

103

爪₁¹⁰³ ─ 抓₂¹⁰³

妥₃¹⁰³ ┬ 綏₄¹⁰³
         └ 餒₅¹⁰³

奚₆¹⁰³ ┬ 溪₇¹⁰³
         └ 雞₈¹⁰³

采₉¹⁰³ ┬ 彩₁₀¹⁰³
觅₁₅¹⁰³ ├ 採₁₁¹⁰³
         ├ 睬₁₂¹⁰³
         ├ 踩₁₃¹⁰³
         └ 菜₁₄¹⁰³

妥₁₆¹⁰³ ┬ 受₁₇¹⁰³ ─ 授₁₈¹⁰³
愛₁₉¹⁰³ ┬ 援₂₀¹⁰³
         ├ 緩₂₁¹⁰³
         └ 暖₂₂¹⁰³

預定 yùdìng 🔲 reserve, make a reservation
預防 yùfáng 🔲 prevent
預感 yùgǎn 🔲 premonition
預告 yùgào 🔲 advance notice
預估 yùgū 🔲 estimate
預計 yùjì 🔲 predict, estimate
預料 yùliào 🔲 anticipate, predict
預期 yùqī 🔲 expect
預算 yùsuàn 🔲 budget
預先 yùxiān 🔲 beforehand, in advance
預言 yùyán 🔲 prophecy prophesy: 預言家 prophet
預演 yùyǎn 🔲 preview
預兆 yùzhào 🔲 omen
預知 yùzhī 🔲 know beforehand 🔲 foreknowledge

豫₃ ¹⁰² yù
Elephant 象¹⁷² with 予¹⁰² phonetic. 🔲 hesitate Henan Province ⇔ 猶豫¹⁵⁹

舒₄ ¹⁰² shū
Give 予¹⁰² (phonetic) accommodation 舍⁴³. 🔲 stretch, relax
舒服 shūfú 🔲 comfortable
舒適 shūshì 🔲 comfortable
舒坦 shūtǎn 🔲 comfortable

抒₅ ¹⁰² shū
Hand 手¹⁷ giving 予¹⁰² (phonetic). 🔲 relieve, unburden 🔲 express
抒解 shūjiě 🔲 🔲 relieve: 抒解壓力 relieve pressure
抒情 shūqíng 🔲 express emotions

紓₆ ¹⁰² shū
[纾] Give 予¹⁰² (phonetic) silk 糸⁵³. 🔲 relieve
紓困 shūkùn 🔲 relieve, aid

序₇ ¹⁰² xù
Shelter 广⁶⁰ offering 予¹⁰² (phonetic). 🔲 altar wall 🔲 sequence ⇔ 順序, 次序, 程序, 秩序, 依序, 排序
序幕 xùmù 🔲 prologue, prelude
序言 xùyán 🔲 preface, foreword

野₈ ¹⁰² yě
Village 里¹⁸⁵ with 予¹⁰² phonetic. 🔲 countryside, wilderness 🔲 wild 🔲 barbaric ⇔ 荒野, 曠野, 分野, 越野, 在野, 朝野, 田野
野餐 yěcān 🔲 picnic
野蠻 yěmán 🔲 savage
野人 yěrén 🔲 savage, barbarian
野生 yěshēng 🔲 grow wild: 野生動物 wildlife
野獸 yěshòu 🔲 wild beast
野外 yěwài 🔲 outdoors
野心 yěxīn 🔲 greed, ambition
野營 yěyíng 🔲 🔲 camp out
野豬 yězhū 🔲 boar

墅₉ ¹⁰² shù
Earthen 土⁷⁰ building in countryside 野¹⁰². 🔲 farmhouse ⇔ 別墅

爪₁ ¹⁰³ zhuǎ zhǎo
Pictograph of a hand or paw facing down. 🔲 claw, talon
爪子 zhuǎzi,zhǎozi 🔲 claw, talon

抓₂ ¹⁰³ zhuā
Hand 手¹⁷ using claws 爪¹⁰³ (phonetic). 🔲 scratch 🔲 grasp, seize 🔲 arrest
抓到 zhuādào 🔲 catch
抓緊 zhuājǐn 🔲 grasp well, pay close attention to

抓住 zhuāzhù 🈟 hold tight

妥 103 tuǒ
3　Hand 爪ᴵº³ on a woman 女ᴵ⁴. 🈺 secure 🈺 appropriate.
妥當 tuǒdàng 🈺 appropriate, proper
妥善 tuǒshàn 🈺 appropriate, proper: 妥善安排 make appropriate arrangements
妥協 tuǒxié 🈟 compromise

綏 103 🈺 suī 🈸 suí
4　[绥] Threads 糸ᴵ⁵³ that secure 妥ᴵº³ on a carriage 🈟 appease
綏靖 suījìng 🈟 pacify, appease

餒 103 něi
5　[馁] Food 食ᴵ⁴ with 妥ᴵº³ phonetic. 🈟 starve 🈺 dispirited ⇔ 氣餒ᴵ⁴⁴

奚 103 xī
6　Person 大ᴵ⁸ with an ancient variant of 系ᴵ⁸³ (abbreviated to 爪ᴵº³ and 幺ᴵⁿ) phonetic. 🈺 servant 🈺 🈺 why, how, what
奚落 xīluò 🈟 taunt

溪 103 xī
7　Water 水ᴵ⁴ twisting 奚ᴵº³ (phonetic). 🈺 brook, mountain stream
溪谷 xīgǔ 🈺 valley, gorge
溪流 xīliú 🈺 brook
溪水 xīshuǐ 🈺 brook

雞 103 jī
8　[鸡] Servant 奚ᴵº³ (phonetic) bird 隹ᴵ⁶². Simplified form uses 又ᴵ⁴ and 鳥ᴵ⁷⁸.
🈺 chicken ⇔ 公雞ᴵ⁷, 小雞ᴵ⁸, 母雞ᴵ⁸
雞蛋 jīdàn 🈺 egg (hen's)
雞尾酒 jīwěijiǔ 🈺 cocktail

采 103 cǎi
9　Hand 爪ᴵº³ picking from a tree 木ᴵ⁷. 🈺 gather, pick 🈺 colors ⇔ 喝采ᴵ⁸, 風采ᴵ⁷, 精采ᴵ⁸, 丰采ᴵ⁸

彩 103 cǎi
10　Colorful 采ᴵº³ (phonetic) markings 彡ᴵ⁷. 🈸 essay 🈺 colors ⇔ 五彩ᴵ, 雲彩ᴵ⁴, 光彩ᴵ⁴, 色彩ᴵ⁸, 倒彩ᴵ⁴, 中彩ᴵ⁸, 精彩ᴵⁿ
彩虹 cǎihóng 🈺 rainbow
彩票 cǎipiào 🈺 lottery ticket
彩券 cǎiquàn 🈺 lottery ticket
彩色 cǎisè 🈺 color: 彩色電視 color television
彩雲 cǎiyún 🈺 multi-colored clouds

採 103 cǎi
11　[采ᴵº³] Hand 手ᴵⁿ gathering 采ᴵº³ (phonetic). 🈟 gather, pick 🈟 adopt, utilize
採訪 cǎifǎng 🈟 cover (news) 🈟 interview
採購 cǎigòu 🈟 purchase
採集 cǎijí 🈟 collect, gather
採礦 cǎikuàng 🈟 mine
採納 cǎinà 🈟 adopt, accept
採取 cǎiqǔ 🈟 adopt, take
採行 cǎixíng 🈟 implement, adopt
採用 cǎiyòng 🈟 adopt, utilize

睬 103 cǎi
12　Eye 目ᴵ⁴ gathering 采ᴵº³ (phonetic). 🈟 notice ⇔ 理睬ᴵ⁸

踩 103 cǎi
13　Feet 足ᴵ⁸ with 采ᴵº³ phonetic. 🈟 trample

菜 103 cài
14　Plants 艸ᴵⁿ gathered 采ᴵº³ (phonetic). 🈺 vegetable: 菜市場 vegetable market 🈺 food dishes 🈺 cuisine ⇔ 酸菜ᴵ⁸, 菠菜ᴵ⁴, 泡菜ᴵⁿ, 涼菜ᴵ⁸, 芥菜ᴵⁿ, 鹹菜ᴵ⁸, 蔬菜ᴵ⁸, 青菜ᴵ⁸, 白菜ᴵⁿ, 煮菜ᴵ⁸, 芹菜ᴵⁿ, 滷菜ᴵⁿ⁰, 韭菜ᴵ⁶⁸
菜單 càidān 🈺 menu
菜刀 càidāo 🈺 large Chinese cooking knife
菜館 càiguǎn 🈺 restaurant

菜色 càisè 🈺 emaciated look
菜系 càixì 🈺 cuisine: 八大菜系 eight main regional cuisines of China
菜肴 càiyáo 🈺 food, dishes
菜園 càiyuán 🈺 vegetable garden

覓 103 mì
15　[觅] Hand 爪ᴵº³ and see 見ᴵⁿ. 🈟 seek ⇔ 尋覓ᴵ⁸
覓食 mìshí 🈟 forage

受 103 piāo
16　From hand 爪ᴵº³ above to hand 又ᴵ⁴ below. 🈸 pass down

受 103 shòu
17　Boat 舟ᴵ⁷⁹ (phonetic, abbreviated to 冖 ᴵ⁴), suggesting passage, and pass down 受ᴵº³. 🈟 receive, accept 🈟 suffer, endure: 受不了 cannot endure, unbearable ⇔ 承受ᴵ, 享受ᴵ⁸, 難受ᴵ⁸, 忍受ᴵ⁸, 感受ᴵ⁸, 接受ᴵⁿ, 遭受ᴵ⁸
受挫 shòucuò 🈟 suffer a setback
受到 shòudào 🈟 receive 🈟 be subject to
受罰 shòufá 🈟 be punished
受害 shòuhài 🈟 be victimized, suffer: 受害者 victim
受惠 shòuhuì 🈟 benefit
受苦 shòukǔ 🈟 suffer
受難 shòunàn 🈟 suffer a disaster
受傷 shòushāng 🈟 be hurt, suffer injury
受訓 shòuxùn 🈟 receive training
受益 shòuyì 🈟 benefit: 受益者 beneficiary

授 103 shòu
18　Hand 手ᴵⁿ and receive 受ᴵⁿ (phonetic). 🈟 confer, award 🈟 teach ⇔ 教授ᴵ⁹, 傳授ᴵ⁸
授課 shòukè 🈟 teach
授權 shòuquán 🈟 authorize
授意 shòuyì 🈟 suggest, hint

字譜及字典

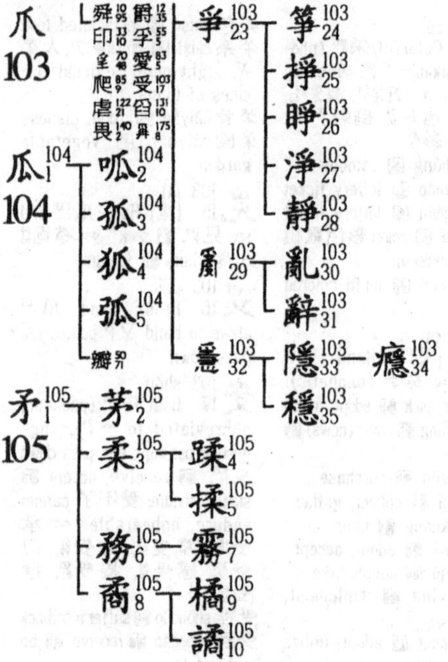
爪 103
舜 10/95
爵 12/35
印 33/10
孚 55/5
𦥑 70/48
愛 83/5
爬 85/9
受 103/17
虐 122/21
舀 131/10
畏 140/2
彝 175/8
争 103/23
箏 103/24
掙 103/25
睜 103/26
淨 103/27
靜 103/28
𤔔 103/29
亂 103/30
辭 103/31
㥯 103/32
隱 103/33
癮 103/34
穩 103/35
瓜 104/1
104
呱 104/2
孤 104/3
狐 104/4
弧 104/5
瓣 50/71
矛 105/1
105
茅 105/2
柔 105/3
蹂 105/4
揉 105/5
務 105/6
霧 105/7
矞 105/8
橘 105/9
譎 105/10

授予 shòuyǔ [動] confer, award

爰 103 yuán
19 Pass down 𠬪[103/16] and exhale 于[7/32]. [古] pull (⇔ 援)

援 103 yuán
20 Hand 手[89/1] and pull 爰[103/19] (phonetic). [動] pull [動] assist ⇔ 聲援[37/8], 支援[71/2], 外援[72/11]

援引 yuányǐn [動] cite

援助 yuánzhù [動] help, assist: 經濟援助 economic aid

緩 103 huǎn
21 [缓] Thread 糸[153/1] and pull 爰[103/19] (phonetic). [名] loose, slack [形] gradual [動] delay ⇔ 趨緩[66/5], 暫緩[96/21]

緩和 huǎnhé [動] mitigate, ameliorate [動] mollify

緩緩 huǎnhuǎn [副] slowly, gradually

緩解 huǎnjiě [動] [簡] relieve: 緩解壓力 relieve pressure

緩慢 huǎnmàn [形] slow

暖 103 nuǎn
22 Sun 日[76/1] with 爰[103/19] phonetic. [形] warm ⇔ 溫暖[69/21], 保暖[77/74].

暖和 nuǎnhuo [形] warm

暖氣 nuǎnqì [名] warm air, heating

爭 103 zhēng
23 [争] Hands 𠬪[103/16] pulling ノ[7/1]. [動] struggle, contend [動] argue, quarrel ⇔ 力爭[34/1], 紛爭[35/6], 競爭[68/82], 百家爭鳴[76/3], 鬥爭[89/10], 戰爭[136/5]

爭辯 zhēngbiàn [動] argue, debate

爭吵 zhēngchǎo [動] quarrel

爭端 zhēngduān [名] cause of a dispute: 邊界爭端 border dispute

爭奪 zhēngdúo [動] struggle for, fight for

爭光 zhēngguāng [動] win honor: 爲國爭光 win honor for one's country

爭論 zhēnglùn [名] dispute, controversy

爭取 zhēngqǔ [動] struggle for

爭議 zhēngyì [名] dispute, controversy

爭執 zhēngzhí [動] argue, dispute

箏 103 zhēng
24 [筝] Bamboo 竹[71/11] and pull 爭[103/23] (phonetic). [名] zither [名] kite ⇔ 風箏[47/4]

掙 103 zhēng zhèng
25 [挣] Hands 手[89/1] struggling 爭[103/23] (phonetic). zhēng: [動] struggle zhèng: [動] earn

掙錢 zhèngqián [動] make money

掙脫 zhēngtūo [動] shake off, liberate

掙扎 zhēngzhá [動] struggle

睜 103 zhēng
26 [睁] Eye 目[114/1] with 爭[103/23] phonetic. [動] open (eyes)

睜開 zhēngkāi [動] open (eyes): 睜開眼睛 open one's eyes

淨 103 jìng
27 [净] Water 水[2/21] with 爭[103/23] phonetic. [形] clean [副] completely [形] net ⇔ 純淨[69/55], 乾淨[76/68], 潔淨[79/6]

淨利 jìnglì [名] net profit

淨值 jìngzhí [名] net value

靜 103 jìng
28 [静] Think vividly 青[70/66] and pull 爭[103/23] (phonetic) at truth. [古] examine [形] tranquil, serene ⇔ 沈靜[23/57], 平靜[27/44], 鎮靜[31/33], 冷靜[44/38], 安靜[54/10], 幽靜[59/3], 恬靜[68/77], 動靜[76/98], 寧靜[116/5], 寂靜[121/6]

靜靜 jìngjìng [形] quiet

靜脈 jìngmài 图 vein
靜態 jìngtài 图 static, motionless
靜止 jìngzhǐ 图 static, motionless
靜坐 jìngzuò 图 sit in silence 图 have a sit-down strike

亂 103 luàn
29 Threads 糸 |⁵³ (plus lines at side resembling 冂 |⁷ʲ) untangled by two hands 叉 |⁰⁸. 图 control, govern

亂 103 luàn
30 [乱] Control 爲 |⁵⁷ with 乙|? redundantly representing thread. Simplified form uses 舌 兜. 图 control 图 chaos, anarchy: 怕亂 fear anarchy 图 chaotic, disorderly 图 rebellion ⇔ 混亂 忠, 暴亂 以, 戡亂 兜, 胡亂 兜, 凌亂 兜, 淫亂 兜, 動亂 兜, 叛亂 兜, 紊亂 兜, 迷亂 兜, 擾亂 兜, 雜亂 兜, 霍亂 兜, 搞亂 兜
亂丟 luàndiū 图 litter
亂講 luànjiǎng 图 speak nonsensically 图 Nonsense!
亂七八糟 luànqībāzāo 图 topsy-turvy
亂扔 luànrēng 图 litter
亂想 luànxiǎng 图 think crazy thoughts

辭 103 cí
31 [辞] Resolve 爲 |⁵⁷ a sin 辛 兜. Simplified form uses 舌 兜. 图 confession 图 words, phrase 图 resign 图 depart ⇔ 卜辭 兜, 歌辭 兜, 託辭 兜, 措辭 兜, 告辭 兜
辭別 cíbié 图 say good-bye
辭呈 cíchéng 图 letter of resignation
辭典 cídiǎn 图 dictionary
辭去 cíqù 图 resign
辭行 cíxíng 图 say farewell
辭職 cízhí 图 resign, quit

懚 103 yǐn
32 Heart 心 |⁹³ and an ancient character composed of hands 叉 |⁰⁹ working 工 |³¹. 图 careful

隱 103 yǐn
33 [隐] Hills 阜 |⁶⁷ and careful 爲 兜 (phonetic). Simplified form uses 急 兜. 图 concealed, hidden
隱蔽 yǐnbì 图 conceal, cover up
隱藏 yǐncáng 图 hide, conceal
隱諱 yǐnhuì 图 hush up, avoid mentioning
隱瞞 yǐnmán 图 cover up, conceal
隱情 yǐnqíng 图 secrets
隱士 yǐnshì 图 recluse, hermit
隱私 yǐnsī 图 private matters: 隱私權 privacy
隱形 yǐnxíng 图 invisible: 隱形眼鏡 contact lenses
隱憂 yǐnyōu 图 latent danger
隱喻 yǐnyù 图 metaphor
隱約 yǐnyuē 图 indistinct, faint

癮 103 yǐn
34 [瘾] Hidden 隱 兜 (phonetic) sickness 疒 兜. 图 addiction ⇔ 上癮 兜, 過癮 |³³
癮者 yǐnzhě 图 addict

穩 103 wěn
35 [稳] Grain 禾 |⁰⁸ and careful 隱 (phonetic, abbreviated to 爲 兜). Simplified form uses 急 兜. 图 security 图 stable, steady ⇔ 平穩 兜, 安穩 兜
穩定 wěndìng 图 stable
穩固 wěngù 图 firm, solid
穩健 wěnjiàn 图 firm, steady

瓜 104 guā
1 Pictograph of a melon-bearing plant. 图 melon ⇔ 傻瓜 兜, 黃瓜 兜, 哈密瓜 兜, 木瓜 兜, 葵瓜子 兜, 西瓜 |⁰⁰
瓜分 guāfēn 图 divide, carve up
瓜葛 guāgé 图 connection, relation 图 complication

呱 104 gū
2 Mouth 口 |⁶ making sound like 瓜 |⁰⁴ (phonetic). 图 cry of a baby
呱呱 gūgū 图 cry of a baby

孤 104 gū
3 Child 子 |⁵ with 瓜 |⁰⁴ phonetic and suggestive of cry 呱 |². 图 fatherless 图 solitary, lonely
孤單 gūdān 图 alone
孤獨 gūdú 图 alone, solitary 图 lonely
孤兒 gūér 图 orphan
孤寂 gūjì 图 lonely
孤立 gūlì 图 isolate 图 isolated

狐 104 hú
4 Dog 犬 |ʲ with 瓜 |⁰⁴ phonetic and suggestive of solitary 孤 |⁰⁴. 图 fox
狐狸 húlí 图 fox

弧 104 hú
5 Bow 弓 |⁶ with 瓜 |⁰⁴ phonetic. 图 arc
弧形 húxíng 图 arc

矛 105 máo
1 Pictograph of an ancient hooked lance. 图 lance, spear
矛盾 máodùn 图 contradiction, inconsistency

茅 105 máo
2 Spear-like 矛 |⁰⁵ (phonetic) plant 艸 兜. 图 a type of grass
茅草 máocǎo 图 thatch
茅房 máofáng 图 outhouse
茅台酒 máotáijiǔ 图 Maotai liquor
茅屋 máowū 图 thatched house

柔 105 róu
3 Wood 木 |ʲ with 矛 |ʲ phonetic. 图 flexible 图 tender, gentle ⇔ 溫柔 兜
柔道 róudào 图 judo
柔和 róuhé 图 soft, gentle
柔軟 róuruǎn 图 soft, yielding

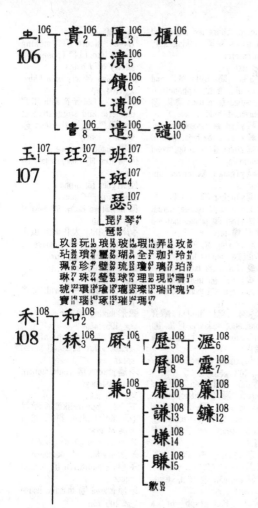

踩 105 róu
4 Feet 足 on tender
柔 105 (phonetic) vegetation.
trample
踩躪 róulìn trample

揉 105 róu
5 Hand 手 and

flexible 柔 105 (phonetic).
rub knead
揉搓 róucuō rub, massage

務 105 wù
6 [务] Strength 力
and an ancient character for
exert from lance 矛 105 and strike

夊. duties, affairs,
business attend to ⇔ 公
務, 商務, 特務, 勤
務, 服務, 國務, 義
務, 任務, 財務, 職
務, 事務, 債務, 勞
務, 家務, 雜務, 業
務

霧 105 wù
7 [雾] Modern form
shows rain 雨 161 with 務 105
phonetic. mist, fog ⇔ 雲
霧
霧氣 wùqì mist, fog

矞 105 yù
8 Spear 矛 105 piercing
冏 pierce

橘 105 jú
9 Tree 木 with 矞 105
phonetic. tangerine ⇔
柑橘
橘子 júzi mandarin orange,
tangerine: 橘子汁 orange juice

譎 105 jué
10 [谲] Words 言 that
pierce 矞 105 (phonetic).
deceive ⇔ 詭譎

虫 106 kùi
1 Pictograph of a
basket.

貴 106 gùi
2 [贵] Basket 虫 106
(phonetic) of money/shells
貝 150. expensive, valuable:
太貴了! Too expensive!
esteemed, honored: 您貴姓?
May I ask your (family) name?
⇔ 高貴, 富貴, 可貴,
昂貴, 珍貴, 寶貴, 權
貴
貴賓 gùibīn honored guest,
VIP
貴方 gùifāng you, your side
貴重 gùizhòng valuable
貴州 gùizhōu Guizhou
Province
貴族 gùizú nobility, aristocrat

匱
106 kùi

3 [匱] Container 匚 for valuables 貴 (phonetic). 图 cabinet

匱乏 kùifá 酬 short of, shortage, deficiency

櫃
106 gùi

4 [櫃] Wooden 木 cabinet 匱 (phonetic). Simplified form uses 巨. 图 cabinet ⇔ 貨櫃, 櫥櫃, 衣櫃

櫃台 gùitái 图 counter

櫃子 gùizi 图 cabinet 图 locker

潰
106 kùi

5 [溃] Water 水 rising high 貴 (phonetic). 酬 burst (through a dike) ⇔ 崩潰

潰瘍 kùiyáng 图 ulcer

饋
106 kùi

6 [馈] Food 食 to the honored 貴 (phonetic). 酬 present a gift ⇔ 反饋, 回饋

饋贈 kùizèng 酬 present (a gift)

遺
106 yí

7 [遗] Movement 辵 with 貴 phonetic. 酬 lose 酬 bequeath ⇔ 後遺症

遺產 yíchǎn 图 inheritance

遺傳 yíchuán 酬 inherit 图 heredity

遺憾 yíhàn 酬 regret 图 regrettable

遺跡 yíjī 图 historic remains, vestiges

遺留 yílíu 酬 bequeath, hand down

遺棄 yíqì 酬 abandon, forsake

遺失 yíshī 酬 lose

遺孀 yíshuāng 图 widow

遺忘 yíwàng 酬 forget

遺址 yízhǐ 图 ruins

遺囑 yízhǔ 图 final wishes, will

蕢
106 qiàn

8 Basket 土 of earth

遣
106 qiǎn

9 Movement 辵 with phonetic. 酬 dispatch ⇔ 差遣, 消遣, 派遣

遣送 qiǎnsòng 酬 send

譴
106 qiǎn

10 [谴] Words 言 with phonetic. 酬 reprimand

譴責 qiǎnzé 酬 accuse, reprimand

玉
107 yù

1 Three pieces of jade strung together. Dot, not added in composition, distinguishes it from 王. 图 jade ⇔ 碧玉, 寶玉

玉米 yùmǐ 图 corn: 玉米粥 corn porridge

玉器 yùqì 图 jadeware

玉山 yùshān 图 Mount Yu - the tallest mountain in Taiwan

玉鐲 yùzhúo 图 jade bracelet

玨
107 jué

2 Pieces of jade 玉.

班
107 bān

3 Knife 刀 splitting jade into two 玨. 图 group, team, squad, class 图 shift: 夜班 night shift 酬 run, flight ⇔ 上班, 下班, 同班, 加班, 交班, 輪班, 西班牙

班代 bāndài 图 class representative

班底 bāndǐ 图 core of a group

班機 bānjī 图 scheduled flight

班級 bānjí 图 class, grade

班長 bānzhǎng 图 class leader

斑
107 bān

4 Modern form shows jade pieces 玨 and lines 文. 图 spots, speckles ⇔ 雀斑

斑白 bānbái 图 graying (hair)

斑點 bāndiǎn 图 spot, stain

斑馬 bānmǎ 图 zebra

斑紋 bānwén 图 stripes, dots

瑟
107 sè

5 Modern form shows jade pieces 玨 and necessity 必. 图 se - a large string instrument ⇔ 蕭瑟, 琴瑟和鳴

禾
108 hé

1 Pictograph of a grain-bearing plant. 图 grain on the stalk

禾苗 hémiáo 图 grain seedling

和
108 hé huo

2 Mouth 口 with 禾 phonetic. hé: harmony, peace 酬 Japanese hé,hàn: 图 and ⇔ 隨和, 共和, 飽和, 琴瑟和鳴, 義和團, 溫和, 調和, 緩和, 暖和, 柔和, 祥和, 總和, 頤和園

和藹 héǎi 图 amiable

和服 héfú 图 kimono

和解 héjiě 图 reconciliation, amicable settlement 酬 reconcile

和睦 hémù 图 at peace, on friendly terms

和平 hépíng 图 peace

和氣 héqì 图 friendly

和善 héshàn 图 kind, amiable

和尚 héshàng 图 monk (Buddhist)

和式 héshì 图 图 Japanese style

和談 hétán 图 peace talks

和諧 héxié 图 harmonious

秝
108 lì

3 Sheaves of grain 禾. 图 grain

厤
108 lì

4 Grain 秝 (phonetic) covered 厂. 图 manage

歷
108 lì

5 [历] Stop 止 with 厤 phonetic. Simplified form uses 力. 酬 experience, undergo 图 previous, past ⇔ 經歷, 資歷, 閱歷, 學歷, 履歷, 遊歷, 來

禾
108

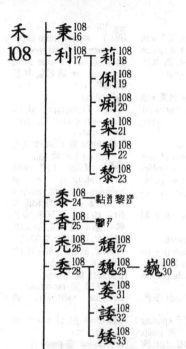

秉 108 16

利 108 17 — 莉 108 18

俐 108 19

痢 108 20

梨 108 21

犁 108 22

黎 108 23

黍 108 24 — 黏 26 黎 108 23

香 108 25 — 馨 27

禿 108 26 — 頹 108 27

委 108 28 — 魏 108 29 — 巍 108 30

萎 108 31

諉 108 32

矮 108 33

稀 108 21 年 108 6 稅 108 12 穎 108 稽 108 秦 108 25 籴 108 13
私 108 11 稿 108 22 秤 108 7 秀 108 2 秒 108 秒 108 穆 108
穀 108 秧 108 稔 108 穢 108 秘 108 穗 108 穗 108
稜 108 粟 108 困 108 稠 108 程 108 移 108 種 108
積 108 秋 108 科 108 秩 108 穗 108 租 108 稻 108
稼 108 酥 108 稚 108 種 108 稱 108 酥 108

瓦 109 1 — 瓷 109 瓶 109

甄 109

歷 160

歷程 lìchéng 图 process, course

歷次 lìcì 图 each time previously

歷代 lìdài 图 past dynasties

歷經 lìjīng 图 experience successively

歷年 lìnián 图 past years

歷時 lìshí 图 last, continue

歷史 lìshǐ 图 history

瀝 108 6 [沥] Water 水 with 歷 108 phonetic. 图 trickle ⇔ 淅瀝

靂 108 7 [雳] Rain 雨 with 歷 108 phonetic. 图 thunder ⇔ 霹靂

曆 108 8 [历] Sun 日 with 厤 108 phonetic. 图 calendar ⇔ 農曆, 陰曆, 日曆, 陽曆, 月曆

曆書 lìshū 图 almanac

兼 108 9 jiān Hand 又 holding two sheafs of grain 秝 (altered). 图 unite concurrently, simultaneously

兼併 jiānbìng 图 annex, merge

兼差 jiānchāi 图 moonlight, work part-time

兼顧 jiāngù 图 consider equally

兼職 jiānzhí 图 part-time job

廉 108 10 lián Joins 兼 (phonetic) a shelter 广. 图 corner 图 honest 图 cheap ⇔ 清廉, 低廉

廉價 liánjià 图 bargain price

簾 108 11 lián [帘] Bamboo 竹 with 廉 108 phonetic. Simplified form, an ancient form, shows window/hole 穴 cloth 巾. 图 blinds, curtain ⇔ 窗簾

鎌 108 12 lián [镰] Metal 金 with 廉 108 phonetic. 图 sickle

鎌刀 liándāo 图 sickle

謙 108 13 qiān [谦] Words 言 uniting 兼 108 (phonetic). 图 self-effacing

謙卑 qiānbēi 图 humble

謙讓 qiānràng 图 yield, defer

謙虛 qiānxū 图 modest, unassuming, self-effacing

謙遜 qiānxùn 图 humble, modest, unassuming

嫌 108 14 xián Woman 女 and simultaneously 兼 108 (phonetic). 图 suspicion 图 dislike, mind, be bothered by ⇔ 涉嫌

嫌犯 xiánfàn 图 suspect

嫌棄 xiánqì 图 reject in disgust

嫌隙 xiánxì 图 enmity, grudge
嫌疑 xiányí 图 suspect: 嫌疑犯 a suspect

賺 108 zhuàn
15 [賺] Modern form shows shells/money 貝 |⁵⁰ together 兼 |⁶ (phonetic). 動 earn: 賺一大筆錢 earn a large sum of money
賺錢 zhuànqián 動 make money 形 lucrative

秉 108 bǐng
16 Hand 又 |⁴ holding sheaf of grain 禾 |⁰⁸. 名 sheaf 動 hold
秉承 bǐngchéng 動 act on instructions

利 108 lì
17 Grain 禾 |⁰⁸ and knife 刀 |⁵. 名 an ancient tool 形 sharp 图 advantage, benefit 形 beneficial 動 benefit 图 interest ⇔ 不利ᵇᵘ, 順利ᶜˣ, 水利ᵏˣ, 匈牙利ᵃˣ, 銳利ˣˣ, 比利時ˣˣ, 暴利ᶻˣ, 便利ᵇᵘ, 私利ᵇᵘ, 福利ᵇˣ, 盈利ᵇˣ, 吉利ᵇˣ, 互利ᵇˣ, 義大利ᵇˣ, 功利ᵇˣ, 紅利ᵇˣ, 流利ᵇˣ, 專利ᵇˣ, 純利ᵇˣ, 意大利ᵇˣ, 鋒利ᵇˣ, 名利ᵇˣ, 營利ᵇˣ, 毛利ᵇˣ, 犀利ᵇˣ, 牟利ᵇˣ, 淨利ᵇˣ, 蠅頭小利ᵇˣ, 勝利ᵇˣ, 西伯利亞ᵇˣ, 奧地利ᵇˣ, 澳大利亞ᵇˣ, 獲利ᵇˣ, 權利ᵇˣ
利弊 lìbì 图 pros and cons, advantages and disadvantages
利比亞 lìbǐyà 图 Libya
利害 lìhài 图 pros and cons, advantages and disadvantages
利率 lìlǜ 图 interest rate
利潤 lìrùn 图 profit, earnings
利息 lìxí 图 interest
利益 lìyì 图 benefit
利用 lìyòng 動 use, utilize: 被利用了 used, taken advantage of

莉 108 lì
18 Plant 艸 |⁶ with 利 |⁷ phonetic. 图 jasmine ⇔ 茉莉ᵇˣ

俐 108 lì
19 Person 人 |⁰ who is sharp 利 |⁷ (phonetic). 形 clever ⇔ 伶俐ᵇˣ

痢 108 lì
20 Sickness 疒 |⁷⁴ with 利 |⁷ phonetic. 图 dysentery
痢疾 lìjí 图 dysentery

梨 108 lì
21 Tree 木 |⁷ with 利 |⁷ phonetic. 图 pear ⇔ 鳳梨ᵇˣ
梨子 lízi 图 pear

犁 108 lì
22 Ox 牛 |⁷² and sharp 利 |⁷ (phonetic). 動 plow
犁田 lítián 動 plow

黎 108 lì
23 Millet 黍 |²⁴ with 利 |⁷ phonetic (old form, left part merged with top of 黍). 形 dark 图 a surname ⇔ 巴黎ᵇˣ
黎明 límíng 图 dawn
黎族 lízú 图 the Li people

黍 108 shǔ
24 Grain 禾 |⁰⁸ put in 入 |² water 水 |⁴ to ferment. 图 millet

香 108 xiāng
25 Millet 黍 |²⁴ (now abbreviated to 禾 |⁰⁸) and sweet 甘 |⁸. 形 fragrant 图 incense ⇔ 點香ᵇˣ, 馨香ᵇˣ, 口香糖ᵇˣ, 燒香ᵇˣ, 百香果ᵇˣ, 檀香ᵇˣ, 焚香ᵇˣ, 芳香ᵇˣ
香檳酒 xiāngbīnjiǔ 图 champagne
香草 xiāngcǎo 图 vanilla
香腸 xiāngcháng 图 sausage
香港 xiānggǎng 图 Hong Kong: 香港腳 athlete's foot
香菇 xiānggū 图 mushroom
香蕉 xiāngjiāo 图 banana
香氣 xiāngqì 图 aroma, fragrance
香肉 xiāngròu 图 dog meat
香水 xiāngshuǐ 图 perfume
香味 xiāngwèi 图 flavor
香煙 xiāngyān 图 cigarette
香菸 xiāngyān 图 cigarette
香油 xiāngyóu 图 sesame oil 图 balm
香皂 xiāngzào 图 scented soap

禿 108 tū
26 [禿] Person 儿 |¹ with head shining like ripening grain 禾 |⁰⁸. 形 bald
禿頭 tūtóu 形 baldheaded

頹 108 tuí
27 [頹] Balding 禿 |²⁶ (phonetic) head 頁 |¹⁸. 動 decay, decline
頹廢 tuífèi 形 decadent, degenerate
頹勢 tuíshì 图 declining tendency

委 108 wěi
28 Grain 禾 |⁰⁸ and woman 女 |⁴. 動 yield 動 entrust, commission
委屈 wěiqū 動 wronged 動 inconvenience 動 demean
委曲 wěiqū 形 winding
委託 wěituō 動 entrust
委員 wěiyuán 图 committee member: 委員會 committee

魏 108 wèi
29 Ghost 鬼 |¹⁴⁰ with 委 |²⁸ phonetic. 國 an ancient kingdom in China 图 a surname: 魏徵 Wei Zheng - a Tang Dynasty statesman

巍 108 wéi
30 Modern form shows mountain 山 |⁴⁷ with 魏 |²⁹ phonetic. 形 lofty

萎 108 wěi
31 Plant 艸 |⁶ with 委 |²⁸ phonetic. 動 wither ⇔ 枯萎ᵇˣ
萎縮 wěisuō 動 wither, atrophy

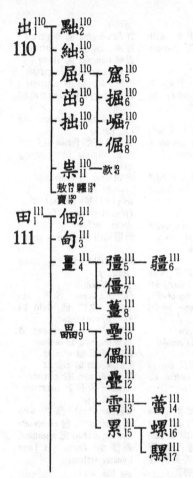

出 110 | 黜 110 | |
絀 110 | |
屈 110 | 窟 110 |
苗 110 | 掘 110 |
拙 110 | 崛 110 |
| 倔 110 |
祟 110 — 款 |
救 羅 124 |
賣 |
田 111 | 佃 111 |
甸 111 |
畺 111 | 疆 111 — 疆 111 |
僵 111 |
薑 111 |
晶 111 | 壘 111 |
儡 111 |
疊 111 |
雷 111 — 蕾 111 |
累 111 — 螺 111 |
騾 117 |

出 110 chū

出 1 Pictograph of a sprouting plant. 🔲 produce 🔲 exit 🔲 issue, put forward: 出意見 offer suggestions 🔲 happen, occur 🔲 exceed (indicating outward movement) 跑出 run out 🔲 (indicating completion) 看不出來 can't discern ⇔ 露出, 傑出, 脫口而出, 指出, 付出, 伸出, 認出, 超出, 拉出, 送出, 拿出, 找出, 刊出, 撤出, 流出, 傳出, 突出, 演出, 噴出, 使出, 凸出, 支出, 日出, 查出, 揪出, 發出, 提出, 放出, 產出, 看出, 想出, 溢出, 派出所, 輸出, 騰出, 取出, 顯出, 播出, 進出口

出版 chūbǎn 🔲 publish, issue: 出版社 publisher, publishing house

出差 chūchāi 🔲 go on a business trip

出場 chūchǎng 🔲 appear

出動 chūdòng 🔲 start out

出發 chūfā 🔲 set out: 出發點 point of departure

出國 chūgúo 🔲 go abroad

出汗 chūhàn 🔲 perspire, sweat

出境 chūjìng 🔲 exit a country

出口 chūkǒu 🔲 图 export

出來 chúlái 图 come out

出路 chūlù 图 exit, escape

出賣 chūmài 🔲 betray, sell out

出門 chūmén 🔲 go out, exit

出面 chūmiàn 🔲 appear in public

出名 chūmíng 🔲 become famous

出納 chūnà 图 cashier

出品 chūpǐn 🔲 produce 图 product

出氣 chūqì 🔲 vent anger

出去 chūqù 🔲 go out

出入 chūrù 🔲 come and go 图

諉 108 wěi

諉 32 [诿] Words 言 and entrust 委 (phonetic). 🔲 shirk ⇔ 推諉

矮 108 ǎi

矮 33 Arrow/dart 矢 with 委 phonetic. 🔲 short ⇔ 高矮

瓦 109 wǎ

瓦 1 Pictograph of interlocking roof tiles. 图 tile

瓦解 wǎjiě 🔲 crumble, disintegrate

瓦礫 wǎlì 图 rubble, ruins

瓦片 wǎpiàn 图 tile

瓦斯 wǎsī 图 natural gas

瓦特 wǎtè 图 watt

discrepancy

出色 chūsè 圈 remarkable, outstanding

出身 chūshēn 圈 background, experience

出生 chūshēng 動 be born

出師 chūshī 動 dispatch troops

出示 chūshì 動 show, produce

出世 chūshì 動 be born

出事 chūshì 動 have an accident

出手 chūshǒu 動 offer, reach out a hand

出售 chūshòu 動 sell

出庭 chūtíng 動 appear in court

出席 chūxí 動 be present, attend

出現 chūxiàn 動 appear, emerge

出血 chūxiě 動 bleed

出於 chūyú 動 come from

出租 chūzū 動 rent out: 出租汽車 rental car; 出租車 taxi

黜 110 chù 2 Expel 出 |10 (phonetic) into the dark 黑 |7. 動 demote, dismiss ⇔ 罷黜 |12

絀 110 chù 3 [绌] Threads 糸 |53 exiting 出 |10 (phonetic). 圈 inadequate ⇔ 短絀 |9

屈 110 qū 4 Tail 尾 |9 (abbreviated to 尸 |8) with 出 |10 phonetic. 動 bend 動 submit, humiliate 圈 a surname: 屈原 Qu Yuan - Warring States poet who committed suicide to protest government policies ⇔ 委屈 |28, 冤屈 |64

屈從 qūcóng 動 submit

屈服 qūfú 動 submit, yield, accept defeat

屈辱 qūrù 圈 humiliation, disgrace 動 humiliate

窟 110 kū 5 Hole 穴 |9 that bends 屈 |10 (phonetic). 圈 cave ⇔ 石窟 |24, 洞窟 |24

窟窿 kūlong 圈 hole

掘 110 jué 6 Hand 手 |9 and bent over 屈 |10 (phonetic). 動 dig ⇔ 挖掘 |9, 發掘 |28

崛 110 jué 7 Modern form shows mountain 山 |7 with 屈 |10 phonetic. 動 rise suddenly

崛起 juéqǐ 動 stand out 動 rise suddenly

倔 110 jué 8 Person 人 |10 who will not bend 屈 |10 (phonetic). 圈 stubborn

倔強 juéjiàng 圈 stubborn

茁 110 zhuó 9 Plant 艸 |66 sprouting 出 |10 (phonetic). 圈 vigorous

茁壯 zhuózhuàng 圈 vigorous

拙 110 zhuó 拙 zhūo 10 Hand 手 |9 moving like sprouting plant 出 |10 (phonetic). 圈 clumsy, awkward ⇔ 笨拙 |27

拙見 zhuójiàn 圈 謙 humble opinion

拙劣 zhuóliè 圈 inferior

拙作 zhuózùo 圈 謙 my work: 請看我的拙作. Please look at my work.

祟 11 suì 11 Spirits/omens 示 |16 sprouting 出 |10 from below. 圈 evil spirit ⇔ 作祟 |9, 鬼祟 |10

田 111 tián 1 Pictograph of a field with irrigation channels. 圈 field 圈 a surname ⇔ 農田 |14, 梯田 |57, 屯田 |68, 耕田 |7, 犁田 |33, 稻田 |31

田地 tiándì 圈 field, farmland

田埂 tiángěng 圈 embankment between fields

田徑 tiánjìng 圈 track and field

田野 tiányě 圈 cultivated fields

佃 111 diàn 2 Person 人 |10 who works the fields 田 |11 (phonetic). 圈 tenant farmer

佃戶 diànhù 圈 tenant farmer

佃農 diànnóng 圈 tenant farmer

甸 111 diàn 3 Encompassed 勹 |8 fields 田 |11 (phonetic). 圈 land owned by the emperor ⇔ 緬甸 |8

畺 111 jiāng 4 Lines 三 |9 separating fields 田 |11. 圈 boundary (⇒ 疆 |11)

彊 111 qiáng 5 [強] Bow 弓 |65 solid like well-defended border 畺 |11 phonetic. 圈 strong bow 圈 powerful (⇒ 強 |65)

疆 111 jiāng 6 Land 土 |7 with 彊 |11 phonetic. 圈 boundary ⇔ 新疆 |9, 邊疆 |9

疆界 jiāngjiè 圈 border

疆域 jiāngyù 圈 territory

僵 111 jiāng 7 Person 人 |10 immobile like field boundaries 畺 |11 (phonetic). 動 lie still 圈 stiff, numb 動 stalemate

僵持 jiāngchí 動 deadlock

僵化 jiānghuà 動 ossify 動 be deadlocked

僵局 jiāngjú 圈 deadlock

僵硬 jiāngyìng 圈 rigid, inflexible

薑 111 jiāng 8 [姜/薑] Plant 艸 |66 with 畺 |11 phonetic. 圈 ginger

畾 111 léi 9 Fields 田 |11. In composition can represent objects piled up.

壘 111 lěi 10 [垒] Piled up 畾 |11 (phonetic) earth 土 |7. 圈 rampart 動 pile up 圈 base (in baseball) ⇔ 全壘打 |27, 壁壘 |9, 堡壘 |7

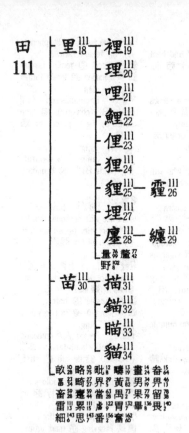

重疊²⁶, 摺疊¹²⁴

雷 111 léi
13 Rain 雨¹⁶¹ over fields 晶¹¹¹ (phonetic, abbreviated to 田¹¹¹). 圖 thunder 圍 a surname: 雷鋒 Lei Feng - a Chinese worker-hero of the 1950s
雷達 léidá 圖 radar
雷電 léidiàn 圖 thunder and lightning
雷根 léigēn 囚 圙 Reagan
雷厲風行 léilìfēngxíng 圐 act decisively, act drastically
雷射 léishè 圖 圙 laser: 雷射印表機 laser printer
雷聲 léishēng 圖 thunder
雷同 léitóng 圐 similar, identical
雷雨 léiyǔ 圐 thunderstorm

蕾 111 lěi
14 Plant 艸⁹⁴ bursting like thunder 雷¹¹¹ (phonetic). 圖 bud ⇔ 蓓蕾⁴⁹, 芭蕾⁹⁴

累 111 léi lěi lèi
15 Thread 糸¹⁵³ with 晶¹¹¹ (abbreviated to 田¹¹¹) phonetic. léi: 圖 bind lěi: 圖 accumulate lèi: 圙 tired 圖 work hard ⇔ 疲累⁴⁹, 積累⁷⁶, 連累¹⁹⁸
累積 lěijī 圖 accumulate
累累 lěilěi 圙 one after another
累贅 léizhui 圖 burden 圙 verbose

螺 111 lúo
16 Modern form shows insect 虫¹²⁵ and accumulate 累¹¹¹ (phonetic). 圖 spiral shell ⇔ 陀螺¹²⁵
螺絲 lúosī 圖 screw: 圙 螺絲起子 screwdriver
螺旋 lúoxuán 圖 spiral

騾 111 lúo
17 [骡] Modern form shows horse 馬¹⁷⁷ and work hard 累¹¹¹ (phonetic). 圖 mule
騾子 lúozi 圖 mule

壘球 lěiqíu 圖 softball

偏 111 lěi
11 Person 人¹⁰ with 晶¹¹¹ phonetic. 圖 puppet ⇔ 傀偏¹⁴⁰

疊 111 dié
12 [叠] Modern form shows fitting 宜¹⁴ and pile up 晶¹¹¹ (formerly 晶²⁶). 圙 overlap 圖 fold 圖 stack ⇔

里 111 lǐ
里 18 Field 田|¹¹ and earth 土|⁶. 图 hamlet, village 图 li – about one-third of a mile ⇔ 千里|², 公里|², 阿里山|³, 英里|³
里根 lǐgēn 囚 爾 Reagan
里長 lǐzhǎng 图 颲 precinct leader

裡 111 lǐ li
裡 19 [里|¹⁸] Clothing 衣|²⁶ with 里|¹⁸ phonetic. 图 lining 爾 inside ⇔ 道裡|⁴, 心裡|⁵, 那裡|², 哪裡|³, 家裡|⁵⁵
裡邊 lǐbiān 颲 inside
裡面 lǐmiàn 颲 inside
裡頭 lǐtóu 颲 inside

理 111 lǐ
理 20 Jade 玉|⁰⁷ with 里|¹⁸ phonetic. 颲 work jade 图 texture, grain 图 reason, logic 颲 manage, administer 颲 arrange 颲 acknowledge, respond ⇔ 不理⁵, 經理|², 原理|³, 公理|², 修理|², 條理|³, 悖理|³, 眞理|³, 處理|³, 大理|³, 合理|³, 代理|³, 辦理|³, 按理|³, 地理|³, 治理|³, 裏理|³, 生理|³, 清理|³, 情理|³, 心理|³, 物理|³, 料理|³, 整理|³, 定理|³, 倫理|³⁵, 助理|³, 總理|³, 道理|³, 推理|³, 管理|⁶⁷
理財 lǐcái 颲 administer finances
理睬 lǐcǎi 颲 notice: 無人理睬 unnoticed
理當 lǐdàng 颲 should, ought to
理髮 lǐfǎ 颲 cut hair: 理髮師 barber, hairdresser
理工 lǐgōng 图 science and engineering
理會 lǐhùi 颲 acknowledge (somebody)
理解 lǐjiě 颲 comprehend
理論 lǐlùn 图 theory: 理論上可以. In theory it's possible.

理念 lǐniàn 图 idea, concept
理事 lǐshì 图 council member: 理事會 council
理想 lǐxiǎng 图 颲 ideal: 理想主義 idealism
理性 lǐxìng 颲 reasonable, rational: 非理性 irrational
理學 lǐxué 图 Neo-Confucianism
理由 lǐyóu 图 reason, logic

哩 111 lǐ
哩 21 Mouth 口|⁶ with 里|¹⁸ phonetic. 图 mile (⇒ 里|¹⁸) ⇔ 咖哩|²⁴

鯉 111 lǐ
鯉 22 [鲤] Fish 魚|⁹⁰ with 里|¹⁸ phonetic. 图 carp
鯉魚 lǐyú 图 carp

俚 111 lǐ
俚 23 Person's 人|⁰ village 里|¹⁸ (phonetic). 图 resources, livelihood 颲 rustic
俚俗 lǐsú 颲 vulgar
俚語 lǐyǔ 图 slang

狸 111 lǐ
狸 24 Modern form shows dog 犬|⁷ with 里|¹⁸ phonetic. 图 fox ⇔ 狐狸|²⁴

貍 111 lí mái
貍 25 [貍|²⁴] Clawed beast 豸|⁴⁶ that lives near villages 里|¹⁸ (phonetic). 图 fox, raccoon (⇒ 狸|²⁴) Also meaning of clawed beast 豸|⁴⁶ that digs inside 里|¹⁸. 图 bury (⇒ 埋|²⁷)

霾 111 mái
霾 26 Rain/storm 雨|⁶¹ that buries 貍|²⁵ (phonetic). 图 duststorm 颲 misty, foggy ⇔ 陰霾|²⁴

埋 111 mái mán
埋 27 In 里|¹⁸ the ground 土|⁶. mái: 颲 bury ⇔ 掩埋|⁵⁵
埋藏 máicáng 颲 bury, stash underground
埋單 máidān 颲 pay the check ⇒ 買單|⁵⁰

埋伏 máifú 颲 ambush 颲 lie in wait
埋沒 máimò 颲 stifle, neglect
埋葬 máizàng 颲 bury
埋怨 mányuàn 颲 blame, complain

廛 111 chán
廛 28 Village 里|¹⁸ land 土|⁶ divided 八|⁷ for houses 广|⁶. 图 plot of land

纏 111 chán
纏 29 [缠] Thread 糸|⁵³ with 廛|²⁸ phonetic. 颲 bind, tangle 颲 pester, bother ⇔ 糾纏|², 難纏|³, 整纏|²⁹
纏繞 chánrào 颲 wind around 颲 harass, bother
纏足 chánzú 图 bound feet

苗 111 miáo
苗 30 Plants 艸|² rising from a field 田|¹¹. 图 sprout 图 a surname ⇔ 疫苗|³, 秧苗|², 禾苗|⁰
苗條 miáotiáo 颲 slender, slim
苗頭 miáotóu 图 portent
苗族 miáozú 图 the Miao people

描 111 miáo
描 31 Hand 手|⁶ generating 苗|³⁰ (phonetic). 颲 copy, trace ⇔ 掃描|³, 素描|³
描繪 miáohùi 颲 depict, portray
描述 miáoshù 颲 describe, portray
描寫 miáoxiě 颲 describe, depict

錨 111 máo
錨 32 [锚] Metal 金|³⁴ with 苗|³⁰ phonetic. 图 anchor 抛錨|⁵

瞄 111 miáo
瞄 33 Eyes 目|¹⁴ with 苗|³⁰ phonetic. 图 aim ⇔ 掃瞄|³
瞄準 miáozhǔn 颲 take aim at

貓 111 máo
貓 34 [猫] Clawed beast 豸|⁴⁶ that makes sound like 苗|³⁰ (phonetic). Simplified character uses 犬|⁷. 图 cat ⇔ 熊貓|³²

字譜及字典

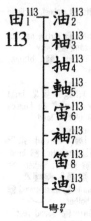

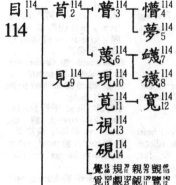

甲 112 jiǎ
1 Pictograph of a seed germinating. 圖 shell 圖 armor 圖 first Heavenly Stem (⇨ 干支²⁰) ⇔ 指甲⁵³, 保甲⁴⁷, 盔甲⁸², 龜甲²³⁹
甲蟲 jiǎchóng 圖 beetle
甲骨文 jiǎgǔwén 圖 oracle bone inscriptions

鴨 112 yā
2 [鸭] Bird 鳥¹⁷⁸ that makes sound like 甲¹¹² (phonetic). 圖 duck ⇔ 烤鴨³⁷, 填鴨⁵³, 塗鴨⁴³
鴨絨 yāróng 圖 down
鴨子 yāzi 圖 duck

押 112 yā
3 Hand 手⁸⁹ with 甲¹¹² phonetic. 圖 signature, personal mark 圖 pledge, pawn 圖 detain ⇔ 扣押²⁶, 抵押⁵⁰, 羈押¹⁷⁷

押金 yājīn 圖 security deposit
押韻 yāyùn 圖 rhyme

匣 112 xiá
4 Container 匚⁵² with 甲¹¹² phonetic. 圖 box, case
匣子 xiázi 圖 box, case

由 113 yóu
1 Pictograph of fruit, or possibly a basket. 圖 from 圖 by 圖 reason, cause ⇔ 經由⁵, 緣由⁸⁹, 藉由⁵⁹, 理由²⁵, 自由¹⁹
由此 yóucǐ 圖 hence, therefore
由於 yóuyú 圖 because

油 113 yóu
2 Water 水³⁸ with 由¹¹³ phonetic. 圖 oil, grease 圖 oily 圖 stain ⇔ 石油⁸⁵, 奶油²⁹, 黃油⁸⁷, 加油⁴⁸, 萬金油⁵⁹, 柏油⁷⁷, 煉油⁵⁰, 醬油⁵⁶, 汽油³⁷, 柴油⁴⁶, 香油⁹²
油垢 yóugòu 圖 grease stain
油畫 yóuhuà 圖 oil painting
油膩 yóunì 圖 greasy
油漆 yóuqī 圖 paint: 油漆未乾 wet paint
油條 yóutiáo 圖 fried breadstick
油脂 yóuzhī 圖 oil, fat

柚 113 yòu
3 Tree 木⁷ with basket-like 由¹¹³ (phonetic) fruit. 圖 pomelo: 葡萄柚 grapefruit 圖 teak tree
柚木 yòumù 圖 teak

抽 113 chōu
4 Hand 手⁸⁹ pulling from 由¹¹³ (phonetic). 圖 pull out, draw 圖 sprout
抽筋 chōujīn 圖 cramp
抽籤 chōuqiān 圖 draw lots
抽身 chōushēn 圖 get away from work
抽屜 chōuti 圖 drawer
抽象 chōuxiàng 圖 abstract: 抽象畫 abstract painting
抽煙 chōuyān 圖 smoke cigarettes: 謝謝,我不抽煙。 Thank you, I don't smoke.

抽驗 chōuyàn 動 sample and analyze

軸⁵ ¹¹³ zhóu [軸] Chariot 車|⁵⁸ with 由|¹³ phonetic. 图 axle 图 pivot ⇔ 橫軸|³⁴
軸心 zhóuxīn 图 axis: 軸心國 axis powers

宙⁶ ¹¹³ zhòu Roof 宀|⁴³ with 由|¹³ phonetic. 图 universe 图 eternity ⇔ 宇宙|²⁹

袖⁷ ¹¹³ xìu Clothing 衣|²⁶ from which hands extend 由|¹³ (phonetic). 图 sleeve: 長袖 long sleeves ⇔ 領袖|³⁴
袖口 xìukǒu 图 cuff
袖珍 xìuzhēn 形 pocket-sized: 袖珍辭典 pocket dictionary

笛⁸ ¹¹³ dí Bamboo 竹|¹¹ which music comes from 由|¹³ (phonetic). 图 flute
笛子 dízi 图 flute

迪⁹ ¹¹³ dí Movement 辵|⁴⁹ from 由|¹³ (phonetic). 動 advance

目¹ ¹¹⁴ mù Pictograph of an eye. 图 eye 图 category ⇔ 網
目|³¹, 注目|³⁵, 悅目|³⁵, 盲目|¹⁹, 帳目|³⁵, 瞬目|³⁵, 節目|²³, 拭目以待|⁵⁵, 項目|³⁵, 數目|³⁵, 刮目相看|⁴⁷, 頭目|⁴⁵, 名目|⁷, 心目|¹³, 科目|³⁷, 題目|⁹⁵, 眉目|¹⁴, 矚目|¹²⁵, 面目|¹⁴
目標 mùbiāo 图 target, objective
目瞪口呆 mùdèngkǒudāi 成 stunned speechless
目的 mùdì 图 purpose, goal, objective
目睹 mùdǔ 動 witness
目光 mùguāng 图 vision, sight
目擊 mùjí 图 eyewitness
目錄 mùlù 图 catalog
目前 mùqián 副 presently, now

苜² ¹¹⁴ mù Plant 艸|⁴⁶ with eye-shaped 目|¹⁴ (phonetic) leaves. 图 clover
苜蓿 mùsù 图 clover

瞢³ ¹¹⁴ mèng From an ancient character for skewed eye (now written to resemble 苜|²) and a character for rubbing the eye from wrap around 勹|⁸ and eye 目|¹⁴. 图 faulty eyesight

懵⁴ ¹¹⁴ měng Modern form shows mind/heart 心|¹³ unclear 瞢|⁴ (phonetic). 形 confused
懵懂 měngdǒng 形 ignorant

夢⁵ ¹¹⁴ mèng [梦] Unclear 瞢|⁴ (abbreviated, phonetic) at night 夕|⁷². Simplified form uses 林|⁷. 图 dream ⇔ 作夢|⁷, 做夢|⁵², 噩夢|⁵⁵, 惡夢|⁵⁶
夢見 mèngjiàn 動 dream of
夢寐 mèngmèi 图 dream, sleep
夢想 mèngxiǎng 图 dream of
夢魘 mèngyǎn 图 nightmare

蔑⁶ ¹¹⁴ miè Skewed eye (an ancient character resembling 苜|²) and guard 戍|⁴⁶. 會 tired vision 動 disdain
蔑視 mièshì 動 despise, disdain, disregard

衊⁷ ¹¹⁴ miè [蔑|¹⁴] Blood 血|¹⁶ with 蔑|¹⁴ phonetic. 動 stain ⇔ 污衊|²⁹

襪⁸ ¹¹⁴ wà [袜] Clothing 衣|²⁶ looked down on 蔑|¹⁴. Simplified form uses 末|⁷. 图 socks
襪子 wàzi 图 socks

見⁹ ¹¹⁴ jiàn [见] Eye 目|¹⁴ above a standing person 儿|¹. 動 see 動 meet 图 view, opinion ⇔

不見|⁷⁰, 不見得|⁷⁰, 創見|⁵², 望見|³⁷, 乍見|³⁷, 可見|³⁷, 少見|³⁷, 聽見|³⁵, 碰見|³⁵, 成見|⁴³, 參見|⁴⁷, 罕見|²⁹, 瞥見|³⁵, 慶見不鮮|⁴⁵, 灼見|⁵⁶, 意見|⁵⁶, 歧見|⁷², 遇見|⁴⁹, 忽見|⁵⁶, 夢見|¹¹⁴, 定見|⁴³, 拙見|¹⁰⁵, 看見|¹¹⁴, 相見|³⁵, 偏見|¹¹⁵, 遠見|¹⁴⁹, 會見|¹¹⁴, 瞧見|³⁵, 再見|⁷⁵
見到 jiàndào 動 see 動 meet: 很高興見到你. Pleased to meet you.
見地 jiàndì 图 insight
見解 jiànjiě 图 view, opinion
見諒 jiànliàng 動 forgive, excuse
見面 jiànmiàn 動 meet
見識 jiànshì 图 experience
見證 jiànzhèng 图 witness

現¹⁰ ¹¹⁴ xiàn [现] Jade 玉|⁰⁷ visible 見|¹⁴ (phonetic). 動 emerge, appear 形 current, present ⇔ 曇花一現|⁴⁶, 湧現|²⁹, 呈現|⁷², 體現|⁴³, 發現|³⁷, 實現|⁴³, 出現|¹⁰, 表現|²⁶, 顯現|¹³³
現場 xiànchǎng 图 scene, spot 形 on-the-spot 副 live
現鈔 xiànchāo 图 cash
現成 xiànchéng 形 ready-made
現代 xiàndài 图 modern era: 現代化 modernization; 現代詩 modern poetry
現金 xiànjīn 图 cash
現今 xiànjīn 副 present, now
現款 xiànkuǎn 图 cash
現任 xiànrèn 形 incumbent
現實 xiànshí 图 reality 形 realistic, practical, pragmatic: 現實主義 pragmatism
現象 xiànxiàng 图 phenomenon
現有 xiànyǒu 形 available, at hand 形 existing, current
現在 xiànzài 副 now, currently
現狀 xiànzhuàng 图 present condition, status quo

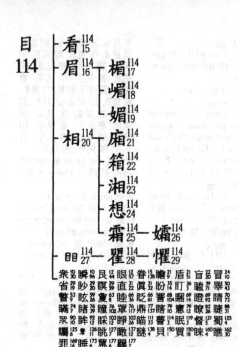

目 114
- 看 114/15
- 眉 114/16 — 楣 114/17, 嵋 114/18, 媚 114/19
- 相 114/20 — 廂 114/21, 箱 114/22, 湘 114/23, 想 114/24, 霜 114/25 — 孀 114/26
- 䀠 114/27 — 瞿 114/28 — 懼 114/29
- 衆 10/30 瞬 10/96 艮 12/44 眼 12/57 眷 15/138 瞻 21/9 盾 21/51 盲 22/20 冒 24/10
省 29/19 眇 29/20 瞑 29/99 直 31/22 眞 31/32 盼 35/14 盯 36/3 瞌 39/71 睪 50/43
瞥 53/9 眩 59/26 夐 63/8 睦 66/36 眨 66/61 睿 68/104 睏 69/14 瞪 69/92 睛 70/73
瞞 74/7 睹 76/39 瞳 76/102 罩 76/117 鼎 77/137 瞎 79/10 憲 79/12 瞭 82/26 睫 88/31
罘 90/10 眸 92/12 睬 103/12 睜 103/26 瞄 111/33 瞢 114/3 眠 119/3 督 121/5 蜀 125/4
矚 125/6 衆 126/11 眺 127/7 瞰 137/12 瞇 138/4 貝 150/1 買 150/18 睞 160/4 瞧 162/30
罪 169/16 睡 173/6 罵 177/6 羈 177/7

莧 114 xiàn
11 [苋] Plant 艸 66/2 with 見 114/9 phonetic. [名] amaranth

寬 114 kuān
12 [宽] Roof 宀 63/1 with an ancient character resembling 莧 114/11 phonetic. [形] wide [形] lenient ⇔ 放寬 94/12

寬敞 kuānchǎng [形] spacious, roomy

寬大 kuāndà [形] spacious [形] magnanimous

寬度 kuāndù [名] breadth, width

寬廣 kuānguǎng [形] vast, extensive

寬闊 kuānkuò [形] spacious, roomy

寬容 kuānróng [形] lenient, tolerant

寬恕 kuānshù [動] forgive

寬裕 kuānyù [形] ample

視 114 shì
13 [视] Show 示 1/46 (phonetic) and see 見 114/9. [動] see, watch [動] consider as, regard as ⇔ 輕視 2/11, 巡視 2/14, 注視 6/7, 檢視 10/15, 藐視 11/25, 電視 15/109, 透視 28/10, 仇視 30/4, 凝視 32/17, 窺視 39/12, 漠視 66/19, 愕視 68/10, 鄙視 69/8, 歧視 71/10, 重視 76/91, 敵視 77/63, 忽視 86/2, 傲視 94/16, 蔑視 114/6, 監視 142/3

視察 shìchá [動] inspect

視覺 shìjué [名] vision

視力 shìlì [名] eyesight, vision

視聽 shìtīng [形] audio-visual: 視聽室 video room

視爲 shìwéi [動] see as

硯 114 yàn
14 [砚] Stone 石 112/17 with 見 114/9 phonetic. [名] ink stone

硯臺 yàntái [名] ink stone

看 114 kàn kān
15 Hand 手 64/1 shading the eye 目 114/1. kàn: [動] see, watch, look [動] read [動] think, consider: 你看怎麼樣? What do you think? [動] visit, see: 明天來看你 visit you tomorrow [動] depend on: 看你 depends on you kān: [動] look after, tend ⇔ 察看 1/53, 眼看 12/57, 小看 29/8, 難看 31/99, 好看 54/7, 刮目相看 68/71, 查看 76/64, 偷看 129/18

看板 kànbǎn [名] sign, billboard

看不起 kànbùqǐ [動] despise, look down on

看成 kànchéng [動] see as, regard as

看出 kànchū [動] see, discern

看穿 kànchuān [動] see through

看到 kàndào [動] see

看懂 kàndǒng [動] understand: 你看得懂嗎? Can you read it?

看法 kànfǎ [名] viewpoint, perspective

看管 kānguǎn [動] watch over, guard

看好 kànhǎo [動] favor

看護 kānhù [名] nurse

看家 kānjiā [動] look after the house

看見 kànjiàn [動] see

看看 kànkàn [動] look and see

看來 kànlái [動] look like

看起來 kànqǐlái [動] look like

看輕 kànqīng [動] underestimate, look down on

看守 kānshǒu [動] watch over, guard

看透 kàntòu [動] see through (a deception)

看相 kànxiàng [名] physiognomy [動] tell fortune through physiognomy

看重 kànzhòng 🅥 value highly, emphasize
看準 kànzhǔn 🅥 foresee

眉 114 méi
16 Eye 目 |¹⁴ with a pictograph of hair above. 🅝 eyebrow ⇔ 皺眉⁶⁶
眉毛 méimáo 🅝 eyebrow
眉目 méimù 🅝 looks, features

楣 114 méi
17 Wooden 木⁷ eyebrow 眉|¹⁴ (phonetic). 🅝 crossbeam above a door or window ⇔ 倒楣³⁵

嵋 114 méi
18 Mountain 山⁶⁷ shaped like eyebrows 眉|¹⁴ (phonetic). ⇔ 峨嵋山³⁷

媚 114 mèi
19 Women 女⁵⁴ using eyebrows 眉|¹⁴ (phonetic). 🅥 fawn on ⇔ 嫵媚³¹, 嬌媚³²
媚外 mèiwài 🅥 obsequious to foreigners, toady to foreigners
媚眼 mèiyǎn 🅝 suggestive glance

相 114 xiàng xiāng
20 Eye 目|¹⁴ behind a tree 木⁷. xiàng: 🅥 examine, study 🅝 appearance 🅝 🅡 prime minister xiāng: 🅟 mutually ⇔ 丞相¹⁶, 長相⁶², 眞相²¹, 照相²⁸, 互相⁹, 宰相⁹, 刮目相看⁹⁷, 識相⁶⁸, 休戚相關⁷⁷, 看相¹⁶, 息息相關¹⁷⁹, 首相¹⁹⁸, 面面相覷¹⁴⁸, 變相¹⁵³
相愛 xiāngài 🅝 mutual love
相比 xiāngbǐ 🅥 compare
相處 xiāngchǔ 🅥 get along with
相傳 xiāngchuán 🅥 according to legend
相當 xiāngdāng 🅐 very, quite
相等 xiāngděng 🅟 equal
相對 xiāngduì 🅟 opposite 🅥 relative to, compared to
相反 xiāngfǎn 🅝 contrary, opposite, converse

相符 xiāngfú 🅥 agree with, conform to
相輔相成 xiāngfǔxiāngchéng 🅟 mutually complementary
相干 xiānggān 🅥 relate to, have to do with
相關 xiāngguān 🅟 related
相互 xiānghù 🅟 mutually
相繼 xiāngjì 🅐 in succession
相機 xiàngjī 🅝 camera
相見 xiāngjiàn 🅥 meet one another
相近 xiāngjìn 🅟 close, proximate
相框 xiàngkuàng 🅝 picture frame
相貌 xiàngmào 🅝 countenance, facial features
相片 xiàngpiàn 🅝 photograph
相撲 xiàngpū 🅝 sumo wrestling
相親 xiàngqīn 🅥 interview a marriage prospect
相聲 xiàngshēng 🅝 comic dialogue
相識 xiāngshì 🅥 mutually acquainted
相思 xiāngsī 🅥 miss, pine for: 相思病 lovesickness
相似 xiāngsì 🅟 resemble, alike, similar
相同 xiāngtóng 🅟 the same, identical
相信 xiāngxìn 🅥 believe
相應 xiāngyīng 🅝 mutual support 🅟 corresponding, relevant

廂 114 xiāng
21 Roof 广⁶⁰ over opposing 相|¹⁴ (phonetic) sides of house. Simplified form uses 厂²¹. 🅝 side room, wing 🅝 train car ⇔ 車廂¹⁵⁸
廂房 xiāngfáng 🅝 side room

箱 114 xiāng
22 Bamboo 竹⁷¹ with 相|¹⁴ phonetic. 🅝 chest, box ⇔ 皮箱²⁹, 冰箱²⁷, 郵箱⁹⁷
箱子 xiāngzi 🅝 chest, box

湘 114 xiāng
23 Water 水³| with 相|¹⁴ phonetic. 🅝 a river in Hunan 🅟 Hunan Province

想 114 xiǎng
24 Examine 相|¹⁴ (phonetic) the mind/heart 心|⁹³. 🅥 think, consider 🅥 think of, miss: 我很想你. I miss you. 🅥 want to: 你想不想去? Do you want to go? ⇔ 妄想⁵⁶, 冥想⁸⁶, 設想⁸⁵, 感想⁸⁵, 試想⁸⁵, 空想¹⁵, 幻想⁸², 回想⁹⁷, 猜想⁸⁹, 休想⁷⁷, 心想⁹³, 料想⁹⁷, 亂想⁸⁷, 理想¹³⁶, 夢想¹¹⁴, 思想¹⁴³, 構想²
想必 xiǎngbì 🅐 presumably, probably
想不到 xiǎngbùdào 🅥 unexpected
想出 xiǎngchū 🅥 figure out
想到 xiǎngdào 🅥 think of
想法 xiǎngfǎ 🅝 view, opinion
想念 xiǎngniàn 🅥 think of, miss
想起 xiǎngqǐ 🅥 think of, remember
想像 xiǎngxiàng 🅥 imagine: 不可想像 unimaginable
想要 xiǎngyào 🅥 want, feel like

霜 114 shuāng
25 Rain 雨|⁶¹ with 相|¹⁴ phonetic. 🅝 frost

孀 114 shuāng
26 Woman 女⁵⁴ in frosty 霜|¹⁴ (phonetic) situation. 🅝 widow ⇔ 遺孀¹⁰⁶

䀎 114 jù
27 Eyes 目|¹⁴ looking left and right.

瞿 114 qū
28 Bird 隹|⁶² looking to both sides 䀎|¹⁴ (phonetic). 🅝 falcon

懼 114 jù
29 [惧] Heart 心|⁹³ and falcon 瞿|¹⁴ (phonetic). Simplified form uses 具|¹²⁶. 🅝

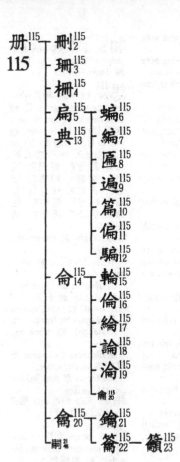

栅⁴ zhà Wood 木⁷ arranged like bamboo strips 册 I¹⁵ (phonetic). 图 fence, railing
栅欄 zhàlán 图 fence, railing
栅門 zhàmén 图 gate

扁⁵ biǎn Inscriptions 册 I¹⁵ by the sides of a door 戶户. 图 tablet 图 flat
扁擔 biǎndan 图 carrying pole

蝙⁶ biān bā biǎn Insect-like 虫 I²⁵ with 扁 I¹⁵ phonetic. 图 bat
蝙蝠 biānfú, biǎnfú 图 bat

編⁷ biān [编] Thread 糸 I⁵³ binding together tablets 扁 I¹⁵ (phonetic). 图 compile, edit 图 compose 图 weave 图 volume ⇔ 改編²⁷, 竹編²⁷, 彙編⁵⁸
編輯 biānjí 图 edit: 編輯者 editor
編排 biānpái 图 arrange, lay out 图 layout
編寫 biānxiě 图 compile
編織 biānzhī 图 weave
編制 biānzhì 图 organization, system
編製 biānzhì 图 draw up (a plan) 图 organization
編撰 biānzhuàn 图 compile
編纂 biānzuǎn 图 compile

匾⁸ biǎn Modern form shows tablet 扁 I¹⁵ (phonetic) in a box 匸²⁸. 图 tablet
匾額 biǎné 图 tablet

遍⁹ biàn Movement 辵⁴⁷ with 扁 I¹⁵ phonetic. 图 everywhere 图 time: 再來一遍 one more time ⇔ 普遍²⁷

篇¹⁰ piān Bamboo 竹⁷¹ tablet 扁 I¹⁵ (phonetic). 图 measure-word for written works 图 sheet

fear, dread ⇔ 恐懼³⁹, 畏懼⁴⁰, 憂懼¹⁹
懼怕 jùpà 图 fear, dread

册¹ cè Pictograph of an ancient book composed of bamboo strips tied together. 图 book, register 图 volume ⇔ 註册⁸⁶, 手册⁹⁹
册子 cèzi 图 pamphlet, booklet

删² shān Erase book 册 I¹⁵ by scraping with knife 刀³⁵. 图 excise, delete
删除 shānchú 图 excise, delete

珊³ shān Jade 玉¹⁰⁷ with 册 I¹⁵, abbreviated from 删 I¹⁵, phonetic. 图 coral
珊瑚 shānhú 图 coral: 珊瑚島 coral island

圐 chapter, section ⇔ 短篇圐
篇幅 piānfú 圐 length (of a written work)

偏 115 piān
11 Person 人[p] with 扁[115] phonetic. 圐 lean, tilt 圐 contrary to expectations ⇔ 不偏不倚

偏愛 piānài 圐 be partial to, favor
偏廢 piānfèi 圐 overemphasize one thing at the expense of another
偏好 piānhào 圐 hobby 圐 preference
偏見 piānjiàn 圐 prejudice, bias
偏離 piānlí 圐 deviate from, diverge from
偏旁 piānpáng 圐 component of a Chinese character
偏僻 piānpì 圐 remote
偏偏 piānpiān 圐 contrary to expectations 圐 deliberately
偏頗 piānpō,piānpǒ 圐 partial, biased
偏袒 piāntǎn 圐 be partial to, favor 圐 partiality, favoritism
偏聽偏信 piāntīngpiānxìn 圐 listen to and believe only one side
偏向 piānxiàng 圐 incline toward
偏心 piānxīn 圐 bias, partiality
偏遠 piānyuǎn 圐 remote
偏執 piānzhí 圐 obstinate
偏重 piānzhòng 圐 overemphasize: 偏重學歷 overemphasize scholastic achievement

騙 115 piàn
12 [骗] Horse 馬[177] with 扁[115] phonetic. 圐 deceive, cheat ⇔ 哄騙, 詐騙, 拐騙, 欺騙, 瞞騙
騙人 piànrén 圐 deceive, cheat

典 115 diǎn
13 Books 冊[115] on pedestal 丌[46]. 圐 classics 圐 ceremony ⇔ 經典, 詞典, 古典, 字典, 辭典, 瑞典, 慶典
典範 diǎnfàn 圐 model

典禮 diǎnlǐ 圐 ceremony
典型 diǎnxíng 圐 typical, model, representative
典雅 diǎnyǎ 圐 refined, elegant

侖 115 lún
14 [仑] Gather documents 冊[115]. Simplified form uses 匕[12]. 圐 reflect on, meditate 圐 orderly ⇔ 加侖

輪 115 lún
15 [轮] Cart 車[58] with 侖[115] phonetic. 圐 wheel 圐 in turns 圐 take turns: 輪到你了 your turn 圐 round ⇔ 三輪車, 齒輪
輪班 lúnbān 圐 in shifts
輪船 lúnchuán 圐 steamship
輪迴 lúnhuí 圐 reincarnation
輪廓 lúnkuò 圐 outline, silhouette
輪流 lúnliú 圐 in turns, alternately
輪胎 lúntāi 圐 tire
輪子 lúnzi 圐 wheel

倫 115 lún
16 [伦] People 人[p] in order 侖[115] (phonetic). 圐 sequence 圐 ethics
倫常 lúncháng 圐 social order governing interpersonal relations
倫次 lúncì 圐 logical sequence
倫敦 lúndūn 圐 London
倫理 lúnlǐ 圐 ethics

綸 115 lún
17 [纶] Thread 糸[153] with 侖[115] phonetic. 圐 decorative silk cord in ancient times 圐 fishing line

論 115 lùn lún
18 [论] Speak 言[9] in logical order 侖[115] (phonetic). lùn: 圐 argue, debate 圐 opinion, theory ⇔ 遑論, 不論, 討論, 輿論, 公論, 評論, 結論, 無論, 無神論, 議論, 辯論, 空論, 言論, 社論, 談論, 定論, 爭論, 理論, 推論, 唯物論, 唯心論
論點 lùndiǎn 圐 thesis, argument
論調 lùndiào 圐 view, argument
論壇 lùntán 圐 forum
論文 lùnwén 圐 paper, treatise 圐 thesis, dissertation: 博士論文 Ph.D. dissertation
論語 lúnyǔ 圐 The Analects of Confucius (⇨ 四書)
論戰 lùnzhàn 圐 debate, polemic

淪 115 lún
19 [沦] Water 水 and sequence 侖[115] (phonetic). 圐 ripples ⇔ 沈淪
淪為 lúnwéi 圐 sink to, reduced to
淪陷 lúnxiàn 圐 be occupied, be subjugated

龠 115 yuè
20 Holes 口[66] arranged 侖[115]. 圐 panpipe

鑰 115 yào
21 [钥] Metal 金[31] with 龠[115] phonetic. Simplified form uses 月[p]. 圐 key
鑰匙 yàoshi 圐 key

籥 115 yuè
22 [龠] Bamboo 竹[71] flute 龠[115] (phonetic). 圐 an ancient short flute

籲 115 yù
23 [吁] Head 頁[18] playing a flute 籥[115] (phonetic) to please the gods. Simplified form is a related character from 口[66] and 于. 圐 beseech ⇔ 呼籲
籲請 yùqǐng 圐 beseech

皿 116 mǐn
1 Pictograph of a serving vessel. 圐 plate, saucer ⇔ 器皿

孟 116 mèng
2 Child 子[55] with 皿[116] phonetic. 圐 eldest child 圐 a surname
孟浪 mènglàng 圐 reckless

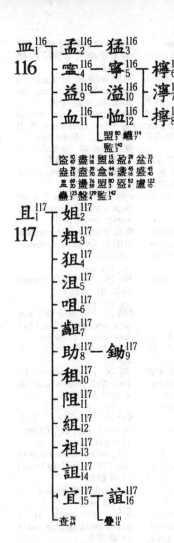

116

皿₁¹¹⁶ ┬ 孟₂¹¹⁶ ─ 猛₃¹¹⁶
├ 寍₄¹¹⁶ ─ 寧₅¹¹⁶ ┬ 檸₆¹¹⁶
├ 益₉¹¹⁶ ─ 溢₁₀¹¹⁶ ├ 濘₇¹¹⁶
└ 血₁₁¹¹⁶ ┬ 恤₁₂¹¹⁶ └ 擰₈¹¹⁶
　　　　　├ 盟₈₀ 衊₁₁₄
　　　　　└ 監₁₄₂

盜₄₀ 盡₁₄₆ 盬₁₅ 盈₅₄ 盆₃₅
益₅₄ 盍₃₀ 盔₆₄ 盞₄₆ 盛₄₀
盅₁₄ 盪₇₆ 盟₈₀ 盃₈₂ 盧₁₂₂
蠱₁₂₅ 盤₁₂₉ 監₁₄₂

117

且₁¹¹⁷ ┬ 姐₂¹¹⁷
├ 粗₃¹¹⁷
├ 狙₄¹¹⁷
├ 沮₅¹¹⁷
├ 咀₆¹¹⁷
├ 齟₇¹¹⁷
├ 助₈¹¹⁷ ─ 鋤₉¹¹⁷
├ 租₁₀¹¹⁷
├ 阻₁₁¹¹⁷
├ 組₁₂¹¹⁷
├ 祖₁₃¹¹⁷
├ 詛₁₄¹¹⁷
├ 宜₁₅¹¹⁷ ┬ 誼₁₆¹¹⁷
└ 查₆₄ 　 └ 疊₁₂¹¹¹

孟子 mèngzǐ [N] [img] Mencius (⇔ 四書)

猛 ³ 116 měng
Dog 犬 ¹ with 孟 ² ¹⁶ phonetic. [img] fierce ⇔ 凶

猛 ³, 兇猛 ³
猛進 měngjìn [img] advance rapidly
猛烈 měngliè [img] violent
猛然 měngrán [img] suddenly

寍 ⁴ 116 níng
Heart 心 ⁶³ satisfied with dish III ¹¹⁶ under shelter 宀 ¹. [img] rest

寧 ⁵ 116 níng
[宁] Rest 主 ⁴⁶ and exhale 丂 ⁷ (altered to resemble 丁 ³⁶). [img] tranquil ⇔ 安寧 ³⁶, 遠寧 ⁸⁹, 列寧 ¹³³
寧靜 níngjìng [img] quiet, still, tranquil
寧可 níngkě [img] would rather, prefer to
寧夏 níngxià [img] Ningxia Province
寧願 níngyuàn [img] would rather, prefer to

檸 ⁶ 116 níng
[柠] Wood 木 ⁷ with 寧 ¹¹⁶ phonetic. [img] lemon
檸檬 níngméng [img] lemon

濘 ⁷ 116 nìng
[泞] Water 水 ⁵¹ that is tranquil 寧 ¹¹⁶ (phonetic). [img] muddy ⇔ 泥濘 ⁴⁵

擰 ⁸ 116 níng nǐng
[拧] Hand 手 ⁴⁹ with 寧 ¹¹⁶ phonetic. níng: [img] wring: 擰乾 wring dry [img] pinch nǐng: [img] twist, screw

益 ⁹ 116 yì
Water 水 ⁵¹ (written sideways) overflowing a saucer III ¹¹⁶. [img] augment [img] benefit, advantage [img] increasingly ⇔ 裨益 ⁵², 收益 ⁵⁷, 公益 ², 效益 ²⁴, 日益 ⁷⁶, 受益 ¹⁹⁷, 利益 ¹⁹², 權益 ¹⁶²
益處 yìchù [img] benefit, good

溢 ¹⁰ 116 yì
Overflow 益 ¹¹⁶ (phonetic) with water 水 ⁵¹ redundant. [img] overflow ⇔ 外溢 ⁷⁷, 洋溢 ¹²³
溢出 yìchū [img] overflow

血 ¹¹ 116 xuè xiě
Vase III ¹¹⁶ containing sacrificial blood (mark on top). [img] blood ⇔ 混血 ⁵², 流

血⁵⁸, 出血¹¹⁰, 捐血¹³²

血管 xiěguǎn 图 blood vessel

血球 xiěqiú 图 blood cell

血統 xiětǒng 图 lineage, blood relations

血腥 xiěxīng 图 bloody

血壓 xiěyā 图 blood pressure

血液 xiěyè,xiěyì 图 blood

恤¹¹⁶ xù
12 Heart 心⁸³ and blood 血¹¹⁶ (phonetic). 📖 worry 📖 sympathize ⇔ 撫恤¹²⁰

且¹¹⁷ qiě
1 Pictograph of a stand with shelves for offerings to ancestors. 📖 offering table 📖 ancestors 📖 moreover 📖 and ⇔ 況且¹¹, 苟且⁵⁶, 並且⁹³, 尚且⁶², 暫且⁹⁸, 而且¹³⁴

姐¹¹⁷ jiě
2 Woman 女³⁴ with 且¹¹⁷ phonetic. 图 sister (elder) 图 young woman ⇔ 學姐⁴⁸, 小姐⁷, 大姐⁷, 堂姐⁶⁹, 表姐¹²⁶

姐姐 jiějie 图 sister (elder)

姐妹 jiěmèi 图 sister, sisters

粗¹¹⁷ cū
3 Rice 米¹³⁸ with 且¹¹⁷ phonetic. 📖 coarse, rough 📖 vulgar, uncultured

粗暴 cūbào 📖 rough, violent

粗糙 cūcāo 📖 rough, unpolished

粗獷 cūguǎng 📖 crude and uncivilized

粗略 cūlüè 📖 rough, preliminary

粗淺 cūqiǎn 📖 superficial, shallow

粗率 cūshuài 📖 careless, rash 📖 coarse, crude

粗俗 cūsú 📖 vulgar

粗心 cūxīn 📖 careless: 粗心大意 careless

狙¹¹⁷ jū
4 Dog-like 犬⁹¹ with 且¹¹⁷ phonetic. 图 monkey

狙擊 jūjí 📖 ambush, snipe: 狙擊手 sniper

沮¹¹⁷ jǔ
5 Water 水²¹ with 且¹¹⁷ phonetic. 📖 prevent, abate

沮喪 jǔsàng 📖 depressed, discouraged

咀¹¹⁷ jǔ
6 Mouth 口⁶⁸ with 且¹¹⁷ phonetic. 📖 chew

咀嚼 jǔjué 📖 chew carefully 📖 ruminate

齟¹¹⁷ jǔ
7 [龃] Teeth 齒⁹⁹ with 且¹¹⁷ phonetic. 图 crooked teeth

齟齬 jǔyǔ 图 bickering, discord

助¹¹⁷ zhù
8 Offerings to ancestors 且¹¹⁷ (phonetic) bringing strength 力⁷⁴. 📖 assist, help ⇔ 贊助⁹³, 有助於¹⁶, 協助²⁶, 互助⁹⁷, 輔助⁸⁰, 補助⁹⁶, 幫助⁶², 救助⁷², 援助³⁰, 捐助¹³², 自助¹⁷⁹, 濟助¹⁸²

助教 zhùjiào 图 teaching assistant

助理 zhùlǐ 图 assistant

助力 zhùlì 图 help, assistance

助手 zhùshǒu 图 assistant

助學金 zhùxuéjīn 图 stipend

助長 zhùzhǎng 📖 foster, encourage

鋤¹¹⁷ chú
9 [锄] Metal 金⁹⁴ that helps 助¹¹⁷ (phonetic). 图 hoe 📖 uproot

鋤頭 chútóu 图 hoe

租¹¹⁷ zū
10 Grain 禾¹⁰⁸ offering 且¹¹⁷ (phonetic). 图 grain tax 📖 rent ⇔ 房租⁹, 出租¹¹⁰

租界 zūjiè 图 concession - Chinese territory forcibly leased to foreign powers

租金 zūjīn 图 rent

租賃 zūlìn 📖 lease

租稅 zūshuì 图 taxes

租用 zūyòng 📖 rent

阻¹¹⁷ zǔ
11 Hill 阜¹⁶⁷ with 且¹¹⁷ phonetic. 📖 block, obstruct ⇔ 梗阻¹²⁶, 遏阻³³, 攔阻⁶², 勸阻⁹⁷

阻礙 zǔài 📖 obstruct, impede

阻擋 zǔdǎng 📖 impede

阻攔 zǔlán 📖 obstruct, prevent

阻力 zǔlì 图 resistance, obstruction

阻撓 zǔnáo 📖 hamper, obstruct 📖 obstruction

阻塞 zǔsè 📖 jam, block up

阻止 zǔzhǐ 📖 obstruct, stop

阻滯 zǔzhì 📖 impeded, blocked

組¹¹⁷ zǔ
12 [组] Threads 糸¹⁵³ added 且¹¹⁷ (phonetic). 📖 braid, plait 📖 organize, arrange 图 group, team, section ⇔ 小組⁷

組成 zǔchéng 📖 constitute, form

組合 zǔhé 📖 combine, assemble

組長 zǔzhǎng 图 section chief

組織 zǔzhī 图 organization 📖 organize: 有組織 organized

祖¹¹⁷ zǔ
13 Omen 示⁴ from ancestors 且¹¹⁷ (phonetic). 图 ancestral tomb 图 ancestors ⇔ 祭祖⁵¹, 鼻祖⁹⁸, 曾祖¹⁴⁴, 媽祖¹⁷, 媽祖³⁷

祖墳 zǔfén 图 ancestral grave

祖父 zǔfù 图 grandfather

祖國 zǔguó 图 homeland

祖母 zǔmǔ 图 grandmother

祖師 zǔshī 图 founder (of a school or sect)

祖先 zǔxiān 图 ancestors

祖宗 zǔzōng 图 ancestors

詛¹¹⁷ zǔ
14 [诅] Words 言⁹⁶ against ancestors 且¹¹⁷ (phonetic). 📖 curse

詛咒 zǔzhòu 📖 curse

字譜及字典

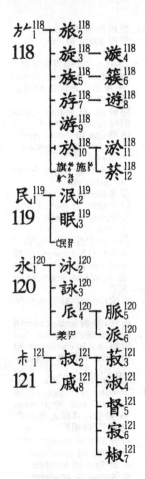

旅[118] lǚ

旅[2] People 人人[旅] marching under banner 方丶[118]. 囶 brigade 囶 囶 travel

旅程 lǚchéng 囶 itinerary, route
旅店 lǚdiàn 囶 tavern, inn
旅館 lǚguǎn 囶 hotel
旅客 lǚkè 囶 traveler, tourist
旅社 lǚshè 囶 inn, hotel
旅途 lǚtú 囶 trip, journey: 祝你旅途愉快! Have a happy trip!
旅行 lǚxíng 囶 tour, travel: 旅行社 travel agency; 旅行團 tourist group
旅遊 lǚyóu 囶 travel, tourism

旋[118] xuán xuàn

旋[3] Feet 足[旋] under waving banner 方丶[118]. xuán: 囶 revolve xuàn: 囶 whirl ⇔ 周旋[旋], 凱旋[旋], 斡旋[旋], 螺旋[旋], 盤旋[旋]
旋風 xuánfēng 囶 whirlwind, tornado
旋律 xuánlù 囶 melody
旋轉 xuánzhuǎn 囶 revolve

漩[118] xuán

漩[4] [漩] Water 水[漩] revolving 旋[118] (phonetic). 囶 whirlpool
漩渦 xuánwō 囶 whirlpool

族[118] zú

族[5] Bundle of arrows 矢[族] for practice shooting at a banner 方丶[118]. 囶 group 囶 clan 囶 ethnic group, people ⇔ 納西族[族], 漢族[族], 彝族[族], 回族[族], 滿族[族], 白族[族], 種族[族], 藏族[族], 壯族[族], 氏族[族], 貴族[族], 黎族[族], 苗族[族], 民族[族], 家族[族], 維吾爾族[族]
族譜 zúpǔ 囶 genealogy

簇[118] cù

簇[6] Bamboo 竹[簇] and group 族[118] (phonetic). 囶 cluster, bunch

斿[118] yóu

斿[7] Child 子[斿] under a

宜[117] yí

宜[15] At home between roof 宀[宜] and floor 一[宜] with 多[宜] (altered to resemble 且[宜]) phonetic. 囶 fitting, appropriate 囶 should, ought to ⇔ 不宜[宜], 便宜[宜], 適宜[宜], 權宜[宜]

誼[117] 囶 yí 囶 yì

誼[16] [誼] Words 言[誼] which make situation appropriate 宜[宜] (phonetic). 囶 friendship ⇔ 友誼[誼], 交誼[誼], 聯誼[誼], 情誼[誼]

方丶[118] yǎn

方丶[1] Pictograph of a waving banner. 囵 banner

banner 方 |⁸. ㊂ flutter 旄 roam

遊 118 yóu
8 [游|⁸] Movement
足⁴ and flutter 斿|⁸ (phonetic). ㊀ roam, travel ⇔ 郊遊㲹, 遨遊㲹, 旅遊㲹|⁸
遊蕩 yóudàng ㊀ bum around
遊記 yóují ㊂ travel notes: 西遊記 Pilgrimage to the West - a Ming dynasty novel
遊客 yóukè ㊂ tourist
遊覽 yóulǎn ㊀ tour: 遊覽車 tour bus
遊歷 yóulì ㊀ travel for research
遊民 yóumín ㊂ vagrant, homeless person
遊說 yóushuì ㊀ lobby, canvass
遊戲 yóuxì ㊂ game
遊行 yóuxíng ㊀ parade, demonstrate ㊂ parade, demonstration
遊學 yóuxué ㊀ study abroad

游 118 yóu
9 Banner 方 |⁸ swimming (ancient character from water 水㲹 and child 子陞, phonetic). ㊁ fluttering banner 旄 float, swim ⇔ 下游㲹
游標 yóubiāo ㊂ ㊄ cursor
游擊 yóují ㊂ guerrilla attack: 游擊隊 guerrillas
游泳 yóuyǒng ㊀ swim: 游泳池 swimming pool; 游泳褲 swim trunks; 游泳衣 swimsuit, bathing suit

於 118 yú
10 [于陞] Now written to resemble 方|⁸, early form suggests a variant of crow 烏陞. ㊀ at, to ⇔ 次於㲹, 限於㲹, 急於㲹, 有助於㲹, 便於㲹, 高於㲹, 等於㲹, 處於陞, 位於陞, 終於陞, 基於陞, 遜於陞, 流於陞, 關於陞, 樂於陞, 在於㲹, 適於㲹, 近於㲹, 低於陞, 出於㲹, 由於陞, 善於陞, 屬

於陞, 至於陞, 過於陞, 耿耿於懷陞, 鑒於㲹, 鑑於㲹, 對於陞
於是 yúshì ㊄ thereupon

淤 118 yū
11 Water 水㲹 with 於|⁸ phonetic. ㊂ silt, sludge ㊀ silt up
淤積 yūjī ㊀ silt up
淤泥 yūní ㊂ silt, sludge

菸 118 yān
12 [烟陞] Plant 艸㲹 with 於|⁸ phonetic. ㊂ damaged plant ㊂ tobacco leaf (⇨煙陞) ⇔ 香菸陞
菸酒 yānjiǔ ㊂ tobacco and alcohol

民 119 mín
1 Pictograph of a sprouting plant. ㊂ people, public ㊃ civilian, private ⇔ 三民主義㲹, 原住民㲹, 人民|⁰, 先民㲹, 村民㲹, 選民㲹, 公民陞, 農民㲹, 平民㲹, 殖民㲹, 居民㲹, 庶民㲹, 難民㲹, 全民陞, 貧民㲹, 賤民㲹, 國民陞, 市民㲹, 移民陞, 榮民㲹, 遊民|⁸, 臣民|⁴², 漁民|⁰⁰
民歌 míngē ㊂ folksong
民國 mínguó ㊂ republic: 中華民國 Republic of China
民間 mínjiān ㊃ of the people, non-governmental ㊅ private: 民間公司 private company
民進黨 mínjìndǎng ㊂ Democratic Progressive Party - a party in Taiwan
民權 mínquán ㊂ civil rights
民生 mínshēng ㊂ people's livelihood
民俗 mínsú ㊂ folk customs
民心 mínxīn ㊂ popular sentiment
民選 mínxuǎn ㊅ popularly elected
民意 mínyì ㊂ public opinion: 民意代表 elected repre-

sentative; 民意調查 public opinion poll
民營 mínyíng ㊀ privately operated: 民營化 privatization
民運 mínyùn ㊂ democracy movement (民主運動)
民眾 mínzhòng ㊂ the people
民主 mínzhǔ ㊂ democracy: 民主黨 Democratic Party, democratic party; 民主牆 Democracy Wall; 民主化 democratization
民族 mínzú ㊂ ethnic group, people, nationality: 民族主義 nationalism

泯 119 mǐn
2 Water 水㲹 drowning the people 民|⁹ (phonetic). ㊀ die out
泯滅 mǐnmiè ㊀ die out

眠 119 mián
3 Eyes 目|⁴ with 民|⁹ phonetic. ㊂ sleep ⇔ 冬眠陞, 安眠陞, 失眠陞, 催眠陞, 睡眠陞

永 120 yǒng
1 Pictograph of a tributary joining a main river 川㲹 (altered). ㊀ forever, eternally ⇔ 雋永㲹
永垂不朽 yǒngchuíbùxiǔ ㊀ immortal
永恆 yǒnghéng ㊅ eternal, permanent
永久 yǒngjiǔ ㊅ permanent
永遠 yǒngyuǎn ㊀ forever, always, eternally

泳 120 yǒng
2 Water 水㲹 with 永|²⁰ phonetic. ㊀ swim ⇔ 游泳|⁸
泳裝 yǒngzhuāng ㊂ swimsuit

詠 120 yǒng
3 [咏] Words 言㲹 unending 永|²⁰ (phonetic). Simplified form is an ancient form using 口㲹. ㊀ recite,

字譜及字典

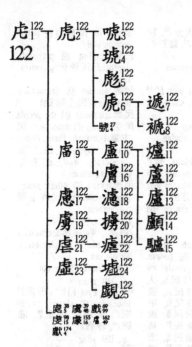

虍 122
122

處³⁹ 虞³⁹ 戲⁶⁹
虔¹⁹ 劇¹⁵⁵ 虚¹⁶²
獻¹⁷⁴₄

chant
詠嘆 yǒngtàn 圖 sigh in admiration

辰 120 pài 4 Joining of rivers 永¹²⁰ reversed.

脈 120 mài 5 [脉] Body's 肉¹³² tributaries 辰¹²⁰ (phonetic). 圖 vein, artery 圖 pulse ⇔ 山脈⁶⁷, 動脈??, 靜脈??
脈搏 màibó 圖 pulse
脈絡 màiluò 圖 system, network

派 120 pài 6 Water 水?? branching off to form a tributary 辰¹²⁰ (phonetic). 圖 faction 圖 dispatch, send ⇔ 宗派¹⁵, 左派¹⁵, 右派??, 學派??, 攤

派??, 幫派??, 氣派??, 正派??
派出所 pàichūsuǒ 圖 police substation
派遣 pàiqiǎn 圖 send, dispatch
派系 pàixì 圖 faction

尗 121 shú 1 Pictograph of a bean sprout. ㊎ beans (⇒ 菽)

叔 121 ㊎ shú 圖 shū 2 Beans 尗¹²¹ (phonetic) collected by hand 又¹⁴. ㊎ pick 圖 uncle (father's younger brother)
叔父 shúfù 圖 uncle (father's younger brother)
叔叔 shúshu 圖 uncle (father's younger brother)

菽 121 shú 3 Plant 艸?? and collect beans 叔¹²¹. 圖 peas and beans

淑 121 shú 4 Water 水?? with 叔¹²¹ phonetic. 圖 clear 圖 virtuous ⇔ 賢淑¹⁴²
淑女 shúnǚ 圖 lady

督 121 dū 5 Eye 目¹¹⁴ and collect beans 叔¹²¹ (phonetic). 圖 supervise ⇔ 基督⁴⁶, 監督¹⁴², 總督¹⁴⁴

寂 121 ㊎ jí 圖 jì 6 House 宀⁶³ with 叔¹²¹ phonetic. 圖 silent 沈寂??, 孤寂??
寂靜 jìjìng 圖 silent, still
寂寞 jímò 圖 lonely

椒 121 jiāo 7 Tree 木?? and pick beans 叔¹²¹. 圖 pepper 胡椒??, 青椒??, 辣椒??

戚 121 qī 8 Lance 戊?? (originally 戊??) with 尗¹²¹ phonetic. 圖 small battle-ax 圖 relatives by marriage 親戚??, 休戚相關??

虍 122 hū 1 Pictograph of a tiger's striped fur. ㊎ tiger

虎 122 hǔ hū 2 [虎] Tiger 虍¹²² crouching on legs 儿¹⁴. hǔ: 圖 tiger ⇔ 老虎??, 壁虎??, 馬虎¹⁷⁷
虎頭蛇尾 hǔtóushéwěi 圖 impressive beginning but poor ending

唬 122 hǔ 3 [嚇] From mouth 口⁶⁸ of a tiger 虎¹²² (phonetic). 圖 howl, roar 圖 scare ⇔ 嚇唬??

琥 122 hǔ 4 [琥] Jade 玉¹⁰⁷ with

虎 122 phonetic. 图 amber
琥珀 hǔpò 图 amber

彪 5 [彪] Tiger 虎 122
stripes 彡 . 图 tiger stripes
图 tiger cub 图 big and tall
彪炳 biāobǐng 图 shining,
splendid

虒 6 Tiger 虎 122 and cliff
厂 . 图 a tiger-like animal

遞 7 [递] Movement 辵
with 虒 122 phonetic. Simplified form uses 弟 . 图
transmit, pass on 图 substitute
⇔ 傳遞 , 郵遞
遞補 dìbǔ 图 fill a vacancy
遞給 dìgěi 图 pass on, hand over
遞減 dìjiǎn 图 gradually
decrease
遞送 dìsòng 图 deliver
遞增 dìzēng 图 gradually
increase

褫 8 [褫] Clothing 衣
with 虒 122 phonetic. 图 strip
褫奪 chǐduó 图 deprive, strip

甎 9 Pottery (ancient
character now written to
resemble 田) with 虍 122
phonetic. 图 earthenware
vessel (⇨ 盧)

盧 10 [卢] Earthenware
vessel 甎 122 with vessel 皿 116
redundant. 图 pot 图 black
图 a surname
盧比 lúbǐ 图 rupee
盧布 lúbù 图 ruble

爐 11 [炉] Modern form
shows fire 火 82 and pot 盧
(phonetic). Simplified
form uses 戶 . 图 stove, oven,
furnace ⇔ 熔爐 , 火爐
爐灶 lúzào 图 stove: 另起爐

灶 make a fresh start
爐子 lúzi 图 stove

蘆 12 [芦] Grass 艸 with
盧 122 phonetic. Simplified
form uses 戶 . 图 reed, rush
图 a surname ⇔ 葫蘆
蘆溝橋 lúgōuqiáo 图 Marco Polo
Bridge: 蘆溝橋事變 Marco
Polo Bridge Incident (1937)
蘆薈 lúhuì 图 aloe
蘆葦 lúwěi 图 reed

廬 13 [庐] Shed 广 with
盧 122 phonetic. Simplified
form uses 戶 . 图 thatched
cottage
廬山 lúshān 图 Lu Mountain - a
sacred Daoist mountain in
Jiangxi Province
廬舍 lúshè 图 farmhouse

顱 14 [颅] Pot-like 盧
(phonetic) and head 頁 . 图
skull
顱骨 lúgǔ 图 skull

驢 15 [驴] Horse 馬 177 with
盧 122 phonetic. 图 donkey

膚 16 [肤] Flesh 肉 132 with
虍 122 phonetic. Simplified
form uses 夫 . 图 skin ⇔
皮膚 , 肌膚
膚淺 fūqiǎn 图 skin-deep, superficial

慮 17 [虑] Think 思
along different lines like tiger
stripes 虍 122 (phonetic). 图
strategize ⇔ 考慮 , 疑
慮 , 顧慮 , 思慮 , 憂
慮 , 焦慮

濾 18 [滤] Water 水 with
strategize 慮 (phonetic).
图 filter ⇔ 過濾
濾清 lùqīng 图 filter

虜 19 [虏] Tie 毌
strongly 力 , with tiger 虍 122
phonetic. 图 capture ⇔ 俘
虜
虜獲 lǔhuò 图 capture

擄 20 [掳] Hand 手
capturing 虜 (phonetic).
图 capture
擄掠 lǔlüè 图 pillage

虐 21 Tiger 虍 122 clawing
爪 103 (written horizontally).
图 cruel ⇔ 肆虐 , 暴虐
虐待 nüèdài 图 mistreat, abuse:
性虐待 sexual abuse

瘧 22 [疟] Cruel 虐
(phonetic) sickness 疒 . 图
malaria
瘧疾 nüèjí 图 malaria

虛 23 [虚] Tiger 虍 122
(phonetic) hill 丘 (altered).
㊣ large hill (⇨ 墟) 图
empty, unoccupied 图 false,
unreal 图 feeble ⇔ 空虛 ,
謙虛
虛構 xūgòu 图 fabricate, make
up
虛榮 xūróng 图 vainglory: 虛
榮心 vanity
虛弱 xūrùo 图 feeble
虛偽 xūwèi 图 false 图 hypo-
critical

墟 24 [墟] Earthen 土
large hill 虛 (phonetic). 图
large hill ⇔ 殷墟 , 廢墟

覷 25 [觑] Modern form
shows see 見 114 with 虛
phonetic. 图 watch ⇔ 小
覷 , 面面相覷

羊 123 yáng
1 Pictograph of a sheep
with horns. 图 sheep ⇔ 羚

羊[123] ─ 洋[123]
　　　├ 佯[123]
　　　├ 養[123] ─ 癢[123]
　　　├ 氧[123]
　　　├ 羕[123] ┬ 樣[123]
　　　├ 恙[123] └ 漾[123]
　　　├ 姜[123]
　　　├ 羌[123]
　　　├ 詳[123]
　　　├ 祥[123]
　　　├ 翔[123]
　　　├ 鮮[123]
　　　├ 善[17][123] ┬ 膳[123]
　　　├ 美[21][123] ┼ 繕[123]
　　　│　　　　　└ 鱔[123]
　　　└ 羔[22][123] ┬ 糕[123]
　　　　　　　　　　└ 窯[123]

羨[10][14] 群[14] 羞[14]
差[15] 羸[27] 宰[17]
羚[13] 義[35]

羊[33], 山羊[67], 綿羊[62], 牧
羊[62], 羔羊[22]

羊肉 yángròu 图 mutton

洋[2][123] yáng
Water 水[24] with
羊[123] phonetic. 图 ocean 图
imported ⇔ 汪洋[17], 崇洋[18],
大西洋[17], 海洋[24], 西洋[10]
洋蔥 yángcōng 图 onion

洋化 yánghuà 图 westernized
洋火 yánghuǒ 图 match
洋片 yángpiàn 图 foreign movie
洋人 yángrén 图 foreigner
洋溢 yángyì 图 brimming, over-flowing
洋芋片 yángyùpiàn 图 潮 potato chip

佯[3][123] yáng
Person 人[10] in sheep's 羊[123] (phonetic) clothing. 图 feign, pretend
佯裝 yángzhuāng 图 feign, pretend

養[4][123] yáng
[养] Sheep 羊[123] (phonetic) for food 食[24]. 图 provide for 图 raise: 養雞 raise chickens 图 cultivate, nourish ⇔ 培養[14], 教養[18], 供養[18], 撫養[14], 涵養[18], 收養[18], 瞻養[11], 飼養[17], 修養[17], 撫養[16], 扶養[23], 領養[14], 滋養[15], 奉養[20], 保養[14], 營養[10], 餵養[10]
養病 yǎngbìng 图 convalesce, recuperate
養成 yǎngchéng 图 develop, cultivate
養分 yǎngfèn 图 nutrient
養老 yǎnglǎo 图 live in retirement: 養老院 retirement home; 養老金 pension
養女 yǎngnǚ 图 foster daughter, adopted daughter
養育 yǎngyù 图 bring up, raise
養殖 yǎngzhí 图 breed, cultivate
養子 yǎngzi 图 foster son, adopted son

癢[5][123] yǎng
[痒] Sickness 疒[24] with 養[123] phonetic. 图 itch ⇔ 搔癢[14]

氧[6][123] yǎng
Air 气[81] with 羊[123] phonetic. 图 oxygen: 有氧 aerobic; 有氧舞蹈 aerobics
氧氣 yǎngqì 图 oxygen

羕[7][123] yàng
Forever 永[20] with 羊[123] phonetic. 图 long river

樣[8][123] yàng
[样] Wood 木[7] with 羕[123] phonetic. 图 model, pattern 图 appearance ⇔ 一模一樣[1], 一樣[1], 各式各

樣⁰, 怎樣²², 同樣²⁴, 兩樣²⁸, 照樣²⁹, 式樣²², 模樣⁵⁸, 這樣⁶⁸, 那樣⁷², 榜樣³⁴

樣板 yàngbǎn 图 model, paragon

樣本 yàngběn 图 sample

樣子 yàngzi 图 appearance

漾 123 yàng
9 Water 水³⁄₄ with 羕¹²³ phonetic. 動 ripple ⇔ 蕩漾⁵⁸

恙 123 yàng
10 Heart 心¹³ with 羊¹²³ phonetic. 图 worry sickness, disease ⇔ 無恙³⁷

姜 123 jiāng
11 Woman 女¹⁴ with 羊¹²³ phonetic. 图 a surname

羌 123 qiāng
12 Sheep 羊¹²³ (phonetic) herding people 儿¹¹. 图 an ancient tribe in western China

詳 123 xiáng
13 [详] Words 言⁹⁸ with 羊¹²³ phonetic. 動 know in detail 图 detailed 图 details, minutia ⇔ 周詳⁹⁵
詳盡 xiángjìn 图 detailed, exhaustive
詳細 xiángxì 图 detailed

祥 123 xiáng
14 Omen 示³⁄₄ from offering sheep 羊¹²³ (phonetic). 图 auspicious ⇔ 吉祥³¹, 慈祥⁵²
祥和 xiánghé 图 peaceful (expression)

翔 123 xiáng
15 Wings 羽¹²⁴ with 羊¹²³ phonetic. 動 soar, glide ⇔ 滑翔³³, 飛翔⁶⁹

鮮 123 xiān xiǎn
16 [鲜] Fish 魚¹⁸⁰ and mutton 羊¹²³. xiān: 图 fresh savory 图 rare ⇔ 新鮮²⁷, 海鮮³⁴, 屢見不鮮⁴⁸, 朝鮮⁵⁹

鮮明 xiānmíng 图 clear, distinct
鮮少 xiānshǎo 图 rare

善 123 shàn
17 Words 言⁹⁸ (altered) gentle like a sheep 羊¹²³. 图 friendly 图 good 動 good at ⇔ 完善¹⁵, 友善²⁷, 改善⁸⁷, 慈善⁵², 妥善¹⁰³, 和善¹⁰⁸, 偽善¹⁷¹

善待 shàndài 動 treat kindly
善良 shànliáng 图 gentle, kind
善意 shànyì 图 good intentions
善於 shànyú 動 good at

膳 123 shàn
18 Meat 肉¹³² that is good 善¹⁷ (phonetic) to have. 图 food, provisions
膳食 shànshí 图 meals
膳宿 shànsù 图 room and board

繕 123 shàn
19 [缮] Thread 糸¹⁵³ that makes good 善¹⁷ (phonetic). 動 mend ⇔ 修繕²⁶
繕寫 shànxiě 動 transcribe

鱔 123 shàn
20 [鳝] Fish 魚¹⁸⁰ that is snake-like but good 善¹⁷ (phonetic). 图 eel

美 123 měi
21 Sheep 羊¹²³ plump and big 大³⁸. 图 tasty 图 nice, good 图 pretty, beautiful ⇔ 完美¹⁵, 讚美⁸ᵉ, 媲美¹²ᵉ, 反美³¹, 秀美²ᵉ, 南美⁷², 十全十美⁷¹, 歐美⁸⁹, 甜美⁵⁸, 中美⁴⁸, 中美洲⁴⁸, 精美⁷⁷, 優美⁸¹
美感 měigǎn 图 sense of beauty, aesthetics
美國 měiguó 图 America: 美國人 American; 美國之音 Voice of America
美好 měihǎo 图 fine, happy
美金 měijīn 图 图 dollar
美麗 měilì 图 beautiful
美貌 měimào 图 beautiful looks
美妙 měimiào 图 wonderful, beautiful

美女 měinǚ 图 beautiful woman
美人 měirén 图 beautiful woman
美容 měiróng 動 beautify: 美容院 beauty parlor; 美容手術 plastic surgery
美食 měishí 图 delicacy
美術 měishù 图 art: 美術館 art museum; 美術展 art exhibition
美味 měiwèi 图 delicacy 图 delicious
美學 měixué 图 aesthetics
美元 měiyuán 图 dollar
美洲 měizhōu 图 America: 北美洲 North America; 南美洲 South America; 中美洲 Central America

羔 123 gāo
22 Sheep 羊¹²³ for roasting on a fire 火¹². 图 lamb
羔羊 gāoyáng 图 lamb: 代罪羔羊 sacrificial lamb

糕 123 gāo
23 Rice 米¹³⁸ soft like a lamb 羔²² (phonetic). 图 cake ⇔ 年糕⁹¹, 精糕⁸⁷, 蛋糕⁸⁸

窯 123 yáo
24 [窑] Pit 穴¹² with 羔²² phonetic. Simplified form is a variant form using crock 缶¹⁴¹. 图 kiln
窯洞 yáodòng 图 cave dwelling

羽 124 yǔ
1 Pictograph of long wing feathers (analogous to 彡¹ᵉ). 图 feather
羽毛 yǔmáo 图 feather: 羽毛球 badminton

翌 124 yì
2 Wings 羽¹²⁴ with 立⁷¹ phonetic. 图 clear 图 next, subsequent
翌年 yìnián 图 following year
翌日 yìrì 图 following day

習 124 xí
3 [习] Wings 羽¹²⁴ and white 白²⁶. 動 flap wings

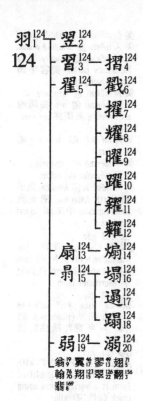

羽 124 1 　翊 124 2

124 　習 124 3 —摺 124 4

　翟 124 5 —戳 124 6

　　—擢 124 7

　　—耀 124 8

　　—曜 124 9

　　—躍 124 10

　　—糴 124 11

　　—糶 124 12

　扇 124 13 —煽 124 14

　翜 124 15 —塌 124 16

　　—遢 124 17

　　—蹋 124 18

　弱 124 19 —溺 124 20

翁 19 9 　翼 42 11 　蓼 48 13 　翅 71 5

翰 76 10 　翔 123 21 　翠 124 22 　翻 156 8

翟 169 6

repeatedly 🔲 practice 🔲
accustomed to 🖾 custom ⇔
學習 21/9, 復習 42/8, 陋習 42/22, 研
習 43/9, 演習 67/8, 補習 93/9, 練
習 120/9, 實習 95/9, 惡習 166/9
習慣 xíguàn 🖾 habit, custom
accustomed to, used to
習俗 xísú 🖾 custom

摺 124 4 zhé
[摺] Hand 手 99 with
習 124 phonetic. 🔲 fold
摺疊 zhédié 🔲 fold
摺扇 zhéshàn 🖾 folding fan
摺紙 zhézhǐ 🖾 origami

翟 124 5 dí zhái
Bird 隹 162 with long
feathers 羽 124. dí: 🖾 a kind
of pheasant zhái: 🖾 a surname

戳 124 6 chuō
Lance 戈 45 with
翟 124 phonetic. 🔲 poke, jab
⇔ 郵戳 37 3
戳穿 chuōchuān 🔲 puncture 🔲
expose
戳記 chuōjì 🖾 stamp, seal

擢 124 7 zhuó
Hand 手 99 with
翟 124 phonetic. 🔲 select
擢升 zhuóshēng 🔲 promote,
advance 🖾 promotion

耀 124 8 yào
Bright 光 42 plumage
of a pheasant 翟 124 (phonetic).
🔲 show off ⇔ 光耀 42, 誇
耀 149, 炫耀 86, 榮耀 75
耀眼 yàoyǎn 🖾 dazzling

曜 124 9 yào
Sun 日 76 with 翟 124
phonetic. 🖾 daylight

躍 124 10 yuè yào
[跃] As feet 足 93 of
pheasant 翟 124 (phonetic).
Simplified form uses 夭 9.🔲
leap, jump ⇔ 雀躍 42, 大躍
進 37, 活躍 85, 踴躍 93, 跳
躍 127
躍躍欲試 yuèyuèyùshì 🔲
anxious to try

糴 124 11 dí
[籴] Bring in 入 9
grain (ancient character from
米 138 and 翟 124). 🔲 buy grain

糶 124 12 tiào
[粜] Send out 出 10
grain (ancient character from
米 138 and 翟 124). 🔲 sell grain

扇 124 13 shàn
Half-door 戶 76 like
feathers 羽 124. 🖾 bamboo or
reed door 🔲 fan ⇔ 電扇 106,
摺扇 124
扇子 shànzi 🖾 fan

煽 124 14 shān
Fire 火 82 fanned
扇 124 (phonetic). 🔲 incite
煽動 shāndòng 🔲 instigate
煽情 shānqíng 🔲 flirt

翜 124 15 tà
Wings 羽 124 covering
日 64 the sky. 🖾 swarming birds

塌 124 16 tā
Earth 土 76 swarming
翜 124 (phonetic). 🔲 cave in,
collapse ⇔ 一塌糊塗 1, 倒
塌 37, 坍塌 37
塌陷 tāxiàn 🔲 cave in

遝 124 tà
17 Walk 足 in a swarm 舄 (phonetic). 圖 march ⇔ 遝遝

蹋 124 tà
18 Feet 足 swarming 舄 (phonetic). 圖 tread on, trample ⇔ 糟蹋踏

弱 124 ruò
19 Pictograph of a fragile plant, or possibly a variation of a young bird's wings 羽. 圖 weak ⇔ 瘦弱, 脆弱, 羸弱, 怯弱, 減弱, 孱弱, 薄弱, 虛弱, 衰弱, 微弱, 懦弱
弱點 ruòdiǎn 圖 weakness, weak point

溺 124 nì
20 Water 水 and weak 弱. 圖 drown
溺愛 nìài 圖 pamper, spoil
溺死 nìsǐ 圖 drown

虫 125 huǐ
1 Pictograph of a small snake or snake-like insect. 圖 reptiles and insects 圖 insect (⇨ 蟲)

蟲 125 chóng
2 [虫] Multiple insects 虫. 圖 insect worm, larva ⇔ 蝗蟲, 昆蟲, 小蟲, 蛔蟲, 螢火蟲, 毛蟲, 甲蟲
蟲子 chóngzi 圖 insect

蠱 125 gǔ
3 [蛊] Worm 蟲 in a plate 皿. 圖 poison
蠱惑 gǔhuò 圖 enchant, bewitch: 蠱惑人心 use demagogy

蜀 125 shǔ
4 Insect 虫 and a pictograph of a silkworm. 圖 a worm 圖 an ancient kingdom in China 圖 Sichuan Province

屬 125 shǔ
5 [属] Tail 尾 with

蜀 phonetic. Simplified form uses 禹. 圖 belong to 圖 category ⇔ 隸屬, 附屬, 眷屬, 金屬, 親屬, 家屬, 歸屬
屬於 shǔyú 圖 be part of, belong to

矚 125 zhǔ
6 [瞩] Eyes 目 connecting 屬 (phonetic). 圖 stare
矚目 zhǔmù 圖 focus attention

囑 125 zhǔ
7 [嘱] Mouth 口 connecting 屬 (phonetic). 圖 exhort ⇔ 叮囑, 遺囑
囑咐 zhǔfù 圖 exhort, instruct

燭 125 zhú
8 [烛] Fire 火 with 蜀 (phonetic). 圖 candle ⇔ 蠟燭
燭光 zhúguāng 圖 candlelight

濁 125 zhuó
9 [浊] Water 水 with 蜀 (phonetic). 圖 muddy 圖 混濁, 污濁

鐲 125 zhuó
10 [镯] Metal 金 with 蜀 (phonetic). 圖 bracelet ⇔ 手鐲, 玉鐲

觸 125 chù
11 [触] Horn 角 with 蜀 (phonetic). 圖 ram, butt 圖 touch ⇔ 感觸, 接觸, 抵觸
觸電 chùdiàn 圖 receive an electric shock
觸發 chùfā 圖 touch off, spark
觸犯 chùfàn 圖 offend
觸礁 chùjiāo 圖 run aground 圖 encounter problems
觸摸 chùmō 圖 touch
觸怒 chùnù 圖 anger, enrage

獨 125 dú
12 [独] Dog 犬 with 蜀 (phonetic). 圖 alone 圖 sole, only ⇔ 孤獨, 單獨

獨裁 dúcái 圖 dictatorial: 獨裁者 dictator
獨創 dúchuàng 圖 original creation
獨到 dúdào 圖 original
獨攬 dúlǎn 圖 monopolize
獨立 dúlì 圖 become independent 圖 independence: 宣佈獨立 declare independence 圖 independent
獨身 dúshēn 圖 single, unmarried
獨特 dútè 圖 special, unique
獨一無二 dúyīwúèr 圖 one and only, unique
獨佔 dúzhàn 圖 monopolize
獨自 dúzì 圖 single-handedly

它 125 tā
13 Snake 虫 (altered) on its tail. 圖 it ⇔ 其它
它們 tāmen 圖 they

駝 125 tuó
14 [驼] Horse 馬 with 它 phonetic. 圖 camel ⇔ 駱駝
駝背 tuóbèi 圖 hunchback

鴕 125 tuó
15 [鸵] Bird 鳥 with 它 phonetic. 圖 ostrich
鴕鳥 tuóniǎo 圖 ostrich

陀 125 tuó
16 Modern form shows hill 阜 with 它 phonetic. 圖 hilly ⇔ 阿彌陀佛, 普陀山, 佛陀
陀螺 tuóluó 圖 spinning top

舵 125 duò
17 Snake-like 它 (phonetic) appendage to boat 舟. 圖 helm, tiller ⇔ 掌舵
舵手 duòshǒu 圖 helmsman: 偉大舵手 the Great Helmsman - a reference to Mao Zedong

蛇 125 shé
18 Snake 它 with insect-like 虫 redundant. 圖 snake, serpent ⇔ 畫蛇

304 字譜及字典

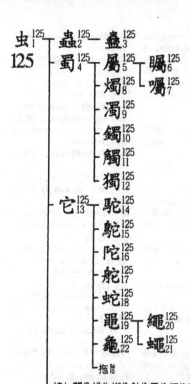

虫 125

蝗 鼉 蛻 蜋 蝕 蚤 蝦 蟲 蟾
蠍 蝠 蜥 蝴 蝶 蚜 蟻 蜜 蜂 蚤
蟹 虹 強 蚓 蟑 蜘 蛙 蜒 蜻
蚌 蜂 蠣 蠶 蛛 閩 蝥 蛋 螃
蜥 蚯 蛭 蚊 螺 蝙 蛇 蠅 蜗 蝸
蚰 蟬 蟹 蟋 雖 蜴 融 螞
蟻

添足, 虎頭蛇尾

黽 125 mǐn
[黾] Pictograph of a tadpole based on snake 它 (early form). 图 tadpole 图 strive

繩 125 shéng
[绳] Thread 糸 with 黽 phonetic. 图 rope

繩索 shéngsuǒ 图 ropes
繩子 shéngzi 图 rope

蠅 125 yíng
[蝇] Insect 虫 with tad-pole 黽 like abdomen. 图 fly ⇔ 蒼蠅, 果蠅
蠅頭小利 yíngtóuxiǎolì 图 miniscule profits

龜 125 guī
[龟] Pictograph of a turtle based on snake 它 (early form). 图 turtle, tortoise ⇔ 海龜, 烏龜
龜甲 guījiǎ 图 tortoiseshell

衣 126 yī
Pictograph of a cloak showing sleeves and flowing lower part. 图 clothing, dress 图 coating, covering ⇔ 洗衣, 便衣, 内衣, 大衣, 成衣, 襯衣, 毛衣, 蓑衣, 雨衣, 睡衣

衣袋 yīdài 图 sack
衣服 yīfú clothing
衣櫃 yīguì 图 wardrobe
衣裳 yīshang 图 clothing
衣著 yīzhuó 图 clothing

依 126 yī
Person 人 wrapped in clothing 衣 (phonetic). 图 depend on, rely on 图 comply with, follow 图 according to ⇔ 飯依

依次 yīcì 图 in sequence, successively
依法 yīfǎ 图 legally
依附 yīfù 图 depend on
依舊 yījiù 图 as before, still
依據 yījù 图 basis, foundation 图 according to
依靠 yīkào 图 depend on
依賴 yīlài 图 depend on
依然 yīrán 图 as before, still
依序 yīxù 图 in sequence
依照 yīzhào 图 according to

裔 126 yì
Clothing 衣 with 商 phonetic. 图 hem 图 descendant: 亞裔美國人 Asian-American ⇔ 後裔, 華裔

哀 126 āi
Mouth 口 with 衣 phonetic. 图 grieve, mourn 图 sorrow, grief

305

sorrowful, lamentable ⇔ 喜怒哀樂, 悲哀

哀悼 āidào 動 mourn
哀憐 āilián 動 commiserate
哀求 āiqiú 動 implore

衰 5 126 shuāi Clothes 衣126 of straw or fur 冉 (altered). 借 rain clothes (⇨ 蓑) 動 decline, wane ⇔ 興衰

衰敗 shuāibài 動 decline, wane
衰老 shuāilǎo 形 aged
衰落 shuāiluò 動 decline
衰弱 shuāiruò 形 weak
衰退 shuāituì 動 decline

蓑 6 126 suō Grass 艸 rain clothes 衰126 (phonetic). 图 straw raincoat

蓑衣 suōyī 图 rain cape made of grass or palm bark

袁 7 126 yuán Clothing 衣126 with ▢ (altered) phonetic. 图 long flowing robe 图 a surname: 袁世凱 Yuan Shih-kai - first president of the Republic of China

園 8 126 yuán [园] Enclosure 囗 with 袁126 phonetic. Simplified form uses 元. 图 garden 图 park ⇔ 花園, 公園, 校園, 茶園, 樂園, 庭園, 果園, 菜園, 桃園, 頤和園

園地 yuándì 图 garden
園子 yuánzi 图 garden

猿 9 126 yuán Dog/beast 犬 with 袁126 phonetic. 图 ape

猿猴 yuánhóu 图 ape
猿人 yuánrén 图 ape-man: 北京猿人 Peking man

遠 10 126 yuǎn [远] Movement 足 and long robes 袁126 (phonetic). Simplified form uses 元. 图 distant, far ⇔ 久遠, 老遠, 望遠鏡, 疏遠, 偏遠, 永遠, 遙遠

遠處 yuǎnchù 图 distant place
遠東 yuǎndōng 地 Far East
遠見 yuǎnjiàn 图 foresight
遠近 yuǎnjìn 图 near and far

睘 11 126 huán Eye 目 with 袁126 (altered) phonetic. 借 alarmed look

還 12 126 huán hái [还] Movement 足 and alarmed look 睘126 (phonetic). Simplified form uses 不. huán: 動 return, go back 動 repay, return, give back hái: 副 still 副 also 副 even passably: 還可以 all right (indicating emphasis) 還不用說. It goes without saying. ⇔ 交還, 償還

還好 háihǎo 形 all right, o.k.
還沒 háiméi 副 not yet
還是 háishì 副 still
還有 háiyǒu 連 moreover, furthermore
還本 huánběn 動 recover original investment

環 13 126 huán [环] Jade 玉 with 睘126 phonetic. Simplified form uses 不. 图 ring 動 surround, encircle ⇔ 循環

環保 huánbǎo 图 environmental protection (環境保護)
環節 huánjié 图 link
環境 huánjìng 图 surroundings, environment: 環境保護 environmental protection
環繞 huánrào 動 surround, encircle, orbit

表 14 126 biǎo Fur 毛 (altered) clothing 衣126. 图 outer garment 图 outside, surface 图 appearance 图 table, chart, gauge ⇔ 印表機, 代表, 外表, 發表

表白 biǎobái 動 explain, clarify
表達 biǎodá 動 express
表弟 biǎodì 图 cousin (younger male on maternal side)
表哥 biǎogē 图 cousin (older male on maternal side)
表格 biǎogé 图 form
表姐 biǎojiě 图 cousin (older female on maternal side)
表露 biǎolù 動 reveal
表妹 biǎomèi 图 cousin (younger female on maternal side)
表面 biǎomiàn 图 surface
表明 biǎomíng 動 express
表情 biǎoqíng 图 expression, look
表示 biǎoshì 動 show, express, indicate
表態 biǎotài 動 state one's position
表現 biǎoxiàn 動 express, indicate 图 showing, performance: 她的表現不錯. She did very well.
表演 biǎoyǎn 動 perform: 表演藝術 performing arts 图 performance
表揚 biǎoyáng 動 commend, praise
表彰 biǎozhāng 動 commend, cite 图 commendation, citation
表徵 biǎozhēng 图 symbol

嫖 15 126 biǎo Woman 女 on the outside 表126 (phonetic). 图 prostitute

嫖子 biǎozi 图 (動) bitch, whore

錶 16 126 biǎo [表] Metal 金 gauge 表126 (phonetic). 图 watch ⇔ 鐘錶, 手錶

裱 17 126 biǎo Cloth 衣126 on surface 表126 (phonetic). 图 scarf 動 mount (paintings or calligraphy) ⇔ 裝裱

裱褙 biǎobèi 動 mount (paintings

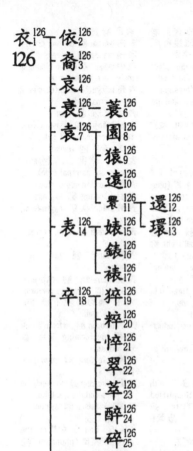

衣 126₁ — 依 126₂
126 — 裔 126₃
— 哀 126₄
— 衰 126₅ — 蓑 126₆
— 袁 126₇ — 園 126₈
— 猿 126₉
— 遠 126₁₀
— 睘 126₁₁ — 還 126₁₂
— 環 126₁₃
— 表 126₁₄ — 嬛 126₁₅
— 鐶 126₁₆
— 褾 126₁₇
— 卒 126₁₈ — 猝 126₁₉
— 粹 126₂₀
— 悴 126₂₁
— 翠 126₂₂
— 萃 126₂₃
— 醉 126₂₄
— 碎 126₂₅

褙¹²⁶ 褪¹⁴ 襪¹³ 裙¹⁴ 衩¹² 被¹⁰ 褲¹² 袍¹⁰
衰²⁷ 褥²⁸ 褐²⁹ 複³² 初³⁰ 袂³¹ 展³⁸ 裁⁴⁵
袋⁵⁷ 衫⁵⁸ 襯⁹⁶ 裘⁹⁷ 褲⁹⁵ 褒⁴⁸ 襄⁴⁹ 裕¹¹⁴
衷¹⁰⁷ 補⁶⁰ 袒⁶¹ 襟⁵⁹ 製⁵⁴ 褓⁷⁷ 褻⁷⁸ 襤¹²²
裸⁵⁷ 裝⁸⁰ 裹⁸¹ 袱⁹³ 裡⁹⁴ 袖¹¹³ 襪¹⁵⁴ 襤¹²²
裱¹²⁷ 襲¹³² 裂¹³³ 襖¹⁵⁵ 褲¹⁶² 雜¹⁶² 裴¹³⁷

or calligraphy)
卒 126 zú
18 Clothing 衣 126 (altered) with a signifying mark 一L [image] slave, servant [image]

soldier
猝 126 cù
19 Dog 犬 [image] attacking like a soldier 卒 126 (phonetic). [image] sudden

猝然 cùrán [image] suddenly

粹 126 cuì
20 Rice 米 [image] with 卒 126 phonetic. [image] pure [image] essence ⇔ 納粹, 國粹, 純粹

悴 126 cuì
21 Heart 心 [image] of a slave 卒 126 (phonetic). [image] worry ⇔ 憔悴

翠 126 cuì
22 Feathers 羽 [image] with 卒 126 phonetic. [image] female kingfisher [image] blue-green [image] green jade ⇔ 蒼翠, 翡翠
翠綠 cuìlǜ [image] blue-green, emerald

萃 126 cuì
23 Plants 艸 [image] with 卒 126 phonetic. [image] dense vegetation ⇔ 薈萃

醉 126 zuì
24 Alcohol 酉 [image] with 卒 126 phonetic. [image] drunk ⇔ 喝醉, 沈醉, 宿醉, 麻醉, 陶醉, 酒醉, 灌醉
醉漢 zuìhàn [image] drunkard
醉心 zuìxīn [image] infatuated with, engrossed in
醉意 zuìyì [image] tipsy feeling

碎 126 suì
25 Stone 石 [image] and slave 卒 126 (phonetic). [image] break, smash ⇔ 破碎, 瑣碎, 粉碎, 心碎, 易碎

兆 127 zhào
1 Pictograph of many cracks on a tortoise shell (⇒ 卜 [26]). [image] omen, portent [image] portend [image] trillion ⇔ 吉兆, 預兆, 朕兆, 徵兆
兆頭 zhàotóu [image] portent, omen

逃 127 táo
2 Move 足 [image] and portent 兆 127 (phonetic). [image] flee ⇔ 潛逃, 叛逃, 竄逃
逃避 táobì [image] evade, avoid

逃犯 táofàn 图 fugitive
逃跑 táopǎo 团 flee, run off
逃税 táoshuì 团 evade taxes
逃亡 táowáng 团 flee, go into hiding
逃逸 táoyì 团 escape
逃走 táozǒu 团 flee, run off

桃 127 táo
3 Tree 木 with 兆 phonetic. 图 peach ⇔ 核
桃儿, 楊桃, 櫻桃
桃花 táohuā 图 peach blossom
桃園 táoyuán 图 Taoyuan - a city in Taiwan
桃子 táozi 图 peach

挑 127 tiāo tiǎo
4 Hand 手 and portend 兆 (phonetic). tiāo: 团 choose 图 choosy, picky tiǎo: 团 raise 团 incite, stir up
挑撥 tiāobō 团 provoke, arouse, incite
挑錯 tiāocuò 团 look for flaws, find fault
挑動 tiǎodòng 团 provoke, incite
挑逗 tiǎodòu 团 seduce, arouse
挑剔 tiāoti 团 picky, choosy
挑釁 tiāoxìn 团 provoke: 軍事挑釁 military provocation
挑選 tiāoxuǎn 团 choose, select
挑戰 tiǎozhàn 团 challenge

窕 127 tiǎo
5 Hole 穴 and omen 兆 phonetic. 图 deep, profound ⇔ 窈窕

跳 127 tiào
6 Foot 足 with 兆 phonetic. 团 jump 团 beat, pulsate 团 skip over, omit ⇔ 心跳
跳槽 tiàocáo 团 change jobs
跳票 tiàopiào 团 bounce a check
跳棋 tiàoqí 图 Chinese checkers
跳傘 tiàosǎn 团 parachute
跳舞 tiàowǔ 团 dance
跳躍 tiàoyuè 团 leap, bound
跳蚤 tiàozao 图 flea: 跳蚤市場 flea market

眺 127 tiào
7 Eyes 目 and portend 兆 (phonetic). 团 look into the distance
眺望 tiàowàng 团 look into the distance

姚 127 yáo
8 Woman 女 with 兆 phonetic. 图 a surname 图 elegant

至 128 zhì
1 Pictograph of a bird swooping down towards the ground. 团 arrive, stop 囧 to, until 团 extremely ⇔ 甚至, 乃至, 多至, 夏至
至今 zhìjīn 圆 up to now, so far
至少 zhìshǎo 图 at least
至於 zhìyú 圆 as to, regarding

致 128 zhì
2 Arrive 至 (phonetic) despite difficulties 夊. 团 send, convey 团 cause, incur 团 achieve ⇔ 一致, 興致, 景致, 招致, 大致, 以致, 引致, 導致
致詞 zhìcí 团 deliver a speech
致富 zhìfù 团 get rich
致敬 zhìjìng 团 pay respects
致力 zhìlì 团 devote oneself to, dedicate oneself to
致命 zhìmìng 图 fatal
致謝 zhìxiè 团 send thanks

緻 128 zhì
3 [致] Thread 糸 with 致 phonetic. 图 fine, delicate ⇔ 別緻, 精緻, 雅緻, 細緻

窒 128 zhì
4 Hole 穴 stopped 至 (phonetic). 团 obstruct
窒礙 zhìài 图 obstacle 团 obstruct
窒息 zhìxí 团 suffocate, choke

桎 128 zhì
5 Wood 木 that stops 至 (phonetic). 图 shackles
桎梏 zhìgù 图 shackles

軽 128 zhì
6 [軽] Chariot 車 with 至 phonetic. 图 rear of a chariot

姪 128 zhì
7 [姪] Woman 女 with 至 phonetic. Simplified form uses person 人. 图 nephew (brother's son), niece (brother's daughter)
姪兒 zhíér 图 nephew (brother's son)
姪女 zhínǚ 图 niece (brother's daughter)
姪子 zhízi 图 nephew (brother's son)

室 128 shì
8 Roof 宀 where one stops 至 (phonetic). 图 room ⇔ 教室, 寢室, 辦公室, 浴室, 囚室, 臥室
室內 shìnèi 图 indoors
室友 shìyǒu 图 roommate

屋 128 wū
9 Stop 至 under roof (written as body 尸). 图 house 图 room ⇔ 草屋, 木屋, 房屋, 茅屋
屋頂 wūdǐng 图 roof
屋簷 wūyán 图 eaves
屋子 wūzi 图 house

握 128 wò
10 In hand 手 residing 屋 (phonetic). 团 grasp ⇔ 掌握, 把握
握手 wòshǒu 团 shake hands
握著 wòzhe 团 hold

漏 128 lòu
11 From water 水 and an ancient character showing rain 雨 in the house 屋 (abbreviated). 圈 mark time with water clock 团 leak 团 divulge 团 neglect, leave out ⇔ 紕漏, 淺漏

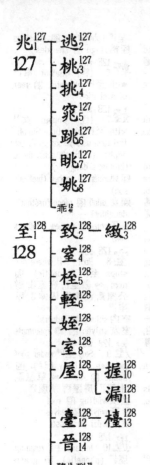

兆₁ 127 逃₂ 127 桃₃ 127 挑₄ 127 窕₅ 127 跳₆ 127 眺₇ 127 姚₈ 127 乖½

至₁ 128 致₂ 128 — 緻₃ 128 室₄ 128 桎₅ 128 輊₆ 128 姪₇ 128 室₈ 128 屋₉ 128 — 握₁₀ 128 / 漏₁₁ 128 臺₁₂ 128 — 檯₁₃ 128 晉₁₄ 128 臻½到½

漏洞 lòudòng 图 leak 图 loophole

臺 12 [台58] tái Tall tower 高37 (abbreviated, altered), grow 之58 (altered), and arrive 至128. 图 lookout tower 图 platform, stage ⇔ 硯臺114

臺階 táijiē 图 steps 图 a way out, a way to save face

臺灣 táiwān 图 Taiwan (⇨ 台灣58)

檯 13 [台58] tái Wood 木7 platform 臺128 (phonetic). 图 table

檯燈 táidēng 图 table lamp

晉 14 [晋] jìn Sun 日76 and swooping birds 至128 (doubled, altered). Simplified form uses 亞166 simplification. 图 advance 图 an ancient kingdom in China 图 Shanxi Province

晉朝 jìncháo 图 Jin Dynasty

晉升 jìnshēng 图 be promoted

舟 1 zhōu Pictograph of a dugout canoe. 图 boat ⇔ 同舟共濟27, 龍舟132

般 2 bān Boat 舟129 propelled by strokes 殳7. 古 move (⇨搬129) 图 kind, sort: 百般 all sorts ⇔ 一般1, 這般58

搬 3 bān Hand 手9 moving 般129 (phonetic). 图 remove, transfer 图 move (house)

搬到 bāndào 图 move

搬家 bānjiā 图 move house

搬運 bānyùn 图 transport

盤 4 [盘] pán Moveable 般129 (phonetic) container 皿116. 图 plate, dish 图 examine ⇔ 鍵盤53, 全盤27, 棋盤36, 地盤26, 磁盤53, 轉盤57, 碗盤73, 算盤30, 飛盤169

盤查 pánchá 图 interrogate

盤纏 pánchán 图 traveling expenses

盤古 pángǔ 图 Pan Ku - god of creation

盤據 pánjù 图 forcibly occupy

盤算 pánsuàn 图 calculate, plan

盤問 pánwèn 图 interrogate

盤旋 pánxuán 图 circle, spiral, hover around

盤子 pánzi 图 plate

亙 5 gèn [亘] Boat 舟129 (altered) traveling between two 二½ banks. Simplified form is conflated with 亘15. 图 extend, cross ⇔ 綿亙76

恆[6] 129 héng [恒] Heart 心[93] that perseveres the crossing 亘[95]. 彤 permanent, constant ⇔ 永恆[90]

恆河 hénghé 彤 Ganges River

恆久 héngjĭu 彤 enduring, lasting

恆山 héngshān 彤 Heng Mountain - a sacred mountain between Hebei and Shanxi Provinces

恆心 héngxīn 彤 perseverance

俞[7] 129 yú Assemble 合[14] a canoe 舟[129] (altered) to cross a river 巜[33]. 彤 make a canoe 彤 a surname

愉[8] 129 yú Heart 心[93] when boating 俞[97] (phonetic). 彤 joyful, pleased

愉快 yúkuài 彤 happy, joyful

愉悅 yúyuè 彤 pleased

逾[9] 129 yú Movement 辵[97] across 俞[97] (phonetic). 彤 pass, exceed

逾越 yúyuè 彤 exceed, transgress

瑜[10] 129 yú Jade 玉[107] with 俞[97] phonetic. 彤 flawless gem

瑜珈 yújiā 彤 yoga

覦[11] 129 yú [觎] Other bank of river to be crossed 俞[97] (phonetic) in sight 見[14]. 彤 covet ⇔ 覬覦[95]

揄[12] 129 yú Hand 手[99] and dugout canoe 俞[97] (phonetic). 彤 scoop out 彤 praise ⇔ 揶揄[92]

愈[13] 129 yú Heart 心[93] with 俞[97] phonetic. 彤 improve 彤 the more ... the more ⇔ 每況愈下[98]

愈來愈 yùláiyù 彤 more and more, increasingly

癒[14] 129 yù [愈[97]] Sick 疒[76] period crossed 俞[97] (phonetic, changed to 愈[97]). 彤 cure 彤 痊癒[92]

喻[15] 129 yù Mouth 口[68] conveying 俞[97] (phonetic). 彤 explain, make known 彤 understand, know 彤 compare, liken ⇔ 比喻[93], 隱喻[93]

諭[16] 129 yù [谕] Words 言[96] conveying 俞[97] (phonetic). 彤 notify

諭知 yùzhī 彤 notify by edict 彤 edict

輸[17] 129 shū [输] Cart 車[58] conveying 俞[97] (phonetic). 彤 transport 彤 lose, be defeated 彤 loss ⇔ 運輸[58], 灌輸[62]

輸出 shūchū 彤 output 彤 export

輸入 shūrù 彤 input

偷[18] 129 tōu Person 人[10] conveying 俞[97] (phonetic). 彤 steal ⇔ 小偷[97]

偷渡 tōudù 彤 immigrate illegally: 偷渡客 illegal immigrant

偷看 tōukàn 彤 peek, cheat (on a test)

偷懶 tōulăn 彤 lazy

偷竊 tōuqiè 彤 steal

偷聽 tōutīng 彤 eavesdrop

偷偷 tōutōu 彤 secretly

前[19] 129 qián Feet 止[98] on a boat 舟[129] (altered), with knife 刀[75] added later as early form of 剪[97]. 彤 float forward 彤 front, forward: 向前走 walk forward 彤 before 彤 preced-ing, former ⇔ 上前[95], 從前[95], 先前[95], 跟前[95], 眼前[95], 空前[95], 以前[95], 向前[95], 當前[95], 之前[95], 事前[95], 生前[95], 日前[76], 提前[95], 目前[14], 面前[48]

前輩 qiánbèi 彤 previous generations

前邊 qiánbiān 彤 in front, ahead

前後 qiánhòu 彤 front and back

前進 qiánjìn 彤 go forward, advance

前科 qiánkē 彤 criminal record

前面 qiánmiàn 彤 front

前年 qiánnián 彤 year before last

前驅 qiánqū 彤 forerunner, pioneer, vanguard, precursor

前任 qiánrèn 彤 predecessor: 前任總統 former President

前生 qiánshēng 彤 previous life

前世 qiánshì 彤 previous life

前天 qiántiān 彤 day before yesterday: 大前天 three days ago

前頭 qiántóu 彤 ahead

前途 qiántú 彤 prospects, future: 他的前途很好. He has a great future.

前往 qiánwǎng 彤 leave for, go to

前夕 qiánxì 彤 eve, night before

前言 qiányán 彤 preface, foreword

前者 qiánzhě 彤 the former

剪[20] 129 jiǎn Forward-cutting 前[97] (phonetic) knife 刀[75]. 彤 shear, clip

簡報 jiǎnbào 彤 newspaper clipping

剪刀 jiǎndāo 彤 scissors

剪輯 jiǎnjí 彤 film editing

剪紙 jiǎnzhĭ 彤 paper cutting

箭[21] 129 jiàn Bamboo 竹[71] cutting forward 前[97] (phonetic). 彤 arrow ⇔ 擋箭牌[95], 弓箭[65], 火箭[82]

箭頭 jiàntóu 彤 arrowhead

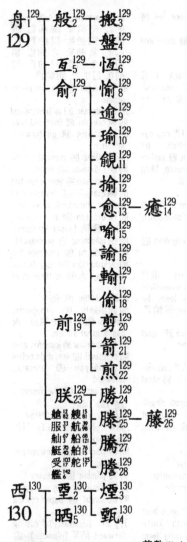

ancient character comprised of hands 廾异 and fire 火⁶². ㉗ caulk a boat 朕 I (emperor) 朕兆 zhènzhào ㊦ omen, portent

勝 129 shèng ㊄ shēng
24 [胜] Strength 力⁷⁴ with 朕⁵⁷ phonetic. Simplified form uses 生⁵⁶ shēng: ㊦ competent shèng: ㊦ win ㊦ victory ㊦ excellent ⇔ 不勝 búshèng, 取勝 qǔshèng, 獲勝 huòshèng
勝敗 shèngbài ㊦ victory or defeat, success or failure
勝地 shèngdì ㊦ scenic spot
勝過 shèngguò ㊦ excel, prevail
勝利 shènglì ㊦ victory
勝任 shēngrèn ㊦ competent, qualified
勝算 shèngsuàn ㊦ chance of success

滕 129 téng
25 Water 水⁴⁰ with 朕⁵⁷ phonetic. ㊦ an ancient kingdom in China

藤 129 téng
26 Plant 艸³⁰ with 滕⁵⁷ phonetic. ㊦ cane, rattan, wicker ⇔ 長春藤 chángchūnténg
藤器 téngqì ㊦ wickerwork

騰 129 téng
27 [腾] Horse 馬¹⁷⁷ with 朕⁵⁷ phonetic. ㊦ leap, soar ⇔ 沸騰 fèiténg, 奔騰 bēnténg
騰出 téngchū ㊦ make room, vacate

謄 129 téng
28 [誊] Words 言⁶⁹ with 朕⁵⁷ phonetic. ㊦ transcribe
謄本 téngběn ㊦ manuscript
謄寫 téngxiě ㊦ copy by hand

西 130 xī
1 Early forms show a bird roosting, suggesting sunset and the direction thereof. ㊦ west ⇔ 紐西蘭 Niǔxīlán, 納西族 Nàxīzú, 廣西 Guǎngxī, 大西洋 Dàxīyáng, 陝西 Shǎnxī, 新西蘭 Xīnxīlán, 江西 Jiāngxī, 山西 Shānxī, 東西 dōngxī, 巴西 Bāxī, 墨西

煎熬 jiānáo ㊦ ㊦ torment

朕 129 zhèn
23 Boat 舟¹²⁹ and an

煎 129 jiān
22 Fire 火⁶² with 前¹²⁹ phonetic. ㊦ fry

西安 xiān 地 Xian - capital of Shaanxi Province

西岸 xiàn 名 West Coast

西班牙 xībānyá 地 Spain

西伯利亞 xībólìyǎ 地 Siberia

西部 xībù 名 western region: 西部片 a Western (movie genre)

西餐 xīcān 名 Western food

西方 xīfāng 名 west 地 the West, Occident: 西方人 Westerner

西貢 xīgòng 地 Saigon

西瓜 xīguā 名 watermelon

西歐 xīōu 地 Western Europe

西雙版納 xīshuāngbǎnnà 地 Xishuangbanna - a region in Yunnan Province

西天 xītiān 地 Buddhist paradise

西洋 xīyáng 形 Western

西醫 xīyī 名 Western medicine

西元 xīyuán 名 A.D.: 西元前 B.C.

西藏 xīzàng 地 Tibet

西裝 xīzhuāng 名 Western clothing 服 suit

垔 130 yīn
2 Nest 西[130] and dirt 土[70]. 名 dam, block

煙 130 yān
3 [烟] Fire 火[82] and block 垔[130] (phonetic). Simplified form is an ancient form with 因[47] phonetic. 名 smoke ⇨ 吸煙..., 戒煙..., 香煙..., 抽煙...

煙草 yāncǎo 名 tobacco

煙囪 yāncōng 名 chimney, stovepipe

煙蒂 yāndì 名 cigarette butt

煙斗 yāndǒu 名 pipe

煙灰 yānhuī 名 ashes: 煙灰缸 ashtray

煙火 yānhuǒ 名 smoke and fire 名 fireworks

甄 130 zhēn
4 Tile 瓦[109] with 垔[130] phonetic. 動 make pottery

甄別 zhēnbié 動 differentiate, screen

甄選 zhēnxuǎn 動 select

晒 130 shài
5 A variant of 曬[154] from sun 日[76] with 西[130] phonetic.

洒 130 sǎ
6 Water 水[32] with 西[130] phonetic. 動 spray (⇨ 灑[154])

鹵 130 lǔ
7 [卤] Dots of something from the West 西[130] (altered). 名 salt

滷 130 lǔ
8 [卤90] Water 水[32] containing salt 鹵[130] (phonetic). 形 salty 名 sauce

滷菜 lǔcài 名 marinated dish

滷肉 lǔròu 名 marinated meat

臼 131 jiù
1 Pictograph of a mortar. Used to represent a head in some derivatives. 名 mortar ⇨ 脫臼..., 窠臼...

臼齒 jiùchǐ 名 molar

舊 131 jiù
2 [旧] Owl 萑[162] with 臼[131] phonetic. 名 a bird name 形 old, past 形 former ⇨ 破舊..., 仍舊..., 照舊..., 陳舊..., 折舊..., 依舊...

舊金山 jiùjīnshān 地 San Francisco

舊日 jiùrì 名 old times

舅 131 jiù
3 Male 男[94] with 臼[131] phonetic. 名 uncle (mother's brother)

舅舅 jiùjiu 名 uncle (mother's brother)

舅媽 jiùmā 名 aunt (mother's brother's wife)

臽 131 xiàn
4 Person 人[9] falling into a hole/mortar 臼[131]. 名 pit, trap

陷 131 xiàn
5 From hill 阜[167] down into a hole 臽[131] (phonetic). 動 sink, submerge 動 entrap ⇨ 缺陷..., 誣陷..., 淪陷..., 塌陷...

陷害 xiànhài 動 frame, set up

陷阱 xiànjǐng 名 trap, pitfall

陷入 xiànrù 動 sink into

餡 131 xiàn
6 [馅] Food 食[59] trapped 臽[131] (phonetic). 名 filling, stuffing: 素餡 vegetarian filling

焰 131 yàn
7 Fire 火[82] with 臽[131] phonetic. 名 flame ⇦ 火焰[82]

閻 131 yán
8 [阎] Gate 門[169] enclosing 臽[131] (phonetic). 名 village gate 姓 a surname

掐 131 qiā
9 Hand 手[90] sinking in 臽[131] (phonetic). 動 pinch 動 grasp

掐死 qiāsǐ 動 strangle

掐住 qiāzhù 動 seize, grasp

舀 131 yǎo
10 Hand 爪[108] reaching into mortar 臼[131] to dehull rice. 動 ladle out

稻 131 dào
11 Grain 禾[108] to be dehulled 舀[131] (phonetic). 名 rice ⇦ 水稻[32]

稻米 dàomǐ 名 rice

稻穗 dàosuì 名 spike of the rice plant

稻田 dàotián 名 paddy field

蹈 131 動 dào 動 dǎo
12 Feet 足[85] churning like hands in mortar 舀[131] (phonetic). 動 stamp, trample ⇦ 舞蹈..., 重蹈覆轍...

滔 131 tāo
13 Water 水[32] churning like hands in mortar 舀[131] (phonetic). 動 inundate

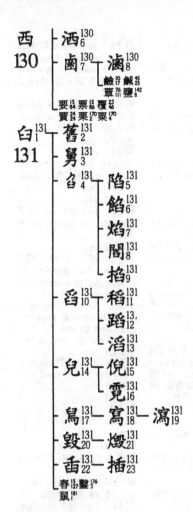

滔滔 tāotāo 🔲 torrential
滔天大罪 tāotiāndàzùi 🔲 heinous crime

兒 ér
14 [儿] Person 儿 with head 囟 not fully closed (written as 臼). 🔲 child 🔲

son ⇔ 一會兒, 一塊兒, 小孩兒, 女兒, 女孩兒, 胎兒, 幼兒, 托兒所, 模特兒, 遺兒, 碴兒, 那兒, 哪兒, 孤兒, 姪兒, 寵兒, 嬰兒

兒女 érnǔ 🔲 children
兒童 értóng 🔲 child
兒戲 érxì 🔲 child's play
兒子 érzi 🔲 son

倪 ní
15 Person 人 and child 兒 (phonetic). 🔲 small child 🔲 a surname ⇔ 端倪

霓 ní
16 Rain 雨 with 兒 phonetic. 🔲 rainbow
霓虹 níhóng 🔲 neon: 霓虹燈 neon light

舃 xì
17 Pictograph of a bird 鳥 with head written as 臼. 🔲 magpie 🔲 clogs

寫 xiě
18 [写] Roof 宀 with 舃 phonetic. Simplified form uses 宀 and 与. 🔲 write ⇔ 書寫, 撰寫, 抄寫, 填寫, 大寫, 改寫, 縮寫, 描寫, 編寫, 繕寫, 謄寫
寫信 xiěxìn 🔲 correspond, write a letter
寫照 xiězhào 🔲 portrayal, description
寫眞 xiězhēn 🔲 portrait
寫字 xiězì 🔲 write characters
寫作 xiězuò 🔲 writing write, compose

瀉 xiè
19 [泻] Water 水 with 寫 phonetic. 🔲 flow out: 瀉肚子 have diarrhea

毀 huǐ
20 Dirt 土 destroyed (rare character including mortar 臼 and pound 殳). 🔲 destroy ⇔ 炸毀, 擊毀, 撕毀, 詆毀, 墜毀, 摧毀
毀謗 huǐbàng 🔲 slander, libel
毀滅 huǐmiè 🔲 demolish, destroy

燬 huǐ
21 [毁] Firey 火

destruction 毀²⁹ (phonetic). 動 burn down ⇔ 燒燬²⁹, 焚燬²⁹

舂¹³¹ chā
22 Stem 干⁹⁵, used as pestle, in mortar 臼¹³¹. 動 dehull rice 動 insert

插¹³¹ chā
23 Hand 手⁹⁹ inserting 舂²² (phonetic). 動 insert ⇔ 穿插²⁴

插隊 chāduì 動 cut in line
插花 chāhuā 图 arrange flowers:
插花藝術 flower arranging
插進 chājìn 動 stick in, insert
插曲 chāqǔ 图 interlude 图 episode
插入 chārù 動 insert
插手 chāshǒu 動 participate 動 have a hand in, meddle
插頭 chātóu 图 plug
插圖 chātú 图 illustration
插秧 chāyāng 動 transplant rice seedlings
插嘴 chāzuǐ 動 get a word in
插座 chāzuò 图 socket, outlet

肉¹³² ròu
1 Pictograph of a carcass cut open. In composition can resemble month 月⁹⁰. 图 meat, flesh ⇔ 烤肉¹⁹, 肥肉²², 肌肉⁷, 豬肉³⁵, 牛肉¹², 香肉⁹², 羊肉¹²³, 滷肉⁵⁰

肉串 ròuchuàn 图 kebab
肉桂 ròuguì 图 cinnamon
肉類 ròulèi 图 meat
肉絲 ròusī 图 shredded meat
肉體 ròutǐ 图 body, flesh
肉眼 ròuyǎn 图 naked eye

肙¹³² yuān
2 Round (now written as 口⁶⁸) flesh 肉¹³². 图 larvae

捐¹³² juān
3 Hand 手⁹⁹ with 肙² phonetic. 動 discard 動 donate ⇔ 稅捐⁹

捐給 juāngěi 動 donate

捐款 juānkuǎn 動 donate money
捐血 juānxiě 動 donate blood
捐助 juānzhù 動 contribute, donate

娟¹³² juān
4 Woman 女¹⁴ curved like larvae 肙² (phonetic). 图 beautiful

娟秀 juānxiù 图 graceful

鵑¹³² juān
5 [鹃] Bird 鳥¹⁷⁸ with 肙² phonetic. 图 cuckoo ⇔ 杜鵑⁵⁷

絹¹³² juàn
6 [绢] Threads 糸⁵³ with 肙² phonetic. 图 silk

絹帛 juànbó 图 silk
絹畫 juànhuà 图 silk painting
絹子 juànzi 图 handkerchief

胃¹³² wèi
7 Flesh 肉¹³² and a pictograph of a stomach containing food (written as 田⁸¹). 图 stomach

胃口 wèikǒu 图 appetite

謂¹³² wèi
8 [谓] Words 言⁹⁸ with 胃³² phonetic. 動 name, call 图 meaning ⇔ 無所謂⁷⁵, 無謂⁷⁵, 所謂⁷⁴

脊¹³² jǐ
9 Flesh 肉¹³² with a pictograph of a spine and ribs on top. 图 spine, backbone 图 ridge ⇔ 背脊⁸⁹

脊椎 jǐzhuī 图 spine, vertebrae

炙¹³² zhì
10 Flesh 肉¹³² over fire 火⁸². 動 roast

炙手可熱 zhìshǒukěrè 图 popular and influential

能¹³² néng
11 Body 肉¹³² and claws (resembling daggers 匕¹²) with 㠯⁹⁷ (resembling 厶 ¹²) phonetic. 動 bear (⇒ 熊¹²) 图 can, able to 图 ability 图 energy ⇔ 不能⁵⁰, 不能不⁵⁰, 潛

能⁵², 核能¹³⁵, 可能⁵⁷, 無能⁷⁵, 全能³⁷, 效能⁸², 功能²⁰, 機能⁸⁵, 才能¹⁷, 性能⁶², 體能⁷⁵, 技能⁹⁹, 未能¹²², 本能⁷⁰, 產能¹³⁵, 賢能¹⁴²

能否 néngfǒu 動 can or cannot
能幹 nénggàn 图 capable, competent
能夠 nénggòu 動 able to, capable of
能力 nénglì 图 ability: 有能力 capable
能量 néngliàng 图 energy, power
能耐 néngnài 图 ability, talent
能手 néngshǒu 图 expert hand
能源 néngyuán 图 energy, energy resources

熊¹³² xióng
12 Bear 能¹² with 炎⁸⁷ (abbreviated to 火⁸²) phonetic. 图 bear 图 a surname
熊貓 xióngmāo 图 panda
熊熊 xióngxióng 图 flaming
熊掌 xióngzhǎng 图 bear paw

態¹³² tài
13 [态] Can 能¹² show the heart 心⁸³. Simplified form uses 太²⁸. 图 attitude, manner ⇔ 姿態³², 神態¹³⁵, 形態⁶², 型態³², 生態⁹⁰, 動態⁹⁴, 狀態⁷³, 心態¹⁷, 靜態⁹², 表態¹²⁶, 變態⁵³

態度 tàidù 图 attitude

罷¹³² bà
14 [罢] Person of ability 能¹² caught in web 网⁹² (altered) of accusations. Simplified form uses 去²⁸. 動 dismiss, fire 图 merely, only
罷黜 bàchù 動 dismiss, fire
罷工 bàgōng 動 strike
罷課 bàkè 動 strike classes
罷了 bàle 图 only
罷免 bàmiǎn 動 recall, impeach

擺¹³² bǎi
15 [摆] Hand 手⁹⁹ with 罷¹² phonetic. 動 place,

肉₁ 132

132

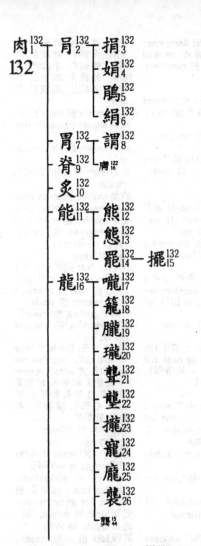

肉₁ 132
冐₂ 132 — 捐₃ 132
— 娟₄ 132
— 鵑₅ 132
— 絹₆ 132
胃₇ 132 — 謂₈ 132
脊₉ 132 — 膌 12
炙₁₀ 132
能₁₁ 132 — 熊₁₂ 132
— 態₁₃ 132
— 罷₁₄ 132 — 擺₁₅ 132
龍₁₆ 132 — 嚨₁₇ 132
— 籠₁₈ 132
— 朧₁₉ 132
— 瓏₂₀ 132
— 聾₂₁ 132
— 壟₂₂ 132
— 攏₂₃ 132
— 寵₂₄ 132
— 龐₂₅ 132
— 襲₂₆ 132
— 冀 15 44

a pictograph of a dragon in flight with 童恣 (abbreviated) phonetic. 圀 dragon 圀 a surname ⇔ 沙龍??, 舞龍舞獅??, 恐龍??, 黑龍江??, 烏龍茶??

龍捲風 lóngjuǎnfēng tornado
龍頭 lóngtóu 圀 faucet 圀 first on a list
龍蝦 lóngxiā 圀 lobster
龍舟 lóngzhōu 圀 dragonboat

嚨 132 lóng
17 [咙] Mouth 口⁶⁹ with dragon 龍¹³² phonetic and suggestive of long. 圀 throat ⇔ 喉嚨??

籠 132 lóng lǒng
18 [笼] Bamboo 竹⁷? with 龍¹³² phonetic. lóng: 圀 coop, cage lǒng: 圀 include, encompass ⇔ 燈籠??, 牢籠??, 鳥籠??

籠絡 lǒngluò 圀 entice, tempt
籠統 lǒngtǒng 圀 vague
籠罩 lǒngzhào 圀 cover, envelop, shroud

朧 132 lóng
19 [胧] Moon 月⁸⁰ with 龍¹³² phonetic. 圀 moonlight ⇔ 朦朧¹⁵⁵

瓏 132 lóng
20 [珑] Jade 玉¹⁰⁷ with 龍¹³² phonetic. 圀 tinkle of jade ⇔ 玲瓏??

聾 132 lóng
21 [聋] Ear 耳¹⁷? with 龍¹³² phonetic. 圀 deaf
聾啞 lóngyǎ 圀 deaf mute
聾子 lóngzi 圀 deaf person

壟 132 lǒng
22 [垄] Earth 土⁷? with 龍¹³² phonetic. 圀 mound
壟斷 lǒngduàn 圀 monopolize

攏 132 lǒng
23 [拢] Hand 手⁹? with 龍¹³² phonetic. 圀 gather 圀 approach ⇔ 拉攏??, 靠攏??

arrange 圀 swing, sway 圀 pendulum ⇔ 鐘擺??
擺佈 bǎibù 圀 manipulate
擺動 bǎidòng 圀 swing, sway
擺架子 bǎijiàzi 圀 put on airs

擺設 bǎishè 圀 furnish 圀 furnishings
擺脫 bǎituō 圀 extricate oneself
龍 132 lóng
16 [龙] Flesh 肉¹³² and

寵 132 chǒng
24 [宠] Roof 宀⁶³ with
龍¹³² phonetic. 動 favor ⇔
嘩衆取寵¹⁷
寵愛 chǒngài 動 dote on
寵兒 chǒngér 名 favorite
寵壞 chǒnghuài 動 spoil
寵物 chǒngwù 名 pet

龐 132 páng
25 [庞] Open roof 广⁶⁰
and dragon 龍¹³² (phonetic).
形 large
龐大 pángdà 形 huge, enormous

襲 132 xí
26 [袭] Clothing 衣¹²⁶
and dragon 龍¹³². 動 wear 動
attack ⇔ 侵襲¹³⁷, 承襲¹⁴⁷,
抄襲²⁶², 空襲¹⁴⁹, 沿襲⁶⁹
襲擊 xíjí 動 assault, attack, raid

冎 133 guǎ
1 Pictograph of a skull
and vertebrae.

骨 133 gǔ
2 [骨] Skeleton 冎¹³³
(phonetic) at core of flesh
肉¹¹². 名 bone ⇔ 撿骨³³,
露骨²⁷², 刻骨¹⁰⁵, 腑骨³⁷, 肋
骨²⁴, 筋骨²⁷, 甲骨文¹¹², 顱
骨¹²⁷
骨幹 gǔgàn 名 backbone,
mainstay
骨骼 gǔgé 名 skeleton
骨牌 gǔpái 名 dominoes
骨氣 gǔqì 名 pluck, spirit
骨髓 gǔsuǐ 名 marrow
骨頭 gǔtou, gútou 名 bone
骨子 gǔzi 名 skeleton, framework

滑 133 huá
3 [滑] Water 水⁴¹ and
bones 骨¹³³ (phonetic). 形
slippery ⇔ 光滑⁴², 潤滑⁴¹
滑板 huábǎn 名 skateboard
滑冰 huábīng 動 ice-skate
滑稽 huájī 形 farcical, ludicrous
滑溜 huáliū 形 smooth and
slippery
滑鼠 huáshǔ 名 computer mouse

滑翔 huáxiáng 動 glide: 滑翔
機 glider
滑雪 huáxuě 動 ski

猾 133 huá
4 [猾] Dog 犬⁷¹ with
骨¹³³ phonetic and sugges-
tive of slippery 滑¹³³. 形
cunning ⇔ 狡猾²⁵

咼 133 kuā wāi
5 Mouth 口⁶⁸ with
冎¹³³ phonetic. 古 twisted
mouth

蝸 133 guā
6 [蜗] Insect 虫¹²⁵ and
twisted 咼¹³³ (phonetic). 名
snail
蝸牛 guāníu 名 snail

鍋 133 guō
7 [锅] Metal 金⁴⁴ with
咼¹³³ phonetic. 名 pot, pan
⇔ 電鍋¹³⁵, 飯鍋¹³⁵, 火鍋⁹²
鍋貼 guōtiē 名 fried dumpling

過 133 guò
8 [过] Move 辵⁵⁹ with
咼¹³³ phonetic and sugges-
tive of whirlpool 渦¹³³. Simplified form uses 寸³⁵. 動 ford
動 cross, pass 動 spend, pass:
過暑假 spend summer
vacation 動 go over, pass
through 動 exceed 副 exces-
sively, too 名 mistake ⇔ 不
過²⁶, 經過²⁴, 考過¹⁰³, 反過
來²⁷, 掠過²⁴², 透過²⁶², 難
過²⁶³, 超過²⁶², 去過²⁶, 越
過⁸⁵, 悔過²²³, 通過²⁶, 錯
過²⁶², 穿過⁸⁴, 勝過²⁷
過程 guòchéng 名 process
過度 guòdù 副 excessively: 過
度反應 overreact
過渡 guòdù 動 cross a river 名
transition: 過渡時期 tran-
sitional period
過分 guòfèn 副 excessively: 你
太過分! You're too much!
You've gone too far!
過關 guòguān 動 pass a barrier
or test

過獎 guòjiǎng 動 overpraise
過節 guòjié 動 celebrate a
holiday
過境 guòjìng 動 transit, pass
through
過來 guòlái 動 come over
過量 guòliàng 動 overdo 名
overdose
過濾 guòlǜ 動 filter, filtrate
過敏 guòmǐn 形 allergic: 過敏
症 allergy
過年 guònián 動 celebrate New
Year's
過去 guòqù 副 formerly, in the
past 動 pass by 名 past
過熱 guòrè 動 overheat
過剩 guòshèng 名 excess,
surplus
過失 guòshī 名 mistake, error
過時 guòshí 動 become outdated,
expire
過世 guòshì 動 pass away, die
過夜 guòyè 動 spend the night
過癮 guòyǐn 動 satiate
過於 guòyú 副 excessively
過重 guòzhòng 動 overweight

禍 133 huò
9 [祸] Omen 示⁴⁰
twisted 咼¹³³ (phonetic). 名
misfortune, disaster 動 harm,
ruin ⇔ 災禍⁸⁵, 惹禍⁸⁹, 肇
禍⁷⁸, 嫁禍¹⁵⁵, 車禍¹⁵⁸, 闖
禍⁷⁷
禍害 huòhài 名 disaster
禍患 huòhuàn 名 disaster
禍首 huòshǒu 名 culprit

窩 133 wō
10 [窝] Hole 穴⁶⁷ which
twists 咼¹³³ (phonetic). 名
den, nest ⇔ 燕窩²⁴⁵
窩囊 wōnang 形 cowardly

渦 133 wō
11 [涡] Water 水⁴¹
twisting 咼¹³³ (phonetic). 名
whirlpool ⇔ 漩渦⁴⁸

歹 133 dǎi
12 Bones 冎¹³³ (alter-
ed) broken in half. 形 evil ⇔

316

字譜及字典

肉
132

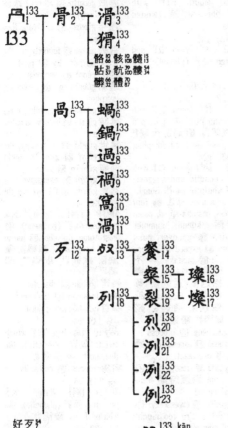

好歹
歹徒 dǎitú 图 hoodlum, gangster

叞 133 kān
13 Hand 又 crushing bones 歹. 围 crush

餐 133 cān
14 Crush 奴丯 (phonetic) food 食忩. 围 eat 图 food 图 meal ⇔ 快餐忩, 中餐忩, 早餐忩, 午餐忩, 野餐忩, 西餐忩, 素餐忩, 晚餐忩
餐館 cānguǎn 图 restaurant
餐巾 cānjīn 图 napkin
餐具 cānjù 图 utensils
餐廳 cāntīng 图 cafeteria, dining room, canteen

粲 133 càn
15 Crushed 奴丯 (phonetic) rice 米. 图 polished rice

璨 133 càn
16 Jade 玉 like polished rice 粲 (phonetic). 圈 lustrous ⇔ 璀璨

燦 133 càn
17 [灿] Fire 火 and polished rice 粲 (phonetic). Simplified form uses 山. 圈 bright
燦爛 cànlàn 圈 brilliant, resplendent

列 133 liè
18 Modern form shows cut 刀 to the bare bone 歹. 围 separate 围 arrange 围 line up 图 row, line, series measureword for things in a row ⇔ 並列, 行列, 以色列, 陳列, 系列, 排列
列車 lièchē 图 train
列國 lièguó 图 various countries
列舉 lièjǔ 围 enumerate, list
列寧 lièníng 囚 Lenin
列強 lièqiáng 图 powerful countries
列入 lièrù 围 include, incorporate
列爲 lièwéi 围 list as

裂 133 liè
19 Separated 列 (phonetic) cloth 衣. 围 split ⇔ 破裂, 分裂, 決裂,

迸裂

烈 133 liè
20   Fire 火 with 列 phonetic. intense, fiery virtuous ⇔ 先烈, 暴烈, 强烈, 熱烈, 熾烈, 激烈, 猛烈, 劇烈
烈酒 lièjiǔ liquor
烈士 lièshì martyr

洌 133 liè
21   Water 水 with 列 phonetic. clear

冽 133 liè
22   Splitting 列 (phonetic) cold 冫. frigid ⇔ 凜冽

例 133 lì
23   Person 人 lining things up 列 (phonetic). compare example, instance precedent rules, regulations ⇔ 比例, 舉例, 範例, 條例, 照例, 慣例, 實例
例如 lìrú for example
例外 lìwài exception
例證 lìzhèng illustration, example
例子 lìzi example, instance

死 133 sǐ
24   Crushed bones 歹 and inverted person 匕. die dead extremely 該死, 淹死, 打死, 餓死, 拼死, 弔死, 生死, 害死, 氣死, 殺死, 溺死, 掐死, 垂死
死板 sǐbǎn inflexible, rigid
死鬼 sǐguǐ devil
死活 sǐhuó life or death
死路 sǐlù dead end
死傷 sǐshāng casualties
死亡 sǐwáng die
死心 sǐxīn lose hope
死刑 sǐxíng death penalty
死者 sǐzhě the dead

而 134 ér
1   Pictograph of a beard. and and yet (indicating effect or means) 為錢 而工作 work for money ⇔ 從而, 久而久之, 脫口 而出, 反而, 迎刃而 解, 幸而, 偶 而, 然而, 半途而廢, 總而言之
而後 érhòu and then
而今 érjīn now, currently
而且 érqiě moreover, furthermore
而是 érshì but rather
而已 éryǐ only: 只是開玩 笑而已. It's only a joke.

耑 134 duān zhuān
2   [专] Pictograph of a plant growing above ground (written as 山) and below ground (written as 而). duān: tip (⇨ 端) zhuān: special (⇨ 專)

端 134 duān
3   Stand 立 like a growing plant 耑 (phonetic). upright end, tip cause hold level ⇔ 極端, 尖端, 弊端, 事端, 開 端, 爭端
端倪 duānní clue, inkling
端午節 duānwǔjié Dragonboat Festival
端正 duānzhèng correct, proper rectify

喘 134 chuǎn
4   Mouth 口 with 耑 phonetic and suggestive of air rising through respiratory tract. gasp, pant ⇔ 氣喘
喘氣 chuǎnqì gasp, pant
喘息 chuǎnxí pause for breath

揣 134 chuāi
5   Hand 手 measuring plant growth 耑 (phonetic). estimate

揣測 chuǎicè conjecture, surmise
揣摩 chuǎimó ponder, speculate

攵 134 wēi
6   Person 人 (bottom left, altered) striking 攵 at a plant 耑 to remove fibers. slender, fine

微 134 wéi wēi
7   Small 攵 (phonetic) steps 彳. tiny, slight ⇔ 輕微, 稍微, 式微, 顯微鏡
微波 wéibō microwave: 微 波爐 microwave oven
微妙 wéimiào delicate, subtle
微弱 wéiruò frail, weak
微微 wéiwéi slight, tiny
微小 wéixiǎo tiny, minute
微笑 wéixiào smile

薇 134 wéi
8   Small 微 (phonetic) plant 艸. a type of fern ⇔ 薔薇

徽 134 huī
9   Thread 糸 with 微 (abbreviated) phonetic. pennant, emblem ⇔ 安 徽
徽章 huīzhāng badge, medal

徵 134 zhēng
10   [征] Request good 壬 services of one who steps lightly 微 (abbreviated). summon prove indication solicit levy ⇔ 特徵, 表徵, 應徵, 象 徵
徵兵 zhēngbīng conscription, draft: 徵兵制 draft system conscript
徵求 zhēngqiú seek, solicit
徵稅 zhēngshuì collect taxes
徵信社 zhēngxìnshè detective agency
徵詢 zhēngxún solicit opinion, consult

字譜及字典

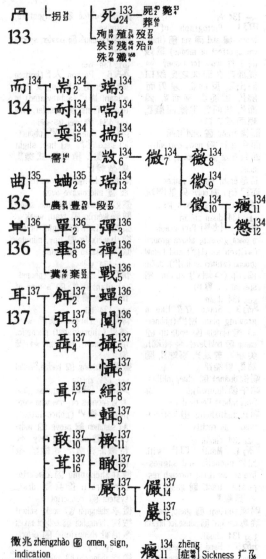

tinal obstruction

癥結 zhēngjié [图] crux, key

懲 134 chéng
12 [惩] Heart 心¹³ with
徵¹³⁴ phonetic. [动] punish

懲罰 chéngfá [动] penalize

瑞 134 rùi
13 Jade 玉¹⁷ that
measures status (揣¹³⁴ abbreviated as 耑¹³⁴). [图] jade tablet
symbolizing rank of princes
[图] lucky ⇔ 人瑞¹⁰

瑞典 rùidiǎn [图] Sweden

瑞士 rùishì [图] Switzerland

耐 134 nài
14 Beard 而¹³⁴ required
by law 寸¹³. [动] punishment
forbidding shaving [动] endure
⇔ 不耐煩.., 忍耐.., 能
耐¹²

耐力 nàilì [图] endurance

耐心 nàixīn [图] patience [形]
patient

耐性 nàixìng [图] patience, tolerance, endurance

耐用 nàiyòng [形] durable

耍 134 shuǎ
15 Beard 而¹³⁴ and
woman 女³⁴. [动] play ⇔ 玩
耍..

曲 135 qū qǔ
1 Pictograph of wood
curved into cup shape. qū: [形]
bent, twisted [图] bend, twist [图]
a surname qǔ: [图] song, melody
⇔ 歪曲.., 扭曲.., 作曲..,
歌曲.., 譜曲.., 戲曲.., 委
曲.., 挿曲.., 彎曲¹..

曲阜 qūfù [图] Qufu - Confucius's
hometown in Shandong Province

曲棍球 qūgùnqíu [图] hockey

曲解 qūjiě [动] misinterpret

曲線 qūxiàn [图] curve

曲折 qūzhé [图] winding [图] complication

曲子 qǔzi [图] song, melody

蛐 135 qū
2 Insect 虫¹²⁵ which is

徵兆 zhēngzhào [图] omen, sign, indication

癥 134 zhēng
11 [症] Sickness 疒²⁴
with 徵¹³⁴ phonetic. [图] intes-

twisted 曲 |³⁵ (phonetic). 圖 maggot, worm

單 136 fán
1 Pictograph of a winnowing basket or pitchfork with a handle.

單 136 dān
2 [单] Cries 吅 ⁹ from shovel 羋 |³⁶ (phonetic). 圖 big 圖 single: 單人床 single bed 圖 singly, separately 圖 only, solely 圖 sheet, slip ⇔ 被單²⁶, 帳單⁴⁸, 床單⁹⁷, 清單⁴⁶, 名單²⁴, 簡單²⁴, 菜單¹⁰³, 孤單¹⁰⁴, 埋單¹¹⁷, 買單¹⁵⁰

單純 dānchún 圖 pure, innocent
單詞 dāncí 圖 word
單調 dāndiào 圖 monotonous
單獨 dāndú 圖 alone, individually
單方 dānfāng 圖 unilaterally
單身 dānshēn 圖 single, unmarried: 單身貴族 singles; 單身漢 bachelor
單數 dānshù 圖 singular 圖 odd number
單位 dānwèi 圖 unit 圖 work unit
單一 dānyī 圖 unique, unitary
單字 dānzì 圖 word

彈 136 tán dàn
3 [弹] Bow 弓⁶⁵ shooting a single 羋 |³⁶ (phonetic) pellet. dàn: 圖 bullet tán: 圖 spring, rebound 圖 play, pluck: 彈琴 play a stringed instrument ⇔ 氫彈¹²?, 砲彈¹?, 反彈?, 炸彈?, 子彈⁵⁵, 動彈?, 榴彈?, 導彈¹⁴⁶, 飛彈¹⁶⁹

彈頭 dàntóu 圖 bullet
彈藥 dànyào 圖 ammunition
彈子 dànzi 圖 bullet
彈劾 tánhé 圖 impeach
彈簧 tánhuáng 圖 spring
彈性 tánxìng 圖 flexibility

禪 136 chán shàn
4 [禅] Omen 示⁴⁶ with 羋 |³⁶ phonetic. shàn: 圖 abdicate chán: 圖 Zen Buddhism

禪寺 chánsì 圖 Zen temple
禪悟 chánwù 圖 realize through meditation
禪宗 chánzōng 圖 Zen Buddhism
禪讓 shànràng 圖 abdicate

戰 136 zhàn
5 [战] Lance 戈⁵⁸ with 羋 |³⁶ phonetic. Simplified form uses 占²⁸. 圖 war, battle ⇔ 作戰³⁶, 內戰⁴³, 大戰², 抗戰²⁹, 冷戰³⁹, 論戰¹⁴³, 挑戰¹⁴⁷

戰場 zhànchǎng 圖 battlefield
戰鬥 zhàndòu 圖 fight, combat
戰犯 zhànfàn 圖 war criminal
戰俘 zhànfú 圖 prisoner of war
戰國 zhànguó 圖 Warring States:
戰國時代 Warring States Period - 475-221 B.C.
戰機 zhànjī 圖 fighter plane
戰慄 zhànlì 圖 tremble
戰略 zhànlüè 圖 military strategy
戰事 zhànshì 圖 warfare
戰線 zhànxiàn 圖 battle line
戰役 zhànyì 圖 military campaign
戰爭 zhànzhēng 圖 war

蟬 136 chán
6 [蝉] Insect 虫¹²⁵ with 羋 |³⁶ phonetic. 圖 cicada
蟬聯 chánlián 圖 continue to hold a position

闡 136 chǎn
7 [阐] Gate 門⁷⁹ with 羋 |³⁶ phonetic. 圖 clarify
闡明 chǎnmíng 圖 clarify
闡釋 chǎnshì 圖 explain
闡述 chǎnshù 圖 expound

畢 136 bì
8 [毕] Like winnowing basket 羋 |³⁶ in field 田¹¹. Simplified form uses 比⁴² and 十⁴. 圖 trapping net 圖 finish, complete ⇔ 完畢⁴⁵ 圖 completely 圖 a surname
畢竟 bìjìng 圖 after all

畢生 bìshēng 圖 all one's life
畢業 bìyè 圖 graduate: 畢業證書 diploma; 畢業生 alum

耳 137 ěr
1 Pictograph of an ear. 圖 ear ⇔ 土耳其²⁶, 木耳⁷⁷, 刺耳²⁴, 牛耳²⁷, 酒酣耳熱¹⁵⁹

耳朵 ěrduo 圖 ear: 小耳朵 satellite dish
耳機 ěrjī 圖 earphone
耳語 ěryǔ 圖 圖 whisper

餌 137 ěr
2 [饵] Food 食⁵⁶ with 耳¹³⁷ phonetic. 圖 cake 圖 bait

弭 137 mǐ
3 Bow's 弓⁶⁵ ears 耳¹³⁷. 圖 ends of a bow 圖 stop ⇔ 消弭⁴²

聶 137 niè
4 [聂] Ears 耳¹³⁷ together. Simplified form uses double 雙¹⁶² simplification. 圖 whisper 圖 a surname

攝 137 shè
5 [摄] Hand 手⁹⁹ pulling together 聶 |³⁷ (phonetic). 圖 absorb 圖 shoot (a picture or movie) ⇔ 拍攝²⁹
攝取 shèqǔ 圖 absorb, assimilate
攝氏 shèshì 圖 Celsius, centigrade: 攝氏二十度 twenty degrees Celsius
攝影 shèyǐng 圖 shoot a movie: 攝影機 movie camera; 攝影師 cameraman

懾 137 zhé
6 [慑] Heart 心⁸³ affected by whispered rumors 聶 |³⁷ (phonetic). 圖 fearful

聑 137 qī
7 Mouth 口⁶⁸ close to ear 耳¹³⁷. 圖 whisper

緝 137 qì jī
8 [缉] Thread 糸⁵³ close 咠 |³⁷ (phonetic). 圖

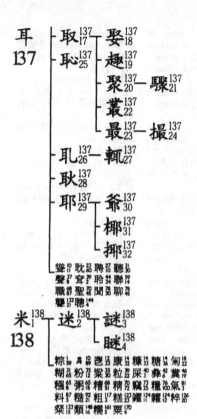

瞰 137
12 [瞰] Eyes 目|⁴ with 敢|³⁷ phonetic. 🔲 overlook ⇔ 俯瞰⅗, 鳥瞰|⁷⁸

嚴 137
13 [嚴] Cries 口口 ⁶⁶ and dangerous mountain (phonetic, ancient character from cliff 厂²¹ and courage 敢|³⁷). 🔲 strict, rigorous, severe 🔲 a surname ⇔ 戒嚴²⁹, 威嚴³⁶, 森嚴²⁶, 莊嚴²⁶, 解嚴|⁸⁰, 尊嚴|⁵⁹

嚴格 yángé 🔲 strict
嚴謹 yánjǐn 🔲 strict, rigorous
嚴峻 yánjùn 🔲 stern, rigorous
嚴厲 yánlì 🔲 stern, severe
嚴密 yánmì 🔲 tight, close
嚴肅 yánsù 🔲 strict, rigorous
嚴刑 yánxíng 🔲 severe punishment
嚴正 yánzhèng 🔲 solemn and just
嚴重 yánzhòng 🔲 serious, critical

儼 137
14 [儼] Person 人|³ strict 嚴|³⁷ (phonetic) with self. 🔲 dignified
儼然 yǎnrán 🔲 dignified 🔲 just like, as if

巖 137
15 [岩] Severe 嚴|³⁷ (phonetic) mountain 山⁶⁷. 🔲 cliff ⇒ 岩⁶⁷ ⇔ 攀巖⁷⁷

茸 137
16 Grass 艸²⁶ with ear 耳|³⁷ phonetic. 🔲 soft and lush ⇔ 鹿茸|⁷⁸

取 137
17 Grab ear 耳|³⁷ with the hand 又|⁴. 🔲 take, obtain 🔲 choose ⇔ 汲取⁸⁴, 吸取³², 收取|⁷, 詐取⁴⁸, 榨取⁹⁶, 可取²⁶, 索取⁸⁶, 竊取⁵⁸, 牟取⁶⁶, 予取予求|²², 採取|²², 爭取⁵³, 攝取|³⁷, 奪取|³², 獲取|³², 嘩衆取寵|⁷, 獵取|⁸¹

entwine 🔲 arrest
緝拿 qíná 🔲 arrest, apprehend
緝私 qìsī 🔲 arrest smugglers 🔲 seize contraband

輯 137
9 [輯] Cart 車|⁵⁸ with 咠|³⁷ phonetic. 🔘 carriage compile ⇔ 編輯|⁷⁵, 剪輯|²⁶, 邏輯|⁹²
輯錄 jílù 🔲 compile

敢 137
10 [敢] Modern form shows a variant of ear 耳|³⁷ and strike 攴²⁵. 🔲 dare 🔲 daring, courageous ⇔ 不敢¾₀, 膽敢⁶¹, 勇敢|⁴², 果敢⁷⁹
敢當 gǎndāng 🔲 dare to accept: 敢做敢當 bravely accept consequences

橄 137
11 [橄] Tree 木⁷ with 敢|³⁷ phonetic. 🔲 olive tree
橄欖 gǎnlǎn 🔲 olive: 橄欖球 rugby

取出 qǔchū take out, remove
取代 qǔdài replace
取得 qǔdé obtain
取締 qǔdì ban, outlaw
取捨 qǔshě choose, select, tradeoff
取勝 qǔshèng win, be victorious
取向 qǔxiàng orientation
取消 qǔxiāo cancel, revoke
取悅 qǔyuè please

娶 137 qǔ
18 Take 取 (phonetic) a woman 女. marry (a woman) ⇔ 迎娶

趣 137 qù
19 Walk 走 to obtain 取 (phonetic). hasten interest 有趣, 興趣, 風趣, 樂趣, 逗趣, 情趣
趣味 qùwèi interest, fun

聚 137 jù
20 Bring 取 together people assemble, gather ⇔ 凝聚, 團聚
聚會 jùhuì meet, assemble, gather
聚集 jùjí assemble, gather

驟 137 zòu zhòu
21 [骤] Horse 馬 with 聚 phonetic. gallop ⇔ 步驟
驟然 zòurán suddenly

叢 137 cóng
22 [丛] Foliage 丵 gathered 取 (phonetic). Simplified form uses 人 and 一. thicket crowd together a measureword for flowers
叢林 cónglín jungle
叢書 cóngshū book series

最 137 zuì
23 Cover and take 取. steal most
最初 zuìchū earliest at first
最大 zuìdà biggest

最低 zuìdī lowest
最多 zuìduō most
最高 zuìgāo tallest, highest
最好 zuìhǎo best should:
你最好不去. It is best that you don't go.
最後 zuìhòu last finally, at last
最佳 zuìjiā finest, best
最近 zuìjìn recently
最早 zuìzǎo at the earliest
最終 zuìzhōng finally, at last

撮 137 cuō zuǒ
24 Hand 手 with 最 phonetic. cuō: pick up with fingers pinch zuǒ: tuft
撮合 cuōhé matchmake

恥 137 chǐ
25 [耻] Ear 耳 disturbing the heart 心. Simplified form uses 止. shame ⇔ 羞恥, 無恥, 知恥
恥辱 chǐrù humiliation, shame
恥笑 chǐxiào mock, ridicule

耴 137 zhé
26 Ears 耳 drooping as suggested by additional stroke.

輒 137 zhé
27 [辄] Chariot's 車 drooping ears 耴 (phonetic). sides of a chariot ⇔ 動輒

耿 137 gěng
28 Ears 耳 and fire 火. anxious honest
耿耿於懷 gěnggěngyúhuái deeply concerned
耿直 gěngzhí fair and just, upright

耶 137 yé yē
29 A variant of 邪 from ear 耳 and city 邑. a county name yé: a particle indicating a question
耶誕 yēdàn Christmas: 耶誕

節 Christmas holiday
耶穌 yēsū Jesus

爺 137 yé
30 [爷] Father 父 with 耶 phonetic. Simplified form uses 㸊. grandfather father ⇔ 老爺
爺爺 yéyé grandpa

椰 137 yé yē
31 Tree 木 with 耶 phonetic. coconut tree
椰子 yēzi coconut

揶 137 yé
32 Hand 手 with 耶 phonetic. tease
揶揄 yéyú tease, ridicule

米 138 mǐ
1 Pictograph of grains of rice. rice kernel meter a surname ⇔ 爆米花, 舂米, 小米, 大米, 蓬米, 玉米, 稻米, 糯米
米飯 mǐfàn rice
米粉 mǐfěn rice noodles rice flour
米酒 mǐjiǔ rice wine, sake
米粥 mǐzhōu rice porridge

迷 138 mí
2 Movement 辵 with 米 phonetic and graphically suggestive of multiple directions. be confused, be lost enchanted by, crazy about fan, enthusiast ⇔ 著迷, 球迷, 低迷, 昏迷
迷糊 míhú clueless
迷幻藥 míhuànyào hallucinogen
迷惑 míhuò perplex, baffle
迷戀 míliàn blinded with love, infatuated with
迷路 mílù lose way, be lost
迷亂 míluàn confused, dazed
迷你 mínǐ mini
迷人 mírén charming
迷失 míshī enchant

字譜及字典

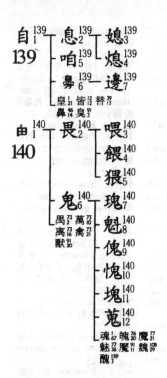

自給自足 zìjǐzìzú 🀄 self-sufficient

自家 zìjiā oneself

自覺 zìjué 🀄 self-awareness

自誇 zìkuā 🀄 boast

自來水 zìláishuǐ 🀄 running water, tap water

自力更生 zìlìgèngshēng 🀄 self-reliance

自滿 zìmǎn 🀄 self-satisfied

自然 zìrán 🀄 nature: 大自然 Mother Nature 🀄 natural: 自然而然 naturally; 自然科學 natural science

自殺 zìshā 🀄 commit suicide 🀄 suicide

自首 zìshǒu 🀄 turn oneself in

自私 zìsī 🀄 selfish: 不自私 unselfish

自衛 zìwèi 🀄 self-defense

自我 zìwǒ 🀄 ego, self: 自我批評 self-criticism; 自我介紹 self-introduction

自信 zìxìn 🀄 self-confidence

自行 zìxíng 🀄 by oneself: 自行車 🀄 bicycle

自省 zìxǐng 🀄 self-examination

自言自語 zìyánzìyǔ 🀄 talk to oneself

自由 zìyóu 🀄 free 🀄 freedom, liberty: 學術自由 academic freedom; 自由化 liberalization, liberalized, open; 自由派 liberal

自娛 zìyú 🀄 amuse oneself

自願 zìyuàn 🀄 willingly, voluntarily

自在 zìzài at ease, natural

自知 zìzhī 🀄 self-knowledge

自治 zìzhì 🀄 self-government, home-rule: 自治區 autonomous region

自重 zìzhòng 🀄 self-respect, self-esteem

自主 zìzhǔ 🀄 independence, self-determination

自助 zìzhù 🀄 self-help: 自助

迷信 míxìn 🀄 superstition

謎3 138 mí [谜] Words 言 that confuse 迷 (phonetic). 🀄 riddle, puzzle

謎語 míyǔ 🀄 riddle

瞇4 138 mī [眯] Eyes 目 and confuse 迷 (phonetic). 🀄 squint 🀄 nap: 瞇一下眼 take a nap

自1 139 zì Pictograph of a nose. 🀄 self 🀄 personal 🀄 since, from 🀄 naturally ⇔ 逕自, 源自, 各自, 畫地自封, 親自, 擅自, 獨

自, 來自

自卑 zìbēi 🀄 self-loathing: 自卑感 inferiority complex

自稱 zìchēng 🀄 claim to be

自此 zìcǐ 🀄 since then

自從 zìcóng 🀄 since then

自大 zìdà 🀄 arrogant, conceited

自動 zìdòng 🀄 automatic: 自動化 automation

自費 zìfèi 🀄 self-financed: 自費生 self-financed student

自焚 zìfén 🀄 self-immolate

自負 zìfù 🀄 conceited 🀄 assume personally: 自負責任 assume responsibility

自豪 zìháo 🀄 pride 🀄 proud of

自己 zìjǐ 🀄 oneself

餐 buffet, cafeteria
自傳 zìzhuàn 图 autobiography
自尊 zìzūn 图 self-respect

息 139 國 xí 粵 xī
2 Heart's 心⁸³ life force exhaling through the nose 自¹³⁹ (phonetic). 图 breath 图 news 粵 cease 图 interest (on funds) 粵 rest ⇔ 樓息, 歇息, 平息, 消息, 姑息, 嘆息, 鼻息, 訊息, 屏息, 孳息, 信息, 休息, 氣息, 利息, 窒息, 喘息
息息相關 xíxíxiāngguān 图 closely related

媳 139 xí
3 Woman 女 with 息 phonetic. 图 daughter-in-law
媳婦 xífù 图 daughter-in-law

熄 139 國 xí 粵 xī
4 Fire 火 stopped 息 (phonetic). 粵 extinguish
熄滅 xímiè 粵 extinguish

咱 139 zán
5 Spoken 口 of self 自. 國 I 粵 we (inclusive of the listener)
咱們 zánmen 粵 we (inclusive of the listener)

臬 139 yān
6 From 自, hole 穴 and cover (altered to 方). 图 disappear, edge

邊 139 biān
7 [边] Movement 辵 on edge 臬 (phonetic). Simplifie form uses 力. 图 border, edge, frontier 图 side ⇔ 一邊, 下邊, 路邊, 左邊, 右邊, 兩邊, 河邊, 無邊, 後邊, 海邊, 這邊, 外邊, 那邊, 旁邊, 裡邊, 前邊, 身邊
邊陲 biānchúi 图 borderland, frontier
邊際 biānjì 图 boundary
邊疆 biānjiāng 图 frontier
邊界 biānjiè 图 border
邊緣 biānyuán 图 fringe, periphery

由 140 fú
1 Pictograph of a spirit's large head.

畏 140 wèi
2 Spirit's head 由 and an altered form of tiger's claws 爪. 粵 fear, dread ⇔ 敬畏
畏懼 wèijù 粵 fear, be afraid

喂 140 wèi
3 Mouth 口 with 畏 phonetic. 國 hello (telephone usage), hey

餵 140 wèi
4 [喂] Food 食 with 畏 phonetic. 粵 feed
餵奶 wèinǎi 粵 breast-feed
餵養 wèiyǎng 粵 raise, feed

猥 140 wèi
5 Dog 犬 inducing fear 畏 (phonetic). 图 bark
猥褻 wěixiè 图 obscene, indecent 粵 behave indecently

鬼 140 gǔi
6 Legs 儿 with large spirit's head 由 and vapor (resembling 厶). 图 ghost, demon, spirit ⇔ 搞鬼, 色鬼, 魔鬼, 死鬼, 酒鬼
鬼怪 gǔiguài 图 demon
鬼魂 gǔihún 图 ghost, spirit
鬼混 gǔihùn 粵 fool around, make mischief
鬼佬 gǔilǎo 口 gwailo, foreign devil (Cantonese)
鬼祟 gǔisùi 粵 surreptitious
鬼月 gǔiyuè 图 ghost month - seventh month of the lunar calendar
鬼子 gǔizi 图 ghost, demon 粵 foreigner (particularly Japanese): 洋鬼子 foreign devil

瑰 140 gūi
7 Jade 玉 with 鬼 phonetic. 粵 magnificent ⇔ 玫瑰
瑰麗 gūilì 粵 magnificent, gorgeous

魁 140 kúi
8 Dipper 斗 with 鬼 phonetic. 國 large dipper 粵 large leader ⇔ 黨魁
魁 140 kǔi
9 Person 人 with 鬼 phonetic. 图 puppet
傀儡 kǔiléi 图 puppet: 傀儡政府 puppet government

愧 140 kùi
10 Heart 心 and spirit 鬼 (phonetic). 粵 ashamed, guilt-ridden ⇔ 羞愧, 慚愧
愧色 kùisè 图 look of shame

塊 140 kùai
11 [块] Earth 土 with 鬼 phonetic. Simplified form uses 夬. 图 piece, chunk, clump: 一塊土地 a piece of land 粵 ⊟ yuan, dollar: 三塊美金 three dollars ⇔ 一塊兒, 石塊, 冰塊, 方塊

蒐 140 sōu
12 Plant 艸 with 鬼 phonetic. 图 madder - a plant used for dyeing 粵 gather, collect
蒐集 sōují 粵 collect (⇨ 搜集, 收集)

缶 141 fǒu
1 Pictograph of a covered clay vessel. 图 crock

匋 141 táo
2 Earthenware 缶 encased 勹. 图 furnace

陶 141 táo
3 Hill-like 阜 furnace 匋 (phonetic). 粵

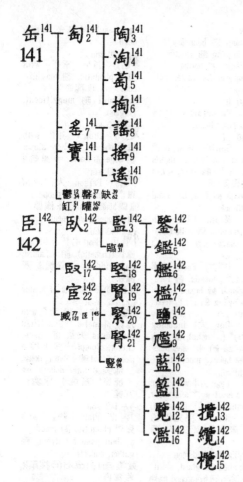

supplant

萄5 táo Plant 艸 with 匋 phonetic. a plant name ⇔ 葡萄, 葡萄牙

掏6 táo Hand 手 in pot 匋 (phonetic). pull out, take out
掏錢 táoqián spend money

䍃7 yáo Meat 肉 (phonetic) in a crock 缶. crock

謠8 yáo [谣] Words 言 with 䍃 phonetic. song, rumor ⇔ 歌謠, 闢謠
謠傳 yáochuán spread rumors
謠言 yáoyán rumor

搖9 [摇] Hand 手 shaking contents of crock 䍃 (phonetic). shake, rock ⇔ 動搖
搖動 yáodòng shake, rock
搖滾 yáogǔn rock and roll
搖晃 yáohuàng shake, swing shaky, unsteady
搖籃 yáolán cradle: 文明的搖籃 cradle of civilization
搖頭 yáotóu shake one's head in disagreement
搖曳 yáoyì waver, sway

遙10 [遥] Movement 辵 with 䍃 phonetic. distant, remote ⇔ 逍遙
遙控 yáokòng remote control
遙遠 yáoyuǎn remote, distant

寶11 [宝] Jade 玉, earthenware 缶 (phonetic), and shells 貝 under the roof 宀. treasure, precious ⇔ 法寶, 國寶, 財寶, 珠寶
寶貝 bǎobèi precious object baby, sweetheart

make pottery, pottery happy a surname: 陶潛 Tao Qian - Eastern Jin Dynasty poet ⇔ 薰陶
陶瓷 táocí ceramics
陶器 táoqì pottery
陶冶 táoyě mold and smelt cultivate, shape
陶醉 táozuì infatuated with, drunk with

淘4 táo Water 水 with 匋 phonetic. wash, rinse: 淘米 wash rice
淘金 táojīn pan for gold
淘氣 táoqì naughty, mischievous
淘汰 táotài supersede,

寶貴 bǎoguì 图 precious, valuable
寶石 bǎoshí 图 precious stone, jewel: 紅寶石 ruby
寶玉 bǎoyù 图 precious jade

臣 142 chén
1 Pictograph of a kneeling person. 图 subject, servant 图 minister, official ⇔ 大臣
臣民 chénmín 图 subjects

臥 142 wò
2 Prostrate 臣 person 人. lie down
臥車 wòchē 图 sleeping car
臥房 wòfáng 图 bedroom
臥舖 wòpù 图 sleeping berth
臥室 wòshì 图 bedroom

監 142 jiān jiàn
3 [监] Prostrate person 臥 looking into sacrificial vase 血 (note dislocation of mark representing blood). jiān: inspect imprison jiàn: 图 eunuch ⇔ 太監
監察 jiānchá inspect
監督 jiāndū supervise, oversee, monitor
監牢 jiānláo 图 jail
監視 jiānshì watch over
監獄 jiānyù 图 jail, prison

鑒 142 jiàn
4 [鉴] Metal 金 for inspecting 監 (phonetic). 图 bronze mirror (⇒ 鑑) examine ⇔ 鉤鑒
鑒於 jiànyú in view of (⇒ 鑑於)

鑑 142 jiàn
5 [鉴] Metal 金 for inspecting 監 (phonetic). 图 bronze mirror examine ⇔ 年鑑
鑑別 jiànbié differentiate
鑑定 jiàndìng authenticate appraise
鑑賞 jiànshǎng appreciate
鑑於 jiànyú in view of

艦 142 jiàn
6 [舰] Boat 舟 with 監 phonetic. Simplified form uses 见. 图 warship, naval vessel
艦隊 jiànduì 图 fleet
艦艇 jiàntǐng 图 warship, naval vessel

檻 142 kǎn
7 [槛] Wood 木 with 監 phonetic. 图 threshold ⇔ 門檻

鹽 142 yán
8 [盐] Salt 鹵 with 監 phonetic. Simplified form uses 土 and 卜. 图 salt

尷 142 gān
9 [尴] Modern form shows walk unevenly 尤 with 監 phonetic. embarrassed
尷尬 gāngà embarrassed, awkward

藍 142 lán
10 [蓝] Plant 艸 with 監 phonetic. 图 indigo plant 图 blue: 藍調音樂 blues (music) ⇔ 蔚藍
藍色 lánsè 图 blue
藍天 lántiān 图 blue sky
藍圖 lántú 图 blueprint

籃 142 lán
11 [篮] Bamboo 竹 that imprisons 監 phonetic. 图 basket ⇔ 花籃, 竹籃, 搖籃
籃球 lánqiú 图 basketball
籃子 lánzi 图 basket

覽 142 lǎn
12 [览] See 見 and examine 監 phonetic. sightsee read ⇔ 閱覽, 展覽, 流覽, 瀏覽, 遊覽

攬 142 lǎn
13 [揽] Hand 手 with 覽 phonetic. hold, grab

⇔ 延攬, 獨攬
攬權 lǎnquán seize power

纜 142 lǎn
14 [缆] Thread 糸 with 覽 phonetic and suggestive of hold 攬. 图 cable ⇔ 電纜
纜車 lǎnchē 图 cable car

欖 142 lǎn
15 [榄] Tree 木 worth viewing 覽 (phonetic). 图 olive tree ⇔ 橄欖

濫 142 làn
16 [滥] Water 水 from tipped vase 監 (phonetic). overflow recklessly ⇔ 氾濫, 陳腔濫調
濫調 làndiào hackneyed
濫情 lànqíng sentimental
濫用 lànyòng abuse, misuse: 濫用權力 abuse power; 濫用職權 abuse one's position

臤 142 jiān
17 Hand 又 controlling servant 臣 (phonetic). firm

堅 142 jiān
18 [坚] Firm 臤 (phonetic) earth 土. firm, solid
堅持 jiānchí insist
堅定 jiāndìng resolute, firm, staunch
堅固 jiāngù firm, solid
堅決 jiānjué resolute
堅強 jiānqiáng strong, firm strengthen
堅實 jiānshí substantial, solid
堅守 jiānshǒu stand firm
堅硬 jiānyìng hard, solid

賢 142 xián
19 [贤] Solid 臤 (phonetic) money/shells 貝. worthy, virtuous versatile, talented
賢才 xiáncái 图 virtuous and talented person

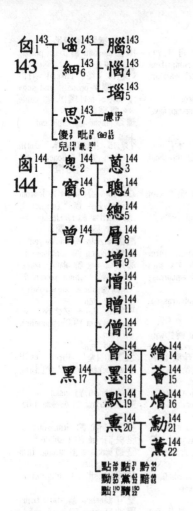

緊引, 抓緊引

緊急 jǐnjí 囲 urgent
緊緊 jǐnjǐn 囲 tightly, closely
緊密 jǐnmì 囲 compact, close
緊迫 jǐnpò 囲 urgent
緊縮 jǐnsūo 囲 tighten
緊要 jǐnyào 囲 important
緊張 jǐnzhāng 囲 nervous 囲 stressful

腎 142 shèn
21 [腎] Tight 臤 phonetic) flesh 肉 |³². 囲 kidney 囲 testicle
腎臟 shènzàng 囲 kidney

宦 142 huàn
22 Minister 臣 |⁴² under palace roof 宀 |³. 囲 official 囲 eunuch ⟺ 仕宦 ³
宦官 huànguān 囲 eunuch

囟 143 xìn
1 Pictograph of a skull with brain inside.

𡿺 143 nǎo
2 Head 囟 |⁴³ with hair 川 |³ on a person 匕 |². ㊇ brain (⟹ 腦 |⁴³)

腦 143 nǎo
3 [脑] Flesh 肉 |³² and brain 𡿺 |⁴³ (phonetic, abbreviated). 囲 brain ⟺ 電腦 ᵇ, 頭腦 ᵇ
腦袋 nǎodài 囲 head
腦海 nǎohǎi 囲 mind, head
腦筋 nǎojīn 囲 brains, mind, head: 傷腦筋 troublesome; 動腦筋 think
腦瘤 nǎolíu 囲 brain tumor
腦子 nǎozi 囲 brains, mind

惱 143 nǎo
4 [恼] Heart 心 |⁴³ and brain 𡿺 |⁴³ (phonetic, abbreviated). 動 annoy, exasperate ⟺ 苦惱 ᵇ, 煩惱 ᵇ, 懊惱 ᵇ
惱怒 nǎonù 囲 angry, furious
惱人 nǎorén 囲 annoying

瑙 143 nǎo
5 Jade 玉 |⁰⁷ with 𡿺 |⁴³ (abbreviated) phonetic.

賢德 xiándé 囲 virtue
賢惠 xiánhùi 囲 virtuous and dutiful (woman)
賢明 xiánmíng 囲 capable and wise
賢能 xiánnéng 囲 virtuous and talented
賢淑 xiánshú 囲 virtuous (woman)

緊 142 jǐn
20 [紧] Tied firmly 臤 |⁴² with thread 糸 |⁵³. 囲 tight, taut urgent ⟺ 要緊 ᵇ, 加緊 ²⁴, 趕緊 ᵇ, 吃

图 agate ⇔ 瑪瑙[77]

細 143 xì
6 [细] Threads 糸[53] with 囟[143] (altered to resemble 田[1]) phonetic. 形 thin, fine 形 detailed ⇔ 仔細[34], 精細[54], 底細[100], 詳細[53]
細胞 xìbāo 名 cell: 沒有運動細胞 bad at sports
細節 xìjié 名 details
細菌 xìjùn 名 germ, bacterium
細膩 xìnì 形 delicate, fine, detailed
細小 xìxiǎo 形 tiny, minute
細心 xìxīn 形 careful, attentive
細緻 xìzhì 形 meticulous

思 143 sī
7 Head 囟[143] (written as 田[1]) and heart 心[93]. 動 think, contemplate 動 long for, think of ⇔ 不可思議[6], 沈思[24], 好意思[34], 意思[64], 心思[35], 相思[61], 匪夷所思[20], 馬克思[77]
思潮 sīcháo 名 thoughts
思考 sīkǎo 動 consider, think over, ponder
思慮 sīlù 動 consider
思索 sīsuǒ 動 deliberate, think over, ponder
思維 sīwéi 名 thought, thinking
思想 sīxiǎng 名 thought, ideology: 毛澤東思想 Maoism

囪 144 cōng
1 [囱] Pictograph of a window with lattices. ⇔ 煙囪[30]

悤 144 cōng
2 Heart 心[93] and window 囪[144] (phonetic). 古 alarmed (⇨ 匆[5])

蔥 144 cōng
3 [葱] Plant 艸[92] with 悤[144] phonetic. Simplified form uses 匆[5]. 名 onion 大蔥[3], 青蔥[8], 洋蔥[23]

聰 144 cōng
4 [聪] Ear 耳[37] with 悤[144] phonetic. Simplified form uses 總[144] simplification. 形 clever
聰慧 cōnghùi 形 intelligent, clever
聰明 cōngmíng 形 intelligent, bright, clever
聰穎 cōngyǐng 形 bright, precocious

總 144 zǒng
5 [总] Thread 糸[53] with 悤[144] phonetic. 動 assemble, sum up 形 general, overall 形 principal, chief: 總經理 general manager 副 always 副 eventually
總裁 zǒngcái 名 chief executive officer
總督 zǒngdū 名 governor (of a colony)
總額 zǒngé 名 total
總而言之 zǒngéryánzhī 成 in summation
總共 zǒnggòng 副 in total, in all
總和 zǒnghé 名 total, sum
總結 zǒngjié 名 summary 動 sum up
總理 zǒnglǐ 名 premier, prime minister
總是 zǒngshì 副 always
總數 zǒngshù 名 total
總算 zǒngsuàn 副 finally 副 on the whole
總統 zǒngtǒng 名 president
總之 zǒngzhī 副 in short, in summation

窗 144 chuāng
6 Window 囪[144] (phonetic) with hole 穴[52] for emphasis. 名 window ⇔ 紗窗[58], 櫥窗[22]
窗戶 chuānghù 名 window
窗口 chuāngkǒu 名 ticket window
窗簾 chuānglián 名 curtain, blinds

窗子 chuāngzi 名 window

曾 144 céng zēng
7 Separate 八[9] words 曰[52] with window 囪[144] (altered) phonetic and suggestive of clarity. 古 assent zēng: 囧 repeated, doubled 囮 a surname céng: 副 previously ⇔ 未曾[9]
曾經 céngjīng 副 previously
曾孫 zēngsūn 名 great-grandchild
曾祖 zēngzǔ 名 great-grandparent (on father's father's side)

層 144 céng
8 [层] Roof 屋[28] (abbreviated to 尸[9]) doubled 曾[144] (phonetic). Simplified form uses 云[42]. 名 floor, story 名 stratum, layer 名 shelf ⇔ 上層[43], 階層[19], 基層[8], 岩層[97]
層層 céngcéng 副 layer after layer
層次 céngcì 名 order, arrangement 名 level

增 144 zēng
9 Earth 土[9] doubled 曾[144] (phonetic). 動 increase, add ⇔ 遞增[72]
增補 zēngbǔ 動 supplement
增加 zēngjiā 動 increase, augment
增進 zēngjìn 動 enhance, promote
增強 zēngqiáng 動 strengthen
增添 zēngtiān 動 increase, add
增長 zēngzhǎng 動 grow, increase

憎 144 zēng
10 Heart 心[93] with 曾[144] phonetic. 動 hate
憎惡 zēngè 動 loathe, detest
憎恨 zēnghèn 動 detest, hate

贈 144 zèng
11 [赠] Shells/money 貝[90] doubled 曾[144] (phonet-

328　　　　　　　　　　　　　字譜及字典

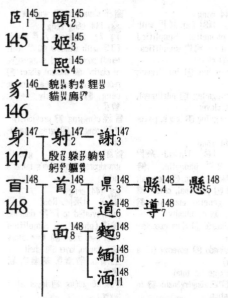

臣 145₁　頤 145₂
145
　　姬 145₃
　　熙 145₄

豸 146₁　貌 146⁴⁷　豹 146⁴⁸　狸 146⁴⁹
146　　貓 146⁵⁰　廌 146⁵¹

身 147₁　射 147₂　謝 147₃
147　殷 147⁷⁷　躲 147⁷⁸　躺 147⁷⁹
　　躬 147⁶⁵　軀 147⁶⁶

百 148₁　首 148₂　県 148₃　縣 148₄　懸 148₅
148　　　道 148₆　導 148₇
　　面 148₈　麵 148₉
　　　　緬 148₁₀
　　　　酒 148₁₁

ic). 🔵 donate, give ⇔ 饋
贈 ¹⁰⁶
贈品 zèngpǐn 🔵 present, gift
贈送 zèngsòng 🔵 donate, give

僧 144 sēng
12 Person 人¹⁰ with
曾 ¹⁴⁴ phonetic. 🔵 monk
僧侶 sēnglǚ 🔵 monks
僧人 sēngrén 🔵 monk

會 144 huì huǐ kuài
13 [会] Double 曾 ¹⁴⁴
(abbreviated) together ∧ ⁴⁴.
Simplified form uses 云 ²⁵. huì:
🔵 meet 🔵 meeting, conference
🔵 association, society 🔵 can,
be able to 🔵 will huǐ: 🔵
moment kuài: 🔵 add ⇔ 一
會兒 ¹, 三合會 ⁴⁵, 不會 ¹⁰,
教會 ¹⁴, 學會 ²², 標會 ²⁵, 公
會 ¹⁷, 省會 ²⁹, 舞會 ³⁰, 協
會 ³¹, 大會 ³², 誤會 ⁵³, 國
會 ⁵², 議會 ⁵³, 幸會 ⁵⁵, 工
會 ³⁷, 宴會 ⁵⁴, 幽會 ⁵⁷, 機

會 ⁵⁷, 約會 ⁶¹, 社會 ⁵⁹, 幫
會 ²³, 體會 ²⁷, 散會 ²², 休
會 ⁷⁶, 開會 ²⁹, 理會 ²⁹, 聚
會 ⁵⁷, 集會 ¹⁶², 晚會 ¹⁴⁴
會合 huìhé 🔵 assemble, meet
會話 huìhuà 🔵 conversation
會見 huìjiàn 🔵 meet
會面 huìmiàn 🔵 meet face to
face
會商 huìshāng 🔵 consult
會社 huìshè 🔵 society, association
會談 huìtán 🔵 talks
會晤 huìwù 🔵 meet face to face
會議 huìyì 🔵 meeting
會意 huìyì 🔵 understand 🔵
type of Chinese character in
which the meaning is derived
from the meanings of component parts (⇒ 六書)
會員 huìyuán 🔵 club member:
會員卡 membership card
會計 kuàijì 🔵 accountancy: 會

計師 accountant; 會計學
accounting

繪 144 huì
14 [绘] Thread/silk
糸 ⁵³ with 會 ¹³ phonetic. 🔵
paint, draw ⇔ 描繪 ³¹¹
繪畫 huìhuà 🔵 painting, drawing

薈 144 huì
15 [荟] Plants 艸 ²⁶
gathered 會 ¹³ (phonetic). 🔵
dense vegetation ⇔ 蘆薈 ¹⁵³
薈萃 huìcuì 🔵 thriving, flourishing 🔵 assemble (distinguished
people)

燴 144 huì
16 [烩] Food gathered
會 ¹³ (phonetic) over fire
火 ¹². 🔵 braise, stew

黑 144 hēi
17 Window 囱 ¹⁴⁴ (alter-
ed) darkened by fire 炎 ⁸² (altered). 🔵 black 🔵 dark 🔵
illicit ⇔ 黝黑 ⁸⁵, 漆黑 ²³, 曬
黑 ⁵⁴, 烏黑 ⁷⁶
黑暗 hēiàn 🔵 dark: 黑暗時代
dark ages
黑白 hēibái 🔵 black and white:
黑白照片 black and white
picture
黑板 hēibǎn 🔵 blackboard
黑道 hēidào 🔵 underworld
黑龍江 hēilóngjiāng 🔵
Heilongjiang Province
黑人 hēirén 🔵 black person
黑色 hēisè 🔵 black
黑市 hēishì 🔵 black market
黑手黨 hēishǒudǎng 🔵 mafia

墨 144 mò
18 Earthy 土 ⁷⁰ material
from soot 黑 ¹⁴⁴ (phonetic).
🔵 ink stick, ink ⇔ 筆墨 ¹²,
翰墨 ²⁶
墨水 mòshuǐ 🔵 ink
墨西哥 mòxīgē 🔵 Mexico
墨子 mòzǐ 🅰 Mozi - an ancient
philosopher

默 144 mò
19 Dog 犬 ⁹¹ tracking in

dark 黑 (phonetic). silent ⇔ 沈默, 緘默, 幽默

默默 mòmò silently

默契 mòqì tacit understanding

默然 mòrán silently

默認 mòrèn tacitly approve

熏 144 xūn
20 Black 黑 vapor rising 屮 (altered). smoke

勳 144 xūn
21 [勛] Strength 力 with 熏 phonetic. Simplified form is ancient form using clerk 員. achievement ⇔ 功勳

薰 144 xūn
22 [薰] Plant 艸 fragrant like smoke 熏 (phonetic). a fragrant herb

薰陶 xūntáo nurture, edify

臣 145 yí
1 Pictograph of a face. cheeks (⇨ 頤)

頤 145 yí
2 Cheeks 臣 with head 頁 redundant. cheeks

頤和園 yíhéyuán Summer Palace (of Qing Dynasty)

姬 145 jī
3 Woman 女 with 臣 phonetic. imperial concubine

熙 145 xī
4 Fat cheeks (ancient character from cheek 臣 and embryo 巳) and fire 火. firey glorious ⇔ 康熙

豸 146 zhì
1 Pictograph of a clawed beast. a mythical animal legless insect or reptile

身 147 shēn
1 Pictograph of a human profile. body life oneself ⇔ 人身, 脫身, 樓身, 隨身, 全身, 終身, 親身, 起身, 轉身, 熱身, 本身, 紋身, 出身, 抽身, 獨身, 單身, 翻身, 渾身

身邊 shēnbiān at one's side on hand

身材 shēncái figure, body, build: 身材很好 a great body

身份 shēnfèn personal status, identity: 身份證 I.D. card

身旁 shēnpáng at one's side

身軀 shēnqū body

身世 shēnshì life experiences

身體 shēntǐ body

身心 shēnxīn mind and body

身形 shēnxíng body shape

身子 shēnzi body

射 147 shè
2 Body 身 and measure 寸 (originally arrow 矢). shoot ⇔ 注射, 反射, 輻射, 投射, 噴射, 發射, 放射, 雷射

射門 shèmén shoot (a ball at a goal)

謝 147 xiè
3 [谢] Words 言 and shoot 射 (phonetic). part, take leave thank decline, wither ⇔ 酬謝, 答謝, 感謝, 凋謝, 多謝, 致謝, 道謝, 鳴謝

謝絕 xièjué decline, refuse

謝謝 xièxiè thank you

百 148 shǒu
1 Pictograph of a face (note similarity to nose 自).

首 148 shǒu
2 Face 百 with river/hair 川 (abbreviated) on top. head chief measureword for songs and poems ⇔ 部首, 匕首, 俯首, 榜首, 斬首, 禍首, 自首

首次 shǒucì first time

首都 shǒudū capital city

首度 shǒudù first time

首肯 shǒukěn nod approval

首領 shǒulǐng chief, leader

首位 shǒuwèi first

首先 shǒuxiān first

首相 shǒuxiàng prime minister, premier

首要 shǒuyào most important

首長 shǒuzhǎng chief, senior officer

梟 148 jiāo
3 Head 首 hanging upside down.

縣 148 xiàn
4 [县] Inverted head 首 tied 系. hang, suspend (⇨ 懸) prefecture, county

懸 148 xuán
5 [悬] Heart 心 in suspense 縣 (phonetic). suspend, hang

懸掛 xuánguà hang (a picture)

懸殊 xuánshū vastly different: 貧富懸殊 vastly unequal distribution of wealth

懸崖 xuányá cliff, precipice

懸疑 xuányí suspense

道 148 dào
6 Movement 辵 ahead 首. road, path way, means doctrine Daoism, Taoism ⇔ 一道, 人道, 人行道, 劍道, 衛道, 說道, 北海道, 孝道, 跑道, 殉道, 河道, 軌道, 志同道合, 難道, 知道, 報道, 大道, 赤道, 交道, 航道, 陰道, 合氣道, 空手道, 渠道, 穴道, 通道, 街

字譜及字典

面積 miànjī 图 area

面頰 miànjiá 图 cheek

面具 miànjù 图 mask

面孔 miànkǒng 图 face

面臨 miànlín 图 facing, confronting

面貌 miànmào 图 facial features 图 appearance

面面相覷 miànmiànxiāngqù 图 gaze warily at each other

面目 miànmù 图 countenance: 真正面目 true face

面前 miànqián 图 in front

面容 miànróng 图 facial features, visage

面紗 miànshā 图 veil

面談 miàntán 图 interview

面子 miànzi 图 face, pride: 面子的問題 a problem of face; 太沒有面子 humiliating; 給面子 give face; 要面子 anxious to save face

麵 9 148 miàn [面] Wheat 麥 with 面 phonetic. 图 flour ⇔ 下麵, 泡麵, 炸麵, 炒麵, 撈麵

麵包 miànbāo 图 bread: 烤麵包 toast, to toast; 麵包車 van

麵粉 miànfěn 图 flour

麵條 miàntiáo 图 noodles

緬 10 148 miǎn [缅] Thread 糸 with 面 phonetic. 图 distant

緬甸 miǎndiàn 图 Burma, Myanmar

緬懷 miǎnhuái 图 cherish, memorialize

酒 11 148 miǎn Liquid 水 affecting face 面 (phonetic). 图 drunk ⇔ 沈湎

頁 12 148 yè [页] Face 首 upon a person 儿 (altered): head. 图 page ⇔ 扉頁

道, 鐵道, 味道, 步道, 頻道, 柔道, 黑道, 隧道, 車道, 霸道, 管道

道別 dàobié 图 bid farewell

道德 dàodé 图 morals

道地 dàodì 图 genuine, authentic

道教 dàojiào 图 Daoism

道理 dàolǐ 图 truth

道路 dàolù 图 road

道歉 dàoqiàn 图 apologize: 你應該跟他道歉。 You should apologize to him.

道瓊 dàoqióng 图 Dow-Jones: 道瓊指數 Dow-Jones index

道士 dàoshì 图 Daoist priest

道謝 dàoxiè 图 thank

導 7 148 dǎo [导] Follow path 道 (phonetic) in measured 寸 way. Simplified form uses 巳. 图 lead, guide 图 transmit, conduct ⇔ 宣導, 訓導, 主導, 指導, 播導, 教導, 誘導, 報導, 領導, 疏導, 引導, 輔導, 勸導

導彈 dǎodàn 图 图 guided missile: 洲際導彈 ICBM

導師 dǎoshī 图 adviser

導體 dǎotǐ 图 conductor: 半導體 semiconductor; 超導體 superconductor

導向 dǎoxiàng 图 guide: 導向飛彈 guided missile

導演 dǎoyǎn 图 director (of a film or play)

導致 dǎozhì 图 result in, lead to, induce

面 8 148 miàn Face 首 with circle (resembling 口) for emphasis. 图 face 图 aspect, side 图 surface 图 area ⇔ 一面, 晤面, 上面, 下面, 露面, 背面, 書面, 局面, 反面, 四面, 全面, 迎面, 後面, 海面, 地面, 當面, 封面, 體面, 外面, 場面, 片面, 正面, 方面, 顏面, 出面, 裡面, 見面, 表面, 前面, 會面, 側面, 負面, 對面

面對 miànduì 图 facing, faced with

字譜及字典

331

憂 13 [忧] Walk slowly 夊 with troubled head 頁 (phonetic, altered) and heart 心. Simplified form uses especially 尤. 形 anxious, worried 動 worry ⇔ 擔憂, 隱憂

憂愁 yōuchóu 形 depressed
憂懼 yōujù 形 apprehensive
憂慮 yōulù 形 worried, anxious
憂傷 yōushāng 名 sadness
憂鬱 yōuyù 形 depressed: 憂鬱症 depression

優 148 yōu
14 [优] Person 人 with 憂 phonetic. Simplified form uses especially 尤. 形 excellent

優待 yōudài 名 privilege
優點 yōudiǎn 名 strong point, merits
優厚 yōuhòu 形 liberal, generous: 待遇優厚 generous compensation
優美 yōuměi 形 beautiful
優生 yōushēng 名 eugenics
優勢 yōushì 名 advantage
優先 yōuxiān 名 形 priority: 第一優先 first priority
優秀 yōuxiù 形 excellent, outstanding
優異 yōuyì 形 excellent, outstanding
優越 yōuyuè 形 superior: 優越感 superiority complex

擾 148 rǎo
15 [扰] Hand 手 troubling 憂. Simplified form uses especially 尤. 動 disturb ⇔ 騷擾, 攪擾, 紛擾, 打擾, 干擾, 困擾, 煩擾

擾亂 rǎoluàn 動 disturb

類 148 lèi
16 [类] Dog 犬 with an ancient character from rice 米 and head 頁 pho-netic. 名 type, kind 動 resemble ⇔ 人類, 詞類, 同類, 分類, 種類, 肉類, 歸類

類別 lèibié 名 classification
類似 lèisì 形 similar, analogous
類推 lèituī 動 reason by analogy
類型 lèixíng 名 type

煩 148 fán
17 [烦] Fire 火 in the head 頁. 動 annoy, trouble: 別煩人 "cut it out" 形 annoying, troubling ⇔ 不耐煩, 麻煩, 勞煩, 厭煩

煩惱 fánnǎo 形 vexing, annoying 名 worries
煩擾 fánrǎo 動 bother, disturb 動 be bothered, be annoyed
煩躁 fánzào 形 agitated, irritable, impatient

夏 148 xià
18 Modern form shows person 頁 (abbreviated) walking 夊. 名 summer 名 Xia Dynasty 名 a surname ⇔ 寧夏, 華夏

夏季 xiàjì 名 summer
夏天 xiàtiān 名 summer
夏威夷 xiàwēiyí 名 Hawaii
夏至 xiàzhì 名 summer solstice

廈 148 xià 廈 shà
19 [厦] Large roof 广 with 夏 phonetic. Simplified form uses 厂. 名 tall building ⇔ 大廈

廈門 xiàmén 名 Xiamen (Amoy) - a city in Fujian Province

戛 148 jiá
20 Head 首 like lance 戈. 名 halberd, lance 動 strike, tap

戛然 jiárán 動 sharp, clear: 戛然而止 stop abruptly

角 148 jiǎo jué
1 Pictograph of a horn. jiǎo: 名 horn jué: 動 contend 名 character, role ⇔ 三角, 主角, 直角, 菱角, 稜角, 口角, 牆角, 鹿角

角度 jiǎodù 名 angle
角落 jiǎoluò 名 corner
角力 juélì 動 wrestle
角色 juésè 名 role, character
角逐 juézhú 動 contend for, contest

解 149 jiě
2 Ox's 牛 horn 角 cut with knife 刀. 動 separate, divide 動 solve 動 untie 動 relieve, alleviate ⇔ 註解, 迎刃而解, 分解, 誤解, 辯解, 了解, 費解, 調解, 瞭解, 抒解, 緩解, 和解, 瓦解, 理解, 見解, 曲解, 講解

解除 jiěchú 動 relieve, eliminate 動 fire, dismiss
解答 jiědá 動 answer, solution
解放 jiěfàng 動 liberate, free: 人民解放軍 People's Liberation Army
解決 jiějué 動 settle, resolve
解開 jiěkāi 動 untie, undo
解剖 jiěpōu 動 dissect: 解剖學 anatomy
解散 jiěsàn 動 disband, dissolve, adjourn
解釋 jiěshì 動 explain 名 explanation
解脫 jiětuō 動 set free
解析 jiěxī 動 analyze: 解析度 (screen) resolution
解嚴 jiěyán 動 lift martial law

懈 149 xiè
3 Heart/mind 心 separated 解 (phonetic). 形 inattentive ⇔ 鬆懈

懈怠 xièdài 形 lax

蟹 149 xiè
4 Insect-like 虫 with 解 phonetic. 名 crab ⇔ 螃蟹

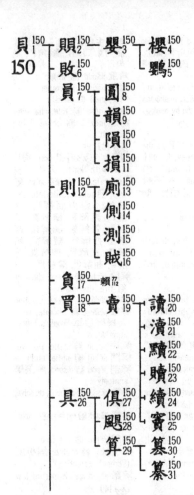

🈀 cherry
櫻花 yīnghuā 🈀 cherry blossom
櫻桃 yīngtáo 🈀 cherry

鸚 150 yīng
5 [鹦] Bird 鳥170 pretty like necklace 嬰150 (phonetic). 🈀 parrot
鸚鵡 yīngwǔ 🈀 parrot

敗 150 bài
6 [败] Shell money 貝150 (phonetic) struck 攵 and destroyed. 🈀 defeat defeat be defeated, lose ⇔ 腐敗, 打敗, 擊敗, 成敗, 慘敗, 失敗, 衰敗, 勝敗
敗北 bàiběi be defeated
敗壞 bàihuài ruin

員 150 yuán
7 [员] Shell 貝150 with 口 phonetic. 🈀 objects round 🈀 clerk 🈀 member of a group ⇔ 人員, 閣員, 教員, 教職員, 警員, 幅員, 店員, 冗員, 成員, 議員, 海員, 團員, 黨員, 演員, 職員, 動員, 球員, 委員, 會員, 隊員, 官員
員工 yuángōng 🈀 employees, staff

圓 150 yuán
8 [圆] Encircle 口 and round 員150 (phonetic). 🈀 round 🈀 yuan, dollar (⇨ 元) ⇔ 橢圓, 日圓, 湯圓
圓滿 yuánmǎn 🈀 satisfactory
圓圈 yuánquān 🈀 circle, ring
圓形 yuánxíng 🈀 circular, spherical
圓周 yuánzhōu 🈀 circumference
圓珠筆 yuánzhūbǐ 🈀 🈀 ball-point pen

韻 150 yùn
9 [韵] Sound 音 that

貝 150 bèi
1 [贝] Pictograph of a shell. 🈀 shell 🈀 cowrie, shell money ⇔ 拷貝, 寶貝
貝殼 bèiké 🈀 shell

賏 150 yīng
2 Shells 貝150 strung together. 🈀 necklace

嬰 150 yīng
3 [婴] Woman 女 wearing shells 賏150 (phonetic). 🈀 necklace 🈀 infant ⇔ 殺嬰
嬰兒 yīngér 🈀 infant

櫻 150 yīng
4 [樱] Tree 木75 pretty like necklace 嬰150 (phonetic).

is round 員¹⁵⁰ (phonetic). Simplified form uses even 勻⁷⁶. 形 rhyme 韻 charming ⇔ 風韻⁷, 押韻¹²。韻律 yùnlǜ 名 rhythm, meter

隕¹⁵⁰10 [陨] Hill 阜¹⁶⁷ with 員¹⁵⁰ phonetic. 動 fall 隕石 yǔnshí 名 meteorite

損¹⁵⁰11 [损] Hand 手⁹⁷ with 員¹⁵⁰ phonetic. 動 damage, harm ⇔ 折損⁸⁷, 虧損⁸⁹。損害 sǔnhài 動 injure, damage, harm 損壞 sǔnhuài 動 damage 損失 sǔnshī 動 lose 名 loss

則¹⁵⁰12 [则] Shell money 貝¹⁵⁰ cut 刀³⁵ in standard pieces. 名 law, rule 量 item (of news) 連 consequently, then ⇔ 否則⁷⁶, 原則⁷⁵, 規則⁷⁷, 法則³³, 通則⁷⁷, 定則⁹⁴, 準則⁹⁷, 雖則⁴⁹。

廁¹⁵⁰13 [厕] Shed 广⁶⁰ with 則¹⁵² phonetic. Simplified form uses 厂¹. 名 toilet 廁所 cèsuǒ 名 形 bathroom, toilet, latrine: 上廁所 go to the bathroom

側¹⁵⁰14 [侧] Person 人¹⁰ with 則¹⁵² phonetic. 名 side 側面 cèmiàn 名 side, profile

測¹⁵⁰15 [测] Estimate water 水⁸⁴ depth according to rule 則¹⁵² (phonetic). 動 measure ⇔ 不測⁷⁶, 叵測, 臆測⁶⁶, 猜測⁴⁷, 揆測⁹⁴, 預測⁵², 揣測³⁴, 推測¹², 觀測⁶⁶。測定 cèdìng 動 survey 測量 cèliáng 動 measure 測試 cèshì 動 test 測驗 cèyàn 動 test 測字 cèzì 動 tell fortune from handwriting

賊¹⁵⁰16 [贼] Use lance 戈²⁵ against the law 則¹⁵² (phonetic, altered). 名 thief ⇔ 盜賊⁶², 竊賊²³

負¹⁵⁰17 [负] Person 人¹⁰ working for shell money 貝¹⁵⁰. 動 bear, shoulder: 負責任 assume responsibility 形 negative 動 owe ⇔ 背負², 抱負², 擔負², 辜負⁶, 欺負², 肩負²⁹, 自負³⁹。負擔 fùdān 名 burden 負荷 fùhè 動 bear, sustain 名 burden 負面 fùmiàn 形 negative: 負面的影響 negative influence 負數 fùshù 名 negative number 負責 fùzé 動 be responsible: 負責人 person responsible 負債 fùzhài 動 incur debt

買¹⁵⁰18 [买] Catch 网⁵² (altered) with shell money 貝¹⁵⁰. Simplified form uses 頭⁵⁸ simplification. 動 buy ⇔ 收買⁷, 購買⁷⁵。買辦 mǎibàn 名 comprador 買單 mǎidān 動 pay the check ⇒ 埋單⁷⁷。買賣 mǎimài 動 buy and sell 名 business: 做買賣 do business 買下 mǎixià 動 buy up

賣¹⁵⁰19 [卖] Outward 出¹⁰ (altered to resemble 士³) purchase 買¹⁵⁰ (phonetic). Listed derivatives are based on a related ancient character for peddling with different pronunciation. 動 sell ⇔ 盜賣⁶², 販賣³⁴, 炒賣², 燒賣², 拍賣³⁵, 叛賣²⁷, 出賣¹⁰, 買賣¹⁸。賣春 màichūn 動 engage in prostitution

賣給 màigěi 動 sell to 賣淫 màiyín 動 engage in prostitution

讀²⁰ [读] Words 言⁴⁸ with 賣¹⁵⁰ phonetic. 動 read aloud, read study ⇔ 閱讀⁵¹, 朗讀³⁸, 就讀⁴⁵, 工讀⁵¹。讀書 dúshū 動 study, be a student: 讀書人 intellectual 讀者 dúzhě 名 reader

瀆²¹ [渎] Water 水⁸⁴ with 賣¹⁵⁰ phonetic. 名 gutter 貪瀆⁴⁷, 褻瀆⁴⁶。瀆職 dúzhí 名 malfeasance

黷²² [黩] Dark 黑¹⁹ with 賣¹⁵⁰ phonetic. 動 tarnish rash 黷武 dúwǔ 形 trigger-happy, militaristic

贖²³ [赎] Shells/money 貝¹⁵⁰ and peddle 賣¹⁵⁰ (phonetic). 動 redeem 贖金 shújīn 名 ransom 贖罪 shúzuì 動 atone for sins

續²⁴ [续] Thread 糸¹⁵³ with 賣¹⁵⁰ phonetic. 動 continue, extend: 續約 renew a contract ⇔ 持續⁸, 斷續⁸², 繼續⁸⁹, 陸續⁶⁸, 延續⁸⁹, 手續, 連續。

竇²⁵ [窦] Hole 穴⁹¹ with 賣¹⁵⁰ phonetic. 名 hole, burrow ⇔ 疑竇⁷³

具²⁶ Hands 廾¹⁹ accumulating shell money 貝¹⁵⁰ (abbreviated). 動 prepare 動 own, possess 名 tool 量 measureword for equipment ⇔ 炊具, 玩具, 茶具, 工具, 用具, 陽具, 文具, 餐具, 面具, 家

字譜及字典

貝 150 (character tree)
貳₁₁ 賠₁₂₉ 資₇₉ 賂₁₂₈ 賓₁₅₅ 貨₇₂ 舅⁴ 賄₁₂₂
賽₁₃₄ 贍₁₇₈ 販₁₀₈ 賑₂₃₈ 贏₇₁ 眼₄₅ 寶₂₄ 貼₁₃₅
貞₃₄ 貿₈₂ 賀₆₇ 貧₅₇ 貯₂₀ 貪⁷⁷ 賒₄₄ 賤₄₆
貸₅₆ 賣⁵¹ 質₇₃ 貽₁₇ 賞₁₇⁰ 財³¹ 費⁶⁶ 賁₆₆
貶₇₈ 實₃₃ 賭₁₆₀ 貴³⁹ 賴⁵⁶ 臟₁₁₇ 貶 賦₁₃₄
贅₂₄₅ 賢₂₆ 質₃₉ 賺₃₇ 賺₁₅ 貴 賢¹⁹ 贈¹⁴⁴
頁₁₄₆ 賊₁₂₅ 贖₁₅₀ 賡₁₆₂ 賜⁷ 購₁₇₅

呂 151 / 侶 151₂ / 鋁 151₃ / 閭 151₄ — 櫚 151₅ / 宮 151₆

克 152₁ / 剋 152₂ / 兢 152₃

糸 153₁ / 絲 153₂ / 繼 153₃ / 戀 153₄ / 變 153₅ / 蠻 153₆ / 彎 153₇ — 灣 153₈ / 顯 153₁₀ / 濕 153₁₁ / 系 153₁₂ / 係 153₁₃ / 素 153₁₄ / 孫⁵⁵ 縣₁₄₆ / 率 153₁₅ / 摔 153₁₆ / 蟀 153₁₇
聯⁵⁹ 玆⁷⁵ 昴 153₉

具₁₅₅
具備 jùbèi 🈯 have, possess
具體 jùtǐ 🈺 concrete, specific
具有 jùyǒu 🈯 have, possess

俱 150 27 People 人 ₁₀ have
具₁₅₀ (phonetic). 🈺 all ⇔

傢俱₁₅₅
俱樂部 jùlèbù 🈺 club

颶 150 28 [飓] Wind 風 ⁴⁷ with
具₁₅₀ phonetic. 🈺 hurricane
颶風 jùfēng 🈺 hurricane,
cyclone

算 150 suàn
算 29 Bamboo 竹 ⁷₁ abacus
for counting hoard 具₁₅₀. 🈺
calculate, count 🈺 count as
⇔ 就算⁴₆, 計算₃₁, 估算⁴₆,
打算³⁶, 合算⁴⁵, 划算₅₀, 淸
算⁷₉, 預算₁₀², 盤算⁴⁷, 勝
算₁₂⁷, 總算₁₄₄

算錯 suàncuò 🈺 miscalculate
算法 suànfǎ 🈺 calculation
method
算計 suànjì 🈺 calculate 🈺
scheme
算了 suànle 🈺 Forget it!
算命 suànmìng 🈺 tell fortunes:
算命人 fortune teller; 手相
算命 palmistry
算盤 suànpán 🈺 abacus
算數 suànshù 🈺 count, stand:
他說話是算數的. His word
counts.
算術 suànshù 🈺 arithmetic
算帳 suànzhàng 🈺 settle
accounts

篡 150 cuàn
篡 30 Calculate 算₁₅₀ (pho-
netic) for one's selfish 厶 ₁₉
ends. 🈺 usurp
篡奪 cuàndúo 🈺 usurp, seize
篡位 cuànwèi 🈺 usurp: 篡位者
usurper

纂 150 zuǎn
纂 31 Thread 糸₁₅₃ with
算₁₅₀ phonetic. 🈺 compile
⇔ 編纂¹₁₅

呂 151 lǚ
呂 1 [呂] Pictograph of
vertebrae. 🈺 a surname

侶 151 lǚ
侶 2 [侣] People 人 ₁₀
linked like vertebrae 呂₁₅₁
(phonetic). 🈺 spouse, companion ⇔ 情侶⁸₆, 伴侶⁹⁷,
僧侶¹²⁴

鋁 151 lǚ
鋁 3 [铝] Metal 金 ³⁴ with
呂₁₅₁ phonetic. 🈺 aluminum

閭 151 lú
4 [闾] People linked like vertebrae 呂|51 (phonetic) behind gate 門7. 图 ⑰ village gate 图 ⑰ group of twenty-five households

櫚 151 lú
5 [榈] Tree 木7 in groups like villagers 閭|51 (phonetic). 图 palm tree ⇔ 棕櫚5,

宮 151 gōng
6 [宫] Connected rooms 口6" (written as 呂|51) under a roof 宀63. 图 palace ⇔ 皇宮2?, 故宮3?, 子宮15, 白宮76

宮殿 gōngdiàn 图 palace

克 152 kè
1 Pictograph of roof on supports. ⑪ shoulder, bear ⑪ repress, subdue ⑪ overcome 图 gram ⇔ 尼克森?, 伊拉克?, 公克?, 巧克力?, 夾克?, 坦克?, 休克?, 捷克?, 撲克?, 馬克?, 馬克思?, 烏克蘭?

克服 kèfú ⑪ overcome
克制 kèzhì ⑪ restrain

剋 152 kè
2 [克152] Subdue 克152 (phonetic) with knife 刀|52 (originally strength 力74). ⑪ overcome

剋星 kèxīng 图 unlucky star, nemesis

兢 152 jīng
3 Brothers 兄12 with ?7 (altered) phonetic. ⑪ dread

兢兢業業 jīngjīngyèyè ⑱ cautious and fearful

糸 153 mì
1 Pictograph of threads twisted together. 图 fine thread

絲 153 sī
2 [丝] Threads 糸|53 twisted together. 图 silk 图

thread, fiber ⇔ 鋼絲?, 真絲?, 鐵絲?, 仿絲?, 螺絲?, 肉絲|52

絲綢 sīchóu 图 silk: 絲綢之路 Silk Road

絲毫 sīháo 图 the slightest, the least bit: 絲毫無關 completely unrelated

絲絨 sīróng 图 velvet

繼 153 lián
3 Words 言? tangled like threads 糸|53. ㊀ continuous ㊀ chaotic

戀 153 liàn
4 [恋] Unbroken ?|53 (phonetic) heart 心? (originally woman 女7). ⑪ love ⇔ 眷戀?, 畸戀?, 初戀?, 留戀?, 迷戀?

戀愛 liànài 图 love: 談戀愛 fall in love

戀棧 liànzhàn ⑪ refuse to leave a position

變 153 biàn
5 [变] Strike 攵74 with ?|53 phonetic. ⑪ change, alter ⑪ transform, become ⇔ 蛻變?, 衍變?, 改變?, 轉變?, 演變?, 事變?, 政變?, 叛變|?, 嘩變|?

變成 biànchéng ⑪ become, transform into
變得 biànde ⑪ become
變動 biàndòng ⑪ change, vary 图 fluctuation, variance
變法 biànfǎ 图 political reform
變革 biàngé ⑪ reform
變更 biàngēng ⑪ change, modify
變化 biànhuà ⑪ change, transform 图 change, transformation
變壞 biànhuài ⑪ deteriorate, worsen
變換 biànhuàn ⑪ convert (money) ⑪ vary, switch
變幻 biànhuàn ⑪ fluctuate
變節 biànjié ⑪ desert (a cause), betray

變遷 biànqiān ⑪ change, evolve
變數 biànshù 图 variable
變態 biàntài ⑱ abnormal, perverted
變通 biàntōng ⑪ adjust to fit specific conditions
變為 biànwéi ⑪ change into
變相 biànxiàng ⑱ disguised
變壓器 biànyāqì 图 transformer

蠻 153 mán
6 [蛮] Chaos ?|53 (phonetic) in land of snakes and insects 虫|25. 图 barbarians to the south ⑱ barbaric ⑱ very, extremely: 蠻好 very good ⇔ 刁蠻?, 野蠻|52

蠻橫 mánhèng ⑱ unreasonable, arbitrary: 蠻橫的態度 unreasonable attitude

彎 153 wān
7 [弯] Bow 弓65 with ?|53 phonetic. ⑱ bent ⑪ bend, curve ⇔ 拐彎?, 轉彎?

彎曲 wānqū ⑱ winding, bent

灣 153 wān
8 [湾] Water 水? curved 彎|53 (phonetic). 图 bay, gulf 图 bend in a stream ⇔ 海灣?, 台灣?, 臺灣|?

顯 153 xiǎn
9 Silk threads 糸|53 in the sunlight 日76. ㊀ visible, apparent (⇨ 顯|53)

顯 153 xiǎn
10 [显] Prominent ?|53 (phonetic) forehead 頁|?. ⑱ eminent ⑱ apparent, evident ⑪ show, display ⇔ 彰顯?, 凸顯?, 明顯?

顯出 xiǎnchū ⑪ appear, show, highlight
顯得 xiǎnde ⑪ appear, look
顯赫 xiǎnhè ⑱ influential, illustrious, prominent
顯露 xiǎnlù ⑪ unveil, reveal
顯明 xiǎnmíng ⑱ obvious

糸 153

綜 縕 經 線 繡 網 綱 紫 縱 絡
緯 紕 綴 紐 級 紳 糾 絢 納 紗
索 結 絕 紛 紉 紹 縈 緞 緣 彝
綠 終 給 緘 絨 繹 辮 紅 繁 統
紀 繼 約 純 織 緝 緬 縛 網 繞
絆 絹 綱 絹 紳 綽 緻 綢 綿 繞
絮 縈 紮 綻 絆 紡 緻 紋 素 紙
紓 絞 綬 紬 絮 纍 編 繪 組 綰
繩 緞 絹 徽 繳 織 繁 紮 細 總 繪
緬 續 纂 維 續 繡 纈 纖 緋

丽 154

丽 麗 儷
灑
曬

豕 155

豕 家 傢
嫁
稼

冢 蒙 檬
琢 朦
啄 濛
家 塚

豪 劇
逐 據
遽

象 遂 隧
豚 邃
隊 墜

狼 豢 豪
毅 象 豬

顯著 xiǎnzhù marked, remarkable

濕 11 [溼] Water 水 with 㬎 phonetic. damp, moist, humid, wet dampen, wet ⇔ 潮濕

濕度 shīdù humidity
濕潤 shīrùn moist, damp moisten, dampen

系 153 xì 12 Pull ノ (phonetic) a thread 糸. line, connection series department: 經濟系 economics department ⇔ 語系, 父系, 母系, 星系, 體系, 茶系, 派系

系列 xìliè series, sequence
系統 xìtǒng system: 系統化 systematize, systematic

係 153 xì 13 [系] People 人 connected 系 (phonetic). belong to tie, bind be ⇔ 關係

係數 xìshù coefficient

素 153 sù 14 Thread 糸 shining like berry-laden branches 主. raw silk simple, pure vegetarian diet ⇔ 元素, 酵素, 要素, 因素, 吃素, 激素, 樸素

素材 sùcái source material
素餐 sùcān vegetarian meal
素來 sùlái always usually
素描 sùmiáo sketch, outline
素食 sùshí vegetarian food: 素食餐館 vegetarian restaurant
素質 sùzhí quality

率 153 shuài lǜ 15 Pictograph showing threads, based on 糸, surrounded by marks representing frame. net shuài: lead, command rash,

hasty 📖 generally lǜ: 📖 rate, ratio: 增長率 growth rate ⇔ 輕率 🗝, 稅率 🗝, 比率 🗝, 效率 🗝, 機率 🗝, 坦率 🗝, 草率 🗝, 頻率 🗝, 利率 🗝, 粗率 🗝, 匯率 🗝
率領 shuàilǐng 🗝 lead

摔 153 shuāi
16 Hand 手 🗝 acting rashly 率 🗝 (phonetic). 🗝 throw to the ground 🗝 break 🗝 fall down, stumble
摔倒 shuāidǎo 🗝 fall down
摔跤 shuāijiāo 🗝 trip and fall down 🗝 wrestle

蟀 153 shuài
17 Modern form shows insect 虫 🗝 with 率 🗝 phonetic. 📖 cricket ⇔ 蟋蟀 🗝

丽 154 lì
1 Pictograph of two objects, possibly deer skins or antlers.

麗 154 lì
2 [丽] Deer 鹿 🗝 moving in pairs 丽 🗝 (phonetic). 🗝 elegant, beautiful 🗝 絢麗 🗝, 秀麗 🗝, 俏麗 🗝, 豔麗 🗝, 壯麗 🗝, 美麗 🗝, 瑰麗 🗝, 華麗 🗝

儷 154 lì
3 [俪] People 人 🗝 in elegant pair 麗 🗝 (phonetic). 📖 pair, couple ⇔ 伉儷 🗝

灑 154 sǎ
4 [洒 🗝] Water 水 🗝 dispersed like prancing deer 麗 🗝. 🗝 splash, sprinkle ⇔ 瀟灑 🗝
灑脫 sǎtuō 📖 carefree 📖 generous

曬 154 shài
5 [晒 🗝] Sun's 日 🗝 rays like prancing deer 麗 🗝. Simplified form uses 西 🗝. 🗝 dry by sunlight: 曬太陽 to sun
曬乾 shàigān 🗝 dry by sunlight
曬黑 shàihēi 🗝 tan

豕 155 shǐ
1 Pictograph of a boar. 📖 boar, pig

家 155 jiā
2 Roof 宀 🗝 over pig 豕 🗝 (phonetic from 豭 abbreviated). 📖 household, family 📖 home, house 📖 specialist: 經濟學家 economist 📖 a measureword for stores ⇔ 住家 🗝, 人家 🗝, 客家 🗝, 老人家 🗝, 畫家 🗝, 作家 🗝, 持家 🗝, 世家 🗝, 全家 🗝, 分家 🗝, 大家 🗝, 法家 🗝, 行家 🗝, 成家 🗝, 國家 🗝, 我家 🗝, 親家 🗝, 專家 🗝, 回家 🗝, 百家爭鳴 🗝, 看家 🗝, 搬家 🗝, 自家 🗝, 酒家 🗝, 儒家 🗝
家常 jiācháng 🗝 relating to ordinary domestic life
家畜 jiāchù 🗝 domestic animal
家電 jiādiàn 🗝 household appliances
家計 jiājì 📖 family livelihood
家教 jiājiào 📖 tutor 📖 upbringing
家境 jiājìng 📖 family financial situation
家具 jiājù 📖 furniture
家眷 jiājuàn 📖 dependents
家裡 jiālǐ 📖 home 📖 family: 你家裡有幾個人？ How many people are in your family?
家譜 jiāpǔ 📖 family tree, genealogy
家人 jiārén 📖 family members
家事 jiāshì 📖 family affairs
家書 jiāshū 📖 letter home 📖 letter from home
家屬 jiāshǔ 📖 family members
家庭 jiātíng 📖 family: 家庭主婦 housewife
家務 jiāwù 📖 household chores
家鄉 jiāxiāng 📖 hometown
家長 jiāzhǎng 📖 head of household: 家長風格 paternalistic
家族 jiāzú 📖 clan

傢 155 jiā
3 [家 🗝] Person 人 🗝 and home 家 🗝 (phonetic). 📖 furniture
傢伙 jiāhuǒ 📖 tools, equipment 📖 guy
傢俱 jiājù 📖 furniture (⇨ 家具 🗝)

嫁 155 jià
4 Woman 女 🗝 and family 家 🗝 (phonetic). 🗝 marry (a man) ⇔ 陪嫁 🗝
嫁給 jiàgěi 🗝 marry (a man)
嫁禍 jiàhuò 🗝 shift blame
嫁妝 jiàzhuāng 📖 dowry

稼 155 jià
5 Grain 禾 🗝 requiring work of whole family 家 🗝 (phonetic). 🗝 sow ⇔ 莊稼 🗝

冡 155 méng
6 Boar 豕 🗝 covered/ trapped 冂 🗝. 🈁 cover

蒙 155 méng 🈁 měng mǒng
7 Plant 艸 🗝 that covers 冡 🗝. 📖 a parasitic plant 🗝 cover 🗝 deceive, cheat ⇔ 荷爾蒙 🗝, 啟蒙 🗝
蒙古 ménggǔ 🈁 Mongolia: 蒙古包 yurt
蒙混 ménghùn 🗝 hoodwink
蒙羞 méngxiū 🗝 be humiliated

檬 155 méng
8 Tree 木 🗝 with 蒙 🗝 phonetic. 🗝 lemon ⇔ 檸檬 🗝

朦 155 méng
9 Moon 月 🗝 covered 蒙 🗝 (phonetic). 📖 moon's appearance at moonset
朦朧 ménglóng 🈁 hazy, dim

濛 155 méng
10 Water 水 🗝 covering 蒙 🗝 (phonetic). 🈁 misty
濛濛 méngméng 🈁 misty

豖 155 zhuó
11 Boar 豕 🗝 with two bound legs.

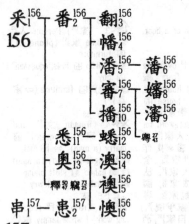

采₁156 番₂156 翻₃156
156
幡₄156
潘₅156 藩₆156
審₇156 嬸₈156
播₁₀156 潘₉156
悉₁₁156 蟋₁₂156 粵₄₃27
奧₁₃156 澳₁₄156
襖₁₅156
釋₃₉27 癇₄₁27
串₁157 患₂157 懊₁₆156

157

琢₁₂ 155 zhuó
Jade 玉₁₀₇ with 豖₁₅₅ phonetic and suggestive of slowness. 🔒 carve
琢磨 zhuómó 🔒 cut and polish (jade) 🔒 polish (written work)

啄₁₃ 155 zhuó
Mouth 口₆₈ with 豖₁₅₅ phonetic. 🔒 peck
啄木鳥 zhuómùniǎo 🔒 woodpecker

冢₁₄ 155 zhǒng
Bound boar 豖₁₅₅ enwrapped 勹₁₈. 🔒 grave

塚₁₅ 155 zhǒng
[冢] Earth 土₇₆ grave 冢₁₅₅ (phonetic). 🔒 grave ⇔ 荒塚₈₆, 義塚₅₉

豦₁₆ 155 qú
Tiger 虍₁₂₂ and boar 豖₁₅₅ fighting. 🔒 ceaseless fighting

劇₁₇ 155 jù
[剧] Ceaseless fight 豦₁₅₅ (phonetic) and knife 刀₈₅. Simplified form uses 居₇₁. 🔒 intense drama, play ⇔ 急劇₄₄, 京劇₆, 歌劇₈₇, 平劇₄₁, 加劇₂₁, 國

劇₃₆, 慘劇₂₆, 戲劇₈₉, 喜劇₆₆, 悲劇₁₀₉
劇本 jùběn 🔒 script
劇場 jùchǎng 🔒 theater
劇烈 jùliè 🔒 fierce, severe
劇院 jùyuàn 🔒 theater

據₁₈ 155 jù
[据] Hand 手₉₉ and vicious fight 豦₁₅₅ (phonetic). Simplified form uses 居₇₁. 🔒 seize, occupy 🔒 according to: 據我所知 as far as I know ⇔ 根據₆₃, 收據₃₁, 憑據₈₇, 佔據₄₂, 數據₉₅, 證據₉₂, 依據₁₂₆, 盤據₁₂₉
據稱 jùchēng 🔒 it is said, reportedly
據點 jùdiǎn 🔒 base, stronghold
據說 jùshuō 🔒 it is said, reportedly
據悉 jùxī 🔒 reportedly

遽₁₉ 155 jù
Movement 辵₉₁ with 豦₁₅₅ phonetic. 🔒 stagecoach 🔒 hurriedly ⇔ 急遽₄₄
遽然 jùrán 🔒 suddenly

逐₂₀ 155 zhú
Movement 辵₉₁ after boar 豕₁₅₅. 🔒 chase, pursue

🔒 gradually ⇔ 驅逐₈₉, 放逐₉₂, 角逐₁₄₉, 追逐₆₇
逐步 zhúbù 🔒 step by step
逐漸 zhújiàn 🔒 gradually
逐年 zhúnián 🔒 year by year
逐一 zhúyī 🔒 one by one
逐字 zhúzì 🔒 word by word, verbatim

彖₂₁ 155 suì
Split up 八₇ pigs 豕₁₅₅ into groups. 🔒 follow

遂₂₂ 155 suì
Movement 辵₉₁ and follow 彖₁₅₅ (phonetic). 🔒 proceed 🔒 succeed, satisfy ⇔ 未遂₂₇

隧₂₃ 155 suì
[隧] Proceed 遂₁₅₅ (phonetic) through a hill 阜₁₆₇. 🔒 tunnel
隧道 suìdào 🔒 tunnel

邃₂₄ 155 suì
Hole 穴₈₁ with 遂₁₅₅ phonetic. 🔒 deep, profound ⇔ 深邃₄₃

隊₂₅ 155 duì
[队] Follow 彖₁₅₅ from hill 阜₁₆₇. Simplified form uses person 人₁₀. 🔒 fall 🔒 troops 🔒 group, team ⇔ 神風隊₇₅, 大隊₂₉, 啦啦隊₂₇, 樂隊₈₇, 捕隊₉₉, 艦隊₁₄₂, 軍隊₅₈, 排隊₉₉
隊伍 duìwǔ 🔒 troops
隊員 duìyuán 🔒 team member
隊長 duìzhǎng 🔒 captain

墜₂₆ 155 zhuì
[坠] Fall 隊₁₅₅ (phonetic) to ground 土₇₆. 🔒 fall, sink, crash
墜毀 zhuìhuǐ 🔒 crash to the ground
墜落 zhuìluò 🔒 fall, drop

豚₂₇ 155 tún
Flesh 肉₁₃₂ and pig 豕₁₅₅. 🔒 piglet ⇔ 海豚₉₄

采₁ 156 biàn
Pictograph of claw

marks. ㊁ differentiate, determine

番2 fān Impression of claws 采|⁵⁶ and sole (resembling 田|'). ㊀ paw (now 蹯) type ㊁ time: 三番五次 repeatedly ㊂ ㊃ barbarian ⇔ 翻番|⁵⁶

番茄 fānqié ㊁ tomato: 番茄醬 ketchup

番薯 fānshǔ ㊁ sweet potato, yam

翻3 fān Repeated 番|⁵⁶ (phonetic) flapping of wings 羽|²⁴. ㊀ fly ㊁ flip ㊂ search through, skim ㊃ translate ㊄ double ⇔ 推翻|¹⁶²

翻案 fānàn ㊁ overturn a ruling

翻船 fānchuán ㊁ capsize

翻番 fānfān ㊀ ㊃ double

翻臉 fānliǎn ㊀ turn hostile

翻身 fānshēn ㊀ turn over ㊁ ㊃ be liberated

翻譯 fānyì ㊁ translation ㊂ translate: 翻譯成英文 translate into English; 同步翻譯 simultaneous translation

幡4 fān Cloth 巾|⁵³ with 番|⁵⁶ phonetic. ㊁ pennant

幡然 fānrán ㊂ suddenly

潘5 pān Water 水|³₂ changed repeatedly 番|⁵⁶ (phonetic). ㊀ water in which rice is washed ㊁ a surname

藩6 fān Plant 艸|⁹⁶ with 潘|⁵⁶ phonetic. ㊁ hedge

藩籬 fánlí ㊁ fence, hedge ㊂ barrier

審7 shěn [审] Cover 宀|⁶³ and differentiate 番|⁵⁶. Simplified form uses 申|³₆. ㊀ know thoroughly ㊁ examine, study ⇔ 陪審|⁶², 評審|²⁷

審查 shěnchá ㊁ investigate, examine

審核 shěnhé ㊁ audit

審判 shěnpàn ㊁ try (a case) ㊂ trial

審慎 shěnshèn ㊃ cautious, careful, prudent

審訊 shěnxùn ㊀ try, interrogate: 秘密審訊 secret trial

審議 shěnyì ㊀ review, deliberate, consider

嬸8 shěn [婶] Woman 女|⁵⁴ with 審|⁵⁶ phonetic. ㊁ aunt, sister-in-law

嬸嬸 shěnshen ㊁ aunt (wife of father's younger brother)

瀋9 shěn [沈] Water 水|³₂ with 審|⁵⁶ phonetic. ㊁ juice

瀋陽 shěnyáng ㊁ Shenyang (Mukden) - capital of Liaoning Province: 瀋陽事件 Mukden Incident

播10 bō bò Hand 手|⁹⁷ with 番|⁵⁶ (alternate pronunciation) phonetic. bō,bò: ㊀ sow ⇔ 主播|₂, 廣播|⁴⁰, 轉播|⁹², 傳播|²², 散播|⁴⁸

播出 bōchū ㊀ broadcast

播放 bōfàng ㊀ broadcast

播送 bōsòng ㊀ transmit

播音 bōyīn ㊀ broadcast

播種 bōzhǒng,bòzhòng ㊀ sow seeds

悉11 xī Mind/heart 心|⁸³ determining 采|⁵⁶. ㊁ know ⇔ 熟悉|⁴⁸, 洞悉|²⁴, 據悉|¹⁶⁵

蟋12 xī Insect 虫|¹²⁵ with 悉|⁵⁶ phonetic. ㊁ cricket

蟋蟀 xīshuài ㊁ cricket

奥13 ào [奥] Differentiate 采|⁵⁶ in house 宀|⁶³ with hands 廾|⁴⁹. Simplified form uses 米|³⁸. ㊁ dark corner of a house ㊃ mysterious

奥地利 àodìlì ㊁ Austria

奥祕 àomì ㊁ profound mystery

奥妙 àomiào ㊂ mysterious ㊃ marvelous ㊄ subtle

奥運 àoyùn ㊁ Olympics

澳14 ào [澳] Water 水|³₂ deep and mysterious 奥|⁵⁶ (phonetic). ㊁ deep inlet ⇔ 港澳|¹⁶

澳大利亞 àodàlìyǎ ㊁ Australia

澳門 àomén ㊁ Macau

澳洲 àozhōu ㊁ Australia

襖15 ǎo [袄] Clothing 衣|²⁶ with 奥|⁵⁶ phonetic. Simplified form uses 夭|⁹⁷. ㊁ short traditional coat ⇔ 棉襖|⁷⁶

懊16 ào [懊] Heart 心|⁸³ in darkness 奥|⁵⁶ (phonetic). ㊃ remorseful

懊惱 àonǎo ㊃ displeased

串1 chuàn Pictograph of objects strung together. ㊁ string together ㊂ string, cluster ㊃ run about: 串門子 chat with neighbors ⇔ 肉串|¹⁷², 連串|⁹⁸

串連 chuànlián ㊀ ally with

串通 chuàntōng ㊀ collude, conspire

患2 huàn String 串|⁵⁷ (phonetic) of troubles for the heart 心|⁸³. ㊀ worry ㊁ suffer from ⇔ 病患|⁴⁸, 禍患|¹³³, 罹患|¹⁶²

患病 huànbìng ㊀ fall ill, get sick

患難 huànnàn ㊁ adversity, troubles

患友 huànyǒu ㊀ fall ill with

患者 huànzhě ㊁ sufferer, patient

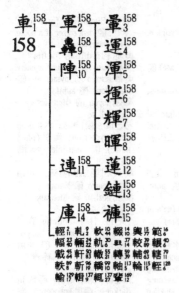

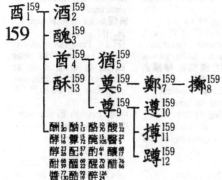

車把 chēbǎ 图 handle bars
車道 chēdào 图 lane
車費 chēfèi 图 transit fare
車禍 chēhùo 图 traffic accident
車間 chējiān 图 workshop
車庫 chēkù 图 garage
車輛 chēliàng 图 vehicle
車票 chēpiào 图 ticket (for bus or train)
車廂 chēxiāng 图 train car
車站 chēzhàn 图 station: 火車站 train station
車子 chēzi 图 car, vehicle

軍 2 [军] jūn Encompassing 勹 (altered to resemble 冖) chariots 車 (phonetic). army, military ⇔ 駐軍, 冠軍, 殿軍, 紅軍, 空軍, 海軍, 聯軍, 陸軍, 將軍

軍備 jūnbèi 图 armaments
軍隊 jūndùi 图 troops, army, military
軍閥 jūnfá 图 warlord
軍費 jūnfèi 图 military expenses
軍官 jūnguān 图 military officer
軍火 jūnhǔo 图 armaments
軍人 jūnrén 图 soldier
軍事 jūnshì 图 military matters
軍裝 jūnzhuāng 图 military uniform

暈 3 [晕] yùn yūn Circles sun 日 like an army 軍 (phonetic). yùn: 图 halo 图 dizzy yūn: 图 feel faint 图 feel dizzy ⇔ 頭暈

暈車 yùnchē 图 feel carsick
暈倒 yūndǎo 图 faint
暈眩 yūnxuàn 图 dizzy

運 4 [运] yùn Troops 軍 (phonetic) on the move 辵. 图 transport Simplified form uses 云. 图 use 图 luck,

車, 列車, 臥車, 纜車, 暈車, 馬車

車 1 [车] chē jū [车] Pictograph of a chariot viewed from above with wheels at top and bottom. chē: 图 cart, chariot 图 vehicle jū: 图 a chesspiece ⇔ 三輪車, 卡車, 水車, 客車, 貨車, 煞車, 塞車, 公車, 騎車, 計程車, 招車, 停車, 搭便車, 拖車, 機車, 吊車, 腳踏車, 堵車, 撞車, 開車, 汽車, 火車, 飆車, 牛車, 轎

fortune ⇔ 貨運[13], 學運[58], 厄運[58], 航運[86], 命運[57], 幸運[58], 好運[58], 營運[87], 捷運[58], 民運[19], 搬運[175], 奧運[19]

運動 yùndòng 動 exercise sports, athletics: 運動員 athlete 图 movement, campaign: 學生運動 student movement

運河 yùnhé 图 canal: 大運河 Grand Canal

運氣 yùnqì 图 luck

運輸 yùnshū 動 transport

運用 yùnyòng 動 utilize, apply

運作 yùnzuò 動 operations

渾 158 hún
5 [浑] Water 水[58] with 軍[58] phonetic. 形 muddy 形 complete

渾蛋 húndàn 图 ⓤ damn fool

渾沌 húndùn 图 chaos

渾身 húnshēn 副 all over, head to toe

揮 158 huī
6 [挥] Hand 手[99] leading an army 軍[58] (phonetic). 動 dispatch (an army) 動 wield, brandish 動 wave 動 wipe away ⇔ 指揮[58], 發揮[82]

揮動 huīdòng 動 wield, brandish

揮霍 huīhuò 動 squander

揮手 huīshǒu 動 wave

輝 158 huī
7 [辉] Bright 光[42] army 軍[58] (phonetic). 图 splendor, luster ⇔ 光輝[42]

輝煌 huīhuáng 形 glorious

輝映 huīyìng 動 reflect, shine

暉 158 huī
8 [晖] Sun 日[76] shining like an army 軍[58] (phonetic). 图 sunshine 形 radiant

轟 158 hōng
9 [轰] Sound of many carts 車[158]. Simplified form uses 雙[162] simplification. 動 rumble 動 bomb

轟動 hōngdòng 動 cause a sensation

轟炸 hōngzhà 動 bomb

陣 158 zhèn
10 [阵] Modern form shows hill 阜[167] and chariot 車[158]. 图 battle formation gust, spell, burst, puff ⇔ 一陣子, 矩陣[35]

陣腳 zhènjiǎo 图 position, situation

陣容 zhènróng 图 cast, lineup

陣線 zhènxiàn 图 battle line

陣營 zhènyíng 图 camp

陣雨 zhènyǔ 图 rainstorm, shower

連 158 lián
11 [连] Carts 車[158] moving 足[9]. 動 connect, join 動 successively 介 with, including 副 even ⇔ 接連[91], 流連忘返[55], 牽連[80], 株連[22], 串連[57]

連串 liánchuàn 图 series, string of

連詞 liáncí 图 conjunction

連帶 liándài 形 involved, related:
連帶責任 joint responsibility

連貫 liánguàn 動 link up 形 coherent, continuous: 連貫性 continuity

連接 liánjiē 動 link, connect

連結 liánjié 動 join together

連累 liánlèi 動 bring trouble

連忙 liánmáng 副 hurriedly

連綿 liánmián 形 unbroken, continuous

連任 liánrèn 動 serve another term

連鎖 liánsuǒ 图 chain: 連鎖反應 chain reaction; 連鎖商店 chain store

連繫 liánxì 動 contact 動 stay in touch

連續 liánxù 形 continuous: 連續劇 drama series, soap opera 副 continually

蓮 158 lián
12 [莲] Plant 艸[26] that is interconnected 連[158] (phonetic). 图 lotus ⇔ 花蓮[57]

蓮花 liánhuā 图 lotus

鏈 158 liàn
13 [链] Metal 金[14] connecting 連[158] (phonetic). 图 a metal alloy 图 chain

鏈條 liàntiáo 图 chain

鏈子 liànzi 图 chain

庫 158 kù
14 [库] Chariot 車[158] in a shed 广[97]. 图 storehouse ⇔ 水庫[58], 倉庫[52], 國庫[10], 車庫[158]

庫存 kùcún 图 stock

褲 158 kù
15 [裤] Modern form shows clothing 衣[126] with 庫[158] phonetic. 图 pants ⇔ 短褲[49]

褲子 kùzi 图 pants

酉 159 yǒu
1 Pictograph of a wine vase. 图 liquor (⇨ 酒[159]) 图 tenth Earthly Branch (⇨ 干支[1])

酒 159 jiǔ
2 Alcohol 酉[159] (phonetic) with water 水[58] redundant. 图 liquor, wine, alcohol ⇔ 陪酒[82], 酗酒[85], 嗜酒[13], 啤酒[45], 敬酒[85], 私酒[17], 喝酒[45], 汾酒[37], 戒酒[75], 喜酒[50], 白酒[77], 雞尾酒[103], 茅台酒[105], 香檳酒[49], 菸酒[12], 烈酒[55], 米酒[138]

酒吧 jiǔbā 图 bar

酒保 jiǔbǎo 图 bartender

酒店 jiǔdiàn 图 tavern, bar

酒鬼 jiǔguǐ 图 alcoholic

酒酣耳熱 jiǔhāněrrè 成 inebriated

酒家 jiǔjiā 图 bar: 酒家女 图 bar girl 图 restaurant

酒精 jiǔjīng 图 alcohol: 酒精度 proof; 酒精含量 alcohol content

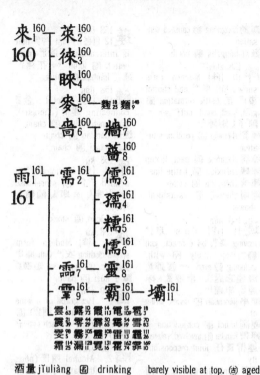

來₁ 160 — 萊₂ 160
160 — 徠₃ 160
— 睞₄ 160
— 麥₅ 160 — 麴₁₈₂₃ 麵₉ 146
— 嗇₆ 160 — 牆₇ 160
— 薔₈ 160

雨₁ 161 — 需₂ 161 — 儒₃ 161
161 — 孺₄ 161
— 糯₅ 161
— 懦₆ 161
— 霝₇ 161 — 靈₈ 161
— 霍₉ 161 — 霸₁₀ 161 — 壩₁₁ 161

雲 63 露 173 霞 114 電 72 霜 73
霽 84 雰 74 霹 50 霖 84 雪 70
雯 90 霧 105 靂 108 雷 113 霾 111
霜 114 漏 11 霓 16 霍 74 罪 10

酒量 jǐuliàng 图 drinking capacity

酒色財氣 jǐusècáiqì 图 material temptations - wine, sex, wealth, and power

酒肆 jǐusì 图 图 tavern

酒席 jǐuxí 图 feast, banquet

酒醉 jǐuzùi 图 drunk

醜₃ 159 chǒu [丑] Alcohol 酉 159 (phonetic) and demon 鬼 ?. 图 vile 图 ugly

醜惡 chǒuè 图 repulsive

醜陋 chǒulòu 图 ugly

醜聞 chǒuwén 图 scandal: 性醜聞 sex scandal

酋₄ 159 qíu 图 Wine vase 酉 159 (phonetic) with liquid 水 ?

barely visible at top. 图 aged rice wine 图 chief

酋長 qíuzhǎng 图 chief

猶₅ 159 yóu [犹] Animal/dog 犬 ? with 酋 159 phonetic. Simplified form uses 尤 ?. 图 a kind of monkey 图 like, as if

猶如 yóurú 图 like, as if

猶太 yóutài 图 Judaea 图 Jewish: 猶太教 Judaism; 猶太人 Jew

猶豫 yóuyù 图 hesitate

奠₆ 159 diàn Wine 酋 159 offering on a pedestal 丌 ? (altered to resemble 大 ?). 图 offer libations 图 establish

奠定 diàndìng 图 establish

奠儀 diànyí 图 funeral gift money

鄭₇ 159 zhèng [郑] City 邑 ? with 奠 159 phonetic. 图 name of an ancient city Simplified form uses 關 ? simplification. 图 solemn, serious 图 a surname

鄭重 zhèngzhòng 图 serious, earnest

擲₈ 159 图 zhí 图 zhì [掷] Modern form shows hand 手 ? with 鄭 159 phonetic. 图 throw ⇔ 投擲 ?

尊₉ 159 zūn Hand 寸 ? offering wine 酋 159. 图 respect, esteem ⇔ 自尊 ?

尊敬 zūnjìng 图 respect

尊嚴 zūnyán 图 dignity, respectability

尊重 zūnzhòng 图 revere, respect, venerate

遵₁₀ 159 zūn Move 辵 ? respectfully 尊 159 (phonetic). 图 abide by

遵從 zūncóng 图 follow, adhere to

遵守 zūnshǒu 图 obey

遵循 zūnxún 图 follow, abide by

撙₁₁ 159 zūn Hand 手 ? with 尊 159 phonetic. 图 economize, save

撙節 zǔnjié 图 economize

蹲₁₂ 159 dūn Foot 足 ? with 尊 159 phonetic. 图 squat

蹲下 dūnxià 图 squat

酥₁₃ 159 sū Vase 酉 159 with 禾 ?, abbreviated from 酥 ? phonetic. 图 shortening

酥餅 sūbǐng 图 shortcake cookies

來₁ 160 lái [来] Pictograph of ears of wheat hanging from a

wheat plant. Original meaning of wheat has been assumed by its derivate 麥¹⁶⁰, while modern meaning is from its derivative 徠¹⁶⁰. ⇔ come, arrive ⊛ next ⇔ 往來⁴⁸, 上來⁴⁵, 下來⁵⁶, 原來⁵⁶, 從來⁹⁵, 反過來⁶⁷, 少來⁹⁷, 邇來⁴⁹, 胡來⁵⁹, 到來⁷⁷, 後來⁸¹, 拿來⁷⁸, 越來越⁶², 趕來⁸⁰, 帶來⁶⁷, 起來⁹⁷, 以來⁹⁸, 向來⁶⁹, 回來⁹⁷, 用來⁶⁸, 醒來⁵³, 外來⁷⁷, 舶來品⁷⁶, 未來⁷⁴, 本來⁷⁸, 將來⁷⁴, 爬起來⁷⁹, 近來⁹⁵, 出來¹¹⁰, 看來¹⁴⁵, 看起來¹⁴⁵, 愈來愈¹²⁷, 過來¹³⁷, 自來水¹³⁹, 素來¹²³, 進來¹⁶², 歸來¹⁶⁷

來賓 láibīn ⊛ guest

來不及 láibùjí ⊛ too late, impossible

來到 láidào ⊛ arrive

來訪 láifǎng ⊛ come to visit

來回 láihúi ⊛ round-trip: 來回票 round-trip ticket

來歷 láilì ⊛ background, history

來臨 láilín ⊛ arrive, approach

來往 láiwǎng ⊛ contact, interaction

來信 láixìn ⊛ letter ⊛ send a letter here

來源 láiyuán ⊛ source, origin

來自 láizì ⊛ come from

萊 160 lái
2 [莱] Grass 艸⁹⁶ with grain 來¹⁶⁰ phonetic. ⊛ an edible grass times. ⊛ a surname

徠 160 lái
3 [徕] Step 彳⁷⁴ with 來¹⁶⁰ phonetic. ⊛ come (⇔ 來¹⁶⁰) ⊛ solicit ⇔ 招徠²³⁵

睞 160 lài
4 [睐] Eye 目¹¹⁴ with 來¹⁶⁰ phonetic. ⊛ cockeyed ⊛ glance ⇔ 青睞²³

麥 160 mài
5 [麦] Wheat 來¹⁶⁰

(phonetic) crop slowly progressing ⋏ ㈵. ⊛ wheat ⊛ a surname ⇔ 小麥⁴⁷, 丹麥⁹⁷

麥當勞 màidāngláo ⊛ McDonald's

麥片 màipiàn ⊛ oatmeal

嗇 160 sè
6 [啬] Wheat 來¹⁶⁰ stored in granary 靣 ⁸ (abbreviated to 回⁹⁷). ⊛ stingy ⇔ 吝嗇⁶⁴

牆 160 qiáng
7 [墙] Planks 片⁷⁰ (phonetic) protecting hoard 嗇¹⁶⁰. ⊛ wall ⇔ 圍牆⁸⁹, 城牆⁹⁵

牆壁 qiángbì ⊛ wall

牆角 qiángjiǎo ⊛ corner

薔 160 qiáng
8 [蔷] Plant 艸⁹⁶ with 嗇¹⁶⁰ phonetic. (pronunciation altered).

薔薇 qiángwéi ⊛ rose

雨 161 yǔ
1 Pictograph of raindrops falling through a cloud. ⊛ rain ⇔ 下雨⁴⁶, 酸雨⁵³, 暴雨⁶⁵, 豪雨⁹⁷, 風雨⁸⁷, 梅雨⁸⁰, 雷雨¹¹⁵, 陣雨¹⁵⁸

雨季 yǔjì ⊛ rainy season

雨林 yǔlín ⊛ rain forest

雨傘 yǔsǎn ⊛ umbrella

雨水 yǔshuǐ ⊛ rain water, rainfall

雨衣 yǔyī ⊛ raincoat

需 161 xū
2 Rains 雨¹⁶¹ arriving as slow as a growing beard 而¹³⁴. ⊛ need, require ⇔ 急需¹⁴, 供需⁴³, 無需⁷¹, 必需⁷⁹

需求 xūqiú ⊛ need, request

需要 xūyào ⊛ need

儒 161 rú
3 People 人¹⁰ needed 需¹⁶¹ (phonetic). ⊛ scholars ⊛ weak ⊛ Confucian ⇔ 焚書坑儒⁷⁶, 侏儒⁴⁷

儒家 rújiā ⊛ Confucian: 儒家思想 Confucianism

孺 161 rú
4 Children 子⁵⁵ and need 需¹⁶¹ (phonetic). ⊛ breast-feeding infant ⇔ 婦孺³¹

糯 161 nùo
5 Modern form shows rice 米¹³⁸ with 需¹⁶¹ phonetic. ⊛ glutinous rice

糯米 nùomǐ ⊛ glutinous rice

懦 161 nùo
6 Heart 心⁸³ with 需¹⁶¹ phonetic. ⊛ cowardly ⇔ 怯懦²³

懦弱 nùoruò ⊛ cowardly and weak

霝 161 líng
7 Drops (resembling 口⁴⁸) of rain 雨¹⁶¹. ⊛ rainfall

靈 161 líng
8 [灵] Sorcerers 巫³¹ praying for rain 霝¹⁶¹ (phonetic). Simplified form is conflated with a rare character for warmth showing hand 又¹⁴ over fire 火¹². ⊛ spirit, soul ⊛ clever, quick ⊛ good, effective ⇔ 幽靈⁹⁷, 通靈⁹³, 心靈⁸³, 失靈¹⁰⁰

靈丹 língdān ⊛ panacea

靈感 línggǎn ⊛ inspiration

靈魂 línghún ⊛ soul

靈活 línghúo ⊛ flexible ⊛ clever

靈敏 língmǐn ⊛ agile ⊛ clever

靈通 língtōng ⊛ well-informed

鞾 161 bà
9 Leather 革²⁴ in the rain 雨¹⁶¹. ⊛ stretch

霸 161 bà
10 Moon 月⁹⁰ waxing 鞾¹⁶¹ (phonetic). ⊛ dominate ⊛ feudal prince ⇔ 稱霸¹⁷⁵

霸道 bàdào ⊛ tyrannical

霸權 bàquán ⊛ hegemony

霸王 bàwáng ⊛ overlord: 霸王

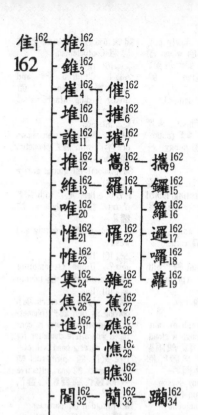

佳₁ 162
162

椎₂ 162
錐₃ 162
崔₄ 162 — 催₅ 162
堆₁₀ 162 — 摧₆ 162
誰₁₁ 162 — 璀₇ 162
推₁₂ 162 — 巂₈ 162 — 攜₉ 162
維₁₃ 162 — 羅₁₄ 162 — 鑼₁₅ 162
唯₂₀ 162 — 籮₁₆ 162
惟₂₁ 162 — 儸₂₂ 162 — 邏₁₇ 162
帷₂₃ 162 — 囉₁₈ 162
集₂₄ 162 — 雜₂₅ 162 — 蘿₁₉ 162
焦₂₆ 162 — 蕉₂₇ 162
進₃₁ 162 — 礁₂₈ 162
憔₂₉ 162
瞧₃₀ 162
闍₃₂ 162 — 蘭₃₃ 162 — 躪₃₄ 162

龍 Tyrranosaurus Rex
霸佔 bàzhàn 🈪 forcibly occupy
霸主 bàzhǔ 🈪 hegemon

壩₁₁ 161 bà
[坝] Earth 土¹⁰ that dominates 霸¹⁶¹₁₀ (phonetic). Simplified form uses 貝¹⁵⁰. 🈐 dam, dike ⇔ 水壩 ₃₃

佳₁ 162 zhūi
Pictograph of a bird with a short tail. 🈐 pigeons and other short-tailed birds

椎₂ 162 zhūi
[槌] Wood 木⁷⁵ with 佳 phonetic. 🈐 mallet 🈐 vertebra ⇔ 脊椎¹³²

錐₃ 162 zhūi
[锥] Metal 金¹⁶⁷ pointy like a bird 佳¹⁶² (phonetic). 🈐 awl 🈐 bore ⇔ 改錐⁵⁷

崔₄ 162 cūi
Mountain 山⁶⁷ with 佳¹⁶² phonetic. 🈐 lofty 🈐 a surname

催₅ 162 cūi
Push person 人⁹ to heights 崔¹⁶² (phonetic). 🈐 press, urge

催促 cūicù 🈪 press, urge
催眠 cūimián 🈪 lull to sleep 🈪 hypnotize

摧₆ 162 cūi
Hand 手⁹⁷ applying high 崔¹⁶² (phonetic) pressure. 🈐 destroy
摧殘 cūicán 🈪 trample
摧毀 cūihǔi 🈪 destroy

璀₇ 162 cūi
Jade 玉¹⁰⁷ with 崔¹⁶² phonetic. 🈐 luster
璀璨 cūicàn 🈐 luster

巂₈ 162 xī
Bird 佳¹⁶² with a crest (altered to resemble 崔¹⁶²) with 罔¹²² phonetic. 🈐 cuckoo

攜₉ 162 🈐 xī 🈐 xié
[携] Hand 手⁹⁷ with 巂¹⁶² phonetic. Simplified form uses 巂⁶⁶₈. 🈐 carry, take ⇔ 提攜⁸³
攜帶 xīdài 🈪 carry along 🈐 portable
攜手 xīshǒu 🈪 join hands, cooperate

堆₁₀ 162 dūi
Dirt 土⁷⁰ with 佳¹⁶² phonetic. 🈐 stack, pile: 一大堆 a big pile 🈐 🈐 stack, pile
堆積 dūijī 🈪 pile up

誰₁₁ 162 shéi shúi
[谁] Words 言⁹⁸ with 佳¹⁶² phonetic. 🈐 who

推₁₂ 162 tūi
Hand 手⁹⁷ with 佳¹⁶² phonetic. 🈐 push 🈐 procrastinate, postpone ⇔ 類推¹⁴⁸
推測 tūicè 🈪 infer, conjecture
推崇 tūichóng 🈪 esteem, praise highly
推動 tūidòng 🈪 push forward, propel 🈪 promote
推斷 tūiduàn 🈪 predict, infer
推翻 tūifān 🈪 overthrow
推廣 tūiguǎng 🈪 propagate,

字譜及字典

popularize, promote

推薦 tuījiàn 動 recommend
推開 tuīkāi 動 push away 動 push open
推理 tuīlǐ 動 deduce, infer
推論 tuīlùn 動 infer 名 inference
推拿 tuīná 名 massage
推敲 tuīqiāo 動 weigh, consider, deliberate
推諉 tuīwěi 動 shirk
推銷 tuīxiāo 動 promote, market
推卸 tuīxiè 動 evade, shirk
推行 tuīxíng 動 implement, carry out
推選 tuīxuǎn 動 elect, choose

維 162 wéi
13 [维] Thread 糸¹⁵³ with 隹¹⁶² phonetic. 動 tie ⇔ 恭維, 思維, 纖維
維持 wéichí 動 maintain
維護 wéihù 動 support
維他命 wéitāmìng 名 vitamin
維吾爾族 wéiwúěrzú 名 Uygur people
維繫 wéixì 動 maintain
維新 wéixīn 動 reform: 明治維新 Meiji Restoration
維修 wéixiū 動 maintain, repair

羅 162 luó
14 [罗] Catch with a net 网½ (altered) and tie 維¹⁶². Simplified form uses 夕⁷³. snare birds 名 net 名 a surname ⇔ 網羅, 俄羅斯
羅馬 luómǎ 地 Rome
羅斯福 luósīfú 人 Roosevelt
羅網 luówǎng 名 snare, trap

鑼 162 luó
15 [锣] Metal 金⁹ with 羅¹⁶² phonetic and suggestive of basket 籮¹⁶² shape. 名 gong ⇔ 銅鑼, 開鑼
鑼聲 luóshēng 名 gong

籮 162 luó
16 [箩] Bamboo 竹⁷¹ 羅¹⁶² (phonetic). 名 bamboo basket

籮筐 luókuāng 名 bamboo basket

邏 162 luó
17 [逻] Move 辵⁹¹ about like net 羅¹⁶² (phonetic). 動 patrol ⇔ 巡邏
邏輯 luójí 名 logic

囉 162 luō
18 [罗] Mouth 口⁶⁶ with 羅¹⁶² phonetic. 動 chatter
囉嗦 luōsuō 形 bothersome, repetitive, long-winded

蘿 162 luó
19 [萝] Plant 艸⁹⁶ with 羅¹⁶² phonetic. 名 wisteria ⇔ 菠蘿
蘿蔔 luóbo 名 radish 名 turnip: 紅蘿蔔 carrot; 胡蘿蔔 carrot; 白蘿蔔 daikon

唯 162 wéi
20 Mouth 口⁶⁶ with 隹¹⁶² phonetic. 嘆 promise 副 only
唯物論 wéiwùlùn 名 materialism
唯心論 wéixīnlùn 名 idealism
唯一 wéiyī 形 only, unique
唯有 wéiyǒu 副 only, unique

惟 162 wéi
21 Heart 心⁸³ with 隹¹⁶² phonetic. 動 consider 副 only 連 but, however
惟恐 wéikǒng 連 lest, for fear that
惟一 wéiyī 形 only, unique ⇔ 唯一¹⁶²

罹 162 lí
22 Think 惟¹⁶² of being trapped by net 网½ (alter/ed). 動 sorrow 動 suffer from
罹患 líhuàn 動 get sick, fall ill
罹難 línàn 動 die tragically

帷 162 wéi
23 Cloth 巾⁵³ with 隹¹⁶² phonetic. 名 curtain, screen
帷幕 wéimù 名 tent

集 162 jí
24 Birds 隹¹⁶² (early form shows three) perched on a

tree 木⁷⁷. 動 assemble, gather 名 collection 名 market, fair 名 part: 第一集 part one ⇔ 籌集, 群集, 選集, 搜集, 收集, 詩集, 召集, 密集, 募集, 邀集, 採集, 聚集, 蒐集, 匯集
集合 jíhé 動 assemble, gather
集會 jíhuì 動 assemble: 集會自由 freedom of assembly
集權 jíquán 名 centralize power: 集權主義 totalitarianism
集體 jítǐ 名 collective: 集體企業 collective enterprise
集團 jítuán 名 group
集郵 jíyóu 動 collect stamps
集中 jízhōng 動 concentrate, centralize

雜 162 zá
25 [杂] Clothing 衣¹²⁶ (altered) assembled 集 with variegated pieces. Simplified form uses 九⁹. 形 miscellaneous ⇔ 混雜, 複雜, 冗雜, 夾雜, 拉雜, 繁雜, 嘈雜, 錯雜, 攙雜
雜草 zácǎo 名 weeds
雜貨 záhuò 名 groceries: 雜貨店 grocery store
雜技 zájì 名 juggling and acrobatics
雜亂 záluàn 形 disorderly
雜事 záshì 名 complications, distractions
雜務 záwù 名 chores, miscellaneous duties
雜音 záyīn 名 noise, static
雜誌 zázhì 名 magazine

焦 162 jiāo
26 Bird 隹¹⁶² roasted 火⁸². 形 charred 形 anxious 名 a surname ⇔ 心焦⁸³
焦點 jiāodiǎn 名 focal point 名 key issue
焦急 jiāojí 形 anxious
焦距 jiāojù 名 focus

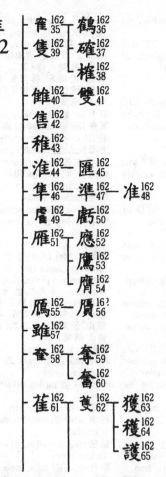

焦慮 jiāolǜ 图 be anxious, worry
焦躁 jiāozào 图 anxious, fretful

蕉 162 jiāo
27 Plant 艸⁹ with 焦 phonetic. 图 a type of hemp 图 banana, plantain ⇔ 芭蕉, 香蕉

礁 162 jiāo
28 Stone 石 with 焦 phonetic. 图 reef ⇔ 觸礁
礁石 jiāoshí 图 reef

憔 162 qiáo
29 Heart 心|³ and worry 焦 (phonetic). 图 haggard
憔悴 qiáocuì 图 distressed 图 haggard

瞧 162 qiáo
30 Eyes 目|⁴ with 焦 phonetic. 图 look, see: 瞧不起 look down on
瞧見 qiáojiàn 图 see, catch sight of

進 162 jìn
31 Move 辵辶 with bird 隹|⁶² phonetic. 图 rise 图 advance, progress 图 enter 图 receive 图 (verb complement) into: 走進 enter ⇔ 先進, 冒進, 大躍進, 改進, 引進, 凹進, 邁進, 促進, 激進, 猛進, 民進黨, 前進, 挿進, 增進, 擠進

進步 jìnbù 图 progress 图 progressive
進程 jìnchéng 图 process
進出口 jìnchūkǒu 图 imports and exports, foreign trade
進口 jìnkǒu 图 import 图 imports
進來 jìnlái 图 come in
進去 jìnqù 图 enter
進入 jìnrù 图 enter
進行 jìnxíng 图 proceed, advance
進展 jìnzhǎn 图 progress

閵 162 lìn
32 Bird 隹|⁶² with 門 phonetic. 图 a bird name

藺 162 lìn
33 [蔺] Grass 艸⁹ with 閵 phonetic. 图 rush used to make mats 图 a surname

躪 162 lìn
34 [躏] Feet 足 with 藺 phonetic. 图 trample ⇔ 蹂躪

隺 162 hào
35 Bird 隹|⁶² heading into the distance 冂. 图 soar

鶴 162 hè
36 Soaring 隺 (phonetic) bird 鳥|⁷⁶. 图 crane

確 162 què
37 [确] Stone 石 with

soaring bird 隹 舝 suggesting persistence. Simplified form is based on an ancient form with 角|⁴⁹. 國 certain, reliable 囤 firmly ⇔ 的確⁴', 精確⁴², 明確⁴⁶, 正確⁶³, 準確⁴⁷
確保 quèbǎo 囯 ensure, guarantee
確定 quèdìng 囯 decide, make certain, confirm
確切 quèqiè 國 accurate
確認 quèrèn 囯 confirm
確實 quèshí 國 definite, true, certain 囯 actually, really
確鑿 quèzáo, quèzùo 國 accurate, precise

榷 162 què
38 Wood 木|⁷ and soar 隹 舝. 圄 plank across a stream 囯 monopolize ⇔ 商榷⁸³

隻 162 zhī
39 [只³⁸] One bird 隹|⁶² in the hand 又|⁴. 囯 single 囯 measureword for certain animals

雔 162 chóu
40 Two birds 隹|⁶². 圄 pair of birds

雙 162 shuāng
41 [双] Pair of birds 隹|⁶² in the hand 又|⁴. 國 both, double 囯 pair ⇔ 西雙版納|³⁰
雙胞胎 shuāngbāotāi 囯 twins
雙重 shuāngchóng 國 double, twofold: 雙重標準 double standard
雙方 shuāngfāng 國 both sides 國 bilateral
雙關 shuāngguān 國 ambiguous: 雙關語 pun, double entendre
雙軌 shuānggǔi 國 two-track
雙數 shuāngshù 國 even number

售 162 shòu
42 Mouth 口|⁶⁰ with 隹|⁶² (abbreviated from 雔³⁹) phonetic. 囯 sell ⇔ 兜售³⁵, 銷售⁸⁷, 沽售³⁵, 抛

售³⁷, 零售³⁹, 蠆售|³, 發售¹⁵, 出售|¹⁰
售貨 shòuhuò 囯 sell goods
售價 shòujià 囯 selling price
售票 shòupiào 囯 sell tickets: 售票處 ticket office

稚 162 zhì
43 Grain 禾|⁰⁸ like short-tailed bird 隹|⁶² (phonetic). 國 immature ⇔ 幼稚³⁷
稚嫩 zhìnèn 國 young and tender
稚氣 zhìqì 囯 childlike

淮 162 huái
44 Water 水|³ with 隹|⁶² phonetic. 囵 Huaihe River
淮河 huáihé 囵 Huaihe River

匯 162 hùi
45 [汇] River 淮⁴⁴ (phonetic) within containment 匚|³² dikes. 囯 converge 囯 remit ⇔ 電匯⁷³, 外匯²⁷
匯集 hùijí 囯 gather, converge
匯款 hùikuǎn 囯 remit 囵 remittance
匯率 hùilǜ 囵 exchange rate
匯票 hùipiào 囵 bank draft
匯入 hùirù 囯 remit

隼 162 zhǔn sǔn
46 Bird 隹|⁶² with mark (originally written as 一|¹, now as 十⁷') suggesting sharpness of claw. zhǔn,sǔn: 囵 falcon

準 162 zhǔn
47 [准⁴⁸] Water 水|³ with 隼⁴⁶ phonetic. 國 level 囵 standard, criterion 國 correct: 我的發音不準. My pronunciation is incorrect. 國 para-, quasi- 囯 certainly, definitely ⇔ 水準³¹, 標準³⁵, 瞄準⁸³, 看準|¹⁵, 對準|⁷⁶
準備 zhǔnbèi 囯 prepare
準確 zhǔnquè 國 accurate
準時 zhǔnshí 囯 on time
準則 zhǔnzé 囵 norm, standard

准 162 zhǔn
48 A variation on 準⁴⁷. 囯 allow, permit ⇔ 核准⁰⁵,

批准|², 獲准⁹⁰
准許 zhǔnxǔ 囯 allow, permit
准予 zhǔnyǔ 囯 permit, approve

隺 162 hū
49 Bird 隹|⁶² with 冖|²² phonetic. 囵 bird

虧 162 kūi
50 [亏] Bird 隺⁴⁹ (phonetic) and exhale 于⁵³. 囵 wind damage 囯 lose 囯 lack ⇔ 盈虧⁶⁵, 幸虧⁶², 吃虧⁹¹
虧本 kūiběn 囯 lose money
虧損 kūisǔn 囵 loss, deficit

雁 162 yàn
51 Birds 隹|⁶² that fly in 人|⁰ shape from home on cliffs 厂|⁷' (phonetic). 囵 wild goose

應 162 yìng yīng
52 [应] Heart 心|⁶³ of birds flying together 雁⁵² (variant form). yīng: 囯 comply with, agree to, meet 囯 respond yìng: 囯 should ⇔ 供不應求⁴², 供應³⁵, 反應³¹, 呼應⁸', 報應⁷⁴, 因應²⁷, 答應³⁸, 適應²², 相應³⁵, 對應|⁷⁶
應酬 yìngchóu 囵 obligatory social activities
應當 yīngdāng 囯 should, ought to
應對 yìngdùi 囯 respond
應付 yìngfù 囯 cope with
應該 yīnggāi 囯 should
應用 yìngyòng 囯 utilize, apply
應允 yìngyǔn 囯 consent, assent
應徵 yìngzhēng 囯 be enlisted, be recruited

鷹 162 yīng
53 [鹰] Bird 鳥|⁷⁸ with 雁|⁶² (variant form) phonetic. 囵 hawk, falcon: 貓頭鷹 owl ⇔ 兀鷹³⁵, 老鷹|³
鷹架 yīngjià 囵 scaffolding

膺 162 yīng
54 Flesh 肉|³² with 雁|⁶² (variant form) phonetic.

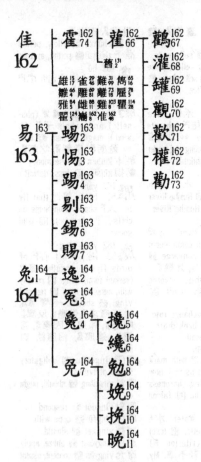

佳
162

易
163

兔
164

囷 breast 咠 undertake (responsibility)
膺任 yīngrèn 咠 be appointed
膺選 yīngxuǎn 咠 be elected

鷹 162 55 Variant of 雁162 showing birds 鳥178 that fly in 人10 shape from home on cliffs 厂21 (phonetic). 囲 wild goose

贋 162 yàn
56 [赝] Modern form shows money/shells 貝150 with 鴈162 phonetic. Alternative form has 雁162 phonetic. 囮 counterfeit

贋品 yànpǐn 咠 forgery, counterfeit good

雖 162 suī
57 [虽] Insect-like 虫25 (altered) with 隹162 phonetic. 囲 a type of lizard 咠 although

雖然 suīrán 咠 although

雖則 suīzé 咠 although, even if

162 suī
奞 58 Bird 隹162 (phonetic) stretching wings large 大37.

162 dúo
奪 59 [夺] Bird 奞162 from hand 寸46. 咠 snatch, seize ⇔ 搶奪.., 掠奪.., 剝奪.., 爭奪.., 褫奪122, 篡奪..

奪取 dúoqǔ 咠 seize, wrest

162 fèn
奮 60 [奋] Bird stretching wings 奞162 over a field 田111. 咠 take flight 咠 arouse, invigorate ⇔ 興奮.., 振奮.., 勤奮.., 亢奮..

奮鬥 fèndòu 咠 struggle
奮發 fènfā 咠 rouse oneself
奮力 fènlì 咠 spare no effort

162 huán
萑 61 Bird 隹162 with horn-like Y74 (written as abbreviated form of 艸59) feathers. 囧 a type of owl

162 hùo
蒦 62 Bird 萑162 in the hand 又1. 囧 capture

162 hùo
獲 63 [获] Beast 犬94 captured 蒦162 (phonetic). 咠 capture, catch 咠 obtain ⇔ 查獲.., 擄獲..

獲得 hùodé 咠 acquire, obtain
獲利 hùolì 咠 profit, gain advantage
獲取 hùoqǔ 咠 obtain
獲勝 hùoshèng 咠 triumph, be victorious
獲准 hùozhǔn 咠 receive permission

162 hùo
穫 64 [获] Grain 禾108 captured 蒦162 (phonetic). 咠 reap, harvest ⇔ 收穫..

162 hù
護 65 [护] Words 言149 securing 蒦162 (phonetic). Simplified form uses 手97 and

戶[78]. □ protect, shield ⇔ 庇
護[72], 守護[59], 掩護[64], 擁
護[74], 辯護[37], 袒護[85], 保
護[24], 愛護[31], 救護[22], 看
護[119], 維護[197]
護士 hùshì □ nurse
護送 hùsòng □ escort
護照 hùzhào □ passport

蒦 162 guàn
66 Screeching ᵒᵒ 🔲 bird
萑[162]. □ stork (⇒ 鸛[67])

鸛 162 guàn
67 [鹳] Stork 蒦[162]
(phonetic) with bird 鳥[178]
redundant. □ stork

灌 162 guàn
68 Water 水[57] with
蒦[162] phonetic. □ irrigate
⇔ 澆灌[40]
灌溉 guàngài □ irrigate
灌木 guànmù □ bush, shrub
灌輸 guànshū □ imbue with
灌注 guànzhù □ pour
灌醉 guànzuì □ get somebody drunk

罐 162 guàn
69 Pottery 缶[141] with
蒦[162] phonetic. □ can, jar
罐頭 guàntóu □ can

觀 162 guān
70 [观] As a stork 蒦[162]
(phonetic) sees 見[104]. Simplified form uses 又[14]. □ observe
□ view ⇔ 綜觀[56], 主觀[5],
客觀[38], 宏觀[5], 景觀[67], 可
觀[72], 參觀[87], 樂觀[72], 旁
觀[95], 悲觀[109]
觀測 guāncè □ observe, survey
觀察 guānchá □ observe
觀點 guāndiǎn □ viewpoint
觀感 guāngǎn □ impressions
觀光 guānguāng □ tour,
sightsee: 觀光客 tourist
觀念 guānniàn □ idea
觀賞 guānshǎng □ appreciate
觀望 guānwàng □ hesitate, wait
and see
觀音 guānyīn □ Goddess of
Mercy
觀照 guānzhào □ look after
觀眾 guānzhòng □ audience,
spectators

歡 162 huān
71 [欢] Bird 萑[162] (pho-
netic) exhaling 欠[65]. Simplified form uses 又[14]. □ joyfully
⇔ 狂歡[60], 聯歡[27], 喜歡[66]
歡呼 huānhū □ cheer
歡樂 huānlè □ happiness
歡喜 huānxǐ □ happy
歡笑 huānxiào □ laugh heartily
歡欣 huānxīn □ joy, jubilation
歡迎 huānyíng □ Welcome! □
welcome

權 162 quán
72 [权] Tree 木[7] with
萑[162] phonetic. Simplified
form uses 又[14]. □ a tree name
□ right, authority, power
⇔ 極權[62], 主權[5], 人權[13],
君權[56], 父權[55], 版權[51], 特
權[34], 加權[34], 股權[27], 威
權[55], 女權[44], 海權[64], 集
權[24], 強權[54], 職權[55], 債
權[75], 政權[104], 產權[71], 授
權[102], 民權[119], 攬權[192], 霸
權[161], 集權[24]
權貴 quánguì □ influential
people
權力 quánlì □ power, authority
權利 quánlì □ right, privilege
權勢 quánshì □ power and
influence
權威 quánwēi □ authority
權宜 quányí □ expedient: 權宜
之計 expediency
權益 quányì □ rights and interests

勸 162 quàn
73 [劝] Strength 力[34]
with 萑[162] phonetic. Simplified form uses 又[14]. □ advise,
urge ⇔ 規勸[77]
勸導 quàndǎo □ advise, urge
勸告 quàngào □ warn, urge
勸阻 quànzǔ □ dissuade, advise
against

霍 162 huò
74 Rain 雨[161] over birds
雒[62] (phonetic, abbreviated
to 隹[162]). □ suddenly ⇔ 揮
霍[58]
霍亂 huòluàn □ cholera

易 163 yì
1 Pictograph of a
lizard, head resembling 日[76]
and legs resembling 勿[14].
Now 蜴[163]. □ easy □ change
□ exchange ⇔ 輕易[5], 交
易[52], 容易[56], 周易[92], 簡
易[72], 貿易[53]
易懂 yìdǒng □ easily under-
stood, simple
易經 yìjīng □ I-Qing, Book of
Changes
易如反掌 yìrúfǎnzhǎng □ as
easy as flipping one's hand
易碎 yìsuì □ fragile
易學 yìxué □ easy to study

蜴 163 yì
2 Lizard 易[163] (pho-
netic) with insect-like 虫[125]
redundant. □ lizard ⇔ 蜥
蜴[68]

惕 163 tì
3 Heart 心[63] changed
易[163] (phonetic). □ cautious
⇔ 警惕[37]

踢 163 tī
4 Change 易[163] (pho-
netic) with the foot 足[88]. □
kick

剔 163 tī
5 Change 易[163] (pho-
netic) with a knife 刀[35].
□ scrape meat from bones ⇔ 挑
剔[127]
剔除 tīchú □ reject, pick out

錫 163 xī
6 [锡] Metal 金[94] that
changes 易[163] (phonetic)
easily. □ tin

賜 163 sì cì
7 [赐] Money/shells

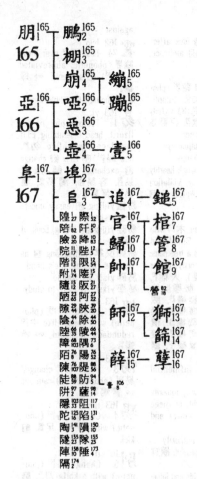

冤獄 yuānyù 图 injustice, frame-up

黿4 chán
Rabbit 兔[164] below and an ancient character for a rabbit-like animal above. 图 crafty

攙5 chān
[撑] Hand 手[97] with 毚[164] phonetic. Simplified form shows 免[164] doubled 二[.]. 图 mix 图 lead by the hand
攙扶 chānfú 图 lead by the hand
攙雜 chānzá 图 mix, adulterate

纔6 cái
[才艹] Thread 糸[153] with 毚[164] phonetic. 图 just now 图 only (⇨ 才艹) ⇦ 剛
纔⅛, 方纔[%]

免7 miǎn
Rabbit 兔[164] that escapes, as represented by missing dot. 图 avoid, escape 图 excuse from, exempt from ⇦ 不免[%], 難免[%], 赦免[%], 避免[%], 以免[%], 未免[%], 豁免[?], 罷免[%]
免不了 miǎnbùliǎo 图 cannot help but
免除 miǎnchú 图 dismiss
免得 miǎndé 图 so as not to
免費 miǎnfèi 图 free of charge
免稅 miǎnshuì 图 tax-free, duty-free

勉8 miǎn
Strength 力[19] to escape 免[164] (phonetic). 图 strive 图 encourage ⇦ 勤
勉⅛
勉勵 miǎnlì 图 urge, encourage
勉強 miǎnqiǎng 图 force, compel

娩9 miǎn
From woman 女[38] escape 免[164] (phonetic). 图 give birth ⇦ 分娩[%]

挽10 Hand 手[97] with

貝[150] exchanged 易[163] (phonetic). sì: 图 grant, bestow 图 grant, favor ⇦ 恩賜[%], 賞賜[%]
賜予 sìyǔ 图 grant, bestow

兔1 tù
Pictograph of a rabbit. 图 rabbit
兔子 tùzi 图 rabbit

逸2 yì
Rabbit 兔[164] running off 辵[]. 图 escape 图 leisure, idleness ⇦ 飄逸[%], 逃逸[127]

冤3 yuān
Rabbit 兔[164] covered 冖[14] in a trap. 图 injustice
冤屈 yuānqū 图 injustice
冤枉 yuānwǎng 图 wrong, treat

免 phonetic. 🔲 draw, pull
挽回 wǎnhúi 🔲 save, redeem
挽救 wǎnjìu 🔲 save, rescue
挽留 wǎnlíu 🔲 urge to stay

晚 164 wǎn
11 Sun 日 escaping 免 (phonetic). 🔲 evening late ⟺ 昨晚, 今晚, 當晚, 夜晚, 早晚, 傍晚
晚安 wǎnān 🔲 Good night!
晚餐 wǎncān 🔲 dinner
晚飯 wǎnfàn 🔲 dinner
晚會 wǎnhùi 🔲 party
晚上 wǎnshàng 🔲 evening, night: 今天晚上 tonight
晚霞 wǎnxiá 🔲 clouds of sunset
晚裝 wǎnzhuāng 🔲 evening dress

朋 165 péng
1 Pictograph of a legendary phoenix-like bird (altered to resemble 月). Now 鳳 or 鵬. 🔲 friend
朋友 péngyǒu 🔲 friend: 男朋友 boyfriend; 女朋友 girlfriend; 小朋友 child

鵬 165 péng
2 [鹏] Phoenix 朋 (phonetic) with bird 鳥 redundant. 🔲 phoenix

棚 165 péng
3 Wood 木 arranged closely 朋 (phonetic). 🔲 shed ⟺ 帳棚
棚架 péngjià 🔲 scaffolding

崩 165 bēng
4 Mountain 山 roaring like phoenix 朋 (phonetic). 🔲 collapse ⟺ 山崩, 雪崩
崩潰 bēngkùi 🔲 collapse

繃 165 bēng běng bèng
5 [绷] String 糸 and burst 崩 (phonetic). bēng: 🔲 stretch taut: 繃著臉 tighten face when upset běng: 🔲 endure bèng: 🔲 split, crack

繃帶 bēngdài 🔲 bandage
繃斷 bèngduàn 🔲 snap

蹦 165 bèng
6 Foot 足 bursting 崩 (phonetic). 🔲 leap, jump

亞 166 yǎ yà
1 [亚] Pictograph of a deformed person. yà: 🔲 inferior, second-rate ⟺ 東亞, 利比亞, 西伯利亞, 澳大利亞
亞太 yàtài 🔲 Asian Pacific
亞洲 yàzhōu 🔲 Asia: 亞洲人 Asian

啞 166 yǎ
2 [哑] Mouth 口 with 亞 phonetic and suggestive of laughing sound. 🔲 mute ⟺ 沙啞, 聾啞, 啞巴 yǎbā 🔲 mute person

惡 166 è ě wù
3 [恶] Deformed 亞 (phonetic) heart 心. è: 🔲 evil, wicked ě: 🔲 be disgusted wù: 🔲 hate ⟺ 凶惡, 兇惡, 險惡, 可惡, 邪惡, 厭惡, 憎惡, 醜惡, 罪惡
惡毒 èdú 🔲 vicious, malicious
惡化 èhuà 🔲 deteriorate
惡劣 èliè 🔲 bad
惡夢 èmèng 🔲 nightmare
惡魔 èmó 🔲 demon
惡習 èxí 🔲 bad habit
惡心 ěxin 🔲 be disgusted, disgusting
惡性 èxìng 🔲 malignant
惡意 èyì 🔲 malice, malicious

壺 166 hú
4 [壶] Pictograph of a pot with lid resembling 士 and bottom resembling 亞. 🔲 pot ⟺ 水壺, 茶壺

壹 166 yī
5 Vase 壺 with 吉 (now resembling 豆) phonetic. 🔲 one (complex form)

阜 167 fù
1 Pictograph of three steps, the bottom one altered. 🔲 hill ⟺ 曲阜

埠 167 bù
2 Earth 土 hill 阜 (phonetic) at water's edge. 🔲 dock, moor ⟺ 華埠

𠂤 167 dūi
3 Smaller hill 阜. 🔲 small hill, ramparts (⟹ 堆) 🔲 legion

追 167 zhūi
4 Legion 𠂤 (phonetic) moving 辵. 🔲 chase
追查 zhūichá 🔲 investigate
追悼 zhūidào 🔲 mourn: 追悼會 memorial service
追趕 zhūigǎn 🔲 chase, run after
追究 zhūijìu 🔲 seek the root cause
追求 zhūiqíu 🔲 pursue
追溯 zhūisù 🔲 trace back
追隨 zhūisúi 🔲 follow (a leader): 追隨者 follower
追問 zhūiwèn 🔲 question repeatedly
追尋 zhūixún 🔲 search for, track
追逐 zhūizhú 🔲 pursue, chase
追蹤 zhūizōng 🔲 trace, trail, track

鎚 167 chúi
5 [锤] Metal 金 chasing 追 (phonetic). 🔲 hammer ⟺ 鐵鎚

官 167 guān
6 Legion 𠂤 (abbreviated) in a hall 宀. 🔲 government official ⟺ 檢察官, 教官, 做官, 法官, 感官, 當官, 器官, 清官, 文官, 宦官, 軍官
官場 guānchǎng 🔲 officialdom
官倒 guāndǎo 🔲 official profiteering
官邸 guāndǐ 🔲 official residence

字譜及字典

168
韭 168₁ — 韱 168₂ ┬ 纖 168₃
├ 殲 168₄
├ 籤 168₅
└ 懺 168₆

169
飛 169₁ — 非 169₂ ┬ 啡 169₃
├ 菲 169₄
├ 緋 169₅
├ 扉 169₆
├ 匪 169₇
├ 翡 169₈
├ 斐 169₉
├ 霏 169₁₀
├ 悲 169₁₁
├ 辈 169₁₂
├ 裴 169₁₃
├ 排 169₁₄
├ 徘 169₁₅
└ 罪 169₁₆
└ 靡⅗ 靠⅞

棺 167₇ guān Wood 木⁷ with 官₆¹⁶⁷ phonetic. 图 coffin
棺材 guāncái 图 coffin

管 167₈ guǎn Bamboo 竹⁷ with 官₆¹⁶⁷ phonetic. 图 pipe, tube 动 manage, take care of 动 mind, bother about: 别管我 leave me alone ⇔ 不管₆, 水管᷍, 主管⅖, 儘管⅗, 吸管⅘, 看管⅗, 血管⅙
管道 guǎndào 图 pipeline 图 communications channel
管教 guǎnjiào 动 discipline and instruct
管理 guǎnlǐ 动 manage
管轄 guǎnxiá 动 rule over: 管轄權 jurisdiction
管制 guǎnzhì 动 图 control

館 167₉ [馆] Food 食⅛ for officials 官₆¹⁶⁷ (phonetic). 图 guesthouse 图 consulate 图 hall ⇔ 飯館⅗, 茶館⅗, 茶藝館⅗, 圖書館⁹⁷, 使館⅗, 賓館⁷, 菜館¹⁰³, 旅館¹⁰, 餐館¹⁴⁷
館子 guǎnzi 图 restaurant

歸 167₁₀ [归] Wife 婦⅗ (abbreviated to broom 帚⅘), arriving 止⁷⁷ with ⅝¹⁶⁷ phonetic. 动 marry (a man) 动 belong to 动 return to 动 return ⇔ 回歸⁹
歸咎 guījiù 动 blame
歸來 guīlái 动 return
歸類 guīlèi 动 categorize
歸納 guīnà 动 induce: 歸納法 induction
歸屬 guīshǔ 动 belong to: 歸屬感 sense of belonging

帥 167₁₁ [帅] Hill ⅝¹⁶⁷ and banner 巾⁵⁷. 图 commander 形 handsome ⇔ 元帥⅗
帥哥 shuàigē 图 图 口 handsome

官方 guānfāng 动 authorities 形 official: 非官方 unofficial
官話 guānhuà 图 Mandarin
官吏 guānlì 图 officialdom
官僚 guānliáo 图 bureaucrat: 有官僚作風 bureaucratic (person); 官僚化 bureaucratic (system); 官僚資本主義 bureaucratic capitalism

官商 guānshāng 图 officials and businesspeople 图 bureaucrat-business
官署 guānshǔ 图 official bureau
官司 guānsī 图 lawsuit: 打官司 sue
官員 guānyuán 图 government official

man

師 167 shī
12 [师] Legion 自 ¹⁶⁷ surrounding 匝总 (altered). 图 legion 图 teacher, master 图 specialist 图 老師吗, 教師吗, 律師吗, 醫師吗, 大師吗, 恩師吗, 廚師吗, 牧師吗, 出師吗, 祖師吗, 導師吗, 講師吗

師弟 shīdì 图 classmate (younger male student of same teacher)

師範 shīfàn 图 teacher-training: 師範大學 normal university, teachers university

師傅 shīfù 图 teacher, master

師父 shīfù 图 teacher, master

師姊 shījiě 图 classmate (elder female student of same teacher)

師妹 shīmèi 图 classmate (younger female student of same teacher)

師母 shīmǔ 图 teacher's wife

師娘 shīniáng 图 teacher's wife

師徒 shītú 图 teacher and pupil

師兄 shīxiōng 图 classmate (elder male student of same teacher)

師長 shīzhǎng 图 teacher

師丈 shīzhàng 图 teacher's husband

獅 167 shī
13 [狮] Beast/dog 犬吗 and master 師吗 (phonetic). 图 lion ⇔ 舞龍舞獅吗

獅子 shīzi 图 lion

篩 167 shāi
14 [筛] Modern form shows bamboo 竹吗 with 師吗 phonetic. 图 screen, sieve 图 screen, sift out

篩選 shāixuǎn 图 screen, sift out

薛 167 xuē
15 [薛] Grass 艸吗 with an ancient character for sin from hill 自 ¹⁶⁷ and bitterness 辛吗 phonetic. 图 a marsh

grass 图 a surname

孽 167 niè
16 Child 子吗 of sin 薛吗 (phonetic). 图 concubine's son ⇔ 作孽吗, 罪孽吗

韭 168 jǐu
1 Pictograph of a plant with diverging stems. 图 scallions, chives

韭菜 jǐucài 图 scallions, chives

韯 168 xiān
2 Scallions 韭吗 with an ancient character from two men 从吗 and lance 戈吗 phonetic. 图 wild scallion

纖 168 xiān
3 [纤] Thread 糸吗 thin like wild scallion 韯吗 (phonetic). Simplified form uses 千吗. 图 slender ⇔ 光纖吗

纖維 xiānwéi 图 fiber: 玻璃纖維 fiberglass

殲 168 jiān
4 [歼] Corpse 歹吗 with 韯吗 phonetic. Simplified form uses 千吗. 图 destroy

殲滅 jiānmiè 图 annihilate

籤 168 qiān
5 [签图] Bamboo 竹吗 with 韯吗 phonetic. 图 bamboo slip ⇔ 標籤吗, 牙籤吗, 抽籤吗

懺 168 chàn
6 [忏] Heart 心吗 with 韯吗 phonetic. Simplified form uses 千吗. 图 repent

懺悔 chànhuǐ 图 repent

飛 169 fēi
1 [飞] Pictograph of a crane flying with feathers spread out. Modern form resembles character for rise 升吗. 图 fly ⇔ 起飛吗

飛奔 fēibēn 图 dash away, run off

飛彈 fēidàn 图 图 missile: 洲際飛彈 ICBM

飛機 fēijī 图 airplane

飛盤 fēipán 图 frisbee

飛翔 fēixiáng 图 hover, glide

飛行 fēixíng 图 fly

非 169 fēi
2 Opposing wings from lower half of 飛吗 (altered). 图 not 图 wrongs, evils ⇔ 南非吗, 無非吗, 並非吗, 除非吗, 安非他命吗, 莫非吗, 啼笑皆非吗, 是非吗

非常 fēicháng 图 very, extremely 图 extraordinary, emergency

非但 fēidàn 图 not only

非法 fēifǎ 图 illegal

非難 fēinàn 图 reproach

非洲 fēizhōu 图 Africa: 非洲人 African; 非洲裔美國人 African-American

啡 169 fēi
3 Mouth 口吗 with 非吗 phonetic. Used in transliterations of foreign words. ⇔ 咖啡吗, 嗎啡吗

菲 169 fēi
4 Plant 艸吗 with 非吗 phonetic. fěi: 图 a type of radish 图 meager fēi: 图 fragrant

菲薄 fěibó 图 underestimate, slight

菲律賓 fēilǜbīn 图 Philippines

緋 169 fēi
5 [绯] Silk 糸吗 with 非吗 phonetic. 图 red

緋聞 fēiwén 图 sex scandal

扉 169 fēi
6 Door 戶吗 with 非吗 phonetic and suggesting opposition. 图 door leaf

扉頁 fēiyè 图 page

匪 169 fěi
7 Container 匚吗 with 非吗 phonetic. 图 bamboo basket (⇨ 篚) 图 bandit 盜匪吗, 共匪吗, 土匪吗, 劫匪吗

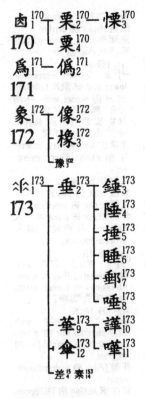

170
鹵[170] ┬ 栗[170] ─ 慄[170]
　　　└ 粟[170]

171
爲[171] ─ 僞[171]

172
象[172] ┬ 像[172]
　　　├ 橡[172]
　　　└ 豫[102]

173
𠂢[173] ┬ 垂[173] ┬ 錘[173]
　　　　　　　├ 陲[173]
　　　　　　　├ 捶[173]
　　　　　　　├ 睡[173]
　　　　　　　├ 郵[173]
　　　　　　　└ 唾[173]
　　　　├ 華[173] ┬ 譁[173]
　　　　│　　　　└ 嘩[173]
　　　　├ 傘[173]
　　　　└ 差[15] 棄[153]

匪徒 fěitú 图 bandit
匪夷所思 fěiyísuǒsī 图 unimaginably strange

翡 169 fěi
8 Feathers 羽[124] with 非[169] phonetic. 图 male kingfisher
翡翠 fěicùi 图 kingfisher 图 emerald 图 blue-green, emerald

斐 169 fěi
9 Writing 文[198] with 非[169] phonetic. 图 elegant, beautiful

霏 169 fēi
10 Rain 雨[161] with 非[169] phonetic. 图 falling snow and rain

悲 169 bēi
11 Contradicted 非[169] (phonetic) heart 心[1]. 图 sorrowful ⇔ 慈悲[2]
悲哀 bēiāi 图 sorrowful
悲慘 bēicǎn 图 tragic
悲觀 bēiguān 图 pessimistic
悲劇 bēijù 图 tragedy
悲傷 bēishāng 图 sad, miserable
悲痛 bēitòng 图 grief, sorrow

輩 12 [辈] Carts 車[198] with 非[169] phonetic and suggestive of line up 排[14]. 图 row of chariots 图 rank 图 generation ⇔ 一輩子[1], 長輩[2], 後輩[3], 前輩[4]
輩子 bèizi 图 lifetime: 下輩子 next life

裴 169 péi
13 Clothing 衣[126] in opposition 非[169] (phonetic). 图 look of flowing gown 图 a surname

排 169 pái
14 Hand 手[89] in opposition 非[169] (phonetic). 图 push 图 expel 图 arrange, line up 图 line, row ⇔ 安排[5], 木排[7], 牛排[?], 編排[15]
排場 páichǎng 图 ostentation, extravagance
排斥 páichì 图 expel, ostracize
排除 páichú 图 exclude, remove, eliminate
排隊 páidùi 图 line up, stand in line
排擠 páijǐ 图 expel, ostracize 图 push aside
排課 páikè 图 arrange classes
排列 páiliè 图 arrange
排名 páimíng 图 rank
排球 páiqiú 图 volleyball
排水 páishǔi 图 drain
排他 páitā 图 exclude 图 exclusionary
排外 páiwài 图 anti-foreign, xenophobic
排序 páixù 图 sequence, arrangement, ordering

徘 169 pái
15 Step 彳[61] or not 非[169] (phonetic). 图 hesitate
徘徊 páihuái 图 hesitate 图 pace back and forth

罪 169 zùi
16 Net 网[?] (altered) over a wrong 非[169] (phonetic). 图 crime ⇔ 得罪[?], 犯罪[?], 無罪[?], 認罪[?], 恕罪[?], 滔天大罪[?], 贖罪[?]

罪惡 zuìè 图 crime
罪犯 zuìfàn 图 criminal
罪戾 zuìlì 图 crime, vice 图 evil
罪名 zuìmíng 图 criminal charge
罪孽 zuìniè 图 sin
罪證 zuìzhèng 图 evidence of guilt

肉1 170 tiáo Pictograph of fruit hanging from a tree. 图 fruit

栗2 170 lì Tree 木⁷ that produces nuts/fruit 肉¹⁷⁰ (altered to resemble 西¹³⁰). 图 chestnut tree
栗樹 lìshù 图 chestnut tree
栗子 lìzi 图 chestnut

慄3 170 lì Heart 心⁸³ with 栗¹⁷⁰ phonetic. 图 tremble ⇔ 戰慄¹³⁶

粟4 170 sù Rice 米¹³⁸ hanging like fruit 肉¹⁷⁰ (altered to resemble 西¹³⁰). 图 paddy 图 millet

爲1 171 wéi wèi [为] Pictograph of a female monkey. Early form and some modern forms show claws 爪¹⁰³ on top. wéi: 图 do 图 serve as, act as 图 become wèi: 团 for: 爲你的方便 for your convenience ⇔ 極爲¹⁴, 人爲¹⁴⁶, 頗爲¹⁵⁸, 更爲¹⁵³, 甚爲²⁷, 作爲²⁷, 認爲²⁸, 因爲²⁷, 較爲²⁸, 行爲⁵⁸, 成爲⁵⁸, 視爲¹¹⁵, 淪爲¹¹⁵, 列爲¹³⁷, 變爲¹⁵⁷, 稱爲⁹
爲此 wèicǐ 图 for this reason
爲何 wèihé 团 why
爲了 wèile 团 for the sake of
爲人 wéirén 图 behave
爲什麼 wèishéme 团 why
爲甚麼 wèishéme 团 why
爲止 wéizhǐ 图 up to, until: 到

現在爲止 until now

偽2 171 wèi 团 wěi [伪] Person-like 人¹⁰ monkey 爲¹⁷¹ (phonetic). 图 fake, bogus ⇔ 虛偽⁹⁷
偽鈔 wèichāo 图 counterfeit money
偽善 wèishàn 图 hypocrisy 图 hypocritical
偽造 wèizào 图 forge, counterfeit
偽裝 wèizhuāng 图 pretend, feign 图 disguise, camouflage

象1 172 xiàng Pictograph of an elephant. 图 elephant 图 image ⇔ 假象¹²⁶, 景象⁶⁷, 印象²⁷, 大象²⁷, 跡象²⁵, 形象²⁵, 幻象³⁵, 星象²⁷, 氣象⁵¹, 抽象¹³, 現象¹⁵, 對象¹⁷⁶
象棋 xiàngqí 图 chess (Chinese): 西洋象形 chess (Western)
象形 xiàngxíng 图 pictograph (⇨六書)
象牙 xiàngyá 图 ivory
象徵 xiàngzhēng 图 symbol: 象徵性 symbolic

像2 172 xiàng Person 人¹⁰ with 象¹⁷² phonetic. 图 resemble 图 image ⇔ 影像⁹², 肖像⁸⁵, 錄像⁹², 好像⁵⁴, 佛像⁸⁵, 雕像⁸¹, 偶像⁷, 想像¹¹⁴, 顯像¹⁵³
像是 xiàngshì 图 seem, look like
像章 xiàngzhāng 图 badge with a person's likeness: 毛澤東像章 Mao button

橡3 172 xiàng Modern form shows wood 木⁷ with 象¹⁷² phonetic. 图 oak 图 rubber tree
橡膠 xiàngjiāo 图 rubber
橡皮 xiàngpí 图 eraser 图 rubber: 橡皮印章 rubberstamp: 橡皮擦 图 eraser

垂1 173 chuí Pictograph of a plant

with drooping leaves or fruit.

垂2 173 chuí Ground 土⁶ with 叒¹⁷³ (altered) phonetic. 图 frontier (⇨ 陲¹⁷³) 图 hang, droop ⇔ 永垂不朽¹²⁰
垂青 chuíqīng 团 treat specially
垂死 chuísǐ 图 dying, last-ditch
垂涎 chuíxián 团 drool over, covet
垂直 chuízhí 图 perpendicular, vertical

錘3 173 chuí [锤] Metal 金¹⁴ with 垂¹⁷³ phonetic. 图 hammer
錘鍊 chuíliàn 团 forge, temper 团 polish

陲4 173 chuí Mountains 阜¹⁶⁷ with 垂¹⁷³ phonetic. 图 border, frontier ⇔ 邊陲¹⁷³

捶5 173 chuí Hand 手⁷ bringing staff down 垂¹⁷³ (phonetic). 团 beat, pound

睡6 173 shuì Eyes 目¹⁴ drooping 垂¹⁷³ (phonetic). 团 sleep: 睡飽 图 sleep a full night's sleep ⇔ 熟睡⁴², 沈睡⁸⁹, 入睡², 瞌睡⁸⁹, 酣睡⁸⁹, 午睡⁹³
睡覺 shuìjiào 团 go to bed, sleep: 睡不好覺 sleep poorly
睡眠 shuìmián 图 sleep
睡醒 shuìxǐng 团 wake up
睡衣 shuìyī 图 pajamas
睡著 shuìzháo 团 fall asleep

郵7 173 yóu [邮] Walled city 邑⁴² on empire's fringe 垂¹⁷³. Simplified form uses 由¹³. 图 postal station 图 postal ⇔ 集郵¹²⁴
郵差 yóuchāi 图 mailman
郵戳 yóuchuō 图 postmark
郵遞 yóudì 图 postal service 图 post, mail: 郵遞區號 图 zip code
郵寄 yóujì 团 mail

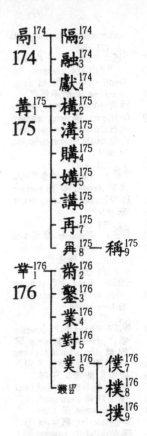

華埠 huábù 图 Chinatown
華府 huáfǔ 图 American government
華麗 huálì 圈 ornate
華南 huánán 圈 southern China
華僑 huáqiáo 图 overseas Chinese
華人 huárén 图 Chinese person (ethnically)
華山 huàshān 圈 Hua Mountain - a sacred Daoist mountain in Shaanxi Province
華盛頓 huáshèngdùn 凡 圈 Washington
華氏 huáshì 图 Fahrenheit: 華氏三十度 thirty degrees Fahrenheit
華夏 huáxià 圈 China
華裔 huáyì 圈 Chinese descent: 華裔美國人 Chinese-American
華語 huáyǔ 图 Chinese, Mandarin

譁 173 huá
10 [哗] Flashy 華¹⁷³ (phonetic) words 言⁹. 图 clamor, uproar ⇔ 喧譁₁
譁然 huárán 图 uproar, commotion

嘩 173 huā huá
11 [哗] Flashy 華¹⁷³ (phonetic) mouth 口⁶⁸. 图 clamor, uproar
嘩變 huábiàn 图 mutiny, revolt
嘩啦 huālā 图 crash, splash
嘩眾取寵 huázhòngqǔchǒng engage in demagogy

傘 173 sǎn
12 [伞] Pictograph of an umbrella. 图 umbrella ⇔ 陽傘₂₈, 紙傘¹⁰⁰, 跳傘², 雨傘¹⁶¹

鬲 174 lì gé
1 Pictograph of a bronze caldron. lì: 图 a type of caldron gé: 圈 an ancient kingdom

隔 174 gé
2 Hill 阜¹⁶⁷ with 鬲¹⁷⁴

郵件 yóujiàn 图 mail: 電子郵件 e-mail
郵局 yóujú 图 post office
郵票 yóupiào 图 postage stamp
郵筒 yóutǒng 图 mailbox
郵箱 yóuxiāng 图 mailbox
郵政 yóuzhèng 图 postal system: 郵政編號 图 zip code

唾 173 tuò
8 Hang 垂¹⁷³ from the mouth 口⁶⁸. 图 spit, saliva
唾罵 tuòmà 图 excoriate, revile
唾沫 tuòmò 图 spit, saliva
唾棄 tuòqì 图 spurn, spit at contemptuously

華 173 huá huà
9 [华] Emerging 𠂢⁷⁷ (altered) flowers and leaves 𥝌¹⁷³ (altered) of a plant 屮⁶. Simplified form uses 化¹² and 十⁹. huá: 图 flowery, showy 圈 magnificent, splendid 图 China huà: 图 a surname ⇔ 反華₁, 豪華₂₇, 繁華₂₃, 浮華₂₇, 才華⁶⁴, 中華₆, 精華₂₆, 昇華₃₇

字譜及字典

phonetic. ▥ divide, partition ▥ at an interval of, at a distance from ⇔ 分隔³⁷, 間隔³⁷
隔壁 gébì ▦ next door
隔斷 géduàn ▥ separate, cut off
隔閡 géhé ▦ misunderstanding
隔絕 géjué ▥ isolate
隔離 gélí ▥ isolate, segregate
隔年 génián ▦ following year
隔天 gétiān ▦ following day
隔音 géyīn ▩ soundproof

融 174 róng
3 Caldron 鬲¹⁷⁴ with 虫¹²⁵ phonetic. ▩ rising fumes melt ▥ blend, fuse ⇔ 金融³⁷
融合 rónghé ▥ blend, fuse
融化 rónghuà ▥ melt, fuse
融洽 róngqià ▩ harmonious, on friendly terms

獻 174 xiàn
4 [献] Dog 犬⁹¹ offered in a sacrificial vessel (ancient character from 鬲¹⁷⁴ and 虍¹²²). Simplified form uses 南³⁷. ▥ donate, offer ⇔ 貢獻³⁷, 奉獻³⁷, 文獻³⁷
獻給 xiàngěi ▥ dedicate to
獻金 xiànjīn ▥ contribute to contribution

冓 175 gòu
1 Pictograph of interlocking framework of a house.

構 175 gòu
2 [构] Wooden 木⁷ framework 冓¹⁷⁵ (phonetic). Simplified form uses 勾³⁷. ▥ construct, form ⇔ 結構³⁷, 架構³⁷, 機構³⁷, 虛構³⁷
構成 gòuchéng ▥ constitute, compose, form
構想 gòuxiǎng ▩ idea, plan, scheme
構造 gòuzào ▩ structure

溝 175 gōu
3 [沟] Waterways 水³⁷ with interlocking structure 冓¹⁷⁵ (phonetic). Simplified form uses 勾³⁷. ▩ irrigation canal ditch ▩ groove ⇔ 水溝³⁷, 壕溝²⁷, 代溝³⁷, 鴻溝³⁷, 蘆溝橋¹²²
溝渠 gōuqú ▩ irrigation canal
溝通 gōutōng ▥ communicate ▥ get through, connect

購 175 gòu
4 [购] Money/shells 貝⁵⁰ interlocking/exchanging 冓¹⁷⁵ (phonetic). Simplified form uses 勾³⁷. ▥ purchase ⇔ 搶購³⁷, 收購³⁷, 訂購³⁷, 添購³⁷, 賒購³⁷, 採購³⁷
購買 gòumǎi ▥ purchase
購物 gòuwù ▥ shop: 購物中心 shopping center
購置 gòuzhì ▥ purchase

媾 175 gòu
5 Woman 女⁹¹ forming framework 冓¹⁷⁵ (phonetic). ▩ marry within the family marry ▥ copulate ⇔ 交媾³⁷

講 175 jiǎng
6 [讲] Words 言⁹⁸ forming a structure 冓¹⁷⁵. Simplified form uses 井⁹⁷. ▩ mediate, harmonize ▥ speak, talk ▥ emphasize ▥ explain ⇔ 演講³⁷, 亂講³⁷
講話 jiǎnghuà ▥ speak
講價 jiǎngjià ▥ bargain
講解 jiǎngjiě ▥ explain in detail
講究 jiǎngjiu ▥ emphasize, be particular about ▩ tasteful
講求 jiǎngqiú ▥ demand, insist on, strive for
講師 jiǎngshī ▩ lecturer
講台 jiǎngtái ▩ lectern, rostrum

再 175 zài
7 Structure 冓¹⁷⁵ folded over into one 一³⁷ again ▨ then ⇔ 一再³⁷, 不再³⁷
再次 zàicì ▥ once more, again
再度 zàidù ▥ once more, again
再見 zàijiàn ▥ Good-bye!

再三 zàisān ▥ repeatedly
再生 zàishēng ▥ rebirth
再者 zàizhě ▩ furthermore

爯 175 chèn
8 Hand 爪¹⁰³ reaching over a structure 冓¹⁷⁵ (abbreviated). ⓥ weigh

稱 175 chēng chèn
9 [称] Weigh 爯¹⁷⁵ (phonetic) grain 禾⁹⁸. Simplified form uses 尒³⁷. chēng: ▥ weigh, measure ▥ call, name chèn: ▥ suit, fit ⇔ 宜稱³⁷, 勻稱³⁷, 號稱³⁷, 聲稱³⁷, 統稱³⁷, 職稱³⁷, 稱稱³⁷, 名稱³⁷, 簡稱³⁷, 自稱³⁷, 據稱³⁷, 對稱¹⁷⁶
稱霸 chēngbà ▥ dominate, hegemonize
稱呼 chēnghū ▥ call, name name, form of address
稱爲 chēngwéi ▥ called
稱讚 chēngzàn ▥ praise
稱職 chēngzhí ▩ competent

丵 176 zhuó
1 Pictograph of branches and foliage.

黹 176 zhǐ
2 Cloth pierced 市⁵³ with foliage-like 丵¹⁷⁶ (altered) marks. ▩ embroidery

鑿 176 záo zuò
3 [凿] Metal 金³⁷ with an ancient character for grinding rice phonetic (abbreviated to foliage 丵¹⁷⁶, mortar 臼¹³¹ and strike 殳⁹⁷). záo: ▥ chisel, bore ▩ chisel zuò: ▩ authentic ⇔ 確鑿³⁷
鑿開 záokāi ▥ bore through

業 176 yè
4 [业] Tree 木⁷ and the foliage 丵¹⁷⁶ it produces. ▩ industry ▩ profession, occupation ▩ estate ⇔ 創業³⁷, 就業³⁷, 學業³⁷, 農業³⁷, 作業³⁷, 商業³⁷, 同業³⁷, 待業³⁷, 肆業³⁷, 行

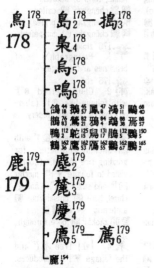

業 $^{51}_4$, 工業 $^{51}_1$, 專業 $^{89}_7$, 職 業 $^{99}_7$, 產業 $^{89}_{11}$, 畢業 $^{136}_8$, 兢兢
業 $^{68}_5$, 事業 $^{89}_8$, 林業 $^{7}_0$, 開 業業 $^{152}_2$
業 $^{28}_0$, 營業 $^{67}_9$, 企業 $^{83}_6$, 失   業務 yèwù 图 business affairs

業餘 yèyú 图 amateur

對 $_5^{176}$ duì [对] Foliage 丰 $^{176}_4$, sage 士 $^{3}_0$, and measure 寸 $^{43}_0$. Simplified form uses 又 $^1_0$. 图 correct, right, proper 图 face, oppose 图 treat: 他對我很好. He is very good to me. 图 compare, check 介 as for, regarding: 對我來說 as far as I'm concerned; 對這個問題 regarding this question 介 to, towards, at 图 couple ⇔ 不對 $^{14}_0$, 不對勁 $^{14}_0$, 核對 $^{15}_6$, 反對 $^{9}_3$, 作對 $^{9}_8$, 針對 $^{8}_3$, 絕 對 $^{29}_7$, 校對 $^{7}_6$, 配對 $^{37}_3$, 查 對 $^{74}_4$, 相對 $^{103}_2$, 面對 $^{148}_1$, 應 對 $^{67}_9$

對比 dùibǐ 图 comparison, contrast 图 compare, contrast
對不起 dùibùqǐ 图 I'm sorry, excuse me 图 treat improperly
對策 dùicè 图 counterplan
對稱 dùichèn 图 symmetric
對待 dùidài 图 treat, deal with
對等 dùiděng 图 equal, reciprocal: 對等待遇 equal treatment
對方 dùifāng 图 the other party
對付 dùifù 图 deal with
對話 dùihuà 图 dialogue
對抗 dùikàng 图 resist: 對抗性 antagonism
對立 dùilì 图 be in opposition, stand opposed
對聯 dùilián 图 couplet written on a pair of scrolls
對面 dùimiàn 图 directly opposite, across
對手 dùishǒu 图 opponent
對數 dùishù 图 logarithm
對象 dùixiàng 图 object, target 图 (图) boyfriend, girlfriend
對應 dùiyìng 图 corresponding
對於 dùiyú 介 regarding, as to
對照 dùizhào 图 check against
對著 dùizhe 图 toward
對峙 dùizhì 图 confront

對準 duìzhǔn 动 aim 图 adjust, tune

業 6 176 pú Gather firewood/twigs 芈 176 with hands 廾 55 (altered).

僕 7 176 pú [仆] Person 人 10 who does chores 業 176 (phonetic). Simplified form uses 卜 9. 图 servant ⇔ 公僕 37, 奴僕 81 僕人 púrén 图 servant

樸 8 176 pú 图 pǔ [朴羚] Wood 木 7 with 業 176 phonetic. 台 plain wood 图 plain, simple ⇔ 儉 樸 12, 純樸 88 樸素 púsù 图 plain, simple

撲 176 pū [扑羚] Hand 手 97 with 業 176 phonetic. 动 strike, beat 动 spring at, rush at ⇔ 反撲 31, 相撲 55 撲克 pūkè 图 poker, cards: 撲克牌 playing cards 撲滅 pūmiè 动 put out, extinguish

馬 1 177 mǎ [马] Pictograph of a horse showing head, mane, legs and tail. 图 horse 图 a surname ⇔ 司馬 35, 騎馬 25, 巴拿馬 85, 兵馬 22, 斑馬 107, 羅馬 142 馬鞍 mǎ'ān 图 saddle 馬車 mǎchē 图 wagon, cart 馬虎 mǎhū 图 careless: 馬馬虎虎 mediocre, so-so 馬克 mǎkè 图 mark: 德國馬克 German mark 馬克思 mǎkèsī 人 Marx: 馬克思主義 Marxism 馬勒 mǎlè 图 bridle 馬鈴薯 mǎlíngshǔ 图 potato 馬路 mǎlù 图 street 馬匹 mǎpī 图 horses 馬上 mǎshàng 动 immediately 馬桶 mǎtǒng 图 chamber pot 图 toilet

馬戲 mǎxì 图 circus: 馬戲團 circus troupe 馬祖 mǎzǔ 地 Matsu Islands

嗎 177 ma mǎ [吗] Mouth 口 68 with 馬 177 phonetic. 图 ma: 助 particle indicating a question 嗎啡 mǎfēi 图 morphine

媽 3 177 mā [妈] Woman 女 94 with 馬 177 phonetic. 图 mom, mother ⇔ 奶媽 27, 姑媽 43, 他媽的 9, 姨媽 65, 舅媽 31 媽媽 māma 图 mama, mother 媽祖 māzǔ 人 Goddess of the Sea

瑪 4 177 mǎ [玛] Jade 玉 107 with 馬 177 phonetic. 图 agate 瑪瑙 mǎnǎo 图 agate

碼 5 177 mǎ [码] Stone 石 57 with 馬 177 phonetic. 图 yard 图 symbol ⇔ 籌碼 53, 號碼 27, 密碼 65, 起碼 97 碼頭 mǎtóu 图 wharf

罵 6 177 mà [骂] Net 网 122 (sometimes altered to ⺌ 9) with 馬 177 phonetic. 动 scold, curse ⇔ 辱罵 51, 詬罵 63, 謾罵 75, 挨罵 27, 咒罵 89, 責罵 27, 唾罵 173 罵人 màrén 动 swear (at people): 罵人話 swearword

羈 7 177 jī [羁] Modern form shows leather 革 24 net 网 122 for a horse 馬 177. 图 bridle 动 restrain 羈絆 jībàn 动 restrain, fetter 图 restraints 羈押 jīyā 动 detain, arrest

螞 177 mǎ [蚂] Insect 虫 125 with 馬 177 phonetic. 图 ant 螞蟻 mǎyǐ 图 ant

闖 177 chuǎng 9 [闯] Horse 馬 177 charging out of a gate 門 79. 动 rush, charge: 闖紅燈 run a red light 闖蕩 chuǎngdàng 动 venture out 闖禍 chuǎnghuò 动 cause an accident, get into trouble

鳥 1 178 niǎo [鸟] Pictograph of a bird with long tailfeathers. 图 bird ⇔ 水鳥 81, 鴕鳥 137, 啄木鳥 159 鳥巢 niǎocháo 图 bird's nest 鳥瞰 niǎokàn 图 bird's eye view 鳥籠 niǎolóng 图 bird cage

島 2 178 dǎo [岛] Mountain 山 67 inhabited by birds 鳥 178 (abbreviated, phonetic). 图 island ⇔ 群島 42, 荒島 82, 冰島 27, 廣島 25, 關島 27, 青島 27, 半島 97 島嶼 dǎoyǔ 图 islands

搗 3 178 dǎo [捣] Hand 手 97 with 島 178 phonetic. A variant of 擣 35. 动 pound, hit 搗蛋 dǎodàn 动 make trouble 搗亂 dǎoluàn 动 make trouble, cause a disturbance

梟 4 178 xiāo [枭] Bird 鳥 178 (abbreviated, phonetic) perched on a tree 木 7. 图 owl ⇔ 毒 梟 89 梟雄 xiāoxióng 图 ambitious and unscrupulous person

烏 5 178 wū [乌] Pictograph of a bird 鳥 178 with stroke representing eye omitted to indicate absence of contrast with color of feathers. 图 crow 图 black 烏龜 wūguī 图 tortoise 烏黑 wūhēi 图 jet black 烏克蘭 wūkèlán 地 Ukraine 烏龍茶 wūlóngchá 图 oolong tea

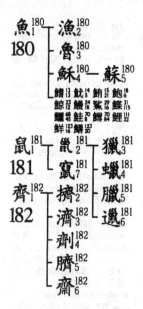

魚₁ 180 ─┬─ 漁₂ 180
180   ├─ 魯₃ 180
         ├─ 穌₄ 180 ── 蘇₅ 180
         │
鰭₁₃¹⁸⁰ 魷₁⁴ 鮪₁⁵ 鮑₁⁶
鯨₁₈ 鰻₂₄ 鯊₂₇ 鰈₃₁
鱷₄₂ 鮭₈₇ 鱈₉₂ 鯉₁₁₁
鮮₁₂₇ 鱔₁₂₃

鼠₁ 181 ─┬─ 鼠₁ 181 ─── 獵₃ 181
181   └─ 竄₇ 181 ─── 蠟₄ 181

齊₁ 182 ─┬─ 擠₂ 182 ─┬─ 臍₁ 181
182   ├─ 濟₃ 182 └─ 遘₆ 181
         ├─ 劑₄ 182
         ├─ 臍₅ 182
         └─ 齋₆ 182

烏魯木齊 wūlǔmùqí 图 Urumqi
- capital of Xinjiang Province
烏托邦 wūtuōbāng 图 utopia
烏鴉 wūyā 图 crow, raven
烏有 wūyǒu 图 nothing

鳴₆ 178 míng [鸣] Mouthing 口⁶⁶
by birds 鳥 i⁷⁸. 🔊 chirp, sing
图 birdcalls ⇔ 共鳴₃₅, 琴
瑟和鳴₈₆, 百家爭鳴₃₆
鳴鼓 mínggǔ 🔊 beat a drum
鳴謝 míngxiè 🔊 thank formally

鹿₁ 179 lù
🌀 Pictograph of a deer.
图 deer ⇔ 長頸鹿₈₃
鹿角 lùjiǎo 图 deer antler
鹿茸 lùróng 图 deer antler

塵₂ 179 chén [尘] Deer 鹿 i⁷⁹
(early form shows group of
three) kicking up dirt 土 i⁷⁰.
Simplified form, an ancient
variant, shows small 小₈⁷ dirt

土 i⁷⁰. 图 dust ⇔ 吸塵器₆₅,
灰塵₉²
塵埃 chénāi 图 dust
塵土 chéntǔ 图 dust

麓₃ 179 lù Forest 林₉⁷ with
鹿 i⁷⁹ phonetic. 图 foothill
⇔ 山麓⁶⁷

慶₄ 179 qìng [庆] Go 夂 i³₈ and
offer heartfelt 心₈³ gift of
deerskin 鹿 i⁷⁹ (abbreviated).
Simplified form uses 大 i⁷.
🔊 congratulate, celebrate ⇔
國慶₄₈, 重慶₂₇
慶典 qìngdiǎn 图 celebration
慶賀 qìnghè 🔊 congratulate,
celebrate
慶幸 qìngxìng 🔊 rejoice
慶祝 qìngzhù 🔊 celebrate

麃₅ 179 jiān
🌀 Pictograph of a yak-
like animal with deer-like 鹿 i⁷⁹

head and body from 彡 i⁴⁶. 图
a mythical animal

薦₆ 179 jiàn [荐₅⁴] Grass 艸⁹⁶
eaten by a mythical animal 麃₅⁷⁹
(phonetic). 图 fodder 🔊
recommend ⇔ 推薦₁₂²

魚₁ 180 yú [鱼] Pictograph of a
fish. 图 fish ⇔ 魷魚₁⁴, 鮪
魚₁⁵, 鮑魚 i⁶, 鯨魚₈², 鰻
魚₂⁴, 鯊魚₂⁷, 黃魚₉₂, 金
魚₁⁷, 鹹魚₈₉, 釣魚₉⁷, 鱷
魚₄²
魚叉 yúchā 图 harpoon
魚池 yúchí 图 fishpond
魚翅 yúchì 图 shark fin
魚刺 yúcì 图 fishbone
魚鉤 yúgōu 图 fishhook
魚卵 yúluǎn 图 roe

漁₂ 180 yú [渔] Fish 魚 i⁸⁰
(phonetic) from water 水₃₁.
🔊 fish
漁船 yúchuán 图 fishing boat
漁夫 yúfū 图 fisherman
漁港 yúgǎng 图 harbor
漁民 yúmín 图 fishermen

魯₃ 180 lǔ [鲁] Fish 魚 i⁸⁰
(phonetic) and mouth 口⁶⁶
(now written as 曰₄₈). 图 dull,
stupid 🌀 a surname: 魯迅 Lu
Xun - a 20th century writer 图
an ancient kingdom in China 🗺
Shandong Province ⇔ 秘魯₈₃,
烏魯木齊 i⁷⁸
魯莽 lǔmǎng 🔊 rude 图 rash,
careless

穌₄ 180 sū [稣] Grain 禾 i⁰⁸ with
魚 i⁸⁰ phonetic. 🌀 glean grains
of rice 🔊 revive (⇒ 甦 i⁰⁹) ⇔
耶穌₈⁷

蘇₅ 180 sū [苏] Plant 艸⁹⁶ with
穌 i⁸⁰ phonetic. Simplified

字譜及字典

361

form uses 辦㕘 simplification. 图 perilla 团 revive (⇨ 胜㑆) 地 Jiangsu Province a surname ⇔ 江蘇㕘

蘇丹 sūdān 地 Sudan
蘇俄 sūé 地 Soviet Russia
蘇格蘭 sūgélán 地 Scotland
蘇聯 sūlián 地 Soviet Union
蘇醒 sūxǐng 动 regain consciousness (⇨ 胜醒㑆)
蘇州 sūzhōu 地 Suzhou - a city in Jiangsu Province

鼠 181 shǔ
1   Pictograph of animal with prominent tail and teethy head (written as 臼㌔). 图 rat ⇔ 老鼠㌔, 松鼠㌔, 袋鼠㌔, 滑鼠㌔

鼠疫 shǔyì 图 plague

鼣 181 liè
2   Rat 鼠㛦 (head altered to 凶㌔) with fur 川㌔ raised.

獵 181 liè
3   [猎] Dog 犬㌔ with raised fur 鼣㛦 (phonetic). Simplified form uses 昔㝏. 团 hunt ⇔ 狩獵㌔, 打獵㌔, 弋獵㌔

獵取 lièqǔ 团 pursue, hunt

蠟 181 là
4   [蜡] Insect 虫㌔ with 鼣㛦 phonetic. Simplified form uses 昔㝏. 图 wax

蠟筆 làbǐ 图 crayon
蠟染 làrǎn 图 batik
蠟燭 làzhú 图 candle

臘 181 là
5   [腊] Flesh 肉㌔ with 鼣㛦 phonetic and suggestive of hunt 獵㛦. Simplified form uses 昔㝏. 团 meat sacrifice at end of lunar year 图 last month of lunar year ⇔ 希臘㌔

臘腸 làcháng 图 sausage

邋 181 lā
6   Movement 辵㌔ with 鼣㛦 phonetic. 团 pull 形 slovenly

邋遢 lātà 形 slovenly: 我的字很邋遢. My characters are very poorly written.

竄 181 cuàn
7   [窜] Rat 鼠㛦 in its den 穴㌔. Simplified form uses 串㌔. 团 hide 团 flee

竄改 cuàngǎi 团 interpolate, alter: 竄改歷史 rewrite history

竄逃 cuàntáo 团 flee in disorder

齊 182 qí
1   [齐] Pictograph of stalks of grain in a field. Simplified form uses 文㌔. 形 even, orderly, neat 副 together 形 complete 动 a surname ⇔ 一齊㌔, 百花齊放㌔, 整齊㌔, 烏魯木齊㌔

擠 182 jǐ
2   [挤] Hand 手㌔ with 齊㛦 phonetic. 团 squeeze 团 push 形 crowded ⇔ 擁擠㌔, 排擠㌔

擠進 jǐjìn 团 crowd in

濟 182 jì jǐ
3   [济] Water 水㌔ with 齊㛦 phonetic. jǐ: 地 an ancient river 形 numerous jì: 团 ford a river 团 aid ⇔ 經濟㌔, 賑濟㌔, 同舟共濟㌔, 接濟㌔, 救濟㌔

濟濟 jǐjǐ 形 numerous (people)
濟南 jǐnán,jìnán 地 Jinan - capital of Shandong Province
濟助 jìzhù 团 assist

劑 182 jì
4   [剂] Make even 齊㛦 (phonetic) with knife 刀㌔. 动 cut even 团 prepare (medicine) 图 团 dose ⇔ 調劑㌔

劑量 jìliàng 图 dosage

臍 182 jí
5   [脐] Flesh 肉㌔ with 齊㛦 phonetic. 图 navel ⇔ 肚臍㌔

齋 182 zhāi
6   [斋] Omen 示㌔ with 齊㛦 phonetic. Simplified form uses 而㌔. 形 pious, pure 图 vegetarian meal 图 study ⇔ 書齋㌔, 吃齋㌔

齋飯 zhāifàn 图 Buddhist vegetarian dish

英 漢 索 引 表

This English-Chinese index is an inversion of the Chinese-English section, indexing the English definitions of Chinese words and characters. All word definitions are included, but rare character definitions are excluded. Translations of longer examples are also excluded. Since this is merely an index, rather than an English-Chinese dictionary, the Chinese following an English listing will not always be the most common Chinese definition of that English word. For this same reason, many common English words are not included. These problems can be mitigated by checking the synonyms of missing or partial English listings.

The top number to the right of a Chinese word is the 文 reference number and the bottom number is the 字 reference number.

actual 眞實 實
actually 究竟 其實 確實 事實上
acupuncture 針灸
acupuncture points 穴道
acute 銳
adapt 適應
add 加 添 添加 增 增添
add on 加上
addict 癮者
addicted to 上癮 嗜酒 沈醉 耽溺
addicted to alcohol 酗酒 嗜酒
addiction 癖好 癮
addition 加法
additional 額外
address 住址 地址
address book 通訊錄
adept 拿手 嫻熟
adhere to 遵從
adhesiveness 黏性
adjacent 毗鄰
adjective 形容詞
adjoin 鄰接
adjourn 休會 解散
adjourn a meeting 散會
adjust 調節 調劑 調節 調整 對準
administer 治理 轄理
administer finances 理財
administration 行政 施政 政
administrative region 轄區
admire 欽佩 讚賞 嘆服 嘆賞 仰仗 仰慕 仰望 佩服 欣賞
admire sincerely 心服
admission ticket 門票
admit 承認 認
admit an error 認錯
admonish 訓誡 警戒

規勸
adopt 收養 領養 採 採納 採取 採行 採用
adopted daughter 養女
adopted son 養子
adorable 可愛
adore 愛慕
adorn 飾 修 修飾 點綴 裝扮 裝飾
adult 大人 成年 成人
adulterate 攙雜
adultery 姦淫 通姦
advance 提昇 提升 前進 進 進行
advance money 墊款
advance notice 預告
advance rapidly 邁進 猛進
advanced 先進
advantage 上風 長處 好處 利 益 優勢
advantageous 有利 便
adventure 冒險
adverb 副詞
adversity 不幸 逆境 患難
advertise 登廣告 (⇨廣告)
advertisement 廣告
advise 指教 教 勸告 勸導
advise against 勸阻
adviser 參謀 顧問 導師
advocate 主張 鼓吹 提倡
aerobic 有氧 (⇨氧)
aerobics 有氧舞蹈 (⇨氧)
aesthetics 美感 美學
afar 老遠

affair 事 事情
affairs 事務
affect 影響
affected 做作
affection 感情 慈愛 情意 心意
affectionate 親暱 親熱 體貼
affiliated 隸屬 附屬
affirm 肯定
afforest 綠化
affront 侮辱
Afghanistan 阿富汗
afraid 畏懼
afresh 重新
Africa 非洲
African 非洲人
African-American 非洲裔美國人
after 之後
after all 究竟 到底 畢竟
after-effect 後勁 後遺症
afternoon 下午 午後
aftertaste 回味
afterwards 後 後來 以後 事後 然後
again 又 再 再次 再度
again and again 一再 頻頻
agate 瑪瑙
age 年代 年紀 年齡 年歲 壽 世 齡
aged 陳年 衰老
agenda 議程
agent 經紀人 代理
aggravate 加劇 加重
agile 輕快 敏捷 靈敏
agitate 攪擾 鬧
agitated 激動 煩躁
agitatedly 勃然

agitation 風潮
agony 痛楚
agree 同意 情願 契合 肯
agree to 答應 約定 約好 應
agree with 贊成 相符
agreement 協定
agriculture 農業
ah 啊
ahead 前邊 前頭
ahead of schedule 提前 提早
aid 賑濟 協助 扶救 救濟 紓困 濟
aikido 合氣道
aim 瞄 對準
aimed at 針對
air 空氣 氣
air current 氣流
air force 空軍
air raid 空襲
air route 航線
air temperature 氣溫
air-conditioner 空調 冷氣機
air-conditioning 冷氣 空調
aircraft carrier 航空母艦
airline 航空公司
airmail 航空信
airplane 飛機
airport 機場
airs 氣
alarm 驚 驚動 警報
alarm clock 鬧鐘
Alas! 哉
alcohol 酒 酒精
alcohol content 酒精含量
alcoholic 酒鬼
alcoholism 酗酒
alert 警惕
alertness 警覺
alias 化名 別名

alien 外僑[67] 外星人[75]
alienated 疏遠[40]
alike 同樣[71] 相似[40]
alimony 贍養費[71]
Alishan 阿里山[23]
alive 活著[71]
alkaline 鹼性[19]
all 一概[1] 一律[1] 僉[120]
皆[121] 均[61] 個個[60] 全[67]
全部[67] 全體[67] 咸[120]
凡[47] 統[87] 通[87] 通通[87]
諸[40] 都[39] 所有[40]
俱[110]
all along 一向[40] 從來[60]
向來[40]
all around 四周[62] 周[62]
all at once 一下[1] 一下
子[1]
all day 終日[87] 整天[77]
all night 通宵[87]
all of a sudden 一下[1] 一
下子[1]
all one's life 畢生[136]
all one's strength 全力[67]
all over 渾身[58]
all right 普通[77] 行[71] 好[71]
還好[71] 還可以 (⇨
可以[47])
all sorts 百般 (⇨般[97])
all the way 一路[1]
all things 凡事[47]
all year 四季[62] 終年[87]
Allah 真主[25]
allergic 過敏[133]
allergy 敏感[47] 過敏
症[133]
alleviate 減輕[40] 解[109]
alley 巷[71] 巷子[75] 弄[47]
衖[71] 衚衕[40]
alliance 同盟[71] 聯盟[71]
盟[71]
alliance treaty 盟約[9]
allied armies 聯軍[71]
allocate 調[62] 調撥[40] 調
配[62] 支配[40] 撥[40]
allow 允許[67] 給予 任[71]
讓[40] 容許[67] 許可[67]
准[162] 准許[162]

allowance 貼補[40] 補助
金[40]
alloy 合金[71]
ally 同盟[71] 聯盟[71] 聯手[71]
掛鉤[67] 盟國[71]
ally with 串連[157]
alma mater 母校[67]
almanac 年鑑[47] 曆書[108]
almond 杏仁[77]
almost 殆[47] 幾乎[47] 將
近[60]
aloe 蘆薈[47]
alone 孑然[60] 孤單[67] 孤
獨[40] 獨[62] 單獨[67]
alone in the world 孑然
一身[40]
along 沿[67]
along with 隨著[40]
aloof 冷漠[40] 淡漠[40]
alphabet 字母[47]
already 既[40] 就[47] 已[40]
已經[40] 早已[40]
already known 已知[47]
already so 已然[40]
also 又[40] 亦[40] 并[40] 也[40]
還[40]
altar 祭壇[40] 壇[40]
alter 更易[40] 更改[40] 移[40]
變[40] 竄改[40]
alternate 更[40] 更迭[40]
alternate member 候補[40]
alternately 交互[40] 迭[40]
輪流[40]
although 縱[40] 即使[40]
雖[40] 雖然[40] 雖則[40]
altitude 海拔[40]
altogether 一共[1] 一起[1]
alum 校友[40] 畢業生[136]
aluminum 鋁[51]
always 一直[1] 從來[60] 老
是[40] 始終[40] 常常[40]
朝夕[40] 永遠[120] 總[40]
總是[40] 素來[40]
amateur 業餘[176]
amaze 驚奇[40]
amazing 不得了[40]
ambassador 大使[40]
amber 琥珀[122]

ambiguous 曖昧[40] 雙
關[47]
ambition 抱負[40] 志[40] 志
向[40] 野心[102]
ambulance 救護車[40]
ambush 伏擊[40] 埋伏[40]
狙擊[47]
ameliorate 改善[40] 緩
和[40]
amend 修正[40]
America 美國[40] 美洲[40]
American 美國人[40] 美
籍 (⇨籍[40])
American football 美式足
球 (⇨足球[40])
American government 華
府[40]
amiable 隨和[40] 和藹[40]
和善[108]
amicable settlement 和
解[40]
Amitabha 阿彌陀佛[40]
ammunition 彈藥[40]
amnesty 特赦[40] 赦免[40]
among 之中[40] 中間[40] 間[40]
among which 其中[40]
amoral 卑鄙[40]
amount 份量[40] 數目[40]
多寡[7] 量[40]
amount of money 款項[40]
金額[40]
amphetamine 安非他
命[40]
ample 充分[40] 充足[40] 寬
裕[40]
amplify 擴音[40]
amuse 逗趣[40] 逗人[40]
逗笑[40]
amuse oneself 自娛[40]
amusement 娛樂[40]
amusing 好笑[40] 逗[40]
analogous 類似[40]
analogy 比擬[40] 比喻[40]
analysis 分析[40]
analyze 剖析[40] 分解[40]
分析[40] 解析[40]
anarchy 亂[40] 無政府狀
態 (⇨政府[40])

anatomy 解剖學[40]
ancestors 宗[40] 祖[40] 祖
先[40] 祖宗[40]
ancestral grave 祖墳[40]
ancestral hall 祠堂[40]
anchor 錨[40]
ancient 久遠[40] 古[40] 古
老[40] 昔[40]
ancient books 古籍[40]
ancient bronze tripod 鼎[40]
ancient times 古代[40] 古
時[40]
ancients 先民[40] 古人[40]
and 曁[40] 及[40] 並[40] 并[40]
以及[40] 和[40] 且[40]
而[40]
and even 乃至[40]
and not 並非[40]
and so on 等等[40]
and then 然後[40] 而後[134]
anecdote 軼事[40] 軼聞[40]
anesthetize 麻醉[40]
anew 重新[40]
angel 天使[40]
anger 憤怒[40] 氣[40] 氣
死[40] 觸怒[40]
angered 氣死[40]
angle 稜角[40] 角度[40]
angry 生氣[40] 氣憤[40] 惱
怒[143]
anguished 苦澀[40]
Anhui Province 安徽[40]
animal 動物[40] 獸[40]
animal husbandry 畜牧[40]
animals 禽獸[40]
animation 動畫[40]
anime 動畫[40]
ankle 腳踝[40] 足踝[40]
annals 紀[40]
annex 鯨吞[40] 吞併[40] 併
吞[40] 兼併[40]
annihilate 殲滅[40]
anniversary 週年[40] 紀
念日[40]
annotate 註解[40]
annotation 註[40] 註解[40]
註釋[40] 批註[40] 詮釋[40]
annotations 訓詁[40]

announce 宣佈 宣佈 宣布 宣告 公佈 公布 公告 揭示 佈 通告 發布 發佈
announcement 佈告 通告
annoy 攪 惱 煩
annoyed 煩擾
annoyed by 厭煩
annoying 無聊 惱人 煩 煩惱
anonymous 匿名 無名 無名氏
anonymous letter 匿名信
another 另外 他
another time 下次
answer 搭腔 答案 回答 解答
ant 螞蟻
antagonism 對抗性
antagonize 作對
Antarctica 南極洲
antelope 羚羊
antenna 天線
anthology 選 選集
anthropology 人類學
anti-American 反美
anti-Chinese 反華
anticipate 期盼 意料 企盼 企望 預料
anti-communist 反共
anti-foreign 排外
antipathy 反感
antique 古董 古玩
anti-rightist 反右
anti-rightist campaign 反右運動
anus 肛門
anxiety 疑慮 虞
anxious 急 心焦 憂慮 憂慮 焦慮 急 焦慮 焦躁
anxious to 急於
anxious to try 躍躍欲試

anxiously 亟
any 任何
anyhow 反正 好歹
anyone 任何人
anytime 隨時
anyway 反正 橫豎
apartment 公寓 套房
apathetic 淡漠
ape 猿 猿猴
ape-man 猿人
apologize 道歉
apology 歉意
apparatus 儀器 器械
apparel 成衣
apparent 昭著 著明 顯 顯
apparently 好像 似乎
appeal 上訴 申訴 號召 情趣 陳請書 (⇒ 陳情)
appeal for 呼籲
appear 起 呈 呈現 出場 出現 顯出 顯得
appear in court 出庭
appear in public 露面 出面
appear to be 貌似
appearance 神氣 神情 長相 形態 模樣 外貌 狀 狀態 相 樣 樣子 表 面貌
appease 苟安 姑息 綏靖
append 附帶 附加 加
appendicitis 盲腸炎 闌尾炎
appendix 附錄 盲腸 闌尾
appetite 食量 食慾 胃口
appetizer 開味菜

applaud 喝采 鼓掌 拍手
apple 蘋果
appliance 用具
application form 申請表
apply 申請 施 敷 著 適用 運用 應用
apply makeup 化妝 打扮
apply mechanically 套用
appoint 指定 聘請 任 任命
appointed 膺任
appointment 約會
appointment letter 聘書
apportion 攤派 分攤
appraisal 評價
appraise 評價 估 估價 品 鑑定
appreciable 可觀
appreciate 讚賞 賞 賞識 升值 欣賞 鑑賞 觀賞
apprehend 緝拿
apprehension 顧慮
apprehensive 忐忑 憂懼
apprentice 學徒
approach 立意 接近 走近 靠近 來臨
appropriate 佔用 合 合適 恰當 當 適 適當 適度 適合 正當 妥 妥當 妥善 宜
appropriate for 適於
appropriations 經費
approve 核准 允 批准 認可 准予
approve of 贊成 贊同
approved 通過

approximate 略 大概 近似
approximately 大約 約
apricot 杏
April 四月 (⇒ 月)
apron 圍裙
aptitude 才能
Arab 阿拉伯
arbitrarily 任意
arbitrary 武斷 蠻橫
arbitrate 評議 仲裁
arc 弓形 弧 弧形
arch 拱 拱門 弓
arched bridge 拱橋
archenemy 宿敵
archeology 考古學
archipelago 群島
architect 建築師
archway 拱門
Arctic 北極
ardent 殷 殷切 熱心
arduous 艱鉅 艱苦
area 區 面 面積
Argentina 阿根廷
argue 議論 爭 爭辯 爭執
argument 論點 論調
arid 燥 乾旱
arise 起來
aristocrat 貴族
aristocratic family 世家
arithmetic 算術
arm 胳臂 胳膊 臂 武裝 手臂
arm and shoulder 臂膀
armaments 干戈 武器 武裝 兵備 軍火
armor 盔甲 甲
armpit 腋
arms and legs 四肢
army 陸軍 兵 軍 軍隊

aroma 馨香[37] 香氣[42]
around 光景[42]
arouse 啓發[37] 激發[37] 激發[37] 激起[37] 挑撥[137] 挑逗[137]
arouse suspicion 啓人疑竇 (⇨疑竇[37])
arrange 訂[?] 佈置[67] 安排[26] 支配[42] 措[?] 料理[67] 理[63] 編排[115] 組[12] 擺[12] 列[133] 排[169] 排列[169]
arrange classes 排課[?]
arrange flowers 插花[28]
arrange for 安置[?]
arrange to 約定[?] 約好[?]
arrange with 接洽[67]
arranged marriage 包辦婚姻[19]
arrangement 條理[37] 安排[36] 層次[144] 排序[?]
arrest 拘留[37] 拘捕[67] 扣押[?] 捉拿[?] 逮捕[90] 抓[121] 緝[?] 緝拿[137] 羈押[?]
arrest smugglers 緝私[137]
arrive 降臨[?] 到[25] 到達[?] 趕到[?] 止[?] 抵達[?] 至[128] 來[140] 來到[160] 來臨[160]
arrive late 遲到[97]
arrogant 高傲[37] 傲[?] 傲慢[?] 驕傲[?] 驕傲[?] 自大[139]
arrogant and aggressive 囂張[48]
arrow 箭[37]
arrowhead 箭頭[37]
art 藝術[98] 藝術品[?] 美術[?]
art exhibition 畫展[37] 美術展[?]
art museum 美術館[97] 藝術館[?]
artemisa 蕭[?]
artery 動脈[37] 脈[120]
article 冠詞[114] 條[37] 條款[37] 報導[37] 報道[37] 報告[37] 文章[98]

artificial 人工[10] 人為[10] 人造[10]
artillery 砲兵[19]
artist 藝術家[98]
arts and literature 文藝[98]
as a group 一併[?]
as a rule 照例[?]
as before 照舊[126] 依舊[126] 依然[126]
as can be seen 可見[?]
as everyone well knows 眾所周知[?]
as expected 果然[?] 果真[?]
as follows 如下[?]
as for 對[176]
as hard as one can 盡量[18] 儘量[18]
as if 有如[?] 如[?] 如同[?] 似乎[?] 宛如[?] 儼然[?] 猶[?] 猶如[159]
as of old 如昔[?]
as scheduled 如期[?] 按時[?]
as soon as 一旦[?]
as soon as possible 儘快[?] 及早[?]
as time passes 久而久之[24]
as to 至於[128] 對於[176]
as usual 仍舊[?] 照常[?] 照舊[?] 照樣[?]
as well as 以及[38]
as wished 如意[?] 如願[?]
as you please 隨意[15]
ascend 上升[13] 昇[37]
ashamed 羞[?] 羞慚[38] 羞愧[?] 羞澀[?] 汗顏[?] 慚愧[?]
ashen 鐵青[?]
ashes 餘燼[44] 灰[37] 灰燼[37] 煙灰[?]
ashtray 煙灰缸[?]
Asia 亞洲[?]
Asian 亞洲人[166]
Asian Pacific 亞太[166]
Asian-American 亞裔美國人 (⇨裔[26])

aside from 除外[30]
ask 打聽[37] 訊[37] 請問[37]
ask a question 發問[?]
ask for 要[37]
ask for advice 領教[?] 請教[37]
ask for help 伸手[?]
ask off 請假[?]
ask the way 問路[37]
askew 歪[?] 歪斜[?]
aspect 局面[37] 方面[37] 面[?]
asphalt 柏油[37]
aspiration 願望[37] 抱負[37] 志[37] 志向[37] 職志[37] 意願[?]
aspirations 襟懷[72]
aspire to 嚮往[?]
ass 屁[?] 屁股[?] 臀部[?]
assassin 刺客[37]
assassinate 暗殺[37] 刺殺[37]
assault 突擊[37] 襲擊[37]
assemble 召集[37] 裝配[37] 組合[112] 聚[37] 聚會[37] 聚集[37] 會合[?] 薈萃[?] 集[162] 集合[162] 集會[162]
assent 應允[162]
assert 宣稱[?] 斷言[?]
assess 評估[37]
assess and decide 核定[?]
assets 資產[37] 財產[37] 產[?]
assiduous 刻苦[15]
assign 指定[37] 分配[37]
assimilate 吸取[37] 同化[37] 攝取[37]
assist 協助[37] 接濟[37] 輔助[37] 輔佐[37] 援助[37] 助[117] 濟助[?]
assistance 贊助[37] 助力[117]
assistant 副[?] 幫手[37] 助理[117] 助手[117]
assistant manager 襄理[68]

associate 掛鉤[?]
association 公會[17] 協會[?] 社[?] 社團[?] 會[?] 會社[?]
assorted 什錦[?]
assortment 品種[?]
assume 就[?] 假定[116] 設[?] 擔[?] 擔當[?] 假設[?]
assume a post 任[34]
assume office 就職[14]
assume personally 自負[139]
assume responsibility 自負責任[139] 負責任[139]
assumption 假設[116]
assure 保證[37]
assured 篤定[12]
assuredly 固然[37]
asteroid 小行星 (⇨行星[?])
asthma 氣喘病[?]
astigmatism 散光[?]
astonish 震驚[?]
astonished 駭異[37] 驚訝[37] 驚異[37] 詫異[37] 發愣[?]
astonishing 驚人[18]
astringent 澀[?]
astrologist 星象家[?]
astrology 星象[?] 星象學[?]
astronaut 太空人[?]
astronomy 天文[37] 天文學[?]
at 于[37] 在[?] 於[10] 對[176]
at a distance from 隔[174]
at an interval of 隔[174]
at ease 坦然[?] 自在[?]
at every turn 動輒[?]
at first 原先[?] 起初[37] 最初[37]
at hand 現有[10]
at last 最後[37] 最終[37]
at least 起碼[37] 至少[?]
at once 趕快[?] 當即[?]
at one's convenience 順

匪 匪徒
bang 砰 碰
Bangkok 曼谷
banish 驅逐 放逐
banister 欄杆
bank 銀行 岸
bank account 帳戶
bank draft 匯票
banknote 鈔 鈔票
banner 旗 旗幟 旗子
banquet 宴 宴會 筵席 酒席
bar 吧 酒吧 酒店 酒家
bar girl 吧女
barbarian 野人 番
barbaric 野
barbecue 烤肉
barber 理髮師
bare 赤 赤裸
barefoot 赤腳
bargain 討價 談判 殺價 講價
bargain price 廉價
bargaining chip 籌碼
baritone 低沈
bark 樹皮 吠
barn 穀倉
barrel 桶
barren 荒 荒涼
barrier 屏障 壁壘 藩籬
bartender 酒保
base 卑鄙 基地 底 底子 壘 據點
baseball 棒球
based on 憑
basement 地下室
basic 初級 基本
basin 盆 盆地
basis 憑據 基 本 依據
basket 筐子 簍子 籃 籃子
basketball 籃球
bat 棒子 蝙蝠

batch 批 撥
bath 澡 浴
bathe 洗澡 浴 沐浴 洗個澡 (⇨澡)
bathroom 浴室 廁所 洗手間
bathtub 浴缸
batik 蠟染
battalion 營
battery 電池
battle 仗 役 搏鬥 戰
battle formation 陣
battle line 戰線 陣線
battlefield 戰場
bay 灣
be 是 係 為
beach 沙灘 灘 海濱 海灘
bead 珠 顆粒
beak 喙 嘴
beam 梁
bean 豆
bean sprout 豆芽
bear 承受 擔 擔負 堪 生 生育 肩負 熊 負 荷
bear fruit 結 結實
bear paw 熊掌
beard 鬍子
bearing 姿態 舉止
beast 畜生 獸
beasts 禽獸
beat 拷 揍 贏 敲擊 扑 打 跳 捶 撲
beat a drum 鳴鼓
beat to death 打死
beat up 拷打 毆 毆打
beaten up 挨打 挨揍
beautiful 漂亮 美 美麗 美妙 娟 優美
beautiful and charming 嬌豔

beautiful looks 美貌
beautiful woman 仙女 仙子 美女 美人
beautify 美容
beauty parlor 美容院
because 既然 因 因為 由於
beckon 召喚 招 招呼
become 就 成 成為 形成 發 變 變成 變得 為
bed 床 床鋪
bedroom 寢 寢室 臥房 臥室
bee 蜜蜂 蜂
beef 牛肉
been to 去過
beeper 呼叫器
beer 啤酒
beer hall 啤酒屋
beetle 甲蟲
before 先 先前 以前 之前
before one's eyes 眼前
beforehand 事前 事先 預先
befriend 結交 親近
beg 丐 乞 乞求 乞討
beggar 乞丐
begin 下手 起 始 著手 動手 開 開闢 開幕 開始 開演
begin classes 開學
begin school 開學
begin suddenly 勃發
begin to study 初學
beginner 初學者
beginning 初 始 頭 開始
beginning of the month 月初
beginning of the year 年初
behave 做人 為人

behave indecently 猥褻
behavior 舉動 作為 行為
behead 斬首
behind 後 後邊 後面 之後
Beijing 北京 北平
Belgium 比利時
belief 信念 信仰
believe 認為 以為 相信
believe in 信奉 信服 信仰
believer 教徒 信徒
belittle 輕 輕忽 輕視 藐視 小看
bell 鈴 鐘
belly 肚 肚子
belong to 隸屬 屬 屬於 係 歸屬
beloved 親愛的
below 下 下邊 下面 以下 之下 低於
below zero 零下
belt 皮帶 腰帶 帶
bench 板凳 凳 凳子
bend 傾 屈 曲 彎
beneath 之下
beneficial 利
beneficial to 有助於
beneficiary 受益者
benefit 裨益 受惠 受益 利 利益 益 益處
benevolence 仁 仁愛 仁慈 恩
bent 彎 彎曲
bequeath 遺留
berate 詬罵
bereavement money 撫恤金
Berlin 柏林
berth 床鋪 船艙

舖[94] 舖位[94]
beseech 懇求[114] 籲請[113]
besides 除[93] 除外[93] 以外[93] 此外[89]
besiege 圍攻[150]
besmirch 褻瀆[74]
best 最好[197] 最佳[18]
bestial behavior 獸行[76]
bestial desire 獸慾[76]
bestir 振作[9]
bestow 頒[17] 施[75] 賞賜[69] 賦予[57] 賦與[57] 賜予[63]
bestseller 暢銷書[25]
bet 打賭[35]
betel nut 檳榔[7]
betray 背叛[5] 叛[5] 叛賣[7] 出賣[110] 變節[153]
betrothal gifts 聘禮[73]
between 介[7] 之間[63] 中間[31] 間[63]
beverage 飲料[182]
beware 當心[36]
bewitch 蠱惑[125]
beyond the Great Wall 賽外[114] 關外[149]
bias 偏見[115] 偏心[115]
biased 偏頗[115]
Bible 聖經[73]
bibliography 參考文獻[22]
bickering 齟齬[197]
bicycle 腳踏車[178] 自行車[139]
bid farewell 離別[?] 道別[?]
bide time 守候[76]
big 大[37]
Big Dipper 北斗七星 (⇨ 斗[87])
big character 大字[37]
big fellow 大漢[37]
big stir 軒然大波[?]
big toe 拇趾[?]
big-character poster 大字報[?]
biggest 最大[197]
bilateral 雙方[162] 雙[41]

bill 票[?] 帳單[?] 法案[?] 喙[?]
billboard 看板[114]
billiards 台球[?] 撞球[?]
billion 十億 (⇨ 億[?])
billow 滾[?] 滾滾[?] 冒[?]
bind 紮[?] 約束[?] 捆[?] 縛[?] 綁[?] 裹[?] 束[?] 束縛[?] 裝訂[?] 纏[?] 保[?]
bind feet 裹腳[?]
biochemistry 生物化學[?]
biography 傳[?] 傳記[?]
biology 生物學[?]
bird 禽[?] 鳥[176]
bird cage 鳥籠[176]
bird's eye view 鳥瞰[176]
bird's nest 鳥巢[176]
birdcalls 鳴[?]
birth control 節育[?] 避孕[?]
birth control pills 避孕藥[?]
birthday 冥誕[?] 生日[?] 誕辰[?]
birthday party 慶生會[?]
birthday person 壽星[?]
biscuit 餅[?] 餅乾[?]
bishop 主教[?]
bit 一點[?]
bitch 婊子[?]
bite 叮[?] 咬[?]
biting cold 凜冽[?]
bitter 苦[?] 苦澀[?] 慘痛[?]
bizarre 奇異[?]
black 黔[?] 盧[?] 黑[?] 黑色[?] 烏[176]
black and white 黑白[?]
black market 黑市[?] 黑市場 (⇨ 市場[?])
black pepper 胡椒[?]
black person 黑人[?]
black tea 紅茶[?]
blackboard 黑板[?]
blacklist 黑名單 (⇨ 名單[?])

blade 刀口[?] 刀刃[?] 刃[?]
blame 咎[?] 指責[?] 怨[?] 責[?] 責備[?] 責怪[?] 埋怨[?] 歸咎[?]
bland 乏味[?] 味如嚼蠟 (⇨ 嚼[?])
blank 空白[?] 白[?]
blanket 被子[?] 毯子[?]
blasphemy 褻瀆[?]
blazing 熾[?] 熾烈[?] 熾熱[?]
blazing hot 炎熱[?]
bleach 漂白[?] 漂白劑[?]
bleak 蕭瑟[?] 淒涼[?] 慘淡[?]
bleed 流血[?] 出血[110]
blemish 瑕疵[?]
blend 混合[?] 調配[?] 融[?] 融合[?]
bless 祝福[?] 保佑[?]
blessing 保佑[?]
blind 盲[?] 盲目[?] 瞎[?] 失明[?]
blind person 盲人[?] 瞎子[?]
blinded with love by 迷戀[138]
blindly 盲目[?]
blinds 簾[?] 窗簾[144]
blink 瞬[?] 眨[?] 眨眼[?]
bloat 脹[?]
block 卡[?] 梗阻[?] 塞[?] 遮[?] 截[?] 截斷[?] 擋[?] 閉塞[?] 封[?] 攔[?] 攔住[?] 阻[117]
block up 堵塞[?] 堵住[?] 阻塞[?]
blockade 封鎖[?]
blocked 阻滯[117]
blond hair 金髮[?]
blood 血[?] 血液[116]
blood cell 血球[116]
blood pressure 血壓[116]
blood relations 血統[116]
blood vessel 血管[116]
bloody 血腥[116]
bloom 開放[?] 開花[?]

blow 吹[?] 颳[?]
blow up 炸毀[?]
blow-dry 吹風[?]
blow-dryer 吹風機[?]
blowing wind 颳風[?]
blue 青[?] 青色[?] 藍[?] 藍色[?]
blue sea 滄海[?] 碧海[?]
blue sky 青天[?] 藍天[?]
blue-green 翠[?] 翠綠[?] 翡翠[?]
blueprint 藍圖[?]
blues 藍調音樂[?]
blunt 唐突[?] 鈍[?]
blurred 模糊[?]
blurt out 脫口而出[?]
blush 臉紅[?]
boar 野豬[?]
board 板[?] 寄宿[?] 木板[?]
board a plane 登機[?]
board of directors 董事會[?]
boarding pass 登機證[?]
boast 吹[?] 吹牛[?] 誇[?] 自誇[?]
boast of 標榜[?]
boat 航[?] 船[?] 舟[129]
bode ill 不妙[?] 凶多吉少[?]
Bodhidharma 達摩[?]
Bodhisattva 菩薩[?]
body 軀[?] 軀體[?] 體[?] 肉體[132] 身[147] 身材[147] 身軀[147] 身體[147] 身子[147]
body shape 體型[?] 身形[147]
body temperature 體溫[?]
body weight 體重[?]
bodyguard 侍衛[?] 保鏢[?]
bogus 假[?] 偽[171]
Bohai Sea 渤海[?]
boil 滾[?] 煮[?] 開[?]
boil thin slices of meat 涮[?]

check against 對照	裁	chip 片	circuit 線路 周
check in 報到	child 孩 孩子 小孩 小孩兒 小孩子 子 童 兒 兒童 小朋友 (⇨ 朋友)	chirp 鳴	circuitous 迂迴
check out 退房		chisel 鑿	circular 圓形
checkpoint 關卡		chivalry 俠 武俠	circulate 循環 流通
cheek 臉皮 面頰		chives 大蔥 韭 韭菜	circulation 循環 通風
cheer 吶喊 歡呼		chocolate 巧克力	circumference 周圍 圓周
cheerful 快活	child prodigy 神童	choice 選擇 抉擇 精選 精選	circumstances 局勢 處境 風頭 境地 情況
cheerleading squad 啦啦隊	child's play 兒戲	choke 窒息	circus 馬戲
Cheers! 乾杯	childbirth 分娩	cholera 霍亂	circus troupe 馬戲團
cheese 奶酪 乳酪 乾酪	childhood 小時候 幼年 童年	cholesterol 膽固醇	citation 表彰
chef 大廚師 (⇨ 廚師)	childish 幼稚	Chongqing 重慶	cite 引 引述 引用 援引 表彰
chemical compound 化合物	childlike 稚氣 孩子氣	choose 遴選 選 選 拔 選擇 抉擇 挑 挑選 取 取捨 推選	citizen 公民 國民 市民
chemical fertilizer 化肥	children 子女 兒女	choose words 措辭	citizenry 市民
chemistry 化學	chime 鈴 風鈴	choosy 挑 挑剔	city 城 城市 市 都市
chemotherapy 化學療法	chimney 煙囪	chop 砍 印章 剁 圖章 斬	city center 城中心
cheongsam 旗袍	chimpanzee 黑猩猩 (⇨ 猩猩)	chop down 砍伐	city council 市議會 (⇨ 議會)
cherish 胸懷 抱 珍惜 鍾愛 心懷 愛護 愛惜 懷 緬懷	chin 下巴	chop off 砍掉	city gate 城門
	China 神州 中國 中華 華 夏	chopsticks 筷子	city god 城隍
cherry 櫻 櫻桃	china 瓷器	chores 雜務	city wall 城牆
cherry blossom 櫻花	China own 唐人街 華埠	chorus 合唱團	city-founded 市立
chess 棋 象棋 西洋象棋 (⇨ 象棋)	Chinese 漢語 國文 國語 中文 華語	chow mein 炒麵	civil rights 民權
chess piece 棋 棋子	Chinese calendar 農曆	Christ 基督	civil servant 公僕 文官
chessboard 棋盤	Chinese characters 漢字 方塊字 中文字	Christian 基督徒	civil service exam 科舉
chest 胸 胸部 胸膛 箱 箱子	Chinese checkers 跳棋	Christianity 基督教	civil war 內戰
chestnut 栗子	Chinese date tree 棗樹	Christmas 聖誕 耶誕 耶誕節 聖誕節	civilian 民
chestnut tree 栗樹	Chinese descent 華裔	chronicle 傳	civilian clothes 便衣
chew 嚼 嚼食	Chinese edition 中文版 (⇨ 版)	chrysanthemum 菊 菊花 黃花	civilians 平民
chew carefully 咀嚼	Chinese food 中餐	Chungking 重慶	civilities 客套
Chiang Kai-Shek 蔣介石	Chinese gown 旗袍	chunk 丁 塊	civilization 文明
Chicago 芝加哥	Chinese macrame 中國結 (⇨ 結)	church 教會 教堂	civilized 文明
chick 小雞	Chinese person 華人 中國人	cicada 蟬	claim to be 自稱
chicken 雞	Chinese-American 華裔美國人	cigar 雪茄	clam 蚌
chickenpox 水痘	Chinese-to-English 漢英	cigarette 香煙 香菸	clam shell 蚌殼
chief 頭領 頭目 總 首 首領 首 長 酋長		cigarette butt 煙蒂	clamber 攀 攀爬 爬
chief culprit 元兇		cinema 電影院	clamor 叫囂
chief executive officer 總		cinnamon 肉桂	clamorous 鬧
		circle 圈 圈子 繞 盤旋 圓圈	clan 氏族 族 家族

clan system 氏族制度

clap 鼓掌 拍手 拍手

clarify 澄清 釐清 表白 闡明 弄清楚 (⇒清楚) 搞清楚

clarity 清晰度

clash 衝突

class 階級 等別 流課 門類 班 班級

class leader 班長

class representative 班代

class struggle 階級鬥爭

classic 高尚

classical 經典 古典

classical Chinese 文言 文言文

classical literature 古典文學

classical music 古典音樂

classics 經典 經書 典

classification 類別

classified 內部

classmate 師弟 師姊 師妹 師兄 同班同學

classroom 教室 課堂

classy 高貴

clause 條款

claw 爪 爪子

clay 黏土

clean 擦拭 清白 清潔 乾淨 潔淨

cleanse 清洗

clear 朗 亮 透徹 分明 昭彰 澄清 清 清澈 清楚 清晰 晴 白 開朗 開通 明 明瞭 明確 明晰 鮮明 戛然

clear away 廓清

clear enunciation 口齒清楚

clear sky 晴天

clear statement 明文

clear-headed 清醒

clearly 截然 明明

cleave 劈

clerical script 隸書

clerk 幹事

clever 穎慧 乖巧 巧妙 伶俐 心靈 聰慧 聰明 靈 靈活 靈敏

cliche 陳腔濫調 窠臼

cliff 山崖 崖 巖 懸崖

cliffside 峭壁

climate 氣候

climax 高潮

climb 登 攀 攀登 爬

climb a tree 爬樹

climb off 爬下

climb on 爬上

clinic 診所

clinical 臨床

clip 夾子 剪

clitoris 陰核

cloak 披風

clock 時鐘 鐘 鐘錶

clog 塞 填塞

clogged 壅塞

clogs 木屐

close 附近 掩 截止 密切 接近 關 閉 封閉 近相近 嚴密 緊密

close down 關閉

close friend 知己 密友 摯友

close in 逼近

close off 密封

close relatives 親人 近親

close shop 關門

close to 挨 挨近 靠近 近於

closed-minded 囿於成見

closely 緊緊

closely related 息息相關

closet 壁櫥

cloth 巾 布

cloth sack 布袋

clothes dryer 烘乾機

clothes hanger 衣架子 (⇒架子)

clothing 服裝 成衣 裝 穿著 衣 衣服 衣裳 衣著

clothing apparel 服飾

clothing store 服裝店

clouds 雲 雲彩

clouds of sunset 晚霞

cloudy 陰

cloudy day 陰天

clover 苜蓿

clown 小丑

club 棍 棍子 社團 棒子 俱樂部

club member 會員

clue 線索 頭緒 端倪

clueless 迷糊

clump 塊

clumsily written 生澀

clumsy 笨拙

cluster 簇 串

clutch 揪

coach 教練

coal 煤 煤炭

coal mine 煤礦

coalition 聯盟

coarse 粗 粗率

coast 海岸 岸

coastal 沿岸 沿海

coat 大衣 外套

Coca-Cola 可口可樂 (⇒可樂)

cockroach 蟑螂

cocktail 雞尾酒

coconut 椰子

cod 鱈魚

code of honor 義氣

codeword 暗號

coefficient 係數

coerce 脅迫

coexist 共處 共存

coffee 咖啡

coffin 棺 棺材

cognition 認知

cohabitate 同居

coherent 通 連貫

coin 錢幣

coincide 吻合

coincidental 巧 巧合

coincidentally 恰巧 偶

cola 可樂

cold 寒冷 冷 冷酷 感冒 凍

cold dish 涼菜

cold war 冷戰

cold water 冷水

collaborate 勾結 合作

collapse 垮 垮台 倒塌 坍塌 塌 崩潰

collar 領

collateral 抵押品

colleague 同僚 同仁 同事

collect 搜集 收 收藏 收集 收取 拾 珍藏 採集 蒐 蒐集

collect fees 收費

collect stamps 集郵

collect taxes 徵稅

collection 集

collective 集體

collective enterprise 集體企業

collectively 共

collectively known as 統稱

college 學院

collide 撞 撞擊

compradore 買辦
comprehend 悟 領悟 理解
comprehension 悟性
comprehensive 全盤
compress 壓縮
compromise 遷就 調和 將就 妥協
computer 電腦 計算機
computer chip 晶片
computer mouse 滑鼠
computer program 程式
computer virus 電腦病毒 (⇨病毒)
comrade 同志
concave 凹陷 凹進
conceal 謊言 匿 匿藏 掩 掩蔽 掩蓋 遮 蔽 藏 藏匿 隱蔽 隱藏 隱瞞
concede 服氣 讓步
conceited 自大 自負
conceive 設想 懷 懷孕
concentrate 注 潛心 濃縮 凝神 集中
concentrated 濃 密集
concept 概念 理念
conception 立意
concern 干 關 顧慮
concerned about 關懷 關切 關心
concerning 攸關 關於
concession 讓步 租界
concise 扼要 簡潔
conclude 簽訂 結束 認定 了結 斷定 締結

conclusion 結論 終結
concrete 具體
concubine 妾 姨太太
concurrent 當時
concurrently 兼
condemn 判處
condense 濃縮 凝結 凝聚
condiment 佐料
condition 條件 境地 情形 狀況 狀態 步地
condole 弔唁 弔喪
condom 保險套 避孕套
condone 縱容
conduct 舉動 舉行 作為 行徑 導
conduct oneself 做人
conductor 導體
confer 頒 授 授予
conference 大會 會 座談會
confess 供認 認罪
confession 供詞 口供
confidence 信心
confident 篤定 把握
confidential 秘密 心腹
confine 圄 圈 禁錮
confirm 證實 確定 確認
confiscate 沒收 充公 扣留 查扣
conflagration 火災
conflict 衝突
conflict with 抵觸
conflicting opinions 歧見
conform to 符合 合乎 相符
confront 對峙
confronting 面臨

Confucian 儒 儒家
Confucian teacher 夫子
Confucian temple 孔廟
Confucianism 儒家思想
Confucius 孔子 孔夫子 (⇨夫子)
confuse 混淆 混淆
confused 胡亂 糊塗 惑 迷亂
confusing 生澀
confusion 混亂
congeal 結 凝結 凝聚
congested 壅塞
congratulate 祝賀 恭賀 恭喜 賀 慶 慶賀
Congratulations! 恭喜
congratulatory card 賀卡
congress 大會 國會
conical bamboo hat 斗笠
conjecture 臆測 揣測 推測
conjunction 連詞
connect 繫 銜接 接 聯 連 連接 溝通
connected 關聯
connection 聯繫 瓜葛 系
connections 關係
conquer 擊敗 征服
conquered nation 亡國
conscience 良心
conscious 省
consciousness 覺悟 知覺 意識
conscript 徵兵
conscription 徵兵
consent 允 允諾 肯 應允
consent to 願 願意
consequently 乃 以致 則

conservative 保守
conserve 節約
consider 考慮 斟酌 酌 照顧 試想 顧及 看 想 思考 思慮 審議 推敲
consider as 當作 當做 視
consider equally 兼顧
considerable 雄厚
considerate 周到 體貼
consign 付 寄託 交付 托 託 託付
consistent 一貫 一致 契合
consolation 安慰
consolation prize 安慰獎
console 慰 慰藉 安慰
consolidate 鞏固
conspire 同謀 串通
constant 常數 恆
constellation 星宿 星座
constitute 佔 組成 構成
constitution 憲法
constrain 牽制
construct 建 建設 建造 建築 蓋 築 施工 營建 營造 構
construct sentences 造句
construction company 營造企業
consul 領事
consulate 館 領事館
consult 諮詢 協商 洽 洽談 參 參考 徵詢 會商
consult and consider 參酌
consultant 顧問

curfew 宵禁	**D d**	data 資料 數據	decadent music 靡靡之音
curio 古玩	dad 爹	database 資料庫 數據庫	decay 蛻變
curious 好奇	daddy 爹爹	date 約會 日期	decayed 腐朽
curl 捲	dagger 匕首	daughter 女兒 女孩 女孩兒 女孩子	deceive 詐 詐騙 欺瞞 欺騙 瞞 騙 騙人
currency 貨幣 幣 通貨	daikon 白蘿蔔	daughter-in-law 媳婦	decelerate 趨緩
current 水流 時 今 現 現有	daily necessities 日用品	dawn 晨 清晨 曙光 黎明	December 十二月 (⇨ 月)
current affairs 時事	daily newspaper 日報	dawn's light 曙光	decentralized 分散
currently 今 當今 現在 而今	Dalai Lama 達賴喇嘛 (⇨ 喇嘛)	day 天 日	deception 欺騙
curriculum 課程	Dali 大理	day after tomorrow 後天	decide 認定 決 決定 斷 定 確定
curry 咖哩	dam 水壩	day and night 晝夜 日夜 朝夕	decided 既定
curry favor 巴結	damage 折損 損 害 損壞	day before yesterday 前天	decision 決策 決定
curse 咒 咒罵 詛咒 罵	damn 該死 他媽的	daybreak 晨	decisive 果斷
cursor 光標 游標	damn fool 混蛋 渾蛋	daydream 空想	decisively 果斷
curtain 幕 簾 窗簾	Damn! 糟糕	daylight 日光 白晝	declaration 宣言 聲明
curve 曲線 彎	damned 該死的	days 日子	declare 宣佈 宣布 聲稱 聲明
cushion 墊 墊子	damp 潮濕 濕 濕潤	daytime 晝 白天 白晝	decline 落 降 沒落 式微 回絕 衰 衰敗 衰落 衰退 謝絕
custom 風氣 俗 習 習慣 習俗	dampen 濕 濕潤	dazed 迷亂	declining tendency 頹勢
customer 客 客戶 用戶 顧客	dance 舞 舞蹈 跳舞	dazzling 耀眼	decommissioned 退伍
customs 風俗 海關 俗尚	dancing party 舞會	dead 亡故 死 死者	decorate 飾 修 修飾 佈置 陳設 裝潢 裝飾 裝修
customs house 海關	dandelion 蒲公英	dead end 死路	decorations 飾物 陳設 裝飾
cut 切 削 剁 裁 裁減 截 縮減 傷口 刺 割	dandruff 頭皮屑	deadline 限期 期限	decorum 禮
cut and polish 琢磨	danger 危 風險	deadlock 僵持 僵局	decrease 降低 減 減少
cut down 砍掉 削減 伐	dangerous 險 險惡 危險	deadlocked 膠著 僵化	decree 法令 令
cut hair 理髮	dangerously close to 險些	deaf 聾	dedicate oneself to 致力
cut in line 插隊	Daoism 道 道教	deaf mute 聾啞	dedicate to 獻給
Cut it out! 少來	Daoist priest 道士	deaf person 聾子	deduce 演繹 推理
cut off 切斷 截斷 斷絕 割斷 隔斷	dare 膽敢 敢	deal 版	deduct 扣 扣除
cut out 割除	dare not 不敢	deal with 接洽 周旋 對待 對付	deduction 演繹法
cut prices 削價	dare to accept 敢當	dealings 往來	
cut through 穿 穿過	daring 敢	dean 院長	
cute 可愛	dark 黝黑 黑 黑暗	dear 親愛的	
cycle 循環 週期	dark ages 黑暗時代	death penalty 死刑	
cyclone 颶風	dark complexion 黝黑皮膚	debate 辯論 爭辯 論戰	
cypress 柏樹	darling 心肝	debauched 荒淫 放浪	
Czech Republic 捷克	Darwin 達爾文	debt 債 債務	
	dash away 飛奔	decade 年代	
	dashing 洶湧 風采 丰采	decadent 頹廢	

deed 舉動 勞役

deep 窈窕 深沈 深厚 深刻 深邃

deep impression 印象很深

deep of night 深夜

deepen 加深 深化

deeply 深

deeply concerned 耿耿於懷

deeply engrained 刻骨

deep-rooted 根深蒂固

deer 鹿

deer antler 鹿角 鹿茸

defame 詆毀

defeat 打敗 擊敗 敗

defeated 輸 敗 敗北 被打敗 (⇨ 打敗)

defect 投誠 缺陷 毛病 叛逃

defend 駐守 守 守衛 捍衛 保衛 防 防守 防衛 防禦

defendant 被告

defense 提防

defer 暫緩 謙讓

deficiency 匱乏

deficient 殘 短缺

deficit 赤字 逆差 虧損

define 訂定

definite 確實

definite article 定冠詞 (⇨ 冠詞)

definitely 千萬 明明 準

definition 定義

defraud 哄 哄騙

defy 違 違抗

degenerate 不肖 蛻化 墮落 頹廢

degenerate into 流於

degree 度 程度

delay 攔阻 耽擱 挨 拖 留 延 延遲 緩

delegation 代表團

delete 刪 刪除

deliberate 斟酌 蓄意 思索 審議 推敲

deliberately 刻意 偏偏

delicacy 美食 美味

delicate 精緻 嫩 嬌嫩 微妙 細膩

delicate and attractive 綽約

delicious 好吃 美味

delight 樂趣

delighted 痛快 欣慰

delimit 劃

delinquent 流氓

delinquent debt 呆帳

deliver 送 送交 傳遞 遞送

deliver a speech 致詞

delta 三角洲

delude 惑

delude oneself 妄想 休想

deluded 狂妄

delusion 妄想 幻想

demand 要 索 索取 責 講求

demand compensation 索賠

demanding 苛求

demean 委屈

democracy 民主

Democracy Wall 民主牆

democracy movement 民運

Democratic Party 民主黨

democratization 民主化

demolish 拆 拆除 拆

掉 毀滅

demon 魔 魔鬼 妖 妖怪 妖精 鬼 鬼怪 鬼子 惡魔

demonstrate 示範 示威 彰顯 遊行

demonstration 遊行 示威遊行

den 書房 書齋 窩

Deng Xiaoping 鄧小平

dengue fever 登革熱 (⇨ 熱)

denial 否定 否認

Denmark 丹麥

denominator 分母

denounce 檢舉 斥責

dense 濃 濃厚 密 密集 稠 稠密

density 密度

dentist 牙醫

dentistry 牙科

deny 否 否定 否認

deny history 抹殺歷史

depart 離 離開 走

depart for 往

department 部 處 科 系

department chair 系主任 (⇨ 主任)

department chief 處長

department store 百貨公司 百貨商店

depend on 附 倚賴 賴 看 依 依附 依靠 依賴

dependable 可靠

dependents 眷屬 家眷

depict 刻畫 描繪 描寫

deploy 部署 布署 調度 調配

deport 驅逐出境

deportment 姿態

deposit 存

deposits 儲量

depraved 卑鄙

depreciate 貶值 折舊

depressed 鬱悶 納悶 沈悶 消沈 苦悶 悶 低沈 沮喪 憂愁 憂鬱

depression 蕭條 盆地 憂鬱症

deprive 剝奪 褫奪

depth 深度

depth of winter 隆冬

depths 深處

deranged 狂妄

deride 譏評

derive 汲取 衍生

derogatory 貶義

desalinate 淡化

descend 下降

descendants 後裔 子孫

describe 敘述 形容 狀 描述 描寫

description 寫照

desert 沙漠 變節

desert island 荒島

design 設計

desirable 可取

desire 貪圖 欲 欲望 慾望 覬覦

desist 收起

desk 書桌 桌 桌子

desolate 蕭瑟 荒 荒涼

desolate and remote 荒僻

despair 絕望 喪氣

desperately 要命

despise 藐視 鄙視 鄙夷 蔑視 看不起

despite 儘管

despot 暴君

despotic 暴虐

dessert 點心

destined 有緣分的 (⇨

do time in prison 坐牢　docile 溫順　doctor 醫 醫生 醫師 大夫 博士　doctorate 博士學位　doctrine 主義 教義 道　Doctrine of the Mean 中庸　document 書 文件　documentary 文獻片 紀錄片　documents 文獻　dodge 躲開 避開 閃　dog 狗 犬　dog meat 香肉　dogma 教條　dogmatic 教條　doll 玩偶 洋娃娃(⇨娃娃)　dollar 元 美金 美元 塊 圓　dolphin 海豚　domain 領域　domestic 國內　domestic animal 畜生 家畜　domestic goods 國產　dominant 主導　dominate 主宰 稱霸　dominoes 骨牌　don't care 無所謂　don't feel like 懶得　don't mind 不介意(⇨介意)　don't worry 別著急(⇨著急)　donate 布施 捐 捐給 捐助 贈 贈送 獻　donate blood 捐血　donate money 捐款　donkey 驢　doodle 塗抹　doomed 完蛋　doomed to 註定 注定　door 戶 門 房門

door guard 門衛　door-god 門神　doorway 門口　dorm room 寢室　dormitory 宿舍　dosage 劑量　dose 劑　dot 點　dote on 鍾愛 寵愛　dots 斑紋　double 加倍 翻 翻番 雙 雙重　Double Nine Festival 重九　double bed 雙人床(⇨床)　double entendre 雙關語　double eyelids 雙眼皮(⇨眼皮)　double standard 雙重標準　doubt 置疑 疑 疑竇 疑問 疑心 懷疑 質疑　doubtless 無疑　Dow-Jones 道瓊　Dow-Jones index 道瓊指數　down 絨 絨毛 鴨絨　down with 打倒　downcast 低落　downfall 失敗　downstairs 樓下　downstream 下游　dowry 陪嫁 嫁妝　dozen 打　draft 稿 稿子 擬定 擬訂 徵兵　draft beer 扎啤 生啤酒　draft plan 草案　draft system 徵兵制　drag 曳 拽 拉 攆 拖 牽　drag in 拉扯 牽扯　dragon 龍

dragonboat 龍舟　Dragonboat Festival 端午節　dragonfly 蜻蜓　drain 水溝 排水　drama 戲 戲劇 劇　drape 披　drastic 斷然　draw 畫 畫圖 畫圖 汲取 牽引 抽 繪　draw close 靠攏　draw in 捲入　draw lots 抽籤　draw near 靠近　draw out 拉長　draw up 擬定 擬訂 編製　draw water 汲水　drawback 缺陷 弊病　drawer 抽屜　drawing 畫 畫圖 圖 圖畫 繪畫　dread 恐 恐懼 懼 懼怕　dream 作夢 做夢 夢 夢寐　dream of 休想 夢見 夢想　dreary 淒涼　dredge 疏導 疏通　dredge for 撈　dregs 渣滓 渣子　drench 淋　dress 穿著 衣　dress and put on make-up 梳妝　dress store 服飾店　dress up 打扮　dress up as 扮　dressing table 妝台　dried tofu 豆腐乾　dried up 枯竭　drift 漂浮 漂流 流浪　drill 鑽 操　drill ground 操場　drink 飲 喝

drink a toast 乾杯　drink alcohol 喝酒　drink tea 飲茶　drink water 飲水　drink with patron 陪酒　drinking capacity 酒量　drinking fountain 飲水機　drinking water 飲水　drip 滴　dripping wet 淋漓　drive 駕駛 駕馭 行駛 趕 帶動 開　drive a car 開車　drive out 趕走 驅趕　drive up 哄抬　drivel 胡說　driver 司機　driver's license 駕照 駕執照　drool over 垂涎　droop 耷拉 垂　drop 下降 落下 點 點滴 丟 掉 掉下 滴 墜落　drop anchor 拋錨　drop in the ocean 九牛一毛　drop of water 水滴　drop out of school 輟學　drought 旱災　drown 淹死 沈淪 溺 溺死　drug 毒 毒品 藥品 藥物　drug pusher 毒販　druglord 毒梟　drugstore 藥店 藥房　drum 鼓　drunk 喝醉 醉 酒醉　drunk with 陶醉　drunkard 醉漢　dry 枯燥 乾 乾燥　dry by fire 烘 烘乾　dry by sunlight 曬 曬乾

dry up 乾枯[83]
dry-clean 乾洗[26]
Du Fu 杜甫[9]
dubious 可疑[81] 曖昧[83]
duck 閃躲[112] 鴨[112] 鴨子[112]
dull 枯燥[18] 乏味[48] 呆板[9] 魯[10]
dump 傾倒[29] 傾銷[9] 拋開[9] 拋棄[9] 拋售[9]
dumpling 餃子[27]
Dunhuang 敦煌[61]
dupe 愚弄[9]
duplicate 複製[9] 重複[9]
durable 結實[9] 牢[62] 耐用[14]
duration 長[62]
during lifetime 生前[80]
dusk 黃昏[83] 暮色[80] 夕[79] 傍晚[80]
dust 灰塵[9] 塵[9] 塵埃[9] 塵土[9]
dustpan 簸箕[16] 畚箕[16]
duty 勤務[29] 義務[29] 職務[29] 職責[29] 責任[29]
duty-free 免稅[64]
dwarf 侏儒[9]
dye 染[9]
dying 垂死[17]
dynamic 活潑[86] 動態[29]
dynasty 代[9] 朝[9] 朝代[9]
dysentery 痢疾[82]

E e

each 各[9] 各個[9] 各自[9] 個個[9] 每[9]
each other 彼此[9]
each place 各地[9]
each time previously 歷次[108]
eager 殷[77] 殷切[77]
eagle 老鷹[9]
ear 耳[137] 耳朵[137]
earlier times 早期[9]
earliest 最初[9]
early 初[63] 早[76]
early in the morning 一早[1]
early morning 凌晨[83] 清

晨[83] 早晨[76]
early times 初期[9]
earn 掙[9] 賺[9]
earnest 認真[83] 誠懇[83] 熱忱[99] 鄭重[99]
earnings 收入[9] 盈利[9] 利潤[9]
earphone 耳機[137]
earth 大地[79] 地[9] 地球[9] 土[9]
Earthly Branches 地支[9]
earthquake 地震[9]
earthworm 蚯蚓[9]
easily 好[94]
easily spoken 上口[43] 順口[43]
easily understood 易懂[163]
east 東[9]
East Asia 東亞[61]
East Asian 黃種人[31]
East Coast 東岸[9]
Eastern Europe 東歐[9]
Eastern Orthodox Church 東正教[9]
eastern region 東部[9]
easy 輕易[9] 容易[9] 易[163]
easy to please 打發[16]
easy to study 易學[163]
easy-going 瀟灑[9]
eat 吃[9] 吃飯[9]
eat until full 吃飽[9]
eat up 吃掉[9] 吃光(⇨光[42])
eaves 簷[14] 屋簷[28]
eavesdrop 竊聽[9] 偷聽[9]
eccentric 怪僻[9] 古怪[11]
echo 響[61] 回響[9] 回音[9] 迴響[9]
ecology 生態學[9]
economic aid 經濟援助(⇨援助[32])
economic prosperity 景氣[9]
economic recovery 經濟復甦(⇨復甦[9])
economic reform 經濟改

革 (⇨改革[9])
economical 經濟[9] 省錢[9]
economics 經濟學[9]
economist 經濟學家[9]
economize 省[9] 節省[9] 節約[9] 撙節[9]
economy 經濟[9]
ecosystem 生態[9]
edge 刃[9] 邊[9]
edible 食用[9]
edible tree mushroom 木耳[9]
edict 飭令[9] 諭知[9]
edify 薰陶[9]
edit 彙編[9] 編[9] 編輯[9]
edition 版[9] 版本[9] 本[9]
editor 編輯者[9]
editorial 社論[9]
educate 教育[9] 栽培[9]
education 教育[9] 學業[9]
educational background 學歷[9]
eel 鰻魚[9] 鱔[9]
effect 作用[9] 效[9] 效果[9] 效力[9] 成效[9] 功效[9] 功用[9]
effective 有效[9] 奏效[9] 靈[9]
efficacy 效[9] 效力[9] 效能[9] 功效[9]
efficiency 效率[9] 效益[9]
effort 工夫[9]
egg 子[9] 蛋[9] 雞蛋[103]
egg white 蛋白[9]
eggplant 茄子[34]
eggs 卵[9]
ego 自我[9]
Egypt 埃及[9]
eight 八[9] 捌[9]
Eight Diagrams 八卦[9]
eighth Earthly Branch 未[9]
eighth Heavenly Stem 辛[9]
eke out a living 餬口[9]
elbow 肘[9] 掣肘[9]
elder statesman 元老[9]

elderly 老人[9] 老者[9] 老[9] 老年人[9]
elders 父老[9] 長輩[9] 長老[9]
eldest sibling 老大[9]
elect 選[9] 選舉[9] 推選[9]
elected 當選[9] 膺選[9]
election 選舉[9]
electorate 選民[9]
electric appliances 電器[9]
electric bill 電費 (⇨費[9])
electric cable 電纜[9]
electric fan 電扇[9]
electric light 電燈[9]
electric power 電力[9]
electric powered 電動[9]
electric wire 電線[9]
electricity 電[9]
electron 電子[9]
electronic 電子[9]
electronic dictionary 電子字典[9]
electronic games 電子遊戲[9]
electronic organ 電子琴[9]
electronics 電子品[9]
elegance 雅緻[9]
elegant 飄逸[9] 高貴[9] 秀[9] 秀麗[9] 秀美[9] 大方[9] 精美[9] 雅[9] 雅緻[9] 典雅[9] 姚[127]
element 元件[9]
elementary 初級[9] 起碼[9]
elementary school 小學[9] 國小[9]
elephant 大象[9] 象[172]
elevation 海拔[9]
eleventh Earthly Branch 戌[9]
eliminate 廓清[9] 掃除[9] 破除[9] 消除[9] 去除[9] 除掉[9] 摒除[9] 清除[9] 革除[9] 解

忧 熱情[99] 幹勁[99]
enthusiast 迷[178]
enthusiastic 熱烈[99] 熱情[99] 熱心[99] 熱
enthusiastically 踴躍[99]
entice 勾引[99] 誘引 誘[99] 籠絡[99]
entire 全[92] 全體[92] 整[99] 整個[99]
entire family 全家[92]
entirely 盡[99] 全[92]
entirety 整體[99]
entrance 入口[92] 口[98] 門口[99]
entreat 央求[99]
entrepreneur 企業家[99]
entrust 倚重[99] 托[92] 託[99] 託付[92] 信託[99] 委[99] 委託[99]
entwine 糾纏[99]
enumerate 列舉[123]
enunciation 口齒[68]
envelop 籠罩[132]
envelope 信封[99]
envious 眼紅[99]
environment 環境[99]
environmental damage 公害[92]
envision 設想[99]
envoy 代表[99] 使節[99]
envy 羨[99] 羨慕[99] 眼紅[99] 嫉妒[99] 忌[99] 妒[99] 妒忌[99]
enzyme 酵素[12]
epidemic 疫[99]
epilogue 尾聲[99]
episode 片段[99] 插曲[99]
equal 均[99] 匹[92] 平等[99] 等[99] 當[99] 相等[99] 對等[99]
equal of 匹敵[92]
equal treatment 對等待遇[176]
equality sign 等號[99]
equals 等於[99]
equation 等式[99] 方程式[99]
equator 赤道[99]

equilibrium 均衡[99] 平衡[92]
equip 配備[97] 裝備[99] 裝設[99] 裝置[99]
equipment 設備[99] 器[99] 裝備[99] 傢伙[99]
equivalent to 不啻[99]
era 年代[99] 時代[99] 世代[99]
eradicate 根除[99] 杜絕[99] 剷除[99]
eraser 橡皮[97] 橡皮擦[97]
erect 建[99] 勃起[99] 架[99] 設立[97] 立[99] 豎立[99] 挺[97]
erection 勃起[99]
erhu 二胡[99]
err 弄錯[99] 犯錯[99] 做錯[99]
error 舛誤[99] 紕漏[99] 差[99] 誤[99] 誤差[99] 錯誤 錯[99] 誤[99] 失誤[99] 過失[131]
erupt 爆發[99]
escape 出路[110] 逃逸[127] 免[99]
escort 護送[99]
escort out 送[99]
especially 尤其[99] 尤其是[99] 特意[99] 別外[99]
espionage 特務活動[99]
esprit de corps 團體感[99]
essay 散文[99]
essence 根本[99] 精華[99] 精華[99] 本質[99] 實質[99]
essence of China 國粹[99]
establish 創立[99] 建[99] 建立[99] 設[99] 立足[99] 成立[99] 締結[99] 奠定[99]
estate 產業[99]
esteem 崇敬[99] 尊[99] 推崇[99]
esteemed 貴[106]
estimate 估[99] 估計[99] 估量[99] 估算[99] 預估[99] 預計[99] 揣[99]
estimation 估算[99]
estranged 疏遠[99]

etc. 等[99] 等等[99]
eternal 永恆[120]
eternally 永[120] 永遠[120]
ethics 倫理[99]
ethnic group 種族[99] 族[99] 民族[99]
etiquette 禮節[99]
eugenics 優生[99]
eulogy 頌[99]
eunuch 太監[99] 宦官[99]
euphonious 上口[99]
Europe 歐[99] 歐洲[99]
Europe and America 歐美[99]
European 歐洲人[99]
European Union 歐洲聯盟 (⇒ 聯盟[99])
evade 避[99] 迴避[99] 逃避[99] 推卸[99]
evade taxes 逃稅[99]
evaluate 考核[99] 評價[99] 評審[99] 褒貶[99]
evaporate 破滅[99] 蒸發[99]
eve 前夕[99]
even 勻[99] 均[99] 均勻[99] 平[99] 尚且[99] 還[99] 連[99] 齊[182]
even if 縱然[99] 就[99] 就算[99] 即[99] 即便[99] 雖則[99]
even more 更加[99]
even number 偶數[99] 雙數[92]
even though 即便[99] 即使[99]
even to the point that 甚至[99] 乃至[99]
evening 宵[99] 夕[99] 傍晚[99] 晚[99] 晚[99] 晚上[99]
evening dress 晚裝[99]
evening paper 晚報 (⇒ 報[99])
event 事件[99]
eventually 早晚[99] 總[99]
every 各[99] 皆[99] 凡是[99] 每[99]
every day 天天[99]

every kind of 各式各樣[99] 各種[99]
every time 每次[99]
every year 年年[99] 每年[99]
everybody 大家[99] 諸位[99]
everyday 每日[99] 每天[99] 日常[76]
everyday life 日常生活[76]
everyday use 日用[76]
everyone 人人[99] 各位[99]
everything 一切[99] 事事[99]
everywhere 四處[99] 四下[99] 到處[99] 處處[99] 遍[115]
evidence 憑[99] 證[99] 證據[99]
evidence of guilt 罪證[99]
evident 昭[99] 昭彰[99] 明[99] 顯[153]
evil 凶[99] 邪[99] 邪惡[99] 壞[99] 惡[99] 罪戾[99]
evil deed 壞事[99]
evil ways 邪路[99]
evolution 衍變[99] 演變[99] 演化[99]
evolve 衍變[99] 衍生[99] 演為[99] 演變[99] 演化[99] 變遷[153]
ex ante 事前[99] 事先[99]
ex post 事後[99]
exacerbate 加劇[99]
exact 索[99] 精確[99]
exacting 苛求[99]
exactly 剛[99] 就[99] 就是[99] 正是[99]
exaggerate 誇大[99] 誇張[99]
exaggeratedly feminine 三八[99]
exalt 讚揚[99]
exam 考試[99]
examine 察[99] 檢[99] 檢視[99] 檢驗[99] 驗[99] 考察[99] 省[99] 診[99] 查[99]

盤[129] 審[56] 審查[95]
examinee 考生[17]
example 範例[95] 實例[95]
例[57] 例證[57] 例子[57]
exasperate 惱[143]
excavate 挖[22] 挖掘[22] 刨[22]
發掘[12]
exceed 超過[22] 超出[22] 超
過[22] 越[22] 越過[22] 浮[97]
出[110] 逾[97] 逾越[97]
過[133]
exceed a quota 超額[22]
excel 勝過[22]
excel at 擅[22] 擅長[22]
excellent 嘉[24] 好棒[97]
了得[22] 挺好[97] 勝過[22]
優[124] 優秀[124] 優異[124]
多麼好[21] 好極了
(⇨極[14]) 特好[97]
except 除[36] 除了[36]
excepted 除外[36]
exception 例外[57]
exceptional 不凡[76] 格
外[36] 特殊[36] 特異[133]
excess 餘[44] 過剩[133]
excessive 多[77]
excessively 太[77] 過[133]
過度[133] 過分[133] 過
於[6]
exchange 兌[57] 兌換[57] 退
換[36] 交換[36] 交流[36]
換[57] 易[163]
exchange rate 匯率[162]
excise 刪[115] 刪除[115]
excited 興奮[97] 亢奮[97]
激動[97]
excitement 快感[97]
exclaim 驚歎[97] 歎[97] 感
歎[97]
exclamation 嘆詞[76]
exclamation point 驚歎
號[97] 感嘆號[97]
exclamatory particle 乎[97]
啦[97]
exclude 排除[36] 排他[97]
excluding 以外[97]
exclusionary 排他[97]
exclusive right 專利[97]

excoriate 唾罵[173]
excrement 屎[95] 糞便[95]
excrete 拉[22]
excursion 郊遊[22]
excuse 託辭[97] 擋箭牌[97]
藉口[97] 見諒[97]
excuse from 免[164]
excuse me 抱歉[97] 對不
起[176]
execute by firing squad 槍
斃[22]
executive 幹事[97]
Executive Yuan 行政院[41]
exemplary 模範[97]
exempt from 豁免[97] 免[164]
exercise 鍛鍊[97] 行使[97]
操[22] 課題[22] 運動[158]
exercise book 練習簿[97]
exert 施加[97] 使出[97]
勞[97]
exert all one's strength 使
勁[97]
exert self 用力[97]
exhale 呼[22] 呼[97]
exhaust 盡[97] 罄盡[97] 廢
氣[97] 耗竭[97]
exhausted 疲乏[97] 疲
勞[97] 乏[97] 困頓[97] 凋
敝[97] 精光[97]
exhaustive 詳盡[97]
exhibit 陳列[97]
exhibition 展覽[97]
exhort 叮囑[97] 囑咐[97]
exhortation 忠告[97]
exile 放逐[97]
exist 有[97] 在[97] 存[97] 存
在[97] 生存[97]
existence 存有[97]
existentialism 存在主
義[97]
existing 現有[114]
exit 出[110] 出路[97] 出
門[110]
exit a country 離境[97] 出
境[97]
exorbitant profits 暴
利[97]
expand 脹[97] 擴充[22] 擴充[97]

擴展[97] 擴張[97] 弘
揚[97] 壯大[41]
expand and develop 拓
展[97]
expect 指望[97] 望[97] 期[97]
期待[97] 期望[97] 意[97]
料[97] 料[97] 料想[97] 預
期[97]
expectation 期望[97] 期
許[97]
expediency 權宜之
計[97]
expedient 權宜[97]
expel 趕[97] 趕走[97] 驅
趕[97] 驅逐[97] 革除[74]
開除[97] 排[97] 排斥[97]
排擠[97]
expenditure 消費[97] 支
出[97] 開支[97]
expenses 費用[97]
expensive 昂貴[97] 貴[106]
高消費 (⇨消費[97])
價格高昂 (⇨高
昂[97])
experience 經[97] 經歷[97]
經驗[97] 資歷[97] 閱歷[97]
領教[97] 歷[108] 出身[110]
見識[114]
experience personally
體驗[97]
experience successively
歷經[108]
experienced 資深[97] 熟[97]
練達[97] 有經驗 (⇨
經驗[97])
experiment 試驗[97] 實
驗[97]
expert 高手[97] 內行[97]
家[97] 好手[97] 專家[97]
通[97]
expert hand 能手[97]
expire 屆滿[97] 到期[97] 過
時[133]
explain 說[41] 說明[97] 介
紹[97] 述[97] 表白[97] 闡
釋[96] 解釋[97] 講[97]
explain in detail 講解[175]
explain one's situation 陳

explanation 說明[41] 解
釋[97]
explanatory note 詮釋[97]
explode 爆[97] 爆發[97] 爆
炸[97] 炸[97]
exploit 剝削[97]
exploitation 剝削[97]
explore 勘探[97] 探[97] 探
索[97]
explosive 炸藥[97]
exponent 指數[97]
export 外銷[97] 出口[97]
輸出[97]
expose 暴露[97] 揭[97] 揭
穿[97] 揭發[97] 揭露[97]
戳穿[97]
exposed 裸露[97]
exposure 曝光[97]
expound 闡述[96]
express 達[97] 發[97] 表
達[97] 表明[124] 表示[124]
表現[124]
express appreciation 答
謝[97]
express emotions 抒情[97]
express regrets 表示歉
意 (⇨歉意[97])
express support for 聲
援[97]
expression 神氣[97] 神
色[97] 神態[97] 表情[124]
expressway 高架橋[97]
expropriate 沒收[97] 充
公[97]
exquisite 精[97] 精巧[97]
精湛[97] 精緻[97]
extend 伸展[97] 蔓延[97]
擴大[97] 擴展[97] 延[97]
延長[97] 延伸[97] 續[124]
extension 分[97] 延伸[97]
extension cord 延長線[97]
extensive 廣[97] 廣泛[97]
恢弘[97] 浩瀚[97] 寬
廣[97]
extent 地步[97] 程度[97]
extent of a country 幅員[97]
exterminate 根除[97] 消

滅[?] 滅[?]

extinct 絕跡 絕種 滅絕

extinction 絕種

extinguish 滅熄 熄滅 撲滅

extol 頌揚

extort 詐取 敲詐 索取 勒索 攫取 壓榨 攫錢

extra 額外 多 多餘

extract 搾取 索取

extracurricular 課外

extradite 引渡

extraordinary 不凡 非常

extravagance 排場

extravagant 闊綽 奢侈

extreme 極 極度 極端

extreme limit 極限

extremely 極 極其 極為 不得了 不堪 不勝 要命 絕頂 太 萬分 酷 死 蠻 非常

extremely hot 酷熱

extremist 極端

extricate oneself 擺脫

extroverted 外向

eye 眼 眸子 目

eyebrow 眉 眉毛

eyeglasses 眼鏡

eyelashes 睫毛

eyelid 眼皮

eyes 眼睛

eyesight 視力

eyewitness 目擊

F f

fable 寓言

fabricate 杜撰 捏造 虛構

facade 幌子

face 臉 臉皮 向 當 臨 體面 朝 嘴臉 顏 顏面 面 面孔 面子 對

faced with 面對

facemask 口罩

face-to-face 當面

facial expression 臉色 神情

facial features 相貌 面貌 面容

facile and smooth 流暢

facilitate 促成

facilities 設施

facing 向著 朝著 面對 面臨

fact 事實 實

faction 黨 派 派系

factor 因素

factory 工廠 廠

factory director 廠長

factory premises 廠房

faculty 教員

faculty and staff 教職員

fade 褪 褪色 失色

fade away 消逝

Fahrenheit 華氏

fail 砸 失敗

failure 故障 失敗

faint 淡薄 昏倒 昏厥 隱約 暈倒

fair 均 均等 公 公平 公正 正當 正直 集

fair and just 耿直

fairy 仙 仙女 仙子

faith 信仰

faithful 忠誠 忠實

faithfulness 忠心

fake 假 充 偽

falcon 鷹

fall 落 墮 掉 秋 秋天 跌 跌下 墜 墜落

fall asleep 入睡 睡著

fall behind 落後 跟不上 (⇨ 跟上)

fall down 倒 跌倒 摔 摔倒

fall equinox 秋分

fall for 傾倒

fall ill 生病 患病 罹患

fall ill with 患有

fall in love 鍾情 談戀愛 (⇨ 戀愛)

fall in love with 愛上

fall into 落入

fall into a coma 昏迷

fall into water 落水

fall off 掉下

fall overboard 落水

fall short 差

fall sick 得病

fall through 落空 破滅

fallen 落

false 虛 虛偽

falsehood 謬誤

falter 動搖

fame 聲 聲名 名

fame and wealth 名利

familiar with 熟 熟悉

family 家 家裡 家庭

family affairs 家事

family and given name 姓名

family livelihood 家計

family members 家人 家屬

family name 姓 姓氏

family planning 節育 計劃生育 (⇨ 生育)

family reunion 全家團聚 (⇨ 團聚)

family status 門第

family tree 家譜

famine 災荒 荒 饑荒 饑餓

famished 飢餓

famous 有名 知名 成名 馳名 名 出名

famous product 名產

famous work 名著

fan 扇 扇子 迷 愛好者

fanatic 狂熱

fanaticism 狂熱

fang 犬齒

fantasize 空想

fantasy 空想

far 遠

Far East 遠東

farcical 滑稽

farewell dinner 餞行

farm 農場 場

farm goods 莊稼

farmer 農民 農夫 農人

farmer household 農戶

farmhouse 廬舍

farming 耕作

farmland 農地 農田 耕地 田地

fart 屁 放屁

fascinated 著迷

fashion 熱門

fashion model 模特兒

fashion show 服裝表演 時裝展覽

fashionable 時髦 盛行 風靡 紅 流行

fashionable clothing 時裝

fast 絕食 快 快速 迅 速

fast asleep 沈睡

fast food 快餐 速食

fasten 拴

fast-food restaurant 快餐廳

fat 脂 脂肪 肥 肥胖 胖 油脂

fat person 胖子

fatal 致命

fate 緣分 命 命運 造化

father 老爸 父 父親 翁 爸 爸爸

father of the nation 國父

father-in-law 公公 岳父

fatigued 疲憊 疲倦 疲軟 困倦 困倦

fatty meat 肥肉

fatuous 昏庸

faucet 龍頭

fault 缺點

fauna 動物

favor 人情 恩惠 青睞 看好 偏愛 偏袒

favorable impression 好感

favorite 寵兒

favoritism 偏袒

fax 傳真

fear 恐 恐懼 恐怕 生怕 怕 害怕 懼 懼怕 畏 畏懼

fearful 可怕

feasibility 可行性

feasible 可行

feast 宴會 酒席

feather 羽 羽毛

feature 特點

features 容貌 容顏 嘴臉 眉目

February 二月 (⇨ 月)

federal 聯邦

federal government 聯邦政府

fee 費

feeble 虛弱 虛弱

feed 飼料 餵 餵養

feedback 反饋 回饋

feel 覺 覺得 感 感到 感覺 感受

feel attached to 眷戀

feel bad 難受

feel carsick 暈車

feel deeply 深感

feel faint 發昏 暈

feel helpless 束手無策

feel like 想要

feel nostalgic about 眷念

feel remorse 悔恨

feel sentimental about 眷戀

feel sick 難受

feel sorry 難受

feeling 感覺 感覺 情緒

feeling of safety 安全感

feelings 情 襟懷 心

feign 裝 裝作 佯 佯裝 偽裝

feign innocence 撒清

fell 伐

fell trees 伐木

fellow 院士 佬 漢

fellow villager 老鄉

fellowship 獎學金

female 陰性 女 女性 女子 雌 雌性

female and male 雌雄

female infanticide 殺女嬰

feminism 女權主義

feminist 女權主義者

fence 圍牆 柵欄 藩籬

fengshui 風水

fenjiu 汾酒

ferment 釀 醞釀 發酵

ferocious 凶猛 兇猛

ferret out 揪出

fertile 肥 肥沃 豐腴

fertilizer 肥料

fervent 慷慨 熱切

fervor 氣勢

fester 爛

festival 祭 節 節日

fetch 拿來

fetter 羈絆

fetus 胎 胎兒

feudal 封建

feudal title 爵位

feudalism 封建主義

fever 熱

few 少 些 兩三 幾

few days ago 日前

fiance 未婚夫

fiancee 未婚妻

fiber 絲 纖維

fiberglass 玻璃纖維 (⇨ 纖維)

field 田 田地

field of study 科目

fierce 凶 兇 兇狠 暴烈 強暴 厲害 激烈 激烈 猛 劇烈

fiery 烈

fifth Earthly Branch 辰

fifth Heavenly Stem 戊

fight 打 打架 打伏 搏鬥 戰鬥

fight for 爭奪

fighter 鬥士

fighter plane 戰機

figure 位 數字 身材

figure out 想出

file 案 檔 檔案

file a complaint 投訴

filename 檔名

filial 孝順

filial piety 孝 孝道

filial son 孝子

fill 彌 填 充

fill a vacancy 遞補

fill out 填寫

fill up 填補 填塞

filling 餡

film 影片 拍 拍攝 片子 底片

film a movie 拍電影

film editing 剪輯

film festival 影展

film roll 膠捲

filter 濾 濾清 過濾

filth 垢 污垢 污垢

filtrate 過濾

fin 鰭

final conclusion 定論

final exam 期末考

final stage 末期

final wishes 遺囑

finally 終 終究 終於 最後 最終 總算

finance 金融 財務

finance and economics 財經

find 找到

find fault 挑錯

find fault with 詬病

find out 找出 查出

fine 嘉 罰 罰款 罰錢 佳 精 精細 精緻 美好 細 細膩

fine jade 瓊瑤

finely crafted 精巧

finest 最佳

finger 指 手指

fingernail 指甲

fingerprint 指紋 手印

finish 完 完畢 做好 做完 終 了 已 畢

Finland 芬蘭

fir tree 杉

fire 開除 火 火災 罷黜 解除

fire alarm 火警

fire department 消防隊

fire extinguisher 滅火器

fire fighting 消防

fire pit 火坑

firecracker 爆竹 鞭

炮[69]
firefly 螢火蟲[99]
firelight 火光[62]
firewood 柴[66]
fireworks 煙火[130]
firm 剛[5] 剛強[5] 行[5]
廠商[51] 牢固[78] 牢
靠[78] 穩固[97] 穩健[97]
堅[142] 堅定[142] 堅固[142]
堅強[142]
firmly 毅然[?] 確[?]
first 先[?] 初[?] 頭[?] 首
位[?] 首先[?] 第一[?]
first Earthly Branch 子[12]
first Heavenly Stem 甲[12]
first aid 急救[?]
first love 初戀[?]
first on a list 龍頭[128]
first place 第一名 (⇨
名[?])
first priority 第一優先
(⇨ 優先[?])
first step 初步[?] 第一
步 (⇨ 步[?])
first time 首次[?] 首
度[148]
first-class 頭等[?]
first-rate 一流[1]
fiscal year 會計年度
(⇨ 年度[?])
fish 釣[?] 釣魚[?] 魚[?]
漁[80]
fish pond 魚池 (⇨ 池[?])
fishbone 魚刺[?]
fisherman 漁夫[80]
fishermen 漁民[80]
fishhook 魚鉤[?]
fishing boat 漁船[80]
fishpond 魚池[80]
fissure 隙[?]
fist 拳[?] 拳頭[?]
fit 容納[?] 適合[?]
fitting 合適[?] 恰[?] 恰
當[?] 適當[?] 宜[?]
five 五[?] 伍[?]
Five Classics 五經[?]
five primary elements 五
行[?]

fix 修[?] 固定[?] 訂定[?]
fixed 額定[?] 固定[?]
fixed opinion 定見[?]
fixed period 定期[?]
fixed quantity 定量[?]
fixed term 定期[?]
flabby 鬆弛[?]
flag 旗[?] 旗幟[?] 旗子[?]
flagpole 旗杆[?]
flagrantly 悍然[?]
flake 屑[?]
flame 火[?] 火焰[?] 焰[?]
flaming 熊熊[?]
flank 旁邊[?]
flap 振[?]
flash 閃[?] 閃光[?] 閃
閃[?]
flash in the pan 曇花一
現[?]
flash of light 閃亮[?]
flashlight 手電筒[?]
flat 平[?] 平坦[?] 扁[115]
flatter 恭維[?] 阿諛[?] 奉
承[?] 拍馬屁[?]
flaunt 誇耀[?] 炫耀[?]
flavor 滋味[?] 口味[?] 調
味[?] 味道[?] 香
味[?]
flavorless 淡[?]
flaw 破綻[?] 瑕疵[?]
flax 麻[?]
flea 蚤[?] 跳蚤[127]
flea market 跳蚤市場[127]
flee 跑[?] 跑走[?] 遁走[?] 投
奔[?] 逃[?] 逃跑[127] 逃
亡[127] 逃走[?] 竄[181]
flee in disorder 竄逃[191]
flee to freedom 投奔自
由[?]
fleet 艦隊[142]
flesh 肉[132] 肉體[132]
flexibility 彈性[136]
flexible 機動[?] 靈活[161]
flickering 幢幢[?]
flight 班[97]
flighty 輕浮[?]
flip 反[?] 翻[156]
flip-flops 拖鞋[?]

flirt 調情[?] 煽情[124]
float 漂[?] 漂浮[?] 飄[?]
浮[?] 浮動[?] 游[?]
flock 群[?]
flood 洪水[?] 氾濫[?] 充
斥[?]
floor 樓[?] 地[?] 地板[?]
層[144]
flora 植物[?]
florid 花[?]
flounder 鰈[?]
flour 粉[?] 麵[?] 麵粉[?]
flourishing 興隆[?] 勃
勃[?] 茂盛[?] 盛[?] 繁
華[?] 昌[?] 昌明[?] 蓬
勃[?] 欣欣向榮[?] 薈
萃[?]
flow 水流[?] 流[?] 流動[?]
flow out 流出[?] 瀉[?]
flower 花[?] 花朵[?]
flower arranging 插花
藝術[?]
flower basket 花籃[?]
flower bud 蕊[?]
flower store 花店[?]
flower terrace 花壇[?]
flower vase 花瓶[?]
flowering plants 花卉[?]
flowery 花[?]
flowing 順[?]
flowing water 流水[?]
fluctuate 波動[?] 變
幻[53]
fluctuation 變動[53]
fluent 流利[?]
fluid 通順[?] 液[?]
flunk 當[?] 當掉[?]
fluorescence 螢光[?]
fluorescent light 日光
燈[76]
flush 沖[?]
flustered 發慌[?]
flute 笛[113] 笛子[113]
flutter 飄[?]
fly 蒼蠅[?] 飛[169] 飛行[169]
fly a kite 放風箏 (⇨ 風
箏[?])
foam 泡沫[?]

focal point 焦點[62]
focus 焦距[62]
focus attention 矚目[125]
fodder 飼料[?]
fog 霧[105] 霧氣[105]
fold 折[24] 疊[?] 摺[124] 摺
疊[?]
folding fan 摺扇[124]
folk customs 民俗[119]
folksong 歌謠[?] 民歌[119]
follow 順[?] 從[?] 跟[?]
隨[?] 承襲[?] 繼[?] 沿
襲[?] 尾隨[?] 依[?] 遵
從[?] 遵循[?] 追隨[167]
follow behind 跟隨[?]
follow example of 效法[?]
follow in a line 貫[?]
follower 追隨者[167]
follower of a religion 教
徒[?]
following day 翌日[124]
隔天[?]
following year 翌年[124]
隔年[?]
fond of 熱中[?] 惜[?]
font 字體[?] 字形[?]
food 食[?] 食物[?] 糧
食[?] 菜肴[?] 餐[?]
food and beverages 飲
食[?]
food container 器皿[?]
food dishes 菜[?]
foods 食品[?]
fool 傻瓜[?] 傻子[?] 哄
瞞[?]
fool around 鬼混[140]
fooled 上當[?]
foolish 愚[?] 愚笨[?] 愚
蠢[?]
foot 尺[?] 腳[?] 足[?]
football 足球[?]
foot-binding 裹腳[?]
foothill 山麓[67]
footnote 註[?] 註釋[?] 詮
釋[?]
footpath 步道[?]
footprint 腳印[?]
footstep 腳步[?]

for 給 為	foreign expert 外國專家 (⇨ 專家)	formality 形式	fountainhead 泉源 源
for example 比如 例如	foreign firm 外商	former 原 原來 前 前者 舊	four 肆 四
for fear that 惟恐	foreign guest 外賓	former days 昔日	Four Books 四書
for imperial use 御用	foreign language 外語	former palace 故宮	four seasons 四季
for incidental use 零用	foreign movie 洋片	former times 往昔	four tones of Mandarin 四聲
for instance 比方 譬如	foreign nationality 外籍	formerly 從前 以往 曩昔 過去	fourth Earthly Branch 卯
for the moment 暫且	foreign student 僑生	formula 公式 模式	fourth Heavenly Stem 丁
for the sake of 為了	foreign trade 外貿 進出口	formulaic 八股	fourth place 殿軍
for this reason 故此 為此	foreigner 老外 外僑 洋人 鬼子 外國人	formulate 釐定	fox 狐 狐狸
for what reason 何故	foreknowledge 預知	forsake 背叛 遺棄	fraction 分 分數
forage 覓食	forerunner 前驅	fort 堡壘	fragile 脆 嬌嫩 易碎
forbid 禁 禁止	foresee 看準	fortress 要塞	fragment 碴 碴兒
Forbidden City 紫禁城	foreshadowing 伏筆	fortuitous 湊巧	fragmentary 瑣碎 零星
forbidding 森嚴	foresight 遠見	fortuitous meeting 幸會	fragrance 馨香 芳香 香氣
force 逼 逼迫 力 勒 脅迫 威力 威武 強 強迫 迫 迫使 壓迫 勉強	forest 樹林 林 森林	fortuitously 湊巧	fragrant 芬芳 馨香 芳 香馥
force down 壓低	forestry 林業	fortunate 幸運	frail 瘦弱 羸弱 孱弱 薄弱 微弱
forced 被逼 被迫 強制	foretell 卜卦	fortunately 恰好 恰巧 幸虧 幸而 好彩 僥倖	frame 框 架 架子 誣陷 陷害
force-feed ducks 填鴨	forever 永 永遠	fortune 福 財富 運	frame-up 冤獄
forceful 威武	foreword 序言 前言	fortune cookie 幸運籤餅	framework 架子 骨子
forcibly demand 強求	forge 鍊 偽造 錘鍊	fortune teller 筮人 算命人	franc 法郎
forcibly occupy 盤據 霸佔	forgery 贗品	forum 論壇	France 法國
ford 渡 過	forget 忘 忘掉 忘懷 忘記 遺忘	forward 向前 前	frank 坦白 坦率
forearm 肱	Forget it! 算了	fossil 化石	frank and sincere 坦誠
forecast 展望 預報 預測	forgive 原諒 包容 諒 恕 恕罪 饒恕 見諒 寬恕	foster 培養 發揚 助長	fraternity 博愛 兄弟會
forehead 額 額頭	forgiveness 饒恕	foster daughter 養女	fraud 詐欺 弊
foreign 外 外來	fork 叉 岔	foster father 義父	freckles 雀斑
foreign affairs office 外辦	form 格局 格式 形局 形式 形態 形象 形狀 造成 組成 表格 構 構成	foster mother 義母	free 鬆 自由 解放
foreign aggression 外侮	form gradually 釀成	foster son 養子	free market 自由市場 (⇨ 市場)
foreign aid 外援	form of address 稱呼	found 創立 創辦 創立 創始 建立 設立 立 成立 締造 開創	free of charge 無償 白 免費
foreign capital 外資	formal 沈重 正式	found a nation 建國	free throw 罰球
foreign country 外國	formal dress 禮服	foundation 根基 基 基礎 底 底子 依據 基金會	free time 暇 空 空閒
foreign currency 外幣	formalities 手續	founder 鼻祖 祖師	freedom 自由
foreign debt 外債		fountain pen 鋼筆	freedom of assembly 集會自由
foreign devil 鬼佬 洋鬼子 (⇨ 鬼子)			
foreign exchange 外匯			

freedom of religion 宗教自由[46]

freedom of speech 言論自由[49]

freedom of the press 新聞自由[49]

freeze 冰凍[14] 冷凍[14] 凍[58] 凍結[58]

freezer 冰箱[9] 冷凍庫[58]

freight 貨運[12]

French 法文 (⇨ 文[49])

french fries 薯條[49]

frequency 頻道[58] 頻率[58]

frequently 往往[11] 時常[11] 時時[11] 屢次[49] 常常[49] 動輒[64] 頻[58] 頻繁[58]

fresco 壁畫[49]

fresh 新[49] 新鮮[49] 生[49] 鮮[12]

fresh and cool 清涼[29]

fresh water 淡水[12]

freshman 一年級學生 (⇨ 年級[49])

fretful 焦躁[62]

friction 摩擦[29]

Friday 星期五[9] 禮拜五[9]

fried breadstick 油條[13]

fried dumpling 鍋貼[13]

fried noodles 炒麵[49]

fried rice 炒飯[49]

friend 友[12] 友人[12] 熟人[49] 朋友[65]

friendly 友[12] 友好[12] 友善[12] 隨和[49] 親切[49] 和氣[19] 善[49]

friends and relatives 親友[49]

friendship 友情[14] 友誼[12] 交情[49] 交誼[49] 情誼[49]

friendship society 聯誼會[49]

frighten 駭[62] 驚嚇[49] 嚇[49] 嚇唬[49]

frightened 惶恐[49] 驚恐[49] 吃驚[49]

frigid 寒冷[13]

frigid zone 寒帶[13]

fringe 邊緣[13]

fringe benefit 津貼[58]

frisbee 飛盤[69]

frivolous 輕浮[49]

frog 蛙[12] 青蛙[58]

from 從[49] 由[13] 自[19]

from now on 從此[14] 今後[14]

from the very start 劈頭[49]

from then on 嗣後[58]

front 前[19] 前面[19]

front and back 前後[19]

front door 大門[49]

front page 頭版[58]

front side 正面[49]

frontier 邊境[19] 邊陲[19] 邊疆[49]

frost 霜[14]

froth 泡沫[49]

frown 皺眉[49]

fruit 水果[14] 果[49] 果實[49] 果子[49]

fruit juice 果汁[49]

fruitfly 果蠅[49]

fruition 成果[49]

fruits 結果[49] 果實[49]

fruits and vegetables 蔬果[49]

frustrate 挫折[49]

frustration 挫折感[49]

fry 炸[49] 炒[49] 煎[49]

fu 賦[49]

Fu Xi 伏羲[78]

fuck 姦[49] 幹[49]

fuel 燃料[49]

fugitive 逃犯[27]

Fujian Province 福建[49] 閩[49]

Fukienese 台語[49] 福建話[49] 閩南話[49]

fulfill 滿[49]

full 客滿[49] 飽[49] 飽滿[49] 充分[49] 充份[49] 滿[24]

full name 姓名[49]

full of 富有[49] 充滿[49]

full of smiles 滿面笑容 (⇨ 笑容[77])

full-figured 身材豐滿 (⇨ 豐滿[49])

full-time 專任[49]

fumble 摸索[49]

fun 好玩[49] 趣味[49]

function 函數[13] 作用[49] 功能[49] 功用[49] 機能[49] 性能[49]

fundamental 基本[46]

funds 資源[49] 資金[49] 款[49] 基金[49]

funeral 葬禮[49] 喪禮[49]

funeral gift money 奠儀[59]

fungus 菌[49]

funny 好笑[49] 逗[65] 詼諧[49]

fur 皮毛[49] 毛[90]

furious 猖狂[49] 氣憤[49] 憤怒[43]

furnace 爐[12]

furnish 裝備[75] 擺設[49]

furnishings 擺設[49]

furniture 家具[155] 傢俱[55]

further 更[49]

furthermore 還有[42] 而且[34] 再者[75]

fury 狂怒[49] 怒氣[49] 怒亂[34]

fuse 熔[49] 熔化[49] 鎔融[49] 融合[49] 融化[49]

futilely 枉然[15]

future 未來[49] 前途[49]

future generations 後輩[49] 後代[49] 後世[49]

futures 期貨[49]

futures market 期貨市場[49]

G g

gain 得[49] 收入[49] 贏[49] 贏得[49]

gain advantage 獲利[49]

gain power 得勢[49]

gain weight 胖[49]

gains 收穫[49] 果實[49]

galaxy 銀河[49] 星系[49]

gall bladder 膽[19]

gallant 雄赳赳[49]

gallon 加侖[49]

gallop 奔騰[49]

gallop about 馳騁[49]

gamble 打賭[49] 賭[49] 賭博[49] 賭錢[49]

game 比賽[12] 局[49] 戲[49] 遊戲[49]

Gandhi 甘地[49]

gang 黨[49] 幫[49] 幫會[49] 幫派[49]

gang leader 老大[12] 大哥[12] 幫主[49]

Gang of Four 四人幫 (⇨ 幫[49])

gang up 聯手[49]

Ganges River 恆河[49]

gangster 歹徒[12] 幫派分子[49]

Gansu Province 甘肅[49]

gap 差距[15]

garage 車庫[58]

garbage 垃圾[49]

garden 花園[12] 庭園[49] 園[126] 園地[126] 園子[126]

garden pond 池塘[58]

gargle 漱口[49]

garlic 蒜[12] 大蒜[12]

garrison 駐守[49]

gas 煤氣[49] 氣[9] 氣體[49]

gas station 汽油站[49]

gasoline 汽油[49]

gasp 氣喘[9] 喘[34] 喘氣[34]

gasp in admiration 讚歎[15]

gate 門[49] 門戶[49] 柵門[49]

Gate of Heavenly Peace 天安門[49]

gateway 門口[49]

gather 撿[49] 收[49] 收取[49] 扒[49] 攏[49] 團聚[49] 採[12] 採集[12] 聚[49] 聚會[49] 蒐[12] 集[24] 集合[49] 匯集[49]

gather data 收集資料 (⇨資料[界])

gauge 表[汁]

gauze 紗[汁]

gaze at 望[汁]

gear 齒輪[汁]

gecko 壁虎[汁]

geisha 藝妓[汁]

gender 性[汁] 性別[汁]

gender equity 男女平等[汁]

gene 基因[汁]

genealogy 族譜[汁] 家譜[155]

general 普遍[汁] 將軍[汁] 將領[汁] 總[144]

general idea 大意[汁]

general manager 總幹事 (⇨幹事[汁]) 總經理[144]

general merchandise 百貨[汁]

general rule 通則[汁]

general situation 大勢[汁]

general term 統稱[汁]

generally 一般[汁] 大抵[汁] 大體[汁]

generally acknowledged 公認[汁]

generally believed 咸信[汁]

generally speaking 大體說來[汁] 一般來說[汁]

generate electricity 發電[汁]

generation 世代[汁] 世代[汁] 代[汁] 輩[汁]

generation gap 代溝[汁]

generous 慨然[汁] 慷慨[汁] 大方[汁] 豐厚[汁] 優厚[汁] 灑脫[汁]

genitals 生殖器[汁]

genius 天才[汁]

gentle 軟[汁] 溫和[汁] 溫柔[汁] 柔[汁] 柔和[汁] 善良[汁]

gentleman 先生[汁] 君子[汁] 君子[汁] 紳士[汁] 士[汁]

genuine 道地[汁]

geography 地理[汁]

geology 地質[汁] 地質學[汁]

geomancer 風水先生[汁]

geomancy 風水[汁]

geometry 幾何[汁] 幾何學[汁]

germ 細菌[143]

Germany 德國[汁]

gesture 手勢[汁]

get 得[汁] 得到[汁] 拿[汁] 領[汁]

get a word in 插嘴[汁]

get along with 處[汁] 相處[汁]

get away 脫身[汁]

get away from work 抽身[汁]

get caught on 掛[汁]

get hold of 拿到[汁]

get in touch with 聯絡[汁]

get into trouble 闖禍[汁]

get involved 介入[汁]

Get lost! 走開[汁]

get married 結婚[汁]

get off 下[汁]

get off work 下班[汁]

get on 上[汁]

get rich 發財[汁] 致富[汁]

get rich suddenly 暴發[汁]

get sick 生病[汁] 患病[汁]

get somebody drunk 灌醉[汁]

get started 著手[汁] 動手[汁]

get through 溝通[汁]

get to know 結識[汁]

get up 起[汁] 起床[汁] 來[汁] 起身[汁] 爬起來[汁]

get up the courage 鼓起勇氣[汁]

Ghengis Khan 成吉思汗 (⇨汗[汁])

ghost 鬼[汁] 鬼魂[汁] 鬼子[140]

ghost month 鬼月[140]

ghostwrite 捉刀[汁]

giant 巨人[汁]

gift 才華[汁] 禮[汁] 禮物[汁] 贈品[144]

giggle 嘻[汁] 嘻笑[汁]

gigolo 牛郎[汁]

ginger 薑[汁]

ginseng 人參[汁]

giraffe 長頸鹿[汁]

girl 娘[汁] 妞[汁] 姑娘[汁] 女孩[汁] 女孩兒[汁] 女孩子[汁] 女郎[汁] 女生[汁]

girlfriend 女友[汁] 對象[汁] 女朋友 (⇨朋友[165])

gist 梗概[汁]

give 與[汁] 送[汁] 送給[汁] 給[汁] 給予[汁] 予以[汁] 贈[汁] 贈送[汁]

give a speech 發言[汁]

give back 還[汁]

give birth 生育[汁]

give birth to 生[汁] 產[汁]

give examples 舉例[汁]

give face 給面子 (⇨面子[汁])

give full play to 發揮[汁]

Give me a break! 少來[汁] 拜託[汁]

give up 戒除[汁] 放棄[汁]

give up halfway 半途而廢[汁]

give way 讓路[汁]

given name 名字[汁]

glacier 冰河[汁]

gladly 欣然[汁]

glamour 魅力[汁]

glance at 瞥[汁]

gland 腺[汁]

glass 玻璃[汁]

glass window 玻璃窗[汁]

glaze 琉璃[汁]

glazed tiles 琉璃瓦[汁]

gleam 閃光[汁]

gleam in one's eyes 眼神[汁]

glide 滑翔[汁] 飛翔[169]

glider 滑翔機[汁]

glimpse 乍見[汁]

glitter 閃光[汁]

glittering 絢爛[汁]

globe 球[汁]

gloomy 陰森[汁] 慘淡[汁] 黯然[汁]

glorify 讚揚[汁]

glorious 隆[汁] 昌明[汁] 輝煌[汁]

glory 榮[汁] 榮耀[汁] 榮譽[汁]

glossy 光[汁]

gloves 手套[汁]

glow 燦發[汁] 發亮[汁]

glue 黏貼[汁] 貼[汁] 膠[汁] 膠水[汁] 糨糊[汁]

glutinous rice 糯米[汁]

glutinous rice ball 湯圓[汁]

gnaw 啃[汁]

go 圍棋[汁] 去[汁]

go abroad 出國[110]

go around 繞[汁] 繞路[汁]

go ashore 登陸[汁]

go astray 走上斜路 (⇨斜路[汁])

go bankrupt 破產[汁] 倒閉[汁]

go commercial 下海[汁]

go crazy 發瘋[汁] 發狂[汁]

go down 下[汁] 下去[汁]

go down south 南下[汁]

go first 先行[汁]

go forward 前進[汁]

go into action 發作[汁]

go into exile 流亡[汁]

go into hiding 逃亡[汁]

go on 下去[汁]

go on a business trip 出差[110]

go on foot 徒步[汁]

go on holiday 放假[汁]

go on stage 上台[汁]

go on the market 上市[汁]

go out 出門[110] 出去[110]

go over 過[汁]

go to 赴[汁] 到[汁] 前往[汁]

go to bed 上床[汁] 睡覺[汁]

go to college 念大學[汁]

go to one's doom 送命

go to sea 下海

go to the bathroom 上廁所 (⇨ 廁所)

go to the countryside 下鄉

go to the office 上班

go to war 打仗

go to work 上班

go toward 往

go up 上

go up north 北上

go up to 上去

goal 目的

goat 山羊

goatee 山羊鬍

go-between 媒介

Gobi Desert 戈壁沙漠 (⇨ 沙漠)

God 上帝 天

god 神 仙

goddess 女神

Goddess of Mercy 觀音

Goddess of the Sea 媽祖

godfather 大哥大

going to 要 將 將要

gold 黃金 金

gold color 金色

gold medal 金牌 (⇨ 牌)

golden mean 中庸之道

goldfish 金魚

golf 高球

gong 銅鑼 鑼 鑼聲

good 不錯 良 良好 商品 可以 吉 好 佳 產品 益處 靈

good and bad 好歹 好壞

good at 善於

good friend 良友 好友

good intentions 好意 善意

good life 好生

good luck 好運

Good luck! 祝你好運! (⇨ 好運)

Good morning! 早

good neighbors 睦鄰

Good night! 晚安

good omen 吉兆

good point 好處

good will 好感

Good-bye! 再見

good-looking 好看

goods 貨品

goose 鵝

goose feather 鵝毛

gorge 峽 谷 溪谷

gorgeous 絢麗 艷 艷麗 瑰麗

gorilla 大猩猩 (⇨ 猩猩)

go-slow strike 怠工

gossip 閒話

gouge 挖

gourd 葫蘆

govern 執政 治 轄

government 政 政府

government and public 朝野

government bonds 公債

government in exile 流亡政府

government office 衙門 院 府 司 署

government official 官 官員

government seal 國璽

government-operated 公營

governor 州長 省長 總督

gown 袍

grab 揪 把握

grace 恩惠 風韻

graceful 飄逸 秀 秀麗 秀美 雍容 娟秀

grade 年級 級 等級 成績 品 班

級

gradient 坡度 斜度

gradually 日漸 冉冉 漸 漸漸 緩緩 逐漸 逐漸

gradually decrease 遞減

gradually increase 遞增

graduate 畢業

graduate school 研究所

graduate student 研究生

graffiti 塗鴉

graft 貪污

grain 粒 糧 顆粒

grain coupon 糧票

grain seedling 禾苗

grains 穀 穀物

gram 公克 克

granary 穀倉 糧倉

grand 隆 隆重 宏 宏大 宏偉 大 盛 堂皇

Grand Canal 大運河 (⇨ 運河)

Grand Canyon 大峽谷 (⇨ 峽谷)

grand occasion 盛況

grandchild 孫

granddaughter 孫女 外孫女

grandfather 公 公公 祖父 爺

grandma 奶奶

grandmother 外婆 祖母

grandpa 爺爺

grandson 孫子 外孫

grandstand 作秀

grant 批准 給予 施 賞賜 予以 賜予

granted that 就算

granular sugar 砂糖

grape 葡萄

grapefruit 葡萄柚

graph 圖 圖形

grasp 持 執 把 把握 捉 抓 握 掐住 掐住

grasp well 抓緊

grass 草

grassland 草地

grasslands 草原

grassroots 基層 草根

grateful 領情 感恩 感激

gratified 欣慰

grating 刺耳

gratitude or resentment 恩怨

gratuity 小費

grave 墳墓 墓

grave rob 盜墓

gravel 砂石

gravestone 墓碑

graveyard 墳地 墓地

gravity 引力 重力

gray 灰 灰色

gray market 灰市

graying 斑白

grease 油

grease stain 油垢

greasy 膩 油膩

great 偉 偉大 大 鉅

Great Harmony 大同

Great Helmsman 偉大舵手 (⇨ 舵手)

Great Leap Forward 大躍進

Great Wall 長城

great master 大師

greater part 大部

greatest 莫大

great-grandchild 曾孫

great-grandparent 曾祖

greatly 大

Greece 希臘

greed 貪心 野心

greedy 貪婪 貪心 愛錢

欣喜 美好 愉快 陶 歡喜
Happy New Year! 恭賀新禧! 新年快樂!
happy to 樂於
harass 騷擾 纏繞
Harbin 哈爾濱
harbor 港 港口 抱 心懷 漁港
hard 硬 堅硬
hard of hearing 重聽
hard to deal with 難纏
hard to say 難說
hard to swallow 夠嗆
hard up 拮据
hard work 苦力
hardbound 精裝
hard-drive 硬碟
hard-pressed 窘迫
hardship 苦難 艱辛
hardware 硬件 硬體
harm 作孽 傷 害 妨害 禍 損 損害
harm others 害人
harmonica 口琴
harmonious 雍 和諧 融洽
harmonize 協調
harpoon 魚叉
harsh 苛 苛刻
harvest 收成
hastily 貿然
hat 冠 弁 帽 帽子
hatch 孵化
hatchet 斧頭 斧子
hate 恨 仇恨 怨恨 憎恨 惡
hate bitterly 痛恨
hate life 厭世
hatred 仇 仇恨 怨氣
haul 曳
have 有 具備 具有
have a child 生孩子
have a hand in 插手

have a headache 頭痛
have a party 聯歡
have a sense of shame 知恥
have a showdown 攤牌
have a sit-down strike 靜坐
have always been 向來
have an accident 出事
have children 生兒育女
have diarrhea 拉肚子
have insight into 洞察
have no choice 無奈
have not 沒 沒有 未
have peace of mind 安心
have sex 上床 交合 性交
have the advantage 得勢 佔上風 (⇨ 上風)
have the nerve to 好意思
have to 要 只得 只好
have to do with 相干
having no alternative 無可奈何
Hawaii 夏威夷
hawk 兜售 鷹
hayfever 花粉熱
haze 陰霾
hazy 朦朧
he 伊 其 他
head 頭 頭部 腦袋 腦海 腦筋 首
head of household 家長
head to toe 渾身
headache 頭痛
headline 標題
head-on 迎面 劈頭
headwaters 水源
heal 醫治
healed 痊癒

health 健康
health care 保健
health insurance 健康保險
healthy 健 健康 康 無恙
hear 聽 聽見 聽說 聞
heart 內心 心 心目 心頭 心臟
heart disease 心臟病
heartbeat 心跳
heart-broken 心碎
heartfelt 深切 衷心
heartland 腹地
heartless 無情
heated 激
heating 暖氣
heaven 上天 天 天堂 穹蒼
heaven and earth 乾坤
Heavenly Stems 天干
heavy 沈重 重
Hebei Province 河北
hectare 頃 公頃
hectic 繁忙
hedge 藩籬
heed 介意 聽
heel 跟 腳跟
hegemon 霸主
hegemonize 稱霸
hegemony 霸權
height 高矮 高低 個子
heighten 提高
Heilongjiang Province 黑龍江
heinous crime 滔天大罪
held up 滯留
helicopter 直昇機
hell 地獄
hellish situation 火坑
hello 你好 喂
helm 舵
helmet 頭盔 盔
helmsman 舵手
help 扶 幫 幫忙

幫助 救助 援助 助 助力
Help! 救命
hemp 麻
hen 母雞
Henan Province 河南 豫
hence 乃 是以 由此
henceforth 爾後 此後
Heng Mountain 恆山
hepatitis 肝炎
herbal tea 花茶
herd 群
here 這邊 這裡 這兒 此
heredity 遺傳
heresy 邪說
hermit 隱士
hero 英烈 英雄 好漢 壯士
heroic act 壯舉
hertz 赫
hesitate 躊躇 遲疑 彷徨 徬徨 猶豫 觀望 徘徊
hesitation 遲疑
heterosexual 異性
heterosexuality 異性戀
hey 喂
hibernate 蟄伏
hibernation 多眠
hidden 潛伏 潛在 陰
hide 遮 遮蔽 躲 躲藏 伏 隱藏
hide embarrassment 遮羞
high 崇高 高 高昂 快感
high altitude 高空
high degree 高度
high level 高 高等
high mountains 山岳
high official 大夫
high tide 高潮

human affairs 世事

human body 人身／人體

human feelings 人情

human life 人生／人世

human nature 人性

human resources 人才／人力資源

human rights 人權

human shadow 人影

human tide 人潮

human world 人間

humanism 人本主義

humanitarianism 人道主義

humanities 人文

humanity 人道／人類／仁愛

humankind 人類

humble 謙卑／謙遜

humble opinion 拙見

humid 潮濕／濕

humidity 濕度

humiliate 羞辱／污辱／欺負／欺侮／侮辱／凌辱／屈辱

humiliated 蒙羞

humiliating 太沒有面子 (⇨ 面子)

humiliation 羞辱／屈辱／恥辱

humor 風趣

humorous 幽默／詼諧

Hunan Province 湖南／湘

hunchback 駝背

hundred 百／佰

hundred million 億

hundred points 百分

Hungary 匈牙利

hunger 飢餓

hunger strike 絕食

hungry 飢餓／餓

Huns 匈奴

hunt 狩獵／打獵／弋獵／獵／獵取

hurricane 狂飆／颶風

hurriedly 倉促／慌忙／趕緊／匆匆／匆促／匆忙／連忙

hurry 忙／趕／趕來

hurry after 趕

hurt 被害／疼／痛／傷害／受傷

husband 先生／老公／丈夫／夫

husband and wife 夫婦／夫妻

hush money 遮羞費

hush up 隱諱

hush up scandal 遮羞

hydrogen 氫

hydrogen bomb 氫彈

hygiene 衛生

hymen 處女膜

hypnotize 催眠

hypocrisy 偽善

hypocrite 偽君子

hypocritical 虛偽／偽善

hypothesis 假說

I i

I 吾／俺／余／我／本人／咱

I'm sorry 對不起

I.D. card 身份證

ICBM 洲際飛彈 (⇨ 飛彈)／洲際導彈 (⇨ 導彈)

I-Qing 周易／易經

ice 冰

ice cream 冰淇淋

ice cube 冰塊

ice skates 冰鞋

iceberg 冰山

ice-cream cone 甜筒

iced tea 冰茶

Iceland 冰島

ice-skate 溜冰／滑冰

icicle 冰柱

idea 主意／概念／點子／念頭／意念／理念／觀念／構想

ideal 志願／理想

idealism 唯心論／理想主義

identical 一模一樣／雷同／相同

identify 認／認出／同／辨認／辨識／識別

identity 身份

ideology 主義／思想／意識型態

idiom 成語

idiot 傻瓜／傻子／獃子／白痴／白癡／笨蛋／呆子

idle talk 空話

idle 閒／閒置

idol 偶像

idolize 崇／崇拜

if 假如／假若／假使／若是／若／要是／要／設／如／如果／倘若／倘使

if by any chance 萬一

if only 但願

ignite 點／點燃

ignorance 愚昧

ignorant 茫然／無知／愚昧／懵懂

ignore 不理／小覷／漠視／忽視

ill 病了

illegal 非法

illegal buildings 違建

illegal immigrant 非法移民 (⇨ 移民)／偷渡客

illicit 私／黑

illiquid 週轉不靈

illiteracy 文盲

illiterate person 文盲

illness 病

illuminate 照／照亮

illusion 幻覺／幻想／幻象／錯覺

illusory 幻

illustration 插圖／例證

illustrious 顯赫

image 影像／形象／顯像／象

imagine 設想／試想／料想／想像

imbalance 失調

imbecile 笨蛋

imbue with 灌輸

imitate 模仿／仿效

imitation silk 仿絲

immature 幼稚／幼稚／不成熟 (⇨ 成熟)

immediately 就／隨即／即／即刻／立即／立刻／劈頭／當即／馬上

immediately following 接著

immense 宏大

immerse 沈浸／沒

immigrant 移民

immigrate 移民

immigrate illegally 偷渡

imminently 即將

immortal 不朽／神仙／仙人／仙子／永垂不朽

impact 份量／衝擊

impartial 客觀／均等

impassable 不通

impatient 不耐煩／煩躁

impeach 罷免／彈劾

impede 攔阻／阻礙／阻擋

impeded 阻滯

impel 促使

imperceptibly 不知不覺

imperial 御

imperial concubine 姬

imperial court 廷／朝／朝廷

imperial decree 敕令

imperial palace 皇宮

imperial seal 璽／國璽

imperialism 帝國主義

impermanent 無常

India 印度[72]
Indian 印第安[72]
Indian Ocean 印度洋[72]
indicate 指示[91] 標明[91] 表示[124] 表現[124]
indication 跡象[76] 徵兆[163]
indicator 指針[91]
indifferent 冷淡[88] 冷漠[88] 淡漠[82]
indignation 憤慨[62]
indirect 間接[53]
indiscreet 輕率[76]
indistinct 隱約[73]
indistinguishable 分別不出來[35]
individual 個別[51] 個人[51] 個體[51]
individualism 個人主義[51]
individually 一一[1] 各自[69] 單獨[136]
indolent 怠惰[59]
indomitable 剛強[55]
Indonesia 印尼[72]
indoors 室內[127]
induce 誘導[69] 引發[67] 引起[67] 導致[190] 歸納[167]
inducement 誘因[69]
induction 歸納法[167]
indulge 姑息[39] 放縱[57]
industrialization 工業化[51]
industrious 勤奮[59] 勤快[59] 勤勞[59] 勤勉[59]
industry 工業[51] 產業[176] 業[4]
inebriated 酒醉耳熱[199]
ineffective 無效[117]
inertia 惰性[15]
inevitably 必然[97]
inexpensive 便宜[16]
infancy 襁褓[95]
infant 幼兒[69] 嬰兒[150]
infanticide 殺嬰[151]
infatuated with 傾倒[9]

醉心[124] 迷戀[98] 陶醉[14]
infect 感染[55] 傳染[26]
infected 發炎[95]
infection 炎[97]
infectious disease 傳染病[26]
infer 推測[192] 推斷[192] 推理[192] 推論[192]
inference 推論[192]
inferior 次等[30] 卑下[53] 陋劣[14] 劣等[14] 遜[57] 遜色[57] 低劣[90] 拙劣[195] 亞[166]
inferior to 不及[1] 不如[1] 次於[30] 遜於[57]
inferiority complex 自卑感[139]
infiltrate 滲透[97]
infinite 無邊[117] 無窮[117] 無窮無盡[117] 無限[117]
inflamed 發炎[95]
inflammation 炎[97]
inflate 膨脹[96]
inflation 通貨膨脹[88]
inflexible 刻版[59] 拘泥[55] 機械[97] 僵硬[98] 死板[139] 硬[165]
influence 左右[195] 影響[?] 感染[55] 勢力[?] 影響力[?]
influential 顯赫[183] 有影響力[?] (⇨影響[?])
influential people 權貴[?]
influenza 流行性感冒[?]
inform 通知[88] 奉告[?] 告知[?]
inform and guide 宣導[?]
inform on 檢舉[?] 告發[?] 告密[?]
informal 便[116]
information 資料[?] 資訊[?] 消息[?] 訊[?] 信息[?] 情報[?]
information desk 諮詢台[?]
informed 知情[87]

infrastructure 基礎建設 (⇨建設[?])
infringe on a patent 剽竊專利權[?]
infringe upon 侵犯[?]
infuriate 氣死[?] 激怒[?]
infuriated 氣死[?]
infuriating 氣死人[?]
infuse 沏[?] 沖[?]
ingenious 乖巧[?] 巧妙[?]
ingredient 成分[?]
inhabit 住[?]
inhale 吸[?]
inherent 內在[?]
inherent nature 本性[?]
inherit 繼承[?] 遺傳[?]
inheritance 遺產[?]
inhibit 壓制[?]
inhibition 抑制[?] 壓制[?]
inhospitable 怠慢[?]
initial 初[?]
initiate 開創[?] 發起[?]
initiative 主動[?]
initiator 發起人[?]
inject 注射[?] 打針[?]
injure 傷[?] 傷害[?] 損害[?]
injustice 冤[?] 冤屈[?] 冤獄[?]
ink 墨[?] 墨水[?]
ink stick 墨[?]
ink stone 硯臺[?]
inkling 端倪[?]
inland 內陸[?]
inlay 鑲[?]
inn 旅店[?] 旅社[?]
innate 天生[?]
innocent 無辜[?] 無罪[?] 天真[?] 清白[?] 單純[136]
innovation 革新[?]
innumerable 無數[117]
input 輸入[?]
inquire 諮詢[?] 詢問[?] 打聽[?] 訊[?]
inquire about 探聽[?] 查

詢[?]
inquire into 探究[?] 探討[?]
insane 瘋[?] 瘋狂[?]
inscribe 銘刻[?]
inscription 銘記[?] 銘文[?]
insect 蟲[?] 蟲子[?]
insecticide 農藥[?]
insects 昆蟲[?]
insert 插[?] 插進[?] 插入[?]
inside 內[?] 裡[?] 裡邊[?] 裡面[?] 裡頭[?]
inside and outside 內外[?]
insight 灼見[?] 啟示[?] 見地[?] 洞察力[?]
insist 執意[?] 堅持[?]
insist on 講求[75]
insomnia 失眠病[?]
inspect 視察[?] 監察[?]
inspiration 啟示[?] 靈感[161]
inspire 振奮[?] 鼓舞[?] 啟發[?]
install 安裝[?] 裝[?] 設[?] 裝置[?]
instance 實例[?] 例[?] 例子[?]
instant 須臾[?] 片刻[?]
instant noodles 泡麵[?] 快餐麵[?] 速食麵[?]
instantaneously 瞬時[?]
instantly 頃刻[?] 刹那[?]
instigate 慫恿[?] 唆使[?] 教唆[?] 策動[?] 煽動[?]
instinct 本能[?]
institute 學院[?]
instruct 指點[?] 指示[?] 教[?] 教導[?] 吩咐[?] 囑咐[?]
instrument 儀器[?] 器械[?]
insufficient 不敷[?] 短缺[?] 不充分 (⇨充分[?])
insult 辱罵[?] 污辱[?] 凌

辱 [48]
insurance 保險 [74]
insurrection 叛亂 [97]
intact 完整 [15] 全 [17]
integrate 結合 [83] 整合 [83]
integrity 操守 [27] 情操 [89]
intellectual 知識份子 [17] 讀書人 [120]
intelligence 智 [87] 智慧 [87] 智力 [87] 心智 [93]
intelligence report 情報 [89]
intelligent 慧 [83] 聰慧 [144] 聰明 [144]
intelligentsia 士林 [?] 知識介 [27]
intend 有意 [16] 擬 [?] 打算 [?]
intense 強烈 [65] 激烈 [?] 烈 [?]
intensify 加緊 [34]
intensity 強度 [65]
intention 打算 [?] 意思 [89] 意圖 [89] 心聲 [?] 心意 [?]
intentional 有意的 [16]
intentionally 有心 [?] 特意 [?] 故意 [?] 存心 [?]
interaction 來往 [160]
intercalary month 閏月 [?]
intercept 攔截 [?]
interest 興趣 [?] 興致 [?] 孳息 [?] 意思 [?] 利 [?] 利息 [?] 趣 [137] 趣味 [137] 息 [139]
interest rate 利率 [?]
interesting 有趣 [?] 雋永 [?]
interfere 干擾 [50] 干涉 [?] 干預 [?]
interflow 交流 [?]
interior 內部 [?]
interjection 嘆詞 [?]
interlude 插曲 [?]
intermittent 斷續 [?] 間歇 [?]
intern 實習 [95]

internal 內 [83] 內部 [83] 內在 [83]
internal organs 內臟 [?] 臟 [74]
international 國際 [43]
internationalization 國際化 [43]
internet 網際網路 網路 (⇒ 網路 [34]) 互聯網 [?]
interpersonal 人際 [10]
interpolate 竄改 [91]
interrogate 詰問 [?] 訊問 [?] 盤查 [129] 盤問 [129] 審訊 [156]
interrupt 打岔 [?] 打斷 [?]
interrupted 間斷 [?]
intersect 交會 [?] 交叉 [?]
intersection 十字路口 [?]
intervene 調停 [?]
interview 口試 [?] 訪問 [?] 探訪 [103] 面談 [148]
intestine 腸 [?]
intimacy 親密 [?]
intimate 貼心 [?] 密友 [?] 密切 [?] 親友 [?] 親密 [?] 親暱 [?] 溫馨 [?]
intimate relations 肌膚之親 [?]
intimidate 嚇 [?] 恐嚇 [?]
intolerable 難堪 [?]
intonation 腔調 [?]
intricate 錯綜 [?] 錯綜複雜 [?]
intriguing 奇妙 [?] 雋永 [?]
introduce 介紹 [?] 引進 [95]
introduction 介紹 [?] 緒言 [?]
introspection 反省 [?]
introverted 內向 [?]
intuition 直覺 [?]
inundate 淹 [?] 淹沒 [?] 充斥 [?]
invade 侵 [?] 侵略 [?] 侵入 [?] 入侵 [32]
invalid 無效 [?]
invariably 無不 [?]

invent 發明 [98]
invention 發明 [98]
inventory 存貨 [?] 清單 [?]
invert 顛倒 [?] 倒 [15]
invest 投資 [77]
investigate 察 [?] 偵查 [?] 偵訊 [?] 探究 [?] 探索 [?] 探討 [?] 調查 [?] 審查 [156] 追查 [167]
investigate thoroughly 深究 [63]
investment 投資 [77]
invincible 所向披靡 [?]
invisible 無形 [?] 隱形 [?]
invitation 請帖 [?]
invite 邀 [?] 邀請 [?]
invite bids 招標 [?]
invite to a gathering 邀集 [?]
involve 牽扯 [?] 牽連 [?] 牽涉 [?] 株連 [?] 涉及 [?]
involved 連帶 [158]
Iran 伊朗 [?]
Iraq 伊拉克 [?]
Ireland 愛爾蘭 [?]
iron 熨 [?] 熨斗 [?] 鐵 [?]
Iron Curtain 鐵幕 [?]
iron and steel 鋼鐵 [?]
iron clothes 熨衣服 [?]
iron rice bowl 鐵飯碗 (⇒ 飯碗 [?])
iron staff 鐵棒 [?]
irrational 悖理 [?] 非理性 (⇒ 理性 [?])
irregular 參差 [?]
irrelevant 無關 [?]
irresponsible 不負責任 (⇒ 責任 [?])
irrigate 澆 [?] 澆灌 [?] 灌 [?] 灌溉 [?]
irrigation canal 溝渠 [175]
irrigation projects 水利 [?]
irritable 煩躁 [?]
is 乃 [?] 乃是 [?] 呈 [?]

is it 豈 [114]
Islam 伊斯蘭 [?] 回教 [?]
Islamic 清真 [?]
island 島 [?]
islands 島嶼 [?]
isolate 孤立 [104] 隔絕 [174] 隔離 [174]
isolated 孤立 [104]
Israel 以色列 [?]
issue 頒佈 [?] 頒發 [?] 發佈 [?] 發表 [?] 題目 [?] 出 [110] 出版 [?]
issue funds 撥款 [?]
it 其 [?] 牠 [?] 之 [?] 它 [?]
it doesn't matter 沒關係 (⇒ 關係 [?])
it is said 據稱 [?] 據說 [155]
it seems 似的 [?] 似乎 [?]
Italy 義大利 [?] 意大利 [?]
itch 癢 [?]
item 條 [?] 項 [?] 項目 [?] 事項 [?] 則 [?]
itinerant 江湖 [?]
itinerary 日程 [76] 旅程 [118]
ivory 象牙 [172]
ivy 長春藤 [?]
Ivy League 長春藤大學 [?]

J j

jab 刺 [?] 戳 [124]
jacket 夾克 [?]
jade 玉 [107]
jade bracelet 玉鐲 [107]
jade pendant 珮 [?]
jade ring 璧 [?]
jadeware 玉器 [107]
jail 獄 [?] 牢 [?] 監牢 [142] 監獄 [142]
jam 果醬 [?] 醬 [?] 阻塞 [117]
January 元月 [?] 一月 (⇒ 月 [?])
Japan 日本 [76]
Japanese food 日本料理 (⇒ 料理 [97])
Japanese style 和式 [?]

jar 罐	帶責任	才 正 正義	key point 重點
jargon 術語	joint venture 合資	just a little 一點點 (⇨	keyboard 鍵盤
jasmine 茉莉	jointly owned 共有	點點)	khan 汗
jasmine tea 茉莉花茶	joke 玩笑 笑話 開	just before 臨	kick 踢
jasper 碧玉	玩笑 (⇨ 玩笑)	just going to 正要	kickback 回扣 佣金
javelin 標槍	jolt 顛簸	just like 儼然	kidnap 拐 劫持 綁
jazz 爵士	jottings 隨筆	just now 剛 剛纔 剛	架
jealous 吃醋	journey 路程 路途	纔 方才 方纔	kidney 腎 腎臟
jealous of 忌妒 妒忌	程 旅途	just right 剛好 恰好	kill 戕害 殺 殺害
jealously suspect 猜忌	joy 悅 喜悅 歡欣	正好	殺人 殺死
jealousy 嫉妒 醋意	joy ride 飆車	just when 正當	kill time 消磨時間
jeans 牛仔褲	joyful 樂 痛快 開	justice 義 正義	kilogram 公斤
jeep 吉普	心 欣喜 愉快	juvenile 少年	kilometer 公里
jeer 起鬨	joyous matter 樂事	juvenile delinquency 少	kimchee 泡菜
jellyfish 海蜇	joyous occasion 喜事	年犯罪	kimono 和服
Jesus 耶穌	joyride 兜風		kind 慈祥 種 類
jet 噴射	jubilant 士氣高昂 (⇨	**K k**	和善 善良 般
jet black 烏黑	高昂)	kamikaze 神風隊	類
Jew 猶太人	jubilation 歡欣	kang 炕	kindergarten 幼稚園
jewel 寶石	Judaea 猶太	Kang-Hsi 康熙	kindle 點燃
jewelry 珠寶	Judaism 猶太教	kanji 漢字	kindling 火種
Jewish 猶太	judge 批判 評斷 評	Kaohsiung 高雄	kindness 仁慈 恩
Jiang Qing 江青	分 評估 評判	karate 空手道	情 慈愛
Jiangsu Province 江蘇	評審 法官 裁	karma 報應 因果	king 王 大王 國
蘇	判 斷 判 判斷	kebab 肉串	君 國王
Jiangxi Province 贛 江	judgment 判決	Keelung 基隆	kingdom 王國
西	judiciary 司法	keen 敏銳 鋒利	kingfisher 翡翠
Jiayi 嘉義	judo 柔道	keep 保持 保存	kiss 親吻 接吻 吻
jigsaw puzzle 拼圖	juggling 把戲	keep a secret 保密	kiss lightly 親
Jilin Province 吉林	juggling and acrobatics	keep as a memento 留念	kitchen 廚房 灶
Jin Dynasty 晉朝	雜技	keep company 陪伴	kitchen god 灶神
Jinan 濟南	juice 汁	keep in mind 記 記住	kite 風箏
job 工作	jujube tree 棗樹	留意	kiwi 奇異果
jog 慢跑	July 七月 (⇨ 月)	keep in touch 保持聯繫	knapsack 背包
john 嫖客	jumbled 錯雜	(⇨ 聯繫)	knead 揉
join 結合 繫 銜接	jump 躍 跳 蹦	keep silent 緘口 緘	knee 膝
合 參加 參與	jump for joy 雀躍	默	kneecap 膝蓋
接 聯 連	juncture 關頭	keep warm 保暖 保	kneel 跪 跪下
join a partnership 入	June 六月 (⇨ 月)	溫	knife 刀 刀子
夥	jungle 叢林	kelp 海帶	knife and fork 刀叉
join forces 戮力	junior 三年級學生 (⇨	kendo 劍道	knight 騎士 武士
join hands 攜手	級)	kernel 核仁 米	knit 織
join together 連結	junior high school 初中	ketchup 番茄醬	knock 敲 敲打 敲
joint 節 關節	國中	kettle 水壺	擊 磕 叩
joint examination 聯	jurisdiction 管轄權	key 鍵 關鍵 癥結 門	knock down 打倒
考	juror 陪審員	鑰匙	knock on the door 敲門
joint responsibility 連	jury 陪審團	key issue 焦點	knot 結 結扣
	just 剛 剛剛 公		know 得知 知 知

leave behind 擱置 甩掉 留下 留下
leave blank 空格
leave for 到 開往 前往
leave out 落掉 漏掉
lectern 講台
lecture 演講
lecturer 講師
leeward 下風
leeway 餘地 空間
left 左
left hand 左手
left over 剩 剩下
left side 左邊
left wing 左派 左翼
leftist 左傾
leftover 多餘
leg 腿 足
legal 合法
legal case 案
legal studies 法學
legal system 法制
Legalism 法家
legally 依法
legation 使館
legend 傳奇 傳說
legislate 立法
Legislative Yuan 立法院
legislator 議員 立法員
Lei Feng 雷鋒
leisure 暇 空閒 休閒
leisure time 閒暇 閒暇
leisurely 悠閒
lemon 檸檬
lend 貸款 借貸 借給
length 長 長度 長短 篇幅
lengthy 冗長
lenient 寬 寬容
Lenin 列寧
leopard 豹
leprosy 痲瘋
lesson 教訓 課
lest 要不然 惟恐

let 給 任 讓
let alone 何況
let go 放 放開 放手 放下
let out 發洩 放出
letter 書 書信 函 字 字母 信 信件 來信
letter from home 家書
letter home 家書
letter of introduction 介紹信
letter of reply 回信
letter of resignation 辭呈
level 水平 水準 級 均 平 平坦 削 層次
lever 槓桿
lewd 淫蕩
Lhasa 拉薩
li 里
Li Bai 李白
Li people 黎族
liability 債務
Liaoning Province 遼寧
liar 說謊者
libel 毀謗
liberal 優厚 自由派
liberalization 自由化
liberate 掙脫 解放
liberated 翻身
liberty 自由
libido 性慾
library 圖書館
Libya 利比亞
lice 蝨 蝨子
license 牌照 執照
license plate 牌照
licentious 淫蕩
lick 舔
lid 蓋子
lie 說謊 謊 謊話 躺
lie down 臥

lie in wait 埋伏
lie prone 爬
lie waste 荒廢
lies in 在於
lieutenant 中尉
life 命 生活 生命 性命 身
life experiences 身世
life or death 存亡 生死 死活
life span 壽命
life story 生平
lifelike 逼真
lifelong 終身 終生
lifestyle 生活作風 (⇒ 作風)
lifetime 一輩子 一生 世 輩子
lift 舉 扛 抬 提 掀
lift martial law 解嚴
lift off 起飛
lift open 掀開
lift up 抬起
ligament 韌帶
light 輕 光 光線 點 點燃 燈 清淡 明 淡 淡淡
light rain 零
light ray 光線
light up 亮
lighter 打火機
light-hearted 輕快
lighthouse 燈塔
lightning 閃電
lights 燈火
like 有 如 若 如 同 好 好比 喜 喜愛 喜好 喜歡 猶 猶如
like that 那麼
like this 如此 這般 這麼 這樣
likewise 亦然
lily 百合
limb 肢
limbs 四肢 肢體
lime 石灰

limit 限 限度 限制 止境
limit oneself 畫地自封
limited 有限
limitless 無邊 無限 無涯 無止境 (⇒ 止境)
limp 鬆弛
line 線 線路 線條 格 條 行 列 系 排
line of business 行
line up 列 排 排隊
lineage 血統
linear 線性
lines 紋
lineup 陣容
linger 逗留
link 環節 連接
link up 掛鉤 連貫
lion 獅 獅子
lip 唇 嘴唇
lipstick 口紅
liquid 液 液體
liquidate 清除
liquor 烈酒 酒 白酒
list 清單 列舉
list as 列為
list price 牌價 定價
listen 聽
listen carefully 傾聽
listen respectfully 聆聽
listless 懶散
litchi 荔枝
liter 公升 升
literacy rate 識字率
literary circles 文壇
literary works 詩文
literate 識字
literati 士林 文人
literature 書籍 文獻 文學
litigation 訴訟
litter 亂丟 亂扔

lunar calendar 農曆[34] 陰曆[7] 月曆[10]
lunar eclipse 月蝕[10]
lunatic 狂人[5] 瘋子[7]
lunch 中餐[9] 午餐[3] 午飯[3]
lunch box 便當[16]
lung 肺臟[20]
lung cancer 肺癌[8]
lure 誘惑[8] 誘惑[8]
lush 郁郁[18] 豐盛[9] 榮[9]
lust 色[8] 色情[8] 慾[6]
luster 光澤[8] 璀璨[62]
lute 琵琶[9]
luxuriant 郁郁[15] 茂盛[9] 熒熒[8]
luxurious 豪華[9] 奢侈[8]
luxury goods 奢侈品[8]
lye 鹼[9]
lyrics 歌辭[7]

M m

MSG 味精[20]
MTV 音樂電視[88]
Macau 澳門[14]
machine 機器[7] 機器[7] 機械[7] 器械[9]
machine gun 機槍[9]
macho 有男子氣概(⇒氣概[9])
macroeconomics 宏觀經濟[18]
macroscopic 宏觀[18]
Madame Chiang Kai-Shek 宋美齡[87]
madman 狂人[5] 瘋子[7]
mafia 黑手黨[19]
magazine 雜誌[20]
maggot 蛆[35]
magic 魔術[7]
magic weapon 法寶[9]
magnanimous 寬大[14]
magnate 大王[9] 財閥[9]
magnet 吸鐵石[9] 磁鐵[9]
magnetic disk 磁碟[9]
magnificent 光耀[9] 宏偉[18] 雄偉[19] 絢麗[9] 壯麗[75] 瑰麗[10]
magnolia 木蘭[7]
magpie 喜鵲[80]
mahjong 麻將[7] 麻雀[7]
maid 侍女[9]
maidservant 婢[45] 婢女[45]
mail 寄[9] 信件[9] 郵遞[7] 郵寄[7] 郵件[7]
mail a letter 寄信[9]
mail to 寄給[9]
mailbox 郵筒[9] 郵箱[7]
mailman 郵差[73]
maimed 殘廢[78]
main 主[9] 主要[9]
main entrance 大門[9] 正門[9]
main factor 要素[14]
mainland 大陸[9]
mainland China 中國大陸 (⇒大陸[9])
mainstay 柱石[9] 骨幹[9]
mainstream 主流[2]
maintain 保持[9] 保養[9] 維持[19] 維繫[19] 維修[9]
majestic 威嚴[19]
majesty 威嚴[19]
major 主修[9] 少校[9] 專業[9]
major in 主修[9]
majority 大多數[9] 多數[7]
majority opinion 眾議[9]
make 弄[18] 作[9] 做[9] 打[9] 令[80] 施[9] 使[88] 使得[89] 製[9] 造[9]
make a fool of 愚弄[9]
make a living 謀生[9]
make a mistake 犯錯[9]
make a reservation 預定[102]
make a sneak attack 侵襲[9]
make an all-out effort 卯勁[9]
make an appointment 約[9] 約會[61]
make an inspection tour 巡視[24]
make certain 確定[19]
make difficulties for 刁難[9]
make do with 將就[95]
make every effort 極力[14]
make excuses 辯解[9] 託辭[9]
make excuses for 袒護[9]
make friends 交朋友[9]
make instant noodles 泡麵[19]
make into 作成[9] 製成[9]
make love 做愛[9]
make mischief 作祟[9] 鬼混[10]
make money 掙錢[9] 賺錢[9]
make noodles 下麵[9]
make payments 付款[9]
make public 公佈[9] 公布[9] 公告[9] 揭示[9]
make reservations 定位[9]
make room 騰出[9]
make soup 泡湯[9]
make steel 煉鋼[9]
make stone rubbings 拓[9]
make stuck 卡[4]
make tea 沏茶[4] 泡茶[19] 沖茶[9]
make the best of 將就[95]
make trouble 作怪[9] 搞鬼[9] 鬧事[9] 搗蛋[9] 搗亂[9]
make up 彌補[9] 虛構[9]
make war 作戰[9]
makeup 化妝[9]
malaria 瘧疾[9]
male 雄[9] 雄性[9] 公[9] 男[9] 男性[9] 男子[9] 陽性[9] 牡[9]
malfeasance 舞弊[31] 瀆職[19]
malfunction 失靈[9]
malice 惡意[66]
malicious 兇狠[9] 毒[9]
malicious talk 壞話[9]
malign 謾罵[9] 誣害[9] 中傷[9]
malignant 惡性[66]
malignant tumor 毒瘤[9]
mama 媽媽[9]
mammal 哺乳動物[9]
man 先生[9] 漢子[9] 男子[9] 男人[9] 男子[9] 夫[9]
manage 經理[9] 經營[9] 司[9] 處[9] 辦理[9] 辦理[9] 治理[9] 操持[9] 料理[9] 管[9] 管理[67]
manage the household 持家[9]
manager 經理[9]
Manchu people 滿族[9]
Manchukuo 滿州國[9]
Manchuria 滿州[9]
Mandarin 漢語[9] 國語[9] 官話[67] 華語[9] 普通話[9]
mandarin orange 柑橘[9] 橘子[105]
mandate of heaven 天命[9]
mandatory 強制[9]
maneuver 駕馭[9]
manga 漫畫[9]
mango 芒果[9]
manifest 彰顯[9]
manifesto 宣言[9]
manipulate 操縱[9] 擺佈[9]
mannequin 模特兒[9]
manner 舉止[9] 架子[9] 風格[9] 氣[9] 氣派[9]
mansion 大廈[9]
mantou 饅頭[9]
manual 譜[9] 手冊[9]
manual labor 勞力[9]
manual worker 工友[9]
manufacture 製[9] 製造[9] 製作[9]
manufacturing industry 製造業[9]
manuscript 原稿[9] 稿[9]

稿子[2] 底稿[100] 謄本[...]
many 不少[...] 多[7] 諸多[...] 許多[...]
many thanks 多謝[...]
Mao Zedong 毛澤東[...]
Mao button 毛澤東像章 (⇨ 像章[172])
Mao suit 中山裝[...]
Maoism 毛澤東思想 (⇨ 思想[43])
Maotai liquor 茅台酒[105]
map 地圖[...]
maple 楓[...]
maple syrup 楓糖[...]
maple tree 楓樹[...]
marble 大理石[...]
March 三月 (⇨ 月[...])
march toward 邁向[...]
Marco Polo Bridge 盧溝橋[...]
marijuana 大麻[...]
marinated dish 滷菜[130]
marinated meat 滷肉[...]
marital bliss 琴瑟和鳴[...] 鶼鰈[...]
marital love 恩愛[...]
mark 痕[...] 痕跡[...] 符號[...] 標[...] 勾[...] 號[...] 評分[...] 跡象[...] 馬克[177]
mark clearly 標明[...]
marked 顯著[...]
market 銷[...] 銷售[...] 行銷[...] 市[...] 市場[...] 推銷[...] 集[...]
market demand 銷路[...]
market directly 直銷[...]
market economy 市場經濟[...]
market place 商場[...]
market price 行情[...] 市價[...]
market system 市場機制 (⇨ 機制[...])
marketing channels 銷路[...]
marketing strategy 行銷策略[...]

marquis 侯爵[...]
marriage 婚事[...] 婚姻[100]
married couple 伉儷[...]
married woman 婦人[...]
marrow 骨髓[...]
marry 娶[...] 嫁[155] 嫁給[155]
marsh 沼澤[...]
marshal 元帥[...]
marshland 窪地[...]
martial arts 武打[...] 武術[...]
martial arts movie 武打片[...]
martial arts novel 武俠小說[...]
martial arts skill 武功[...] 武藝[...]
martial law 戒嚴[...]
martial law period 戒嚴時期[...]
martyr 先烈[...] 烈士[...] 殉道者[...]
marvel 驚歎[...] 納罕[...]
marvellous 奇妙[...] 奧妙[...]
Marx 馬克思[177]
Marxism 馬克思主義[177]
mash 砸[...]
mask 面具[...]
masquerade 裝扮[...]
mass movement 群衆運動[...]
massacre 殘殺[...] 屠殺[...] 殺戮[100]
massage 按摩[...] 揉搓[105] 推拿[...]
masses 衆人[...] 群衆[...] 大衆[...]
mast 桅杆[...]
master 主[...] 主人[...] 老爺[...] 掌握[...] 師[...] 師傅[...] 師父[...]
master of ceremonies 主持人[...]
master's degree 碩士[...]
master's student 碩士班學生[...]

masterpiece 傑作[...] 名著[...]
mastery 技能[...]
masturbation 手淫[...]
mat 席[...] 草席[...]
match 比賽[...] 符[...] 符合[...] 賽[...] 匹[...] 搭配[...] 配[...] 配對[...] 火柴[...] 球賽[...] 洋火[...]
matchless 無比[...] 絕[...]
matchmake 撮合[...]
matchmaker 媒人[...]
mate 交配[...] 配偶[...]
material 材[...] 材料[...] 物質[...] 料[...]
material temptations 酒色財氣[199]
materialism 唯物論[...] 物質主義[...]
mathematics 數學[...]
matrilineal 母系[...]
matrilineal society 母系社會[...]
matrix 矩陣[...]
Matsu Islands 馬祖[177]
matter 事[...] 事情[...]
mattress 床墊[...]
mature 長大[...] 成熟[...]
mausoleum 陵[...] 陵墓[...]
maxim 座右銘[...]
May 五月 (⇨ 月[...])
may 可[...] 可以[...]
May I ask...? 請問[...]
May I trouble you...? 勞駕[...]
maybe 說不定[...] 可能[...] 或許[...]
mayor 市長[...]
McDonald's 麥當勞[100]
meal 飯[...] 頓[...] 餐[133]
meals 膳食[...]
mean 刻薄[...] 平均[...] 壞[...]
mean person 小人[...]
meaning 義[...] 意義[...] 意思[...] 意味[...] 意義[...]
meaningless 空虛[...] 沒

有意義 (⇨ 意義[...])
means 手段[...] 道[...]
measles 疹子[...] 痳疹[...]
measure 計量[...] 度[...] 尺度[...] 衡量[...] 措施[...] 步驟[...] 測[...] 測量[...] 稱[...]
measurements 尺寸[...]
measureword for buildings 幢[...]
measureword for horses 匹[...]
meat 肉[132] 肉類[...]
mechanical 機械[...]
mechanics 力學[...]
medal 牌[...] 獎牌[...] 徽章[...]
meddle 干涉[...] 插手[...]
media 傳媒[...] 媒體[...]
mediate 疏通[...] 仲介[...] 調停[...] 調和[...] 調解[...] 調停[...] 幹旋[...]
mediate with spirits 通靈[...]
medical school 醫學院[...]
medical science 醫學[...] 醫學[...]
medical treatment 醫療[...]
medicinal plaster 膏藥[...]
medicine 醫[...] 醫學[...] 醫藥[...] 藥[...] 藥[...] 藥品[...] 藥物[...]
mediocre 平平[...] 中庸[...] 庸碌[...] 馬馬虎虎 (⇨ 馬虎[177])
meditation 冥想[...]
Mediterranean Sea 地中海[...]
medium 媒介[...] 中[...]
meet 晤[...] 碰到[...] 碰見[...] 碰頭[...] 接[...] 接頭[...] 逢[...] 遇[...] 遇到[...] 遇見[...] 見[...] 見到[...] 見面[...] 聚會[...] 會[...] 會合[...] 會見[...] 應接[...]
meet and talk 晤談[...]
meet face to face 晤面[...] 會面[...] 會晤[...]

meet one another 相見[126]
meet with 遭[66]
meet with calamity 遭殃[66]
meeting 會[101] 會議[101]
megaphone 擴音器[56]
Meiji Restoration 明治維新 (⇒ 維新[87])
mellow 醇厚[22]
melodious 悠揚[20]
melody 旋律[116] 曲[135] 曲子[135]
melon 瓜[104]
melt 溶[62] 溶化[62] 融[74] 融化[74]
melting pot 熔爐[66]
member 份子[3] 成員[55]
membership card 會員卡[11]
membrane 膜[62]
memento 紀念品[37]
memoir 回憶錄[9]
memorandum 備忘錄[9]
memorial hall 紀念堂[37]
memorial service 追悼會[167]
memorial tablet 牌位[15]
memorialize 緬懷[16]
memorize 背[13]
memory 記憶[37] 回憶[9]
men and women 男女[34]
men's team 男子隊[34]
Mencius 孟子[16]
mend 褪[9] 修補[9] 補[66]
menses 月經[9]
mental handicap 智障[9]
mental illness 精神病[?] 神經病[126]
mental power 心智[83]
mental state 心理[83] 心情[?]
mentality 心理[83] 心態[?]
mentally 心裡[?]
mentally unstable 心裡不平衡[83]
mention 提起[13] 提到[13]
mention in passing 順口[?]
mentor 恩師[22] 提拔[83]

menu 菜單[107]
mercenary 傭兵[20]
merchandise 貨物[?]
merciless 苛刻[?] 慘[66]
merciless and vicious 心狠手辣[?]
mercy 慈悲[?]
merely 光是[?] 就[?] 空[?] 只[?] 只是[?] 罷[?]
merge 並[?] 合併[?] 併[?] 入[?] 兼併[?]
meritorious deeds 功德[?]
merits 功績[?] 優點[?]
message 訊息[?]
messed up 糟糕[?]
messenger 差役[15]
metallurgy 冶金[?]
metals 金[?] 金屬[?]
metamorphose 蛻變[?]
metaphor 比擬[?] 比喻[?] 隱喻[?]
meteor 流星[?]
meteorite 隕石[120]
meter 公尺[?] 米[?] 韻律[?]
method 作法[?] 做法[?] 法[?] 法子[?] 辦法[?] 手段[?] 方[?] 方法[?] 術[?]
methodology 方法論[?]
meticulous 精細[?] 細緻[143]
meticulously 精心[?]
metric system 公制[?]
Mexico 墨西哥[144]
Miao people 苗族[?]
Mickey Mouse 米老鼠 (⇒ 老鼠[?])
microscope 顯微鏡[?]
microwave 微波[?]
microwave oven 微波爐[134]
Mid-Autumn Festival 中秋節[?]
mid-air 空中[?]
middle 中[?] 心[83]

Middle Ages 中古時代 (⇒ 時代[?])
Middle East 中東[?]
middle age 中年[?]
middle school 國中[?] 中學[?]
middle-aged person 中年人[?]
middle-class 小康[?]
middleman 仲介人[?]
midnight 零時[?] 半夜[?] 午夜[?]
midway 中途[?]
might as well 索性[?] 無妨[?]
mighty 威武[?]
migrate 遷居[?] 遷移[?] 移居[?]
mildew 霉[?]
mildewed 發霉[?]
mile 英里[?]
militaristic 黷武[?]
military 武[?] 軍[?] 軍隊[?]
military campaign 戰役[36]
military dress 戎裝[?]
military expenses 軍費[?]
military force 武力[?]
military forces 兵馬[?]
military instructor 教官[?]
military matters 軍事[?]
military officer 軍官[?]
military police 憲兵[?]
military service 服役[?] 兵役[?]
military strategy 戰略[?]
military strength 兵力[?]
military uniform 軍裝[?]
milk 牛奶[?]
milk tea 奶茶[?]
Milky Way 銀河[?]
mill 碾[?] 礱[?] 水車屋[?]
mill rice 碾米[?]
millet 小米[?] 粟[170]
millimeter 公釐[?] 毫

米[?]
million 百萬[?]
millionaire 百萬富翁 (⇒ 富翁[?])
millions and millions 億萬[?]
mimic 模擬[?]
mind 介意[?] 計較[?] 心[?] 心目[?] 心頭[?] 嫌[?] 腦海[143] 腦筋[143] 腦子[143] 管[167]
mind and body 身心[147]
mine 礦場[?] 採礦[103]
miner 礦工[?]
mineral resources 礦藏[?]
mineral springs 礦泉[?]
mineral water 礦泉水[?]
Ming Tombs 明朝十三陵 (⇒ 陵[?])
mingle 混雜[?]
mini 迷你[?]
miniature 模型[?]
minimally 起碼[?]
minimum 起碼[?]
mining pit 礦坑[?]
miniscule profits 蠅頭小利[?]
minister 部長[?] 卿[?] 大臣[?] 牧師[?] 臣[142]
minor 輕微[?] 枝節[?]
minor complication 枝節問題[?]
minority 少數[?]
minority peoples 少數民族[?]
minute 分[?] 分鐘[35] 微小[?] 細小[143]
minutes 紀錄[?]
miracle 奇蹟[?]
miraculous 神奇[15]
mirage 幻象[?]
mire 泥濘[?]
mirror 鏡[?] 鏡子[?]
miscalculate 算錯[150]
miscarriage 流產[?]
miscellaneous 雜[?]
miscellaneous duties 雜務[?]

mischievous 頑皮 作怪 淘氣
misconception 錯覺
miserable 悽慘 悲傷
miserable situation 慘狀
misfortune 好歹 害 禍
misgivings 疑慮 顧忌
misinterpret 誤解 曲解
misplace 丟 丟掉
Miss 小姐 姑娘
miss 惦念 念 錯過 錯失 失掉 相思 想 想念
missile 飛彈
missing 不見 少 缺失
mission 任務 職志 使命
missionary 傳教士
missionary school 教會學校
misstep 失足
mist 雲霧 霧 霧氣
mistake 舛誤 紕漏 弄錯 誤 謬誤 錯 錯誤 過失
mistaken 錯
mistreat 虐待
mistress 姨太太 情婦 小老婆 (⇨老婆)
misty 濛濛
misunderstand 搞錯 誤會 誤解
misunderstanding 誤會 誤解 隔閡
misuse 濫用
mitigate 緩和
mix 混 混合 混雜 攪 攪拌 攪動 調配 拌 攙雜
mix up 夾雜
mixed 什錦

mixed race 混血
mixed up 錯雜
moan 呻吟
moat 壕溝
mobile 機動
mobilize 調動 動員 發動
mock 訕笑 嘲弄 笑 恥笑
model 楷模 範例 型 模範 模式 模型 造型 榜樣 典範 典型 樣 樣板
model worker 勞動模範 (⇨模範)
modem 數據機
moderate 適度
moderation 中庸
modern era 近代 現代
modern history 近代史
modern people 近人
modern poetry 現代詩
modernization 現代化
modest 謙虛 謙遜
modify 變更
moist 濕 濕潤
moisten 濕潤
molar 臼齒
mold 鑄 鑄造 塑型 塑造 捏 造型
mold and smelt 陶冶
molecule 分子
mollify 緩和
mom 媽
mom and dad 爸爸媽媽
moment 刻 時刻 須臾 關頭 片刻 會 一會兒
momentarily 一時
monarch 君 君主 國君 帝王
monarchy 君權
monastery 寺院
monastery gate 山門

Monday 星期一 禮拜一
money 金 金錢 錢 錢財
money order 電匯
money politics 金錢政治
Mongolia 蒙古
monitor 監督
monk 和尚 僧 僧人
monkey 猴子
Monkey King 孫悟空
monks 僧侶
monopolize 獨攬 獨佔 壟斷
monosodium glutamate 味精
monotonous 單調
monster 怪物 魔鬼 妖怪
monstrous 妖邪
month 月 月份
monthly salary 月薪 (⇨薪)
mood 氣氛 心境 心情
moon 月 月亮 月球
Moon Festival 中秋節
moon cake 月餅
moon goddess 嫦娥
moonlight 月光 兼差
mop 拖把
mop up 掃蕩
moral 教訓 寓意
moral character 品德 品格
moral education 德育
moral strength 操守 氣魄
morale 人心 士氣 氣
morals 道德
more 更 更多
more ... the more 越愈

more and more 越發 越來越 愈來愈
more or less 差不多 多少
more so 更為
more than 餘 多
more...the more 越...越
moreover 況且 加以 並且 且 還有 而且
morning 上午 早晨 早上
morning exercises 早操
morning sun 旭日 朝陽
morphine 嗎啡
mortals 世人
mortgage 抵押
Moscow 莫斯科
Mosque 清真寺
mosquito 蚊 蚊子
mosquito larvae 孑孓
mosquito net 蚊帳
most 大半 大部份 大部分 多半 多數 最 最多
most important 首要
mostly 大半 大都 大多 大致
mother 娘 母 母親 媽 媽媽
Mother Nature 大自然 (⇨自然)
mother tongue 母語
Mother's Day 母親節
mother-in-law 婆婆 岳母
motherland 母國
motionless 靜態 靜止
motivate 刺激 策動
motivation 動力
motive 動機
motor 摩托
motorcycle 機車 摩托車
motorized 機動
motto 座右銘

natural 天然[9] 天生[9] 自然[19] 自在[19]

natural endowment 天分[9]

natural environment 水土[4]

natural gas 瓦斯[19] 天然瓦斯[9] 天然氣[9]

natural resources 自然資源 (⇨ 資源[9])

natural scenery 山水[67]

natural science 博物[6] 自然科學[19]

natural talent 稟賦[6]

naturalized 入籍[12]

naturally 自然而然[19]

nature 天性[9] 性[9] 性質[9] 質地[9] 自然[19]

naughty 頑皮[4] 皮[4] 淘氣[141]

naval power 海權[9]

naval vessel 艦[142] 艦艇[142]

navel 肚臍[9]

navigate 航[9] 航行[9]

navy 海軍[9]

Naxi 納西族[9]

Nazi 納粹[9]

near 接近[9] 靠[9] 靠近[9] 近[9]

near and far 遠近[9]

near to 挨近[9] 近於[9]

nearby 鄰近[9] 附近[14]

nearly 殆[9] 幾乎[9] 將近[9]

nearly exhausted 殆盡[58]

neat 整[9] 整齊[9] 齊[102]

neat and clean 整潔[9]

necessarily 必[9] 必定[9]

necessary 必需[9] 必要[9]

necessity 必要性[9] 必需品[9]

neck 頸[9] 頸部[9] 脖子[9] 領[9]

necklace 項鍊[9] 項圈[9]

need 得[9] 要[14] 必要[9] 需[161] 需求[9] 需要[161]

---

need not 不必[9] 不用[9] 無需[9]

need to 須[9] 須要[9]

need urgently 急需[14]

needle 針[9]

negate 否定[9]

negation 否定[9]

negative 消極[9] 陰性[9] 零下[9] 底片[100] 負[9] 負面[19]

negative influence 負面的影響[9]

negative number 負數[19]

neglect 輕忽[9] 輕率[9] 荒廢[9] 疏忽[9] 忽[9] 忽略[9] 忽視[9] 埋沒[9] 漏[129]

neglect a guest 怠慢[9]

neglectfully 輕忽[9]

negligent 疏失[9]

negligible 渺小[9]

negotiate 磋商[9] 商議[9] 協商[9] 協議[9] 交涉[9] 洽[9] 談判[9]

negotiations 談判[9]

neighbor 鄰居[9] 鄰人[9]

neighboring country 鄰國[9]

nemesis 剋星[152]

Neo-Confucianism 理學[111]

neologism 新語[9]

neon 霓虹[9]

neon light 霓虹燈[9]

Nepal 尼泊爾[9]

nephew 甥[9] 外甥[9] 姪[9] 姪兒[9] 姪子[9]

nerd 書呆子 (⇨ 呆子[9])

nerve 神經[9]

nervous 緊張[9]

nest 巢[9] 窩[9]

net 網[9] 絡[9]

net profit 純利[9] 淨利[9]

net value 淨值[9]

network 網路[9] 網絡[9] 脈絡[9]

neutral tone 輕聲[9]

---

neutralize 抵銷[9]

never 從未[9] 未曾[9] 從來沒有[9]

never again 不再[9]

nevertheless 卻是[9]

new 新[9]

New Year 春節[15] 新年[9]

New Year's Day 元旦[9]

New Year's Eve 除夕[9]

New Year's cake 年糕[9]

New Year's card 新年卡[9]

New Year's couplet 春聯[9]

New York 紐約[9]

New Zealand 紐西蘭[9] 新西蘭[9]

new student 新生[9]

newborn 新生[9]

news 消息[9] 訊[9] 新聞[9] 息[9]

news anchor 主播[9]

newspaper 報[9] 報紙[9]

newspaper clipping 簡報[24]

newspaper column 專欄[9]

newspaper company 報社[9]

newspaper page 版[9]

newspapers 報章[9]

next 下[9] 次[9] 其次[9] 翌[124] 來[9]

next day 次日[9]

next door 鄰舍[9] 隔壁[9]

next life 下輩子 (⇨ 輩子[9])

next time 下次[9]

next year 明年[9]

nibble 啃[9]

nice 友善[9]

nickname 外號[9] 綽號[9]

niece 甥女[9] 姪[9] 姪女[9] 外甥女[9]

night 夜[9] 夜晚[9] 宿[9] 晚上[9]

night before 前夕[9]

night market 夜市[9]

night school 夜校[9]

---

night shift 夜班 (⇨ 班[9])

night soil 糞便[9]

nightmare 噩夢[9] 夢魘[14] 惡夢[9]

nighttime 夜間[9]

nimble 敏捷[9]

nine 玖[9] 九[9]

nineties 九十年代 (⇨ 年代[9])

Ningxia Province 寧夏[16]

ninja 忍者[9]

ninth Earthly Branch 申[9]

ninth Heavenly Stem 壬[9]

nip 切斷[9]

nipple 奶頭[9]

Nixon 尼克森[9]

no 不[9] 否[9]

no comment 無可奉告 (⇨ 奉告[9])

no doubt 固然[9]

no harm in 不妨[9] 無妨[9]

no longer 不再[9]

no matter 憑[9]

no matter what 任憑[9]

no one 莫不[9]

no problem 沒事[9]

no wonder 怪不得[9] 難怪[9]

Nobel Prize 諾貝爾獎 (⇨ 獎[9])

nobility 貴族[106]

noble 高貴[9] 高尚[9]

noble sentiments 情操[9]

nod 點頭[9]

nod approval 首肯[9]

noise 噪音[9] 雜音[9]

noise pollution 噪音污染[9]

noisy 響[9] 吵[9] 嘈[9] 雜[9] 鬧[9]

nominal 掛名[9] 名目[9] 名義[9]

nominate 提名[9]

non-governmental 民間[119]

non-party 黨外[9]

non-profit 非牟利 (⇨
牟利㊗) 非營利 (⇨
營利㊗)
nonsense 狗屁㊐ 胡說㊐
Nonsense! 廢話㊏ 亂
講㊏
nonsensical 胡說八
道㊐
nonstop 不停㊐
noodles 麵條㊐
nook 隅㊝
noon 中午㊐ 午㊐
noon nap 午覺㊐ 午睡㊐
norm 規範㊐ 準則㊐
normal 正常㊏
normally 經常㊏ 通常㊏
日常㊐
North 北方㊐
north 北㊐ 北方㊐
North America 北美洲
(⇨ 美洲㊐)
North China plain 華北平
原 (⇨ 平原㊐)
North Korea 北朝鮮 (⇨
朝鮮㊐) 北韓 (⇨
韓㊐)
North Pole 北極點㊐
north wind 朔風㊐
northeast 東北㊐
northern part 北部㊐
Norway 挪威㊐
nose 鼻㊐ 鼻子㊐
nostalgic 感慨㊐
nostril 鼻孔㊐
not 不㊐ 無㊐ 弗㊐ 莫㊐
非㊐
not a few 不少㊐
not at all 好不㊐ 毫不㊐
not bad 不錯㊐
not conform to 不合㊐
not in sight 不見㊐
not limited to 不止 (⇨
止㊐)
not long 不久㊐
not necessarily 不見
得㊐ 未必㊐ 不一定
(⇨ 一定㊐)
not only 不但㊐ 不僅㊐

非但㊐
not to mention 遑論㊐ 何
況㊐
not worthwhile 不值 (⇨
值㊐)
not yet 尚未㊐ 未㊐ 還
沒㊐
notation 符號㊐
note 注意㊐ 帖㊐ 字條㊐
notebook 簿子㊐ 本子㊐
notes 筆記㊐
notice 佈告㊐ 睬㊐ 理
睬㊐
notify 通知㊐ 告知㊐
notify by edict 諭知㊐
notify publicly 通告㊐
noun 名詞㊐
nourish 滋補㊐ 滋養㊐
養㊐
nourishment 營養㊐
nouveau riche 暴發戶㊐
novel 小說㊐ 別緻㊐ 新
穎㊐
novelist 小說家㊐
November 十一月 (⇨
月㊐)
novice 新手㊐ 生手㊐
now 就此㊐ 今㊐ 茲㊐
茲㊐ 目前㊐ 現今㊐
現在㊐ 而今㊐
now that 既㊐
nowadays 如今㊐ 當今㊐
nuclear bomb 核子彈㊐
nuclear energy 核能㊐
nuclear family 核心家
庭㊐
nuclear power 核電㊐
nuclear weapons 核武㊐
nucleus 核心㊐ 核子㊐
nude 裸體㊐
nude body 天體㊐
numb 麻痺㊐ 麻痺㊐ 麻
木㊐ 僵㊐
number 號㊐ 號碼㊐ 數㊐
數目㊐

number of people 人數㊐
人頭㊐
number of times 次數㊐
number one on a list 榜
首㊐
numbness 麻痺㊐ 麻痺㊐
numeral 數字㊐
numerator 分子㊐
numerous 衆多㊐ 濟
濟㊐
numerous and complex 繁
雜㊐
nun 尼姑㊐ 尼姑㊐ 修女㊐
姑㊐
nunnery 庵㊐ 庵堂㊐
nuptial chamber 洞房㊐
nurse 哺乳㊐ 看護㊐ 護
士㊐
nursemaid 奶媽㊐
nursery 托兒所㊐
nurture 培養㊐ 孕育㊐
薰陶㊐
nut 果㊐
nutmeg 荳蔻㊐
nutrient 養分㊐
nutrify 滋補㊐
nutrition 營養㊐

O o

o'clock 點㊐ 點鐘㊐ 時㊐
鐘㊐
o.k. 可以㊐ 行㊐ 還好㊐
oak 橡㊐
oar 槳㊐
oasis 綠洲㊐
oath 誓言㊐
oatmeal 麥片㊐
obedient 乖㊐ 乖乖㊐ 聽
話㊐
obese 臃腫㊐
obey 順㊐ 順從㊐ 從㊐
聽話㊐ 服㊐ 服從㊐
遵守㊐
obey authority 服從權
威㊐
obey orders 聽命㊐
obey the law 守法㊐
obituary 訃告㊐
object 物㊐ 物體㊐ 對

象㊐
objection 異議㊐ 意見㊐
objective 宗旨㊐ 客觀㊐
目標㊐ 目的㊐
obligation 義務㊐
obliged to 只得㊐
obliging 隨和㊐
obliterate 塗抹㊐
obscene 下流㊐ 黃色㊐
淫穢㊐ 猥褻㊐
observatory 天文台㊐
observe 察看㊐ 考察㊐
觀㊐ 觀測㊐ 觀察㊐
obsessively 一味㊐
obsolete 陳舊㊐
obstacle 波折㊐ 障礙㊐
絆腳石㊐ 窒礙㊐
obstinate 頑㊐ 頑固㊐
硬㊐ 冥頑㊐ 刁蠻㊐
偏執㊐
obstruct 梗阻㊐ 攔住㊐
攔阻㊐ 阻㊐ 阻礙㊐
阻攔㊐ 阻撓㊐ 阻
止㊐ 窒礙㊐
obstructed 不通㊐
obstruction 阻力㊐ 阻
撓㊐
obtain 得㊐ 搞㊐ 取㊐
取得㊐ 獲㊐ 獲得㊐
獲取㊐
obverse 正面㊐
obvious 明顯㊐ 顯明㊐
obviously 顯然㊐
occasion 場合㊐
occasional 不定期 (⇨
定期㊐)
occasionally 不時㊐ 偶
而㊐ 偶爾㊐
Occident 西方㊐
occupation 職業㊐
occupied 淪陷㊐
occupy 佔㊐ 佔據㊐ 佔
領㊐ 佔有㊐ 據㊐
occur 發生㊐ 出㊐
ocean 大海㊐ 海㊐ 海
洋㊐ 洋㊐
ocean surface 海面㊐
October 十月 (⇨ 月㊐)

odd 詭異⁷ 奇⁶³ 離奇⁷⁰
odd number 奇數⁶³ 單數¹³⁶
ode 頌⁸⁵ 之頌⁸⁵
of 的⁹¹ 之⁸⁵
of course 當然⁸⁵
of one mind 志同道合³⁵
of the people 民間¹¹⁹
of the same kind 同類⁸⁴
of the same profession 同業⁸⁴
of which 其中⁴⁵
off season 淡季⁷²
offend 得罪²⁵ 觸犯¹⁶⁵
offensive 唐突⁸ 攻勢⁵²
offer 貢獻³¹ 讓⁶⁶ 出手¹¹⁰ 獻¹⁷⁴
offer in tribute 奉獻³¹
offer one's seat 讓座⁶⁶
offer sacrifices 祭祀¹
offer suggestions 出意見¹¹⁰
office 局⁷⁶ 處³⁸ 辦公室⁴⁸
office workers 上班族⁴³
official 仕⁸ 吏⁷ 幹部⁵⁶ 臣¹⁴² 官方⁶⁷
official bureau 官署⁶⁷
official business 公務²⁷
official career 仕途⁸¹
official document 文書²⁷
official profiteering 官倒⁶⁷
official rank 職等⁶⁹
official residence 府²⁵ 官邸⁶⁷
officialdom 政界⁹⁴ 官場⁶⁷ 官吏⁶⁷
offset 抵銷¹⁰⁰
offshoot 支⁷¹
often 時常¹⁵ 常⁸⁵ 頻繁¹⁴⁶
Oh! 哦⁸⁵
oil 油¹³ 油脂¹¹³
oil painting 油畫¹¹³
oily 油¹¹³
ointment 荇⁸
old 蒼老⁷⁰ 老⁶ 陳⁴⁸

old 舊¹³⁴ 年紀大⁶⁵
old age 老年⁶⁵
old friend 老友²⁵
old man 老人⁶ 老頭¹³ 翁⁸⁵
old person 老人家⁶
old times 舊日¹³⁴
old woman 老太太¹³
olive 橄欖¹⁷
Olympics 奧運⁶⁸
omelet 蛋包⁸⁵
omen 預兆⁶⁸ 兆¹²⁷ 兆頭¹²⁷ 朕兆⁶⁸ 徵兆⁸⁵
omit 略⁹⁵ 落⁸⁹ 省⁶ 省略⁵⁶ 跳¹²⁷
omnipotent 全能⁸⁷
on 在⁵⁴
on all sides 四面⁸² 四周⁸²
on friendly terms 和睦⁵⁸ 融洽¹⁷⁴
on guard 戒備¹⁹
on hand 手下⁹⁹ 手中⁹⁹ 身邊¹⁴⁷
on purpose 有心¹⁸
on the basis of 因⁴⁵ 基於⁴⁶ 按照⁸⁵
on the contrary 反而⁴⁸
on the ground 地上³⁶
on the market 坊間²⁷
on the one hand 一方面⁴⁹ (⇨方面⁴⁹)
on the other hand 反過來⁴⁸ 反之而言⁴⁸
on the road 路上¹²⁹
on the scene 在場⁵⁴
on the street 街上⁵⁵
on the whole 總算⁵⁴
on time 及時⁵⁵ 按時⁸⁵ 準時¹⁵²
once 一旦¹ 一度¹ 一回¹ 一下子¹
once more 再次¹⁷⁵ 再度¹⁷⁵
one 一¹ 一個¹ 個個⁶⁸ 壹¹⁶⁶
one after another 重重⁶⁸ 累累¹¹
one and only 獨一無二¹²⁵

one aspect 一面¹
one by one 一一¹ 各個⁶⁸ 逐一⁹⁷
one hundred percent 百分之百⁹⁷
one or two 一二¹
one side 一邊¹ 一面¹
one with 打成一片⁵³
one's self 本身⁶⁶
one's turn 該⁶⁶
one-child policy 一胎化政策 (⇨胎⁹⁰)
oneself 自己¹⁷⁹ 自家¹⁷⁹ 身¹⁴⁷
one-sided 片面⁷⁶
onion 洋蔥¹²³ 蔥¹⁴⁴
only 就⁴⁶ 僅⁵³ 僅僅⁵³ 無非⁵³ 才⁴⁵ 只⁸⁵ 只是⁴⁶ 祇⁴⁶ 祇要⁴⁶ 祇有¹⁰⁰ 獨¹³¹ 龍⁷³ 龍了¹² 而已¹³⁴ 單¹³⁶ 唯⁸⁵ 唯一⁸⁵ 唯有⁵³ 惟⁸⁵ 惟一⁸⁵ 纔¹⁶⁴
only if 只有⁸⁵
on-the-spot 實地⁹⁵ 現場⁹⁵
oolong tea 烏龍茶¹⁷⁵
open 光明⁵² 公開²⁷ 張⁴⁸ 開⁸⁵ 打開⁵³ 敞開¹⁴⁴ 開放⁸⁵ 開幕⁸⁵ 開啓⁸⁵ 睜⁹⁵ 睜開⁹⁵
open and clear 豁然⁵⁵
open and honest 光明磊落¹¹
open door policy 開放政策⁸⁵
open one's mouth 開口²⁵
open space 場⁴⁸
open to traffic 通行⁹⁷
open up 開發⁸⁵ 開闢⁸⁵ 開拓⁸⁵
open wide 敞開¹⁴⁴
opening 孔⁸⁵ 口⁸⁵
openly 公開²⁷ 公然²⁷
open-minded 開明⁸⁵ 開通⁸⁵ 豁達⁵⁵
opera 歌劇⁸³

operate 經營¹⁶⁶ 操⁹⁵ 操縱⁹⁵ 操作⁹⁵ 駛⁶⁷ 開⁸⁵ 開刀⁸⁵
operating profit 營利¹⁶⁶
operation 作業⁵⁸
operations 營運¹⁶⁶ 運作¹⁵⁸
opinion 見¹¹⁴ 見解¹¹⁴ 想法¹⁴
opium 鴉片⁸⁴
Opium War 鴉片戰爭⁸⁴
opponent 對手¹⁷⁶
opportune moment 時機¹⁵
opportunism 機會主義⁷³
opportunist 投機分子⁷³ 機會主義者⁷³
opportunistic 投機⁷³
opportunity 機會⁷³ 機遇⁷³ 契機⁷³
oppose 反對³¹ 作對³¹ 對¹⁷⁶
opposite 相對⁹⁵ 相反⁹⁵
opposite direction 反向⁴⁸
opposite sex 異性⁸⁵
opposition party 在野黨⁵⁴
oppress 欺負⁶⁸ 欺壓⁶⁸ 壓⁸⁹ 壓迫⁸⁹ 壓榨⁸⁹
oppressive 沈悶⁸⁷
optical fiber 光纖⁵²
optimistic 樂觀⁸⁹
or 抑或⁸⁵ 或⁵⁵ 或是⁵⁵ 或者⁵⁵
or so 左右¹³
oracle bone inscriptions 卜辭²⁶
oral examination 口試²⁵
oral report 口頭報告²⁵
oral sex 口交⁶⁸
orally 口頭⁶⁸
orange 柳橙²⁴
orange juice 橘子汁¹⁰⁵ 柳橙汁²⁴
orangutan 猩猩⁶⁵
orbit 軌道⁷⁷ 軌跡⁷⁷ 繞行¹⁷ 環繞¹⁷
orchard 果園²⁴

orchestra 樂隊

orchid 蘭花 蘭花兒

Orchid Island 蘭嶼

order 順序 次第 次序 指令 條理 令 命 命令 驅使 程 秩序 層次

order dishes 點菜

ordering 排序

orderly 整齊 整齊 井然 齊

ordinance 法令

ordinary 平凡 普通 常

ore 礦

organ 器官

organization 機構 機關 團體 社 編制 編製 組織

organize 搞 組 組織

organized 有條理(⇒條理) 有組織(⇒組織)

orgasm 性高潮(⇒高潮)

orgy 性狂歡會(⇒狂歡)

Orient 東方

orientation 取向

origami 摺紙

origin 淵源 緣起 起因 起源 本 來源

origin and development 源流

original 不俗 原本 原稿 原來 元 初 新穎 本 獨到

original creation 獨創

original idea 創見

original intention 本意

original language 原文

original text 原文

originally 原先 當初 本來

originally possessed 原有

originate 手創

originate from 源自

ornaments 飾物

ornate 華麗

orphan 孤兒

orthodox 正統 正宗

Osaka 大阪

oscillate 震盪

ossify 僵化

ostentation 排場

ostentatious 浮華

ostracize 排斥 排擠

ostrich 鴕鳥

other 別 別的 其他 其它 他

other party 對方

others 人家 別人 他人

otherwise 不然 否則 要不 要不然

ought to 理當 宜 應當

our country 我國

out of order 失靈

out of power 在野

out of practice 生疏

out of tune 失調

outcome 結果 結局 分曉

outdated 落後 落伍 過時

outdoor 戶外

outdoors 野外

outer space 外太空(⇒太空)

outflow 流出 外流

outhouse 茅房

outing 郊遊

outlaw 取締

outlet 插座

outline 綱領 綱目 綱要 架子 大綱 大意 題綱 輪廓 素描

out-patient service 門診

output 產出 產量 輸出

outrageous 離譜

outside 外 外邊 外面 外頭 外在 表

outsider 外人

outsiders 外界

outstanding 傑 傑出 偉 突出 卓越 出色 優秀 優異

outward appearance 外表

ova 卵

oval 橢圓

ovary 卵巢

oven 爐

over 餘

overall 概 總

overbearing 架子大

overcast 陰 低沈

overcoat 大衣

overcome 克服

overcooked 爛

overdo 過量

overdose 過量

overemphasize 偏重

overestimate 高估

overflow 氾濫 漫 溢出 濫

overflowing 瀰漫 盎然 洋溢

overheat 過熱

overlap 重疊 疊

overlook 忽視

overlord 霸王

overpass 高架橋 天橋

overpower 制伏

overpraise 過獎

overreact 過度反應

override 凌駕

overseas 海外

overseas Chinese 華僑

oversee 監督

overstay 滯留

overstep 超出

overthrow 顛覆 打倒 推翻

overturn a ruling 翻案

overview 綜觀

overweight 超重 過重

overwhelm 壓倒

owe 欠 負

owl 貓頭鷹(⇒鷹)

own 本 所有 具

owner 老闆 老板

ox 黃牛 牛

ox ears 牛耳

oxcart 牛車

oxygen 氧 氧氣

oyster 牡蠣

P p

PIN 密碼

pa 爸

pace 踱步 節奏 步調 步伐

pace back and forth 彷徨 徬徨 徘徊

Pacific Ocean 太平洋

Pacific War 太平洋戰爭

pacify 安撫 綏靖

pack 包裝

package 包 包裹 包裝

packed 擁擠

packet 包

paddle 划 划船

paddy field 稻田

paddy rice 水稻

page 傳呼 頁 扉頁

pager 傳呼機

pagoda 塔

paid 收訖

pain 苦 苦痛 痛苦

pained 痛心

painful 疼 慘痛

painful love 酷愛

painstakingly 苦

paint 渲染 畫 畫

畫[34] 畫圖[34] 油漆[173] 繪畫[14]
painter 畫家[34]
painting 畫[34] 畫圖[34] 繪畫[14]
pair 配對[162] 雙[162]
pajamas 睡衣[173]
Pakistan 巴基斯坦[85]
palace 宮[151] 宮殿[151]
palace hall 殿堂[151]
palanquin 轎子[93]
pale 蒼白[51] 白[51]
Palestine 巴勒斯坦[85]
palm 掌[99] 巴掌[99] 手掌[99]
palm tree 棕櫚[67]
palmistry 手相算命[120] (⇨ 算命[120])
palpitate with fear 悸動[?]
palpitations 心跳[?]
paltry 渺小[?]
pamper 溺愛[?]
pamphlet 冊子[115]
pan 鍋[133]
Pan Ku 盤古[129]
pan for gold 淘金[141]
panacea 靈丹[161]
Panama 巴拿馬[85]
pancake 烙餅[?]
panda 熊貓[?]
panic 恐慌[51]
panicky 恐慌[51]
panpipe 笙[?] 簫[?]
pant 氣喘[134] 喘[134] 喘氣[134]
pants 褲子[173]
papa 爸爸[?]
papaya 木瓜[77]
paper 文章[?] 紙[100] 論文[115]
paper cutting 剪紙[?]
paper tiger 紙老虎(⇨ 老虎[?])
paper umbrella 紙傘[100]
para- 準[?]
parachute 跳傘[127]
parade 遊行[116]

paradigm 模型[?]
paradise 天堂[?] 樂園[?]
paragon 模範[?] 樣板[123]
paragraph 段落[?]
paralysis 癱瘓[?] 麻痺[77] 麻痺[77]
parameter 參數[?]
paraphrase 改寫[?]
parasite 寄生蟲[?]
parasitic 寄生[?]
parasol 陽傘[?] 紙傘[100] 太陽傘[?]
pardon 特赦[?] 赦免[?] 恕罪[?] 饒恕[?]
pare 削[?]
parentheses 括號[?]
parents 父母[?] 父母親[?] 爸爸媽媽[?]
Paris 巴黎[?]
park 公園[?] 停車[?] 停車[?]
parking lot 停車場[?]
parliament 議會[?] 議院[?]
parole 假釋[?]
parrot 鸚鵡[?]
parrot others 人云亦云 (⇨ 云[62])
part 部[?] 部分[?] 部份[?] 元件[?] 局部[?] 分別[?] 份[?] 段[?] 離別[?] 集[24]
part of 屬於[125]
part of speech 詞類[?]
part reluctantly 惜別[?]
partial 局部[?] 偏頗[115]
partial to 偏愛[115] 偏袒[115]
partiality 偏袒[115] 偏心[115]
participate 加入[?] 參加[?] 參與[?] 插手[?]
particle 粒子[?]
particular 特定[?]
particular about 講究[175]
partition 分割[?] 屏風[?] 間隔[?] 隔[174]
partner 夥伴[?] 伙伴[?] 伴[?]

partnership 合夥[?]
part-time job 兼職[108]
party 晚會[?] 聯歡會[?]
party leader 黨魁[?]
party member 黨員[?]
pass 及格[?] 度[?] 傳[?] 逾[?] 過[133]
pass a barrier or test 過關[133]
pass a test 考過[?] 考上[?]
pass away 去世[?] 凋零[?] 凋謝[?] 逝世[?] 過世[?]
pass by 錯過[?] 過去[?]
pass off as 冒充[?]
pass on 流傳[?] 轉達[?] 轉告[?] 傳出[?] 遞[?] 遞給[?]
pass through 經[?] 經過[?] 通過[?] 通行[?] 穿越[?] 貫[?] 貫穿[?] 過[133] 過境[133]
passable 通[?] 通行[?]
passably 還[?]
passage 片段[77]
passageway 通道[?]
passed along 輾轉[?]
passenger 乘客[?]
passenger cabin 客艙[?]
passion 慾念[?] 情[?]
passion fruit 百香果[76]
passionate 熱烈[?]
passionate love 熱愛[?]
passive 被動[?] 消極[?]
passive tense 被動態[?]
passport 護照[?]
password 口令[?] 暗號[?]
past 往[?] 歷[?] 舊[?] 過去[?]
past dynasties 歷代[108]
past years 歷年[108]
paste 黏貼[?] 糊[?] 糨糊[?] 漿[?] 醬[?]
pastime 消遣[?]
pastor 牧師[?]
pasture 牧場[?]
pat 拍[?]
patch 襪[?] 補[?]

patent 專利[?]
paternalistic 家長風格[155]
path 徑[?] 逕[?] 路[?] 路徑[?] 道[140]
patience 耐心[?]
patient 耐性[?] 病人[?] 耐心[?] 患者[157]
patient's condition 病情[?]
patriarchal 父權[?]
patriarchy 父權制[?]
patrilineal 父系[?]
patriotic 愛國[?]
patrol 巡[?] 巡查[?] 巡邏[?]
patronize 光顧[?]
patronize prostitutes 嫖[?] 嫖妓[?]
patter of raindrops 淅瀝[?]
pattern 格[?] 格式[?] 楷模[?] 型式[?] 模式[?] 圖案[?] 方式[?] 樣[?]
pause 停頓[?] 頓[?] 逗息[?]
pause for breath 喘息[134]
pave the way 鋪路[?]
pavilion 閣[?] 亭[?] 亭閣[?] 亭子[?]
paw 掌[?]
pawn 當[?] 抵押[?] 押[172]
pawn shop 當舖[?]
pay 付[?] 付出[?] 付錢[?] 支[?] 繳納[?]
pay a bill 付帳[?]
pay a visit 拜[?] 拜訪[?]
pay a visit to 探[?]
pay attention 注意[?] 關注[?]
pay close attention to 抓緊[103]
pay homage 憑弔[?]
pay imperial tribute 朝貢[?]
pay off debts 清償[?]
pay out 支付[?]
pay respects 請安[?] 拜[?] 致敬[128]

pole 杆[?] 竿[?] 桿[?]

polemic 論戰[?]

police 警察[?] 警方[?] 公安[?]

police officer 警員[?] 警察員[?]

police station 警察局[?]

police substation 派出所[?]

policy 政策[?]

polio 小兒麻痺症 (⇨ 麻痺[7])

polish 琢磨[?] 錘鍊[?]

polite 客氣[?] 恭敬[?] 禮貌[?] 彬彬有禮[?]

polite words 客套話[?]

politely refuse 婉拒[?]

political asylum 政治庇護 (⇨ 庇護[?])

political career 仕途[?]

political circles 政壇[?]

political party 黨[?] 政黨[?]

political power 政權[?]

political prisoner 政治犯[?]

political reform 變法[?] 政治改革[?]

political science 政治學[?]

political situation 政局[?] 政情[?]

political views 政見[?]

politician 政客[?] 政治家[?]

politics 政[?] 政治[?]

pollen 花粉[?]

pollute 污染[?]

pollution 污染[?]

polygamy 重婚[?]

pomegranate 榴[?]

pond 水池[?] 水塘[?] 池[?]

ponder 沈思[?] 揣摩[?] 思考[?] 思索[?]

ponder aloud 沈吟[?]

pool 水塘[?] 湊[?] 池[?] 台球[?] 撞球[?]

poor 貧[?] 貧乏[?] 貧困[?]

貧民[?] 貧窮[?] 窮[?] 窮人[?] 爛[?] 壞[?]

poor harvest 歉收[?]

popcorn 爆米花[?]

pope 教皇[?] 教宗[?]

poplar 楊[?]

popsicle 冰棒[?] 冰棍[?]

popular 紅[?] 流行[?] 熱門[?] 通俗[?]

popular culture 大眾文化[?]

popular saying 俗語[?]

popular sentiment 民心[?]

popularity 人緣[?] 聲望[?]

popularize 普及[?] 推廣[?]

popularly elected 民選[?]

population 人口[?] 戶口[?]

porcelain 瓷器[?]

pork 豬肉[?]

pornographic 黃色[?] 色情[?]

porridge 粥[?]

port 港[?] 港口[?] 海口[?]

portable 隨身[?] 挾帶[?] 手提[?] 攜帶[?]

portend 兆[?]

portent 苗頭[?] 兆[?] 兆頭[?] 朕兆[?]

portion 份[?] 份額[?]

portrait 肖像[?] 寫真[?]

portray 描繪[?] 描述[?]

portrayal 寫照[?]

Portugal 葡萄牙[?]

pose 姿勢[?] 姿態[?] 架式[?]

pose as 冒充[?]

position 位[?] 位置[?] 職位[?] 職位[?] 陣腳[?]

positive 陽性[?] 積極[?] 正[?]

positive number 正數[?]

possess 有[?] 持有[?] 擁有[?] 所有[?] 具備[?] 具有[?]

possession 保有[?]

post 椿[?] 杆[?] 桿[?] 職[?] 職位[?] 職務[?] 郵遞[?]

post office 郵局[?]

postage stamp 郵票[?]

postal service 郵遞[?]

postal system 郵政[?]

poster 海報[?]

posterity 後代[?]

postmark 郵戳[?]

postpone 延期[?] 延後[?] 延期[?] 暫緩[?] 推[?]

posture 姿勢[?]

pot 鍋[?] 壺[?]

potato 土豆[?] 馬鈴薯[?]

potato chip 洋芋片[?]

potential 潛力[?]

potted landscape 盆景[?]

pottery 陶器[?]

pound 搗[?] 砸[?] 磅[?] 斤[?] 捶[?] 搗[?]

pound rice 舂米[?]

pound sterling 鎊[?]

pour 灌注[?]

pour out 倒[?]

pour out one's heart 傾訴[?]

pour tea 倒茶[?]

pouring rain 豪雨[?]

poverty 窘境[?] 貧窮[?]

powder 粉[?]

powdered milk 奶粉[?]

power 力[?] 力量[?] 強權[?] 勢力[?] 動力[?] 能量[?] 權[?] 權力[?]

power and influence 權勢[?]

power and prestige 威風[?]

power supply 電源[?]

power vacuum 權力真空 (⇨ 真空[?])

powerful 勁[?] 有力[?] 強[?] 強大[?] 強勁[?]

powerful adversary 勁敵[?]

powerful countries 列強[?]

practical 踏實[?] 實用[?]

現實[?]

practical value 實用價值[?]

practice 演習[?] 演習[?] 練[?] 練習[?] 實習[?] 習[?]

practice by copying 臨摹[?]

practice shooting 打靶[?]

pragmatic 現實[?]

pragmatism 現實主義[?]

prairie 草原[?]

praise 讚[?] 讚美[?] 恭維[?] 頌揚[?] 誇獎[?] 好話[?] 褒揚[?] 表揚[?] 稱讚[?]

praise highly 讚歎[?] 推崇[?]

pray 禱告[?] 祈禱[?]

pray for 祝[?] 祈求[?]

pray for luck 祈福[?]

precedent 慣例[?] 例[?]

preceding 前[?]

precinct leader 里長[?]

precious 珍[?] 珍貴[?] 寶[?] 寶貴[?]

precious jade 寶玉[?]

precious object 寶貝[?]

precious stone 寶石[?]

precipice 崖[?] 懸崖[?]

precipitate 沈澱[?] 沈澱[?]

precipitous 陡峭[?]

precise 精密[?] 精確[?] 確鑿[?]

precisely 就是[?]

precocious 聰穎[?]

precursor 前驅[?]

pre-dawn hours 凌晨[?]

predecessor 前任[?]

predestined 註定[?] 注定[?]

predicament 困境[?]

predict 料[?] 預測[?] 預計[?] 預料[?] 推斷[?]

predestined 註定[?]

preface 弁言[?] 序言[?] 前言[?]

prefecture 郡⁴⁶ 府⁵⁵ 縣¹⁴⁸

prefer to 情願⁵⁶ 寧可¹¹⁶ 寧願¹¹⁶

preference 偏好¹¹⁵

pregnant 懷孕⁷²

pregnant woman 孕婦⁷²

prejudice 成見³⁹ 偏見¹¹⁵

preliminary 粗略¹¹⁷

preliminary report 快報⁸⁹

prelude 序幕¹⁰²

premeditated 蓄意⁸⁹

premier 總理⁵¹⁴⁴ 首相⁹⁷

premonition 預感¹⁰²

prepare 籌備³⁵ 備⁹ 預備¹⁰² 準備⁹⁷

prepare against 防備⁹⁴

preposition 介詞⁵⁸

preposterous 荒唐⁸³

prescription 處方⁹ 藥方³⁹ 方³⁹

presence 光臨⁴⁶

present 有⁹⁸ 在場¹⁸ 呈現⁵² 發表⁹⁷ 饋贈¹¹⁰ 出席¹¹⁰ 現¹⁶ 現今¹⁶ 贈品¹¹⁴

present a paper 發表文章⁹⁶

present condition 現狀¹¹⁴

presently 眼前³⁹ 當前⁹⁶ 目前¹¹⁴

preserve 保存⁷⁴ 保存⁷⁴ 保守⁷⁴

president 總統⁵¹⁴⁴

press 熨⁷⁵ 按⁵⁸ 催¹⁶² 催促¹⁶²

press down 按住⁵⁸ 壓⁷⁵

press in 逼近⁴⁸

pressed for time 勾促時間⁸⁶

pressing 迫切⁴⁸

pressure 壓力⁷⁵ 施加壓力⁷⁵

prestige 聲望⁹⁷ 威信⁹⁹

信響⁹⁷

presumably 想必²⁴

presume to 冒昧⁵⁸

presumptuous 冒昧⁵⁸

pretend 假裝¹⁶ 作勢⁶⁴ 充裝⁵⁵ 裝作⁵⁵ 伴¹⁷ 伴裝¹⁷ 假裝¹⁷

pretentious 做作⁶⁴

pretext 託辭⁵⁷ 擋箭牌⁸⁹

pretty 俏⁸⁹ 俏麗⁸⁹ 好看³⁹ 美³⁹

prevail 得逞³⁹ 勝過⁸⁸

prevent 防⁹⁴ 防止⁹⁴ 預防⁹⁴ 阻攔¹¹¹

prevention and cure 防治⁹⁴

preview 預演¹⁰²

previous 往¹⁶ 上¹⁶ 歷⁵⁸

previous generations 前輩¹⁷

previous life 前生⁵⁹ 前世¹⁶

previously 先前¹⁶ 以前³⁹ 曾¹⁶ 曾經¹⁶

price 價⁵⁵ 價格⁵⁵ 價錢⁵⁵ 代價⁵⁵

price estimate 估價³⁵

prices 物價⁹⁵

prick 扎⁵⁰ 刺⁴⁹

pride 驕傲⁸⁵ 自豪¹⁷⁹ 面子¹⁴⁸

priest 神父⁴⁶ 牧師⁹⁷

primary 主⁵ 元⁵⁸

primary cause 主因⁵

primary emotions 喜怒哀樂⁸⁶

primary level 基層⁸⁶

prime minister 丞相⁵⁶ 宰相⁵⁶ 摸⁵⁶ 相⁵⁸ 總理¹⁴⁴ 首相⁹⁷

prime of life 壯年⁷⁵

primitive 原始⁵⁶

primordial chaos 混沌⁸⁹

prince 王子⁵⁶ 太子⁵⁶

princess 王妃⁵⁶ 公主⁵⁶

principal 主要⁵ 校長⁸⁶ 本⁵⁶ 本金⁵⁶ 總⁵¹⁴⁴

principle 原理⁵⁶ 原則⁵⁶

principled 有原則 (⇨ 原則⁵⁶)

print 印刷⁵⁸ 印刷⁵⁸

printer 印表機⁵⁸ 打印機⁹⁷

printing plate 版⁵⁵

priority 優先¹⁴⁸

prison 牢⁵⁸ 監獄¹⁴²

prison cell 囚室⁸⁹

prison sentence 徒刑⁵⁸

prisoner 囚犯⁵⁸ 囚犯⁵⁸

prisoner of war 俘虜⁸⁵ 戰俘⁸⁵

privacy 隱私權⁵⁹

private 私⁵⁹ 私立⁵⁹ 私人⁵⁹ 民⁵⁹ 民間¹¹⁹

private company 私營公司⁵⁹ 民間公司⁵⁹

private interest 私利⁵⁹

private matters 私事⁵⁹ 隱私⁵⁹

private property 私產⁵⁹

private school 私塾⁵⁹

private university 私立大學⁵⁹

private worries 心事⁸³

privately 私下⁵⁹

privately operated 私營⁵⁹ 民營¹¹⁹

privately owned 私有⁵⁹

privatization 民營化¹¹⁹ 私營化⁵⁹

privilege 特權⁵⁵ 優待¹⁴⁸ 權利⁹²

prize 獎⁷⁷

probability 機率⁹⁷ 可能性⁹⁷

probably 大概⁵⁹ 想必²⁴

problem 岔子⁵⁵ 課題²¹ 問題⁵⁷ 毛病⁹⁷

procedure 程序⁹⁷ 程序⁵⁵

procedures 手續¹⁹⁷

proceed 進行¹⁶²

proceed rashly 冒進⁵⁸

proceed smoothly 亨通⁸⁵

process 加工⁵⁶ 處理⁹⁷ 程序⁹⁷ 歷程¹⁰⁸ 過程¹⁷³ 進程¹⁶²

proclaim 宣⁸⁶ 宣告¹⁶

procrastinate 拖延⁵⁸ 推¹⁶²

prodigal son 浪子¹⁷²

produce 生⁵⁹ 生產⁸⁹ 製造⁹⁸ 產⁸⁹ 產生⁸⁹ 出品¹¹⁰ 出品¹¹⁰ 出示¹¹⁰

product 貨物⁷⁹ 品⁸⁹ 產品⁸⁹ 出品¹¹⁰

production 生產⁸⁹ 產出⁸⁹

production capacity 產能⁸⁹

production value 產值⁸⁹

profession 行業⁵⁴ 行業⁵⁹ 專業⁵⁹

professional title 職稱⁵⁹

professor 教授¹⁹

proficient 純熟⁵⁹ 練達⁵¹

profile 側面¹⁵⁶

profit 贏⁸⁹ 盈利⁸⁹ 營利⁸⁹ 利潤⁸⁹ 獲利⁸⁹

profit and loss 盈虧²⁸

profit share 紅利⁸⁹

profitable 合算⁸⁹ 划算⁵⁶

profound 窈窕⁵⁹ 玄妙⁵⁹ 深厚⁶⁷ 深邃⁵⁹

profound mystery 奧祕¹⁵⁹

profoundly 深深⁶⁷

program 節目⁹⁷

progress 進⁶² 進步¹⁶² 進展¹⁶²

progressive 進步¹⁶²

prohibit 禁⁷⁷ 禁止⁷⁷

project 投射⁷⁷ 投影⁷⁷ 方案¹¹ 放映⁷²

projector 投影機⁷⁷ 放映機⁷²

proletariat 無產階級³⁷

prologue 序幕¹⁰²

prolong 拉長⁵⁹ 延⁸⁹ 延長⁸⁹

prominence 風頭⁴⁷

prominent 突出⁶³ 顯

赫[153]
promiscuous 淫亂[22]
promise 允諾[13] 諾言[15] 諾言[15] 承諾[14] 答應[15]
promote 主張[9] 振興[73] 提昇[9] 提升[9] 促進[14] 擢升[74] 增進[44] 推動[162] 推廣[162] 推銷[162]
promote friendship 聯誼[74]
promoted 升遷[87] 晉升[14]
promotion 擢升[74]
prompt 提示[9]
promptly 及時[44]
promulgate 頒佈[73]
pronoun 代名詞 (⇨ 名詞[92])
pronounce 發音[88]
pronunciation 發音[88]
proof 憑據[25] 證據[88] 證明[88] 酒精度[159]
proofread 校[88] 校對[88] 校稿[88] 校正[88]
prop up 扶植[88] 撐[87] 支[87] 支撐[87]
propaganda 宣傳[16]
propagate 揚[84] 推廣[162]
propel 推動[162]
proper 衷[88] 適當[27] 正[73] 正當[73] 正經[74] 安[99] 當[99] 妥善[99] 端正[73] 對[76]
properly 好好[54]
property 資產[89] 財產[94] 產業[99]
property rights 產權[99] 所有權[74]
prophecy 預言[102]
prophesy 預言[102]
prophet 預言家[102]
proportion 比例[92]
proposal 案[92] 提案[99] 提議[99]
propose 提案[99] 提案[99] 提出[99] 提議[99]
propose a toast 敬酒[89]
propose marriage 求婚[92]

proposition 命題[92]
proprietress 老板娘[14]
propriety 禮[22] 禮儀[22]
pros and cons 利弊[9] 利害[9]
proscription 諱[88]
prose 散文[9]
prosecutor 檢察官[9]
proselytize 傳教[92]
prospects 景象[9] 展望[9] 前途[9]
prosperous 旺[16] 旺盛[16] 興旺[16] 繁榮[89] 昌盛[89] 欣欣向榮[9]
prostitute 娼妓[9] 妓女[9]
protect 守護[16] 保[74] 保護[74] 保佑[74] 愛護[9] 護[62]
protein 蛋白質[89]
protest 抗議[88]
Protestant 新教徒[9]
Protestantism 新教[9]
protrude 凸[88]
proud 神氣[16] 驕[9] 驕傲[9]
proud of 自豪[9]
proudly and boldly 昂然[74]
prove 證[88] 證明[88]
proverb 格言[9] 歇後語[9] 成語[9] 諺語[9]
provide 供[47] 配備[9] 提供[9]
provide for 供養[47] 養[47]
provided that 只要[99]
province 州[99] 省[99]
provincial capital 省會[99]
provincial citizenship 省籍[99]
provincial government 省府[99]
provincial native 本省人[9]
provisional 臨時[99] 暫行[99]
provoke 惹[99] 挑撥[127] 挑動[127] 挑釁[127]

proximate 相近[45]
prudent 慎重[94] 謹慎[99] 審慎[156]
pry into 窺探[127] 刺探[127]
pseudo- 假[116]
psychological warfare 心理戰[83]
psychologist 心理學家[83]
psychology 心理學[83]
Pu Yi 溥儀[99]
pubic hair 陰毛[24]
public 衆人[9] 公[9] 公共[9] 公開[9] 公衆[9] 公民[119]
public affairs 公事[9]
public anger 衆怒[99]
public bus 公車[9] 公共汽車[9]
public cemetery 義塚[99]
public expense 公費[9]
public finance 財政[94]
public funds 公款[9]
public good 公益[9]
public granary 義倉[99]
public housing 國宅[99]
public notice 通告[99]
public official 公務人員[9] 公務員[9]
public opinion 輿論[9] 公論[9] 民意[119]
public opinion poll 民意調查[119]
public order 治安[99]
public phone 公用電話[9]
public relations 公關[9] 公共關係[9]
public school 公立學校[9]
public security 公安[9] 保安[74]
public sentiment 輿情[99]
public square 廣場[99]
public use 公用[9]
publication 刊物[99] 刊物[99]
publicity 聞名[99]
publicize 宣傳[16] 宣揚[16]
publicly 公開[9] 當衆[99]

publicly established 公立[9]
publicly owned 公有[9]
publish 刊出[99] 刊登[99] 發表[99] 發行[99] 出版[110]
publisher 出版社[110]
puckery 澀[88]
Pudong 浦東[99]
puff 股[97] 陣[158]
pull 扳[99] 拉[24] 摟[99] 拖[99] 牽[99] 牽引[99] 引[99] 掣[99] 扯[99]
pull along 帶動[99]
pull and drag 拉扯[24]
pull apart 掰[99]
pull open 拉開[24]
pull out 拔[99] 抽[413] 掏[141]
pull up 拉出[99]
pulsate 跳[127]
pulse 脈[120] 脈搏[120]
pun 雙關語[162]
punch 打[9]
punctual 守時[44]
punctuate 標點[15]
punctuation 標點符號[15]
puncture 戳穿[124]
punish 處罰[9] 處分[38] 懲[124]
punished 受罰[93]
punishment 刑罰[93]
pupil 弟子[99] 瞳孔[99] 門生[9] 眸子[92]
puppet 木偶[77] 傀儡[140]
puppet government 傀儡政府[140]
puppet show 布袋戲[99]
purchase 收購[99] 收買[9] 採購[99] 購[175] 購買[175] 購置[175]
pure 純[89] 純粹[89] 純真[89] 清[9] 清白[9] 清澈[9] 白[76] 單純[136] 素[153]
pure and clean 純淨[99]
pure and clear 清明[9]
pure and honest 純潔[99]

rattan 藤[122]
ravage 肆虐[44]
raven 烏鴉[175]
raw 原[21] 生[32]
raw material 原料[24]
rays of light 光芒[43]
raze 剷[112]
razor 剃刀[85] 刮臉刀[91]
刮鬍刀[91]
reach 及[13] 達[27] 達成[27]
達到[27]
reach agreement 達成協
議[27]
reach for 伸手[13]
reach out a hand 出手[110]
react 反應[21]
reaction 反應[21] 感想[22]
reactionary 反動[21]
reactionary elements 反
動份子[21]
reactionary faction 反
動派[21]
read 閱[10] 閱讀[10] 閱覽[10]
就讀[14] 看[15] 讀[150]
read aloud 唸[34] 讀[150]
reader 讀者[5]
readily 甘心[49]
readily solved 迎刃而
解[49]
reading room 閱覽室[4]
ready-made 現成[10]
Reagan 雷根[10] 里根[11]
real 眞實[32] 眞正[32] 實
際[49] 實在[32]
real estate 房地產[17]
real situation 眞實狀
況[32]
realistic 踏實[24] 逼眞[32]
現實[10]
reality 實[9] 實際[49] 現
實[10]
realization 省悟[22]
realize 悟[6] 省悟[22] 明
白[22] 發覺[22] 發現[22]
實現[9]
really 眞[32] 當眞[32] 未
免[9] 果眞[32] 實在[32]
確實[32]

realm 界[3] 領域[84]
rear 豢養[14] 撫養[14] 撫
育[14] 後方[4]
reason 原故[21] 原因[21]
因[21] 緣由[17] 情理[29]
理由[11] 由[13]
reason by analogy 類推[2]
rebel 悖逆[89] 叛逆[91]
rebellion 暴動[15] 暴亂[15]
叛亂[91] 亂[58]
rebirth 再生[32]
rebound 反彈[21] 彈[105]
rebuke 申斥[15] 責備[27]
斥責[57]
rebut 反駁[21]
recall 收回[17] 召回[17] 回
收[17] 回溯[17] 回想[17]
罷免[117]
recapture 光復[44]
recede 退[84]
receipt 收據[17]
receive 承[17] 收[17] 收到[17]
納[32] 領接[32] 接待[32]
接洽[32] 接收[32] 接
受[32] 受[17] 受到[17]
進[92]
receive permission 獲
准[82]
receive training 受訓[17]
recent 今[2]
recent years 近年[90]
recently 邇來[92] 日前[16]
近來[92] 近日[16] 最
近[92]
recession 經濟不景氣
(⇨景氣[89])
recharge 充電[50]
recipe 食譜[14]
reciprocal 互惠[9] 對
等[176]
reciprocate 互惠[9]
recite 朗讀[91] 朗誦[91]
吟[34] 吟誦[34] 詠[90]
recite from memory 背
誦[58]
reckless 玩命[15] 冒失[15]

莽撞[14] 孟浪[116]
recline 躺[81]
recluse 隱士[17]
recognize 認[32] 認出[32]
認得[32] 認識[32] 辨
認[32] 辨識[32]
recoil 縮回[8]
recollect 回憶[17]
recollection 回憶[17]
recollections 感慨[22]
recommend 介紹[17] 推
薦[12]
reconcile 疏通[32] 調[37]
調和[37] 調解[37] 和
解[108]
reconciliation 和解[108]
reconnaissance 勘察[92]
reconnoiter 偵察[85]
record 錄[83] 錄音[83] 成
績[85] 載案[84] 紀錄[83]
記[37] 記錄[37] 記載[37]
檔[82] 檔案[82] 唱片[89]
登[84]
record clearly 載明[84]
recorder 錄音機[83]
records 紀錄[83] 記錄[37]
recount 敘述[90] 述說[90]
recover 光復[44] 復[84] 復
甦[84] 拿回[8] 恢復[44]
recover from illness 康
復[44]
recovery 復甦[84]
recruit 網羅[4] 招募[58]
recruited 應徵[82]
rectify 匡正[11] 糾正[42] 改
正[37] 補救[42] 整[88] 整
頓[88] 整肅[88] 矯正[90]
端正[114]
recuperate 修養[14] 養
病[14]
recycle 回收[17]
red 赤[89] 紅[83] 紅色[83]
朱[21] 丹[27]
Red Army 紅軍[83]
red guard 紅衛兵 (⇨衛
兵[85])
red ink 赤字[89]
red ink paste for seals 印

泥[32]
redeem 挽回[8]
red-hot 熾熱[89]
redress 糾正[42] 平反[21]
reduce 降低[90] 削減[90]
減[90] 減低[90] 減少[90]
裁減[90] 縮減[76] 縮
小[76]
reduce prices 減價[32]
reduced to 淪爲[115]
redundant workers 冗
員[8]
reed 蘆葦[122]
reeducation 再教育
(⇨教育[9])
reeducation camp 勞改
營[83]
reef 礁石[122]
refer to 說到[11] 參考[3] 參
見[3] 參考[3]
referee 裁判[85]
reference book 參考
書[3]
refine 精煉[37] 煉[76]
refine oil 煉油[76]
refined 斯文[91] 彬彬[7]
雅[91] 雅緻[91] 文雅[91]
典雅[91]
reflect 反射[21] 反映[21] 體
現[32] 輝映[158]
reflect back on 回想[17]
reflect on 省[43]
reflection 反射[21] 反
省[43]
reform 改革[37] 改造[37]
革新[2] 變革[153] 維
新[2]
refrain from 節制[42]
refreshed 爽快[4]
refreshing 爽[4] 涼快[42]
清新[2]
refrigerate 冷藏[88]
refrigerator 冰箱[25]
refuel 加油[34]
refugee 難民[4]
refuse 駁回[8] 拒絕[17] 拒
絕[17] 回絕[8] 謝絕[147]
refute 駁[83] 駁斥[83] 反

救[] 救護[] 挽救[] | resonance 共鳴[] | restricted to 限於[] | 重[]
research 研究[] | resort to violence 動武[] | restroom 洗手間[] | reverse 反[] 倒[]
research and study 研習[] | resound 迴響[] | restructure 改編[] 改 | reverse a sentence 平反[]
research institute 研究 | resounding 高亢[] | 造[] | reverse effect 反效果
院[] | resourcefulness 智謀[] | rests in 在於[] | (⇨ 效果[])
researcher 研究員[] | resources 資源[] 物 | result 結果[] 效果[] 後 | reverse side 背面[] 反
resemble 肖[] 好像[] 彷 | 資[] | 果[] 成效[] 回事[] | 面[]
佛[] 相似[] 像[] | respect 敬[] 尊[] 尊 | result in 造成[] 導致[] | review 復習[] 評論[]
resent 怨恨[] | 敬[] 尊重[] | results 收穫[] | 審議[]
resentful 憤懣[] | respect and admire 敬佩[] | resume 履歷[] | review troops 閱兵[]
resentment 怨恨[] | respectability 尊嚴[] | retail 零售[] | revile 唾罵[]
reservation 保護區[] | respectfully 敬[] | retail goods 零售貨[] | revise 修訂[] 修改[] 修
reserve 儲備[] 保留[] | respectfully request 敬 | retain 保留[] | 正[]
定位[] 預定[] | 請[] | retake an exam 補考[] | revisionism 修正主
reserved 拘謹[] 含蓄[] | respective 各自[] | reticent 沈默寡言[] | 義[]
恬靜[] | resplendent 琳琅[] 燦 | retina 網膜[] | revive 甦醒[] 復甦[]
reserves 存底[] 儲備[] | 爛[] | retire 退休[] | 復興[] 蘇[]
reservoir 水庫[] | respond 反應[] 報[] 搭 | retirement home 養老 | revoke 撤銷[] 取消[]
reside 住[] 居[] 居留[] | 腔[] 答應[] 理[] | 院[] | revolt 悖逆[] 起義[] 叛
reside temporarily 棲 | 應[] 應對[] | retract 縮回[] | 亂[] 嘩變[]
身[] | respond favorably 響 | retreat 退[] 撤退[] | revolution 轉[] 革命[]
residence 住處[] 住家[] | 應[] | retrieve 拿回[] 拿來[] | Revolution of 1911 辛亥
住所[] 住宅[] | response 反應[] | retrocession 回歸[] | 革命[]
residence permit 居留 | responsibility 職責[] | retrospective 回顧[] | revolutionary 紅[] 革
證[] | 責[] 責任[] | return 退換[] 返[] 返 | 命家[]
resident 居民[] | responsible 負責[] | 回[] 復[] 交還[] 回[] | revolve 迴轉[] 旋[] 旋
residential area 住宅 | rest 棲息[] 歇[] 歇息[] | 回報[] 回去[] 重 | 轉[]
區[] | 休[] 休息[] 息[] | 返[] 還[] 歸[] 歸 | revolve around 圍繞[]
residue 殘渣[] 渣滓[] | rest assured 放心[] | 來[] | reward 嘉獎[] 賞[]
渣子[] | restaurant 飯店[] 飯 | return a ticket 退票[] | 獎[] 獎勵[]
resign 辭去[] 辭職[] | 館[] 菜館[] 餐館[] | return change 找錢[] | rewrite 改寫[]
resigned to fate 認命[] | 酒家[] 館子[] | return home 返鄉[] 回 | rewrite history 竄改歷
resist 反抗[] 抗[] 抗 | restore a monarchy 復 | 家[] | 史[]
拒[] 抵[] 抵擋[] 抵 | 辟[] | return to 回到[] 歸[] | rhinocerous 犀牛[]
抗[] 抵禦[] 抵制[] | restrain 拘束[] 遏制[] | return triumphant 凱旋[] | rhyme 押韻[] 韻[]
對抗[] | 節[] 按[] 按住[] 約 | reunite 團聚[] | rhythm 節奏[] 韻律[]
resistance 阻力[] | 束[] 箝制[] 束縛[] | revalue 升值[] | rib 肋骨[]
resistance army 反抗 | 壓制[] 克制[] 羈 | reveal 露[] 露出[] 披 | rice 大米[] 白飯[] 稻[]
軍[] | 絆[] | 露[] 暴露[] 淺露[] | 稻米[] 米[] 米飯[]
resistance war 抗戰[] | restrain oneself 收斂[] | 揭示[] 透露[] 流 | rice bowl 飯碗[]
resolute 斷然[] 果斷[] | 忍耐[] 禁[] | 露[] 表露[] 顯露[] | rice cooker 電飯鍋[]
堅定[] 堅決[] | restrained 有涵養(⇨涵 | 顯現[] | rice flour 米粉[]
resolute and courageous | 養[]) | revel 狂歡[] | rice gruel 粥[]
果敢[] | restraint 束縛[] | revenge 報仇[] 報復[] | rice noodles 米粉[]
resolutely 果斷[] | restraints 羈絆[] | revenue 收益[] | rice porridge 稀飯[] 米
resolution 決議[] 解析 | restrict 限[] 限制[] | revenue and expenditure | 粥[]
度[] | restricted 內部[] | 收支[] | rice pot 飯鍋[]
resolve 決心[] 解決[] | restricted area 禁區[] | revere 崇敬[] 仰[] 尊 | rice seedlings 秧苗[]

run after 追趕[67]
run aground 觸礁[115]
run for office 競選[68]
run into 碰撞[49] 逢[79] 遇了[7] 遇到[7] 遇見[29]
run off 跑走[18] 流失[95] 逃跑[37] 逃走[17] 飛奔[160]
running dog 走狗[88]
running path 跑道[18]
running water 自來水[139]
rupee 盧比[127]
rupture 破裂[16] 決裂[48]
rush 搶[68] 衝[96] 闖[77]
rush about 奔波[60]
rush at 撲[76]
rush hour 交通高峰時間 (⇨ 高峰[47])
rush to buy 搶購[35]
Russia 俄[95] 俄國[95] 俄羅斯[95]
rust 鏽[16] 生鏽[52]
rusty 生疏[52]
ruthless 殘酷[45]
Ryukyu 琉球[93]

S s

sack 袋[96] 囊[69] 衣袋[126]
sacred 神聖[16] 聖[69]
sacrifice 祭[61] 犧牲[97]
sacrificial lamb 代罪羔羊 (⇨ 羔羊[67])
sad 難過[35] 傷心[89] 悲傷[191]
saddle 鞍[69] 馬鞍[177]
sadness 憂傷[198]
safe 平安[43] 安全[59] 保險[74]
safe and stable 安穩[66]
safeguard 保衛[74] 保障[74]
safety 安全[16]
sage 智叟[97] 聖[69] 聖人[69] 哲人[66]
Saigon 西貢[130]
sail 航[66] 帆[67]
sailboat 帆船[67]
sailor 水手[55] 海員[54]
sake 米酒[138]

salacious 色[59] 淫穢[92]
salad 涼菜[67] 沙拉[67]
salary 薪[69] 薪俸[69] 薪水[69] 薪資[69]
salary and benefits 待遇[31]
salary and rank 祿位[67]
salesclerk 店員[86]
saliva 唾沫[45]
salmon 鮭魚[68]
salon 沙龍[67]
salt 醃[55] 鹵[76] 鹽[142]
salted fish 鹹魚[55]
salty 鹹[55]
salute 行禮[61]
same 一樣[1] 同[194] 同樣[95] 同一[34] 等[15] 半斤八兩[27] 相同[19] 沒有兩樣 (⇨ 兩樣[36])
same profession 同行[34]
same sex 同性[34]
sampan 舢板[82]
sample 樣本[123]
sample and analyze 抽驗[113]
sample tea 品茶[91]
samurai 武士[98]
San Francisco 舊金山[831]
sanction 認可[69]
sanctions 制裁[49]
sand 砂[69] 沙[69] 沙子[69]
sand dune 沙丘[69]
sandals 涼鞋[67]
sandalwood 檀香[66]
sandalwood fan 檀香扇[66]
sandwich 三明治[16]
sanitary 清潔[89]
Sanskrit 梵文[96]
Santa Claus 聖誕老人[69]
sarcastic 俏皮[89] 諷刺[97]
sash 帶[67]
sashimi 刺生[82] 生魚片[82]
satellite 衛星[65]
satellite dish 小耳朵 (⇨ 耳朵[137]) 衛星天線[165]

satiate 過癮[133]
satin 緞[69] 緞子[69]
satirical 諷刺[97]
satirize 諷[97] 諷刺[97] 譏諷[97]
satisfactory 圓滿[65]
satisfied 飽[19] 滿[65] 滿意[65] 滿足[65]
satisfy 滿足[65]
saturate 浸透[65]
saturated 飽和[65]
saturation 飽和[65]
Saturday 星期六[58] 禮拜六[59]
saunter 逍遙[65]
sausage 香腸[195] 臘腸[191]
saute 炮[79] 炒[66]
savage 野蠻[97] 野人[102]
save 省[88] 節省[58] 省[88] 蓄[69] 儲[69] 儲蓄[69] 積[66] 積蓄[69] 藏[55] 挽回[65] 挽救[16]
save a life 救活[52]
save money 省錢[88]
save time 省時間[88]
save trouble 省事[88]
savings 存款[94] 存量[67] 儲備[69] 儲蓄[69] 積蓄[69]
savory 鮮[123]
saw 鋸[76]
say 云[52] 說[11] 說道[11] 曰[99]
say farewell 辭行[97]
say good-bye 惜別[76] 告別[79] 告辭[97] 辭別[97]
saying 成語[65] 諺語[96]
sayings 語錄[6]
scaffolding 鷹架[195] 棚架[195]
scald 燙[69]
scalding 滾燙[95] 燙[69]
scale 秤[79] 規模[79] 尺度[89]
scallions 韮[168] 韮菜[168]
scalp 頭皮[66]
scalped tickets 黃牛票[65]
scan 掃瞄[85] 掃描[165] 流

覽[35] 瀏覽[35]
scandal 醜聞[159]
scanner 掃描器[85]
scar 痕[65] 創痕[65] 傷痕[65] 疤痕[65]
scarce 希罕[45] 稀[61] 稀少[45] 罕見[67]
scarcity 空缺[31]
scare 嚇[95] 唬[67] 唬[122]
scared 慌[59]
scarf 圍巾[89] 領巾[14]
scarlet 朱紅[69]
scatter 分散[49] 驅散[69] 散[49] 散開[49]
scattered 分散[49] 散[49]
scene 光景[42] 景[67] 鏡頭[89] 情景[67] 場[55] 場面[55] 現場[164]
scenery 景色[67] 景色[67] 景致[67] 風景[47]
scenic area 風景區[47]
scenic spot 勝地[129]
scented soap 香皂[158]
schedule 日程[76]
scheduled flight 班機[197]
scheme 計[58] 陰謀[24] 算計[58] 構想[175]
scholar 學人[15] 學者[15] 士[97] 文人[76]
scholarly manner 學者氣派 (⇨ 氣派[91])
scholar-official 士大夫[97]
scholarship 獎學金[76]
school 學堂[15] 學校[15] 校[59]
school children 學童[15]
school of thought 學派[15] 門戶[79]
school president 校長[59]
schoolboy 男生[52]
schoolgirl 女生[54]
schoolmate 學弟[15] 學姐[15] 學妹[15] 學長[15] 同學[34]
science 科學[97]
science and engineering 理工[111]
scientist 科學家[97]

scissors 剪刀⁵²

scold 咒罵⁵⁵ 咒罵責⁵⁵
罵⁵³ 罵⁵⁷

scolded 挨罵⁵⁴

scope 範圍⁵⁵ 規模⁵⁶

score points 得分⁵³

scorn 鄙夷⁵²

scorpion 蠍子⁵⁰

Scotland 蘇格蘭¹⁸⁰

scout 偵察⁵⁹

scout for 物色⁵⁶

scrambled egg 炒蛋⁵⁵

scrap paper 廢紙¹⁹

scrape 刮⁵⁷

scratch 擦傷⁵⁵ 抓¹⁰³

scratch an itch 搔癢⁴⁴

scream 呼嘯⁵⁵

screen 掩護¹⁵⁵ 遮蔽³⁴
屏風⁵⁹ 屏幕⁵⁹ 甄
別⁴⁷⁰ 篩選¹⁴⁷ 螢光
屏⁵⁹ 螢光幕⁵⁹

screen window 紗窗⁷⁸

screw 螺絲¹¹⁵ 擰¹¹⁶

screwdriver 起子⁵² 改
錐⁵² 螺絲起子¹¹⁵

scribble 塗抹⁴²

scribbles 塗鴉⁴²

script 文⁹⁸ 文字⁹⁸ 劇
本¹⁹⁹

scriptures 經書¹⁵

scrub 洗刷⁵⁵ 刷⁵⁹ 刷
洗⁵⁹

scruples 顧忌⁷³

sculpt 雕塑⁶⁷

sculpture 雕刻⁶⁷ 雕
塑⁶⁷

se 瑟⁹⁷

sea 海⁵⁴

sea area 海域⁵⁴

sea cucumber 海參⁵⁴

sea gull 沙鷗⁵⁴ 海鷗⁵⁴

sea of clouds 雲海⁶³

sea of people 人海¹⁰

sea turtle 海龜⁵⁴

seafood 海鮮⁵⁴

seal 印⁵⁵ 印章⁵⁵ 密封⁵⁷
海豹⁵⁴ 章⁵⁵ 圖章⁵⁵
封⁵⁷ 封閉⁵⁷ 戳記¹²⁴

seal carving 篆刻⁴²

seal characters 篆書⁴²

seam 縫⁵⁹

seaman 水手⁵⁵ 海員⁵⁴

search 搜尋¹⁵ 搜查⁵⁹ 找
尋⁹ 探尋⁹ 查⁵⁹ 延攬⁸⁹
尋求⁵⁵ 尋找⁵⁵ 搜
索⁵⁹ 探求⁹ 追尋¹⁶⁷

search for a job 謀職⁵⁵

search out 查出⁵⁹

search through 翻⁴⁵

search warrant 搜查
證⁵⁵

seaside 海邊⁵⁴

season 節⁵⁵ 季⁵⁵ 季節⁵⁵
調味⁵⁵

seat 席⁵⁶ 位子⁵⁵ 坐位⁵⁵
座⁵⁵ 座位⁵⁵

seatbelt 安全帶⁵⁵

seats 席位⁷⁶

seawater 海水⁵⁴

seaweed 海苔⁵⁴

secluded 幽⁵⁹ 幽靜⁵⁹

second 次⁵⁵ 秒⁵⁵ 秒鐘⁵⁵

second Earthly Branch
丑⁵⁵

second Heavenly Stem 乙⁹

second hand 二手½

second name 別名⁵⁴

second to 次於⁵⁵

secondary 枝節⁹

second-hand goods 二手
貨½

secondly 其次⁴⁶

second-rate 次等¹⁶⁶ 亞¹⁶⁶

secret 私⁷¹ 陰⁴¹ 密⁵⁵ 祕
密⁵⁵ 秘密⁵⁵ 機密⁵⁵
特務⁵⁵

secret agent 特務⁵⁵

secret number 密碼⁵⁵

secret recipe 秘方⁵⁵

secret rendezvous 幽會⁵⁹

secret trial 秘密審訊⁵⁵
(⇨ 審訊⁴⁹)

secret trick 秘訣⁴⁹

secret vote 匿名投票⁵⁵

secretary 秘書⁵⁵

Secretary of State 國務

卿 國務卿 (⇨ 卿⁴⁵)

secrete 分泌⁷⁵ 泌⁷⁵

secretive 詭祕⁴¹

secretly 悄悄⁵⁹ 暗中⁴⁵
偷偷⁵¹

secrets 隱情⁵⁵

sect 宗派⁵

section 部⁵⁵ 部分⁵⁵ 部
份⁵⁵ 部門⁵⁵ 款⁵⁵ 節⁵⁵
段⁵⁵ 瓣⁵⁹ 章⁵⁵ 片段⁷⁶
科⁵⁵ 篇¹⁵ 組¹⁴

section chief 部長⁵⁵ 組
長⁵⁵

secure 安全⁵⁵ 妥⁹³

securities markets 證券
市場⁵⁵

security 安全⁵⁵ 證券⁵⁵

Security Council 安全理
事會⁵⁵

security deposit 押金¹⁵⁷

sedan 轎車⁵⁵

sedan-chair 轎⁵⁵ 轎子⁵⁵

sediment 沈澱⁵⁹

seduce 姦淫⁸⁹ 引誘⁹
挑逗⁵⁵

see 眼看⁵⁵ 見⁵⁹ 見到⁵⁴
視⁵⁵ 看⁵⁵ 看出⁵⁵ 看
到⁵⁵ 看見¹⁵ 瞧⁵⁵ 瞧
見⁵⁵

see as 視為¹⁵ 看成⁵⁵

see from afar 望見⁵⁵

see off 送⁵⁵

see suddenly 忽見⁵⁵

see through 透視⁷⁷ 看
穿⁵⁵ 看透¹⁵

See you later! 回頭見!⁵⁵

seed 子⁵⁵ 種⁵⁵ 種子⁵⁵

seedling 秧⁵⁵

seek 尋求⁵⁵ 尋覓⁵⁵ 尋
求⁵⁵ 尋找⁵⁵ 找⁹ 探
求⁹ 摸⁹⁹ 謀⁵⁵ 謀求⁵⁵
求⁹ 牟⁷⁷ 牟取⁷⁷
覓⁹⁷ 徵求¹⁵

seek advice 諮詢⁵⁵

seek patronage of 投靠⁵⁹

seek profits 牟利⁷⁷

seek refuge 避難⁵⁵

seek the root cause 追

seek truth from facts 實
事求是⁵⁵

seem 若⁵⁵ 似⁵⁵ 像是⁵⁷

seem to 彷彿⁵⁵

seemingly 好像⁵⁴

seep 泌⁷⁵

seep in 滲⁷⁷ 滲透⁷⁷

seething 沸騰⁵⁹

segment 瓣⁵⁹

segregate 隔離¹⁷⁴

seize 佔⁵⁵ 佔領⁵⁵ 抄⁵²
捕⁵⁵ 捉⁵⁵ 抓¹⁰³ 搶
住⁵⁷ 簒奪¹⁵⁰ 據¹⁵
奪⁵⁵ 奪取⁵⁵

seize contraband 緝私⁵⁵

seize power 攬權⁵⁵

seize the opportunity 乘
機⁵⁵ 趁機⁵⁵

select 遴選⁵⁹ 選⁵⁵ 選
拔⁵⁵ 點選⁵⁵ 擇⁵⁵ 精⁵⁵
摘⁵⁵ 揀⁵⁵ 揀選⁵⁵ 挑
選⁴⁷ 甄選⁴⁷ 取捨⁵⁵

selected 精選⁵⁵

selected writings 文選⁹⁸

selection 選⁵⁵ 選集⁵⁵

self 己⁹⁷ 自¹⁹⁹ 自我¹⁹⁹

self-awareness 自覺¹⁹⁹

self-confidence 自信¹⁹⁹

self-criticism 檢討¹⁹ 自
我批評¹⁹⁹

self-criticize 檢討¹⁹

self-defense 自衛¹⁹⁹

self-determination 自
主¹⁹⁹

self-effacing 謙虛¹⁹⁹

self-esteem 自重¹⁹⁹

self-examination 自省¹⁹⁹

self-financed 自費¹⁹⁹

self-financed student 自
費生¹⁹⁹

self-government 自治¹⁹⁹

self-help 自助¹⁹⁹

self-immolate 自焚¹⁹⁹

self-introduction 自我介
紹¹⁹⁹

selfish 私¹⁹⁹ 私心¹⁹ 自
私¹⁹⁹

serve jury duty 陪審[42]
serves you right 活該[9]
service 勤務[31] 服務[37] 役[41] 勞[52] 勞務[52]
sesame 芝麻[9]
sesame oil 香油[25]
session 屆[9]
set 套[2] 固定[32] 訂定[39] 鑲[9]
set a price 定價[39]
set an example 示範[4]
set at 定為[39]
set exam questions 命題[35]
set free 釋放[9] 釋放[9] 放開[2] 解脫[19]
set off 襯托[9] 掀起[9]
set out 啓程[7] 出發[110]
set to music 譜曲[5]
set up 架[9] 設[7] 設置[7] 陷害[9]
setback 挫折[9]
setting sun 夕陽[72]
settle 沈澱[9] 結[8] 訂[9] 安置[9] 解決[19]
settle accounts 清理[29] 清算[29] 算帳[9]
settle down 成家[9]
settle new land 墾荒[9]
seven 七[9] 柒[9]
seventh Earthly Branch 午[9]
seventh Heavenly Stem 庚[9]
sever 絕[9] 截[9] 斷[9] 斷絕[9]
several 若干[9] 數[9] 幾[9]
severe 嚴[9] 嚴厲[9] 劇烈[9]
severe injury 重傷[9]
severe punishment 酷刑[9] 嚴刑[9]
sew 縫[9]
sewage 污水[9]
sewing 縫紉[9]
sewing machine 縫紉機[9]
sex 性[9] 性別[9]
sex maniac 色鬼[9] 色狼[9]

sex scandal 緋聞[9] 性醜聞 (⇨ 醜聞[9])
sexual abuse 性虐待 (⇨ 虐待[9])
sexual desire 性慾[9]
sexual harassment 性騷擾 (⇨ 騷擾[9])
sexual intercourse 交媾[9] 性交[9]
sexual passion 色情[9]
sexual relations 性關係[9]
sexy 性感[9]
Shaanxi Province 陝西[9]
shackles 枷鎖[9] 桎梏[9]
shade 陰[9]
shadow 影[9] 影子[9] 盯梢[9] 陰影[9] 尾隨[9]
shake 振[9] 振動[9] 震[9] 撼[9] 抖[9] 抖動[9] 搖[141] 搖動[141] 搖晃[141]
shake hands 握手[128]
shake off 掙脫[9]
shaky 搖晃[141]
shallow 淺[9] 粗淺[9]
shallow and ignorant 鄙陋無知[9]
shame 羞恥[9] 恥[9] 恥辱[9]
shameless 無恥[9] 不知羞恥 (⇨ 羞恥[9]) 臉皮很厚[9]
Shandong Province 山東[9] 魯[9]
Shang Dynasty 商朝[9] 殷[9] 殷商[9]
Shanghai 上海[9] 滬[9]
Shanghaiese 滬語[9]
Shanxi Province 山西[9] 晉[126]
Shaolin temple 少林寺[9]
Shaoxing 紹興[9]
shape 形[9] 捏塑[9] 陶冶[9]
share 共享[9] 攤[9] 分攤[9] 分享[9] 份額[9] 股[9] 股份[9]
shared 共同[9]
shared values 共識[9]

self-knowledge 自知[139]
selfless 無私 (⇨ 私[17])
self-loathing 自卑[139]
self-reliance 自力更生[139]
self-respect 自重[139] 自尊[139]
self-restraint 涵養[113] 抑制力[139]
self-satisfied 得意[139] 自滿[139]
self-sufficient 自給自足[139]
sell 販賣[24] 銷[99] 銷售[99] 行銷[99] 發售[99] 出售[110] 賣[150] 售[162]
sell below cost 傾銷[99] 抛售[8]
sell drugs 販毒[24]
sell goods 售貨[42]
sell out 出賣[110]
sell tickets 售票[162]
sell to 賣給[150]
sell wholesale 批發[12]
selling price 售價[162]
semblance 假象[16]
semester 學期[53]
semi- 半[12]
semicolon 分號[35]
semiconductor 半導體 (⇨ 導體[46])
Senate 參議院 (⇨ 議院[53])
Senator 參議員[9]
send 寄[26] 遣送[106] 派[120] 派遣[120] 致[128]
send a letter here 來信[160]
send away 打發[9]
send back 送回[6]
send one's regards to 問好[9] 問候[9]
send out 送出[6] 發出[9]
send thanks 致謝[128]
send to 送到[6]
senility 老年癡呆[13]
senior 資深[9] 長[53]
senior high school 高中[9]
senior officer 首長[146]

sense 覺[53] 感[55]
sense of beauty 美感[55]
sense of belonging 歸屬感[67]
sense of mission 使命感[55]
sense of quality 眼光[55]
sense of smell 嗅覺[91]
senseless 無謂[117]
senses 感官[55]
sensitive 敏感[54]
sentence 句[53] 句子[53] 判處[9] 判刑[9]
sentimental 濫情[62]
sentry 崗哨[9] 警衛[9]
sentry post 崗位[9]
Seoul 漢城[9]
separate 脫節[116] 另[33] 另外[33] 分[35] 分別[35] 分隔[35] 分離[35] 分手[35] 解[9] 隔斷[9]
separate from 脫離[116]
separated 暌違[9]
separately 另[33] 另外[33] 分別[35] 單[36]
September 九月 (⇨ 月[9])
sequence 順序[9] 次第[9] 次序[9] 秩序[9] 系列[9] 排序[9]
serendipitous 巧合[9]
serene 靜[9]
series 列[9] 系[9] 系列[9] 連串[9]
serious 沈重[9] 認真[9] 重[9] 嚴重[9] 鄭[9] 鄭重[9]
serious injury 重傷[9]
seriously injure 重傷[9]
serpent 蛇[9]
servant 小厮[9] 奴僕[9] 僕人[9] 服務員[9]
serve 伺候[9] 服[9] 服侍[9]
serve another term 連任[9]
serve as 擔任[9] 作為[9] 充當[9] 為[9]

shareholder 股東³⁷
shark 鯊魚⁸²
shark fin 魚翅¹⁸⁰
sharp 銳⁴⁴ 銳利⁴⁴ 尖⁸⁹
　尖銳⁸⁹ 敏銳³¹ 鋒
　利⁴⁴ 犀利⁸⁵ 利⁴⁴⁴ 戛
　然⁸⁰
shatter 破滅⁴⁶ 粉碎⁷²
shattered 破碎¹⁶²
shave 剃⁴⁶ 刮⁴⁹ 刮鬍⁴⁹
　子⁴⁹ 刮臉⁴⁹
shawl 披肩⁴⁴
she 伊¹⁸ 其²¹ 她⁵⁶
shear 剪⁴⁸²
shed 棚¹⁶⁵
shed leaves 落葉⁵⁵
shed tears 流淚⁴⁶
sheen 光澤⁴²
sheep 綿羊²⁹ 羊¹²³
sheepish 低聲下氣²⁰⁰
sheet 被單⁴⁴ 張⁶⁶ 床
　單⁴⁴ 篇¹¹⁵ 單¹³⁶
shelf 格⁶⁹ 層¹⁴⁴
shell 砲彈⁵⁷ 殼⁵⁶ 剝⁵¹
　甲¹¹² 貝⁵⁰ 貝殼⁵⁰
shelled shrimp 蝦仁⁴¹
shelter 庇護⁴⁷ 包庇¹⁸⁶
Shen Nong 神農⁵⁶
Shenyang 瀋陽¹⁵⁶
Shenzhen 深圳⁴⁷
shepherd 牧者⁴² 牧羊⁴² 牧
　羊者⁴²
shield 庇護⁴⁷ 掩護⁵⁶
　盾⁸¹ 盾牌⁸¹ 遮蔽⁵⁶
　擋⁴⁹ 擋箭牌⁴⁹ 袒
　護⁴⁷ 護⁴⁷²
shift 更動¹⁴⁵ 轉移³¹ 調
　動⁴² 移⁸⁷ 移動⁸⁷ 挪
　動⁸⁴ 挪移⁸⁴ 班⁴¹
shift blame 嫁禍¹⁵⁵
shine 煥發⁴⁷ 發光⁴⁷ 輝
　映⁵⁸
shining 彪炳¹²²
shining clean 皎潔⁴²
shiny 光亮⁴²
ship 航海⁵⁷ 船舶⁹⁴
shipping 航運⁵⁷
shipping container 貨櫃⁴⁷

shipping route 航線⁵⁷
ships 船舶⁹⁴
shirk 躲開³⁹ 推諉¹⁶² 推
　卸¹⁶²
shirt 衫⁹⁴ 襯衫⁹⁴
shit 大便⁷³ 拉屎²⁹ 屎²⁹
shiver 哆嗦⁷⁹ 顫抖⁴⁶
　抖⁴⁷ 抖動⁴⁷ 發抖⁴⁷
shock 振動⁴⁷ 震驚⁵⁹ 衝
　擊⁵⁶ 刺激⁵⁹ 休克⁷⁷
shocked 駭異⁵⁶
shoelaces 鞋帶²⁹
shoes 鞋¹⁴ 鞋子¹⁴
shoot 拍⁴⁹ 拍攝⁴⁹ 發⁵⁶
　發射⁵⁶ 攝¹³⁷ 射¹⁴⁷ 射
　門¹⁴⁷
shoot a movie 攝影¹³⁷
shoot dead 槍殺⁵⁶
shop 商店⁵⁹ 店⁸⁶ 店
　鋪⁸⁶ 鋪⁸⁶ 購物¹⁴⁵
shopping center 購物中
　心¹⁷⁵
shore 海岸⁴² 陸⁶⁷ 岸⁶⁷
short 少⁴⁷ 短⁴⁶ 矮⁶⁹
short article 短篇⁴⁶
short distance 短程⁴⁶
short of 匱乏¹⁹⁶
short of money 拮据⁴⁷ 缺
　錢²³
short stories 短篇小說⁴⁶
short traditional coat
　襖¹⁸⁶
short wave 短波⁴⁶
shortage 供不應求⁴⁴ 匱
　乏¹⁹⁶
shortcake cookies 酥
　餅¹⁹
shortcoming 短處⁴⁶ 短
　絀⁴⁹
shortcut 捷徑⁴⁸
shorten 縮短⁷⁶
shortly 快⁸⁹
shorts 短褲⁴⁹
short-term 短期⁴⁶
should 該¹⁶ 要⁵² 理當⁴⁸
　宜¹³ 最好¹³ 應²² 應
　當²² 應該²²
shoulder 背⁴⁹ 背負³⁹

shoulders 肩頭²⁹
shout 叫⁴⁷ 喝⁸⁹ 呼⁴⁷
　喊⁴⁷ 喊叫⁴⁷ 嚷⁸⁹ 嚷
　嚷⁸⁹
shout a command 喝令⁸⁹
shout to 呼喚⁴⁷ 呼叫⁴⁷
shouts 呼聲⁴⁷
shovel 鏟⁴⁶ 鏟子¹⁹
show 示⁴⁷ 示範⁵⁶ 秀⁴⁷
　節目⁴⁵ 呈²⁹ 出示⁴⁷
　表示⁴⁷ 顯⁸⁵ 顯出⁸⁵
　顯示⁸⁵ 顯現⁸⁵
show cards 攤牌³⁵
show mercy 可憐²³
show off 作秀⁴⁷ 誇耀⁸⁹
　秀⁸⁷ 炫耀⁸⁹ 逞⁴²
show respect to 瞻仰²⁸
shower 洗澡¹¹ 淋浴⁴⁷
　陣雨⁵⁸
shower room 浴室⁴⁵
showing 表現¹²⁸
showy 浮華⁴⁹
shredded meat 肉絲¹³²
shrew 潑婦²⁹
shriek 尖叫⁴⁷
shrimp 蝦⁴¹
shrink 收縮⁴⁷ 縮⁷⁶
shroud 籠罩¹⁶²
shrub 灌木⁵⁶
Shun 舜⁵⁶
shut 掩⁵⁶ 關閉⁴⁷ 閉⁹⁴
shut off 關掉⁴⁷
shut the door 關門⁷⁹ 閉
　門⁷⁹
Shut up! 住口⁴ 閉嘴⁴⁷
shuttle 梭¹¹
shuttle back and forth 穿
　梭⁸⁴
shy 害羞⁴⁷
shyness 害羞⁴⁷
Siberia 西伯利亞³⁰
siblings 兄弟姊妹¹²
Sichuan Province 四川⁴⁶
　蜀¹²⁵
sick 病了⁴⁴
sickle 鐮刀¹⁰²

sickness 病患⁴⁴
sickroom 病房⁴⁴
side 方¹⁴ 方面¹⁴⁴ 旁⁴⁷
　旁邊⁴⁷ 邊⁴⁷ 面¹⁴⁸
　側¹⁷ 側面¹⁷
side room 廂¹⁴ 廂房¹⁴
side-effect 副作用 (⇒
　作用⁴⁷)
sidewalk 人行道¹⁹ 步
　道⁴⁴
siesta 午覺⁴⁷ 午睡⁴⁷
sift out 篩選⁴²
sigh 歎⁴⁶ 嘆³⁴ 嘆息⁴⁶
　感慨⁵⁹
sigh in admiration 詠
　嘆¹²⁰
sigh in relief 鬆口氣⁴²
sight 目光⁴⁴
sightsee 觀光⁴⁸
sign 簽訂¹² 簽名¹² 簽
　署¹² 簽字¹² 符⁴² 符
　號⁴² 標誌⁴⁵ 號⁴⁷ 招
　牌⁴⁵ 迹象⁴⁷ 署名¹²
　手勢⁴⁷ 看板¹¹⁴ 徵
　兆⁴⁴
sign language 手語⁴⁷
signal 訊號⁴⁷ 信號⁴⁷
signature 簽名¹² 簽名¹²
　簽字¹² 署名¹²
signboard 牌⁴⁵
signs of improvement 起
　色⁴⁷
silence 沈默³⁹
silent 沈寂⁴⁹ 寂靜⁴⁹
　默⁴⁴
silently 悄悄⁴² 默默¹⁴⁴
　默然¹⁴⁴
silhouette 輪廓¹¹⁵
silicon 矽⁴²
Silicon Valley 矽谷⁴²
silk 蠶絲⁴⁶ 真絲⁴⁴ 綢
　絹¹³² 絹帛¹³² 絲⁵³ 絲
　綢⁵³
Silk Road 絲綢之路¹⁵³
silk and satin 綢緞⁴⁹
silk cocoon 繭²⁵
silk painting 絹畫¹³²
silkworm 蠶⁵⁹ 桑蠶⁵⁹

silkworm cocoon 蠶繭
silly smile 傻笑
silt 淤 淤泥
silt up 淤 淤積
silver 銀 銀色 銀子
Sima Guang 司馬光
similar 同 同樣 雷同 相似 類似
similarly 同 亦然
simple 輕易 儉樸 容易 簡 簡單 明瞭 素 易懂 模素
simple and crude 簡陋
simple and easy 簡易
simple and frugal 刻苦
simplify 簡化
simplify matters 省事
simply 純粹 乾脆 簡直
simulate 模擬
simulation 模擬
simultaneously 一邊 一面 一齊 並 兼
sin 罪孽
since 既 既然 既是 以來 自
since then 自此 自從
sincere 敦厚 忱 眞誠 眞心 眞摯 誠 誠懇 誠摯 純眞 哀
sincerely 眞心
sincerely believe 篤信
sincerity 誠意
sing 歌唱 唱 唱歌 鳴
sing in chorus 合唱
Singapore 新加坡
singer 歌手
singing star 歌星
single 獨身 單 單身
single bed 單人床
single people 單身貴族

single-handedly 獨自
single-mindedly 專心
singly 單
singular 單數
sinicize 漢化
sinister 險惡
sink 水槽 墮 沈 沒落 墜
sink into 陷入
sink to 淪爲
Sino-American 中美
sinologist 中國通 (⇨ 通) 漢學家
sinology 漢學
sip 啜
sir 先生
sister 大姐 姊 姊姊 姊妹 妹 妹妹 姐 姐姐 姐妹
sister-in-law 嫂 嫂嫂 姑 大嫂 姨
sisters 姊妹 姐妹
sit 坐
sit down 坐下
sit in on 旁聽
sit in silence 靜坐
site 地點 場 場地 場所
situated at 位於
situation 況 局 局面 形勢 地步 境 情 情況 情勢 情形 場合 狀況 步 陣腳
six 六 陸
six feet square 坪
sixth Earthly Branch 巳
sixth Heavenly Stem 己
sizable 可觀
size 大小 尺寸
skateboard 滑板
skeleton 骷髏 骨骼 骨子
sketch 圖形 素描
sketchy 簡略
ski 滑雪

skill 工夫 技 伎倆 手法
skilled 熟練 純熟 嫻熟
skilled worker 技工
skillful 巧 巧妙
skim 流覽 瀏覽
skin 皮 皮膚 肌膚
skin-deep 膚淺
skinny 瘦
skip class 曉課
skip out 溜走
skip over 跳
skirt 裙 裙子
skull 顱骨 骷髏頭
sky 天空
sky-blue 蔚藍
skyscraper 摩天大樓 (⇨ 大樓)
slack 清淡
slander 汙衊 誣賴 詆毀 毀謗
slang 俚語
slant 傾斜
slanting 斜
slap 打巴掌 (⇨ 巴掌)
slash 刺
slaughter 殘殺 戮 宰殺 屠 屠殺 屠宰 殺戮
slave 奴隸
slay 戕害
sleep 夢寐 眠 睡 睡覺 睡眠
sleep peacefully 安眠
sleep soundly 熟睡 酣睡
sleeping berth 臥舖
sleeping car 臥車
sleeping mat 涼蓆
sleeping pill 安眠藥
sleepy 睏
sleeve 袖
slender 苗條
slice 切
slide 溜 幻燈片

slide projector 幻燈機
slide show 幻燈
slight 輕 輕忽 輕微 稍 微 微微 菲薄
slightest 絲毫
slightly 稍微
slim 苗條
slim and graceful 輕盈
slip 失手 失足 單
slip away 溜 溜走
slip of paper 字條
slippers 拖鞋
slippery 滑
slit 刺 開衩
slogan 標語 口號
slope 坡 坡度 斜度 斜坡
sloppy 草率
slot 槽
slovenly 邋遢
slow 慢 徐徐 遲 遲鈍 遲滯 緩慢
slowdown 怠工
slowly 遲遲 緩緩
sludge 淤 淤泥
sluggish 遲滯
slut 賤貨
small 小
small boat 艇
small business 中小企業 (⇨ 企業)
small cup 盞
small hill 丘
small plate 碟子
small-scale 小型
smash 擊毀 砸破 碎
smash to pieces 粉碎
smear 玷污 塗
smear over 塗抹
smell 味 聞 嗅
smelly 臭
smelt 冶煉 熔 熔化 鎔 煉
smile 笑 微笑
smiling 莞 莞爾

spare part 零件[39]

spark 觸發[35]

sparkle 閃閃[29]

sparkling 晶瑩[69]

sparrow 雀[39] 麻雀[74]

sparse 稀[31] 疏[35]

spawn 孵化[9]

speak 云[&] 說[11] 說話[11] 言[96] 開口[39] 發音[92] 講[175] 講話[175]

speak in defense of 辯護[39]

speak nonsensically 亂講[100]

speak of 談到[87]

speaker 喇叭[77]

special 特[39] 特別[39] 特殊[39] 獨特[125]

special case 專案[39]

special characteristic 特性[39]

special course of study 專科[39]

special district 特區[39]

special economic zone 經濟特區[39]

special envoy 特使[39]

special feature 特色[39] 特徵[39]

special service 特務[39]

special skill 專長[39]

specialist 家[155] 師[162]

specialize 專攻[39]

specially 特地[39] 特別[39] 專門[39]

specialty 拿手[39] 專長[39]

specific 特定[39] 具體[120]

specification 規格[77]

specified 額定[108]

specify 指定[77]

speck 點子[107]

speckles 斑[107]

spectators 觀眾[95] 旁觀者[95]

speculate 炒賣[22] 投機[37] 揣摩[194]

speech 演說[95] 話[95] 言論[96]

speechless 無話可說 (⇨ 說話[6])

speed 奔馳[68] 速[63] 速度[63]

speed per hour 時速[72]

spell 拼[39] 拼音[39] 陣[15]

spelling 拼法[39]

spend 花[9] 度[31] 過[133]

spend money 花錢[9] 掏錢[141]

spend the night 過夜[133]

spending 開支[39]

sperm 精子[39]

sphere 球[39]

spherical 球形[39] 圓形[40]

spicy 麻辣[74] 辣[74]

spicy tofu 麻辣豆腐[74]

spider 蜘蛛[39]

spider web 蛛網[74] 蜘蛛網[76]

spike of the rice plant 稻穗[31]

spillover 外溢[77]

spin into yarn 紡紗[77]

spinach 菠菜[34]

spine 背脊[39] 脊[132] 脊椎[77]

spinning top 陀螺[125]

spiral 螺旋[125] 盤旋[29]

spirit 神[155] 幽靈[39] 意氣[69] 精神[39] 氣[9] 氣概[39] 氣魄[9] 心靈[83] 妖精[27] 骨氣[37] 鬼[39] 鬼魂[140] 靈[161]

spirited 激昂[22]

spiritual pollution 精神污染[39]

spit 吐[39] 吐痰[39] 痰[39] 唾沫[173]

spit at contemptuously 唾棄[39]

spiteful 潑辣[99]

splash 灑[154] 嘩啦[17]

spleen 脾[59]

splendid 精采[39] 精彩[39] 錦繡[76] 彪炳[19]

split 劈[39] 裂[137] 綳[165]

split apart 分裂[35]

split open 迸裂[39] 劈開[39]

spoil 攪局[39] 糟蹋[69] 溺愛[39] 寵壞[132]

spoiled 腐[39] 腐爛[39]

spoils 贓物[39]

spoke 輻[39]

spoken language 口語[69] 言語[96]

spokesperson 發言人[92]

sponsor 主辦[39]

spoon 勺子[41] 杓子[41] 匙[99]

sports 運動[8]

sports fan 球迷[39]

sports ground 操場[39]

spot 點[39] 污點[39] 斑點[107] 現場[114]

spotless 潔白[9]

spots 斑[107]

spouse 配偶[39] 愛人[93]

spray 噴[39]

spray paint 噴漆[69]

spread 波及[35] 張[39] 蔓延[39] 擴散[39] 擴張[39] 普及[39] 流行[39] 傳播[39] 揚[39] 散播[39] 撒[39]

spread lies 撒謊[39]

spread out 攤[39] 鋪[39]

spread over 敷[69]

spread rumors 謠傳[141]

spring 泉[39] 春[135] 春天[135] 彈[136] 彈簧[136]

Spring Festival 春節[135]

spring and autumn 春秋[135]

spring at 撲[176]

spring equinox 春分[135]

spring roll 春捲[135]

spring water 泉水[39]

sprinkle 澆[39] 撒[39] 潑[99] 灑[154]

sprout 萌[92] 芽[92] 發芽[92] 苗[39] 抽[113]

sprout 蒙[?] 萌芽[95]

spry 輕快[37]

spur 刺[39] 刺激[39] 策[39] 促使[88]

spur on 帶動[39]

spur to action 激發[22]

spurn 唾棄[173]

spurt 噴[39] 噴射[69]

spy 間諜[39]

spy on 窺[39] 窺視[39] 窺探[39]

squad 班[197]

squander 揮霍[158]

square 平方[39] 方[39] 方塊[?] 方形[39]

square meter 平方公尺[39] 平方米[39]

squat 蹲[192] 蹲下[192]

squeeze 擁擠[39] 夾[39] 擠[2]

squid 魷魚[14]

squint 瞇[138]

squirrel 松鼠[39]

stabilize 平定[39] 安定[68]

stable 平穩[39] 牢靠[39] 穩[39] 穩定[39]

stack 疊[39] 堆[68]

staff 杖[39] 員工[90]

staff member 職員[39]

stage 階段[39] 舞台[39] 台[39] 場[39] 臺[?]

stagnant sales 滯銷[39]

stagnate 停滯[39]

stain 玷污[39] 污點[39] 漬[39] 斑點[107] 油[113]

stainless steel 不鏽鋼 (⇨ 鏽[35])

staircase 梯[39]

stairs 階梯[39] 樓梯[39]

stake 注[9] 樁[135] 賭注[39] 木樁[77]

stale 陳[39] 陳腐[39]

stalk 莖[39] 梗[114]

stamen 蕊[59]

stamina 後勁[39] 精力[39]

stammer 口吃[39]

stamp 印[39] 蓋章[39] 章[39] 戳記[124]

stance 架式[34]

stand 承受[39] 站[39] 站立[39] 攤[39] 立[39] 豎立[39] 算數[39]

stand firm 堅守[142]

stand guard 把風[35]

straits 海峽

strange 怪 奇 奇怪 離奇 陌生

stranger 陌生人

strangle 扼殺 掐死

strategize 謀略 慮

strategy 略 策 策略

stratum 階層 層

straw 吸管

straw mat 蓆 蓆子

streak 條紋

street 街 街道 馬路

street committee 街道

street corner 街頭

streetwalker 流鶯

strength 長處 力 力量 勢力 實力

strengthen 健 加強 鞏固 壯 壯大 堅強 增強

stress 注重 重音

stressful 緊張

stretch 伸 伸展 張

stretch open 張開

stretch out 伸出

stretch taut 繃

strict 整飭 嚴 嚴格 嚴謹 嚴厲

stride 跨 邁

stride across 跨越

stride forward 邁進

strike 扑 打 擊 擊中 罷工 撲

strike classes 罷課

string 線 弦 串

string music 弦樂

string of 連串

string together 串

stringed instrument 弦樂器

strip 脫 條 扒 剝 剝奪 褫奪

strip bare 脫光

strip of cloth 布條

stripe 條紋

stripes 紋 斑紋

strive for 力求 求 講求

strive to 力圖

stroke 撫摸 摸 中風

stroll 逛 逛逛 漫步 踱步 散步 閒逛

strong 勁 強 強壯 壯 壯大 堅強

strong breeze 狂風

strong point 優點

strong reaction 軒然大波

stronghold 據點

struck dumb 愣住

structure 格局 建築 結構 架構 構造

struggle 搏 鬥 門爭 爭鬥 掙扎 奮鬥

struggle for 力爭 爭奪 爭取

stubborn 頑固 頑強 固執 執拗 倔強

stuck 卡住了

student 學生

student I.D. 學生證 (⇒ 證)

student movement 學運 學生運動 (⇒ 運動)

student studying abroad 留學生

studies 學業

study 就學 書房 書齋 學 學習 修 念 念書 唸書 求學 讀 讀書 審

study abroad 留學 遊學

study and discuss 研討

study at a school 肄業

study from each other 互相學習

study thoroughly 鑽研

stuffing 餡

stuffy 悶

stuffy air 悶氣

stuffy nose 鼻塞

stumble 絆 摔

stumbling block 絆腳石

stunned 驚愕 愕然

stunned speechless 目瞪口呆

stupa 塔 佛塔

stupefied 發呆 愣住

stupid 傻 頑 癡呆 獸 愚笨 愚蠢 笨 呆 呆呆 遲鈍 魯

sturdy 扎實 結實 固 強勁 壯 牢 牢固

stutter 口吃

sty 圈

style 款式 作風 式 式樣 風格 方式

style of speech 談吐

subconscious 下意識 (⇒意識) 潛意識 (⇒意識)

subdue 鎮 制伏

subdued 就範

subject 主題 科目 題

subject to 遭受 受到

subjective 主觀

subjects 臣民

subjugated 淪陷

sublimation 昇華

submarine 潛艇

submerge 淹沒 沈沒

submit 順從 交 屈從 屈服

submit for publication 投稿

subscribe 訂 預訂

subsequent 翌

subside 平息 減弱

subsidize 貼補 補助

subsidy 津貼 貼 補貼

substantial 充實 堅實

substitute for 替 替代 代替 代

subterfuge 狡計

subtitle 字幕

subtle 妙 微妙 奧妙

subtract 減

subtraction 減法

subtropics 亞熱帶 (⇒ 熱帶)

suburbs 郊區 市郊

subversive activities 顛覆活動

subvert 顛覆

subway 地鐵 地下鐵

success 成功 成績

success or failure 成敗 勝敗

successively 先後 依次 連

succinct 簡潔

such 何等 如此

such as 諸如

suck 吸

Sudan 蘇丹

sudden 急劇 急遽

suddenly 恍然 暴 乍 驀忽 勃 突 突然 突兀 驀 驀地 驀然 頓時 忽 忽然 陡然 猛然 猝然 驟然 遽然 幡然

suddenly understand 恍然大悟

sue 控訴 告 打官司 (⇒ 官司)

suffer 挨 忍受 遭受 吃 吃苦 受 受

sweep ancestors' graves 掃墓

sweep away 掃除

sweep the floor 掃地

sweet 甘 甜 甜美 甜蜜

sweet and sour 糖醋 甜酸

sweet and sour fish 糖醋魚

sweet potato 甘薯 番薯

sweetheart 心肝 寶貝

swell 漲 膨脹 腫

sweltering 悶熱

swift 疾

swift and powerful 凌厲

swim 游 游泳 泳

swim trunks 游泳褲

swimming pool 游泳池

swimsuit 泳裝 游泳衣

swindle 拐騙 欺 欺詐

swing 甩 秋千 鞦韆 擺 擺動 搖晃

swirl around 縈繞

switch 更換 開關 變換

Switzerland 瑞士

sword 劍 刀

sycophant 哈巴狗

syllable 音節

symbol 符 符號 標誌 表徵 象徵

symbolic 象徵性

symbolize 標誌

symmetric 勻稱 對稱

sympathize 同情

sympathy 人情 同情

symposium 研討會

symptom 病症 症候 症狀

synergy 交互作用

synopsis 梗概 簡介 提要

synthesize 綜 綜合 合成

system 機制 體系 體制 制 制度 編制 脈絡 系統

systematic 系統化

T t

table 擱置 譜 台 桌 桌子 表 檯

table lamp 檯燈

table tennis 桌球

tablet 扁 匾 匾額

taboo 諱 忌諱 禁忌

tacit understanding 默契

tacitly approve 默認

tactful 識相

tactful words 婉言

tactfully 婉轉

tactless 不識相 (⇨識相)

tael 兩

tag 標籤

taichi 太極拳

Taihu lake 太湖

tail 盯梢 尾 尾巴

tailor 裁縫

tailoring 成衣

Tainan 台南

Taipei 台北

Taiping Rebellion 太平天國起義

Taishan 泰山

Taiwan 台灣 臺灣

Taiwan Straits 台灣海峽

Taiwan dollar 台幣

Taiwanese 台語

take 吸食 捎 服 服用 照 拿 拿走 帶 帶走 採取 取 攔

take a class 修課

take a nap 打瞌睡 (⇨瞌睡) 眯一下眼

take a stroll 走動

take a walk 逛逛走走

take action 行動

take advantage of 趁 趁著 佔便宜

take aim at 瞄準

take at will 予取予求

take back 收回

take bribes 貪贓

take care of 照料 辦理 管

Take care! 慢走!

take drugs 吸毒

take effect 生效

take for 當

take hold of 拿住

take into account 加以 顧及

take kickbacks 收取佣金 (⇨佣金)

take leave 請假

take medicine 吃藥

take notes 筆錄 記錄 記錄

take off 脫 脫下 起飛

take office 就任

take out 拿出 帶走 取出 掏

take over 接收

take place 發生

take precautions 戒備

take risks 冒風險

take root 紮根 生根

take the trouble 費心

take to 帶給

take turns 輪

take vacation 放假

talent 天分 才華 才能 藝 本領 能耐

talented 有天分的 (⇨天分)

talented person 人才

talisman 符

talk 聊 聊天 談話 講

talk glibly 侈談

talk incessantly 喋喋不休

talk nonsense 胡說

talk to oneself 自言自語

talks 會談

tall 高

tall and straight 挺拔

tallest 最高

tally 吻合

talon 爪 爪子

tan 曬黑

Tang Dynasty 唐朝 唐代

Tang poetry 唐詩

tangerine 柑橘 橘子

tangle 纏

Tangshan 唐山

tank 坦克

tantamount to 不啻

Tao Qian 陶潛

Taoism 道

Taoyuan 桃園

tap water 自來水

tape 膠帶 磁帶 錄音帶

tardy 遲

target 指標 目標 對象

tariff 關稅

taro 芋頭

task 作業

taste 眼光 滋味 嘗 口味 品嘗 味道

tasteful 講究

tasty 可口 好吃

tattered 破爛

tattoo 刺青 紋身

taunt 嘲諷 奚落

taut 緊

tavern 旅店 酒店 酒肆

tax 稅 賦

tax rate 稅率

以 是以 由此

thereupon 於是
thermometer 溫度計
thermos 保溫杯 保溫瓶
these 這些
thesis 論點 論文
they 他們 她們 牠們 它們
thick 濃厚 厚 稠
thicket 叢
thickness 厚薄 厚度
thick-skinned 皮很厚
thief 竊盜 竊犯 賊 賊仔
thigh 腿 股 大腿
thin 瘦 消瘦 疏 薄 細
thin and weak 瘦弱
thing 事物 者 東西 物
things of the past 往事
think 認為 以為 看 想 思 動腦筋 (⇨ 腦筋)
think crazy thoughts 亂想
think of 惦記 念 掛念 想 想到 想念 想起 思
think of a way 設法
think over 思考 思索
thinking 心聲 心思 思維
third Earthly Branch 寅
third Heavenly Stem 丙
thirst 渴
thirst for 渴望
thirsty 渴
this 今 其 茲 茲 這 這個 本 此
this article 本文
this evening 今晚
this kind 這種
this locality 本地
this province 本省

this time 這次
this year 今年
thorn 刺
thorns 荊棘
thorny 荊棘 棘手
thorough 深入
thoroughfare 通道
thoroughly 透 好好 徹底
those 那些
though 儘管
thought 思維 思想
thoughtful 周到 周全
thoughts 感想 心思 思潮
thoughts of love 春意
thoughts of spring 春意
thousand 千 仟
thousandth 毫
thousand-year-old egg 皮蛋
thread 線 絲
threaten 恫嚇 嚇 威脅 恐嚇 揚言
threatening force 聲勢
three 三 參
Three Gorges 三峽
Three Kingdoms 三國
three-dimensional 立體
threshold 門檻
thrifty 儉樸 節儉
thrilling 暢快
thriving 熾盛 薈萃
throat 頸 頸部 嗓子 喉嚨 喉嘴 咽喉
through 經由 藉由 藉著
throughout a journey 沿途
throw 扔 投 投擲 拋 擲
throw away 扔掉 拋開 丟掉
throw down 丟下
throw into 投入
throw off 甩

throw up 吐
thumb 拇指
thunder 雷 雷聲
thunder and lightning 雷電
thunderbolt 霹靂
thunderstorm 雷雨
Thursday 星期四 禮拜四
thus 從而
Tiananmen Square 天安門廣場
Tianjin 天津
Tibet 藏 西藏
Tibetan people 藏族
ticket 票 券 車票
ticket office 售票處
ticket scalper 黃牛
ticket window 窗口
tidal current 潮流
tidal wave 海嘯
tide 浪潮 潮 潮汐
tidy up 收拾 清理
tie 紮 結 拴 繫 捆 總 束 保
tie up 綁
tiger 老虎 虎
tight 嚴密 緊
tighten 緊縮
tightly 緊緊
tile 瓦 瓦片
till 耕 耕田
tiller 舵
tilt 傾斜 偏
tilted 斜
timber 木材
time 光陰 時日 時代 時光 時候 時間 時刻 時期 期間 工夫 功夫 遍 番
time difference 時差
time lag 時差
time-consuming 很花時間 (⇨ 花)
times 倍 次 度 回
timetable 時刻表

timid 膽怯 怯弱
tin 錫
tinkle of bells 鈴聲
tiny 微 微微 微小 細小
tip 小費 末 端
tip off 告密
tipsy feeling 醉意
tire 輪胎
tired 疲乏 疲勞 疲累 疲軟 困倦 累
tired of 厭倦
title 書名 標題 號
title of address 抬頭 頭銜 名目
titular 掛名
to 往 于 給 於 至 對
to the contrary 然而
to the utmost 儘
toad 蟾
toady to foreigners 媚外
toast 烤
tobacco 煙草
tobacco and alcohol 菸酒
tobacco leaf 菸
today 今日 今天
tofu 豆腐
together 一併 一道 一塊兒 一齊 一起 一同 共 同 聯袂 齊
toilet 廁所 馬桶
toilet paper 衛生紙
toilsome 辛苦
token of appreciation 意思
Tokyo 東京
tolerance 耐性
tolerant 寬容
tolerate 包容 忍受 接受 容納 容忍
tomato 番茄
tomb 陵 陵墓

treat kindly 善待[17]
treat specially 垂青[17]
treat unjustly 冤枉[164]
treatise 論文[115]
treatment 待遇[71]
treaty 公約[12] 條約[12] 約[41]
tree 樹[66] 樹木[66] 木[77]
tree branch 樹枝[66]
tree trunk 樹幹[66]
trek 跋涉[94]
tremble 震[28]哆嗦[27]顫[28] 戰慄[170]慄[170]
trench 壕溝[12]
trenchant 犀利[20]
trend 趨勢[65]趨向[65]潮流[74]動態[65]
triad 三合會[10]幫會[12]
trial 考驗[21]審判[156]
trials and tribulations 風雨[17]
triangle 三角[10]
tribe 部落[41]
tributary 支流[27]
trick 圈套[65]詭計[27]狡計[27]
trick of the trade 訣竅[27]
tricycle 三輪車[10]
trigger 扳機[83]
trigger-happy 黷武[150]
trillion 兆[127]
trip 趟[67]絆[97]絆倒[97]旅途[118]
trip and fall down 摔跤[153]
trip over 絆倒[97]
tripe 肚子[70]
trite 迂腐[67]陳腐[76]
triumph 獲勝[25]
trivial 瑣屑[87]區區[83]
trivial matter 小事[27]
trivial matters 瑣事[87]
troops 隊[135]隊伍[135]軍隊[156]
trophy 錦標[76]
Tropic of Cancer 北回歸線 (⇨回歸[27])
Tropic of Capricorn 南回

歸線 (⇨回歸[27])
tropics 熱帶[65]
trouble 麻煩[71]害死[27]煩[17]
troubles 患難[157]
troublesome 傷腦筋 (⇨腦筋[143])
troubling 煩[17]
trough 槽[66]
truck 卡車[14]貨車[21]
true 眞[28]眞正[28]實[27]實在[27]確實[27]
true details 底細[100]
true face 眞正面目 (⇨面目[?])
true situation 眞相[28]
truly 眞[28]眞是[28]的確[71]
trump card 王牌[10]
trumpet 喇叭[77]
trunk 幹[66]
trunk line 幹線[66]
trust 信[99]信賴[99]信任[99]信託[99]
trustee 董事[?]
trustworthiness 信用[99]
trustworthy 守信[99]
truth 眞理[28]道理[148]
try 設法[27]試[28]試試[28] 試圖[28]嘗[28]嘗試[28] 企圖[28]審判[125]審訊[125]
try and see 試試看[28]
try for 謀取[?]
try in vain 枉費[16]
try out 試用[28]
tryst 幽會[27]
tsunami 海嘯[34]
tube 管[67]
tuberculosis 肺病[21]
Tuesday 星期二[28]禮拜二[28]
tuft 撮[37]
tug 拉[27]
tuition 學費[15]
tumble 跌倒[87]
tumor 腫瘤[28]瘤[28]
tuna 鮪魚[31]
tune 調[22]對準[176]

tunnel 隧道[135]
turbid 混[37]混濁[37]低迷[17]
turf 地盤[36]
Turkey 土耳其[70]
turmoil 動亂[65]
turn 拐[28]拐彎[28]轉[65]轉變[65]
turn around 扭轉[65]轉身[65]回頭[27]
turn for the better 好轉[65]轉機[65]
turn for the worse 逆轉[65]
turn hostile 翻臉[156]
turn in 繳[37]
turn off 關[57]關掉[57]
turn on 開[28]
turn on the light 開燈 (⇨燈[65])
turn oneself in 自首[27]
turn over 反[21]反過來[21]翻身[156]
turn pale 失色[27]
turning point 轉捩[65]
turnip 蘿蔔[162]
turnover 週轉[65]
turtle 龜[28]
tutor 家教[155]
tweezers 鉗子[?]
twelfth Earthly Branch 亥[126]
twenty 廿[?]
twig 條[?]樹梢[66]枝[27]
twilight 暮色[65]
twins 雙胞胎[162]
twist 歪曲[?]扭[37]擰[37]曲[135]
twists and turns 波折[37]
two 二[2]貳[11]兩[28]倆[?]
two of them 他倆[?]
twofold 雙重[162]
two-track 雙軌[41]
two-way radio 無線電[17]
tycoon 財閥[27]
type 打字[?]式[28]形態[28]型[28]型態[28]種[28]種類[28]類[148]類型[148]番[156]

types 品種[?]
typestyle 字體[?]字形[?]
typewriter 打字機[?]
typhoon 颱風[?]
typical 典型[115]
tyrannical 暴戾[28]暴虐[28]霸道[28]
tyranny 暴政[28]
tyrant 暴君[28]
Tyrranosaurus Rex 霸王龍[28]

U u

ugly 難看[28]醜[59]醜陋[57]
Ukraine 烏克蘭[176]
ulcer 潰瘍[106]
ultimatum 最後通牒 (⇨通牒[65])
umbrella 雨傘[161]傘[12]
unadulterated 純粹[65]
unassuming 謙虛[17]謙遜[17]
unavoidable 不免[10]難免[28]無可奈何[71]
unavoidably 不免[10]
unbalanced 畸形[28]
unbearable 不堪[10]夠嗆[28]難堪[28]
unbiased 不偏不倚[10]
unbridled 猖獗[65]
unbroken 綿延[?]連綿[?]
uncertain 茫然[?]疑惑[?]
uncertainty 疑問[?]
uncivilized 非文明 (⇨文明[?])
uncle 伯伯[?]伯父[?]叔父[17]叔叔[17]舅舅[17]
unclear 含糊[?]模糊[?]
uncommon 不俗[10]
unconsciously 不知不覺[10]
uncontrolled 漫[28]
unconvinced 疑惑[?]
uncover 揭[57]揭開[57]揭露[57]
uncrowded 鬆動[17]
uncultivated 荒[28]

英漢索引表

viewpoint 看法[115] 觀點[99]

vigilance 戒心[19]

vigilant 警惕[99]

vigor 勁[56] 元氣[13] 幹勁[56] 朝氣[56]

vigorous 健壯[56] 勃勃[56] 起勁[56] 強壯[56] 蓬勃[56] 茁壯[110]

vilify 辱罵[55] 謾罵[76] 中傷[56]

villa 別墅[67] 山莊[67]

village 鄉[95] 鄉鎮[95] 村[95] 村落[95] 村莊[95] 村子[95] 農村[95] 莊[95]

village elder 鄉長[95]

villagers 村民[95] 鄉下人[95]

vinegar 醋[13]

vintage 陳年[15]

violate 違背[99] 違反[99] 違犯[99] 背[95] 侵犯[99]

violate a prohibition 違禁[96]

violate the rules 違規[96]

violence 暴力[99]

violent 兇猛[99] 暴[99] 暴力[95] 暴烈[95] 強暴[99] 強烈[95] 猛烈[99] 粗暴[99]

virgin 處男[76] 處女[76]

virtue 德[95] 賢德[12]

virtuous 衷[95] 烈[95] 賢[12] 賢淑[95]

virtuous and dutiful 賢惠[12]

virtuous and talented 賢能[12]

virtuous path 大道[76]

virus 病毒[13]

visa 簽證[55]

visage 面容[18]

vision 目光[114] 視覺[99] 視力[115]

visit 參觀[99] 探望[95] 造訪[95] 訪[95] 看[115]

visit parents 省親[95]

visit relatives 探親[95]

visitor 客人[95] 賓[76]

vista 景觀[99]

visually appealing 悅目[14]

vita 履歷[55]

vital 蓬勃[56]

vitality 元氣[13] 活力[99] 精力[99] 朝氣[56] 生命力[95]

vitamin 維他命[18]

vivacious 活潑[99]

vivid 生動[99]

vivid portrayal 傳神[95]

vocabulary 詞彙[55]

voice 嗓音[14] 聲音[14]

Voice of America 美國之音[14]

volcano 火山[12]

volleyball 排球[99]

volt 伏特[13]

voltage 電壓[13]

volume 卷[115] 冊[115] 編[95]

voluntarily 自願[13]

volunteer 志願[55] 志願者[55]

vomit 嘔吐[99] 吐[99]

vote 投票[99]

voters 選民[95]

vow 發誓[56]

voyage 航程[95]

vulgar 卑俗[99] 俗[99] 俗氣[99] 庸俗[99] 俚俗[113] 粗[117] 粗俗[113]

vulture 兀鷹[113]

W w

wages 工資[13]

wagon 馬車[77]

waist 腰[95] 腰部[95]

wait 守候[95] 待[95] 等[99] 等等[99] 俟[95] 俟候[95]

wait a moment 稍候[99] 等一會兒 (⇨ 一會兒[99])

wait and see 拭目以待[95] 觀望[99]

wait for 等待[99] 等候[99] 等著[99]

wait until 等到[95]

wait upon 伺候[95] 侍候[95]

waiter 跑堂[95] 侍者[95]

waive a right 棄權[95]

wake up 醒[55] 醒來[55] 睡醒[113]

Wales 威爾斯[95]

walk 行[95] 行走[95] 散步[95] 步履[95] 步行[95] 走[95] 走路[95]

walk forward 向前走 (⇨ 前[99])

walk off with 拿走[95] 帶走[95]

walk straight ahead 一直走[1]

walking stick 拐杖[95]

walkman 隨身聽[55]

wall 壁[95] 牆[95] 牆壁[95]

wallet 皮包[95]

wallow in 沈湎[95]

walnut 核桃[95]

wander 流浪[95] 遨遊[95]

wane 衰[95] 衰敗[99]

want 願意[95] 要[95] 欲[99] 想要[115]

want to 想[115]

wantonly 肆意[95] 大肆[95]

war 仗[95] 大戰[95] 戰[95] 戰爭[95]

war criminal 戰犯[95]

ward off 祛[95]

ward off evil 祛邪[99] 避邪[95]

ward off the cold 禦寒[95]

wardrobe 衣櫃[126]

warehouse 倉庫[95]

warfare 干戈[95] 戰事[95]

warlord 軍閥[95]

warm 殷勤[95] 慇懃[95] 親切[95] 親熱[95] 溫[95] 溫暖[95] 暖[95] 暖和[99]

warm air 暖氣[95]

warm and fed 溫飽[95]

warm up 熱身[95]

warmth 熱情[95]

warm-up exercises 熱身運動[95]

warn 警[95] 警告[99] 警戒[95] 告誡[95] 勸告[95]

warning 警報[95]

warp 經[95]

warp and woof 經緯[95]

Warring States 戰國[95]

Warring States Period 戰國時代[95]

warrior 壯士[95] 武士[95]

warship 艦[95] 艦艇[95]

wash 洗[95] 洗滌[95] 盥洗[95] 清洗[95] 淘[114]

wash away 滌除[95]

wash one's face 洗臉[95]

wash one's hands 洗手[95]

wash rice 淘米[114]

wash up 洗臉[95]

washbasin 臉盆[95] 盆子[95]

washing machine 洗衣機[95]

Washington 華盛頓[95]

washroom 盥洗室[95] 洗手間[95]

waste 浪費[95] 荒廢[95] 費[95] 糟蹋[95] 白費[95] 耗費[95]

waste away 消瘦[95]

waste material 廢物[95]

waste time 費時間[95]

wasteland 荒地[95]

watch 望[95] 視[115] 看[115] 錶[126]

watch and wait 窺伺[95]

watch from a distance 瞭望[95]

watch from the sidelines 旁觀[95]

watch over 看管[115] 看守[115] 監視[95]

water 水[95] 澆[95]

water and soil 水土[95]

water buffalo 水牛[95]

water chestnut 菱角[95]

water conservancy 水利[95]

water flowers 澆花[95]

water pipe 水管[95]

water plants 澆水[95]

water power 水力[3]
water tower 水塔[3]
waterfall 瀑布[13]
waterfowl 水鳥[3]
watermelon 西瓜[30]
waterway 航道[3]
waterwheel 水車[3]
watt 瓦特[109]
wave 浪[3] 浪潮[3] 波[63] 揮[58] 揮手[58]
waver 動搖[66] 搖曳[44]
wavering 幢幢[66]
waves 波浪[63]
wax 蠟[81]
way 做法[50] 法子[50] 途[49] 途徑[49] 方式[5] 道[46]
way of speaking 說法[11]
way out 臺階[5]
we 吾[5] 俺[120] 我們[43] 咱[5] 咱們[5]
weak 軟[3] 脆弱[85] 薄弱[3] 淡[82] 淡薄[82] 淡淡[82] 弱[184] 衰弱[3] 微弱[194]
weak point 破綻[12] 弱點[184]
weaken 減弱[3]
weakness 缺點[6] 弱點[184]
wealth 錢財[12] 財[24] 財富[24]
wealth and status 富貴[43]
wealthy 富有[43] 富裕[43]
weapons 武器[43] 武裝[81] 兵[12] 兵刃[12] 兵戎[81]
wear 戴[46] 佩帶[47] 著[81] 穿[81] 穿戴[81] 穿上[81]
wear glasses 戴眼鏡[46]
weary 疲勞[3] 疲憊[3] 疲倦[3] 疲累[3] 倦[120] 困[93]
weary of 厭倦[91]
weather 天氣[3] 天色[3] 氣候[3] 氣象[3]
weather forecast 天氣預報 (⇨ 預報[92])
weather report 氣象報告[91]

weave 織[93] 紐[93] 編[15] 編織[15]
weave in 穿插[84]
web 網[43] 絡[43]
website 網站[43]
wedding banquet 喜酒[66] 喜筵[66]
wedding ceremony 婚禮[100]
Wednesday 星期三[8] 禮拜三[8]
weeds 荒草[8] 雜草[8]
week 週[49] 星期[8] 禮拜[8]
weekend 週末[49]
weekly magazine 週刊[49]
weep 泣[8] 哭[8] 哭泣[8]
Wei Zheng 魏徵[89]
weigh 衡[4] 衡量[4] 推敲[84] 稱[8]
weight 加重[4] 份量[4] 重量[4]
weighted 加權[4]
weighted index 加權指數[4]
weird 怪[83] 詭異[9] 奇怪[83]
welcome 迎[43] 接[43] 歡迎[142]
Welcome! 歡迎[142] 歡迎光臨! (⇨ 光臨[4])
weld 焊接[9]
welfare 福利[43] 福祉[43]
well 井[97]
well-behaved 乖[43] 乖乖[43] 規規矩矩 (⇨ 規矩[7])
well-experienced 資歷很深[9]
well-informed 靈通[161]
well-known 有名[13] 名[27] 著名[8]
wellspring 泉源[3]
well-trained 熟練[8]
well-versed 熟[8]
West 西方[30]
west 西[30] 西方[30]
West Coast 西岸[30]

Western 西洋[30] 西部片[30]
Western Europe 西歐[30]
Western clothing 西裝[30]
Western food 西餐[30]
Western medicine 西醫[30]
western region 西部[30]
Westerner 西方人[30] 歐美人[9]
westernized 洋化[27]
wet 濕[93]
wet paint 油漆未乾[15]
whale 鯨魚[9]
wharf 碼頭[17]
what 甚麼[7] 怎麼[7] 怎麼[7] 何[7] 什麼[7] 啥[43] 那[16] 哪[16]
what kind 何等[7]
what time 何時[7] 幾時[7]
what's the harm 何妨[7]
wheat 小麥[7] 麥[60]
wheel 輪[15] 輪子[15]
when 何時[7] 幾時[7] 當[8]
when the time comes 屆時[7]
whenever 每次[16]
where 何處[7] 那裡[16] 哪裡[16] 哪兒[16]
whereabouts 下落[16]
whereabouts unknown 下落不明[16]
whet 磨[7]
whet the appetite 開味[3]
whether or not 是否[9]
which 孰[43] 何[7] 所[8] 那[16] 那個[16] 哪[16] 哪個[16] 哪些[16]
whichever 任何[31]
whiff 股[7]
while 一下[1] 一陣子[1]
while away 消磨[7]
while it's not too late 趁早[7]
whip 鞭撻[8] 鞭子[15]
whirlpool 漩渦[118]
whirlwind 旋風[118]
whisk 拂[93]

whisper 私語[17] 耳語[177]
whistle 嘯[3] 口哨[8] 吹口哨 (⇨ 口哨[8])
white 白[26] 白色[26]
White House 白宮[26]
white person 白人[26]
white rice 白飯[26]
white wine 白酒[26]
white-out fluid 修正液[93]
whitewash 粉刷[93]
who 孰[43] 何人[7] 誰[17]
whole 全[2] 整[88] 整個[88] 整體[88]
whole body 全身[2]
whole world 四海[63] 全球[2]
wholehearted 衷心[88]
wholeheartedly 一心[1] 全心[2] 專心[9]
wholesale 躉售[9]
whoop 吶喊[43]
whore 婊子[19]
why 怎[43] 怎麼[43] 何故[7] 何以[7] 為何[7] 為什麼[17] 為甚麼[17]
why is it necessary 何必[7]
why not 何妨[7]
wick 炷[9]
wicked 妖邪[9] 惡[166]
wicker 藤[127]
wickerwork 藤器[9]
wide 廣[43] 闊[89] 寬[114]
wide gap 鴻溝[31]
widely rumored 盛傳[9]
widespread 普遍[9]
widow 寡婦[9] 遺孀[95]
width 幅[89] 寬度[9]
wield 揮[58] 揮動[58]
wife 娘[9] 老婆[9] 妻[9] 妻子[9] 婦[9] 夫人[9] 太太[9]
wild 荒[8] 猖狂[9] 野[102]
wild beast 野獸[102]
wilderness 荒野[8] 曠野[9] 野[102]
wildlife 野生動物[102]
wildlife protection 保

育[74]

wilful 刁蠻[89] 任性[34]	wise 高明[81]	women's team 女子隊[14]	world war 世界大戰[26]
will 要[5] 志[16] 意願[88]	wish 願望[6] 願意[6] 心	wonder 納罕[88]	world wide web 萬維網
意志[65] 將[42] 將要[42]	想[81] 心願[83]	wonderful 妙[87] 美妙[87]	(⇨ 網[34])
遺囑[89] 會[14]	wish anxiously 巴不得[85]	wonton 餛飩[35]	worlds apart 迥然不同[87]
will of the people 人心[10]	wish but that 但願[88]	wood 木[17] 木頭[17]	worldwide 舉世[25]
will to fight 戰鬥意志[65]	wish well 祝[12]	woodpecker 啄木鳥[85]	worm 蟲[125] 蚰[135]
(⇨ 意志[65])	wistful 感慨[88]	wool blanket 毛毯[77]	worn-out 破[12] 破舊[12]
willing 願[6] 願意[6] 情	wit 風趣[89]	word 言[88] 單詞[12] 單	破爛[12]
願[89]	witch 巫婆[89]	字[136]	worried 著急[28] 憂[19] 憂
willing to give up 捨得[44]	witchdoctor 術士[10]	word by word 逐字[89]	慮[19]
willingly 樂意[88] 甘[89] 甘	with 跟[49] 與[49] 連[58]	word processor 文字處	worries 煩惱[19]
心[89] 甘願[89] 自願[89]	with all one's might 拼	理[19] 文書處理	worry 擔心[21] 擔憂
willow 楊柳[89] 柳[89]	命[89]	wording 字眼[89] 措辭[89]	慮[19] 操心[19] 愁[82]
willpower 毅力[79]	with own eyes 親眼[89]	words 語[9] 筆墨[13] 話[89]	憂[19] 焦慮[19]
win 贏[85] 贏得[85] 勝[12]	with own hands 親手[89]	辭[89]	worry about 惦念[89] 掛[73]
取勝[12]	with pleasure 欣然[89]	words and actions 言行[89]	掛念[72]
win a lottery prize 中彩[88]	withdraw 退[15] 撤[38] 撤	work 做事[89] 打工[89] 辦	worsen 變壞[153]
中獎[88]	出[38] 迴避[89]	事[89] 工[1] 工夫[9] 工	worship 崇[40] 崇拜[40] 膜
win an award 得獎[14]	withdraw funds 提款[89]	作[89] 功夫[9]	拜[40]
win honor 爭光[89]	withdraw troops 撤兵[88]	work as 當[49]	worship foreign things 崇
win over 拉攏[89]	wither 凋零[89] 乾枯[88] 萎	work hard 努力[79] 累[89]	洋[89]
wind 風[47]	縮[89]	下功夫 (⇨ 功夫[9])	worth 值[89]
wind around 纏繞[89]	wither away 枯萎[89]	work harder 加油[89]	worthwhile 值得[89] 合
wind of 風聲[47]	withered 枯[89] 枯竭[89] 乾	work in concert 呼應[89]	算[89] 划算[89]
winding 委曲[89] 曲折[135]	枯[89]	work on the computer 打	worthy 值得[89] 賢[89]
彎曲[153]	without 無[49] 沒[49]	電腦[89]	would it not be 豈不[89]
window 窗[144] 窗戶[144] 窗	without a hitch 順利[89]	work overtime 加班[89]	would rather 情願[89] 寧
子[144]	without authorization 逕	work part-time 打工[89] 兼	可[19] 寧願[19]
window shop 逛街[14]	自[89] 擅自[89]	差[89]	wound 創[85] 創傷[85] 傷
windstorm 暴風[89]	without basis 憑空[89]	work station 工作站[89]	口[89]
windward 上風[89]	without exception 無不[117]	work stoppage 停工[89]	wrap 包[18]
wine 酒[89] 葡萄酒[89]	通通[89]	work unit 單位[136]	wrath 憤怒[89]
wing 翼[49] 翅[49] 翅膀[89]	without restraint 肆意[89]	worker 工人[1]	wreath 花圈[89]
廂[114]	without the least 毫無[89]	workers and staff 職工[89]	wreck 擊毀[87]
wink 眨眼[89]	withstand 抵禦[89]	working class 工人階	wreckage 殘骸[89]
winter 冬[41] 冬季[41] 冬	witness 證人[89] 目睹[11]	級[51]	wrench 扭[89] 扳手[89]
天[41]	見證[14]	works 書籍[89] 著作[89]	wrest 奪取[89]
winter solstice 冬至[41]	witticism 俏皮話[89]	workshop 廠[89] 坊[89] 車	wrestle 搏[89] 搏鬥[89] 角
winter vacation 寒假[14]	witty 俏皮[89] 機敏[89] 機	間[58]	力[19] 摔跤[153]
wipe 擦[12] 揩[12] 拭[89] 抹[89]	智[89]	work-study 工讀[89]	wriggle 蠕動[89]
wipe away 揮[89]	wolf 狼[89]	world 界[9] 世[25] 世間[89]	wring 擰[116]
wipe out 抹殺[89]	woman 娘[89] 婦人[89] 女[51]	世界[89] 天地[89] 天	wring dry 擰乾[116]
wire 線[89] 鐵絲[89]	女人[89] 女子[54]	下[89]	wrinkle 皺[89] 皺紋[89]
wire fence 鐵絲網[89]	womb 子宮[55]	World Cup 世界杯 (⇨	wrinkle one's brow 皺眉[89]
wired 有線[89]	women 婦女[89]	杯[7])	wrist 腕[89] 腕子[89] 手
wireless 無線[71]	women and children 婦	World War II 第二次世	腕[89]
wisdom 智[32]	孺[14]	界大戰 (⇨ 大戰[26])	wristwatch 手錶[89]
	women's rights 女權[54]	world view 世界觀[86]	write 書寫[89] 撰寫[89]

著 寫 寫作
write a check 開支票 (⇨ 支票)
write a letter 寫信
write characters 寫字
write vertically 直著寫 豎著寫
writer 筆者 作者
writhe 蠕動
writing 筆墨 文 文字 寫作
writing brush 筆 毛筆
writing reform 文字改革
writing style 筆
writings 著作
written 書面
written invitation 請柬
written test 筆試
wrong 不對 錯 冤枉
wrong path 斜路
wronged 委屈
Wu Zetian 武則天

yard 院子 碼
yawn 哈欠
year 年 年度 年級 級 春秋 載
year after next 後年
year before last 前年
year by year 逐年
yearbook 年鑑
year-end 年底
year-end employee dinner 尾牙
yearn for 渴望
years 歲月
years old 歲
yeast 酵母
yell 嚷 嚷嚷
yellow 黃 黃色
Yellow Emperor 黃帝
Yellow River 黃河
yellow croaker 黃魚
yellow-brown 黃
yen 日幣 日圓
yes 是 是的
yesterday 昨 昨日 昨天
yesterday evening 昨晚
yet 尚 只是 卻 而
Yi people 彝族
yield 退讓 就範 讓 產量 謙讓 屈服
yielding 柔軟
yin 陰
yin and yang 陰陽
yoga 瑜珈
yogurt 酸奶
yoke 枷鎖
Yokohama 橫濱
you 你 您 妳 貴方
you all 你們 妳們
young 年輕 年青 年少 少 青
Young Pioneers 少年先鋒隊 (⇨ 先鋒)
young and tender 稚嫩
young girl 少女
young wife 少婦

young woman 小姐 女郎 女生 姐
young woman's heart 芳心
youngest child 么
Your Excellency 閣下
Your Majesty 陛下
your side 貴方
your turn 該你
your work 大作
youth 少年 青春 青年 年輕人
youthful 年青
yo-yo 扯鈴
yuan 元 塊 圓
Yuan Shih-kai 袁世凱
Yungang grottoes 雲岡石窟 (⇨ 石窟)
Yunnan Province 雲南
yurt 蒙古包

拼 音 索 引 表

This Romanized pronunciation index lists characters under all pronunciations which appear in the dictionary, including the Mandarin standards in both mainland Chinese and Taiwan. Ordering is first alphabetical and second by tone according to the 漢語拼音 standard.

In addition to individual characters, multi-characters words are also indexed, allowing the user to quickly locate an overheard word composed of unknown characters. Rather than looking through the dictionary character-by-character, the word can be found directly in this index.

The top number to the right of a character is the 文 reference number and the bottom number is the 字 reference number.

a	ānhuī 安徽	àonǎo 懊惱	bàzhàn 霸佔	bān 版 板 阪 闆
a 啊	ànjiàn 案件	àoshì 傲視	bāzhǎng 巴掌	bàn 扮 辦 瓣 片 半 伴 絆 拌
ābīnggē 阿兵哥	ānjìng 安靜	áoyè 熬夜	bàzhǔ 霸主	bànàn 辦案
āfùhàn 阿富汗	ānmián 安眠	àoyóu 遨遊	bai	bānbái 斑白
āgēntíng 阿根廷	ànmó 按摩	àoyùn 奧運	bāi 掰	bǎnběn 版本
ālābó 阿拉伯	ànnà 按捺	àozhōu 澳洲	bái 白	bāndài 班代
ālǐshān 阿里山	ānníng 安寧	ba	bǎi 百 佰 擺	bàndǎo 半島 絆倒
āyí 阿姨	ànnǐu 按鈕	bā 八 叭 扒 捌 巴 吧 疤 芭 笆	bài 拜 敗	bàndào 搬到
ai	ānpái 安排	bá 犮 拔 跋	bàibài 拜拜	bǎndèng 板凳
āi 哎 挨 埃 哀	ānquán 安全	bǎ 把 靶	bàiběi 敗北	bāndǐ 班底
ái 挨 癌	ànrán 黯然	bà 把 爸 龍 罷 霸 壩	bǎibù 擺佈	bàndiǎn 半點
ǎi 藹 毒 矮	ànshā 暗殺	ba 吧	báicài 白菜	bāndiǎn 斑點
ài 艾 礙 愛 曖	ànshì 暗示	bàba 爸爸	báichī 白痴 白癡	bànfā 頒發
āidǎ 挨打	àntáng 庵堂	bǎbǐng 把柄	bǎidòng 擺動	bànfǎ 辦法
āidào 哀悼	ānwèi 安慰	bābude 巴不得	báifàn 白飯	bàngōngshì 辦公室
àiěrlán 愛爾蘭	ānwěn 安穩	bàchù 罷黜	bàifǎng 拜訪	bānjī 扳機 班機
àifǔ 愛撫	ānxīn 安心	bàdào 霸道	báifèi 白費	bānjí 班級
àiguó 愛國	ànzhào 按照	bǎfēng 把風	bǎifēn 百分	bānjiāoshí 絆腳石
àihào 愛好	ànzhe 按著	bàgōng 罷工	bǎigōng 白宮	bànjīnbāliǎng 半斤八兩
àihù 愛護	ānzhì 安置	bāgǔ 八股	bǎihé 百合	bànjìng 半徑
āijí 埃及	ànzhōng 暗中	bāguà 八卦	báihuà 白話	bànlǐ 辦理
āijìn 挨近	ànzhù 按住	bāhén 疤痕	bǎihuāqífàng 百花齊放	bànlǚ 伴侶
āilián 哀憐	ānzhuāng 安裝	bājīsītǎn 巴基斯坦	bàihuài 敗壞	bānmǎ 斑馬
āimà 挨罵	ànzi 案子	bājiāo 芭蕉	bǎijiāzhēngmíng 百家爭鳴	bǎnquán 版權
àimèi 曖昧	ang	bājiè 八戒	bǎijiàzi 擺架子	bànshǎng 半晌
àimù 愛慕	āng 骯	bājié 巴結	báijǐu 白酒	bànshì 辦事
àiqián 愛錢	áng 卬 昂	bàkè 罷課	bǎikēquánshū 百科全書	bànshǒu 扳手
àiqíng 愛情	àng 盎	bālè 芭樂	bàinián 拜年	bànshù 半數
āiqiú 哀求	ánggùi 昂貴	bàle 罷了	báirén 白人	bànsúi 伴隨
àirén 愛人	ángrán 昂然	bālèsītǎn 巴勒斯坦	báisè 白色	bàntiān 半天
àishàng 愛上	ángrán 盎然	bǎlěi 芭蕾	bǎishè 擺設	bàntúérfèi 半途而廢
àixí 愛惜	āngzāng 骯髒	bālí 巴黎	báitiān 白天	bānwén 斑紋
àixīn 愛心	ao	bàmiǎn 罷免	bàituō 拜託	bànyǎn 扮演
āiyā 哎呀	āo 凹	bānámǎ 巴拿馬	bǎituō 擺脫	bànyè 半夜
áizhèng 癌症	áo 敖 熬 遨	bàquán 霸權	báiwàn 百萬	bānyùn 搬運
àizībìng 愛滋病	ǎo 拗 襖	báshè 跋涉	bǎixiānggǔo 百香果	bānzhǎng 班長
āizòu 挨揍	ào 拗 傲 奧 澳 懊	bǎshǒu 把守 把手	bǎixìng 百姓	
an	àodàlìyǎ 澳大利亞	bàwáng 霸王	báizhòu 白晝	
ān 庵 安 鞍	àodìlì 奧地利	bǎwò 把握	báizì 白字	
ǎn 俺	āojìn 凹進	bāxī 巴西	báizú 白族	
àn 按 案 岸 暗 黯	àomàn 傲慢	bǎxì 把戲	ban	
āndìng 安定	àomén 澳門		bān 扳 頒 班	
ānfēitāmìng 安非他命	àomì 奧祕			
ānhào 暗號	àomiào 奧妙			

bǐlì 比例	biān 編 邊	biǎnyì 貶義	biǎozi 婊子	bìngqì 摒棄
bǐlìshí 比利時	biǎn 貶 扁 蝙	biànyú 便於	**bie**	bīngqílín 冰淇淋
bǐlòu 鄙陋	匾	biānyuán 邊緣	bié 別	bìngqiě 並且
bǐlù 筆錄	biàn 升 便 辨	biànzhèng 辯證	biéchù 別處	bìngqíng 病情
bǐlǜ 比率	辯 辨 辨	biǎnzhí 貶值	biéde 別的	bìngrén 病人
bìlǜ 碧綠	遍 變 釆	biānzhī 編織	biémíng 別名	bīngrèn 兵刃
bìmén 閉門	biànbié 辨別	biānzhì 編制 編製	biérén 別人	bīngróng 兵戎
bìmiǎn 避免	biànchéng 變成	biānzhuàn 編撰	biéshù 別墅	bīngrù 併入
bǐmíng 筆名	biānchuí 邊陲	biānzi 鞭子	biéwài 別外	bīngshān 冰山
bǐmò 筆墨	biǎndan 扁擔	biànzi 辮子	biézhì 別緻	bìngshì 病逝
bìnàn 避難	biàndāng 便當	biānzuǎn 編纂	**bin**	bìngtūn 併吞
bǐnǐ 比擬	biànde 變得	**biao**	bīn 賓 檳 瀕	bǐngxī 屏息
bīnǚ 婢女	biàndòng 變動	biāo 標 鏢 彪	彬 瀕 斌	bīngxiāng 冰箱
bīpò 逼迫	biǎné 匾額	森 飆 彪	bīn 鬢	bīngxié 冰鞋
bǐqǐ 比起	biànfǎ 變法	biǎo 表 婊	bīnbīn 彬彬	bīngyì 兵役
bìrán 必然	biànfú 便服	鋲 裱	bīnfà 鬢髮	bìngzhèng 病症
bǐrú 比如	biānfú 蝙蝠	biǎobái 表白	bīnguǎn 賓館	bìngzhòng 並重
bǐsà 比薩	biǎnfú 蝙蝠	biāobǎng 標榜	bīnláng 檳榔	bīngzhù 冰柱
bǐsài 比賽	biàngé 變革	biǎobèi 裱褙	bīnlín 瀕臨	**bo**
bìsè 鼻塞	biàngēng 變更	biāobǐng 彪炳	bìnmáo 鬢毛	剝 撥 播
bìsè 閉塞	biànhù 辯護	biāochē 飆車	**bing**	bó 駁 葡 脖
bìshè 敝舍	biànhuà 變化	biǎodá 表達	bīng 冰 兵	勃 渤 薄
bìshēng 畢生	biànhuài 變壞	biǎodì 表弟	bǐng 丙 柄	博 膊 搏
bǐshì 筆試	biànhuàn 變換	biāodiǎn 標點	炳 餅 屏	白 帛 柏
bǐshí 彼時	變幻	biǎogē 表哥	bǐng 稟 秉 並	伯 舶 泊
bǐshì 鼻視	biānjí 編輯	biǎogé 表格	bìng 病 並 并	bǒ 簸
bǐshǒu 匕首	biānjì 邊際	biāohuì 標會	併 摒	bǒ 簸 風 播
bíshuǐ 鼻水	biānjiāng 邊疆	biǎojiě 表姐	bīngbàng 冰棒	bóài 博愛
bítì 鼻涕	biànjiě 辯解	biǎolù 表露	bǐngbǎo 冰雹	bóbo 伯伯
bíxí 鼻息	biānjiè 邊界	biǎomèi 表妹	bìngbào 稟報	bōcài 菠菜
bìxià 陛下	biànjié 變節	biǎomiàn 表面	bīngchá 冰茶	bóchì 駁斥
bìxié 避邪	biànlì 便利	biāomíng 標明	bǐngchéng 秉承	bōchū 播出
bìxū 必須 必需	biànlùn 辯論	biǎomíng 表明	bìngchú 摒除	bōdòng 波動
bìyào 必要	biānpái 編排	biāoqiān 標籤	bīngdǎo 冰島	bódòu 搏鬥
bìyè 畢業	biānpào 鞭炮	biāoqiāng 標槍	bīngdòng 冰凍	bōduó 剝奪
bǐyì 神益	biànqiān 變遷	biǎoqíng 表情	bìngdú 病毒	bōfā 勃發
bǐyí 鄙夷	biànrèn 辨認	biǎoshì 表示	bìngfáng 病房	bōfàng 播放
bǐyù 比喻	biànshì 辨識	biǎotài 表態	bìngfēi 並非	bófù 伯父
bìyù 碧玉	biànshù 變數	biāotí 標題	bǐngfù 稟賦	bóhǎi 渤海
bìyùn 避孕	biāntà 鞭撻	biǎoxiàn 表現	bǐnggān 餅乾	bóhuí 駁回
bǐzhě 筆者	biàntài 變態	biǎoyǎn 表演	bǐnggào 稟告	bōjí 波及
bīzhēn 逼真	biàntōng 變通	biǎoyáng 表揚	bīnggùn 冰棍	bójì 簸箕
bízi 鼻子	biànwéi 變為	biāoyǔ 標語	bīnghé 冰河	bójué 伯爵
bízǔ 鼻祖	biànxiàng 變相	biǎozhāng 表彰	bìnghuàn 病患	bōkuǎn 撥款
bìzuǐ 閉嘴	biānxiě 編寫	biǎozhēng 表徵	bīngkuài 冰塊	bóláipǐn 舶來品
bian	biànyàqì 變壓器	biāozhì 標誌	bīnglì 兵力	bōlán 波蘭
biān 鞭 蝙	biànyán 弁言	biāozhǔn 標準	bìngliè 並列	
	biànyī 便衣		bīngmǎ 兵馬	

bōlàng 波浪	bùfá 步伐	bǔrǔ 哺乳	cáibǎo 財寶	cánfèi 殘廢
bōlí 玻璃	bùfán 不凡	bùshǎo 不少	cāicè 猜測	cānguān 參觀
bólín 柏林	bùfáng 不妨	bùshèng 不勝	cáichǎn 財產	cānguǎn 餐館
bōluó 菠蘿	bùfèn 部分 部份	bùshí 不時	càidān 菜單	cánhái 殘骸
bómǔ 伯母	bùfū 不敷	bǔshì 卜筮	càidāo 菜刀	cánjí 殘疾
bóqǐ 勃起	bùgǎn 不敢	bùshī 布施	cáifá 財閥	cānjiā 參加
bórán 勃然	bùgào 佈告	bùshǒu 部首	cǎifǎng 採訪	cānjiǎn 蠶繭
bóruò 薄弱	bùgù 不顧	bùshǔ 部署	cáiféng 裁縫	cānjiàn 參見
bóshì 博士	bǔguà 卜卦	bùsú 不俗	cáifù 財富	cānjīn 餐巾
bōshìdùn 波士頓	bùguǎn 不管	bùtiáo 布條	cáigàn 才幹	cǎnjù 慘劇
bóshù 柏樹	bùguò 不過	bùtíng 不停	cǎigòu 採購	cānjù 餐具
bōsòng 播送	bùhé 不合	bùtōng 不通	càiguǎn 菜館	cānkǎo 參考
bōtāo 波濤	bùhuì 不會	bùtóng 不同	cǎihóng 彩虹	cánkù 殘酷
bówù 博物	bùjí 不及	bǔxí 補習	cáihuá 才華	cánkuì 慚愧
bōxuē 剝削	bùjiàn 不見	bùxiào 不肖 不孝	cāijì 猜忌	cànlàn 燦爛
bōyīn 播音	bùjiàndé 不見得	bùxíng 不行	cǎijí 採集	cānmóu 參謀
bóyóu 柏油	bùjīn 不禁	bùxìng 不幸	cáijiǎn 裁減	cánrěn 殘忍
bōzhé 波折	bùjǐn 不僅	bùxíng 步行	cáijīng 財經	cánshā 殘殺
bōzhǒng 播種	bùjìn 不盡	bùxiǔ 不朽	cǎikuàng 採礦	cānshù 參數
bōzhǒng 播種	bùjiǔ 不久	bǔyào 補藥	cáiliào 材料	cánsī 蠶絲
bózi 脖子	bǔjiù 補救	bùyī 不一	cǎinà 採納	cāntīng 餐廳
bu	bùjú 佈局	bùyí 不宜	cáinéng 才能	cǎntòng 慘痛
bǔ 卜 哺 補 捕	bùkān 不堪	bùyǐ 不已	cáipàn 裁判	cānyì 參議
bù 不 部 布 佈 怖 簿 步 埠	bǔkǎo 補考	bùyòng 不用	cǎipiào 彩票	cányú 殘餘
bùān 不安	bùkěsīyì 不可思議	bùyuè 不悅	cǎiqǔ 採取	cānyù 參與
bùbì 不必	bùkěn 不肯	bùzài 不再 不在	cǎiquàn 彩券	cánzhā 殘渣
bùbiàn 不便	bùkuài 不快	bùzhǎng 部長	cǎisè 彩色	cānzhǎn 參展
bùcè 不測	bùlǐ 不理	bùzhì 佈置	càisè 菜色	cánzhàng 殘障
bǔcháng 補償	bùlì 不利	bùzhībùjué 不知不覺	cáiwù 財務	cǎnzhòng 慘重
bùchì 不啻	bùliào 不料	bùzhù 補助	càixì 菜系	cǎnzhuàng 慘狀
bǔchōng 補充	bùlùn 不論	bǔzhuō 捕捉	cāixiǎng 猜想	cānzhuó 參酌
bǔcí 卜辭	bùluò 部落	bùzi 簿子	cǎixíng 採行	**cang**
bùcuò 不錯	bùlǚ 步履	bùzōu 步驟	càiyáo 菜肴	cāng 倉 滄 蒼 艙
bùdài 布袋	bùmǎn 不滿	**ca**	cāiyí 猜疑	cáng 藏
bùdàn 不但	bùmén 部門	cā 擦	cǎiyòng 採用	cāngbái 蒼白
bùdàng 不當	bùmiǎn 不免	cāshāng 擦傷	cáiyuán 財源	cāngcù 倉促
bùdào 步道	bùmiào 不妙	cāshì 擦拭	cǎiyún 彩雲	cāngcuì 蒼翠
bùdé 不得	bùnàifán 不耐煩	**cai**	cáizhèng 財政	cānghǎi 滄海
bùdébù 不得不	bùnéng 不能	cāi 猜	cáizhì 才智	cāngjié 倉頡
bùdéliǎo 不得了	bùnéngbù 不能不	cái 才 材 裁 財 纔	**can**	cāngkù 倉庫
bùdéyǐ 不得已	bùpiānbùyǐ 不偏不倚		cān 參 餐	cānglǎo 蒼老
bùdiào 步調	bǔpǐn 補品	cǎi 采 彩 採 睬 踩	cán 蠶 殘 慚	cāngmáng 蒼茫
bùduàn 不斷	bùrán 不然		cǎn 慘	cángnì 藏匿
bùduì 不對	bùrěn 不忍		càn 粲 璨 燦	cángshū 藏書
bùduìjìn 不對勁	bùrú 不如	cài 蔡 菜	cǎnbài 慘敗	cāngyíng 蒼蠅
			cǎndàn 慘淡	**cao**
			cándòu 蠶豆	cāo 操 糙

cáo 曹 嘈 槽
cǎo 艸 草
cào 肏
cǎoàn 草案
cāochǎng 操場
cǎodì 草地
cǎogēn 草根
cǎopíng 草坪
cāoshǒu 操守
cǎoshū 草書
cǎoshuài 草率
cǎowū 草屋
cǎoxí 草席
cāoxīn 操心
cǎoyuán 草原
cáozá 嘈雜
cāozòng 操縱
cāozuò 操作

ce

cè 㿝 策 冊
廁 側 測
cèdìng 測定
cèdòng 策動
cèhuà 策劃
cèliáng 測量
cèlüè 策略
cèmiàn 側面
cèshì 測試
cèsuǒ 廁所
cèyàn 測驗
cèzi 冊子
cèzì 測字

cen

cēn 參差
cēncī 參差

ceng

céng 曾 層
céngcéng 層層
céngcì 層次
céngjīng 曾經

cha

chā 叉 杈 差
臿 插
chá 察 茶 查
碴
chà 杈 差 岔
詫 剎
chábēi 茶杯

chābié 差別
chābùduō 差不多
cháchū 查出
chádùi 查對
chādùi 插隊
chāé 差額
cháfáng 茶房
cháguǎn 茶館
cháhú 茶壺
chāhuā 插花
cháhùo 查獲
chájǐ 茶几
chājìn 插進
chājù 差距
chájù 茶具
chájué 察覺
chákàn 察看, 查看
chákòu 查扣
chàlù 岔路
chànà 剎那
chànuó 剎那
chāqū 插曲
chár 碴兒
chārù 插入
chāshǒu 插手
chātóu 插頭
chātú 插圖
cháxún 查詢
chāyāng 插秧
cháyè 茶葉
chāyì 差異
chāyì 詫異
cháyìguǎn 茶藝館
cháyuán 茶園
chàzi 岔子
chāzǔi 插嘴
chāzùo 插座

chai

chāi 釵 差 拆
cháichú 拆除
cháidiào 拆掉
cháikāi 拆開
chāiqiǎn 差遣
chāisàn 拆散
chāiyì 差役

cháiyóu 柴油

chan

chān 攙
chán 蟾 孱 潺
廛 纏 禪
蟬 毚
chǎn 產 剷 鏟
闡
chàn 顫 懺
chánchán 潺潺
chǎnchū 產出
chǎnchú 剷除
chàndòng 顫動
chàndǒu 顫抖
chānfú 攙扶
chànhùi 懺悔
chánlián 蟬聯
chǎnliàng 產量
chǎnmíng 闡明
chǎnnéng 產能
chǎnpǐn 產品
chǎnquán 產權
chánrào 纏繞
chánrùo 孱弱
chǎnshēng 產生
chǎnshì 闡釋
chǎnshù 闡述
chánsì 禪寺
chánwù 禪悟
chǎnyè 產業
chānzá 攙雜
chǎnzhí 產值
chǎnzi 鏟子
chánzōng 禪宗
chánzú 纏足

chang

chāng 昌 猖
娼
cháng 長 償
裳 常 嫦
嘗 腸 場
chǎng 敞 廠
場
chàng 悵 悵
唱 倡 暢

chángcháng 常常
chángchéng 長程
長城
chángchù 長處
chángchūn 長春
chángchūnténg 長春藤
chǎngdì 場地
chángdù 長度
chángduǎn 長短
chángé 嫦娥
chǎngfáng 廠房
chángfù 償付
chànggē 唱歌
chǎnghé 場合
chánghuán 償還
chāngjì 娼妓
chángjiāng 長江
chángjǐnglù 長頸鹿
chángjiǔ 長久
chángjué 猖獗
chǎngkāi 敞開
chángkè 常客
chàngkuài 暢快
chāngkuáng 猖狂
chǎngmiàn 場面
chāngmíng 昌明
chàngpiàn 唱片
chángqī 長期
chángrèn 常任
chángshā 長沙
chǎngshāng 廠商
chángshèng 昌盛
chángshì 常識 嘗試
chángshòu 長壽
chángshù 常數
chǎngsuǒ 場所
chàngtōng 暢通
chángtú 長途
chàngxiāo 暢銷
chángzhài 償債
chángzhǎng 廠長
chángzhēng 長征

chao

chāo 抄 鈔 超

cháo 朝 潮 嘲
巢
chǎo 炒 吵
chāochū 超出
cháodài 朝代
chāoé 超額
chǎofàn 炒飯
cháofèng 嘲諷
cháogòng 朝貢
chāoguò 超過
chāojí 超級
cháoliú 潮流
chǎomài 炒賣
chǎomiàn 炒麵
cháonòng 嘲弄
chāopiào 鈔票
chāoqiáng 超強
chǎorǎng 吵嚷
chāorén 超人
cháoshī 潮濕
cháotíng 朝廷
chāoxí 抄襲
cháoxì 潮汐
cháoxiān 朝鮮
cháoxiào 嘲笑
chāoxiě 抄寫
cháoyě 朝野
cháoyuè 超越
cháozhe 朝著
chāozhòng 超重

che

chē 車
chě 扯
chè 徹 撤 撤
轍 屮 掣
chèbǎ 車把
chèbīng 撤兵
chèchū 撤出
chēdào 車道
chèdǐ 徹底
chēfèi 車費
chēhuò 車禍
chējiān 車間
chēkù 車庫

gèbié 個別　　gēbó 胳膊　　gēcǎo 割草　　gēchàng 歌唱　　géchú 革除　　gēchú 割除　　gēcí 歌辭　　gèdì 各地　　géduàn 割斷　　géduàn 隔斷　　gège 各個　　gēgē 哥哥　　gègè 個個　　géhé 隔閡　　géjú 格局　　gējù 歌劇　　géjué 隔絕　　gélí 隔離　　gélóu 閣樓　　gémìng 革命　　génián 隔年　　gēqǔ 歌曲　　gèrén 個人　　géshì 格式　　gèshìgèyàng 各式各樣　　gēshǒu 歌手　　gètǐ 個體　　gétiān 隔天　　gētīng 歌廳　　géwài 格外　　gèwèi 各位　　géxià 閣下　　géxīn 革新　　gēxīng 歌星　　gèxìng 個性　　géyán 格言　　géyáo 歌謠　　géyīn 隔音　　géyuán 閣員　　gēzhì 擱置　　gèzhǒng 各種　　gèzì 各自　　gèzi 個子　　gēzi 鴿子

gei
gěi 給　　gěiyǔ 給予

gen
gēn 根　跟　　gèn 艮　亙　　gēnběn 根本　　gēnchú 根除　　gēnjī 根基　　gēnjù 根據　　gēnqián 跟前　　gēnshàng 跟上　　gēnshēndìgù 根深蒂固　　gēnsuí 跟隨　　gēnyuán 根源　　gēnzi 根子

geng
gēng 庚　更　耕　　gěng 梗　埂　耿　　gèng 更　　gēngdì 耕地　　gēngdié 更迭　　gēngdòng 更動　　gèngduō 更多　　gēnggǎi 更改　　gěnggài 梗概　　gěnggěngyúhuái 耿耿於懷　　gēnghuàn 更換　　gèngjiā 更加　　gēngtián 耕田　　gèngwéi 更為　　gēngxīn 更新　　gēngyún 耕耘　　gēngzhèng 更正　　gěngzhí 耿直　　gēngzǐzhīyì 庚子之役　　gēngzǔ 梗阻　　gēngzuò 耕作

gong
gōng 工　肱　供　恭　龔　公　弓　躬　宮　　gǒng 汞　拱　鞏　　gòng 共　供　貢　　gōngān 公安　　gōngbào 公報　　gōngbù 公佈　公布　　gōngbùyìngqíu 供不應求　　gòngchǎn 共產　　gòngchǎng 工廠　　gōngchē 公車　　gōngchéng 工程　　gōngchǐ 公尺　　gòngchǔ 共處　　gòngcí 供詞　　gòngcún 共存　　gōngdé 功德　　gōngdì 工地　　gōngdiàn 宮殿　　gōngdú 工讀　　gòngfěi 共匪　　gōngfèi 公費　　gōngfèn 公分　　gòngfèng 供奉　　gōngfū 工夫　功夫　　gōnggào 公告　　gōnggòng 公共　　gōnggù 鞏固　　gōngguān 公關　　gōnghài 公害　　gònghé 共和　　gōnghè 恭賀　　gōnghùi 公會　工會　　gōngjǐ 供給　　gōngjī 公雞　　gōngjí 攻擊　　gōngjì 功績　　gōngjiàn 弓箭　　gōngjiàng 工匠　　gōngjīn 公斤　　gōngjìng 恭敬　　gōngjù 工具　　gōngkāi 公開　　gōngkè 公克　功課　　gōngkuǎn 公款

gōngláo 功勞　　gōnglǐ 公釐　　gōnglǐ 公理　公里　　gōnglì 公立　功利　　gōnglù 公路　　gònglùn 公論　　gōngmén 공門　　gōngmín 公民　　gòngmíng 共鳴　　gōngnéng 功能　　gōngníu 公牛　　gōngpíng 公平　　gōngpú 公僕　　gǒngqiáo 拱橋　　gōngqǐng 公頃　　gōngrán 公然　　gòngrèn 供認　　gōngrèn 公認　　gōngrén 工人　　gōngshè 公社　　gōngshēng 公升　　gòngshì 共識　　gōngshì 公事　公式　攻勢　　gǒngshǒu 拱手　　gōngsī 公司　　gōngsūn 公孫　　gòngtōng 共通　　gòngtóng 共同　　gōngwéi 恭維　　gōngwù 公務　　gōngxǐ 恭喜　　gòngxiàn 貢獻　　gòngxiǎng 共享　　gōngxiào 功效　　gōngxíng 弓形　　gōngxū 供需　　gōngxūn 功勳　　gōngyǎng 供養　　gōngyè 工業　　gōngyì 公益　　gōngyìng 供應　　gōngyíng 公營　　gōngyòng 公用　功用　　gòngyǒu 共有

gōngyǒu 公有　工友　　gōngyù 公寓　　gōngyuán 公元　公園　　gōngyuē 公約　　gòngzhài 公債　　gōngzhèng 公正　　gōngzhì 公制　　gōngzhòng 公眾　　gōngzhǔ 公主　　gōngzī 工資　　gōngzuò 工作

gou
gōu 句　鉤　勾　溝　　gǒu 苟　狗　　gòu 夠　詬　垢　構　購　媾　　gǒuān 苟安　　gòubìng 詬病　　gòuchéng 構成　　gòuduō 夠多　　gòujié 勾結　　gòumà 詬罵　　gòumǎi 購買　　gǒupì 狗屁　　gòuqiàng 夠嗆　　gǒuqiě 苟且　　gōuqú 溝渠　　gōutōng 溝通　　gòuwù 購物　　gòuxiǎng 構想　　gōuyǐn 勾引　　gòuzào 構造　　gòuzhì 購置

gu
gǔ 及　估　姑　菇　辜　沽　呱　孤　　gǔ 賈　古　詁　股　穀　谷　鼓　蠱　骨　　gù 故　固　錮　雇　僱　顧　楛　　gǔbā 古巴

huà 匕 化 畫	huásuàn 划算	句話說	huāngliáng 荒涼	húiguó 回國
劃 話 華	huātán 花壇	huànjué 幻覺	huánglùn 謬論	húihé 回合
huābàn 花瓣	huàtí 話題	huānlè 歡樂	huāngmáng 慌忙	hùihé 會合
huábǎn 滑板	huàtú 畫圖	huǎnmàn 緩慢	huāngmiù 荒謬	hùihèn 悔恨
huàbào 畫報	huáxià 華夏	huànnàn 患難	huángniú 黃牛	huīhóng 恢弘
huábiàn 嘩變	huáxiáng 滑翔	huànqián 換錢	huángpí 黃錢	húihuà 回話
huábīng 滑冰	huàxué 化學	huánrào 環繞	huǎngrán 恍然	hùihuà 會話 繪
huábù 華埠	huáxuě 滑雪	huānxǐ 歡喜	huángsè 黃色	畫
huáchá 花茶	huáyì 華裔	huànxiǎng 幻想	huāngtáng 荒唐	huīhuáng 輝煌
huáchuán 划船	huáyǔ 華語	huànxiàng 幻象	huángtóng 黃銅	huīhuò 揮霍
huàdìzìfēng 畫地自封	huāyuán 花園	huānxiào 歡笑	huāngyě 荒野	húijí 匯集
huādiàn 花店	huàzhǎn 畫展	huānyíng 歡迎	huángyín 荒淫	húijiā 回家
huāduǒ 花朵	huázhòngqǔchǒng	huànyǒu 患有	huángyóu 黃油	húijiàn 會見
huàféi 化肥	嘩眾取寵	huànzhě 患者	huángyú 黃魚	húijiào 回教
huāfèi 花費	huàzhuāng 化妝		huángzhǒng 荒塚	huījìn 灰燼
huāfěn 花粉		huang	huángzhǒngrén 黃	húijué 回絕
huàfēn 劃分	huai	huāng 喪 荒	種人	hùikòu 回扣
huáfǔ 華府	huái 徊 踝 褢	慌	huǎngzi 幌子	hùikuǎn 匯款
huàhéwù 化合物	懷 淮	hui		húikuì 回饋
huàhuà 畫畫	huái 壞	huáng 皇 凰	hui	húilai 回來
huāhuāgōngzǐ 花花	huàichù 壞處	蝗 惶 遑	灰 恢 詼	hùilù 賄賂
公子	huáihé 淮河	徨 隍 煌	徽 揮 輝	húilǜ 匯率
huāhuì 花卉	huàihuà 壞話	王 黃 磺	暉	hùimiàn 會面
huájī 滑稽	huàishì 壞事	潢 簧	huí 回 迴 蛔	hǔimiè 毀滅
huàjiā 畫家	huáiyí 懷疑	huǎng 晃 幌	huǐ 悔 誨 虫	húipiào 匯票
huālā 嘩啦	huáiyùn 懷孕	恍 謊	毀 燬 會	hùiqí 晦氣
huālán 花籃	huan	huàng 晃	huì 諱 賄 喙	húiqù 回去
huálì 華麗	huān 歡	huāngcǎo 荒草	穢 誨 晦	hùirù 匯入
huālián 花蓮	huán 景 還 環 隼	huángchóng 蝗蟲	惠 卉	húisè 灰色
huáliū 滑溜	huǎn 緩	huàngdàng 晃蕩	彗 慧 彙	hùishāng 會商
huàmíng 化名	huàn 豢 幻	huāngdǎo 荒島	會 繪 薈	hùishè 會社
huánán 華南	奐 換 喚 宦	huángdì 皇帝	燴 薈	húishì 回事
huāpíng 花瓶	瘓 煥 宦	huāngdì 荒地	huǐbàng 毀謗	hùishì 灰市
huáqián 花錢	患	huángdì 黃帝	huǐbào 回報	hùishōu 回收
huáqiáo 華僑	huánbǎo 環保	huángdòu 黃豆	huíbì 迴避	huīshǒu 揮手
huāquān 花圈	huánběn 還本	huāngfèi 荒廢	hùibiān 彙編	húisù 回溯
huárán 譁然	huànbìng 患病	huánggōng 皇宮	huíbǐng 回稟	hùitán 會談
huárén 華人	huànchéng 換成	huángguā 黃瓜	hūichén 灰塵	húitóu 回頭
huàshān 華山	huàndēng 幻燈	huánghé 黃河	húichóng 蛔蟲	húiwèi 回味
huàshétiānzú 畫蛇	huànfā 煥發	huánghòu 皇后	hùicì 薈萃	hùiwù 會晤
添足	huànguān 宦官	huǎnghū 恍惚	huídá 回答	húixiǎng 回響 迴
huāshēng 花生	huǎnhé 緩和	huǎnghuà 謊話	huídào 回到	想 迴想
huáshèngdùn 華盛	huānhū 歡呼	huánghuā 黃花	huīdòng 揮動	hùixié 詼諧
頓	huǎnhuǎn 緩緩	huánghūn 黃昏	huífù 回覆	húixìn 回信
huàshí 化石	huànjiě 緩解	huángjīn 黃金	huīfù 恢復	hùixīn 灰心
huàshì 華氏	huánjié 環節	huángkǒng 惶恐	hùigù 回顧	húixīng 彗星
huáshǔ 滑鼠	huánjìng 環境		hùiguǐ 回歸	hùixuǎn 賄選
	huànjùhuàshuō 換		hǔiguò 悔過	hùiyán 諱言

jìsuàn 計算　jítā 吉他　jìtán 祭壇　jítǐ 集體　jítuán 集團　jìtuō 寄託　jìwàng 寄望　jíwéi 極爲　jīwěijiǔ 雞尾酒　jíxiàn 極限　jíxiáng 吉祥　jīxiàng 跡象　jīxiào 譏笑 績效　jīxiè 機械　jìxìn 寄信　jīxíng 畸形　jíxǔ 幾許　jìxù 繼續　jīxù 積蓄　jīyā 羈押　jìyì 記憶 技藝　jīyīn 基因　jíyóu 集郵　jìyù 覬欲　jíyú 急於　jīyú 基於　jīyù 機遇　jǐyú 覬覦　jìyuán 紀元　jìzài 記載　jízào 急躁　jìzhào 吉兆　jìzhě 記者　jízhěn 急診　jīzhì 機制 機智　jīzhòng 擊中　jízhōng 集中　jìzhù 記住 濟助　jǐzhuī 脊椎　jìzǔ 祭祖

jia
jiā 加 珈 嘉 枷 茄 夾　jiāshàng 加上　jiāshè 假設　jiāshēn 加深

jiā 佳 家 傢　jiá 夾 頰 戛　jiǎ 限 假 賈 甲　jià 假 價 架 駕 嫁 稼　jiābān 加班　jiābèi 加倍　jiābīn 嘉賓　jiācháng 家常　jiāchóng 甲蟲　jiāchù 家畜　jiādiàn 家電　jiādìng 假定　jiāfǎ 加法　jiàgé 價格　jiàgěi 嫁給　jiāgōng 加工　jiàgòu 架構　jiǎgǔwén 甲骨文　jiāhuǒ 傢伙　jiàhuò 嫁禍　jiàjì 家計　jiǎjiǎng 嘉獎　jiāzhōu 加州　jiàjiào 家教　jiǎjiè 假借　jiājǐn 加緊　jiājìng 家境　jiājù 加劇 家具 傢俱　jiājuàn 家眷　jiākè 夾克　jiākuài 加快　jiālǐ 家裡　jiālún 加侖　jiāpǔ 家譜　jiàqián 價錢　jiāqiáng 加強　jiàquán 家權　jiárán 戛然　jiārén 家人　jiàrì 假日　jiǎrú 假如　jiārù 加入　jiǎruò 假若

jiǎshǐ 假使　jiǎshì 假釋　jiàshì 架式　jiàshǐ 駕駛　jiāshì 家事　jiāshū 家書　jiāshǔ 家屬　jiǎshuō 假說　jiāsù 加速　jiāsuǒ 枷鎖　jiātíng 家庭　jiāwù 家務　jiāxiàng 假象　jiāxiāng 家鄉　jiāyǐ 加以　jiāyì 嘉義　jiāyóu 加油　jiāyù 駕馭　jiázá 夾雜　jiāzhǎng 家長　jiāzhào 駕照　jiàzhí 價值　jiāzhòng 加重　jiǎzhuāng 假裝　jiàzhuāng 嫁妝　jiàzi 架子　jiázi 夾子　jiāzú 家族

jian
jiān 尖 殲 姦 箋 緘 奸 奸 肩 姦 兼 煎 監 取 堅 殲 鷹　jiǎn 檢 儉 鹼 撿 減 繭 柬 揀 簡 剪　jiàn 劍 建 鍵 健 踐 賤 餞 荐 諫 間 件 漸 見 箭 監 鑒 鑑 艦 鷹
jiānáo 煎熬

jiǎndāo 剪刀　jiǎndī 減低　jiàndì 見地　jiàndié 間諜　jiàndìng 鑑定　jiàndìng 堅定　jiāndū 監督　jiānduān 尖端　jiànduàn 間斷　jiānduǎn 間短　jiànduì 艦隊　jiǎnfǎ 減法　jiǎnféi 減肥　jiānfù 肩負　jiàngé 間隔　jiāngú 撬骨　jiāngù 兼顧 堅固　jiànguó 建國　jiǎnhuà 簡化　jiànhuò 賤貨　jiǎnjí 剪輯　jiǎnjià 減價　jiànjiàn 漸漸　jiànjiāo 建交　jiānjiào 尖叫　jiànjiē 間接　jiǎnjié 簡潔　jiǎnjiè 簡介　jiànjiě 見解　jiǎnjǔ 檢舉　jiānjù 艱鉅　jiānjué 堅決　jiànkāng 健康

jiānbǎng 肩膀　jiǎnbào 簡報　jiànbié 鑑別　jiānbìng 兼併　jiǎnchá 檢查　jiānchá 監察　jiǎncháguān 檢察官　jiānchāi 兼差　jiǎnchēng 簡稱　jiānchí 堅持　jiǎndān 簡單　jiàndào 劍道 見到　jiānkǒu 緘口　jiānkǔ 艱苦　jiānláo 監牢　jiànlì 建立　jiànliàng 見諒　jiǎnlòu 簡陋　jiǎnlüè 簡略　jiànmiàn 見面　jiānmiè 殲滅　jiànmín 賤民　jiānmò 緘默　jiānnán 艱難　jiǎnpàn 減盤　jiǎnpú 儉樸　jiǎnpǔzhài 柬埔寨　jiānqiáng 堅強　jiànqiáo 劍橋　jiǎnqīng 減輕　jiànquán 健全　jiānruì 尖銳　jiǎnruò 減弱　jiànshǎng 鑑賞　jiǎnshǎo 減少　jiànshè 建設　jiǎnshì 檢視　jiànshì 見識　jiānshì 監視　jiānshí 堅實　jiānshǒu 堅守　jiàntà 踐踏　jiǎntǎo 檢討　jiǎntǐzì 簡體字　jiàntǐng 艦艇　jiāntóu 肩頭　jiàntóu 箭頭　jiànxiē 間歇　jiānxīn 艱辛　jiànxìng 鹼性　jiànxíng 餞行　jiǎnxuǎn 揀選　jiǎnyàn 檢驗　jiànyì 建議　jiǎnyì 簡易　jiānyín 姦淫　jiānyìng 堅硬　jiānyù 監獄　jiànyú 鑑於 鑑

jiùdú 就讀　jiǔérjiǔzhī 久而久之　jiūfàn 就範　jiūfēn 糾紛　jiǔguǐ 酒鬼　jiǔhāněrrè 酒酣耳熱　jiùhù 救護　jiùhúo 救活　jiùjì 救濟　jiǔjiā 酒家　jiùjīnshān 舊金山　jiùjìng 究竟　jiǔjīng 酒精　jiùjiu 舅舅　jiǔliàng 酒量　jiùmā 舅媽　jiùmìng 救命　jiǔníuyīmáo 九牛一毛　jiùrèn 就任　jiùrì 舊日　jiǔsècáiqì 酒色財氣　jiùshì 就是　jiǔsì 酒肆　jiùsuàn 就算　jiǔxí 酒席　jiùxù 就緒　jiùxué 就學　jiùyào 就要　jiùyè 就業　jiǔyuǎn 久遠　jiūzhèng 糾正　jiùzhí 就職　jiùzhù 救助　jiǔzùi 酒醉

ju
jū 鞠 拘 居 据 狙 車　jú 白 知 菊 鞠 局 橘　jǔ 舉 矩 沮 咀 齟　jù 句 鋸 巨

jùyǒu 具有　jùyǔ 齟齬　jùbèi 具備　jùběn 劇本　jūbǔ 拘捕　jùbù 局部　jùchǎng 劇場　jùchēng 據稱　jùdà 巨大　jùdiǎn 據點　jǔdòng 舉動　jué 巨額 鉅額　jùfēng 颶風　júgōng 鞠躬　jùhào 句號　júhuā 菊花　jùhùi 聚會　jùjī 狙擊　jùjí 聚集　jūjǐn 拘謹　jūjìn 拘禁　jùjué 拒絕　jǔjué 咀嚼　jùlèbù 俱樂部　jǔlì 舉例　jùlí 距離　jùliè 劇烈　jūlíu 拘留居留　júmiàn 局面　jūmín 居民　jūnì 拘泥　jùpà 懼怕　jǔqǐ 舉起　jūrán 居然　jùrán 遽然　jùrén 巨人　jǔsàng 沮喪　jǔshì 舉世　jùshì 局勢　jùshù 拘束　jùshūo 據說　jǔtǐ 具體　jùxì 據悉　jǔxíng 舉行

juan
juān 圈 鎸　juān 捐 娟 鵑　juǎn 捲　juǎn 卷　juàn 圈 卷 雋 絹

juànbó 絹帛　juāngěi 捐給　juàngù 眷顧　juànhuà 絹畫　juānkè 鎸刻　juānkuǎn 捐款　juànliàn 眷戀　juànniàn 眷念　juǎnrù 捲入　juànshǔ 眷屬　juānxiě 捐血　juānxìu 娟秀　juànyǒng 雋永　juānzhù 捐助　juànzi 絹子

jue
juē 噘　jué 爵 嚼 覺 絕 決 抉 訣 厥 獗 子 譎 玨 掘 崛 佩 角

juécè 決策　juédé 覺得　juédìng 決定　juéduì 絕對　juéjì 絕跡　juéjiàng 倔强　juélì 角力　juéliè 決裂　juéqǐ 崛起

juéqiào 訣竅　juésè 角色　juéshì 爵士　juéshí 嚼食 絕食　juéwàng 絕望　juéwèi 爵位　juéwù 覺悟　juéxīn 決心　juéxǐng 覺醒　juéyì 決議　juézé 抉擇　juézhǒng 絕種　juézhú 角逐

jun
jūn 君 均 鈞 困 菌 軍　jùn 圳 俊 峻 竣 郡 菌

jūnbèi 軍備　jūnděng 均等　jūnduì 軍隊　jūnfá 軍閥　jūnfèi 軍費　jùngōng 竣工　jūnguān 軍官　jūnhéng 均衡　jūnhǔo 軍火　jùnjiàn 鈞鑒　jùnlǐng 峻嶺　jūnqí 鈞啓　jūnquán 君權　jūnrén 軍人　jūnshì 軍事　jūnyún 均勻　jūnzhǔ 君主　jūnzhuāng 軍裝　jūnzǐ 君子

ka
kā 咖　kǎ 卡　kǎchē 卡車　kāfēi 咖啡　kǎpiàn 卡片　kǎtōng 卡通

kai
kāi 揩 開　kǎi 慨 楷 凱

kāichā 開杈　kāichē 開車　kāichú 開除　kāichuàng 開創　kāidāo 開刀　kāiduān 開端　kāifā 開發　kāifàng 開放　kāiguān 開關　kāihuā 開花　kāihùi 開會　kāikǒu 開口　kāilǎng 開朗　kāilúo 開鑼　kāimíng 開明　kāimó 楷模　kāimù 開幕　kāipī 開闢　kāiqǐ 開啓　kǎirán 慨然　kāishǐ 開始　kāishū 楷書　kāishǔi 開水　kāitōng 開通　kāituò 開拓　kāiwǎng 開往　kāiwèi 開胃　kāixīn 開心　kǎixuán 凱旋　kāixué 開學　kāiyǎn 開演　kāiyè 開業　kāizhǎn 開展　kāizhī 開支

kan
kān 堪 戡 勘　kǎn 坎 砍 凵 檻　kānbǎn 看板　kànbùqǐ 看不起　kānchá 勘察　kànchéng 看成　kānchū 刊出　kànchū 看出　kànchuān 看穿　kàndào 看到

kāndēng 刊登	kàojìn 靠近	kēmù 科目	kōngjiān 空間	kòutóu 叩頭
kǎndiào 砍掉	kǎojuàn 考卷	kěnéng 可能	kǒngjù 恐懼	kǒuwèi 口味
kàndǒng 看懂	kàolǒng 靠攏	kěpà 可怕	kōngjūn 空軍	kǒuxiāngtáng 口香
kānfá 砍伐	kǎolǜ 考慮	kèqì 客氣	kōngkuàng 空曠	糖
kànfǎ 看法	kǎoròu 烤肉	kěqiú 苛求	kǒnglóng 恐龍	kùxīn 苦心
kānguǎn 看管	kǎoshàng 考上	kěqǔ 可取	kōnglùn 空論	kòuyā 扣押
kànhǎo 看好	kǎoshēng 考生	kèrén 客人	kǒngmiào 孔廟	kǒuyīn 口音
kānhù 看護	kǎoshì 考試	kěshì 可是	kǒngpà 恐怕	kǒuyǔ 口語
kānjiā 看家	kǎotí 考題	kēshuì 瞌睡	kōngqì 空氣	kǒuzhào 口罩
kànjiàn 看見	kǎowèn 拷問	késòu 咳嗽	kōngqián 空前	kòuzi 扣子
kànkàn 看看	kǎoyā 烤鴨	kètáng 課堂	kòngquē 空缺	
kānkě 坎坷	kǎoyàn 考驗	kètào 客套	kōngquè 孔雀	**ku**
kànlái 看來		kètí 課題	kōngshǒudào 空手	kū 圣 枯 骷 哭 窟
kānluàn 戡亂	**ke**	kètīng 客廳	道	kǔ 苦
kànqǐlái 看起來	kē 刻 柯 苛	kètóu 磕頭	kòngsù 控訴	kù 酷 庫 褲
kànqīng 看輕	瞌 磕 棵	kèwài 課外	kōngtiáo 空調	kù'ài 酷愛
kānshǒu 看守	顆 窠 科	kěwàng 渴望	kòngwèi 空位	kùcún 庫存
kāntàn 勘探	ké 咳 殼	kěxī 可惜	kōngxì 空隙	kūjié 枯竭
kàntòu 看透	kě 渴 可 坷	kěxí 可惜	kòngxián 空閒	kǔlì 苦力
kānwù 刊物	kè 客 刻 嗑	kěxiào 可笑	kōngxiǎng 空想	kùlì 酷吏
kànxiàng 看相	課 克 剋	kěxíng 可行	kōngxū 空虛	kūlong 窟窿
kànzhòng 看重	kě'ài 可愛	kèxīng 剋星	kōngzhōng 空中	kūlóu 骷髏
kànzhǔn 看準	kèbǎn 刻版	kēxué 科學	kǒngzǐ 孔子	kǔmèn 苦悶
	kèběn 課本	kěyí 可疑		kǔnàn 苦難
kang	kèbó 刻薄	kěyǐ 可以	**kou**	kǔnǎo 苦惱
kāng 康 糠	kècāng 客艙	kěyìn 刻印	kǒu 口	kūqì 哭泣
慷	kèchē 客車	kèzhì 克制	kòu 寇 蔻 扣	kùrè 酷熱
káng 扛	kèchéng 課程		釦 叩	kǔsè 苦澀
kàng 亢 抗	kèdiàn 客店	**ken**	kǒucái 口才	kūshēng 哭聲
炕 伉	kèfú 克服	kěn 狠 懇 墾	kǒuchǐ 齒	kǔtòng 苦痛
kàngfèn 亢奮	kěgǔ 刻骨	肯 啃	kòuchú 扣除	kūwěi 枯萎
kāngfù 康復	kěguān 客觀/可觀	kěndìng 肯定	kòudài 口袋	kùxíng 酷刑
kànghéng 抗衡	kěguì 可貴	kěnhuāng 墾荒	kǒufú 口福	kūzào 枯燥
kàngjù 抗拒	kèhù 客戶	kěnqiú 懇求	kǒugōng 口供	kùzi 褲子
kāngkǎi 慷慨	kèhuà 刻畫		kǒuhào 口號	
kànglì 伉儷	kējì 科技	**keng**	kǒuhóng 口紅	**kua**
kāngxī 康熙	kèjiā 客家	kēng 坑	kǒují 口吃	kuā 夸 誇 侉
kàngyì 抗議	kějiàn 可見		kǒujiāo 口交	kuǎ 垮
kàngzhàn 抗戰	kèlòu 寠臼	**kong**	kǒujiǎo 口角	kuà 屮 胯 跨
	kējǔ 科舉	kōng 空	kǒujìng 口徑	kuàdà 誇大
kao	kěkào 可靠	kǒng 恐 孔	kòulíng 口令	kuàgǔ 胯骨
kǎo 考 烤 拷	kěkǒu 可口	kòng 空 控	kòuliú 扣留	kuājiǎng 誇獎
攷	kèkǔ 刻苦	kòngbái 空白	kǒuqì 口氣	kuǎtái 垮台
kào 銬 靠	kělè 可樂	kǒngbù 恐怖	kǒuqín 口琴	kuāyào 誇耀
kǎobèi 拷貝	kēlì 顆粒	kòngdì 空地	kǒushào 口哨	kuàyuè 跨越
kǎochá 考察	kělián 可憐	kōngdòng 空洞	kǒushì 口試	kuāzhāng 誇張
kǎodǎ 拷打	kèmǎn 客滿	kònggào 控告	kǒutóu 口頭	
kǎogǔxué 考古學		kǒnghè 恐嚇		**kuai**
kǎoguò 考過		kōnghuà 空話		kuài 《 快
kǎohé 考核		kǒnghuāng 恐慌		筷 塊 會

kuàibào 快報勁
kuàicān 快餐勁
kuàigǎn 快感勁
kuàihúo 快活勁
kuàijì 會計⁹¹ → kuàijì 會計
kuàilè 快樂勁
kuàisù 快速勁
kuàizi 筷子勁

kuan
kuān 寬
kuǎn 款
kuānchǎng 寬敞
kuāndà 寬大
kuǎndài 款待
kuāndù 寬度
kuānguǎng 寬廣
kuānkùo 寬闊
kuānróng 寬容
kuǎnshì 款式
kuānshù 寬恕
kuānxiàng 款項
kuānyù 寬裕

kuang
kuāng 匡 筐
kuáng 狂 ... 況
礦 曠
kuángbiāo 狂飆
kuàngcáng 礦藏
kuàngchǎng 礦場
kuángfēng 狂風
kuànggōng 礦工
kuànghuān 狂歡
kuàngkēng 礦坑
kuángnù 狂怒
kuàngqiě 況且
kuàngquán 礦泉
kuángrè 狂熱
kuángrén 狂人
kuángwàng 狂妄
kuàngyě 曠野
kuàngzhèng 匡正
kuāngzi 筐子

kui
kūi 窺 盔 虧
kúi 奎 揆 暌
葵 魁
kǔi 傀

kùi 匱 匱
潰 饋 愧
kūiběn 虧本
kúicè 揆測
kùifá 匱乏
kúiguāzi 葵瓜子
kúihuā 葵花
kúijiǎ 盔甲
kǔilěi 傀儡
kùisè 愧色
kūishì 窺視
kūisì 窺伺
kūisǔn 虧損
kūitàn 窺探
kúiwéi 暌違
kùiyáng 潰瘍
kùizèng 饋贈

kun
kūn 昆 崑 坤
kǔn 捆 綑
kùn 困 睏
kūnchóng 昆蟲
kùndùn 困頓
kùnhùo 困惑
kùnjìng 困境
kùnjuàn 困倦
kūnlún 崑崙
kūnmíng 昆明
kùnnán 困難
kùnrǎo 困擾
kūnzhòng 昆仲

kuo
kùo 廓 擴 闊
括
kùobié 闊別
kùochōng 擴充
kùochùo 闊綽
kùodà 擴大
kùolǎo 闊佬
kùoqīng 廓清
kùosàn 擴散
kùoyīn 擴音
kùozhǎn 擴展
kùozhāng 擴張

la
lā 拉 啦 垃
邋
lá 剌

lǎ 剌 喇
là 落 辣 蠟
臘
la 啦
lābā 喇叭
làbǐ 蠟筆
lācháng 拉長
làcháng 臘腸
lāchě 拉扯
lāchū 拉出
lādīng 拉丁
lādùzi 拉肚子
làjiāo 辣椒
lākāi 拉開
lālādùi 啦啦隊
lāliàn 拉鍊
lālǒng 拉攏
lǎma 喇嘛
lāpiào 拉票
làrǎn 蠟染
lāsā 拉撒
lāshǐ 拉屎
lātà 邋遢
lāzá 拉雜
làzhú 蠟燭

lai
lái 來 萊 徠
lài 賴 睞
láibīn 來賓
láibùjí 來不及
láidào 來到
láifǎng 來訪
láihúi 來回
láilì 來歷
láilín 來臨
láiwǎng 來往
láixìn 來信
láiyuán 來源
làizhàng 賴帳
láizì 來自

lan
lán 婪 闌 攔
欄 蘭 藍
籃
lǎn 懶 覽 攬
纜
làn 爛 濫
lǎnchē 纜車

lǎnde 懶得
làndiào 濫調
lǎndùo 懶惰
lángān 欄杆
lánhuā 蘭花
lánjié 攔截
lànmàn 爛漫
lànqíng 濫情
lánqíu 籃球
lánquán 攬權
lǎnsàn 懶散
lánsè 藍色
lántián 藍天
lántú 藍圖
lánwěi 闌尾
lànyòng 濫用
lányǔ 蘭嶼
lánzhù 攔住
lánzi 籃子
lánzǔ 攔阻

lang
láng 狼 郎 榔
廊 螂 琅
lǎng 朗
làng 浪
làngcháo 浪潮
lǎngdú 朗讀
làngfèi 浪費
làngmàn 浪漫
lǎngsòng 朗誦
làngzǐ 浪子

lao
lāo 撈
láo 勞 牢
lǎo 老 佬
lào 酪 烙
lǎobǎn 老闆 老板
lǎobǐng 烙餅
lǎobīng 老兵
lǎodà 老大
lǎodiē 老爹
láodòng 勞動
láofán 勞煩
láogǎi 勞改
lǎogōng 老公
láogōng 勞工
láogù 牢固

lǎohǔ 老虎
láojià 勞駕
lǎojiǎn 老繭
lǎojūn 老君
láokào 牢靠
láolì 勞力
láolóng 牢籠
láomiàn 撈麵
lǎonián 老年
lǎopó 老婆
lǎorén 老人
lǎorénjiā 老人家
láosāo 牢騷
lǎoshī 老師
lǎoshí 老實
lǎoshì 老是
lǎoshǔ 老鼠
lǎotàitài 老太太
lǎotiān 老天
lǎotóu 老頭
lǎowài 老外
láowù 勞務
lǎoxiāng 老鄉
lǎoyé 老爺
làoyìn 烙印
lǎoyīng 老鷹
lǎoyǒu 老友
lǎoyuǎn 老遠
lǎozhě 老者
lǎozǐ 老子

le
lè 肋 勒 垃
樂
le 了
lègǔ 肋骨
lèguān 樂觀
lèqù 樂趣
lèsè 垃圾
lèshì 樂事
lèsuǒ 勒索
lèyì 樂意
lèyú 樂於
lèyuán 樂園

lei
lēi 勒
léi 羸 晶 雷
累
lěi 磊 耒 壘

偏榴 蕾累 lì 隸 力 lìlù 利率 liàntiáo 鏈條
lèi 肋 淚 累 荔 茘 立 lǐmào 禮貌 lǐzi 李子 liánxī 憐惜
類 粒 笠 礫 límǐ 釐米 lízi 梨子 liánxì 聯繫
léibié 類別 署 吏 屬 lǐmiàn 裡面 lìzi 例子 栗 liánxí 練習
léidá 雷達 勵 蠣 戾 límíng 黎明 子 liánxí 連繫
léidiàn 雷電 秝 麻 歷 línán 罹難 lízú 黎族 liánxù 連續
léigēn 雷根 瀝 靂 曆 lìnián 歷年 lia liányì 聯誼
lěijī 累積 利 莉 俐 lǐniàn 理念 liǎ 倆 liányóu 煉油
lěilěi 累累 痢 例 俐 líniú 犛牛 lian liànzhàn 戀棧
léilìfēngxíng 雷厲 麗 儷 栗 lípǔ 離譜 lián 憐 聯 廉 liànzi 鏈子
風行 慄 离 lìqì 力氣 簾 鐮 連 liang
léiqiú 壘球 li 裡 lìqí 離奇 蓮 臉 liángliáng 涼 梁
léiruò 羸弱 lìbā 籬笆 lìqīng 釐清 liǎn 臉 樑 梁 量
léishè 雷射 lǐbài 禮拜 lìqiú 力求 liàn 斂 練 糧
léishēng 雷聲 lìbì 利弊 lìrú 例如 煉 鍊 鏈 liǎng 兩
lèishuǐ 淚水 lǐbǐyǎ 利比亞 lìrùn 利潤 戀 鏈 倆
lèisì 類似 lǐbiān 裡邊 lìshēng 厲聲 liànài 戀愛 liàng 涼 諒
léitóng 雷同 lìbié 離別 lìshí 歷時 liánbāng 聯邦 亮 輛 量
lèituī 類推 lǐcái 理財 lìshí 歷史 liánchuàn 連串 liǎngbiān 兩邊
lèixíng 類型 lǐcǎi 理睬 lìshì 理事 liáncí 連詞 liángcài 涼菜
léiyǔ 雷雨 lìchǎng 立場 liàndá 練達 liángcāng 糧倉
lèizhū 淚珠 lìchéng 歷程 liándài 連帶 liánghǎo 良好
léizhuì 累贅 lìcì 歷次 liándāo 鐮刀 liángkuài 涼快
leng lìdài 歷代 lìshū 隸書 liànggāng 煉鋼 liángpiào 糧票
léng 稜 棱 lǐdàng 理當 lìshǔ 隸屬 liánguàn 連貫 liǎngsān 兩三
lěng 冷 lǐdìng 釐定 lìshū 曆書 liánhé 聯合 liángshí 糧食
lèng 愣 lìfǎ 立法 lìshù 栗樹 liǎnhóng 臉紅 liángxí 涼蓆
lěngcáng 冷藏 lǐfà 理髮 lìsú 俚俗 liánhuā 蓮花 liángxié 涼鞋
lěngdàn 冷淡 lǐfú 禮服 lìtǐ 立體 liánhuān 聯歡 liángxīn 良心
lěngdòng 冷凍 lǐgēn 里根 lítí 離題 liánjià 廉價 liǎngyàng 兩樣
lěngjiǎo 稜角 lǐgōng 理工 lìtián 犁田 liánjiē 連接 liángyǒu 良友
lěngjìng 冷靜 lìhài 厲害 利 lǐtóu 裡頭 liánjié 連結 liao
lěngkù 冷酷 害 lìwài 例外 liánjūn 聯軍 liáo 蓼 聊 嘹
lěngmò 冷漠 lǐhuàn 罹患 lìwù 禮物 liánkǎo 聯考 療 寮 遼
lěngqì 冷氣 lǐhuì 理會 lìxī 利息 liánlèi 連累 僚
lěngquè 冷卻 lǐhūn 離婚 lǐxiǎng 理想 liánluò 聯絡 liǎo 了 瞭
lěngshuǐ 冷水 lǐjí 立即 lǐxìng 理性 liánmáng 連忙 liào 撂 廖 瞭
lěngzhàn 冷戰 lǐjì 禮記 lìxué 力學 liánmèi 聯袂 料
lèngzhù 愣住 lìjí 痢疾 lǐxué 理學 liánméng 聯盟 liǎobùqǐ 了不起
li lǐjiàn 離間 lìyì 立誓 liánmián 連綿 liǎodé 了得
li 离 璃 離 lǐjié 禮節 lǐyí 禮儀 liánmǐn 憐憫 liáofǎ 療法
籬 漓 犛 lǐjiě 理解 lìyì 利益 liǎnpén 臉盆 liáoguó 寮國
犛 罹 梨 lǐjìng 離境 lìyòng 利用 liǎnpí 臉皮 liǎojié 了結
犁 黎 狸 lìjīng 歷經 lǐyóu 理由 liǎnpǔ 臉譜 liǎojiě 了解 瞭
貍 罹 lǐkāi 離開 lǐyú 鯉魚 liánrèn 連任 liáokāi 撂開
lǐ 李 豊 禮 lìkè 立刻 lǐyǔ 俚語 liǎnsè 臉色 liáokuò 遼闊
里 裡 理 lǐliàng 力量 lǐzhǎng 里長 liànshǒu 聯手 liàolǐ 料理
哩 鯉 俚 lǐlùn 理論 lìzhēng 力爭 liánshǒu 聯手
lìzhèng 例證
lìzhī 荔枝 liánsuǒ 連鎖

28

羅 鑼 籮 / 邏 蘿

lǜsè 綠色	mǎlíngshǔ 馬鈴薯	蔓 饅	màojìn 冒進	
lǚshè 旅社	luǒ 裸	mànbù 漫步	mǎojìn 卯勁	
lùshī 律師	mǎlù 馬路	màncháng 漫長	máojīn 毛巾	
lǚtú 旅途	māma 媽媽	mǎnfēn 滿分	máolì 毛利	
lǚxíng 履行 旅行	mámù 麻木	màngǔ 曼谷	màomèi 冒昧	
lǚyóu 旅遊	mǎnǎo 瑪瑙	mánhèng 蠻橫	màorán 貿然	
lǜzhōu 綠洲	mǎpī 馬匹	mànhuà 漫畫	màoshèng 茂盛	

[luan]
luǎn 卵
luàn 亂
luàncháo 卵巢
luàndiū 亂丟
luànjiǎng 亂講
luànqībāzāo 亂七八糟
luànrēng 亂扔
luànxiǎng 亂想

[lue]
lüè 略 掠
lüèduó 掠奪
lüèguò 掠過

[lun]
lún 侖 輪 倫 綸 論 淪
lùn 論
lúnbān 輪班
lúncháng 倫常
lúnchuán 輪船
lúncì 倫次
lùndiǎn 論點
lùndiào 論調
lúndūn 倫敦
lúnhuí 輪迴
lúnkuò 輪廓
lúnlǐ 倫理
lúnliú 輪流
lúntāi 輪胎
lùntán 論壇
lúnwéi 淪為
lùnwén 論文
lúnxiàn 淪陷
lúnyǔ 論語
lùnzhàn 論戰
lúnzi 輪子

[luo]
luō 囉
luó 羅 螺 騾

luòbo 蘿蔔
luòhòu 落後
luójí 邏輯
luòkōng 落空
luókuāng 籮筐
luǒlù 裸露
luómǎ 羅馬
luòmò 落寞
luòrù 落入
luòshānjī 洛杉磯
luóshēng 鑼聲
luòshuǐ 落水
luósī 螺絲
luósīfú 羅斯福
luōsūo 囉嗦
luǒtǐ 裸體
luòtuó 駱駝
luówǎng 羅網
luòwǔ 落伍
luòxià 落下
luóxuán 螺旋
luòyè 落葉
luózi 騾子

[ma]
mā 媽 嬤
má 麻 嘛 痲
mǎ 馬 嗎 / 瑪 碼 螞
mà 罵
ma 嘛 麼 嗎
mǎān 馬鞍
mábì 麻痺 麻痹
mǎchē 馬車
máfan 麻煩
mǎfēi 嗎啡
máfēng 痲瘋
mǎhǔ 馬虎
májiàng 麻將
mǎkè 馬克
mǎkèsī 馬克思
málà 麻辣
mǎlè 馬勒

mámù 麻木
mǎnǎo 瑪瑙
mǎpī 馬匹
máquè 麻雀
màrén 罵人
mǎshàng 馬上
mǎtǒng 馬桶
mǎtóu 碼頭
mǎxì 馬戲
mǎyǐ 螞蟻
mázhěn 痲疹
mǎzǔ 馬祖
māzǔ 媽祖
mázuì 麻醉

[mai]
mái 貍 霾 埋
mǎi 買
mài 邁 脈 / 賣 麥
mǎibàn 買辦
màibó 脈搏
màibù 邁步
máicáng 埋藏
màichūn 賣春
máidān 埋單
màidān 買單
màidāngláo 麥當勞
máifú 埋伏
màigěi 賣給
màijìn 邁進
màiluò 脈絡
mǎimài 買賣
máimò 埋沒
màipiàn 麥片
máixià 埋下
màixiàng 邁向
màiyín 賣淫
máizàng 埋葬

[man]
mán 饅 鰻 蠻 / 瞞 埋 蠻
mǎn 滿
màn 曼 慢 漫

màncháng 漫長
mǎnfēn 滿分
màngǔ 曼谷
mánhèng 蠻橫
mànhuà 漫畫
mànmà 謾罵
mànpǎo 慢跑
mànpiàn 瞞騙
mǎnqīng 滿清
màntán 漫談
mántou 饅頭
mànyán 蔓延
mǎnyì 滿意
mányú 鰻魚
mǎnyuàn 埋怨
mǎnzhōu 滿州
mǎnzú 滿族 滿足

[mang]
máng 忙 芒 / 茫 盲 氓
mǎng 蟒 莽
mángcháng 盲腸
mángguǒ 芒果
mánglù 忙碌
mángmáng 茫茫
mángmù 盲目
mángrán 茫然
mángrén 盲人
mǎngzhuàng 莽撞

[mao]
māo 貓
máo 毛 髦 矛 / 茅 錨
mǎo 卯
mào 兒 貌 冃 / 冒 帽
màochōng 冒充
máochóng 毛蟲
máodùn 矛盾
máofáng 茅房
màohào 冒號

màoshī 冒失
màosì 貌似
máotáijiǔ 茅台酒
máotǎn 毛毯
máowū 茅屋
màoxiǎn 冒險
màoyì 貿易
máoyī 毛衣
màozi 帽子

[me]
me 麼
me 麼

[mei]
méi 枚 玫 沒 / 霉 梅 煤 / 媒 眉 楣 / 嵋
měi 每 美
mèi 妹 魅 媚 寐
měicì 每次
méicuò 沒錯
měigǎn 美感
měiguī 玫瑰
měiguó 美國
měihǎo 美好
méihuā 梅花
méijiè 媒介
měijīn 美金
méikuàng 煤礦
měikuàngyùxià 每況愈下
mèilì 魅力
měilì 美麗
méimáo 眉毛
měimào 美貌
mèimei 妹妹
měimiào 美妙
méimù 眉目
měinián 每年

míngxīn 銘心[92]	然[144]	mùdì 墓地[92] 目	nàhǎn 納罕[57] 吶
míngxīng 明星[97]	mòrèn 默認[144]	的[114]	喊[57]
míngyì 名義[92]	mǒshā 抹殺[57]	mùdǔ 目睹[114]	náhuí 拿回[57]
míngyù 名譽[92]	mòshēng 陌生[57]	mùěr 木耳[77]	nálái 拿來[57]
míngyùn 命運[92]	mòshì 漠視[57]	mùgōng 木工[77]	nǎlǐ 那裡[57]
míngzhǐ 冥紙[92]	móshì 模式[92]	mùguā 木瓜[77]	nàlǐ 那裡[57]
míngzhī 明知[92]	mòshōu 沒收[57]	mùguāng 目光[114]	nǎlǐ 哪裡[57]
míngzhù 名著[92]	móshù 魔術[92]	mǔguó 母國[77]	nàme 那麼[57]
míngzì 名字[92]	mòshuǐ 墨水[144]	mǔjī 母雞[77]	nàmèn 納悶[57]
miu	mòsīkē 莫斯科[57]	mùjí 募集[92]	náqǐ 拿起[57]
miù 謬[78]	mòsuǒ 摸索[57]	mùjí 木屐[77]	nàr 那兒[57]
miùwù 謬誤[78]	mótèr 模特兒[92]	mùjī 木擊[114]	nǎr 哪兒[57]
mo	mótuō 摩托[57]	mùjiàng 木匠[77]	nàrù 納入[57]
mō 摸[57]	mówáng 魔王[92]	mùlán 木蘭[77]	náshǒu 拿手[57]
mó 膜[92] 模[92] 摹[92]	mòxīgē 墨西哥[144]	mǔlì 牡蠣[77]	nàshuì 納稅[57]
磨[92] 蘑[92] 摩[92]	móxíng 模型[92]	mùlín 睦鄰[114]	nàxīzú 納西族[57]
魔[92]	mòzǐ 墨子[144]	mùlù 目錄[114]	nàxiē 那些[57]
mǒ 抹[57]	**mou**	mùǒu 木偶[77]	nǎxiē 哪些[57]
mò 沒[57] 歿[57] 莫[57]	móu 謀[57] 牟[57] 眸[57]	mùpái 木排[77]	nàyàng 那樣[57]
寞[92] 漠[92] 驀[92]	mǒu 某[57]	mùqián 目前[114]	názhe 拿著[57]
陌[92] 磨[92] 末[57]	móulì 牟利[57]	mǔqīn 母親[77]	názhù 拿住[57]
沫[57] 茉[57] 抹[57]	móulüè 謀略[57]	mùsè 暮色[92]	názǒu 拿走[57]
墨[144] 默[144] 默[144]	mǒumǒu 某某[57]	mùshī 牧師[114]	**nai**
móbài 膜拜[92]	mùsīlín 穆斯林[114]		nǎi 乃[8] 奶[57]
mòbù 莫不[57]	móuqiú 謀求[57]	nǎi 乃[8] 奶[57]	nài 奈[8] 奈[57] 耐[57]
mǒbù 抹布[57]	móuqǔ 牟取[57]	nàisù 耐素[57]	nǎichá 奶茶[57]
mócā 摩擦[57]	mǒurén 某人[57]	mùtóu 木頭[77]	nǎifáng 奶房[57]
mòdà 莫大[57]	móushā 謀殺[57]	mùwū 木屋[77]	nǎifěn 奶粉[57]
mòdài 末代[57]	móushēng 謀生[57]	mǔxì 母系[77]	nǎilào 奶酪[57]
mòdì 驀地[92]	mǒuxiē 某些[57]	mùxiào 母校[77]	nàilì 耐力[114]
mófàn 模範[92]	móuzhí 謀職[57]	múyàng 模樣[92]	nǎimā 奶媽[57]
mófǎng 模仿[92]	móuzi 眸子[57]	mùyáng 牧羊[114]	nǎinai 奶奶[57]
mòfēi 莫非[57]	**mu**	mǔyǔ 母語[77]	nǎishì 乃是[8]
mógu 蘑菇[92]	mú 模[92]	mùyù 沐浴[57]	nǎitou 奶頭[57]
móhú 模糊[92]	mǔ 畝[77] 母[77] 拇[57]	mǔzhǐ 拇指[57] 拇	nàixīn 耐心[114]
mòlì 茉莉[57]	姆[57] 牡[77]	趾[57]	nàixìng 耐性[114]
móliàn 磨練[92]	mù 穆[114] 叉[92] 慕[92]	mùzhuāng 木樁[77]	nàiyòng 耐用[114]
mòluò 沒落[57]	幕[92] 墓[92] 暮[92]	**na**	nǎiyóu 奶油[57]
mòmíng 莫名[57]	沐[57] 牧[114] 目[114]	ná 拿[57]	nǎizhī 乃至[8]
mòmíngqímiào 莫名	苜[114]	nǎ 那[57] 哪[57]	nǎizi 奶子[57]
其妙[57]	mùbǎn 木板[77]	nà 捺[57] 納[57] 吶[57]	**nan**
mòmò 默默[144]	mùbēi 墓碑[92]	悶[57] 那[57]	nàbiān 那邊[57] 喃[57] 難[57]
móní 模擬[92]	mùbiāo 目標[114]	nàbiān 那邊[57]	nán 南[57] 男[57]
mònián 末年[57]	mùcái 木材[77]	náchū 拿出[57]	nàn 難[57] 疒[87]
mòqī 末期[57]	mùchǎng 牧場[114]	nàcuì 納粹[57]	nánbù 南部[57]
mòqì 默契[144]	mǔdān 牡丹[77]	nàdào 拿到[57]	nánchán 難纏[57]
mòrán 驀然[92] 默	mùdèngkǒudāi 目瞪	nǎge 那個[57]	nándào 難道[57]
	口呆[114]	nàge 那個[57]	nándé 難得[57]

nànfāng 南方[57]	nándé 難得[57]
nánfēi 南非[57]	
nánguài 難怪[57]	
nánhái 男孩[57]	
nánháizǐ 男孩子[57]	
nánjí 南極[57]	
nánjīng 南京[57]	
nánkān 難堪[57]	
nánkàn 難看[57]	
nánměi 南美[57]	
nánmiǎn 難免[57]	
nánmín 難民[57]	
nánnán 喃喃[57]	
nánnǚ 男女[57]	
nánrén 男人[57]	
nánshēng 男生[57]	
nánshòu 難受[57]	
nánshuō 難說[57]	
nántí 難題[57]	
nánxià 南下[57]	
nánxìng 男性[57]	
nányǐ 難以[57]	
nányǒu 男友[57]	
nánzǐ 男子[57]	
nang	
náng 囊[57]	
nǎng 曩[57]	
nángguā 囊括[57]	
nǎngxī 曩昔[57]	
nao	
náo 撓[57]	
nǎo 惱[143] 腦[143]	
惱[143] 瑙[143]	
nào 鬧[57]	
nǎodài 腦袋[143]	
nǎohǎi 腦海[143]	
nǎojīn 腦筋[143]	
nǎolíu 腦瘤[143]	
nǎonù 惱怒[143]	
nǎorén 惱人[143]	
nàoshì 鬧事[57]	
nàozhōng 鬧鐘[57]	
nǎozi 腦子[143]	
ne	
ne 呢[57]	
nei	
něi 餒[103]	

páiliè 排列	pāng 乓	péijiǔ 陪酒	僻 闢	piānlí 偏離
páilóu 牌樓	páng 彷 旁	pèiǒu 配偶	píbāo 皮包	piànmiàn 片面
pāimài 拍賣	螃 徬 龐	péiqián 賠錢	píbèi 疲憊	piānpáng 偏旁
páimíng 排名	pàng 胖	péishěn 陪審	pídài 皮帶	piānpì 偏僻
pàiqiǎn 派遣	pángbiān 旁邊	pēitāi 胚胎	pídàn 皮蛋	piānpō 偏頗
páiqiú 排球	pángdà 龐大	péiyǎng 培養	pǐdí 匹敵	piānpǒ 偏頗
pāishè 拍攝	pángguān 旁觀	péiyù 培育	pīfā 批發	piànrén 騙人
pāishǒu 拍手	pánghuáng 彷徨	péizhí 培植	pífá 疲乏	piāntǎn 偏袒
páishuǐ 排水	徬徨		pīfēng 披風	piāntīngpiānxìn 偏
páitā 排他	pángtīng 旁聽	pen	pífū 皮膚	聽偏信
páiwài 排外	pángxiè 螃蟹	pēn 噴	pīgǎi 批改	piānxiàng 偏向
páiwèi 牌位	pàngzi 胖子	pén 盆	pígé 皮革	piānxīn 偏心
pàixì 派系		pēnchū 噴出	pìgǔ 屁股	piányí 便宜
páixù 排序	pao	péndì 盆地	pǐhào 癖好	piànyǔ 片語
páizhào 牌照	pāo 抛	pénjǐng 盆景	pījiān 披肩	piānyuǎn 偏遠
pāizhào 拍照	páo 袍 刨 炮	pēnqī 噴漆	píjiǔ 啤酒	piānzhí 偏執
pāizi 牌子	pǎo 跑	pēnshè 噴射	píjuàn 疲倦	piānzhòng 偏重
pāizi 拍子	pào 泡 炮 砲	pēntì 噴嚏	pīkāi 劈開	piànzi 片子
	pǎobīng 跑兵	pénzi 盆子	píláo 疲勞	
pan	pǎobù 跑步		pílèi 疲累	piao
pān 攀 潘	pàocài 泡菜	peng	pīlì 霹靂	piāo 漂 飄 剽
pán 盤	pàochá 泡茶	pēng 烹 砰	pílín 毗鄰	piáo 嫖
pàn 盼 判 叛	pàodàn 砲彈	抨 澎	pīlòu 紕漏	piào 票 漂 剽
pànbiàn 叛變	pǎodào 跑道	péng 彭 膨	pīlù 披露	piāobái 漂白
pánchá 盤查	pāokāi 抛開	澎 蓬 蓬	pímáo 皮毛	piāofú 漂浮
pánchán 盤纏	pāomáo 抛錨	朋 鵬 棚	pìměi 媲美	piáojì 嫖妓
pànchǔ 判處	pàomiàn 泡麵	pěng 捧	pīpàn 批判	piáokè 嫖客
pāndēng 攀登	pàomò 泡沫	pèng 碰	pīpíng 批評	piàoliàng 漂亮
pànduàn 判斷	pāoqì 抛棄	péngbó 蓬勃	píqi 脾氣	piāoliú 漂流
pángǔ 盤古	pāoshòu 抛售	pèngdào 碰到	pírú 譬如	piàoqiè 剽竊
pànguó 叛國	pàotáng 泡堂	pénghú 澎湖	píruǎn 疲軟	piāoyì 飄逸
pánjù 盤據	pàotāng 泡湯	pēngjià 抨擊	pītóu 劈頭	
pànjué 判決	pǎozǒu 跑走	péngjià 棚架	píxiāng 皮箱	pie
pànluàn 叛亂		pèngjiàn 碰見	pìyáo 闢謠	piē 撇 瞥
pànmài 叛賣	pei	pēngpài 澎湃	pīzhù 批註	piě 丿 撇
pànnì 叛逆	pēi 胚	pēngrèn 烹飪	pīzhǔn 批准	piējiàn 瞥見
pānpá 攀爬	péi 蓓 陪 賠	pēngtiáo 烹調		piēkāi 撇開
pānshēng 攀升	培 裴	pèngtóu 碰頭	pian	piēqīng 撇清
pánsuàn 盤算	pèi 沛 佩 珮	péngyǒu 朋友	piān 篇 偏	
pāntán 攀談	配	péngzhàng 膨脹	pián 便	pin
pàntáo 叛逃	péibàn 陪伴	pèngzhuàng 碰撞	piàn 片 騙	pīn 拼 姘
pàntú 叛徒	pèibèi 配備		piānài 偏愛	pín 貧 頻
pànwàng 盼望	péicháng 賠償	pi	piànduàn 片段	pǐn 品
pánwèn 盤問	pèidài 佩帶	pī 丕 批 紕	piānfèi 偏廢	pìn 聘
pànxíng 判刑	pèiduì 配對	披 匹 劈	piānfú 偏幅	pǐncháng 品嘗
pánxuán 盤旋	pèié 配額	霹	piānhào 偏好	píndào 頻道
pānyán 攀巖	pèifu 佩服	pí 琵 毗 皮	piānjiàn 偏見	pǐndé 品德
pánzi 盤子	pèihé 配合	疲 啤 脾	piànkè 片刻	pínfá 貧乏
	pèijǐ 配給	pǐ 匹 癖 劈		pīnfǎ 拼法
pang	péijià 陪嫁	庀		
		pì 媲 屁 譬		

pínfán 頻繁　pǐngé 品格　pínkǔ 貧苦　pínkùn 貧困　pìnlǐ 聘禮　pínlǜ 頻率　pínmín 貧民　pīnmìng 拼命　pínpín 頻頻　pìnqǐng 聘請　pínqióng 貧窮　pìnrèn 聘任　pìnshū 聘書　pīnsǐ 拼死　pīntóu 姘頭　pīntú 拼圖　pīnyīn 拼音　pìnyòng 聘用　pǐnzhí 品質　pǐnzhǒng 品種

[ping]
pīng 乒
píng 馮 憑 軬 甹 平 坪 評 屏 瓶 蘋
píngān 平安　píngcháng 平常　píngděng 平等　píngdiào 憑弔　píngdìng 平定　píngfán 平凡　píngfǎn 平反　píngfāng 平方　píngfēn 評分　píngfēng 屏風　pínggài 瓶蓋　pínggū 評估　píngguǒ 蘋果　pínghéng 平衡　píngjià 評價　píngjiè 憑藉　píngjìng 平靜　píngjǐng 瓶頸　píngjù 憑據 平劇　píngjūn 平均　píngkōng 憑空　pínglùn 評論

píngmín 平民　píngmù 屏幕　píngpàn 評判　pīngpāng 乒乓　píngpíng 平平　píngrǎng 平壤　píngrì 平日　píngshěn 評審　píngshí 平時　píngtǎn 平坦　píngwěn 平穩　píngxī 平息　píngyì 評議　píngyǔ 評語　píngyuán 平原　píngzhàng 屏障　píngzi 瓶子

[po]
pō 頗 坡 潑
pó 婆
pǒ 頗 叵
pò 破 珀 迫 魄
pòàn 破案　pòcè 叵測　pòchǎn 破產　pòchú 破除　pòdù 坡度　pōfù 潑婦　pòhài 迫害　pòhuài 破壞　pòjiù 破舊　pōlà 潑辣　pòlàn 破爛　pòlì 魄力　pòliè 破裂　pòmiè 破滅　pópo 婆婆　pòqiè 迫切　pòshǐ 迫使　pòsuì 破碎　pósuō 婆娑　pǒwéi 頗爲　pòyīnzì 破音字　pòzhàn 破綻

[pou]
pōu 剖
pǒu 剖

pōuxī 剖析

[pu]
pū 攵 扑 鋪 撲
pú 菩 朴 匍 蒲 僕 樸
pǔ 普 譜 溥
pǔ 埔 樸
pù 暴 瀑 曝 鋪 舖
pǔbiàn 普遍　pùbù 瀑布　pǔdōng 浦東　púfú 匍匐　púgōngyīng 蒲公英　pùguāng 曝光　pǔjí 普及　pūkè 撲克　pùlù 暴露　pūlù 鋪路　pūmiè 撲滅　pǔqǔ 譜曲　púrén 僕人　púsà 菩薩　púsù 樸素　pútáo 葡萄　pútáoyá 葡萄牙　pǔtōng 普通　pǔtuóshān 普陀山　pùwèi 舖位　pǔyí 溥儀

[qi]
qī 七 柒 沏 妻 悽 淒 棲 期 欺 桼 漆 戚 戺
qí 耆 鰭 奇 騎 崎 其 期 棋 旗 淇 歧 祈 衹 齊
qǐ 起 豈 啓 乞 企
qì 泣 棄 器 切 契 气 汽 氣 迄 訖 企 緝

qǐcǎn 悽慘　qíchá 沏茶　qǐchē 騎車　qìchē 汽車　qǐchéng 啓程　qǐchū 起初　qìchuǎn 氣喘　qǐchuáng 起床　qícì 其次　qídài 期待　qídǎo 祈禱　qǐdòng 啓動　qǐfā 啓發　qǐfēi 起飛　qìfēn 氣氛　qìfèn 氣憤　qīfù 欺負　qǐfú 起伏　qífú 祈福　qìgài 氣概　qǐgài 乞丐　qígān 旗杆　qìgōng 氣功　qíguài 奇怪　qìguān 器官　qìhé 契合　qīhēi 漆黑　qǐhòng 起鬨　qìhòu 氣候　qíhuò 期貨　qǐhuǒ 起火　qíjī 奇蹟　qìjī 契機　qíjiàn 期間 歧見　qǐjìn 起勁　qìjīn 迄今　qíkān 期刊　qǐlái 起來　qílǎo 耆老　qìlì 氣力　qíliáng 淒涼　qìliú 氣流　qímǎ 騎馬

qǐmǎ 起碼　qīmán 欺瞞　qǐméng 啓蒙　qímiào 奇妙　qìmǐn 器皿　qímò 期末　qìná 緝拿　qìněi 氣餒　qìpài 氣派　qīpàn 期盼　qípán 棋盤　qǐpàn 企盼　qípáo 旗袍　qìpào 氣泡　qīpiàn 欺騙　qìpò 氣魄　qìqì 漆器　qìqiú 氣球　qǐqiú 乞求　qíqiú 祈求　qíqū 崎嶇　qìquán 棄權　qǐsè 起色　qǐshēn 棲身　qǐshēn 起身　qíshì 騎士　qíshí 其實　qíshì 歧視　qìshì 氣勢　qìshuǐ 汽水　qìsǐ 氣死　qìsī 緝私　qítā 其他 其它　qǐtǎo 乞討　qítè 奇特　qìtǐ 氣體　qìtú 企圖　qīwàng 期望　qìwàng 企望　qìwēn 氣溫　qīwǔ 欺侮　qīxī 棲息　qìxī 氣息　qíxiàn 期限　qìxiàng 氣象　qìxiè 器械　qīxǔ 期許

qīyā 欺壓	qiāndìng 簽訂	qiānzhèng 簽證	qiáo 喬 僑 橋	qíncài 芹菜
qǐyè 企業	qiánfú 潛伏	qiānzhì 牽制	蕎 憔 瞧	qíncháo 秦朝
qíyì 奇異	qiánhòu 前後	qiánzhì 箝制	qiǎo 巧 悄	qīnfàn 侵犯
qǐyì 起義	qiánjìn 前進	qiánzhuāng 錢莊	qiào 俏 峭 殼	qínfèn 勤奮
qíyì 歧異	qiānjiù 遷就	qiānzi 簽字	蹺 竅	qínjiǎn 勤儉
qǐyīn 起因	qiánjū 遷居	qiánzi 鉗子	qiàobì 峭壁	qīnjìn 親近
qìyóu 汽油	qiánkè 掮客	**qiang**	qiáocuì 憔悴	qīnkuài 勤快
qíyú 其餘	qiánkē 前科	qiāng 槍 鏘	qiáodǎ 敲打	qínláo 勤勞
qǐyuán 起源	qiánkūn 乾坤	腔 羌	qiáodūn 橋墩	qīnlüè 侵略
qìyuē 契約	qiānlǐ 千里	qiáng 強 爿	qiǎohé 巧合	qīnmì 親密
qīzhà 欺詐	qiánlì 潛力	戕 疆 牆	qiāojī 敲擊	qínmiǎn 勤勉
qízhì 旗幟	qiānlián 牽連	薔	qiáojiàn 瞧見	qínná 擒拿
qìzhì 棄置	qiánmiàn 前面	qiǎng 搶 強	qiàokè 蹺課	qīnnì 親暱
qìzhì 氣質	qiánmíng 簽名	襁	qiǎokèlì 巧克力	qínpèi 欽佩
qízhōng 其中	qiānmò 阡陌	qiàng 嗆	qiàolì 俏麗	qīnqī 親戚
qīzi 妻子	qiánnéng 潛能	qiǎngàn 搶案	qiáoliáng 橋樑 橋	qīnqiè 親切
qízi 棋子 旗子	qiánnián 前年	qiángbào 強暴	梁	qīnrè 親熱
qǐzi 起子	qiánqū 前驅	qiǎngbǎo 襁褓	qiàomén 竅門	qīnrén 親人
qia	qiànquē 欠缺	qiāngbì 槍斃	qiáoqiān 喬遷	qīnrù 侵入
qiā 掐	qiānràng 謙讓	qiángbì 牆壁	qiāoqiāo 悄悄	qínsèhémíng 琴瑟
qià 恰 洽	qiánrèn 前任	qiángdà 強大	qiǎorán 悄然	和鳴
qiàdāng 恰當	qiánshè 牽涉	qiángdào 強盜	qiáoshēng 僑生	qīnshēn 親身
qiàhǎo 恰好	qiánshēng 前生	qiāngdiào 腔調	qiāozhà 敲詐	qǐnshì 寢室
qiàqiǎo 恰巧	qiánshì 前世	qiángdiào 強調	qiáozhuāng 喬裝	qīnshǒu 親手
qiàshāng 洽商	qiānshōu 歉收	qiángdù 強度	**qie**	qínshòu 禽獸
qiāsǐ 掐死	qiānshǔ 簽署	qiāngduó 搶奪	qiē 切	qīnshǔ 親屬
qiàtán 洽談	qiánshuǐ 潛水	qiǎnggòu 搶購	qié 茄	qīnwěn 親吻
qiāzhù 掐住	qiǎnsòng 遣送	qiánghài 戕害	qiě 且	qínwù 勤務
qian	qiántáo 潛逃	qiángjiān 強姦	qiè 切 怯 妾	qīnxí 侵襲
qiān 千 仟 阡	qiántiān 前天	qiángjiǎo 牆角	竊	qīnyǎn 親眼
僉 簽 遷	qiántǐng 潛艇	qiǎngjié 搶劫	qiēcuō 切磋	qīnyǒu 親友
韆 牽	qiántóu 前頭	qiángjìng 強勁	qièdào 竊盜	qīnzì 親自
鉛 謙 籤	qiántú 前途	qiǎngjiù 搶救	qiēduàn 切斷	**qing**
qián 潛 黔 錢	qiānwàn 千萬	qiángliè 強烈	qièfàn 竊犯	qīng 輕 氫 傾
拑 箝 鉗	qiánwǎng 前往	qiángpò 強迫	qièqǔ 竊取	卿 卿 青
乾 揵 虔	qiānxǐ 遷徙	qiángpò 強迫	qiètīng 竊聽	清 蜻
前	qiánxī 前夕	qiángqiú 強求	qièzéi 竊賊	qíng 擎 晴 情
qiǎn 淺 圡	qiānxīn 潛心	qiǎngqiú 強求	qiézi 茄子	qǐng 頃 請
遣 譴	qiānxū 謙虛	qiángquán 強權	**qin**	qìng 罄 親
qiàn 欠 歉	qiānxùn 謙遜	qiāngshā 槍殺	qīn 欽 侵 親	慶
qiānbēi 謙卑	qiányán 前言	qiángshèng 強盛	qín 秦 董 勤	qíngài 情愛
qiánbèi 前輩	qiànyì 歉意	qiángwēi 薔薇	懃 琴 禽	qǐngān 請安
qiánbì 錢幣	qiānyí 遷移	qiángyìng 強硬	擒 覃 芹	qīngbái 清白
qiānbǐ 鉛筆	qiānyǐn 牽引	qiāngzhī 槍枝	qǐn 寢	qíngbào 情報
qiánbiān 前邊	qiánzài 潛在	qiángzhì 強制	**qiao**	qīngcài 青菜
qiáncái 錢財	qiǎnzé 譴責	qiángzhuàng 強壯	qiāo 敲 悄 蹺	qíngcāo 情操
qiānchě 牽扯	qiánzhě 前者	**qiao**	qǐn 寢	qīngcháng 清償
qiánchéng 虔誠		qiāo 敲 悄 蹺	qīnàide 親愛的	qīngcháo 清朝

qīngchè 清澈　qīngshì 輕視　qiújìn 囚禁　qǔshèng 取勝　quánxīn 全心
qīngchén 清晨　qíngshì 情勢　qiújiù 求救　qùshì 去世　quányí 權宜
qīngchú 清除　qīngshuài 輕率　qiūlíng 丘陵　qūshì 趨勢　quányì 權益
qīngchūn 青春　qīngshuǎng 清爽　qiúmí 球迷　qūshǐ 驅使　quányù 痊癒
qīngcōng 青蔥　qīngsōng 輕鬆　qiūqiān 秋千 鞦韆　qùwèi 趣味　quányuán 泉源
qīngdàn 氫彈　qīngsù 傾訴　qiúsài 球賽　qūxiàn 曲線　quānzi 圈子
qīngdàn 清單　qīngsuàn 清算　qiūsè 秋色　qūxiàng 趨向　quànzǔ 勸阻
qīngdàn 清淡　qīngtiān 青天　qiúshì 囚室　qǔxiàng 取向
qīngdǎo 傾倒　qíngtiān 晴天　qiūtiān 秋天　qǔxiāo 取消

qīngdǎo 傾倒　qǐngtiě 請帖　qiúxié 球鞋　qūxié 祛邪　quē 缺
qīngdǎo 青島　qīngtīng 傾聽　qiúxíng 球形　qūyù 區域　què 雀 怯 卻 鵲 確 雀斑
qīngdiǎn 慶典　qīngtíng 蜻蜓　qiúxué 求學　qǔyuè 取悅
qīngfú 輕浮　qīngtóng 青銅　qiūyǐn 蚯蚓　qūzhé 曲折　quèbān 雀斑
qīngfù 情婦　qīngwā 青蛙　qiúyuán 球員　qūzhú 驅逐　quèbǎo 確保
qīnggǎn 情感　qīngwēi 輕微　qiúzhǎng 酋長　qūzi 曲子　quèbù 卻步
qīngguān 清官　qǐngwèn 請問　　　　　quēdiǎn 缺點

　　quèdìng 確定

qīnghǎi 青海　qīngxī 清晰　qū 麴 祛 趨 區 驅 軀 嶇 屈 瞿 曲 蛆　quān 圈　quēfá 缺乏
qìnghè 慶賀　qīngxǐ 清洗　　　　quán 泉 拳 全 詮 痊 權　quènuò 怯懦
qīnghū 輕忽　qīngxiàng 傾向　　　　　　quèqiè 確切
qīngjiā 親家　qīngxiāo 傾銷　qú 麴 渠 癯　quǎn 犬　quèrèn 確認
qǐngjià 請假　qīngxié 傾斜　qǔ 曲 取 娶　quàn 券 勸　quèruò 怯弱
qǐngjiǎn 請柬　qīngxīn 清新　qù 去 覷 趣　quánbù 全部　quēshǎo 缺少
qīngjiāo 青椒　qīngxǐng 清醒　qūbié 區別　quánchǐ 犬齒　quēshī 缺失
qǐngjiào 請教　qíngxíng 情形　qùchú 去除　quàndǎo 勸導　quèshí 卻是 確實
qīngjié 清潔　qìngxìng 慶幸　qùchù 去處　quàngào 勸告　quèxí 缺席
qíngjié 情節　qíngxù 情緒　qǔchū 取出　quánguì 權貴　quēxiàn 缺陷
qìngjìn 罄盡　qīngyì 輕易　qūcóng 屈從　quánguó 全國　quèyuè 雀躍
qǐngjǐng 情景　qíngyì 情誼　qǔdài 取代　quánjiā 全家　quèzáo 確鑿
qǐngkè 頃刻 請客　qíngyì 情意　qúdào 渠道　quánlěidǎ 全壘打

qīngkuài 輕快　qíngyíng 輕盈　qǔdé 取得　quánlì 全力 權力 權利　qūn 夋
qíngkuàng 情況　qíngyuàn 情願　qǔdì 取締　　　　qún 群 裙
qīnglài 青睞　qíngyuàn 請願　qūfēn 區分　quánmiàn 全面　qúndǎo 群島

qīnglǐ 清理　qīngzhēn 清真　qūfú 屈服　quánmín 全民　qúnjí 群集
qínglǐ 情理　qìngzhù 慶祝　qūfù 曲阜　quánnéng 全能　qúntǐ 群體
qīnglián 清廉　qióng 瓊 窮 穹　qǔgǎn 取趕　quánpán 全盤　qúnzhòng 群眾
qīngliáng 清涼　qióngcāng 穹蒼　qūgùnqiú 曲棍球　quánqiú 全球　qúnzi 裙子
qínglǚ 情侶　qióngrén 窮人　qùguò 去過　quánshēn 全身

qīngmíng 清明　qióngyáo 瓊瑤　qùhuǎn 趨緩　quánshénguànzhù 全神貫注　rán 然 燃
qīngnián 青年　　　　　qūjiān 區間　　　　rǎn 染 冉

qǐngqiú 請求　qiū 秋 鞦 丘 邱 蚯　qūjiě 曲解　quánshì 詮釋 權勢　ránér 然而
qíngqù 情趣　　　　　qùnián 去年　quánshuǐ 泉水　ránhòu 然後
qíngrén 情人　qiú 囚 求 球 酋　qūqū 區區　quāntào 圈套　ránliào 燃料
qīngsè 青色　　　　　qǔrù 屈辱　quántǐ 全體　rǎnrǎn 冉冉
qīngshàonián 青少年　qiúfàn 囚犯　qùsàn 驅散　quántóu 拳頭　rǎnshàng 染上
qiūfēn 秋分　qǔshě 取捨　quánwēi 權威　ránshāo 燃燒

qīngshēng 輕聲　qiúhūn 求婚

shàofù 少婦	shèxián 涉嫌	shēnrù 深入	shēngdiào 聲調
shāohòu 稍候	shèxiǎng 設想	shénsè 神色	shēngdòng 生動
shāohǔi 燒燬	shèyǐng 攝影	shēnshēn 深深	shěngfǔ 省府
shǎojiàn 少見	shèzhì 設置	shěnshèn 審慎	shēnggēn 生根
shǎolái 少來		shēnshen 嬸嬸	shèngguò 勝過
shàolínsì 少林寺	**shei**	shénshèng 神聖	shēnghuá 昇華
shāomài 燒賣	shéi 誰	shēnshì 紳士 身世	shěnghùi 省會
shàonián 少年		shēnshǒu 伸手	shēnghúo 生活
shàonǔ 少女	**shen**	shēnsù 申訴	shěngjí 省籍
shǎoshù 少數	shēn 申 伸 紳 呻 參 柔 深 身	shēnsùi 深邃	shēngjì 生計
shāowēi 稍微	shén 神 什	shéntài 神態	shēngjí 升級
shāoxiāng 燒香	shěn 沈 審 嬸 瀋	shēntǐ 身體	shèngjīng 聖經
shàoxiào 少校	shèn 甚 慎 滲 腎	shéntóng 神童	shèngkuàng 盛況
sháoxīng 紹興	shēnbiān 身邊	shèntòu 滲透	shēnglǐ 生理
sháozi 勺子 杓子	shēncái 身材	shènwéi 甚為	shènglì 勝利
	shēnchá 身查	shénxiān 神仙	shěnglüè 省略
she	shēnchén 深沈	shēnxīn 身心	shēngmíng 聲名 聲明
shē 賒 奢	shēnchì 申斥	shēnxíng 身形	shēngmìng 生命
shé 甚 折 余 舌 蛇	shēnchū 伸出	shěnxùn 審訊	shēngnǔ 甥女
shě 捨	shēnchù 深處	shěnyáng 瀋陽	shēngpà 生怕
shè 設 赦 舍 社 涉 攝 射	shēndù 深度	shēnyè 深夜	shēngpíng 生平
shèbèi 設備	shēnfèn 身份	shěnyì 審議	shēngqì 生氣
shěbùdé 捨不得	shénfēngdùi 神風隊	shēnyín 呻吟	shěngqián 省錢
shēchǐ 奢侈	shénfù 神父	shènzàng 腎臟	shēngqián 生前
shědé 捨得	shēngǎn 深感	shēnzào 深造	shēngqiān 升遷
shèfǎ 設法	shěnhé 審核	shēnzhǎn 伸展	shèngrén 聖人
shēgòu 賒購	shēnhòu 深厚	shènzhì 甚至	shèngrèn 勝任
shèhùi 社會	shénhuà 神話	shènzhòng 慎重	shēngrì 生日
shèjì 設計	shēnhuà 深化	shénzhōu 神州	shēngsè 生色
shèjí 涉及	shénjīng 神經	shēnzi 身子	shèngshì 省事
shèlì 設立	shēnjiù 深究		shēngshì 聲勢
shèlùn 社論	shēnjùn 深圳	**sheng**	shēngshǒu 生手
shéme 甚麼 什麼	shēnkè 深刻	shēng 聲 生 牲 甥 笙 升 昇 勝	shēngshū 生疏
shèmén 射門	shénmì 神秘	shéng 繩	shēngsǐ 生死
shèmiǎn 赦免	shénnóng 神農	shěng 省	shèngsuàn 勝算
shěqì 捨棄	shěnpàn 審判	shèng 剩 盛 聖 勝	shéngsǔo 繩索
shēqiàn 賒欠	shēnpáng 身旁	shèngbài 勝敗	shēngtài 生態
shèqū 社區	shénqí 神奇	shèngbìng 生病	shēngwàng 聲望
shèqǔ 攝取	shénqì 神氣	shēngchǎn 生產	shēngwù 生物
shèshī 設施	shēnqiè 深切	shēngchēng 聲稱	shèngxià 剩下
shèshì 攝氏	shēnqǐng 申請	shēngchù 牲畜	shēngxiǎng 聲響
shétou 舌頭	shénqíng 神情	shèngchuán 盛傳	shēngxiào 生肖 生效
shètuán 社團	shēnqū 身軀	shēngcún 生存	shèngxíng 盛行
shēwàng 奢望	shénrén 神人	shèngdàn 聖誕	shēngxiù 生鏽
	shēnrù 滲入	shèngdì 勝地	shēngxué 升學
			shēngyá 生涯

shēngyì 生意	
shēngyīn 聲音	
shèngyú 剩餘	
shēngyù 聲譽 生育	
shēngyuán 聲援	
shěngzhǎng 省長	
shēngzhǎng 生長	
shēngzhí 生殖 升值	
shéngzi 繩子	
shi	
shī 詩 尸 屍 蝨 施 失 濕 師 獅	
shí 食 拾 蝕 石 十 時 什 拾 識 實	
shǐ 矢 屎 始 史 駛 使 豕	
shì 示 飾 嗜 士 仕 侍 恃 世 式 試 拭 釋 筮 噬 勢 市 識 事 適 是 誓 逝 氏 視 室	
shi 匙	
shībài 失敗	
shìbàn 試辦	
shíbēi 石碑	
shíběn 蝕本	
shìbì 石壁	
shìbì 勢必	
shìbiàn 事變	
shìbié 識別	
shìbīng 士兵	
shíchā 時差	
shìchá 視察	
shícháng 時常	
shìcháng 市場	
shícháng 失常	
shíchén 時辰	
shǐchū 使出	

shǒushí 守時
shōushí 收拾
shǒushì 手勢
shǒushù 手術
shóushuì 熟睡
shòusī 壽司
shǒusuì 守歲
shōusuō 收縮
shǒutào 手套
shǒutí 手提
shǒuwàn 手腕
shǒuwèi 守衛 首位
shǒuxī 熟悉
shǒuxià 手下
shǒuxiān 首先
shǒuxiàng 首相
shòuxìn 守信
shòuxīng 壽星
shòuxíng 獸行
shǒuxù 手續
shòuxùn 受訓
shǒuyǎng 收養
shǒuyào 首要
shòuyì 收益
shòuyī 獸醫
shòuyì 受益 授意
shǒuyín 手淫
shǒuyìn 手印
shǒuyǔ 手語
shòuyù 獸慾
shòuyǔ 授予
shǒuzhǎng 手掌 首長
shōuzhī 收支
shǒuzhǐ 手指
shǒuzhōng 手中
shǒuzhù 守住
shǒuzhuó 手鐲
shǒuzú 手足

shu
shū 書 殳 疏 蔬 梳 樞 尌 殊 舒 抒 紓 叔 輸
shú 孰 熟 塾

几 朮 叔
菽 淑 贖
shǔ 數 暑 署
薯 曙 黍
蜀 屬 鼠
shù 倏 庶 戍
恕 數 豎
樹 署 曙
束 漱 尤
術 述 墅
shūbāo 書包
shūběn 書本
shūcài 蔬菜
shūchū 輸出
shūdǎo 疏導
shūdiàn 書店
shùé 數額
shūfǎ 書法
shūfáng 書房
shùfú 束縛
shūfú 舒服
shūfù 叔父
shùgàn 樹幹
shǔguāng 曙光
shǔguǒ 蔬果
shūhū 倏忽
shūhū 疏忽
shūjí 書籍
shūjià 書架
shǔjià 暑假
shūjiě 抒解
shújīn 贖金
shūjīng 書經
shùjù 數據
shùkǒu 漱口
shūkùn 紓困
shùlì 豎立
shùliàng 數量
shùlín 樹林
shūmiàn 書面
shùmín 庶民
shūmíng 書名
shǔmíng 署名
shùmù 數目 樹木
shūnyu 樞紐
shūnǚ 淑女
shùpí 樹皮

shūqíng 抒情
shūrù 輸入
shùshāo 樹梢
shūshī 疏失
shùshì 術士
shūshì 舒適
shùshǒu 戍守
shùshǒuwúcè 束手無策
shúshu 叔叔
shùshuō 述說
shūtǎn 舒坦
shǔtiáo 薯條
shūtōng 疏通
shùwèi 數位
shūxiě 書寫
shūxìn 書信
shùxué 數學
shǔyì 鼠疫
shùyǔ 術語
shǔyú 屬於
shūyuǎn 疏遠
shūzhāi 書齋
shùzhī 樹枝
shūzhuāng 梳妝
shūzhuō 書桌
shùzì 數字
shūzi 梳子
shùzuì 恕罪
shúzuì 贖罪

shua
shuā 刷
shuǎ 耍
shuākǎ 刷卡
shuāxǐ 刷洗
shuāyá 刷牙
shuāzi 刷子

shuai
shuāi 衰 摔
shuǎi 甩
shuài 率 蟀 帥
shuāibài 衰敗
shuāidǎo 摔倒
shuàigē 帥哥
shuāijiāo 摔跤
shuāilǎo 衰老
shuàilǐng 率領

shuāiluò 衰落
shuāiruò 衰弱
shuāituì 衰退

shuan
shuān 拴 閂
shuàn 涮

shuang
shuāng 霜 孀 雙
shuǎng 爽
shuāngbāotāi 雙胞胎
shuāngchóng 雙重
shuāngfāng 雙方
shuāngguān 雙關
shuāngguǐ 雙軌
shuǎngkuài 爽快
shuāngshù 雙數

shui
shuí 誰
shuǐ 水
shuì 稅 說 睡
shuǐbà 水壩
shuǐcáo 水槽
shuǐchē 水車
shuǐchí 水池
shuǐdào 水稻
shuǐdī 水滴
shuǐdòu 水痘
shuìfú 說服
shuǐgōu 水溝
shuǐguǎn 水管
shuǐguǒ 水果
shuǐhú 水壺
shuǐjiǎo 水餃
shuìjiào 睡覺
shuǐjīng 水晶
shuìjuān 稅捐
shuìkè 睡客
shuǐkù 水庫
shuǐlì 水力 水利
shuǐliú 水流
shuìlǜ 稅率
shuìmián 睡眠
shuǐní 水泥
shuǐniǎo 水鳥

shuǐniú 水牛
shuǐpíng 水平
shuǐshǒu 水手
shuìshōu 稅收
shuǐtǎ 水塔
shuǐtáng 水塘
shuǐtǔ 水土
shuìxǐng 睡醒
shuìyī 睡衣
shuǐyuán 水源
shuìzháo 睡著
shuìzhì 稅制
shuǐzhǔn 水準

shun
shùn 順 舜 瞬
shùnbiàn 順便
shùncóng 順從
shùnjiān 瞬間
shùnkǒu 順口
shùnlì 順利
shùnshí 瞬時
shùnshǒu 順手
shùnxù 順序

shuo
shuō 說
shuò 碩 朔 欷
shuōbùdìng 說不定
shuōdà 碩大
shuōdào 說道 說到
shuōfǎ 說法
shuòfēng 朔風
shuōfú 說服
shuōhuà 說話
shuōhuǎng 說謊
shuōmíng 說明
shuòshì 碩士

si
sī ㄙ 私 司 斯 撕 廝 虒 思 絲
sǐ 死
sì 肆 伺 飼 嗣 四 寺 俟 巳 祀 似 賜
sǐbǎn 死板

táijiē 臺階	tànqíu 探求	táo 逃 桃 匋	tèzhì 特質	tǐxì 體系
tàikōng 太空	tǎnrán 坦然	陶 淘 萄	**teng**	tíxī 提攜
táinán 台南	tànshǎng 嘆賞	tǎo 討	téng 疼 滕	tǐxiàn 體現
tàipíng 太平	tǎnshuài 坦率	tào 套	藤 騰 謄	tǐxíng 體型
táiqǐ 抬起	tànsuǒ 探索	táobì 逃避	téngběn 謄本	tíxǐng 提醒
táiqíu 台球	tāntā 坍塌	táocí 陶瓷	téngchū 騰出	tíyào 提要
tàirán 泰然	tántán 談談	táofàn 逃犯	téngqì 藤器	tíyì 提議
tàishān 泰山	tàntǎo 探討	tàofáng 套房	téngtòng 疼痛	tǐyù 體育
tàitai 太太	tǎntè 忐忑	táohuā 桃花	téngxiě 謄寫	tízǎo 提早
táitóu 抬頭	tàntīng 探聽	tǎojià 討價	**ti**	tǐzhì 體制
táiwān 台灣 臺灣	tántú 貪圖	táojīn 淘金	tī 梯 踢 剔	tǐzhòng 體重
tàiyáng 太陽	tántǔ 談吐	tàoláo 套牢	tí 啼 提 題	**tian**
táiyǔ 台語	tànwàng 探望	tàolù 套路	tǐ 體 体	tiān 天 添
tàizǐ 太子	tānwū 貪污	táopǎo 逃跑	tì 屜 替 嚏	tián 填 甜 恬
tan	tànxí 嘆息	táoqì 陶器 淘氣	剃 涕 惕	田
tān 癱 攤 灘	tánxiāng 檀香	táoqián 掏錢	tíàn 提案	tiǎn 忝 舔
貪 坍	tānxīn 貪心	táoshuì 逃稅	tíbá 提拔	tiānānmén 天安門
tán 疊 壇 檀	tánxìng 彈性	táotài 淘汰	tícái 題材	tiánbǔ 填補
罈 潭 譚	tánzāng 貪贓	tāotāo 滔滔	tǐcāo 體操	tiáncái 天才
談 疲 彈	tǎnzi 毯子	tāotiāndàzuì 滔天	tíchàng 提倡	tiāndì 天地
tǎn 忐 坦 袒	**tang**	大罪	tíchū 提出	tiāndǐ 天底
後	tāng 湯	táowáng 逃亡	tíchú 剔除	tiāné 天鵝
tàn 歎 嘆 探	táng 唐 糖 塘	tǎoyàn 討厭	tìdài 替代	tiānfèn 天分
炭 碳	堂 膛	táoyě 陶冶	tìdāo 剃刀	tiāngān 天干
tǎnbái 坦白	tǎng 躺 倘	táoyì 逃逸	tídào 提到	tiángěng 田埂
tǎnchéng 坦誠	tàng 趟 燙	tàoyòng 套用	tífáng 提防 堤	tiángòu 添購
tàncí 嘆詞	tángcháo 唐朝	táoyuán 桃園	防 隄防	tiānhuābǎn 天花
tándào 談到	tāngchí 湯匙	táozi 桃子	tígāng 題綱	板
tāndú 貪瀆	tángcù 糖醋	táozǒu 逃走	tígāo 提高	tiānhuáng 天皇
tānfàn 攤販	tángdài 唐代	táozuì 陶醉	tígōng 提供	tiānjiā 添加
tānfāng 坍方	tángdì 堂弟	**te**	tǐhuì 體會	tiānjīn 天津
tànfú 嘆服	tánggē 堂哥	tè 忑 特	tǐjiǎn 體檢	tiánjìng 恬靜 田
tánhé 彈劾	tángguǒ 糖果	tèbié 特別	tíkū 啼哭	徑
tǎnhù 袒護	tánghuáng 堂皇	tèchǎn 特產	tíkuǎn 提款	tiānkōng 天空
tánhuà 談話	tángjiě 堂姐	tèdì 特地	tǐlì 體力	tiānměi 甜美
tánhuāyīxiàn 曇花	tángmèi 堂妹	tèdiǎn 特點	tǐmiàn 體面	tiánmì 甜蜜
一現	tángniàobìng 糖尿	tèdìng 特定	tímíng 提名	tiānmìng 天命
tānhuàn 癱瘓	病	tèqū 特區	tímù 題目	tiānqì 天氣
tánhuáng 彈簧	tángrénjiē 唐人	tèquán 特權	tǐnéng 體能	tiānqiáo 天橋
tànjìu 探究	街	tèsè 特色	tíqián 提前	tiānrán 天然
tǎnkè 坦克	tǎngruò 倘若	tèshè 特赦	tǐrèn 體認	tiánsài 填塞
tānlán 貪婪	tángshān 唐山	tèshǐ 特使	tíshēng 提昇 提	tiānsè 天色
tánlùn 談論	tángshī 唐詩	tèshū 特殊	升	tiānshēng 天生
tānpái 攤牌	tǎngshǐ 倘使	tèwù 特務	tíshì 提示	tiānshǐ 天使
tānpài 攤派	tángtū 唐突	tèxìng 特性	títián 梯田	
tánpàn 談判	tángyuán 湯圓	tèyì 特意 特異	tǐtiē 體貼	
tànqīn 探親	**tao**	tèzhēng 特徵	tǐwēn 體溫	
	tāo 濤 滔 掏			

tiánsuān 甜酸	tiǎoxìn 挑釁	**tong**	tōngxìn 通信
tiāntán 天壇	tiāoxuǎn 挑選	tōng 通	tòngxīn 痛心
tiāntáng 天堂	tiáoyuē 條約	tóng 同 銅 童	tóngxìng 同性
tiāntǐ 天體	tiàoyuè 跳躍	瞳	tōngxíng 通行
tiāntiān 天天	tiàozǎo 跳蚤	tǒng 筒 統 桶	tóngxué 同學
tiántǒng 甜筒	tiǎozhàn 挑戰	tòng 衕 痛	tōngxùn 通訊
tiānwén 天文	tiáozhěng 調整	tóngbān 同班	tóngyàng 同樣
tiānxià 天下	**tie**	tóngbàn 同伴	tóngyè 同業
tiānxiàn 天線	tiē 貼	tóngbāo 同胞	tóngyī 同一
tiānxiě 填寫	tiě 帖 鐵	tōngcháng 通常	tóngyì 同意
tiānxìng 天性	tiè 帖 鐵	tǒngchēng 統稱	tǒngyī 統一
tiányā 填鴨	tiěbàng 鐵棒	tòngchǔ 痛楚	tōngzé 通則
tiányě 田野	tiēbǔ 貼補	tōngdào 通道	tóngzhì 同志
tiānzhēn 天真	tiěchuí 鐵鎚	tóngdié 通牒	tǒngzhì 統治
tiānzhǔjiào 天主	tiědào 鐵道	tōngfēng 通風	tōngzhī 通知
教	tiělù 鐵路	tōnggào 通告	tóngzhōugòngjì 同
tiānzǐ 天子	tiěmù 鐵幕	tōngguò 通過	舟共濟
tiao	tiěqīng 鐵青	tóngháng 同行	**tou**
tiāo 挑	tiěsī 鐵絲	tònghèn 痛恨	tōu 偷
tiáo 條 調 白	tiēxīn 貼心	tōnghóng 通紅	tóu 投 頭
tiāo 挑 宛	tiēzhǐ 貼紙	tōnghuà 同化	tòu 透
tiào 糶 跳	**ting**	tōnghuò 通貨	tou 頭
眺	tīng 聽 廳	tǒngjì 統計	tóubǎn 頭版
tiāobō 挑撥	tíng 亭 停 廷	tōngjiān 通姦	tóubèn 投奔
tiàocáo 跳槽	庭 蜓 挺	tóngjìng 銅鏡	tóubù 頭部
tiāocuò 挑錯	tǐng 艇 挺	tóngjū 同居	tòuchè 透徹
tiāodòng 挑動	tìng 聽	tóngkǒng 瞳孔	tóuchéng 投誠
tiāodòu 挑逗	tǐngbá 挺拔	tòngkǔ 痛苦	tóuděng 頭等
tiáohé 調和	tíngchē 停車	tòngkuài 痛快	tóudù 偷渡
tiáojì 調劑	tīngdào 聽到	tónglèi 同類	tóufà 頭髮
tiáojiàn 條件	tíngdùn 停頓	tóngliáo 同僚	tóugǎo 投稿
tiáojié 調節	tínggé 亭閣	tónglíng 通靈	tōuguò 偷渡過
tiáojiě 調解	tínggōng 停工	tónglóu 銅鑼	tóujī 投機
tiáokuǎn 條款	tǐnghǎo 挺好	tóngméng 同盟	tōukàn 偷看
tiáolǐ 條理	tínghuà 聽話	tóngmóu 同謀	tóukào 投靠
tiáolì 條例	tínghuǒ 停火	tóngnián 童年	tóukuī 頭盔
tiáopèi 調配	tīngjiàn 聽見	tóngqì 銅器	tōulǎn 偷懶
tiàopiào 跳票	tīngkè 聽課	tóngqián 銅錢	tóulǐng 頭領
tiàoqí 跳棋	tíngliú 停留	tōngqín 通勤	tōulù 偷漏
tiáoqíng 調情	tīngmìng 聽命	tóngqíng 同情	tòumíng 透明
tiàosǎn 跳傘	tīngshuō 聽說	tóngrén 同仁	tóumù 頭目
tiāoti 挑剔	tíngyuán 庭園	tóngshí 同時	tóunǎo 頭腦
tiáotíng 調停	tíngyuàn 庭院	tóngshì 同事	tóupí 頭皮
tiàowàng 眺望	tíngzhǐ 停止	tōngshùn 通順	tóupiào 投票
tiáowèi 調味	tíngzhì 停滯	tōngsú 通俗	tōuqiè 偷竊
tiáowén 條文 條	tíngzhí 挺直	tōngtōng 通通	tóurù 投入
紋	tīngzhòng 聽眾	tóngxiāng 同鄉	tóushè 投射
tiàowǔ 跳舞	tíngzi 亭子	tōngxiāo 通宵	tòushì 透視

tóushǒu 投手
tóusù 投訴
tōutīng 偷聽
tóutòng 頭痛
tōutōu 偷偷
tóuxián 頭銜
tóuxiáng 投降
tóuxù 頭緒
tóuyǐng 投影
tóuyūn 頭暈
tóuzhí 投擲
tóuzī 投資
tu
tū 突 凸 禿
tú 涂 塗 途
圖 凸 徒
tǔ 土 吐
tù 吐 兔
tuán 團
túbù 徒步
tūchū 突出 凸
出
tǔdì 土地
túdì 徒弟
tǔdòu 土豆
tǔěrqí 土耳其
tǔfěi 土匪
túhuà 圖畫
tǔhuà 土話
tújí 突擊
tújìng 途徑
túmǒ 塗抹
túpò 突破
túrán 突然 徒
然
tǔrǎng 土壤
túshā 屠殺
túshūguǎn 圖書
館
tǔtán 吐痰
tūtóu 禿頭
túwù 突兀
túxiǎn 凸顯
túxíng 圖形 徒
刑
túyā 塗鴉

túzǎi 屠宰	tún 臀 屯 囤	wá 娃	人	wánwù 玩物
túzhāng 圖章	tún 飩 豚	wǎ 瓦	wàiyì 外溢	wànxī 惋惜
túzhōng 途中	tùn 褪	wà 襪	wàiyǔ 外語	wǎnxiá 晚霞
tùzi 兔子	tūnbìng 吞併	wādì 窪地	wàiyù 外遇	wánxiào 玩笑
tuan	túnbù 臀部	wājiě 瓦解	wàiyuán 外援	wányán 婉言
tuán 團	túnjī 囤積	wājué 挖掘	wàizài 外在	wànyī 萬一
tuàn 彖	tùnsè 褪色	wǎlì 瓦礫	wàizhài 外債	wánzhěng 完整
tuánjié 團結	tūnshì 吞噬	wǎpiàn 瓦片	wàizī 外資	wǎnzhuǎn 婉轉
tuánjù 團聚	túntián 屯田	wāsī 瓦斯	**wan**	wǎnzhuāng 晚裝
tuántǐ 團體	tūnxià 吞下	wǎtè 瓦特	wān 彎 灣	wànzi 腕子
tuányuán 團員	**tuo**	wáwa 娃娃	wán 完 玩 頑 丸	**wang**
tui	tuō 脫 拖 托 託	wàzi 襪子	wǎn 莞 宛 碗 婉 惋 挽 晚	wāng 汪 尢
tuī 推	túo 駝 鴕 陀	**wai**	wàn 玩 腕 惋 萬	wáng 王 亡
túí 頹	tuǒ 橢 妥	wāi 歪 喎	wǎnān 晚安	wǎng 枉 往 网 罔 網
tǔí 腿	tuò 拓 唾	wài 外	wánbì 完畢	wàng 旺 妄 望 忘
tùí 蛻 退 褪	tuōba 拖把	wàibàn 外辦	wǎncān 晚餐	wángbā 王八
tuībiàn 蛻變	tuōbèi 駝背	wàibì 外幣	wánchéng 完成	wàngběn 忘本
tuìbù 退步	tuōchē 拖車	wàibiān 外邊	wándàn 完蛋	wǎngcháng 往常
tuīcè 推測	tuōcí 託辭	wàibiǎo 外表	wǎněr 莞爾	wàngdiào 忘掉
tuīchóng 推崇	tuǒdàng 妥當	wàibīn 外賓	wánfàn 晚飯	wàngdòng 妄動
tuīdòng 推動	tuōérsuǒ 托兒所	wàiguó 外國	wànfēn 萬分	wángfēi 王妃
tuīduàn 推斷	tuōfù 託付	wàihào 外號	wángù 頑固	wángfèi 枉費
tuìfáng 退房	tuōguāng 脫光	wàihuì 外匯	wǎnhuí 挽回	wànggù 亡故
tuífèi 頹廢	tuòhuāng 拓荒	wàijí 外籍	wǎnhuì 晚會	wángguó 王國 亡國
tuīguǎng 推廣	tuōjié 脫節	wàijiāo 外交	wànjīnyóu 萬金油	wànghòu 往後
tuìhuà 蛻化 退化	tuōjiù 脫臼	wàijiè 外界	wǎnjiù 挽救	wànghuái 忘懷
tuìhuàn 退換	tuōkǒuérchū 脫口而出	wàikē 外科	wánjù 玩具	wàngjì 旺季 忘記
tuījiàn 推薦	tuōlājī 拖拉機	wàikuài 外快	wǎnjù 婉拒	wàngjiàn 望見
tuīkāi 推開	tuōlí 脫離	wàilái 外來	wǎnliú 挽留	wǎnglái 往來
tuīlǐ 推理	túoluó 陀螺	wàiliú 外流	wánměi 完美	wǎnglù 網路
tuīlùn 推論	tuòmà 唾罵	wàimào 外貿 外貌	wánmìng 玩命	wǎngluó 網羅
tuīná 推拿	tuòmò 唾沫	wàimiàn 外面	wánnòng 玩弄	wǎngluò 網絡
tuìpiào 退票	túoniǎo 鴕鳥	wàipó 外婆	wánǒu 玩偶	wángpái 王牌
tuīqiāo 推敲	tuòqì 唾棄	wàiqiáo 外僑	wǎnpán 碗盤	wǎngqiú 網球
tuìràng 退讓	tuǒshàn 妥善	wāiqū 歪曲	wánpí 頑皮	wǎngrán 枉然
tuìsè 褪色	tuōshēn 脫身	wàirén 外人	wánqiáng 頑強	wàngrì 往日
tuíshì 頹勢	tuōxià 脫下	wàishāng 外商	wānqū 彎曲	wàngshèng 旺盛
tuīwěi 推諉	tuōxié 拖鞋	wàishēng 外甥	wánquán 完全	wàngshì 往事
tuìwǔ 退伍	tuǒxié 妥協	wàisūn 外孫	wánrú 宛如	wǎngwǎng 往往
tuīxiāo 推銷	tuōyán 拖延	wàitào 外套	wánshàn 完善	wǎngxí 往昔
tuīxiè 推卸	tuǒyuán 橢圓	wàitou 外頭	wǎnshàng 晚上	wàngxiǎng 妄想
tuìxíng 推行	tuòzhǎn 拓展	wàiwǔ 外侮	wánshuǎ 玩耍	wāngyáng 汪洋
tuìxiū 退休	**wa**	wàixiàng 外向	wànsuì 萬歲	wàngyuǎnjìng 望遠
tuīxuǎn 推選	wā 窪 挖 蛙	wàixiāo 外銷		
tun	注 窪	wāixié 歪斜		
tūn 吞		wàixiè 外洩		
		wàixīngrén 外星		

46　　　　　　　　　　　　　拼音索引表

wūlài 誣賴 51/28
wúlǐ 無禮 31/117
wùlǐ 物理 86/5
wǔlì 武力 88/36
wúliáo 無聊 31/117
wūlóngchá 烏龍茶 178/5
wǔlóngwǔshī 舞龍舞獅 31/119
wūlǔmùqí 烏魯木齊 178/5
wúlùn 無論 31/117
wǔmèi 嫵媚 31/118
wùmiàn 晤面 1/7
wūmiè 污衊 27/37
wúmíng 無名 31/117
wúmíngshì 無名氏 31/117
wúnài 無奈 31/117
wúnéng 無能 31/117
wūní 污泥 27/37
wūpó 巫婆 51/27
wǔqì 武器 88/36
wùqì 霧氣 105/5
wúqíng 無情 31/117
wúqíong 無窮 31/117
wúqíongwújìn 無窮無盡 31/117
wūrǎn 污染 27/37
wūrù 污辱 27/37
wǔrù 侮辱 54/23
wùsè 物色 86/5
wúshénlùn 無神論 31/117
wǔshì 武士 88/36
wúshù 無數 31/117
wūshù 巫術 51/27
wǔshù 武術 88/36
wūshǔi 污水 27/37
wǔshùi 午睡 93/1
wúsǔowèi 無所謂 31/117
wǔtái 舞台 31/119
wùtán 晤談 1/7
wùtǐ 物體 86/5
wūtūobāng 烏托邦 178/5
wúwèi 無謂 31/117
wǔxiá 武俠 88/36
wúxiàn 無限 31/117 無線 31/117
wūxiàn 誣陷 51/28
wúxiào 無效 31/117
wǔxíng 五行 1/3
wùxìng 悟性 1/6
wúxíng 無形 31/117
wúxū 無需 31/117
wúyá 無涯 31/117
wūyā 烏鴉 178/5
wūyán 屋簷 128/9
wúyàng 無恙 31/117
wǔyè 午夜 93/1
wúyí 無疑 31/117
wúyì 無意 31/117
wǔyì 武藝 88/36
wùyīng 兀鷹 11/35
wūyǒu 烏有 178/5
wúzhī 無知 31/117
wùzhí 物質 86/5
wǔzhuāng 武裝 88/36
wūzhúo 污濁 27/37
wùzī 物資 86/5
wūzi 屋子 128/9
wúzùi 無罪 31/117

xi

xī 希 3/20 稀 3/21 吸 14/92 兮 27/5 羲 27/6 犧 27/7 嘻 69/112 嬉 69/113 夕 72/1 汐 72/2 昔 76/77 惜 76/78 膝 77/93 犀 90/6 析 96/7 晰 96/8 淅 96/9 蜥 96/10 奚 103/6 溪 103/7 西 130/1 息 139/2 熄 139/4 熙 145/4 悉 156/11 蟋 156/12 巂 162/8 攜 162/9
xí 席 31/78 蓆 31/79 昔 76/77 惜 76/78 習 124/3 襲 132/26 息 139/2 媳 139/3 熄 139/4 錫 163/6
xǐ 洗 11/37 匚 22/2 璽 29/30 喜 69/109 禧 69/110 囍 69/111 徙 88/35
xì 糸 29/13 隙 29/44 卌 31/116 繫 77/16 戲 69/99 夕 72/1 汐 72/2 矽 72/3 舄 131/5 細 143/6 系 153/12 係 153/13
xǐài 喜愛 69/109
xīān 西安 130/1
xīàn 西岸 130/1
xībānyá 西班牙 130/1
xìbāo 細胞 143/6
xíbié 惜別 76/78
xībólìyǎ 西伯利亞 130/1
xībù 西部 130/1
xīcān 西餐 130/1
xīchénqì 吸塵器 14/92
xīdài 攜帶 162/9
xǐdí 洗滌 11/37
xìdì 隙地 29/44
xīdú 吸毒 14/92
xīfàn 稀飯 3/21
xīfāng 西方 130/1
xífù 媳婦 139/3
xīgài 膝蓋 77/93
xīgòng 西貢 130/1
xīgǔ 溪谷 103/7
xīguā 西瓜 130/1
xīguǎn 吸管 14/92
xíguàn 習慣 124/3
xīhǎn 希罕 3/20
xǐhào 喜好 69/109
xǐhuān 喜歡 69/109
xíjí 襲擊 132/26
xìjié 細節 143/6
xǐjǐu 喜酒 69/109
xìjù 戲劇 69/99
xǐjù 喜劇 69/109
xíjuǎn 席捲 31/78
xìjùn 細菌 143/6
xīlà 希臘 3/20
xīlì 犀利 90/6 淅瀝 96/9
xǐliǎn 洗臉 11/37
xìliè 系列 153/12
xīlíu 溪流 103/7
xīlùo 奚落 103/6
xīmiè 熄滅 139/4
xìnì 細膩 143/6
xīníu 犀牛 90/6
xǐnùàilè 喜怒哀樂 69/109
xīōu 西歐 130/1
xīpí 嬉皮 69/113
xīqí 稀奇 3/21
xīqǔ 吸取 14/92
xìqǔ 戲曲 69/99
xǐquè 喜鵲 69/109
xīrì 昔日 76/77
xīshǎo 稀少 3/21
xīshēng 犧牲 27/7
xīshí 吸食 14/92
xǐshì 喜事 69/109
xǐshǒu 洗手 11/37
xīshōu 吸收 14/92
xīshǒu 攜手 162/9
xìshù 係數 153/13
xǐshuā 洗刷 11/37
xīshuài 蟋蟀 156/12
xīshuāngbǎnnà 西雙版納 130/1
xīshǔi 溪水 103/7
xísú 習俗 124/3
xītèlè 希特勒 3/20
xītiān 西天 130/1
xītiěshí 吸鐵石 14/92
xìtǒng 系統 153/12
xīwàng 希望 3/20
xíwèi 席位 31/78
xīxì 嬉戲 69/113
xíxíxiāngguān 息息相關 139/2
xīxiào 嘻笑 69/112
xìxiǎo 細小 143/6
xìxīn 細心 143/6
xīyān 吸煙 14/92
xǐyán 喜筵 69/109
xīyáng 夕陽 72/1
xīyáng 西洋 130/1
xǐyī 洗衣 11/37
xīyì 蜥蜴 96/10
xīyī 西醫 130/1
xīyǐn 吸引 14/92
xìyuàn 戲院 69/99
xīyuán 西元 130/1
xǐyuè 喜悅 69/109
xīzàng 西藏 130/1
xǐzǎo 洗澡 11/37
xìzhì 細緻 143/6
xīzhuāng 西裝 130/1
xízi 蓆子 31/79

xia

xiā 蝦 14/111 瞎 79/10
xiá 瑕 14/112 霞 14/113 暇 14/114 黠 31/9 俠 39/16 峽 39/17 狹 39/18 挾 39/19 轄 79/11 匣 112/4
xià 下 1/68 嚇 39/82 夏 148/18 廈 148/19
xiàbā 下巴 1/68
xiàbān 下班 1/68
xiàbiān 下邊 1/68
xiáchí 挾持 39/19
xiàcì 下次 1/68
xiácī 瑕疵 14/112
xiádài 挾帶 39/19
xiàfēng 下風 1/68
xiágǔ 峽谷 39/17
xiáguāng 霞光 14/113
xiàhǎi 下海 1/68
xiàhu 嚇唬 39/82
xiàjì 夏季 148/18
xiàjiàng 下降 1/68
xiàkè 下課 1/68
xiàlái 下來 1/68
xiàlíu 下流 1/68
xiàlùo 下落 1/68
xiàmén 廈門 148/19
xiàmiàn 下面 1/68 下麵 1/68
xiàqí 下棋 1/68
xiàqù 下去 1/68
xiáqū 轄區 79/11
xiārén 蝦仁 14/111
xiàrén 嚇人 39/82
xiàshǒu 下手 1/68
xiàtiān 夏天 148/18
xiàwēiyí 夏威夷 148/18
xiàwǔ 下午 1/68
xiàxiāng 下鄉 1/68
xiàxún 下旬 1/68
xiáyì 狹義 39/18
xiàyóu 下游 1/68
xiàyǔ 下雨 1/68
xiázhǎi 狹窄 39/18
xiàzhì 夏至 148/18
xiāzi 瞎子 79/10
xiázi 匣子 112/4

xian

xiān 先 11/36 暹 15/93 仙 67/4 掀 96/5 鮮 123/16 厶 131/4

xiàolì 效力　xiàolù 銷路　xiàolù 效率　xiǎomài 小麥　xiǎomǐ 小米　xiāomǐ 消弭　xiāomiè 消滅　xiāomó 消磨　xiàomǔ 酵母　xiàonéng 效能　xiǎoqì 小氣　xiāoqiǎn 消遣　xiǎoqù 小覷　xiǎorén 小人　xiàoróng 笑容　xiāosǎ 瀟灑　xiāosè 蕭瑟　xiǎoshí 小時　xiǎoshì 小事　xiāoshì 消失　xiāoshì 消逝　xiǎoshíhòu 小時候　xiāoshòu 消瘦 銷售　xiàoshùn 孝順　xiǎoshuō 小說　xiǎosī 小斯　xiàosù 酵素　xiāotiáo 蕭條　xiǎotōu 小偷　xiāoxí 消息　xiàoxiàng 肖像　xiǎoxīn 小心　xiǎoxíng 小型　xiāoxióng 梟雄　xiǎoxué 小學　xiāoyáo 逍遙　xiāoyè 宵夜　xiàoyì 效益　xiàoyòng 效用　xiàoyǒu 校友　xiàoyuán 校園　xiāozhǎng 消長　xiàozhǎng 校長　xiāozhāng 囂張　xiǎozhuàn 小篆　xiàozǐ 孝子

xiǎozi 小子　xiǎozǔ 小組

xie

xiē 歇 蠍 些　xié 諧 點 協 脅 挾 斜 鞋 絮 邪 擷　xiě 血 寫　xié 淺 屑 械 褻 卸 瀉 謝 懈 蟹　xiédài 挾帶 鞋帶　xièdài 懈怠　xiédìng 協定　xiédù 斜度　xièdú 褻瀆　xié'è 邪惡　xiěguǎn 血管　xiēhòuyǔ 歇後語　xiéhuì 協會　xièhuò 卸貨　xiéjué 絕絕　xièlòu 洩漏　xièlù 洩露　xiélù 斜路 邪路　xiépò 脅迫　xiépō 斜坡　xiěqì 洩氣　xiěqiú 血球　xiéshāng 協商　xiéshuō 邪說　xiēsù 歇宿　xiétiáo 協調　xiětǒng 血統　xièxì 歇息　xièxiè 謝謝　xiěxìn 寫信　xiěxīng 血腥　xiěyā 血壓　xiěyè 血液　xiéyì 協議　xiěyì 血液　xiězhào 寫照　xiězhēn 寫真

xiézhù 協助　xiēzi 蠍子

xie

xiézi 鞋子　xiězì 寫字　xiězuò 寫作

xin

xīn 馨 鑫 辛 新 薪 心 芯 欣　xìn 釁 R 信 芯 凶　xīnbùzàiyān 心不在焉　xīnfèng 薪俸　xìnfēng 信封　xìnfèng 信奉　xìnfú 信服　xīnfú 心服　xìnfù 心腹　xīngān 心肝　xīnhài 辛亥　xìnhào 信號　xīnhěnshǒulà 心狠手辣　xīnhuái 心懷　xīnjiāpō 新加坡　xìnjiān 信箋　xìnjiàn 信件　xīnjiāng 新疆　xīnjiào 新教　xīnjiāo 心焦　xīnjìng 心境　xīnkǔ 辛苦　xìnlài 信賴　xīnláng 新郎　xīnlǐ 心理 心裡　xīnlíng 心靈　xīnmù 心目　xīnnián 新年　xìnniàn 信念　xīnniáng 新娘　xīnqí 新奇　xīnqíng 心情　xīnrán 欣然　xìnrèn 信任　xīnshǎng 欣賞　xīnshēng 新生 心

擊　xīnshì 心事　xīnshǒu 新手　xīnshuǐ 薪水　xīnsī 心思　xīnsuì 心碎　xīntài 心態　xīnténg 心疼　xīntiào 心跳　xīntóu 心頭　xìntú 信徒　xìntuō 信託　xìnwèi 欣慰　xīnwén 新聞　xìnxì 釁隙　xìnxí 信息　xīnxǐ 欣喜　xīnxīlán 新西蘭　xīnxiān 新鮮　xīnxiāng 馨香　xīnxiǎng 心想　xìnxīn 信心　xīnxīnxiàngróng 欣欣向榮　xīnxīng 新興　xìnyǎng 信仰　xīnyì 心意　xīnyǐng 新穎　xìnyòng 信用　xīnyǔ 新語　xìnyù 信譽　xīnyuàn 心願　xīnzàng 心臟　xìnzhǐ 信紙　xīnzhì 心智　xīnzhōng 心中　xīnzī 薪資

xing

xīng 興 星 猩 腥　xíng 行 形 刑 型 邢　xǐng 省 醒　xìng 興 幸 倖 姓 性 杏　xìngbié 性別　xìngbìng 性病　xīngchén 星辰

xíngchéng 形成　xìngcún 倖存　xíngdòng 行動　xìng'ér 幸而　xíngfá 刑罰　xíngfǎ 刑法　xìngfèn 興奮　xìngfú 幸福　xìnggǎn 性感　xìnggé 性格　xìnghǎo 幸好　xínghuì 行賄　xìnghuì 幸會　xīngjiàn 興建　xìngjiāo 性交　xíngjìng 行徑　xìngkuī 幸虧　xínglái 醒來　xínglǐ 行李 行禮　xìnglóng 興隆　xìngmíng 姓名　xìngmìng 性命　xíngnáng 行囊　xìngnéng 性能　xīngqǐ 興起　xīngqī 星期　xǐngqīn 省親　xìngqíng 性情　xíngqiú 刑求　xīngqiú 星球　xìngqù 興趣　xíngrén 行人　xìngrén 杏仁　xíngróng 形容　xíngshēng 形聲　xíngshǐ 行駛 行使　xíngshì 形式 形勢 刑事 型式　xìngshì 姓氏　xīngshuāi 興衰　xīngsù 星宿　xíngtài 形態 型態　xīngwàng 興旺　xíngwéi 行為

xǐngwù 省悟 醒悟
xīngxì 星系
xíngxiàng 形象
xíngxiàng 星象
xíngxiāo 行銷
xíngxīng 行星
xīngxing 猩猩
xíngxiōng 行兇
xīngxiù 星宿
xìngyù 性慾
xìngyùn 幸運
xíngzhě 行者
xíngzhèng 行政
xìngzhì 興致
xìngzhì 性質
xíngzhuàng 形狀
xíngzǒu 行走
xíngzuò 星座

xiong
xiōng 凶 兇 匈 胸 洶 兄
xióng 雄 熊
xiòng 敻
xiōngbù 胸部
xiōngdì 兄弟
xiōngduōjíshǎo 凶多吉少
xiōnggè 凶惡 兇惡
xiōnghěn 兇狠
xiónghòu 雄厚
xiōnghuái 胸懷
xióngjiūjiū 雄赳赳
xióngmāo 熊貓
xiōngměng 凶猛 兇猛
xiōngnú 匈奴
xiōngpú 胸脯
xiōngshǒu 兇手
xiōngtáng 胸膛
xióngwěi 雄偉
xióngxìng 雄性
xiōngxiōng 洶洶
xióngxióng 熊熊
xiōngyálì 匈牙利
xiōngyǒng 洶湧

xiōngzhǎng 兄長
xióngzhǎng 熊掌
xiōngzhào 胸罩
xiōngzhēn 胸針

xiu
xiū 羞 修 休
xiǔ 朽 宿
xiù 繡 鏽 秀 宿 嗅 袖
xiūbǔ 修補
xiūcán 羞慚
xiūchǐ 羞恥
xiūdìng 修訂
xiūgǎi 修改
xiùhuā 繡花
xiūhuì 休會
xiūjià 休假
xiùjué 嗅覺
xiūkè 修課 休克
xiùkǒu 袖口
xiūkuì 羞愧
xiūlǐ 修理
xiùlì 秀麗
xiūnǚ 修女
xiūqìxiāngguān 休戚相關
xiūrù 羞辱
xiūsè 羞澀
xiūshàn 修繕
xiūshì 修飾
xiūxí 休息
xiūxián 休閒
xiūxiǎng 休想
xiūxíng 修行
xiūxué 休學
xiūyǎng 修養
xiùzhēn 袖珍
xiūzhèng 修正
xiūzhǐ 休止

xu
xū 戌 須 鬚 胥 虛 墟 需
xú 徐
xǔ 許
xù 酗 旭 敘

畜 蓄 緒
婿 序 恤
續
xǔduō 許多
xūgòu 虛構
xùjiǔ 酗酒
xǔjiǔ 許久
xǔkě 許可
xùmù 畜牧 序幕
xūqiú 需求
xùrì 旭日
xūróng 虛榮
xūruò 虛弱
xùshù 敘述
xūwèi 虛偽
xúxú 徐徐
xùyán 緒言 序言
xūyào 須要 需要
xùyì 蓄意
xūyú 須臾
xūzhī 須知
xúzhōu 徐州

xuan
xuān 亘 宣 喧 軒 玄 旋 漩 懸
xuǎn 選
xuàn 渲 絢 炫 眩 旋
xuǎnbá 選拔
xuānbù 宣佈 宣布
xuānchēng 宣稱
xuānchuán 宣傳
xuāndǎo 宣導
xuànfēng 旋風
xuāngào 宣告
xuánguà 懸掛
xuānhuá 喧譁
xuǎnjí 選集
xuǎnjǔ 選舉
xuànlàn 絢爛
xuànlì 絢麗
xuánlǜ 旋律

xuánmiào 玄妙
xuǎnmín 選民
xuànrǎn 渲染
xuānrándàbō 軒然大波
xuǎnshǒu 選手
xuánshū 懸殊
xuánwō 漩渦
xuányái 懸崖
xuānyán 宣言
xuānyáng 宣揚
xuànyào 炫耀
xuányí 懸疑
xuǎnzé 選擇
xuánzhuǎn 旋轉

xue
xuē 靴 削 薛
xué 學 穴
xuě 雪 鱈
xuè 削 穴 血
xuěbái 雪白
xuébào 學報
xuěbēng 雪崩
xuédào 學到
xuédào 穴道
xuédé 學得
xuédì 學弟
xuéfèi 學費
xuéhǎo 學好
xuěhuā 雪花
xuéhuì 學會
xuéjiā 雪茄
xuéjiě 學姐
xuélì 學歷
xuémèi 學妹
xuépài 學派
xuéqí 學期
xuěqiú 雪球
xuérén 學人
xuéshēng 學生
xuéshì 學識 學士
xuéshù 學術
xuétáng 學堂
xuétóng 學童
xuétú 學徒
xuéwèi 學位
xuéwèn 學問

xuéxí 學習
xuéxiào 學校
xuéyè 學業
xuéyú 鱈魚
xuéyuàn 學院
xuéyùn 學運
xuézhǎng 學長
xuézhě 學者
xuēzi 靴子

xun
xūn 熏 勳 薰
xún 巡 尋 旬 詢 循
xùn 訓 巽 殉 訊 迅 遜
xúnchá 巡查
xúncháng 尋常
xùndǎo 訓導
xùndào 殉道
xùngǔ 訓詁
xúnháng 巡航
xùnhào 訊號
xúnhuán 循環
xúnhuí 巡迴
xùnjiè 訓誡
xùnliàn 訓練
xúnluó 巡邏
xúnmì 尋覓
xúnqiú 尋求
xùnsè 遜色
xúnshì 巡視
xùnsù 迅速
xūntáo 薰陶
xúnwèn 詢問
xùnwèn 訊問
xùnxí 訊息
xúnyì 巡弋
xùnyú 遜於
xúnzhǎo 尋找

ya
yā 呀 鴉 壓 鴨 押
yá 衙 崖 涯 牙 芽
yǎ 雅 亞 啞
yà 軋 亞 訝 亞

yē 耶 椰	奕 弋 義	yìhéyuán 頤和園	yíqì 遺棄	yíxiàzi 一下子
yé 耶 爺 椰 挪	議 異 翼	yǐhòu 以後	yǐqián 以前	yíxiàng 一向
yě 也 冶 野	翠 譯 驛	yìhuí 一回	yíqiè 一切	yíxiàodàfāng 貽笑 大方
yè 曳 謁 枼	繹 埶 藝	yìhuì 議會	yìqún 一群	
葉 夜 液	意 億 憶	yìhuǐer 一會兒	yìrán 毅然 亦然	yìxiē 一些
腋 頁 業	膽 液 吃	yíhuò 疑惑	yìrán 已然	yìxīn 一心
yěcān 野餐	軼 益 溢	yìhuò 抑或	yìrán 依然	yíxīn 疑心
yēdàn 耶誕	誼 翌 裔	yìjí 亦即	yìrì 翌日	yìxìng 異性
yèjiàn 夜間	易 蜴 逸	yǐjí 以及	yìrúfǎnzhǎng 易如 反掌	yìxù 依序
yějīn 冶金	yíàn 疑案	yìjì 藝妓		yīxué 醫學
yěliàn 冶煉	yìbān 一般	yìjì 遺跡	yǐsèliè 以色列	yìxué 易學
yěmán 野蠻	yíbàn 一半	yìjiàn 意見	yǐshàng 以上	yíyàng 一樣
yěrén 野人	yíbèizi 一輩子	yǐjīng 已經	yīshang 衣裳	yìyào 醫藥
yěshēng 野生	yìbiān 一邊	yìjīng 易經	yìshēng 一生 醫 生	yìyè 肄業
yèshì 夜市	yǐbiàn 以便	yījiù 依舊		yīyī 一一
yěshòu 野獸	yíbìng 一併	yíjū 移居	yìshí 一時	yìyì 異議 意義
yēsū 耶穌	yǐcāng 義倉	yījù 依據	yīshī 醫師	yīyuàn 醫院
yètǐ 液體	yìcè 臆測	yīkào 依靠	yìshì 義士	yìyuán 議員
yěwài 野外	yíchǎn 遺產	yíkuàier 一塊兒	yíshì 儀式	yìyuàn 議院 意 願
yèwǎn 夜晚	yìcháng 異常	yīlākè 伊拉克	yìshí 意識 軼 事	
yèwù 業務	yìchéng 議程	yīlài 倚賴		yízài 一再
yèxiào 夜校	yìchù 益處	yǐlái 以來	yíshī 遺失	yìzǎo 一早
yěxīn 野心	yìchū 溢出	yīlài 依賴	yìshù 藝術	yìzhàn 驛站
yěxǔ 也許	yíchuán 遺傳	yīlǎng 伊朗	yíshuāng 遺孀	yīzhào 依照
yéyé 爺爺	yīcì 依次	yìlì 毅力 吃立	yìsi 意思	yízhènzi 一陣子
yěyíng 野營	yídàlì 義大利 意 大利	yìliáo 醫療	yīsīlán 伊斯蘭	yìzhí 一致 醫治
yēyú 椰揄		yìliào 意料	yìsuì 易碎	yìzhì 抑制
yèyú 業餘	yīdài 衣袋	yìliè 弋獵	yìtāhútú 一塌糊 塗	yǐzhī 已知
yězhū 野豬	yídàn 一旦	yìliú 一流		yìzhì 意志
yēzi 椰子	yídào 一道	yíliú 遺留	yítàitài 姨太太	yízhí 移植
yi	yìdiǎn 一點	yílù 一路	yìtí 議題	yízhǐ 遺址
yī 一 伊 醫 衣 依 壹	yídìng 一定	yìlùn 議論	yìtǐ 液體	yǐzhòng 倚重
	yídòng 移動	yílǜ 一律	yìtóng 一同	yìzhǒng 義塚
yí 疑 彝 儀 台 怡 貽 夷 宜 誼 遺 宜 頤	yìdǒng 易懂	yílǜ 疑慮	yìtú 意圖	yízhǔ 遺囑
	yídòu 疑竇	yímā 姨媽	yǐwài 以外	yīzhuó 衣著
yǐ 乙 倚 椅 矣 蟻 已 以	yídù 一度	yímiàn 一面	yìwài 意外	yǐzi 椅子
	yìèr 一二	yǐmiǎn 以免	yìwàn 億萬	yízú 彝族
yì 义 刈 丿 曳 医 肄 抑 邑 毅 役 疫 亦	yīfǎ 依法	yìmiáo 疫苗	yǐwǎng 以往	**yin**
	yìfù 義父	yímín 移民	yìwàng 遺忘	yīn 殷 慇 因 姻 愛 陰 音 至
	yīfú 衣服	yīmóyíyàng 一模 一樣	yíwèi 一味	
	yīfù 依附		yǐwéi 以為	yín 銀 齦 尤 吟 寅 淫
	yígài 一概	yìmǔ 義母	yìwèi 意味	
	yīgè 一個	yìnián 翌年	yíwèn 疑問	yǐn 飲 尹 L 引 蚓
	yígòng 一共	yìqí 一齊	yìwù 義務	
	yìguàn 一貫	yìqǐ 一起	yíxià 一下	
	yīguì 衣櫃	yìqì 義氣	yǐxià 以下	
	yíhàn 遺憾	yìqì 儀器		
	yìhétuán 義和團	yìqì 意氣		

yóupài 右派 / yóupiào 郵票 / yóuqí 尤其 / yóuqī 油漆 / yǒuqián 有錢 / yǒuqíng 友情 / yòuqīng 右傾 / yǒuqù 有趣 / yǒurén 友人 / yǒurú 有如 / yóurú 猶如 / yǒushàn 友善 / yōushāng 憂傷 / yōushēng 優生 / yǒushí 有時 / yōushì 優勢 / yòushǒu 右手 / yóushuì 遊說 / yòutài 猶太 / yóutiáo 油條 / yóutǒng 郵筒 / yóuxì 遊戲 / yǒuxiàn 有限 有線 / yōuxián 悠閒 / yōuxiān 優先 / yóuxiāng 郵箱 / yǒuxiào 有效 / yǒuxiē 有些 / yǒuxīn 有心 / yóuxíng 遊行 / yōuxiù 優秀 / yóuxué 遊學 / yōuyáng 悠揚 / yǒuyì 友誼 / yǒuyì 有意 / yǒuyì 有翼 / yòuyì 優異 / yòuyīn 誘因 / yǒuyòng 有用 / yóuyǒng 游泳 / yóuyú 魷魚 由於 / yōuyù 憂鬱 / yóuyù 猶豫 / yōuyuè 優越 / yóuzhèng 郵政 / yòuzhì 幼稚

yóuzhī 油脂 / yǒuzhùyú 有助於

[yu]
yū 迂 淤
yú 昇 輿 臾 映 諛 于 虞 娛 余 餘 愚 隅 於 俞 偷 逾 瑜 覦 揄 魚 漁
yǔ 語 嶼 與 嶼 宇 与 禹 予 羽 雨
yù 鬱 取 聿 郁 與 譽 芋 域 育 毓 谷 欲 慾 裕 浴 禺 遇 寓 獄 御 禦 預 豫 喬 玉 籲 愈 癒 迂 論
yùbào 預報 / yùbèi 預備 / yúbèn 愚笨 / yùcè 預測 / yúchā 魚叉 / yúchí 魚池 / yúchì 魚翅 / yúchuán 漁船 / yúchǔn 愚蠢 / yúcì 魚刺 / yùdào 遇到 / yúdì 餘地 / yùdìng 預訂 預定 / yúé 餘額 / yùfáng 預防 / yúfū 漁夫 / yùgǎn 預感 / yùgāng 浴缸 / yúgǎng 漁港 / yùgào 預告 / yúgōu 魚鉤

yùgū 預估 / yùhán 禦寒 / yūhuí 迂迴 / yùjì 預計 / yūjī 淤積 / yǔjì 雨季 / yújiā 瑜珈 / yùjiàn 遇見 / yújìn 餘燼 / yúkuài 愉快 / yùláiyù 愈來愈 / yúlè 娛樂 / yùliào 預料 / yǔlín 雨林 / yǔlù 語錄 / yúluǎn 魚卵 / yúlùn 輿論 / yǔmáo 羽毛 / yúmèi 愚昧 / yùmèn 鬱悶 / yùmǐ 玉米 / yúmín 漁民 / yùnàn 遇難 / yūní 淤泥 / yúnòng 愚弄 / yǔqì 語氣 / yùqī 預期 / yùqì 玉器 / yúqíng 輿情 / yùqǐng 籲請 / yǔqǔyǔqiú 予取予求 / yǔsǎn 雨傘 / yùshān 玉山 / yùshì 浴室 / yúshì 於是 / yǔshuǐ 雨水 / yùsuàn 預算 / yùsuǒ 寓所 / yùtóu 芋頭 / yùwàng 欲望 慾望 / yǔwén 語文 / yǔxì 語系 / yùxiān 預先 / yùyán 語言 / yùyán 寓言 預言

yùyǎn 預演 / yùyì 寓意 / yǔyǐ 予以 / yǔyī 雨衣 / yùyòng 御用 / yùyù 郁郁 / yúyuè 愉悅 逾越 / yùzhào 預兆 / yùzhī 預知 諭知 / yǔzhòu 宇宙 / yùzhuó 玉鐲

[yuan]
yuān 爿 淵 昌 冤
yuán 原 源 元 緣 愛 援 袁 員 猿 員 圓
yuǎn 遠
yuàn 願 院 夗 怨
yuánběn 原本 / yuǎnchù 遠處 / yuándàn 元旦 / yuándì 園地 / yuǎndōng 遠東 / yuánfèn 緣分 / yuángǎo 原稿 / yuángōng 員工 / yuángù 原故 緣故 / yuànhèn 怨恨 / yuánhóu 猿猴 / yuánjiàn 元件 / yuǎnjiàn 遠見 / yuǎnjìn 遠近 / yuánlái 原來 / yuánlǎo 元老 / yuánlǐ 原理 / yuánliàng 原諒 / yuánliào 原料 / yuánliú 源流 / yuánmǎn 圓滿 / yuánqì 元氣 / yuánqǐ 緣起

yuànqì 怨氣 / yuānqū 冤屈 / yuánquān 圓圈 / yuánrén 猿人 / yuánshǐ 原始 / yuànshì 院士 / yuánshuài 元帥 / yuánsǒu 淵藪 / yuánsù 元素 / yuànwàng 願望 / yuānwǎng 冤枉 / yuánwén 原文 / yuánxiān 原先 / yuánxiāo 元宵 / yuánxíng 圓形 / yuánxiōng 元兇 / yuànyì 願意 / yuányīn 原因 / yuányǐn 援引 / yuányǒu 原有 / yuányóu 緣由 / yuānyù 冤獄 / yuányuán 淵源 / yuányuè 元月 / yuánzé 原則 / yuànzhǎng 院長 / yuánzhōu 圓周 / yuánzhù 援助 / yuánzhūbǐ 圓珠筆 / yuánzhùmín 原住民 / yuánzǐ 原子 / yuánzì 源自 / yuànzi 院子 / yuànzi 園子

[yue]
yuē 約 曰
yuè 閱 悅 說 粵 戊 越 樂 月 嶽 岳 龠 籥 躍
yuèbīng 閱兵 / yuèbǐng 月餅 / yuèchū 月初 / yuèdǐ 月底 / yuēdìng 約定

zhèngmíng 證明　zhèngpài 正派　zhēngqì 蒸汽　zhěngqí 整齊　zhèngqián 掙錢　zhèngqíng 政情　zhēngqiú 徵求　zhēngqǔ 爭取　zhèngquàn 證券　zhèngquán 政權　zhèngquè 正確　zhèngrén 證人　zhèngshí 證實　zhèngshì 正式　zhēngshuì 徵稅　zhěngsù 整肅　zhèngtán 政壇　zhěngtǐ 整體　zhěngtiān 整天　zhèngtǒng 正統　zhēngtuō 掙脫　zhēngxìnshè 徵信社　zhēngxún 徵詢　zhèngyào 正要　zhèngyì 正義　zhēngyì 爭議　zhèngzài 正在　zhēngzhá 掙扎　zhēngzhào 徵兆　zhèngzhí 正直　zhèngzhì 政治　zhēngzhí 爭執　zhèngzhòng 鄭重　zhèngzhuàng 症狀　zhèngzōng 正宗

zhi

zhī 脂 汁 知　蜘 之 芝　織 支 枝　肢 隻　zhí 直 值 殖　植 執 質　戟 職　姪 擲　zhǐ 旨 指　只 咫 止

zhǐ 趾 址 祉　紙 祇 瓣　zhì 峙 志 誌　置 智 摯　滯 治 緻　幟 制 製　秩 質 至　致 緻 窒　桎 輊 炙　多 擲 稚

zhìài 窒礙　zhìān 治安　zhìào 執拗　zhǐbǎn 紙板　zhǐbiāo 指標　zhǐbù 止步　zhìchēng 職稱　zhīchēng 支撐　zhìchéng 製成　zhīchǐ 知恥　zhǐchǐ 咫尺　zhīchí 支持　zhǐchū 指出　zhīchū 支出　zhìcí 致詞　zhǐdǎo 指導　zhídào 直到　zhīdào 知道　zhíde 值得　zhídé 只得　zhíděng 職等　zhǐdiǎn 指點　zhǐdìng 指定　zhìdù 制度　zhíér 姪兒　zhīfáng 脂肪　zhīfěn 脂粉　zhìfú 蟄伏　zhīfù 支付　zhìfú 制伏 制服　zhìfù 致富　zhígōng 職工　zhìgù 桎梏　zhǐhǎo 只好　zhìhéng 制衡　zhìhòu 之後

zhǐhuī 指揮　zhìhuì 智慧　zhījǐ 知己　zhǐjiǎ 指甲　zhījiāgē 芝加哥　zhījiān 之間　zhǐjiào 指教　zhíjiǎo 直角　zhíjiē 直接　zhījié 枝節　zhìjīn 至今　zhǐjìng 止境　zhìjìng 致敬　zhìjú 支局　zhíjué 直覺　zhījué 知覺　zhìliàng 質量　zhìliáo 治療　zhǐlìng 指令　zhìliú 滯留　zhīliú 支流　zhīmá 芝麻　zhímín 殖民　zhǐmíng 指明　zhīmíng 知名　zhìmìng 致命　zhìmóu 智謀　zhǐnán 指南　zhìnèn 稚嫩　zhínǚ 姪女　zhīpèi 支配　zhīpiào 支票　zhìqì 稚氣　zhīqián 之前　zhǐqián 紙錢　zhīqīng 知青　zhīqíng 知情　zhíquán 職權　zhǐsǎn 紙傘　zhīshàng 之上　zhìshǎo 至少　zhíshēngjī 直昇機　zhǐshì 指示 指

事　zhīshí 知識　zhǐshì 只是　zhìshǒukěrè 炙手可熱　zhǐshù 指數　zhìsǒu 智叟　zhìtǐ 肢體　zhìtóngdàohé 志同道合　zhǐwàng 指望　zhíwèi 職位　zhǐwén 指紋　zhìwèn 質問　zhíwù 植物 職務　zhìxī 窒息　zhíxiá 直轄　zhìxià 之下　zhíxiàn 直線　zhìxiàng 志向　zhíxiāo 直銷　zhīxiǎo 知曉　zhìxiè 致謝　zhíxíng 執行　zhìxù 秩序　zhíxún 質詢　zhǐyào 只要 祇要　zhíyè 職業　zhìyí 置疑　zhíyì 執意　zhíyí 質疑　zhìyǒu 摯友　zhǐyǒu 只有 祇有　zhìyú 至於　zhìyuàn 志願　zhíyuán 職員　zhīyuán 支援　zhìzào 製造　zhízé 指責　zhízé 職責　zhìzhàng 智障　zhízhào 執照　zhǐzhēn 指針　zhízhèng 執政

zhìzhì 職志　zhǐzhǐ 制止　zhīzhōng 之中　zhīzhū 蜘蛛　zhízhuó 執著　zhízi 姪子　zhìzuò 製作

zhong

zhōng 終　中 忠 衷　鍾 鐘　zhǒng 種 腫　冢 塚　zhòng 眾　中 仲 重　種

zhōngài 鍾愛　zhòngbǎi 鐘擺　zhōngbiǎo 鐘錶　zhòngcǎi 中彩　zhòngcái 仲裁　zhōngcān 中餐　zhōngchéng 忠誠　zhòngdà 重大　zhōngdiǎn 終點　zhòngdiǎn 重點　zhōngdiǎn 鐘點　zhōngdōng 中東　zhòngdú 中毒　zhòngduō 眾多　zhòngduàn 中斷　zhòngfēng 中風　zhōnggào 忠告　zhōnggòng 中共　zhōngguó 中國　zhōnghòu 忠厚　zhōnghuá 中華　zhōngjiān 中間　zhòngjiǎng 中獎　zhōngjié 終結　zhòngjiè 仲介　zhōngjiù 終究　zhǒnglèi 種類　zhònglì 重力　zhòngliàng 重量　zhōngliú 腫瘤　zhōngměi 中美　zhōngměizhōu 中美

洲

zhōngnián 終年 / 中年
zhòngnù 衆怒
zhōngqíng 鍾情
zhōngqiūjié 中秋節
zhòngrén 衆人
zhōngrì 終日
zhōngshān 中山
zhòngshāng 中傷 / 重傷
zhōngshēn 終身
zhōngshēng 終生
zhōngshí 忠實
zhòngshì 重視
zhōngshū 中樞
zhòngsǒzhōuzhī 衆所周知
zhòngtīng 重聽
zhōngtóu 鐘頭
zhōngtú 中途
zhōngwèi 中尉
zhōngwén 中文
zhōngwǔ 中午
zhōngxiào 忠孝
zhōngxīn 中心 / 忠心 / 衷心
zhōngxué 中學
zhōngxún 中旬
zhōngyāng 中央
zhòngyào 重要
zhòngyì 衆議
zhòngyīn 重音
zhōngyōng 中庸
zhōngyú 終於
zhōngzhǐ 終止 / 中止
zhòngzhí 種植
zhǒngzhǒng 種種
zhǒngzǐ 種子
zhǒngzú 種族

zhou
zhōu 州 / 洲 / 粥 / 周 / 週 / 舟
zhóu 軸
zhǒu 帚 / 肘
zhòu 晝 / 皺 / 咒

宙 / 驟
zhōudài 周代
zhōudào 周到
zhōukān 週刊
zhòumà 咒罵
zhòuméi 皺眉
zhòumì 周密
zhōumò 週末
zhōunián 週年
zhōuquán 周全
zhōuwéi 周圍
zhòuwén 皺紋
zhōuxiáng 周詳
zhóuxīn 軸心
zhōuxuán 周旋
zhòuyè 晝夜
zhōuyì 周易
zhōuzhǎng 州長
zhōuzhuǎn 週轉

zhu
zhū 諸 / 豬 / 朱 / 珠 / 蛛 / 株 / 侏
zhú 筑 / 築 / 竹 / 燭 / 逐
zhǔ 主 / 貯 / 拄 / 煮 / 囑 / 嘱
zhù 炷 / 住 / 駐 / 註 / 注 / 柱 / 祝 / 鑄 / 宁 / 佇 / 苧 / 筑 / 築 / 著 / 助
zhǔbàn 主辦
zhūbǎo 珠寶
zhúbiān 竹編
zhǔbō 主播
zhúbù 逐步
zhǔcài 煮菜
zhùcáng 貯藏
zhùcè 註冊
zhǔchí 主持
zhùchù 住處
zhǔcún 貯存
zhǔdǎo 主導
zhùdìng 註定 / 注定
zhǔdòng 主動

zhūduō 諸多
zhǔfàn 煮飯
zhùfáng 駐防
zhùfù 主婦
zhùfú 祝福
zhǔfù 囑咐
zhúgān 竹竿
zhǔguān 主觀
zhǔguǎn 主管
zhúguāng 燭光
zhùhǎi 珠海
zhùhè 祝賀
zhūhóng 朱紅
zhùjiā 住家
zhújiàn 逐漸
zhūjiāng 珠江
zhǔjiǎo 主角
zhǔjiào 主教
zhùjiào 助教
zhùjiě 註解
zhùjūn 駐軍
zhùkǒu 住口
zhúlán 竹籃
zhùlì 佇立
zhùlǐ 助理
zhùlì 助力
zhūlián 株連
zhúlín 竹林
zhǔliú 主流
zhúlù 築路
zhùmá 苧麻
zhùmíng 著名
zhùmù 注目
zhǔmù 矚目
zhúnián 逐年
zhǔquán 主權
zhǔrén 主人
zhūròu 豬肉
zhūrú 諸如 / 侏儒
zhùshè 注射
zhùshì 註釋 / 注視
zhùshí 柱石
zhùshǒu 住手 / 助手
zhúsǔn 竹筍

zhùsuǒ 住所
zhǔtí 主題
zhūwǎng 蛛網
zhūwèi 諸位
zhúxí 竹蓆
zhùxiū 主修
zhùxuéjīn 助學金
zhǔyǎn 主演
zhǔyào 主要
zhǔyì 主義 / 主意
zhùyì 注意
zhúyī 逐一
zhǔyīn 主因
zhùyīn 注音
zhùyuàn 住院
zhǔzǎi 主宰
zhùzào 鑄造
zhúzhái 竹寨
zhùzhái 住宅
zhǔzhāng 主張
zhùzhǎng 助長
zhùzhǐ 住址
zhùzhòng 注重
zhúzi 竹子
zhúzì 逐字
zhùzuò 著作

zhua
zhuā 抓
zhuǎ 爪
zhuādào 抓到
zhuājǐn 抓緊
zhuāzhù 抓住
zhuǎzi 爪子

zhuai
zhuāi 拽

zhuan
zhuān 專 / 磚 / 耑
zhuǎn 轉
zhuàn 撰 / 饌 / 篆 / 轉 / 傳 / 賺
zhuānàn 專案
zhuǎnbiàn 轉變
zhuǎnbō 轉播
zhuāncháng 專長

zhuǎndá 轉達
zhuāngào 轉告
zhuāngōng 專攻
zhuǎnhuàn 轉換
zhuǎnjī 轉機
zhuànjì 傳記
zhuānjiā 專家
zhuānkè 篆刻
zhuānkē 專科
zhuānlán 專欄
zhuānlì 專利
zhuǎnliè 轉捩
zhuānmén 專門
zhuǎnpán 轉盤
zhuànqián 賺錢
zhuānrèn 專任
zhuǎnshēn 轉身
zhuànshù 撰述
zhuànshū 篆書
zhuāntóu 磚頭
zhuǎnwān 轉彎
zhuànxiě 撰寫
zhuānxīn 專心
zhuānyè 專業
zhuǎnyí 轉移
zhuānzhèng 專政
zhuānzhì 專制
zhuǎnzhù 轉注

zhuang
zhuāng 樁 / 莊 / 裝 / 妝
zhuàng 撞 / 幢 / 壯 / 狀
zhuāngbàn 裝扮
zhuāngbèi 裝備
zhuāngbiāo 裝裱
zhuàngchē 撞車
zhuàngdà 壯大
zhuāngdìng 裝訂
zhuānghuáng 裝潢
zhuàngjī 撞擊
zhuāngjià 莊稼
zhuàngjǔ 壯舉
zhuàngkuàng 狀況
zhuànglì 壯麗
zhuàngnián 壯年

zhuāngpèi 裝配	zhūodāo 捉刀	城	zìzhī 自知
zhuàngqiú 撞球	zhúojiàn 灼見 拙	zìjué 自覺	zìzhì 自治
zhuāngshè 裝設	見	zìkuā 自誇	zìzhòng 自重
zhuàngshì 壯士	zhúoliè 拙劣	zìláishuǐ 自來水	zìzhǔ 自主
zhuāngshì 裝飾	zhúomó 琢磨	zìlì 資歷	zìzhù 自助
zhuāngtài 狀態	zhúomùniǎo 啄木	zìlìgèngshēng 自力	zìzhuàn 自傳
zhuāngtái 妝台	鳥	更生	zìzìbùjuàn 孜孜不
zhuāngxiū 裝修	zhūoná 捉拿	zìliào 資料	倦
zhuāngyán 莊嚴	zhúoqiú 桌球	zìmǎn 自滿	zìzūn 自尊
zhuāngzhì 裝置	zhúoshāng 灼傷	zìmǔ 字母	
zhuāngzǐ 莊子	zhúoshēng 擢升	zìmù 字幕	**zong**
zhuàngzú 壯族	zhúoshǒu 著手	zǐnǚ 子女	zōng 宗 棕
zhuāngzuò 裝作	zhúoyuè 卓越	zìrán 自然	綜 蹤
	zhúozhòng 著重	zǐsè 紫色	zǒng 總
zhui	zhúozhuàng 茁壯	zìshā 自殺	zòng 綜 粽 從
zhuī 佳 椎	zhúozi 桌子	zìshēn 資深	縱
錐 追		zìshēng 滋生 孳	**zu**
zhuì 綴 贅 墜	**zi**	生	zū 租
zhuīchá 追查	zī 資 姿 咨	zìshì 姿勢	zú 足 族 卒
zhuīdào 追悼	諮 孜 茲	zìshǒu 自首	阻 組 祖
zhuīgǎn 追趕	茲 滋 孳	zìsī 自私	詛
zhuìhuǐ 墜毀	zǐ 滓 子 仔	zìsūn 子孫	zǔài 阻礙
zhuījiù 追究	姊 紫	zìtài 姿態	zǔchéng 組成
zhuìluò 墜落	zǐ 字 漬 自	zìtǐ 字體	zǔdǎng 阻擋
zhuīqiú 追求	zǐ 子	zìtiáo 字條	zǔfén 祖墳
zhuìshù 贅述	zìbēi 自卑	zìtiè 字帖	zǔfù 祖父
zhuīsù 追溯	zīběn 資本	zìwèi 滋味	zúgòu 足夠
zhuīsuí 追隨	zībǔ 滋補	zìwèi 自衛	zǔguó 祖國
zhuīwèn 追問	zīchǎn 資產	zìwǒ 自我	zǔhé 組合
zhuīxún 追尋	zīchēng 自稱	zǐxì 仔細	zúhuái 足踝
zhuīzhú 追逐	zìcǐ 自此	zìxí 孳息	zūjiè 租界
zhuīzōng 追蹤	zìcóng 自從	zìxìn 自信	zūjīn 租金
zhun	zìdà 自大	zìxíng 字形 自	zǔlán 阻攔
zhǔn 隼 準	zǐdàn 子彈	行	zǔlì 阻力
准	zìdiǎn 字典	zìxǐng 自省	zūlìn 租賃
zhǔnbèi 準備	zìdòng 自動	zìxùn 資訊	zǔmǔ 祖母
zhǔnquè 準確	zìfèi 自費	zīxún 諮詢	zǔnáo 阻撓
zhǔnshí 準時	zìfén 自焚	zìyǎn 字眼	zúpǔ 族譜
zhǔnxǔ 准許	zìfù 自負	zìyánzìyǔ 自言自	zúqiú 足球
zhǔnyǔ 准予	zīgé 資格	語	zǔsè 阻塞
zhǔnzé 準則	zǐgōng 子宮	zìyǎng 滋養	zǔshī 祖師
zhuo	zìháo 自豪	zìyóu 自由	zūshuì 租稅
zhūo 桌 捉	zìjǐ 自己	zìyú 自娛	zúxià 足下
拙	zìjǐzìzú 自給自	zìyuán 資源	zǔxiān 祖先
zhúo 灼 酌 著	足	zìyuán 字源	zúyǐ 足以
卓 擢 茁	zìjiā 自家	zìyuàn 自願	zúyòng 租用
拙 擢 濁	zījīn 資金	zìzài 自在	zǔzhǎng 組長
鐲 豕 琢	zǐjìnchéng 紫禁	zīzhǎng 滋長	**zou**
啄 晢			zǔzhǐ 阻止
		zōu 鄒	zǔzhì 阻滯
		zǒu 走	zǔzhī 組織
	zou		
	zòu 奏 揍		
		zǒudòng 走動	
		zǒugǒu 走狗	
		zòujié 奏捷	
		zòujìn 走近	
		zǒukāi 走開	
		zǒuláng 走廊	
		zǒulù 走路	
		zòurán 驟然	
		zǒusī 走私	
		zòuxiào 奏效	
		zòuyuè 奏樂	
		zǒuzou 走走	

注 音 索 引 表

This character pronunciation index lists characters under all pronunciations which appear in the dictionary, including the Mandarin standards in both mainland Chinese and Taiwan, according to the 注音符號 phoneticization system used in Taiwan.

The top number to the right of a character is the 文 reference number and the bottom number is the 字 reference number.

注音索引表

注音索引表

注音索引表

ㄊㄧㄝ 貼 帖 鐵 帖
ㄊㄧㄠ 挑 條 調 窕 跳 眺
ㄊㄧㄢ 天 添 填 甜 恬 田 忝 舔
ㄊㄧㄥ 聽 廳 亭 停 廷 庭 蜓 艇 挺
ㄊㄨ 突 凸 禿 涂 塗 途 荼 突 圖 凸 徒 屠 土 吐 兔
ㄊㄨㄛ 脫 拖 托 託 鴕 駝 陀 橢 妥 拓 唾
ㄊㄨㄟ 推 頹 腿 蛻 退 褪
ㄊㄨㄢ 團 彖
ㄊㄨㄣ 吞 臀 屯 囤 飩 豚
ㄊㄨㄥ 通 同 銅 童 瞳 統 桶 衛 痛

ㄋㄚ 拿 那 哪 捺 納 呐 囡 那
ㄋㄜ ·呢
ㄋㄞ 乃 奶 奈 奈 耐
ㄋㄟ 內
ㄋㄠ 那 撓 鳥 尿 撓 妞 牛 紐 扭 鈕 拗 南 喃 難 男 難 念 恁 您 嫩 囊 囊 娘 釀 能 嚀 凝 寧 檸 濘 擰
ㄋㄩ 女 虐 瘧

ㄌㄚ 拉 啦 垃 邋 撈 婁 樓 摟 簍 漏 露 滷 擄 魯
ㄌㄜ 肋 勒 垃 樂 藍 籃 懶 覽 攬 纜 攬 纜
ㄌㄞ 來 萊 徠 賴 睞
ㄌㄟ 濫 贏 晶 雷 累 磊 耒 壘 儡 蕾 累
ㄌㄠ 肋 淚 棱 冷 愣 离 璃 離 籬 儷 栗 慄 茘 連 蓮 臉 斂 變 練 煉 鍊 陵 菱 靈 鏈 靈 領 嶺 另 令 鄰 遴 臨 爐 蘆 廬 驢 慮 濾 率 略 掠
ㄌㄤ 狼 郎 廊 螂 朗 浪
ㄌㄥ 稜 棱 冷 愣
ㄌㄧ 離 璃 離 籬 儷 栗 慄 莉 俐 荊 俐 陸 陸 例
ㄌㄧㄚ 倆
ㄌㄧㄝ 劣 列 裂 烈 劣 獵
ㄌㄧㄡ 溜 流 硫 琉 留 榴 量 量 柳 涼 諒 亮 輛 量 聯 廉 簾 鐮 連 蓮 臉 斂 變 練 煉 鍊 戀 鏈 領 嶺 另 令 鄰 遴 臨 林 琳 淋 磷 鱗
ㄌㄧㄤ 良 涼 梁 樑 粱 量 糧 兩 倆 涼 諒 亮 輛 量
ㄌㄧㄥ 零 齡 玲 鈴 羚 聆 伶 凌 陵 菱 靈 鏈 靈 領 嶺 另 令
ㄌㄨ 路 露 鹿 陸 祿 戮 祿 陸 露 綠 律 慮 濾 率 略 掠
ㄌㄨㄛ 曬 羅 騾 螺 裸 洛 落 絡 駱 卵 亂 輪 倫 綸 淪 論 論
ㄌㄨㄢ 卵 亂
ㄌㄨㄣ 輪 倫 綸 淪 論 論
ㄌㄨㄥ 隆 窿 聾 龍 嚨 籠 朧 瓏
ㄌㄩ 呂 侶 鋁 律 綠 慮 濾 率
ㄌㄩㄝ 略 掠

ㄍㄚ 咖 尬
ㄍㄜ 胳 哥 歌 鴿 戈 割 格 閣 骼 革 萵 隔 葛 各 個
ㄍㄞ 該 改

鑾 籠 攣 攏 弄
鐘 閭 欄 闌 履 屨 旅 呂 侶 鋁 律 綠 縷

3

注音索引表（ㄍ・ㄎ・ㄏ）

注音索引表（接續）

ㄓㄨㄤ 椿 莊 裝 妝 撞 幢 壯 狀 蔡 茶 查 碴 杈 岔 詫 剎

ㄓㄨㄥ 終 中 忠 衷 鍾 鐘 種 腫 冢 塚 眾 中 仲 重 種

ㄔ 痴 癡 喫 吃 持 池 馳 弛 匙 遲 尺 侈 齒 褫 恥 飭 赤

ㄔㄞ 叉 杈 差 丑 醜 臭 插 察 茶 查 碴 岔 詫 剎 蟲 產

ㄔㄜ 車 扯 徹 撤 澈 掣 砌 犁 辰 晨 沈 忱 沉 陳 臣 塵 趁 襯

ㄔㄢ 摻 蟾 孱 潺 廛 纏 禪 蟬 饞 產 鏟 闡 顫 懺 少

ㄔㄥ 撐 稱 乘 承 丞 成 誠 城 盛 澄 橙 程 懲 騁 逞 秤

ㄔㄨ 初 出 除 趁 雛 廚 櫥 醇 躇 儲 楚 儲 處 窗 床 幢 广 闖

ㄔㄨㄣ 春 唇 醇 純 蠢

ㄔㄨㄤ 創 窗 床 幢 闖

ㄔㄨㄥ 春 充 沖 衝 憧 崇 重 蟲 寵 衝

ㄕ 詩 尸 屍 蝨 施 失 濕 師 獅 食 鈒 殺 啥 傻 煞 啥 廈 拾 識 實 矢 屎 始 史 駛 使 豕 示 飾 嗜 士 仕 侍 恃 世 式 篩

ㄕㄚ 煞 砂 沙 鯊 紗 剎 殺 啥 傻 煞

ㄕㄠ 稍 梢 捎 燒 韶 勺 杓 少 少 哨 紹 邵

ㄕㄣ 申 伸 紳 呻 參 深 身 什 沈 審 嬸 瀋 甚 慎 滲 腎 參

ㄕㄨ 疏 蔬 梳 樞 紓 抒 紆 叔 輸 孰 塾 叔 菽 淑 贖 數 暑 署 薯 曙 黍 蜀 屬 鼠 庶 戍 恕 數 豎 樹 署 束 漱 術 墅 述 書

ㄕㄤ 商 裳 傷 賞 晌 上 尚 售 授 受

ㄕㄥ 生 牲 甥 笙 升 昇 勝 繩 省 剩 聖 勝 盛 聲

ㄕㄜ 賒 奢 甚 什 余 舌 蛇 舢 刪 珊 煽 陝 閃 贍 訕 擅 善 膳

ㄕㄡ 收 熟 守 手 首 壽 狩 瘦 獸 賞 晌

ㄕㄨㄚ 刷

ㄕㄨㄞ 衰 摔 甩 蟀 帥

ㄕㄨㄟ 誰 水 稅 睡

ㄕㄨㄛ 說 碩 欶

ㄕㄨㄣ 拴 閂 涮

ㄕㄨㄢ 順 舜 瞬

ㄕㄨㄤ 霜 孀 雙 爽

ㄖ 日

ㄖㄜ 惹 熱

ㄖㄠ 曙 擾 繞

ㄖㄡ 內 柔 蹂 揉 肉

ㄖㄢ 耍

注音索引表（接續）

第一欄

執 勢
藝
意
億
憶
臆
液
吃
軼
益
溢
誼
翌
裔
易
蜴
逸

【一ㄚ】
呀
鴉
壓
鴨
押
衙
崖
涯
牙
芽
雅
亞
啞
軋
兩
訝
亞

【一ㄝ】
耶
椰
耶
爺
椰
揶
也
冶
野
曳
謁
枼

第二欄

葉
夜
液
腋
頁
業

【一ㄞ】
厓
崖

【一ㄠ】
的
要
腰
么
邀
夭
妖
爻

【一ㄢ】
奄
垚
堯
窯
姚
名
謠
搖
遙
咬
窈
夭
窅
要
藥
鑰
耀
曜
躍

【一ㄡ】
攸
悠
絲
幽
憂
優
尤
就
由

第三欄

油
斿
遊
游
猶
郵

【一ㄢ】
友
有
勤
嚥
酉
又
圉
右
佑
誘
幼
柚
彦
硯
焰
雁
燕
咽
焉
獻
恭
煙
【一ㄣ】
簷
研
岩
嵒
癌
言
沿
炎
延
顏
閻
嚴
嚴
邐
眼
由

第四欄

广
演
合
魘
㕑
儼
乙
驗
燕
嚥
瘍
羊
洋
佯
仰
養
瘍
氧
央
樣
漾
恙

【一ㄥ】
英
鶯
嬰
櫻
鸚
應
鷹
膺
鷹
臐
盈
音
堊
銀
齦
螢
尤
吟
寅
室
淫
飲
ㄩ
辵
引
蚓
量
掩
衍

第五欄

瘴
印
【一ㄤ】
央
殃
秧
易
陽
楊
揚
瘍
羊
舞
侮
武
鵡
午
悟
晤
兀
誤
戊
勿
物
務
霧
惡
忢
猥
【一ㄚ】
穵
挖
蛙
洼
窪
娃
瓦
襪
【1ㄛ】
魏
渦
我
幹
沃
握
臥
偽
歪
【1ㄞ】
彎
灣
外

第六欄

污
巫
誣
屋
烏
吾
無
吳
母
五
伍
嫵
舞
侮
晦
薇
維
唯
惟
帷
為
偉
葦
緯
鮪
尾
委
萎
諉
猥
衛
位
尉
慰
蔚
未
味
畏
喂
餵
為
偽
翁
蓊
【ㄨㄢ】
迂

第七欄

ㄨㄟ
危
威
嵗
微
韋
違
圍
㦱
危
桅
口
巍
微
薇
ㄨㄣ
溫
聞
文
紋
蚊
雯
【ㄨㄢ】
汪
尢
王
亡
枉
往
網
罔
網
旺
妄
望
忘
【ㄨㄥ】
翁
蓊

第八欄

完
玩
頑
丸
莞
苑
碗
婉
惋
挽
晚
玩
腕
惋
萬
俞
愉
逾
瑜
覦
魚
漁
語
齬
與
嶼
宇
与
禹
予
羽
雨
鬱
取
聿
冤
原
源
元
緣
援
袁
園
猿
員
遠
願

第九欄

淤
舁
輿
臾
臾
映
于
虞
喬
玉
籲
愈
癒
喻
論
【ㄩㄝ】
約
曰
閱
悅
說
粵
越
月
嶽
岳
俞
籥
躍

【ㄩㄢ】
雨
汙

第十欄

遇
寓
獄
御
禦
【ㄩㄣ】
云
雲
紜
耘
勻
允
隕
孕
熨
醞
縕
蘊
韻
暈
運
【ㄩㄥ】
尹
雍
擁
臃
塞
庸
傭
擁
甬
勇
湧
踴
俑
愿
永
泳
詠
用
佣

第十一欄（右）

院
宛
怨
【ㄩㄣ】
云
紜
耘
勻
允
隕
孕
慰
醞
縕
蘊
韻
暈
運
【ㄩㄥ】
尹
雍
擁
臃
塞
庸
傭
擁
甬
勇
湧
踴
俑
愿
永
泳
詠
用
佣

注音索引表　　　　9

筆 劃 索 引 表

This stroke count index serves as a last resort when a character cannot
be located through the 字譜 or other indexes. Characters are indexed under
the number of strokes in the standard form of the character.

The top number to the right of a character is the 文 reference number and
the bottom number is the 字 reference number.

筆劃索引表

彷 兵 折 阱 坍 吝 妖 沃 低 抒 序 抓 妥 利 秃 佃 甸 里 匣 見 刪 助 肖 汽 迄 耽 囪 豸 身 角 貝 呂 克 系 豕 采 串 車 酉 免

八
枉 旺 往 奈 宗 杯 沓 肴 岡

肚 杜 廷 呈 坐 灶 邦 牟 技 妓 伯 皂 体 呆 杏 束 壯 妝 妒 卵 汽 孚 呀 邪 吧 把 吻 抖 址 扯 步 走 足 尾 求 那 吠 狄 伴 判 牢 告 坊 妨 防

冷 余 佘 找 戒 我 迅 杉 肝 杆 旱 罕 彤 邢 辛 攻 矣 抑 即 邑 男 別 吲 汾 忿 岔 忍 盯 伶 均 投 役 沒 沉 扶 夾 辰 位 汰 吞 吳 快 吶 沌 言 谷 困 沖 佣 甬 佈 莆 豆

吹 坎 兌 完 阮 庇 坐 批 你 沛 孚 李 究 罕 形 估 矣 杈 汲 吸 佐 宏 佑 弄 伸 再 創 伃 均 局 私 役 沒 沉 扶 夾 辰 伺 忘 芒 作 吭 吶 沈 忱 赤 抗 估 住 粵 何 伶

伏 件 牟 仿 阰 屁 羊 孝 君 虫 扭 妞 志 杖 估 村 肘 杈 西 臼 肉 列 死 而 曲 耳 朿 自 缶 均 囟 呈 糸

七
吾 狂 汪 沏 志 否 坚 巡 災 尿 希 灰 此 玖 灸

汗 开 井 刑 江 任 如 荒 同 兩 冰 朴 杅 宇 汗 污 夸 尖 旭 吉 寺 全 仰 印 色 肋 劣 姦 份 吐 圭 伎 竹 汐 多 亦 交 优 行 合 伐 戌 成 戍 戎 划 式 帆 奸

曳 丞 收 旬 危 后 妄 忙 荒 冱 回 两 池 弛 地 她 妃 宅 托 向 在 存 夷 吊 艸 扣 舌 回 仲 吏 凶 糸 朵 肌 因 丟 氿 多 名 百 早 朱 朱 束 休 吃 屹 尿 伙 灰 此 企

半 丘 斥 氏 氿 瓜 矛 玉 禾 瓦 出 田 甲 由 目 冊 皿 且 民 永 它

六
伍 匡 圳 州 艾 兇 匈 网 宄 阡 年 次 各 舛 亥 先 光 旨 良 考 聿 伊 守 有 戎

代 必 刊 功 叵 布 奴 母 仔 充 他 以 台 幼 玄 穴 弘 弗 卉 之 匝 市 仙 叩 甘 只 囚 史 用 仗 天 世 冊 外 処 內 白 且 卯 匆 正 失 冉 犮

左 右 弁 申 犯 叫 包 句 石 乍 丙 占 巧 可 叵 乎 奶 扔 孕 叭 氽 四 仕 汁 仸 甩 凹 凸 生 矢 加 另 召 叮 叼 打 寧 立 央 去 令 戊 戊 皮

丰 支 丏 日 木 片 爿 戶 月 气 火 心 牙 毛 犬 牛 午 毋 斤 丹 文 夬 尺 爪 歹 戈

五
卡 示 丕 叶 叮 卌 札 主 尼 北 付 皮

父 及 勾 公 厄 反 仄 匹 丐 內 尤 兮 仍 及 介 少 六 市 仇 什 廿 卅 卬 分 父 冗 夫 太 天 夬 尺 互 今 戈

亍 弋 兀 凡 干 工 巾 反 仄 女 子 孑 也 已 巳 么 勺 弓 屮 山 口 土 夕 乞 冗

二
一
乙

三
七 乂 人 儿 匕 又 凵 厂 乃 八 九 十 入 力 刀 刁 丁 几 匸 了

三
三 上 下 川 千 久 兀 寸 叉 廾 丸 亡 于 小 士 丈 刃 大 尤 尸 彳

四
五 王 切 云 不 水 刈 凶 互 今 戈 五 壬 仁 欠 无 元 允 比 化 友 尤 尹 丑

1

十一

十二

筆劃索引表 — 此為部首／筆劃索引頁，內容為密集排列之漢字與頁碼（按筆劃分欄），包含下列筆劃分類標記：

十八　十九　二十　廿一　廿二　廿三　廿四　廿五　廿六　廿七　廿八　廿九　卅二

部 首 索 引 表

All characters are listed under one of the 214 radicals in the following standard 部首 index. The top number to the right of a character is the 文 reference number and the bottom number is the 字 reference number.

Radical indexes arbitrarily place each character under one and only one radical, even if the character has several components which are radicals, or even if it has no components which are a standard radical. While radicals can be used to find characters in this dictionary just as in any other dictionary, this dictionary is structured around the 字譜 rather than the 部首. The 字譜 method generalizes the radical method by allowing a character to be found via any of its components, radical or not, and even via any collaterally related characters which share one of the same components.

【一】
1 一　2 丨　3 丶　4 丿　5 乙　6 亅

【二】
7 二　8 亠　9 人　10 儿　11 入　12 八　13 冂　14 冖　15 冫　16 几　17 凵　18 刀　19 力　20 勹　21 匕　22 匚　23 匸　24 十　25 卜　26 卩　27 厂　28 厶　29 又

【三】
30 口　31 囗　32 土　33 士　34 夂　35 夊　36 夕　37 大　38 女　39 子　40 宀　41 寸　42 小　43 尢　44 尸　45 屮　46 山　47 川　48 工　49 己　50 巾　51 干　52 幺　53 广　54 廴　55 廾　56 弋　57 弓　58 彐　59 彡　60 彳

【四】
61 心　62 戈　63 戶　64 手　65 支　66 文　67 攵　68 斗　69 斤　70 方　71 无　72 日　73 曰　74 月　75 木　76 欠　77 止　78 歹　79 殳　80 毋　81 比　82 毛　83 氏　84 气　85 水　86 火　87 爪　88 父　89 爻　90 爿　91 片　92 牙　93 牛　94 犬

【五】
95 玄　96 玉　97 瓜　98 瓦　99 甘　100 生　101 用　102 田　103 疋　104 疒　105 癶　106 白　107 皮　108 皿　109 目　110 矛　111 矢　112 石　113 示　114 禸　115 禾　116 穴　117 立

【六】
118 竹　119 米　120 糸　121 缶　122 网　123 羊　124 羽　125 老　126 而　127 耒　128 耳　129 聿　130 肉　131 臣　132 自　133 至　134 臼　135 舌　136 舛　137 舟　138 艮　139 色　140 艸　141 虍　142 虫　143 血　144 行　145 衣　146 襾

【七】
147 見　148 角　149 言　150 谷　151 豆　152 豕　153 豸　154 貝　155 赤　156 走　157 足　158 身　159 車　160 辛　161 辰

【八】
162 辵　163 邑　164 酉　165 釆　166 里　167 金　168 長　169 門　170 阜　171 隶　172 隹　173 雨　174 靑　175 非

【九】
176 面　177 革　178 韋　179 韭　180 音　181 頁　182 風　183 飛　184 食　185 首　186 香

【十】
187 馬　188 骨　189 高　190 髟　191 鬥　192 鬯　193 鬲　194 鬼

【十一】
195 魚　196 鳥　197 鹵　198 鹿　199 麥　200 麻

【十二】
201 黃　202 黍　203 黑　204 黹

【十三】
205 黽　206 鼎　207 鼓　208 鼠

【十四】
209 鼻　210 齊

【十五】
211 齒

【十六】
212 龍　213 龜

【十七】
214 龠

部首索引表

[1] 一	一 丁 七 丈 三 上 下 丌 不 与 丏 丐 丑 且 丕 世 丘 丙 丞 丟 並
[2] 丨	中 丮 丰 串
[3] 丶	丸 丹 主
[4] 丿	乂 乃 久 乇 么 之 乍 乎 乏 乒 乓 乖 乘
[5] 乙	乙 九 乞 也 乳 乾 亂
[6] 亅	了 事
[7] 二	二 于 云 五 井 互 些 亞 亟
[8] 亠	亡 亢 交 亥 亦 亨 享 京 亮 童
[9] 人	人 什 仁 仄 仇 今 介 仍 仔 仕 他 仗 付 仙 仟 代 令 以 仰 仲 件 任 份 仿 企 优 伊 伍 伎 伏 伐 休 伙 伯 估 伴 伶 伸 伺 似 佃 但 佇 佈 位 低 住 佐 佑 体 佔 何 余 佘 佛 作 你 佝 佟 佬 佯 佰 佳 併 使 來 多 例 侍 侏 侖 侔 供 依 侮 侯 侵 侶 便 係 促 俄 俊 俏 俐 俑 俗 俘 俚 保 俞 俟 俠 信 修 俱 俸 俺 俾 倆 倉 個 倍 候 們 倒 倖 倘 倚 借 倡 倦 倪 倫 值 假 偉 偏 做 停 健 側 偵 偶 偷 傀 傅 傍 傑 傘 備 傢 催 傲 傳 債 傷 傻 傾 僅 僉 僑 像 僚 僕 僧 僵 價 儀 億 儆 儉 儐 儒 儔
[10] 儿	儿 元 允 兄 充 兆 兇 先 光 克 免 兒 兔 兜 兢
[11] 入	入 內 全 兩
[12] 八	八 公 六 兮 共 兵 其 具 典 兼
[13] 冂	冉 冊 再 冏 冒
[14] 冖	冗 尤 冠 冢 冤 冥 冪
[15] 冫	冬 冰 冶 冷 冽 冼 凋 凌 凍 凝 凜
[16] 几	几 凡 凰 凱 凳
[17] 凵	凶 凸 凹 出 函
[18] 刀	刀 刁 分 切 刈 刊 划 列 初 判 別 刨 利 刪 到 制 刷 券 刺 刻 剁 削 剋 剌 前 剎 剔 剖 剛 剝 剪 副 割 創 劇 剽 劂 劈 劊 劍 劑
[19] 力	力 功 加 劣 劫 助 努 劾 勁 勃 勇 勉 勒 動 勘 務 勝 勞 募 勢 勤 勳 勵 勸
[20] 勹	勺 勾 勿 包 匈 匍 匐 匏
[21] 匕	匕 化 北 匙
[22] 匚	匹 匝 匠 匣 匪 匯 匱 匾
[23] 匸	匹 匿 區
[24] 十	十 千 卅 升 午 卉 半 卌 卑 卒 卓 協 南 博
[25] 卜	卜 占 卡 卦
[26] 卩	卯 印 危 即 卵 卷 卸 卻 卿
[27] 厂	厄 厚 原 厭 厲 厝 厥
[28] 厶	去 參
[29] 又	又 叉 及 友 反 叔 取 受 叛 叟 叢
[30] 口	口 古 句 另 叩 只 叫 召 叭 叮 可 台 史 右 叵 司 叼 吃 各 合 吉 吊 同 名 后 吏 吐 向 君 吝 吞 吟 吠 否 吧 吩 含 吳 吵 吶 吸 吹 吻 吾 呀 呆 呈 告 呢 周 味 呵 呻 呼 命 咀 和 咎 咐 咒 咖 咢 咨 咫 咬 咱 咳 咸 咼 咽 哀 品 哄 哆 哈 哉 員 哥 哦 哨 哩 哪 哭 哲 哺 哼 唁

1

部首索引表（續）

各部首（方框內為部首序號與部首）：

32 土　31 口　33 士　34 夂　35 夊　36 夕　37 大　38 女　39 子　40 宀　41 寸　42 小　43 尢　44 尸　45 屮　46 山　47 巛　48 工　49 己　50 巾　51 干　52 幺　53 广

部首索引表（部首54～76）

54 廴
延 廷 建

55 廾
廾 廿 弁 弄 弊

56 弋
弋 式

57 弓
弓 弔 引 弗 弘 弛 弟 弦 弧 弨 弱 張 強 弼 彈 彊 彌 彎

58 彐
彖 彗 彙 彝

59 彡
形 彥 彩 彪 彬 彭 影 彰 彫

60 彳
彳 彷 役 彼 彿 往 征 待 很 徊 律 後 徐 徑 徒 得 徘 徙 從 御 徨 復 循 徬 微 德 徵 徹 徽

61 心
心 必 忌 忍 志 忐 忘 忙 忖 忠 快 忱 念 忿 怒 怕 怖 思 怠 急 性 怨 怪 怯 恆 恍 恐 恕 恙 恢 恤 恥 恨 恩 恫 恬 恭 息 恰 惠 悄 悅 悉 悍 悔 悟 悠 患 您 悲 悴 情 悽 惆 惋 惑 惕 惜 惟 惡 惦 惰 惱 想 惶 惹 愁 愈 愉 意 愕 愚 愛 慨 感 愣 愧 愴 慄 慈 慌 慎 慕 慘 慚 慢 慣 慧 慰 慮 慫 慶 慷 憂 慾 憋 憔 憤 憧 憬 憫 憐 憶 懂 憨 憾 懇 應 懊 懈 懦 懣 懲 懷 懸 懼 懾 戀

62 戈
戈 戊 戌 戍 成 我 戒 戔 戕 或 戚 戛 戟 戡 截 戮 戰 戲 戴

63 戶
戶 戾 房 所 扁 扇 扈 扉

64 手
手 才 扎 扑 扒 打 扔 托 扛 扣 扭 扮 扯 扳 扶 批 扼 找 承 技 抄 抉 把 抑 抒 抓 投 抖 抗 折 抨 披 抬 抱 抵 抹 押 抽 拂 拇 拉 拋 拌 拍 拐 拒 拓 拔 拖 拗 拘 拙 招 拜 括 拭 拮 拯 拱 拳 拴 拷 接 拼 拽 拾 捅 拿 持 指 按 挑 挖 挨 挪 挫 振 挺 挽 挾 捆 捉 捐 捕 捨 捫 捶 捷 掃 掀 捲 捧 掉 掌 掏 掐 排 掘 掙 掛 採 探 掣 控 掠 掩 措 捻 掬 揉 描 提 插 揭 搖 搞 損 搏 搓 搗 搜 搭 搶 摧 摩 摯 摞 摺 撤 撈 撐 撥 撮 撒 播 撞 撩 撬 撰 撲 撕 擋 擇 擊 擂 撻 擦 擔 擁 搬 據 擄 攏 攔 攙 攝 攘 攢 攪

65 支
支

66 攴（攵）
收 攻 改 政 故 效 啓 敏 救 敕 敗 敘 敢 敞 敦 敬 敲 整 斂 斃

67 文
文 斌 斐 斑

68 斗
斗 料 斜 斟 斡

69 斤
斤 斥 斧 斬 斯 新 斷

70 方
方 於 施 旁 旅 旋 族 旗

71 无
无 旣

72 日
日 旦 旨 早 旬 旭 旱 旺 昂 昆 昇 昌 明 香 易 昔 昏 昧 昨 是 時 晃 晉 晌 晒 晚 晝 晤 晦 晨 普 景 晰 晴 晶 智 暇 暈 暉 曉 暑 暖 暗 暢

部首索引表 (continued)

（日部 續）
暫 96　暮 97　曛　暴 123　曋　曆 112　曇　曉　曖　曜 124　曝　曠　曩　曬 154

[73] 曰
曰　曲 135　曳　更　曷　書　曹　曼　曾 144　替　最　會

[74] 月
月 80　有　朋　服　朔 125　朕　朗　望　朝 79　期　朦 155　朧

[75] 木
木 77　未　末　本　札　朱　朴　朵　朽　束　杆　杉　李　杏　材　村　杓　杖　杜　束　杭 175　杯　杜　東　杵　松　板　枉　析　枕　林　枚　果　枝　枯　架　枷　柄　柏　某　柑　柴　染　柔　柚　查　柬　柯　柰　柱　柳　柴
柵 115　栗　校　株　核　根　格　栽　梆　楊　楓　椰　楚　楣　業　極　楷　概　椰　榨　榴　椎　構　槍　槓　槐　槤　樣　樞　標　樓　標　樘　樟　模　樣　樸　模　棋　棍　棒　棕　橘　橙　棘　棚 165　機　橡　橢　橫　檀　檔　檢
棺 167　椅　植　椎　椒　棣　櫃　楊　楓　楔　楚　楣　業　極　楷　概　椰　榨　榴　椎　構　槍　梅　梧　梗　條　梟　梢　梁　梅　梯　械　梳　梵　棄　柄　棉　棋　棍　棒　棕　柔　棗　棘　棚　棟　棧　森　棲　楝　樓　槳

[76] 欠
欠　次　欣　欲　欺　歇　歉　歌　歐　歡

[77] 止
止　正　此　步　武　歧　歪　歲　歷　歸

[78] 歹
歹　死　殃　殆　殉　殊　殖　殘

[79] 殳
殳　段　殷　殺　殿　毀　毅

[80] 毋
毋　母　每　毒　毓

[81] 比
比　毗　毖

[82] 毛
毛　毫　毯

[83] 民
民　氏　氓

[84] 气
气　氛　氣　氧

[85] 水
水　永　氾　汁　求　汐　汗　江　池　污　汪　汰　汲　決　汽　汾　沃　沈　沉　沌　沏　沐　沒　沓　沖　沙　沛　沫　沮　河　沸　油　治　沼　沽　沿　況　泉　泊　泌　法　泛　泡　波　泣　泥　注　泯　泰　泳　洄　洋　洌　洒　洗　洛
洞　津　淺　洪　洲　洵　活　洼　洽　派　流　浙　浦　浩　浪　浮　浴　海　浸　涂　消　涉　涎　涕　涮　淚　涼　淅　淆　淇　淋　淑　淒　淘　淚　淞　淨　淪　淫　淮　漓　深　淵　混　淹　淺
添　清　減　渠　渡　渣　渤　渦　測　渴　游　湮　渾　湃　湖　湊　涸　湘　湛　湧　湯　溉　源　準　溜　溝　溢　溥　溪　溫　溶　溺　滄　淚　滑　滓　滔　滕　漓　滾　滿　漁　漂　漆　漏　演　漠　漢　漩　漫　漬　漱　漲　漸　漾
濃　滯　滬　潘　漯　潛　滾　藩　潺　瀑　瀕　潮　漏　澀　瀾　灌　澆　漠　漢　澎　潑　漱　瀉　潤　潭　潮　潰　潺　溏　澄　澆　澈　澎　溫　潮　澡　澤　濺　澳　激　濁　濃　濕　濘　濱　濟　濤　濫　濾　濱
濾 122　漬　瀉　藩 156　瀏　瀑　瀨　瀚　瀝　瀟　瀾 153　灣　瀠

[86] 火
火　灰 68　灶　灸　灼　災　炎　炒　炕　炙　炫　炭　炮　炳　炷　炸　為　烏　烘　烙　烝　烤　烹　焉　焊　焙　焚　無　焦　焰
然 96　煮 76　煉 70　煌 69　煎 137　煞 118　煤 138　煥 61　照 124　煩 131　熄 115　熊 122　熏 144　熒　熔 68　熙 145　熟　熨　熬　熱　熾　燃　燈　燐　燒　燕　燙　營　燥　燦　燧　燭　燴　爐　爆　爛

[87] 爪
爪 103　爬 85　爭　爱 103　爵

[88] 父
父　爸 85

4　部首索引表

六 爹 72 6
九 爺 137 30

89 爻

爻 3 14
七 爽 3 16
十 爾 29 46

90 爿

爿 77 119
十三 牆 160 7

91 片

片 77 118
四 版 21 25
八 牌 15 36
九 牒 31 111

92 牙

牙 84 1
八 牚 63 26

93 牛

牛 92 1
二 牟 92 11
三 牠 56 9
牡 92 13
牢 92 10
四 牧 92 14
物 86 5
五 牲 70 57
六 特 31 19
七 牽 59 30
犁 108 22
八 犀 90 6
十一 犛 77 41
十六 犧 27 7

94 犬

犬 91 1
一 犮 91 12
二 犯 16 2
四 狀 77 134
狂 1 33
狄 91 23
五 狐 104 4
狗 18 33
狙 117 4
六 狠 12 53
狡 39 66
狩 14 77
七 狸 111 24
狹 39 18
狼 12 62
八 猋 91 16
猒 91 8
猖 68 53
猛 116 3
猜 70 75
猝 126 19
九 猥 140 5
猩 70 63
猴 32 27
猶 159 5
十 猾 133 4
猿 126 9
獃 69 117
獄 91 21
獅 167 13
十二 獗 50 38
十三 獨 125 12
十四 獲 162 63
十五 獵 181 3
獷 31 87
獸 91 20
十六 獻 174 4

95 玄

玄 59 24
五 玆 59 31
六 率 153 13

96 玉

玉 107 1
王 1 20
三 玖 10 25
四 玨 107 2
玩 11 20
玫 26 10
五 玲 44 31
玷 26 22
玻 14 106
珀 76 17
珈 34 3
珊 115 3
珍 49 7
六 珠 77 44
琉 55 25
班 107 3
珮 47 10
七 現 114 10
球 90 15
琅 12 70
理 111 20
八 琢 155 12
琥 122 4
琳 77 4
琴 44 9
琵 12 7
琶 85 10
九 瑕 14 112
瑙 143 5
瑚 31 64
瑜 129 10
瑞 134 13
瑟 107 5
十 瑣 29 41
瑩 82 20
瑪 177 4
瑰 140 7
十一 璀 162 7
璃 73 17
十三 璧 50 59
璨 133 16
環 126 13
十四 璽 28 50
十五 瓊 63 9
十六 瓏 132 20

97 瓜

瓜 104 1
十四 瓣 50 71

98 瓦

瓦 109 1
六 瓶 50 24
瓷 10 36
九 甄 130 4

99 甘

甘 66 57
四 甚 22 7
六 甜 68 64

100 生

生 70 56
六 產 98 11
七 甥 70 58
甦 15 119

101 用

用 69 35
甩 69 75
二 甫 69 52
甬 69 37
四 甭 1 75

102 田

田 111 1
由 113 1
甲 112 1
申 15 96
二 男 34 19
甸 111 3
甹 27 9
三 畀 46 13
四 界 29 5
畏 140 2
五 留 78 38
畚 15 64
畜 59 28
畝 10 28
六 畢 136 8
略 10 75
七 番 156 2
畫 14 24
異 46 16
八 當 63 28
畸 27 27
十 畾 111 9
十四 疆 111 6
疇 13 19
十七 疊 111 12

103 疋

疋 88 63
三 疌 88 29
七 疏 55 26
九 疐 59 44
疑 32 13

104 疒

三 疚 10 27
四 疤 85 3
疫 37 19
五 疲 14 97
疵 88 5
疹 49 6
疼 43 4
疾 32 22
病 23 64
症 88 48
六 痊 32 4
痕 12 50
七 痘 69 86
痛 69 45
痢 108 20
八 痰 82 15
痲 77 23
痴 32 11
痹 46 15
痺 15 35
九 瘋 47 5
瘍 76 55
瘓 63 13
十 瘤 78 41
瘦 15 80
瘧 122 22
十二 療 82 27
癌 68 30
十三 癒 129 14
癖 50 63
十四 癡 32 16
十五 癢 123 5
癥 134 11
十七 癰 103 34
十九 癱 31 100

105 癶

四 癸 88 20
七 登 69 89
發 88 16

106 白

白 76 2
一 百 76 3
二 皂 76 110
三 的 61 7
四 皆 12 12
皇 1 21
皈 21 29
六 皎 39 88

107 皮

皮 14 96
十 皺 66 6

108 皿

皿 116 1
四 盆 35 15
盈 28 6
五 益 116 9
盍 39 70
盎 39 55
六 盒 44 16
盔 82 6
七 盛 45 40
盜 10 47
八 盞 45 16
盟 80 3
九 盡 14 18
監 142 3
十 盤 129 4
十一 盥 15 66
盧 122 10
十二 盪 76 59

109 目

目 114 1
二 盯 36 3
三 盲 22 20
直 31 22
四 相 114 20
盼 35 14
盾 21 51
省 29 19
眇 39 20
眉 114 16
看 114 15
五 眞 31 32
眠 119 3
眨 66 61
眩 39 26
六 眷 15 138
眸 92 12
眺 127 7
眼 13 57
衆 10 30
七 睏 69 14
八 睛 70 73
睜 103 26
睞 160 4
睡 173 6
督 121 5
睦 66 36
睪 50 43
睫 88 31
睬 103 12
九 睹 76 39
瞄 111 33
十 瞇 138 4
瞌 39 71
瞎 79 10
瞑 39 59
十一 瞞 74 7
瞢 114 3
十二 瞥 53 9
瞧 162 30
瞪 69 92
瞬 10 96
瞭 82 28
瞰 137 12
瞳 76 102
十三 瞻 21 9
瞿 114 28
十九 矗 31 27
廿一 矚 125 6

110 矛

矛 105 1
七 矞 105 8

111 矢

矢 32 7
二 矣 32 18
三 知 32 8
五 矩 51 32
七 短 69 97
八 矮 108 33
十二 矯 99 9

112 石

石 21 17
三 矽 72 3
四 砂 29 14
砍 10 42
五 砰 27 45
砲 18 13
破 14 102
砸 66 63
六 研 50 25
七 硫 55 24
硬 15 118
硯 114 14
八 碌 42 10
碎 126 25
碑 15 31
碗 72 15
碰 39 30
九 碟 31 110
碧 76 18
碩 21 18
碳 67 8
碴 76 66
十 磁 59 34
確 162 37
碼 177 5
碾 40 7
磅 94 30
磊 21 20
磋 15 6
磕 39 72
十一 磚 59 38
磨 77 18
十二 磯 59 7
磷 10 91
磺 31 83
礁 162 28
十三 礎 88 65
十四 礙 32 15
十五 礦 31 88
礫 59 16

113 示

示 1 46
三 社 70 6
祀 58 2
四 祇 100 9
祈 96 11
祉 88 13
五 祕 45 76
祖 117 13
祛 39 65
祝 11 12
神 15 100
祟 110 11
祠 21 80
六 祥 123 14
票 15 86
祭 1 51
八 祿 42 11
禁 77 11
九 禍 133 9
福 23 36
十一 禦 93 7
十二 禧 69 110
禪 136 4
十三 禮 70 66
十四 禱 13 24

114 禸

禸 73 1
四 禹 73 23
禺 73 2
六 离 73 16
八 禽 73 21

115 禾

禾 108 1
二 禿 108 26
秀 28 8
私 19 11
三 秉 108 16
四 秋 82 7
科 87 4
秒 29 22
五 秘 45 77
秣 108 3
租 117 10
秤 27 49
秦 15 129
秧 39 52
秩 89 5
六 移 72 7
七 稀 3 21
稅 11 7
程 70 43
稍 29 31
八 稔 44 14
稚 162 43
稜 66 46
稟 69 10
稠 69 79
九 種 76 94
稱 175 9
十 稻 131 11
稼 155 5
稽 12 32
稿 23 4
穀 37 11
十一 穆 29 45
穌 180 4
積 77 70
穎 12 28
十二 穗 59 43
十三 穢 46 35
十四 穩 103 35
穫 162 64

116 穴

穴 63 2
一 穵 8 2
二 究 30 2
三 穹 65 4
空 51 15
四 穿 84 8
突 63 6
五 窄 22 47
窈 59 21
六 窒 128 4
窕 127 5
七 窗 144 6
窖 14 44
八 窟 110 5
窠 77 85
九 窩 133 10
窪 70 19
十 窮 65 3
窯 123 24
十一 窺 39 12
十二 窿 10 85
十三 竄 181 7
竅 94 20
十五 竇 150 25
十七 竊 73 25

117 立

立 39 21
五 站 26 19
六 竟 68 92
章 68 99
七 竣 11 31
童 76 101
九 竭 22 38
端 134 3
十五 競 68 82

118 竹

竹 71 11
三 竿 50 4
四 笆 85 5
笑 99 11
五 笙 70 59
笛 113 8
笠 39 23
符 14 69
笨 77 51
第 65 20
笵 16 5
六 筆 14 22
等 31 18
筋 34 12
筍 18 20
筏 45 5
筐 1 31
筑 51 21
筒 24 5
答 44 22
策 77 55
七 筮 51 29
筵 88 40
筷 39 58
節 33 12
八 箋 45 8
箏 103 24
箕 46 12
算 150 29
箝 68 66
管 167 8
九 箭 129 21
箱 114 22
範 16 6
篆 42 4
篇 115 10
十 築 51 22
篡 150 30
篤 71 12
篩 167 14
十一 篷 70 94
簇 118 6
簍 54 35
十二 簡 78 24
簣 31 85
簪 10 57
簫 2 38
十三 簽 21 14
簸 14 107
簷 10 14
簾 108 11
簿 69 59
十四 籃 142 11
籌 13 20
籍 76 80
十六 籠 132 18
十七 籤 168 5
籥 115 22
十九 籬 73 19
籮 162 16
廿六 籲 115 23

119 米

米 138 1
四 粉 35 12
五 粒 39 22
粗 117 3
六 粟 170 4
粥 65 18
粵 27 43
七 粱 35 30
粲 133 15
八 粹 126 20
粽 1 59
精 70 72
九 糊 31 65
十 糕 123 23
糖 14 36
十一 糙 92 21
糞 46 19
糟 68 51
糠 14 33
糨 65 8
十二 糧 76 100
十四 糯 161 5
十六 糴 124 11
十九 糶 124 12

120 糸

糸 153 1
一 系 153 12
二 糾 17 2
三 紀 57 2
約 61 8
紅 51 13
紉 35 24
四 紊 98 3
紋 98 2
納 23 51
紐 14 56
紓 102 6
純 66 55
紕 12 10
紗 29 18
紙 100 8
級 14 90
紛 35 6
紜 1 65
素 153 14
紡 94 11
索 29 70
五 紫 88 7
紮 9 4
累 111 15
細 143 6
紳 15 98
紹 35 37
紺 110 3
終 43 3
組 117 12

絆	總	羚	聖	胳	臘	艙	荊	蓄	蘭	蝦	衰
結	續	羞	聘	胸	臟	艦	荸	蓆	蘆	蚕	袁
絕	繁	群	聚	能	臥	**138 艮**	荒	蒿	蘇	蝴	快
絮	繃	羨	聞	脂	**131 臣**	艮	荔	蓋	蘊	蝶	袋
絡	織	義	聯	脅	臣	良	荐	蓑	蘋	蝸	袍
絢	繕	羹	聰	脆	臨	**139 色**	荷	蔗	蘭	螃	袖
給	繞	贏	聲	脈	**132 自**	色	莉	蓮	蘿	融	衮
絨	繡	**124 羽**	聳	脊	自	艷	莊	蓿	**141 虍**	螞	被
統	繩	羽	聶	脖	臭	**140 艸**	莖	蔑	虎	螢	袱
絲	繪	翁	職	脫	**133 至**	艸	莞	蔓	虐	螺	袄
絹	繫	翅	聽	脯	至	艾	莫	蓬	虜	蟀	裁
綳	繭	翌	龔	腋	致	芋	莽	蔗	虞	蟄	裂
綏	繳	翏	**129 聿**	脾	臺	芒	菇	蔚	虔	蟋	裕
綑	繹	習	聿	腴	臻	芝	菊	蔡	處	蟑	裙
綜	繼	翔	肆	腐	芽	芥	菌	蔣	虛	蟬	補
綠	纂	翟	肅	腑	**134 臼**	芬	菜	蕙	虜	蟲	裝
維	續	翠	肇	腔	臼	芭	菠	蔬	號	蟹	裡
綱	纏	翡	**130 肉**	腥	與	芮	苦	蔻	虧	蟻	襯
網	纖	翰	肉	腺	舂	芯	華	蔽	**142 虫**	蟾	褄
綴	纜	翱	肋	腦	舅	花	菱	蕉	虫	蠅	裟
綸	**121 缶**	翼	肌	腫	舉	芳	菲	蕊	虹	蠍	裹
缶	缶	耀	肓	腰	舊	芹	萎	蕩	蚊	蠔	裴
缸	**125 老**	肖	腳	舛	莉	莢	蕾	蚌	蠕	裸
缺	老	考	肘	腋	**135 舌**	芽	萃	薔	蚵	蠟	褒
罄	者	耆	肖	腸	舌	苞	荷	薄	蚤	蠢	褰
罐	耘	耋	肚	腹	舍	苔	萊	薇	蚯	蠶	製
122 网	耙	**126 而**	肛	腺	舒	苗	萌	薔	蛇	**143 血**	複
网	而	肝	腿	舐	苟	萎	薑	蛋	血	褐
罔	耍	股	膀	舔	首	崔	薈	蚰	衊	褙
罕	耐	肢	膊	舖	若	蓍	蕾	蛔	**144 行**	褌
罩	耑	肥	臍	**136 舛**	苦	萬	薛	蛙	行	褂
罪	**127 耒**	肩	膚	舛	苓	落	肅	蛛	衍	褪
置	耒	肪	膛	舜	英	葉	薪	蛻	術	褓
署	耕	肯	膜	舞	苗	葛	薯	蜀	衙	褒
罰	耗	肱	膝	范	茂	董	薰	蜂	街	褲
罷	耘	育	膠	茄	范	葷	藍	蜒	衛	褥
羅	耦	肴	膨	茅	葫	藏	蛾	衝	襄
羈	**128 耳**	肺	膩	**137 舟**	茉	葬	蕷	蜘	衡	襖
123 羊	耳	胃	膳	舟	范	葵	藐	蜜	**145 衣**	襟
羊	耶	背	膺	航	茲	蒂	藕	蜥	衣	襪
羌	耽	胎	膽	般	茶	藝	蜴	表	**146 襾**	
牟	耿	胖	臀	舵	茸	蕙	藤	蜻	衫	西
美	聆	胚	臃	舶	草	蒲	藥	蝕	衩	要
羔	聊	胞	臆	船	蓄	蒸	藩	蝗	衰	
羹	聒	胡	臍	艇	茍	藹	蝙	蝠		
羨	聰	胥	臍	艘	草	蒼	蝠			

部首索引表（續）

第一欄

八 陪 162
陰 24
陸 173
陳 161
陶
陷
陸
九 陽
隄
隅
隆
隊
隋 15
隍 27
階
陸 17
隔 174
隙
際
十 際
障
士 陵
隨
險
十 隱

〔171〕隸
九 隸 6

〔172〕隹
隹
隻
隼
三 雀
四 雁 162
雄
雅
集 162
雁
八 雋
雌
雍
八 雎 162
雕
九 雖 162
十 雙 162
雚
雛 162
雜 162

第二欄

雞 103
七 離 78
難 78
難 78

〔173〕雨
雨 161
三 雪
四 雯 168
雲
五 零
雷 161
電
雹
六 需 161
震
霄 54
八 霍 162
霏
霓 131
十 霜 161
露 161
霞
十 霧 105
十 露
十 霸
霹
十 霾
靈 161
靂 108
靉 161

〔174〕青
青
七 靖 169
八 靜 103

〔175〕非
非 169
七 靠 77
十 靡 77

〔176〕面
面

〔177〕革
革 74
四 靴 17
靶 95
六 鞋 74
鞍
鞏
九 鞠
鞦
鞭

第三欄

士 韃
士 韁
三 靭
〔178〕韋
韋
三 韌
五 韓
〔179〕韭
韭
八 韱
〔180〕音
音 63
二 韶
十 韻 150
十 響
〔181〕頁
頁 148
二 頂
三 項
順
須
頌
預 102
十 頑
頒
頏
頗
領
頡
頤 145
頭 66
煩
頸
類
頰
頷
顆
題
額
顏
顧
類
類
顫
十 顰

〔182〕風
風

第四欄

六 颺
颼
十 飄
飆
飆
〔183〕飛
飛
〔184〕食
食
二 飢
四 飩
飪
飭
飯
飲
五 飼
飽
飾
六 餃
餅
養 123
餌
七 餐
餃
餓
餘
八 餛
餞
館
館 167
九 餬
餚
餵
十 饅
饉
饌
饒
饒
〔185〕首
首
〔186〕香
香
十 馨
〔187〕馬
馬 177
五 馭
馮
馳
四 駁
駐

第五欄

駕 34
駛
駝 125
六 駭
駱
駢
駟
駒
魃
七 魏
十 魔
十 魘
〔195〕魚
魚 180
四 魯 180
鮏
鮑
六 鮒
鮭
鮮 123
七 鯉
鯊
鯨
鰈
鰭
鰻
鱈
鰥
鰭
鱸
〔196〕鳥
鳥 178
三 鳳 47
鳴 178
四 鴉
鴕 125
鴨 112
六 鴻
鴿
七 鵑 132
鵝
鵡
九 鶴
十 鶩
鷹 150
鷺 162
鷗

第六欄

〔194〕鬼
鬼 140
九 魃 193
十 魁 140
魂 67
〔198〕鹿
鹿
麂
麗 154
〔199〕麥
麥 160
八 麴
十 麵
〔200〕麻
麻 74
三 麼 77
〔201〕黃
黃 31
〔202〕黍
黍
黎
黏
〔203〕黑
黑
黔
默
黝
黜
點
六 黠
黨
十 黯
黷
〔204〕黹
黹
〔205〕黽
黽 125
〔206〕鼎
鼎
〔207〕鼓
鼓 108
〔208〕鼠
鼠 181
〔209〕鼻
鼻 46
軒 14

〔210〕齊
齊 182

第七欄

〔211〕齒
齒
齟 117
齡 33
六 齦
七 齧
〔212〕龍
龍 132
六 龔
〔213〕龜
龜 122
〔214〕龠
龠 115
龠